CENTRAL STATISTICAL OFFICE

Annual Abstract of Statistics

1993

No 129

Editor: GEOFF DENNIS

London: HMSO

© *Crown copyright 1993*
First published 1993

Proposals for reproduction of tables or contents should be addressed to Copyright Section, CSO Publications, Room D.140, Government Buildings, Cardiff Road, Newport, Gwent NP9 1XG. (Telephone: 0633 812101)

ISBN 0 11 620553 9

ISSN 0072 5730

HMSO

Standing order service

Placing a standing order with HMSO BOOKS enables a customer to receive future editions of this title automatically as published.

This saves the time, trouble and expense of placing individual orders and avoids the problem of knowing when to do so.

For details please write to HMSO BOOKS (PC13A/1), Publications Centre, PO Box 276, London SW8 5DT and quoting reference 02.02.027.

The standing order service also enables customers to receive automatically as published all material of their choice which additionally saves extensive catalogue research. The scope and selectivity of the service has been extended by new techniques, and there are more than 3,500 classifications to choose from. A special leaflet describing the service in detail may be obtained on request.

Introduction

The *Annual Abstract of Statistics* is prepared by the Central Statistical Office in collaboration with statistics divisions of other government departments. The name of the department or organisation providing the statistics is given under each table. Some of the statistics provided by government departments are actually collected by other organisations such as the national associations. The assistance provided by these organisations is gratefully acknowledged.

In addition, an Index of Sources is given on pages 337 to 343, which sets out the official publications or other sources from which tables in this issue contain the latest statistics available, even though they may not yet have appeared in departmental publications.

Most of the tables in this *Abstract of Statistics* give annual figures, so far as they are available, for each of the years 1981 to 1991 and some include figures for the early months of 1992. Current data for many of the series appearing in the *Abstract* are contained in *Economic Trends*, the *Monthly Digest of Statistics* and in *Financial Statistics*, all prepared by the Central Statistical Office. Regional information, supplementary to the national figures in this *Abstract*, is published in *Regional Trends* also prepared by the Central Statistical Office. These publications are available from HMSO at the address given on the inside back cover.

Definitions

Area covered. Except where otherwise stated all statistics relate to the United Kingdom of Great Britain and Northern Ireland.

Time Series. So far as possible annual totals are given throughout, but quarterly or monthly figures are given where these are more suitable to the type of series. Except where it is stated to the contrary all statistics are for calendar years ended 31 December.

For some series, weekly data are collected and not figures for calendar years. In such cases the figures appearing for particular years are cumulative totals for 52 or 53 weeks and attention to this is drawn by the footnotes to the tables. Since the series have not been adjusted to make them equivalent to a calendar year, care must be taken in making comparisons between annual figures for periods of differing numbers of weeks.

Explanatory notes. Several sections of the *Abstract* are preceded by explanatory notes which should be read in conjunction with the tables. Definitions of many of the terms occurring in the *Abstract* and the *Monthly Digest of Statistics* are given in the *Supplement of Definitions and Explanatory Notes* to the *Monthly Digest*, published annually. Detailed notes on items which appear in both the *Abstract* and *Financial Statistics* are given in an annual supplement to the latter entitled *Financial Statistics: Explanatory Handbook*. The original sources listed in the Index of Sources may also be consulted.

Consumption and stocks. Statistics of consumption and stocks should be used with care. The terms 'consumption', 'disposals' and 'stocks' are defined in details given in the *Supplement* to the *Monthly Digest of Statistics*. The stocks figures given may often relate to only part of the total stocks in the country.

Standard Industrial Classification

The Standard Industrial Classification has been prepared as a means of securing uniformity and comparability in the statistics published by government departments in the United Kingdom. It is a system of classification according to industry; it does not relate to commodities or occupations for which other systems of classification have been devised. It was compiled to conform with the organisation and structure of industry within the United Kingdom.

A revised Classification, which replaced the 1968 Classification was published in 1979 and came into general use in 1983. One of the principal objectives of this revision was to eliminate such differences, as the structure of British industry allows, between the activity classification of the European Community, ('Nomenclature Generale des Activites Economiques dans les Communautes Europeennes (NACE)') and the 1968 Classification. The 1980 Classification is a different structure from its predecessor with 10 Divisions, 60 Classes, 22 Groups and 334 Activity Headings. Full details are available from *Standard Industrial Classification Revised 1980* (HMSO 1979, price £5.50 net) and *Indexes to the Standard Industrial Classification Revised 1980* (HMSO 1981, price £12.95 net).

Revisions and changes in content

Readers will notice that due to the new computerised method of producing the *Abstract* some changes in layout and design have been necessary. In addition, four digit identifiers are shown at the top of the column or start of the row of figures. Please see note on CSO Databank for further details.

Revisions. The scope of the *Abstract* is revised from time to time to include new statistical information as it becomes available. Some of the figures, particularly for the latest year, are provisional and are revised in a subsequent issue of the *Abstract*.

Table 1.2 - Information on the climate does not appear in this section. It is hoped to include this data in future editions. Further information can be obtained from the Meteorological Office, Sutton House, London Road, Bracknell, Berkshire

Table 2.12A - This is a new table for this edition, detailing applications for Asylum into the United Kingdom

Table 8.20 - Wood pulp, paper and paper-making materials - these statistics are no longer collected and the table has been deleted.

Symbols and conventions used

Change of basis. Where consecutive figures have been compiled on different bases and are not strictly comparable, a footnote is added indicating the nature of the difference.

Units of measurement. A table showing the various units of measurement used in this *Abstract* is given on page 336.

Rounding of figures. In tables where figures have been rounded to the nearest final digit, there may be an apparent slight discrepancy between the sums of the constituent items and the total as shown.

Symbols. The following symbols have been used throughout:

.. = not available
- = nil or less than half the final digit shown
nes = not elsewhere specified

Central Statistical Office
Great George Street

February 1993

CSO Databank

Most tables in this publication contain data which is available on the Annual Abstract dataset, one of the datasets in the CSO Databank. The appropriate four digit identifier is included at the top of the column or start of the row of figures. This is to facilitate access to the data in computer-readable form and make available longer runs of data than appear in these tables.

The CSO Databank is a collection of mostly macro-economic time-series available on magnetic tape or disk. The tape format, unlabelled EBCDIC, is the same for all the datasets. Details about availability and prices, or to place your order please telephone, write to the Databank Marketing, Room D.134, CSO, Cardiff Road, Newport, Gwent, NP9 1XG (Telephone: 0633 812915). For further information on the content and technical details please telephone, write to the Databank Service, Room 52/4, CSO, Great George Street, London SW1P 3AQ (Telephone: 071-270 6386 or 6387).

Contents

Introduction   Page

1 Area
1.1	Area of the United Kingdom	1

2 Population and Vital statistics
	Explanatory notes	3

Population
2.1	Population summary	4
2.2	Population changes	5
2.3	Age distribution of the enumerated population: census figures	6
2.4	Age distribution of the enumerated population: census figures	8
2.5	Age distribution of the resident population: mid-year estimates and projections	10
2.6	Marital condition: census figures	12
2.7	Marital condition of the resident population: mid-year estimates and projections	14
2.8	Geographical distribution of the enumerated population: census figures	15
2.9	Geographical distribution of resident population: mid-year estimates	16
2.10	Migration into and out of the United Kingdom: by occupation and sex	17
2.11	by citizenship and country of residence	18
2.12	Acceptances for settlement by nationality	20
*2.12A	Applications for asylum	21

Vital statistics
2.13	Marriages	22
2.14	Divorce	24
2.15	Divorce proceedings	25
2.16	Births	27
2.17	Birth occurrence inside and outside of marriage by age of mother	29
2.18	Live births by age of mother	30
2.19	Deaths: analysis by age and sex	32
2.20	analysed by cause	36
2.21	Infant and maternal mortality	39
2.22	Death rates per 1000 population	41
2.23	Life tables	42

3 Social conditions
	Explanatory notes	43

Social services
3.1	Summary of government expenditure on social services and housing	44
3.2	Government expenditure on education	45
3.3	Government expenditure on the National Health Service	46
3.4, 3.5	Government expenditure on welfare services and social security benefits	47
3.6	Government and other public sector expenditure on housing	48
3.7, 3.8	Stock of dwellings: renovations	49
3.9	Slum clearance: dwellings demolished or closed	49
3.10	Permanent dwellings completed	50

National Insurance and other social security
3.11	National Insurance Fund	51
3.12	National Insurance Acts: persons for whom contributions were payable	51
3.13	Weekly rates of principal social security benefits	52
3.14	National Insurance: contributions	54
3.15	Social Security Acts: number of persons receiving benefit	55
3.16	Unemployed claimants analysed by benefit entitlement	56
3.17	Sickness and invalidity benefit: claimants by age and duration of spell	57
3.18	days of certified incapacity by age	57
3.19	Widow's benefit (excluding widow's allowance: widow's payment)	58
3.20	Family allowances/Child benefits	58
3.21	Contributory and non-contributory retirement pensions	59
3.22	Family income supplement/Family credit	59
3.23	Income support: number of beneficiaries receiving weekly payment	60
3.24	Income support	60
3.25	Income support: average weekly amounts of benefit	61
3.26	War pensions	61

* New or revised in this edition of the *Annual Abstract*

Contents (contd)   Page

National Health Service
3.27	Hospital and family health services	62
3.28	Hospital and primary care services	63
3.29	Hospital and general health services	64
3.30	Health and personal social services: manpower summary	65
3.31	NHS hospitals: selected diagnoses of in-patients treated in non-psychiatric departments (excluding maternity)	67

Public health
3.32	Notifications of infectious diseases	68
3.33	Deaths due to occupationally-related lung disease	69
3.34	New cases of occupational diseases diagnosed under the Industrial Injuries Pneumoconiosis, Byssinosis and Miscellaneous Diseases benefits schemes	69
3.35	Injuries at work	70

Other
3.36	Private households with usual residents: census 1981	71
3.37	Parliamentary elections	72
3.38	Parliamentary by-elections	72

4 Law enforcement
Explanatory notes   73

England and Wales
4.1	Notifiable offences recorded by the police	73
4.2	Police forces: authorised establishment and strength	74
4.3	Offenders found guilty: by offence group	75
4.4	Offenders cautioned: by offence group	76
4.5	Offenders found guilty of offences: by sex and age	77
4.6	Offenders cautioned by the police: by sex and age	77
4.7	Sentence or order passed on offenders sentenced for indictable offences: by sex	78
4.8	Receptions into prison: by number of previous convictions	78
4.9	Receptions and average population in custody	79
4.10	Prison population serving sentences: analysis by age and offence	80
4.11	Expenditure on prisons	81

Scotland
4.12	Crimes and offences recorded by the police	81
4.13	Persons proceeded against	82
4.14	Persons called to court	82
4.15,4.16	Persons with charge proved	83
4.17	Penal establishments: average daily population and receptions	84
4.18	Expenditure on penal establishments	85

Northern Ireland
4.19	Offences known to police, proceedings taken and results of proceedings	85
4.20	Persons found guilty: analysis by type of offence	86
4.21	Juveniles found guilty of offences	86
4.22	Prisons, Young Offenders' Centres and borstal institutions: receptions and average population	87

5 Education
Explanatory notes   88

5.1	Number of schools or departments by type and establishments of higher and further education	89
5.2	Pupils in school by age and sex, number and as a percentage of the population	90
5.3	Number of pupils and teachers: pupil/teacher ratios	91
5.4	Pupils with special needs in public sector and assisted schools	92
5.5	Pupils leaving school by sex and highest qualification held	93
5.6	Numbers and percentages continuing education aged 16 and over by age, sex and type of course	94
5.7	Students in further and Higher education at public sector and assisted establishments by mode of study	95
5.8	Full-time students from abroad	96
5.9	Students in education by type of course, mode of study, sex and subject	98
5.10	Students obtaining qualifications by subject of study, sex and awarding body in the year ended 31 December 1989	99
5.11	Lecturers and teachers by type of establishment, sex and graduate status	100
5.12	Initial training of teachers by sex, type of course and stage	101
5.13	Full-time academic teaching and research staff at universities	101
5.14	Students at universities	102
5.15	Students at universities: UK new admissions	103
5.16	Universities: full-time students analysed by subject group of study	104
5.17	Universities: degrees and diplomas obtained by full-time students	104
5.18	Scientific research: postgraduate awards and special grants	105
5.19	Student awards: new and current by type	107

6 Employment
6.1	Distribution of the workforce	108
6.2	Employees in employment	109
6.3	Males/Females employed in engineering industries	112
6.4	Administrative, technical and clerical workers in manufacturing industries	114

Contents (contd)   Page

	6.5	Number of workers employed in agriculture	114
	6.6	Rates of unemployment	114
	6.7	Civil Service staff	115
	6.8	Unemployment figures by region	116
	6.9	Vacancies at Jobcentres in the United Kingdom	117
	6.10	Vacancies unfilled in Northern Ireland	118
	6.11	Industrial stoppages	119
	6.12	Economic activity: 1981	120
	6.13	Size of manufacturing units 1992	121
	6.14	Average weekly earnings and hours of manual workers	122
	6.15	Average weekly and hourly earnings and hours of full-time employees on adult rates	123
	6.16	Average earnings index: all employees	124
	6.17	Gross weekly and hourly earnings of full-time adult employees	126
	6.18	Gross weekly and hourly earnings of full-time adults	128
	6.19	Average earnings by age group of full-time employees whose pay for the survey pay-period was not affected by absence	130
	6.20	Trade unions	131
7		**Defence**	
		Explanatory notes	132
	7.1	Formation of the Armed Forces	133
	7.2	Defence expenditure	133
	7.3	Defence manpower strengths	134
	7.4	Recruitment of UK Service personnel to each Service	134
	7.5	Outflow of UK Service personnel from each Service	135
	7.6	Deployment of service personnel	135
	7.7	Service married accommodation and Defence land holdings	136
	7.8	Defence civilian manpower strengths	136
	7.9	Service hospitals	137
	7.10	Strength of uniformed medical staff	137
	7.11	Sickness medical discharges and deaths of UK Service personnel	138
	7.12	Search and rescue operations at home	139
	7.13	Defence services and the civilian community	139
	7.14	Defence energy consumption	139
8		**Production**	
		Explanatory notes	140
	8.1	Censuses of production: summary table	140
		Energy	
	8.2	Total inland energy consumption	146
	8.3	Coal: supply and demand	147
	8.4	Coal production	148
	8.5	Coal: average number of wage earners on colliery books	148
	8.6	Coal: output per manshift	149
	8.7	Fuel input and gas output: gas sales	150
8.8 - 8.10		Electricity: production; capacity of generating plant and sales	151
	8.11	Indigenous production, refinery receipts, arrivals and shipments of oil	153
	8.12	Throughput of crude and process oils and output of refined products from refineries	153
	8.13	Deliveries of petroleum products for inland consumption	154
		Iron and steel	
	8.14	Steel supplies, deliveries and stocks	155
	8.15	Iron ore, manganese ore, pig iron and iron and steel scrap	156
	8.16	Number of furnaces and production of steel	157
		Industrial materials	
	8.17	Non-ferrous metals	158
	8.18	Cotton, man-made fibres and wool	160
	8.19	Packaging products of paper and board: manufacturers' sales	161
	8.20	Timber	161
	8.21	Synthetic rubber, carbon black and rubber products	162
	8.22	Fertilisers	162
	8.23	Synthetic dyestuffs, colours, paint, varnish and allied products	163
8.24, 8.25		Chemicals: inorganic and organic	164
	8.26	Synthetic resins, production of synthetic resins	165
	8.27	Minerals: production	166
		Building and construction	
	8.28	Building materials and components: production	167
	8.29	Construction: value of output in Great Britain	168
	8.30	Construction: value of new orders obtained by Contractors	168
		Manufactured goods	
	8.31	Manufacturers' sales of metal goods, etc	169
	8.32	Volume index: engineering industries	171

Contents (contd)

		Page
8.33	Merchant shipbuilding	172
8.34	Motor vehicles production	172
8.35	Alcoholic drink	173
8.36	Tobacco products	173

9 Agriculture, fisheries and food

Agriculture
	Explanatory notes	174
9.1	Outputs, inputs and net product at current prices	175
9.2	Agricultural output, input and net product at constant prices	178
9.3	Agricultural land use	180
9.4	Quantity of crops and grass harvested	181
9.5	Cattle, sheep, pigs and poultry on agricultural holdings	182
9.6	Forest area	183
9.7	Weekly earnings and hours of agricultural workers	183
9.8	Distribution of hired regular full-time men in agriculture by earnings band, *Great Britain*	183
9.9	Sales of food for agricultural produce and livestock	184
9.10	Stocks of food and feedingstuffs	184
9.11	Processed food and animal feedingstuffs	185
9.12	Disposals of food and animal feedingstuffs	186

Fisheries
9.13	Landings of fish of British taking: weight and value	187
9.14	Fishing fleet	188
9.15	Scottish Fishing Vessels	188

Food consumption
9.16	Estimated household food consumption	189

10 Transport and communications

10.1	Goods transport in Great Britain	190
10.2	Passenger transport in Great Britain	190

Road transport
Great Britain
10.3	Length of public roads	190
10.4	Estimated traffic on all roads	191
10.5	Motor vehicles currently licensed	191
10.6	New vehicle registrations	192
10.7	Driving tests: applications and results	192
10.8, 10.9	Vehicles: licences current and new registrations, *Northern Ireland*	193
10.10	Buses and coaches	194
10.11	Indices of local stage bus service fares	194
10.12	Road accidents, vehicles involved and casualties	195
10.13	Casualties in road accidents	196
10.14	Road goods transport	196

Rail transport
Great Britain
10.15-10.17	British Rail: assets; passenger and freight receipts and traffic; operations	197
10.18	London Regional Transport: receipts, operations and assets	199
10.19	Accidents on railways	200
	Northern Ireland	
10.20	Railways: permanent way and rolling stock	201
10.21	Operating statistics of railways	201

Air transport
10.22	Main output of UK airlines	202
10.23	Air traffic between the United Kingdom and abroad	202
10.24	UK airlines	203
10.25	Non-scheduled services by UK airlines	204
10.26	Trends in major UK airlines: operating costs and revenues	205
10.27	UK airlines: accidents on scheduled services	206
10.28	Activity at civil aerodromes	206

Sea transport
10.29-10.30	UK and Crown Dependency registered trading vessels of 500 and 100 gross tons and over	207
10.31	UK and Crown Dependency registered trading vessels of 100 gross tons and over	209
10.32-10.34	International seaborne trade of the United Kingdom	210
10.35	Seaport traffic of Great Britain	213

Passenger movement
10.36	UK International passenger movement by sea and air: by countries	214

Contents (contd)   Page

Communications
10.37	Postal services and television licences	215

11 Distributive trades, Research and Development
	Explanatory notes	216
11.1	Retail trades by form of organisation and kind of business	217
11.2	Retail trade: index numbers of value and volume of sales	218
11.3	Motor trades: commodity sales	219
11.4	Catering and allied trades 1981-1990	220
11.5	Cost of research and development: analysis by sector	221
11.6	Gross central government expenditure on research and development	221
11.7	Net central government expenditure on research and development, using European Community objectives for R&D expenditure	222
11.8	Intra-mural expenditure on industrial research and development, 1985 to 1990	222
11.9	Sources of funds for R and D within industry in the United Kingdom, 1985 to 1990	223

12 External trade
	Explanatory notes	224
12.1	Visible trade of the UK on a balance of payments basis	224
12.2	Import penetration and export sales ratios for products of manufacturing industry	225
12.3	Value of UK exports (fob): Analysis by sections and divisions	227
12.4	Value of UK imports (cif): Analysis by sections and divisions	229
12.5	Value of UK exports (fob): Analysis by destination	231
12.6	Value of UK imports (cif): Analysis by source	233

13 Balance of payments
	Explanatory notes	235
13.1, 13.2	Balance of payments: summary	237
	current account	238
13.3	Levels of UK external assets and liabilities	239
13.4	UK public expenditure on overseas aid: summary; gross aid-analysis by major components	239
13.5	UK public expenditure on overseas aid: summary; gross bilateral aid-analysis	240

14 National income and expenditure
	Explanatory notes	241
14.1	National product: categories of expenditure and factor incomes	243
14.2	Personal income and expenditure	244
14.3	Corporate sector: appropriation account	245
14.4	General government summary account	245
14.5	Summary capital account	246
14.6	Gross domestic product: output-based measure by industry at constant factor cost	247
14.7	Gross domestic product by industry	248
14.8	Gross national product by category of expenditure at 1985 prices	249
14.9	Consumers' expenditure: at current prices classified by function	250
14.10	Consumers' expenditure: at 1985 market prices, classified by function	252
14.11	Consumers' expenditure: at current market prices classified by commodity	254
14.12	Consumers' expenditure at 1985 market prices: classified by commodity	254
14.13	National accounts aggregates: national disposable income and volume indices	255
14.14	Value of physical increase in stocks and work in progress	256
14.15	Goss domestic fixed capital formation	257
14.16	Gross capital stock at 1985 replacement cost	258

15 Personal income, expenditure and wealth
	Explanatory notes	259
15.1	Average incomes of households before and after taxes and benefits: 1989	259
15.2	Distribution of total incomes before and after tax	260
15.3	Sources of household income	262
15.4	Availability in households of certain durable goods	262
15.5	Households and their expenditure	263

16 Home finance
Central government
	Explanatory notes	264
16.1, 16.2	Public sector financial account; borrowing requirement	264
16.3	Debt of the public sector: nominal amount outstanding	266
16.4	Consolidated Fund: revenue and expenditure	268
	: and National Loans Fund summary of receipts and payments	
16.5	Central government borrowing requirement (net balance)	269
16.6	Borrowing and repayment of debt	270
16.7	Consolidated Fund and National Loans Fund: assets and liabilities	271
16.8	British government and government guaranteed marketable securities	273
16.9	National savings	274
16.10	Income tax: allowances and reliefs	276
16.11	Rates of income tax	277
16.12	Rateable values	278

Contents (contd) Page

Local authorities
United Kingdom
16.13	Local authorities: gross loan debt outstanding	279
16.14	Expenditure and income of local authorities: summary	279

England and Wales
16.15	Revenue account expenditure of local authorities	280
16.16	Capital account expenditure of local authorities	281
16.17	Water authority expenditure	281
16.18	Income of local authorities: classified according to source	282
16.19	Income of local authorities from government grants including capital grants	283

Scotland
16.20	Expenditure of local authorities	284
16.21, 16.22	Income: according to source; from government grants	285

Northern Ireland
16.23	Expenditure of local authorities	286
16.24	Income of local authorities: classified according to source	287
16.25	Income of local authorities from government grants: classified according to services	287

17 Banking, Insurance, etc
Banking and capital markets
17.1	Bank of England	288
17.2	Value of Inter-bank clearings	288
17.3	UK Banks: liabilities and assets outstanding	289
17.4	Banks: summary of monthly reporting institutions	290
17.5	Analysis of bank lending to UK residents	291
17.6	Discount houses	292
17.7	Public sector borrowing requirement and other counterparts to changes in money stock during the year	292
17.8	Money stock and liquidity	293
17.9	Money and bill rates	294
17.10	Security yields and prices	295
17.11	Securities quoted on The Stock Exchange	296
17.12	Capital issues and redemptions in the United Kingdom	297

Other financial institutions
17.13	Building societies	298
17.14	Consumer Credit	299
17.15	Finance houses and other credit companies in Great Britain: assets and liabilities	299
17.16	End-year assets and liabilities of investment trust companies, unit trusts and property unit trusts	300
17.17	Self-administered pension funds market value of assets	300
17.18	Insurance companies: balance sheet	301
17.19, 17.20	Industrial and provident societies and co-operative trading societies	303
17.21, 17.22	Collecting societies and friendly societies	304

Insurance
17.23	Life assurance	305
17.24	Returns of industrial assurances taken up and discontinued	305

Companies
17.25	Acquisitions and mergers of UK companies	306
17.26	Income and finance of large companies	307

Insolvency
17.27, 17.28	Insolvencies: individual, Company	309
17.29	Industry analysis: bankruptcies and deeds of arrangement	310
17.30	: Company insolvencies	310

18 Prices
Explanatory notes 311

18.1	Producer price index numbers: of materials and fuel purchased	312
18.2	index numbers of output (home sales)	312
18.3	Price index numbers of materials and fuel purchased by detailed sectors of Industry	313
18.4	index numbers: of products manufactured in the United Kingdom (home sales)	317
18.5	index: of commodities wholly or mainly imported into the United Kingdom	328
18.6	Internal purchasing power of the pound (based on RPI)	330
18.7	Index of retail prices	331
18.8	Tax and price index	332
18.9	Index of purchase prices of the means of agricultural production	333
18.10	Index of producer prices of agricultural products	334
18.11	Commodity price trends	335

Index of sources 337

Alphabetical index 344

GOVERNMENT STATISTICS IN COMPUTER READABLE FORM
via

THE CSO DATABANK

The CSO Databank is the service offered by the Government's Central Statistical Office to customers who need data in computer readable form.

Datasets available NOW on magnetic tape or floppy disk are:

Economic Trends	Monthly
National Accounts Quarterly Article	Quarterly
Balance of Payments Quarterly Article	Quarterly
Acquisitions and Mergers within the UK	Quarterly
Index of Production	Monthly
Cyclical Indicators	Monthly
GDP(O)	Quarterly
Employment and Earnings	Monthly
Unemployment	Monthly
RPI/TPI and Producer Price Indices	Monthly (aggregates)
Financial Statistics and PSBR	Monthly
Monthly Digest of Statistics	Monthly
Monthly Review of External Trade Statistics	Monthly
UK Balance of Payments (CSO Pink Book)	Annually
UK National Accounts (CSO Blue Book)	Annually
Economic Trends Annual Supplement	Annually
Consumers' Expenditure (floppy disk only)	Quarterly
Trade by Industry	Monthly
Index of Manufacturing (IOM)	Monthly

Also available shortly:

- Retail sales
- Credit Business
- Quarterly Capital Expenditure (CAPEX)
- Annual Census of Production
- Company Liquidity
- Insurance Companies & Pension Funds Investment (MQ5)
- Institutional Investment
- Dividends and Interest
- Producer Price Indices (detailed)
- Cross-border Acquisitions & Mergers

The service is available to:

Host bureaux for incorporation in their client services
End users who require the data for their own use

The service is flexible:

Hosts may choose to receive specific datasets
End users may buy individual tapes or disks

For more details about availability and prices, or to place your order you can telephone, write or fax to:

Databank Marketing
Room D134
Central Statistical Office
Cardiff Road
Newport, Gwent NP9 1XG
Telephone (0633) 812915
Fax (0633) 812599

For further information on the CSO Databank technical details you can telephone or write to:

The Databank Service
Room 52/4
Central Statistical Office
Great George Street
London SW1P 3AQ
Telephone 071-270 6386 or 6387

The CSO does not offer direct on-line access to the data, but a list of host bureaux offering this service is available from Databank Marketing on request.

A leaflet **More about the CSO Databank** gives more details of the contents and number of series under each heading; this is also available from Databank Marketing on request.

For more general inquiries about UK government statistics, and the work of the Central Statistical Office, you can telephone our Public Inquiry Service on 071-270 6363 or 6364 (London) or (0633) 812973 (Newport).

Central Statistical Office
An executive agency of government

1. Area

1.1 Area of the United Kingdom[1]
At 31st March 1981

	Metric measure					
	Thousand hectares			Square kilometres		
	Total	Land	Inland water[2]	Total	Land	Inland water[2]
United Kingdom	24 415	24 093	322	244 157	240 939	3 218
Great Britain	23 003	22 745	258	230 033	227 453	2 580
England and Wales	15 125	15 036	89	151 244	150 356	888
England	13 048	12 972	76	130 478	129 720	758
Wales	2 077	2 064	13	20 766	20 636	130
Scotland	7 879	7 710	169	78 789	77 097	1 692
Northern Ireland[3]	1 414	1 350	64	14 144	13 506	638

	Imperial measure					
	Thousand acres			Square miles		
	Total	Land	Inland water[1]	Total	Land	Inland water[1]
United Kingdom	60 331	59 535	796	94 269	93 027	1 242
Great Britain	58 842	56 204	638	88 816	87 820	996
England and Wales	37 375	37 155	219	58 395	58 052	343
England	32 242	32 054	188	50 377	50 085	293
Wales	5 132	5 100	32	8 018	7 968	50
Scotland	19 469	19 051	418	30 420	29 767	653
Northern Ireland[3]	3 493	3 336	157	5 461	5 215	246

	Standard regions											
	United Kingdom	North	Yorkshire & Humberside	East Midlands	East Anglia	South East	South West	West Midlands	North West	Wales	Scotland	Northern Ireland
Thousand Square Kilometres	244.1	15.4	15.4	15.6	12.6	27.2	23.9	13.0	7.3	20.8	78.8	14.0

1 Based on 1:50 000 digital information for 1984 Boundaries Commission.
2 Excluding tidal water.
3 Excluding certain tidal waters that are parts of statutory areas in Northern Ireland.

Sources: Central Statistical Office;
Ordnance Survey of Northern Ireland;
Ordnance Survey

THE STANDARD INDUSTRIAL CLASSIFICATION IS CHANGING

Have you been using this book during the last twelve years?

The Standard Industrial Classification (SIC) is being changed as a result of the Single European Market. These changes are extensive and the 1980 SIC will be obsolete. The latest version is now available from HMSO - demand will be high so we suggest you order your copy as soon as possible. You can telephone your order to the HMSO Publications Centre on 071-873 9090, Fax it on 071-873 8200, or buy the book at any HMSO bookshop or accredited agent.

STANDARD INDUSTRIAL CLASSIFICATION 1992

From 1 January 1993 you will need this book instead

Published by HMSO for the Central Statistical Office.
Price £18.00 net
ISBN 0 11 620550 4
From HMSO and through good booksellers

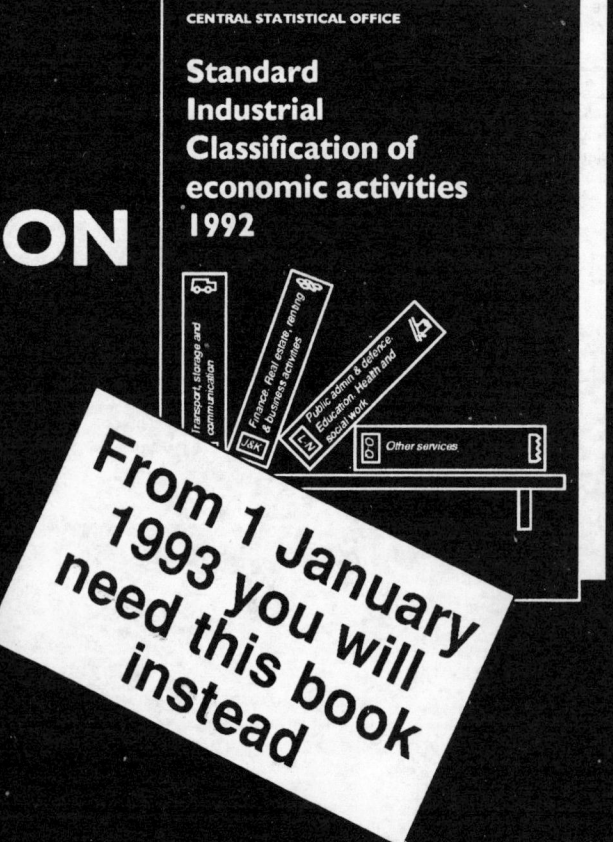

2 Population and Vital Statistics

This section begins with a summary of population figures for the United Kingdom and constituent countries from 1851 to 2031 and for Great Britain from 1801 (Table 2.1). Table 2.2 analyses the elements of population change. Tables 2.3-2.4 give details of the national sex and age structure for years up to the present date. The marital condition of the population is given in Tables 2.6 and 2.7. Table 2.5 gives projections of the population by sex and age up to the year 2031. The distribution of population at local and regional level is summarised in Tables 2.8 and 2.9.

In the main, historical series relate to census information while mid-year estimates which make allowance for underenumeration and absences abroad in the latest census are given for the recent past and the present.

Population *(Tables 2.1-2.4).*

Figures shown in these tables relate to the population enumerated at successive censuses, mid-year estimates and population projections.

Definition of resident population
The estimated population of an area includes all those usually resident in the area, whatever their nationality. Members of HM and non-UK Armed Forces are taken to be resident at their stationed address. Students are taken to be resident at their term-time address.

The current series of estimates are updated annually, starting with those derived from the 1981 Census of Population and then allowing for subsequent births, deaths and migration.

Results of the 1991 Census of Population, and estimates based upon them, were not available in time for incorporation within this volume.

Projected resident population of the United Kingdom and constituent countries *(Tables 2.1, 2.2 and 2.5).*

These projections are prepared by the Government Actuary, in consultation with the Registrars General, as a common framework for use in national planning in a number of different fields. New projections are made at least every second year on a set of assumptions which seems most appropriate on the basis of the statistical evidence available at the time. The population projections in Tables 2.1, 2.2 and 2.5 are 1989 based. The base population is as estimated for mid-1989 by the Registrars General, and the assumptions for mortality, fertility and migration reflect statistical evidence up to mid-1989.

Geographical distribution of the enumerated population: census figures *(Table 2.8).*

The urban and rural districts and the conurbations shown in the table are based on local government administrative areas as they were prior to reorganisation in England and Wales in 1974 and in Scotland in 1975. Preliminary population counts from the 1981 Census were prepared for these areas in England and Wales, but it was not possible to continue the series to 1981 in Scotland or in Northern Ireland.

A new study of urban land and population based on the 1981 Census of Population has been made in Great Britain and the results published in *1981 Census, Key Statistics for Urban Areas, Great Britain*. This gives the total population in Great Britain in urban areas in 1981 as 48 655 thousand and the population in remaining rural areas as 5 630 thousand, indicating that the division by administrative areas underestimated the urban population. However, it is not possible to give statistics of population in earlier years for the new urban areas, so the series based on administrative areas is given in Table 2.8.

Migration into and out of the United Kingdom *(Tables 2.10 and 2.11).*

A migrant into the United Kingdom is defined as a person who has resided abroad for a year or more and on entering has declared the intention to reside here for a year or more; and *vice versa* for a migrant from the United Kingdom. Estimates are derived from the International Passenger Survey (IPS), a sample survey covering the principal air and sea routes between the United Kingdom and overseas but excluding routes to and from the Irish Republic. Migration between the Channel Islands and the Isle of Man and the rest of the world has been excluded from these tables. The figures include British citizens as well as people subject to immigration control.

Acceptances for settlement in the United Kingdom *(Table 2.12).*

This table presents in geographic regions the statistics of individual nationalities, arranged alphabetically within each region. The figures are on a different basis from those derived from the IPS (Tables 2.10 and 2.11) and relate only to people subject to immigration control. It should be noted that information is not separately available for all nationalities and countries and therefore the group sub-totals shown are simply the totals of the countries listed.

Applications received in the United Kingdom for asylum, excluding dependants *(Table 2.12A).*

This table shows statistics of applications for asylum in the United Kingdom. Figures are shown of the main applicant nationalities, by geographic region. The basis of assessing asylum applications, and hence of deciding whether to grant asylum in the United Kingdom, is the 1951 United Nations Convention on Refugees.

Divorces *(Tables 2.14 and 2.15).*

Table 2.14 gives figures for dissolutions and annulments by duration of marriage and age of wife. Scottish figures prior to 1979 relate only to marriages which took place in Scotland. Data in Table 2.15 give petitions filed for divorce, divorces by fact proven and separations.

Births *(Tables 2.16, 2.17 and 2.18).*

For Scotland and Northern Ireland the number of births relate to those registered during the year. For England and Wales the figures up to and including 1930-32 are for those registered while later figures relate to births occurring in each year.

Deaths *(Tables 2.19-2.22).*

The figures relate to the number of deaths registered during the calendar year, the normal time lag between occurrence and registration being a matter of days only.

Life tables *(Table 2.23).*

The interim life tables are constructed from the estimated home population in 1988-90 and the total deaths registered in those years.

Population

2.1 Population summary

Thousands

	United Kingdom			England and Wales			Wales	Scotland			Northern Ireland		
	Persons	Males	Females	Persons	Males	Females	Persons	Persons	Males	Females	Persons	Males	Females

Enumerated population: census figures

1801	..	..	..	8 893	4 255	4 638	587	1 608	739	869	..	..	..
1851	22 259	10 855	11 404	17 928	8 781	9 146	1 163	2 889	1 376	1 513	1 442	698	745
1901	38 237	18 492	19 745	32 528	15 729	16 799	2 013	4 472	2 174	2 298	1 237	590	647
1911	42 082	20 357	21 725	36 070	17 446	18 625	2 421	4 761	2 309	2 452	1 251	603	648
1921[1]	44 027	21 033	22 994	37 887	18 075	19 811	2 656	4 882	2 348	2 535	1 258	610	648
1931[1]	46 038	22 060	23 978	39 952	19 133	20 819	2 593	4 843	2 326	2 517	1 243	601	642
1951	50 225	24 118	26 107	43 758	21 016	22 742	2 599	5 096	2 434	2 662	1 371	668	703
1961	52 709	25 481	27 228	46 105	22 304	23 801	2 644	5 179	2 483	2 697	1 425	694	731
1966[2]	53 788	26 044	27 745	47 136	22 841	24 295	2 663	5 168	2 479	2 689	1 485	724	761
1971	55 515	26 952	28 562	48 750	23 683	25 067	2 731	5 229	2 515	2 714	1 536	755	781
1981	55 848	27 104	28 742	49 155	23 873	25 281	2 792	5 131	2 466	2 664	1 533[4]	750	783
1991	56 467	27 344	29 123	49 890	24 182	25 707	..	4 999	2 392	2 606	1 578	769	809

Usually resident

1981	55 089	26 803	28 286	48 522	23 625	24 897	2 750	5 035	2 428	2 607	1 532	749	783

Resident population: mid-year estimates

	DYAY	BBAB	BBAC	BBAD	BBAE	BBAF	KGJM	BBAG	BBAH	BBAI	BBAJ	BBAK	BBAL
1959	51 956	25 043	26 913	45 386	21 885	23 501	2 623	5 163	2 472	2 690	1 408	686	722
1960	52 372	25 271	27 102	45 775	22 097	23 678	2 629	5 178	2 482	2 696	1 420	692	728
1961	52 807	25 528	27 279	46 196	22 347	23 849	2 635	5 184	2 485	2 698	1 427	696	732
1962	53 292	25 826	27 465	46 657	22 631	24 026	2 652	5 198	2 495	2 703	1 437	700	737
1963	53 625	25 992	27 633	46 973	22 787	24 186	2 664	5 205	2 500	2 705	1 447	705	741
1964	53 991	26 191	27 800	47 324	22 978	24 346	2 677	5 208	2 501	2 707	1 458	711	747
1965	54 350	26 368	27 982	47 671	23 151	24 521	2 693	5 210	2 501	2 709	1 468	716	752
1966	54 643	26 511	28 132	47 966	23 296	24 671	2 702	5 201	2 496	2 704	1 476	719	757
1967	54 959	26 673	28 286	48 272	23 451	24 821	2 710	5 198	2 496	2 702	1 489	726	763
1968	55 214	26 784	28 429	48 511	23 554	24 957	2 715	5 200	2 498	2 702	1 503	733	770
1969	55 461	26 908	28 553	48 738	23 666	25 072	2 722	5 208	2 503	2 706	1 514	739	776
1970	55 632	26 992	28 641	48 891	23 738	25 153	2 729	5 214	2 507	2 707	1 527	747	781
1971	55 928	27 167	28 761	49 152	23 897	25 255	2 740	5 236	2 516	2 720	1 540	755	786
1972	56 097	27 259	28 837	49 327	23 989	25 339	2 755	5 231	2 513	2 717	1 539	758	782
1973	56 223	27 332	28 891	49 459	24 061	25 399	2 773	5 234	2 515	2 719	1 530	756	774
1974	56 236	27 349	28 887	49 468	24 075	25 393	2 785	5 241	2 519	2 722	1 527	755	772
1975	56 226	27 361	28 865	49 470	24 091	25 378	2 795	5 232	2 516	2 716	1 524	753	770
1976	56 216	27 360	28 856	49 459	24 089	25 370	2 799	5 233	2 517	2 716	1 524	754	770
1977	56 190	27 345	28 845	49 440	24 076	25 364	2 801	5 226	2 515	2 711	1 523	754	769
1978	56 178	27 330	28 849	49 443	24 067	25 375	2 804	5 212	2 509	2 704	1 523	754	770
1979	56 240	27 373	28 867	49 508	24 113	25 395	2 810	5 204	2 505	2 699	1 530	755	773
1980	56 330	27 411	28 919	49 603	24 156	25 448	2 816	5 194	2 501	2 693	1 533	755	778
1981	56 352	27 409	28 943	49 634	24 160	25 474	2 814	5 180	2 495	2 685	1 538	754	784
1982	56 306	27 386	28 920	49 601	24 143	25 459	2 807	5 167	2 490	2 677	1 538	754	784
1983	56 347	27 417	28 931	49 654	24 176	25 478	2 808	5 150	2 485	2 665	1 543	756	788
1984	56 460	27 487	28 973	49 764	24 244	25 519	2 807	5 146	2 484	2 662	1 551	760	791
1985	56 618	27 574	29 044	49 924	24 330	25 594	2 812	5 137	2 481	2 656	1 558	763	795
1986	56 763	27 647	29 116	50 075	24 403	25 672	2 821	5 121	2 475	2 646	1 567	768	798
1987	56 930	27 737	29 193	50 243	24 493	25 750	2 836	5 112	2 471	2 641	1 575	773	802
1988	57 065	27 813	29 253	50 393	24 576	25 817	2 857	5 094	2 462	2 632	1 578	774	804
1989	57 236	27 907	29 330	50 562	24 669	25 893	2 873	5 091	2 460	2 630	1 583	777	806
1990	<u>57 411</u>	<u>28 013</u>	<u>29 398</u>	<u>50 719</u>	<u>24 766</u>	<u>25 953</u>	<u>2 881</u>	<u>5 102</u>	<u>2 467</u>	<u>2 636</u>	<u>1 589</u>	<u>780</u>	<u>809</u>
1991[5]	57 649	28 132	29 517	50 955	24 892	26 063	2 886	5 100	2 462	2 638	1 594	778	817

Resident population: projections (mid-year)[3]

1991	57 561	28 099	29 463	50 903	24 865	26 038	2 899	5 068	2 452	2 615	1 590	781	809
1996	58 413	28 604	29 809	51 752	25 358	26 394	2 946	5 051	2 452	2 598	1 610	794	817
2001	59 174	29 069	30 105	52 526	25 819	26 708	2 987	5 026	2 449	2 577	1 622	802	820
2006	59 681	29 397	30 284	53 084	26 161	26 922	3 012	4 973	2 430	2 543	1 625	805	819
2011	60 033	29 630	30 403	53 510	26 423	27 087	3 029	4 900	2 400	2 500	1 623	806	816
2021	60 743	30 049	30 694	54 411	26 927	27 484	3 062	4 727	2 322	2 405	1 605	800	805
2031	61 068	30 213	30 855	54 977	27 208	27 769	3 062	4 524	2 224	2 300	1 567	782	785

1 Figures for Northern Ireland are estimated. The population at the Census of 1926 was 1 257 thousand (608 thousand males and 649 thousand females).
2 Except for Northern Ireland, where a full census was taken, figures are based on the 10 per cent sample census.
3 These projections are 1989 based. More detail given in Table 2.5.
4 The figures include 44 500 non-enumerated persons.
5 The population estimates for mid-1991 are provisional. They are based on early 1991 Census results, and are therefore not comparable with estimates for 1982 to 1990 which were based on the 1981 Census and will be revised in due course.

Sources: Office of Population Censuses and Surveys; General Register Office (Northern Ireland); General Register Office (Scotland); Government Actuary's Department

2.2 Population changes

Thousands

	Population at beginning of period[1]	Average annual change				
		Total increase or decrease (-)	Births	Deaths[2]	Excess of births over deaths	Net civilian migration	Other adjustments[3]
United Kingdom							
1901-1911	38 237	385	1 091	624	467		-82
1911-1921	42 082	195	975	689	286		-92
1921-1931	44 027	201	824	555	268		-67
1931-1951	46 038	213	793	603	190		+22
1951-1961	50 290	252	839	593	246	-7	+13
1961-1971	52 807	310	962	638	324	-32	+18
1971-1981	55 928	42	736	666	69	-44	+17
1981-1991	56 352	130	757	655	103	21	6
1991-2001[4]	57 649	161	800	639	161		0
2001-2011	59 174	86	736	650	86		0
2011-2021	60 033	71	750	679	71		0
England and Wales							
1901-1911	32 528	354	929	525	404		-50
1911-1921	36 070	182	828	584	244		-62
1921-1931	37 887	207	693	469	224		-17
1931-1951	39 952	193	673	518	155		+38
1951-1961	43 815	238	714	516	197	+30	+10
1961-1971	46 196	296	832	560	272	+7	+16
1971-1981	49 152	48	638	585	53	-18	+13
1981-1991	49 634	132	664	576	89	36	8
1991-2001[4]	50 955	162	709	564	145		17
2001-2011	52 526	98	656	574	81		17
2011-2021	53 510	90	674	600	73		17
Scotland							
1901-1911	4 472	29	131	76	54		-25
1911-1921	4 761	12	118	82	36		-24
1921-1931	4 882	-4	100	65	35		-39
1931-1951	4 843	13	92	67	25	-11	-1
1951-1961	5 102	8	95	62	34	-28	+2
1961-1971	5 184	3	97	63	34	-32	+2
1971-1981	5 236	-6	70	64	6	-15	+4
1981-1991	5 180	-8	66	63	3	-10	0
1991-2001[4]	5 100	-4	65	60	5		-10
2001-2011	5 026	-13	58	60	-2		-10
2011-2021	4 900	-17	55	62	-7		-10
Northern Ireland							
1901-1911	1 237	1	31	23	8		-6
1911-1921	1 251	1	29	22	7		-6
1921-1931	1 258	-2	30	21	9		-11
1931-1951	1 243	6	28	18	10		-4
1951-1961	1 373	5	30	15	15	-9	-
1961-1971	1 427	11	33	16	17	-7	+1
1971-1981	1 540	0	28	17	11	-11	0
1981-1991	1 538	6	27	16	12	-5	1
1991-2001[4]	1 594	3	26	15	11		-7
2001-2011	1 622	0	23	16	7		-7
2011-2021	1 623	-2	22	17	5		-7

1 Census enumerated population up to 1951; mid-year estimates of resident population from 1951 to 1991 and mid-1989 based projections of resident population thereafter.
2 Including deaths of non-civilians and merchant seamen who died outside the country. These numbered 577,000 in 1911-1921 and 240,000 in 1931-1951 for England and Wales; 74,000 in 1911-1921 and 34,000 in 1931-1951 for Scotland; and 10,000 in 1911-1926 for Northern Ireland.
3 For England and Wales, changes in Armed Forces, in visitor balance and other adjustments.
4 Population at the beginning of the period is the provisional rebased mid-year Estimate for 1991 and is therefore not fully consitent with the total increase/decrease figures which are calculated from the 1989 based projections of the population at mid-1991.

Sources: Office of Population Censuses and Surveys; General Register Office (Scotland); General Register Office (Northern Ireland); Government Actuary's Department

Population

2.3 Age distribution of the enumerated population: census figures
United Kingdom

Thousands

		1901	1931[1]	1951	1971	1981[2,3]	1991[3]
Persons: all ages	KGUA	38 237	46 038	50 225	55 515	55 089	56 467
Under 5	KGUB	4 381	3 531	4 326	4 505	3 349	3 766
Under 16	KGUC	..	..	11 975	14 168	12 384	11 434
Under 18	KGUD	..	..	13 248	15 705	14 272	12 863
5 - 14	KGUE	8 040	7 643	6 999	8 882	8 106	6 997
15 - 29	KGUF	10 808	11 853	10 328	11 678	12 409	12 383
30 - 44	KGUG	7 493	9 717	11 125	9 759	10 760	11 974
45 - 64	KGUH	5 706	9 877	11 980	13 384	12 296	12 341
65 - 74	KGUI	1 278	2 461	3 689	4 713	5 049	5 062
75 and over	KGUJ	531	957	1 777	2 594	3 120	3 748
Pensionable age aggregate	KFIA	2 387	4 421	6 828	9 015	9 680	10 512
Under 1	KGUK	938	712	773	891	713	766
1 and under 2	KGUL	857	699	805	878	714	759
2 - 4	KGUM	2 586	2 119	2 748	2 736	1 923	2 237
5 - 9	KGUN	4 106	3 897	3 689	4 670	3 685	3 569
10 - 14	KGUO	3 934	3 746	3 310	4 213	4 420	3 427
15 - 19	KGUP	3 826	3 989	3 175	3 832	4 611	3 665
20 - 24	KGUQ	3 674	4 024	3 393	4 237	4 081	4 232
25 - 29	KGUR	3 308	3 841	3 761	3 610	3 717	4 486
30 - 34	KGUS	2 833	3 494	3 515	3 259	4 114	4 111
35 - 39	KGUT	2 494	3 195	3 786	3 169	3 485	3 745
40 - 44	KGUU	2 165	3 028	3 825	3 331	3 162	4 117
45 - 49	KGUV	1 837	2 901	3 603	3 544	3 051	3 461
50 - 54	KGUW	1 566	2 713	3 209	3 273	3 151	3 077
55 - 59	KGUX	1 236	2 365	2 746	3 360	3 242	2 910
60 - 64	KGUY	1 067	1 897	2 422	3 206	2 852	2 893
65 - 69	KGUZ	743	1 455	2 069	2 707	2 730	2 802
70 - 74	KGVA	535	1 005	1 620	2 005	2 318	2 260
75 - 79	KGVB	313	581	1 049	1 331	1 635	1 860
80 - 84	KGVC	157	263	506	790	920	1 241
85 and over	KGVD	61	113	224	473	565	847
Males: all ages	KGWA	18 492	22 060	24 118	26 952	26 803	27 344
Under 5	KGWB	2 190	1 784	2 215	2 312	1 717	1 925
Under 16	KGWC	..	..	6 110	7 275	6 352	5 857
Under 18	KGWD	..	..	6 753	8 064	7 318	6 590
5 - 14	KGWE	4 024	3 859	3 566	4 561	4 159	3 586
15 - 29	KGWF	5 191	5 804	5 073	5 915	6 294	6 172
30 - 44	KGWG	3 597	4 495	5 461	4 909	5 401	5 952
45 - 64	KGWH	2 705	4 647	5 554	6 452	6 003	6 195
65 - 74	KGWI	565	1 099	1 561	1 976	2 210	2 266
75 and over	KGWJ	219	372	687	828	1 019	1 349
Pensionable age aggregate	KFIB	785	1 471	2 247	2 804	3 228	3 615
Under 1	KGWK	471	361	397	457	364	392
1 and under 2	KGWL	429	353	412	451	366	388
2 - 4	KGWM	1 290	1 070	1 406	1 404	987	1 144
5 - 9	KGWN	2 052	1 967	1 885	2 395	1 893	1 828
10 - 14	KGWO	1 972	1 892	1 681	2 166	2 266	1 757
15 - 19	KGWP	1 898	1 987	1 564	1 961	2 356	1 871
20 - 24	KGWQ	1 737	1 958	1 648	2 132	2 067	2 093
25 - 29	KGWR	1 556	1 860	1 861	1 822	1 871	2 209
30 - 34	KGWS	1 349	1 636	1 725	1 652	2 065	2 040
35 - 39	KGWT	1 200	1 462	1 856	1 598	1 750	1 862
40 - 44	KGWU	1 048	1 397	1 881	1 659	1 586	2 050
45 - 49	KGWV	886	1 348	1 764	1 750	1 528	1 729
50 - 54	KGWW	747	1 274	1 495	1 591	1 556	1 535
55 - 59	KGWX	582	1 131	1 234	1 614	1 577	1 440
60 - 64	KGWY	490	894	1 061	1 497	1 342	1 391
65 - 69	KGWZ	332	663	885	1 196	1 234	1 294
70 - 74	KGXA	233	436	675	779	976	972
75 - 79	KGXB	133	237	428	461	608	715
80 - 84	KGXC	63	98	189	244	278	415
85 and over	KGXD	23	36	70	124	133	208

1 Figures included for Northern Ireland are estimated.
2 The figures for Northern Ireland have been revised using a new estimate of 44 500 non-enumerated persons in the 1981 Census.
3 1981 and 1991 data cover the 'resident' population. The 1991 figures include the population resident in absent households not included in 1981.

Sources: Office of Population Censuses and Surveys;
General Register Office (Northern Ireland);
General Register Office (Scotland)

Population

2.3 Age distribution of the enumerated population: census figures
United Kingdom
continued

Thousands

		1901	1931[1]	1951	1971	1981[2,3]	1991[3]
Females: all ages	KGYA	19 745	23 978	26 107	28 562	28 286	29 123
Under 5	KGYB	2 190	1 747	2 111	2 194	1 632	1 837
Under 16	KGYC	..	..	5 864	6 893	6 032	5 577
Under 18	KGYD	..	..	6 495	7 641	6 954	6 273
5 - 14	KGYE	4 016	3 784	3 433	4 321	3 946	3 411
15 - 29	KGYF	5 618	6 049	5 255	5 764	6 115	6 211
30 - 44	KGYG	3 895	5 222	5 663	4 850	5 359	6 021
45 - 64	KGYH	3 001	5 229	6 425	6 931	6 293	6 247
65 - 74	KGYI	713	1 361	2 128	2 737	2 839	2 796
75 and over	KGYJ	312	586	1 091	1 765	2 102	2 599
Pensionable age aggregate	KFIC	1 601	2 950	4 580	6 211	6 451	6 897
Under 1	KGYK	466	351	376	434	349	374
1 and under 2	KGYL	428	347	393	428	348	370
2 - 4	KGYM	1 296	1 050	1 342	1 332	936	1 092
5 - 9	KGYN	2 054	1 930	1 804	2 274	1 793	1 741
10 - 14	KGYO	1 962	1 854	1 629	2 047	2 154	1 670
15 - 19	KGYP	1 928	2 002	1 611	1 872	2 255	1 752
20 - 24	KGYQ	1 938	2 066	1 744	2 105	2 014	2 139
25 - 29	KGYR	1 752	1 981	1 900	1 788	1 846	2 277
30 - 34	KGYS	1 484	1 858	1 790	1 607	2 049	2 072
35 - 39	KGYT	1 294	1 733	1 930	1 572	1 735	1 884
40 - 44	KGYU	1 117	1 631	1 943	1 672	1 575	2 067
45 - 49	KGYV	951	1 553	1 839	1 794	1 523	1 732
50 - 54	KGYW	819	1 439	1 714	1 683	1 594	1 543
55 - 59	KGYX	654	1 234	1 512	1 746	1 665	1 470
60 - 64	KGYY	577	1 003	1 361	1 709	1 510	1 502
65 - 69	KGYZ	411	792	1 183	1 511	1 497	1 509
70 - 74	KGZA	302	569	944	1 226	1 342	1 288
75 - 79	KGZB	180	344	620	870	1 028	1 134
80 - 84	KGZC	94	165	317	546	642	825
85 and over	KGZD	38	77	154	349	432	639

1 Figures included for Northern Ireland are estimated.
2 The figures for Northern Ireland have been revised using a new estimate of 44 500 non-enumerated persons in the 1981 Census.
3 1981 and 1991 data covers the 'resident' population. The 1991 figures include the population resident in absent households not included in 1981.

Sources: Office of Population Censuses and Surveys;
General Register Office (Northern Ireland);
General Register Office (Scotland)

Population

2.4 Age distribution of the enumerated population[1]: census figures
Constituent countries

Thousands

		England and Wales					Scotland					Northern Ireland			
		1961	1971	1981[1]	1991[1]		1961	1971	1981[1]	1991[1]		1961	1971	1981[1,2]	1991[1]
Persons: all ages	KFIR	46 105	48 750	48 522	49 890	KFIS	5 179.3	5 229.0	5 035.3	4 998.6	KFIT	1 425.0	1 536.1	1 532.2	1 577.8
Under 5	KIDF	3 597	3 905	2 910	3 316	KIJA	469.2	444.3	308.4	317.2	KFIU	146.5	156.2	130.8	128.3
Under 16	KIDG	11 233	12 246	10 773	10 013	KIJB	1 413.9	1 438.1	1 167.0	1 010.3	KFIV	437.0	483.9	443.3	409.9
Under 18	KIDH	12 576	13 574	12 418	11 263	KIJC	1 567.5	1 596.7	1 350.8	1 139.8	KFIW	487.5	534.9	502.9	460.6
5 - 14	KIDI	6 987	7 671	7 053	6 110	KIJD	869.9	910.5	769.6	629.5	KFIX	265.6	300.8	283.1	257.0
15 - 29	KIDJ	8 925	10 236	10 859	10 908	KIJE	1 034.1	1 099.2	1 183.1	1 099.2	KFIY	299.2	343.2	366.9	375.9
30 - 44	KIDK	9 263	8 593	9 541	10 593	KIJF	1 000.3	912.7	947.2	1 069.9	KFIZ	262.5	253.4	272.4	310.7
45 - 64	KIDL	11 836	11 849	10 884	10 919	KIJG	1 256.9	1 217.9	1 116.3	1 115.4	KFPK	307.3	316.5	295.2	306.9
65 - 74	KIDM	3 520	4 178	4 488	4 505	KIJH	358.4	426.5	443.4	440.3	KFPL	92.3	108.2	116.2	117.1
75 and over	KIDN	1 976	2 318	2 786	3 539	KIJI	190.5	217.9	266.5	326.7	KFPM	51.6	57.8	67.8	82.0
Pensionable age aggregate	KIDO	6 858	8 007	8 611	9 367	KIJJ	695.3	803.7	847.6	908.5	KFPN	180.1	204.9	220.6	236.4
Under 1	KIFE	764	774	619	677	KIJK	97.8	86.0	66.1	63.9	KFPO	30.8	31.1	27.1	24.7
1 and under 2	KIFF	725	761	622	671	KIJL	94.3	86.4	65.0	62.4	KFPP	29.8	30.9	27.4	25.2
2 - 4	KIFG	2 107	2 370	1 669	1 968	KIJM	277.1	271.9	177.3	190.8	KFWA	86.0	94.2	76.2	78.3
5 - 9	KIFH	3 262	4 044	3 207	3 123	KIJN	420.7	468.4	344.4	317.6	KFWB	132.4	157.1	134.3	129.1
10 - 14	KIFI	3 725	3 627	3 846	2 988	KIJO	449.1	442.1	425.2	311.9	KFWC	133.2	143.7	148.8	127.8
15 - 19	KIFJ	3 201	3 314	4 020	3 205	KIHF	374.1	392.3	446.6	332.1	KFWD	120.2	126.4	144.5	127.5
20 - 24	KIFK	2 878	3 731	3 564	3 731	KIHG	333.0	390.4	394.3	374.5	KFWE	93.8	114.9	122.3	126.1
25 - 29	KIFL	2 846	3 191	3 275	3 971	KIHH	327.0	316.4	342.2	392.6	KFWF	85.2	101.9	99.9	122.2
30 - 34	KIFM	2 984	2 871	3 656	3 623	KIHI	332.5	300.6	358.7	375.2	KFWG	86.5	86.7	98.7	113.4
35 - 39	KIFN	3 242	2 786	3 092	3 308	KIHJ	347.3	300.8	300.3	337.9	KFWH	90.9	82.4	92.5	99.3
40 - 44	KIFO	3 037	2 935	2 792	3 662	KIHK	320.5	311.3	288.1	356.7	KFWI	85.1	84.3	81.2	97.9
45 - 49	KFII	3 229	3 135	2 689	3 074	KIHL	342.6	322.8	285.7	297.4	KFWJ	87.0	86.0	76.1	89.9
50 - 54	KFIJ	3 221	2 897	2 785	3 720	KIHM	342.2	295.8	289.6	280.8	KFWK	82.0	80.0	76.0	76.5
55 - 59	KFIK	2 928	2 976	2 877	2 567	KIHN	312.5	306.3	289.8	272.0	KFWL	72.5	78.5	75.1	71.0
60 - 64	KFIL	2 458	2 841	2 533	2 559	KIHO	259.5	293.0	251.3	265.0	KFWM	65.7	72.0	68.0	69.3
65 - 69	KFIM	1 979	2 400	2 426	2 491	KFID	204.6	247.2	240.8	246.8	KFWN	52.2	60.3	63.4	64.9
70 - 74	KFIN	1 542	1 778	2 062	2 014	KFIE	153.9	179.3	203.5	193.4	KFWO	40.1	47.9	52.8	52.1
75 - 79	KFIO	1 069	1 185	1 458	1 663	KFIF	105.4	115.2	142.5	156.0	KFWP	27.0	29.9	34.6	40.2
80 - 84	KFIP	605	707	821	1 113	KFIG	57.9	65.6	78.3	102.7	KFWQ	16.2	17.5	20.5	25.0
85 and over	KFIQ	302	425	507	763	KFIH	27.2	37.2	45.6	67.9	KFWR	8.4	10.4	12.7	16.6
Males: all ages	KICA	22 304	23 683	23 625	24 183	KIGA	2 482.7	2 514.6	2 428.5	2 392.0	KFWS	694.2	754.7	749.5	769.1
Under 5	KICB	1 846	2 003	1 492	1 696	KIGB	240.1	228.5	158.3	162.4	KFWT	75.4	80.3	66.8	65.9
Under 16	KICC	5 756	6 288	5 526	5 129	KIGC	723.5	737.9	598.3	517.6	KFWU	224.4	249.0	227.6	209.9
Under 18	KICD	6 440	6 971	6 368	5 770	KIGD	800.7	818.7	691.9	583.8	KFWV	249.8	275.2	258.3	236.0
5 - 14	KICE	3 578	3 940	3 619	3 132	KIGE	445.2	466.7	394.5	322.5	KFWW	136.2	154.9	145.6	131.3
15 - 29	KICF	4 502	5 184	5 506	5 438	KIGF	507.8	554.4	599.7	543.4	KFWX	148.8	176.0	187.9	190.1
30 - 44	KICG	4 612	4 337	4 794	5 270	KIGG	486.5	446.9	471.2	527.8	KFWY	127.1	124.9	135.8	154.2
45 - 64	KICH	5 663	5 728	5 331	5 409	KIGH	588.6	573.5	531.9	537.4	KFWZ	145.5	151.2	140.3	148.2
65 - 74	KICI	1 419	1 755	1 971	2 023	KIGI	143.7	174.5	188.9	191.4	KFXA	40.0	45.9	50.0	51.5
75 and over	KICJ	684	737	912	1 215	KIGJ	71.0	70.3	83.9	106.6	KFXB	21.3	21.4	23.0	27.8
Pensionable age aggregate	KICK	2 102	2 492	2 882	3 238	KIGK	214.6	244.8	272.8	298.1	KFXC	61.3	67.4	73.0	79.3
Under 1	KICL	393	397	317	346	KIGL	49.9	44.2	33.8	32.7	KFXD	15.9	15.9	13.8	12.7
1 and under 2	KICM	372	390	319	343	KIGM	48.4	44.5	33.4	31.8	KFXE	15.4	15.9	14.1	13.0
2 - 4	KICN	1 080	1 215	857	1 006	KIGN	141.8	139.8	91.0	98.0	KFXF	44.1	48.5	38.9	40.2
5 - 9	KICO	1 671	2 074	1 647	1 600	KIGO	215.1	240.1	176.3	162.5	KFXG	68.1	81.1	69.3	66.2
10 - 14	KICP	1 907	1 865	1 972	1 532	KIGP	230.1	226.5	218.2	160.0	KFXH	68.1	73.7	76.4	65.1
15 - 19	KICQ	1 622	1 696	2 054	1 636	KIGQ	187.4	199.4	227.8	168.7	KFXI	60.3	65.1	74.4	65.7
20 - 24	KICR	1 434	1 876	1 805	1 845	KIGR	159.4	196.6	199.8	184.4	KFXJ	46.9	59.3	62.5	63.8
25 - 29	KICS	1 446	1 612	1 648	1 958	KIGS	161.0	158.3	172.2	190.3	KFXK	41.6	51.6	51.0	60.4
30 - 34	KICT	1 502	1 460	1 835	1 801	KIGT	162.8	148.1	180.5	183.3	KFXL	41.6	43.5	49.7	55.7
35 - 39	KICU	1 616	1 410	1 554	1 646	KIGU	170.5	147.4	149.5	167.0	KFXM	43.9	40.7	46.1	49.7
40 - 44	KICV	1 494	1 467	1 405	1 824	KIGV	153.2	151.4	141.3	177.3	KFXN	41.6	40.7	40.0	48.6
45 - 49	KICW	1 584	1 552	1 351	1 537	KIGW	163.9	157.0	139.5	146.9	KFXO	42.1	41.7	37.1	44.5
50 - 54	KICX	1 575	1 412	1 381	1 361	KIGX	164.3	139.6	139.6	136.3	KFXP	39.6	39.1	36.3	37.5
55 - 59	KICY	1 408	1 434	1 403	1 275	KIGY	147.3	143.2	138.4	130.4	KFXQ	34.4	37.7	35.5	34.1
60 - 64	KICZ	1 096	1 330	1 196	1 236	KIGZ	113.2	133.7	114.4	123.7	KFXR	29.4	33.1	31.4	31.9
65 - 69	KIDA	819	1 063	1 100	1 153	KIHA	83.4	106.6	105.7	111.3	KFXS	23.0	26.4	28.2	29.2
70 - 74	KIDB	600	692	871	870	KIHB	60.2	67.9	83.2	80.0	KFXT	17.0	19.5	21.8	22.2
75 - 79	KIDC	389	410	544	651	KIHC	40.2	39.4	50.9	58.4	KFXU	11.3	11.6	12.8	15.4
80 - 84	KIDD	205	217	248	375	KIHD	21.7	20.5	22.5	32.6	KFXV	6.7	6.4	6.7	8.2
85 and over	KIDE	90	110	119	189	KIHE	9.0	10.4	10.5	15.5	KFXW	3.2	3.5	3.5	4.0

See footnotes on page 9.

Sources: Office of Population Censuses and Surveys;
General Register Office (Northern Ireland);
General Register Office (Scotland)

2.4 Age distribution of the enumerated population[1]: census figures
Constituent countries continued

Population

Thousands

		England and Wales					Scotland					Northern Ireland			
		1961	1971	1981[1]	1991[1]		1961	1971	1981[1]	1991[1]		1961	1971	1981[1,2]	1991[1]
Females: all ages	KIEA	23 801	25 067	24 897	25 707	KIIA	2 696.6	2 714.3	2 606.8	2 607.0	KFXX	730.8	781.4	782.7	808.8
Under 5	KIEB	1 751	1 902	1 418	1 620	KIIB	229.1	215.8	150.1	154.7	KFXY	71.2	75.9	64.0	62.3
Under 16	KIEC	5 477	5 958	5 248	4 884	KIIC	690.5	700.2	568.6	492.6	KFXZ	212.6	234.8	215.7	200.0
Under 18	KIED	6 136	6 603	6 050	5 493	KIID	766.9	778.0	658.9	556.0	KHMI	237.8	259.7	244.6	224.6
5 - 14	KIEE	3 410	3 732	3 434	2 979	KIIE	424.8	443.8	375.1	307.0	KHMJ	129.4	145.9	137.5	125.7
15 - 29	KIEF	4 423	5 052	5 353	5 469	KIIF	526.4	544.8	583.4	555.7	KHMK	150.4	167.2	178.8	185.8
30 - 44	KIEG	4 651	4 256	4 747	5 323	KIIG	513.8	465.7	475.9	542.1	KHML	135.4	128.5	136.6	156.5
45 - 64	KIEH	6 172	6 122	5 554	5 510	KIIH	668.3	644.4	584.4	577.9	KHMM	161.9	165.3	154.9	158.7
65 - 74	KIEI	2 102	2 423	2 517	2 482	KIII	214.8	252.0	255.4	248.9	KHMN	52.3	62.2	66.2	65.6
75 and over	KIEJ	1 292	1 581	1 875	2 325	KIIJ	119.5	147.7	182.5	220.0	KHMO	30.3	36.4	44.8	54.2
Pensionable age aggregate	KERZ	4 756	5 515	5 729	6 130	KETV	480.7	559.0	574.8	610.4	KETW	118.9	137.5	147.5	157.1
Under 1	KIEK	371	377	303	331	KIIK	47.9	41.8	32.3	31.2	KLGY	14.9	15.1	13.4	12.0
1 and under 2	KIEL	353	371	303	328	KIIL	45.9	41.9	31.6	30.5	KLGZ	14.4	15.0	13.3	12.2
2 - 4	KIEM	1 027	1 154	812	962	KIIM	153.3	132.1	86.2	93.0	KLHY	41.9	45.8	37.3	38.1
5 - 9	KIEN	1 592	1 970	1 560	1 523	KIIN	205.7	228.3	168.1	155.1	KLHZ	64.3	76.0	65.0	62.9
10 - 14	KIEO	1 818	1 762	1 875	1 456	KIIO	219.1	215.5	207.0	151.8	KLIA	65.0	69.9	72.4	62.7
15 - 19	KIEP	1 579	1 618	1 966	1 569	KIIP	186.7	192.9	218.8	163.4	KLIB	60.0	61.2	70.1	61.8
20 - 24	KIEQ	1 444	1 855	1 760	1 887	KIIQ	173.3	193.8	194.6	190.1	KLIC	46.9	55.6	59.8	62.2
25 - 29	KIER	1 400	1 579	1 627	2 013	KIIR	166.0	158.1	170.0	202.2	KLID	43.6	50.3	48.9	61.7
30 - 34	KIES	1 483	1 411	1 822	1 822	KIIS	169.7	152.4	178.3	191.8	KLIE	44.9	43.2	49.0	57.6
35 - 39	KIET	1 626	1 376	1 538	1 663	KIIT	176.9	153.4	150.8	170.8	KLIF	47.0	41.7	46.4	49.5
40 - 44	KIEU	1 543	1 468	1 387	1 838	KIIU	167.2	159.9	146.9	179.3	KLIG	43.4	43.6	41.2	49.3
45 - 49	KIEV	1 645	1 584	1 338	1 536	KIIV	178.8	165.8	146.2	150.4	KLIH	44.9	44.4	39.0	45.4
50 - 54	KIEW	1 646	1 485	1 404	1 359	KIIW	177.9	156.2	150.1	144.5	KLII	42.5	41.0	39.7	39.0
55 - 59	KIEX	1 520	1 542	1 474	1 292	KIIX	165.2	163.1	151.3	141.5	KLIJ	38.2	41.1	39.6	36.8
60 - 64	KIEY	1 362	1 511	1 337	1 323	KIIY	146.4	159.3	136.8	141.3	KLIK	36.3	39.0	36.6	37.3
65 - 69	KIEZ	1 160	1 336	1 326	1 338	KIIZ	121.1	140.6	135.1	135.4	KLIL	29.2	33.8	35.2	35.7
70 - 74	KIFA	942	1 086	1 191	1 144	KLIQ	93.7	111.4	120.3	113.4	KLIM	23.1	28.4	31.0	29.8
75 - 79	KIFB	680	776	914	1 012	KLIR	65.2	75.8	91.6	97.5	KLIN	15.7	18.3	21.8	24.8
80 - 84	KIFC	401	490	573	739	KLIS	36.2	45.1	55.8	70.0	KLIO	9.4	11.1	13.8	16.7
85 and over	KIFD	212	315	388	574	KLIT	18.2	26.8	35.1	52.4	KLIP	5.2	6.9	9.2	12.5

1 1981 and 1991 data cover the 'resident' population. The 1991 figures include the population resident in absent households not included in 1981.
2 The figures for Northern Ireland have been revised using a new estimate of 44 500 non-enumerated persons in the 1981 census.

Sources: Office of Population Censuses and Surveys;
General Register Office (Northern Ireland);
General Register Office (Scotland)

Population

2.5 Age distribution of the resident population: mid-year estimates and projections
United Kingdom

Thousands

		Estimates						Projections[1]				
		1971	1976	1981	1986	1991[2]		1996	2001	2011	2021	2031
Persons all ages	KLIU	55 928	56 216	56 352	56 763	57 649	KOAY	58 413	59 174	60 033	60 743	61 068
0 - 4	KLIV	4 553	3 721	3 455	3 642	3 882	KOAZ	4 019	3 927	3 605	3 783	3 732
5 - 9	KLIW	4 684	4 483	3 677	3 467	3 670	KOBA	3 879	4 020	3 712	3 679	3 803
10 - 14	KLIX	4 232	4 693	4 470	3 690	3 498	KOBB	3 677	3 888	3 938	3 617	3 789
15 - 19	KLIY	3 862	4 244	4 735	4 479	3 727	KOBC	3 517	3 703	4 056	3 748	3 699
20 - 24	KLIZ	4 282	3 881	4 284	4 784	4 484	KOBD	3 752	3 547	3 944	3 995	3 667
25 - 29	KLJA	3 686	4 239	3 828	4 237	4 740	KOBE	4 457	3 711	3 693	4 045	3 756
30 - 34	KLJB	3 284	3 629	4 182	3 787	4 225	KOBF	4 698	4 414	3 467	3 863	3 923
35 - 39	KLJC	3 187	3 225	3 589	4 158	3 790	KOBG	4 182	4 666	3 646	3 629	3 981
40 - 44	KLJW	3 325	3 136	3 185	3 561	4 142	KOBH	3 750	4 150	4 358	3 422	3 817
45 - 49	KLJX	3 532	3 262	3 090	3 142	3 519	KOBI	4 088	3 706	4 579	3 584	3 574
50 - 54	KLJY	3 304	3 423	3 179	3 023	3 074	KOBJ	3 462	4 016	4 028	4 239	3 338
55 - 59	KLJZ	3 365	3 151	3 271	3 055	2 920	KOBK	2 991	3 363	3 536	4 378	3 435
60 - 64	KLYG	3 222	3 131	2 935	3 055	2 894	KOBL	2 765	2 838	3 706	3 732	3 939
65 - 69	KLYH	2 736	2 851	2 801	2 641	2 793	KOBM	2 618	2 531	2 944	3 107	3 866
70 - 74	KLYI	2 029	2 260	2 393	2 364	2 282	KOBN	2 381	2 279	2 292	3 014	3 062
75 - 79	KLYJ	1 356	1 499	1 708	1 837	1 864	KOBO	1 818	1 925	1 821	2 152	2 287
80 - 84	KLYK	803	849	968	1 132	1 248	KOBP	1 306	1 319	1 372	1 407	1 864
85 and over	KLYL	485	538	602	709	897	KOBQ	1 054	1 171	1 337	1 351	1 538
Males all ages	KLYM	27 167	27 360	27 409	27 647	28 132	KOBR	28 604	29 069	29 630	30 049	30 213
0 - 4	KLYN	2 336	1 912	1 772	1 867	1 992	KOBS	2 059	2 012	1 847	1 938	1 911
5 - 9	KLYO	2 401	2 302	1 889	1 780	1 885	KOBT	1 990	2 063	1 905	1 889	1 951
10 - 14	KLYP	2 175	2 409	2 295	1 897	1 798	KOBU	1 889	1 998	2 024	1 860	1 947
15 - 19	KLYQ	1 976	2 167	2 424	2 296	1 913	KOBV	1 810	1 906	2 088	1 931	1 904
20 - 24	KLYR	2 161	1 979	2 172	2 431	2 282	KOBW	1 923	1 821	2 025	2 051	1 886
25 - 29	KMCX	1 863	2 144	1 931	2 138	2 396	KOBX	2 261	1 893	1 887	2 067	1 923
30 - 34	KMCY	1 667	1 837	2 104	1 907	2 120	KOBY	2 368	2 232	1 765	1 968	2 001
35 - 39	KMCZ	1 612	1 632	1 807	2 081	1 896	KOBZ	2 099	2 347	1 850	1 884	2 026
40 - 44	KMDA	1 659	1 582	1 602	1 791	2 070	KOCA	1 875	2 077	2 196	1 735	1 938
45 - 49	KMDB	1 747	1 623	1 549	1 574	1 758	KOCB	2 037	1 847	2 291	1 811	1 810
50 - 54	KMDC	1 607	1 684	1 572	1 506	1 533	KOCC	1 727	1 991	2 000	2 122	1 683
55 - 59	KMDD	1 616	1 513	1 590	1 496	1 445	KOCD	1 479	1 667	1 742	2 169	1 720
60 - 64	KMDE	1 507	1 466	1 376	1 458	1 393	KOCE	1 349	1 387	1 804	1 823	1 941
65 - 69	KOAA	1 209	1 276	1 261	1 198	1 291	KOCF	1 230	1 207	1 413	1 485	1 859
70 - 74	KOAB	790	927	1 003	1 002	983	KOCG	1 055	1 030	1 059	1 391	1 422
75 - 79	KOAC	468	522	630	698	727	KOCH	730	799	791	948	1 006
80 - 84	KOAD	248	253	290	362	419	KOCI	449	476	532	565	751
85 and over	KOAE	126	133	141	166	230	KOCJ	272	317	410	452	536
Females all ages	KOAF	28 761	28 856	28 943	29 116	29 517	KOCK	29 809	30 105	30 403	30 694	30 855
0 - 4	KOAG	2 217	1 808	1 682	1 775	1 891	KOCL	1 960	1 915	1 758	1 845	1 821
5 - 9	KOAH	2 283	2 181	1 788	1 687	1 785	KOCM	1 889	1 957	1 806	1 791	1 852
10 - 14	KOAI	2 057	2 284	2 175	1 793	1 701	KODA	1 788	1 890	1 914	1 757	1 843
15 - 19	KOAJ	1 887	2 078	2 311	2 183	1 814	KODB	1 707	1 797	1 968	1 818	1 795
20 - 24	KOAK	2 121	1 903	2 112	2 353	2 202	KODC	1 829	1 726	1 919	1 943	1 780
25 - 29	KOAL	1 824	2 095	1 897	2 099	2 344	KODD	2 196	1 818	1 806	1 977	1 833
30 - 34	KOAM	1 617	1 792	2 078	1 881	2 105	KODE	2 329	2 181	1 702	1 894	1 922
35 - 39	KOAN	1 575	1 593	1 782	2 077	1 894	KODF	2 082	2 319	1 796	1 784	1 955
40 - 44	KOAO	1 667	1 554	1 583	1 770	2 072	KODG	1 874	2 072	2 162	1 687	1 879
45 - 49	KOAP	1 785	1 639	1 541	1 569	1 761	KODH	2 051	1 859	2 288	1 773	1 764
50 - 54	KOAQ	1 697	1 739	1 608	1 516	1 541	KODI	1 735	2 024	2 028	2 117	1 655
55 - 59	KOAR	1 749	1 638	1 681	1 559	1 475	KOEA	1 512	1 696	1 794	2 209	1 715
60 - 64	KOAS	1 715	1 665	1 559	1 598	1 501	KOEB	1 416	1 451	1 902	1 909	1 998
65 - 69	KOAT	1 527	1 575	1 540	1 443	1 503	KOEC	1 388	1 324	1 531	1 622	2 007
70 - 74	KOAU	1 238	1 333	1 390	1 361	1 299	KOED	1 325	1 250	1 232	1 623	1 639
75 - 79	KOAV	888	977	1 078	1 138	1 136	KOEE	1 088	1 127	1 030	1 204	1 281
80 - 84	KOAW	555	597	677	770	829	KOEF	857	843	840	841	1 113
85 and over	KOAX	359	405	461	543	667	KOEG	782	853	927	899	1 002

1 These 1989-based projections are made as described in the introductory note on page 3.
2 The population estimates for mid-1991 are provisional. They are based on early 1991 Census results, and are therefore not comparable with estimates for 1986 which were based on the 1981 Census and will be revised in due course.

Sources: Office of Population Censuses and Surveys;
General Register Office (Northern Ireland);
General Register Office (Scotland);
Government Actuary's Department

Population

2.5 Age distribution of the resident population: mid-year estimates and projections
United Kingdom
continued

Thousands

		Estimates						Projections[1]			
Age		1971	1976	1981	1986	1991[2]		1996	2001	2011	2021	2031
England and Wales												
Persons all ages	KOEH	49 152	49 459	49 634	50 075	50 955	KOLE	51 752	52 526	53 510	54 411	54 977
0 - 4	KOEI	3 951	3 226	3 006	3 183	3 427	KOLF	3 561	3 488	3 219	3 406	3 379
5 - 9	KOFA	4 056	3 895	3 196	3 025	3 219	KOLG	3 429	3 567	3 312	3 204	3 439
10 - 14	KOFB	3 649	4 071	3 889	3 214	3 057	KOLH	3 229	3 443	3 508	3 240	3 420
15 - 19	KOFC	3 344	3 681	4 130	3 911	3 260	KOLI	3 083	3 261	3 612	3 357	3 330
20 - 24	KOFD	3 773	3 395	3 744	4 203	3 943	KONA	3 301	3 131	3 521	3 587	3 304
25 - 29	KOFE	3 267	3 758	3 372	3 724	4 200	KONB	3 941	3 288	3 296	3 646	3 400
30 - 34	KOFF	2 897	3 220	3 715	3 341	3 723	KONC	4 176	3 915	3 095	3 484	3 554
35 - 39	KOFG	2 804	2 845	3 185	3 700	3 347	KOND	3 698	4 154	3 249	3 257	3 606
40 - 44	KOFH	2 932	2 763	2 811	3 163	3 686	KONE	3 320	3 673	3 876	3 065	3 452
45 - 49	KOFI	3 126	2 879	2 723	2 776	3 128	KONF	3 645	3 284	4 083	3 200	3 213
50 - 54	KOGA	2 925	3 034	2 809	2 667	2 717	KONG	3 081	3 583	3 570	3 775	2 994
55 - 59	KOGB	2 982	2 795	2 901	2 703	2 576	KONH	2 647	2 995	3 137	3 908	3 070
60 - 64 Males	KOGC	1 337	1 304	1 227	1 299	1 237	KONI	1 197	1 233	1 614	1 621	1 732
60 - 64 Females	KOGD	1 516	1 473	1 380	1 415	1 322	KOOA	1 245	1 280	1 697	1 692	1 781
65 - 69	KOGE	2 428	2 530	2 490	2 351	2 482	KOOB	2 322	2 239	2 627	2 762	3 459
70 - 74	KOGF	1 801	2 010	2 129	2 107	2 034	KOOC	2 123	2 026	2 036	2 701	2 727
75 - 79	KOGG	1 208	1 334	1 524	1 640	1 667	KOOD	1 628	1 722	1 620	1 930	2 042
80 - 84	KOGH	718	759	865	1 015	1 119	KOOE	1 173	1 186	1 228	1 258	1 681
85 and over	KOGI	438	486	541	639	812	KOOF	953	1 059	1 210	1 217	1 392
Scotland												
Persons all ages	KOHA	5 236	5 233	5 180	5 121	5 100	KOOG	5 051	5 026	4 900	4 727	4 524
0 - 4	KOHB	443	357	318	325	326	KOOH	328	318	276	272	258
5 - 9	KOHC	469	438	348	313	321	KOOI	319	325	289	269	265
10 - 14	KOHD	444	466	433	344	313	KOPA	317	317	313	271	268
15 - 19	KOHE	393	432	459	424	339	KOPB	308	314	321	285	266
20 - 24	KOHF	388	374	415	446	410	KOPC	331	298	305	302	264
25 - 29	KOHG	318	378	355	396	416	KOPD	389	312	286	293	264
30 - 34	KOHH	300	315	368	346	388	KOPE	401	375	267	273	274
35 - 39	KOHI	301	296	310	361	343	KOPF	374	393	292	266	275
40 - 44	KOIA	311	295	293	306	358	KOPG	334	368	363	256	263
45 - 49	KOIB	322	304	291	287	300	KOPH	351	328	382	283	259
50 - 54	KOIC	298	311	295	282	280	KOPI	294	343	355	351	248
55 - 59	KOID	306	282	295	280	272	KOQA	271	285	311	362	269
60 - 64 Males	KOIE	134	128	118	126	124	KOQB	120	121	151	158	158
60 - 64 Females	KOIF	160	154	142	145	141	KOQC	136	135	163	168	165
65 - 69	KOIG	249	258	248	230	246	KOQD	236	232	246	270	315
70 - 74	KOIH	181	202	211	204	195	KOQE	206	202	202	249	260
75 - 79	KOII	116	131	149	157	156	KOQF	151	162	160	173	191
80 - 84	KOJA	66	71	83	95	103	KOQG	106	106	115	118	146
85 and over	KOJB	38	42	49	57	69	KOQH	82	90	103	108	116
Northern Ireland												
Persons all ages	KOJC	1 540	1 524	1 538	1 567	1 594	KOQI	1 610	1 622	1 623	1 605	1 567
0 - 4	KOJD	158	137	131	136	130	KQEA	130	121	110	105	95
5 - 9	KOJE	160	150	133	130	130	KQEB	131	127	111	106	98
10 - 14	KOJF	139	156	148	132	129	KQEC	131	128	116	105	101
15 - 19	KOJG	126	131	146	144	129	KQED	126	129	123	107	102
20 - 24	KOJH	121	112	125	136	130	KQEE	120	117	118	106	99
25 - 29	KOJI	102	103	101	117	124	KQEF	127	111	111	105	92
30 - 34	KOKA	88	94	99	100	115	KQEG	121	123	105	105	94
35 - 39	KOKB	82	84	94	97	100	KQEH	110	119	105	105	100
40 - 44	KOKC	83	79	81	92	98	KQEI	96	108	119	100	101
45 - 49	KOKD	84	79	76	79	91	KQEJ	92	94	114	101	101
50 - 54	KOKE	81	78	76	74	77	KQEK	87	90	103	113	96
55 - 59	KOKF	78	74	75	72	72	KQEL	74	84	87	107	95
60 - 64 Males	KOKG	36	34	32	32	32	KQEM	31	33	39	45	51
60 - 64 Females	KOKH	39	38	37	37	38	KQEN	35	36	42	49	52
65 - 69	KOKI	59	63	63	60	65	KQHV	60	60	72	75	92
70 - 74	KOLA	47	48	53	52	53	KQHW	52	51	54	64	74
75 - 79	KOLB	32	33	35	40	41	KQYY	40	41	41	50	53
80 - 84	KOLC	18	19	21	22	26	KRPG	27	28	29	31	37
85 and over	KOLD	17	10	13	14	17	KRPH	19	21	24	26	30

1 These 1989-based projections are made as described in the introductory note on page 3.
2 The population estimates for mid-1991 are provisional. They are based on early 1991 Census results, and are therefore not comparable with estimates for 1986 which were based on the 1981 Census and will be revised in due course.

Sources: Office of Population Censuses and Surveys; General Register Office (Northern Ireland); General Register Office (Scotland); Government Actuary's Department

Population

2.6 Marital condition: census figures

Thousands

			United Kingdom								England and Wales				
			Males				Females				Males			Females	
			1971	1981[1]	1991[1]		1971	1981[1]	1991[1]		1971	1981[1]	1991[1]	1971	1981[1]	1991[1]

All ages:																
	Single	KQCA	12 014	11 860	12 306	KQDP	11 055	10 585	11 047	KRPL	10 399	10 363	10 827	KUBS	9 513	9 199	9 677
	Married	KQCB	13 976	13 563	13 071	KQDQ	14 050	13 630	13 209	KRPM	12 433	12 042	11 585	KVCC	12 488	12 093	11 691
	Widowed	KQCC	762	749	818	KQDR	3 139	3 182	3 306	KRPN	666	657	720	KVCD	2 773	2 808	2 918
	Divorced	KQCD	200	606	1 149	KQDS	318	863	1 560	KRPO	185	563	1 051	KVCE	293	797	1 421
Age groups:																
0 - 14:	Single	KQCE	6 873	5 861	5 510	KQDT	6 515	5 564	5 248	KRPP	5 942	5 111	4 828	KVCF	5 633	4 852	4 599
15 - 19:	Single	KQCF	1 921	2 328	1 861	KQDU	1 713	2 152	1 763	KRPQ	1 661	2 031	1 628	KVCG	1 477	1 878	1 542
	Married	KQCG	40	26	9	KQDV	159	101	29	KRPR	35	22	8	KVCH	140	88	21
	Widowed	KQCH	–	–	–	KQDW	–	1	1	KRPS	–	–	–	KVCI	–	–	1
	Divorced	KQCI	–	–	1	KQDW	–	1	1	KRPT	–	–	–	KVCJ	–	1	1
20 - 24:	Single	KQCJ	1 350	1 536	1 844	KQDY	848	1 080	1 613	KRPU	1 186	1 350	1 629	KVCK	737	945	1 425
	Married	KQCK	779	517	238	KQDZ	1 244	896	493	KRPV	687	443	205	KVCL	1 107	782	431
	Widowed	KQCL	–	1	–	KQYZ	2	2	2	KRPW	–	1	–	KVCM	2	2	2
	Divorced	KQCM	3	12	11	KQZA	10	34	32	KRPK	3	11	49	KVCN	9	31	29
25 - 34:	Single	KQCN	703	973	1 748	KQZB	374	534	1 246	KRPY	617	866	1 567	KVCO	320	471	1 111
	Married	KQCO	2 727	2 802	2 286	KQZC	2 940	3 113	2 751	KRPZ	2 414	2 469	1 998	KVCP	2 597	2 753	2 408
	Widowed	KQCP	4	5	4	KQZD	14	15	14	KRQA	3	4	5	KVCQ	12	13	12
	Divorced	KQCQ	41	154	210	KQZE	67	230	337	KRQB	38	143	190	KVCR	61	212	304
35 - 44:	Single	KQCR	363	346	753	KQZF	247	195	326	KRQC	315	304	485	KVEH	206	167	286
	Married	KQCS	2 828	2 806	3 001	KQZG	2 868	2 836	3 109	KRQD	2 502	2 487	2 651	KVEI	2 525	2 505	2 749
	Widowed	KQCT	15	13	15	KQZH	57	48	48	KRQE	13	11	13	KVEJ	48	41	41
	Divorced	KQCU	51	169	352	KQZI	72	230	468	KRQF	47	157	322	KVEK	66	212	425
45 - 54:	Single	KQCV	325	288	289	KQZJ	298	200	170	KRQG	278	251	253	KVEL	248	167	145
	Married	KQCW	2 913	2 617	2 647	KQZK	2 885	2 577	2 616	KUAR	2 593	2 319	2 348	KVEM	2 565	2 276	2 312
	Widowed	KQCX	53	44	38	KQZL	218	176	135	KUBA	46	38	32	KVEN	187	149	118
	Divorced	KQCY	50	134	290	KQZM	75	164	351	KUBB	46	124	265	KVEO	69	151	321
55 - 59:	Single	KQCZ	140	148	118	KQZN	177	127	82	KUBC	118	128	102	KVEP	148	105	69
	Married	KQDA	1 397	1 326	1 180	KQZO	1 290	1 259	1 115	KUBD	1 248	1 184	1 045	KVEQ	1 151	1 124	983
	Widowed	KQDB	56	53	40	KQZP	246	214	156	KUBE	48	46	34	KVER	213	186	134
	Divorced	KQDC	21	50	102	KQZQ	33	65	117	KUBF	20	47	94	KVES	30	60	107
60 - 64:	Single	KQDD	125	115	121	KQZR	207	125	99	KUBG	105	98	105	KVET	173	104	82
	Married	KQDE	1 268	1 120	1 122	KQZS	1 095	1 018	1 027	KUBH	1 135	1 003	998	KVEU	982	911	912
	Widowed	KQDF	87	72	72	KQZT	380	316	284	KUBI	75	62	62	KVEV	330	274	245
	Divorced	KQDG	16	35	76	KQZU	27	51	92	KUBJ	15	33	70	KVEW	25	47	84
65 - 74:	Single	KQDH	158	183	178	KQZV	392	305	213	KUBK	130	154	152	KMGN	328	254	176
	Married	KQDI	1 550	1 732	1 751	KQZW	1 242	1 403	1 477	KUBL	1 391	1 558	1 572	KMGO	1 122	1 266	1 329
	Widowed	KQDJ	253	252	255	KQZX	1 075	1 062	993	KUBM	220	220	223	KMGP	948	934	871
	Divorced	KQDK	15	41	82	KQZY	27	67	114	KUBN	14	38	76	KMGQ	26	62	105
75 and over:	Single	KQDL	58	82	93	KQZZ	285	304	288	KUBO	47	69	78	KMGR	243	257	243
	Married	KQDM	474	616	837	KRPI	326	426	591	KUBP	428	558	760	KMGS	298	389	540
	Widowed	KQDN	294	310	394	KRPJ	1 148	1 348	1 671	KUBQ	259	276	352	KMGT	1 034	1 208	1 496
	Divorced	KQDO	3	10	25	KRPK	3	11	49	KUBR	2	9	24	KMGU	6	20	46

1 1981 and 1991 data cover the 'resident' population. The 1991 figures include the population resident in absent households not included in 1981. The 1971 data covers the enumerated population.

Sources: *Office of Population Censuses and Surveys;*
General Register Office (Northern Ireland);
General Register Office (Scotland)

2.6 Marital condition: census figures (continued)

Population

Thousands

			Scotland							Northern Ireland						
			Males				Females			Males				Females		
			1971	1981[1]	1991[1]		1971	1981[1]	1991[1]		1971	1981[1]	1991[1]		1971	1981[1]	1991[1]
All ages:	Single	KJPS	1 197.6	1 113.0	1 073.3	KJVG	1 153.8	1 034.2	2 606.6	KJWV	417.5	384.7	406.4	KJYK	388.5	352.3	368.3
	Married	KJPT	1 225.9	1 201.5	1 152.3	KJVH	1 241.8	1 211.3	1 173.4	KJWW	317.6	319.3	334.1	KJYL	320.4	318.1	344.8
	Widowed	KJPU	78.0	74.4	79.9	KJVI	295.2	301.5	309.4	KJWX	18.5	17.3	18.3	KJYM	70.4	73.0	78.4
	Divorced	KJPV	13.2	39.6	86.4	KJVJ	23.6	59.9	122.3	KJWY	1.1	3.9	11.3	KJYN	2.0	6.2	17.3

			Scotland							Northern Ireland						
			Males				Females			Males				Females		
			1961	1971	1981[1]		1961	1971	1981[1]		1961	1971	1981[1]		1961	1971	1981[1]
Age groups:																	
0 - 14:	Single	KJPW	685.3	695.1	552.8	KJVK	653.8	659.7	525.1	KJWZ	211.6	235.2	197.2	KJYO	200.6	221.8	187.1
15 - 19:	Single	KJPX	185.2	194.8	224.2	KJVL	175.9	177.6	207.8	KJXA	59.9	64.3	72.3	KJYP	58.0	58.2	66.1
	Married	KJPY	2.2	4.6	3.6	KJVM	10.8	15.2	10.9	KJXB	0.4	0.9	0.8	KJYQ	2.0	3.0	2.7
	Widowed	KJPZ	–	–	–	KJVN	–	–	–	KJXC	–	–	–	KJYR	–	–	–
	Divorced	KJQQ	–	–	–	KJVO	–	–	–	KJXD	–	–	–	KJYS	–	–	–
20 - 24:	Single	KJQR	112.2	121.2	140.2	KJVP	83.6	81.5	101.7	KJXE	37.0	42.3	45.9	KJYT	28.7	29.7	33.1
	Married	KJQS	47.1	75.0	58.3	KJVQ	89.6	111.2	89.8	KJXF	9.8	17.0	15.5	KJYU	18.1	25.9	24.8
	Widowed	KJQT	–	–	–	KJVR	0.2	0.2	0.3	KJXG	–	–	–	KJYV	–	–	–
	Divorced	KJQU	–	0.4	1.2	KJVS	0.2	1.0	2.7	KJXH	–	–	0.1	KJYW	–	–	0.2
25 - 34:	Single	KJQV	80.4	60.7	80.7	KJVT	56.0	37.0	47.4	KJXI	30.6	25.0	26.4	KJYX	22.9	16.2	15.7
	Married	KJQW	242.1	242.6	261.1	KJVU	276.1	266.8	282.8	KJXJ	52.4	69.8	71.4	KJYY	65.1	76.5	76.6
	Widowed	KJQX	0.5	0.4	0.6	KJVV	1.8	1.6	1.7	KJXK	0.1	0.1	0.1	KJYZ	0.4	0.4	0.6
	Divorced	KJQY	0.9	2.8	10.4	KJVW	1.8	5.2	16.5	KJXL	0.1	0.2	1.0	KJZA	0.1	0.4	1.6
35 - 44:	Single	KJQZ	46.4	34.9	30.9	KJVX	46.1	29.6	20.0	KJXM	18.7	13.5	10.9	KJZB	16.5	11.3	7.7
	Married	KJRW	273.2	259.0	247.4	KJVY	284.9	271.3	256.1	KJXN	66.1	67.2	71.9	KJZC	71.4	71.8	73.1
	Widowed	KJRX	2.3	1.6	1.6	KJVZ	8.9	6.8	5.6	KJXO	0.5	0.4	0.5	KJZD	2.2	1.7	1.9
	Divorced	KJRY	1.8	3.3	11.0	KJWA	4.3	5.6	16.0	KJXP	0.2	0.3	1.1	KJZE	0.4	0.5	1.7
45 - 54:	Single	KJRZ	40.2	33.7	27.7	KJWB	55.1	37.3	24.5	KJXQ	15.0	13.6	10.0	KJZF	17.2	13.2	8.9
	Married	KJTD	278.3	253.8	237.2	KJWC	268.1	254.4	239.6	KJXR	64.8	65.4	60.4	KJZG	62.9	65.3	60.6
	Widowed	KJTE	7.5	5.9	5.2	KJWD	29.7	24.6	20.5	KJXS	1.7	1.4	1.2	KJZH	7.0	6.2	5.7
	Divorced	KJTF	2.2	3.2	8.8	KJWE	3.8	5.7	11.6	KJXT	0.2	0.3	0.9	KJZI	0.3	0.6	1.2
55 - 59:	Single	KJTG	17.9	15.7	14.8	KJWF	31.8	22.0	16.3	KJXU	6.2	6.2	5.4	KJZJ	8.7	7.2	5.7
	Married	KJTH	121.4	119.9	114.6	KJWG	104.5	111.9	108.1	KJXV	26.5	29.6	28.8	KJZK	23.3	27.1	26.3
	Widowed	KJTI	7.2	6.4	5.9	KJWH	27.6	27.1	22.4	KJXW	1.5	1.5	1.4	KJZL	6.1	6.5	6.2
	Divorced	KJTJ	0.8	1.3	3.2	KJWI	1.4	2.2	4.5	KJXX	0.1	0.1	0.3	KJZM	0.1	0.2	0.5
60 - 64:	Single	KJTK	13.5	14.7	11.7	KJWJ	29.7	26.0	15.7	KJXY	5.3	5.6	4.9	KJZN	8.6	7.9	5.8
	Married	KJTL	89.6	108.2	92.9	KJWK	77.5	91.6	84.7	KJXZ	21.8	25.3	24.3	KJZO	18.5	21.4	20.8
	Widowed	KJTM	9.6	9.7	7.7	KJWL	38.3	39.9	33.2	KJYA	2.3	2.1	1.9	KJZP	9.1	9.4	8.6
	Divorced	KJTN	0.5	1.0	2.0	KJWM	1.0	1.8	3.3	KJYB	–	0.1	0.2	KJZQ	0.1	0.2	0.4
65 - 74:	Single	KJUY	16.4	19.5	20.6	KJWN	46.3	49.8	38.2	KJYC	7.7	8.2	7.9	KJZR	12.7	14.4	12.3
	Married	KJUZ	101.3	127.6	140.2	KJWO	79.2	97.4	109.9	KJYD	26.3	31.7	34.7	KJZS	19.0	23.4	25.8
	Widowed	KJVA	25.6	26.4	25.7	KJWP	88.4	103.2	103.4	KJYE	6.0	6.0	5.9	KJZT	20.6	24.2	24.8
	Divorced	KJVB	0.4	1.0	2.3	KJWQ	0.9	1.7	3.9	KJYF	–	0.1	0.3	KJZU	0.1	0.2	0.4
75 and over:	Single	KJVC	8.7	7.2	9.6	KJWR	27.5	33.3	37.5	KJYG	3.9	3.7	3.8	KJZV	7.4	8.6	9.9
	Married	KJVD	32.6	35.3	46.2	KJWS	18.5	22.2	29.4	KJYH	9.8	10.7	12.2	KJZW	4.7	5.9	7.8
	Widowed	KJVE	29.6	27.5	27.7	KJWT	73.3	91.8	114.4	KJYI	7.5	7.0	6.3	KJZX	18.3	21.9	25.1
	Divorced	KJVF	0.1	0.2	0.6	KJWU	0.2	0.4	1.2	KJYJ	–	–	–	KJZY	–	–	0.1

1 1981 and 1991 data cover the 'resident' population. The 1991 figures include the population resident in absent households not included in 1981. The 1961 and 1971 data cover the enumerated population.

Sources: General Register Office (Northern Ireland); General Register Office (Scotland)

Population

2.7 Marital condition of the resident population: mid-year estimates and projections [1]
Great Britain

Thousands

			Males						Females			
		1981	1985	1989	1990	2001		1981	1985	1989	1990	2001
All ages	KEYD	26 655	26 810	27 129	27 232	28 268	KEYE	28 160	28 250	28 524	28 589	29 284
Single	KKIT	11 762	11 964	12 242	12 335	13 213	KKJZ	10 490	10 554	10 716	10 771	11 310
Married	KKIU	13 465	13 154	12 944	12 890	12 261	KKLP	13 524	13 254	13 098	13 059	12 514
Widowed	KKIV	775	774	771	770	819	KKLQ	3 256	3 263	3 244	3 222	3 148
Divorced	KKIW	653	918	1 172	1 237	1 975	KKLR	890	1 178	1 466	1 537	2 312
Age groups:												
0 - 14: Single	KKIX	5 744	5 389	5 350	5 397	5 879	KKLS	5 445	5 109	5 080	5 127	5 579
15 - 19: Single	KEWV	2 325	2 240	2 011	1 933	1 831	KEXT	2 136	2 077	1 874	1 801	1 695
Married	KKIY	23	14	10	8	8	KKLT	104	66	48	42	40
Widowed	KKIZ	–	–	–	–	–	KKLU	–	–	–	–	–
Divorced	KKJA	–	–	–	–	–	KKLV	2	–	–	–	–
20 - 24: Single	KEWW	1 569	1 922	1 958	1 936	1 491	KEXU	1 116	1 459	1 552	1 543	1 205
Married	KKJB	526	405	323	299	252	KKLW	904	779	631	593	435
Widowed	KKJC	1	–	–	–	–	KKLX	2	1	1	1	1
Divorced	KKJD	11	13	15	14	16	KKLY	30	31	34	33	30
25 - 34: Single	KEWX	993	1 225	1 669	1 793	1 985	KEXV	547	737	1 082	1 179	1 345
Married	KKJE	2 774	2 427	2 297	2 273	1 759	KKLZ	3 080	2 767	2 734	2 730	2 220
Widowed	KKJF	5	4	3	3	2	KKMA	15	12	10	9	6
Divorced	KKJG	162	210	246	255	258	KKMB	235	279	319	328	316
35 - 44: Single	KEWY	348	418	483	500	1 100	KEXW	190	225	274	289	759
Married	KKJH	2 771	2 984	2 975	2 945	2 649	KKMC	2 801	3 057	3 078	3 058	2 885
Widowed	KKJI	13	13	13	13	10	KKMD	47	45	41	40	30
Divorced	KKJJ	190	289	374	394	553	KKME	238	349	441	460	604
45 - 54: Single	KEWZ	282	262	265	271	427	KEXX	194	166	155	156	253
Married	KKJK	2 579	2 519	2 534	2 560	2 727	KKMF	2 535	2 475	2 509	2 541	2 782
Widowed	KKJL	43	39	36	36	34	KKMG	170	151	136	132	132
Divorced	KKJM	143	208	279	299	560	KKMH	170	238	317	340	622
55 - 59: Single	KEXP	143	133	120	116	128	KEXY	125	104	86	81	73
Married	KKJN	1 308	1 222	1 172	1 162	1 248	KKMI	1 270	1 160	1 112	1 100	1 192
Widowed	KKJO	51	46	40	39	37	KKMJ	209	187	164	157	150
Divorced	KKJP	52	71	93	100	213	KKMK	67	83	107	113	238
60 - 64: Single	KEXQ	110	125	118	116	98	KEXZ	125	122	100	96	62
Married	KKJQ	1 125	1 202	1 113	1 107	1 044	KKML	1 024	1 091	1 006	1 003	949
Widowed	KKJR	72	81	71	69	60	KKMM	319	328	285	277	233
Divorced	KKJS	38	53	67	71	151	KKMN	54	73	83	88	171
65 - 74: Single	KEXR	170	161	168	170	160	KEYA	302	246	217	210	135
Married	KKJT	1 738	1 661	1 710	1 712	1 640	KKMO	1 404	1 359	1 416	1 418	1 323
Widowed	KKJU	261	240	236	234	224	KKMP	1 087	1 018	976	958	847
Divorced	KKJV	45	55	72	77	163	KKMQ	72	88	113	118	207
75 and over: Single	KEXS	77	88	100	102	114	KEYB	309	308	296	289	203
Married	KKJW	621	719	811	824	934	KKMR	432	501	564	574	688
Widowed	KKJX	329	351	372	376	452	KKMS	1 406	1 501	1 631	1 649	1 748
Divorced	KKJY	11	18	26	28	61	KKMT	24	36	52	56	125

Note: Figures may not add due to rounding.

1 1989 - based projections.

Sources: Office of Population Censuses and Surveys;
General Register Office (Scotland);
Government Actuary's Department

Population

2.8 Geographical distribution of the enumerated population: census figures[1]

Thousands

			Area in square kilometres[2]	1911	1931	1951	1961	1971	1981[3]	1991
Urban and rural districts										
England and Wales:										
Urban areas	KKMU	KHWR	21 765	28 163	31 952	35 336	36 872	38 151	37 324	49 194
Rural districts	KKMV		129 360	7 908	8 000	8 422	9 233	10 598	11 687	
Scotland:										
Cities and burghs	KKMW	KEZJ	1 300	3 140	3 362	3 563	3 646	3 705	5 131	4 962
Landward areas	KKMX		75 879	1 620	1 481	1 534	1 533	1 524		
Northern Ireland:										
Urban areas	KKMY	KEZK	240	587	678[4]	728	770	846	1 532	1 578
Rural districts	KKMZ		13 330	664	602[4]	643	655	690		
Standard regions of England and Wales										
England	KKOJ			33 650	37 359	41 159	43 461	46 018	46 363	46 382
North	KKNA		19 349	2 815	3 038	3 137	3 250	3 296	3 104	3 019
Yorkshire and Humberside	KKNB		14 196	3 877	4 285	4 522	4 635	4 799	4 860	4 797
East Midlands	KKNC		12 179	2 263	2 531	2 893	3 100	3 390	3 819	3 919
East Anglia	KKND		12 565	1 192	1 232	1 382	1 470	1 669	1 872	2 018
South East	KKNE		27 408	11 744	13 539	15 127	16 271	17 230	16 796	16 794
South West	KKNF		23 660	2 687	2 794	3 229	3 411	3 781	4 349	4 600
West Midlands	KKNG		13 013	3 277	3 743	4 423	4 758	5 110	5 148	5 089
North West	KKNH		7 993	5 796	6 197	6 447	6 567	6 743	6 414	6 147
Wales	KKNI		20 763	2 421	2 593	2 599	2 644	2 731	2 792	2 812
Conurbations										
Greater London	KKNJ		1 580	7 160	8 110	8 197	7 992	7 452	6 696	..
West Midlands	KKNK		678	1 651	1 951	2 260	2 378	2 372	2 244	..
West Yorkshire	KKNL		1 255	1 590	1 655	1 693	1 704	1 728	1 682	..
South East Lancashire	KKNM		983	2 328	2 427	2 423	2 428	2 393	2 245	..
Merseyside	KKNN		394	1 157	1 347	1 386	1 384	1 267	1 127	..
Tyneside	KKNO		235	761	827	836	856	805	738	..
Central Clydeside	KKNP		778	..	1 690	1 759	1 802	1 728	1 718	..
Cities										
Birmingham	KKNQ		209	526	1 003	1 113	1 107	1 015	1 007	938
Liverpool	KKNR		113	746	856	789	746	610	510	450
Manchester	KKNS		110	714	766	703	662	544	449	400
Sheffield	KKNT		184	455	512	513	494	520	538	503
Leeds	KKNU		164	446	483	505	511	496	705	677
Bristol	KKNV		110	357	397	443	437	427	391	372
Coventry	KKNW		81	106	167	258	306	335	314	295
Nottingham	KKNX		74	260	269	306	312	301	272	262
Bradford	KKNY		103	288	298	292	296	294	457	451
Kingston-upon-Hull	KKNZ		71	278	314	299	303	286	270	253
Leicester	KKOA		73	227	239	285	273	284	280	272
Cardiff	KKOB		80	182	224	244	257	279	274	277
Wolverhampton	KKOC		69	95	133	163	151	269	255	241
Stoke-on-Trent	KKOD		93	235	277	275	265	265	253	244
Glasgow	KKOE		157	784	1 088	1 090	1 055	897	766	654
Edinburgh	KKOF		135	320	439	467	468	454	437	422
Dundee	KKOG		50	165	176	177	183	182	180	166
Aberdeen	KKOH		50	164	167	183	185	182	204	201
Belfast	KKOI		73	387	438[4]	444	416	362	314	279

1 Populations of urban and rural districts and cities are for the administrative areas as constituted at the time of each census from 1911 to 1981. So some changes in population may be the result of changes in the constitutions of the areas; details can be found in the reports of the censuses. The cities shown do not include all urban areas with populations of 180 000 or more in 1981. Populations of standard regions and conurbations relate to approximately the same area throughout the period 1911 to 1981.

2 The statistics of area in square kilometres are for areas as constituted in 1971. The areas of urban and rural districts and of conurbations have not been measured since 1971, but there have been some changes in the areas of standard regions and cities.

3 Figures for the urban and rural districts in England and Wales and for the conurbations are from the *Census 1981 Preliminary Report for Towns*.

Figures for Scotland, standard regions, and cities (administrative districts) are persons present on census night from *Census 1981, Key Statistics for Local Authorities, Great Britain*.

In Northern Ireland it is estimated that some 44 500 persons were not enumerated. These are included in the above figures.

4 Figures for Northern Ireland and the City of Belfast relate to the 1987 Census.

Source: Office of Population Censuses and Surveys

Population

2.9 Geographical distribution of resident population: mid-year estimates

Thousands

		1981	1982	1983	1984	1985	1986	1987	1988	1989	1990	1991[2]
England and Wales	KGJA	49 634	49 601	49 654	49 764	49 924	50 075	50 243	50 393	50 562	50 719	50 955
Scotland	KGJB	5 180	5 167	5 150	5 146	5 137	5 121	5 112	5 094	5 091	5 102	5 100
Northern Ireland	KGJC	1 538[1]	1 538[1]	1 543[1]	1 550[1]	1 558	1 567	1 575	1 578	1 583	1 589	1 594
Standard regions of England and Wales												
North	KGJD	3 118	3 107	3 100	3 093	3 086	3 080	3 077	3 071	3 073	3 075	3 084
Yorkshire and Humberside	KGJE	4 918	4 910	4 908	4 904	4 903	4 899	4 900	4 913	4 940	4 952	4 954
East Midlands	KGJF	3 853	3 852	3 860	3 874	3 897	3 920	3 942	3 970	3 999	4 019	4 026
East Anglia	KGJG	1 895	1 911	1 925	1 940	1 965	1 992	2 014	2 034	2 045	2 059	2 091
South East	KGJH	17 010	17 006	17 042	17 112	17 192	17 265	17 318	17 344	17 384	17 458	17 558
Greater London	KGJI	*6 806*	*6 766*	*6 754*	*6 756*	*6 768*	*6 775*	*6 770*	*6 735*	*6 756*	*6 794*	*6 803*
South West	KGJJ	4 381	4 398	4 424	4 461	4 501	4 543	4 588	4 634	4 652	4 666	4 723
West Midlands	KGJK	5 186	5 180	5 176	5 176	5 183	5 181	5 198	5 207	5 216	5 219	5 255
North West	KGJL	6 460	6 431	6 410	6 396	6 386	6 374	6 370	6 364	6 380	6 389	6 377
Wales	KGJM	2 814	2 807	2 808	2 807	2 812	2 821	2 836	2 857	2 873	2 881	2 886
Metropolitan counties												
Tyne and Wear	KGJN	1 155	1 150	1 145	1 142	1 140	1 135	1 136	1 131	1 128	1 127	1 126
South Yorkshire	KGJO	1 317	1 313	1 310	1 305	1 303	1 298	1 296	1 293	1 295	1 296	1 293
West Yorkshire	KGJP	2 067	2 063	2 059	2 056	2 053	2 053	2 052	2 057	2 067	2 070	2 066
West Midlands	KGJQ	2 673	2 666	2 658	2 647	2 642	2 632	2 624	2 617	2 615	2 615	2 619
Greater Manchester	KGJR	2 619	2 605	2 598	2 588	2 583	2 579	2 580	2 578	2 582	2 591	2 562
Merseyside	KGJS	1 522	1 510	1 501	1 491	1 481	1 468	1 457	1 448	1 448	1 444	1 441
London boroughs and county districts (with about 275 000 or more population)												
Tyne and Wear												
Newcastle-upon-Tyne	KGJT	284	281	281	281	282	281	283	280	278	278	273
Sunderland	KGJU	297	300	299	299	299	298	297	296	296	296	296
South Yorkshire												
Sheffield	KGJV	548	546	543	540	539	534	532	528	527	526	520
Doncaster	KGJW	291	289	290	288	289	289	290	292	293	294	294
West Yorkshire												
Leeds	KGJX	718	716	714	712	711	711	709	710	712	712	706
Bradford	KGJY	465	465	464	464	464	463	462	464	468	469	469
Kirklees	KGJZ	377	377	377	378	377	377	376	375	376	376	381
Wakefield	KGKA	314	314	312	311	310	309	310	312	314	316	316
Greater London												
Croydon	KGKB	321	322	321	319	319	319	319	317	317	319	317
Barnet	KGKC	295	295	294	298	301	305	306	301	310	310	298
Bromley	KGKD	298	298	299	298	298	297	298	298	299	300	293
Ealing	KGKE	282	282	284	289	292	296	297	297	294	293	280
West Midlands												
Birmingham	KGKF	1 021	1 017	1 013	1 009	1 008	1 004	998	994	992	993	994
Coventry	KGKG	319	317	316	314	312	310	309	306	304	304	306
Sandwell	KGKH	310	309	307	305	303	301	298	296	296	295	295
Dudley	KGKI	301	301	301	301	301	301	303	304	305	307	309
Greater Manchester												
Manchester	KGKJ	463	459	458	455	451	451	450	446	444	447	433
Wigan	KGKK	310	309	308	307	307	307	307	308	310	310	311
Stockport	KGKL	290	290	289	289	291	290	291	291	291	290	288
Merseyside												
Liverpool	KGKM	517	510	502	497	492	483	476	470	466	463	475
Wirral	KGKN	341	339	338	338	337	335	335	335	336	335	336
Sefton	KGKO	300	299	300	299	298	298	297	298	300	300	295
Avon												
Bristol	KGKP	401	400	399	397	394	391	384	378	373	374	393
Leicestershire												
Leicester	KGKQ	283	282	282	282	283	281	280	279	280	278	280
South Glamorgan												
Cardiff	KGKS	281	280	280	281	279	280	281	284	285	287	290
City of Glasgow local government district	KGKT	774	762	751	744	734	725	716	703	696	689	688
City of Edinburgh local government district	KGKU	446	444	441	440	440	438	439	433	433	435	439
Belfast	KGKV	315[1]	310[1]	306[1]	304[1]	302	304	304	300	296	295	287

1 The figures for Northern Ireland have been revised using a new estimate of 44 500 non-enumerated persons in the 1981 Census.
2 The population estimates for mid-1991 are provisional. They are based on early 1991 Census results, and are therefore not comparable with estimates for 1982 to 1990 which were based on the 1981 Census and will be revised in due course.

Sources: Office of Population Censuses and Surveys; General Register Office (Northern Ireland); General Register Office (Scotland)

2.10 Migration into and out of the United Kingdom
Analysis by usual occupation[1] and sex

Thousands

	Total			Professional and managerial			Manual and clerical			Not gainfully employed[2]		
	Persons	Males	Females	Persons	Males	Females	Persons	Males	Females	Persons	Males	Females
Inflow												
	KGOA	KGOB	KGOC	KGOD	KGOE	KGOF	KGOG	KGOH	KGOI	KGOJ	KGOK	KGOL
1981	153	82	70	45	32	13	23	14	9	84	37	48
1982	201	100	101	43	34	9	38	18	20	120	48	72
1983	202	107	95	55	40	15	36	21	15	110	46	64
1984	201	102	99	59	41	18	32	15	17	110	46	64
1985	232	99	133	65	38	26	32	16	16	134	44	90
1986	250	120	130	76	52	24	46	21	25	128	47	81
1987	211	104	107	62	43	18	48	21	27	101	39	62
1988	216	109	107	67	44	23	44	26	18	105	40	66
1989	250	110	140	75	47	28	49	22	26	126	40	86
1990	267	135	132	93	61	32	53	26	27	121	48	72
1991	267	122	144	80	51	29	56	23	33	131	48	83
Outflow												
	KGPA	KGPB	KGPC	KGPD	KGPE	KGPF	KGPG	KGPH	KGPI	KGPJ	KGPK	KGPL
1981	232	133	100	67	50	17	60	38	22	105	44	60
1982	257	133	124	66	47	19	65	36	29	126	50	76
1983	184	90	94	51	32	18	35	19	16	98	38	60
1984	164	80	83	51	32	19	34	16	19	78	32	46
1985	174	91	83	51	36	15	36	18	17	87	36	50
1986	213	107	106	77	55	21	38	17	22	98	35	63
1987	209	107	102	63	38	26	56	28	28	90	41	48
1988	237	125	113	68	44	23	52	25	27	118	55	63
1989	205	108	97	70	44	27	49	23	26	86	41	45
1990	231	113	118	75	47	27	56	25	31	100	41	59
1991	239	120	119	82	48	34	50	28	21	108	44	63
Balance												
	KGRA	KGRB	KGRC	KGRD	KGRE	KGRF	KGRG	KGRH	KGRI	KGRJ	KGRK	KGRL
1981	−79	−50	−29	−22	−19	−4	−37	−24	−13	−20	−8	−13
1982	−56	−33	−23	−23	−13	−10	−27	−18	−9	−6	−2	−4
1983	17	17	–	5	8	−3	1	1	−1	12	8	4
1984	37	22	16	8	8	–	−3	−1	−2	32	14	18
1985	58	8	51	13	2	11	−3	−2	−1	48	8	40
1986	37	13	24	−1	−4	3	8	5	3	30	12	18
1987	2	−3	5	−1	6	−7	−8	−7	−1	12	−2	13
1988	−21	−15	−6	−1	−1	–	−8	1	−9	−13	−16	3
1989	44	1	43	5	4	1	−1	−1	1	40	−1	41
1990	36	22	14	19	14	5	−3	1	−4	21	7	13
1991	28	2	26	−2	3	−5	6	−5	11	24	4	19

See note on page 3.

Source: Office of Population Censuses and Surveys

1 Refers to regular occupation before migration.
2 Includes housewives, students, children and retired persons.

Migration

2.11 Migration into and out of the United Kingdom
Analysis by citizenship and country of last or next residence

Thousands

	All migrants Total	British citizens Total	European[1] Community	Old Common-wealth	New[2] Common-wealth	United States of America	Other countries	European Community citizens[1] (excl British) Total	European[1] Community	Other Europe	Other countries
Inflow											
	KEZR	KGLA	KGLB	KGLC	KGLD	KGLE	KGLF	KGLG	KGLH	KGLI	KGLJ
1981	153	60	12	9	19	6	14	11	10	–	–
1982	201	97	38	10	19	8	21	18	17	–	1
1983	202	94	22	20	22	11	19	13	11	–	3
1984	201	95	24	13	22	6	30	19	17	–	2
1985	232	110	37	12	22	11	27	21	17	–	4
1986	250	120	36	14	25	10	35	35	31	–	3
1987	211	98	32	13	19	11	23	25	21	1	2
1988	216	89	26	15	17	8	23	26	24	1	1
1989	250	104	23	24	18	12	27	29	28	–	2
1990	267	106	28	23	22	10	22	35	31	–	4
1991	267	117	40	23	23	10	21	31	27	–	3
Outflow											
	KEZS	KGMA	KGMB	KGMC	KGMD	KGME	KGMF	KGMG	KGMH	KGMI	KGMJ
1981	232	164	17	66	15	13	52	15	12	–	3
1982	257	186	31	60	22	15	58	11	7	–	4
1983	184	121	26	31	18	16	30	12	10	–	2
1984	164	102	26	19	18	12	28	10	7	–	3
1985	174	108	26	21	17	12	33	12	8	–	3
1986	213	132	47	34	15	13	23	10	8	–	1
1987	209	130	40	39	12	18	20	19	16	–	3
1988	237	143	41	48	16	15	23	22	16	3	3
1989	205	122	26	42	18	13	23	21	17	–	4
1990	231	135	34	43	15	22	22	28	25	–	3
1991	239	137	47	36	19	13	23	32	23	2	7
Balance											
	KEZT	KGNA	KGNB	KGNC	KGND	KGNE	KGNF	KGNG	KGNH	KGNI	KGNJ
1981	–79	–104	–6	–56	4	–7	–39	–4	–1	–	–3
1982	–56	–88	7	–49	–3	–6	–37	7	9	–	–3
1983	17	–27	–4	–11	5	–5	–11	2	–	–	1
1984	37	–7	–2	–6	4	–6	2	9	10	–	–1
1985	58	1	11	–8	5	–1	–6	10	9	–	–
1986	37	–11	–11	–19	10	–3	12	25	23	–	2
1987	2	–32	–8	–26	7	–7	2	6	5	1	–1
1988	–21	–54	–15	–33	1	–7	–	4	8	–2	–2
1989	44	–18	–3	–18	–	–	4	9	11	–	–2
1990	36	–30	–6	–20	7	–12	1	7	6	–	1
1991	28	–20	–7	–13	4	–3	–1	–1	4	–2	–4

See note on page 3.

Source: Office of Population Censuses and Surveys

1 Figures for the European Community have been revised for all the years in this table to show the Community as it was constituted on 1 January 1991.
2 Figures for all years include Pakistan in the New Commonwealth.

2.11 Migration into and out of the United Kingdom
Analysis by citizenship and country of last or next residence

Thousands

	Commonwealth citizens[2] Country of last/next residence										Other foreign citizens Country of last/next residence				
	Total	Australia	Canada	New Zealand	Bangladesh, India, Sri Lanka	Pakistan	African Commonwealth	Caribbean Commonwealth	Other Commonwealth	Other countries	Total	European[1] Community	Other Europe	United States of America	Other countries

Inflow

	KGLK	KGLL	KGLM	KGLN	KGLO	KGLP	KGLQ	KGLR	KGLS	KGLT	KGLU	KGLV	KGLW	KGLX	KGLY
1981	47	5	2	3	14	7	6	2	7	1	36	2	3	10	21
1982	49	5	1	3	14	8	7	1	6	3	37	1	4	11	22
1983	54	5	2	4	10	8	7	3	13	1	40	2	2	14	22
1984	49	7	2	5	12	7	7	1	8	1	37	2	2	16	17
1985	54	8	3	7	10	7	5	1	11	2	47	4	10	11	22
1986	50	7	2	6	11	6	5	2	9	2	46	1	6	14	24
1987	54	7	3	8	12	6	5	1	9	3	35	1	3	14	18
1988	53	11	2	7	9	5	4	1	10	3	47	1	7	14	25
1989	67	10	3	10	12	6	7	1	13	4	49	2	5	18	24
1990	70	17	3	10	11	4	8	2	10	4	57	6	10	17	23
1991	67	12	4	7	10	7	8	2	13	3	52	4	10	14	24

Outflow

	KGMK	KGML	KGMM	KGMN	KGMO	KGMP	KGMQ	KGMR	KGMS	KGMT	KGMU	KGMV	KGMW	KGMX	KGMY
1981	29	6	3	3	2	–	4	1	7	4	25	3	3	8	10
1982	32	6	3	4	3	–	4	2	8	3	28	–	4	13	11
1983	26	5	1	2	2	–	4	1	8	3	25	–	2	14	8
1984	25	6	1	2	2	1	2	1	6	2	27	–	2	14	10
1985	28	5	3	4	1	2	3	1	8	1	26	1	4	11	11
1986	31	9	3	4	2	–	3	1	7	3	40	1	8	20	12
1987	30	9	5	4	2	1	2	1	4	3	30	2	4	13	12
1988	36	6	2	3	3	2	5	2	9	5	36	–	6	14	16
1989	26	6	2	2	3	2	3	1	5	2	36	2	4	16	14
1990	29	8	3	5	1	1	4	1	5	2	38	–	6	18	13
1991	34	7	4	5	2	2	2	–	10	3	36	1	3	16	17

Balance

	KGNK	KGNL	KGNM	KGNN	KGNO	KGNP	KGNQ	KGNR	KGNS	KGNT	KGNU	KGNV	KGNW	KGNX	KGNY
1981	17	–	-1	-1	13	6	1	1	–	-2	11	-1	–	1	11
1982	17	-1	-2	-1	12	8	3	-1	-2	–	9	–	–	-3	11
1983	28	–	1	1	8	8	3	2	6	-2	15	1	–	–	14
1984	24	1	1	3	9	5	5	–	2	-2	10	2	–	2	7
1985	27	3	–	4	9	5	3	–	3	1	21	3	6	–	12
1986	18	-2	-1	2	9	5	2	1	3	-1	5	1	-2	-5	12
1987	23	-2	-2	4	10	5	3	–	5	–	5	–	-1	1	6
1988	17	5	–	4	6	3	–	-1	1	-2	11	1	1	-1	10
1989	41	4	2	8	9	4	4	–	8	2	13	–	1	2	9
1990	40	9	–	5	10	3	4	2	5	2	19	6	4	-1	10
1991	32	5	–	2	7	5	6	2	4	–	16	4	6	-2	8

See footnotes on page 18.

Source: Office of Population Censuses and Surveys

Acceptances for Settlement

2.12 Acceptances for settlement by nationality
United Kingdom

Number of persons

Geographical region and nationality		All acceptances for settlement 1989	1990	1991	Geographical region and nationality		All acceptances for settlement 1989	1990	1991
All nationalities	KGFA	49 650	53 200	53 900	**Africa**-continued				
					Mauritius	KGHC	230	330	310
Europe					Morocco	KGHD	390	580	790
European Community					Nigeria	KGHE	1 380	2 080	2 870
Belgium	KGFB	60	50	50	Sierra Leone	KGHF	170	240	290
Denmark	KGFC	90	130	100					
France	KGFD	350	340	250	Somalia	KGHG	160	500	510
Germany[1]	KGFE	310	280	270	South Africa	KGHH	730	850	1 050
Greece	KGFF	100	60	40	Sudan	KGHI	90	100	100
Italy	KGFG	240	250	170	Tanzania	KGHJ	260	210	260
Luxembourg	KGFH	–	–	–	Tunisia	KGHK	60	100	120
Netherlands	KGFI	220	180	170					
Portugal[2]	KGFJ	210	200	150	Uganda	KGHL	100	100	110
Spain[2]	KGFK	340	270	210	Zambia	KGHM	180	180	170
					Zimbabwe	KGHN	460	330	240
European Community	KGFL	1 920	1 760	1 420					
					Africa	KGHO	6 480	8 310	9 580
Other Western Europe									
Austria	KGFM	110	100	120	**Asia**				
Cyprus	KGFN	350	350	320	**Indian Sub-Continent**				
Finland	KGFO	120	160	130	Bangladesh	KGHP	3 790	3 040	2 780
Malta	KGFP	100	100	80	India	KGHQ	4 580	5 100	5 680
Norway	KGFQ	130	200	220	Pakistan	KGHR	4 150	5 040	5 820
Sweden	KGFR	370	380	520					
Switzerland	KGFS	150	160	180	Indian Sub-Continent	KGHS	12 520	13 170	14 290
Turkey	KGFT	700	910	1 050	**Middle East**				
Yugoslavia	KGFU	250	370	390	Iran	KGHT	2 020	1 500	1 170
Other Western Europe	KGFV	2 280	2 730	3 000	Iraq	KGHU	600	430	580
					Israel	KGHV	320	360	430
Eastern Europe					Jordan	KGHW	180	160	180
Bulgaria	KGFW	20	30	60					
Czechoslovakia	KGFX	20	20	60	Kuwait	KGHX	10	10	40
German Democratic Republic[3]	KGFY	10	10	–	Lebanon	KGHY	370	330	330
					Saudi Arabia	KGHZ	50	100	40
Hungary	KGFZ	20	70	90	Syria	KGIA	120	130	120
Poland	KGGA	600	450	700					
Romania	KGGB	10	20	60	Middle East	KGIB	3 670	3 030	2 900
USSR	KGGC	20	50	140	**Remainder of Asia**				
Eastern Europe	KGGD	690	640	1 110	China	KGIC	170	320	390
					Indonesia	KGID	70	50	80
Europe	KGGE	4 880	5 130	5 530	Japan	KGIE	1 430	1 770	1 970
Americas					Malaysia	KGIF	920	880	690
Argentina	KGGF	30	40	50	Philippines	KGIG	760	1 090	1 190
Barbados	KGGG	40	60	60	Singapore	KGIH	150	150	190
Brazil	KGGH	130	250	260	Sri Lanka	KGII	800	840	660
Canada	KGGI	1 050	890	680	Thailand	KGIJ	240	570	660
Chile	KGGJ	40	50	60	BDTC Hong Kong[4]	KGIK	1 400	1 760	1 890
Columbia	KGGK	180	220	270	Remainder of Asia	KGIL	5 950	7 430	7 720
Cuba	KGGL	–	–	–					
Guyana	KGGM	120	170	190	Asia	KGIM	22 140	23 630	24 900
Jamaica	KGGN	530	920	1 310	**Australasia**				
Mexico	KGGO	40	90	90	Australia	KGIN	3 870	3 110	1 450
Peru	KGGP	60	60	100	New Zealand	KGIO	2 980	2 240	990
Trinidad and Tobago	KGGQ	180	220	210					
USA	KGGR	3 070	3 750	3 910	Australasia	KGIP	6 840	5 350	2 440
Uruguay	KGGS	10	–	10					
Venezuela	KGGT	40	50	30	British Overseas citizens	KGIQ	1 450	1 480	1 350
					Other countries not elsewhere specified	KGIR	840	1 110	1 430
Americas	KGGU	5 570	6 800	7 220	Stateless[5]	KGIS	1 510	1 410	1 430
Africa									
Algeria	KGGV	170	210	240	**All nationalities**	KGIT	49 650	53 200	53 900
Egypt	KGGW	340	320	380					
Ethiopia	KGGX	70	60	70	Commonwealth[6]	KGIV	31 050	32 210	31 060
Ghana	KGGY	1 160	1 550	1 480					
Kenya	KGHA	370	440	480	Old Commonwealth	KGIW	7 890	6 230	3 120
Libya	KGHB	160	130	100	New Commonwealth[4]	KGIX	23 160	25 980	27 930
					Foreign	KGIU	18 600	20 990	22 850

1 Includes nationals of the former GDR recorded after the unification of Germany on 3 October 1990.
2 Portugal and Spain joined the European Community on 1 January 1986.
3 Acceptances recorded prior to the unification of Germany on 3 October 1990.
4 British Dependent Territories citizens.
5 Includes refugees from South-East Asia.
6 Includes Pakistan throughout the period covered.

Source: Home Office

Applications for Asylum

2.12A Applications received in the United Kingdom for asylum

Number of principal applicants

Nationality		1985	1986	1987	1988	1989[3]	1990[3]	1991[3]
Europe								
Bulgaria	KEAU	6	5	5	4	30	135	375
Romania	KEAV	6	11	20	12	20	300	555
Turkey	KEAW	27	86	121	337	2 415	1 185	2 110
USSR	KEAX	4	1	4	5	30	100	245
Other Europe	KEAY	89	80	88	121	135	65	360
Total	KEAZ	132	183	238	479	2 630	1 780	3 645
Americas								
Colombia	KEBZ	4	13	15	33	90	170	140
Other	KECS	21	24	24	21	45	75	90
Total	KECT	25	37	39	54	135	245	230
Africa								
Angola	KECU	7	8	22	47	235	1 160	5 780
Congo	KECV	..	1	1	5	20	70	370
Ethiopia	KECW	177	179	223	227	560	1 975	1 685
Ghana	KECX	141	196	125	172	330	1 020	2 405
Nigeria	KECY	17	8	10	10	20	115	335
Somalia	KECZ	192	152	202	305	1 850	1 920	1 995
Sudan	KEEE	16	18	20	22	110	255	1 150
Togo/Ivory Coast	KEEF	..	..	..	..	20	110	1 910
Uganda	KEEG	170	174	318	414	1 235	1 905	1 450
Zaire	KEEH	7	26	53	157	525	1 730	7 010
Others[1]	KEEI	201	288	290	205	205	560	3 405
Total	KEEJ	928	1 050	1 264	1 564	5 095	10 820	27 500
Middle East								
Iran	KEEK	861	897	649	393	350	365	530
Iraq	KEEL	251	210	210	163	215	890	915
Lebanon	KEGW	22	31	93	148	180	1 020	755
Others	KEGX	13	30	39	26	35	80	340
Total	KEGY	1 147	1 168	991	730	780	2 355	2 540
Asia								
China	KEGZ	1	2	6	5	85	240	525
India	KEIL	32	114	126	293	630	1 430	2 075
Pakistan	KEIM	134	287	446	328	250	1 315	3 245
Sri Lanka	KEIN	1 893	1 275	992	402	1 790	3 215	3 765
Others[2]	KEIO	52	102	68	69	130	285	890
Total	KEJO	2 112	1 780	1 638	1 097	2 885	6 490	10 495
Other, and nationality not recorded	KEJP	45	48	86	74	110	315	435
Grand Total	KEJQ	4 389	4 266	4 256	3 998	11 640	22 000	44 840

1 In addition, about 40 applications in 1991 by nationals of Liberia to the British High Commission in Lagos were processed locally.
2 In addition, about 1695 applications in 1988, 35 in 1989, 55 in 1990 and 15 in 1991 by nationals of Afghanistan to the British High Commission in New Delhi were processed locally.
3 Provisional.

Source: Home Office

Marriages

2.13 Marriages

Numbers

		1980	1981	1982	1983	1984	1985	1986	1987	1988	1989	1990[2]
United Kingdom												
Marriages	KKAA	418 446	397 846	387 021	389 286	395 797	393 117	393 939	397 937	394 049	392 042	375 410
Persons marrying per 1 000 resident population	KKAB	*15.0*	*14.1*	*13.4*	*13.8*	*14.0*	*13.9*	*13.9*	*14.0*	*13.8*	*13.7*	*13.1*
Previous marital status												
Bachelors	KKAC	314 849	297 589	288 408	288 713	293 645	291 171	290 144	296 290	289 493	288 478	276 512
Divorced men	KKAD	87 663	85 141	84 110	86 484	88 691	88 981	91 006	89 814	92 755	92 033	88 199
Widowers	KKAE	15 934	15 116	14 503	14 089	13 461	12 965	12 789	11 833	11 801	11 531	10 699
Spinsters	KKAF	319 088	302 354	293 068	293 554	299 256	296 797	294 564	301 073	293 551	291 516	279 442
Divorced women	KKAG	80 370	80 755	80 148	82 314	83 477	83 921	87 080	85 238	89 066	89 234	85 608
Widows	KKAH	15 982	14 737	13 805	13 418	13 064	12 399	12 295	11 626	11 612	11 294	10 360
First marriage for both partners	KMGH	278 608	263 209	254 868	254 620	258 997	256 594	254 237	260 459	253 150	251 572	240 729
First marriage for one partner	KMGI	76 721	73 525	71 740	73 027	74 913	74 780	76 254	76 445	76 744	76 850	74 496
Remarriage for both partners	KMGJ	63 117	61 112	60 413	61 639	61 890	61 743	63 458	61 033	64 155	63 620	60 185
Males												
Under 21 years	KKAI	52 644	46 197	41 544	37 141	33 447	30 243	25 828	24 269	20 608	19 070	15 930
21-24	KKAJ	141 776	133 522	127 833	127 149	127 351	123 242	119 464	118 355	109 482	102 977	92 270
25-29	KKAK	98 831	96 062	96 194	99 855	105 799	109 896	114 007	119 808	120 939	123 491	122 800
30-34	KKAL	48 104	46 873	45 266	45 794	47 325	47 594	49 287	51 389	53 865	56 442	56 966
35-44	KKAM	39 427	39 366	41 111	43 538	45 955	46 265	48 583	48 598	51 329	51 411	49 984
45-54	KKAN	19 360	18 333	18 286	18 990	19 358	19 652	20 376	19 788	21 544	22 329	21 996
55 and over	KKAO	18 304	17 493	16 787	16 819	16 562	16 225	16 394	15 730	16 282	16 322	15 464
Females												
Under 21 years	KKAP	127 542	114 540	104 642	96 859	90 301	82 209	72 466	68 629	59 284	54 256	45 626
21-24	KKAQ	133 309	129 565	128 446	132 020	136 244	137 437	138 219	140 509	134 122	128 411	119 037
25-29	KKAR	65 818	65 131	66 293	70 284	76 566	80 105	85 316	90 911	95 338	100 531	103 209
30-34	KKAS	34 064	32 786	31 306	32 163	32 998	33 424	35 237	36 643	39 680	41 989	42 794
35-44	KKAT	30 699	30 493	31 795	33 156	34 854	35 380	37 515	36 978	39 534	40 290	38 983
45-54	KKAU	15 011	14 091	13 857	14 325	14 716	14 892	15 414	15 001	16 570	17 172	16 825
55 and over	KKAV	12 003	11 240	10 682	10 479	10 118	9 670	9 772	9 260	9 521	9 393	8 936
England and Wales												
Marriages	KKBA	370 022	351 973	342 166	344 334	349 186	346 389	347 924	351 761	348 492	346 697	331 150
Persons marrying per 1 000 resident population	KKBB	*14.9*	*14.2*	*13.8*	*13.9*	*14.0*	*13.9*	*13.9*	*14.0*	*13.8*	*13.7*	*13.1*
Previous marital status												
Bachelors	KKBC	274 140	259 106	250 999	251 845	255 469	253 296	252 953	258 750	252 780	252 230	241 274
Divorced men	KKBD	81 396	79 099	78 040	79 678	81 448	81 370	83 401	82 315	84 991	84 035	80 282
Widowers	KKBE	14 486	13 768	13 127	12 811	12 269	11 723	11 570	10 696	10 721	10 432	9 594
Spinsters	KKBF	277 826	263 368	255 171	256 214	260 359	258 089	256 767	262 958	256 221	254 763	243 825
Divorced women	KKBG	77 595	75 147	74 418	75 909	76 899	77 031	79 964	78 219	81 691	81 702	77 994
Widows	KKBH	14 601	13 458	12 577	12 211	11 928	11 269	11 193	10 584	10 580	10 232	9 331
First marriage for both partners	KMGK	241 001	227 713	220 427	220 949	224 015	221 927	220 372	226 308	219 791	218 904	209 043
First marriage for one partner	KMGL	69 964	67 048	65 316	66 161	67 798	67 531	68 976	69 092	69 419	69 185	67 013
Remarriage for both partners	KMGM	59 057	57 212	56 423	57 224	57 373	56 931	58 576	56 361	59 282	58 608	55 094
Males[1]												
Under 21 years	KKBI	44 062	38 660	34 809	31 216	27 941	25 496	21 758	20 541	17 578	16 312	13 772
21-24	KKBJ	123 080	115 924	110 972	110 537	110 351	106 089	103 651	102 907	95 029	89 263	79 818
25-29	KKBK	88 067	85 391	85 333	88 470	93 227	96 804	100 360	105 458	106 349	108 834	107 784
30-34	KKBL	43 854	42 696	41 084	41 402	42 563	42 532	44 125	46 063	48 112	50 409	50 600
35-44	KKBM	36 323	36 312	37 712	39 882	42 064	42 120	44 309	44 237	46 688	46 549	45 038
45-54	KKBN	17 842	16 862	16 812	17 389	17 790	17 968	18 681	18 055	19 754	20 365	19 991
55 and over	KKBO	16 794	16 128	15 444	15 438	15 250	14 861	15 040	14 500	14 982	14 965	14 147
Females[1]												
Under 21 years	KKBP	110 288	99 246	90 669	84 125	78 026	71 394	62 831	59 705	51 717	47 529	40 022
21-24	KKBQ	116 618	113 149	112 314	115 641	118 928	119 707	120 769	122 999	117 239	112 048	103 653
25-29	KKBR	58 767	58 183	58 932	62 288	67 567	70 495	75 224	80 062	88 833	88 662	90 629
30-34	KKBS	31 259	30 122	28 510	29 194	29 917	30 055	31 658	32 932	35 609	37 452	38 032
35-44	KKBT	28 258	28 011	29 240	30 381	31 969	32 296	34 375	33 818	36 135	36 678	35 315
45-54	KKBU	13 709	12 842	12 596	13 007	13 401	13 549	14 054	13 690	15 173	15 661	15 290
55 and over	KKBV	11 123	10 420	9 905	9 698	9 378	8 893	9 013	8 555	8 786	8 667	8 209

1 The figures for England and Wales include an assumed distribution of 'Age not stated'.
2 1991 figures not yet available.

Source: Office of Population Censuses and Surveys

2.13 Marriages
continued

Marriages

Numbers

		1980	1981	1982	1983	1984	1985	1986	1987	1988	1989	1990[1]
Scotland												
Marriages	KKCA	38 501	36 237	34 942	34 962	36 253	36 385	35 790	35 813	35 599	35 326	34 672
Persons marrying per 1 000 population	KKCB	*14.9*	*14.1*	*13.5*	*13.6*	*14.1*	*14.2*	*14.0*	*14.0*	*14.0*	*13.9*	*13.6*
Previous marital status												
Bachelors	KKCC	31 472	29 622	28 357	27 765	28 753	28 475	27 860	28 126	27 622	27 186	26 636
Divorced men	KKCD	5 777	5 462	5 416	6 111	6 488	6 876	6 890	6 740	7 062	7 224	7 108
Widowers	KKCE	1 252	1 153	1 169	1 086	1 012	1 034	1 040	947	915	916	928
Spinsters	KKCF	31 968	30 103	28 736	28 185	29 358	29 208	28 414	28 588	28 150	27 606	26 940
Divorced women	KKCG	5 355	5 065	5 163	5 755	5 948	6 233	6 452	6 349	6 574	6 832	6 869
Widows	KKCH	1 178	1 069	1 043	1 022	947	944	924	876	875	888	863
First marriage for both partners	KEZV	28 692	27 012	25 752	24 991	25 951	25 674	24 968	25 147	24 628	24 032	23 529
First marriage for one partner	KEZW	6 056	5 701	5 589	5 968	6 209	6 335	6 358	6 420	6 516	6 728	6 518
Remarriage for both partners	KEZX	3 753	3 524	3 601	4 003	4 093	4 376	4 474	4 246	4 455	4 566	4 625
Males												
Under 21 years	KKCI	6 798	5 930	5 190	4 491	4 172	3 591	3 028	2 780	2 259	2 042	1 626
21-24	KKCJ	14 700	13 736	12 986	12 806	12 996	12 689	12 015	11 742	10 956	10 295	9 454
25-29	KKCK	8 263	8 273	8 215	8 590	9 602	9 903	10 322	10 883	11 140	11 122	11 430
30-34	KKCL	3 448	3 362	3 333	3 503	3 752	4 052	4 125	4 191	4 609	4 831	5 061
35-44	KKCM	2 639	2 524	2 818	3 021	3 235	3 515	3 624	3 655	3 953	4 135	4 210
45-54	KKCN	1 354	1 243	1 259	1 375	1 371	1 466	1 483	1 509	1 558	1 721	1 760
55 and over	KKCO	1 299	1 169	1 141	1 176	1 125	1 169	1 193	1 053	1 124	1 180	1 131
Females												
Under 21 years	KKCP	13 575	12 019	10 752	9 685	9 336	8 224	7 245	6 665	5 692	4 951	4 161
21-24	KKCQ	13 091	12 847	12 439	12 627	13 255	13 531	13 316	13 338	12 801	12 386	11 666
25-29	KKCR	5 476	5 347	5 594	6 105	6 922	7 393	7 720	8 314	8 959	9 163	9 755
30-34	KKCS	2 326	2 175	2 251	2 394	2 502	2 746	2 926	3 044	3 311	3 728	3 925
35-44	KKCT	2 127	2 086	2 166	2 320	2 472	2 652	2 720	2 686	2 964	3 120	3 194
45-54	KKCU	1 147	1 070	1 083	1 165	1 130	1 180	1 157	1 209	1 233	1 345	1 351
55 and over	KKCV	759	693	657	666	636	659	654	609	639	633	620
Northern Ireland												
Marriages	KKDA	9 923	9 636	9 913	9 990	10 358	10 343	10 225	10 363	9 960	10 019	9 588
Persons marrying per 1 000 population	KKDB	*12.8*	*12.3*	*12.6*	*12.8*	*13.1*	*13.3*	*13.1*	*13.2*	*12.6*	*12.7*	*12.1*
Previous marital status												
Bachelors	KKDC	9 237	8 861	9 052	9 103	9 423	9 400	9 331	9 414	9 093	9 062	8 602
Divorced men	KKDD	490	580	654	695	755	735	715	759	702	774	809
Widowers	KKDE	196	195	207	192	180	208	179	190	165	183	177
Spinsters	KKDF	9 294	8 883	9 161	9 155	9 539	9 500	9 383	9 527	9 182	9 147	8 677
Divorced women	KKDG	426	543	567	650	630	657	664	670	621	700	745
Widows	KKDH	203	210	185	185	189	186	178	166	157	172	166
First marriage for both partners	KEZY	8 915	8 484	8 689	8 680	9 031	8 993	8 897	9 004	8 733	8 636	8 157
First marriage for one partner	KEZZ	701	776	835	898	906	914	920	933	809	937	965
Remarriage for both partners	KFBI	307	376	389	412	424	436	408	426	418	446	466
Males												
Under 21 years	KKDI	1 784	1 607	1 545	1 435	1 334	1 156	1 042	948	771	716	532
21-24	KKDJ	3 996	3 862	3 875	3 806	4 004	3 945	3 798	3 706	3 497	3 419	2 998
25-29	KKDK	2 501	2 398	2 646	2 794	2 970	3 189	3 325	3 467	3 452	3 535	3 586
30-34	KKDL	802	815	849	889	1 010	1 010	1 037	1 135	1 144	1 202	1 305
35-44	KKDM	465	530	581	635	656	630	650	706	688	727	736
45-54	KKDN	164	228	215	226	197	218	212	224	232	243	245
55 and over	KKDO	211	196	202	205	187	195	161	177	176	177	186
Females												
Under 21 years	KKDP	3 679	3 275	3 221	3 050	2 939	2 591	2 390	2 259	1 875	1 776	1 443
21-24	KKDQ	3 600	3 569	3 693	3 751	4 061	4 199	4 134	4 172	4 082	3 977	3 718
25-29	KKDR	1 575	1 601	1 767	1 891	2 077	2 217	2 372	2 535	2 547	2 706	2 825
30-34	KKDS	479	489	545	575	579	623	653	667	761	809	837
35-44	KKDT	314	396	389	455	413	432	420	474	435	492	474
45-54	KKDU	155	179	178	153	185	163	151	154	164	166	184
55 and over	KKDV	121	127	120	115	104	118	105	102	96	93	107

1 1991 figures not yet available.

Sources: General Register Office (Scotland);
General Register Office (Northern Ireland)

Divorce

2.14 Divorce
England and Wales, Scotland

Numbers

		1980	1981	1982	1983	1984	1985	1986	1987	1988	1989	1990	1991
England and Wales													
Decrees absolute[1], granted:													
Number[1]	KKEA	148 301	145 713	146 698	147 479	144 501	160 300	153 903	151 007	152 633	150 872	153 386	..
Rate per 1 000 married couples	KKEB	*12.0*	*11.9*	*12.0*	*12.2*	*12.0*	*13.4*	*12.9*	*12.7*	*12.8*	*12.7*	*12.9*	..
Duration of marriage:													
0-4 years	KKEC	28 517	28 640	30 262	31 097	30 500	45 776	38 637	35 423	35 582	35 719	36 299	..
5-9 years	KKED	45 152	43 808	42 499	42 041	40 866	41 537	42 187	43 150	42 617	42 108	42 061	..
10-14 years	KKEE	28 620	28 242	28 737	28 432	27 336	27 087	26 718	26 194	26 545	26 281	27 310	..
15-19 years	KKEF	18 541	18 499	18 855	19 103	19 108	18 460	19 547	19 576	20 132	19 418	19 819	..
20 years and over	KKEG	27 471	26 499	26 301	26 769	26 681	26 427	26 805	26 664	27 747	27 327	27 881	..
Not stated	KKEH	..	25	44	37	10	13	9	–	10	19	16	..
Age of wife at marriage:													
16-19 years	KKEI	55 946	54 424	54 067	52 547	49 610	52 858	48 621	46 097	44 693	42 612	41 116	..
20-24 years	KKEJ	64 786	63 034	62 955	63 382	62 642	69 663	68 387	68 345	69 489	69 424	71 489	..
25-29 years	KKEK	15 060	15 281	15 714	16 351	16 811	18 689	18 990	19 049	20 267	20 369	21 701	..
30-34 years	KKEL	5 638	5 813	6 317	7 092	7 125	8 544	8 189	7 983	8 441	8 590	8 909	..
35-39 years	KKEM	2 893	3 091	3 312	3 502	3 729	4 612	4 497	4 403	4 501	4 643	4 880	..
40-44 years	KKEN	1 672	1 757	1 975	2 081	2 090	2 609	2 378	2 416	2 530	2 541	2 598	..
45 years and over	KKEO	2 306	2 313	2 358	2 524	2 494	3 325	2 841	2 714	2 712	2 693	2 693	..
Age of wife at divorce:													
16-24 years	KKEP	20 905	20 095	19 987	19 440	18 232	26 170	21 713	19 066	17 693	16 628	15 454	..
25-29 years	KKEQ	34 308	33 299	32 995	32 695	31 800	35 680	34 478	34 209	34 504	34 483	35 121	..
30-34 years	KKER	31 765	31 104	30 023	28 958	27 734	28 668	28 452	28 995	29 406	29 757	31 295	..
35-39 years	KKES	21 436	22 459	24 567	25 673	25 522	26 554	25 956	24 934	24 685	24 170	24 421	..
40-44 years	KKET	15 423	15 276	15 587	16 336	16 712	17 767	18 519	19 403	20 873	20 647	21 263	..
45 years and over	KKEU	24 464	23 455	23 495	24 340	24 491	25 448	24 776	24 400	25 462	25 168	25 816	..
Not stated	KKEV	..	25	44	37	10	13	9	–	10	19	16	..
Divorces in which there were:													
No children[2]	KKEW	45 334	42 292	42 174	42 458	41 831	51 912	47 330	46 770	47 049	46 910	47 119	..
1 or more children[2]	KKEX	102 967	103 421	104 524	105 021	102 670	108 388	106 573	104 237	105 584	103 962	106 267	..
Scotland													
Decrees absolute, granted[3,4]:													
Number[1]	KKFA	10 528	9 894	11 288	13 238	11 906	13 371	12 800	12 133	11 472	11 659	12 272	12 399
Rate per 1 000 married[5] couples	KKFB	*8.6*	*8.0*	*9.2*	*11.0*	*9.9*	*11.2*	*10.7*	*10.2*	*9.8*	*10.0*	*10.5*	*10.6*
Duration of marriage:													
0-4 years	KKFC	1 807	1 699	1 991	2 267	2 157	2 364	2 233	2 173	1 986	2 013	2 208	2 142
5-9 years	KKFD	3 134	3 014	3 493	4 008	3 455	3 882	3 735	3 544	3 353	3 420	3 546	3 508
10-14 years	KKFE	2 090	1 944	2 272	2 419	2 284	2 684	2 536	2 351	2 227	2 245	2 361	2 484
15-19 years	KKFF	1 359	1 224	1 401	1 655	1 578	1 868	1 804	1 670	1 592	1 633	1 617	1 718
20 years and over	KKFG	2 138	2 013	2 131	2 889	2 433	2 573	2 492	2 395	2 314	2 348	2 540	2 547
Age of wife at marriage:													
16-20 years	KKFH	5 988	5 584	6 423	7 089	6 384	7 143	6 767	6 134	5 660	5 565	5 600	5 592
21-24 years	KKFI	2 935	2 769	3 159	3 813	3 510	3 914	3 768	3 778	3 577	3 708	4 185	4 147
25-29 years	KKFJ	902	853	929	1 218	1 093	1 246	1 257	1 274	1 236	1 363	1 377	1 545
30-34 years	KKFK	314	293	322	470	404	461	458	423	466	479	497	514
35-39 years	KKFL	150	167	184	252	182	247	250	224	219	235	275	249
40-44 years	KKFM	78	86	105	144	123	143	120	142	124	131	139	148
45 years and over	KKFN	161	142	127	178	162	170	174	158	153	143	159	142
Age not stated	KKFO	..	..	39	74	57	49	6	–	37	35	40	62
Age of wife at divorce:													
16-24 years	KKFP	1 702	1 525	1 831	1 909	1 682	1 881	1 674	1 504	1 285	1 139	1 199	1 038
25-29 years	KKFQ	2 625	2 428	2 820	3 154	2 865	3 152	3 001	2 920	2 676	2 818	2 938	2 932
30-34 years	KKFR	2 027	2 012	2 285	2 494	2 291	2 628	2 597	2 443	2 378	2 442	2 611	2 741
35-39 years	KKFS	1 431	1 345	1 543	1 850	1 852	2 183	2 136	1 942	1 917	1 927	1 891	2 037
40-44 years	KKFT	1 053	1 000	1 112	1 382	1 247	1 440	1 370	1 482	1 381	1 436	1 614	1 665
45 years and over	KKFU	1 690	1 584	1 658	2 375	1 921	2 040	2 016	1 842	1 798	1 862	1 979	1 924
Age not stated	KKFV	..	..	39	74	57	49	6	–	37	35	40	62
Actions[6] in which there were:													
No children	KKFW	4 325	4 148	4 603	6 774	5 488	6 040	6 046	5 989	5 887	6 091	6 555	6 521
1 or more children	KKFX	6 622	6 099	7 079	6 863	6 418	7 331	6 754	6 144	5 585	5 568	5 717	5 878

1 Includes decrees of divorce and of nullity.
2 Children of the family as defined by the Matrimonial Causes Act 1973.
3 For divorces under pre-1976 legislation these figures relate only to persons who were married in Scotland, and obtained their decree of divorce from the Court of Session. Also with effect from 1 May 1984 the jurisdiction of the Sheriff Courts was extended to include divorce.
4 With effect from 1984 these statistics are being collected on the basis of divorces granted only and any difference in the number of divorces brought and granted relates to nullity of marriages.
5 Rates are calculated using the average of the estimated married male and female populations.
6 These Actions relate to all persons divorced or separated in Scotland, irrespective of the country of marriage.

Sources: Office of Population Censuses and Surveys;
General Register Office (Scotland);
Scottish Courts Administration

2.15 Divorce proceedings

Divorce

Number

England and Wales

		1981	1982	1983	1984	1985	1986	1987	1988	1989	1990	1991
Dissolution of Marriage[1]												
Petitions filed[2]	KKGA	169 076	173 452	168 428	178 940	190 481	179 844	182 934	182 804	184 610	191 615	179 103
On grounds of:[4]												
Adultery	KKGB	47 250	48 010	47 130	50 720	53 330	51 730	52 780	50 250	51 650	..	..
Behaviour	KKGC	66 940	72 320	69 850	73 340	81 220	81 590	85 410	88 260	89 040	..	..
Desertion	KKGD	3 740	3 080	2 450	3 060	8 000	2 580	2 153	2 180	2 040	..	..
Separation (2 years and consent)	KKGE	38 480	37 700	36 930	38 950	36 460	32 760	31 150	30 860	30 610	..	..
Separation (5 years)	KKGF	11 690	11 390	11 320	10 780	10 210	10 200	10 420	9 830	10 100	..	..
Adultery and behaviour	KKGG	720	710	580	1 890	970	750	760	1 000	820	..	..
Adultery and desertion	KKGH	10	30	20	10	130	50	90	120	100	..	..
Behaviour and desertion	KKGI	40	70	30	20	70	50	70	70	160	..	..
Other	KKGJ	210	140	120	170	100	140	120	240	70	..	..
By husbands[4]	KKGK	46 220	46 470	45 150	48 940	52 090	49 480	49 780	49 130	49 150	..	..
By wives	KKGL	122 850	126 980	123 280	130 000	138 390	130 370	133 150	133 670	135 090	..	..
Decrees nisi granted	KKGM	147 226	147 763	149 189	147 136	161 409	152 073	149 272	154 788	151 309	157 344	153 258
Decrees absolute granted	KKGN	144 763	145 802	146 669	143 746	159 693	153 418	150 557	152 139	150 477	155 239	155 927
Nullity of marriage[3]												
Petitions filed[2]	KKGO	1 050	921	887	1 036	574	554	542	604	478	665	619
By husbands[4]	KKGP	430	400	320	480	220	240	250	260	220	..	..
By wives	KKGQ	620	520	570	560	360	310	290	350	260	..	..
Decrees nisi granted	KKGR	894	803	819	871	589	461	444	389	365	430	508
Decrees absolute granted	KKGS	950	896	810	755	607	485	443	494	395	467	417
Judicial separation												
Petitions filed[2]	KKGT	6 036	7 480	7 430	6 098	3 479	3 428	3 199	2 925	2 741	2 900	2 588
By husbands[4]	KKGU	600	840	880	1 190	350	480	360	270	270	..	..
By wives	KKGV	5 430	6 640	6 550	4 910	3 130	2 950	2 840	2 660	2 470	..	..
Decrees granted	KKGW	3 334	4 026	4 852	4 445	2 344	1 768	1 659	1 917	1 678	1 794	1 747

1 Excluding petitions in which divorce is asked for as alternative to nullity.
2 The breakdown of petitions filed is based on actual figures for The Principal Registry of the Family Division and the county courts (from 1990)
3 Including cases in which dissolution is asked for in the alternative.
4 This data is no longer available.

Source: Lord Chancellor's Department

Divorce

2.15 Divorce proceedings continued

Number

Scotland

		1981	1982	1983	1984	1985	1986	1987	1988	1989	1990	1991
Divorce[1]												
Actions in which final judgment given	KKHA	10 247	11 682	13 637	11 915	13 373	13 063	12 133	11 472	11 659	12 272	12 399
On grounds of[2]:												
Adultery	KKHB	6	2	–	–	–	–	–	–	–	–	–
Desertion	KKHC	–	–	–	–	–	–	–	–	–	–	–
Insanity	KKHD	–	–	–	–	–	–	–	–	–	–	–
Cruelty	KKHE	8	2	–	–	–	–	–	–	–	–	–
Sodomy	KKHF	–	–	–	–	–	–	–	–	–	–	–
On grounds of[3]:												
Adultery	KKHG	1 749	1 926	1 844	1 415	1 760	1 610	1 531	1 309	1 291	1 232	1 198
Desertion	KKHH	242	252	207	142	120	129	79	83	100	68	82
Behaviour	KKHI	4 382	5 096	4 900	4 351	5 020	4 620	4 180	3 559	3 532	3 847	3 622
2 years non-cohabitation	KKHJ	2 470	2 844	4 250	4 250	4 665	4 950	4 738	4 879	5 076	5 360	5 274
5 years non-cohabitation	KKHK	1 389	1 556	2 428	1 741	1 791	1 729	1 591	1 626	1 632	1 757	1 919
Other	KKHL	1	4	7	7	15	16	5	5	6	8	4
At instances of: Husbands	KKHM	2 584	2 833	3 847	3 198	3 401	3 389	3 333	3 195	3 226	3 410	3 469
Wives	KKHN	7 663	8 849	9 790	8 708	9 970	9 665	8 800	8 277	8 439	8 862	8 930
Divorce granted	KKHO	9 889	11 275	13 235	11 906	13 371	13 054	12 130	11 472	11 659	12 272	12 399
Separation												
Action in which final judgment given	KKHP	–	–	–	–	–	–	–	–	–	–	–
Separation granted	KKHQ	–	–	–	–	–	–	–	–	–	–	–
Duration of marriages where divorce or separation granted												
Under 1 year	KKHR	9	9	3	12	42	31	31	24	27	26	24
1 - 2 years	KKHS	146	173	140	158	200	202	170	173	168	198	179
2 - 5 years	KKHT	1 542	1 801	2 121	1 987	2 122	2 039	1 972	1 789	1 818	1 987	1 939
5 - 10 years	KKHU	3 014	3 490	4 008	3 455	3 882	3 822	3 544	3 353	3 420	3 546	3 508
10 - 20 years	KKHV	3 169	3 671	4 074	3 862	4 552	4 415	4 021	3 819	3 878	3 978	4 202
20 years and over	KKHW	2 009	2 131	2 880	2 432	2 573	2 545	2 395	2 314	2 348	2 540	2 547
Actions[4] in which there were:												
Children of marriage	KKHX	6 099	7 079	6 863	6 418	7 331	6 910	6 144	5 585	5 568	5 717	5 878
No children	KKHY	4 148	4 603	6 774	5 488	6 040	6 144	5 989	5 887	6 091	6 555	6 521

1 With effect from 1984 these statistics are being collected on the basis of divorces granted only and any difference in the number of divorces brought and granted relates to nullity of marriage.
2 Prior to the divorce (Scotland) Act 1976. Figures do not exist after 1982.
3 The grounds given show the allegations made-divorce is granted on the grounds of irretrievable breakdown of marriage under the Divorce (Scotland) Act 1976.
4 Divorce and separation.

Northern Ireland

		1981	1982	1983	1984	1985	1986	1987	1988	1989	1990	1991
Petitions filed												
Nullity of marriage	KKHZ	9	5	–	6	6	6	4	1	6	7	5
Divorce	KKIA	1 645	1 734	1 577	1 749	1 986	1 630	1 834	2 217	2 385	2 258	2 591
Judicial separation	KKIB	2	2	9	5	15	17	7	6	16	16	23

Sources: Scottish Courts Administration; Northern Ireland Court Service

Vital statistics

2.16 Births
Annual averages or calendar years

Thousands

	Live births			Sex ratio	Rates[1] Crude birth rate[2]	General fertility rate[3]	TPFR[4]	Still-births	Still-birth rate
	Total	Male	Female						

United Kingdom

1900 - 02	1 095	558	537	1 037	28.6	115.1	..	..	..
1910 - 12	1 037	528	508	1 039	24.6	99.4	..	..	..
1920 - 22	1 018	522	496	1 052	23.1	93.0	..	..	..
1930 - 32	750	383	367	1 046	16.3	66.5	..	..	..
1940 - 42	723	372	351	1 062	15.0	..	1.89	26	..
1950 - 52	803	413	390	1 061	16.0	73.7	2.21	18	..
1960 - 62	946	487	459	1 063	17.9	90.3	2.80	18	..
1970 - 72	880	453	427	1 064	15.8	82.5	2.36	12	13
1980 - 82	735	377	358	1 053	13.0	62.5	1.83	5	7
	BBCA	KBCZ	KBCY	KMFW	KBCT	KBCS	KBCR	KBCQ	KMFX
1978	687	353	334	1 059	12.2	60.8	1.76	6	8
1979	735	378	356	1 061	13.1	64.1	1.86	6	8
1980	754	386	368	1 050	13.4	64.9	1.89	6	7
1981	731	375	356	1 053	13.0	62.1	1.81	5	7
1982	719	369	350	1 054	12.8	60.6	1.78	5	6
1983	721	371	351	1 058	12.8	60.2	1.77	4	6
1984	730	373	356	1 049	12.9	60.3	1.77	4	6
1985	751	385	366	1 053	13.3	61.4	1.80	4	6
1986	755	387	368	1 053	13.3	61.1	1.78	4	5
1987	776	398	378	1 053	13.6	62.3	1.82	4	5
1988	788	403	384	1 049	13.8	63.2	1.84	4	5
1989	777	398	379	1 051	13.6	62.4	1.81	4	5
1990	799	409	390	1 049	13.9	64.2	1.84	4	5
1991	793	406	386	1 052	13.8	63.8	1.82	4	5

England and Wales

1900 - 02	932	475	458	1 037	28.6	114.7	..	..	..
1910 - 12	884	450	433	1 040	24.5	98.6	..	..	..
1920 - 22	862	442	420	1 051	22.8	91.1	..	..	..
1930 - 32	632	323	309	1 047	15.8	64.4	..	27	..
1940 - 42	607	312	295	1 057	15.6	61.3	1.81	22	..
1950 - 52	683	351	332	1 058	15.6	72.1	2.16	16	..
1960 - 62	812	418	394	1 061	17.6	88.9	2.77	16	..
1970 - 72	764	394	371	1 061	15.6	81.4	2.31	10	13
1980 - 82	639	328	311	1 053	12.9	61.8	1.81	4	7
	BBCB	KMFY	KMFZ	KMGA	KMGB	KMGC	KMGD	KMGE	KMGF
1978	596	307	289	1 061	12.1	60.1	1.73	5	8
1979	638	328	310	1 060	12.9	63.3	1.84	5	8
1980	656	336	320	1 049	13.2	64.2	1.88	5	7
1981	634	326	309	1 055	12.8	61.3	1.80	4	7
1982	626	321	305	1 055	12.6	59.9	1.76	4	6
1983	629	323	306	1 056	12.7	59.7	1.76	4	6
1984	637	326	311	1 049	12.8	59.8	1.75	4	6
1985	656	337	320	1 054	13.1	61.0	1.78	4	6
1986	661	339	322	1 052	13.2	60.6	1.77	4	5
1987	682	350	332	1 053	13.6	62.0	1.81	3	5
1988	694	355	339	1 048	13.8	63.0	1.82	3	5
1989	688	352	335	1 051	13.6	62.5	1.80	3	5
1990	706	361	345	1 048	13.9	64.3	1.84	3	5
1991	699	358	341	1 052	13.7	63.8	1.82	3	5

See footnotes on page 28.

Vital statistics
2.16 Births
Annual averages or calendar years
continued

Thousands

	Live births				Rates[1]				Still-birth rate
	Total	Male	Female	Sex ratio	Crude birth rate[2]	General fertility rate[3]	TPFR[4]	Still-births	

Scotland

1900 - 02	132	67	65	1 046	29.5	120.6	..	..	..
1910 - 12	123	63	60	1 044	25.9	107.4	..	..	..
1920 - 22	125	64	61	1 046	25.6	105.9	..	..	..
1930 - 32	93	47	45	1 040	19.1	78.8	..	..	..
1940 - 42	89	46	43	1 051	18.5	73.7	..	4	..
1950 - 52	91	47	44	1 060	17.9	81.4	2.41	2	..
1960 - 62	102	53	50	1 060	19.7	97.8	2.98	2	..
1970 - 72	84	43	41	1 057	16.1	83.3	2.46	1	13
1980 - 82	68	35	33	1 051	13.1	62.2	1.80	-	6
	BBCD	KMEU	KMEV	KMEW	KMEX	KMEY	KMEZ	KMFM	KMFN
1978	64	33	31	1 058	12.3	60.1	1.75	1	8
1979	68	35	33	1 071	13.1	63.4	1.85	–	7
1980	69	35	33	1 057	13.3	63.3	1.84	–	7
1981	69	35	34	1 045	13.3	63.1	1.83	–	6
1982	66	34	32	1 050	12.8	60.1	1.74	–	6
1983	65	34	31	1 071	12.6	58.9	1.70	–	6
1984	65	33	32	1 037	12.7	58.4	1.68	–	6
1985	67	34	33	1 048	13.0	59.5	1.71	–	5
1986	66	34	32	1 061	12.9	58.5	1.68	–	6
1987	66	34	32	1 053	13.0	58.8	1.68	–	5
1988	66	34	32	1 059	13.0	59.1	1.68	–	5
1989	63	33	31	1 049	12.5	56.9	1.61	–	5
1990	66	34	32	1 057	12.9	58.8	1.67	–	5
1991	67	34	33	1 056	13.1	59.8	1.70	–	6

Northern Ireland

1900 - 02	..	..	..	..	..	..	..	..	..
1910 - 12	..	..	..	..	..	..	..	..	..
1920 - 22	31	16	15	1 048	24.2	105.9	..	..	..
1930 - 32	26	13	12	1 047	20.5	78.8	..	..	..
1940 - 42	27	14	13	1 078	20.8	73.7	..	..	..
1950 - 52	29	15	14	1 066	20.9	81.4	..	..	..
1960 - 62	31	16	15	1 068	22.5	111.5	3.47	7	23
1970 - 72	31	16	15	1 074	20.4	105.7	3.13	3	14
1980 - 82	28	14	13	1 048	18.0	87.5	2.59	-	8
	BBCE	KMFO	KMFP	KMFQ	KMFR	KMFS	KMFT	KMFU	KMFV
1978	26	13	13	1 007	17.1	85.4	2.64	–	9
1979	28	14	14	1 058	18.4	92.2	2.80	–	9
1980	29	15	14	1 057	18.6	91.6	2.78	–	9
1981	27	14	13	1 041	17.8	86.3	2.59	–	9
1982	27	14	13	1 045	17.6	84.6	2.52	–	7
1983	27	14	13	1 068	17.7	84.0	2.56	–	7
1984	28	14	13	1 069	17.9	84.2	2.49	–	6
1985	28	14	13	1 054	17.7	83.1	2.45	–	6
1986	28	15	14	1 075	18.0	83.7	2.46	–	4
1987	28	14	14	1 056	17.7	82.2	2.41	–	6
1988	28	14	14	1 055	17.6	82.0	2.39	–	5
1989	26	13	13	1 061	16.5	76.9	2.23	–	5
1990	26	14	13	1 048	16.7	78.0	2.26	–	4
1991	26	14	13	1 065	16.5	76.0	2.18	–	5

1 Rates are based on a new series of population estimates which use a new definition and population base taking into account the 1981 Census results.
2 Rate per 1 000 population.
3 Rate per 1 000 women aged 15 - 44.
4 Total period fertility rate is the average number of children which would be born per woman if women experienced the age-specific fertility rates of the period in question throughout their child-bearing life span. UK figures for the years 1970-72 and earlier are estimates.

Sources: Office of Population Censuses and Surveys;
General Register Office (Northern Ireland);
General Register Office (Scotland)

Vital statistics

2.17 Birth occurrence inside and outside marriage by age of mother

Thousands

	Inside marriage						Outside marriage					
	All ages	Under 20	20 - 24	25 - 29	Over 30	Mean age (Years)	All ages	Under 20	20 - 24	25 - 29	Over 30	Mean age (Years)
Year												
United Kingdom												
	KKEY	KKEZ	KKFY	KKFZ	KKGX	KKGY	KKGZ	KKIC	KKID	KKIE	KKIF	KKIG
1961	890	55	273	280	282	27.7	54	13	17	10	13	25.5
1971	828	70	301	271	185	26.4	74	24	25	13	12	23.8
1981	640	36	193	231	180	27.3	91	30	33	16	13	23.4
1985	609	24	169	233	183	27.7	142	42	54	27	19	23.6
1986	597	21	159	231	185	27.9	158	45	60	31	22	23.7
1987	598	18	153	235	192	28.1	178	48	68	37	26	23.9
1988	590	16	144	235	195	28.2	198	51	76	42	29	24.1
1989	571	14	130	229	198	28.4	207	49	79	46	32	24.3
1990	576	13	121	233	209	28.6	223	51	83	53	37	24.5
1991	556	10	109	224	213	28.9	236	50	87	58	41	24.8
Great Britain												
	KKIH	KKII	KKIJ	KKIK	KKIL	KKIM	KKIN	KKIO	KKIP	KKIQ	KKIR	KKIS
1961	859	53	264	270	272	27.7	53	13	17	10	13	25.5
1971	797	68	293	261	176	26.4	73	24	25	13	12	23.8
1981	614	34	186	223	171	27.2	89	29	32	16	13	23.3
1985	584	23	162	224	175	27.7	139	41	52	27	19	22.7
1986	572	20	153	222	177	27.9	155	44	59	30	22	22.9
1987	574	17	147	227	184	28.0	174	46	66	36	25	23.4
1988	566	16	138	226	186	28.2	194	49	74	42	29	23.6
1989	549	13	125	220	190	28.4	202	48	77	45	32	24.2
1990	554	12	116	225	201	28.6	218	49	81	52	36	24.6
1991	535	10	105	216	205	28.9	231	48	85	57	41	24.8

Source: Office of Population Censuses and Surveys

Vital statistics

2.18 Live births by age of mother

Number

All live births - United Kingdom

Year	Age-group:	Under 20	20 - 24	25 - 29	30 - 34	35 - 39	40 - 44	45 and over	All ages
		KMDV	KMDW	KMDX	KMDY	KMDZ	KMES	KMET	KMBZ
1980		70 115	232 606	255 731	147 881	39 526	7 156	693	753 708
1981		65 362	225 673	247 461	144 472	39 893	7 241	744	730 848
1982		64 239	222 200	242 495	137 689	44 919	6 932	681	719 155
1983		62 354	221 029	244 952	137 811	47 296	7 315	710	721 467
1984		62 784	220 230	249 799	139 555	48 962	7 687	600	729 617
1985		65 435	222 614	260 192	143 385	50 590	7 884	628	750 728
1986		65 892	219 749	261 889	147 190	51 612	8 075	575	754 982
1987		65 952	220 377	271 897	154 982	52 667	9 176	566	775 617
1988		66 961	219 965	276 869	159 821	53 802	9 590	548	787 566
1989		63 173	208 972	274 882	164 215	55 537	9 966	540	777 285
1990		63 007	203 490	286 014	176 826	58 425	10 301	549	798 612
1991		59 722	196 243	282 186	182 739	60 583	10 453	580	792 506

Age-specific fertility rates - United Kingdom

Year	Age-group:	Under 20	20 - 24	25 - 29	30 - 34	35 - 39	40 - 44	45 and over	All ages
		KMBR	KMBS	KMBT	KMBU	KMBV	KMBW	KMBX	KMBY
1980		30.5	113.5	134.9	71.4	23.1	4.5	0.4	64.9
1981		28.3	106.8	130.4	69.5	22.4	4.6	0.5	62.1
1982		27.8	102.7	127.1	69.8	23.3	4.4	0.4	60.6
1983		27.1	99.5	127.0	72.1	23.6	4.5	0.5	60.2
1984		27.8	96.4	126.8	74.0	24.0	4.6	0.4	60.3
1985		29.6	95.3	128.2	76.7	24.5	4.6	0.4	61.4
1986		30.2	93.4	124.7	78.3	24.8	4.6	0.4	61.1
1987		30.9	93.9	125.5	81.3	26.6	4.8	0.4	62.3
1988		32.3	94.9	124.4	82.6	28.0	4.8	0.3	63.1
1989		31.8	91.5	120.3	83.2	29.3	4.9	0.3	62.4
1990		33.0	91.1	122.7	87.0	31.0	5.0	0.3	64.2
1991		32.9	89.1	120.4	86.8	32.0	5.1	0.3	63.8

All live births - England and Wales

Year	Age-group:	Under 20	20 - 24	25 - 29	30 - 34	35 - 39	40 - 44	45 and over	All ages
		KGSA	KGSB	KGSC	KGSD	KGSE	KGSF	KGSG	KGSH
1980		60 754	201 541	223 438	129 908	33 893	6 075	625	656 234
1981		56 570	194 500	215 760	126 590	34 210	6 170	690	634 492
1982		55 435	192 322	211 905	120 758	38 992	5 886	633	625 931
1983		54 059	191 852	214 078	120 996	41 277	6 210	662	629 134
1984		54 058	191 455	218 031	122 774	42 921	6 576	553	636 818
1985		56 929	193 958	227 486	126 185	44 393	6 882	584	656 417
1986		57 406	192 064	229 035	129 487	45 465	7 033	528	661 018
1987		57 545	193 232	238 929	136 558	46 604	8 112	531	681 511
1988		58 741	193 726	243 460	140 974	47 649	8 520	507	693 577
1989		55 543	185 239	242 822	145 320	49 465	8 845	491	687 725
1990		55 541	180 136	252 577	156 264	51 905	9 220	497	706 140
1991		52 396	173 356	248 727	161 259	53 644	9 316	519	699 217

Age-specific fertility rates - England and Wales

Year	Age-group:	Under 20	20 - 24	25 - 29	30 - 34	35 - 39	40 - 44	45 and over	All ages
		KGSI	KGSJ	KGSK	KGSL	KGSM	KGSN	KGSO	KGSP
1980		30.4	112.7	133.6	70.5	22.3	4.3	0.5	64.2
1981		28.1	105.3	129.1	68.6	21.7	4.4	0.5	61.3
1982		27.4	101.6	126.4	69.1	22.8	4.2	0.5	59.9
1983		26.9	98.5	126.4	71.5	23.1	4.4	0.5	59.7
1984		27.6	95.5	126.2	73.6	23.6	4.5	0.4	59.8
1985		29.5	94.5	127.6	76.4	24.1	4.6	0.4	61.0
1986		30.1	92.7	124.0	78.1	24.6	4.5	0.4	60.6
1987		30.9	93.4	125.1	81.3	26.5	4.8	0.4	62.0
1988		32.4	94.9	123.8	82.7	27.9	4.8	0.4	63.0
1989		31.9	92.2	120.0	83.7	29.4	4.9	0.3	62.5
1990		33.3	91.7	122.4	87.3	31.2	5.0	0.3	64.3
1991		33.0	89.6	119.9	87.0	32.1	5.1	0.3	63.8

Sources: Office of Population Censuses and Surveys;
General Register Office (Northern Ireland);
General Register Office (Scotland)

2.18 continued Live births by age of mother

Vital statistics

Number

All live births - Scotland

Year	Under 20	20 - 24	25 - 29	30 - 34	35 - 39	40 - 44	45 and over	All ages
	KGTA	KGTB	KGTC	KGTD	KGTE	KGTF	KGTG	KGTH
1980	7 237	22 598	23 235	12 129	3 109	557	27	68 892
1981	6 880	23 050	23 170	12 134	3 238	555	27	69 054
1982	6 891	21 855	22 133	11 333	3 408	550	26	66 196
1983	6 348	21 319	22 110	11 216	3 533	530	22	65 078
1984	6 251	20 728	22 816	11 227	3 517	543	24	65 106
1985	6 528	20 809	23 511	11 600	3 692	512	24	66 676
1986	6 390	19 853	23 357	12 013	3 654	519	26	65 812
1987	6 398	19 534	23 511	12 593	3 643	542	20	66 241
1988	6 166	18 836	23 947	12 844	3 863	534	22	66 212
1989	5 729	17 191	22 936	13 131	3 852	619	22	63 480
1990	5 608	16 970	24 227	14 393	4 147	604	24	65 973
1991	5 537	16 753	24 196	15 225	4 595	686	32	67 024

Age-specific fertility rates - Scotland

Year	Under 20	20 - 24	25 - 29	30 - 34	35 - 39	40 - 44	45 and over	All ages
	KGTI	KGTJ	KGTK	KGTL	KGTM	KGTN	KGTO	KGTP
1980	32.0	112.5	132.7	66.8	20.3	3.7	0.2	63.3
1981	30.6	112.5	131.5	66.2	20.8	3.7	0.2	63.1
1982	30.8	104.9	123.2	64.7	20.5	3.7	0.2	60.1
1983	28.8	101.0	121.3	65.5	20.7	3.5	0.1	58.9
1984	28.8	96.2	122.2	65.9	20.1	3.6	0.2	58.4
1985	30.9	95.2	123.3	68.0	20.7	3.4	0.2	59.5
1986	30.8	91.4	120.0	70.0	20.3	3.4	0.2	58.5
1987	31.7	90.5	118.9	71.9	21.2	3.3	0.1	58.8
1988	31.9	88.6	120.3	72.2	22.9	3.2	0.1	59.1
1989	31.2	82.5	113.7	72.1	22.9	3.6	0.1	56.9
1990	31.9	82.5	117.3	76.8	24.5	3.4	0.2	58.8
1991	33.4	82.4	116.6	78.5	26.8	3.8	0.2	59.8

All live births - Northern Ireland

Year	Under 20	20 - 24	25 - 29	30 - 34	35 - 39	40 - 44	45 and over	All ages
	KMDF	KMDG	KMDH	KMDI	KMDJ	KMDK	KMDL	KMDM
1980	2 124	8 467	9 058	5 844	2 524	524	41	28 582
1981	1 912	8 123	8 531	5 748	2 445	516	27	27 302
1982	1 913	8 023	8 457	5 598	2 519	496	22	27 028
1983	1 947	7 858	8 764	5 599	2 486	575	26	27 255
1984	2 025	8 047	8 952	5 554	2 524	568	23	27 693
1985	1 978	7 847	9 195	5 600	2 505	490	20	27 635
1986	2 096	7 832	9 497	5 690	2 493	523	21	28 152
1987	2 009	7 611	9 457	5 831	2 420	522	15	27 865
1988	2 054	7 403	9 462	6 003	2 790	536	19	27 767
1989	1 900	6 542	9 124	5 764	2 220	502	27	26 080
1990	1 858	6 384	9 210	6 169	2 373	477	28	26 499
1991	1 789	6 134	9 263	6 255	2 344	451	29	26 265

Age-specific fertility rates - Northern Ireland

Year	Under 20	20 - 24	25 - 29	30 - 34	35 - 39	40 - 44	45 and over	All ages
	KMDN	KMDO	KMDP	KMDQ	KMDR	KMDS	KMDT	KMDU
1980	29.2	143.3	191.5	122.0	56.6	12.9	1.0	91.6
1981	27.3	134.9	172.7	117.8	52.2	12.6	0.7	86.3
1982	27.6	131.5	163.6	116.4	52.2	12.1	0.6	84.6
1983	28.1	125.5	164.1	116.2	51.4	13.5	0.7	84.0
1984	29.1	125.9	163.4	114.8	52.1	13.0	0.6	84.2
1985	28.7	121.8	162.7	114.1	51.8	10.9	0.5	83.1
1986	30.3	122.2	164.3	112.5	51.7	11.2	0.5	83.7
1987	29.4	118.0	160.8	112.6	50.7	10.9	0.4	82.2
1988	30.8	115.1	159.3	113.7	48.0	11.2	0.5	82.0
1989	29.1	101.7	151.5	107.1	46.3	10.5	0.6	76.8
1990	29.3	99.9	152.0	111.6	48.7	10.0	0.6	78.0
1991	28.8	96.4	148.6	107.5	46.9	9.1	0.6	76.0

Sources: Office of Population Censuses and Surveys;
General Register Office (Northern Ireland);
General Register Office (Scotland)

Vital statistics
2.19 Deaths: analysis by age and sex
Annual averages or calendar years

Number

	All ages[1]	Under 1 year	1-4	5-9	10-14	15-19	20-24	25-34	35-44	45-54	55-64	65-74	75-84	85 and over
						United Kingdom								
Males														
1900 - 02	340 664	87 242	37 834	8 429	4 696	7 047	8 766	19 154	24 739	30 488	37 610	39 765	28 320	6 563
1910 - 12	303 703	63 885	29 452	7 091	4 095	5 873	6 817	16 141	21 813	28 981	37 721	45 140	29 397	7 283
1920 - 22	284 876	48 044	19 008	6 052	3 953	5 906	6 572	13 663	19 702	29 256	40 583	49 398	34 937	7 801
1930 - 32	284 249	28 840	11 276	4 580	2 890	5 076	6 495	12 327	16 326	29 376	47 989	63 804	45 247	10 022
1940 - 42	314 643	24 624	6 949	3 400	2 474	4 653	4 246	11 506	17 296	30 082	57 076	79 652	59 733	12 900
1950 - 52	307 312	14 105	2 585	1 317	919	1 498	2 289	5 862	11 074	27 637	53 691	86 435	79 768	20 131
1960 - 62	318 850	12 234	1 733	971	871	1 718	1 857	3 842	8 753	26 422	63 009	87 542	83 291	26 605
1970 - 72	335 166	9 158	1 485	1 019	802	1 778	2 104	3 590	7 733	24 608	64 898	105 058	82 905	30 027
1980 - 82	330 495	4 829	774	527	652	1 999	1 943	3 736	6 568	19 728	54 159	105 155	98 488	31 936
	KHUA	KHUB	KHUC	KHUD	KHUE	KHUF	KHUG	KHUH	KHUI	KHUJ	KHUK	KHUL	KHUM	KHUN
1971	328 537	9 366	1 439	1 055	834	1 802	2 091	3 524	7 735	24 242	63 657	102 139	81 183	29 470
1972	342 605	8 393	1 460	1 024	801	1 779	2 092	3 661	7 629	25 184	64 379	109 448	85 535	31 220
1973	338 788	7 783	1 438	978	790	1 819	2 213	3 953	7 530	25 434	61 970	108 871	85 172	30 837
1974	337 263	7 180	1 307	858	775	1 895	1 968	3 820	7 448	25 864	59 703	110 718	84 491	31 236
1975	335 006	6 392	1 139	829	842	1 871	2 018	3 845	7 006	24 630	58 581	110 126	86 653	31 074
1976	341 910	5 706	1 036	798	769	1 978	1 994	3 867	6 976	23 663	59 703	112 234	90 710	32 476
1977	329 924	5 350	918	744	702	1 892	1 947	3 864	6 752	22 787	57 214	108 677	88 569	30 508
1978	336 395	5 220	866	726	729	2 067	2 055	3 944	6 912	22 439	57 381	110 384	92 574	31 098
1979	339 568	5 447	748	708	707	2 042	1 969	4 012	6 868	21 828	56 944	110 172	96 026	32 097
1980	332 370	5 174	792	609	659	2 022	1 940	3 786	6 698	20 577	55 176	107 089	96 301	31 547
1981	329 145	4 759	771	517	666	2 008	1 919	3 761	6 544	19 740	53 770	104 950	97 881	31 859
1982	329 971	4 555	760	456	632	1 966	1 971	3 661	6 462	18 867	53 531	103 426	101 281	32 403
1983	328 824	4 230	695	469	609	1 834	1 899	3 601	6 537	18 238	54 493	100 469	103 038	32 712
1984	321 095	3 995	725	423	580	1 708	1 999	3 595	6 425	17 647	53 715	95 420	102 513	32 350
1985	331 562	4 003	728	393	583	1 612	2 031	3 452	6 728	17 316	52 502	97 458	109 241	35 515
1986	327 160	4 219	653	384	444	1 676	2 067	3 668	6 712	16 814	50 352	95 987	108 123	36 061
1987	318 282	4 105	657	377	470	1 612	2 125	3 776	6 793	15 950	47 675	93 348	105 773	35 621
1988	319 119	4 110	680	433	460	1 525	2 160	3 983	6 860	16 016	46 001	91 893	107 082	37 916
1989	320 193	3 799	699	414	398	1 537	2 118	3 968	6 832	15 560	43 693	90 304	109 450	41 421
1990	314 601	3 614	674	376	406	1 487	2 197	4 354	6 991	15 507	41 983	88 458	107 451	41 103
1991[2]	314 427	3 377	636	395	404	1 417	2 049	4 270	7 102	15 493	40 256	88 014	107 416	43 598
Females														
1900 - 02	322 058	68 770	36 164	8 757	5 034	6 818	8 264	18 702	21 887	25 679	34 521	42 456	34 907	10 099
1910 - 12	289 608	49 865	27 817	7 113	4 355	5 683	6 531	15 676	19 647	24 481	32 813	46 453	37 353	11 828
1920 - 22	274 772	35 356	17 323	5 808	4 133	5 729	6 753	14 878	18 121	24 347	34 026	48 573	45 521	14 203
1930 - 32	275 336	21 072	9 995	3 990	2 734	4 721	5 931	12 699	15 373	24 695	39 471	59 520	56 250	18 886
1940 - 42	296 646	17 936	5 952	2 743	2 068	4 180	5 028	11 261	14 255	23 629	42 651	70 907	71 377	24 658
1950 - 52	291 597	10 293	2 098	880	625	1 115	1 717	5 018	8 989	18 875	37 075	75 220	92 848	36 844
1960 - 62	304 871	8 887	1 334	627	522	684	811	2 504	6 513	16 720	36 078	73 118	105 956	51 117
1970 - 72	322 968	6 666	1 183	654	459	718	900	2 110	5 345	15 594	36 177	75 599	109 539	68 024
1980 - 82	330 269	3 561	585	355	425	733	772	2 099	4 360	12 206	32 052	72 618	117 760	82 743
	KIUA	KIUB	KIUC	KIUD	KIUE	KIUF	KIUG	KIUH	KIUI	KIUJ	KIUK	KIUL	KIUM	KIUN
1971	316 541	6 798	1 129	649	493	721	866	2 105	5 267	15 358	35 621	73 502	107 056	66 976
1972	331 333	6 198	1 238	665	416	770	878	2 107	5 267	15 897	36 260	77 261	113 076	71 300
1973	330 904	5 646	1 060	610	455	803	847	2 166	5 145	15 822	34 733	77 067	113 393	73 157
1974	330 096	5 172	981	581	503	736	805	2 070	5 038	15 972	34 342	76 929	112 492	74 475
1975	327 471	4 798	860	540	405	751	813	2 211	4 897	15 054	33 904	75 459	112 838	74 941
1976	338 889	4 070	735	516	484	724	786	2 264	4 737	14 912	34 468	76 950	118 246	79 997
1977	325 219	3 933	720	431	450	750	839	2 148	4 583	13 905	33 395	74 573	113 872	75 620
1978	330 782	3 908	715	480	497	818	823	2 343	4 719	13 914	33 353	75 433	115 730	78 049
1979	336 009	4 026	617	428	462	701	738	2 244	4 544	13 667	33 274	75 610	118 859	80 839
1980	329 149	3 938	596	409	442	771	811	2 157	4 460	12 583	32 349	73 672	116 461	80 500
1981	328 829	3 402	599	352	424	738	737	2 083	4 309	12 275	31 625	72 476	117 458	82 351
1982	332 830	3 342	561	304	410	689	767	2 057	4 312	11 759	32 183	71 705	119 362	85 379
1983	330 277	3 126	568	318	374	719	698	1 914	4 318	11 384	32 197	69 266	118 940	86 455
1984	323 823	3 005	537	304	344	665	722	1 932	4 269	10 947	32 262	66 432	116 649	85 756
1985	339 094	3 027	574	314	355	626	729	1 852	4 397	10 581	32 010	68 505	122 445	93 679
1986	333 575	2 961	561	275	307	635	769	1 882	4 387	10 211	29 954	67 313	120 663	93 657
1987	326 060	2 972	550	265	288	614	733	1 974	4 454	10 177	29 037	65 570	117 266	92 160
1988	330 059	2 951	552	264	251	612	745	1 915	4 615	9 887	28 154	65 020	117 731	97 362
1989	337 540	2 743	551	271	268	598	773	1 955	4 506	9 834	27 324	64 575	120 975	103 167
1990	327 198	2 658	489	249	273	534	700	1 967	4 463	9 718	26 350	62 019	116 357	101 421
1991[2]	331 754	2 448	512	280	264	538	738	2 005	4 295	9 699	24 952	62 200	116 924	106 899

1 In some years the totals include a small number of persons whose age was not stated.
2 Provisional.

Sources: Office of Population Censuses and Surveys;
General Register Office (Northern Ireland);
General Register Office (Scotland)

2.19 Deaths: analysis by age and sex
continued — Annual averages or calendar years

Vital statistics

Number

England and Wales

	All ages[1]	Under 1 year	1-4	5-9	10-14	15-19	20-24	25-34	35-44	45-54	55-64	65-74	75-84	85 and over
Males														
1900 - 02	288 886	76 095	32 051	7 066	3 818	5 611	7 028	15 869	21 135	26 065	31 600	33 568	23 835	5 144
1910 - 12	257 253	54 678	24 676	5 907	3 348	4 765	5 596	13 603	18 665	24 820	32 217	38 016	24 928	6 036
1920 - 22	240 605	39 796	15 565	5 151	3 314	4 901	5 447	11 551	17 004	25 073	34 639	42 025	29 685	6 455
1930 - 32	243 147	23 331	9 099	3 844	2 435	4 354	5 580	10 600	14 041	25 657	41 581	54 910	39 091	8 624
1940 - 42	268 876	19 393	5 616	2 834	2 051	3 832	3 156	9 484	14 744	25 983	50 058	68 791	51 779	11 158
1950 - 52	266 879	11 498	2 131	1 087	778	1 248	1 947	4 990	9 489	23 815	46 948	75 774	69 496	17 677
1960 - 62	278 369	10 157	1 444	812	742	1 523	1 624	3 278	7 524	22 813	54 908	77 000	73 180	23 364
1970 - 72	293 934	7 818	1 259	860	677	1 524	1 788	3 079	6 637	21 348	56 667	92 389	73 365	26 522
1980 - 82	290 352	4 168	657	452	555	1 716	1 619	3 169	5 590	16 909	47 144	92 485	87 338	28 551
	KHVA	KHVB	KHVC	KHVD	KHVE	KHVF	KHVG	KHVH	KHVI	KHVJ	KHVK	KHVL	KHVM	KHVN
1971	288 359	7 974	1 228	916	690	1 538	1 771	3 046	6 683	21 046	55 699	89 802	71 907	26 059
1972	300 389	7 210	1 235	847	693	1 482	1 757	3 103	6 511	21 837	56 202	96 329	75 564	27 619
1973	296 546	6 599	1 203	817	677	1 510	1 836	3 336	6 455	21 923	53 976	95 605	75 300	27 309
1974	295 315	6 137	1 095	720	649	1 582	1 666	3 241	6 222	22 388	51 883	97 331	74 770	27 631
1975	294 174	5 430	983	677	692	1 584	1 697	3 229	5 935	21 337	51 088	96 934	76 879	27 709
1976	300 058	4 879	876	676	639	1 660	1 663	3 245	5 928	20 449	52 048	98 654	80 348	28 993
1977	289 773	4 519	769	635	598	1 620	1 599	3 270	5 695	19 600	49 855	95 873	78 528	27 212
1978	295 505	4 513	739	628	619	1 776	1 761	3 325	5 849	19 307	49 976	97 194	82 067	27 751
1979	297 862	4 731	641	602	605	1 727	1 649	3 426	5 822	18 607	49 586	96 764	85 091	28 611
1980	291 869	4 471	668	517	546	1 745	1 613	3 203	5 710	17 693	48 053	94 188	85 300	28 162
1981	289 022	4 119	651	447	573	1 734	1 576	3 181	5 535	16 889	46 858	92 189	86 774	28 496
1982	290 166	3 914	652	391	546	1 669	1 668	3 122	5 526	16 144	46 521	91 079	89 940	28 994
1983	289 419	3 654	604	391	514	1 580	1 635	3 071	5 581	15 632	47 315	88 622	91 531	29 289
1984	282 357	3 443	610	348	501	1 484	1 728	3 033	5 512	15 113	46 904	83 728	90 983	28 970
1985	292 327	3 510	638	328	503	1 374	1 738	2 953	5 776	14 838	45 704	85 695	97 362	31 908
1986	287 894	3 724	573	325	380	1 429	1 746	3 104	5 767	14 370	43 637	84 437	96 201	32 201
1987	280 177	3 637	578	309	404	1 389	1 811	3 218	5 823	13 678	41 367	82 021	94 060	31 882
1988	280 931	3 649	587	374	402	1 279	1 802	3 367	5 855	13 701	39 791	80 870	95 306	33 948
1989	281 290	3 368	606	371	337	1 325	1 782	3 380	5 947	13 407	37 680	79 012	97 027	37 048
1990	277 336	3 207	593	333	338	1 295	1 889	3 714	6 060	13 342	36 405	77 604	95 539	37 017
1991	277 582	2 966	554	341	354	1 208	1 760	3 687	6 160	13 316	34 853	77 227	95 815	39 341
Females														
1900 - 02	269 432	60 090	30 674	7 278	4 010	5 265	6 497	15 065	18 253	21 474	28 424	35 307	29 118	7 977
1910 - 12	242 079	42 642	23 335	5 883	3 519	4 522	5 256	12 742	16 363	20 611	27 571	38 489	31 363	9 782
1920 - 22	229 908	29 178	14 174	4 928	3 456	4 719	5 533	12 244	15 142	20 580	28 633	41 010	38 439	11 871
1930 - 32	233 915	16 929	8 013	3 338	2 293	3 969	5 039	10 716	13 022	21 190	33 798	50 844	48 531	16 234
1940 - 42	253 702	14 174	4 726	2 265	1 695	3 426	4 198	9 470	12 093	20 413	36 814	60 987	61 891	21 550
1950 - 52	252 176	8 367	1 727	732	520	893	1 365	4 131	7 586	16 161	31 875	65 087	81 154	32 579
1960 - 62	266 849	7 409	1 103	527	444	591	700	2 147	5 576	14 389	31 083	63 543	93 548	45 789
1970 - 72	284 181	5 677	1 020	562	396	620	806	1 814	4 585	13 417	31 222	65 817	96 952	61 293
1980 - 82	290 026	3 064	511	301	365	635	670	1 821	3 740	10 420	27 606	63 023	103 676	74 194
	KIVA	KIVB	KIVC	KIVD	KIVE	KIVF	KIVG	KIVH	KIVI	KIVJ	KIVK	KIVL	KIVM	KIVN
1971	278 903	5 746	976	568	419	631	787	1 836	4 528	13 274	30 760	64 017	94 958	60 403
1972	291 500	5 288	1 073	579	367	658	783	1 804	4 512	13 686	31 330	67 215	99 980	64 225
1973	290 932	4 808	896	510	393	681	740	1 876	4 362	13 611	29 872	67 137	100 293	65 753
1974	289 977	4 322	827	505	442	630	688	1 785	4 291	13 828	29 471	66 992	99 398	66 798
1975	288 667	4 058	716	463	354	632	711	1 921	4 180	13 053	29 192	65 822	100 000	67 565
1976	298 458	3 455	593	451	417	623	671	1 939	4 041	12 806	29 605	67 107	104 673	72 077
1977	286 155	3 322	614	373	394	616	702	1 870	3 883	11 929	28 828	64 903	100 536	68 185
1978	290 396	3 368	607	417	421	691	710	2 042	4 004	11 911	28 607	65 411	102 058	70 149
1979	295 157	3 447	527	368	386	622	635	1 938	3 868	11 671	28 624	65 646	104 807	72 618
1980	289 516	3 428	518	349	373	667	696	1 861	3 771	10 757	27 857	64 087	102 728	72 424
1981	288 868	2 902	529	302	368	650	642	1 821	3 742	10 513	27 211	62 762	103 554	73 872
1982	291 695	2 861	485	253	353	588	672	1 781	3 708	9 990	27 751	62 221	104 745	76 287
1983	290 189	2 727	489	269	332	629	597	1 655	3 708	9 786	27 792	59 913	104 844	77 448
1984	284 524	2 594	454	260	302	575	621	1 676	3 658	9 343	27 764	57 813	102 744	76 720
1985	298 407	2 631	497	260	308	544	630	1 583	3 803	9 111	27 664	59 285	108 099	83 992
1986	293 309	2 589	491	248	272	562	674	1 646	3 834	8 761	25 785	58 360	106 463	83 624
1987	286 817	2 635	489	237	246	525	639	1 708	3 897	8 774	25 000	56 858	103 354	82 455
1988	290 477	2 621	498	232	218	542	650	1 670	4 025	8 448	24 104	56 567	103 666	87 236
1989	295 582	2 440	472	241	226	531	650	1 678	3 925	8 406	23 336	55 932	106 000	91 745
1990	287 510	2 357	434	220	230	472	616	1 702	3 875	8 337	22 511	53 770	102 440	90 546
1991	292 462	2 192	439	248	222	462	644	1 729	3 703	8 369	21 303	54 156	103 268	95 727

1 In some years the totals include a small number of persons whose age was not stated.

Source: Office of Population Censuses and Surveys

Vital statistics

2.19 Deaths: analysis by age and sex
Annual averages or calendar years
continued

Number

							Scotland							
	All ages[1]	Under 1 year	1-4	5-9	10-14	15-19	20-24	25-34	35-44	45-54	55-64	65-74	75-84	85 and over

Males

1900 - 02	40 224	9 189	4 798	1 083	672	1 069	1 292	2 506	2 935	3 591	4 597	4 531	3 117	834
1910 - 12	35 981	7 510	3 935	962	595	826	910	1 969	2 469	3 325	4 356	5 113	3 182	813
1920 - 22	34 649	6 757	2 847	710	489	747	791	1 616	2 128	3 314	4 785	5 624	3 928	911
1930 - 32	32 476	4 426	1 771	610	365	568	706	1 352	1 848	2 979	5 095	6 906	4 839	1 010
1940 - 42	36 384	3 973	1 011	449	321	668	888	1 643	2 090	3 348	5 728	8 556	6 317	1 337
1950 - 52	32 236	1 949	349	175	105	200	265	693	1 267	3 151	5 574	8 544	8 094	1 871
1960 - 62	32 401	1 578	222	121	102	146	185	456	1 013	2 986	6 682	8 505	7 980	2 425
1970 - 72	32 446	944	168	119	93	178	233	396	875	2 617	6 641	10 176	7 383	2 624
1980 - 82	31 723	451	80	56	71	206	233	423	776	2 280	5 601	10 152	8 804	2 591
	KHWA	KHWB	KHWC	KHWD	KHWE	KHWF	KHWG	KHWH	KHWI	KHWJ	KHWK	KHWL	KHWM	KHWN
1971	31 585	988	155	100	114	197	242	371	832	2 588	6 427	9 945	7 134	2 492
1972	33 215	833	162	133	76	176	226	413	902	2 658	6 573	10 596	7 748	2 719
1973	32 954	841	171	117	76	175	225	381	839	2 789	6 435	10 693	7 603	2 609
1974	32 722	748	148	97	83	202	183	403	953	2 739	6 205	10 757	7 505	2 699
1975	32 168	669	113	112	104	195	216	411	838	2 634	5 994	10 727	7 617	2 538
1976	32 983	568	110	84	97	204	212	448	811	2 621	6 109	10 926	8 146	2 647
1977	31 280	585	103	81	75	181	236	432	817	2 494	5 835	10 173	7 802	2 466
1978	32 432	479	87	63	78	211	210	479	854	2 508	5 888	10 734	8 299	2 542
1979	32 884	490	79	79	71	219	215	442	805	2 599	5 851	10 804	8 543	2 687
1980	31 669	481	93	65	78	190	223	421	778	2 316	5 628	10 248	8 571	2 577
1981	31 700	435	71	50	66	208	250	439	816	2 330	5 506	10 193	8 788	2 548
1982	31 801	436	77	53	69	220	225	410	733	2 195	5 669	10 015	9 052	2 647
1983	31 196	380	67	53	65	185	178	406	764	2 131	5 769	9 414	9 204	2 580
1984	30 731	389	87	53	65	172	202	429	696	2 017	5 493	9 337	9 222	2 569
1985	31 147	342	57	49	58	174	208	390	759	1 959	5 486	9 339	9 569	2 757
1986	31 111	334	66	44	49	177	238	436	757	1 967	5 354	9 169	9 574	2 946
1987	30 384	331	54	46	47	163	212	415	779	1 870	5 131	9 058	9 383	2 895
1988	30 195	324	64	39	42	181	246	475	808	1 915	4 997	8 763	9 314	3 027
1989	31 025	331	62	24	45	150	246	445	719	1 721	4 889	9 028	9 922	3 443
1990	29 617	297	62	31	50	138	240	502	745	1 734	4 512	8 635	9 499	3 172
1991	29 312	299	59	42	34	150	211	441	757	1 741	4 382	8 657	9 209	3 330

Females

1900 - 02	39 891	7 143	4 477	1 162	747	1 058	1 246	2 625	2 732	3 130	4 485	5 273	4 305	1 508
1910 - 12	36 132	5 854	3 674	981	618	836	910	2 149	2 473	2 909	3 960	5 636	4 588	1 552
1920 - 22	34 449	5 029	2 602	687	489	711	889	1 947	2 266	2 828	4 157	5 587	5 443	1 814
1930 - 32	32 377	3 319	1 602	527	339	568	666	1 508	1 812	2 731	4 380	6 630	6 178	2 117
1940 - 42	33 715	2 852	921	373	283	595	656	1 382	1 672	2 528	4 630	7 674	7 613	2 536
1950 - 52	31 525	1 432	284	115	84	185	293	714	1 127	2 188	4 204	8 157	9 310	3 431
1960 - 62	30 559	1 107	170	80	63	72	87	287	762	1 897	4 115	7 752	9 991	4 177
1970 - 72	30 978	694	118	69	46	73	74	231	608	1 769	4 036	7 823	10 112	5 324
1980 - 82	32 326	337	49	37	44	74	73	213	493	1 456	3 565	7 781	11 333	6 871
	KIWA	KIWB	KIWC	KIWD	KIWE	KIWF	KIWG	KIWH	KIWI	KIWJ	KIWK	KIWL	KIWM	KIWN
1971	30 029	734	107	64	60	64	62	214	590	1 720	4 000	7 603	9 686	5 125
1972	31 802	644	117	62	29	79	67	234	602	1 783	4 001	8 052	10 493	5 639
1973	31 591	571	105	77	46	91	80	224	604	1 796	3 890	7 930	10 355	5 822
1974	32 018	578	109	59	48	73	90	217	613	1 741	3 979	8 037	10 440	6 034
1975	30 957	499	104	56	33	84	77	228	580	1 625	3 792	7 750	10 250	5 879
1976	32 270	391	86	48	49	69	88	235	567	1 708	3 916	7 961	10 795	6 357
1977	31 014	419	73	45	41	97	100	214	557	1 578	3 671	7 761	10 628	5 830
1978	32 691	351	73	37	61	93	86	236	598	1 651	3 871	8 208	11 028	6 398
1979	32 863	388	69	37	58	59	81	247	551	1 635	3 776	8 045	11 309	6 608
1980	31 630	350	51	41	44	77	90	222	547	1 511	3 587	7 673	10 988	6 449
1981	32 128	345	46	35	43	68	69	213	453	1 414	3 556	7 935	11 144	6 807
1982	33 221	317	50	35	45	78	60	203	479	1 444	3 552	7 735	11 867	7 356
1983	32 258	266	51	33	33	67	76	201	504	1 317	3 568	7 558	11 340	7 244
1984	31 614	283	62	32	37	72	78	205	475	1 320	3 703	6 979	11 134	7 234
1985	32 820	282	55	37	34	63	76	207	481	1 179	3 563	7 449	11 604	7 790
1986	32 356	247	50	16	24	50	77	188	441	1 181	3 372	7 251	11 476	7 983
1987	31 630	232	44	21	34	60	70	195	429	1 160	3 301	7 032	11 262	7 790
1988	31 762	219	33	22	21	54	63	197	470	1 115	3 250	6 879	11 361	8 078
1989	33 992	223	56	23	27	54	104	224	470	1 156	3 279	7 052	12 100	9 224
1990	31 910	213	32	16	34	46	68	204	468	1 099	3 109	6 685	11 233	8 703
1991	31 729	174	54	22	31	57	74	225	463	1 070	2 974	6 542	11 059	8 984

1 In some years the totals include a small number of persons whose age was not stated.

Source: General Register Office (Scotland)

Vital statistics

2.19 Deaths: analysis by age and sex
continued Annual averages or calendar years

Number

Northern Ireland

	All ages[1]	Under 1 year	1-4	5-9	10-14	15-19	20-24	25-34	35-44	45-54	55-64	65-74	75-84	85 and over
Males														
1900 - 02	11 554	1 958	985	280	206	367	446	779	669	832	1 413	1 666	1 368	585
1910 - 12	10 469	1 697	841	222	152	282	311	569	679	836	1 148	2 011	1 287	434
1920 - 22	9 622	1 491	596	191	150	258	334	496	570	869	1 159	1 749	1 324	435
1930 - 32	8 626	1 083	406	126	90	154	209	375	437	740	1 313	1 988	1 317	388
1940 - 42	9 383	1 258	322	117	102	153	202	379	462	751	1 290	2 305	1 637	405
1950 - 52	8 197	658	105	55	36	50	77	179	318	671	1 169	2 117	2 178	583
1960 - 62	8 080	499	67	38	27	49	48	108	216	623	1 419	2 037	2 131	816
1970 - 72	8 786	396	58	40	32	76	83	115	221	643	1 590	2 493	2 157	881
1980 - 82	8 420	211	37	20	26	77	92	144	202	539	1 414	2 518	2 346	795
	KHXA	KHXB	KHXC	KHXD	KHXE	KHXF	KHXG	KHXH	KHXI	KHXJ	KHXK	KHXL	KHXM	KHXN
1971	8 593	404	56	39	30	67	78	107	220	608	1 531	2 392	2 142	919
1972	9 001	350	63	44	32	121	109	145	216	689	1 604	2 523	2 223	882
1973	9 288	343	64	44	37	134	152	236	236	722	1 559	2 573	2 269	919
1974	9 226	295	64	41	43	111	119	176	273	737	1 615	2 630	2 216	906
1975	8 664	293	43	40	46	92	105	205	233	659	1 499	2 465	2 157	827
1976	8 869	259	50	38	33	114	119	174	237	593	1 546	2 654	2 216	836
1977	8 871	246	46	28	29	91	112	162	240	693	1 524	2 631	2 239	830
1978	8 458	228	40	35	32	80	84	140	209	624	1 517	2 456	2 208	805
1979	8 822	226	28	27	31	96	105	144	241	622	1 507	2 604	2 392	799
1980	8 832	222	31	27	35	87	104	162	210	568	1 495	2 653	2 430	808
1981	8 423	205	49	20	27	66	93	141	193	521	1 406	2 568	2 319	815
1982	8 004	205	31	12	17	77	78	129	203	528	1 341	2 332	2 289	762
1983	8 209	196	24	25	30	69	86	124	192	475	1 409	2 433	2 303	843
1984	8 007	163	28	22	14	52	69	133	217	517	1 318	2 355	2 308	811
1985	8 088	151	33	16	22	64	85	109	193	519	1 312	2 424	2 310	850
1986	8 155	161	14	15	15	70	83	128	188	477	1 361	2 381	2 348	914
1987	7 721	137	25	22	19	60	102	143	191	402	1 177	2 269	2 330	844
1988	7 993	137	29	20	16	65	112	141	197	400	1 213	2 260	2 462	941
1989	7 878	100	31	19	16	62	90	143	166	432	1 124	2 264	2 501	930
1990	7 648	110	19	12	18	54	68	138	186	431	1 066	2 219	2 413	914
1991[2]	7 533	112	23	12	16	59	78	142	185	436	1 021	2 130	2 392	927
Females														
1900 - 02	12 735	1 537	1 013	317	277	495	521	1 012	902	1 075	1 612	1 876	1 484	614
1910 - 12	11 397	1 369	808	249	218	325	365	785	811	961	1 282	2 328	1 402	494
1920 - 22	10 415	1 149	547	193	188	299	331	687	713	939	1 236	1 976	1 639	518
1930 - 32	9 044	824	380	125	102	184	226	475	539	774	1 293	2 046	1 541	535
1940 - 42	9 229	910	305	105	90	159	174	409	490	688	1 207	2 246	1 873	572
1950 - 52	7 896	494	87	33	21	37	59	173	276	526	996	1 976	2 384	834
1960 - 62	7 463	371	61	20	15	21	24	70	175	434	880	1 823	2 417	1 151
1970 - 72	7 809	295	45	23	17	25	20	65	152	408	919	1 959	2 475	1 407
1980 - 82	7 917	160	26	17	17	23	29	65	127	329	881	1 813	2 752	1 678
	KIXA	KIXB	KIXC	KIXD	KIXE	KIXF	KIXG	KIXH	KIXI	KIXJ	KIXK	KIXL	KIXM	KIXN
1971	7 609	318	46	17	14	26	17	55	149	364	861	1 882	2 412	1 448
1972	8 031	266	48	24	20	33	28	69	153	428	929	1 994	2 603	1 436
1973	8 381	267	59	23	16	31	27	66	179	415	971	2 000	2 745	1 582
1974	8 101	272	45	17	13	33	27	68	134	403	892	1 900	2 654	1 643
1975	7 847	241	40	21	18	35	25	62	137	376	920	1 887	2 588	1 497
1976	8 161	224	56	17	18	32	27	90	129	398	947	1 882	2 778	1 563
1977	8 050	192	33	13	15	37	37	64	143	398	896	1 909	2 708	1 605
1978	7 695	189	35	26	15	34	27	65	117	352	875	1 814	2 644	1 502
1979	7 989	191	21	23	18	20	22	59	125	361	874	1 919	2 743	1 613
1980	8 003	160	27	19	25	27	25	74	142	315	905	1 912	2 745	1 627
1981	7 833	155	24	15	13	20	26	49	114	348	858	1 779	2 760	1 672
1982	7 914	164	26	16	12	23	35	73	125	325	880	1 749	2 750	1 736
1983	7 830	133	28	16	9	23	25	58	106	281	837	1 795	2 756	1 763
1984	7 685	128	21	12	5	18	23	51	136	284	795	1 640	2 770	1 802
1985	7 867	114	22	17	13	19	23	62	113	291	783	1 771	2 742	1 897
1986	7 910	125	20	11	11	23	18	48	112	269	797	1 702	2 724	2 050
1987	7 613	105	17	7	8	29	24	71	128	243	736	1 680	2 650	1 915
1988	7 820	111	21	10	12	16	32	48	120	324	800	1 574	2 704	2 048
1989	7 966	80	23	7	15	13	19	53	111	272	709	1 591	2 875	2 198
1990	7 778	88	23	13	9	16	16	61	120	282	730	1 564	2 684	2 172
1991[2]	7 563	82	19	10	11	19	20	51	129	260	675	1 502	2 597	2 188

1 In some years the totals include a small number of persons whose age was not stated.
2 Provisional.

Source: General Register Office (Northern Ireland)

Vital statistics

2.20 Deaths analysed by cause
International Statistical Classification of Diseases, Injuries and Causes of Death, Ninth Revision, 1979

Number

England and Wales

		ICD 9 code	1984[1]	1985	1986[2]	1987[2]	1988[2]	1989[2]	1990[2]	1991[2]
Infections and total deaths	KHEA		566 881	590 734	581 203	566 994	571 408	576 872	564 846	570 044
Deaths from natural causes [3]	KHEB		548 046	571 725	562 449	545 723	550 051	556 100	543 682	549 706
Infectious and parasitic diseases	KHEC	001-139	2 295	2 381	2 470	2 375	2 480	2 543	2 446	2 406
Intestinal infectious diseases	KJZZ	001-009	193	177	176	162	164	185	187	169
Tuberculosis of the respiratory system	KHEH	010-012	376	408	376	329	384	333	313	334
Other tuberculosis, including late effects	KHEI	013-018,137	377	366	357	296	334	316	264	240
Whooping cough	KHEK	033	1	4	3	5	–	1	7	–
Meningococcal infection	KHEM	036	79	97	141	155	174	203	169	170
Measles	KHEP	055	10	11	10	6	16	3	1	1
Malaria	KHER	084	4	5	3	7	6	4	3	11
Syphillis	KHES	090-097	68	40	38	35	29	17	18	15
Neoplasms	KHET	140-239	140 101	141 618	140 801	142 451	144 260	145 120	144 577	145 355
Malignant neoplasm of stomach	KHEU	151	10 360	9 971	9 714	9 509	9 425	9 062	8 712	8 427
Malignant neoplasm of trachea, bronchus and lung	KHEV	162	35 739	35 792	35 257	35 138	35 302	34 581	34 375	34 190
Malignant neoplasm of breast	KHEW	174-175	13 409	13 592	13 746	13 840	13 723	14 084	13 741	13 869
Malignant neoplasm of uterus	KHEX	179-182	3 381	3 494	3 466	3 377	3 418	3 271	3 235	3 163
Leukaemia	KHEY	204-208	3 572	3 696	3 572	3 650	3 683	3 729	3 488	3 687
Benign and unspecified neoplasms	KHEZ	210-229,239	1 358	1 346	1 311	1 283	1 288	1 275	1 330	1 337
Endocrine, nutritional and metabolic diseases and immunity disorders	KHFA	240-279	8 499	9 798	10 158	9 810	10 106	10 153	10 249	10 538
Diabetes mellitus	KHFB	250	6 369	7 452	7 912	7 637	7 850	7 872	7 933	8 087
Nutritional deficiencies	KHFC	260-269	104	130	123	74	106	120	125	109
Other metabolic and immunity disorders[4]	KMBO	270-279	1 077	1 270	1 253	1 368	1 376	1 497	1 512	1 664
Diseases of blood and blood-forming organs	KHFD	280-289	2 100	2 422	2 366	2 323	2 370	2 424	2 427	2 446
Anaemias	KHFE	280-285	1 363	1 522	1 409	1 329	1 245	1 214	1 217	1 110
Mental disorders	KHFF	290-319	10 744	12 011	12 410	12 437	13 234	13 718	13 395	13 500
Diseases of nervous system and sense organs	KHFG	320-389	10 483	11 414	11 182	10 953	11 220	11 456	11 644	11 889
Meningitis	KHFH	320-322	246	306	271	260	230	246	203	233
Diseases of the circulatory system	KHFI	390-459	278 849	287 054	278 749	271 061	267 927	264 600	259 247	261 834
Rheumatic heart disease	KHFJ	393-398	2 931	2 889	2 616	–	2 543	2 314	2 174	2 193
Hypertensive disease	KHFL	401-405	4 644	4 581	4 173	3 760	3 578	3 526	3 269	3 340
Ischaemic heart disease	KHFM	410-414	157 506	163 104	158 667	155 235	153 084	150 794	148 159	150 090
Diseases of pulmonary circulation and other forms of heart disease	KHFN	415-429	22 425	22 835	21 930	21 112	21 202	21 298	19 847	18 820
Cerebrovascular disease	KHFO	430-438	71 470	73 219	71 454	69 450	68 599	67 692	66 769	68 669
Diseases of the respiratory system	KHFP	460-519	56 828	64 607	63 052	57 075	60 483	66 712	61 018	63 273
Influenza	KHFQ	487	346	662	587	190	285	2 114	791	248
Pneumonia	KHFR	480-486	24 687	27 931	27 624	24 603	26 424	28 777	26 817	28 504
Bronchitis, emphysema	KHFS	490-492	14 009	14 255	12 119	9 821	9 188	8 680	7 081	6 773
Asthma	KHFT	493	1 764	1 972	1 990	1 898	2 006	1 957	1 858	1 884
Diseases of the digestive system	KHFU	520-579	16 980	18 148	17 974	17 669	17 954	18 679	18 429	18 508
Ulcer of stomach and duodenum	KHFV	531-533	4 483	4 861	4 528	4 307	4 279	4 399	4 355	4 304
Appendicitis	KHFW	540-543	147	147	137	115	136	106	148	108
Hernia of the abdominal cavity and other intestinal obstruction	KHFX	550-553,560	1 947	2 001	2 013	1 900	1 991	1 989	1 988	1 967
Chronic liver disease and cirrhosis	KHFY	571	2 280	2 582	2 527	2 709	2 801	3 023	3 063	3 102
Diseases of the genito-urinary system	KHFZ	580-629	7 731	8 012	7 926	7 696	7 589	7 772	7 317	6 964
Nephritis, nephrotic syndrome and nephrosis	KHGA	580-589	4 391	4 640	4 556	4 488	4 381	4 465	3 919	3 234
Hyperplasia of prostate	KHGB	600	689	668	585	530	483	501	450	413
Complications of pregnancy, childbirth, etc	KHGC	630-676	52	46	45	46	41	56	57	45
Abortion	KHGD	630-639	6	9	3	5	7	6	10	6
Diseases of the skin and subcutaneous tissue	KHGE	680-709	601	670	743	734	772	823	823	930
Diseases of the musculo-skeletal system	KHGF	710-739	4 943	5 452	5 448	5 192	5 406	5 374	5 286	5 417
Congenital anomalies	KHGG	740-759	3 017	2 909	1 871	1 794	1 697	1 766	1 621	1 643
Certain conditions originating in the perinatal period	KHGH	760-779	2 289	2 293	225	198	248	240	249	250
Birth trauma, hypoxia, birth asphyxia and other respiratory conditions	KHGI	767-770	1 243	1 293	85	78	90	85	68	78
Signs, symptoms and ill-defined conditions	KHGJ	780-799	2 534	2 890	3 540	3 909	4 264	4 664	4 897	5 208
Sudden infant death syndrome	KMBP	798-0	1 118	1 195	1 315	1 375	1 422	1 190	1 079	912
Deaths from injury and poisoning[3]	KHGK	E800-E999	18 835	19 009	18 754	17 823	17 936	17 500	17 943	17 286
All accidents	KHGL	E800-E929	12 603	12 475	12 369	11 524	11 288	11 491	11 721	11 049
Motor vehicle accidents	KHGM	E810-E825	5 090	4 914	4 900	4 836	4 559	4 880	4 968	4 470
Suicide and self-inflicted injury	KHGN	E950-E959	4 315	4 419	4 126	3 986	4 220	3 717	3 950	3 893
All other external causes	KHGO	(E930-E949) (E960-E999)	1 917	2 115	2 259	2 313	2 428	2 292	2 272	2 344

1 Changes in OPCS coding of underlying cause of death (from 1 January 1984) have led to some differences in the pattern of causes of death for 1984 onwards as compared with previous years.
2 On 1 January 1986, a new certificate for deaths within the first 28 days of life was introduced. It is not possible to assign one underlying cause of death from this certificate. The 'cause' figures in this table for 1986 onwards exclude all deaths at ages under 28 days.
3 Within certain main categories only selected causes of death are shown.
4 Deaths assigned to AIDS & AIDS related diseases are included in ICD 270 279.

Source: Office of Population Censuses and Surveys

2.20 continued
Deaths analysed by cause
International Statistical Classification of Diseases, Injuries and Causes of Death, Ninth Revision, 1979

Vital statistics

Number

			Scotland							
		ICD 9 code	1984[1]	1985	1986	1987	1988	1989	1990	1991
Total deaths	KHHA		62 345	63 967	63 467	62 014	61 957	65 017	61 527	61 041
Deaths from natural causes[2]	KHHB		59 519	61 148	60 562	59 328	58 993	62 206	58 887	58 509
Infectious and parasitic diseases	KHHC	001-139	259	278	268	250	253	307	285	310
Intestinal infectious diseases	KFBP	001-009	..	..	..	7	10	6	13	14
Tuberculosis of respiratory system	KHHH	010-012	46	47	41	29	41	42	31	46
Other tuberculosis, including late effects	KHHI	013-018,137	39	57	47	47	36	39	31	38
Whooping cough	KHHL	033	–	–	–	–	–	–	1	–
Meningococcal infection	KHHN	036	7	9	11	17	9	15	16	10
Measles	KHHQ	055	3	1	–	–	–	–	–	1
Malaria	KHHS	084	1	–	1	1	–	–	–	1
Syphilis	KHHT	090-097	2	2	3	1	2	2	1	2
Neoplasms	KHHU	140-239	14 456	14 618	14 686	14 793	14 889	15 054	15 137	15 031
Malignant neoplasm of stomach	KHHV	151	970	1 010	961	985	946	877	877	833
Malignant neoplasm of the trachea, bronchus and lung	KHHW	162	4 225	4 307	4 149	4 290	4 144	4 234	4 123	4 209
Malignant neoplasm of breast	KHHX	174-175	1 248	1 264	1 326	1 245	1 268	1 363	1 257	1 282
Malignant neoplasm of uterus	KHHY	179-182	379	353	334	327	313	331	298	294
Leukaemia	KHHZ	204-208	306	352	315	312	318	325	312	268
Benign neoplasms	KHIA	210-229,239	109	113	116	111	129	107	140	112
Endocrine, nutritional and metabolic diseases and immunity disorders	KHIB	240-279	669	723	707	730	691	765	733	776
Diabetes mellitus	KHIC	250	477	534	518	540	501	576	512	530
Nutritional deficiencies	KHID	260-269	24	21	15	12	15	10	18	6
Other metabolic and immunity disorders	KMBN	270-279	106	121	116	129	126	137	156	197
Diseases of blood and blood-forming organs	KHIE	280-289	149	181	167	190	175	174	169	170
Anaemias	KHIF	280-285	89	83	89	89	90	75	73	68
Mental disorders	KHIG	290-319	645	965	949	918	1 005	1 105	986	1 110
Diseases of nervous system and sense organs	KHIH	320-389	776	810	827	788	864	887	890	947
Meningitis	KHII	320-322	25	18	20	22	25	33	26	26
Diseases of the circulatory system	KHIJ	390-459	31 489	32 319	31 424	31 057	30 511	31 223	29 437	29 166
Rheumatic heart disease	KHIL	393-398	275	252	258	242	253	246	205	180
Hypertensive disease	KHIM	401-405	411	391	372	324	304	273	260	316
Ischaemic heart disease	KHIN	410-414	18 107	18 758	18 138	18 405	17 963	18 107	17 028	16 866
Diseases of pulmonary circulation and other forms of heart disease	KHIO	415-429	2 549	2 620	2 337	2 222	2 183	2 468	2 305	2 234
Cerebrovascular disease	KHIP	430-438	8 378	8 505	8 590	8 225	8 150	8 437	7 998	7 968
Diseases of the respiratory system	KHIQ	460-519	7 099	7 156	7 469	6 793	6 724	8 668	7 231	7 068
Influenza	KHIR	487	59	54	121	36	25	457	126	28
Pneumonia	KHIS	480-486	3 974	3 880	4 113	3 750	3 691	4 565	3 918	3 785
Bronchitis, emphysema	KHIT	490-492	1 009	969	791	632	558	621	490	378
Asthma	KHIU	493	157	146	152	159	152	174	148	161
Diseases of the digestive system	KHIV	520-579	2 015	2 038	2 011	1 915	1 925	1 961	2 035	2 059
Ulcer of stomach and duodenum	KHIW	531-533	475	470	448	422	359	388	370	368
Appendicitis	KHIX	540-543	13	18	6	8	11	13	7	10
Hernia of abdominal cavity	KHIY	550-553, 560	189	201	165	166	193	166	174	176
Chronic liver disease and cirrhosis	KHIZ	571	423	423	380	401	429	427	490	476
Diseases of the genito-urinary system	KHJA	580-629	804	897	887	842	810	834	817	805
Nephritis, nephrotic syndrome and nephrosis	KHJB	580-589	513	555	538	514	525	544	538	541
Hyperplasia of prostate	KHJC	600	37	37	41	34	25	19	11	12
Complications of pregnancy, childbirth, etc	KHJD	630-676	8	9	7	2	8	4	4	9
Abortion	KHJE	630-639	1	1	2	–	1	–	1	–
Diseases of the skin and subcutaneous tissue	KHJF	680-709	70	89	86	79	76	98	79	82
Diseases of the musculo-skeletal system	KHJG	710-739	239	269	289	252	318	302	301	270
Congenital anomalies	KHJH	740-759	291	265	224	225	237	226	206	193
Certain conditions originating in the perinatal period	KHJI	760-779	278	246	250	230	210	229	206	213
Birth trauma, hypoxia, birth asphyxia and other respiratory conditions	KHJJ	767-770	160	122	142	131	123	123	104	105
Signs, sysptoms and ill-defined conditions	KHJK	780-779[3]	272	285	311	264	297	369	371	300
Sudden infant death syndrome	KMBM	798.0	137	139	153	136	134	143	132	90
Deaths from injury and poisoning[2]	KHJL	E800-E999	2 826	2 819	2 905	2 686	2 964	2 811	2 640	2 532
All accidents	KHJM	E800-E929	2 050	1 981	2 055	1 858	2 020	1 829	1 784	1 734
Motor vehicle accidents	KHJN	E810-E825	612	609	608	582	561	561	547	513
Suicide and self-inflicted injuries	KHJO	E950-E959	519	569	568	522	598	527	535	525
All other external causes	KMBQ	(E930-E949) (E960-E999)	257	269	282	306	346	455	321	273

1 See page 36.
2 Within certain main categories only selected causes of death are shown.
3 See page 3.

Source: General Register Office (Scotland)

Vital statistics

2.20 continued Deaths analysed by cause
International Statistical Classification of Diseases, Injuries and Causes of Death, Ninth Revision, 1979

Number

		ICD 9 code	1984	1985	1986	1987	1988	1989	1990[1]	1991[2]
Total deaths	KHKA		15 692	15 955	16 065	15 334	15 813	15 844	15 426	15 096
Deaths from natural causes[1]	KHKB		14 951	15 209	15 335	14 572	14 979	15 151	14 727	14 377
Infectious and parasitic diseases	KHKC	001-139	42	43	38	63	45	49	46	44
Intestinal and infectious diseases	KHKD	001-009	..	..	..	–	3	–	3	1
Tuberculosis of the respiratory system	KHKE	010-012	10	16	11	13	7	10	11	6
Other tuberculosis, including late effects	KHKF	013-018,137	6	2	3	1	2	3	1	2
Whooping cough	KHKG	033	–	–	–	–	–	–	–	–
Meningococcal infection	KHKH	036	2	5	1	6	2	6	4	6
Measles	KHKI	055	–	–	1	1	1	3	1	–
Malaria	KHKJ	084	–	–	–	–	–	–	–	–
Syphilis	KHKK	090-097	–	1	–	–	1	–	–	–
Neoplasms	KHKL	140-239	3 327	3 254	3 282	3 417	3 409	3 571	3 525	3 551
Malignant neoplasm of stomach	KHKM	151	240	231	243	239	241	246	219	233
Malignant neoplasm of the trachea, bronchus and lung	KHKN	162	788	761	736	759	777	831	771	787
Malignant neoplasm of breast	KHKO	174-175	304	308	294	312	317	305	295	342
Malignant neoplasm of uterus	KHKP	179-182	67	62	78	73	64	75	68	66
Leukaemia	KHKQ	204-208	108	86	77	83	83	79	79	83
Benign neoplasms and neoplasms of unspecified nature	KHKR	210-229,239	22	14	40	42	47	49	51	38
Endocrine, nutritional and metabolic diseases	KHKS	240-279	225	119	116	78	73	83	78	68
Diabetes mellitus	KHKT	250	192	91	85	57	46	38	41	41
Nutritional deficiencies	KHKU	260-269	3	2	–	1	1	9	1	1
Other metabolic and immunity disorders	KHKV	270-279	22	17	22	16	19	29	27	23
Diseases of blood and blood-forming organs	KHKW	280-289	42	31	24	27	18	32	35	31
Anaemias	KHKX	280-285	29	16	13	14	8	18	19	18
Mental disorders	KHKY	290-319	33	13	64	35	35	45	58	68
Diseases of nervous system and sense organs	KHKZ	320-389	221	166	163	174	152	178	177	168
Meningitis	KHLA	320-322	8	8	4	4	4	10	15	10
Diseases of the circulatory system	KHLB	390-459	8 099	8 031	8 064	7 602	7 744	7 421	7 110	6 983
Rheumatic heart disease	KHLC	393-398	60	55	59	53	46	51	70	56
Hypertensive disease	KHLD	401-405	97	57	62	69	49	63	81	67
Ischaemic heart disease	KHLE	410-414	4 825	4 736	4 686	4 538	4 746	4 508	4 327	4 223
Diseases of pulmonary circulation and other forms of heart disease	KHLF	415-429	784	884	874	796	834	665	625	627
Cerebrovascular disease	KHLG	430-438	1 966	1 941	2 008	1 818	1 708	1 804	1 642	1 711
Diseases of the respiratory system	KHLH	460-519	1 936	2 511	2 581	2 269	2 568	2 885	2 781	2 494
Influenza	KHLI	487	15	28	23	2	9	43	48	5
Pneumonia	KHLJ	480-486	1 150	1 651	1 730	1 510	1 678	1 908	1 855	1 684
Bronchitis, emphysema	KHLK	490-492	209	184	168	158	179	150	160	150
Asthma	KHLL	493	43	49	64	50	55	60	49	47
Diseases of the digestive system	KHLM	520-579	424	420	400	368	358	380	392	395
Ulcer of stomach and duodenum	KHLN	531-533	101	96	83	77	88	89	90	98
Appendicitis	KHLO	540-543	3	4	2	3	1	2	3	2
Hernia of the abdominal cavity and other intestinal obstruction	KHLP	550-553,560	45	35	47	41	39	39	41	45
Chronic liver disease and cirrhosis	KHLQ	571	75	69	64	58	59	70	70	60
Diseases of the genito-urinary system	KHLR	580-629	256	304	290	237	250	243	251	272
Nephritis, nephrotic syndrome and nephrosis	KHLS	580-589	156	223	186	147	161	159	159	183
Hyperplasia of prostate	KHLT	600	10	8	9	9	4	6	4	8
Complications of pregnancy, childbirth, etc	KHLU	630-676	3	–	–	1	2	–	–	1
Abortion	KHLV	630-639	–	–	–	–	1	–	–	–
Diseases of the skin and subcutaneous tissue	KHLW	680-709	15	12	15	28	40	31	21	36
Diseases of the musculo-skeletal system	KHLX	710-739	54	36	40	46	50	45	59	54
Congenital anomalies	KHLY	740-759	145	133	113	91	91	92	85	90
Certain conditions originating in the perinatal period	KHLZ	760-779	102	96	99	79	100	56	68	82
Birth trauma, hypoxia, birth asphyxia and other respiratory conditions	KHMA	767-770	44	47	36	31	35	18	37	31
Signs, symptoms and ill-defined conditions	KHMB	780-799[3]	27	40	47	57	44	40	41	40
Sudden infant death syndrome	KHMC	798.0	..	..	..	16	10	6	14	15
Deaths from injury and poisoning[1]	KHMD	E800-E999	741	746	730	762	834	693	699	719
All accidents	KHME	E800-E929	532	527	487	542	540	446	456	492
Motor vehicle accidents	KHMF	E810-E825	178	197	185	228	233	184	186	195
Suicide and self-inflicted injuries	KHMG	E950-E959	109	117	145	86	153	116	158	129
All other external causes	KHMH	(E930-E949) (E960-E999)	100	102	98	134	141	131	85	98

1 Within certain main categories only selected causes of death are shown.
2 Provisional.
3 See page 3.

Source: General Register Office (Northern Ireland)

Vital statistics

2.21 Infant and maternal mortality

| | \multicolumn{12}{c|}{Deaths of Infants under 1 year of age per thousand live births} | \multicolumn{4}{c}{Maternal deaths per thousand live births[2]} |
| | United Kingdom ||| England and Wales[1] ||| Scotland ||| Northern Ireland ||| United Kingdom | England and Wales | Scotland | Northern Ireland |
	Total	Males	Females	Total	Males	Females	Total	Males	Females	Total	Males	Females				
1900 - 02	142	156	128	146	160	131	124	136	111	113	123	103	4.71	4.67	4.74	6.03
1910 - 12	110	121	98	110	121	98	109	120	97	101	110	92	3.95	3.67	5.65	5.28
1920 - 22	82	92	71	80	90	69	94	106	82	86	95	77	4.37	4.03	6.36	5.62
1930 - 32	67	75	58	64	72	55	84	94	73	75	83	66	4.54	4.24	6.40	5.24
1940 - 42	59	66	51	55	62	48	77	87	66	80	89	70	3.29	2.74	4.50	3.79
1950 - 52	30	34	26	29	33	25	37	42	32	40	45	36	0.88	0.79	1.09	1.09
1960 - 62	22	25	19	22	24	19	26	30	22	27	30	24	0.36	0.36	0.37	0.43
1970 - 72	18	20	16	18	20	15	19	22	17	22	24	20	0.17	0.17	0.17	0.12
1980 - 82	12	13	10	11	13	10	12	13	10	13	15	12	0.09	0.09	0.14	0.06
	KKAW	KKAX	KKAY	KKAZ	KKBW	KKBX	KKBY	KKBZ	KKCW	KKCX	KKCY	KKCZ	KKDW	KKDX	KKDY	KKDZ
1978	13.3	14.8	11.7	13.2	14.7	11.6	12.9	14.5	11.2	15.9	17.3	14.5	0.10	0.11	0.06	–
1979	12.9	14.4	11.3	12.8	14.4	11.1	12.8	13.9	11.8	14.8	15.6	13.9	0.11	0.12	0.10	0.04
1980	12.2	13.4	10.6	12.0	13.3	10.7	12.1	13.6	10.4	13.4	15.1	11.5	0.11	0.11	0.15	0.07
1981	11.2	12.7	9.5	11.1	12.6	9.4	11.3	12.3	10.2	13.2	14.7	11.6	0.09	0.09	0.19	0.04
1982	11.0	12.3	9.5	10.8	12.2	9.4	11.4	12.9	9.8	13.6	14.8	12.4	0.07	0.07	0.09	0.07
1983	10.1	11.3	8.9	10.1	11.3	8.9	9.9	11.3	8.5	12.1	13.9	10.1	0.09	0.09	0.12	0.15
1984	9.6	10.7	8.4	9.5	10.6	8.3	10.3	11.7	8.9	10.5	11.4	9.6	0.09	0.08	0.12	0.11
1985	9.4	10.4	8.3	9.4	10.4	8.2	9.4	10.0	8.7	9.6	10.6	8.5	0.07	0.07	0.13	0.07
1986	9.5	10.9	8.1	9.6	11.0	8.0	8.8	9.9	7.7	10.2	11.0	9.2	0.07	0.07	0.11	–
1987	9.1	10.3	7.9	9.2	10.4	7.9	8.5	9.7	7.2	8.7	9.6	7.7	0.06	0.07	0.03	0.04
1988	9.0	10.2	7.7	9.0	10.3	7.7	8.2	9.5	6.8	8.9	9.6	8.2	0.06	0.06	0.12	0.07
1989	8.4	9.5	7.2	8.4	9.6	7.3	8.7	10.2	7.2	6.9	7.4	6.3	0.08	0.08	0.06	–
1990	7.9[3]	8.8[3]	6.8[3]	7.9	8.9	6.8	7.7	8.8	6.6	7.5[3]	8.1[3]	6.8[3]	0.08	0.08	0.06	–
1991	7.4[3]	8.3[3]	6.3[3]	7.4	8.3	6.4	7.1	8.7	5.3	7.4[3]	8.3[3]	6.4	0.07[3]	0.06	0.13	0.04[3]

1 From 1937 to 1956 death rates are based on the births to which they relate in the current and preceding years.
2 Deaths in pregnancy and childbirth.
3 Provisional.

Sources: Office of Population Censuses and Surveys;
General Register Office (Northern Ireland);
General Register Office (Scotland)

Vital statistics

2.21 Infant and maternal mortality (continued)

Deaths per 1 000 live births

		1978	1979	1980	1981	1982	1983	1984	1985	1986	1987	1988	1989	1990[1]	1991[1]
Total															
United Kingdom:																
Stillbirths[2]	KHNQ	8.5	7.9	7.2	6.6	6.2	5.8	5.7	5.5	5.3	5.0	4.9	4.7	4.6	4.7
Perinatal[2]	KHNR	15.6	14.7	13.2	12.0	11.4	10.5	10.2	10.1	9.6	9.0	8.8	8.3	8.1	8.1
Neonatal	KHNS	8.8	8.3	7.7	6.7	6.4	5.9	5.7	5.4	5.3	5.0	4.9	4.7	4.5	4.4
Post Neonatal	KHNT	4.5	4.6	4.4	4.4	4.6	4.3	3.9	4.0	4.2	4.1	4.1	3.7	3.3	3.0
England and Wales:																
Stillbirths[2]	KHNU	8.5	8.0	7.2	6.6	6.3	5.7	5.7	5.5	5.3	5.0	4.9	4.7	4.6	4.6
Perinatal[2]	KHNV	15.5	14.7	13.1	11.8	11.3	10.4	10.1	10.1	9.6	8.9	8.7	8.3	8.1	8.0
Neonatal	KHNW	8.7	8.2	7.7	6.7	6.3	5.9	5.6	5.4	5.3	5.1	4.9	4.8	4.6	4.4
Post Neonatal	KHNX	4.5	4.6	4.4	4.4	4.6	4.3	3.9	4.0	4.3	4.1	4.1	3.7	3.3	3.0
Scotland:																
Stillbirths[2]	KHNY	8.1	6.9	6.7	6.3	5.8	5.8	5.8	5.5	5.8	5.1	5.4	5.0	5.3	5.5
Perinatal[2]	KHNZ	15.4	14.1	13.1	11.6	11.5	10.6	11.0	9.8	10.2	8.9	8.9	8.7	8.7	8.6
Neonatal	KHOA	8.8	8.7	7.8	6.9	7.1	5.8	6.4	5.5	5.2	4.7	4.5	4.7	4.4	4.4
Post Neonatal	KHOB	4.1	4.2	4.3	4.4	4.3	4.1	3.9	3.9	3.6	3.8	3.7	4.0	3.3	2.7
Northern Ireland:																
Stillbirths[2]	KHOC	9.2	8.7	9.2	8.7	6.9	7.4	5.9	6.4	4.4	6.1	5.0	5.1	4.4	4.7
Perinatal[2]	KHOD	18.1	16.6	15.6	15.3	13.3	13.1	10.8	11.1	9.5	9.8	9.3	8.2	7.6	8.1
Neonatal	KHOE	10.5	9.4	8.0	8.3	7.8	7.3	6.7	5.6	6.0	4.8	5.4	4.0	4.0	4.4
Post Neonatal	KHOF	5.4	5.4	5.4	4.9	5.9	4.8	3.8	4.0	4.2	3.8	3.6	2.9	3.5	3.0
Males															
United Kingdom:																
Perinatal[2]	KHOG	16.5	15.7	14.3	12.8	12.3	11.3	11.1	11.2	10.4	9.7	9.5	9.3	8.8	8.7
Neonatal	KHOH	9.7	9.4	8.6	7.7	7.3	6.5	6.4	5.9	6.0	5.7	5.5	5.4	5.0	4.9
Infant mortality	KHOI	14.8	14.4	13.4	12.7	12.3	11.4	10.7	10.4	10.9	10.3	10.2	9.5	8.8	8.3
England and Wales:																
Perinatal[2]	KHOK	16.4	15.7	14.2	12.8	12.2	11.2	11.0	11.3	10.4	9.8	9.4	9.2	8.8	8.6
Neonatal	KHOL	9.6	9.4	8.5	7.7	7.1	6.5	6.3	6.0	6.0	5.7	5.5	5.4	5.1	4.8
Infant mortality	KHOM	14.7	14.4	13.3	12.6	12.2	11.3	10.6	10.4	11.0	10.4	10.3	9.6	8.9	8.3
Scotland:																
Perinatal[2]	KHOO	16.8	15.3	14.2	12.2	13.1	11.6	12.6	10.1	10.9	8.9	9.7	10.0	9.1	9.8
Neonatal	KHOP	10.3	9.7	9.1	7.1	8.1	6.1	7.1	5.5	5.6	5.3	5.3	5.3	4.7	5.5
Infant mortality	KHOQ	14.5	13.9	13.6	12.3	12.9	11.3	11.7	10.0	9.9	9.7	9.5	10.2	8.8	8.7
Northern Ireland:																
Perinatal[2]	KHOS	19.2	16.6	16.9	15.7	13.5	14.3	10.7	11.3	9.7	10.5	10.9	8.7	8.7	7.9
Neonatal	KHOT	11.2	9.9	9.1	8.8	8.4	8.8	7.3	6.3	6.2	5.3	6.0	4.5	4.8	5.5
Infant mortality	KHOU	17.3	15.6	15.1	14.7	14.8	13.9	11.4	10.6	11.0	9.6	9.6	7.4	8.1	8.3
Females															
United Kingdom:																
Perinatal[2]	KHOW	14.7	13.6	12.0	11.0	10.4	9.7	9.2	9.1	8.8	8.1	8.0	7.4	7.4	7.5
Neonatal	KHOX	7.7	7.1	6.8	5.8	5.6	5.2	4.9	4.8	4.6	4.3	4.3	4.0	4.0	3.8
Infant mortality	KHOY	11.7	11.3	10.7	9.6	9.5	8.9	8.4	8.3	8.1	7.9	7.7	7.2	6.8	6.3
England and Wales:																
Perinatal[2]	KHPA	14.7	13.5	12.0	10.9	10.3	9.6	9.1	8.9	8.7	8.0	8.0	7.4	7.4	7.5
Neonatal	KHPB	7.7	7.0	6.8	5.6	5.4	5.2	4.8	4.8	4.5	4.3	4.3	4.0	4.0	3.9
Infant mortality	KHPC	11.6	11.0	10.7	9.4	9.4	8.9	8.3	8.2	8.0	7.9	7.7	7.3	6.8	6.4
Scotland:																
Perinatal[2]	KHPE	14.0	12.9	11.9	11.1	9.8	9.6	9.3	9.5	9.4	9.0	8.1	7.3	8.2	7.4
Neonatal	KHPF	7.2	7.6	6.4	6.7	6.1	5.5	5.7	5.5	4.8	4.1	3.7	4.1	4.1	3.2
Infant mortality	KHPG	11.2	11.8	10.4	10.2	9.8	8.5	8.9	8.7	7.7	7.2	6.8	7.2	6.6	5.3
Northern Ireland:																
Perinatal[2]	KHPI	17.1	16.6	14.2	15.0	13.1	11.8	10.9	10.9	9.2	9.2	7.6	7.6	6.4	9.0
Neonatal	KHPJ	9.7	8.9	6.9	7.8	7.1	5.7	6.1	4.9	5.8	4.4	4.7	3.5	3.2	3.7
Infant mortality	KHPK	14.5	13.9	11.5	11.6	12.4	10.1	9.6	8.5	9.2	7.7	8.2	6.3	6.8	6.4

1 Provisional.
2 Deaths per 1 000 live and stillbirths.

Sources: Office of Population, Censuses and Surveys;
General Register Office (Northern Ireland);
General Register Office (Scotland)

Vital statistics

2.22 Death rates per 1 000 population[1]
Analysis by age and sex
United Kingdom

	All ages	0-4	5-9	10-14	15-19	20-24	25-34	35-44	45-54	55-64	65-74	75-84	85 and over
Males													
1900 - 02	18.4	57.0	4.1	2.4	3.7	5.0	6.6	11.0	18.6	35.0	69.9	143.6	289.6
1910 - 12	14.9	40.5	3.3	2.0	3.0	3.9	5.0	8.0	14.9	29.8	62.1	133.8	261.5
1920 - 22	13.5	33.4	2.9	1.8	2.9	3.9	4.5	6.9	11.9	25.3	57.8	131.8	259.1
1930 - 32	12.9	22.3	2.3	1.5	2.6	3.3	3.5	5.7	11.3	23.7	57.9	134.2	277.0
1940 - 42	..	..	..	..	..	..	..	..	..	..	..	..	..
1950 - 52	12.6	7.7	0.7	0.5	0.9	1.4	1.6	3.0	8.5	23.2	55.2	127.6	272.0
1960 - 62	12.5	6.4	0.5	0.4	0.9	1.1	1.1	2.5	7.4	22.2	54.4	123.4	251.0
1970 - 72	12.4	4.6	0.4	0.4	0.9	1.0	1.0	2.4	7.3	20.9	52.9	116.3	246.1
1980 - 82	12.1	3.2	0.3	0.3	0.8	0.9	0.9	1.9	6.3	18.2	46.7	107.1	224.9
	KHZA	KHZB	KHZC	KHZD	KHZE	KHZF	KHZG	KHZH	KHZJ	KHZK	KHZL	KHZM	KHZN
1971	12.2	4.7	0.4	0.4	0.9	1.0	1.0	2.4	7.3	20.6	52.3	118.2	251.0
1972	12.6	4.4	0.4	0.4	0.9	1.0	1.0	2.4	7.5	21.0	53.8	119.8	248.0
1973	12.4	4.2	0.4	0.3	0.9	1.1	1.0	2.3	7.4	20.8	51.9	117.5	240.9
1974	12.3	4.2	0.4	0.3	0.9	1.0	1.0	2.3	7.4	20.6	51.6	115.3	240.3
1975	12.2	3.7	0.4	0.3	0.9	1.0	1.0	2.2	7.3	19.9	50.5	115.2	237.2
1976	12.5	3.5	0.3	0.3	0.9	1.0	1.0	2.2	7.2	20.1	51.0	117.5	246.0
1977	12.1	3.5	0.3	0.3	0.9	1.0	1.0	2.1	7.0	19.2	49.0	110.7	229.4
1978	12.3	3.4	0.3	0.3	0.9	1.0	1.0	2.1	7.0	19.3	49.3	111.8	232.0
1979	12.4	3.8	0.3	0.3	0.9	1.0	1.0	2.1	6.9	19.2	48.8	112.0	236.0
1980	12.1	3.4	0.3	0.3	0.8	0.9	0.9	2.0	6.5	18.7	47.2	108.6	227.0
1981	12.3	3.2	0.3	0.3	0.9	0.9	1.0	2.0	6.4	18.4	47.5	110.6	239.5
1982	12.0	2.9	0.3	0.3	0.8	0.9	0.9	1.8	6.1	17.9	46.4	106.4	225.0
1983	12.0	2.7	0.3	0.3	0.8	0.8	0.9	1.8	5.9	18.0	46.3	104.6	221.0
1984	11.7	2.6	0.3	0.3	0.7	0.9	0.9	1.7	5.7	17.5	44.9	100.9	212.8
1985	12.0	2.6	0.2	0.3	0.7	0.8	0.9	1.8	5.6	17.5	45.0	104.8	223.4
1986	11.8	2.6	0.2	0.2	0.7	0.9	0.9	1.7	5.5	17.0	43.6	102.0	217.1
1987	11.5	2.5	0.2	0.3	0.7	0.9	0.9	1.7	5.2	16.4	42.0	97.3	194.3
1988	11.5	2.5	0.2	0.3	0.7	0.9	0.9	1.7	5.1	16.0	41.2	96.6	193.9
1989	11.5	2.3	0.2	0.2	0.7	0.9	0.9	1.7	4.9	15.3	40.4	97.0	199.0
1990	11.2	2.2	0.2	0.2	0.7	0.9	1.0	1.8	4.8	14.8	39.5	94.3	187.8
1991[2]	11.2	2.0	0.2	0.2	0.7	0.9	1.0	1.8	4.8	14.2	39.3	94.3	199.2
Females													
1900 - 02	16.3	47.9	4.3	2.6	3.5	4.3	5.8	9.0	14.4	27.9	59.3	127.0	262.6
1910 - 12	13.3	34.0	3.3	2.1	2.9	3.4	4.4	6.7	11.5	23.1	50.7	113.7	234.0
1920 - 22	11.9	26.9	2.8	1.9	2.8	3.4	4.1	5.6	9.3	19.2	45.6	111.5	232.4
1930 - 32	11.5	17.7	2.1	1.5	2.4	2.9	3.3	4.6	8.3	17.6	43.7	110.1	246.3
1940 - 42	..	..	..	..	..	..	..	..	..	..	..	..	..
1950 - 52	11.2	6.0	0.5	0.4	0.7	1.0	1.4	2.3	5.3	12.9	35.5	98.4	228.8
1960 - 62	11.2	4.9	0.3	0.3	0.4	0.5	0.8	1.8	4.5	11.0	30.8	87.3	218.5
1970 - 72	11.3	3.6	0.3	0.2	0.4	0.4	0.6	1.6	4.5	10.5	27.5	76.7	196.1
1980 - 82	11.4	2.3	0.2	0.2	0.3	0.4	0.5	1.3	3.9	9.9	24.8	67.2	179.5
	KHZO	KHZP	KHZQ	KHZR	KHZS	KHZT	KHZU	KHZV	KHZW	KHZX	KHZY	KHZZ	KHZI
1971	11.1	3.6	0.3	0.2	0.4	0.4	0.6	1.6	4.4	10.4	26.9	76.6	209.1
1972	11.5	3.5	0.3	0.2	0.4	0.4	0.6	1.6	4.6	10.7	27.8	78.2	197.3
1973	11.5	3.2	0.3	0.2	0.4	0.4	0.6	1.6	4.5	10.5	27.1	76.5	192.5
1974	11.4	3.1	0.3	0.2	0.4	0.4	0.6	1.6	4.5	10.6	26.7	74.8	191.0
1975	11.3	3.0	0.2	0.2	0.4	0.4	0.6	1.5	4.4	10.4	26.0	73.4	188.3
1976	11.7	2.6	0.2	0.2	0.3	0.4	0.6	1.5	4.4	10.4	26.5	75.2	198.0
1977	11.3	2.7	0.2	0.2	0.4	0.4	0.5	1.5	4.2	10.1	25.5	71.0	183.1
1978	11.5	2.8	0.2	0.2	0.4	0.4	0.6	1.5	4.3	10.1	25.7	70.5	184.5
1979	11.6	2.8	0.2	0.2	0.3	0.4	0.6	1.4	4.3	10.2	25.6	70.8	187.1
1980	11.4	2.7	0.2	0.2	0.3	0.4	0.5	1.3	4.0	10.0	25.0	67.7	181.3
1981	11.6	2.5	0.2	0.2	0.3	0.4	0.5	1.3	3.9	10.0	25.5	70.4	190.6
1982	11.5	2.3	0.2	0.2	0.3	0.4	0.5	1.2	3.8	9.9	24.8	66.8	179.4
1983	11.4	2.1	0.2	0.2	0.3	0.3	0.5	1.2	3.6	9.8	24.7	65.1	177.2
1984	11.2	2.0	0.2	0.2	0.3	0.3	0.5	1.2	3.5	9.7	24.3	62.6	170.2
1985	11.7	2.0	0.2	0.2	0.3	0.3	0.5	1.2	3.4	9.9	24.7	64.8	178.4
1986	11.5	2.0	0.2	0.2	0.3	0.3	0.5	1.1	3.3	9.5	24.0	63.2	172.4
1987	11.2	2.0	0.2	0.2	0.3	0.3	0.5	1.1	3.3	9.4	23.3	60.8	159.9
1988	11.3	1.9	0.2	0.2	0.3	0.3	0.5	1.2	3.2	9.2	23.2	60.4	162.3
1989	11.5	1.8	0.2	0.2	0.3	0.3	0.5	1.1	3.1	9.1	23.2	61.4	164.7
1990	11.1	1.7	0.1	0.2	0.3	0.3	0.5	1.1	3.0	8.8	22.4	58.9	156.7
1991[2]	10.6	1.6	0.2	0.2	0.3	0.3	0.5	1.1	3.0	8.3	22.5	59.2	165.2

1 The figures 1974 to 1980 incorporate the revised intercensal estimates for England and Wales, and Northern Ireland, but the old series for Scotland.
2 Provisional.

Sources: Office of Population Censuses and Surveys;
General Register Office (Northern Ireland);
General Register Office (Scotland)

Vital statistics
2.23 Life tables

United Kingdom
Interim Life Table, 1988-90

Age$_x$	Males l_x	Males $\overset{\circ}{e}_x$	Females l_x	Females $\overset{\circ}{e}_x$
0 years	100 000	72.7	100 000	78.3
5 "	98 882	68.5	99 142	73.9
10 "	98 777	63.6	99 072	69.0
15 "	98 662	58.7	98 995	64.0
20 "	98 315	53.9	98 856	59.1
25 "	97 876	49.1	98 699	54.2
30 "	97 453	44.3	98 518	49.3
35 "	96 963	39.5	98 250	44.4
40 "	96 301	34.8	97 820	39.6
45 "	95 312	30.1	97 140	34.9
50 "	93 587	25.6	96 005	30.3
55 "	90 716	21.3	94 187	25.8
60 "	85 844	17.4	91 132	21.6
65 "	77 805	13.9	86 099	17.7
70 "	66 176	10.9	78 672	14.1
75 "	50 986	8.4	68 049	10.9
80 "	33 817	6.4	53 724	8.1
85 "	18 017	4.8	35 900	5.8

England and Wales
Interim Life Table, 1988-90

Age$_x$	Males l_x	Males $\overset{\circ}{e}_x$	Females l_x	Females $\overset{\circ}{e}_x$
0 years	100 000	73.0	100 000	78.5
5 "	98 876	68.8	99 139	74.2
10 "	98 770	63.9	99 068	69.2
15 "	98 658	58.9	98 994	64.3
20 "	98 319	54.1	98 853	59.4
25 "	97 898	49.3	98 700	54.4
30 "	97 491	44.5	98 524	49.5
35 "	97 021	39.7	98 261	44.6
40 "	96 377	35.0	97 842	39.8
45 "	95 421	30.3	97 175	35.1
50 "	93 752	25.8	96 071	30.5
55 "	90 968	21.5	94 310	26.0
60 "	86 236	17.5	91 347	21.7
65 "	78 355	14.0	86 452	17.8
70 "	66 892	11.0	79 185	14.2
75 "	51 774	8.4	68 693	11.0
80 "	34 505	6.4	54 461	8.2
85 "	18 515	4.9	36 594	5.9

Scotland
Interim Life Table, 1988-90

Age$_x$	Males l_x	Males $\overset{\circ}{e}_x$	Females l_x	Females $\overset{\circ}{e}_x$
0 years	10 000	70.8	10 000	76.6
5 "	9 887	66.6	9 919	72.2
10 "	9 877	61.6	9 912	67.2
15 "	9 863	56.7	9 903	62.3
20 "	9 823	51.9	9 890	57.4
25 "	9 768	47.2	9 871	52.5
30 "	9 714	42.4	9 848	47.6
35 "	9 651	37.7	9 817	42.7
40 "	9 570	33.0	9 762	38.0
45 "	9 440	28.4	9 683	33.2
50 "	9 216	24.0	9 541	28.7
55 "	8 851	19.9	9 318	24.3
60 "	8 247	16.2	8 937	20.2
65 "	7 316	12.9	8 325	16.5
70 "	6 018	10.2	7 439	13.2
75 "	4 456	7.8	6 264	10.2
80 "	2 824	5.9	4 760	7.6
85 "	1 411	4.4	3 036	5.4

Northern Ireland
Interim Life Table, 1988-90

Age$_x$	Males l_x	Males $\overset{\circ}{e}_x$	Females l_x	Females $\overset{\circ}{e}_x$
0 years	10 000	71.3	10 000	77.2
5 "	9 898	67.1	9 912	72.9
10 "	9 885	62.2	9 904	67.9
15 "	9 872	57.2	9 895	63.0
20 "	9 831	52.5	9 883	58.1
25 "	9 769	47.8	9 866	53.2
30 "	9 717	43.0	9 845	48.3
35 "	9 648	38.3	9 820	43.4
40 "	9 575	33.6	9 781	38.6
45 "	9 462	29.0	9 700	33.8
50 "	9 272	24.5	9 581	29.2
55 "	8 961	20.2	9 354	24.9
60 "	8 408	16.4	9 021	20.7
65 "	7 514	13.0	8 451	16.9
70 "	6 227	10.2	7 666	13.4
75 "	4 632	7.8	6 573	10.2
80 "	2 985	5.7	5 089	7.4
85 "	1 480	4.1	3 246	5.1

Note Column l_x shows the number who would survive to exact age x, out of 100 000 or 10 000 born, who were subject throughout their lives to the death rates experienced in the three-year period indicated.

Column e°_x is 'the expectation of life', that is, the average future lifetime which would be lived by a person aged exactly x if likewise subject to the death rates experienced in the three-year period indicated. (See introductory note on page 3.)

Source: Government Actuary's Department

3 Social Conditions

Government expenditure on social services and housing

The following tables of general government expenditure on the social services and housing in the United Kingdom comprise a summary table followed by separate tables for each of the social services and housing. The definition of government expenditure used in these tables follows that in Table 9.4 of *United Kingdom National Accounts 1991 Edition*, the CSO Blue Book, and covers both current and capital expenditure of the central government (including the National Insurance Fund) and local authorities. The housing table also includes the capital expenditure of public corporations concerned with housing. As in the Blue Book government expenditure is measured after deducting fees and charges for services. Expenditure on administration includes the cost of common services (accommodation, stationery and printing, superannuation, etc) some of which is not directly borne by the departments administering each service. Transfers from one part of government to another have been eliminated to avoid double counting. The figures relate to years ended 31 March. Figures for the latest two years are the most recent estimates available and are subject to revision.

It should be noted that the figures no longer include imputed rents for the use of fixed assets owned and used by general government. In the Blue Book imputed rents have been replaced by capital consumption. Capital consumption, however, cannot be allocated to individual services and is therefore not included in these tables.

The following notes give brief descriptions of each of the main services shown in the tables.

Education
This covers expenditure by the Education Departments, local education authorities and the University Grants Committee on education in schools, training colleges, technical institutions and universities. It includes expenditure on school meals and milk.

The education statistics in Table 3.2 are provided by the Department of Education and Science. They are not normally able to provide a full set of estimates, from their sources, for the latest financial year. The CSO has in the past made estimates from a variety of sources but, following a review of their accuracy, it has been decided that they do not give a reliable guide to the final outcome and have therefore been withdrawn.

National Health Service
This covers expenditure by central government on hospital and community health, family practitioner and other health services. The expenditure by local authorities on the provision of health centres, health visiting, home nursing, ambulance services, vaccination and immunisation, etc, was transferred to central government on 1 April 1974. Only the net costs of providing these services are included in total government expenditure, receipts from patients being shown separately.

Personal social services
This covers local authority expenditure on the aged, handicapped and homeless, child care, care of mothers and young children, mental health, domestic help, etc. Also included are central government grants to voluntary approved schools.

Welfare foods
This covers the cost of providing welfe foods at reduced prices to children and expectant mothers. Only the net costs of providing these services are included in the total government expenditure, payments by the recipients of the services being shown separately.

Social security
This comprises both benefits under the Social Security schemes and non-contributory benefits and allowances, administered by the Department of Social Security. The analysis by type of Income Support is not exact; the estimates are derived from average numbers in receipt of benefit and average amounts paid. Unified housing benefit (rent rebates and allowances) is also included as social security expenditure and not as housing expenditure. This is now mainly administered by local authorities who receive grants from central government.

Housing

The table shows, in addition to government expenditure on housing, the capital expenditure of public corporations and the total expenditure of the public sector on housing. The government expenditure figures cover subsidies paid by the housing departments towards the provision of housing by local authorities, new town development corporations and housing associations; subsidies by local authorities to their housing revenue accounts; rent rebates for tenants of housing owned by local authorities and new towns; rent allowances for tenants of privately-owned housing; grants to persons for the reduction of mortgage interest payments; capital expenditure on the provision of houses for letting; capital grants to housing associations; grants by local authorities towards the cost of conversion and improvement of privately-owned houses; net lending by the central government and local authorities for private house purchase and improvement and loans for first time purchases. The public corporations' figures cover capital expenditure on the provision of houses for letting and lending by the Housing Corporation to housing associations.

Social Security

Tables 3.12 to 3.16, 3.20 to 3.28 give details of contributors and beneficiaries under the National Insurance and Industrial Injury Acts, supplementary benefits and war pensions.

There are three types of contributor:

Class 1   Employed persons, that is, persons working for employers. Their contributions are paid partly by themselves and partly by their employers. They are covered for all benefits.

Class 2   Self-employed persons, that is, persons working on their own account. They are covered for all benefits other than unemployment and industrial injuries.

Class 3   Non-employed persons, that is, persons who do not work for gain. They are covered for benefits other than unemployment, sickness, industrial injuries and maternity allowances.

Class 4   Payable, in addition to Class 2 by self-employed persons, and the amount payable is proportionate to profits or gains between a lower and upper limit in any one year.

An employer must pay a contribution for every employee whose earnings exceed a base level. Most employed persons pay the full employee's contribution, but retirement pensioners working for an employer do not and some married women and some widows who are working need not, unless they so wish, contribute except for industrial injuries benefit. Thus the total numbers in the analysis by benefit for which the contributions were payable are less than the total numbers in the analysis by class of contributor.

Sickness benefit and Invalidity (Tables 3.17 and 3.18)
The population at risk for sickness benefit is the working population apart from men over age 65 and women over age 60 who are retirement pensioners and all men over 70 and women over 65, members of the Armed Forces, mariners while at sea, most non-industrial civil servants and Post Office employees (who do not normally claim sickness benefit until an illness has lasted six months) and married women and certain widows who have chosen not to be insured for sickness benefit. The tables exclude periods of incapacity, covered by Statutory Sick Pay from 6 April 1983. In general SSP was for a maximum of 8 weeks for the tax year 1983/84 to 1985/86. From 6 April 1986 the SSP period has been extended to 28 weeks.

Fatal injuries at work (Table 3.35)
Under the Notification of Accidents and Dangerous Occurrences Regulations, in force from 1 January 1981 to 30 March 1986, most fatal injuries at or resulting from work activities were reported to HSC enforcement authorities. Prior to 1981, fatal injuries were reported on a less comprehensive basis, and are not therefore comparable with the totals given in the table. Deaths of self-employed people and members of the public are included in the table. Some of these were reported voluntarily prior to 1981.

From 1 April 1986 the Reporting of Injuries, Diseases and Dangerous Occurrences Regulations required the direct reporting of injuries arising from work activity by employers to Health and Safety Commission enforcing authorities. Details of those fatal, major and other injuries causing incapacity for work for more than 3 days, involving employees and self-employed persons are shown in the table. The reporting of fatal injuries is a continuation of the requirement under the Notification of Accidents and Dangerous Occurrences Regulations, 1980 for which data has been presented in previous publications. However, RIDDOR extended the coverage of the major injury definition making comparisons with data for earlier years possible. With the direct reporting of over 3 day injuries being an effectively new requirement, it is suspected that widespread under-reporting of as much as 50%, may have taken place.

3.1 Summary of government expenditure on social services and housing
Years ended 31 March

£ million

		1981/82	1982/83	1983/84	1984/85	1985/86	1986/87	1987/88	1988/89	1989/90	1990/91	1991/92
Education[1]	KJAA	14 041	15 037	15 946	16 516	17 288	18 802	20 401	22 137	24 102	..	..
National health service	KJAB	13 267	14 385	15 383	16 312	17 434	18 729	20 585	22 802	24 828	28 615	31 286
Personal social services	KJAC	2 420	2 552	2 789	2 940	3 467	3 414	3 856	4 355	4 901	5 594	6 103
Welfare foods	KJAD	52	70	86	98	113	120	124	104	107	119	145
Social security benefits	KJAE	29 968	33 946	37 190	39 030	42 310	45 393	47 188	48 130	50 939	53 823	60 649
Housing	KJAF	4 764	4 353	4 744	4 648	4 354	3 963	4 136	3 840	4 106	3 956	5 333
Total government expenditure	KJAG	64 512	70 343	76 138	79 544	84 966	90 421	96 290	101 368	108 983	..	..
Current expenditure	KJAH	60 329	66 142	71 166	74 536	80 093	85 798	91 332	96 652	102 716	..	..
Capital expenditure	KJAI	4 123	4 201	4 972	5 008	4 873	4 623	4 958	4 716	6 267	..	..
Total government expenditure	KJAG	64 512	70 343	76 138	79 544	84 966	90 421	96 290	101 368	108 983	..	..
Central government	KJAK	47 976	52 883	57 222	60 094	64 573	69 039	72 691	76 476	81 725		
Local authorities	KJAL	16 536	17 460	18 916	19 450	20 393	21 382	23 599	24 892	27 258		
Total government expenditure	KJAG	64 512	70 343	76 138	79 544	84 966	90 421	96 290	101 368	108 983	..	..

1 Includes school meals and milk.

Source: Central Statistical Office

Social services

3.2 Government expenditure on education
Years ended 31 march

£ million

			1980/81	1981/82	1982/83	1983/84	1984/85	1985/86	1986/87	1987/88	1988/89	1989[7]/90	1990/91
Current expenditure													
Nursery schools	KJBA	KEZN	52	57	63	67	70	74	81	4 771	5 259	5 694	..
Primary schools	KJBB		2 840	3 093	3 255	3 377	3 483	3 702	4 157				
Secondary schools	KJBC		3 695	4 143	4 435	4 675	4 850	5 061	5 583	6 027	6 437	6 483	..
Special schools	KJBD		444	500	544	583	620	667	727	812	888	989	..
Further and adult education[1]	KJBE	KEZO	1 591	1 812	1 987	2 157	2 260	2 375	2 625	2 895	3 277	2 705	..
Training of teachers: tuition	KJBF		78	83	93	86	88	100	91	156			
PCFC Sector[2]	KEZM		..	..	..	..	..	..	..	..	..	1 024	..
Universities[1]	KJBG		1 265	1 332	1 388	1 497	1 562	1 605	1 654	1 824	1 958	2 104	..
Other education expenditure	KJBH		516	553	599	661	697	736	871	900	1 009	1 195	..
Related current expenditure:													
Training of teachers: residence[3]	KJBI		15	15	18	20	18	19	19	..	..	..	..
School welfare[4]	KJBJ		20	23	27	30	33	37	40	56	70	91	..
Meals and milk	KJBK		479	480	499	519	527	532	559	546	469	485	..
Youth service and physical training	KJBL		148	169	192	209	227	239	211	246	277	328	..
Maintenance grants and allowances to pupils and students	KJBM		630	702	759	825	850	838	806	764	900	934	..
Transport of pupils	KJBN		215	234	253	262	268	279	290	300	311	304	..
Miscellaneous expenditure	KJBO		3	3	4	4	5	5	5	6	10	17	..
Total current expenditure[5]	KJBQ		11 989	13 200	14 115	14 971	15 558	16 267	17 719	19 240	20 865	22 353	..
Capital expenditure													
Nursery schools	KJBR	KEZP	6	4	4	6	7	8	7	192	246	314	..
Primary schools	KJBS		174	136	128	141	154	164	180				
Secondary schools	KJBT		275	233	239	232	217	223	187	213	195	397	..
Special schools	KJBU		26	22	21	20	12	17	23	11	33	38	..
Further and adult education	KJBV	KEZQ	129	108	139	141	144	149	149	174	180	164	..
Training of teachers	KJBW		2	2	3	2	3	3	3	3			
PCFC Sector[2]	KEZL		..	..	..	..	..	..	..	..	..	90	..
Universities	KJBX		117	117	116	139	121	140	156	158	172	196	..
Other education expenditure	KJBY		10	10	13	14	12	11	10	32	22	41	..
Related capital expenditure	KJBZ		24	19	20	22	23	23	24	21	25	33	..
Total capital expenditure[5]	KJCA		763	651	682	716	693	738	739	804	873	1 273	..
VAT refunds to local authorities	KJBP		189	189	240	259	266	284	345	357	399	477	..
Total expenditure													
Central government	KJCB		1 779	1 852	2 022	2 227	2 283	2 378	2 567	2 746	3 025	4 337	..
Local authorities	KJCC		11 162	12 187	13 015	13 719	14 233	14 911	16 235	17 655	19 112	19 765	..
Total government expenditure[6]	KJAA		12 941	14 041	15 037	15 946	16 516	17 288	18 802	20 401	22 137	24 102	..
Gross domestic product (average estimate) at market prices	KLJV		237 713	260 858	285 628	309 606	331 655	362 991	390 613	432 322	481 081	522 297	582 859
Expenditure as a percentage of GDP	KJCE		*5.4*	*5.4*	*5.3*	*5.1*	*5.0*	*4.8*	*4.8*	*4.7*	*4.6*	*4.6*	..

1 Including tuition fees.
2 The Polytechnics and Colleges Funding Council Sector, (PCFC), applicable from 1989/90.
3 With effect from 1987/8 included with maintenance grants and allowances.
4 Expenditure on the school health service is included in the National Health Service.
5 Due to rounding constituent figures may not sum to totals.
6 Excludes additional adjustment to allow for capital consumption made for National Accounts purposes amounting to £1 040m in 1989/90.
7 Provisional

Sources: Department of Education and Science; Central Statistical Office

Social services

3.3 Government expenditure on the National Health Service
Years ended 31 March

£ million

		1984/85	1985/86	1986/87	1987/88	1988/89	1989/90	1990/91	1991/92
Current expenditure									
Central government:									
Hospitals and Community Health Services[1] and Family Health Services[2]	KJQA	14 976	15 932	17 086	18 870	21 110	22 197	25 540	28 278
Administration	KJQB	473	475	553	627	682	855	979	1 113
less Payments by patients:									
Hospital services	KJQC	−84	−92	−99	−106	−347	−407	−95	−369
Pharmaceutical services	KJQD	−149	−158	−204	−256	−202	−242	−228	−240
Dental services	KJQE	−197	−225	−261	−290	−282	−340	−395	−502
Ophthalmic services	KJQF	−52	−14	−1	−1	−	−	−	−
Total	KJQG	−482	−489	−565	−653	−831	−989	−743	−1 111
Departmental administration	KJQH	137	142	171	193	206	223	264	320
Other central services	KJQI	218	283	324	336	326	471	535	658
Total current expenditure	KJQJ	15 322	16 343	17 569	19 373	21 493	23 757	26 575	29 258
Capital expenditure									
Central government	KJQK	990	1 091	1 160	1 212	1 309	2 071	2 040	2 028
Total expenditure									
Central government	KJAB	16 312	17 434	18 729	20 585	22 802	24 828	28 615	31 286

1 Including the school health service.
2 General Medical Services have been included in the expenditure of the Health Authorities. Therefore, Hospitals and Community Health Services and Family Practitioner Services (now Family Health Services) are not identifiable separately.

Source: Central Statistical Office

Social services

3.4 Government expenditure on welfare services[1]
Years ended 31 March

£ million

		1981/82	1982/83	1983/84	1984/85	1985/86	1986/87	1987/88	1988/89	1989/90	1990/91	1991/92
Personal social services												
Central government current expenditure	KJCG	99	93	101	106	115	123	125	126	142	161	182
Local authorities current expenditure:												
Running expenses	CTKQ	2 212	2 372	2 595	2 725	3 229	3 163	3 593	4 077	4 552	5 199	5 728
Capital expenditure	KJCI	109	87	93	109	123	128	138	152	207	234	193
Total	KJAC	2 420	2 552	2 789	2 940	3 467	3 414	3 856	4 355	4 901	5 594	6 103
Welfare foods service												
Central government current expenditure on welfare foods (including administration)	KJCK	52	70	86	98	113	120	124	104	107	119	145
less Receipts from the public	KJCL	–	–	–	–	–	–	–	–	–	–	–
Total	KJAD	52	70	86	98	113	120	124	104	107	119	145

1 School meals and milk are included in Table 3.2.

Source: Central Statistical Office

3.5 Government expenditure on social security benefits
Years ended 31 March

£ million

		1981/82	1982/83	1983/84	1984/85	1985/86	1986/87	1987/88	1988/89	1989/90	1990/91	1991/92
Central government current expenditure												
National insurance fund:												
Retirement pensions	CSDG	12 303	13 766	14 809	15 268	16 584	17 779	18 648	19 237	20 697	22 715	25 533
Lump sums to pensioners	KJDB	103	105	106	102	105	107	107	109	112	114	115
Widows' benefits and guardians' allowances	CSDH	718	755	789	787	801	827	840	851	853	880	948
Unemployment benefit	CSDI	1 758	1 561	1 544	1 578	1 589	1 734	1 468	1 107	733	808	978
Sickness benefit	CSDJ	644	514	255	279	276	179	193	192	204	218	240
Invalidity benefit	CSDK	1 441	1 724	1 965	2 142	2 349	2 673	2 968	3 359	3 837	4 459	5 311
Maternity benefit	CSDL	181	158	146	161	164	168	51	27	30	34	40
Death grant	CSDM	17	17	16	17	18	18	3	–	–	–	–
Injury benefit	CSDN	45	47	–	–	–	–	–	4	4	4	4
Disablement benefit	CSDO	329	355	380	381	407	440	453	451	470	510	547
Industrial death benefit	CSDP	48	51	56	55	58	61	56	59	59	62	69
Statutory sick pay	CSDQ	–	–	440	523	561	779	864	900	1 004	986	..
Statutory maternity pay	GTKZ	–	–	–	–	–	–	199	264	300	348	..
Redundancy Fund	GTKN	463	439	438	344	358	256	92	82	67	130	276
Maternity Fund	GTKO	49	53	59	57	65	71	31	–	–	–	–
Non-contributory benefits:												
War pensions	KJDP	479	504	524	544	581	590	599	610	641	699	761
Family benefits:												
Child benefit	KJDQ	3 497	3 799	4 137	4 276	4 468	4 513	4 598	4 515	4 537	4 636	5 074
One parent benefit	KJDR	76	91	110	120	134	148	163	179	199	216	234
Family credit	KAAA	–	–	–	–	–	–	–	394	425	484	543
Family income supplement	KJDS	73	103	133	126	130	161	180	–	–	–	–
Maternity grants	KJDT	17	17	18	18	17	14	–	–	–	–	–
Income support/Supplementary benefits:												
Supplementary pensions	KJDU	1 450	1 482	752	890	1 009	1 178	1 321	–	–	–	–
Supplementary allowances	KJDV	3 569	5 023	5 121	5 581	6 437	6 789	6 635	–	–	–	–
Income support	KAAB	–	–	–	–	–	–	–	7 582	7 675	8 545	9 850
Social fund	GTLQ	–	–	–	–	–	–	29	149	130	156	161
Other non-contributory benefits:												
Old persons' pensions	KJDX	42	43	44	39	41	37	37	36	35	35	37
Lump sums to pensioners	KJDY	6	6	6	6	7	8	9	9	9	8	9
Attendance allowance	KJDZ	346	422	517	576	686	779	897	1 003	1 159	1 406	1 708
Invalid care allowance	KJEA	7	9	11	11	13	104	184	173	184	213	248
Mobility allowance	KJEB	177	241	310	356	422	514	596	675	769	887	1 060
Invalidity pension and severe disablement allowance	KJEC	138	163	193	236	266	285	295	316	346	433	578
RPI Adjustment	KAAC	–	–	–	–	–	–	94	3	–	–	–
Housing benefit[1]	KJED	572	1 018	2 540	2 833	3 017	3 307	3 473	3 600	3 904	2 059	2 235
Administration	KJEE	1 325	1 437	1 607	1 724	1 735	1 860	2 117	2 270	2 564	2 784	2 994
Total government expenditure	KJAE	29 968	33 946	37 190	39 030	42 310	45 393	47 188	48 130	50 939	53 823	60 649

1 From 1981-82 comprises expenditure by the Department of Health and Social Security under the unified housing benefit scheme.

Source: Central Statistical Office

Social services

3.6 Government and other public sector expenditure on housing
Years ended 31 March

£ million

		1981/82	1982/83	1983/84	1984/85	1985/86	1986/87	1987/88	1988/89	1989/90	1990/91	1991/92
Government expenditure												
Current expenditure												
Central government												
housing subsidies:												
to local authorities	KGVI	1 064	567	417	451	554	513	496	604	713	1 273	1 142
to public corporations	KGVJ	291	260	276	304	295	298	306	304	286	285	274
to housing associations	KJRC	40	46	21	18	17	29	38	41	41	67	41
grants to housing associations	KJRD	115	120	200	182	157	129	109	97	106	163	117
Local authorities												
housing subsidies	KJVK	553	584	649	620	562	542	492	554	487	5	2
Grants under the option mortgage scheme	KJRF	254	299	–	–	–	–	–	–	–	–	–
Administration, etc	KGVL	109	140	168	122	131	200	248	257	233	303	373
Total current expenditure	KJRH	2 426	2 016	1 731	1 697	1 716	1 711	1 689	1 857	1 866	2 096	1 949
Capital expenditure												
Investment in housing by local authorities	KGVM	287	61	794	1 016	1 151	948	999	79	1 387	620	881
Capital grants to housing associations	KJRJ	471	607	983	940	927	894	929	949	525	1 425	2 088
Improvement grants	ADCE	269	561	1 214	982	641	614	757	809	886	862	1 155
Net lending for house purchase	KJRL	807	640	–320	–357	–354	–448	–283	–148	–259	–585	–717
Capital grants to public corporations	KJRM	13	17	20	26	17	23	25	440	16	247	440
Net lending to public corporations	KJRN	491	451	322	344	256	221	20	–146	–315	–709	–315
Total capital expenditure	KJRO	2 338	2 337	3 013	2 951	2 638	2 252	2 447	1 983	2 240	1 860	3 532
Total expenditure												
Central government	KJRP	2 739	2 367	2 239	2 265	2 223	2 107	1 923	2 289	1 372	2 751	3 787
Local authorities	KJRQ	2 025	1 986	2 505	2 383	2 131	1 856	2 213	1 551	2 734	1 205	1 546
Total government expenditure	KJAF	4 764	4 353	4 744	4 648	4 354	3 963	4 136	3 840	4 106	3 956	5 333
Public corporations' capital expenditure												
Investment in housing	KGVN	408	395	411	448	428	398	381	391	377	355	352
Net lending to private sector	AAFR	33	–15	–32	–16	–7	–16	–10	–8	–2	–5	–2
Total	KJRU	441	362	379	432	421	382	371	383	375	350	350
Total public sector expenditure[1]	KJRV	4 714	4 264	4 801	4 736	4 519	4 124	4 487	4 369	4 796	5 015	5 998

1 Total government expenditure *less* grants and loans to public corporations *plus* public corporations' capital expenditure.

Source: Central Statistical Office

Housing

3.7 Stock of dwellings
Great Britain

		1983	1984	1985	1986	1987	1988	1989	1990	1991[2]
Estimated annual gains and losses (Thousands)										
Gains: New construction	KGAA	199.3	210.1	196.9	205.8	216.3	231.8	211.0	189.8	177.8
Other	KGAB	16.2	17.3	16.6	18.3	18.2	15.5	15.5	13.3	13.1
Losses: Slum clearance	KGAC	14.7	11.8	10.6	8.7	8.3	6.8	6.8	7.1	6.9
Other	KGAD	9.6	15.3	11.4	9.6	9.8	11.9	9.2	9.5	10.2
Net gain	KGAE	191.2	200.3	191.4	205.8	216.3	228.7	210.5	186.5	173.8
Stock at end of year[1]	KGAF	21 433	21 633	21 825	22 030	22 247	22 476	22 686	22 872	23 046
Estimated tenure distribution at end of year (percentage)										
Owner occupied	KGAG	59.5	60.6	61.7	62.7	63.8	65.1	66.3	67.2	67.7
Rented: From local authorities and new towns	KGAH	28.3	27.5	26.9	26.2	25.4	24.4	23.2	22.3	21.8
From housing associations	KGAI	2.3	2.4	2.5	2.5	2.6	2.6	2.8	3.0	3.1
From private owners including other tenures	KGAJ	9.9	9.5	9.0	8.6	8.2	7.9	7.6	7.5	7.4

Note: For statistical purposes the stock estimates are expressed to the nearest thousand, but should not be regarded as accurate to the last digit.

1 Estimates are based on data from the 1971 and 1981 Censuses.
2 Provisional.

Sources: Department of Environment; Scottish Development Department; Welsh Office

3.8 Renovations
Great Britain

Number of dwellings

		1981	1982	1983	1984	1985	1986	1987	1988	1989	1990[5]	1991[6]
England												
Local authorities and new towns[1]	KGBA	52 931	57 722	85 461	86 612	96 482	133 661	148 362	169 001	194 928	226 517	177 167
Housing associations[2]	KGBB	11 243	17 364	14 513	18 455	11 350	12 714	10 936	11 237	13 020	10 511	16 413
Private owners: grants paid[3]	KGBC	68 941	104 028	219 826	229 107	136 412	113 328	108 908	105 303	98 217	96 643	86 921
Wales												
Local authorities[1]	KGBE	..	..	..	2 390	1 728	2 788	5 886	8 333	8 444	10 987	11 031
Housing associations[2]	KGBF	694	1 009	993	760	945	907	948	867	812	358	256
Private owners: grants paid[3]	KGBG	7 100	10 989	27 323	29 978	17 152	18 571	19 097	20 187	20 074	26 546	21 047
Scotland												
Local authorities and new towns[4]	KGBI	20 065	51 214	41 583	33 774	58 993	71 397	86 912	72 373	53 699	77 724	76 541
Housing associations[2]	KGBJ	1 833	3 422	2 530	1 424	1 124	1 414	1 262	1 225	1 122	816	..
Private owners: grants paid[3]	KGBK	18 036	23 957	45 498	60 661	46 286	31 453	30 668	31 512	26 870	23 557	23 478
Great Britain												
Local authorities and new towns[1,4]	KGBM	78 996	108 936	127 044	122 776	157 203	207 846	241 160	249 707	257 071	315 228	264 739
Housing associations[2]	KGBN	13 770	21 795	18 036	20 639	13 419	15 035	13 146	13 329	14 954	11 685	..
Private owners: grants paid[3]	KGBO	94 077	138 974	292 647	319 746	199 850	163 352	158 673	157 002	145 161	146 746	131 446

1 Work completed. Includes improvement for sale. Figures for Wales not available before 1984.
2 Figures for England are of work completed funded by the Housing Corporation and Local Authorities. Figures for Wales are for work completed by Housing Corporation funded housing associations only. Figures for Scotland are of work approved under specific housing association legislation. Figures from Scottish Homes not available for 1991.
3 Including grants paid to housing associations under private owner grant legislation. Figures include a small number of grants to tenants in both public and private sectors.
4 Work approved in Scotland.
5 Of the 123 189 renovation grants paid in 1990 to private owners and tenants in England and Wales, 114 192 were paid under the Housing Act 1985 and 8 997 were paid under the Local Government and Housing Act 1989.
6 Of the 107 968 renovation grants paid in 1991 to private owners and tenants in England and Wales, 36 416 were paid under Housing Act 1985 and 71 552 were paid under the Local Government and Housing Act 1989.

Sources: Department of Environment; Scottish Development Department; Welsh Office

3.9 Slum clearance: dwellings demolished or closed

Number

		1981/82	1982/83	1983/84	1984/85	1985/86	1986/87	1987/88	1988/89	1989/90	1990/91
England and Wales: total	KGCA	23 485	17 074	11 622	10 319	9 120	7 026	6 614	5 509	6 083	3 595
Demolished: In clearance areas	KGCB	19 139	14 310	7 272	6 390	5 278	4 161	3 637	2 290	3 351	1 954
Elsewhere	KGCC	2 414	1 944	2 450	2 142	2 439	1 663	1 588	1 456	2 023	1 354
Closed[1]	KGCD	1 932	820	1 900	1 787	1 403	1 202	1 389	1 763	709	287
Scotland[2]: total	KGCE	4 976	3 712	1 987	1 736	1 615	1 735	1 801	1 175	1 007	2 224
Unfit[3]	KGCF	2 710	2 518	1 737	1 040	640	704	794	373	447	..
Other[1,3]	KGCG	2 266	1 194	250	696	975	1 031	1 007	802	560	..

1 Less dwellings included in numbers demolished which had previously been reported as closed.
2 Action under the Housing Acts, Town and Country Planning Acts and other specific statutory powers and other action. Unfit houses comprise houses failing to meet the tolerable standard introduced by the Housing (Scotland) Act 1969 and houses dealt with under earlier statutory provisions as being unfit for human habitation.
3 Figures after 31 March 1990 no longer include information about unfit or other dwellings demolished, as data collection on above and below tolerable standard demolitions ceased.

Sources: Department of Environment; Scottish Development Department; Welsh Office

Housing

3.10 Permanent dwellings completed

Number

United Kingdom

	Total	For local housing authorities[1]	For private owners	Housing Associations and other[2]
	KAAD	KAAE	KAAF	KAAG
1968	425 835	187 984	226 068	11 783
1969	378 324	180 958	185 916	11 450
1970	362 226	176 926	174 342	10 958
1971	364 475	154 894	196 313	13 268
1972	330 936	120 431	200 755	9 750
1973	304 637	102 604	191 080	10 953
1974	279 582	121 017	145 777	13 388
1975	321 936	150 526	154 528	16 882
1976	324 769	151 824	155 229	17 716
1977	314 093	143 250	143 905	26 938
1978	288 603	112 340	152 166	24 097
1979	251 816	88 495	144 055	19 276
1980	241 986	87 974	131 974	22 038
1981	206 625	68 050	118 579	19 996
1982	182 845	39 960	129 004	13 881
1983	209 016	38 921	153 021	17 074
1984	220 548	37 417	165 593	17 538
1985	207 633	30 333	163 447	13 853
1986	216 023	25 110	177 509	13 404
1987	226 140	21 129	191 182	13 829
1988	241 801	21 162	206 842	13 797
1989	221 335	18 641	187 447	15 247
1990	198 103	17 799	162 551	17 753
1991	184 726	10 961	153 412	20 353

England and Wales

	Total	For local housing authorities[1]	For private owners	Housing Associations and other[2]
	KAAH	KAAI	KAAJ	KAAK
1968	371 726	148 049	213 273	10 404
1969	324 165	139 850	173 377	10 938
1970	307 266	134 874	162 084	10 308
1971	309 776	117 215	179 998	12 563
1972	287 294	93 635	184 622	9 037
1973	264 047	79 289	174 413	10 345
1974	241 173	99 423	129 626	12 124
1975	278 694	122 857	140 381	15 456
1976	278 660	124 152	138 477	16 031
1977	276 011	121 246	128 688	26 077
1978	254 001	96 752	134 578	22 671
1979	220 722	77 192	125 306	18 224
1980	224 919	78 012	116 164	20 743
1981	179 783	58 126	104 001	17 656
1982	159 389	33 430	113 875	12 084
1983	181 380	31 391	134 882	15 107
1984	191 244	31 196	145 301	14 747
1985	178 436	24 289	142 072	12 075
1986	187 187	20 343	155 557	11 287
1987	198 672	16 870	169 827	11 975
1988	213 588	16 720	185 152	11 716
1989	190 858	14 667	163 249	12 942
1990	169 890	14 564	139 837	15 489
1991	158 378	8 461	132 264	17 653

Scotland

	Total	For local housing authorities[1]	For private owners	Housing Associations and other[2]
	KAAL	KAAM	KAAN	KAAO
1968	41 989	32 011	8 720	1 258
1969	42 628	33 932	8 326	370
1970	43 126	34 360	8 220	546
1971	40 783	28 577	11 614	592
1972	31 992	19 593	11 835	564
1973	30 033	17 349	12 215	469
1974	28 336	16 182	11 239	915
1975	34 323	22 784	10 371	1 168
1976	36 527	21 154	13 704	1 669
1977	27 320	14 328	12 132	860
1978	25 759	9 907	14 443	1 409
1979	23 782	7 857	15 175	750
1980	20 611	7 455	12 242	914
1981	20 015	7 065	11 021	1 929
1982	16 423	3 716	11 523	1 184
1983	17 931	3 486	13 168	1 277
1984	18 838	2 633	14 115	2 090
1985	18 411	2 811	14 435	1 165
1986	18 637	2 187	14 870	1 580
1987	17 707	2 495	13 904	1 308
1988	18 272	2 730	14 179	1 363
1989	20 173	2 266	16 287	1 620
1990	20 286	1 936	16 551	1 799
1991	19 450	1 546	15 984	1 920

Northern Ireland

	Total	For local housing authorities[1]	For private owners	Housing Associations and other[2]
	KAAP	KAAQ	KAAR	KAAS
1968	12 120	7 924	4 075	121
1969	11 531	7 176	4 213	142
1970	11 834	7 692	4 038	104
1971	13 916	9 102	4 701	113
1972	11 650	7 203	4 298	149
1973	10 557	5 966	4 452	139
1974	10 073	5 412	4 312	349
1975	8 919	4 885	3 776	258
1976	9 582	6 518	3 048	16
1977	10 762	7 676	3 085	1
1978	8 843	5 681	3 145	17
1979	7 312	3 436	3 574	302
1980	6 456	2 507	3 568	381
1981	6 827	2 859	3 557	411
1982	7 033	2 814	3 606	613
1983	9 705	4 044	4 971	690
1984	10 466	3 588	6 177	701
1985	10 786	3 233	6 940	613
1986	10 199	2 580	7 082	537
1987	9 761	1 764	7 451	546
1988	9 941	1 712	7 511	718
1989	10 304	1 708	7 911	685
1990	7 927	1 299	6 163	465
1991	6 898	954	5 164	780

1 Including the Commission for the New Towns and New Towns Development Corporations, the Scottish Special Housing Association, the Northern Ireland Housing Trust and the Northern Ireland Housing Executive.
2 Dwellings provided by housing associations other than the Scottish Special Housing Association and the Northern Ireland Housing Trust and provided or authorised by government departments for the families of police, prison staffs, the Armed Forces and certain other services.

Sources: Scottish Development Department; Department of the Environment (Northern Ireland); Department of the Environment; Welsh Office

National Insurance

3.11 National Insurance Fund
Years ended 31 March

£ thousands

		1982/83	1983/84	1984/85	1985/86	1986/87	1987/88	1988/89	1989/90	1990/91
Receipts										
Opening balance	KJFB	4 194 593	4 164 605	4 742 324	5 165 213	5 400 988	5 858 038	7 481 237	10 634 672	10 852 343
Contributions	KJFC	16 663 862	18 167 156	19 421 972	21 222 636	22 778 266	26 050 756	27 928 396	29 970 364	32 098 174
Compensation for SSP and SMP payments	KJQM	..	..	..	..	..	..	..	..	40 600[5]
Consolidated Fund supplement	KJFD	2 642 891	2 866 800	2 654 055	2 210 245	2 463 600	2 184 725	1 686 175		1 308 600
Reimbursement for Industrial Injury benefit payments	KJQN	..	..	..	..	..	..	..	..	17 342[5]
Income from investments	KJFE	514 038	506 882	533 732	557 951	619 805	607 863	794 860	1 060 702	1 048 515
Other receipts	KJFF	87 859	92 792	96 196	61 778	176 987	194 333	1 081	1 018	965 763
Total	KAAT	24 103 244	25 798 236	27 448 278	29 217 824	31 439 646	28 207 398	38 076 800	41 666 756	47 236 816
Expenditure										
Total benefits[1]	KJFG	19 073 084	20 220 928	21 333 736	22 929 064	24 611 824	25 442 704	28 352 408	30 126 298	33 339 702
Unemployment	KJFH	1 550 329	1 544 726	1 623 021	1 637 596	1 787 975	1 516 649	1 147 832	764 593	928 086
Sickness	KJFI	514 251	267 108	287 455	280 026	190 643	203 623	202 078	214 228	237 644
Invalidity	KJFJ	1 672 580	1 959 334	2 239 461	2 451 527	2 791 026	3 098 571	3 500 571	3 993 974	4 794 989
Maternity	KETY	157 100	145 400	166 727	169 820	174 117	53 216	27 873	31 140	35 515
Widows' pensions	KEWU	751 204	798 752	812 834	829 160	854 709	869 360	880 456	883 822	951 918
Guardians' allowances[2] / Child's special allowance	KJFK	2 240	2 130	1 824	1 542	1 680	1 534	1 449	1 452	1 735
Retirement pensions	KJFL	13 844 825	14 932 644	15 622 324	16 949 264	18 162 400	19 057 884	19 951 518	23 634 712	25 800 660
Death grants	KJFM	17 335	17 132	17 422	18 661	18 842	2 694	–	–	–
Injury	KJFN	47 564	7 573	342	–	–	–	–	–	–
Disablement[3]	KAAU	353 326	379 730	392 235	419 054	453 052	466 658	464 466	483 320	419 756
Death[3]	KAAV	52 430	55 550	56 640	60 279	63 163	58 602	60 760	61 469	47 920
Pensioners' lump sum payments	KAAW	104 500	105 500	107 600	107 618	109 660	109 690	111 710	114 780	118 259
Other benefits	KAAX	5 400	5 400	5 000	4 516	4 017	4 224	3 695	4 278	3 222
Payments in lieu of benefits foregone[4]	KAAY	31 176	11 569	10 825	9 775	–	–	–	–	–
Other payments	KAAZ	287	316	10 736	1 709	7 782	4 785	8 262	7 322	9 623
Administration	KABE	749 321	746 097	833 569	838 124	765 699	830 539	896 458	891 925	1 056 787
Transfers to Northern Ireland	KABF	84 700	77 000	95 000	60 000	175 000	155 000	185 000	210 000	225 000
Personal pensions	KJQO	..	..	..	..	..	..	..	..	42 224[5]
Total	KABG	19 938 638	21 055 912	22 283 064	23 838 672	25 559 764	26 438 028	27 442 128	31 289 692	34 706 980
Accumulated funds	KABH	4 164 605	4 742 324	5 165 213	5 379 151	5 879 881	7 481 287	10 634 672	10 579 741	12 530 598

1 The total benefits figure for Northern Ireland in 1984/85 and 1985/86 includes payments in lieu of benefit foregone.
2 Including figures of Child's special allowance for Northern Ireland.
3 From 1.4.90, industrial injury benefits are no longer paid for out of the National Insurance Fund; this amount is reimbursement for expenditure incurred by the fund for the period 1.4.90 to 31.12.90.
4 Payments to the Post Office, British Telecommunications, Consolidated and Trading Funds, (from 1986/7 Estains payments not shown separately and are included with Sickness Benefit together with Injury Benefit. Estains arrangements were abolished on 25.8.86).
5 Figures provided for Northern Ireland only.

Sources: Department of Social Security; Department of Health and Social Services (Northern Ireland)

3.12 National Insurance Acts: persons for whom contributions were payable
Persons who paid contributions in a tax year ending April[1]

Millions

		Total				Men				Married women				Single, widowed and divorced women		
		1988	1989	1990		1988	1989	1990		1988	1989	1990		1988	1989	1990
Total[2]	KABI	24.69	25.37	25.73	KEYF	14.82	15.03	15.09	KEYP	5.85	6.10	6.28	KEYZ	4.02	4.23	4.37
Class 1 Standard rate	KABJ	21.11	21.81	22.26	KEYG	12.74	12.88	12.92	KEYQ	4.54	4.88	5.15	KEZA	3.84	4.05	4.19
Contracted in	KABK	11.61	11.64	12.14	KEYH	6.33	6.10	6.28	KEYR	2.89	3.05	3.21	KEZB	2.39	2.49	2.65
Contracted out	KABL	8.11	8.24	8.49	KEYI	5.61	5.64	5.73	KEYS	1.37	1.46	1.59	KEZC	1.13	1.15	1.17
Mixed contracted in/out	KABM	1.40	1.93	1.63	KEYJ	0.80	1.13	0.91	KEYT	0.28	0.38	0.35	KEZD	0.32	0.42	0.37
Class 1 Reduced rate	KABN	1.13	1.01	0.85	KEYK	–	–	–	KEYU	1.06	0.94	0.80	KEZE	0.07	0.06	0.05
Mixed Class 1 Standard and Reduced rate	KABO	0.06	0.05	0.08	KEYL	–	–	–	KEYV	0.05	0.05	0.07	KEZF	0.01	–	–
Class 2	KABP	1.96	2.04	2.09	KEYM	1.74	1.79	1.81	KEYW	0.15	0.18	0.20	KEZG	0.07	0.07	0.08
Mixed Class 1 and Class 2	KABQ	0.34	0.37	0.36	KEYN	0.28	0.30	0.29	KEYX	0.03	0.04	0.04	KEZH	0.03	0.03	0.03
Class 3[3]	KABR	0.09	0.08	0.09	KEYO	0.06	0.06	0.06	KEYY	0.02	0.02	0.02	KEZI	0.01	0.01	0.01

1 The tax year commences on 6 April and ends on 5 April of the following year. The years shown at the head of the column refer to the end of the tax year. Persons who paid any contributions at any time in the tax year are shown.
2 Not all figures agree because of rounding.
3 Persons who paid a mixture of Class 3 contributions and others are not included in 'Class 3' but are shown according to the type of the additional contribution.

Source: Department of Social Security

National Insurance

3.13 Weekly rates of principal social security benefits

£

		1980 Nov	1981 Nov	1982 Nov	1983 Nov	1984 Nov	1985 Nov	1986 Jul	1987 Apr	1988 Apr	1989 Apr	1990 Apr	1991 Apr	1992 Apr
Unemployment benefit:[1] Men and women	KJNA	20.65	22.50	25.00	27.05	28.45	30.45	30.80	31.45	32.75	34.70	37.35	41.40	43.10
Sickness benefit:[1] Men and women	KJNB	20.65	22.50	25.00	25.95	27.25	29.15	29.45	30.05	31.30	33.20	35.70	39.60	41.20
Invalidity benefit: Invalidity pension	KJNC	26.00	28.35	31.45	32.60	34.25	38.30	38.70	39.50	41.15	43.60	46.90	52.00	54.15
Invalidity allowance:														
High rate	KJND	5.45	6.20	6.90	7.15	7.50	8.05	8.15	8.30	8.65	9.20	10.00	11.10	11.55
Middle rate	KJNE	3.45	4.00	4.40	4.60	4.80	5.10	5.20	5.30	5.50	5.80	6.20	6.90	7.20
Low rate	KJNF	1.75	2.00	2.20	2.30	2.40	2.55	2.60	2.65	2.75	2.90	3.10	3.45	3.60
Increase for dependants:														
Adult	KJNG	15.60	17.00	18.85	19.55	20.55	23.00	23.25	23.75	24.75	26.20	28.20	31.25	32.55
Each child	KJNH	7.50	..	7.95	7.60	7.65	8.05	8.05	8.05	8.40	8.95	9.65	10.70	10.85
Attendance allowance:														
Higher rate	KJNI	21.65	23.65	26.25	27.20	28.60	30.60	30.95	31.60	32.95	34.90	37.55	41.65	43.35
Lower rate	KJNJ	14.45	15.75	17.50	18.15	19.10	20.45	20.65	21.10	22.00	23.30	25.05	27.10	28.95
Mobility allowance[2]	KJNK	14.50	16.50	18.30	19.00	20.00	21.40	21.65	22.10	23.05	24.40	26.25	29.80	..
Maternity benefit: Maternity allowances for insured women	KJNL	20.65	22.50	25.00	25.95	27.25	29.15	29.45	30.05	31.30	33.20	35.70	40.60	46.30
Death grant[3]	KJNM	30.00	30.00	30.00	30.00	30.00	30.00	30.00	30.00	–	–	–	–	–
Guardian's allowance	KJNN	7.50	7.70	7.95	7.60	7.65	8.05	8.05	8.05	8.40	8.95	9.65	10.70	10.85
Widow's benefit:														
Widow's pension	KJNO	27.15	29.60	32.85	34.05	35.80	38.30	38.70	39.50	41.15	43.60	46.90	52.00	54.15
Widowed mother's allowance	KJNP	27.15	29.60	32.85	34.05	..	38.30	38.70	39.50	41.15	43.60	46.90	52.00	54.15
Addition for each child	KJNQ	7.50	7.70	7.95	7.60	7.65	8.05	8.05	8.05	8.40	8.95	9.65	10.70	10.85
Retirement pension:[4]														
Single person	KJNR	27.15	29.60	32.85	34.05	35.80	38.30	38.70	39.50	41.15	43.60	46.90	52.00	54.15
Married couple	KJNS	43.45	47.35	52.55	54.50	57.30	61.30	61.95	63.25	65.90	69.80	75.10	83.25	86.70
Non-contributory retirement pension:														
Man or woman	KJNT	16.30	17.75	19.70	20.45	21.50	23.00	23.25	23.75	24.75	26.20	28.20	31.25	32.55
Married woman	KJNU	9.80	10.65	11.80	12.25	12.85	13.75	13.90	14.20	14.80	15.65	16.85	18.70	19.45
Industrial injuries benefit:														
Injury benefit	KJNV	23.40	25.25	27.75	–[6]	–	–	–	–	–	–	–	–	–
Disablement pension at 100 per cent rate	KJNW	44.30	48.30	53.60	55.60	58.40	62.50	63.20	64.50	67.20	71.20	76.60	84.90	88.40
Widow's or widower's pension	KJNX	27.70	30.15	33.40	34.60	36.35	38.85	39.25	40.05	41.15	43.60	46.90	52.00	54.15
Increase for dependants:[5]														
Adult	KJNY	12.75	13.90	15.45	16.70	17.55	18.80	19.00	19.40	20.20	21.40	23.05	25.55	26.60
Each child	KJNZ	1.25	0.80	0.30	0.15	–[7]	–	–	–	–	–	–	–	–

1 Persons under the age of 18 are entitled to the appropriate adult rate.
2 Mobility allowance was introduced from 1 January 1976 at the £5.00 rate. Disability living allowance has replaced Mobility allowance from April 1992.
3 Death grant is not payable in respect of the death of a person who on 4 July 1948 was aged 65 or over (men) and 60 or over (women). This benefit was abolished from April 1987 and replaced by payments from Social Fund.
4 Retirement pensioners over 80 receive 25p addition.
5 An allowance for one adult dependant is payable, where appropriate, with unemployment benefit, sickness benefit, retirement pension, injury benefit and maternity allowance. Allowances for dependent children are payable with any of these benefits. Changes in these increases take effect from the same date as the main benefit.
6 Injury benefit ceased on 6 April 1983.
7 Child dependency addition was abolished from 24 November 1984.

Source: Department of Social Security

National Insurance

3.13 Weekly rates of principal social security benefits
continued

£

		1980 Nov	1981 Nov	1982 Nov	1983 Nov	1984 Nov	1985 Nov	1986 Jul	1987 Apr	1988 Apr	1989 Apr	1990 Apr	1991 Apr	1992 Apr
Child benefit:[15]														
First child	KJOA	4.75	5.25	5.85	6.50	6.85	7.00	7.10	7.25	7.25	7.25	7.25	8.25	9.65
Subsequent children	KETZ	–	–	–	–	–	–	–	–	–	–	–	–	7.80
Family Credit[8]														
(maximum awards payable):														
Families with 1 child														
Child under 11	KJOB	17.00	18.50	21.00	22.00	23.00	25.00	25.30	25.85	38.15	40.90	44.60	48.00	51.40
Child 11-15	KJOC	17.00	18.50	21.00	22.00	23.00	25.50	25.80	26.40	43.50	46.50	50.50	54.40	58.25
Child 16 and over	KJOD	17.00	18.50	21.00	22.00	23.00	26.00	26.30	26.90	46.80	49.95	54.15	58.35	62.45
Child age 18	KJOE	–	–	–	–	–	–	–	–	53.45	56.90	61.45	66.25	70.90
Increase for each additional child														
Child under 11	KJOF	1.50	1.50	2.00	2.00	2.00	2.50	2.55	2.60	6.05	7.30	8.25	9.70	10.40
Child 11-15	KJOG	1.50	1.50	2.00	2.00	2.00	3.00	3.05	3.15	11.40	12.90	14.15	16.10	17.25
Child 16 and over	KJOH	1.50	1.50	2.00	2.00	2.00	3.50	3.55	3.65	14.70	16.35	17.80	20.05	21.45
Child age 18	KJOI	–	–	–	–	–	–	–	–	21.35	23.30	25.10	27.95	29.90
War pension:														
Ex-private (100 per cent assessment)	KJOJ	44.30	48.30	53.60	55.60	58.40	62.50	63.20	64.50	67.20	71.20	76.60	84.90	89.00
War widow	KJOK	35.30	38.45	42.70	44.25	46.55	49.80	50.30	51.35	53.50	56.65	60.95	67.60	70.35
Supplementary benefits:[9,14]														
Weekly scale rate of requirements[10]														
Married couple[11]														
Ordinary rate	KJOL	34.60	37.75	41.70	43.50	45.55	47.85	48.40	49.35	–	–	–	–	–
Long-term rate	KJOM	43.45	47.35	52.30	54.55	57.10	60.00	60.65	61.85	–	–	–	–	–
Single householder:[12]														
Ordinary rate	KJON	21.30	23.25	25.70	26.80	28.05	29.50	29.80	30.40	–	–	–	–	–
Long-term rate	KJOO	27.15	29.60	32.70	34.10	35.70	37.50	37.90	38.65	–	–	–	–	–
Non-householder aged:														
18 or over														
Ordinary rate	KJOP	17.05	18.60	20.55	21.45	22.45	23.60	23.85	24.35	–	–	–	–	–
Long-term rate	KJOQ	21.70	23.65	26.15	27.25	28.55	30.00	30.35	30.95	–	–	–	–	–
16-17														
Ordinary rate	KJOR	13.10	14.30	15.80	16.50	17.30	18.20	18.40	18.75	–	–	–	–	–
Long-term rate	KEUZ	..	18.15	20.05	20.90	21.90	23.00	23.25	23.70	–	–	–	–	–
Increase for children aged:														
11-15	KJOS	10.90	11.90	13.15	13.70	14.35	15.10	15.30	15.60	–	–	–	–	–
Under 10	KJOV	7.30	7.90	8.75	9.15	9.60	10.10	10.20	10.40	–	–	–	–	–
Income Support:														
Personal allowances[13]														
Single														
aged 16-17 either	KJOW	–	–	–	–	–	–	–	–	19.40	20.80	21.90	23.65[15]	25.55
or depending on their circumstances	KABS	–	–	–	–	–	–	–	–	–	–	28.80	31.15[16]	33.60
aged 18-24	KJOX	–	–	–	–	–	–	–	–	26.05	27.40	28.80	31.15	33.60
aged 25 or over	KJOY	–	–	–	–	–	–	–	–	33.40	34.90	36.70	39.65	42.45
Couple														
both aged under 18	KJOZ	–	–	–	–	–	–	–	–	38.80	41.60	43.80	47.30	50.60
one or both 18 or over	KJPA	–	–	–	–	–	–	–	–	51.45	54.80	57.60	62.25	66.60
Lone parent														
aged 16-17 either	KJPB	–	–	–	–	–	–	–	–	19.40	20.80	21.90	23.65	25.55
or depending on their circumstances	KABT	–	–	–	–	–	–	–	–	..	..	28.80	31.15[16]	33.60
aged 18 or over	KJPC	–	–	–	–	–	–	–	–	33.40	34.90	36.70	39.65	42.45
Dependant children and young people														
aged under 11	KJPD	–	–	–	–	–	–	–	–	10.75	11.75	12.35	13.35[17]	14.55
aged 11-15	KJPE	–	–	–	–	–	–	–	–	16.10	17.35	18.25	19.75	21.40
aged 16-17	KJPF	–	–	–	–	–	–	–	–	19.40	20.80	21.90	23.65	25.65
aged 18	KABU	–	–	–	–	–	–	–	–	26.05	27.40	28.80	31.15	33.60

8 Family credit superseded Family Income Supplement from April 1988.
9 Supplementary pension is paid to people over age 65 (men) or 60 (women). Supplementary allowance is paid to people below those ages. Persons aged 80 years and over are entitled to a further 25p.
10 Scale rates for normal requirements other than rent.
11 Including couples as man and wife.
12 Including any single person who is directly responsible for rent.
13 In addition to personal allowances a claimant may also be entitled to a premium(s). The types of premium are family, lone parent, pensioner, higher pensioner, disability, severe disability and disabled child.
14 Supplementary Benefit was replaced by Income Support from April 1988.
15 From October 1991 the rate is £23.90.
16 From October 1991 the rate is £31.40.
17 From October 1991 each rate increases by 25p.

Source: Department of Social Security

National Insurance

3.14 National Insurance contributions

	Class 1											Others	
	Not contracted out				Contracted out							
	Employee		Employer	Employer only[3]	Employee			Employer		Employer only		
	Standard[1]	Reduced[2]	Standard and reduced	Standard only	Standard		Reduced	Standard and reduced		Standard only		
					Up to LEL[4]	Over LEL		Up to LEL[4]	Over LEL	Up to LEL[4]	Over LEL	Class 2	Class 3
	%	%	%	%	%	%	%	%	%	%	%	£	£
6 April 1989 Weekly earnings (£)													
43.00 - 74.99	5.0	3.85	5.0	5.0	5.0	3.0	3.85	5.0	1.2	5.0	1.2		
75.00 - 114.99	7.0	3.85	7.0	7.0	7.0	5.0	3.85	7.0	3.2	7.0	3.2		
115.00 - 164.99	9.0	3.85	9.0	9.0	9.0	7.0	3.85	9.0	5.2	9.0	5.2		
165.00 - 325.00	9.0	3.85	10.45	10.45	9.0	7.0	3.85	10.45	6.65	10.45	6.65		
over 325.00			10.45	10.45	-	-	-	10.45	10.45	10.45	10.45		
Classes 2 and 3													

	Up to LEL[4]	Over LEL											
5 October 1989 Weekly earnings (£)													
43.00 - 74.99	2.0	9.0	3.85	5.0	5.0	2.0	7.0	3.85	5.0	1.2	5.0	1.2		
75.00 - 114.99	2.0	9.0	3.85	7.0	7.0	2.0	7.0	3.85	7.0	3.2	7.0	3.2		
115.00 - 164.99	2.0	9.0	3.85	9.0	9.0	2.0	7.0	3.85	9.0	5.2	9.0	5.2		
165.00 - 325.00	2.0	9.0	3.85	10.45	10.45	2.0	7.0	3.85	10.45	6.65	10.45	6.65		
over 325	2.0	9.0	3.85	10.45	10.45	2.0	7.0	3.85	10.45	10.45	10.45	10.45	4.25	4.15
Classes 2 and 3														
6 April 1990 Weekly earnings (£)														
46.00 - 79.99	2.0	9.0	3.85	5.0	5.0	2.0	7.0	3.85	5.0	1.2	5.0	1.2		
80.00 - 124.99	2.0	9.0	3.85	7.0	7.0	2.0	7.0	3.85	7.0	3.2	7.0	3.2		
125.00 - 174.99	2.0	9.0	3.85	9.0	9.0	2.0	7.0	3.85	9.0	5.2	9.0	5.2		
175.00 - 350.00	2.0	9.0	3.85	10.45	10.45	2.0	7.0	3.85	10.45	6.65	10.45	6.65		
over 350	2.0	9.0	3.85	10.45	10.45	2.0	7.0	3.85	10.45	10.45	10.45	10.45	4.55	4.15
Classes 2 and 3														
6 April 1991 Weekly earnings (£)														
52.00 - 84.99	2.0	9.0	3.85	4.6	4.6	2.0	7.0	3.85	4.6	0.8	4.6	0.8		
85.00 - 129.99	2.0	9.0	3.85	6.6	6.6	2.0	7.0	3.85	6.6	2.8	6.6	2.8		
130.00 - 184.99	2.0	9.0	3.85	8.6	8.6	2.0	7.0	3.85	8.6	4.8	8.6	4.8		
185.00 - 390.00	2.0	9.0	3.85	10.4	10.4	2.0	7.0	3.85	10.4	6.6	10.4	6.6		
over 390	2.0	9.0	3.85	10.4	10.4	2.0	7.0	3.85	10.4	6.6	10.4	6.6		
Classes 2 and 3													5.15	5.05
6 April 1992 Weekly earnings (£)														
54.00 - 89.00	2.0	9.0	3.85	4.6	4.6	2.0	7.0	3.85	4.6	0.8	4.6	0.8		
90.00 - 134.99	2.0	9.0	3.85	6.6	6.6	2.0	7.0	3.85	6.6	2.8	6.6	2.8		
135.00 - 189.99	2.0	9.0	3.85	8.6	8.6	2.0	7.0	3.85	8.6	4.8	8.6	4.8		
190.00 - 405.00	2.0	9.0	3.85	10.4	10.4	2.0	7.0	3.85	10.4	6.6	10.4	6.6		
over 405	2.0	9.0	3.85	10.4	10.4	2.0	7.0	3.85	10.4	6.6	10.4	6.6		
Classes 2 and 3													5.35	5.25

1 For employees who are under pension age (65 men/60 women), but excluding those married women or widows who are liable for contributions at the reduced rate.
2 For employees who are married women or widows and liable for contributions at the reduced rate.
3 For all employees over pension age. Applicable also to employees who had made other arrangements to pay Class 1 contributions.
4 From 6 April 1989 LEL £43.00 a week, from 6 April 1990 LEL £46.00 a week, from 6 April 1991 LEL £52.00 a week, from 6 April 1992 LEL £54.00 a week.

Source: Department of Social Security

Social security

3.15 Social Security Acts: number of persons receiving benefit[1]
United Kingdom
At any one time

Thousands

		1980	1981	1982	1983	1984	1985	1986	1987	1988	1989	1990	1991
Persons receiving:													
Unemployment benefit	KJHA	753.0	1 206.0[11]	1 041.0	987.0	926.0	901.0[11]	956.0[11]	811.0	630.2	380.8	331.4	569.5
Sickness and Invalidity benefit[2,3]	KJHB	1 197.0	1 156.0	1 198.0	1 202.0	1 044.0	1 098.0	1 141.0	1 168.0	1 278.0	1 394.7	1 515.6	1 479.5
Guardians' allowances	KJHE	4.6	4.4	4.1	3.9	3.3	3.2	2.9	2.7	2.6	1.9	2.0	2.2
Widows' benefits[4]	KJHF	14.0[3]	433.0	426.0	420.0	414.0	398.0	389.0	380.0	388.0	371.0	365.2	362.3
National Insurance retirement pensions[3]:													
Males	KJHH	3 241.0	3 280.0	3 280.0	3 280.0	3 268.0	3 353.0	3 411.0	3 454.0	3 479.1	3 481.7	3 553.9	3 512.8
Females	KJHL	5 866.0	6 010.0	6 105.0	6 208.0	6 259.0	6 379.0	6 455.0	6 490.0	6 523.5	6 520.4	6 625.7	6 515.3
Total	KJHG	9 108.0	9 291.0	9 386.0	9 487.0	9 528.0	9 732.0	9 865.0	9 944.0	10 001.6	10 002.2	10 179.6	10 028.1
Non-contributory retirement pensions[3]:													
Males	KJHI	6.0	6.0	6.0	6.0	6.0	6.0	7.0	7.0	6.0	6.7	6.7	6.1
Females	KJHJ	50.0	45.0	42.0	39.0	38.0	34.0	36.0	35.0	32.6	31.5	29.4	25.3
Total	KJHK	56.0	51.0	48.0	45.0	43.0	39.0	42.0	41.0	39.3	38.2	36.0	31.4
Industrial Injuries disablement pensions assessments[5]	KJHN	201.0	197.0	194.0	191.0	186.0	191.0	189.0	189.0	189.0	193.0	196.9	198.1
Reduced earnings allowance/ Retirement allowance assessments	KEYC	146.8	146.0	145.6	147.1	147.6	148.3	148.7	148.8	150.5	154.9	160.0	156.9
Child benefit[3] Families receiving benefit	KJHO	7 397.0	7 352.0	7 261.0	7 174.0	7 097.0	7 034.0	6 979.0	6 928.0	6 923.0	6 695.0	6 949.5	7 021.5[14]
Family income supplement	KJHP	106	143	179	215	218	214	218	220	..	..	..	..
Family Credit[6]	KHYH	..	..	..	..	..	..	..	..	313.1	311.9	331.7	360.4
Supplementary benefits[7]	KJHQ	3 247	3 873	4 432	4 524	4 788	4 771	5 158	5 088	..	..	..	..
Income Support	KABV	..	..	..	..	..	..	..	..	4 536.0	4 350.0	4 376.0	4 683.0
Housing Benefit and Community Charge Benefit[8]													
Rent rebate[9]	KABY	..	..	..	..	..	..	..	..	3 132.0[12]	2 971.5	2 928.1	2 944.0
Rent allowance[9]	KABZ	..	..	..	..	..	..	..	..	968.7[12]	958.1	1 067.2	1 082.4
Rate rebate[9]	KACA	..	..	..	..	..	..	..	..	5 225.4[12]	4 299.8[13]	..	..
Community charge benefit[9,10]	KACB	..	..	..	..	..	..	..	..	..	–[13]	6 518.4	6 290.7
Community charge rebate[9,10]	KEZU	..	..	..	..	..	..	..	..	..	876.1[13]	..	..
War pensions[9]	KJHR	353.6	340.5	327.4	313.9	302.3	290.9	274.8	266.0	258.3	252.2	248.0	249.6

1 Caseload counts at a specific date in the year which varies from benefit to benefit.
2 A relatively small number of claims do not result in the payment of benefit but are included here because they indicate notified incapacity for work.
3 Includes overseas cases.
4 Excluding widows' allowances paid during the first twenty-six weeks of widowhood the number of such allowances does not exceed 35 000 in a six month period. Widows' allowance was replaced by widows' payment on 11 April 1988.
5 Industrial injuries disablement pension, reduced earnings allowance retirement allowance assesments starting 1 October upto 1986/87: first Monday in April thereafter.
6 Family Income Supplement was replaced by Family Credit from April 1988.
7 From April 1988 Supplementary Benefit was replaced by Income Support.
8 Data prior to 1988 is not available.
9 Great Britain only.
10 Claimants with partners are treated as one recipient.
11 Figures are given at May each year, except for 1981 and 1984, when figures relate to February, and 1985 when figures relate to November. February 1981 data for Great Britain only, due to industrial action.
12 The housing benefit scheme was reformed in April 1988.
13 Rate rebate in Scotland was replaced by community charge rebate (CCR) in April 1989. In April 1990 rate rebate in England and Wales, and CCR in Scotland was replaced by Community Charge Benefit.
14 Provisional.

Sources: Department of Social Security; Department of Health and Social Services (Northern Ireland)

Unemployment benefit

3.16 Unemployed claimants analysed by benefit entitlement
United Kingdom

Thousands

		1983 Nov	1984 Nov	1985 Nov	1986[2] Nov	1987 Nov	1988 Nov	1989 Nov	1990 Nov	1991 Nov
All Persons										
Flat-rate benefit payable - total	KJIB	938.0	926.0	872.0	955.0	676.0	521.6	304.4	356.1	641.7
Flat-rate benefit only	KJIC	709.0	723.0	679.0	768.0	549.0	402.2	220.3	294.0	520.2
Flat-rate benefit and supplementary allowance[3]	KJIF	229.0	203.0	193.0	187.0	127.0	119.3	82.1	62.0	121.5
Supplementary allowance only[3]	KJIG	1 685.0	1 773.0	1 690.0	1 715.0	1 407.0	1 143.0	995.5	1 044.4	1 464.0
No Flat-rate benefit or supplementary allowance[1,3]	KJIH	383.0	420.0	461.0	500.0	425.0	347.3	252.0	2 529.0	306.6
Total	KJIA	3 006.0	3 119.0	3 023.0	3 170.0	2 508.0	1 012.8	1 551.9	1 653.3	2 412.3
Males										
Flat-rate benefit payable - total	KJIJ	613.0	577.0	541.0	596.0	442.0	328.2	200.5	254.1	472.1
Flat-rate benefit only	KJIK	414.0	402.0	375.0	435.0	331.0	227.5	128.9	197.3	362.0
Flat-rate benefit and supplementary allowance[3]	KJIN	199.0	175.0	166.0	161.0	111.0	100.7	71.6	56.9	110.1
Supplementary allowance only [3]	KJIO	1 284.0	1 350.0	1 281.0	1 308.0	1 140.0	886.0	778.2	825.4	1 171.7
No Flat-rate benefit or supplementary allowance[1,3]	KJIP	221.0	234.0	252.0	275.0	279.0	209.9	157.6	166.8	205.3
Total	KJII	2 118.0	2 161.0	2 074.0	2 179.0	1 861.0	1 424.1	1 136.3	1 246.3	1 849.4
Females										
Flat-rate benefit payable - total	KJIR	325.0	349.0	331.0	359.0	250.0	278.0	1 039.0	101.9	169.7
Flat-rate benefit only	KJIS	295.0	321.0	304.0	333.0	231.0	174.8	92.5	96.8	158.1
Flat-rate benefit and supplementary allowance[3]	KJIV	30.0	28.0	27.0	26.0	19.0	18.6	11.5	5.1	11.5
Supplementary allowance only[3]	KJIW	401.0	423.0	409.0	407.0	354.0	258.0	217.3	219.0	291.9
No Flat-rate benefit or supplementary allowance [1,3]	KJIX	162.0	186.0	209.0	225.0	184.0	138.3	95.4	86.1	101.4
Total	KJIQ	888.0	958.0	949.0	991.0	788.0	588.7	416.7	407.0	562.9

Note: Figures are based on a five per cent sample. For Northern Ireland figures are based on a twenty per cent sample.

1 Prior to Novenber 1978 figures for non-recipients of benefit include non-claimants; from 1978 only claimants for benefit or credit are included.

2 Figures are for Great Britain only. Due to industrial action November 1985 figures for Northern Ireland are not available.

3 Supplementary Benefit was replaced by Income Support from April 1988, therefore, all references to Supplementary Benefit should be treated as Income Support from 1988 onwards.

*Sources: Department of Social Security;
Department of Health and Social Services (Northern Ireland)*

Sickness benefit

3.17 Sickness and Invalidity benefit
Claimants analysed by age and duration of spell
At beginning of June/At end of statistical year[1]

Thousands

		1981	1982	1983	1984	1985	1986	1987	1988	1989	1990	1991
Age at 31 May/31 March[2]												
Males												
All durations: All ages	KJJA	834.0	903.0	903.0	840.0	859.0	896.0	913.0	978.3	1 046.3	1 122.6	1 225.1
Under 20	KJJB	14.0	18.0	13.0	7.0	6.0	6.0	7.0	4.2	5.1	6.1	5.9
20-29	KJJC	64.0	73.0	65.0	43.0	42.0	42.0	37.0	41.0	48.6	51.1	63.3
30-39	KJJD	94.0	102.0	95.0	73.0	72.0	78.0	73.0	75.5	81.2	86.7	105.0
40-49	KJJE	132.0	142.0	133.0	123.0	125.0	127.0	128.0	138.4	148.4	160.7	175.6
50-59	KJJF	253.0	269.0	272.0	256.0	259.0	270.0	273.0	295.0	315.0	337.4	359.2
60-64	KJJG	228.0	246.0	268.0	277.0	279.0	284.0	282.0	290.8	292.4	298.8	309.1
65 and over	KJJH	49.0	53.0	57.0	61.0	76.0	89.0	113.0	134.2	156.0	181.8	207.1
Over six months: All ages	KJJI	528.0	571.0	613.0	655.0	686.0	726.0	769.0	821.7	895.6	972.4	1 057.3
Under 20	KJJJ	1.0	2.0	2.0	1.0	1.0	1.0	3.0	1.0	2.0	2.3	1.8
20-29	KJJK	18.0	17.0	18.0	22.0	22.0	22.0	22.0	23.1	27.8	31.0	39.0
30-39	KJJL	39.0	41.0	44.0	45.0	46.0	51.0	53.0	54.5	60.4	65.2	74.2
40-49	KJJM	73.0	80.0	84.0	87.0	92.0	93.0	100.0	107.2	118.6	126.9	143.3
50-59	KJJN	168.0	179.0	191.0	200.0	206.0	219.0	226.0	243.6	265.2	292.9	310.7
60-64	KJJO	181.0	200.0	218.0	240.0	244.0	251.0	253.0	260.0	266.5	273.1	281.7
65 and over	KJJP	48.0	52.0	56.0	60.0	75.0	89.0	112.0	133.2	155.2	181.1	206.6
Females												
All durations: All ages	KJJQ	249.0	297.0	286.0	246.0	258.0	283.0	294.0	347.3	400.3	452.5	511.6
Under 20	KJJR	11.0	14.0	11.0	5.0	5.0	4.0	5.0	6.2	8.2	8.2	9.2
20-29	KJJS	56.0	65.0	60.0	39.0	35.0	41.0	41.0	43.7	49.4	55.5	58.4
30-39	KJJT	48.0	60.0	53.0	47.0	50.0	53.0	54.0	61.8	65.6	71.0	77.0
40-49	KJJU	51.0	63.0	62.0	55.0	61.0	66.0	67.0	86.0	96.4	108.5	125.1
50-59	KJJV	77.0	86.0	91.0	91.0	94.0	102.0	109.0	128.7	154.4	175.7	200.1
60 and over	KJJW	6.0	8.0	7.0	10.0	13.0	16.0	18.0	22.0	26.3	33.6	41.8
Over six months: All ages	KJJX	122.0	140.0	158.0	173.0	188.0	211.0	229.0	267.0	322.3	370.2	432.9
Under 20	KJJY	1.0	1.0	1.0	1.0	1.0	1.0	1.0	1.0	2.4	3.1	4.0
20-29	KJJZ	15.0	17.0	20.0	20.0	18.0	22.0	24.0	24.4	30.5	34.7	40.5
30-39	KJKA	19.0	24.0	26.0	31.0	36.0	39.0	41.0	44.7	50.9	56.0	60.9
40-49	KJKB	27.0	33.0	36.0	39.0	43.0	49.0	55.0	68.2	79.0	89.4	106.8
50-59	KJKC	55.0	59.0	69.0	72.0	77.0	85.0	90.0	107.8	134.2	154.4	179.7
60 and over	KJKD	5.0	7.0	7.0	8.0	12.0	15.0	18.0	21.9	25.4	32.5	41.2

Note Figures for Great Britain are based on a 1 per cent sample. Figures for Northern Ireland are based on a 20 per cent sample.

Sources: Department of and Social Security; Department of Health and Social Services (Northern Ireland)

1 For Great Britain commencing on first Monday in June up to 1982 and first Monday in April thereafter.
2 From 1984 age at 5 April.

3.18 Sickness and Invalidity benefit[1]: days of certified incapacity
Analysis by age at end of period
Years starting on first Monday in June up to 1982 and from first Monday in April thereafter

Millions

		1980/81	1981/82	1982/83	1983/84	1984/85	1985/86	1986/87	1987/88	1988/89	1989/90	1990/91
Males: All ages	KJKH	272.5	280.5	281.4	251.4	262.8	275.8	275.5	294.8	315.5	338.5	367.7
Under 20	KJKI	5.0	4.8	4.3	1.6	1.7	1.5	1.6	1.1	1.3	1.4	1.6
20 - 29	KJKJ	23.5	23.0	20.7	12.3	13.1	12.7	11.1	11.7	13.4	14.3	17.3
30 - 39	KJKK	32.4	31.9	30.0	21.5	21.7	23.1	21.7	22.1	23.6	25.4	29.1
40 - 49	KJKL	42.3	44.1	42.8	35.6	37.2	37.6	37.7	40.3	43.6	46.5	51.0
50 - 59	KJKM	76.9	79.3	80.7	73.5	74.9	80.0	78.2	84.8	90.6	99.3	104.1
60 - 64	KJKN	68.4	73.9	79.0	81.6	82.9	85.6	83.5	86.6	87.2	88.2	92.2
65 and over	KJKO	23.8	23.4	24.1	25.1	31.2	35.2	41.7	48.3	55.8	63.3	72.2
Females: All ages	KJKP	86.3	91.7	93.9	73.5	78.6	85.2	86.9	101.9	117.7	133.2	153.0
Under 20	KJKQ	4.6	4.0	3.4	1.3	1.4	1.1	1.0	1.5	1.8	2.2	2.3
20 - 29	KJKR	21.7	21.3	20.2	11.5	10.8	12.0	12.1	13.7	14.5	16.0	17.4
30 - 39	KJKS	15.2	15.3	17.7	18.0	13.7	15.1	16.0	17.7	20.0	21.3	23.0
40 - 49	KJKT	16.9	19.0	20.0	16.4	17.5	19.5	19.8	24.2	27.9	30.9	36.2
50 - 59	KJKU	24.7	25.9	28.5	26.4	28.4	29.9	31.0	36.4	44.2	50.8	58.7
60 and over	KJKV	3.1	3.8	3.8	4.2	5.4	6.2	7.0	8.4	9.4	12.1	15.3

See *note* to Table 3.17.

Sources: Department of Social Security; Department of Health and Social Services (Northern Ireland)

57

Allowances and benefits

3.19 Widows' benefit (excluding widows' allowance: widows' payment[1])
United Kingdom
Number in payment analysed by type of benefit and age of widow

Thousands

		September											
		1980[2]	1981	1982	1983	1984[3]	1985	1986	1987	1988	1989	1990	1991[5]
All widows' benefit (excluding widows' allowance)													
All ages	KJGA	15.0	433.0	426.0	420.0	414.0	398.0	389.0	380.0	388.0	371.0	365.2	11.6
Under 30	KJGB	–	3.0	3.0	3.0	3.0	3.0	2.0	2.0	3.0	2.0	2.4	0.1
30 - 39	KJGC	1.0	18.0	18.0	19.0	19.0	18.0	18.0	17.0	17.0	16.0	16.2	0.7
40 - 49	KJGD	3.0	70.0	71.0	69.0	68.0	66.0	65.0	64.0	65.0	62.0	63.7	2.2
50 - 59	KJGE	9.0	293.0	289.0	283.0	279.0	266.0	260.0	253.0	258.0	241.0	239.6	7.2
60 and over	KJGF	2.0	50.0	46.0	47.0	46.0	45.0	44.0	44.0	46.0	49.0	43.3	1.3
Widowed mothers' allowance - with dependant children													
All ages	KJGG	5.0	84.0	79.0	75.0	78.0	66.0	61.0	57.0	59.0	53.0	54.4	3.0
Under 30	KJGH	–	2.0	3.0	3.0	3.0	2.0	2.0	2.0	2.0	2.0	2.3	0.1
30 - 39	KJGI	1.0	16.0	17.0	17.0	17.0	16.0	16.0	15.0	15.0	14.0	14.5	0.6
40 - 49	KJGJ	2.0	36.0	34.0	32.0	33.0	28.0	26.0	25.0	26.0	25.0	25.7	1.2
50 - 59	KJGK	2.0	29.0	27.0	24.0	26.0	20.0	17.0	15.0	15.0	12.0	11.5	1.0
60 and over	KJGL	–	1.0	–	1.0	–	–	–	–	–	–	0.3	–
Widowed mothers' allowance - without dependant children													
All ages	KJGM	1.0	34.0	35.0	35.0	29.0	32.0	31.0	29.0	20.0	21.0	17.8	0.4
Under 30	KJGN	–	–	–	–	–	–	–	–	–	–	0.1	0.1
30 - 39	KJGO	–	1.0	2.0	2.0	2.0	2.0	2.0	2.0	2.0	2.0	1.8	0.2
40 - 49	KJGP	–	11.0	12.0	12.0	10.0	12.0	11.0	11.0	8.0	9.0	8.0	0.1
50 - 59	KJGQ	1.0	20.0	21.0	19.0	16.0	17.0	16.0	15.0	9.0	10.0	7.8	0.1
60 and over	KJGR	–	1.0	1.0	1.0	–	1.0	1.0	–	–	–	0.3	–
Widows' pension													
All ages	KJGS	7.0	208.0	203.0	203.0	201.0	195.0	189.0	185.0	186.0	176.0	157.9	4.8
40 - 49	KJGT	–	–	–	–	–	–	–	–	–	–	–	–
50 - 59	KJGU	5.0	165.0	163.0	162.0	161.0	155.0	152.0	148.0	146.0	133.0	119.2	3.7
60 and over	KJGV	2.0	43.0	40.0	41.0	40.0	40.0	38.0	38.0	40.0	43.0	38.6	1.2
Age-related widows' pension[4]													
All ages	KJGW	3.0	109.0	109.0	108.0	107.0	107.0	108.0	108.0	124.0	121.0	135.0	3.4
40 - 49	KJGX	1.0	24.0	25.0	26.0	26.0	26.0	28.0	28.0	31.0	25.0	30.0	0.8
50 - 59	KJGY	2.0	80.0	79.0	77.0	77.0	75.0	75.0	75.0	88.0	87.0	100.9	2.5
60 and over	KJGZ	–	5.0	5.0	5.0	5.0	5.0	5.0	5.0	6.0	6.0	4.0	0.1

1 This is an especially high rate of benefit which is payable for the first 26 weeks of widowhood, provided that the widow is under pensionable age (age 60) or, if she is over that age, provided that her husband was not entitled to retirement pension. Widows' allowance was replaced by widows' payment on 11/4/88.
2 Northern Ireland data only; Great Britain figures not available due to computer error.
3 For 1984 Great Britain data as at March.
4 Figures for widows' basic pension are included in age-related widows' pension.
5 Northern Ireland data only; Great Britain figures not as yet available.

Sources: Department of Social Security;
Department of Health and Social Services (Northern Ireland)

3.20 Family allowances/Child benefits[1]
At 31 December

Thousands

		1980	1981	1982	1983	1984	1985	1986	1987	1988	1989	1990	1991
Families receiving allowances:													
Total	KJMU	7 397	7 352	7 261	7 175	7 097	7 035	6 979	6 928	6 923	6 695	6 950	7 024
With 1 child	KJMV	2 987	2 996	2 986	2 979	2 970	2 963	2 962	2 948	2 956	2 872	2 955	2 977
2 children[2]	KJMW	3 055	3 048	3 016	2 978	2 939	2 901	2 851	2 817	2 788	2 699	2 788	2 808
3 children[2]	KJMX	1 005	977	947	918	898	882	874	871	878	844	894	918
4 children[2]	KJMY	260	247	234	222	214	213	215	217	222	209	232	238
5 or more children[2]	KJMZ	90	84	79	78	76	76	75	76	79	71	82	83

1 From April 1977 Family allowance has been replaced by Child benefit which is payable for all children in the family, including the first or only child.
2 Until 1976 including the elder or eldest child for whom no allowance was payable, but excluding children over the age limit.

Sources: Department of Social Security;
Department of Health and Social Services (Northern Ireland)

National Insurance

3.21 Contributory and non-contributory retirement pensions
United Kingdom
Numbers in payment analysed by age-group[1]

Thousands (percentages in italics)

		At 30 November 1980	1981	1982	1983	1984[3]	At 30 September[2] 1985	1986	1987	1988[4]	1989[3,4]	1990[5]	1991[4]
Men:													
Age-groups:													
65-69	KJSB	1 170.0	1 157.0	1 130.0	1 072.0	1 046.0	1 066.0	1 102.0	1 143.0	1 178.5	1 194.0	1 163.8	1 124.6
Percentage	KJSC	*36.0*	*35.2*	*34.4*	*32.6*	*32.0*	*31.7*	*32.3*	*33.1*	*33.8*	*34.2*	*32.7*	*31.3*
70-74	KJSD	1 019.0	1 026.0	1 034.0	1 043.0	1 047.0	1 053.0	1 046.0	1 010.0	959.2	936.9	999.2	1 046.0
Percentage	KJSE	*31.4*	*31.2*	*31.5*	*31.8*	*32.0*	*31.4*	*30.6*	*29.3*	*27.5*	*26.9*	*28.1*	*29.1*
75-79	KJSF	629.0	653.0	661.0	684.0	688.0	710.0	720.0	723.0	748.2	750.5	761.4	761.7
Percentage	KJSG	*19.4*	*19.9*	*20.1*	*20.8*	*21.0*	*21.1*	*21.1*	*21.0*	*21.5*	*21.5*	*21.4*	*21.2*
80-84	KJSH	289.0	304.0	315.0	334.0	340.0	363.0	376.0	389.0	403.0	407.2	427.1	437.3
Percentage	KJSI	*8.9*	*9.3*	*9.6*	*10.2*	*10.4*	*10.8*	*11.0*	*11.3*	*11.6*	*11.7*	*12.0*	*12.2*
85-89	KJSJ	109.0	113.0	113.0	117.0	116.0	127.0	133.0	142.0	152.0	155.0	164.0	172.9
Percentage	KJSK	*3.4*	*3.4*	*3.4*	*3.6*	*3.5*	*3.8*	*3.9*	*4.1*	*4.4*	*4.4*	*4.6*	*4.8*
90 and over	KJSL	32.0	34.0	34.0	35.0	36.0	39.0	40.0	42.0	44.0	44.0	46.0	49.1
Percentage	KJSM	*1.0*	*1.0*	*1.0*	*1.1*	*1.1*	*1.2*	*1.2*	*1.2*	*1.3*	*1.3*	*1.3*	*1.4*
Total all ages	KJSA	3 248.0	3 286.0	3 286.0	3 285.0	3 274.0	3 359.0	3 416.0	3 449.0	3 485.8	3 488.0	3 560.5	3 591.5
Women:													
Age-groups:													
60-64	KJSO	945.0	1 007.0	1 110.0	1 210.0	1 274.0	1 217.0	1 195.0	1 154.0	1 117.6	1 099.0	1 138.7	1 124.2
Percentage	KJSP	*16.0*	*16.5*	*18.1*	*19.4*	*20.2*	*19.0*	*18.4*	*17.7*	*17.0*	*16.8*	*17.1*	*16.9*
65-69	KJSQ	1 417.0	1 410.0	1 367.0	1 293.0	1 260.0	1 339.0	1 412.0	1 488.0	1 565.3	1 597.8	1 533.3	1 484.6
Percentage	KJSR	*24.0*	*23.3*	*22.2*	*20.7*	*20.0*	*20.9*	*21.7*	*22.8*	*23.9*	*24.4*	*23.0*	*22.3*
70-74	KJSS	1 358.0	1 373.0	1 377.0	1 378.0	1 380.0	1 379.0	1 369.0	1 319.0	1 257.2	1 225.6	1 285.8	1 336.9
Percentage	KJST	*23.0*	*22.7*	*22.4*	*22.1*	*21.9*	*21.5*	*21.1*	*20.2*	*19.2*	*18.7*	*19.3*	*20.1*
75-79	KJSU	1 055.0	1 085.0	1 095.0	1 122.0	1 127.0	1 149.0	1 151.0	1 160.0	1 161.2	1 164.4	1 170.3	1 161.5
Percentage	KJSV	*17.8*	*17.9*	*17.8*	*18.0*	*17.9*	*17.9*	*17.7*	*17.8*	*17.7*	*17.8*	*17.6*	*17.5*
80-84	KJSW	670.0	690.0	701.0	727.0	736.0	768.0	790.0	807.0	827.7	831.8	855.6	864.2
Percentage	KJSX	*11.3*	*11.4*	*11.4*	*11.6*	*11.7*	*12.0*	*12.2*	*12.4*	*12.6*	*12.7*	*12.9*	*13.0*
85-89	KJSY	336.0	348.0	351.0	362.0	365.0	388.0	398.0	415.0	432.4	438.8	465.7	438.8
Percentage	KJSZ	*5.7*	*5.8*	*5.7*	*5.8*	*5.8*	*6.0*	*6.1*	*6.4*	*6.6*	*6.7*	*7.0*	*6.6*
90 and over	KJTA	130.0	144.0	146.0	155.0	156.0	171.0	177.0	186.0	194.6	195.8	205.7	219.1
Percentage	KJTB	*2.2*	*2.4*	*2.4*	*2.5*	*2.5*	*2.7*	*2.7*	*2.8*	*3.0*	*3.0*	*3.1*	*3.3*
Total all ages	KJSN	5 911.0	6 057.0	6 148.0	6 247.0	6 297.0	6 413.0	6 492.0	6 529.0	6 556.0	6 551.9	6 655.1	6 648.2

1 Including pensions payable to persons residing overseas.
2 Northern Ireland as at 30 November for years 1983 to 1987.
3 Great Britain as at 31 March.
4 Northern Ireland figures are at 30 September
5 Northern Ireland figures are at 31 March.

Sources: Department of Social Security;
Department of Health and Social Services (Northern Ireland)

3.22 Family income supplement[1]/Family credit
United Kingdom
At 31 December

Thousands

		1981	1982	1983	1984	1985	1986[3]	1987[4]	1988[5,6,7]	1989[7]	1990[7]	1991
Families receiving payments:												
Total	KJTO	143.0	179.0	215.0	218.0[2]	214.0[2]	218.0	235.0	298.3	312.3	331.7	360.3
Two-parent families: total	KJTP	78.0	105.0	133.0	121.0[3]	117.0[3]	128.0	140.0	189.9	190.0	201.1	221.5
With 1 child	KJTQ	15.0	21.0	28.0	26.0[3]	25.0[3]	27.0	30.0	44.8	43.3	44.5	52.4
2 children	KJTR	25.0	36.0	47.0	46.0[3]	45.0[3]	50.0	51.0	67.1	65.9	71.3	79.3
3 children	KJTS	19.0	26.0	32.0	29.0[3]	28.0[3]	31.0	34.0	44.8	47.1	49.1	52.4
4 children	KJTT	11.0	13.0	15.0	13.0[3]	12.0[3]	13.0	16.0	21.9	21.4	22.7	23.5
5 children	KJTU	4.0	5.0	6.0	4.0[3]	4.0[3]	5.0	6.0	7.8	8.2	8.5	9.1
6 or more children	KJTV	3.0	3.0	3.0	2.0[3]	2.0[3]	2.0	3.0	3.6	4.1	5.0	4.8
One-parent families: total	KJTW	65.0	74.0	83.0	82.0[3]	82.0[3]	90.0	95.0	108.9	222.3	130.2	138.4
With 1 child	KJTX	34.0	40.0	46.0	46.0[3]	46.0[3]	50.0	54.0	61.8	69.2	72.4	74.7
2 children	KJTY	21.0	24.0	28.0	27.0[3]	27.0[3]	30.0	31.0	34.7	39.7	41.7	45.9
3 or more children	KJTZ	9.0	9.0	10.0	9.0[3]	9.0[3]	10.0	10.0	12.3	14.3	16.1	13.6

1 For weekly rates of Family Income supplement see Table 3.13.
2 Provisional.
3 Great Britain only; Northern Ireland data unavailable.
4 Great Britain figures are for 30.4.87.
5 From April 1988 Family Income Supplement was replaced by Family Credit.
6 For N.I. data 1988 figures are at 1 November and 1989 and 1990 figures are at 31 December.
7 N.I. figures for two-parent families and one-parent families exclude 574 families in 1988, 120 families in 1989 and 315 families in 1990 which cannot be divided into family type.

Sources: Department of Social Security;
Department of Health and Social Services (Northern Ireland)

Supplementary benefits

3.23 Income support: number of beneficiaries receiving weekly payment[1]
Great Britain
On a day in May
Thousands

		1988	1989	1990	1991
All income support	KACC	4 352	4 161	4 180	4 487
All aged 60 and over	KACD	1 719	1 607	1 675	1 575
Retirement pensioners	KACE	1 431	1 314	1 385	1 272
In receipt of other NI benefit	KACF	38	34	45	50
Others	KACG	250	258	244	254
All under 60	KACH	2 632	2 554	2 505	2 912
Unemployed with contributory benefit	KACI	133	97	45	91
Unemployed without contributory benefit	KACJ	1 377	1 118	1 019	1 244
Disabled with contributory benefit	KACK	55	58	62	58
Disabled without contributory benefit	KFBJ	192	232	268	317
Lone parent premium not in other groups[2]	KACL	694	756	793	871
Others	KACM	180	293	319	331

1 Great Britain data is extracted from the Annual Statistical Enquiry undertaken in May 1988, 1989, 1990 and 1991.
2 Figures relate to one-parent families headed by a man also.

Source: Department of Social Security

3.24 Income support
Great Britain[1]
On a day in May
Thousands

		1988	1989	1990	1991
Number of regular weekly payments	KACN	4 352	4 161	4 180	4 487
Total number of persons provided for	KACO	7 388	7 023	7 022	7 747
Number of dependants	KACP	3 036	2 862	2 842	3 260
Partners	KACQ	841	724	691	763
Total children under 16 years	KACR	2 092	2 030	2 045	2 368
Under 11	KACS	1 571	1 565	1 591	1 842
11 - 15 years	KACT	521	465	454	526
16 - 17 years	KACU	91	94	90	110
Other dependents 18 years and over	KACV	13	15	16	19

1 Great Britain data is extracted from the Annual Statistical Enquiry undertaken in May 1988, 1989, 1990, 1991.

Source: Department of Social Security

Benefits and pensions

3.25 Income support: average weekly amounts of benefit
Great Britain[1]
May

Thousands

		1988	1989	1990	1991
All income support	KACW	34.25	35.75	38.52	46.52
All aged 60 and over	KJUB	20.16	23.52	25.44	34.16
Retirement pensioners	KACX	14.69	17.70	19.92	28.12
In receipt of other NI benefit	KJUD	16.10	14.94	18.08	24.57
Others	KACY	52.06	54.28	58.08	66.30
All under 60	KACZ	43.45	43.44	47.27	53.20
Unemployed with contributory benefit	KADA	16.15	14.70	36.98	41.37
Unemployed without contributory benefit	KADB	44.09	43.92	45.01	50.30
Disabled with contributory benefit	KADC	17.00	16.57	21.13	24.78
Disabled without contributory benefit	KADD	38.45	40.14	44.86	47.85
Lone parent premium not in other groups[2]	KADE	49.09	51.01	56.09	62.53
Others	KADF	50.39	39.55	41.12	52.90

1 Great Britain data extracted from the Annual Statistical Enquiry undertaken in May 1988, 1989, 1990 and 1991.
2 Figures relate to one-parent families headed by a man also.

Source: Department of Social Security

3.26 War pensions
Estimated number of pensioners
At 31 March in each year

Thousands

		1980	1981	1982	1983	1984	1985	1986	1987	1988	1989	1990	1991	1992
Total	KADG	362.45	349.36	336.19	323.40	310.34	298.50	287.40	271.72	263.86	256.25	249.96	247.67	249.95
Disablement - 1914 war; 1939 war and later service	KADH	273.00	263.66	253.86	244.50	234.60	225.90	217.80	207.30	201.70	196.45	192.47	192.04	196.19
Widows and dependants - 1914 war; 1939 war and later service	KADI	89.45	85.70	82.34	78.90	75.74	72.60	69.60	64.42	62.16	59.80	57.48	55.63	53.76

Source: Department of Social Security

National Health Service

3.27 Hospital and family health services
England and Wales

			England							Wales					
			1986	1987	1988	1989	1990	1991		1987	1988	1989	1990	1991	1992
Hospital services															
In-patients:															
Average daily number of available beds[1]	KNMY	Thousands	316	297	283	270	255	..	KNHY	21.0	20.7	19.9	19.4	..	..
Average daily occupation of beds:															
All departments	KNMX	"	255	–	–	–	..	..	KNHX	16.0	15.8	15.2	14.8	..	..
Psychiatric departments	KNMW	"	96	–	–	–	..	..	KNGZ	6.0	5.3	4.9	4.7	..	..
Persons waiting for admission at 31 March[2]	KNMV	"	..	..	876	923	959	948	KNGY	46.0	48.0	49.0	53.0	60.0	59.0
Discharges or deaths	KNLZ	"	6 414	6 619	6 586	..	..	..	KNEO	449.0	459.6	470.1	482.5	..	..
Day case attendances	KNLY	"	1 050	881	1 016	1 163	1 261	..	KNBZ	77.0	83.2	86.0	101.1	..	..
Out-patients[3]															
New cases[1]	KNLX	"	19 299	19 409	19 390	19 745	19 718	..	KNBY	1 174.0	1 183.5	1 255.5	1 244.3	..	..
Total attendances[1]	KNLW	"	51 503	51 552	50 820	51 171	50 829	..	KNBX	3 164.0	3 196.8	3 269.7	3 243.9	..	..
Staff at 30 September															
Medical, dental[4]	KNLV	No.(WTE)	37 505	37 575	38 745	40 090	40 961	..	KNBW	2 491	2 545	2 601	2 683	..	..
Professional and technical[5]	KNLU	WTE	76 083	78 975	79 775	81 168	83 987	86 475	KNBV	4 993	5 111	5 318	5 452	5 801	..
Nursing and Midwifery[5,6,7]	KNLT	"	402 690	404 041	403 883	405 281	402 066	394 039	KNBU	27 764	27 920	28 037	28 092	27 991	..
Administrative: clerical[5,7]	KNKZ	"	111 351	114 595	115 951	121 450	129 716	127 367	KNBT	7 087	7 279	7 565	8 069	8 733	..
Other non-medical[5,7,16]	KNKY	"	168 216	158 258	149 034	142 404	133 741	141 861	KNBS	13 567	12 739	12 214	11 721	11 035	..
Family health services															
Medical services:															
Doctors on the list[9]	KNKX	Number	24 460	24 922	25 322	25 608	25 622	25 686	KNBR	1 587	1 599	1 631	1 635	1 647	..
Number of patients per doctor	KNKW	"	2 042	2 020	1 999	1 971	1 942	1 947	KNBQ	1 849	1 851	1 819	1 813	1 794	..
Paid to doctors[18]	KNKV	£ million	1 195.9	1 314.4	1 466.7	1 677.0	1 948.4	..	KNBP	76.3	85.8	95.3	114.6	139.2	..
Pharmaceutical services:															
Prescriptions dispensed	KNKU	Million	322.5	335.3	346.5	351.9	360.5	377.5	KNBO	26.0	27.1	27.8	28.3	29.7	..
Payments to pharmacists[10,11]	KNJV	£ million	1 643.2	1 830.7	2 045.7	2 198.1	2 401.5	2 689.4	KNBN	133.6	149.1	152.2	176.3	198.0	..
Payment by patients[11]	KNJU	"	125.9	138.1	152.7	155.4	173.3	187.4	KNBM	8.4	10.7	10.9	12.4	13.5	..
Paid out of public funds[11]	KNJT	"	1 517.5	1 692.6	1 893.0	2 042.7	2 227.7	2 502.0	KNBL	126.5	138.4	141.3	163.9	184.5	..
Average total cost per prescription	KNJS	£	5.09	5.46	5.90	6.25	6.66	7.12	KNBK	5.13	5.50	5.84	6.23	6.67	..
Dental services:															
Dentists on list at 30 September[12]	KNJR	Number	14 516	14 765	15 070	15 351	15 480	..	KNBJ	780.00	798.00	827.00	837.00	832.00	..
Courses of treatment completed and emergency cases[13]	KNJQ	Thousands	32 279	32 108	33 595	33 580	..	..	KNBI	1 790	1 871	1 826	..	..	..
Payments to dentists[14]	KNJP	£ million	698.7	773.3	881.8	930.2	984.6	..	KNBH	43.1	47.6	48.7	69.6	..	..
Payments by patients	KNJO	"	216.9	233.9	270.2	361.9	382.7	..	KNBG	10.6	12.5	16.5	20.2	..	..
Paid out of public funds	KNJN	"	481.8	539.4	611.6	568.3	601.9	..	KNBF	32.5	35.1	32.2	49.4	..	..
Average gross cost per course and case	KNJM	£	21.64	24.02	26.25	27.70	..	..	KNBE	24.07	25.50	26.67	..	..	..
General ophthalmic services:															
Sight tests, given[15]	KNJL	Thousands	10 502	11 091	12 493	5 280	4 154	4 979	KNBD	651	734	292	271	332	..
Pairs of glasses dispensed/ vouchers issued[17]	KNJK	"	2 214	2 507	2 259	2 270	2 431	2 844	KNBC	176	158	153	176	205	..
Cost of services (gross)[1]	KNJJ	£ million	127.4	141.6	163.4	131.6	104.1	111.0	KNBA	9.7	10.4	8.6	7.6	10.0	..
Payments by patients	KNJI	"	0.9	..	..	..	..	..	KNBB	..	..	..	..	..	..
Paid out of public funds:															
For sight testing[1]	KNJH	"	84.6	95.7	112.9	77.5	43.7	46.9	KMZZ	6.3	6.9	4.8	3.1	4.2	..
For dispensing	KNJG	"	26.4	[8]	..	..	..	..	KMZY	[8]	..	..	..	..	..
For cost of vouchers[1,17]	KNHZ	"	15.5	45.9	50.5	53.8	57.5	63.9	KMZX	3.4	3.5	3.8	4.5	5.8	..

1 For England and Wales from 1987 collection of data changed from year ended 31 Dec to years ended 31 March. Changes in definition mean that these figures are not comparable with data for earlier years.
2 People waiting for admittance as an in-patient or treatment as a day case.
3 At consultant and general practitioner clinics and accident and emergency departments total attendances for England from 1987/88 include ward attenders.
4 Whole-time equivalents (WTE). Excluding locums and general medical practitioners participating in Hospital Staff Fund.
5 From 1987 onwards figures include 'other statutory authorities' (eg Public Health Laboratory Service and Health Education Authority). Figures for these authorities were not collected in the annual non medical-manpower census prior to 1987. Therefore figures for later years are not strictly comparable with those for previous years.
6 Includes Hospital and community staff and agency staff.
7 Provisional data for 1991.
8 Dispensing fees ceased to be paid and charges payable with the introduction to the voucher scheme.
9 Principals providing unrestricted services as at 1 October.
10 The cost of prescriptions dispensed during the calendar year are certified by the pricing authorities.
11 1990 figures have been revised.
12 All assistants are now included.
13 Number scheduled for payment. A new dental contract was introduced in October 1990. Under the contract most children's treatments are now carried out under the capitation scheme and are not separately identifiable.
14 Items of service fees paid to dentists.
15 Number of sight tests paid for by Family Health Service Authorities in the period and not those carried out. From 1.4.89 NHS sight tests were restricted to certain groups in the population.
16 Includes works, maintenance, ancillary and ambulance staff.
17 NHS Voucher scheme commenced 1 July 1986.
18 Taken from audited Department of Health appropriation account figures for 1990/91.

Sources: Department of Health; Welsh Office

3.28 Hospital and primary care services
Scotland

National Health Service

		Unit	1980	1981	1982	1983	1984	1985	1986	1987	1988	1989	1990	1991
Hospital services														
In-patients:														
Average available staffed beds[1]	KDEA	Thousands	58.2	58.0	57.4	57.3	57.3	56.8	56.0	55.3	54.5	53.4	52.1	50.6
Average occupied beds:[1]														
All departments	KDEB	"	48.4	48.1	47.1	46.7	47.0	46.6	46.0	45.1	44.4	43.5	42.5	41.2
Mental and mentally deficient	KDEC	"	21.3	21.0	20.5	20.0	20.1	19.8	19.3	18.8	18.2	17.6	17.0	16.3
Discharges or deaths[1,2]	KDED	"	774	793	764	791	810	822	837	843	871	882	896	912
Outpatients[1,3]:														
New cases	KDEE	"	1 999	2 033	2 021	2 042	2 083	2 144	2 196	2 233	2 275	2 325	2 381	2 403
Total attendances	KDEF	"	5 321	5 434	5 338	5 422	5 519	5 593	5 668	5 693	5 767	5 815	5 925	5 971
Medical and dental staff[4,5]:														
Whole-time	KDEG	Number	4 456	4 479	4 584	4 657	4 690	4 647	4 545	4 565	4 769	4 808	4 935	4 974
Part-time	KDEH	"	1 267	1 465	1 362	1 406	1 415	1 428	1 440	1 421	1 505	1 531	1 508	1 507
Professional and technical staff[4,6]:														
Whole-time	KDEI	"	6 807	7 033	7 113	7 392	7 492	7 591	7 615	7 672	7 676	7 780	7 693	7 536
Part-time	KDEJ	"	1 380	1 417	1 461	1 440	1 465	1 489	1 558	1 672	1 716	1 917	1 996	2 034
Nursing and midwifery staff[4]:														
Whole-time	KDEK	"	37 977	40 218	40 825	41 337	41 080	41 320	41 295	41 388	41 438	41 733	40 149	39 707
Part-time	KDEL	"	23 974	24 407	24 437	24 115	23 850	23 886	24 390	24 640	25 175	25 555	26 048	27 048
Administrative and clerical staff[4]:														
Whole-time	KDEM	"	5 158	5 310	5 410	5 535	5 591	5 653	5 612	5 726	5 683	5 788	5 916	6 084
Part-time	KDEN	"	1 927	2 066	2 156	2 285	2 408	2 584	2 716	2 903	3 075	3 179	3 305	3 521
Domestic, transport, etc. staff[4]:														
Whole-time	KDEO	"	17 289	17 235	17 101	16 604	15 568	14 791	14 089	14 062	13 888	10 177	9 295	8 138
Part-time	KDEP	"	15 209	15 659	16 150	16 310	16 298	16 487	16 913	17 235	16 558	12 993	11 953	11 437
Cost of services (gross)[7]	KDEQ	£ million	964.3	1 117.9	1 212.6	1 290.2	1 376.1	1 461.5	1 537.4	1 592.5	1 828.1	2 004.5	..	2 757.7
Payments by patients[7]	KDER	"	1.0	1.2	1.1	1.3	1.2	1.1	1.3	1.4	1.4	1.4	..	1.3
Payments out of public funds[7]	KDES	"	963.3	1 116.7	1 211.5	1 288.9	1 374.9	1 460.4	1 536.1	1 591.1	1 826.7	2 003.1	..	2 756.4
Primary care services														
Medical services														
Doctors on the list[8]:														
Principals[9]	KDET	Number	2 959	3 001	3 040	3 106	3 169	3 224	3 272	3 305	3 355	3 391	3 360	3 380
Assistants	KDEU	"	28	29	32	31	25	22	21	14	13	10	16	24
Average number of patients per principal doctor[10]	KDEV	"	1 835	1 804	1 778	1 739	1 704	1 668	1 653	1 630	1 605	1 590	1 592	1 580
Payments to doctors	KDEW	£ million	76.7	90.7	102.2	110.8	123.0	133.4	140.5	156.6	165.7	..	..	..
Pharmaceutical services														
Prescriptions dispensed	KDEX	Million	34.30	33.90	35.00	35.70	36.40	36.40	36.70	38.34	39.50	41.02	42.42	44.31
Payments to pharmacists (gross)[11]	KDEY	£ million	111.10	126.70	144.40	161.10	172.20	180.20	196.20	217.70	244.02	269.99	298.16	329.82
Average gross cost per prescription	KDEZ	£	3.242	3.741	4.128	4.514	4.734	4.951	5.348	5.678	6.180	6.580	7.030	7.440
Dental services														
Dentists on list[12]	KDFA	Number	1 251	1 294	1 362	1 407	1 449	1 407	1 488	1 515	1 523	1 585	1 645	..
Number of courses of treatment completed	KDFB	Thousands	2 549	2 595	2 672	2 746	2 792	2 857	2 984	2 987	3 054	3 143	3 057	..
Payments to dentists (gross)	KDFC	£ million	36.6	41.4	46.1	50.9	54.8	59.4	68.0	76.2	86.9	97.7	99.9	..
Payments by patients	KDFD	"	9.5	12.0	15.3	17.9	20.1	24.1	28.3	30.3	33.9	46.4	48.0	..
Payments out of public funds	KDFE	"	27.1	29.4	30.8	32.9	34.6	35.3	39.8	45.9	53.0	51.2	51.8	..
Average gross cost per course	KDFF	£	14.3	15.9	17.3	18.5	19.6	20.8	22.7	25.5	28.5	30.8	33.1	..
General ophthalmic services														
Number of sight tests given	KDFG	Thousands	727	736	761	816	857	918	949	1 022	1 141	716	417	477
Number of pairs of glasses supplied[13]	KDFH	"	546	552	568	570	604	438	305	338	322	313	320	374
Cost of services (gross)[14]	KDFI	£ million	10.0	12.1	18.3	17.5	17.8	15.7	13.9	15.9	17.9	14.5	..	13.7
Payments by patients	KDFJ	"	2.8	3.1	3.6	4.3	4.6	2.1	0.5	–	–	–	–	..
Payments out of public funds: For sight testing and dispensing	KDFK	"	7.2	9.0	14.7	13.2	13.2	13.6	13.4	15.9	17.9	14.5	..	13.7

1 In year to 30 September, from 1984 is to 31 March.
2 Includes transfers out from 1976 onwards.
3 At out-patient and accident and emergency departments.
4 At 30 September.
5 Figures exclude officers holding honorary and locum appointments. Part-time includes maximum part-time and GP hospital appointments.
6 From 1979 onwards, ODAs (Operating Department Assistants) are included in Professional and technical staff; previously ODAs were included in Ancillary staff.
7 Estimated from financial year figures.
8 At 1 October.
9 Unrestricted principals in post.
10 Unrestricted principals: establishment.
11 For prescriptions dispensed in calender year by all general practice pharmacists and appliance suppliers.
12 Assistants are excluded.
13 Supply of spectacles restricted from 1 April 1985, includes hospital eye service.
14 Universal free eyesight testing ended in March 1989.

Source: Scottish Health Service Common Services Agency

National Health Service

3.29 Hospital and general health services
Northern Ireland

		Unit	1981	1982	1983	1984	1985	1986	1987	1988	1989	1990	1991
Hospital services[12]													
In-patients:													
Beds available[1]	KDGA	Number	17 023	..[10]	16 976	16 715	16 595	15 962	15 411	14 686	14 154	13 488	12 551
Average daily occupation of beds	KDGB	Per cent	78.4	..[10]	78.1	77.8	78.6	78.2	78.9	79.8	79.2	77.6	77.4
Discharges or deaths	KDGC	Thousands	249	..[10]	259	261	274	269	267	267	271	274	279
Out-patients[2]:													
New cases	KDGD	"	637	..[10]	685	720	739	756	770	761	780	783	799
Total attendances	KDGE	"	1 746	..[10]	1 893	1 975	2 028	2 025	2 049	1 974	1 985	1 957	1 962
General health services													
Medical services													
Doctors (principals) on the list[3]	KDGF	Number	790	813	838	851	880	908	917	927	933	928	928
Number of patients per doctor[4]	KDGG	"	2 032	1 981	1 951	1 925	1 865	1 823	1 835	1 808	1 794	1 811	1 922
Payments to doctors	KDGH	£ thousand	22 923	24 854	28 539	30 668	33 860	35 856	38 935	43 235	48 651	47 850	53 675
Pharmaceutical services													
Prescription forms dispensed[13]	KDGI	Thousands	7 886	8 077	8 389	8 429	8 319	8 190	8 522	8 915	9 175	9 285	10 144
Number of prescriptions	KDGJ	"	12 691	13 067	13 593	13 667	13 268	13 224	13 920	14 606	15 726	15 404	16 754
Payments to pharmacists (gross)	KDGK	£ thousand	47 699	55 454	61 883	64 349	65 570	70 752	79 662	88 688	97 721	108 144	133 134
Payments by patients	KDGL	"	2 596	2 807	2 936	3 082	3 168	3 298	3 577	3 900	4 185	4 893	4 745
Payments out of public funds	KDGM	"	45 102	52 646	58 947	61 267	62 401	67 454	76 085	84 787	93 536	103 751	119 694
Average gross cost per prescription	KDGN	£	3.8	4.2	4.6	4.7	4.9	5.3	5.7	6.1	6.5	7.0	7.7
Dental services													
Dentists on the list[5]	KDGO	Number	342	363	377	394	420	428	437	460	467	519	513
Number of courses of treatment completed[14]	KDGP	Thousands	752	775	812	838	863	890	909	965	972	986	..
Payments to dentists (gross)	KDGQ	£ thousand	14 669	15 333	16 952	18 540	19 458	21 202	24 226	27 442	31 697	35 026	47 210
Payments by patients	KDGR	"	2 252	2 679	3 034	3 384	3 796	4 517	5 156	5 976	8 009	8 732	9 922
Payments out of public funds	KDGS	"	12 417	12 654	13 917	15 156	15 663	16 686	19 071	21 447	23 688	26 295	37 258
Average gross cost per course[14]	KDGT	£	19.5	19.8	20.9	22.1	22.5	23.8	26.7	28.4	32.6	35.5	..
Ophthalmic services													
Number of sight tests given[6]	KDGU	Thousands	168	161	207	203	219	226	236	281	192	115	135
Number of optical appliances supplied	KDGV	"	144	143	168	167	115[11]	52	5	–	–	96	110
Cost of service (gross)[7]	KDGW	£ thousand	3 085	3 315	6 242	4 892	4 287	3 789	4 484	5 135	4 583	4 158	5 607
Payments by patients	KDGX	"	756.0	908.0	1 210.0	1 244.0	524.0	32.0	0.4	–	–	–	–
Payments out of public funds	KDGY	"	2 329	2 407	5 031	3 648	3 763	3 758	4 425	5 135	4 583	4 158	5 607
Health and social services[8]													
Medical and dental staff													
Whole-time	KDGZ	Number	1 874	1 935	1 988	2 044	2 027	2 040	2 065	2 091	2 218	2 238	2 262
Part-time	KDHA	"	697	661	660	680	692	704	720	719	674	564	560
Nursing and midwifery staff													
Whole-time	KDHB	"	14 971	15 391	15 376	15 288	15 058	14 846	14 634	14 637	14 425	14 071	13 451
Part-time	KDHC	"	5 857	5 811	5 722	5 554	5 549	5 718	5 941	6 207	6 477	6 841	7 144
Administrative and clerical staff													
Whole-time	KDHD	"	4 786	4 833	4 933	5 003	5 079	5 051	5 051	5 175	5 409	5 843	6 398
Part-time	KDHE	"	1 009	1 071	1 113	1 157	1 208	1 317	1 378	1 445	1 583	1 680	1 831
Professional and technical staff													
Whole-time	KDHF	"	2 157	2 172	2 261	2 309	2 334	2 359	2 408	2 477	2 522	2 563	2 673
Part-time	KDHG	"	437	442	419	448	435	432	437	453	475	513	559
Social services staff (excluding casual home helps)													
Whole-time	KDHH	"	3 554	3 728	3 717	3 794	3 791	3 850	3 570	3 601	3 646	3 649	3 641
Part-time	KDHI	"	1 086	1 180	1 240	1 284	1 292	1 357	1 382	1 467	1 546	1 687	1 695
Ancillary and other staff													
Whole-time	KDHJ	"	9 574	9 608	9 279	9 029	8 826	8 424	7 994	7 551	6 960	6 433	5 551
Part-time	KDHK	"	4 949	5 174	5 238	5 403	5 516	5 553	5 659	5 591	5 480	4 989	4 728
Cost of services (gross)	KDHL	£ thousand	438 533	474 189	507 629	534 928	562 636	597 356	639 866[9]	695 515[9]	750 918[9]	822 795	889 422
Payments by recipients	KDHM	"	5 924	7 066	7 850	8 689	9 329	9 684	10 315	10 812	11 125	11 414	12 322
Payments out of public funds	KDHN	"	432 609	467 123	499 779	526 239	553 307	587 670	629 551	684 703	739 793	811 381	877 100

1 Average during year.
2 At out-patients and A & E departments.
3 At 31 September.
4 At 1 July.
5 At 31 December.
6 Excluding sight tests given in hospitals and under the school health service.
7 Figures from 1977 include payments superannuation.
8 Manpower figures refer to 31 December. From 1981, figures for medical and dental staff exclude some joint appointees, information for whom is not held on the computer payroll.
9 Figures relate to the cost of the hospital, community health, and personal social services, and have been estimated from financial year data.
10 Data not available due to industrial action.
11 The decrease in figures is due to legislation introduced on 1 July 1985 which allowed the issue of optical appliances by unregistered suppliers under the 'Voucher Scheme'.
12 From 1/4/91 to 31/3/92.
13 Relates to the number of vouchers supplied.
14 Due to the change in the Dental Contract which came into force in October 1990, dentists are now paid under a combination of headings relating to Capitation and Continuing care patients. Prior to this, payment was simply on an item of service basis, which made statistics such as 'Number of courses of treatment completed' and 'Average gross cost per course' relevant and meaningful. This is no longer the case.

Source: Department of Health and Social Services (Northern Ireland)

National Health Service

3.30 Health and personal social services: manpower summary
Great Britain
At 30 September each year

Number or whole-time equivalent

		1981	1982	1983	1984	1985	1986	1987	1988	1989	1990	1991[8]
Health service staff and practitioners: total	KDBA	1 047 803	1 058 297	1 059 474	1 036 355	1 030 575	1 016 777	1 027 644	1 022 121	1 022 416	1 025 231	1 027 863
Regional and area health authorities/boards and boards of governors staff: total	KDBB	990 572	999 975	999 833	975 411	968 611	956 832	964 016	957 871	957 067	960 214	961 910
Medical staff: total	KDBC	44 706	43 351	46 114	46 375	47 040	47 355	47 119	48 873	50 290	51 502	52 828
Hospital medical staff: total[1]	KDBD	41 152	41 808	42 558	42 848	43 456	43 784	43 741	45 438	46 906	48 418	49 696
Consultant and senior hospital medical officer with allowance	KDBE	13 777	14 017	14 349	14 699	14 978	15 281	15 512	15 974	16 517	17 100	17 470
Staff grade[2]	KADJ	..	..	..	..	..	..	..	..	33	284	518
Associate specialist	KDBF	1 014	1 035	1 019	995	935	884	865	859	877	918	954
Senior registrar	KDBG	3 046	3 079	3 187	3 142	3 254	3 326	3 322	3 351	3 488	3 778	3 916
Registrar	KDBH	6 787	6 995	7 099	7 054	7 014	7 108	7 097	7 385	7 297	7 845	7 246
Senior house officer including post registration house officer	KDBI	10 904	11 023	11 137	11 142	11 351	11 228	10 994	11 623	12 407	12 737	13 331
Pre-registration house officer	KADK	3 419	3 411	3 553	3 483	3 518	3 493	3 478	3 566	3 637	3 748	3 781
Other staff[3]	KDBK	66	58	37	89	36	40	54	23	17	12	17
Hospital practitioner	KDBL	242	251	252	262	257	262	249	231	233	223	207
Part-time medical officer (clinical assistant)	KDBM	1 898	1 940	1 924	1 982	2 113	2 162	2 170	2 426	2 402	2 278	2 256
Community health medical staff[4]	KDBN	3 554	3 543	3 557	3 527	3 586	3 571	3 377	3 435	3 384	3 084	3 132
Dental staff: total	KDBO	3 360	3 397	3 372	3 350	3 370	3 322	3 168	3 128	3 092	3 071	2 954
Hospital dental staff: total[1]	KDBP	1 408	1 440	1 433	1 487	1 498	1 492	1 470	1 465	1 475	1 496	1 478
Consultant and senior hospital dental officer with allowance	KDBQ	477	485	489	506	508	503	517	511	512	497	498
Staff grade[2]	KADL	..	..	..	..	..	..	..	..	–	2	5
Associate specialist	KDBR	91	101	103	105	99	103	93	84	81	82	71
Senior registrar	KDBS	108	106	112	98	97	118	121	118	129	135	123
Registrar	KDBT	199	211	210	229	230	223	201	216	204	197	189
Senior house officer	KDBU	196	197	202	218	232	215	236	223	246	260	266
Dental house officer	KDBV	170	180	166	170	171	168	152	138	129	145	145
Other staff[3]	KDBW	10	8	5	5	3	4	5	4	3	1	1
Hospital practitioner	KDBX	15	17	17	15	14	12	13	12	14	17	15
Part-time medical officer (clinical assistant)	KDBY	142	136	128	142	145	146	134	160	158	161	165
Community health dental staff[4]	KDBZ	1 952	1 957	1 939	1 863	1 872	1 831	1 697	1 663	1 617	1 576	1 476
Nursing and midwifery staff: (excluding agency): total	KDCA	474 497	481 873	483 061	482 215	486 607	487 273	489 038	489 568	490 545	487 001	483 493
Qualified nurses and midwives	KDCB	256 921	265 109	270 736	276 602	284 116	287 715	291 388	294 828	299 527	299 178	298 299
Student and pupil nurses and midwives	KDCC	96 255	97 044	94 167	91 369	86 485	83 148	79 085	77 284	74 929	70 402	59 615
Other nursing and midwifery staff	KDCD	121 321	119 720	118 158	114 244	116 006	116 410	118 566	117 454	116 088	117 432	125 579
Professionals allied to medicine staff	KADM				36 193	37 992	39 215	40 437	41 615	42 834	43 818	45 000
Scientific and professional staff	KADN KEJR	77 887	80 299	82 084	11 433	11 845	12 297	12 653	13 731	14 092	14 776	15 702
Professional and technical (excluding works) staff[5]	KDCF				39 054	38 865	39 402	39 532	38 603	38 528	40 216	40 753
Works and maintenance staff	KDCG	32 977	32 971	32 650	32 087	31 566	30 973	29 972	28 227	26 588	25 050	23 184
Administrative and clerical staff[6,7]	KDCH	124 426	124 863	126 220	126 652	127 594	128 439	131 639	133 563	139 631	153 517	161 526
Ambulance officers, ambulancemen/women and other ambulance staff	KDCI	21 435	21 590	21 697	21 441	21 595	22 465	22 523	22 302	22 443	21 698	21 934
Others[8]	KHWS	..	..	..	..	..	..	..	..	..	..	5 696
Ancillary staff[5]	KDCJ	211 284	209 631	204 635	189 023	175 319	159 109	147 935	138 261	129 024	120 065	108 840

1 Whole-time equivalent. Figures exclude locums and general medical practitioners participating in Hospital Staff Fund.
2 New grade introduced in 1989.
3 Figures include Senior Hospital Medical/Dental Officers (SHMO) without an allowance and other ungraded staff.
4 Whole-time equivalent. Figures exclude locums and occasional seasonal staff.
5 From 1 April 1984, Operating Department Assistants (ODAs) were transferred from Ancillary to Professional and Technical 'B' Staffs Council. Therefore figures for these staff groups prior to September 1984 are not comparable with those for September 1984 onwards (accounting for approximately 3000 WTE in September 1984).
6 Figures exclude ambulance officers.
7 Includes Family Practitioner Service administrative and clerical staff and General Managers.
8 Due to changes in the collection procedure in 1991 a category of "other staff" was introduced for these locally determined payscales. In previous years these staff were included in their respective occupation groups.

Sources: Scottish Health Service Common Services Agency;
Department of Health;
Welsh Office

National Health Service

3.30 Health and personal social services: manpower summary
Great Britain
continued   At 30 September each year

Number or whole-time equivalent

		1981	1982	1983	1984	1985	1986	1987	1988	1989	1990	1991[8]
Family Health services:												
Practitioners: Total	KDCK	52 897	54 136	55 397	56 688	57 755	55 689	56 749	57 639	58 579	58 636	59 199
General medical practitioners[1]: total	KDCL	29 252	29 806	30 422	30 976	31 465	31 854	32 422	32 888	33 310	33 058	33 463
Unrestricted principals	KDCM	26 702	27 256	27 825	28 229	28 783	29 279	29 808	30 277	30 631	30 618	30 713
Restricted principals	KDCN	238	227	204	195	184	175	172	170	179	163	151
Assistants	KDCO	315	301	317	300	258	283	260	276	261	221	471
Trainees	KDCP	1 997	2 022	2 076	2 182	2 240	2 117	2 182	2 165	2 239	2 040	2 102
Associates	KFZX	..	..	..	..	..	..	..	..	..	..	26
General dental practitioners: total	KDCQ	14 803	15 305	15 769	16 185	16 483	16 744	17 083	17 440	17 830	18 011	18 033
Principals	KDCR	14 671	15 181	15 646	16 069	16 375	16 640	16 969	17 144	17 436	17 539	17 440
Assistants	KDCS	132	124	123	116	108	104	114	296	394	472	593
Ophthalmic medical practitioners[2]	KDCT	963	957	951	972	981	1 007	963	930	882	882	862
Ophthalmic opticians[2]	KDCU	5 540	5 608	5 697	5 830	6 011	6 084	6 281	6 381	6 557	6 685	6 841
Dispensing opticians[3]	KDCV	2 338	2 460	2 558	2 725	2 815	..	..	..	..	..	..
Dental Estimates Board staff:[4]												
Total	KDCW	1 626	1 603	1 679	1 698	1 691	1 720	1 637	1 497	1 393	1 020	1 031
Administrative and clerical staff	KDCY	1 579	1 556	1 632	1 653	1 647	1 676	1 592	1 444	1 347	975	994
Ancillary, maintenance and works staff	KDCZ	47	47	48	45	44	44	45	53	47	45	37
Prescription Pricing Authority/ Prescription Pricing Division staff/Welsh Pricing Committee[5]												
Total	KDDA	2 708	2 583	2 565	2 558	2 518	2 512	2 380	2 254	2 302	1 844	1 867
Administrative and clerical staff	KDDC	2 645	2 526	2 506	2 499	2 454	2 446	2 316	2 194	2 227	1 781	1 813
Ancillary, maintenance and works staff	KDDD	63	57	58	59	63	66	64	60	74	63	54
Other Statutory Authorities:[6]												
Total	KADO	..	..	..	..	..	..	2 862	2 860	3 075	3 517	3 856
Nursing and midwifery staff	KADP	..	..	..	..	..	..	6	6	–	5	14
Professional and technical (excluding works) staff	KDCX	..	..	..	..	..	..	1 580	1 572	1 695	1 916	2 117
Administrative and clerical staff	KADQ	..	..	..	..	..	..	686	698	836	1 246	1 134
Ancillary, maintenance and works staff	KADR	..	..	..	..	..	..	590	584	544	350	200
Others[8]	KHWT	..	..	..	..	..	..	..	..	..	..	391
Personal Social Services Staff[7]:												
Total	KDDE	200 945	203 344	209 993	212 856	217 013	223 898	232 019	235 968	238 753	240 342	236 043
Management, administration and ancillary staff	KADS	21 129	20 977	21 325	21 677	22 032	22 921	24 272	24 993	25 801	27 006	28 049
Social work staff	KADT	22 951	22 990	23 714	24 292	24 773	25 914	27 016	27 865	28 598	29 672	30 675
Home help service and other support staff	KADU	50 542	51 462	53 790	55 349	57 008	59 092	62 069	63 151	63 281	62 909	60 521
Day care establishments staff	KADV	21 399	22 318	23 611	24 165	25 072	25 880	27 162	27 962	28 857	28 612	28 442
Residential care staff	KADW	83 117	83 611	85 413	85 058	85 455	86 694	88 242	88 496	88 285	87 858	83 001
All other staff	KADX	1 807	1 987	2 140	2 315	2 673	3 397	3 259	3 502	3 932	4 284	5 355

1 Figures relate to 1 October.
2 Figures relate to 31 December.
3 As from 1 July 1986 the dispensing of spectacles was de-regulated and dispensing opticians no longer have contracts with the General Ophthalmic Service.
4 In Scotland this is the Dentist Practice Division (DPD).
5 The Prescription Pricing Authority in Engalnd is synonymous with the Prescription Pricing Division in Scotland. Figures for the Prescription Pricing Division in Scotland relate to 30 November.
6 Prior to 1987 figures for "other statutory authorities" (eg Public Health Laboratory service and Health Education Authority) were not collected in the annual non-medical manpower census.
7 Figures are for England only.
8 Due to changes in the collection procedure in 1991 a category of "other staff" was introduced for these locally determined payscales. In previous years these staff were included in their respective occupation groups.

Sources: Scottish Health Service Common Services Agency;
Department of Health;
Welsh Office

3.31 NHS hospitals: selected diagnoses of in-patients treated in non-psychiatric departments (excluding maternity) - Great Britain

ICD[1], Injuries and Causes of Death 9th Revision (1975) WHO[2]

National Health Service

Thousands

Diagnostic group		Code numbers	1979	1980	1981	1982	1983	1984	1985[3]
All causes: total	KJLA	001 - 999	4 961.1	5 167.9	5 355.7	5 295.2	5 601.6	5 771.2	6 005.3
Males	KJLB		2 376.4	2 461.4	2 549.5	2 526.7	2 661.4	2 740.9	2 819.8
Females	KJLC		2 584.7	2 706.5	2 806.2	2 768.5	2 940.2	3 030.3	3 185.5
Tuberculosis: total	KJLD	010 - 018	10.9	10.3	9.2	7.5	7.9	6.3	5.7
Males	KJLE		6.6	6.5	5.7	4.3	4.5	3.6	3.2
Females	KJLF		4.3	3.8	3.5	3.2	3.4	2.7	2.5
Malignant neoplasms: total	KJLG	140 - 208	417.0	433.8	451.5	460.9	472.3	475.8	482.9
Males	KJLH		211.3	217.4	226.1	233.1	239.8	239.5	245.5
Females	KJLI		205.7	216.4	225.4	227.8	232.5	236.3	237.4
Benign and unspecified neoplasms: total	KJLJ	210 - 239	95.3	96.7	97.8	93.0	99.5	102.5	106.4
Males	KJLK		26.8	27.0	28.6	26.9	28.3	28.7	28.2
Females	KJLL		68.5	69.7	69.2	66.1	71.2	73.8	78.2
Endocrine, metabolic and nutritional diseases and immunity disorders: total	KJLM	240 - 279	96.9	100.4	101.3	97.5	102.2	100.5	97.0
Males	KJLN		38.1	40.2	40.4	39.7	40.8	40.7	39.9
Females	KJLO		58.8	60.2	60.9	57.8	61.4	59.8	57.1
Diseases of the nervous system: total	KJLP	320 - 359	103.5	109.5	114.9	114.0	119.4	122.2	125.1
Males	KJLQ		48.9	52.0	55.0	54.3	56.5	59.1	59.7
Females	KJLR		54.6	57.5	55.9	59.7	62.9	63.1	65.4
Diseases of the heart, including rheumatic fever and hypertensive disease: total	KJLS	390 - 429	337.1	346.1	359.9	373.7	385.2	401.1	417.2
Males	KJLT		194.4	198.7	206.9	214.8	220.6	230.6	238.9
Females	KJLU		142.7	147.4	153.0	158.9	164.6	170.5	178.3
Cerebrovascular disease and other diseases of circulatory system: total	KJLV	430 - 459	248.7	262.3	271.3	260.6	285.5	293.5	298.5
Males	KJLW		124.4	128.4	131.1	127.6	138.4	140.6	143.2
Females	KJLX		124.3	133.9	140.2	133.0	147.1	152.9	155.3
Diseases of respiratory system: total	KJLY	460 - 519	410.4	444.1	459.3	467.2	489.6	507.8	550.1
Males	KJLZ		232.8	249.4	260.7	261.3	274.3	283.8	305.2
Females	KJMA		177.6	194.7	198.6	205.9	215.3	224.0	244.9
Diseases of the digestive system: total	KJMB	520 - 579	550.8	578.1	595.8	558.6	600.0	604.2	616.9
Males	KJMC		293.9	310.6	316.6	291.4	315.8	316.1	323.9
Females	KJMD		256.9	267.5	279.2	267.2	284.2	288.1	293.0
Diseases of urinary system: total	KJME	580 - 599	96.3	101.5	106.4	110.5	116.9	120.6	126.0
Males	KJMF		52.0	55.8	57.9	62.0	64.2	67.1	55.9
Females	KJMG		44.3	45.7	48.5	48.5	52.7	53.5	70.1
Complications of pregnancy, childbirth and puerperium: Females	KJMH	630 - 676	157.2	159.1	159.6	159.8	160.1	161.9	162.7
Diseases of musculo-skeletal system: total	KJMI	710 - 739	239.0	271.8	292.2	277.1	312.8	326.1	334.2
Males	KJMJ		107.8	123.1	130.4	123.9	137.7	145.3	148.7
Females	KJMK		131.2	148.7	161.8	153.2	175.1	180.8	185.5
Fractures, dislocations and sprains: total	KJML	800 - 848	215.8	209.8	218.7	225.9	228.6	234.6	243.9
Males	KJMM		113.7	108.8	112.0	116.9	116.6	121.3	123.0
Females	KJMN		102.1	101.0	106.7	109.0	112.0	113.3	120.9
Other injuries and reactions: total	KJMO	850 - 999	419.0	412.4	428.4	423.8	417.0	420.5	421.3
Males	KJMP		237.1	232.5	243.0	241.9	241.1	243.9	244.6
Females	KJMQ		181.9	179.9	185.4	181.9	175.9	176.6	176.7
Other causes: total	KJMR		1 563.2	1 632.0	1 689.4	1 665.1	1 804.6	1 893.6	1 966.5
Males	KJMS		688.5	711.0	735.1	728.6	782.8	820.6	845.6
Females	KJMT		874.7	921.0	954.3	936.5	1 021.8	1 073.0	1 120.9

1 International Classification of Diseases.
2 World Health Organisation.
3 Later figures not available.

Sources: Office of Population Censuses and Surveys;
Scottish Health Service;
Department of Health;
Welsh Office

Public health

3.32 Notifications of infectious diseases

Number

		1980	1981	1982	1983	1984	1985	1986	1987	1988	1989	1990	1991
United Kingdom													
Diphtheria	KHQA	5	2	4	4	4	4	4	2	1	2	2	2
Typhoid and paratyphoid fevers	KHQB	307	277	253	269	219	262	260	215	369	273	293	288
Scarlet fever	KHQC	12 936	8 024	8 415	7 609	7 231	7 451	7 881	7 275	7 087	10 385	9 505	6 875
Measles	KHQD	147 938	61 747	105 634	114 945	67 631	104 774	90 207	46 069	90 634	31 045	15 641	11 723
Whooping cough	KHQE	22 873	21 459	70 868	21 589	6 219	24 244	39 939	17 354	5 879	13 550	16 862	6 279
Smallpox	KHQF	–	–	–	–	–	–	–	–	–	–	–	–
Dysentery	KHQG	3 595	3 674	3 256	6 039	8 734	6 111	5 096	3 978	3 946	3 806	3 042	11 527
Food poisoning	KHQH	12 021	12 994	17 478	20 486	23 237	20 242	26 645	32 180	43 004	56 190	55 988	56 114
Tuberculosis: total	KHQI	10 486	9 290	8 449	7 792	7 044	6 648	6 856	5 744	5 775	6 059	5 897	6 078
Respiratory	KHQJ	7 789	6 817	6 696	6 138	5 579	5 293	5 421	4 514	4 491	4 625	4 476	4 468
Other	KHQK	2 697	2 473	1 906	1 764	1 512	1 404	1 489	1 270	1 338	1 475	1 469	1 681
Acute poliomyelitis [1]	KHQL	3	2	4	5	–	5	4	3	2	2	1	5
England and Wales [2]													
Diphtheria	KHRA	5	2	4	4	4	4	4	2	1	2	2	2
Typhoid and paratyphoid fevers	KHRB	290	254	234	259	206	252	239	203	354	252	270	281
Scarlet fever	KHRC	11 116	7 148	7 601	6 539	6 327	6 438	6 888	6 439	5 949	8 294	7 187	5 216
Measles	KHRD	139 485	52 975	94 195	103 700	62 079	97 408	82 054	42 164	86 009	26 222	13 301	9 680
Whooping cough	KHRE	21 131	19 395	65 810	19 340	5 517	22 046	36 506	15 203	5 117	11 646	15 286	5 201
Smallpox	KHRF	–	–	–	–	–	–	–	–	–	–	–	–
Dysentery	KHRG	2 708	3 398	2 850	5 003	6 844	5 334	4 774	3 616	3 692	3 277	2 756	9 935
Food poisoning	KHRH	10 071	9 925	14 242	17 726	20 702	18 114	23 937	29 277	39 704	52 492	52 145	52 540
Ophthalmia neonatorum	KHRI	278	210	201	208	247	258	298	300	374	427	440	433
Tuberculosis [3]: total	KHRJ	9 142	8 128	7 406	6 800	6 141	5 857	5 992	5 085	5 161	5 432	5 204	5 436
Respiratory [4]	KHRK	6 670	5 859	5 827	5 317	4 871	4 660	4 758	4 010	4 019	4 146	3 942	3 950
Other [4]	KHRL	2 472	2 269	1 732	1 593	1 317	1 246	1 288	1 115	1 196	1 327	1 309	1 557
Acute poliomyelitis [1]	KHRM	3	2	2	4	–	4	3	3	2	1	1	4
Acute encephalitis (infective and post infective)	KHRN	91	58	71	56	37	39	51	57	65	40	39	35
Acute meningitis: total	KHRO	1 796	1 393	1 271	1 226	1 230	1 345	2 172	2 542	2 987	2 721	2 572	2 760
Menigococcal	KHRP	509	464	410	428	401	548	870	1 080	1 304	1 132	1 138	1 117
Scotland													
Diphtheria	KHSA	–	–	–	–	–	–	–	–	–	–	–	–
Typhoid and paratyphoid fevers	KHSB	17	20	18	10	13	10	20	11	14	18	20	7
Erysipelas	KHSC	99	87	76	75	69	88	111	120	112	152	125	155
Scarlet fever	KHSD	1 343	592	552	734	512	649	728	562	658	1 345	1 546	1 084
Measles	KHSE	6 646	4 698	10 581	6 193	4 897	4 595	7 073	2 695	2 258	3 359	2 006	1 701
Whooping cough	KHSF	1 366	1 385	4 224	1 870	271	1 118	2 943	1 588	356	659	1 291	838
Smallpox	KHSG	–	–	–	–	–	–	–	–	–	–	–	–
Dysentery	KHSH	854	204	261	871	1 554	512	286	344	196	154	235	1 526
Food poisoning	KHSI	1 836	2 934	3 038	2 632	2 391	1 967	2 436	2 480	2 998	3 197	3 024	2 938
Ophthalmia neonatorum	KHSJ	27	38	45	86	87	61	101	56	9	..	1	..
Puerperal fever and pyrexia	KHSK	2	9	4	6	6	5	9	5	2	3[8]	4	17
Tuberculosis: total [5]	KHSL	1 138	972	902	829	738	707	756	560	528	533	562	546
Respiratory	KHSM	943	799	762	692	586	560	578	425	401	401	440	449
Other	KHSN	195	173	140	137	152	147	178	135	127	132	123	97
Acute poliomyelitis [1]	KHSO	–	–	1	1	–	1	1	–	–	1	–	1
Cholera	KHSP	–	–	–	–	–	3	–	1	–	1	1	1
Northern Ireland													
Diphtheria	KHTA	–	–	–	–	–	–	–	–	–	–	–	–
Typhoid and paratyphoid fevers	KHTB	–	3	1	–	–	–	1	1	1	3	3	–
Scarlet fever	KHTC	477	284	262	336	392	364	265	274	480	746	772	575
Measles	KHTD	1 807	4 074	858	5 052	655	2 771	1 080	1 210	2 376	1 464	334	342
Whooping cough	KHTE	376	679	834	379	431	1 080	490	563	406	1 245	285	240
Smallpox	KHTF	..	..	..	..	..	..	..	..	..	..	..	..
Dysentery	KHTG	33	72	145	165	336	265	36	18	58	375	51	66
Food poisoning	KHTH	114	135	198	128	144	158	272	423	302	501	819	636
Tuberculosis: total	KHTI	206	190	141	163	162	83	108	99	86	94	131	96
Respiratory	KHTJ	176	159	107	129	113	72	85	79	71	78	94	69
Other	KHTK	30	31	34	34	44	11	23	20	15	16	37	27
Acute poliomyelitis [1]	KHTL	–	–	1	–	–	–	–	–	–	–	–	–
Acute encephalitis/meningitis [7]	KHTM	–	–	120	121	184	150	167	104	156	131	158	172
Infective hepatitis	KHTO	–	–	530	252	132	97	153	506	527	402	313	440
Gastro-enteritis (persons under 2 years of age only)	KHTP	–	–	560	598	575	606	806	745	869	1 243	1 157	1 091
Rubella [6]	KHTQ	–	–	–	–	–	–	–	–	124	651	543	357
Mumps	KHTR	–	–	–	–	–	–	–	–	532	696	187	189

1 Including acute polioencephalitis.
2 The figures show the corrected number of notifications, incorporating revisions of diagnosis, either by the notifying medical practitioner or by the medical superintendent of the infectious diseases hospital. Cases notified in Port Health Authorities are excluded.
3 Formal notifications of new cases only. The figures from 1982 exclude chemoprophylaxis.
4 From 1982 catagories overlap and therefore cases will be included in respiratory and other tuberculosis.
5 Figures include cases of tuberculosis not notified before death.
6 From 1 July 1988 only.
7 From 1990 data for Acute encephalitis and meningitis are not available separately. Figures have been combined for earlier years.
8 Figure only includes Puerperal fever. Data for Pyrexia not available.

Sources: Scottish Health Service Common Services Agency;
Department of Health and Social Services (Northern Ireland);
Office of Population Censuses and Surveys

Public health

3.33 Deaths due to occupationally related lung disease [1]

		1980	1981	1982	1983	1984	1985	1986	1987	1988	1989	1990
Asbestosis (without mesothelioma)	KADY	102	137	128	121	129	140	166	144	152	157	163
Mesothelioma [2]	KADZ	458	472	504	573	624	615	702	808	862	900	882
Pneumoconiosis (other than asbestosis)	KAEA	330	341	314	317	314	324	337	279	281	317	328
Byssinosis	KAEB	17	26	22	33	24	25	29	25	22	25	19
Farmer's lung and other occupational allergic alveolitis	KAEC	9	13	15	15	10	7	15	16	9	8	6
Total	KAED	916	989	983	1 059	1 101	1 111	1 249	1 272	1 326	1 407	1 398

1 The data in this table is derived from death certificates. For asbestosis and mesothelioma, the figure shown is the number of certificates mentioning the disease. For the other diseases the figure is the number of deaths coded to the disease as underlying cause.

2 Not all mesothelioma cases are related to occupational exposure to asbestos. The 'natural' rate for mesothelioma is probably about 2 per million per year, equivalent to approximately 100 deaths annually for GB.

Source: Health and Safety Executive

3.34 New cases of occupational diseases diagnosed under the Industrial Injuries and Pneumoconiosis, Byssinosis and Miscellaneous Diseases benefit schemes

Disablement Benefit

		1981	1982	1983	1984	1985	1986	1987	1988	1989	1990	1991
A. Occupational lung diseases and deafness												
Pneumoconiosis (except asbestosis)	KAEE	657	611	540	451	468	480	469	412	437	417[8]	447[8]
Asbestosis	KAEF	153	185	212	200	301	329	282	225	280	306[8]	330[8]
Byssinosis	KAEG	113	135	74	63	37	27	25	15	15	18[8]	7[8]
Farmer's lung	KAEH	12	11	8	4	6	11	8	15	13	7	5
Occupational asthma	KAEI	..[4]	95	183	137	166	166[3]	220	222	220	216	293
Mesothelioma	KAEJ	93	123	148	201	245	305	399	479	441	462	519
Lung cancer (asbestos)	KAEK	..[4]	..[4]	..[4]	..[4]	8	34	55	59	54	58	55
Lung cancer (other prescribed agents)	KAEL	–	–	1	5	2	3	–	–	4	6	6
Bilateral pleural thickening	KAEM	..[4]	..[4]	..[4]	..[4]	61	111	115	114	125	146	149
Other occupational lung disease	KAEN	3	9	6	1	2	5	10	5	–	4	6
Occupational deafness [1]	KAEO	1 022	680	447[3]	1 468	1 492	1 179	1 381	1 515	1 506	1 128	1 041
Total: Occupational lung disease and deafness	KAEP	2 053	1 849	1 619	2 530	2 788	2 650	2 964	3 061	3 095	2 768[8]	2 858[8]

Injury and Disablement Benefit [6] / Disablement Benefit [7]

		1980/81	1981/82	1982/83 [5]	1983/84		1984/85	1985/86	1986/87 [2]	1987/88 [2]	1988/89 [2]	1989/90 [2]	1990/91 [2]
B. Other diseases													
Dermatitis	KAEQ	3 960	3 452	2 110	611	KEAI	619	785	464	368	285	301	432
Tenosynovitis	KAER	2 413	2 282	1 433	337	KEAJ	390	619	376	322	294	423	556
Vibration white finger	KAES	..[4]	..[4]	..[4]	..[4]	KEAK	3	641	1 366	1 673	1 056	2 601	5 401
Beat conditions	KAET	621	525	324	131	KEAL	180	220	57	171	112	95	187
Viral hepatitis	KAEU	40	26	24	3	KEAM	5	9	5	3	1	1	2
Tuberculosis	KAEV	32	29	11	6	KEAN	7	3	13	3	5	–	3
Leptospirosis	KAEW	7	1	4	2	KEAO	–	–	1	–	–	2	–
Other infections	KAEX	9	2	3	4	KEAP	–	1	5	–	1	2	5
Poisonings	KAEY	23	30	14	2	KEAQ	4	3	9	2	16	33	4
Occupational cancers	KAEZ	15	6	5	8	KEAR	6	12	27	29	11	18	17
Other conditions	KAFA	73	55	35	22	KEAS	15	28	58	39	36	55	85
Total: Other diseases	KAFB	7 193	6 408	3 963	1 126	KEAT	1 229	2 321	2 381	2 610	1 817	3 531	6 692

1 For occupational deafness figures to 1982 are for years ending in June; for 1983 ending December; from 1984, years ending September.
2 From October 1986 disablement benefit was paid only for cases with disability assessed at 14% or more; the figures for 1986-87, and subsequent years include cases not qualifying for benefit but assessed at 1-13%.
3 Series affected by changes in prescription benefit rules.
4 The following diseases were first prescribed during the period covered by the table (Year benefit first payable shown in brackets):
 Occupational asthma (1982)
 Lung cancer (asbestos) (1985)
 Bilateral pleural thickening (1985)
 Vibration white finger (1984/85)
5 For year 1982/83 the figures are for 10 months (June 82 to March 83).
6 Years ending in June.
7 Years ending in September.
8 Figures for 1990 and 1991 do not include cases awarded by Medical Appeals Tribunals.

Sources: Health and Safety Executive; Department of Social Security

Public health

3.35 Injuries at work[1]
Standard Industrial Classification 1980

		SIC 1980	Fatal 1988/89	Fatal 1989/90	Fatal 1990/91		Major[2] 1988/89	Major[2] 1989/90	Major[2] 1990/91		Over 3 Days[3] 1988/89	Over 3 Days[3] 1989/90	Over 3 Days[3] 1990/91
Agriculture, forestry and fishing	KMXA	0	46	53	52	KMYR	583	505	558	KMVK	1 615	1 626	1 422
Agriculture and horticulture	KMXB	01	40	48	42	KMYS	527	455	491	KMVL	1 298	1 354	1 215
Forestry	KMXC	02	5	4	10	KMYT	53	45	60	KMVM	291	232	182
Fishing[4]	KMXD	03	1	1	–	KMYU	3	5	7	KMVN	26	40	25
Energy and water supply industries[5,6]	KMXE	1	205	31	27	KMYV	1 267	1 146	1 074	KMVO	13 738	11 705	10 276
Coal extraction and manufacture of solid fuels	KMXF	11	21	20	12	KMYW	769	665	549	KMVP	6 427	5 084	4 253
Coke ovens	KMXG	12	–	1	–	KMYX	8	9	6	KMVQ	104	106	53
Extraction of mineral oil and natural gas[5,6]	KMXH	13	172	2	12	KMYY	64	75	95	KMVR	692	693	701
Mineral oil processing	KMXI	14	2	3	–	KMYZ	33	42	36	KMVS	154	164	147
Nuclear fuels industry	KMXJ	15	–	–	–	KMZA	12	13	9	KMVT	313	288	211
Production and distribution of electricity, gas and other forms of energy	KMXK	16	8	3	3	KMZB	324	273	299	KMVU	4 721	4 224	3 899
Water supply industry	KMXL	17	2	2	–	KMZC	57	69	80	KMVV	1 327	1 146	1 012
Extraction of minerals and ores other than fuels; manufacture of metals, mineral products and chemicals	KMXM	2	35	36	30	KMZD	1 681	1 554	1 414	KMVW	11 150	11 480	10 501
Extraction and preparation of metalliferous ores/extraction of minerals nes	KMXN	21/23	8	3	9	KMZF	180	163	128	KMVY	788	784	687
Metal manufacture	KMXO	22	8	6	5	KMZG	517	415	354	KMVZ	3 430	3 188	2 991
Manufacture of non-metalic mineral products	KMXP	24	11	19	11	KMZH	474	403	408	KMWA	3 251	3 676	3 297
Chemical industry	KMXQ	25	8	8	5	KMZI	498	559	508	KMWB	3 557	3 725	3 439
Man-made fibres industry	KMXR	26	–	–	–	KMZJ	12	14	16	KMWC	124	107	87
Metal goods, engineering and vehicles industries	KMXS	3	33	48	29	KMZK	2 645	2 762	2 609	KMWD	20 076	21 774	20 467
Manufacture of metal goods	KMXT	31	11	9	3	KMZL	682	746	668	KMWE	4 459	5 082	4 573
Mechanical engineering	KMXU	32	11	20	14	KMZM	828	836	772	KMWF	5 043	5 459	5 137
Manufacture of office machinery and data processing equipment	KMXV	33	–	–	–	KMZN	29	40	27	KMWG	205	207	217
Electrical and electronic engineering	KMXW	34	2	9	3	KMZO	366	369	437	KMWH	3 192	3 267	3 087
Manufacture of motor vehicles parts thereof	KMXX	35	5	2	5	KMZP	400	384	333	KMWI	4 019	4 355	4 141
Manufacture of other transport equipment	KMXY	36	4	6	4	KMZQ	303	337	324	KMWJ	2 911	3 097	3 062
Instrument engineering	KMXZ	37	–	2	–	KMZR	37	50	48	KMWK	247	307	250
Other manufacturing industries	KMYA	4	33	31	39	KMZS	3 188	3 181	2 900	KMWL	25 043	26 900	25 581
Food, drink and tobacco industry	KMYB	41/42	7	10	13	KMZT	1 255	1 333	1 192	KMWM	12 932	14 301	13 687
Textile industry	KMYC	43	5	2	6	KMZU	269	248	214	KMWN	1 891	1 989	1 745
Leather and leather goods industry	KMYD	44	–	–	1	KMZV	19	16	20	KMWO	119	144	124
Footwear and clothing industry	KMYE	45	–	–	1	KMZW	106	92	108	KMWP	885	822	723
Timber and wooden furniture industries	KMYF	46	5	11	8	KMVA	631	586	515	KMWQ	2 579	2 602	2 471
Manufacture of paper and paper products; printing and publishing	KMYG	47	10	4	4	KMVB	446	434	395	KMWR	3 289	3 359	3 349
Processing of rubber and plastics	KMYH	48	5	3	6	KMVC	387	415	400	KMWT	2 970	3 257	3 106
Other manufacturing industries	KMYI	49	1	1	–	KMVD	75	57	56	KMWU	378	426	376
Total manufacturing industries	KMYJ	2-4	101	115	98	KMVE	7 514	7 497	6 923	KMWV	56 269	60 154	56 549
Construction	KMYK	5	137	154	124	KMVF	3 660	4 107	3 838	KMWW	17 566	18 487	18 243
Distributive trades, hotels and catering; repairs	KMYL	6	39	35	32	KMVG	2 091	2 244	2 337	KMWX	12 516	14 652	15 991
Transport and communication	KMYM	7	45	46	53	KMVH	1 271	1 324	1 526	KMWY	13 240	14 883	15 817
Banking and finance, insurance, business services and leasing	KMYN	8	10	10	9	KMVI	213	277	316	KMWZ	1 183	1 466	1 593
Other services	KMYO	9	25	31	38	KMVJ	4 359	4 482	4 454	KMUX	44 574	43 655	42 169
Unclassified	KMYP		1	–	–	KMUV	138	124	196	KMUW	3 921	481	828
Total reported to enforcement authorities [6]	KMYQ		609	475	433	KMUZ	21 096	21 706	21 222	KMWS	164 622	167 109	162 888

1 Included work related injuries to employees and self-employed persons reported to enforcing authorities under the Reporting of Injuries. Diseases and Dangerous Occurrences Regulations 1985.
2 As defined in RIDDOR.
3 Injuries causing incapacity for normal work for more than 3 days.
4 Excludes sea fishing.
5 Includes figures for the oil and gas industry collected under offshore safety legislation.
6 Includes the 167 fatalities, 11 major injuries and 50 over 3-day injuries of the Piper Alpha disaster, 6 July 1988.

Source: Health and Safety Executive (HSE)

Households

3.36 Private households with usual residents: Census 1981
Number of families and family type by selected tenures of households in permanent buildings and with no car

Figures are a ten per cent sample

Number of families in household and family type	All households	Owner occupied	Rented From council or new town	Rented Unfurnished	With no car
Great Britain					
All households	1 949 341	1 084 545	607 085	114 553	768 474
Households with no family	516 171	222 685	174 084	53 066	365 946
One person	423 980	178 732	152 025	44 603	322 613
Two or more persons	92 191	43 953	22 059	8 463	43 333
Households with one family	1 416 132	852 256	426 900	60 909	397 726
Married couple family	1 252 564	787 622	345 521	52 289	310 261
With no children	498 920	306 319	133 694	31 371	162 350
With at least one dependent child	595 088	387 713	158 577	15 342	117 754
With non-dependent child(ren) only	158 556	93 590	53 250	5 576	30 157
Lone parent family	163 568	64 634	81 379	8 620	87 465
With at least one dependent child	91 582	31 859	49 605	3 825	53 815
With non-dependent child(ren) only	71 986	32 775	31 774	4 795	33 650
Households with two or more families	17 038	9 604	6 101	578	4 802
England and Wales					
All households	1 770 745	1 022 529	509 678	107 279	681 914
Households with no family	469 089	208 665	148 560	49 763	329 447
One person	384 915	167 373	129 989	41 836	290 990
Two or more persons	84 174	41 292	18 571	7 927	38 457
Households with one family	1 286 201	804 662	356 095	56 972	348 387
Married couple family	1 139 273	743 572	286 554	48 887	271 792
With no children	458 406	290 246	113 575	29 478	145 770
With at least one dependent child	537 926	364 711	129 228	14 201	100 570
With non-dependent child(ren) only	142 941	88 615	43 751	5 208	25 452
Lone parent family	146 928	61 090	69 451	8 085	76 595
With at least one dependent child	83 057	30 327	43 270	3 613	47 667
With non-dependent child(ren) only	63 871	30 763	26 271	4 472	28 928
Households with two or more families	15 455	9 202	5 023	544	4 080
Scotland					
All households	178 596	62 016	97 407	7 274	86 560
Households with no family	47 082	14 020	25 524	3 303	36 499
One person	39 065	11 359	22 036	2 767	31 623
Two or more persons	8 017	2 661	3 488	536	4 876
Households with one family	129 931	47 594	70 805	3 937	49 339
Married couple family	113 291	44 050	58 967	3 402	38 469
With no children	40 514	16 073	20 119	1 893	16 580
With at least one dependent child	57 162	23 002	29 349	1 141	17 184
With non-dependent child(ren) only	15 615	4 975	9 499	368	4 705
Lone parent family	16 640	3 544	11 838	535	10 870
With at least one dependent child	8 525	1 532	6 335	212	6 148
With non-dependent child(ren) only	8 115	2 012	5 503	323	4 722
Households with two or more families	1 583	402	1 078	34	722

Sources: Office of Population Censuses and Surveys; General Register Office (Scotland)

Elections

3.37 Parliamentary elections[1]

Thousands

	23 Feb 1950	25 Oct 1951	26 May 1955	8 Oct 1959	15 Oct 1964	31 Mar 1966	18 June 1970[1]	28 Feb 1974	10 Oct 1974	3 May 1979	9 June 1983	11 June 1987
United Kingdom												
Number of electors	34 412	34 919	34 852	35 397	35 894	35 957	39 615	40 256	40 256	41 573	42 704	43 666
Average-electors per sea	55.1	55.9	55.3	56.2	57.0	57.1	62.9	63.4	63.4	65.5	66.7	67.2
Number of valid votes counted	28 771	28 597	26 760	27 863	27 657	27 265	28 345	31 340	29 189	31 221	30 671	32 530
As percentage of electorate	83.6	81.9	76.8	78.7	77.1	75.8	71.5	77.9	72.5	75.1	71.8	74.5
England and Wales												
Number of electors	30 177	30 626	30 591	31 109	31 610	31 695	34 931	35 509	35 509	36 695	37 708	38 568
Average-electors per seat	55.1	56.5	55.9	56.9	57.8	57.9	63.9	64.3	64.3	66.5	67.2	68.8
Number of valid votes counted	25 483	25 356	23 570	24 619	24 384	24 116	24 877	27 735	25 729	27 609	27 082	28 832
As percentage of electorate	84.4	82.8	77.0	79.1	77.1	76.1	71.2	78.1	72.5	75.2	71.8	74.8
Scotland												
Number of electors	3 370	3 421	3 388	3 414	3 393	3 360	3 659	3 705	3 705	3 837	3 934	3 995
Average-electors per seat	47.5	48.2	47.7	48.1	47.8	47.3	51.5	52.2	52.2	54.0	54.6	55.5
Number of valid votes counted	2 727	2 778	2 543	2 668	2 635	2 553	2 688	2 887	2 758	2 917	2 825	2 968
As percentage of electorate	80.9	81.2	75.1	78.1	77.6	76.0	73.5	77.9	74.5	76.0	71.8	74.3
Northern Ireland												
Number of eligible electors on day of election	865	872	873	875	891	902	1 025	1 027	1 037	1 028	1 050	1 090
Average-electors per seat	72.1	72.5	72.8	72.9	74.2	75.2	85.4	85.6	86.4	85.6	61.8	64.1
Number of valid votes counted	561	463	647	576	638	596	779	718	702	696	765	730
As percentage of electorate	64.9	53.1	74.1	65.8	71.7	66.1	76.0	69.9	67.7	67.7	72.9	67.0
Number of Members of Parliament elected:	625	625	630	630	630	630	630	635	635	635	650	650
Conservative	297	320	344	364	303	253	330	296	276	339	396	375
Labour	315	295	277	258	317	363	287	301	319	268	209	229
Liberal	9	6	6	6	9	12	6	14	13	11	17	17
Social Democratic Party	-	-	-	-	-	-	-	-	-	-	6	5
Scottish National Party	-	-	-	-	-	-	1	7	11	2	2	3
Plaid Cymru	-	-	-	-	-	-	-	2	3	2	2	3
Other[2]	4	4	3	2	1	2	6	15	13	13	18	18

1 The Representation of the People Act 1969 lowered the minimum voting age from 21 to 18 years with effect from 16 February 1970.

2 The Speaker is included in Other.

Sources Home Office: Scottish Home and Health Department; Northern Ireland Office

3.38 Parliamentary by-elections

	March 1974 -Oct 1974	Previous[1] General Election Feb 1974	Oct 1974 -May 1979	Previous[1] General Election Oct 1974	May 1979 -June 1983	Previous[1] General Election May 1979	June 1983 -June 1987	Previous[1] General Election June 1983	June 1987 -April 1992	Previous[1] General Election June 1987
Numbers of by-election	1		30		20		31		24	
Votes recorded										
By party (percentages)										
Conservative	11.1	12.2	45.1	34.8	23.8	33.7	16.0	23.3	23.8	33.7
Labour	62.6	66.1	36.9	44.8	25.7	35.2	14.9	14.8	38.9	41.1
Liberal[2]	12.5	14.8	10.9	17.3	9.0	8.0	15.0	10.9	19.1	18.6
Social Democratic Party[2]	-	-	-	-	14.2	-	5.6	3.0	3.2	0.0
Plaid Cymru	-	-	-	-	0.5	0.4	0.3	0.3	2.3	0.6
Scottish National Party	-	-	2.7	2.6	1.7	1.4	-	-	4.8	1.8
Other	13.7	6.9	4.7	0.5	25.1[3]	21.2[3]	48.2[4]	47.6[4]	7.9	4.2
Total votes recorded										
(percentages)	100.0	100.0	100.0	100.0	100.0	100.0	100.0	100.0	100.0	100.0
(thousands)	15	36	1 058	1 288	715	852	1 235	1 410	878	1 130

1 Votes recorded in the same seats in the previous General Election. Does not apply to June 1983 election in Northern Ireland.
2 The Social Democratic Party was launched on 26 March 1981. An SDP candidate contested a Parliamentary seat for the first time in the by-election held at Warrington on 16 July 1981. From that date, the Liberal and Social putting up a candidate in each. See also note 5.
3 The proportions of votes recorded for 'Other' is high because three of the 20 by-elections were in Northern Ireland. Two were in the same constituency, Fermangh and South Tyrone, and as votes recorded at both by-elections have been included, votes recorded for the 1979 General Election have been included twice in the previous General Election column.
4 The proportion of votes recorded for 'other' is high because 15 of the 31 by-elections were in Northern Ireland.
5 In the 1987 General Election the Liberal Party and the Social Democratic Party contested the election jointly as the Liberal/SDP Alliance. The Alliance subsequently split into its constituent parties and the Liberals are now known as the Liberal Democrats. The future of the SDP, with 3 MPs, is at present uncertain.

Source Home Office

4 Law enforcement

There are differences in the legal and judicial systems of England and Wales, Scotland and Northern Ireland which make it impossible to provide tables covering the United Kingdom as a whole in this section. These differences concern the classification of offences, the meaning of certain terms used in the statistics, the effects of the several Criminal Justice Acts and recording practices.

Court proceedings and police cautions

The statistical basis of the tables of court proceedings is broadly similar in England and Wales, Scotland and Northern Ireland; the tables show the number of persons found guilty, recording a person under the heading of the principal offence of which he is found guilty, excluding additional findings of guilt at the same proceedings. A person found guilty at a number of separate court proceedings is included more than once.

The statistics on offenders cautioned cover only those who, on admission of guilt, were given a formal caution by, or on the instructions of, a senior police officer as an alternative to prosecution; written warnings by the police for motor offences and persons paying fixed penalties for certain motoring offences are excluded. There are no statistics on cautioning available for Northern Ireland.

For England and Wales from 1979 a new offence classification and tabulation procedure was introduced to reflect the changes in the mode of trial introduced by Part III of the Criminal Law Act 1977 which came into force in July 1978. Indictable offences are offences which are a) triable only on indictment (these are the most serious crimes such as murder, manslaughter, rape and robbery) and are tried at the Crown Courts b) triable-either-way offences which may either be tried at the Crown Court or a Magistrates's Court; summary offences are those for which a defendant would normally be tried at a Magistrate's Court. Since 29 March 1982 the courts have had the power to suspend between one quarter and three quarters of a sentence of imprisonment of six months for up to two years; from 31 January 1983 Section 30 of the Criminal Justice Act 1982 reduced the minimum period to three months and allowed a minimum of 28 days to be served. Part 1 of the Criminal Justice Act 1982, with effect from 24 May 1983, abolished borstal training and imprisonment for offenders aged under 21 and introduced youth custody.

On 1 October 1988 section 123 of the Criminal Justice Act 1988 replaced youth custody and detention centre orders by detention in a young offender institution. The Criminal Justice Act 1988 on 20 October 1988 also reclassified certain triable-either-way offences as summary offences.

Section 45 of the Criminal Justice (Scotland) Act 1980 was implemented on 15 November 1983; this introduced unified custodial sentencing for under 21 offenders and abolished borstal training.

The system of magistrates' courts and crown courts in Northern Ireland operates in a similar way to that in England and Wales.

4.1 Notifiable[1] offences recorded by the police
England and Wales

Thousands

		1981	1982	1983	1984	1985	1986	1987	1988	1989	1990	1991
Violence against the person	BEAB	100.2	108.7	111.3	114.2	121.7	125.5	141.0	158.2	177.0	184.7	190.3
Sexual offences[1]	BEAC	19.4	19.7	20.4	20.2	21.4	22.7	25.2	26.5	29.7	29.0	29.4
Burglary	BEAD	723.2	805.4	808.3	892.9	866.7	931.6	900.1	817.8	825.9	1 006.8	1 219.5
Robbery	BEAE	20.3	22.8	22.1	24.9	27.5	30.0	32.6	31.4	33.2	36.2	45.3
Theft and handling stolen goods	BEAF	1 603.2	1 755.9	1 705.9	1 808.0	1 884.1	2 003.9	2 052.0	1 931.3	2 012.8	2 374.4	2 761.1
Fraud and forgery	BEAG	106.7	123.1	121.8	126.1	134.8	133.4	133.0	133.9	134.5	147.9	174.7
Criminal damage	BEAH	386.7	417.8	443.3	497.8	539.0	583.6	589.0	593.9	630.1	733.4	821.1
Other offences[2]	BEAI	8.9	9.0	13.8	15.0	16.7	16.7	19.3	22.7	27.6	31.1	34.6
Total	BEAA	2 963.8	3 262.4	3 247.0	3 499.1	3 611.8	3 847.4	3 892.2	3 715.8	3 870.7	4 543.6	5 276.2

1 Includes from the beginning of 1983 offences of 'Gross indecency with a child'.
2 Includes from the beginning of 1983 offences of 'Trafficking in controlled drugs'.

Source: Home Office

Law enforcement

4.2 Police Forces: authorised establishment and strength
End of year

Number

		1981	1982	1983	1984	1985	1986	1987	1988	1989	1990	1991
England and Wales												
Regular police												
Authorised establishment[1]	KERA	120 008	120 125	120 447	120 679	120 903	121 785	122 648	123 551	124 667	125 646	126 325
Strength:												
Men	KERB	107 379	108 517	108 519	108 102	107 960	108 225	109 773	109 900	110 466	110 790	110 396
Women	KERC	10 702	10 935	10 995	11 001	11 213	11 600	12 492	13 007	13 695	14 352	14 898
Seconded[2]:												
Men	KERD	1 424	1 419	1 407	1 388	1 439	1 617	1 716	1 730	1 815	1 787	1 670
Women	KERE	70	80	82	82	90	108	121	122	134	161	163
Additional constables[3]:												
Men	KERF	90	89	84	83	79	88	70	69	75	85	73
Women	KERG	1	1	2	–	1	1	–	–	1	5	3
Special constables												
Enrolled strength:												
Men	KERH	11 813	11 932	11 743	11 749	11 550	11 140	10 927	10 578	10 390	10 483	11 592
Women	KERI	2 791	3 228	3 588	4 307	4 611	4 930	5 282	5 210	5 199	5 419	6 480
Scotland												
Regular police[4]												
Authorised establishment	KERJ	13 195	13 205	13 261	13 283	13 377	13 489	13 569	13 707	13 813	13 981	14 046
Strength[5]:												
Men	KERK	12 379	12 433	12 435	12 415	12 455	12 504	12 470	12 498	12 656	12 583	12 566
Women	KERL	749	719	713	722	761	838	933	1 020	1 158	1 258	1 357
Central service[5,6]:												
Men	KERM	54	55	65	61	69	70	73	65	69	67	64
Women	KERN	2	2	2	2	1	2	3	3	4	6	6
Seconded[5,7]:												
Men	KERO	78	73	68	67	67	88	85	88	92	98	103
Women	KERP	5	4	3	3	3	4	5	7	8	8	6
Additional regular police:												
Authorised establishment[4]	KERQ	67	62	60	88	88	86	73	64	64	64	91
Strength	KERR	66	62	60	88	88	86	73	64	64	64	93
Part-time auxiliaries[8]												
Strength:												
Men	KERS	2 612	2 528	2 439	2 250	1 846	1 755	1 561	1 514	1 521	1 475	1 436
Women	KERT	202	208	204	203	200	209	216	233	279	312	342
Northern Ireland												
Royal Ulster Constabulary												
Strength:												
Men	KERU	6 622	7 017	7 328	7 487	7 610	7 581	7 591	7 568	7 571	7 535	7 510
Women	KERV	712	701	675	640	649	653	645	659	688	708	707
Royal Ulster Constabulary Reserve												
Strengths												
Men	KERW	4 350	4 385	4 105	4 102	4 199	4 127	4 319	4 268	4 200	4 097	4 069
Women	KERX	520	455	388	337	309	287	325	386	425	449	491

1 Total of establishments of individual forces *plus* the Metropolitan Regional Crime Squad and additional constables in the Metropolitan Police.
2 Regional Crime Squads, other inter-force units and officers in central service.
3 Excluding additional constables in the Metropolitan Police Force.
4 From 1976, officers employed at ports, airports and oil-related industries are no longer included in 'Regular police' but included in 'Additional regular police'.
5 'Strength' includes central service and seconded police.
6 Instructors at Training Establishments, etc formerly shown as secondments.
7 Scottish Crime Squad, officers on courses, etc.
8 Including special constables (enrolled strength).

Sources: Home Office;
Scottish Home and Health Department;
Northern Ireland Office

Law enforcement

4.3 Offenders found guilty: by offence group
Magistrates' courts and the Crown Court
England and Wales

Thousands

		1981	1982	1983	1984	1985	1986	1987	1988	1989	1990	1991[3]
Offenders[1] of all ages found guilty												
						Indictable offences							
Violence against the person:												
Murder	KESB	0.1	0.1	0.1	0.2	0.2	0.2	0.2	0.2	0.2	0.2	0.2
Manslaughter	KESC	0.3	0.2	0.2	0.2	0.3	0.3	0.3	0.3	0.3	0.2	0.2
Wounding	KESD	48.7	49.6	49.5	45.8	45.3	40.9	45.6	50.9	53.7	50.9	45.5
Other offences of violence against the person	KESE	1.7	1.7	1.6	1.6	1.7	1.5	1.8	2.1	1.5	1.2	1.2
Sexual offences	KESF	6.9	6.6	6.4	5.6	6.0	5.5	6.2	7.2	7.3	6.6	5.5
Burglary	KESG	76.4	76.5	72.7	72.7	69.4	56.3	54.2	48.4	43.4	43.6	46.1
Robbery	KESH	4.1	4.4	4.0	4.3	4.4	4.2	4.4	4.3	4.6	4.8	4.8
Theft and handling stolen goods	KESI	232.2	238.7	224.9	219.2	216.3	183.2	175.9	163.4	134.5	134.3	133.5
Fraud and forgery	KESJ	25.7	24.9	25.6	25.7	25.5	22.8	22.5	22.7	22.3	21.9	21.2
Criminal damage	KESK	11.8	11.4	12.1	11.5	11.5	10.1	10.6	11.8	9.4	11.2	10.2
Other offences (excluding motoring)	KESL	29.0	31.2	33.4	33.5	34.3	29.1	35.6	43.7	51.1	56.9	34.4
Motoring offences	KESM	27.7	29.8	30.5	29.2	29.0	27.5	29.1	31.3	11.3	11.1	11.3
Total	KESA	464.6	475.1	461.0	449.4	443.9	381.5	386.4	386.3	339.5	342.8	337.6
						Summary offences							
Assaults	KESO	11.2	11.1	10.7	11.4	10.5	9.6	10.8	11.5	14.7	17.3	16.5
Betting and gaming	KESP	0.5	0.5	0.6	0.3	0.3	0.1	0.1	–	0.1	–	–
Breach of local or other regulations	KESQ	15.8	14.7	14.4	13.3	12.5	13.0	12.6	11.0	10.1	12.6	8.5
Intoxicating Liquor Laws:												
Drunkenness	KESR	97.2	96.4	96.2	60.5	49.2	38.0	42.3	45.3	42.9	37.8	29.4
Other offences	KESS	6.5	4.9	4.5	3.5	2.8	3.0	2.7	3.8	2.8	2.2	1.5
Education Acts	KEST	3.0	2.9	2.5	2.7	2.9	3.1	2.9	2.8	2.8	3.0	2.8
Game Laws	KESU	1.9	1.7	1.9	1.8	1.5	1.4	1.4	1.3	1.2	1.1	1.0
Labour Laws	KESV	0.4	0.3	0.2	0.3	0.2	0.2	0.1	0.1	0.1	0.1	0.1
Summary offences of criminal damage and malicious damage	KESW	37.8	36.6	38.6	39.0	38.5	34.2	35.4	35.2	36.6	33.9	28.5
Offences by prostitutes	KESX	4.1	5.8	10.4	8.6	9.2	9.1	8.2	8.8	11.1	11.5	10.9
Railway offences	KESY	17.4	15.4	15.9	13.3	11.9	9.7	8.3	9.2	9.9	8.3	5.4
Revenue Laws	KESZ	73.6	72.7	107.8	108.7	114.3	121.9	107.4	113.4	108.5	104.9	115.6
Motoring offences (summary)	KETA	1 210.5	1 128.0	1 161.7	1 083.2	1 052.0	1 066.2	738.1	713.9	722.3	704.6	713.1
Vagrancy Acts	KETB	2.9	2.0	1.6	1.3	0.9	0.8	0.9	1.0	1.8	1.9	2.1
Wireless Telegraphy Acts	KETC	49.6	61.9	67.5	77.2	80.6	128.6	120.4	124.3	123.4	126.4	138.7
Other summary offences	KETD	107.5	100.7	99.7	88.3	79.7	72.8	76.6	87.6	104.5	106.1	93.4
Total	KESN	1 640.1	1 555.9	1 634.5	1 513.5	1 467.0	1 510.0	1 168.3	1 169.1	1 193.0	1 171.8	1 167.5
Persons aged under 17 found guilty[2]												
						Indictable offences							
Violence against the person	KETF	7.3	7.3	6.7	6.0	5.6	4.4	4.2	4.3	4.0	3.5	3.2
Sexual offences	KETG	0.6	0.6	0.6	0.5	0.5	0.4	0.4	0.4	0.3	0.3	0.3
Burglary	KETH	25.8	23.0	21.2	20.7	18.1	12.9	11.0	9.1	7.5	6.8	5.9
Robbery	KETI	1.0	1.0	0.8	1.0	0.9	0.8	0.8	0.8	0.4	1.0	1.0
Theft and handling stolen goods	KETJ	44.6	42.9	38.0	36.1	32.7	25.1	21.4	17.6	10.7	9.8	8.6
Fraud and forgery	KETK	1.1	0.9	0.8	0.8	0.8	0.6	0.5	0.4	0.3	0.3	0.2
Criminal damage	KETL	3.1	2.8	2.9	2.6	2.4	1.8	1.6	1.5	1.2	1.3	1.1
Other offences (excluding motoring)	KETM	0.7	0.7	0.6	0.7	0.6	0.5	0.9	1.1	1.2	1.3	0.6
Motoring offences	KETN	2.4	2.5	1.9	1.9	1.6	1.4	1.2	1.2	0.2	0.3	0.3
Total	KETE	86.6	81.1	73.3	70.2	63.2	48.0	42.0	36.5	26.5	24.6	21.9
						Summary offences							
Highway Acts and motoring summary offences:												
Offences with pedal cycles	KETP	2.4	2.1	2.2	1.9	1.3	0.7	0.4	0.2	0.2	0.2	0.1
Other	KETQ	15.5	11.2	10.9	9.1	7.8	7.4	4.5	3.8	3.8	3.6	2.7
Breach of local or other regulations	KETR	0.9	0.8	0.8	0.6	0.5	0.4	0.3	0.1	0.1	0.1	0.1
Summary offences of criminal damage and malicious damage	KETS	7.1	6.0	6.2	5.3	5.0	3.9	3.1	2.5	2.2	1.8	1.4
Railway offences	KETT	0.7	0.7	0.7	0.6	0.4	0.2	0.2	0.2	0.1	0.1	0.1
Other summary offences	KETU	5.1	7.5	6.5	5.6	4.5	2.1	3.2	3.6	7.4	6.9	6.2
Total	KETO	31.7	28.3	27.1	23.1	19.5	14.6	11.6	10.4	13.9	12.7	10.6

1 Includes 'Companies', etc. (see Tables 4.5 and 4.6).
2 Figures for persons aged under 17 are included in the totals for all offenders above.
3 Provisional

Source: Home Office

Law enforcement

4.4 Offenders cautioned: by offence group
England and Wales

Thousands

		1981	1982	1983	1984	1985	1986	1987	1988	1989	1990	1991[4]
Offenders[1] of all ages cautioned												
						Indictable offences						
Violence against the person	KELB	5.6	6.5	7.0	7.8	9.0	9.5	11.3	12.7	14.7	16.8	19.4
Sexual offences	KELC	2.8	2.7	2.9	2.8	2.9	2.9	3.2	3.6	3.5	3.4	3.3
Burglary	KELD	11.5	11.2	12.0	13.5	14.3	12.8	13.0	12.2	12.0	14.3	13.3
Robbery	KELE	0.1	0.2	0.2	0.2	0.2	0.2	0.2	0.2	0.4	0.6	0.6
Theft and handling stolen goods	KELF	79.2	85.9	86.9	92.3	109.0	100.3	106.5	92.6	81.9	99.8	108.5
Fraud and forgery	KELG	1.4	1.4	1.6	1.8	2.2	2.7	3.9	4.0	4.0	4.7	5.6
Criminal damage	KELH	2.1	1.9	2.4	2.6	3.1	3.0	3.5	4.3	3.7	4.2	3.8
Other offences (excluding motoring)	KELI	1.2	1.5	2.1	3.0	4.7	5.5	8.1	11.0	16.0	22.6	25.3
Total	KELA	103.9	111.3	114.9	124.1	145.4	136.9	149.8	140.7	136.0	166.3	179.9
						Summary offences						
Assaults	KELK	0.2	0.2	0.2	0.4	0.6	0.8	0.8	0.9	1.1	1.4	1.6
Betting and gaming	KELL	0.2	0.1	0.1	0.1	0.1	0.1	0.1	0.1	–	–	–
Breach of local or other regulations	KELM	1.3	1.2	1.2	2.1	3.3	3.4	2.0	2.0	1.2	1.2	1.3
Intoxicating Liquor Laws:												
Drunkeness	KELN	0.7	0.8	2.1	21.2	26.1	29.2	40.7	48.6	49.9	48.6	46.0
Other offences	KELO	3.0	2.8	2.2	2.0	2.2	0.5	3.3	4.0	2.6	2.8	1.7
Education Acts	KELP	–	–	–	–	–	–	–	–	–	–	–
Game Laws	KELQ	0.1	0.2	0.2	0.2	0.2	0.2	0.2	0.2	0.1	0.2	0.2
Labour Laws	KELR	–	–	–	–	–	–	0.1	0.1	–	–	–
Summary offences of criminal damage and malicious damage	KELS	8.5	9.2	10.1	11.2	12.7	13.1	13.1	13.5	14.3	16.2	17.3
Offences by prostitutes	KELT	7.9	7.9	7.3	4.9	4.2	4.9	4.7	5.2	5.3	4.5	4.1
Railway offences	KELU	0.1	0.1	0.1	0.1	0.2	0.2	0.4	0.4	0.6	0.4	0.3
Revenue Laws	KELV	1.4	1.6	1.4	1.6	1.7	1.6	1.3	1.0	0.6	0.5	0.7
Highway Act offences	KELW	14.0	12.4	12.9	10.7	9.2	10.0	5.6	5.1	4.5	4.1	1.2
Vagrancy Acts	KELX	0.2	0.2	0.2	0.3	0.3	0.3	0.6	0.6	0.4	0.5	0.7
Wireless Telegraphy Acts	KELY	–	–	–	–	–	–	–	–	–	–	–
Other summary offences	KELZ	12.4	12.5	12.7	11.6	12.6	12.4	13.7	13.1	21.3	22.5	23.8
Total	KELJ	50.0	49.2	50.6	66.3	73.3	76.6	86.7	94.7	102.0	102.8	98.9
Persons aged under 17 cautioned[2]												
						Indictable offences						
Violence against the person	KEMB	3.8	4.4	4.8	5.1	5.7	5.2	5.7	6.2	7.0	7.6	8.1
Sexual offences	KEMC	1.4	1.4	1.5	1.4	1.5	1.2	1.3	1.5	1.5	1.3	1.2
Burglary	KEMD	11.2	10.7	11.5	12.9	13.6	11.7	11.8	10.9	10.0	12.4	11.0
Robbery	KEME	0.1	0.1	0.2	0.2	0.2	0.2	0.2	0.2	0.3	0.5	0.5
Theft and handling stolen goods	KEMF	68.2	73.2	73.2	75.6	86.8	70.8	71.1	57.9	47.3	57.3	55.1
Fraud and forgery	KEMG	0.8	0.8	0.9	0.9	1.1	1.1	1.4	1.3	1.2	1.2	1.2
Criminal damage	KEMH	1.9	1.8	2.2	2.4	2.8	2.5	2.8	3.4	2.9	3.0	2.4
Other offences (excluding motoring)	KEMI	0.3	0.4	0.5	0.5	0.8	0.7	1.3	1.4	2.7	3.2	3.8
Total	KEMA	87.6	93.0	94.6	99.1	112.5	93.5	95.7	82.8	72.8	86.4	83.1
						Summary offences						
Highway Acts offences:												
Offences with pedal cycles	KEMK	5.4	4.8	5.0	4.2	3.1	2.3	1.6	1.5	1.3	1.3	0.7
Other	KEML	1.6	0.8	0.7	0.6	0.7	1.8	0.6	0.4	0.5	0.5	0.3
Breach of local or other regulations	KEMM	0.6	0.6	0.6	0.8	1.0	1.0	0.7	0.6	0.5	0.4	0.4
Summary offences of criminal damage and malicious damage	KEMN	7.5	8.0	8.7	9.4	10.5	9.7	8.5	8.5	8.6	9.4	8.9
Railway offences	KEMO	0.1	0.1	0.1	0.1	0.1	0.1	0.2	0.2	0.2	0.2	0.1
Other summary offences	KEMP	5.5	5.4	5.6	5.7	6.7	5.1	7.1	7.4	12.6	14.0	12.1
Total	KEMJ	20.6	19.8	20.8	20.8	22.1	20.0	18.7	18.6	23.8	25.7	22.6

1 Includes 'Companies', etc. (see Tables 4.5 and 4.6).
2 Figures for persons aged under 17 are included in the figures for all offenders above.
3 Provisional

Source: Home Office

Law enforcement

4.5 Offenders found guilty of offences: by age and sex
Magistrates' courts and the Crown Court
England and Wales

Thousands

		1982	1983	1984	1985	1986	1987	1988	1989	1990	1991[1]
Males						Indictable offences					
All ages	KEFA	407.7	397.0	387.4	382.5	331.7	336.4	337.5	293.7	295.7	293.5
10 and under 14 years	KEFB	13.6	11.6	10.9	9.1	6.1	4.3	3.7	2.8	2.6	2.3
14 and under 17 years	KEFC	59.5	54.4	52.8	48.1	37.7	34.3	29.6	21.2	19.5	17.2
17 and under 21 years	KEFD	119.6	115.3	114.0	114.0	98.9	99.9	97.2	83.0	84.8	83.1
21 years and over	KEFE	215.1	215.8	209.6	211.3	189.0	198.0	207.1	186.8	188.8	190.8
						Summary offences					
All ages	KEFF	1 358.8	1 411.7	1 298.3	1 247.3	1 252.6	972.5	974.5	993.7	968.9	956.3
10 and under 14 years	KEFG	2.2	2.2	1.8	1.5	1.0	0.7	0.6	0.9	0.9	0.8
14 and under 17 years	KEFH	24.5	23.5	20.0	16.9	12.8	10.4	9.2	12.3	11.0	9.2
17 and under 21 years	KEFI	213.2	212.2	192.3	183.1	171.5	148.9	145.6	154.8	149.0	129.5
21 years and over	KEFJ	1 118.9	1 173.8	1 084.2	1 045.7	1 067.3	812.6	819.1	825.7	807.9	816.8
Females						Indictable offences					
All ages	KEFK	66.1	62.7	59.9	59.0	50.0	47.5	46.1	43.0	44.0	41.9
10 and under 14 years	KEFL	1.7	1.3	1.0	0.9	0.5	0.3	0.3	0.2	0.2	0.2
14 and under 17 years	KEFM	7.0	6.1	5.4	5.0	3.7	3.1	2.9	2.3	2.3	2.2
17 and under 21 years	KEFN	15.1	14.8	14.4	14.8	12.7	12.2	11.5	10.7	10.9	10.3
21 years and over	KEFO	42.3	40.5	39.0	38.4	33.1	31.9	31.4	29.8	30.6	29.2
						Summary offences					
All ages	KEFP	169.4	190.4	183.0	189.3	227.4	175.2	176.4	179.1	185.3	194.1
10 and under 14 years	KEFQ	0.1	0.1	0.1	0.1	0.1	–	–	–	–	–
14 and under 17 years	KEFR	1.5	1.4	1.2	1.0	0.7	0.6	0.5	0.5	0.7	0.6
17 and under 21 years	KEFS	14.8	16.7	14.9	14.5	14.9	12.4	12.9	14.2	14.3	13.6
21 years and over	KEFT	153.1	172.3	166.7	173.8	211.6	162.2	163.0	164.3	170.4	179.8
Companies, etc											
Indictable offences	KEFU	1.3	1.4	2.2	2.3	2.4	2.5	2.7	2.9	3.1	2.2
Summary offences	KEFV	29.1	32.4	32.3	30.4	30.0	20.7	18.2	19.6	17.6	17.2

1 Provisional

Source: Home Office

4.6 Offenders cautioned by the police: by age and sex
England and Wales

Thousands

		1982	1983	1984	1985	1986	1987	1988	1989	1990	1991[1]
Males						Indictable offences					
All ages	KEGA	78.5	82.7	91.6	104.2	98.7	111.5	107.0	102.8	124.2	131.4
10 and under 14 years	KEGB	31.6	32.0	33.2	34.4	26.3	26.0	22.9	20.3	22.5	21.0
14 and under 17 years	KEGC	35.4	37.5	42.1	48.0	43.6	48.0	43.0	37.5	44.2	41.0
17 and under 21 years	KEGD	3.8	4.4	5.7	7.5	10.5	14.3	15.0	16.7	22.9	28.0
21 years and over	KEGE	7.7	8.7	10.6	14.4	18.3	23.2	26.1	28.3	34.6	41.4
						Summary offences					
All ages	KEGF	36.2	38.2	54.6	62.0	64.3	73.8	80.6	86.9	88.2	85.3
10 and under 14 years	KEGG	5.9	6.3	6.2	6.1	4.9	4.1	4.0	5.3	5.5	5.2
14 and under 17 years	KEGH	12.0	12.4	12.5	13.9	13.2	12.6	12.5	16.0	17.2	14.7
17 and under 21 years	KEGI	4.6	4.6	7.0	8.3	10.1	12.1	12.4	12.9	13.4	13.5
21 years and over	KEGJ	13.7	14.9	28.9	33.8	36.2	45.0	51.8	52.7	52.1	51.9
Females						Indictable offences					
All ages	KEGK	32.9	32.2	32.4	41.1	38.2	38.3	33.7	33.2	42.1	48.5
10 and under 14 years	KEGL	12.8	12.0	10.4	12.5	8.7	7.5	5.3	4.5	5.9	6.3
14 and under 17 years	KEGM	13.2	13.1	13.3	17.6	14.9	14.2	11.7	10.5	13.8	14.8
17 and under 21 years	KEGN	1.0	1.1	1.6	2.1	3.5	4.2	4.2	4.7	6.6	8.4
21 years and over	KEGO	5.9	6.1	7.0	8.9	11.1	12.4	12.5	13.5	15.8	19.0
						Summary offences					
All ages	KEGP	13.0	12.4	11.6	11.3	12.2	13.0	14.1	15.2	14.6	13.6
10 and under 14 years	KEGQ	0.5	0.6	0.6	0.5	0.4	0.4	0.4	0.4	0.5	0.5
14 and under 17 years	KEGR	1.4	1.6	1.5	1.6	1.6	1.6	1.8	2.1	2.5	2.2
17 and under 21 years	KEGS	3.7	3.1	2.5	2.2	2.6	2.8	2.9	3.2	2.9	2.6
21 years and over	KEGT	7.3	7.1	7.0	7.0	7.7	8.2	9.1	9.5	8.7	8.3
Companies, etc											
Indictable offences	KEGU	..	..	..	..	..	..	..	..	..	..
Summary offences	KEGV	0.1	0.1	0.1	0.1	0.1	..	..	..	..	..

1 Provisional.

Source: Home Office

Law enforcement

4.7 Sentence or order passed on offenders sentenced for indictable offences: by sex Magistrates' courts and the Crown Court
England and Wales

Percentages

		1982	1983	1984	1985	1986	1987	1988	1989	1990	1991[5]
Males											
Sentence or order											
Absolute discharge	KEJB	0.6	0.6	0.5	0.5	0.5	0.5	0.6	0.7	0.7	0.7
Conditional discharge	KEJC	10.2	10.5	11.2	11.0	11.3	11.4	11.1	12.4	14.2	16.1
Probation order	KEJD	5.5	6.0	6.7	7.1	7.7	8.1	8.3	8.5	9.1	9.3
Supervision order	KEJE	3.1	2.8	2.8	2.7	2.4	2.1	1.8	1.6	1.5	1.4
Fine	KEJF	44.0	42.8	41.2	39.7	38.9	38.5	39.4	40.4	40.1	36.0
Community service order	KEJG	6.5	7.5	8.2	8.4	8.6	8.7	8.5	7.6	8.5	9.5
Attendance centre order	KEJH	3.5	3.6	3.4	3.3	2.8	2.5	2.2	1.8	1.9	1.9
Care order	KEJJ	0.7	0.5	0.4	0.3	0.3	0.2	0.1	0.1	0.1	–
Young offender institution[1]	KEJK	5.1	6.5	7.7	7.9	7.5	7.3	6.7	5.4	4.5	4.6
Imprisonment											
Fully suspended[2]	KEJL	7.7	6.7	6.0	6.4	6.6	6.9	7.3	6.4	6.3	6.4
Partly suspended[3]	KAFN	0.3	0.9	0.9	0.9	0.8	0.7	0.7	0.6	0.4	0.3
Unsuspended[4]	KEJM	11.7	10.4	9.7	10.7	11.3	11.8	11.7	11.6	10.7	11.4
Other sentence or order	KEJN	1.2	1.2	1.2	1.2	1.1	1.3	1.5	2.0	2.2	2.3
Total number of offenders (thousands) = 100 per cent	KEJA	409.6	397.8	387.8	383.0	332.5	336.8	337.5	293.2	294.7	291.9
Females											
Sentence or order											
Absolute discharge	KEKB	0.8	0.8	0.8	0.7	0.7	0.8	0.8	0.9	1.0	0.9
Conditional discharge	KEKC	21.7	22.3	23.5	24.5	25.5	26.6	28.1	30.2	33.2	35.9
Probation order	KEKD	15.2	15.8	16.4	16.7	18.0	18.2	18.1	17.4	17.5	17.0
Supervision order	KEKE	3.2	2.5	2.4	2.1	1.6	1.4	1.2	1.1	1.1	1.1
Fine	KEKF	45.0	44.0	41.7	40.0	37.4	35.6	34.4	33.2	30.8	27.2
Community service order	KEKG	2.3	2.6	3.0	3.0	3.5	3.5	3.8	3.3	4.1	4.6
Attendance centre order	KEKH	0.8	0.8	0.7	0.6	0.5	0.4	0.4	0.3	0.3	0.4
Care order	KEKJ	0.6	0.5	0.3	0.3	0.2	0.1	0.1	0.1	0.1	–
Young offender institution[1]	KEKK	0.3	0.9	1.4	1.5	1.5	1.4	1.3	1.1	0.8	0.9
Imprisonment											
Fully suspended[2]	KEKL	5.7	5.0	4.9	5.3	5.4	5.5	5.7	6.0	5.3	5.9
Partly suspended[3]	KAFP	0.2	0.6	0.7	0.6	0.6	0.7	0.6	0.5	0.3	0.3
Unsuspended[4]	KEKM	3.5	3.2	3.3	3.7	3.9	4.5	4.2	4.2	3.5	4.1
Other sentence or order	KEKN	0.9	1.0	1.1	1.0	1.1	1.2	1.4	1.8	1.9	1.5
Total number of offenders (thousands) = 100 per cent	KEKA	66.0	62.7	59.9	59.1	59.1	47.5	46.1	43.0	43.9	41.9

1 Includes borstal training (abolished January 1983), detention centre orders and youth custody (both abolished October 1988).
2 Up until 1982 this was known as Suspended sentence.
3 Introduced on 29 March 1982.
4 Up until 1982 this was known as Immediate imprisonment.
5 Provisional

Source: Home Office

4.8 Receptions into prison[1]: by number of previous convictions
England and Wales

Number of receptions

			1981	1982	1983	1984	1985	1986	1987	1988	1989	1990	1991
Number of previous convictions:													
Males:													
Previous conviction information not recorded	KEES	KHDE	9 860	10 857	13 455	12 985	13 627	11 791	16 370	18 369	21 637	21 723	31 348[2]
None	KEEN		3 290	3 891	3 581	3 545	3 185	3 813	2 923	3 948	3 363	3 579	
1 - 2 sentences	KEEO		8 737	8 576	7 815	8 313	9 137	7 882	7 329	6 354	4 553	3 710	2 789
3 - 5 sentences	KEEP		14 468	14 465	13 701	14 243	15 189	13 231	12 357	9 987	7 832	5 573	4 503
6 - 10 sentences	KEEQ		14 181	14 842	14 373	14 539	16 186	14 167	13 218	12 007	9 626	7 299	5 937
11 or more sentences	KEER		13 614	14 352	14 304	14 192	15 024	12 965	12 354	11 541	9 784	6 852	6 506
Total	KEEM		64 150	66 983	67 229	67 817	72 348	63 849	64 551	62 206	56 795	48 736	51 083
Females:													
Previous conviction information not recorded	KEEZ	KHDF	1 055	1 091	994	1 239	1 534	1 137	1 236	1 058	1 347	1 090	1 504[2]
None	KEEU		199	200	295	347	247	361	313	377	288	162	
1 - 2 sentences	KEEV		310	304	364	363	375	453	389	306	253	250	189
3 - 5 sentences	KEEW		501	514	532	529	482	507	476	463	302	201	195
6 - 10 sentences	KEEX		472	467	451	476	434	407	413	335	249	226	208
11 or more sentences	KEEY		270	326	308	278	276	280	257	274	211	186	161
Total	KEET		2 807	2 902	2 944	3 232	3 348	3 145	3 084	2 813	2 650	2 115	2 257

1 Receptions into Prison Service custody under sentence without the option of a fine.
2 Not separately identifiable.

Source: Home Office

Law enforcement

4.9 Receptions and average population in custody
England and Wales

Number

		1981	1982	1983[2]	1984	1985	1986	1987	1988	1989	1990	1991
Receptions												
Type of inmate:												
Untried	KEDA	47 169	48 474	47 719	51 900	54 718	55 398	59 210	57 876	58 789	53 135	54 676[4]
Convicted, unsentenced	KEDB	24 085	23 268	20 155	18 560	18 523	16 595	18 335	17 280	17 800	20 410	19 927[4]
Remanded for medical examination[1]	KEDC	1 568	1 357	..	..	..	..	..	..	..	..	..
Others	KEDD	22 517	21 911	..	..	..	..	..	..	..	..	..
Sentenced	KEDE	88 110	94 377	93 414	92 810	96 189	86 153	86 358	81 836	76 430	67 510	72 313
Immediate custodial sentence	KEDF	66 957	69 885	70 173	71 049	75 696	66 994	67 635	65 019	59 445	50 851	53 340
Young offenders	KEDG	28 502	28 509	28 382	28 858	29 762	24 801	23 984	21 631	17 674	14 380	15 028
Young offenders(except borstal trainees)												
Up to 18 months	KEDH	19 655	19 938	23 761	26 732	27 025	21 958	20 548	18 268	14 764	11 758	12 447
Over 18 months up to 4 years	KEDJ	1 214	1 135	1 579	1 934	2 477	2 497	3 008	2 966	2 519	2 307	2 270
Over 4 years (including life)	KEDL	174	217	203	192	260	346	428	397	391	315	311
Borstal trainees[2]	KEDK	7 459	7 219	2 839	–	–	–	–	–	–	–	–
Adults	KFBO	38 455	41 376	41 791	42 191	45 934	42 193	43 651	43 388	41 771	36 471	38 312
Up to 18 months	KEDV	31 378	34 235	34 094	34 084	36 043	31 860	31 844	31 005	29 444	25 363	27 159
Over 18 months up to 4 years	KEDW	5 825	5 714	6 203	6 633	7 994	8 068	9 035	9 584	9 270	8 253	8 199
Over 4 years (including life)	KEDX	1 252	1 427	1 494	1 474	1 897	2 265	2 772	2 799	3 057	2 855	2 954
Committed in default of payment of a fine	KEDY	21 153	24 492	23 241	21 761	20 493	19 159	18 723	16 817	16 985	16 659	18 973
Young offenders	KEEA	4 390	5 272	4 849	4 891	4 849	4 676	4 400	3 968	3 671	3 522	4 209
Adults	KAFQ	16 763	19 220	18 392	16 870	15 644	14 483	14 323	12 849	13 314	13 137	14 764
Non-criminal prisoners	KEDM	4 735	4 715	4 050	3 683	3 444	3 665	3 399	3 032	3 021	2 314	2 791
Immigration Act 1971	KEDN	907	963	872	949	1 068	1 422	1 339	1 333	1 448	916	1 225
Others[3]	KEDO	3 828	3 752	3 178	2 734	2 378	2 243	2 060	1 699	1 573	1 398	1 566
Average population												
Total in Custody	KEDP	43 436	43 754	43 772	43 349	46 278	46 889	48 963	49 949	48 610	45 636	45 897
Total in Prison Service establishments	KFBQ	43 311	43 707	43 462	43 295	46 233	46 770	48 426	48 872	48 500	44 975	44 809
Untried	KEDQ	4 804	5 362	6 003	7 173	8 132	8 530	9 074	8 798	8 576	7 625	7 545
Convicted, unsentenced	KEDR	2 101	2 023	1 649	1 514	1 565	1 432	1 551	1 660	1 820	1 815	1 930
Remanded for medical examination[1]	KEDS	138	173	118	77	71	46	37	32	39	20	17
Others	KEDT	1 963	1 850	1 531	1 437	1 494	1 385	1 514	1 628	1 781	1 795	1 913
Police cells[5]	KFBN	125	47	310	54	45	119	537	1 077	110	661	1 088
Sentenced	KEDU	36 022	35 928	35 487	34 321	36 305	36 571	37 531	38 187	37 885	35 336	35 034
Immediate custodial sentence	KFBR	..	..	..	33 568	35 642	36 041	36 998	37 714	37 427	34 972	34 665
Young offenders	KFBS	10 558[6]	10 365[6]	9 929[6]	9 515	9 752	9 080	8 676	8 260	7 160	6 173	5 754
Young offenders(except borstal trainees)	KFBT	4 884[6]	5 077[6]	8 225[6]	9 515	9 752	9 080	8 676	8 260	7 160	6 173	5 754
Up to 18 months	KFBU	3 572[6]	3 673[6]	5 590[6]	7 318	7 164	6 049	5 272	4 523	3 638	3 143	3 095
Over 18 months up to 4 years	KFBV	985	1 086	448	1 597	2 133	2 518	2 748	2 947	2 749	2 328	2 033
Over 4 years (including life)	KFBW	327	318	121	298	406	510	656	790	773	699	623
Young prisoners	KFCN	..	..	2 066	303	49	4	–	–	–	–	–
Borstal trainees[2]	KEDZ	5 674	5 288	1 704	–	–	–	–	–	–	–	–
Adults	KFCO	25 464	25 563	25 557	24 053	25 890	26 961	28 322	29 454	30 267	28 799	28 911
Up to 18 months	KFCP	11 975	12 297	11 861	10 217	10 639	9 764	9 074	8 229	7 646	7 001	7 194
Over 18 months up to 4 years	KFCQ	8 173	7 880	8 087	7 745	8 496	9 534	10 283	11 004	11 191	9 751	9 333
Over 4 years (including life)	KFCR	5 316	5 386	5 609	6 088	6 758	7 664	8 963	10 222	11 430	12 047	12 384
Committed in default of payment of a fine	KFCS	..	..	..	753	663	530	533	473	458	364	369
Young offenders	KFEW	..	..	..	162	141	106	86	78	71	80	85
Adults	KFEX	..	..	..	591	522	424	447	395	387	284	284
Non-criminal prisoners	KEEB	384	394	323	288	231	238	270	227	220	200	300
Immigration Act 1971	KEEC	116	113	141	143	104	132	167	146	157	144	222
Others[3]	KEED	268	281	182	145	126	107	103	81	61	56	78

1 Under section 30, Magistrates' Courts Act 1980.
2 Youth custody for offenders aged 15 to 20 replaced borstal training and imprisonment on 24 May 1983.
3 Mainly persons failing to comply with payment orders.
4 Provisional.
5 Mostly untried prisoners.
6 Including prisoners committed in default of payment of a fine.

Source: Home Office

Law enforcement

4.10 Prison population serving sentences: analysis by age and offence
England and Wales

Number

	Total	14 - 16	17 - 20	21 - 24	25 - 29	30 - 39	40 - 49	50 - 59	60 and over
At 30 June 1989									
Offence									
Males									
Total	36 734	445	6 121	8 554	7 986	8 242	3 752	1 289	345
Violence against the person	8 473	49	1 172	1 913	1 984	2 005	913	357	80
Sexual offences	2 983	9	199	320	516	847	687	270	135
Burglary	7 076	164	1 842	2 086	1 526	1 034	321	88	13
Robbery	4 152	64	839	1 133	968	847	238	55	8
Theft, handling, fraud and forgery	5 120	67	884	1 158	1 042	1 126	596	203	44
Other offences	7 275	73	894	1 516	1 581	2 039	848	271	53
Offence not known	1 655	19	291	428	367	344	149	45	12
Females									
Total	1 279	14	148	258	304	354	148	44	9
Violence against the person	218	4	30	46	42	52	26	14	4
Sexual offences	23	-	1	2	4	10	5	1	-
Burglary	68	1	16	22	11	11	6	1	-
Robbery	82	2	24	24	20	9	3	-	-
Theft, handling, fraud and forgery	296	2	33	72	77	69	34	9	-
Other offences	509	5	33	72	130	183	65	17	4
Offence not known	83	-	11	20	20	20	9	2	1
At 30 June 1990									
Offence									
Males									
Total	33 967	264	5 443	7 456	7 509	7 887	3 712	1 341	355
Violence against the person	7 501	15	877	1 582	1 752	1 932	900	337	106
Sexual offences	3 020	6	168	309	504	863	726	322	122
Burglary	5 896	96	1493	1 718	1 350	890	269	68	12
Robbery	4 052	35	786	1 037	1 048	848	233	60	5
Theft, handling, fraud and forgery	3 902	34	619	834	834	865	492	173	42
Other offences	6 262	33	668	1 201	1 353	1 866	823	270	48
Offence not known	3 334	45	832	766	668	623	269	111	20
Females									
Total	1 253	10	127	228	293	368	169	48	10
Violence against the person	203	2	20	40	35	67	26	9	4
Sexual offences	11	-	2	1	-	6	1	1	-
Burglary	51	1	11	17	12	6	3	1	-
Robbery	51	1	22	8	15	2	3	-	-
Theft, handling, fraud and forgery	255	-	21	57	71	59	32	14	1
Other offences	540	1	32	73	134	194	86	16	4
Offence not known	142	5	19	32	26	34	18	7	1
At 30 June 1991									
Offences									
Males									
Total	33 966	250	5 110	7 305	7 703	8 081	3 743	1 378	396
Violence against the person	6 959	15	754	1 361	1 662	1 857	861	338	111
Sexual offences	3 095	3	151	291	506	860	777	362	145
Burglary	5 100	74	1 231	1 512	1 175	828	207	58	15
Robbery	3 991	21	687	1 005	1 091	891	237	53	6
Theft, handling, fraud and forgery	3 756	63	616	780	814	876	426	156	25
Other offences	5 898	32	688	1 113	1 303	1 675	773	266	48
Offences not known	5 167	42	983	1 243	1 152	1 094	462	145	46
Females									
Total	1 148	5	110	211	253	351	162	44	12
Violence against the person	189	2	17	38	36	58	26	9	3
Sexual offences	16	-	1	1	2	9	2	1	-
Burglary	39	-	6	9	16	6	-	1	1
Robbery	46	-	18	10	8	7	3	-	-
Theft, handling, fraud and forgery	218	1	11	46	59	57	33	9	2
Other offences	449	-	23	68	94	165	77	18	4
Offences not known	191	2	34	39	38	49	21	6	2

Source: Home Office

Law enforcement

4.11 Expenditure on prisons
England and Wales
Years ended 31 March

£ thousand

		1979/80	1980/81	1981/82	1982/83	1983/84	1984/85	1985/86	1986/87	1987/88	1988/89	1989/90	1990/91
Manpower costs[2]	KENA	..	..	..	..	397 558	433 851	451 619	475 871	538 398	544 079	593 670	653 150
Manpower related costs[6]	KENB	..	..	..	..	15 182	14 602	14 591	37 035	43 012	48 530	57 354	68 257
Establishment related costs	KENC	..	..	..	..	64 266	71 712	70 053	63 964	69 937	75 292	88 067	100 912
Inmate related costs[6]	KEND	..	..	..	..	52 871	54 583	58 917	40 776	47 065	53 258	56 678	55 648
Industries and farms:													
Materials	KENE	..	..	..	..	26 471	27 308	25 870	28 931	32 354	30 504	38 268	33 352
Income	KENF	..	..	..	..	−40 259	−40 556	−41 719	−45 891	−48 890	−40 489	−50 976	−38 530
Net income	KENG	..	..	..	..	−13 788	−13 248	−15 849	−16 960	−16 536	−9 985	−12 708	−5 178
Other activities	KENH	..	..	..	..	17 434	18 086	18 650	17 538	13 467	13 918	15 005	17 288
Total establishment operating costs[3]	KENI	..	..	..	..	533 523	579 586	597 981	618 224	695 343	735 092	798 066	890 077
Headquarter/regional office costs	KENJ	..	..	..	..	60 395	53 630	62 215	58 131	78 981	127 906	72 213	117 663
Total net operating costs[3]	KENK	318 420	404 313	466 509	526 440	593 918	633 216	660 196	676 355	774 324	862 998	870 279	1 007 740
Capital expenditure:[4]													
Expenditure	KENL	25 906	33 571	31 915	46 157	59 674	71 210	94 121	121 884	118 198	205 018	386 384	479 822
Receipts	KENM	–	–	–	–	−16 474	−17 309	−11 088	−11 789	−10 181	−54 118	−50 900	−23 335
Total net capital expenditure	KENN	25 906	33 571	31 915	46 157	43 200	53 901	83 033	110 095	108 017	150 900	335 484	456 407
Emergency arrangements[5]	KENO	–	17 220	4 201	–	–	–	–	–	–	–	–	–
Total net expenditure	KENP	344 326	455 104	502 625	572 597	637 118	687 117	743 229	786 450	882 341	1 013 898	1 205 763	1 464 227

1 The Prison Department introduced in 1983/4 a costing system designed to provide line mangers in the Prison Service with better management and financial information. The present table classifies expenditure in the same way as the costing system but differently from earlier years. It follows that the accounting records showing expenditure details from 1983/4 onwards are not comparable, except as regards capital expenditure, with those for previous years.
2 'Costs' differ from actual money spent as they include notional charges, ie superannuation and depreciation.
3 Total net operating costs for 1974/75 to 1982/83 have been calculated by adding maintenance, repairs, rentals etc costs, shown under capital expenditure in earlier volumes of the Annual Abstract to the total net current expenditure for those years. This is consistent with the approach taken in the costing system.
4 Capital expenditure includes Property Services Agency expenditure on behalf of Prison Department.
5 This was the cost of setting up and maintaining camps during the Prison Officers' dispute from October 1980 to February 1981. These costs cannot be attributed to individual groups.
6 Manpower related costs for 1986/87 onwards include Education and Probation Salary costs previously charged to inmate related costs.

Source: Home Office

4.12 Crimes and offences recorded by the police
Scotland

Thousands

		1981	1982	1983	1984	1985	1986	1987	1988	1989	1990	1991
Non-sexual crimes of violence against the person	KAFR	12.2	12.1	13.0	13.7	15.1	15.7	18.4	17.9	18.4	18.2	21.7
Serious assault, etc[1]	KAFS	4.5	4.5	5.0	5.3	6.0	6.4	7.6	7.7	7.3	6.3	7.0
Handling offensive weapons	KAFT	2.9	2.7	3.1	3.0	3.6	3.9	4.7	4.5	4.8	5.1	6.2
Robbery	KAFU	4.2	4.2	4.2	4.5	4.4	4.1	4.6	4.2	4.4	4.7	6.2
Other	KAFV	0.6	0.7	0.8	1.0	1.0	1.3	1.5	1.5	1.9	2.2	2.4
Crimes involving indecency	KAFW	4.8	5.0	5.5	5.7	5.7	5.4	5.3	5.1	5.7	6.0	5.8
Sexual assault	KAFX	1.3	1.1	1.3	1.5	1.4	1.3	1.4	1.3	1.5	1.5	1.4
Lewd and libidinous practices	KAFY	2.2	2.3	2.5	2.4	2.6	2.6	2.4	2.4	2.6	2.6	2.6
Other	KAFZ	1.3	1.6	1.8	1.8	1.7	1.5	1.4	1.4	1.6	2.0	1.8
Crimes involving dishonesty	KAGA	320.0	340.1	342.5	359.2	342.3	342.5	356.5	344.5	355.5	385.0	430.2
Housebreaking	KAGB	95.7	106.3	108.5	112.1	100.7	96.9	98.6	91.4	93.7	101.7	116.1
Theft by opening lockfast places	KAGC	47.3	49.2	50.7	51.9	52.1	61.4	69.0	77.5	84.7	92.4	102.8
Theft of a motor vehicle	KAGD	32.5	33.0	30.0	32.6	29.9	28.0	26.2	26.4	29.1	36.1	44.3
Shoplifting	KAGE	22.6	24.3	24.0	24.8	25.4	26.3	28.4	25.5	26.3	26.8	30.1
Other theft	KAGF	97.4	101.8	101.5	104.5	99.3	94.9	97.8	91.2	92.7	97.8	104.6
Fraud	KAGG	16.9	17.2	17.3	19.6	22.3	23.1	23.5	22.4	19.3	19.6	22.0
Other	KAGH	7.7	8.3	10.5	13.8	12.7	11.9	13.0	10.1	9.7	10.8	10.3
Fire-raising, vandalism, etc	KAGI	61.7	66.0	73.1	79.1	79.5	78.9	76.4	73.5	79.1	86.5	89.7
Fire-raising	KAGJ	3.0	3.4	3.7	4.2	4.1	3.9	3.8	3.7	4.4	4.3	4.8
Vandalism, etc	KAGK	58.7	62.6	69.4	74.8	75.4	75.0	72.6	68.9	74.7	82.1	84.9
Other crimes	KAGL	9.5	11.9	14.3	17.3	19.2	21.4	24.6	29.0	34.7	40.0	45.3
Crimes against public justice	KAGM	7.7	9.3	10.9	12.7	14.0	15.9	19.7	23.6	27.5	30.3	33.1
Drugs	KAGN	1.6	2.5	3.2	4.4	5.1	5.3	4.7	5.2	7.0	9.6	12.0
Other	KAGO	0.2	0.1	0.2	0.2	0.2	0.2	0.2	0.2	0.2	0.2	0.2
Total crimes	KAGQ	402.8	435.1	448.3	474.9	462.0	463.8	481.2	470.0	493.4	535.9	592.8
Miscellaneous offences	KAGR	118.2	115.4	114.8	114.9	118.1	120.4	127.3	124.9	124.9	127.0	122.3
Petty assault[1]	KAGS	27.6	28.5	30.3	31.7	32.2	32.6	35.7	36.6	37.6	39.6	41.0
Breach of the peace	KAGT	53.6	53.0	51.3	51.9	54.4	56.4	59.9	55.9	56.3	57.7	55.3
Drunkenness	KAGU	16.5	15.8	15.0	13.8	12.6	12.4	12.4	12.2	12.2	11.7	10.4
Other	KAGV	20.4	18.1	18.1	17.6	18.9	19.0	19.4	20.2	18.8	18.0	15.6
Motor vehicle offences	KAGW	218.3	212.0	236.5	219.6	220.3	238.1	249.7	260.7	283.8	296.2	305.6
Reckless and careless driving	KAGX	24.4	24.0	25.4	24.3	23.8	23.4	22.7	23.5	25.8	25.3	23.1
Drunk driving	KAGY	13.8	14.0	15.4	15.0	15.4	14.6	13.5	11.4	10.9	11.4	11.0
Speeding	KAGZ	33.9	29.3	37.7	33.7	32.0	41.0	58.7	64.8	81.5	90.0	100.1
Unlawful use of a motor vehicle	KAHA	79.3	86.6	90.7	82.6	84.7	87.0	78.9	68.7	67.6	70.6	75.7
Vehicle defect offences	KAHB	25.1	26.1	29.4	29.4	29.3	33.4	37.5	47.7	48.2	47.5	46.8
Other	KAHC	41.9	32.1	38.0	34.7	35.1	38.6	38.4	44.7	49.8	51.5	48.9
Total offences	KAHD	336.5	327.4	351.3	334.5	338.4	358.5	377.0	385.6	408.6	423.2	427.9
Total crimes and offences	KAHE	744.7	762.5	799.6	809.4	800.4	822.4	858.2	855.6	902.0	959.1	1 020.7

1 The definition of serious assault was changed in January 1990 to improve consistency between forces. It is estimated that the number of serious assaults that would have been recorded in 1989, using the revised definition, is some 1 150 fewer than actually recorded, with a corresponding rise in petty assaults.

Source: The Scottish Office Home and Health Department

Law enforcement

4.13 Persons proceeded against
Scotland

Number of persons

		1980	1981	1982	1983	1984	1985	1986	1987	1988	1989	1990
Non-sexual crimes of violence	KEHC	3 491	3 299	4 740	4 878	4 052	3 984	4 161	4 394	4 334	4 229	4 458
Homicide	KEHD	137	116	132	129	124	127	114	123	118	115	103
Serious assault, etc	KEHE	2 006	1 861	2 451	2 504	1 736	1 443	1 631	1 569	1 454	1 476	1 569
Handling offensive weapons	KEHF	366	460	1 035	1 147	1 174	1 227	1 197	1 340	1 422	1 407	1 418
Robbery	KEHG	657	610	843	776	733	902	883	981	902	779	844
Other violence	KEHH	325	252	279	322	285	285	336	381	438	452	524
Crimes of indecency	KEHI	1 161	1 340	1 799	1 908	1 926	1 829	1 479	1 464	1 358	1 370	1 820
Sexual assault	KEHJ	189	182	178	198	183	226	234	227	220	230	232
Lewd and libidinous practices	KEHK	455	439	420	437	404	489	426	484	444	444	435
Other indecency	KEHL	517	719	1 201	1 273	1 339	1 134	819	753	694	696	1 153
Crimes of dishonesty	KEHM	41 058	44 255	49 824	49 624	47 039	48 891	47 287	45 633	42 906	40 635	40 070
Housebreaking	KEHN	8 061	8 847	11 297	10 871	10 803	10 686	9 543	9 076	8 197	7 631	7 376
Theft by opening lockfast place	KEHO	2 275	2 510	3 351	3 259	3 133	3 726	3 844	3 867	3 825	3 838	3 574
Theft of or from motor vehicle	KEHP	4 678	4 002	4 427	4 205	4 080	4 255	3 957	3 381	3 344	3 047	3 208
Shoplifting[1]	KEHQ	4 588	5 693	5 581	5 783	5 559	6 137	6 784	7 169	6 544	6 623	7 109
Other theft[1]	KEHR	14 741	16 135	17 595	17 425	15 777	15 655	14 644	13 644	12 897	11 556	10 662
Fraud	KEHS	3 254	3 586	4 005	4 501	3 728	3 789	3 945	3 881	3 477	3 494	3 739
Other dishonesty	KEHT	3 461	3 482	3 568	3 580	3 959	4 643	4 570	4 615	4 622	4 446	4 402
Fire-raising, vandalism, etc	KEHU	5 080	6 087	6 441	6 519	7 018	7 120	7 304	7 421	7 568	7 166	6 915
Fire-raising	KEHV	170	185	194	158	248	278	253	279	233	227	215
Vandalism, etc	KEHW	4 910	5 902	6 247	6 361	6 770	6 842	7 051	7 142	7 335	6 939	6 700
Other crime	KEHX	3 584	3 786	5 818	8 124	8 534	9 942	9 907	10 041	9 038	9 388	10 504
Crime against public justice	KFBK	2 052	2 507	4 031	5 984	5 854	6 823	6 739	7 120	6 361	6 613	7 039
Drugs offences	KFBL	1 402	1 183	1 663	1 971	2 584	3 047	3 065	2 842	2 632	2 746	3 424
Other	KFBM	130	96	124	169	96	72	103	79	45	29	41
Total crimes	KEHB	54 374	58 767	68 622	71 053	68 569	71 766	70 138	68 953	65 204	62 788	63 767
Miscellaneous offences	KEHZ	87 540	84 127	75 182	74 700	68 857	67 912	67 301	64 440	67 771	63 642	60 676
Petty assault	KEIA	13 394	13 231	12 639	12 356	12 939	13 387	13 660	14 353	16 277	17 073	16 129
Breach of the peace	KEIB	37 663	39 697	36 798	35 171	31 838	32 652	31 338	30 826	27 376	24 731	23 366
Drunkenness	KEIC	14 459	11 579	10 033	8 324	6 893	5 289	3 815	3 776	3 490	3 043	2 920
Other miscellaneous offences	KEID	22 024	19 620	15 712	18 849	17 187	16 584	18 488	15 485	20 628	18 795	18 261
Motor vehicle offences	KEIE	122 930	103 401	91 648	100 374	72 804	71 070	67 494	66 561	64 363	67 404	73 852
Reckless and careless driving	KEIF	12 380	10 470	8 955	9 125	7 575	7 702	7 040	6 701	7 313	8 547	8 798
Drunk driving	KEIG	12 779	11 460	10 666	11 767	12 500	12 514	12 019	11 438	10 236	8 817	8 854
Speeding	KEIH	37 557	27 296	20 466	22 210	5 692	5 519	6 976	9 803	11 217	13 957	18 198
Unlawful use of vehicle	KEII	29 363	27 066	28 291	33 434	29 306	28 477	27 596	26 639	22 103	20 107	21 079
Vehicle defect offences	KEIJ	10 526	10 024	8 356	8 491	5 269	5 115	5 355	4 740	5 154	5 085	5 047
Other motor vehicle offences	KEIK	20 325	17 085	14 914	15 347	12 462	11 743	8 508	7 240	8 340	10 891	11 876
Total offences	KEHY	210 470	187 528	166 830	175 074	141 661	138 982	134 795	131 001	132 134	131 046	134 528
Total crimes and offences	KEHA	264 844	246 295	235 452	246 127	210 230	210 748	204 933	199 954	197 338	193 834	198 295

1 Only since 1980 has shoplifting been distinguished from 'Other theft'.

Source: Scottish Office Home and Health Department

4.14 Persons called to court[1]
Scotland

Number of persons

		1980	1981	1982	1983	1984	1985	1986	1987	1988[2]	1989	1990
Court procedure												
Solemn	KEIP	4 097	3 443	4 357	4 011	4 067	4 450	4 868	4 556	4 266	4 301	4 597
High Court	KEIQ	576	467	576	557	689	1 036	1 056	1 113	1 024	965	999
Sheriff Court (remit to High Court)	KEIR	101	85	94	122	76	150	127	139	31	80	93
Sheriff Court (other Solemn)	KEIS	3 420	2 891	3 687	3 332	3 302	3 264	3 685	3 304	3 211	3 256	3 505
Summary	KEIT	257 265	238 563	228 690	240 825	205 213	205 617	199 453	194 778	192 330	188 852	192 933
Sheriff Court	KEIU	172 403	143 379	137 575	142 389	106 710	108 628	104 749	100 756	99 441	100 028	98 120
District Court	KEIV	72 839	81 272	75 458	80 918	83 912	78 681	77 728	78 591	81 067	80 137	83 452
Stipendiary Magistrate Court	KEIW	12 023	13 912	15 657	17 518	14 591	18 308	16 976	15 431	11 822	8 687	11 361
Total called to court	KEIZ	261 362	242 006	233 047	244 836	209 280	210 067	204 321	199 334	196 596	193 153	197 530

1 Includes court not known.
2 Revised.

Source: Scottish Office Home and Health Department

Law enforcement

4.15 Persons with charge proved
Scotland

Number of persons

		1981	1982	1983	1984	1985	1986	1987	1988[1]	1989[1]	1990
Main penalty											
Absolute discharge	KEXA	939	792	717	512	527	465	457	563	575	637
Admonition or caution	KEXB	23 101	22 010	22 115	18 422	17 805	16 687	16 500	16 006	15 525	16 382
Probation	KEXC	2 639	2 682	2 757	2 985	3 136	2 931	3 131	3 207	3 715	4 122
Remit to children's hearing	KEXD	99	49	55	121	135	97	68	58	68	52
Community service order	KEXE	1 099	1 950	1 987	2 430	2 658	3 150	3 287	3 368	4 100	4 747
Fine	KEXF	187 308	173 856	183 021	150 047	149 323	144 547	140 752	138 516	133 765	135 104
Compensation order	KEXG	363	909	1 050	953	926	916	794	1 705	1 814	1 727
Guardianship order	KEXH	3	4	4	2	13	8	6	119	123	135
Prison	KEXI	7 060	8 995	9 280	8 965	10 066	9 859	9 293	9 515	9 098	8 838
Young offenders' institution	KEXJ	1 719	2 243	2 147	1 902	2 709	2 964	2 937	4 057	4 546	4 161
Borstal training	KEXK	691	955	894	–	–	–	–	–	–	–
Detention centre	KEXL	949	1 140	1 281	2 826	2 744	2 470	1 881	669	–	–
Detention of child	KEXM	77	88	107	68	68	52	43	34	20	27
Insane and hospital order	KEXN	48	45	83	95	130	130	127	42	24	15
Total persons with charge proved	KEXO	226 095	215 718	225 498	189 328	190 240	184 276	179 276	177 859	173 373	175 947

1 Revised.

Source: Scottish Office Home and Health Department

4.16 Persons with charge proved
Scotland

Number of persons

		1981	1982	1983	1984	1985	1986	1987	1988[3]	1989[3]	1990
Males	KEWA	199 327	191 184	198 705	166 976	166 681	160 708	158 376	152 527	147 660	149 545
Under 16	KEWB	822	642	645	463	495	367	307	261	216	179
16 to 20	KEWC	60 013	59 423	59 162	52 072	52 586	50 548	48 160	43 840	41 076	39 546
21 to 30	KEWD	60 583	60 513	64 856	55 973	57 493	57 282	58 568	57 706	56 272	58 892
Over 30	KEWE	77 909	70 606	74 042	49 616	47 625	46 296	47 343	47 687	46 472	48 220
Not known[1]	KEWF	..	..	..	8 852	8 482	6 215	3 998	3 033	3 624	2 708
Females	KEWG	24 313	22 151	24 097	20 065	20 698	21 535	19 116	22 472	23 006	24 194
Under 16	KEWH	73	25	45	40	21	25	23	17	10	12
16 to 20	KEWI	4 595	4 170	4 444	3 611	3 894	3 952	3 690	3 901	3 697	3 843
21 to 30	KEWJ	7 047	6 794	7 383	6 286	6 423	6 865	6 830	9 080	9 031	10 009
Over 30	KEWK	12 598	11 162	12 225	6 911	6 662	7 044	6 964	8 629	9 164	9 429
Not known[1]	KEWL	..	..	..	3 217	3 698	3 649	1 609	845	1 104	901
Males and Females	KEWM	223 640	213 335	222 802	187 041	187 379	182 243	177 492	174 999	170 666	173 739
Under 16	KEWN	895	667	690	503	516	392	330	278	226	191
16 to 20	KEWO	64 608	63 593	63 606	55 683	56 480	54 500	51 850	47 741	44 773	43 389
21 to 30	KEWP	67 630	67 307	72 239	62 259	63 916	64 147	65 398	66 786	65 303	68 901
Over 30	KEWQ	90 507	81 768	86 267	56 527	54 287	53 340	54 307	56 316	55 636	57 649
Not known[1]	KEWR	..	..	..	12 069	12 180	9 864	5 607	3 878	4 728	3 609
Companies	KEWS	2 455	2 383	2 696	2 287	2 861	2 033	1 784	1 813	2 210	2 023
Total persons with charge proved[2]	KEWT	226 095	215 718	225 498	189 328	190 240	184 276	179 276	177 859	173 373	175 947

1 Prior to 1984, 'Not known' was included in the over 30 total.
2 Includes sex not known.
3 Revised.

Source: Scottish Office Home and Health Department

Law enforcement

4.17 Penal establishments: average daily population and receptions
Scotland

Number

		1981	1982	1983	1984	1985	1986	1987	1988	1989	1990	1991
Average daily population												
Male	KEPB	4 383	4 755	4 917	4 621	5 097	5 394	5 259	5 057	4 838	4 587	4 696
Female	KEPC	135	136	135	132	177	194	187	172	147	137	143
Total	KEPA	4 518	4 891	5 052	4 753	5 273	5 588	5 446	5 229	4 986	4 724	4 839
Analysis by type of custody												
Remand	KEPD	746	844	863	942	1 092	1 017	938	844	770	751	770
Persons under sentence: total	KEPE	3 769	4 044	4 183	3 807	4 178	4 570	4 509	4 385	4 216	3 973	4 069
Adult prisoners[1,4]	KEPF	2 556	2 718	2 851	2 753	3 140	3 448	3 473	3 434	3 342	3 202	3 322
Young offenders[1,4]	KEPI	601	641	578	607	778	913	845	817	814	707	684
Borstal inmates	KEPL	451	493	568	175	2	–	–	–	–	–	–
Detention centre inmates	KEPM	122	142	136	217	210	161	143	85	–	–	–
Persons recalled from supervision/licence	KEPN	33	42	42	36	34	35	31	28	33	40	39
Others	KEPO	6	7	9	18	13	13	17	17	21	13	12
Persons sentenced by court martial	KEPP	2	2	5	3	3	1	–	3	6	11	12
Civil prisoners	KEPQ	1	1	1	1	1	1	1	1	1	1	1
Receptions to penal establishments												
Total[2]												
Remand	KEPR	13 550	16 072	15 286	16 048	18 985	18 107	17 111	15 000	14 281	15 169	13 142
Male	KEPS	12 791	15 265	14 400	15 141	18 088	17 114	16 213	14 225	13 492	14 324	12 360
Female	KEPT	759	807	886	907	897	993	898	775	789	845	782
Persons under sentence: total	KEPU	15 539	20 522	20 183	19 955	24 532	23 220	22 186	20 540	19 484	17 134	18 226
Male	KEPV	14 863	19 749	19 276	19 164	23 310	22 020	20 987	19 427	18 466	16 235	17 033
Female	KEPW	676	773	907	791	1 222	1 200	1 199	1 113	1 018	899	1 193
Imprisoned:												
directly	KEPX	6 311	7 992	7 925	7 634	8 864	8 598	7 975	7 984	7 619	7 551	7 951
in default of fine	KEPY	5 635	7 773	7 572	6 941	8 626	8 139	8 049	7 234	6 801	5 182	6 336
in default of compensation order	KEPZ	1	8	2	1	1	24	2	46	49	23	6
Sentenced to young offenders institution:												
directly	KEQA	1 221	1 542	1 463	1 733	2 359	2 593	2 064	2 160	2 651	2 719	2 356
in default of fine	KEQB	1 120	1 679	1 757	1 903	2 779	2 398	2 882	2 466	2 353	1 653	1 573
in default of compensation order	KEQC	–	1	1	1	2	2	3	6	9	3	2
Sentenced to borstal training	KEQD	490	630	544	–	–	–	–	–	–	–	–
Sentenced to detention centre[3]	KEQE	729	862	889	1 741	1 901	1 462	1 210	642	–	–	–
Recalled to Young Offenders Institutions/ from Borstal supervision	KEQF	31	33	28	1	–	1	1	1	1	1	1
Other sentences	KEQG	1	2	2	–	–	1	–	1	1	2	1
Persons sentenced by court martial	KEQH	10	10	12	5	6	4	11	10	8	10	1
Civil prisoners	KEQI	14	13	15	17	21	13	18	8	15	21	–

1 From 1983 onwards persons detained under Section 205(2) of the Criminal Procedure (Scotland) at 1975 are included as adults or young offenders according to the type of establishment in which they were held. For earlier years they are all included as young offenders.

2 Total receptions cannot be calculated by adding together receptions in each category because there is double counting. This arises because when a person is received on remand and then under sentence in relation to the same set of charges, he is counted in both categories.

3 From 1 November 1988 detention centre sentences were no longer available.

4 Figures were previously provided showing the average daily number in custody for fine default. These figures were found to be unreliable and are now not shown separately.

Source: Scottish Office Home and Health Department

Law enforcement

4.18 Expenditure on penal establishments
Scotland
Years ended 31 March

£ thousand

		1980/81	1981/82	1982/83	1983/84	1984/85	1985/86	1986/87	1987/88	1988/89	1989/90	1990/91
Central charges and costs of staff	KEQP	31 565	36 955	40 661	42 586	46 009	51 575	58 081	70 700	80 331	85 569	91 187
Inmate maintenance	KEQQ	4 267	4 630	5 048	5 686	5 825	6 934	6 295	7 116	7 314	7 148	8 080
Materials for production and training	KEQR	2 605	2 076	2 627	2 372	2 210	2 565	2 459	2 551	2 635	3 229	3 101
Miscellaneous	KEQS	1 490	1 807	2 139	2 355	2 746	3 117	3 362	4 099	4 210	4 746	5 682
Maintenance of establishments	KEQT	2 469	3 273	3 917	4 568	5 065	5 920	5 684	6 345	8 996	7 204	7 305
Capital expenditure	KEQU	4 410	5 339	4 752	7 227	12 641	12 761	7 182	7 474	9 841	14 760	13 088
Cost of central administration	KEQV	1 547	1 865	1 954	2 006	2 106	2 141	2 248	3 883	4 100	4 800	5 800
Total	KEQW	48 353	54 945	61 152	66 800	76 602	84 813	85 311	101 978	117 427	128 426	134 243
Receipts from sales, etc	KEQX	2 769	2 050	2 583	1 957	2 053	2 023	3 950	1 981	2 254	2 127	2 535
Net total	KEQY	45 584	52 895	58 569	64 843	74 549	82 790	81 361	99 997	115 173	126 299	131 708
Average daily number of inmates	KEQZ	4 822	4 455	5 036	4 956	4 823	5 398	5 564	5 421	5 168	4 886	4 739

Source: Scottish Office Home and Health Department

4.19 Offences known to police, proceedings taken and results of proceedings
Northern Ireland

Number

		1981	1982	1983	1984	1985	1986	1987	1988	1989	1990	1991
Offences known to police[1]	KEUP	59 157	62 020	63 984	66 779	64 584	68 255	63 860	55 890	55 147	57 198	63 492
Indictable offences[1]												
Persons proceeded against	KEUB	8 854	8 864	9 007	8 665	9 308	11 245	11 609	10 602	9 864	10 569	10 053
Tried in Courts of Summary Jurisdiction	KEUC	7 086	6 872	7 138	7 037	7 277	9 386	9 686	9 116	8 497	9 147	8 711
Tried at Crown Courts	KEUD	1 768	1 992	1 869	1 928	2 031	1 859	1 923	1 469	1 367	1 422	1 342
Results of proceedings:												
Found guilty	KEUE	7 932	8 244	8 317	8 077	8 568	10 312	10 649	9 571	8 922	9 320	8 893
Absolute discharge	KEUF	204	178	115	74	76	109	109	99	91	103	81
Probation order	KEUG	638	600	580	547	649	775	668	740	720	812	742
Conditional discharge	KEUH	1 289	1 403	1 461	1 322	1 409	1 713	1 717	1 581	1 345	1 377	1 482
Committed to training schools	KEUI	270	181	187	179	161	246	210	154	160	142	169
Fine	KEUJ	1 811	1 904	2 000	2 083	2 044	2 830	2 696	2 555	2 543	2 786	2 294
Sentenced to:												
Imprisonment[2]	KEUL	1 724	1 813	1 806	1 625	1 809	1 976	2 149	1 870	1 660	1 659	1 772
Suspended sentence	KEUM	1 354	1 491	1 488	1 472	1 687	1 829	2 108	1 766	1 780	1 684	1 567
Otherwise dealt with	KEUN	642	674	680	775	733	834	992	806	1 623	757	786
Non-indictable offences[1]												
Persons proceeded against	KEUO	31 641	33 555	34 687	35 137	37 784	34 003	36 581	36 941	33 472	33 758	26 353
Results of proceedings:												
Found guilty	KEUQ	30 181	31 505	32 444	33 171	35 601	32 103	34 273	34 624	31 209	31 500	24 410
Absolute discharge	KEUR	1 482	1 555	1 290	1 166	1 521	1 359	1 551	1 562	1 215	1 173	769
Probation order	KEUS	201	169	157	139	177	111	116	97	130	127	100
Conditional discharge	KEUT	1 037	1 201	1 134	958	1 057	907	936	1 191	728	642	673
Committed to training schools	KEUU	94	98	77	66	58	37	23	18	18	15	21
Fine	KEUV	24 954	26 267	27 433	28 738	29 075	27 984	29 804	30 250	27 866	28 236	21 469
Sentenced to:												
Imprisonment[3]	KEUX	1 745	1 704	1 844	1 601	1 998	1 194	1 777	943	771	831	836
Otherwise dealt with	KEUY	668	511	509	503	1 715	511	66	564	481	476	542

1 Offences known to the police consist mainly of indictable offences and include some hybrid offences. From 1975 to 1981 hybrid offences were included under non-indictable offences; for 1982 onwards, they are included under indictable offences. Indictable offences also include motoring offences.

2 Includes those awarded periods of detention in young offenders centres.

3 Includes those awarded periods of detention in the young offenders centres and those awarded suspended sentences.

Source: Northern Ireland Office

Law enforcement

4.20 Persons found guilty: analysis by type of offence
Northern Ireland

Number

		1981	1982	1983	1984	1985	1986	1987	1988	1989	1990	1991
All offences	KEVA	38 113	39 749	40 762	41 248	44 169	43 249	44 922	44 197	40 131	40 820	33 303
Indictable offences[1]	KEVB	8 291	8 244	8 318	8 077	8 568	10 312	10 649	9 573	8 902	9 320	8 893
Burglary and robbery	KEVC	2 556	2 514	2 619	2 535	2 562	2 318	2 806	1 849	1 636	1 582	1 370
Fraud[2] and forgery	KEVD	341	351	382	362	440	467	728	687	783	699	648
Handling stolen goods	KEVE	390	390	406	476	419	413	417	347	398	482	455
Theft	KEVF	2 901	3 023	2 962	2 944	3 426	3 697	3 690	3 267	2 900	2 917	2 974
Sexual offences	KEVG	134	119	124	151	170	189	210	228	226	275	193
Offences against the person: total	KEVH	642	769	771	772	818	1 362	1 534	1 491	1 424	1 750	1 634
Murder	KEVI	34	21	15	10	39	25	45	30	15	9	11
Manslaughter	KEVJ	22	22	13	15	16	20	15	22	11	10	5
Wounding	KEVK	555	681	698	705	723	491	81	94	69	153	121
Other offences against the person	KEVL	31	45	45	42	40	826	1 393	1 345	1 329	1 578	1 497
Other offences	KEVM	1 327	1 078	1 054	837	733	1 866	1 264	1 704	1 535	1 615	1 619
Non-indictable offences[1]	KEVN	29 822	31 505	32 444	33 171	35 601	32 103	34 273	34 624	31 229	31 500	24 410
Assaults	KEVO	1 230	1 454	1 555	1 501	1 608	943	985	1 015	1 054	1 021	1 011
Betting and gaming	KEVP	21	81	104	54	40	23	31	71	18	24	22
Public Order Offences	KEVQ	3 017	3 038	3 212	3 072	3 391	3 205	2 962	3 034	2 186	1 819	1 779
Intoxication Liquor Laws:												
Drunkenness	KEVR	284	259	317	322	274	244	189	282	227	127	138
Other offences	KEVS	474	538	567	454	437	381	541	558	486	331	401
Malicious damage	KEVT	764	739	767	737	897	264	251	151	124	116	62
Offences by prostitutes	KEVU	11	8	37	44	39	35	50	53	52	60	43
Traffic offences	KEVV	22 585	23 459	24 145	25 417	27 255	26 010	28 201	28 553	26 114	27 207	20 133
Vagrancy Acts	KEVW	27	25	22	10	4	7	9	11	42	6	9
Wireless Telegraphy Acts	KEVX	1	–	–	1	–	32	–	–	–	23	28
Education Acts[3]	KEVY	–	–	–	–	–	–	–	–	–	–	–
Game Laws	KEVZ	2	7	15	12	2	10	5	13	–	–	–
Labour Laws[3]	KEFW	3	5	1	5	–	–	–	–	–	–	–
Railway offences[3]	KEFX	–	3	–	–	–	–	–	–	–	–	–
Revenue Laws[3]	KEFY	45	65	71	27	17	–	–	–	–	–	–
Other offences	KEFZ	1 358	1 824	1 631	1 515	1 637	949	1 049	883	924	766	784

1 From 1975 to 1981 hybrid offences were included under non-indictable offences. From 1982 they are included under indictable offences.
2 Including offences in connection with bankruptcy.
3 These offence headings are brought to court by other government departments and are not collated by police.

Source: Northern Ireland Office

4.21 Juveniles found guilty of offences
Northern Ireland

Number

		1982	1983	1984	1985	1986	1987	1988	1989	1990	1991
Juveniles found guilty											
All offences	KEBA	2 052	1 784	1 616	1 523	1 866	1 373	1 199	1 019	978	875
Indictable offences	KEBB	1 132	1 009	978	921	1 169	983	909	752	748	693
Handling stolen goods	KEBC	49	45	41	28	43	14	40	17	40	32
Theft[2]	KEBD	379	296	354	390	487	421	417	291	289	296
Burglary and robbery	KEBE	518	532	469	404	385	285	270	239	242	201
Sexual offences	KAHF	7	5	3	7	22	12	15	14	17	8
Fraud and forgery	KEBF	12	12	17	12	10	21	6	10	10	10
Offences against the person	KEBG	39	28	32	26	47	55	57	33	44	38
Other offences	KEBH	128	91	62	54	175	189	144	148	106	108
Non-indictable offences	KEBI	920	775	638	602	697	390	290	267	230	182
Assaults	KEBJ	100	124	113	105	94	78	80	82	59	53
Offences connected with motor vehicles	KEBK	374	247	248	213	370	128	100	81	92	71
Malicious damage	KEBL	123	139	77	120	28	29	9	10	9	3
Disorderly behaviour	KEBM	258	168	127	103	123	90	49	47	47	41
Offences against the Education Act	KEBN	..	..	..	..	..	..	..	..	–	–
Other offences	KEBO	65	97	73	61	82	65	52	47	23	14
Disposal by Courts											
Total dealt with	KEBP	2 052	1 784	1 616	1 523	1 866	1 374	1 196	1 019	978	875
Absolute discharge	KEBQ	84	76	28	24	40	23	19	12	15	10
Conditional discharge	KEBR	667	572	493	449	454	375	264	215	221	222
Placed on probation	KEBS	354	275	291	294	304	221	249	213	229	174
Fine	KEBT	306	310	307	282	548	270	202	174	135	91
Remand home order	KEBU	10	23	18	21	16	3	3	2	8	10
Training school order	KEBV	248	232	214	189	259	223	166	173	144	174
Otherwise dealt with	KEBY	383	296	265	264	245	259	293	230	226	194

1 Persons under 17 years of age.
2 Including unauthorised taking of motor vehicles.

Source: Northern Ireland Office

Law enforcement

4.22 Prisons, Young Offenders Centres and Borstal Institutions: receptions and average population[1]
Northern Ireland

Number

		1982	1983	1984	1985	1986	1987	1988	1989	1990	1991
Receptions:											
Reception of untried prisoners	KEOA	2 159	2 175	2 179	2 008	2 250	2 138	1 853	1 795	1 773	1 851
Reception of sentenced prisoners:											
Imprisonment without the option of a fine[2]	KEOB	1 198	1 156	1 038	1 139	1 107	1 288	1 136	1 029	952	974
Imprisonment in default of payment of a fine	KEOC	415	620	731	1 091	1 448	1 379	1 493	1 291	1 264	1 282
Total	KEOD	1 613	1 776	1 769	2 230	2 555	2 667	2 629	2 320	2 216	2 256
Reception into Young Offender Centres:[1]											
Detention without the option of a fine	KEOE	632	651	600	605	583	577	437	422	371	348
Detention in default of payment of a fine	KEOF	207	305	399	450	580	562	457	378	309	356
Total	KEOG	839	956	999	1 055	1 163	1 139	894	800	680	704
Other receptions:											
Sentenced to Borstal training[3]	KEOH	–	–	–	–	–	–	–	–	–	–
Civil committals	KEOI	43	22	22	22	16	24	50	46	21	17
Persons detained or interned	KEOJ	–	–	–	–	–	–	–	–	–	–
Other receptions	KEOK	–	–	–	–	–	–	–	–	–	–
Total	KEOL	43	22	22	22	16	24	50	46	21	17
Daily average population:											
Total	KEOM	2 481	2 453	2 248	2 043	1 900	1 947	1 901	1 815	1 785	1 796
Unconvicted[4]	KEON	428	430	404	338	310	283	270	307	361	349
Convicted	KEOP	2 053	2 023	1 844	1 705	1 590	1 664	1 631	1 508	1 424	1 447

1 1980 was is the first full year of operation of the Young Offenders Centres
2 Includes those detained under Section 73 of the Children and Young Persons (NI) Act 1968.
3 Borstal institutions closed down in October 1980.
4 Prisoners on remand or awaiting trial and prisoners committed by civil process.

Source: Northern Ireland Office

5 Education

In general the education services of the United Kingdom are not subject to detailed central control. Standards are maintained by an Inspectorate with advisory functions having access to all institutions except the universities and related bodies. Within this framework detailed control is exercised by local education authorities or by various forms of independent governing bodies, in association with the teaching staff. In all sectors, such matters as engaging teachers and selection of textbooks and curricula are part of these detailed local responsibilities.

The four government departments dealing with education statistics are:

Department of Education and Science:
  which deals with all sectors of education in England, and with the Government's responsibilities towards universities in Great Britain.
Welsh Office, Education Department:
  which deals with schools and (from April 1978) higher and further education in Wales, excluding matters connected with universities and with the qualifications, probation, remuneration, superannuation and misconduct of teachers.
Scottish Office Education Department:
  schools and further education in Scotland.
Department of Education, Northern Ireland:
  schools, further education and universities in Northern Ireland.

The Universities Funding Council (UFC) is responsible for administering funds made available to it by the Secretary of State for Education and Science to provide financial support for education and research in universities in Great Britain and for advising, when necessary, the Departments of Education and Agriculture in Northern Ireland on matters relating to universities in Northern Ireland.

The Polytechnics and Colleges Funding Council (PCFC) which came into being on 1 April 1989 has a remit for England only. It performs a similar function to the UFC with regard to those polytechnics and colleges which come within the PCFC sector. The PCFC also plans and funds certain courses in English colleges remaining under LEA control.

Statistics for the separate systems obtaining in England, Wales, Scotland and Northern Ireland are collected and processed separately in accordance with the particular needs of the responsible Departments and, particularly where there are structural differences, the assembly of statistics covering the United Kingdom as a single unit presents considerable problems and in some fields is impossible at present.

Stages of education

There are three main stages of education: primary, secondary, and further and higher education. The first two stages are compulsory for all children between the ages of five and sixteen years and the transition from primary to secondary education is usually made at the age of eleven. The third stage of education is voluntary and includes all education provided after full-time schooling ends.

Primary education

Primary education provides for pupils aged five to eleven. The great majority of public sector primary schools take both boys and girls in mixed classes.

Middle schools

In England middle schools take children from first schools and generally lead on, in turn, to comprehensive upper schools. They cover varying age ranges between eight and fourteen. Depending on their individual age range they are deemed either primary or secondary by Order of the Secretary of State for Education and Science or (for age range nine to thirteen) by choice of the local education authority.

Secondary education

Provision of secondary education in an area may include any combination of types of schools. The pattern is a reflection of historical circumstance and of the policy adopted by the local education authority. There is a growing trend to comprehensive schools, on a variety of patterns as to forms of organisation and the age range of the pupils attending. In their 'pure' form, comprehensive schools admit pupils without reference to ability and aptitude, and cater for all the children in a neighbourhood. In 1989/90, some 90% of secondary schools in England were comprehensive. Scotland has some schools which are part comprehensive/part selective; these are comprehensive in intake but selective as regards level of courses offered (typically not beyond 'O' grade).

Special schools, both day and boarding, provide education for handicapped children who cannot be educated satisfactorily in an ordinary school. Hospital special schools provide education for children who are spending a period in hospital.

Further education

The term 'further education' covers post-school education below higher education. It can include study of courses undertaken by those staying on in school, eg A-level GCE.

Higher education

The term higher education includes students on all courses provided by universities (including the Open University, but not the independent University of Buckingham), and courses at polytechnics, Scottish central institutions, and other institutions of further and higher education which lead to qualifications of a standard higher than A-level GCE, BTEC National Certificate/Diploma or Scottish Higher Certificate.

Education

5.1 Number of schools[1] or departments by type and establishments of higher and further education
Academic years[2]

		1980/81	1981/82	1982/83	1983/84	1984/85	1985/86	1986/87	1987/88	1988/89	1989/90	1990[12]/91
United Kingdom: Public sector schools												
Nursery	KBFK	1 251	1 254	1 259	1 260	1 257	1 262	1 271	1 298	1 312	1 337	1 364
Primary	KBFA	26 504	26 072	25 755	25 326	24 993	24 756	24 609	24 482	24 344	24 268	24 135
Secondary	KBFF	5 542	5 506	5 437	5 328	5 262	5 161	5 091	5 020	4 894	4 876	4 790
Non-maintained[3]	KBFU	2 640	2 635	2 637	2 619	2 599	2 538	2 544	2 546	2 542	2 492	2 508
Special	KBFP	2 011	1 994	1 989	1 972	1 949	1 923	1 915	1 900	1 873	1 851	1 824
Universities (including Open University)	KAHG	46	46	46	46	46	46	46	46	46	46	48
PCFC Sector: Polytechnics[4]	KAHH	31	31	31	31	30	30	30	30	30	30	32
Other[5]	KAHI	..	..	..	..	..	..	..	..	..	56	53
Other HE/FE: Vocational colleges and C of Ed												
Public sector[6]	KAHJ	744	729	729	728	693	697	677	673	675	594	587
Assisted[7]	KAHK	62	58	57	57	56	56	52	51	51	25	26
Adult education centres (England and Wales)	KAHL	4 628	4 318	4 542	4 513	4 227	2 874[8]	2 523	2 632	2 782	2 669	2 656
England: Public sector schools												
Nursery	KBAK	588	582	575	565	561	560	558	558	559	564	566
Primary	KBAA	21 018	20 650	20 384	20 020	19 734	19 549	19 432	19 319	19 232	19 162	19 047
Secondary	KBAF	4 654	4 622	4 553	4 444	4 382	4 286	4 221	4 153	4 035	3 976	3 897
Non-maintained	KBAU	2 342	2 340	2 344	2 333	2 313	2 274	2 276	2 273	2 271	2 283	2 289
Special	KBAP	1 593	1 571	1 562	1 548	1 529	1 493	1 470	1 443	1 414	1 398	1 380
Universities (including Open University)	KAHM	35	35	35	35	35	35	35	35	35	35	37
PCFC Sector: Polytechnics	KAHN	29	29	29	29	29	29	29	29	29	29	31
Other[5]	KAHO	..	..	..	..	..	..	..	..	..	56	53
Other HE/FE establishments												
Maintained and assisted	KAHP	468	459	450	439	437	436	422	417	415	375	370
Grant-aided	KAHQ	35	34	33	33	32	31	29	29	30	6	6
Adult education centres	KAHR	4 067	3 747	3 958	3 938	3 684	2 616[8]	2 718	2 412	2 494	2 399	2 315
Wales: Public sector schools												
Nursery	KBBK	69	64	64	65	61	59	59	58	56	55	54
Primary	KBBA	1 908	1 873	1 844	1 821	1 796	1 774	1 762	1 753	1 743	1 729	1 717
Secondary	KBBF	239	241	238	236	237	237	234	233	232	231	230
Non-maintained	KBBU	72	71	73	70	67	69	69	67	66	67	71
Special	KBBP	73	73	71	69	68	67	65	65	64	62	61
Universities	KAHS	1	1	1	1	1	1	1	1	1	1	1
Polytechnics	KAHT	1	1	1	1	1	1	1	1	1	1	1
Other major establishments												
Maintained and assisted	KAHU	44	43	43	43	43	39	39	39	40	36	36
Grant-aided	KAHV	1	1	1	1	1	1	1	1	1	1	1
Adult education centres	KAHW	561	571	584	575	543	258[8]	205	220	288	270	341
Scotland: Public sector schools												
Nursery	KBDK	515	527	537	546	551	559	568	596	612	633	659
Primary	KBDA	2 522	2 499	2 489	2 461	2 443	2 425	2 417	2 418	2 384	2 378	2 372
Secondary	KBDF	444	439	442	444	440	440	440	438	434	429	424
Non-maintained[3]	KBDU	138	136	132	127	131	106	111	118	118	123	131
Special[3]	KBDP	319	324	330	330	328	339	356	346	349	345	337
Universities	KALX	8	8	8	8	8	8	8	8	8	8	8
Vocational further education colleges												
Education authority												
Day	KAHY	65	64	67	64	52	50	49	49	49	46	46
Evening	KAHZ	109	105	111	124	104	115	109	111	114	110	110
Central institutions	KAIA	14	14	14	14	14	16	16	15	15	13	13
Voluntary bodies	KAIB	–	–	–	–	–	–	–	–	–	–	–
Colleges of education	KAIC	10	7	7	7	7	7	5	5	5	5	5
Northern Ireland: Public sector schools												
Nursery	KBEK	79	81	83	84	84	84	86	86	85	85	85
Primary	KBEA	1 056	1 050	1 038	1 024	1 020	1 008	998	992	985	999	999
Secondary[9]	KBEF	205	204	204	204	203	198	196	196	193	240	239
Non-maintained[10]	KBEU	88	88	88	89	88	89	87	88	87	19	17
Special[11]	KBEP	26	26	26	25	24	24	24	46	46	46	46
Universities	KAID	2	2	2	2	2	2	2	2	2	2	2
Colleges of education	KAIE	3	3	3	3	3	2	2	2	2	2	2
Polytechnics	KAIF	1	1	1	1	–	–	–	–	–	–	–
Further education colleges	KAIG	26	26	26	26	26	26	26	26	26	26	24

1 Schools (excluding independent) in Scotland and Northern Ireland with more than one department have been counted once for each department.
2 Schools are counted at January except for Scotland and Wales when the count is at September. Further education establishments are counted at 1 November - England and Wales, October - Scotland and Northern Ireland. University establishments at 31 December.
3 Including for Scotland grant-aided nursery schools.
4 Includes the Polytechnic of Wales.
5 56 Institutions transferred from LEA maintained and grant-aided sector wef 89/90.
6 Maintained and assisted colleges in England and Wales, education authority colleges in Scotland, Stranmills College of Education and education authority / education and library board colleges in Northern Ireland.
7 Direct grant colleges in England and Wales, central institutions, voluntary bodies and colleges of education in Scotland, voluntary colleges of education in Northern Ireland.
8 Excludes youth clubs and centres; these were included in years prior to 1985-86.
9 Wef 89/90 includes Voluntary Grammar Schools formerly allocated to the independent sector.
10 Excludes Voluntary Grammar Schools allocated to the maintained sector wef 89/90
11 Wef 1987/88 includes 22 schools which were the responsibility of Northern Ireland Department of Health and Social Security up to 31 March 1987.
12 Provisional.

Source: Education Departments

Education

5.2 Pupils in school by age and sex: number and as a percentage of the population
United Kingdom
All schools at January [1]

		1980[2]	1981	1982[3]	1983	1984	1985	1986[4]	1987[5]	1988	1989	1990	1991[9]
Age at the beginning of January													
Number (thousands)													
England	KBIA	8 933	8 720	8 502	8 276	8 096	7 956	7 830	7 721	7 610	7 553	7 557	7 617
Wales	KBIB	558	545	531	519	510	503	495	487	481	480	480	482
Scotland	KBIC	1 034	1 005	975	945	918	894	..	..	840	828	821	821
Northern Ireland	KBID	367	363	359	354	351	349	346	343	341	341	340	341
United Kingdom	KBIE	10 892	10 633	10 367	10 094	9 876	9 702	9 565	9 392	9 273	9 203	9 199	9 260
Boys and girls													
2 - 4 [6]	KBIF	804	792	794	823	887	915	917	900	912	937	979	1 012
5 - 10	KBIG	4 959	4 752	4 542	4 302	4 140	4 085	4 096	4 134	4 180	4 252	4 312	4 346
11	KBIH	919	903	869	879	825	774	737	692	668	643	658	714
12 - 14	KBII	2 822	2 777	2 727	2 660	2 631	2 565	2 487	2 314	2 199	2 097	2 011	1 975
Total 2 - 14	KBIJ	9 503	9 224	8 932	8 664	8 482	8 340	8 237	8 041	7 960	7 929	7 961	8 046
15	KBIK	943	940	924	903	886	872	845	864	818	764	726	689
16	KBIL	266	280	306	312	297	289	286	285	296	297	289	297
17	KBIM	160	168	181	188	182	174	169	174	171	185	194	197
18 and over	KBIN	19	21	24	27	28	28	28	27	27	27	29	32
Boys													
14	KBIO	488	481	475	465	457	444	452	421	398	376	358	344
15	KBIP	483	481	472	462	453	446	433	443	420	393	373	354
16	KBIQ	130	136	149	152	145	142	141	141	146	146	141	145
17	KBIR	83	85	91	94	91	88	86	88	86	93	96	96
18 and over	KBIS	12	13	14	15	16	16	16	15	15	15	16	17
Girls													
14	KBIT	464	457	450	442	435	420	428	397	375	356	339	326
15	KBIU	461	459	452	440	433	425	412	421	397	372	354	335
16	KBIV	136	144	157	161	152	147	145	143	150	151	147	152
17	KBIW	78	82	90	93	91	86	84	87	85	93	98	100
18 and over	KBIX	8	8	10	12	12	12	12	12	12	12	14	15
As a percentage of population [7]													
Boys and girls													
2 - 4	KBIY	*40.8*	*40.4*	*39.6*	*39.2*	*40.9*	*42.2*	*42.6*	*41.9*	*41.7*	*42.2*	*43.3*	*44.1*
5 - 10	KBIZ	*104.3*	*100.7*	*100.6*	*100.6*	*100.5*	*100.2*	*99.9*	*99.8*	*99.4*	*99.1*	*98.9*	*98.9*
11	KBJA	*103.6*	*101.4*	*100.6*	*100.8*	*101.6*	*101.6*	*102.5*	*100.2*	*100.1*	*100.1*	*99.6*	*99.0*
12 - 14	KBJB	*103.3*	*100.5*	*100.4*	*100.2*	*100.3*	*100.6*	*101.7*	*100.6*	*100.9*	*100.6*	*100.1*	*99.8*
15	KBJC	*100.0*	*97.7*	*98.5*	*97.9*	*98.1*	*97.9*	*97.3*	*98.8*	*100.0*	*99.7*	*100.3*	*99.1*
16	KBJD	*28.0*	*29.0*	*31.7*	*33.1*	*32.2*	*31.9*	*32.1*	*32.9*	*33.7*	*36.3*	*37.5*	*41.0*
17	KBJE	*17.1*	*17.8*	*18.7*	*19.4*	*19.3*	*18.9*	*18.8*	*19.5*	*19.7*	*21.1*	*23.6*	*25.5*
18 and over [8]	KBJF	*2.1*	*2.3*	*2.5*	*2.8*	*2.9*	*3.0*	*3.0*	*3.0*	*3.1*	*3.1*	*3.3*	*3.8*
Boys													
14	KBJG	*102.7*	*100.0*	*100.1*	*100.4*	*100.2*	*100.0*	*100.6*	*100.2*	*100.8*	*101.2*	*100.6*	*99.8*
15	KBJH	*99.8*	*97.3*	*97.9*	*97.2*	*97.7*	*97.7*	*97.4*	*98.6*	*100.6*	*99.4*	*100.1*	*99.0*
16	KBJI	*26.7*	*27.4*	*30.0*	*31.4*	*30.5*	*30.5*	*30.9*	*31.7*	*32.5*	*34.7*	*35.7*	*38.8*
17	KBJJ	*17.3*	*17.6*	*18.3*	*18.8*	*18.8*	*18.5*	*18.5*	*19.2*	*19.4*	*20.6*	*22.7*	*24.3*
18 and over [8]	KBJK	*2.5*	*2.8*	*2.9*	*3.0*	*3.2*	*3.3*	*3.3*	*3.2*	*3.3*	*3.3*	*3.5*	*3.9*
Girls													
14	KBJL	*103.1*	*100.2*	*100.5*	*100.6*	*100.5*	*99.9*	*100.5*	*100.1*	*100.9*	*101.3*	*100.4*	*100.0*
15	KBJM	*100.4*	*98.1*	*99.1*	*98.3*	*98.5*	*98.2*	*97.8*	*98.9*	*100.0*	*100.0*	*100.5*	*99.2*
16	KBJN	*29.4*	*30.6*	*33.5*	*35.2*	*33.9*	*33.4*	*33.4*	*34.2*	*35.0*	*38.0*	*39.5*	*43.1*
17	KBJO	*17.1*	*17.8*	*19.1*	*19.8*	*19.9*	*19.2*	*19.0*	*19.9*	*20.0*	*21.6*	*24.6*	*26.8*
18 and over [8]	KBJP	*1.8*	*1.8*	*2.2*	*2.5*	*2.5*	*2.7*	*2.8*	*2.7*	*2.9*	*2.8*	*3.2*	*3.7*

1 In Wales the school census date is September whereas that for the rest of the United Kingdom remains at January. In Scotland, figures are at the previous September (the same academic session).
2 Age at 31 August from 1980 onwards.
3 For non-maintained schools in England, pupils' ages have been estimated.
4 Estimated; these figures include 1984-85 data for Scotland.
5 Estimated; these figures include 1987-88 data for Scotland.
6 Each part - time pupil (aged 2 - 4, but also small numbers aged 5 in Scotland attending nursery schools) has been counted as one.
7 The Registrars General estimates of resident population have sometimes been slightly below the number of children found to have attended school.
8 As a percentage of the 18 years age - group.
9 Provisional.

Source: Education Departments

Education

5.3 Number of pupils and teachers: pupil/teacher ratios
United Kingdom
At January [1]

Thousands

		1980	1981	1982	1983	1984	1985	1986	1987	1988	1989	1990	1991[7]
All schools or departments[2]													
Total													
Pupils													
Full-time and full-time equivalent of part-time	KBCA	10 770.9	10 525.3	10 234.7	9 949.7	9 724.7	9 544.3	9 384.8[5]	9 245.6[6]	9 100.7	9 022.7	9 010.0	9 062.3
Teachers[3]	KBCB	590.2	579.1	568.1	559.6	554.1	546.0	540.3[5]	537.4[6]	531.1	528.0	532.5	526.8
Pupils per teacher:													
United Kingdom[3]	KBCC	18.2	18.2	18.0	17.8	17.6	17.5	17.4[5]	17.2[6]	17.1	17.1	16.9	17.2
England	KBCD	18.4	18.2	18.1	17.9	17.6	17.6	17.4	17.2	17.2	17.1	17.0	17.3
Wales	KBCE	18.6	18.5	18.5	18.3	18.1	18.2	18.2	18.2	18.0	18.1	18.1	18.2
Scotland	KBCF	16.8	16.7	16.7	16.6	16.4	16.2	..	..	15.8	15.7	15.3	15.2
Northern Ireland	KBCG	19.0	18.9	18.9	18.7	18.7	18.6	18.5	18.4	18.4	18.3	18.3	18.1
Public sector schools or departments													
Nursery													
Pupils													
Full-time and full-time equivalent of part-time	KBFM	54.9	55.5	55.8	56.3	57.2	57.3	56.9[5]	57.5[6]	57.6	58.4	59.4	60.4
Teachers[3]	KBFN	2.5	2.6	2.6	2.6	2.6	2.6	2.6[5]	2.7[6]	2.7	2.7	2.7	2.8
Pupils per teacher	KBFO	21.6	21.5	21.6	21.8	21.7	21.8	21.7[5]	21.2[6]	21.4	21.6	21.8	21.6
Primary													
Pupils													
Full-time and full-time equivalent of part-time	KBFB	5 317.1	5 087.3	4 870.0	4 659.0	4 549.7	4 513.6	4 520.8	4 550.3	4 598.9	4 662.8	4 747.7	4 812.3
Teachers[3]	KBFD	237.0	227.8	218.7	211.1	207.1	205.0	205.8	208.7	210.1	213.3	219.0	219.2
Pupils per teacher	KBFE	22.4	22.3	22.3	22.1	22.0	22.0	22.0	21.8	21.9	21.9	21.7	22.0
Secondary													
Pupils													
Full-time and full-time equivalent of part-time	KBFG	4 636.2	4 606.3	4 558.5	4 493.6	4 384.2	4 243.6	4 080.0	3 902.4	3 701.5	3 551.7	3 491.6	3 473.3
Teachers[3]	KBFH	283.4	281.6	278.5	277.0	274.5	267.7	260.5	253.8	244.9	237.0	236.6	229.1
Pupils per teacher	KBFI	16.4	16.4	16.4	16.2	16.0	15.9	15.7	15.4	15.1	15.0	14.8	15.2
Special schools[4]													
Pupils													
Full-time and full-time equivalent of part-time	KBFQ	149.3	147.2	145.0	142.7	137.3	133.1	130.0	124.9	120.9	117.6	114.6	112.5
Teachers[3]	KBFS	19.8	19.8	19.7	19.7	19.7	19.7	19.6	19.5	19.3	19.2	19.6	19.4
Pupils per teacher	KBFT	7.5	7.4	7.4	7.3	7.0	6.8	6.6	6.4	6.3	6.1	5.8	5.8

1 In Scotland and in Wales the school census date is September whereas that for the rest of the United Kingdom remains at January.
2 From 1980 onwards includes non-maintained schools or departments, including independent schools in Scotland.
3 Figures of teachers and of pupil/teacher ratios take account of the full-time equivalent of part-time teachers.
4 Public sector only up to and including 1979.
5 Includes 1984-85 data for Scotland.
6 Includes 1987-88 data for Scotland.
7 Provisional.

Source: Education Departments

Education

5.4 Pupils with special needs in public sector and assisted schools
United Kingdom
At January[1]

(i) Numbers of public sector and assisted special schools, full-time pupils and teachers

		1980	1981	1982	1983	1984	1985	1986	1987	1988	1989	1990	1991[12]
Hospital schools[2]													
Schools:													
Public sector	KAIH	145	141	132	125	117	111	98	88	79	68	60	48
Assisted	KAII	4	4	3	3	3	2	2	1	1	1	–	–
Total	KAIJ	149	145	135	128	120	113	100	89	80	69	60	48
Full-time pupils (thousands)	KAIK	7.8	7.3	6.7	6.2	5.3	4.8	4.6	3.2	3.0	2.8	1.6	0.9
Teachers (thousands)[3]													
Full-time teachers	KAIL	1.2	1.2	1.1	1.0	0.9	0.8	0.7	0.6	0.6	0.5	0.4	0.4
Other special schools or departments[4]													
Schools:													
Public sector	KAIM	1 760	1 763	1 759	1 763	1 757	1 742	1 726	1 739	1 736	1 723	1 712	1 695
Assisted	KAIN	115	112	109	107	104	103	95	96	92	89	89	87
Day	KAIO	1 412	1 412	1 412	1 393	1 488	1 469	1 464	1 174[5]	1 500	1 499	1 540	1 522
Boarding	KAIP	463	463	456	477	373	376	357	281[5]	328	313	261	260
Total	KAIQ	1 875	1 875	1 868	1 870	1 861	1 845	1 821	1 835	1 828	1 812	1 801	1 782
Full-time pupils (thousands):													
Blind and partially sighted	KAIR	3.7	3.5	3.3	3.2	..[6]	..	..	..	..	..	..	..
Deaf and partially hearing	KAIS	5.6	5.3	5.0	4.7	..[6]	..	..	..	..	..	..	..
Delicate and physically handicapped	KAIT	18.0	17.3	16.8	16.2	..[6]	..	..	..	..	..	..	..
Maladjusted	KAIU	15.0	14.7	14.5	14.8	..[6]	..	..	..	..	..	..	..
Educationally sub-normal and mentally handicapped[6]	KAIV	92.1	92.8	92.9	92.2	..[6]	..	..	..	..	..	..	..
Epileptic	KAIW	1.9	1.8	1.6	1.6	..[6]	..	..	..	..	..	..	..
Speech defect	KAIX	3.5	3.1	2.5	2.3	..[6]	..	..	..	..	..	..	..
Autistic[5]	KAIY	0.6	0.7	0.6	0.6	..[6]	..	..	..	..	..	..	..
Total	KAIZ	140.7	139.2	137.3	135.5	132.1	128.8	126.0	120.4	117.7	114.1	112.1	110.8
Teachers (thousands)													
Full-time teachers	KAJA	17.6	17.7	17.7	17.8	17.9	17.8	17.7	17.7[7]	..[8]	..	..	..
Full-time equivalent of part-time teachers	KAJB	0.7	0.7	0.7	0.7	0.7	0.8	0.8	0.8[7]	18.7	18.7	19.0	19.1

1 In Wales the school census date is September whereas that for the rest of the United Kingdom remains at January.
2 England, Wales and Northern Ireland only.
3 Excluding part-time teachers in hospital schools, full-time equivalent in 1988 was 36.
4 In the 1986 column, data for Scotland relate to 1984/85.
5 England and Wales only.
6 Information on individual handicaps ceased to be collected in 1984.
7 Including 1984-85 data for Scotland.
8 Data on full-time teachers no longer collected separately.

(ii) Pupils with statements of special needs in other public sector schools

		1986	1987	1988	1989	1990	1991[12]
Public sector primary schools[9]	KAJC	22.8[11]	24.0	28.5	31.8	35.0	40.3
Public sector secondary schools[10]	KAJD	15.4[11]	17.4	21.8	25.7	29.4	34.8
Total	KAJE	38.2	41.3	50.2	57.4	64.4	75.2

9 Including middle schools deemed primary.
10 Including middle schools deemed secondary.
11 Including estimated primary/secondary split for Wales.
12 Provisional.

Source: Education Departments

Education

5.5 Pupils leaving school by sex and highest qualification held
Academic years

Thousands

		1980[1]/81	1981/82	1982[1]/83	1983/84	1984[1]/85	1985/86	1986/87	1987/88	1988/89	1989/90
Persons											
Leavers with GCSE 'A' level/SCE 'H' grade passes											
2 or more 'A', 3 or more 'H'	KALP	122	133	131	136	127	127	129	131	137	146
1 'A', or 2 'H'	KALQ	32	36	37	37	34	34	34	33	31	33
Leavers with GCSE/GCE 'O' level/CSE/SCE 'O' grades alone											
5 or more A - C awards/CSE grade 1[2]	KALR	81	90	91	95	93	95	92	97	100	93
1 - 4 A - C awards/CSE grade 1[2]	KALS	228	240	244	243	232	231	233	210	206	190
No higher grades											
1 or more other grades	KALT	284	293	293	295	283	283	284	241	212	184
No GCSE/GCE/SCE or CSE qualifications	KALU	119	121	105	108	98	101	95	86	67	60
Total school leavers	KALV	865	913	902	914	866	871	867	797	753	706
Males											
Leavers with GCSE/GCE 'A' level/SCE 'H' grade passes											
2 or more 'A', 3 or more 'H'	KALW	65	69	68	70	67	66	66	67	69	72
1 'A', 1 or 2 'H'	KALX	15	17	17	17	15	16	16	16	14	16
Leavers with GCSE/GCE 'O' level/CSE/SCE 'O' grades alone											
5 or more A - C awards/CSE grade 1[2]	KALY	37	41	42	44	43	44	42	42	45	41
1 - 4 A - C awards/CSE grade 1[2]	KALZ	109	115	116	114	108	108	109	100	100	93
No higher grades											
1 or more other grades	KAMA	149	154	155	155	151	151	152	132	118	105
No GCSE/GCE/SCE or CSE qualifications	KAMB	68	69	62	64	57	59	56	51	40	36
Total school leavers	KAMC	442	466	460	464	441	444	442	409	387	362
Females											
Leavers with GCSE/GCE 'A' level/SCE 'H' grade passes											
2 or more 'A', 3 or more 'H'	KAMD	57	64	63	65	60	61	62	64	68	74
1 'A', 1 or 2 'H'	KAME	17	19	20	20	19	18	18	17	17	17
Leavers with GCSE/GCE 'O' level/CSE/SCE 'O' grades alone											
5 or more A - C awards/CSE grade 1[2]	KAMF	44	49	49	50	50	51	50	55	55	52
1 - 4 A - C awards/SCE grade 1[2]	KAMG	120	125	128	129	124	123	124	110	106	97
No Higher grades											
1 or more other grades	KAMH	135	139	138	140	131	132	132	108	94	79
No GCSE/GCE/SCE or CSE qualifications	KAMI	51	51	44	45	42	43	39	35	27	24
Total school leavers	KAMJ	423	447	442	450	425	427	425	388	366	344
The numbers of pupils who left school in Great Britain with no GCSE/GCE/SCE or CSE qualifications were as follows:	KAMK	119	113	105	102	98	95	90	81	62	57

1 Great Britain only.
2 'O' grades in Scotland and 'O' levels in England, Wales and Northern Ireland have been awarded in bands A to E; awards in bands A to C can be regarded as equivalent to what were previously rated as passes.

Source: Education Departments

Education

5.6 Numbers and percentages continuing education aged 16 and over by age, sex and type of course
Men and women
1990/91[3]

Home students

				Age at 31 August 1990				
	All students	16	17	18	16-18	19-20	21-24	25 and over
Numbers								
Total population	-	726	771	822	2 319	1 752	3 670	-
Full-time and sandwich students								
Schools	523	295	197	28	519	4	-	-
Further education	472	154	129	71	354	38	24	56
Higher education	666	1	9	102	112	265	182	107
Universities	312	-	5	53	57	134	83	37
Undergraduate	273	-	5	53	57	134	62	20
Postgraduates	39	-	-	-	-	-	22	16
Polytechnics and other HE estabs	355	-	4	50	54	131	99	70
Undergraduates	338	-	4	50	54	131	91	62
Postgraduates	16	-	-	-	-	1	7	8
Total full-time and sandwich students	1 660	449	334	202	985	307	206	163
Part-time students								
Further education	2 988	140	139	119	397	123	265	1 934
Day students	1 294	98	104	77	278	71	168	746
Adult education centres[1]	506	7	2	3	13	29	102	362
Other	788	90	102	74	265	71	65	384
Evening only students	1 694	42	35	42	119	52	97	1 188
Adult education centres[1]	928	24	12	14	51	52	182	644
Other	766	18	23	28	68	52	97	545
Higher education[2]	365	-	1	9	11	36	69	248
Universities	51	-	-	-	-	1	6	45
Undergraduates	11	-	-	-	-	1	2	8
Postgraduates	41	-	-	-	-	-	4	37
Polytechnics and other HE estabs	264	-	1	9	11	35	61	156
Undergraduates	233	-	1	9	11	35	58	128
Postgraduates	31	-	-	-	-	-	3	28
Open University	49	-	-	-	-	-	2	47
Total part-time students	3 353	140	140	128	408	159	333	2 182
All full-time and part-time students	5 013	589	474	330	1 393	466	539	2 345
As percentage of population								
Full-time and sandwich students								
Schools	-	40.6	25.5	3.4	22.4	0.2	-	-
Further education	-	21.2	16.7	8.7	15.3	2.1	0.7	-
Higher education	-	0.1	1.1	12.5	4.8	15.1	5.0	-
Universities	-	-	0.6	6.4	2.5	7.7	2.3	-
Undergraduates	-	-	0.6	6.4	2.5	7.6	1.7	-
Postgraduates	-	-	-	-	-	-	0.6	-
Polytechnics and other HE estabs	-	0.1	0.5	6.1	2.3	7.5	2.7	-
Undergraduates	-	0.1	0.5	6.0	2.3	7.5	2.5	-
Postgraduates	-	-	-	-	-	-	0.2	-
Total full-time and sandwich students	-	61.9	43.3	24.5	42.5	17.5	5.6	-
Part-time students								
Further education	-	19.3	18.0	14.4	17.1	7.0	7.2	-
Day students	-	13.5	13.5	9.3	12.0	4.0	4.6	-
Adult education centres[1]	-	1.0	0.3	0.4	0.6	1.7	2.8	-
Other	-	12.4	13.2	9.0	11.4	4.0	1.8	-
Evening only students	-	5.8	4.6	5.1	5.1	3.0	2.6	-
Adult education centres[1]	-	3.3	1.6	1.7	2.2	2.9	5.0	-
Other	-	2.5	3.0	3.3	2.9	3.0	2.6	-
Higher education[2]	-	-	0.2	1.2	0.5	2.1	1.9	-
Universities	-	-	-	-	-	-	0.2	-
Undergraduates	-	-	-	-	-	-	-	-
Postgraduates	-	-	-	-	-	-	0.1	-
Polytechnics and other HE estabs	-	-	0.2	1.1	0.5	2.0	1.7	-
Undergraduates	-	-	0.2	1.1	0.5	2.0	1.6	-
Postgraduates	-	-	-	-	-	-	0.1	-
Open University	-	-	-	-	-	-	0.1	-
Total part-time students	-	19.3	18.2	15.6	17.6	9.1	9.1	-
All full-time and part-time students	-	81.2	61.5	40.1	60.1	26.6	14.7	-

1 Including estimated age detail for 1 434 500 students aged 16 years in adult education centres; excluding youth clubs and centres, 77 000 in 1984-85 (England). Excluding 618 900 students in 1989/90 on courses run by responsible bodies for whom age detail was not available.

2 Excluding 81 700 students (1990-91) enrolled on nursing and paramedical courses at Department of Health establishments.

3 Provisional.

Source: Education Departments

Education

5.7 Students in further and higher education at public sector and assisted establishments by mode of study[1]
Autumn term
Thousands

		1977	1978	1979[2]	1980	1981	1982	1983	1984	1985	1986	1987	1988	1989
Major establishments														
Full-time[3]	KBJU	499	498	495	510	564	603	595	594	608	624	633	646	690
Sandwich	KBJV	59	62	65	68	74	83	90	90	90	91	93	92	95
Part-time day	KBJW	790	846	836	820	806	787	846	891	914	951	988	1 065	1 095
Evening	KBJX	739	778	698	694	692	720	771	780	807	852	868	957	985
Total	KDZY	2 087	2 184	2 094	2 092	2 136	2 193	2 302	2 354	2 419	2 518	2 581	2 760	2 866
Adult education centres (England and Wales only)	KBJZ	1 708	2 005	1 849	1 645	1 609	1 632	1 734	1 693	1 478[4]	1 519	1 439[5]	1 457	1 586

1 Including PCFC Sector but excluding universities. Excluding students on non-vocational courses in Scotland and Northern Ireland.
2 In previous years this time series was based on ages as at 31 December, from this year the basis has been changed to 31 August.
3 Including from 1977, teacher training colleges of education in Scotland and Northern Ireland.
4 From 1985 onwards, excludes students aged 18 and over in youth clubs and centres.
5 In 1986 contains 36 thousand men and 69 thousand women aged 18 years and under; and 349 thousand men and 985 thousand women aged 19 years and over.

Source: Education Departments

Education

5.8 Full-time students from overseas, 1990/91
Enrolments by type of course, sex and country, in higher and further education

Thousands

		Higher education			All Further education	1990/91 Higher and Further Education		
		Post-graduate	First degree	Other		Males	Females	persons
RANK	TOP FIFTY COUNTRIES BY NAME							
1	Malaysia	1.3	6.0	0.3	0.3	4.7	3.2	7.9
2	Hong Kong	1.3	5.0	0.4	1.0	5.0	2.7	7.7
3	USA	1.5	0.8	3.1	0.1	2.5	3.0	5.5
4	Ireland, Republic of	0.6	3.4	0.7	0.5	2.6	2.7	5.2
5	West Germany	1.0	2.2	1.6	0.2	2.6	2.3	4.9
6	France	0.9	2.1	1.2	0.4	2.3	2.3	4.6
7	Greece	2.0	1.7	0.3	0.3	3.0	1.3	4.3
8	Singapore	0.5	1.9	0.1	-	1.6	0.9	2.5
9	Spain	0.6	0.9	0.4	0.4	1.1	1.1	2.3
10	Cyprus	0.3	1.4	0.2	0.1	1.2	0.7	1.9
11	Japan	0.7	0.4	0.3	0.4	0.7	1.1	1.8
12	Norway	0.3	1.4	0.1	-	1.1	0.7	1.8
13	China, People's Republic of	1.5	0.1	-	0.1	1.3	0.4	1.7
14	Italy	0.4	0.7	0.4	0.1	0.8	0.8	1.6
15	Kenya	0.5	0.8	0.1	0.1	0.9	0.5	1.4
16	Pakistan	0.8	0.3	0.1	0.1	1.1	0.2	1.3
17	India	0.7	0.2	0.1	0.1	0.9	0.3	1.2
18	Turkey	0.8	0.1	-	0.2	0.8	0.3	1.1
19	Canada	0.7	0.3	0.1	-	0.6	0.5	1.1
20	Netherlands	0.3	0.5	0.2	0.1	0.6	0.5	1.1
21	Nigeria	0.6	0.3	0.1	0.1	0.7	0.3	1.1
22	Brazil	0.9	-	-	-	0.6	0.4	0.9
23	Belgium	0.2	0.5	0.1	0.1	0.5	0.4	0.9
24	Israel	0.2	0.6	-	-	0.6	0.2	0.8
25	Brunei	0.1	0.5	0.2	-	0.5	0.3	0.8
26	Taiwan	0.4	0.1	-	0.2	0.4	0.4	0.7
27	Sri Lanka	0.2	0.4	0.1	0.1	0.5	0.2	0.7
28	South Africa	0.3	0.3	0.1	0.1	0.5	0.3	0.7
29	Zambia	0.2	0.3	0.1	0.1	0.5	0.2	0.7
30	Iran	0.4	0.2	-	0.1	0.5	0.1	0.7
31	Denmark	0.2	0.2	0.1	-	0.3	0.3	0.6
32	Oman	-	0.2	0.1	0.2	0.5	0.1	0.6
33	Saudi Arabia	0.4	0.1	-	0.1	0.5	0.1	0.6
34	South Korea	0.4	0.1	-	-	0.5	0.1	0.6
35	Australia	0.4	0.1	-	-	0.3	0.2	0.6
36	Portugal	0.2	0.2	-	0.1	0.3	0.2	0.5
37	Indonesia	0.4	0.1	-	-	0.4	0.1	0.5
38	Thailand	0.3	0.1	-	0.1	0.3	0.3	0.5
39	Zimbabwe	0.2	0.2	0.1	0.1	0.3	0.2	0.5
40	Tanzania	0.3	0.1	0.1	-	0.4	0.1	0.5
41	Mauritius	-	0.3	0.1	-	0.3	0.2	0.5
42	Botswana	0.1	0.2	0.1	-	0.3	0.1	0.4
43	Switzerland	0.1	0.2	-	-	0.2	0.2	0.4
44	Bangladesh	0.3	-	-	-	0.3	0.1	0.4
45	Jordan	0.2	0.2	-	-	0.3	0.1	0.4
46	Sudan	0.3	0.1	-	-	0.3	0.1	0.4
47	Malawi	0.1	0.2	0.1	-	0.3	0.1	0.4
48	Ghana	0.2	0.1	-	-	0.3	0.1	0.4
49	Mexico	0.3	-	-	-	0.3	0.1	0.4
50	Iraq	0.3	0.1	-	-	0.3	-	0.4
	Other/unknown	4.2	2.8	1.0	1.0	6.1	3.0	9.1
	Total	29.1	38.7	12.4	7.3	53.6	33.9	87.6

Source: Department for Education

5.8 (continued) Full-time students from overseas, 1990/91
First Year Students and Enrolments by grouped country of domicile, in higher and further education[1]

Education

Thousands

	First Year Students[2]					All Enrolments[2]				
	1975/76[7]	1980/81[3]	1985/86[4]	1989/90	1990/91	1975/76[7]	1980/81[3]	1985/86[4]	1989/90	1990/91
European Community	2.0	3.0	5.6	13.3	16.3[5]	2.6	5.4	8.9	21.7	26.5[5]
Other Europe	..	1.1	2.1	1.6	3.1	..	3.1	3.8	4.4	5.7
Commonwealth	23.6	18.1	16.9	16.4	17.3[5]	39.8	39.6	30.2	32.9	34.7[5]
Other countries	21.1	13.4	13.9	14.9	13.5	34.1	27.4	20.8	21.4	20.8
All countries[5]	46.7	35.6	38.5	46.3	50.2[5]	76.5	75.6	63.7	80.5	87.6[5]
of which										
Higher education[5]	26.8	23.8	31.0	40.3	44.2	49.8	55.5	53.7	72.8	80.2
Further education	19.9	11.8	7.5	5.9	6.0	26.8	20.2	10.0	7.7	7.3

1 Figures for Scotland are autumn counts for vocational further education.
2 For years not shown, please refer to previously published editions of Annual Abstract.
3 Estimated.
4 See paragraph 11.14 of explanatory notes for the change of definition of a 'student from overseas'.
5 Gibraltar is included in both EC and Commonwealth figures. Numbers in grouped countries do not sum to overall student numbers due to overlap.
6 For 1985-86 and subsequent years, enrolment figures have been adjusted to take account of the change of definition of a 'student from overseas'.
7 Great Britain only.

Source: Department for Education

Education

5.9 Students in further and higher education by type of course, mode of study, sex and subject group [1,2]

Home and overseas students   Academic year 1989 - 90   Thousands

	Postgraduate level		Undergraduate level or equivalent		Other higher education		Total higher education	Further education [3]		All students			
										Full-time [4]		Part-time [5]
	Full-time [4]	Part-time [5]	Full-time [4]	Part-time [5]	Full-time [4]	Part-time [5]		Full-time [4]	Part-time [5]	Home	Home and overseas	Home and overseas [6]
Male												
Subject group												
1 Medicine and dentistry	1.6	1.8	12.8	0.1	0.1	0.1	16.5	0.2	0.5	12.8	14.7	2.5
2 Allied Medicine	1.0	0.9	3.8	0.5	1.0	1.9	9.1	1.0	4.2	6.0	6.8	7.5
3 Biological sciences	2.8	1.4	10.4	0.5	0.7	0.5	16.4	-	0.3	12.6	13.9	2.8
4 Agriculture, forestry and veterinary sciences	1.1	0.3	3.1	-	1.4	0.2	6.1	4.5	18.7	8.9	10.0	19.2
5 Physical science	6.0	1.7	20.4	1.1	1.3	2.5	32.9	0.2	1.7	25.4	27.8	7.0
6 Mathematical sciences	4.1	1.9	23.0	1.4	7.2	6.0	43.4	8.1	22.5	39.2	42.2	31.7
7 Engineering and technology	8.1	4.7	51.3	4.0	12.4	40.2	120.7	30.7	192.0	88.2	102.4	241.0
8 Architecture and related	1.6	1.7	11.7	2.7	3.6	17.2	38.5	20.0	115.4	34.9	36.8	137.1
9 Social sciences	5.5	3.7	32.7	2.8	2.9	2.8	50.5	1.9	12.3	36.7	43.1	21.6
10 Business and administrative studies	4.6	12.7	24.2	3.3	15.1	48.2	108.2	36.1	84.8	73.5	80.0	149.0
11 Documentation	0.6	0.3	1.2	-	0.4	0.3	2.8	0.5	1.8	2.4	2.6	2.4
12 Languages and related	1.5	1.1	11.1	0.3	0.4	1.1	15.5	1.4	40.7	12.3	14.4	43.2
13 Humanities	1.8	2.0	10.0	0.4	0.2	0.3	14.7	-	1.1	10.9	12.0	3.9
14 Creative arts	1.2	0.6	12.4	0.3	5.8	0.6	20.9	18.2	28.2	36.6	37.7	29.6
15 Education [7]	4.6	5.5	4.9	1.1	0.8	3.9	20.8	2.1	19.2	10.5	12.4	29.7
16 Combined, gen	0.8	1.0	33.7	2.3	2.6	1.1	41.5	19.7	119.2	52.7	56.8	123.6
17 GCSE, SCE and CSE	-	-	-	-	-	-	-	50.8	100.1	50.0	50.8	100.1
All subjects [8]	46.9	41.5	266.4	20.8	56.1	126.9	558.5	208.4	800.1	526.7	577.7	989.3
Female												
Subject group												
1 Medicine and dentistry	1.1	1.4	10.8	-	0.1	0.1	13.6	0.2	3.5	11.3	12.2	5.0
2 Allied medicine	1.3	1.3	9.8	1.7	5.5	5.7	25.3	19.4	14.8	35.0	36.0	23.6
3 Biological sciences	2.1	1.3	13.5	0.8	0.8	0.8	19.3	-	0.5	15.1	16.3	3.4
4 Agriculture, forestry and veterinary sciences	0.5	0.2	2.7	-	0.6	0.2	4.1	2.4	14.1	5.8	6.2	14.4
5 Physical sciences	1.6	0.5	8.9	0.5	0.5	1.6	13.6	0.1	0.6	10.3	11.1	3.2
6 Mathematical sciences	1.2	0.6	8.0	0.3	2.4	2.8	15.2	2.7	24.9	12.9	14.1	28.6
7 Engineering and technology	1.0	0.5	6.7	0.2	2.1	2.1	12.6	3.5	17.9	11.9	13.3	20.7
8 Architecture and related	0.8	0.8	3.8	0.6	0.6	2.3	8.7	0.8	5.2	5.1	5.9	8.8
9 Social sciences	4.2	3.4	34.1	2.9	5.1	6.1	55.7	7.6	41.8	46.3	50.9	54.2
10 Business and administrative studies	2.6	5.2	22.3	2.4	17.0	44.2	93.8	68.4	245.0	105.6	110.3	296.8
11 Documentation	0.8	0.5	2.6	0.2	0.5	0.7	5.4	0.4	1.8	4.0	4.3	3.3
12 Languages and related	1.9	1.4	28.4	0.8	1.0	2.6	36.2	2.7	62.5	30.2	34.1	67.3
13 Humanities	1.0	1.3	10.8	0.5	0.3	0.4	14.3	-	2.2	11.1	12.1	4.5
14 Creative arts	1.4	0.6	19.6	0.4	6.4	1.0	29.3	36.3	95.3	61.9	63.6	97.3
15 Education [7]	8.0	7.0	18.6	3.0	2.2	8.5	47.3	2.0	37.4	26.5	30.8	55.9
16 Combined, gen	0.7	1.0	40.5	4.0	3.7	2.0	52.1	20.6	248.3	60.9	65.6	255.4
17 GCSE, SCE and CSE	-	-	-	-	-	-	-	61.3	171.9	60.8	61.3	171.9
All subjects [8]	30.2	27.2	241.1	18.5	48.6	81.0	446.5	242.8	1 018.9	529.3	562.7	1 145.5
Persons												
Subject group												
1 Medicine and dentistry	2.7	3.3	23.6	0.1	0.2	0.2	30.1	0.4	4.0	24.1	26.9	7.5
2 Allied medicine	2.2	2.2	13.7	2.3	6.5	7.6	34.5	20.4	19.0	41.0	42.8	31.1
3 Biological sciences	4.9	2.7	23.8	1.3	1.5	1.3	35.6	-	0.9	27.7	30.3	6.2
4 Agriculture, forestry and veterinary sciences	1.6	0.4	5.8	-	2.1	0.4	10.2	6.9	32.8	14.7	16.3	33.7
5 Physical sciences	7.6	2.3	29.3	1.6	1.8	4.1	46.6	0.2	2.3	35.7	38.8	10.3
6 Mathematical sciences	5.2	2.4	30.9	1.7	9.5	8.8	58.6	10.7	47.3	52.1	56.4	60.2
7 Engineering and technology	9.1	5.2	58.0	4.3	14.4	42.3	133.3	34.2	209.8	100.1	115.7	261.6
8 Architecture and related	2.3	2.6	15.4	3.3	4.1	19.5	47.2	20.7	120.6	40.0	42.6	145.9
9 Social sciences	9.7	7.1	66.8	5.7	8.0	8.9	106.2	9.5	54.1	83.0	94.0	75.8
10 Business and administrative studies	7.2	18.0	46.5	5.7	32.1	92.4	201.9	104.5	329.8	179.1	190.3	445.8
11 Documentation	1.4	0.8	3.8	0.2	0.9	1.0	8.1	0.9	3.7	6.4	7.0	5.7
12 Languages and related	3.4	2.6	39.5	1.1	1.4	3.7	51.7	4.1	103.2	42.5	48.5	110.5
13 Humanities	2.8	3.3	20.8	1.0	0.5	0.7	29.0	-	3.3	22.1	24.1	8.3
14 Creative arts	2.7	1.1	32.0	0.7	12.2	1.6	50.2	54.5	123.6	98.5	101.3	127.0
15 Education [7]	12.7	12.5	23.5	4.1	3.0	12.4	68.1	4.1	56.6	37.1	43.2	85.6
16 Combined, gen	1.5	2.1	74.2	6.3	6.3	3.2	93.6	40.3	367.5	113.6	122.3	379.0
17 GCSE, SCE and CSE	-	-	-	-	-	-	-	112.1	272.0	110.8	112.1	272.0
All subjects [8]	77.0	68.7	507.5	39.2	104.7	207.9	1 004.9	451.2	1 818.9	1 056.1	1 140.4	2 134.7

1 Excluding data for pupils at schools and for the Open University for which subject detail in this format is not available. Also, excluding 84 000 (provisional) students on nursing and paramedical courses at Department of Health establishments.
2 The subject groups have been revised from the 12 groups previously used and therefore individual subjects cannot be compared to earlier years.
3 Including 672.0 thousand students in all modes in England, Wales and Northern Ireland who are taking unspecified courses.
4 Including sandwich students
5 Day and evening.
6 Including 5.6 thousand part-time students from abroad.
7 Includes teacher training enrolments for Universities only. Others are included under the subject of study.
8 Further education totals include students in Scotland who are taking National Certificate Modules (96 000 persons).

Source: Education Departments

Education

5.10 Students obtaining qualifications by subject of study,[1] sex and type of awarding body, 1988-89[2]

Thousands

	Medicine and Dentistry	Allied Medicine	Biological sciences	Agriculture and related	Physical sciences	Mathematical and Computing sciences	Engineering and Technology	Architecture, building	Social studies	Business and admin studies	Communication and Documentation	Languages and related	Humanities	Creative Arts and Design	Education	Combined and General	All Students	Men
Higher degree																		
University[3]	1.3	0.9	2.0	0.9	2.7	1.8	4.0	0.6	4.8	3.8	0.4	1.8	1.4	0.3	3.1	0.6	30.2	20.4
CNAA	-	0.1	0.2	-	0.3	0.3	0.5	0.1	0.2	0.5	0.2	-	0.1	0.2	0.2	-	3.0	2.1
Total	1.3	0.9	2.2	0.9	2.9	2.1	4.5	0.7	5.1	4.3	0.6	1.8	1.5	0.5	3.3	0.6	33.2	22.5
Higher diplomas and certificates[8]																		
University[4,5]	0.5	0.3	0.1	0.1	0.2	0.3	0.3	0.3	1.6	0.8	0.3	0.2	0.1	0.2	6.7	0.1	12.1	5.7
CNAA	-	0.1	-	-	-	0.2	0.2	0.1	0.1	0.7	0.4	-	0.1	0.1	4.3	-	6.4	2.6
Total	0.5	0.3	0.1	0.1	0.2	0.6	0.5	0.4	1.7	1.6	0.8	0.2	0.2	0.3	11.0	0.1	18.6	8.3
First degree																		
University[3]	5.5	2.0	5.4	1.3	6.2	4.5	9.5	1.3	11.9	3.7	0.1	7.6	5.1	1.4	1.2	8.1	75.0	42.8
CNAA[5]	-	1.3	1.3	0.1	2.1	2.2	5.7	2.4	7.0	6.6	0.8	1.4	0.4	6.4	4.9	7.1	49.6	25.9
University validated degrees (GB)[5]	-	0.1	-	-	0.2	0.1	-	-	0.1	0.2	0.1	0.3	0.2	0.4	1.2	2.2	5.1	1.4
Total	5.5	3.3	6.7	1.5	8.4	6.8	15.2	3.7	18.9	10.5	1.0	9.4	5.7	8.2	7.4	17.4	129.6	70.1
First university diplomas and certificates[5,6]	0.3	0.3	0.3	0.1	0.2	0.3	0.5	0.2	1.1	0.5	-	0.9	0.5	0.3	0.3	2.5	8.3	3.9
CNAA diplomas and certificates[7]	-	0.2	0.2	-	0.1	-	-	-	0.4	2.6	-	0.3	0.6	0.4	4.2	-	9.1	4.7
Professional qualifications (public sector)[9]	-	3.7	0.1	0.2	0.6	2.0	3.1	3.8	3.8	27.4	0.7	1.4	0.1	0.9	0.7	0.6	49.2	26.5
BTEC higher diploma	-	0.1	0.3	0.5	0.4	2.1	3.9	0.7	0.2	4.6	-	-	-	1.8	-	0.1	14.7	10.3
BTEC higher certificate	-	0.4	-	-	0.8	0.8	9.0	2.1	0.8	3.0	-	-	-	0.2	-	0.1	17.4	14.6
SCOTVEC higher diploma/certificate	-	-	0.1	0.1	0.1	0.4	0.6	0.1	0.1	1.5	0.1	-	-	0.2	-	-	3.1	1.7
Total[1]	-	0.5	0.6	0.6	1.3	3.3	13.5	2.9	1.1	9.1	0.1	-	-	2.2	-	0.2	35.2	26.6
Total higher education[1]	7.6	9.3	10.1	3.3	13.8	15.1	37.4	11.7	32.2	55.8	3.2	14.1	8.6	12.8	26.8	21.4	283.1	162.6
Further education																		
BTEC first and national diploma	0.3	0.8	-	1.1	-	2.6	7.2	2.4	0.3	16.6	-	-	-	8.0	-	2.7	42.0	23.5
BTEC first and national certificate	0.1	0.9	-	-	0.1	1.3	16.0	4.5	1.5	18.8	-	-	-	0.8	-	4.0	48.0	30.9
Total further education[11]	0.4	1.7	-	1.1	0.1	3.9	23.2	6.9	1.8	35.4	-	-	-	8.8	-	6.7	90.0	54.4
Grand total[10,12]	8.0	10.9	10.1	4.4	13.9	19.0	60.6	18.6	34.0	91.2	3.2	14.1	8.6	21.6	26.8	28.1	373.1	217.0
Men																		
Higher degrees	0.8	0.5	1.3	0.6	2.3	1.6	4.0	0.5	3.1	3.2	0.3	0.9	1.0	0.3	1.7	0.4	22.5	22.5
Higher diplomas and certificates	0.3	0.1	0.1	0.1	0.1	0.4	0.5	0.3	0.9	0.8	0.3	0.1	0.1	0.1	4.1	0.1	8.3	8.3
First degrees (excluding university validated)	3.1	1.0	3.0	0.8	6.0	5.1	13.9	2.9	9.6	5.5	0.3	2.7	2.9	3.2	1.6	7.2	68.7	68.7
First university diplomas and certificates	0.1	-	0.1	0.1	0.2	0.2	0.4	0.1	0.5	0.2	-	0.2	0.3	0.1	0.1	1.1	3.9	3.9
CNAA diplomas and certificates	-	-	0.1	-	0.1	-	-	-	0.2	1.8[8]	-	0.2	0.3	0.2	1.9	-	4.7[8]	4.7[8]
Professional qualifications (public sector)[9]	-	0.7	-	0.1	0.3	1.1	2.9	3.1	1.3	15.5	0.2	0.4	-	0.4	0.2	0.2	26.5	26.5
BTEC higher diploma	-	0.1	0.2	0.3	0.2	1.4	2.5	0.5	0.1	3.7	-	-	-	1.2	-	0.1	10.3	10.3
BTEC higher certificate	-	0.3	0.2	-	0.7	0.7	7.5	1.8	0.7	2.5	-	-	-	0.1	-	0.1	14.6	14.6
BTEC first and national diploma	0.1	0.4	-	0.6	-	1.4	3.8	1.3	0.1	10.2	-	-	-	4.2	-	1.4	23.5	23.5
BTEC first and national certificate	0.1	0.6	-	-	0.1	0.8	11.1	2.9	0.1	12.1	-	-	-	0.5	-	2.6	30.9	30.9

1 Teacher training results are shown in Table 5.12. However these overlap with results shown here.
2 Excluding qualifications from the private sector.
3 Excluding Open University degrees for which subject detail in this format is not available. These numbered 417 higher degrees, 1 681 honours degrees (872 men) and 6 417 ordinary degrees (3 279 men).
4 Including Postgraduate Certificates in Education (PGCEs).
5 Department of Education and Science (DES) estimates based on various sources.
6 Excluding students who successfully completed courses for which formal qualifications are not awarded.
7 Holding Dip HE, Certificates of Education and PGCEs.
8 Including Diploma in Management studies, which is equivalent to First Degree.
9 DES estimates based on final year of course data.
10 In addition, 31 000 students obtained nursing and paramedical qualifications at Department of Health establishments in 1988-89.
11 Excluding about 97 500 students taking the new SCOTVEC National Certificate (52 000 men). Subject detail is not available.
12 Excluding 483 000 City and Guilds of London Institute awards, which cannot be allocated into the above subject groups.

Source: Education Departments

Education

5.11 Lecturers and teachers by type of establishment, sex and graduate status
Percentage trained

(i) Full-time

	1983-84 All 000s	1983-84 % Graduate	1984-85 All 000s	1984-85 % Graduate	1985-86 All 000s	1985-86 % Graduate	1986-87 All 000s	1986-87 % Graduate	1987-88[1] All 000s	1987-88[1] % Graduate	1988-89[1] All 000s	1988-89[1] % Graduate	1989-90[2] All 000s	1989-90[2] % Graduate	1989-90[2] %[3] Graduates trained
United Kingdom															
Males															
Schools[4]															
Public sector															
Primary[5]	43	29.5	42	31.3	41	33.2	41	35.5	40	37.3	41	39.7	38	42.7	97.6
Secondary[6]	150	62.6	147	64.0	144	65.3	140	65.7	135	66.7	130	67.4	125	68.9	90.8
Non-maintained[6]	21	80.8	21	81.6	21	82.4	21	83.4	21	84.3	21	85.1	20	84.9	..
Special	6	31.6	6	33.4	6	35.4	6	36.4	6	37.9	6	39.7	6	43.8	93.3
All schools[4,6]	221	56.9	216	58.5	213	59.9	209	60.7	202	61.8	198	62.8	190	64.5	78.5
Establishments of further education[8]	71	44.3	70	45.2	69	45.9	69	46.6	69	47.0	69	47.4	63	47.4	56.9
Universities[9]	28	98.9	28	98.9	28	99.0	28	99.0	27	99.0	27	99.1	27	99.2	..
All establishments[4,10]	321	57.4	315	58.9	311	60.1	308	60.5	300	61.4	294	62.5	283	63.7	62.9
Females															
Schools[4]															
Public sector															
Primary[5]	160	19.4	159	21.1	160	22.8	162	23.8	166	26.6	169	29.1	171	32.0	97.4
Secondary[6]	126	55.8	124	57.3	123	58.4	120	59.7	118	59.9	115	59.7	114	61.7	91.9
Non-maintained[6]	21	53.7	21	55.4	22	56.1	22	56.9	22	58.0	24	58.6	23	57.8	..
Special	13	26.7	13	28.5	13	30.1	13	30.9	13	31.2	13	32.4	14	34.1	95.0
All schools[4,6]	319	36.3	317	37.9	317	39.1	318	40.0	320	41.3	320	42.4	323	44.5	85.1
Establishments of further education[8]	22	44.2	23	45.3	23	46.7	24	47.1	25	47.8	25	47.6	27	48.8	65.5
Universities[9]	3	98.5	4	98.4	4	98.9	4	98.7	4	98.9	4	99.1	4	99.1	..
All establishments[4,10]	347	37.3	345	39.0	346	40.2	348	40.8	351	42.1	350	43.4	358	45.3	81.0
England and Wales[2]															
All schools[4]															
Males	195	55.8	191	57.5	187	59.0	183	59.9	179	61.2	175	62.0	168	63.8	..
Females	275	36.4	273	38.2	274	39.6	274	40.5	277	42.0	275	42.8	278	45.2	..
Scotland[2]															
All schools[7]															
Males	19	68.0	19	68.6	..	..	..	..	16	69.2	16	70.4	15	70.3	..
Females	33	33.8	32	34.3	..	..	..	..	32	34.2	33	38.7	33	36.8	..
Northern Ireland[2,8]															
All schools															
Males	7	57.9	7	58.8	7	59.9	7	60.7	7	60.7	7	66.4	7	67.9	..
Females	11	39.0	11	40.8	11	42.5	11	44.0	11	44.0	12	47.8	12	50.1	..

(ii) Part-time

	1983-84 All 000s	1983-84 % Graduate	1984-85 All 000s	1984-85 % Graduate	1985-86 All 000s	1985-86 % Graduate	1986-87 All 000s	1986-87 % Graduate	1987-88 All 000s	1987-88 % Graduate	1988-89 All 000s	1988-89 % Graduate	1989-90 All 000s	1989-90 % Graduate	1989-90 % Graduates trained
Great Britain[11]															
Persons	..	..	..	..	..	..	..	..	..	..	..	..	..	..	..
Persons - full-time equivalent	41	..	42	..	43[4]	..	45[4]	..	48	..	50	..	53	..	..
Schools[12]	18	..	19	..	18	..	19	..	21	..	22	..	29	..	..
Establishments of further education[13]	23	..	23	..	23	..	24	..	27	..	28	..	23	..	..

1 Includes estimated data for England and Wales.
2 Includes some estimated data for each of the countries.
3 GB only. In Scotland all teachers are required to be trained.
4 1985-86 and 1986-87 include 1984-85 schools data for Scotland; 1985-86 includes estimated data for the maintained sector in England and Wales.
5 Including nursery schools.
6 Wef 1989-90 Voluntary Grammar Schools in N. Ireland are recorded in the maintained sector.
7 Excluding independent schools in Scotland.
8 Excluding Ulster Polytechnic. Figures include teacher training.
9 Excluding male and female professors and lecturers and 5 705 part-time tutorial and counselling staff employed by the Open University at January 1990.
10 Totals include a number of teachers in England and Wales classified as miscellaneous who are not shown above (about 2 800 men and 3 800 women in 1989-90).
11 Excluding universities.
12 Figures include unqualified teachers in England and Wales up to 1984-85.
13 England and Wales only up to 1983-84.

Source: Education Departments

Education

5.12 Initial training of teachers by type of course and stage
United Kingdom
Men and Women

Thousands

		1979	1980	1981	1982	1983	1984	1985	1986	1987	1988	1989
Admissions to courses of initial training[1]												
University Departments of Education												
Courses for graduates	KBGA	5.1	5.7	5.7	4.9	4.8	4.5	4.3	5.1[2]	5.5[2]	5.9	6.1
Courses for non-graduates	KBGB	0.6	0.6	0.5	0.7	0.6	0.7	0.6	0.6[2]	1.0[2]	1.2	1.3
Total	KBGC	5.7	6.2	6.2	5.5	5.3	5.2	5.0	5.7[2]	6.5[2]	7.1	7.4
Other institutions												
Courses for graduates	KBGD	6.4	7.0	6.8	5.2	4.6	4.6	4.8	5.3	6.0	5.8	6.1
Courses for non-graduates	KBGE	11.2	8.7	9.1	9.7	9.9	9.1	9.5	9.7	10.5	10.6	12.1
Total	KBGF	17.6	15.7	15.9	15.0	14.5	13.6	14.3	15.0	16.5	16.4	18.2
Students on initial training courses[3]												
University Departments of Education												
Courses for graduates	KBGH	5.1	5.7	5.7	4.9	4.8	4.5	4.4	5.2[2]	5.6[2]	5.9	6.1
Courses for non-graduates	KBGI	1.9	2.0	2.2	2.3	2.2	2.3	2.2	2.3[2]	2.6[2]	3.1	3.5
Total	KBGJ	7.0	7.7	7.9	7.2	7.0	6.9	6.6	7.5[2]	8.1[2]	9.0	9.6
Other institutions												
Courses for graduates	KBGK	6.5	7.0	6.8	5.2	4.5	4.5	4.8	5.3	6.0	5.9	6.2
Courses for non-graduates	KBGL	35.1	28.0	25.9	25.0	26.1	25.7	28.1	28.7	30.9	30.7	33.1
Total	KBGM	41.6	35.1	32.7	30.3	30.7	30.3	33.0	34.0	36.9	36.6	39.3
Students successfully completing courses of initial training[4,5]												
University Departments of Education												
Courses for graduates	KBGO	4.9	4.8	5.4	5.4	4.6	4.5	4.3	4.3	4.5	4.8	4.9
Courses for non-graduates	KBGP	0.8	0.6	0.6	0.6	0.6	0.6	0.6	0.5	0.6	0.5	0.6
Total	KBGQ	5.7	5.5	6.0	6.0	5.2	5.1	4.9	4.8	5.0	5.3	5.5
Other institutions												
Courses for graduates	KBGR	6.2	6.2	6.6	6.3	5.0	4.2	4.6	4.0	4.2	5.3	5.5
Courses for non-graduates	KAFC	19.8	13.1	9.6	8.5	7.3	7.0	6.0	6.5	7.1	6.6	6.4
Total	KAFD	26.0	19.4	16.2	14.8	12.3	11.2	10.6	10.5	11.4	11.9	11.9

1 Calendar year.
2 Including a small element of estimated data for England.
3 October/November of year shown.
4 Academic year ending in year shown.
5 Including students in England and Wales who failed their B.Ed. degree course but have received qualified teacher status, on the basis of a non-degree qualification obtained in an earlier year.

Source: Education Departments

5.13 Full-time academic teaching and research staff at universities[1]
United Kingdom
Academic years

Number

	Professors	Readers and senior lecturers	Lecturers and assistant lecturers	Other	Total	Percentage annual change
	KBGU	KBGV	KBGW	KBGX	KBGY	KBGZ
1972/73	3 649	6 475	19 651	969	30 744	3.7
1973/74	3 753	6 972	19 698	1 031	31 454	2.3
1974/75	3 906	7 398	19 883	914	32 101	2.1
1975/76	3 989	7 617	19 722	880	32 208	0.3
1976/77	4 124	7 877	20 022	712	32 735	1.6
1977/78	4 164	8 163	19 980	677	32 984	0.8
1978/79	4 225	8 454	20 302	714	33 695	2.2
1979/80	4 337	8 734	20 518	661	34 250	1.6
1980/81	4 382	8 809	20 460	646	34 297	0.1
1981/82	4 351	8 777	20 045	562	33 735	-1.6
1982/83	4 017	8 284	18 885	456	31 642	-6.2
1983/84	3 893	8 145	18 595	463	31 096	-1.7
1984/85[2]	3 807	7 942	18 737	557	31 043	-0.2
1985/86	3 959	8 025	18 850	578	31 412	1.2
1986/87	4 070	8 074	18 711	577	31 432	0.1
1987/88	4 160	8 291	18 268	542	31 261	-0.5
1988/89	4 093	8 266	17 778	484	30 621	-2.0
1989/90	4 261	8 618	17 903	558	31 340	2.3
1990/91	4 520	8 842	17 830	669	31 861	1.7

1 Full-time teaching and research staff in posts wholly financed from general university funds excluding the Open University.
2 Includes Ulster Polytechnic which merged with the University of Ulster in October 1984.

Source: Universities Funding Council

Education

5.14 Students at university[1,2]
United Kingdom
Academic years

Number

		1980/81	1981/82	1982/83	1983/84	1984[3]/85	1985/86	1986/87	1987/88	1988/89	1989/90	1990/91
Full-time students												
Total full-time students	KBKA	306 614	308 394	303 965	300 593	305 008	310 145	316 290	320 920	333 547	350 981	370 254
of which												
Total overseas students	KBKB	31 275	28 365	27 520	28 732	29 994	34 357	37 208	38 512	39 756	41 532	43 496
Total postgraduate students	KBKC	48 439	47 674	46 232	48 355	50 189	53 805	56 199	56 117	58 354	60 696	65 282
Total women students	KBKD	115 691	118 840	119 381	118 910	122 555	125 203	128 814	132 674	140 647	151 247	161 895
Overseas students as a percentage of total	KBKE	10.2	9.2	9.1	9.6	9.8	11.1	11.8	12.0	11.9	11.8	11.7
Postgraduate students as a percentage of total	KBKF	15.8	15.5	15.2	16.1	16.5	17.3	17.8	17.5	17.5	17.3	17.6
Women students as a percentage of total	KBKG	37.7	38.5	39.3	39.6	40.2	40.4	40.7	41.3	42.2	43.1	43.7
At undergraduate level												
Total	KBKH	258 175	260 720	257 733	252 238	254 819	256 340	260 091	264 803	275 193	290 285	304 972
Men	KBKI	157 335	156 685	152 869	148 633	148 367	148 320	149 516	150 808	154 783	161 126	167 438
Women	KBKJ	100 840	104 035	104 864	103 605	106 452	108 020	110 575	113 995	120 410	129 159	137 534
From United Kingdom												
Total	KBKK	242 771	246 965	244 506	238 751	240 918	240 401	242 546	246 122	255 733	269 590	283 418
Men	KBKL	146 162	146 886	143 580	139 231	138 812	137 715	138 121	139 010	142 722	148 567	154 544
Women	KBKM	96 609	100 079	100 926	99 520	102 106	102 686	104 425	107 112	113 011	121 023	128 874
From overseas												
Total	KBKN	15 404	13 755	13 227	13 487	13 901	15 939	17 545	18 681	19 460	20 695	21 554
Men	KBKO	11 173	9 799	9 289	9 402	9 555	10 605	11 395	11 798	12 061	12 559	12 894
Women	KBKP	4 231	3 956	3 938	4 085	4 346	5 334	6 150	6 883	7 399	8 136	8 660
At postgraduate level												
Total	KBKQ	48 439	47 674	46 232	48 355	50 189	53 805	56 199	56 117	58 354	60 696	65 282
Men	KBKR	33 588	32 869	31 715	33 050	34 086	36 622	37 960	37 438	38 117	38 608	40 921
Women	KBKS	14 851	14 805	14 517	15 305	16 103	17 183	18 239	18 679	20 237	22 088	24 361
From United Kingdom												
Total	KBKT	32 568	33 064	31 939	33 110	34 096	35 388	36 536	36 286	38 058	39 859	43 340
Men	KBKU	21 072	21 354	20 527	21 172	21 502	22 125	22 599	22 124	22 887	23 305	25 171
Women	KBKV	11 496	11 710	11 412	11 938	12 594	13 263	13 937	14 162	15 171	16 554	18 169
From overseas												
Total	KBKW	15 871	14 610	14 293	15 245	16 093	18 417	19 663	19 831	20 296	20 837	21 942
Men	KBKX	12 516	11 515	11 188	11 878	12 584	14 497	15 361	15 314	15 230	15 303	15 750
Women	KBKY	3 355	3 095	3 105	3 367	3 509	3 920	4 302	4 517	5 066	5 534	6 192
Part-time students												
Total part-time students	KBKZ	33 311	34 613	34 942	36 319	40 752	42 274	44 519	46 062	50 097	53 850	58 604
At undergraduate level												
Total	KBLA	4 779	5 258	5 450	6 159	8 806	9 172	9 441	9 927	10 179	10 558	11 692
Men	KBLB	2 421	2 476	2 496	2 839	4 491	4 542	4 514	4 541	4 514	4 640	4 963
Women	KBLC	2 358	2 782	2 954	3 320	4 315	4 630	4 927	5 386	5 665	5 918	6 729
From United Kingdom												
Total	KBLD	4 281	4 909	5 056	5 551	8 168	8 576	8 596	9 405	9 659	10 084	10 983
Men	KBLE	2 227	2 303	2 311	2 575	4 205	4 291	4 252	4 319	4 278	4 428	4 687
Women	KBLF	2 054	2 606	2 745	2 976	3 963	4 285	4 704	5 086	5 381	5 656	6 296
From overseas												
Total	KAJX	498	349	394	608	638	596	485	522	520	474	709
Men	KAJY	194	173	185	264	286	251	262	222	236	212	276
Women	KAJZ	304	176	209	344	352	345	223	300	284	262	433
At postgraduate level												
Total	KAKA	28 532	29 355	29 492	30 160	31 946	33 102	35 078	36 135	39 918	43 292	46 912
Men	KAKB	20 143	20 352	20 072	20 270	21 203	21 720	23 037	23 030	24 494	25 981	27 474
Women	KAKC	8 389	9 003	9 420	9 890	10 743	11 382	12 041	13 105	15 424	17 311	19 438
From United Kingdom												
Total	KAKD	24 571	25 850	26 231	26 923	28 657	29 300	30 734	32 511	35 997	39 129	42 161
Men	KAKE	17 228	17 823	17 729	17 948	18 815	18 914	19 745	20 554	21 854	23 119	24 137
Women	KAKF	7 343	8 027	8 502	8 975	9 842	10 386	10 989	11 957	14 143	16 010	18 024
From overseas												
Total	KAKG	3 961	3 505	3 261	3 237	3 289	3 802	4 344	3 624	3 921	4 163	4 751
Men	KAKH	2 915	2 529	2 343	2 322	2 388	2 806	3 292	2 476	2 640	2 862	3 337
Women	KAKI	1 046	976	918	915	901	996	1 052	1 148	1 281	1 301	1 414

1 Excluding the Open University.
2 Overseas students defined by fee-paying status. From 1980/81 most European Community students paid home fees and are therefore excluded from the overseas figures and are shown as home students.
3 Includes Ulster Polytechnic which merged with the University of Ulster in October 1984.

Source: Universities Funding Council

Education

5.15 Students at universities[1]: UK New admissions taking courses, & numbers of full-time students by country of home residence & university residence

Academic years

Number

			1980/81	1981/82	1982/83	1983/84	1984[2]/85	1985[2]/86	1986/87	1987/88	1988/89	1989/90	1990/91
New students admitted (full-time only)													
Men	KBMA		52 214	50 646	48 387	46 939	50 280	49 108	49 569	49 907	52 409	56 397	58 309
Women	KBMB		34 613	33 879	33 452	32 601	36 178	35 689	36 649	38 721	40 758	46 298	48 797
Students taking courses (full and part-time)													
Men	KBMC		213 487	212 382	207 152	204 792	208 147	211 204	215 027	215 817	221 908	230 355	240 796
Women	KBMD		126 438	130 625	131 755	132 120	137 613	141 215	145 782	151 165	161 736	174 476	188 062
Full-time students													
Total	KBME	Men	190 923	189 554	184 584	181 683	182 453	184 942	187 476	188 246	192 900	199 734	208 359
	KBMF	Women	115 691	118 840	119 381	118 910	122 555	125 203	128 814	132 674	140 647	151 247	161 895
Advanced	KBMG	Men	33 588	32 869	31 715	33 050	34 086	36 622	37 960	37 438	38 117	38 608	40 921
	KBMH	Women	14 851	14 805	14 517	15 305	16 103	17 183	18 239	18 679	20 237	22 088	24 361
First degree	KBMI	Men	155 601	154 991	151 299	146 806	145 434	145 166	146 052	147 707	151 507	157 198	163 003
	KBMJ	Women	99 107	102 416	103 201	101 841	103 976	104 918	107 195	110 474	116 522	124 440	132 093
First diploma	KBMK	Men	281	275	178	212	1 132	211	240	194	185	160	184
	KBML	Women	119	123	93	101	543	272	198	137	109	89	129
Others	KBMM	Men	1 453	1 419	1 392	1 615	1 801	2 943	3 224	2 907	3 091	3 768	4 251
	KBMN	Women	1 614	1 496	1 570	1 663	1 933	2 830	3 182	3 384	3 779	4 630	5 312
Part-time students													
Total	KBMO	Men	22 564	22 828	22 568	23 109	25 694	26 262	27 551	27 571	29 008	30 621	32 437
	KBMP	Women	10 747	11 785	12 374	13 210	15 058	16 012	16 968	18 491	21 089	23 229	26 167
Advanced	KBMQ	Men	20 143	20 352	20 072	20 270	21 203	21 720	23 037	23 030	24 494	25 981	27 474
	KBMR	Women	8 389	9 003	9 420	9 890	10 743	11 382	12 041	13 105	15 424	17 311	19 438
First degree	KBMS	Men	1 644	1 699	1 770	1 896	2 694	2 740	2 770	2 883	3 004	3 179	3 378
	KBMT	Women	1 378	1 751	1 972	2 199	2 785	3 192	3 298	3 638	3 840	4 005	4 309
First diploma	KBMU	Men	84	70	52	70	824	392	175	155	115	108	102
	KBMV	Women	64	48	26	31	263	113	63	79	104	97	108
Occasional	KBMW	Men	693	707	674	873	973	1 410	1 569	1 503	1 395	1 353	1 483
	KBMX	Women	916	983	956	1 090	1 267	1 325	1 566	1 669	1 721	1 816	2 312
Country of home residence:[3]													
United Kingdom	KBMY		270 442	273 443	270 323	266 458	269 872	270 440	273 326	275 365	284 436	297 483	311 515
Foreign and Commonwealth countries	KBMZ		36 172	34 951	33 642	34 135	35 136	39 705	42 964	45 555	49 111	53 498	58 739
University residence[4,5]													
Colleges and hostels	KBNA	Men	87 766	88 974	87 196	86 486	85 588	86 570	87 373	86 442	87 326	87 776	88 632
	KBNB	Women	52 728	53 542	54 569	54 368	54 742	55 520	57 157	58 023	59 948	63 045	65 662
Lodgings	KBNC	Men	69 131	68 016	66 566	65 752	64 311	67 197	65 858	67 576	69 992	75 988	81 625
	KBND	Women	40 568	42 838	42 949	42 941	43 379	45 990	45 857	47 509	51 814	57 439	62 601
At home	KBNE	Men	27 758	26 156	25 340	23 423	23 356	22 950	23 061	23 280	24 693	25 111	26 170
	KBNF	Women	18 029	17 674	17 715	16 680	17 209	17 447	18 134	19 045	20 878	22 144	24 104

1 Excluding the Open university.
2 Includes Ulster Polytechnic which merged with the University of Ulster in October 1984. Data for some courses in the categories first diploma and others have been re-coded in 1985/86.
3 Stateless and unknown domicile included in the overseas figure.
4 Including those students on courses 'not of university standard', but not those sandwich students undertaking the industrial part of their training away from the university or college at the time of the student count, which is the end of the autumn term (31 December).
5 Excludes students whose type of residence is other than those listed or unknown.

Source: Universities Funding Council

Education

5.16 Universities[1]: full-time students analysed by subject group of study
United Kingdom
Academic years

Thousands

			1983/84	1984[2]/85	1985[3]/86	1986/87	1987/88	1988/89	1989/90	1990/91
Medicine and dentistry:										
Men	KFEY	KAKJ	26.5	26.8	15.2	14.9	14.8	14.7	14.5	14.2
Women		KAKK			11.5	11.5	11.5	11.8	12.0	12.2
Subjects allied to medicine:										
Men	KFEZ	KAKL	8.0	8.1	3.0	3.1	3.1	3.3	3.5	3.8
Women		KAKM			5.7	5.8	5.9	6.1	6.7	7.6
Biological sciences:										
Men	KFGI	KAKN	20.0	20.3	10.1	10.4	10.5	10.8	11.2	11.8
Women		KAKO			10.5	10.9	11.3	11.9	13.2	14.4
Agriculture and related subjects:										
Men	KFGJ	KAKP	6.3	6.2	3.6	3.7	3.7	3.7	3.6	3.6
Women		KAKQ			2.6	2.7	2.6	2.7	2.7	2.8
Physical sciences:										
Men	KFGK	KAKR	26.7	27.1	20.9	20.9	20.5	20.6	21.5	22.2
Women		KAKS			6.3	6.4	6.7	6.9	7.6	8.4
Mathematical sciences:										
Men	KFGL	KAKT	17.9	18.1	13.8	14.0	14.7	15.7	16.8	17.9
Women		KAKU			4.7	4.6	4.6	5.0	5.5	6.1
Engineering and technology:										
Men	KFGM	KAKV	39.0	39.4	36.7	37.3	37.4	37.1	37.9	39.2
Women		KAKW			3.6	4.0	4.3	4.7	5.1	5.8
Architecture, building and planning:										
Men	KFGN	KAKX	4.7	5.0	4.0	3.9	4.0	4.0	4.1	4.5
Women		KAKY			1.3	1.4	1.5	1.6	1.8	1.8
Social studies:										
Men	KFGO	KAKZ	41.7	42.9	24.1	24.6	24.7	25.7	26.4	28.0
Women		KALA			19.6	20.6	21.3	22.7	23.4	25.2
Business and administrative studies:										
Men	KFGP	KALB	12.8	13.3	9.2	9.5	10.1	10.7	11.6	12.1
Women		KALC			5.3	5.9	6.5	7.0	7.7	7.9
Mass communications and documentation:										
Men	KFGQ	KALD	0.8	0.9	0.4	0.4	0.4	0.5	0.6	0.7
Women		KALE			0.7	0.7	0.6	0.8	0.9	1.0
Languages and related disciplines:										
Men	KFGR	KALF	31.0	30.9	10.0	9.9	9.8	10.2	10.6	11.4
Women		KALG			21.2	21.2	21.5	22.4	23.7	25.2
Humanities:										
Men	KFGS	KALH	17.4	17.8	9.4	9.8	9.9	10.1	10.7	11.5
Women		KALI			7.9	8.0	8.2	8.5	9.2	10.1
Creative arts:										
Men	KFGT	KALJ	4.0	4.1	1.9	1.9	2.0	2.3	2.3	2.3
Women		KALK			2.5	2.8	2.9	3.4	3.6	3.5
Education:										
Men	KFGU	KALL	11.0	11.0	4.7	5.0	4.4	4.4	4.4	4.4
Women		KALM			6.4	6.6	6.6	7.3	8.2	8.9
Multidisciplinary:										
Men	KFGV	KALN	32.9	33.3	17.8	18.2	18.4	19.2	20.0	20.8
Women		KALO			15.5	15.7	16.6	17.9	19.9	21.1

1 Excludes the Open University.
2 Includes Ulster Polytechnic which merged with the University of Ulster in October 1984.
3 A new subject classification was introduced in 1985 when certain subjects were reclassified and combinations of subjects were classified separately for the first time.

Source: Universities Funding Council

5.17 Universities[1]: degrees and diplomas obtained by full-time students
Calendar years

Number

			1980	1981	1982	1983	1984[2]	1985[2]	1986	1987	1988	1989	1990
Degrees													
First degrees - honours: Men		KBLJ	35 127	36 018	36 696	37 103	36 940	36 119	35 823	35 845	36 735	37 473	38 324
Women		KBLK	21 344	22 563	24 273	25 636	25 577	26 122	25 988	26 601	27 799	28 578	30 121
First degrees - ordinary[3]: Men		KBLL	7 704	7 743	7 387	7 520	7 031	6 057	5 405	5 518	5 520	5 301	4 973
Women		KBLM	3 975	4 218	4 272	4 659	4 293	3 911	3 696	3 853	3 702	3 601	3 745
Higher degrees: Men		KBLN	14 414	14 746	14 864	15 565	15 593	16 802	17 354	18 559	19 176	20 424	20 905
Women		KBLO	4 511	4 803	5 209	5 671	5 936	6 754	7 219	8 008	8 676	9 794	10 419
Total: Men		KBLH	57 245	58 507	58 947	60 188	59 564	58 978	58 582	60 059	61 431	63 198	64 202
Women		KFGW	29 830	31 584	33 754	35 966	35 806	36 787	36 903	38 475	40 177	41 973	44 285
Diplomas and certificates: Men		KBLP	7 044	7 260	7 572	6 853	6 613	6 447	5 867	6 800	6 659	6 621	6 712
Women		KBLQ	5 754	6 015	6 208	5 547	5 587	5 751	5 706	6 303	6 611	6 599	7 000

1 Excluding the Open University
2 Includes Ulster Polytechnic which merged with the University of Ulster in October 1984.
3 Includes some degrees where the class is not recorded.

Source: Universities Funding Council

Education

5.18 Scientific research: postgraduate awards and special grants
At 1 October in each year

		1980[1]	1981	1982	1983	1984	1985	1986	1987	1988	1989	1990	1991
Special research grants													
Number of new awards	KBOA	4 394	2 462	2 355	2 609	2 493	2 901	2 988	3 372	2 219	2 477	3 092	2 320
Number current: total	KBOB	5 056	5 024	5 056	5 476	5 389	5 350	5 824	6 230	5 037	4 651	5 989	5 343
Biological sciences	KBOC	720	752	754	713	644	626	627	714	712	660	719	428
Biotechnology[2]	KBOD	–	–	–	95	103	103	124	130	123	105	103	52
Chemistry/enzyme chemistry	KBOE	670	668	618	572	525	506	535	542	489	346	333	290
Computing science	KBOF	..	..	..	..	154	–	–	–	–	–	–	–
Mathematics	KBOG	73	66	94	136	185	189	255	258	255	247	244	176
Science Board co-operative grants	KBOH	–	–	–	–	–	33	38	45	51	41	–	–
Process engineering[3]	KBOI	–	–	–	–	141	127	227	170	107	125	140	216
Control engineering	KBOJ	–	–	–	–	–	–	–	–	–	–	–	–
Electrical and systems engineering	KBOK	–	–	–	–	–	–	–	–	–	–	–	–
Aeronautical and mechanical engineering	KBOL	–	–	–	–	–	–	–	–	–	–	–	–
Civil and transport engineering	KBOM	–	–	–	–	–	–	–	–	–	–	–	–
Manufacturing technology	KBON	–	–	–	–	–	–	–	–	–	–	–	–
Materials	KBOO	344	381	346	335	300	266	310	301	246	–	–	–
Physics (other than nuclear)	KBOP	357	339	331	508	427	412	415	413	375	213	229	197
Nuclear physics	KBOQ	98	117	143	143	127	118	101	192	70	71	65	71
Astronomy[5]) Planetary } Sciences)	KBOR	397	388	371	355	355	334	330	475	390	386	382	380
Information science	KBOS	82	63	87	78	98	97	75	76	85	65	78	–
Geology and geophysics	KBOT	186	183	178	167	119	123	113	152	156	114	192	–
Social sciences	KBOU	506	319	324	381	420	522	454	473	563	651	645	647
Neutron beam	KBOV	70	77	71	66	66	78	91	81	66	49	39	26
Polymer science/engineering	KBOW	114	117	106	90	82	75	–	–	–	–	–	–
Laser facility	KBOX	14	13	14	26	33	34	31	34	36	34	27	25
Science based archaeology	KBOY	25	22	22	25	31	35	37	37	24	28	28	24
Synchroton radiation facility	KBOZ	51	73	77	98	103	114	117	126	113	100	81	55
Engineering processes	KBPA	224	229	225	212	132	–	–	–	–	–	–	–
Built environment [12]	KBPB	160	172	197	236	270	251	265	274	203	222	272	254
Information technology	KBPC	320	370	378	489	404	379	369	360	272	486	628	715
Alvey Directorate	KBPD	–	–	–	–	–	163	361	351	305	111	22	3
Electro-Mechanical Engineering[6]	KBPE	277	341	349	357	343	331	323	336	246	263	276	246
ACME	KBPF	–	–	–	–	–	142	178	194	153	146	124	130
Marine technology	KBPG	55	61	73	84	73	68	107	95	106	114	110	107
Teaching company	KBPH	38	65	98	146	173	191	251	307	328	339	363	362
Energy	KBPI	27	39	47	52	–	–	–	–	–	–	–	–
Joint SERC/ESRC[4]	KBPJ	19	31	25	28	26	20	16	12	15	20	22	15
IRC[9]	KFHO	–	–	–	–	–	–	–	–	–	9	9	24
LINK [13]	KFHP	..	..	..	..	..	..	..	..	–	–	–	224
MSEC [8]	KFHQ	..	..	..	..	..	..	..	..	–	523	562	543
Science Board Computing [11]	KFHR	..	..	..	..	..	..	..	..	–	–	–	77
Engineering Board Space Engineering [11]	KFHS	..	..	..	..	..	..	..	..	–	–	–	1
Other grants	KBPK	229	138	128	84	55	14	74	82	105	169	296	–
Total expenditure on grants (years beginning 1 April) (£ thousand)	KBPL	67 567	73 769	80 082	88 494	95 958	106 747	116 813	141 527	142 389	155 175	205 624	184 180
Postgraduate awards													
Studentships:													
Number of new awards	KBPM	5 207	4 791	4 501	5 814	5 602	5 960	6 001	5 927	6 129	5 588	6 789[10]	5 776
Number current: total	KBPN	11 173	10 622	10 132	11 278	11 349	11 809	12 036	12 072	12 276	5 082	12 864[10]	12 072
Biological sciences/Biology	KBPO	1 989	1 924	1 861	1 820	1 813	1 891	1 925	1 974	1 922	1 446	1 879	1 476
Biotechnology[2]	KBPP	–	–	–	112	157	194	203	206	241	244	267	278
Chemical engineering	KBPQ	–	–	–	–	71	227	–	–	–	–	–	–
Chemistry/enzyme chemistry	KBPR	1 534	1 488	1 456	1 464	1 507	1 552	1 595	1 599	1 498	1 456	1 423	1 430
Electrical engineering	KBPS	–	–	–	–	–	–	–	–	–	–	–	–
Aeronautical and mechanical engineering	KBPT	–	–	–	–	–	–	–	–	–	–	–	–
Civil and transport engineering	KBPU	–	–	–	–	–	–	–	–	–	–	–	–
Manufacturing technology	KBPV	–	–	–	–	–	–	–	–	–	–	–	–
Materials	KBPW	412	434	477	515	509	468	454	435	460	257	119	8
Total technology	KBPX	–	–	–	81	82	87	83	84	99	–	116	135
Geology and geophysics	KBPY	473	498	499	496	477	1 104	484	485	489	492	494	–
Mathematics	KBPZ	614	587	531	562	551	525	629	673	684	698	718	733
Physics	KBQA	572	521	519	534	535	–	569	584	631	619	576	504
Science - Board Computing	KBQB	–	–	–	–	–	–	–	–	–	–	8	8
Social sciences	KBQC	2 348	1 758	1 727	1 689	1 536	1 481	1 392	1 402	1 336	1 082	1 101	1 166
Control engineering	KBQD	–	–	–	–	–	–	–	–	–	–	–	–
Polymer science/engineering	KBQE	–	27	26	20	21	18	7	4	–	–	–	–
Information science /technology[7]	KBQF	81	51	53	1 130	1 699	2 071	2 532	2 639	2 790	2 643	2 715	2 820
ACME	KBQG	–	–	–	–	103	163	167	155	148	179	209

Note: See footnotes on page 106.

Sources: *The British Library Research and Development Department;*
Science and Engineering Research Council;
Natural Environment Research Council;
Economic and Social Research Council;
Department for Education

Education

5.18 Scientific research: postgraduate awards and special grants
At 1 October in each year
continued

		1980[1]	1981	1982	1983	1984	1985	1986	1987	1988	1989	1990	1991
Postgraduate awards *(continued)*													
Neutron beam	KBQH	5	9	9	7	3	1	–	–	–	–	–	–
Science based archaeology	KBQI	24	27	29	31	32	42	41	43	65	77	94	86
Astronomy, & Planetary Sciences[5]	KBQJ	248	246	232	249	246	253	257	251	258	253	263	280
Nuclear physics	KBQK	179	176	178	180	184	186	194	191	194	195	199	217
Engineering processes[2]	KBQL	370	368	349	360	188	–	–	–	–	–	–	–
Built environment [12]	KBQM	261	535	323	316	318	351	350	324	321	297	380	378
Information engineering	KBQN	770	829	731	667	360	310	19	–	–	–	–	–
Electro-Mechanical Engineering[6]	KBQO	583	415	406	398	384	367	355	320	309	309	396	417
Marine technology	KBQP	76	92	95	107	105	113	100	71	85	56	83	93
Energy	KBQQ	42	42	43	58	66	37	11	–	–	–	–	–
Joint SERC/ESRC[3]	KBQR	313	288	267	201	174	179	204	224	228	218	243	230
Other	KBQS	279	307	321	281	236	231	204	210	324	458	636	130
Production	KBQT	–	–	–	–	95	65	29	5	–	–	–	–
Process engineering	KBQU	–	–	–	–	–	–	267	257	257	246	227	224
MSEC[8]	KEAH	–	–	–	–	–	–	–	–	–	302	673	945
IRC[9]	KEAG	–	–	–	–	–	–	–	–	–	37	75	123
Engineering design [11]	KFGX	–	–	–	–	–	–	–	–	–	–	–	22
TriCouncil [11]	KFGY	–	–	–	–	–	–	–	–	–	–	–	65
DES Switch [11]	KFGZ	–	–	–	–	–	–	–	–	–	–	–	160
Fellowships:													
Number of new awards	KBQV	109	118	96	128	159	51	56	70	133	131	203	182
Number current	KBQW	264	291	275	282	344	227	227	203	185	284	430	392
Bursaries:													
Number of new awards	KBQX	200	159	127	144	–	86	82	81	76	71	70	74
Number current	KBQY	235	178	133	155	–	87	88	86	79	71	70	74
Total expenditure on awards (years beginning 1 April) (£ thousand)	KBQZ	54 930	47 064	49 083	55 322	60 355	64 729	67 837	70 896	73 617	78 153	91 498	86 107

1 The Science Research Council became the Science and Engineering Research Council from mid - 1981, incorporating additional classifications.
2 Biotechnology was included in Other before 1983.
3 Until 1984 Chemical Engineering and Production Engineering were contained within the Engineering Processes Committee. In 1985 Engineering Processes reorganised, forming the Application of Computers to Manufacturing Engineering Directorate (ACME) and Process Engineering, which subsumed Chemical Engineering.
4 The Social Science Research Council became the Economic and Social Research Council on 1 January 1984.
5 Astronomy, Space and Radio became Astronomy & Planetary Sciences from September 1986.
6 Machines & Power became Electro-Mechanical Engineering from May 1987.
7 All SERC I.T. provision is recorded under information technology and includes provision under the DES Engineering and Technology programme (The 'Switch'). At the conclusion of the Alvey programme on 1.9.88 the Joint Framework for Information Technology (JFIT) was formed with the Department of Trade and Industry. This covers all research Grants covered by the Information Technology Directorate.
8 The Materials Science and Engineering Commission was formed on 1.9.88. It subsumed the National Committee for Super Conductivity, the Materials Committee, the Molecular Electronics Committee and part of the areas covered by Chemistry and Physics Committees.
9 Interdisciplinary Research Centres by SERC to provide a focus for the development of research programmes in interdisciplinary topics of strategic importance.
10 Figures are not complete totals for year.
11 Until 1991, Science Board Computing, Engineering Design, Engineering Board Space Engineering, DES Switch and the TriCouncil Initiative in Cognitive Science and Human Computer Interface were included in 'Other'.
12 Environment became Built Environment from September 1990.
13 LINK projects are intended to increase the commercial exploitation of scientific research in HEI's and can cover the entire spectrum of science and technology.

Sources: The British Library Research and Development Department;
Science and Engineering Research Council;
Natural Environment Research Council;
Economic and Social Research Council;
Department for Education

5.19 Student awards
New and current, by type

Education

Thousands

		1978/79	1979/80	1980/81	1981/82	1982/83	1983/84	1984/85	1985/86	1986/87	1987/88	1988/89	1989[5]/90
New awards													
All new awards	KBRA	235.2[4]	241.0[4]	243.4[4]	264.7[4]	267.4[4]	285.3	289.5	296.6	304.5	311.3	309.9	328.6
Postgraduate awards: Made by education departments and the research councils	KBRB	10.3[4]	10.5[4]	10.4[4]	9.3[4]	9.1[4]	9.0	9.4	9.5	9.3	8.7	8.7	9.4
Local education authorities[1]	KBRC	2.4	2.2	2.2	2.4	3.0	3.0	3.5	3.9	4.3	4.6	4.9	4.8[6]
Undergraduate and non-graduate awards at university	KBRD	71.7[4]	72.9[4]	74.5[4]	73.2[4]	70.4[4]	70.7	72.2	71.9	72.2	74.5	76.2	81.0
Teacher training awards	KBRE	24.0	23.5	21.2	21.5	19.7	18.9	18.9	18.9	19.5	21.2	21.8	23.0
Other awards: Including polytechnics and colleges first degree and comparable courses[2], further and higher education courses, state scholarships and adult education bursaries[3]	KBRF	71.7	73.7	79.6	91.6	96.5	102.4	102.0	102.1	104.7	105.9	109.4	124.3
Awards paid at 50 per cent or less of the mandatory rate	KBRG	55.2[4]	58.3[4]	55.5[4]	66.7[4]	68.7[4]	81.3	83.5	90.2	94.5	96.4	88.9	86.0[6]
Current awards													
All current awards[3]	KBRH	529.4	536.8	545.7	586.2	604.4	637.3	656.0	664.3	676.1	690.0	698.2	706.5
Postgraduate awards: Made by education departments and the research councils	KBRI	19.6	19.2	19.0	18.1	17.6	18.2	18.2	18.9	17.3	16.0	17.2	19.1
Local education authorities[1]	KBRJ	2.6	2.4	2.3	2.5	3.1	3.1	4.0	4.4	7.0	7.3	7.0	7.1
Undergraduate and non-graduate awards at university	KBRK	218.5	224.6	231.1	237.1	232.1	231.4	225.2	225.4	232.8	236.3	240.3	240.6
Teacher training awards	KBRL	61.4	50.1	44.1	41.4	37.7	37.0	38.1	39.4	40.5	42.0	43.7	45.6
Other awards: Including polytechnics and other colleges first degree and comparable courses,[2] further and higher education courses, state scholarships and adult education bursaries[3]	KBRM	154.4	160.5	171.8	193.2	212.4	234.5	242.5	244.5	243.3	249.4	261.1	267.9
Awards paid at 50 per cent or less of the mandatory rate	KBRN	72.9	80.1	77.3	93.8	101.5	113.1	127.9	131.6	135.2	139.0	128.9	126.2[6]

1 Postgraduate course awards made under Section 2 of the Education Act 1962 (excluding initial teacher training) in England and Wales (includes estimated numbers of new awards prior to 1975/76).
2 'Comparable courses' are courses at establishments of further and higher education which have been designated under the University and other Awards regulations, 1965, as comparable to first degree courses.
3 The adult education bursary scheme commenced in September 1975 and operates in England, Wales and Scotland.
4 United Kingdom estimate based upon data for England, Wales and Northern Ireland.
5 Revised figures.
6 Includes estimates for Scotland.

Source: Education Departments

6. Employment

6.1 Distribution of the workforce
At mid-June each year

Thousands, seasonally adjusted

		1979	1980	1981	1982	1983	1984	1985	1986	1987	1988	1989	1990	1991[11]
United Kingdom														
Workforce[1]	KAML	26 580	26 759	26 697	26 610	26 633	27 309	27 743	27 877	28 007	28 347	28 480	28 530	28 340
Males	KAMM	16 174	16 247	16 288	16 175	16 113	16 350	16 509	16 442	16 414	16 427	16 346	16 323	16 240
Females	KAMN	10 406	10 511	10 409	10 435	10 519	10 959	11 234	11 435	11 663	11 920	12 134	12 208	12 100
Unemployed[2,3,4,5]	KAMO	1 068	1 274	2 176	2 521	2 905	2 897	3 019	3 121	2 836	2 295	1 785	1 611	2 293
Males	KAMP	770	910	1 605	1 848	2 028	2 040	2 100	2 154	1 979	1 600	1 276	1 189	1 739
Females	KAMQ	297	363	571	673	778	857	919	967	858	695	510	422	554
Workforce in employment[6]	KAMR	25 365	25 301	24 323	23 889	23 611	24 226	24 530	24 559	25 084	25 922	26 693	26 918	26 043
Males	KAMS	15 328	15 242	14 569	14 213	13 961	14 201	14 294	14 173	14 341	14 746	15 069	15 133	14 498
Females	KAMT	10 037	10 059	9 754	9 676	9 650	10 025	10 236	10 386	10 744	11 176	11 624	11 785	11 544
HM Forces[7]	KAMU	314	323	334	324	322	326	326	322	319	316	308	303	297
Males	KAMV	299	307	317	309	306	310	309	305	302	300	291	286	278
Females	KAMW	15	16	17	15	16	16	16	16	16	16	16	18	19
Self-employed persons (with or without employees)[8]	KAMX	1 906	2 013	2 119	2 169	2 219	2 496	2 614	2 633	2 869	2 998	3 253	3 298	3 143
Males	KAMZ	1 550	1 622	1 694	1 699	1 703	1 901	1 976	1 993	2 157	2 264	2 487	2 511	2 396
Females	KANA	357	391	425	471	517	595	637	640	712	734	766	786	747
Employees in employment[9]	KANB	23 145	22 965	21 870	21 395	21 054	21 229	21 414	21 379	21 586	22 266	22 670	22 894	22 259
Males	KANC	13 480	13 313	12 558	12 205	11 944	11 895	11 908	11 748	11 705	11 978	11 999	12 076	11 613
Females	KAND	9 665	9 652	9 312	9 190	9 109	9 334	9 506	9 631	9 881	10 288	10 671	10 818	10 646
of whom														
Total, production and construction industries	KANF	9 215	8 911	8 068	7 621	7 232	7 080	6 992	6 777	6 688	6 746	6 753	6 686	6 247
Total, all manufacturing industries	KANG	7 258	6 944	6 230	5 873	5 538	5 424	5 377	5 242	5 171	5 215	5 208	5 167	4 846
Work Related Government Training Programmes[10]	KANH	..	..	..	..	16	175	176	226	311	343	462	423	343
Males	KANI	..	..	..	..	8	95	100	127	177	205	291	260	211
Females	KANJ	..	..	..	..	8	80	76	99	134	138	171	163	132
Great Britain														
Workforce[1]	KANK	25 916	26 088	26 028	25 944	25 955	26 627	27 050	27 172	27 367	27 631	27 765	27 815	27 616
Males	KANL	15 774	15 844	15 879	15 772	15 705	15 940	16 093	16 020	15 991	16 005	15 928	15 905	15 817
Females	KANM	10 142	10 244	10 150	10 171	10 250	10 688	10 956	11 152	11 376	11 627	11 837	11 910	11 799
Unemployed[2,3,4,5]	KANN	1 015	1 214	2 089	2 424	2 699	2 787	2 907	2 998	2 714	2 181	1 679	1 514	2 193
Males	KANO	734	869	1 542	1 778	1 949	1 960	2 018	2 064	1 889	1 517	1 198	1 116	1 663
Females	KANP	282	345	547	646	750	828	889	934	825	664	482	398	530
Workforce in employment[6]	KANQ	24 767	24 706	23 753	23 329	23 047	23 660	23 954	23 982	24 502	25 324	26 084	26 299	25 419
Males	KANR	14 969	14 886	14 232	13 885	13 635	13 875	13 963	13 845	14 010	14 409	14 729	14 788	14 153
Females	KANS	9 798	9 819	9 521	9 443	9 411	9 785	9 990	10 137	10 492	10 915	11 355	11 511	11 267
HM Forces[7]	KANT	314	323	334	324	322	326	326	322	319	316	308	303	297
Males	KANU	299	307	317	309	306	310	309	305	302	300	291	286	278
Females	KANV	15	16	17	15	16	16	16	16	16	16	16	18	19
Self-employed persons (with or without employees)[8]	KANW	1 842	1 950	2 058	2 109	2 160	2 435	2 550	2 567	2 801	2 926	3 182	3 222	3 066
Males	KANX	1 494	1 567	1 641	1 647	1 652	1 850	1 923	1 937	2 099	2 205	2 428	2 449	2 333
Females	KANY	348	383	417	462	508	586	628	630	701	721	754	773	733
Employees in employment[9]	KANZ	22 611	22 432	21 362	20 896	20 557	20 731	20 910	20 876	21 081	21 748	22 143	22 363	21 734
Males	KAOA	13 176	13 012	12 275	11 930	11 674	11 625	11 637	11 481	11 437	11 706	11 725	11 802	11 344
Females	KAOB	9 435	9 421	9 087	8 966	8 882	9 106	9 273	9 395	9 643	10 042	10 417	10 561	10 390
of whom														
Total, production and construction industries	KAOC	9 022	8 727	7 907	7 470	7 087	6 936	6 848	6 639	6 550	6 606	6 613	6 547	6 114
Total, all manufacturing industries	KAOD	7 113	6 808	6 107	5 761	5 431	5 316	5 269	5 138	5 068	5 109	5 101	5 062	4 744
Work Related Government Training Programmes[10]	KAOE	..	..	..	..	8	168	168	218	303	335	452	410	323
Males	KAOF	..	..	..	..	3	91	94	122	171	199	285	252	198
Females	KAOG	..	..	..	..	5	78	74	96	132	135	167	159	125

Note: Because the figures have been rounded independently totals may differ from the sum of the components. Also the totals may include some employees whose industrial classification could not be ascertained.

1 The workforce is the workforce in employment plus the claimant unemployed.
2 From October 1982 new basis (claimants); article in *Employment Gazette*, December 1982, page S20 refers.
3 From October 1980 the figures are affected by the introduction in Great Britain of fortnightly payment of unemployment benefit. This is estimated to have resulted in an artificial increase of 20 000 (13 000 males and 7 000 females) in the count of the unemployed and therefore a corresponding reduction should be made when comparing the 1980 figures with those of earlier years.
4 From April 1983, the figures of unemployment reflect the effects of the provisions in the Budget for some men aged 60 and over who no longer have to sign on at an unemployment office. It is estimated that 132 500 men were affected over the period April to June 1983, and a further 29 300 were affected in July and August 1983, The total effect was a reduction in the coverage of the unemployment count of 161 800.
5 Due to a change in the compilation of the unemployment statistics to remove over-recording (see *Employment Gazette* March/April 1986, pp107-108), unadjusted figures from February 1986 are not directly comparable with earlier figures. It is estimated that the change reduced the total UK count by 50 000 on average.
6 The workforce in employment comprises employees in employment, the self-employed, HM Forces and work related government training programmes.
7 HM Forces figures, provided by the Ministry of Defence, represent the total number of UK service personnel, male and female, in HM Regular Forces, wherever serving and including those on release leave.
8 Estimates of the self-employed up to mid-1989 are based on the 1981 Census of Population and the results of the Labour Force Surveys. A detailed description of the current estimates is given in the article on p182 of the April 1990 edition of *Employment Gazette*.
9 Estimates of employees in employment from December 1987 to August 1989 include an allowance based on the Labour Force Survey to compensate for persistent undercounting in the regular sample enquiries (*Employment Gazette*, October 1989 p56). For all dates, individuals with two jobs as employees of different employers are counted twice.
10 Includes all participants on government training and employment programmes who are receiving some work experience on their placement but who do not have a contract of employment (those with a contract are included in the employees in employment series). The numbers are not subject to seasonal adjustment.
11 Estimates from September 1989 are based on data provided by the New Panel of employers (see article on p191 of the April 1992 edition of *Employment Gazette*).

Source: Department of Employment

Employment

6.2 Employees in employment
Analysis by industry based on the Standard Industrial Classification 1980
At June in each year

Thousands, not seasonally adjusted

		SIC 1980	United Kingdom								Great Britain						
			1985	1986	1987	1988	1989	1990	1991		1985	1986	1987	1988	1989	1990	1991
All industries and services	KAOH	0 - 9	21 423	21 387	21 584	22 258	22 661	22 898	22 268	KAPN	20 920	20 886	21 080	21 740	22 134	22 369	21 743
Index of production and construction industries	KAOI	1 - 5	6 974	6 760	6 669	6 727	6 634	6 662	6 224	KAPO	6 830	6 622	6 531	6 587	6 594	6 524	6 090
Index of production industries	KAOJ	1 - 4	5 953	5 771	5 660	5 680	5 651	5 593	5 261	KAPP	5 836	5 658	5 548	5 566	5 537	5 480	5 151
of which, manufacturing industries	KAOK	2 - 4	*5 362*	*5 227*	*5 152*	*5 195*	*5 187*	*5 144*	*4 822*	KAPQ	*5 254*	*5 122*	*5 049*	*5 089*	*5 080*	*5 039*	*4 720*
Service industries	KAOL	6 - 9	14 108	14 297	14 594	15 218	15 627	15 938	15 754	KAPR	13 769	13 954	14 247	14 860	15 261	15 567	15 381
Agriculture, forestry and fishing	KAOM	0	341	329	321	313	300	298	291	KAPS	321	310	302	293	280	278	272
Agriculture and horticulture	KAON	01	323	311	303	295	282	279	272	KAPT	304	293	285	276	263	260	254
Energy and water supply	KAOO	1	591	545	508	485	465	449	439	KAPU	582	536	499	477	457	441	431
Coal extraction and solid fuels	KAOP	111	..	..	..	..	..	..	..	KAPV	216	177	145	120	103	91	82
Electricity	KAOQ	161	..	..	..	..	..	..	..	KAPW	146	143	142	143	142	139	136
Gas	KAOR	162	..	..	..	..	..	..	..	KAPX	91	88	84	82	79	76	77
Other mineral and ore extraction	KAOS	2	779	729	694	689	711	722	660	KAPY	768	720	685	680	701	712	650
Metal manufacturing and extraction of metal ores and minerals	KAOT	21 - 23	217	194	177	166	177	191	165	KAPZ	215	192	175	164	174	189	163
Non-metallic mineral products	KAOU	24	220	204	194	196	202	204	188	KAQA	215	200	190	192	197	200	184
Chemical industry/man-made fibres	KAOV	25/26	342	331	323	328	333	327	307	KAQB	339	328	320	324	329	324	303
Basic industrial chemicals	KAOW	251	..	..	..	..	..	..	..	KAQC	123	119	115	115	117	115	..
Other chemical products and preparations	KAOX	255-259/260	..	..	..	..	..	..	..	KAQD	216	209	205	205	209	211	..
Metal goods, engineering and vehicles	KAOY	3	2 443	2 372	2 331	2 359	2 351	2 312	2 148	KAQE	2 410	2 340	2 299	2 327	2 318	2 280	2 117
Metal goods nes	KAOZ	31	329	320	323	335	335	322	300	KAQF	327	318	321	333	333	320	298
Hand tools and finished metal goods including doors and windows	KAPA	314-316	..	..	..	..	..	..	..	KAQG	192	184	191	197	192	184	..
Other metal goods	KAPB	311-313	..	..	..	..	..	..	..	KAQH	135	133	130	137	140	135	..
Mechanical engineering	KAPC	32	764	749	744	764	771	748	685	KAQI	756	741	737	757	763	740	678
Industrial plant and steelwork	KAPD	320	..	..	..	..	..	..	..	KAQJ	86	86	90	96	101	103	..
Machinery for agriculture, metal working, textile, food and printing etc industries	KAPE	321/322/324/ 326/327	..	..	..	..	..	..	..	KAQK	203	195	190	190	189	182	..
Mining and construction machinery etc	KAPG	325	..	..	..	..	..	..	..	KAQM	78	76	74	73	76	77	..
Other machinery and mechanical equipment incl. ordnance, small arms and ammunition	KAPH	323/328/329	..	..	..	..	..	..	..	KAQN	389	384	383	399	397	382	..
Office machinery, data processing equipment	KAPI	33	88	83	82	84	82	80	77	KAQO	88	83	82	84	82	80	76
Electrical and electronic engineering	KAPJ	34	596	573	563	559	561	564	531	KAQP	589	567	556	552	553	557	524
Wires, cables, batteries and other electrical equipment	KAPK	341/342/343	..	..	..	..	..	..	..	KAQQ	218	208	200	199	199	196	189
Telecommunication equipment	KAPL	344	..	..	..	..	..	..	..	KAQR	175	168	165	162	162	161	155
Other electronic and electrical equipment	KAPM	345-348	..	..	..	..	..	..	..	KAQS	195	192	191	190	192	199	180

Sources: Department of Manpower Services (Northern Ireland); Department of Employment

Employment

6.2 Employees in employment
Analysis by industry based on the Standard Industrial Classification 1980
continued   At June in each year

Thousands, not seasonally adjusted

		SIC 1980			United Kingdom								Great Britain				
			1985	1986	1987	1988	1989	1990	1991		1985	1986	1987	1988	1989	1990	1991
Motor vehicles and parts	KAQT	35	274	266	260	271	264	247	223	KASH	271	263	257	268	262	244	220
Motor vehicles and engines	KAQU	351/352	..	..	..	..	..	..	..	KASI	157	156	155	163	161	154	..
Bodies, trailers, caravans, motor vehicle parts	KAQV	353	..	..	..	..	..	..	..	KASJ	114	107	102	105	101	91	..
Other transport equipment	KAQW	36	288	276	256	244	239	257	241	KASK	276	263	244	232	228	247	230
Shipbuilding and repairing	KAQX	361	..	..	..	..	..	..	..	KASL	78	70	58	52	47	53	..
Aerospace and other transport equipment	KAQY	362-365	..	..	..	..	..	..	..	KASM	198	194	186	180	181	195	..
Instrument engineering	KAQZ	37	105	105	103	102	98	93	91	KASN	103	105	102	101	97	92	90
Other manufacturing industries	KARA	4	2 140	2 126	2 128	2 146	2 125	2 109	2 014	KASO	2 075	2 063	2 065	2 082	2 061	2 047	1 953
Food, drink and tobacco	KARB	41/42	596	576	571	561	549	546	563	KASP	575	555	551	541	530	527	544
Meat and meat products, organic oils and fats	KARC	411/412	..	..	..	..	..	..	..	KASQ	93	93	94	97	96	95	..
Bread, biscuits and flour confectionery	KARD	419	..	..	..	..	..	..	..	KASR	133	130	137	130	125	120	..
Alcoholic, soft drink and tobacco manufacture	KARE	424-429	..	..	..	..	..	..	..	KASS	119	108	101	97	90	83	77
All other food and drink manufacture	KARF	413-418/420-423	..	..	..	..	..	..	..	KAST	229	224	219	218	219	221	..
Textiles	KARH	43	245	249	240	240	226	202	186	KASU	234	238	229	229	215	192	177
Footware and clothing	KARI	45	312	314	310	313	311	293	260	KASV	295	297	294	296	294	275	244
Clothing, hats, gloves and fur goods	KARJ	453/4560	..	..	..	..	..	..	..	KASW	213	211	205	204	195	189	170
Timber and wooden furniture	KARK	46	210	220	227	239	246	250	226	KASX	205	215	222	233	242	245	221
Paper, printing and publishing	KARL	47	483	472	480	483	494	492	480	KASY	477	467	474	478	487	486	474
Pulp, paper, board and derived products	KARM	471/472	..	..	..	..	..	..	..	KASZ	134	132	137	140	140	138	134
Printing and publishing	KARN	475	..	..	..	..	..	..	..	KATA	343	335	338	338	347	348	340
Rubber and plastics	KARO	48	195	198	203	214	215	223	211	KATB	192	194	199	210	214	219	207
Other manufacturing	KARP	49	77	76	76	74	73	83	70	KATC	77	76	76	74	76	82	69
Construction	KARQ	5	1 021	989	1 009	1 047	1 058	1 070	962	KATD	994	964	983	1 021	1 056	1 044	939
Distribution, hotels, catering, repairs	KARR	6	4 295	4 298	4 310	4 494	4 645	4 822	4 686	KATE	4 212	4 213	4 223	4 405	4 639	4 728	4 590
Wholesale distribution	KARS	61	904	894	898	924	944	971	928	KATF	883	874	877	903	935	951	909
Agricultural and textile raw materials, fuels, ores, metals, etc	KART	611/612	..	..	..	..	..	..	..	KATG	124	122	119	119	119	118	118
Timber and building materials	KARU	613	..	..	..	..	..	..	..	KATH	126	126	130	139	141	134	122
Machinery, industrial equipment, vehicles and parts	KARV	614	..	..	..	..	..	..	..	KATI	169	169	168	180	191	202	191
Food, drink and tobacco	KARW	617	..	..	..	..	..	..	..	KATJ	234	231	233	230	231	237	232
Other wholesale distribution	KARX	615/616/618/619	..	..	..	..	..	..	..	KATK	230	226	227	236	252	259	145
Retail distribution	KARZ	64/65	2 080	2 097	2 101	2 179	2 289	2 288	2 195	KATM	2 038	2 054	2 057	2 132	2 234	2 237	2 143
Food	KASA	641	..	..	..	..	..	..	..	KATN	583	584	586	615	656	667	632
Confectioners, tobacconists etc.	KASB	642	..	..	..	..	..	..	..	KATO	123	119	113	103	108	109	118
Dispensing and other chemists	KASC	643	..	..	..	..	..	..	..	KATP	109	113	116	121	128	127	124
Clothing, footware and leather goods	KASD	645/646	..	..	..	..	..	..	..	KATQ	235	231	235	244	248	234	224
Household goods, hardware, ironmongery	KASE	648	..	..	..	..	..	..	..	KATR	212	212	214	230	242	237	..
Motor vehicles and parts, filling stations	KASF	651/652	..	..	..	..	..	..	..	KATS	230	235	231	244	260	270	265
Other retail distribution	KASG	653-656	..	..	..	..	..	..	..	KATT	522	533	533	544	562	572	540

*Sources: Department of Manpower Services (Northern Ireland);
Department of Employment*

6.2 Employees in employment
continued
Analysis by industry based on the Standard Industrial Classification 1980
At June in each year

Thousands, not seasonally adjusted

		SIC 1980	\multicolumn{7}{c}{United Kingdom}		\multicolumn{7}{c}{Great Britain}
			1985	1986	1987	1988	1989	1990	1991		1985	1986	1987	1988	1989	1990	1991
Hotels and catering	KDZX	66	1 042	1 042	1 046	1 123	1 140	1 277	1 251	KAVL	1 027	1 026	1 028	1 105	1 198	1 256	1 230
Restaurants, cafes, snack bars etc	KATU	661	..	..	..	..	..	..	..	KAVM	223	229	240	265	290	306	296
Public houses and bars	KATV	662	..	..	..	..	..	..	..	KAVN	266	260	263	289	326	337	317
Night clubs and licensed clubs	KATW	663	..	..	..	..	..	..	..	KAVO	140	138	137	141	140	142	146
Canteens and messes	KATX	664	..	..	..	..	..	..	..	KAVP	129	128	122	129	140	147	146
Hotel trade	KATY	665	..	..	..	..	..	..	..	KAVQ	234	238	231	245	263	283	284
Repair of consumer goods and vehicles	KATZ	67	218	215	213	216	217	228	253	KAVR	215	211	209	213	215	225	251
Motor vehicles	KAUA	671	..	..	..	..	..	..	..	KAVS	186	184	183	187	190	192	..
Transport and communication	KAUB	7	1 327	1 298	1 285	1 321	1 337	1 382	1 349	KAVT	1 308	1 279	1 266	1 301	1 340	1 361	1 328
Railways	KAUC	71	148	143	140	137	134	130	132	KAVU	147	142	139	136	130	129	131
Other inland transport	KAUD	72	416	395	383	388	387	433	421	KAVV	410	389	377	381	407	426	414
Scheduled road passenger transport	KAUE	721	..	..	..	..	..	..	..	KAVW	182	166	158	151	156	168	..
Other including road haulage	KAUF	722-726	..	..	..	..	..	..	..	KAVX	229	223	219	230	251	257	..
Sea transport	KAUG	74	37	34	34	35	36	33	33	KAVY	37	33	34	34	35	33	33
Air transport	KAUH	75	50	52	53	60	61	64	62	KAVZ	49	51	52	59	62	63	61
Supporting services to transport	KAUI	76	95	93	91	92	94	92	89	KAWA	94	92	90	91	92	91	88
Miscellaneous transport and storage	KAUJ	77	154	160	162	171	179	191	188	KAWB	152	159	160	169	177	189	186
Postal services and Telecommunications	KAUK	79	427	420	422	439	447	439	423	KAWC	419	412	413	430	438	431	415
Postal services	KAUL	7901	..	..	..	..	..	..	..	KAWD	192	188	192	200	205	210	204
Telecommunications	KAUM	7902	..	..	..	..	..	..	..	KAWE	227	224	222	231	233	221	211
Banking, finance, insurance etc	KAUN	8	2 068	2 166	2 280	2 460	2 627	2 745	2 693	KAWF	2 039	2 136	2 250	2 428	2 594	2 710	2 658
Banking and finance	KAUO	81	521	534	562	606	631	630	616	KAWG	513	526	554	598	622	621	607
Banking and bill discounting	KAUP	814	..	..	..	..	..	..	..	KAWH	393	400	416	446	461	453	444
Other financial institutions	KAUQ	815	..	..	..	..	..	..	..	KAWI	120	126	138	151	161	168	164
Insurance, except social security	KAUR	82	227	228	236	251	257	262	264	KAWJ	224	225	233	248	254	259	261
Business services	KAUS	83	1 097	1 174	1 253	1 376	1 492	1 573	1 534	KAWK	1 084	1 160	1 239	1 361	1 475	1 556	1 517
Professional business services	KAUT	831-837	..	..	..	..	..	..	..	KAWL	672	713	752	820	876	914	42
Other business services	KAUU	838/839	..	..	..	..	..	..	..	KAWM	412	447	487	541	599	642	586
Renting of movables	KAUV	84	103	108	107	110	120	135	134	KAWN	102	107	106	108	120	134	133
Owning and dealing in real estate	KAUW	85	119	122	122	118	140	145	144	KAWO	116	118	118	113	122	141	140
Other services	KAUX	9	6 418	6 536	6 719	6 943	6 908	6 988	7 026	KAWP	6 209	6 326	6 508	6 726	6 688	6 768	6 805
Public administration and defence	KAUY	91	1 587	1 595	1 633	1 634	1 556	1 601	1 634	KAWQ	1 532	1 539	1 577	1 578	1 501	1 545	1 565
National Government nes social security	KAUZ	9111/9190	..	..	..	..	..	..	..	KAWR	497	516	539	533	520	517	522
Local Government services nes	KAVA	9112	..	..	..	..	..	..	..	KAWS	603	594	606	602	539	597	607
Justice, police, fire services	KAVB	912-914	..	..	..	..	..	..	..	KAWT	307	306	309	317	318	316	322
National defence	KAVC	915	..	..	..	..	..	..	..	KAWU	126	123	122	126	123	115	114
Sanitary services	KAVD	92	334	333	337	351	374	388	364	KAWV	330	329	332	346	369	382	357
Education	KAVE	93	1 616	1 650	1 698	1 748	1 778	1 805	1 799	KAWW	1 557	1 592	1 641	1 691	1 721	1 748	1 741
Research and development	KAVF	94	114	112	110	114	104	96	96	KAWX	113	111	109	113	103	95	95
Medical and other health services	KAVG	95	1 347	1 359	1 383	1 436	1 465	1 479	1 514	KAWY	1 301	1 312	1 337	1 388	1 418	1 431	1 467
Other services	KAVH	96	743	804	870	963	921	893	896	KAWZ	712	772	837	927	882	855	858
Social welfare etc	KAVI	9611	..	..	..	..	..	..	..	KAXA	564	601	647	718	716	715	702
Recreational and culture services	KAVJ	97	490	493	500	507	508	525	529	KAXB	482	484	491	498	499	516	520
Personal services	KAVK	98	186	191	187	190	201	202	205	KAXC	182	187	183	185	196	197	201

Sources: Department of Manpower Services (Northern Ireland);
Department of Employment

Employment

6.3 Persons employed in engineering industries
Analysed by broad occupational category[1]
Great Britain at April 1989

Thousands

	\multicolumn{7}{c}{Males}						
	All employees	Managerial, administrative, technical and clerical	Foremen[3]	Craftsmen (production and maintenance)	All other production and other occupations	All apprentices[5]	Craft apprentices[5]	Others being trained[4,5]

Industry based on the Standard Industrial Classification 1980[2]

	All employees	Managerial etc.	Foremen	Craftsmen	All other production	All apprentices	Craft apprentices	Others being trained
Metal manufacturing	38.99	7.43	2.50	5.08	23.99	0.19	0.19	0.66
Steel tubes	10.62	1.82	0.72	1.43	6.65	0.08	0.08	0.08
Drawing, cold rolling and cold forming of steel	1.00	0.28	0.05	0.10	0.57	-	-	0.02
Non-ferrous metals industry	27.37	5.33	1.72	3.55	16.77	0.11	0.11	0.56
Manufacturing of metal goods nes	231.20	44.50	13.92	43.75	129.03	1.83	1.51	5.00
Foundries	52.09	8.21	2.88	11.80	29.21	0.34	0.28	0.95
Forging, pressing, stamping	25.88	4.29	1.60	4.30	15.69	0.10	0.80	0.40
Bolts, nuts, etc, springs, non-precision chains, metals treatment	27.91	5.51	1.90	3.69	16.81	0.16	0.14	0.36
Metal doors, windows, etc	18.63	4.69	1.13	2.30	10.51	0.06	0.01	0.27
Hand tools and finished metal goods	106.69	21.80	6.41	21.67	56.81	1.17	1.00	3.02
Mechanical engineering	445.18	133.16	24.33	128.98	158.71	5.33	4.29	10.37
Industrial plant and steelwork	45.23	14.20	2.65	15.23	13.16	0.64	0.46	0.76
Agricultural machinery and tractors	17.34	4.79	0.80	2.53	9.23	0.12	0.08	0.22
Metal-working machine tools and engineers' tools	50.01	12.21	2.52	19.19	16.09	0.61	0.57	1.59
Textile machinery	5.53	1.29	0.31	2.11	1.83	0.10	0.10	0.09
Machinery for food, chemical and related industries; process engineering contractors	21.88	8.54	1.31	6.80	5.23	0.40	0.30	0.30
Mining machinery, construction and mechanical handling equipment	57.46	17.21	3.23	17.04	19.98	0.70	0.51	1.47
Mechanical power transmission equipment	17.82	3.84	1.12	3.75	9.12	0.25	0.23	0.58
Machinery for the printing, paper, wood, leather, rubber, glass and related industries; laundry and dry cleaning machinery	16.40	6.70	0.83	5.36	3.51	0.32	0.31	0.19
Other machinery and mechanical equipment	200.35	59.18	10.89	52.97	77.31	1.82	1.39	4.79
Ordnance, small arms and ammunition	13.17	5.21	0.69	4.00	3.27	0.37	0.33	0.39
Manufacture of office machinery and data processing equipment	63.00	45.86	2.21	3.02	11.92	0.26	0.07	1.96
Electrical and electronic engineering	316.35	150.23	17.45	39.94	108.72	3.68	1.86	10.39
Insulated wires and cables	21.19	6.40	1.26	2.17	11.36	0.13	0.07	0.37
Basic electrical equipment	60.21	24.31	3.24	13.39	19.27	0.98	0.64	1.85
Electrical equipment for industrial use, and batteries and accumulators	39.56	16.98	2.18	6.16	14.23	0.26	0.18	0.99
Telecommunications equipment, electrical measuring equipment, electronic capital goods and passive electronics components	123.35	74.99	6.49	11.87	30.01	1.59	0.62	4.81
Other electronic equipment	36.51	18.95	2.17	2.73	12.67	0.47	0.18	1.69
Domestic-type electric appliances	23.04	4.64	1.07	1.94	15.39	0.15	0.11	0.27
Electric lamps and other electric lighting equipment	12.11	3.76	1.02	1.62	5.72	0.10	0.06	0.43
Electrical equipment installation	0.38	0.20	0.02	0.08	0.08	0.01	-	0.01
Manufacture of motor vehicles and parts thereof	203.38	42.08	8.94	32.44	119.93	1.50	1.10	3.16
Motor vehicles and their engines	130.31	28.26	5.49	19.70	76.86	1.04	0.73	2.02
Motor vehicle bodies, trailers and caravans	13.56	1.92	0.64	3.48	7.52	0.05	0.03	0.16
Motor vehicle parts	59.51	11.90	2.81	9.26	35.55	0.42	0.34	0.98
Manufacture of other transport equipment	147.87	60.03	8.06	50.00	29.78	3.14	2.60	3.61
Shipbuilding and repairing	0.48	0.08	0.03	0.02	0.34	-	-	-
Railway and tramway vehicles	18.81	3.86	0.64	9.15	5.16	0.26	0.23	0.36
Cycles and motor cycles	2.46	0.43	0.10	0.11	1.83	-	-	-
Aerospace equipment manufacturing and repairing	125.58	55.57	7.27	40.65	22.10	2.87	2.37	3.24
Other vehicles	0.53	0.08	0.02	0.08	0.35	0.01	-	-
Instrument engineering	49.61	26.37	2.42	7.56	13.26	0.43	0.23	1.48
Measuring, checking and precision instruments and apparatus	29.74	17.30	1.53	4.41	6.50	0.34	0.18	1.08
Medical and surgical equipment and orthopaedic appliances	6.34	2.58	0.32	1.28	2.17	0.01	0.01	0.13
Optical precision instruments and photographic equipment	12.53	6.17	0.50	1.71	4.16	0.07	0.04	0.26
Clocks, watches and other timing devices	0.99	0.32	0.07	0.17	0.43	-	-	0.01
All other engineering industries nes	9.01	7.07	0.25	0.88	0.82	0.13	0.02	0.30
Total	1 504.59	516.73	80.07	311.65	596.15	16.48	11.87	36.93

1 This occupational survey is carried out by the EITB as at April every year, on a sample basis. The final survey in this series was carried out in April 1990. All the figures in this table are estimates based on this survey and other EITB data. For information about the detailed methods used please contact the Statistics Section, EITB, 54 Clarendon Road, Watford, Herts. WD1 1LB. Telephone: Watford (0923) 38441.
2 Only that part of each industry which is within the scope of the EITB is included in the figures.
3 Except works and other senior foremen and office supervisors, who are included in the preceding column.
4 Excluding canteen staff and seafarers.
5 Included in the previous columns.

Source: Engineering Industry Training Board (EITB)

Employment

6.3 continued
Persons employed in engineering industries
Analysed by broad occupational category[1]
Great Britain at April 1989

Thousands

	All employees	Managerial, administrative, technical and clerical	Foremen[3]	Craftsmen (production and maintenance)	All other production and other occupations	All apprentices[5]	Craft apprentices[5]	Others being trained[4,5]
Females								
Industry based on the Standard Industrial Classification 1980[2]								
Metal manufacturing	6.83	3.16	0.15	0.02	3.51	-	-	0.07
Steel tubes	1.70	0.81	0.02	0.01	0.86	-	-	0.02
Drawing, cold rolling and cold forming of steel	0.17	0.14	-	-	0.03	-	-	-
Non-ferrous metals industry	4.96	2.21	0.13	-	2.62	-	-	0.05
Manufacturing of metal goods nes	61.41	23.05	0.86	0.23	37.28	0.03	0.01	1.52
Foundries	6.61	3.29	0.08	0.04	3.20	-	-	0.21
Forging, pressing, stamping	8.25	2.12	0.08	0.07	5.99	-	-	0.12
Bolts, nuts, etc, springs, non-precision chains, metals treatment	9.01	3.42	0.10	0.05	5.45	0.01	-	0.36
Metal doors, windows etc	3.82	2.37	0.09	-	1.36	-	-	0.04
Hand tools and finished metal goods	33.73	11.86	0.52	0.08	21.28	0.02	0.01	0.80
Mechanical engineering	74.28	48.23	1.34	0.47	24.24	0.12	0.05	2.67
Industrial plant and steelwork	4.31	3.83	0.08	0.01	0.39	0.01	-	0.17
Agricultural machinery and tractors	1.57	1.28	0.02	-	0.27	-	-	0.05
Metal-working machine tools and engineers' tools	7.94	5.02	0.17	0.04	2.71	-	-	0.41
Textile machinery	0.87	0.52	-	0.02	0.33	-	-	0.03
Machinery for food, chemical and related industries; process engineering contractors	3.96	3.05	0.09	0.02	0.80	-	-	0.22
Mining machinery, construction and mechanical handling equipment	7.23	6.26	0.12	0.06	0.79	0.02	0.02	0.46
Mechanical power transmission equipment	3.00	1.51	0.03	0.01	1.45	-	-	0.10
Machinery for the printing, paper, wood, leather, rubber, glass and related industries; laundry and dry cleaning machinery	2.70	2.21	0.05	0.01	0.43	0.02	-	0.07
Other machinery and mechanical equipment	39.41	23.04	0.68	0.21	15.48	0.05	0.01	1.10
Ordnance, small arms and ammunition	3.28	1.50	0.10	0.08	1.59	0.02	0.02	0.06
Manufacture of office machinery and data processing equipment	24.54	15.20	0.54	0.16	8.64	0.01	-	1.03
Electrical and electronic engineering	158.74	52.17	4.01	1.51	101.05	0.23	0.04	5.13
Insulated wires and cables	9.84	2.73	0.25	0.03	6.83	0.01	-	0.20
Basic electrical equipment	22.18	7.51	0.44	0.17	14.06	0.03	0.01	0.42
Electrical equipment for industrial use, and batteries and accumulators	16.56	6.58	0.39	0.14	9.46	0.01	-	0.58
Telecommunications equipment, electrical measuring equipment, electronic capital goods and passive electronics components	62.78	23.21	1.85	0.86	36.87	0.16	0.02	2.53
Other electronic equipment	25.08	6.45	0.74	0.12	17.77	0.02	-	0.94
Domestic-type electric appliances	10.85	3.60	0.16	0.01	7.07	-	-	0.24
Electric lamps and other electric lighting equipment	11.35	1.99	0.18	0.19	8.99	0.01	-	0.22
Electrical equipment installation	0.10	0.09	-	-	-	-	-	-
Manufacture of motor vehicles and parts thereof	23.77	10.66	0.35	0.08	12.69	0.05	0.01	0.73
Motor vehicles and their engines	10.55	5.85	0.18	0.05	4.47	0.04	0.01	0.34
Motor vehicle bodies, trailers and caravans	0.83	0.59	0.02	-	0.22	-	-	0.07
Motor vehicle parts	12.39	4.22	0.15	0.03	8.00	0.01	-	0.32
Manufacture of other transport equipment	18.78	14.36	0.52	0.25	3.66	0.12	0.08	0.72
Shipbuilding and repairing	0.03	0.03	-	-	-	-	-	-
Railway and tramway vehicles	1.54	1.03	0.03	-	0.47	-	-	0.02
Cycles and motor cycles	0.47	0.19	-	-	0.27	-	-	-
Aerospace equipment manufacturing and repairing	16.66	13.06	0.49	0.24	2.88	0.11	0.07	0.70
Other vehicles	0.09	0.05	-	-	0.03	-	-	-
Instrument engineering	17.06	8.76	0.43	0.19	7.68	0.03	0.01	0.42
Measuring, checking and precision instruments and apparatus	10.62	5.22	0.29	0.11	5.00	0.01	0.01	0.27
Medical and surgical equipment and orthopaedic appliances	2.04	1.13	0.06	0.06	0.79	-	-	0.03
Optical precision instruments and photographic equipment	3.59	2.20	0.07	0.02	1.29	0.01	-	0.11
Clocks, watches and other timing devices	0.82	0.21	0.01	-	0.60	-	-	0.01
All other engineering industries nes	1.86	1.61	0.02	0.01	0.22	0.01	-	0.10
Total	387.27	177.19	8.22	2.91	198.95	0.59	0.19	12.39

1 This occupational survey is carried out by the EITB as at April every year, on a sample basis. The final survey in this series was carried out in April 1990. All the figures in this table are estimates based on this survey and other EITB data. For information about the detailed methods used please contact the Statistics Section, EITB, 54 Clarendon Road, Watford, Herts. WD1 1LB: Telephone Watford (0923) 38441.
2 Only that part of each industry which is within the scope of the EITB is included in the figures.
3 Except works and other senior foremen and office supervisors, who are included in the preceding column.
4 Excluding canteen staff and seafarers.
5 Included in previous columns.

Source: Engineering Industry Training Board (EITB)

Employment

6.4 Administrative, technical and clerical workers in manufacturing industries [1]
Analysis by industry based on Standard Industrial Classification 1980
Great Britain

Percentage

		Division/class SIC 1980	1986	1987	1988	1989	1990	1991
All manufacturing industries	KAXD	2 - 4	27.3	26.4	26.7	26.7	30.1	31.5
Mineral and ore extraction other than fuels	KAXE	2	29.2	27.7	30.0	27.4	31.7	34.4
Non-metallic mineral products	KAXF	24	21.2	21.1	21.8	21.9	26.4	27.1
Metal goods, engineering etc	KAXG	3	31.7	30.6	30.3	30.6	33.2	34.8
Metal goods nes	KAXH	31	19.5	20.0	19.3	19.0	23.9	23.5
Mechanical engineering	KAXI	32	31.4	30.2	29.3	28.5	34.4	35.3
Office machinery etc	KAXJ	33	49.5	53.4	45.2	57.8	48.1	61.7
Electrical and electronic engineering	KAXK	34	36.4	34.7	34.3	35.7	37.8	39.7
Motor vehicles and parts	KAXL	35	22.6	21.2	22.1	21.4	25.4	22.1
Other transport equipment	KAXM	36	38.9	37.5	41.9	41.4	33.2	38.8
Instrument engineering	KAXN	37	33.0	31.3	34.5	30.9	35.8	37.4
Other manufacturing industries	KAXO	4	21.7	21.3	21.6	22.2	26.0	26.8
Food, drink and tobacco	KAXP	41/42	20.3	19.4	20.2	19.4	22.6	22.7
Textiles	KAXQ	43	17.0	16.3	18.9	18.5	21.2	21.6
Footwear and clothing	KAXR	45	12.7	13.3	12.8	13.3	16.6	16.2
Timber and wooden furniture	KAXS	46	22.2	23.1	20.0	22.6	25.7	26.3
Paper, printing and publishing	KAXT	47	30.6	30.9	31.2	32.4	38.0	40.2
Rubber and plastics	KAXU	48	22.5	20.6	22.0	21.6	24.7	26.9

1 Expressed as a percentage of total number of employees at September.

Source: Department of Employment

6.5 Number of workers employed in agriculture [1,2,3]
United Kingdom
At June in each year

Thousands

	Regular workers					Seasonal or casual workers			All workers			Salaried managers[4]
		Whole - time		Part - time								
	Total	Male	Female	Male	Female	Total	Male	Female	Total	Male	Female	
	KAXV	KAXW	KAXX	KAXY	KAXZ	KAYA	KAYB	KAYC	KAYD	KAYE	KAYF	KAYG
1982	232.2	154.6	16.0	31.9	29.7	98.7	57.3	41.5	331.0	243.8	87.2	7.9
1983	228.3	152.2	15.5	31.3	29.4	97.9	56.9	41.0	326.2	240.3	85.9	7.8
1984	220.8	145.6	15.2	30.7	29.4	95.6	56.7	38.8	316.3	233.0	83.4	7.8
1985	218.0	141.6	15.1	31.5	29.8	97.2	58.1	39.1	315.2	231.1	84.1	8.3
1986	210.3	134.1	14.8	32.2	29.1	95.3	57.2	38.1	305.5	223.5	82.1	8.3
1987	202.1	126.9	14.6	31.5	29.0	93.4	55.8	37.6	295.5	214.2	81.3	7.9
1988	195.5	120.4	14.6	31.5	29.2	92.7	56.1	37.6	288.2	207.8	80.3	7.9
1989	187.7	114.0	15.1	30.8	27.8	88.3	54.0	34.3	276.0	198.8	77.2	7.8
1990	184.8	109.7	15.5	31.5	28.1	90.5	55.5	34.9	275.3	196.7	78.6	8.1
1991	178.3	104.6	14.9	31.1	27.6	86.6	53.8	32.8	264.9	189.6	75.3	7.9

See notes on page 108.
1 Figures exclude school children, farmers, partners and directors and their wives.
2 Figures include estimated figures for Scotland.
3 Includes estimates for minor holdings in England and Wales.
4 Great Britain only.

Source: Ministry of Agriculture, Fisheries and Food

6.6 Rates of unemployment [1]
Analysis by standard regions
Seasonally adjusted [2]

Percentages

		1981	1982	1983	1984	1985	1986	1987	1988	1989	1990	1991
Annual averages												
United Kingdom	KAYH	8.1	9.5	10.5	10.7	10.9	11.1	10.0	8.1	6.3	5.8	8.1
Great Britain	KAYI	8.0	9.4	10.3	10.6	10.8	11.0	9.8	7.9	6.1	5.6	7.9
North	KAYJ	11.7	13.3	14.6	15.2	15.4	15.3	14.1	11.9	9.9	8.7	10.4
Yorkshire and Humberside	KAYK	8.8	10.3	11.4	11.7	12.0	12.5	11.3	9.3	7.4	6.7	8.7
East Midlands	KAYL	7.4	8.4	9.5	9.8	9.8	10.0	9.0	7.1	5.4	5.1	7.2
East Anglia	KAYM	6.3	7.4	8.0	7.9	8.1	8.5	7.3	5.2	3.6	3.7	5.8
South East	KAYN	5.5	6.7	7.5	7.8	8.1	8.3	7.2	5.4	3.9	4.0	7.0
South West	KAYO	6.8	7.8	8.7	9.0	9.3	9.5	8.1	6.2	4.5	4.4	7.1
West Midlands	KAYP	10.0	11.9	12.9	12.7	12.8	12.9	11.4	8.9	6.6	5.9	8.6
North West	KAYQ	10.2	12.1	13.3	13.6	13.7	13.7	12.5	10.4	8.5	7.7	9.4
Wales	KAYR	10.4	12.1	12.9	13.2	13.6	13.5	12.0	9.8	7.3	6.6	8.7
Scotland	KAYS	9.9	11.3	12.3	12.6	12.9	13.3	13.0	11.2	9.3	8.1	8.7
Northern Ireland	KAYT	12.7	14.4	15.5	15.9	15.9	17.2	17.0	15.6	14.6	13.4	13.7

1 The number of claimants unemployed as a percentage of the estimated total work-force (the sum of claimant employees in employment, unemployed, self-employed, participants on work related government training programmes and HM Forces) at mid-year.
2 Seasonally adjusted and excluding claimants under 18, consistent with current coverage.

Sources: Department of Economic Development (Northern Ireland); Department of Employment

Employment

6.7 Civil Service staff [1]
Analysis by ministerial responsibility
At 1 April in each year

Full-time equivalents [2] (thousands)

		1981	1982	1983	1984	1985	1986	1987	1988	1989	1990	1991	1992
Agriculture, Fisheries and Food	BCDA	13.6	13.1	12.7	12.1	12.1	11.7	11.3	11.1	10.9	10.7	11.0	10.8
Chancellor of the Exchequer's Departments:[3,4,5]	BCDB	114.9	121.0	117.4	112.4	111.9	111.0	110.1	108.6	109.1	109.2	109.6	111.6
Customs and Excise	BCDC	26.8	26.2	25.4	25.1	25.4	25.1	25.8	26.3	26.4	26.9	27.0	26.4
Inland Revenue	BCDD	75.6	74.0	73.1	69.8	69.8	69.3	67.8	66.6	67.0	66.0	65.7	68.9
Department for National Savings	BCDE	10.0	9.1	8.3	8.0	7.8	7.8	7.7	7.4	7.3	7.0	6.7	6.3
Treasury and others	BCDF	2.5	11.7	10.6	9.5	8.9	8.8	8.8	8.3	8.3	9.3	10.1	10.0
Education and Science [6]	BCDG	3.6	3.5	3.5	2.4	2.4	2.4	2.4	2.5	2.5	2.6	2.7	2.7
Employment	BCDH	53.8	58.7	57.9	56.4	54.7	55.7	60.5	58.3	55.0	52.4	49.0	57.1
Energy [19]	BCDI	1.2	1.1	1.1	1.1	1.1	1.0	1.0	1.0	1.1	1.2	1.2	1.1
Environment [7,8,9,10]	BCDJ	47.0	42.1	39.4	36.6	35.8	34.9	34.2	33.0	30.6	29.2	25.8	23.2
Foreign and Commonwealth [11]	BCDK	11.4	11.1	11.1	10.0	9.8	9.6	9.5	9.6	9.6	9.5	9.9	10.0
Health [22,23]	BAKR	..	..	..	..	..	..	..	..	10.9	7.5	6.7	6.9
Home [11,12]	BCDL	35.4	34.6	35.1	36.4	36.6	37.5	37.6	39.2	40.8	42.7	44.1	49.7
Industry [13]	KAZI	8.8	8.3	7.7	..	..	..	..	..	..	..	..	..
Scotland [14,15]	BCDN	13.6	13.4	13.1	12.8	13.0	12.9	13.0	13.0	12.3	12.6	12.9	13.1
Social Security [21]	BAKS	..	..	..	..	..	..	..	..	83.4	80.9	79.0	78.3
Health and Social Security [21,22]	KAZL	100.1	98.0	96.4	92.6	94.9	94.9	97.7	102.3	..	..	..	..
Trade [13,16]	KAZM	9.3	8.9	8.9	..	..	..	..	..	..	..	..	..
Trade and Industry [12,13,17]	BCDQ	..	..	..	14.7	14.8	14.8	14.8	14.6	14.7	13.6	13.4	12.7
Transport [8,16]	BCDR	13.7	13.0	13.0	14.2	14.4	14.7	14.3	14.1	14.1	15.5	15.3	15.0
Welsh Office	BCDS	2.3	2.3	2.2	2.2	2.3	2.3	2.3	2.2	2.2	2.3	2.3	2.4
Other civil departments [3,20]	BCDT	31.3	20.2	20.5	20.9	21.2	21.5	25.1	26.7	30.7	31.0	30.9	31.3
Total Ministry of Defence [18]	BCDW	229.6	216.9	208.9	199.2	174.0	169.5	164.0	143.4	141.3	141.4	140.2	139.5
Total civil and defence departments	BCDX	689.6	666.4	648.9	624.0	599.0	594.4	597.8	579.6	569.2	562.4	553.9	565.3
of which Non-industrials	BCDY	*539.9*	*528.0*	*518.5*	*504.3*	*498.0*	*498.2*	*507.5*	*506.6*	*499.8*	*495.2*	*490.0*	*504.2*
Industrials	BCDZ	*149.7*	*138.4*	*130.4*	*119.7*	*101.0*	*96.2*	*90.3*	*73.0*	*69.4*	*67.2*	*63.9*	*61.1*
Total civil departments	BCDU	460.0	449.4	440.0	424.8	425.0	424.9	433.8	436.2	427.9	421.0	413.7	425.9

NOTE: figures may not add up due to rounding.

1 The figures include non-industrial and industrial staff but exclude casual or seasonal staff (normally recruited for short periods of not more than twelve months) and employees of the Northern Ireland Government.
2 Part-time employees are counted as half units.
3 The responsibilities for the Paymaster General's Office transferred from the Chancellor of the Exchequer's Departments to 'Other civil departments' on 1 July 1979 (868 staff) but transferred back to the Chancellor of the Exchequer's Departments on 1 October 1990. The Treasury Solicitor was reclassified to 'Other civil departments' on 1 April 1981.
4 Certain Civil Service Department (CSD) divisions, along with responsibility for CISCO, HMSO, COI and the Government Actuary's Department, were transferred to the Chancellor of the Exchequer (9 873 staff in all) on 7 December 1981. From the same date the Management and Personnel Office became responsible for CSD's work on efficiency and personnel management, recruitment and training (1 378 staff).
5 On 1 April 1982, responsibility for the HMSO binderies was transferred to the British Libraries Board, and in Scotland, to the National Library of Scotland. A total of 160 staff have been excluded from the manpower count.
6 As of 1 April 1984 the Victoria and Albert Museum and the Science Museum became non-manpower count bodies, they have been accorded Trustee Status - around 1 100 staff are involved.
7 From 1 October 1980, certain staff in Property Services Agency (1 276 involved) have been excluded from the manpower count.
8 With effect from 1 April 1981, some 765 non-industrial Environment/Transport common services staff employed on work for the Department of Transport and previously counted in the Department of Environment, were instead included in the former's figures.
9 With effect from 1 April 1982, the Department of Environment transferred to the Countryside Commission 96 staff formerly on secondment to it; and hived-off the Hydraulics Research Station with its 244 staff. A total of 340 staff have been excluded from the manpower count.
10 From 1 April 1984 approximately 1 100 staff of the Directorate of Historic Monuments and Ancient Buildings have been transferred to a new Commission outside the manpower count.
11 From 1 April 1984 responsibility for the Passport Office was passed to the Home Office from the Foreign and Commonwealth Office (around 950 staff involved).
12 279 non-industrial staff employed in the Radio Regulatory Department of the Home Office were transferred to the Department of Trade and Industry in June 1983.
13 Following the General Election in June 1983 the former Departments of Trade and Industry merged.
14 Departments of the Secretary of State for Scotland and the Lord Advocate.
15 The State Hospital, Carstairs, was hived-off on 31 March 1984, around 400 staff were involved.
16 Some 1 454 non-industrial staff employed in the Aviation and Shipping divisions of the Department of Trade were transferred in June 1983 to the Department of Transport.
17 At 1 July 1984 a new department, the Office of Telecommunications, was formed under the responsibility of the Secretary of State for Trade and Industry.
18 On 2 January 1985 the Royal Ordnance Factories were incorporated as a Companies Act company and are no longer included in the manpower count.
19 On 18 August 1986 a new department, the Office of Gas Supply, was formed under the responsibility of the Secretary of State for Energy.
20 On 20 July 1987 the Serious Fraud Office was formed with staff transferred from the Crown Prosecution Service.
21 With effect from 25 July 1988 the Department of Health and Social Security was split into the Department of Health and the Department of Social Security.
22 On 1 April 1990 approximately 3 000 staff of the Department of Health were transferred to the NHS and, therefore, are no longer in the manpower count.
23 Includes Office of Population Censuses and Surveys.

Source: HM Treasury

Employment

6.8 Unemployment figures by region [1]
Seasonally adjusted

Thousands

	South East	Greater London[2]	East Anglia	South West	West Midlands	East Midlands	Yorkshire and Humberside	North West	North	Wales	Scotland	Great Britain	Northern Ireland	United Kingdom
	DPBA	KEJS	DPAZ	DPBB	DPBC	DPAY	DPAX	DPBD	DPAW	DPBE	DPBF	DPAG	DPBG	BCJD
1978 Jan	269.0	133.2	29.4	90.4	101.1	63.9	96.9	165.6	93.6	70.5	148.6	1 128.8	52.0	1 179.1
Apr	258.0	126.9	29.2	86.7	100.6	63.5	96.6	164.4	93.3	71.4	143.9	1 107.3	53.9	1 159.5
Jul	250.5	123.1	28.7	83.8	100.6	63.9	96.4	163.6	93.4	71.5	141.0	1 093.7	54.0	1 146.1
Oct	242.0	119.7	27.6	81.0	99.8	62.2	96.3	160.5	94.7	69.9	140.6	1 074.8	52.9	1 126.1
1979 Jan	230.6	114.7	27.3	78.2	98.6	60.5	95.2	157.7	94.2	69.4	138.6	1 049.9	52.4	1 100.7
Apr	223.5	112.0	26.4	75.9	99.2	58.0	94.2	156.1	94.2	68.4	141.0	1 036.5	52.6	1 087.6
Jul	213.3	106.6	24.9	73.1	100.1	56.8	91.6	154.0	93.4	65.6	139.9	1 012.9	53.2	1 064.6
Oct	205.1	102.4	24.4	70.5	100.3	57.3	90.3	155.1	93.3	63.9	140.5	1 000.9	53.0	1 052.5
1980 Jan	206.2	104.0	24.4	69.4	101.5	58.4	91.7	162.3	95.9	65.4	145.2	1 020.2	53.6	1 072.5
Apr	224.7	112.5	26.9	74.3	113.7	65.9	105.7	180.0	106.9	73.1	157.7	1 128.8	57.1	1 184.5
Jul	259.7	126.8	31.5	84.0	135.7	78.7	120.5	200.4	114.8	83.7	170.7	1 280.1	62.5	1 341.2
Oct	317.5	153.8	38.5	98.1	172.0	96.9	144.9	234.8	127.4	100.0	194.5	1 524.4	72.0	1 595.1
1981 Jan	383.0	185.0	45.0	112.8	210.5	114.3	173.0	269.3	147.8	112.3	213.6	1 781.6	79.5	1 859.8
Apr	438.2	210.7	50.2	126.9	241.0	127.9	191.7	296.0	158.7	121.0	232.6	1 984.3	83.7	2 066.7
Jul	485.6	237.7	54.4	134.1	258.8	133.3	206.6	320.9	167.1	129.1	249.8	2 140.0	86.8	2 225.4
Oct	518.6	252.1	56.2	139.6	275.0	140.7	216.7	337.2	175.8	133.4	259.6	2 252.9	89.3	2 340.8
1982 Jan	541.8	263.9	58.6	144.5	287.5	146.6	222.3	347.5	179.2	138.8	267.5	2 334.2	91.6	2 424.2
Apr	561.4	273.9	60.4	146.7	291.3	146.9	226.0	356.0	182.3	141.3	271.1	2 383.3	94.4	2 475.9
Jul	578.1	284.3	62.4	151.7	297.8	151.0	235.1	367.9	189.3	145.1	277.6	2 456.0	97.4	2 551.6
Oct	601.1	294.0	66.0	156.9	306.3	157.1	244.2	379.7	193.8	148.9	285.7	2 539.8	101.6	2 639.6
1983 Jan	620.1	304.9	68.3	162.9	316.0	163.9	251.5	388.3	198.1	152.4	293.0	2 614.3	103.7	2 715.9
Apr	635.4	318.2	69.2	164.8	322.3	167.9	255.5	395.9	200.3	154.1	296.0	2 661.5	105.3	2 764.6
Jul	650.7	328.5	69.4	168.8	325.1	171.5	258.1	400.9	203.3	154.2	300.7	2 702.6	107.6	2 807.8
Oct	658.3	333.9	70.3	170.9	320.7	171.9	257.4	403.5	205.2	154.6	300.7	2 713.4	108.6	2 819.2
1984 Jan	670.6	341.7	70.0	172.7	318.8	175.0	260.7	408.5	207.0	155.5	305.1	2 743.6	109.8	2 850.4
Apr	677.2	345.5	70.3	175.7	319.9	177.8	264.1	409.3	210.5	158.5	305.1	2 768.5	110.2	2 876.5
Jul	690.5	352.8	71.3	178.7	322.2	181.0	268.3	409.8	215.1	160.7	309.3	2 807.0	110.3	2 913.1
Oct	706.8	361.7	72.2	184.4	326.4	186.0	275.3	414.8	219.1	164.9	313.1	2 862.6	109.6	2 965.8
1985 Jan	719.5	369.1	73.4	186.9	327.1	186.8	276.5	418.8	219.7	166.5	314.8	2 890.2	110.4	2 994.1
Apr	728.2	374.4	74.8	190.2	327.8	188.5	281.2	422.0	221.9	168.2	322.5	2 925.4	111.8	3 031.5
Jul	726.8	376.5	75.1	190.0	326.3	187.8	280.5	420.5	221.5	168.9	323.3	2 921.0	112.3	3 025.0
Oct	732.0	380.4	75.7	191.7	326.3	187.4	283.8	422.1	222.4	169.6	325.3	2 936.4	114.3	3 040.9
1986 Jan	740.8	385.2	77.6	194.1	327.0	189.9	291.5	422.3	224.1	171.5	324.9	2 963.8	117.5	3 076.2
Apr	757.3	394.0	78.6	196.7	329.0	190.5	294.1	425.0	222.7	171.6	327.5	2 993.2	121.4	3 111.5
Jul	759.3	396.6	79.7	198.1	329.9	192.4	296.8	427.1	221.9	170.3	334.0	3 009.4	123.8	3 124.0
Oct	745.4	390.7	78.4	194.9	325.5	191.5	294.2	419.6	218.2	165.9	337.7	2 971.0	125.3	3 080.4
1987 Jan	728.8	384.5	77.5	189.9	319.1	189.2	289.5	413.0	216.3	162.3	340.6	2 917.6	125.2	3 042.8
Apr	693.5	367.1	73.7	182.2	306.5	184.5	283.6	401.6	212.0	155.3	337.6	2 816.4	123.6	2 940.0
Jul	654.4	351.3	69.2	171.5	290.8	175.6	270.2	383.6	202.9	149.2	323.2	2 671.1	122.1	2 793.2
Oct	612.5	333.5	64.1	159.7	273.6	165.7	256.2	365.3	194.8	142.6	309.4	2 525.6	120.4	2 646.0
1988 Jan	563.5	316.0	58.4	151.2	257.9	156.5	243.9	349.9	186.3	135.7	299.7	2 394.8	116.7	2 511.5
Apr	530.2	301.8	54.3	142.4	244.2	150.7	236.7	334.4	189.9	132.0	288.9	2 268.6	114.5	2 383.1
Jul	484.6	279.5	49.3	131.7	227.4	141.5	223.7	317.6	172.6	124.4	276.9	2 126.0	113.0	2 239.0
Oct	453.0	267.4	45.1	122.8	210.9	128.3	208.7	305.3	163.1	117.6	267.9	2 029.8	110.9	2 140.7
1989 Jan	409.1	244.3	39.1	110.5	192.0	117.5	194.0	289.1	155.7	109.0	255.6	1 873.8	110.0	1 983.8
Apr	376.2	222.8	35.7	102.1	174.4	108.1	180.7	272.0	146.8	100.0	241.9	1 729.5	107.8	1 837.3
Jul	363.6	216.4	34.6	97.0	164.9	103.0	173.2	260.3	138.4	94.8	230.9	1 655.4	105.2	1 760.6
Oct	343.3	205.7	33.4	90.3	155.1	97.7	165.3	245.4	130.3	88.1	219.2	1 579.3	102.7	1 682.0
1990 Jan	339.2	200.7	33.3	88.3	152.0	95.2	160.1	234.8	123.4	85.0	208.8	1 520.3	99.3	1 619.6
Apr	340.9	198.6	34.7	89.0	147.5	94.1	155.8	230.4	119.6	82.7	203.5	1 498.1	97.9	1 596.0
Jul	358.2	204.2	36.4	94.6	148.1	96.9	157.6	230.0	120.7	84.7	199.7	1 527.2	96.7	1 623.9
Oct	406.8	226.3	40.9	105.1	156.4	104.1	165.3	237.6	124.2	88.9	198.7	1 627.9	95.7	1 723.6
1991 Jan	477.4	258.5	46.7	124.7	173.0	115.3	178.0	252.2	129.9	96.4	202.6	1 796.2	97.4	1 893.6
Apr	586.9	306.5	55.2	149.3	206.0	133.3	199.2	274.8	140.0	108.6	214.4	2 067.4	99.2	2 166.6
Jul	663.4	343.7	61.0	166.6	226.8	146.6	213.8	293.6	147.0	117.1	225.6	2 261.7	100.8	2 362.5
Oct	717.6	370.3	64.3	178.6	240.1	154.4	220.4	304.0	149.6	119.9	225.7	2 374.6	102.5	2 477.1
1992 Jan	776.2	395.5	70.5	192.4	254.4	164.1	225.9	313.4	152.2	123.3	230.9	2 503.3	103.8	2 607.1
Apr	820.0	414.3	74.8	201.9	263.2	170.0	230.7	319.2	153.6	123.6	233.9	2 590.8	104.5	2 695.3
Jul	848.1	427.6	77.0	208.1	268.2	173.5	234.3	321.6	155.8	125.9	240.3	2 652.8	107.3	2 760.1

1 The figures are based on the number of claimants at Unemployment Benefit Offices and are adjusted for seasonality and discontinuities to be consistant with current coverage.
2 Included in South East.

Source: Department of Employment

Employment

6.9 Vacancies at jobcentres in the United Kingdom[1]
Seasonally adjusted

Thousands

	January	February	March	April	May	June	July	August	September	October	November	December
Numbers of vacancies remaining unfilled KAZV												
1980	193 400	183 900	174 500	160 900	152 500	138 000	122 500	112 800	104 700	92 200	86 500	88 900
1981	91 000	89 800	90 000	85 600	83 300	76 600	85 700	91 300	93 900	98 200	102 500	105 000
1982	111 100	114 900	113 900	114 500	113 300	112 900	114 300	113 900	110 900	112 400	115 300	119 100
1983	121 500	124 600	126 800	132 500	131 500	136 700	141 400	146 200	146 700	147 100	146 100	146 600
1984	148 000	147 500	149 100	147 300	153 400	151 200	152 300	149 400	151 100	148 300	150 100	154 300
1985	155 600	157 700	160 300	165 700	163 500	164 200	162 600	162 500	162 900	163 500	163 700	162 800
1986	165 500	172 100	175 400	175 500	174 400	185 100	194 200	201 400	202 000	203 000	207 200	209 800
1987	214 600	213 300	218 100	219 400	232 500	231 900	235 100	238 700	245 500	254 600	263 500	257 300
1988	253 000	250 800	251 300	255 400	254 700	252 300	249 700	244 100	241 300	245 000	243 800	242 500
1989	231 800	229 100	225 500	220 800	217 500	222 700	220 600	217 600	218 700	215 300	212 700	201 700
1990	200 200	197 100	196 400	197 100	193 900	184 300	171 900	166 300	159 400	145 500	138 200	133 500
1991	143 600	143 600	141 500	121 800	109 300	101 500	104 000	106 600	106 500	103 500	109 700	123 700
1992	122 000	124 300	127 500	119 600	114 600	109 500	110 800	..	..	..	..	..
Inflow of vacancies KAZW												
1980	200 600	209 200	209 200	193 600	192 700	178 100	170 400	163 600	162 200	150 400	144 800	145 000
1981	168 400	142 700	142 000	140 000	139 200	144 200	142 100	149 100	158 100	157 700	156 100	159 700
1982	174 800	166 700	169 100	167 400	167 300	165 900	166 800	162 500	160 600	161 100	161 000	166 300
1983	176 000	173 400	170 100	174 600	175 300	183 200	182 600	197 600	185 400	184 800	189 000	188 300
1984	188 100	188 000	187 300	195 400	197 000	191 300	195 500	193 200	195 200	196 000	198 700	201 300
1985	198 600	194 100	199 800	195 100	196 700	204 600	206 000	209 100	203 800	206 200	203 400	202 000
1986	187 200	205 200	195 900	212 600	213 800	208 300	219 100	220 400	220 900	219 500	222 100	221 300
1987	224 900	206 200	229 800	223 200	223 700	230 000	221 900	225 200	229 300	233 300	233 300	235 900
1988	232 100	231 700	234 900	231 600	231 400	231 200	231 800	228 400	226 200	229 300	232 200	233 100
1989	227 600	230 700	228 900	221 100	220 100	233 000	229 400	227 700	226 800	227 800	222 300	217 200
1990	211 000	219 800	218 200	215 300	213 700	202 200	198 200	195 800	193 800	186 600	182 500	177 400
1991	198 200	161 100	168 800	182 500	180 700	165 600	166 800	165 600	166 500	167 600	161 900	168 700
1992	181 500	158 100	171 900	162 000	160 100	170 700	165 900	..	..	..	..	..
Outflow of vacancies KAZX												
1980	206 600	219 800	220 400	205 000	204 200	191 000	188 300	172 400	170 400	163 900	148 700	142 700
1981	162 000	145 400	142 500	143 800	143 100	151 000	135 100	143 400	155 400	151 900	151 300	157 600
1982	166 300	163 600	171 100	168 700	168 700	167 600	168 500	160 900	163 900	159 200	159 100	162 700
1983	172 500	170 900	168 900	173 700	174 400	176 900	179 200	189 500	184 500	184 400	191 300	188 200
1984	187 300	189 700	186 800	194 300	195 800	193 300	195 200	194 000	194 300	198 900	198 300	196 000
1985	198 800	194 100	197 900	190 200	191 700	204 100	207 700	207 500	204 100	205 500	202 300	201 500
1986	188 200	202 100	192 800	212 000	213 300	199 100	209 400	212 200	218 500	217 700	217 100	217 500
1987	222 600	209 600	225 100	216 500	217 100	229 100	218 700	220 000	220 600	222 500	225 000	241 100
1988	235 900	236 100	234 900	230 600	230 600	232 300	232 400	234 300	228 000	227 200	236 400	234 400
1989	235 200	234 300	233 800	226 000	225 300	225 800	229 100	231 200	228 300	231 300	227 600	222 000
1990	211 000	222 400	220 300	218 800	217 600	210 700	211 600	202 400	201 800	202 400	192 600	177 500
1991	185 100	159 800	172 700	200 300	198 800	172 500	164 500	163 400	168 200	172 000	154 000	157 500
1992	180 900	154 000	170 200	170 100	168 500	174 500	164 900	..	..	..	..	..
Number of placings KAZY												
1980	148 200	153 400	153 500	145 400	145 000	137 600	133 100	123 300	124 100	119 200	111 400	108 700
1981	125 100	109 900	109 100	109 100	108 900	115 400	107 100	111 600	118 400	119 200	116 600	121 100
1982	130 200	127 500	131 400	130 500	130 800	130 100	130 900	124 000	126 200	122 300	122 700	125 900
1983	132 500	132 100	128 500	132 300	133 100	135 800	136 300	144 700	141 300	140 300	144 300	143 400
1984	142 700	143 300	142 600	150 800	152 000	148 400	151 800	150 100	151 500	155 400	155 800	153 100
1985	152 500	149 900	153 300	143 100	144 100	158 000	160 600	162 000	158 100	159 100	157 400	156 800
1986	143 200	155 000	147 500	162 000	162 700	150 400	158 100	159 100	162 300	162 900	163 000	162 300
1987	162 100	155 200	165 600	157 400	157 600	164 700	156 200	156 500	157 200	158 000	157 100	166 200
1988	165 600	162 000	160 800	159 500	159 200	158 200	157 500	158 200	155 300	153 400	159 800	159 100
1989	161 500	162 200	161 700	156 400	155 800	157 900	158 100	160 100	157 600	158 200	157 200	154 600
1990	147 400	155 200	154 200	152 000	151 100	146 600	148 900	145 000	145 200	147 000	140 500	130 700
1991	133 100	115 900	127 200	149 000	148 100	126 900	123 400	119 800	122 600	125 300	112 500	115 600
1992	129 300	110 900	122 200	123 100	122 200	131 200	126 100	..	..	..	..	..

Note: Vacancies notified to and placings made by jobcentres do not represent the total number of vacancies/engagements in the economy. Latest estimates suggest that about a third of all vacancies are notified to job centres: and about a quarter of all engagements are made through jobcentres. Inflow, outflow and placings figures are collected for four or five-week periods between count dates; the figures in this table are converted to a standard 4 $^1/_3$ week month.

1 Excluding vacancies on government programmes (except vacancies on Enterprise Ulster and Action for Community Employment (ACE) which are included in the seasonally adjusted figures for Northern Ireland). Note that Community Programme vacancies handled by jobcentres were excluded from the seasonally adjusted series when the coverage was revised in September 1985. The coverage of the the seasonally adjusted series is therefore not affected by the cessation of C.P. vacancies with the introduction of Employment Training in September 1988. For further details, see the October 1985 *Employment Gazette*, p 143.

Source: Department of Employment

Employment

6.10 Vacancies unfilled in Northern Ireland[1]

Number

	January	February	March	April	May	June	July	August	September	October	November	December
Adults KAZZ												
1978	1 757	1 907	1 929	1 810	1 863	1 941	1 713	1 604	1 608	1 460	1 366	1 155
1979	1 098	1 160	1 237	1 489	1 558	1 517	1 398	1 314	1 388	1 318	1 210	1 109
1980	1 054	1 177	1 289	1 228	1 284	1 334	1 001	993	825	759	669	639
1981	595	603	619	732	728	741	714	735	791	811	859	795
1982	752	847	875	900	937	957	1 022	1 079	1 123	1 207	1 072	1 019
1983	1 017	1 037	1 160	1 171	1 237	1 380	1 351	1 334	1 298	1 203	1 070	1 113
1984	1 109	1 203	1 294	1 331	1 543	1 779	1 756	1 746	1 628	1 701	1 776	1 419
1985	1 216	1 349	1 609	1 669	1 876	1 912	1 766	1 651	1 662	1 627	1 516	1 502
1986	1 545	1 836	1 924	2 206	2 160	2 202	2 151	2 180	2 097	2 100	2 005	1 723
1987	1 766	1 952	1 985	2 162	2 147	2 223	2 130	2 111	2 148	2 222	2 326	2 728
1988	2 891	2 848	2 824	3 003	2 800	2 795	2 836	2 646	2 562	2 667	2 741	2 781
1989	2 748	3 654	3 511	3 820	3 671	3 722	3 837	3 739	4 302	4 326	3 997	3 585
1990	3 673	4 150	4 126	4 752	5 179	5 370	4 764	4 617	4 819	4 665	4 369	3 921
1991	3 809	4 228	3 949	4 108	4 317	4 539	4 177	4 076	4 496	3 953	3 696	3 477
1992	3 539	3 912	4 115	4 116	4 406	4 353	4 198	4 314	4 646	4 965	4 596	..
Young Persons KBAZ												
1978	364	359	303	349	344	338	307	316	505	406	341	278
1979	243	252	261	286	306	240	261	294	308	250	228	182
1980	170	187	165	164	163	164	149	135	182	123	109	64
1981	71	64	66	109	61	62	54	82	135	158	120	124
1982	136	190	167	158	170	190	157	162	221	206	214	210
1983	193	208	243	295	340	282	240	227	309	352	371	330
1984	309	330	377	400	469	595	542	576	574	673	744	746
1985	709	766	797	837	887	967	758	628	691	651	605	489
1986	445	480	530	576	592	695	572	589	662	675	662	567
1987	546	598	703	635	737	893	814	806	846	978	921	819
1988	777	787	812	996	1 196	1 096	1 005	993	1 038	1 238	1 235	1 140
1989	1 083	1 150	1 271	1 373	1 300	1 284	1 240	1 250	1 491	1 491	1 487	1 302
1990	1 175	1 119	1 064	553	512	466	377	379	454	452	407	342
1991	318	256	277	258	290	287	280	238	302	306	295	319
1992	303	306	332	338	329	374	324	302	376	409	393	..

1 The figures refer to vacancies notified to the local offices of the Training and Employment Agency, and remaining unfilled on the day of the count.

Source: Training and Employment Agency (Northern Ireland)

Employment

6.11 Industrial stoppages
United Kingdom

Thousands

		1985	1986	1987	1988	1989	1990	1991
Working days lost through all stoppages in progress: total	KBBZ	6 402	1 920	3 546	3 702	4 128	1 903	761
Analysis by industry								
Coal extraction	KBCH	4 142	143	217	222	50	59	29
Other energy and water	KBCI	57	6	9	16	20	39	4
Metals, minerals and chemicals	KBCJ	167	192	60	70	42	42	27
Engineering and vehicles	KBCK	481	744	422	1 409	617	922	160
Other manufacturing industries	KBCL	261	135	115	151	91	106	35
Construction	KBCM	50	33	22	17	128	14	14
Transport and communication	KBCN	197	190	1 705	1 491	624	177	60
Public admin., sanitary services and education	KBCO	957	449	939	254	2 237	175	362
Medical and health services	KBDZ	33	11	6	36	151	345	1
All other industries and services	KBEZ	54	20	53	30	167	20	69
Analysis by number of working days lost in each stoppage								
Under 250 days	KBFC	39	48	48	33	30	28	15
250 and under 500 days	KBFJ	46	50	54	34	28	24	16
500 and under 1 000 days	KBFL	100	89	88	78	51	45	34
1 000 and under 5 000 days	KBFY	400	369	360	310	221	216	123
5 000 and under 25 000 days	KBFZ	499	381	388	325	365	286	205
25 000 and under 50 000 days	KBGS	281	258	118	127	234	216	190
50 000 days and over	KBGT	5 037	726	2 490	2 795	3 198	1 087	178
Working days lost per 1 000 employees all industries and services	KBHA	299	90	164	166	182	83	34
Workers directly and indirectly involved: total	KBHB	791	720	887	790	727	298	176
Analysis by industry								
Coal extraction	KBHC	177	87	98	92	25	15	6
Other energy and water	KBHD	6	2	2	2	10	18	2
Metals, minerals and chemicals	KBHE	17	17	9	10	7	5	2
Engineering and vehicles	KBHF	163	147	174	137	99	92	34
Other manufacturing industries	KBHG	34	30	19	29	12	11	15
Construction	KBHH	6	8	4	4	20	5	6
Transport and communication	KBHI	104	72	207	321	112	68	12
Public admin., sanitary services and education	KBHJ	261	348	361	161	414	70	87
Medical and health services	KBHK	10	4	4	31	9	10	–
All other industries and services	KBHL	14	6	10	4	19	3	11
Analysis by duration of stoppage								
Not more than 5 days	KBHM	335	369	308	381	194	185	133
Over 5 but not more than 10 days	KBHN	67	47	66	280	97	24	2
Over 10 but not more than 20 days	KBJQ	40	24	153	19	388	27	11
Over 20 but not more than 30 days	KBJR	170	58	25	22	8	21	3
Over 30 but not more than 50 days	KBJS	13	17	23	57	12	22	1
Over 50 days	KBJT	167	206	313	32	29	19	26
Numbers of stoppages in progress: total	KBLG	903	1 074	1 016	781	701	630	369
Analysis by industry								
Coal extraction	KBLR	160	351	296	154	146	87	32
Other energy and water	KBLS	9	10	6	6	7	7	3
Metals, minerals and chemicals	KBLT	86	62	36	50	40	36	17
Engineering and vehicles	KBLU	198	202	209	162	126	132	67
Other manufacturing industries	KBLV	104	85	98	75	63	45	30
Construction	KBLW	27	26	24	16	40	12	18
Transport and communication	KBLX	143	145	191	176	79	124	37
Public admin., sanitary services and education	KBLY	107	132	99	104	154	164	124
Medical and health services	KBLZ	28	35	24	21	18	13	6
All other industries and services	KBNG	45	34	41	31	31	16	35
Analysis of number of stoppages by duration								
Not more than 5 days	KBNH	622	836	784	587	553	476	270
Over 5 but not more than 10 days	KBNI	115	108	103	89	52	44	20
Over 10 but not more than 20 days	KBNJ	93	65	78	60	45	45	24
Over 20 but not more than 30 days	KBNK	35	23	23	17	18	20	15
Over 30 but not more than 50 days	KBNL	22	18	12	12	18	22	10
Over 50 days	KBNM	16	24	16	16	15	23	30

NOTES These figures exclude details of stoppages involving fewer than ten workers or lasting less than one day except any in which the aggregate number of working days lost exceeded 100.
There may be some under-recording of small or short stoppages; this would have much more effect on the total of stoppages than of working days lost.
Some stoppages which affected more than one industry group have been counted under each of the industries but only once in the totals.
Stoppages have been classified using Standard Industrial Classification 1980.

The figures have been rounded to the nearest 100 workers and 1 000 working days; the sum of the constituent items may not, therefore, agree precisely with the totals shown.
Classifications by size are based on the full duration of stoppages where these continue into the following year.
Working days lost per thousand employees are based on the latest available mid-year (June) estimates of employees in employment.

Source: Department of Employment

Employment

6.12 Economic activity: 1981[1]
Great Britain
All residents

Thousands

	Total	Under 20	20-24	25-34	35-44	45-54	55-59	60-64	65 and over
Males: total population (aged 16 and over)	19 929	1 821	2 004	3 835	3 250	3 011	1 542	1 310	3 155
Total economically inactive (aged 16 and over)	4 430	645	218	110	71	109	130	333	2 815
Students	896	627	193	60	13	4	-	-	-
Retired	2 923	-	-	-	3	10	28	181	2 702
Permanently sick	512	8	13	31	43	86	98	147	85
Other	99	10	11	18	12	9	5	5	28
Total economically active	15 499	1 177	1 787	3 725	3 180	2 902	1 412	977	340
Self-employed (included above)	1 840	23	103	435	496	407	160	120	95
In employment	13 736	949	1 492	3 326	2 902	2 648	1 263	822	333
Working full-time	13 374	933	1 476	3 299	2 881	2 625	1 243	788	130
Working part-time	362	17	17	27	21	24	20	33	203
Out of employment	1 763	227	294	399	278	253	149	156	7
Seeking work	1 595	222	285	374	246	214	122	129	5
Temporarily sick	168	5	9	25	32	39	27	27	3
Females: total population (aged 16 and over)	21 687	1 746	1 954	3 797	3 223	3 039	1 625	1 474	4 830
Total economically inactive (aged 16 and over)	11 809	760	602	1 733	1 112	1 032	776	1 144	4 651
Students	862	672	139	34	13	4	-	-	-
Retired	1 785	-	-	-	3	10	38	298	1 437
Permanently sick	357	6	11	26	33	62	58	31	130
Other	8 806	82	451	1 673	1 064	958	680	815	3 083
Total economically active	9 878	986	1 352	2 064	2 110	2 007	849	330	179
Self-employed (included above)	457	5	23	100	128	107	43	26	26
In employment	9 146	814	1 196	1 909	2 014	1 912	802	324	174
Working full-time	5 602	776	1 092	1 163	975	1 013	417	117	50
Working part-time	3 543	38	104	746	1 039	899	385	207	125
Out of employment	732	172	157	155	96	95	47	6	5
Seeking work	645	165	147	139	79	72	36	4	3
Temporarily sick	88	7	10	16	17	22	11	2	2

1 During the week before the census (5 April 1981). For definition of terms used see *Census 1981, Definitions, Great Britain* (HMSO 1981).

Sources: *Office of Population Censuses and Surveys: General Register Office (Scotland)*

Employment

6.13 Size of manufacturing units 1992

| | Total | \multicolumn{8}{c}{Analysis by number of employees} |
		1-9	10-19	20-49	50-99	100-199	200-499	500-999	1 000 and over
Number of units									
All manufacturing industries	152 824	99 767	18 994	17 389	7 563	4 690	3 165	873	383
Extraction and preparation of metalliferous ores and metal manufacturing	1 524	603	213	281	181	120	84	..	..
Extraction of minerals not elsewhere specified and manufacture of non-metallic mineral products	7 295	4 610	951	847	445	238	151	47	6
Chemical industry and production of man-made fibres	3 848	1 900	487	526	359	248	207	79	42
Manufacture of metal goods not elsewhere specified	14 372	8 663	2 228	2 063	764	403	209	37	5
Mechanical engineering	25 227	16 932	3 202	3 034	994	579	352	99	35
Manufacture of office machinery and data processing equipment	1 469	997	165	143	61	49	26	16	12
Electrical and electronic engineering	11 038	6 956	1 217	1 230	639	412	362	149	73
Manufacture of motor vehicles and parts thereof	2 412	1 187	335	337	219	140	122	38	34
Manufacture of other transport equipment	2 543	1 605	273	255	145	85	81	41	58
Instrument engineering	2 889	1 713	382	401	215	102	62	..	..
Food, drink and tobacco manufacturing industries	10 252	5 756	1 476	1 228	643	491	447	144	67
Textile industry	4 709	2 644	528	642	393	292	178	29	3
Manufacture of leather and leather goods	1 051	723	136	110	51	22	9	-	-
Footwear and clothing industries	10 009	6 421	1 314	1 146	489	373	235	27	4
Timber and wooden furniture industries	14 294	10 602	1 583	1 278	474	247	91	19	-
Manufacture of paper and paper products; printing and publishing	24 741	17 723	2 901	2 388	831	500	310	74	14
Processing of rubber and plastics	5 851	2 891	856	1 035	521	315	195	27	11
Other manufacturing industries	9 300	7 841	747	445	139	74	44	9	1
Number of employees (thousands)									
All manufacturing industries	4 618.2	324.7	259.9	535.9	526.1	651.3	958.0	591.0	771.4
Extraction and preparation of metalliferous ores and metal manufacturing	129.5	2.1	2.9	8.9	13.1	17.5	25.8	..	..
Extraction of minerals not elsewhere specified and manufacture of non-metallic mineral products	203.5	15.3	12.9	26.4	31.0	32.8	45.7	32.0	7.6
Chemical industry and production of man-made fibres	277.2	6.4	6.8	16.6	25.5	34.8	63.5	55.5	67.9
Manufacture of metal goods not elsewhere specified	321.1	30.7	30.9	62.5	51.7	54.7	60.1	24.9	5.5
Mechanical engineering	571.6	55.0	44.0	92.8	68.5	80.4	108.9	67.9	54.1
Manufacture of office machinery and data processing equipment	60.6	2.9	2.3	4.2	4.4	6.6	8.2	10.4	21.6
Electrical and electronic engineering	507.0	21.0	16.8	38.2	44.2	57.1	110.7	100.7	118.1
Manufacture of motor vehicles and parts thereof	238.5	4.1	4.6	10.5	15.3	20.1	39.0	26.9	118.1
Manufacture of other transport equipment	268.6	4.7	3.7	7.9	10.4	12.3	24.3	28.7	176.5
Instrument engineering	82.3	5.2	5.3	12.3	15.0	13.8	18.8	..	..
Food, drink and tobacco manufacturing industries	538.2	22.0	20.1	37.8	44.4	68.6	139.3	96.7	109.1
Textile industry	180.8	8.9	7.1	20.5	28.6	40.6	53.4	18.3	3.4
Manufacture of leather and leather goods	17.1	2.5	1.9	3.6	3.4	3.1	2.7	-	-
Footwear and clothing industries	254.6	23.4	17.8	35.7	34.0	51.9	69.2	17.2	5.3
Timber and wooden furniture industries	196.0	31.3	21.8	39.1	32.2	33.2	25.7	12.7	-
Manufacture of paper and paper products; printing and publishing	458.1	55.9	39.2	72.6	58.3	70.6	92.3	50.2	18.8
Processing of rubber and plastics	228.7	10.4	11.7	32.4	36.3	43.2	58.4	16.5	19.6
Other manufacturing industries	84.9	22.8	10.0	13.7	9.6	10.0	11.9	5.9	1.0

Source: Central Statistical Office

Notes
(i) The analysis follows the Classes of the *Standard Industrial Classification 1980*.
(ii) The employment information is drawn from CSO production inquiries (in particular the Annual Census of Production and the inquiries into manufacturers' sales) and relates generally to 1990.
(iii) Disclosive data has been suppressed.
(iv) Figures may not always add up to total owing to rounding.

Employment

6.14 Average weekly earnings and hours of manual workers
UK: *Standard Industrial Classification 1980*
At October

	Manufacturing and certain other industries[1]					
	All workers on adult rates Full-time	Males on adult rates Full-time	Males on other rates Full-time	Females on adult rates Full-time	Females on adult rates Part-time	Females on other rates Full-time

Average weekly earnings[2] (£)

	KBNN	KBNO	KBNP	KBNQ	KBNR	KBNS
1984	148.69	159.30	80.33	97.34	50.91	61.27
1985	160.39	..	..	..	..	..
1986	171.02	..	..	..	..	..
1987	184.10	..	..	..	..	..
1988	198.57	..	..	..	..	..
1989	214.47	..	..	..	..	..
1990	231.85	..	..	..	..	..
1991[4]	244.14	..	..	..	..	..

Manufacturing industries

	KBNT	KBNU	KBNV	KBNW	KBNX	KBNY
1984	143.09	157.50	80.38	96.30	51.54	61.17
1985	155.04	170.58	84.73	103.21	54.91	64.39
1986	164.74	182.25	88.68	110.48	59.04	70.59
1987	178.54	197.92	94.86	118.79	63.46	75.06
1988	192.55	213.59	101.30	128.82	68.36	77.22
1989	207.53	229.87	108.07	139.93	73.24	84.67
1990	223.75	247.15	117.83	150.44	79.78	91.44
1991[4]	235.61	260.00	..	160.52	85.13	..

	Manufacturing and certain other industries[1]					
	All workers on adult rates Full-time	Males on adult rates Full-time	Males on other rates Full-time	Females on adult rates Full-time	Females on adult rates Part-time	Females on other rates Full-time

Average weekly hours worked[3]

	KBNZ	KBRO	KBRP	KBRQ	KBRR	KBRS
1984	42.5	43.4	39.8	38.2	21.5	37.90
1985	42.8	..	..	..	..	..
1986	42.7	..	..	..	..	..
1987	43.1	..	..	..	..	..
1988	43.5	..	..	..	..	..
1989	43.4	..	..	..	..	..
1990	42.9	..	..	..	..	..
1991	..	..	..	..	..	..

Manufacturing industries

	KBRT	KBRU	KBRV	KBRW	KBRX	KBRY
1984	41.7	42.8	39.5	38.1	21.7	37.9
1985	41.8	43.0	39.7	38.1	21.7	37.9
1986	41.6	42.7	39.4	38.1	21.9	37.9
1987	42.2	43.5	39.7	38.4	22.0	38.0
1988	42.4	43.6	39.8	38.7	22.2	37.5
1989	42.2	43.4	39.7	38.6	21.9	37.7
1990	41.6	42.6	39.3	38.3	22.0	37.1
1991	..	..	..	..	..	..

1 The coverage of the 'certain other industries' changed in 1984.
2 The figures represent the average earnings, including bonus, overtime etc and before deduction of income tax or insurance contributions, in one week in the month indicated. Administrative and clerical workers and other salaried persons have been excluded, together with short-time workers.
3 The figures include overtime and correspond with those for average earnings.
4 The annual October Survey of the weekly earnings and hours of full-time manual employees has now been discontinued. Therefore estimates of gross weekly earnings in October 1991 are based on projections of the 1990 survey as explained in an article in the *Employment Gazette*, April 1992. Estimates of average weekly hours worked are not available for October 1991 but the equivalent figures for April 1991 are available from the New Earnings Survey.

Source: Department of Employment

Employment

6.15 Average weekly and hourly earnings and hours of full-time employees on adult rates - Great Britain
New Earnings Survey April of each year

	All Industries				Manufacturing industries[1]			
	Average weekly earnings[2]	Average hours[3]	Average hourly earnings[2,3] including overtime	Average hourly earnings[2,3] excluding overtime	Average weekly earnings[2]	Average hours[3]	Average hourly earnings[2,3] including overtime	Average hourly earnings[2,3] excluding overtime
	£		P	P	£		P	P
All adults	KBRZ	KBSA	KBSB	KBSC	KBSD	KBSE	KBSF	KBSG
1986	184.7	40.4	450.8	446.8	188.6	41.9	444.4	437.7
1987	198.9	40.4	484.7	481.1	202.0	42.0	474.1	467.6
1988	218.4	40.6	529.2	525.9	219.4	42.3	509.4	501.7
1989	239.7	40.7	580.7	578.5	239.5	42.5	555.3	547.9
1990	263.1	40.5	636.8	634.4	262.8	42.4	609.1	601.1
1991	284.7	40.0	700.2	698.3	280.7	41.3	669.0	661.9
All men	KBSH	KBSI	KBSJ	KBSK	KBSL	KBSM	KBSN	KBSO
1986	207.5	41.8	488.9	486.6	207.8	42.9	479.1	474.0
1987	224.0	41.9	527.3	526.2	223.2	43.0	511.0	506.5
1988	245.8	42.1	573.6	573.1	242.3	43.3	549.8	544.1
1989	269.5	42.3	627.6	629.0	264.6	43.6	598.4	593.7
1990	295.6	42.2	687.8	689.2	289.2	43.4	655.0	649.7
1991	318.9	41.5	755.3	756.9	308.1	42.1	720.4	715.4
Manual men[4]	KBSP	KBSQ	KBSR	KBSS	KBST	KBSU	KBSV	KBSW
1986	174.4	44.5	392.6	380.8	183.4	44.5	411.6	398.5
1987	185.5	44.6	416.5	404.3	195.9	44.7	437.6	423.8
1988	200.6	45.0	445.7	431.5	212.3	45.2	468.5	451.7
1989	217.8	45.3	480.9	466.2	230.6	45.5	506.2	488.7
1990	237.2	45.2	524.6	508.5	250.0	45.2	551.3	532.4
	KFHX	KFHY	KFHZ	KFJS	KFJT	KFJU	KFJV	KFJW
1990	239.5	45.4	528.3	512.2	251.4	45.3	554.6	535.5
1991	253.1	44.4	569.9	554.1	261.8	43.7	598.4	580.2
Non-manual men[4]	KBSX	KBSY	KBSZ	KBTA	KBTB	KBTC	KBTD	KBTE
1986	244.9	38.6	627.3	625.8	255.7	39.3	641.0	640.0
1987	265.9	38.7	679.9	679.3	273.7	39.4	684.1	684.0
1988	294.1	38.7	748.8	748.3	300.5	39.4	744.9	744.1
1989	323.6	38.8	823.3	824.0	331.5	39.6	821.9	822.8
1990	354.9	38.7	901.6	902.1	364.1	39.6	903.4	903.8
	KFJX	KFJY	KFJZ	KFMT	KFMU	KFMV	KFMW	KFMX
1990	346.4	38.9	872.3	873.6	351.0	40.1	856.6	858.9
1991	375.7	38.7	954.9	956.3	379.2	39.5	942.9	944.5
All women	KBTF	KBTG	KBTH	KBTI	KBTJ	KBTK	KBTL	KBTM
1986	137.2	37.3	362.5	360.7	123.2	38.8	316.1	313.3
1987	148.1	37.5	388.4	386.2	133.4	39.0	339.2	335.9
1988	164.2	37.6	431.3	429.0	144.3	39.2	365.8	362.3
1989	182.3	37.6	480.2	478.2	159.1	39.1	403.9	400.2
1990	201.5	37.5	530.1	527.9	177.1	39.1	447.5	443.5
1991	222.4	37.4	591.1	589.1	192.9	38.8	494.4	490.6
Manual women[4]	KBTN	KBTO	KBTP	KBTQ	KBTR	KBTS	KBTT	KBTU
1986	107.5	39.5	273.0	269.2	111.6	40.0	278.9	274.6
1987	115.3	39.7	292.0	287.4	119.6	40.3	297.2	291.9
1988	123.6	39.8	310.5	305.6	127.9	40.5	315.5	309.6
1989	134.9	39.9	338.7	333.3	138.2	40.4	341.8	335.0
1990	148.0	39.8	372.4	366.1	152.8	40.5	377.1	369.3
	KFMY	KFMZ	KFPQ	KFPR	KFPS	KFPT	KFRW	KFRX
1990	148.4	40.0	371.2	364.7	152.8	40.5	377.0	369.1
1991	159.2	39.7	401.4	395.2	162.1	40.0	405.6	398.3
Non-manual women[4]	KBTV	KBTW	KBTX	KBTY	KBTZ	KBUA	KBUB	KBUC
1986	145.7	36.7	390.6	388.8	136.7	37.4	363.2	361.2
1987	157.2	36.8	418.0	415.9	149.1	37.5	391.6	389.4
1988	175.5	36.9	467.7	465.3	163.3	37.6	430.0	427.5
1989	195.0	36.9	521.9	519.7	182.8	37.6	481.6	479.5
1990	215.5	36.9	575.5	573.1	202.8	37.6	530.8	528.5
	KFRY	KFRZ	KFUW	KFUX	KFUY	KFUZ	KFZU	KFZV
1990	214.3	36.9	572.4	570.0	201.2	37.7	525.4	523.0
1991	236.8	36.8	638.1	636.0	221.8	37.6	585.6	583.1

1 Results for manufacturing industries relate to Division 2,3 and 4 of the 1980 SIC.
2 The figures are gross before deductions. Generally they exclude the value of earnings in kind, but include payment such as overtime (except where otherwise stated), bonus, commission and shift premiums for the pay period.
3 The estimates given relate only to employees for whom normal basic hours were reported.
4 Manual and non-manual results for 1986 - 1989 inclusive and the first row of figures for 1990 are based on the list of Key Occupations for Statistical Purposes (KOS). Results for 1991 and the second row of figures for 1990 are based on the Standard Occupational Classification (SOC).

Source: Department of Employment

Employment

6.16 Average earnings index: all employees
Great Britain
Analyses by industry based on Standard Industrial Classification 1980

1988 = 100

Unadjusted

	Annual averages	January	February	March	April	May	June	July	August	September	October	November	December
Whole economy (Division 0 - 9)													
KBUD													
1985	100.0	95.1	95.8	97.8	98.6	98.6	100.0	101.1	100.9	102.5	101.2	102.9	104.8
1986	107.9	102.9	103.5	106.2	107.1	106.1	108.1	109.4	109.0	108.7	109.6	111.2	112.5
1987	116.3	110.8	111.2	113.2	114.0	115.3	116.4	118.2	117.3	117.2	118.4	120.6	122.4
1988	100.0	95.4	95.5	98.3	97.8	98.4	99.8	101.3	100.3	100.9	101.7	103.7	106.9
1989	109.1	104.2	104.6	107.3	107.3	107.5	109.1	110.3	109.1	110.7	111.7	113.2	114.7
1990	119.7	113.8	114.0	117.4	117.3	118.5	120.5	121.2	120.9	121.3	121.7	123.8	126.3
1991	129.3	124.3	124.7	127.5	127.4	128.1	129.2	130.5	130.8	130.8	130.9	133.3	134.5
Manufacturing industries (Revised definition Divisions 2 - 4)													
KBUQ													
1985	100.0	96.0	96.1	97.9	99.1	98.9	100.8	101.5	99.7	101.2	101.1	103.6	104.3
1986	107.7	103.7	103.9	105.3	106.6	106.1	108.6	108.4	107.4	108.2	109.2	111.7	113.0
1987	116.3	111.7	112.3	113.2	114.0	114.7	117.2	118.1	116.0	117.2	118.8	120.5	122.4
1988	100.0	95.8	95.6	98.0	98.8	99.3	100.6	101.1	99.5	100.2	101.8	103.6	105.5
1989	108.7	104.2	105.0	105.7	107.8	108.0	109.4	110.3	108.3	109.5	110.6	112.2	113.8
1990	118.9	112.7	113.9	116.8	117.2	117.9	120.1	120.8	118.8	120.2	120.8	123.0	125.1
1991	128.1	123.4	124.3	126.1	128.0	127.7	129.7	130.0	128.7	129.2	130.8	132.6	134.1
Production industries (Revised definition Divisions 1 - 4)													
KBVD													
1985	100.0	94.0	94.2	97.2	98.7	98.7	100.8	101.8	100.0	101.8	101.5	103.9	104.4
1986	108.0	104.2	104.4	105.7	106.7	106.3	108.4	108.8	108.0	108.6	109.6	112.0	113.1
1987	116.7	112.3	112.7	113.6	114.4	114.8	117.1	118.2	116.9	117.6	119.1	120.9	122.3
1988	100.0	95.8	95.3	97.8	98.9	99.5	100.4	101.3	99.9	100.5	101.9	103.7	105.3
1989	109.1	104.2	104.9	106.0	107.9	108.1	109.6	110.8	109.2	109.8	111.0	112.9	114.3
1990	119.4	113.2	114.3	117.0	117.4	118.2	120.7	121.3	119.7	121.0	121.6	123.7	125.2
1991	129.7	124.3	125.2	126.8	128.6	129.2	130.3	130.8	130.2	130.9	131.7	133.8	134.8

Seasonally adjusted

	Annual averages	January	February	March	April	May	June	July	August	September	October	November	December
Whole economy (Divisions 0 - 9)													
KBVQ													
1985	100.0	96.2	96.9	97.9	99.0	98.7	99.4	100.2	100.7	102.4	101.4	102.5	103.5
1986	107.9	104.2	104.9	106.2	107.4	106.2	107.4	108.3	108.8	108.8	109.9	110.9	111.2
1987	116.2	112.1	112.8	113.2	114.2	115.4	115.7	117.0	117.1	117.4	118.8	120.2	121.0
1988	100.0	96.1	96.7	97.5	97.9	98.6	99.3	100.2	100.9	101.5	102.6	103.5	105.2
1989	109.1	105.0	105.9	106.5	107.4	107.7	108.4	109.1	109.6	111.3	112.6	112.9	112.9
1990	119.7	114.7	115.4	116.5	117.5	118.8	119.9	120.0	121.6	122.0	122.7	123.5	124.2
1991	129.3	125.2	126.2	126.5	127.5	128.4	128.5	129.1	131.5	131.7	132.0	133.0	132.3
Manufacturing Industries (Revised definition Divisions 2 - 4)													
KBWD													
1985	100.0	96.5	96.8	97.9	99.5	98.9	99.5	100.4	100.5	101.9	102.0	102.7	103.6
1986	107.7	104.2	104.6	105.2	107.0	106.0	107.2	107.3	108.3	109.0	110.0	110.9	112.1
1987	116.3	112.2	113.1	113.2	114.4	114.7	115.7	116.9	117.0	118.2	119.4	119.8	121.4
1988	100.0	96.6	96.3	97.7	98.0	98.9	99.5	99.9	100.9	101.3	102.6	103.5	104.4
1989	108.7	105.1	105.8	105.4	106.9	107.6	108.2	109.1	109.8	110.7	111.5	112.1	112.7
1990	119.0	113.6	114.7	116.5	116.2	117.5	118.8	119.5	120.5	121.6	121.7	122.9	123.8
1991	128.7	124.4	125.1	125.8	126.9	127.3	128.3	128.5	130.6	130.6	131.8	132.4	132.7
Production Industries (Revised definition Divisions 1 - 4)													
KBWQ													
1985	100.0	94.4	95.0	97.1	98.9	98.6	99.6	100.7	100.7	102.6	102.1	103.3	103.9
1986	108.0	104.7	105.2	105.6	106.9	106.4	107.1	107.5	108.8	109.5	110.3	111.3	112.4
1987	116.7	112.7	113.5	113.4	114.6	115.2	115.7	116.9	117.7	118.6	119.9	120.1	121.5
1988	100.0	96.5	96.0	97.8	98.2	99.2	99.5	100.1	100.9	101.5	102.7	103.4	104.3
1989	109.1	105.0	105.8	106.0	107.2	107.8	108.6	109.5	110.3	110.9	111.8	112.5	113.3
1990	119.4	114.1	115.1	117.0	116.6	117.8	119.7	119.9	120.9	122.1	122.4	123.3	124.1
1991	129.7	125.2	126.1	126.9	127.7	128.9	129.2	129.3	131.4	132.1	132.6	133.4	133.7

Note: The seasonal adjustment factors currently used for the SIC 1980 series are based on data up to April 1991.

The 1985 = 100 series was discontinued after July 1989 and is printed here for reference purposes. It has been superseded by the 1988 = 100 series which begins in January 1988. For a detailed account of the revised Average Earnings Index based on 1988 = 100 please see the article in *Employment Gazette* November 1989.

Source: Department of Employment

6.16 Average earnings index: all employees
Great Britain
Analyses by industry based on Standard Industrial Classification 1980

Employment

1988 = 100

	Agriculture and forestry[1]	Coal and coke[2]	Mineral oil and natural gas	Electricity, gas, other energy and water supply	Metal processing and manufacturing	Mineral extraction and manufacturing	Chemicals and man-made fibres	Mechanical engineering	Electrical and electronic engineering	Motor vehicles and parts	Other transport equipment	Metal goods and instruments	Food drink and tobacco
SIC 1980 Class	(01-02)	(11-12)	(13-14)	(15-17)	(21-22)	(23-24)	(25-26)	(32)	(33-34, 37)	(35)	(36)	(31)	(41-42)
	KBXD	KBXE	KBXF	KBXG	KBXH	KBXI	KBXJ	KBXK	KBXL	KBXM	KBXN	KBXO	KBXP
1988	100.0	100.0	100.0	100.0	100.0	100.0	100.0	100.0	100.0	100.0	100.0	100.0	100.0
1989	108.0	113.3	110.3	109.8	107.2	109.4	109.0	109.8	109.5	109.9	112.7	107.9	109.3
1990	120.0	125.0	126.7	121.6	115.5	119.1	122.6	119.3	119.3	119.5	125.6	117.5	121.7
1991	132.1	141.9	140.4	134.2	122.8	125.9	134.0	130.2	129.5	129.1	136.2	124.7	134.6
1991 Jan	118.7	137.8	139.6	125.7	123.2	122.3	126.3	124.2	123.6	124.5	135.0	119.9	127.0
Feb	122.0	141.0	131.5	127.8	114.9	121.9	129.7	126.6	125.3	124.8	132.4	121.8	128.4
Mar	120.9	142.7	136.0	126.4	116.9	122.2	135.4	127.8	127.3	124.9	135.7	122.0	131.3
Apr	129.9	139.3	140.0	127.8	127.2	123.7	129.9	129.1	127.1	139.4	139.2	122.6	135.5
May	126.4	140.6	140.8	140.9	119.5	125.8	130.7	129.2	129.4	126.7	133.2	123.9	135.9
Jun	127.1	142.2	141.7	129.0	119.8	128.0	131.6	131.6	132.1	131.2	135.5	124.4	135.5
Jul	134.4	139.7	145.1	133.4	128.6	127.5	132.4	131.0	131.0	131.3	136.0	127.4	134.5
Aug	160.4	141.5	140.8	140.8	125.9	126.5	134.6	130.5	129.3	124.9	136.2	124.3	134.3
Sep	147.6	140.7	140.4	146.1	120.8	127.2	135.5	130.6	129.6	127.0	135.3	126.7	134.7
Oct	137.6	141.8	141.1	136.2	130.1	127.3	136.8	132.6	131.7	129.1	139.8	125.9	135.0
Nov	130.4	152.7	141.1	139.1	121.8	128.5	140.6	134.5	133.0	131.5	139.0	128.0	141.3
Dec	129.7	142.8	146.5	137.6	125.2	130.2	144.4	135.1	134.6	134.3	137.6	129.4	141.5

	Textiles	Leather, footwear and clothing	Paper products, printing and publishing	Rubber, plastics, timber and other manufacturing	Construction	Distribution and repairs	Hotels and catering	Transport and communication[3]	Banking, finance and insurance	Public administration	Education and health	Other services[4]	Whole economy
SIC 1980 Class	(43)	(44-45)	(47)	(46, 48-49)	(50)	(61-65, 67)	(66)	(71-72, 75-77, 79)	(81-82 83pt.- 84pt.)	(91-92pt.)	(93,95)	(92pt.- 93,96pt.) (97pt.- 98pt.)	
	KBXQ	KBXR	KBXS	KBXT	KBXU	KBXV	KBXW	KBXX	KBXY	KBXZ	KBYA	KBYB	KBYC
1988	100.0	100.0	100.0	100.0	100.0	100.0	100.0	100.0	100.0	100.0	100.0	100.0	100.0
1989	107.4	107.1	106.1	107.7	111.8	108.6	107.6	107.6	109.9	108.8	108.6	111.3	109.1
1990	117.6	115.8	113.5	117.5	124.6	117.3	118.4	118.8	121.2	120.7	118.0	122.9	119.7
1991	128.1	123.7	121.6	126.0	134.6	124.7	128.8	128.6	129.4	130.0	129.1	132.7	129.3
1991 Jan	120.8	119.1	117.0	120.3	129.7	120.1	123.6	125.1	126.5	125.7	122.3	125.8	124.3
Feb	121.9	120.1	116.1	122.8	130.8	120.8	124.3	124.8	123.7	126.5	122.6	128.5	124.7
Mar	123.1	121.9	118.0	122.9	131.9	125.5	124.3	125.9	134.9	126.9	123.5	130.7	127.5
Apr	124.5	122.6	119.1	123.7	133.4	124.3	125.0	126.5	126.8	125.7	126.4	129.7	127.4
May	126.7	123.6	120.1	125.6	132.1	124.8	127.6	126.8	127.6	127.5	127.9	130.6	128.1
Jun	129.7	125.8	122.5	127.9	137.4	125.7	129.8	125.7	129.4	126.9	129.1	132.3	129.2
Jul	132.9	124.8	123.4	127.2	137.0	125.5	128.7	127.8	129.0	131.7	133.9	130.8	130.5
Aug	130.6	123.3	122.9	125.4	132.5	124.8	132.1	130.6	128.3	131.1	136.3	134.9	130.8
Sep	129.7	123.9	124.0	126.8	134.8	125.1	129.6	133.7	127.5	133.7	131.5	133.4	130.8
Oct	131.6	125.5	123.5	128.1	135.5	123.6	129.6	131.7	128.3	136.0	130.0	135.6	130.9
Nov	132.0	126.7	125.5	129.3	137.8	128.4	131.8	133.2	135.2	134.5	131.4	138.2	133.3
Dec	133.9	126.6	127.2	132.1	142.4	128.1	138.6	131.9	135.7	134.2	134.1	142.1	134.5

1 England and Wales only.
2 The index series for this group has been based on average 1985 excluding January and February figures which were seriously affected by a dispute in the coal mining industry.
3 Excluding sea transport.
4 Excluding private domestic and personal services.

Source: Department of Employment

Employment

6.17 Gross weekly and hourly earnings of full-time adult employees
Great Britain
New Earnings Survey April of each year

	\multicolumn{5}{c}{Gross weekly earnings[1]}	\multicolumn{5}{c}{Gross hourly earnings[1,2]}
	Lowest decile £	Lower quartile £	Median £	Upper quartile £	Highest decile £	Lowest decile p	Lower quartile p	Median p	Upper quartile p	Highest decile p
All men	KBYD	KBYE	KBYF	KBYG	KBYH	KBYI	KBYJ	KBYK	KBYL	KBYM
1985	105.1	132.9	172.8	226.3	296.3	255.8	313.8	402.9	537.8	740.7
1986	111.4	141.8	185.1	243.7	320.8	271.6	334.6	432.9	581.5	806.4
1987	117.9	150.1	198.4	262.8	349.5	286.1	354.4	462.1	627.7	875.6
1988	127.1	162.7	215.5	288.7	384.2	305.9	380.0	498.2	686.8	963.8
1989	137.8	176.9	235.5	315.6	423.7	330.7	412.9	543.0	751.6	1 061.3
1990	150.5	193.4	258.2	347.5	467.5	360.4	450.5	595.6	828.0	1 168.5
1991	160.7	206.9	277.5	376.5	507.8	387.4	488.3	653.2	911.8	1 298.8
Manual men	KBYN	KBYO	KBYP	KBYQ	KBYR	KBYS	KBYT	KBYU	KBYV	KBYW
1985	100.4	122.9	153.3	191.8	237.1	242.4	288.3	350.2	425.7	509.2
1986	105.5	130.2	163.4	205.5	253.9	256.1	305.9	373.2	457.2	546.4
1987	110.6	137.8	173.9	218.8	272.2	268.5	322.4	395.1	486.0	585.4
1988	119.4	148.6	188.0	237.2	295.4	286.3	343.4	422.4	521.1	627.3
1989	128.8	160.9	203.9	257.4	321.4	308.7	372.2	457.0	561.8	675.2
1990	139.4	174.3	221.3	280.9	350.7	334.1	402.9	498.6	613.3	743.0
	KFZY	KFZZ	KGAK	KGAL	KGAM	KGAN	KGAO	KGAP	KGAQ	KGAR
1990	140.5	176.0	223.1	282.8	354.7	335.7	405.4	501.7	617.9	746.9
1991	149.3	186.0	235.4	298.2	375.5	360.1	436.1	540.2	670.0	809.9
Non-manual men	KBYX	KBYY	KBYZ	KBZA	KBZB	KBZC	KBZD	KBZE	KBZF	KBZG
1985	116.6	153.7	202.4	266.2	348.9	298.2	393.0	523.7	696.2	924.4
1986	124.6	165.9	219.4	289.2	383.2	319.9	424.3	567.1	761.7	1 012.3
1987	132.5	176.8	235.7	312.1	416.4	339.7	450.4	608.0	820.9	1 101.3
1988	143.9	191.9	259.7	345.3	466.1	368.8	489.9	667.6	905.3	1 225.0
1989	154.9	211.2	285.7	378.1	516.0	399.3	539.0	728.3	991.6	1 353.6
1990	171.6	231.5	312.1	414.6	568.8	438.3	592.2	800.7	1 087.5	1 477.2
	KGAS	KGAT	KGAU	KGAV	KGAW	KGAX	KGAY	KGAZ	KGBQ	KGBR
1990	164.6	223.8	305.4	405.4	555.8	415.9	561.1	775.5	1 060.9	1 444.5
1991	178.7	242.1	332.2	440.2	602.0	449.1	611.5	850.4	1 170.6	1 594.8

As percentages of the corresponding median — Percentage

All men	KBZH	KBZI	KBZJ	KBZK	KBZL	KBZM	KBZN	KBZO	KBZP	KBZQ
1985	60.8	76.9	100.0	131.0	171.5	63.5	77.9	100.0	133.5	183.9
1986	60.2	76.6	100.0	131.6	173.3	62.7	77.3	100.0	134.3	186.3
1987	59.4	75.7	100.0	132.5	176.2	61.9	76.7	100.0	135.8	189.5
1988	59.0	75.5	100.0	134.0	178.3	61.4	76.3	100.0	137.9	193.5
1989	58.5	75.1	100.0	134.0	179.9	60.9	76.0	100.0	138.4	195.5
1990	58.3	74.9	100.0	134.6	181.1	60.5	75.6	100.0	139.0	196.2
1991	57.9	74.6	100.0	135.7	183.0	59.3	74.8	100.0	139.6	198.8
Manual men	KBZR	KBZS	KBZT	KBZU	KBZV	KBZW	KBZX	KBZY	KBZZ	KCAQ
1985	65.5	80.1	100.0	125.1	154.6	69.2	82.3	100.0	121.5	145.4
1986	64.5	79.7	100.0	125.8	155.4	68.6	82.0	100.0	122.5	146.4
1987	63.6	79.2	100.0	125.8	156.5	67.9	81.6	100.0	123.0	148.2
1988	63.5	79.1	100.0	126.2	157.1	67.8	81.3	100.0	123.4	148.5
1989	63.2	78.9	100.0	126.2	157.6	67.5	81.4	100.0	122.9	147.7
1990	63.0	78.8	100.0	126.9	158.5	67.0	80.8	100.0	123.0	149.0
	KGBS	KGBT	KGBU	KGBV	KGBW	KGBX	KGBY	KGBZ	KGCH	KGCI
1990	63.0	78.9	100.0	126.8	159.0	66.9	80.8	100.0	123.2	148.9
1991	63.4	79.0	100.0	126.7	159.5	66.7	80.7	100.0	124.0	149.9
Non-manual men	KCAR	KCAS	KCAT	KCAU	KCAV	KCAW	KCAX	KCAY	KCAZ	KCBJ
1985	57.6	75.9	100.0	131.6	172.4	57.0	75.1	100.0	132.9	176.5
1986	56.8	75.6	100.0	131.8	174.7	56.4	74.8	100.0	134.3	178.5
1987	56.2	75.0	100.0	132.4	176.6	55.9	74.1	100.0	135.0	181.1
1988	55.4	73.9	100.0	133.0	179.5	55.2	73.4	100.0	135.5	183.5
1989	54.2	73.9	100.0	132.3	180.6	54.8	74.0	100.0	136.1	185.8
1990	55.0	74.2	100.0	132.8	182.2	54.7	74.0	100.0	135.8	184.5
	KGCJ	KGCQ	KGCR	KGCS	KGCT	KGCU	KGCV	KGCW	KGCX	KGCY
1990	53.9	73.3	100.0	132.7	182.0	53.6	72.4	100.0	136.8	186.3
1991	53.8	72.9	100.0	132.5	181.2	52.8	71.9	100.0	137.7	187.5

1 Of those whose pay for the survey pay period was not affected by absence. See also note 2 to Table 6.15.

2 Including overtime hours and overtime pay, of persons for whom normal basic hours were reported and for whom hourly earnings could, therefore, be calculated.

Source: Department of Employment

Employment

6.17 Gross weekly and hourly earnings of full-time adult employees
Great Britain
continued
New Earnings Survey April of each year

	Gross weekly earnings[1]					Gross hourly earnings[1,2]				
	Lowest decile	Lower quartile	Median	Upper quartile	Highest decile	Lowest decile	Lower quartile	Median	Upper quartile	Highest decile
	£	£	£	£	£	p	p	p	p	p
All women	KCBK	KCBL	KCBM	KCBN	KCBO	KCBP	KCBQ	KCBR	KCBS	KCBT
1985	75.7	90.6	115.2	150.8	189.5	201.1	238.5	301.1	394.3	534.1
1986	80.3	97.0	123.4	163.8	209.8	213.1	255.9	323.9	427.9	589.2
1987	85.3	103.8	132.9	177.5	228.3	226.7	272.8	347.7	459.4	625.8
1988	92.2	112.1	145.3	198.5	258.0	244.4	294.8	379.8	515.6	708.5
1989	101.0	123.4	160.1	220.9	288.8	266.9	324.6	418.2	580.5	805.8
1990	110.9	136.2	177.5	244.7	317.1	292.6	357.9	464.9	640.2	882.2
1991	120.8	150.6	195.7	271.6	353.3	320.3	396.3	516.4	719.7	997.4
Manual women	KCBU	KCBV	KCBW	KCBX	KCBY	KCBZ	KCCA	KCCB	KCCC	KCCD
1985	66.1	78.5	95.3	116.4	143.2	178.5	205.6	244.1	292.3	345.4
1986	69.9	83.3	101.1	124.6	151.3	188.0	217.7	259.1	313.1	366.6
1987	74.0	88.1	108.2	133.7	165.5	200.0	231.1	276.7	334.1	397.5
1988	80.1	94.2	115.6	143.0	178.0	212.6	246.0	293.1	355.7	424.2
1989	86.9	102.4	125.9	156.3	196.0	229.9	266.5	319.0	387.8	468.2
1990	93.4	112.2	137.3	171.4	215.9	251.0	291.4	349.2	426.6	517.6
	KGCZ	KGDA	KGDB	KGDC	KGDD	KGDE	KGDF	KGDG	KGDH	KGDI
1990	93.3	111.5	136.2	172.3	217.9	250.3	289.2	345.8	422.1	518.0
1991	100.5	119.9	147.4	185.5	233.8	268.1	311.7	375.9	459.0	566.7
Non-manual women	KCCO	KCCP	KCCQ	KCCR	KCCS	KCCT	KCCU	KCCV	KCCW	KCCX
1985	79.9	95.7	122.0	161.4	199.0	212.6	254.8	323.1	430.7	577.4
1986	85.0	102.9	131.5	175.3	219.7	226.7	274.7	349.0	466.8	635.9
1987	90.4	110.4	142.2	188.9	237.9	241.7	294.0	374.4	498.7	676.2
1988	98.3	120.9	157.1	213.0	269.9	262.5	322.0	414.1	564.9	758.1
1989	108.1	133.7	173.5	236.5	301.9	289.0	356.9	461.4	635.5	855.0
1990	119.4	147.6	191.8	264.5	331.6	319.5	394.3	507.8	700.0	939.2
	KGDJ	KGDK	KGDL	KGDM	KGDN	KGDO	KGDP	KGDQ	KGDR	KGDS
1990	119.0	146.9	190.7	262.5	330.4	318.7	392.9	504.1	695.1	934.6
1991	131.0	162.8	211.1	289.8	365.4	352.4	436.7	562.0	782.0	1 054.5

As percentages of the corresponding median
Percentage

All women	KGEO	KGEP	KGEQ	KGER	KGES	KGET	KGEU	KGEV	KGEW	KGEX
1985	65.8	78.7	100.0	130.9	164.5	66.8	79.2	100.0	131.0	177.4
1986	65.1	78.6	100.0	132.7	170.0	65.8	79.0	100.0	132.1	181.9
1987	64.2	78.1	100.0	133.5	171.7	65.2	78.5	100.0	132.2	180.0
1988	63.4	77.2	100.0	136.6	177.5	64.3	77.6	100.0	135.7	186.5
1989	63.1	77.1	100.0	138.0	180.5	63.8	77.6	100.0	138.8	192.7
1990	62.5	76.7	100.0	137.9	178.6	62.9	77.0	100.0	137.7	189.8
1991	61.7	76.9	100.0	138.8	180.6	62.0	76.7	100.0	139.4	193.2
Manual women	KCCY	KCCZ	KCDA	KCDB	KCDC	KCDD	KCDE	KCDF	KCDG	KCDH
1985	69.4	82.4	100.0	122.2	150.4	73.1	84.2	100.0	119.8	141.5
1986	69.2	82.4	100.0	123.3	149.7	72.6	84.0	100.0	120.8	141.5
1987	68.3	81.4	100.0	123.5	152.9	72.3	83.5	100.0	120.8	143.7
1988	69.2	81.4	100.0	123.7	153.9	72.6	83.9	100.0	121.4	144.7
1989	69.0	81.3	100.0	124.1	155.7	72.1	83.5	100.0	121.6	146.7
1990	68.0	81.7	100.0	124.9	157.3	71.9	83.4	100.0	122.2	148.2
	KGDT	KGDU	KGDV	KGDW	KGDX	KGDY	KGDZ	KGEA	KGEB	KGEC
1990	68.5	81.9	100.0	126.5	160.0	72.4	83.6	100.0	122.1	149.8
1991	68.2	81.4	100.0	125.9	158.7	71.3	82.9	100.0	122.1	150.8
Non-manual women	KCDI	KCDJ	KCDK	KCDL	KCDM	KCDN	KCDO	KCDP	KCDQ	KCDR
1985	65.5	78.5	100.0	132.3	163.1	65.8	78.9	100.0	133.3	178.7
1986	64.6	78.2	100.0	133.3	167.1	65.0	78.7	100.0	133.8	182.2
1987	63.6	77.6	100.0	132.8	167.3	64.6	78.5	100.0	133.2	180.6
1988	62.6	77.0	100.0	135.6	171.8	63.4	77.8	100.0	136.4	183.1
1989	62.3	77.1	100.0	136.3	174.0	62.6	77.4	100.0	137.7	185.3
1990	62.3	77.0	100.0	137.9	172.9	62.9	77.7	100.0	137.9	185.0
	KGED	KGEE	KGEF	KGEG	KGEH	KGEI	KGEJ	KGEK	KGEL	KGEM
1990	62.4	77.0	100.0	137.7	173.3	63.2	77.9	100.0	137.9	185.4
1991	62.1	77.1	100.0	137.3	173.1	62.7	77.7	100.0	139.1	187.6

1 Of those whose pay for the survey pay period was not affected by absence. See also note 2 to Table 6.15.
2 Including overtime hours and overtime pay, of persons for whom normal basic hours were reported and for whom hourly earnings could, therefore, be calculated.

Source: Department of Employment

Employment

6.18 Gross weekly and hourly earnings of full-time adults[1]
Northern Ireland
April of each year

	Gross weekly earnings[2]					Gross hourly earnings[2]				
	Lowest decile	Lower quartile	Median	Upper quartile	Highest decile	Lowest decile	Lower quartile	Median	Upper quartile	Highest decile
	£	£	£	£	£	p	p	p	p	p
All men										
	KCIF	KCIG	KCIH	KCII	KCIJ	KCIK	KCIL	KCIM	KCIN	KCIO
1983	83.9	102.3	133.2	175.6	240.0	208.7	246.4	307.1	410.9	518.3
1984	85.4	107.3	144.6	194.9	273.3	210.1	258.6	332.4	447.1	587.3
1985	91.9	115.7	153.7	205.1	279.4	222.8	274.6	347.6	465.8	617.1
1986	95.5	119.1	160.6	216.6	297.5	234.4	289.1	363.8	506.6	663.5
1987	103.3	130.4	176.3	242.0	324.8	253.6	313.6	404.9	551.0	714.5
1988	105.6	138.2	189.5	263.7	359.4	262.7	328.4	426.1	595.8	759.7
1989	116.4	150.0	204.1	278.1	382.4	287.9	356.9	469.2	638.4	823.3
1990	121.7	157.1	223.7	311.8	427.4	304.1	375.5	503.4	739.6	945.5
1991	128.7	170.9	237.9	337.5	460.3	318.8	409.2	544.0	808.7	1 042.2
Manual men										
	KCIP	KCIQ	KCIR	KCIS	KCIT	KCIU	KCIV	KCIW	KCIX	KCIY
1983	80.5	94.8	117.4	146.4	174.6	201.1	232.0	276.5	334.7	392.1
1984	80.8	98.0	123.6	160.4	199.2	202.1	236.6	292.2	352.4	427.4
1985	88.5	105.7	131.6	168.6	208.2	214.9	256.8	307.1	378.6	451.1
1986	90.4	110.3	137.1	177.5	220.6	226.5	267.9	322.6	387.6	482.0
1987	98.4	119.1	151.6	191.8	236.7	244.4	296.4	349.2	423.3	511.4
1988	99.8	123.1	156.5	206.6	259.6	250.7	300.1	367.5	450.3	552.4
1989	106.5	132.1	166.0	216.1	272.0	267.6	324.3	396.4	483.0	572.7
1990	113.7	138.8	179.2	239.0	303.9	284.2	339.3	419.7	529.6	672.7
1991	122.4	153.9	195.9	254.5	323.0	308.7	377.4	463.7	571.5	734.7
Non-manual men										
	KCIZ	KCJO	KCJP	KCJQ	KCJR	KCJS	KCJT	KCJU	KCJV	KCJW
1983	97.0	124.2	165.6	225.0	290.7	241.1	305.1	419.3	514.7	680.3
1984	100.6	133.2	181.0	250.6	328.5	247.6	329.0	450.3	569.3	725.8
1985	102.4	140.1	187.4	250.6	327.7	255.5	340.4	460.4	593.4	744.5
1986	104.6	149.1	198.5	274.7	348.0	253.9	357.4	497.3	628.7	809.0
1987	116.7	166.7	226.9	302.6	381.8	292.4	411.5	552.5	690.6	859.1
1988	126.7	177.2	245.2	326.6	429.8	309.0	429.8	601.3	732.0	922.8
1989	145.4	193.4	263.6	355.6	454.3	360.7	489.0	644.2	797.7	1 057.9
1990	146.9	209.8	287.3	393.7	486.2	364.3	514.5	733.9	883.7	1 127.2
1991	141.6	215.4	309.4	421.1	523.4	353.9	519.1	785.0	974.6	1 270.1

As percentages of the corresponding median
Percentage

All men										
	KCJX	KCJY	KCJZ	KCKA	KCKB	KCKC	KCKD	KCKE	KCKF	KCKG
1983	63.0	76.8	100.0	131.8	180.2	68.0	80.2	100.0	133.8	168.8
1984	59.1	74.2	100.0	134.8	189.0	63.2	77.8	100.0	134.5	176.7
1985	59.8	75.3	100.0	133.5	181.8	64.1	79.0	100.0	134.0	177.5
1986	59.5	74.2	100.0	134.9	185.2	64.4	79.5	100.0	139.3	182.4
1987	58.6	74.0	100.0	137.3	184.2	62.6	77.5	100.0	136.1	176.5
1988	55.7	72.9	100.0	139.2	189.7	61.7	77.1	100.0	139.8	178.3
1989	57.0	73.5	100.0	136.6	187.4	61.4	76.1	100.0	136.1	175.5
1990	54.4	70.2	100.0	139.4	191.1	60.4	74.6	100.0	146.9	187.8
1991	54.1	71.8	100.0	141.9	193.5	58.6	75.2	100.0	148.7	191.6
Manual men										
	KCKH	KCKI	KCKT	KCKK	KCKL	KCKM	KCKN	KCKO	KCKP	KCKR
1983	68.5	80.7	100.0	124.7	148.7	72.7	83.9	100.0	121.0	141.8
1984	65.4	79.3	100.0	129.8	161.2	69.2	81.0	100.0	120.6	146.3
1985	67.3	80.4	100.0	128.2	158.3	70.0	83.6	100.0	123.3	146.9
1986	65.9	80.5	100.0	129.5	160.9	70.2	83.0	100.0	120.1	149.4
1987	64.9	78.6	100.0	126.5	156.1	70.0	84.9	100.0	121.2	146.4
1988	63.8	78.7	100.0	132.0	165.9	68.2	81.7	100.0	122.5	150.3
1989	64.2	79.6	100.0	130.2	163.9	67.5	81.8	100.0	121.9	144.5
1990	63.5	77.5	100.0	133.4	169.6	67.7	80.8	100.0	126.2	160.3
1991	62.5	78.6	100.0	129.9	164.9	66.6	81.4	100.0	123.2	158.4
Non-manual men										
	KCKQ	KCKS	KFZW	KCKU	KCKV	KCKW	KCKX	KCKY	KCKZ	KCLA
1983	58.6	75.0	100.0	135.9	175.5	57.5	72.8	100.0	122.7	162.3
1984	55.6	73.6	100.0	138.4	181.5	55.0	73.1	100.0	126.4	161.2
1985	54.7	74.8	100.0	133.8	174.9	55.5	73.9	100.0	128.9	161.7
1986	52.7	75.1	100.0	138.4	175.3	51.1	71.9	100.0	126.4	162.7
1987	51.4	73.5	100.0	133.4	168.2	52.9	74.5	100.0	125.0	155.5
1988	51.7	72.3	100.0	138.2	175.3	51.4	71.5	100.0	121.7	153.5
1989	55.2	73.4	100.0	134.9	172.4	56.0	75.9	100.0	123.8	164.2
1990	51.1	73.0	100.0	137.0	169.2	49.6	70.1	100.0	120.4	153.6
1991	45.8	69.6	100.0	136.1	169.2	45.1	66.1	100.0	124.2	161.8

1 For 1978 to 1983 men aged 21 and over, women aged 18 and over. For 1984 onwards men and women on adult rates.
2 Those whose pay in the survey period was not affected by absence.

Weekly earnings figures refer to April in each year and are gross before deductions excluding, generally, the value of incomes in kind, but including bonus and commission payments for the pay period.

Source: Department of Economic Development (Northern Ireland)

6.18 continued Gross weekly and hourly earnings of full-time adults[1]
Northern Ireland
April of each year

	Gross weekly earnings[2]					Gross hourly earnings[2]				
	Lowest decile	Lower quartile	Median	Upper quartile	Highest decile	Lowest decile	Lower quartile	Median	Upper quartile	Highest decile
	£	£	£	£	£	p	p	p	p	p
All women	KCDS	KCDT	KCDU	KCDV	KCDW	KCDX	KCDY	KCDZ	KCFF	KCFG
1983	60.9	73.4	95.4	126.8	166.8	160.7	188.5	235.7	297.8	390.0
1984	66.0	77.3	99.6	134.9	178.1	173.6	202.1	248.2	321.0	418.3
1985	72.2	85.9	109.6	148.9	184.3	183.4	216.4	268.3	349.0	447.4
1986	72.4	89.3	114.4	158.5	199.4	187.1	226.2	279.4	370.5	495.2
1987	75.2	92.1	123.3	170.7	220.2	199.5	238.4	301.6	400.1	539.8
1988	80.5	97.7	129.9	181.9	247.0	209.1	248.5	316.6	423.2	567.0
1989	90.0	109.1	143.7	215.4	285.9	239.0	280.0	356.9	500.0	687.4
1990	95.7	118.7	157.7	234.9	305.2	251.2	306.2	402.7	568.9	794.4
1991	101.3	128.5	176.2	263.8	336.6	264.9	327.9	446.7	626.9	866.7
Manual women	KCFH	KCFI	KCFJ	KCFK	KCFL	KCFM	KCFN	KCFO	KCFP	KCFQ
1983	55.9	65.7	77.5	95.5	115.1	147.0	169.1	198.6	241.3	291.5
1984	60.8	68.7	81.3	97.4	117.4	162.3	181.6	208.8	248.4	294.5
1985	65.5	75.8	90.0	109.4	143.8	169.5	193.2	228.3	275.9	345.2
1986	63.7	75.4	93.3	111.6	144.6	176.1	198.3	235.6	282.9	336.6
1987	70.9	79.7	99.6	121.2	157.0	187.0	213.7	250.6	305.7	371.4
1988	75.8	85.6	106.4	129.6	149.2	200.6	225.7	270.1	325.7	383.4
1989	82.2	94.5	114.7	139.5	178.4	224.9	253.5	295.5	349.8	427.7
1990	89.5	99.9	122.1	150.2	187.7	234.9	262.9	309.7	377.5	465.5
1991	91.8	107.2	129.0	158.9	201.4	251.9	278.7	335.0	401.8	507.8
Non-manual women	KCFR	KCFS	KCFT	KCFU	KCFV	KCFW	KCFX	KCFY	KCFZ	KCHA
1983	66.1	81.9	103.6	141.3	176.4	170.1	207.0	256.5	332.5	434.4
1984	71.4	87.3	109.9	149.2	188.8	186.5	218.5	275.3	356.9	454.8
1985	77.3	92.2	121.4	163.9	200.4	197.4	236.5	294.8	383.4	472.6
1986	79.6	98.4	128.7	179.9	210.1	204.5	250.9	316.0	418.4	524.1
1987	82.0	100.8	137.1	191.8	234.3	209.6	255.0	338.8	442.7	584.0
1988	86.2	106.4	147.4	213.7	264.7	227.0	269.3	361.3	476.7	630.4
1989	98.4	121.3	158.2	239.3	294.0	259.9	313.3	398.9	570.8	736.4
1990	102.3	131.1	174.3	260.5	313.7	274.9	340.1	444.8	652.2	846.8
1991	111.0	145.1	200.6	292.2	349.1	291.7	373.9	493.6	684.7	909.7

As percentages of the corresponding median Percentage

All women	KCHB	KCHC	KCHD	KCHE	KCHF	KCHG	KCHH	KCHI	KCHJ	KCHK
1983	63.9	77.0	100.0	132.9	174.9	68.2	80.0	100.0	126.4	165.5
1984	66.3	77.6	100.0	135.4	178.7	70.0	81.4	100.0	129.3	168.5
1985	65.9	78.4	100.0	135.9	168.2	68.4	80.7	100.0	130.1	166.7
1986	63.3	78.1	100.0	138.5	174.3	67.0	81.0	100.0	132.6	177.2
1987	60.9	74.7	100.0	138.4	178.6	66.1	79.0	100.0	132.7	178.9
1988	62.0	75.2	100.0	140.0	190.1	66.0	78.5	100.0	133.7	179.1
1989	62.6	75.9	100.0	149.9	199.0	67.0	78.5	100.0	140.1	192.6
1990	60.7	75.3	100.0	149.0	193.5	62.4	76.0	100.0	141.3	197.3
1991	57.5	72.9	100.0	149.7	191.0	59.3	73.4	100.0	140.3	194.0
Manual women	KCHL	KCHM	KCHN	KCHO	KCHP	KCHQ	KCHR	KCHS	KCHT	KCHU
1983	72.1	84.8	100.0	123.2	148.5	74.0	85.2	100.0	121.5	146.8
1984	74.7	84.5	100.0	119.8	144.4	77.8	87.0	100.0	119.0	141.1
1985	72.8	84.2	100.0	121.5	159.8	74.3	84.6	100.0	120.9	151.2
1986	68.3	80.8	100.0	119.6	155.0	74.7	84.2	100.0	120.1	142.9
1987	71.2	80.0	100.0	121.7	157.6	74.6	85.3	100.0	122.0	148.2
1988	71.2	80.5	100.0	121.8	140.2	74.3	83.6	100.0	120.6	141.9
1989	71.7	82.4	100.0	121.6	156.4	76.1	85.8	100.0	118.4	144.7
1990	73.3	81.8	100.0	123.0	153.7	75.9	84.9	100.0	121.9	150.3
1991	71.2	83.1	100.0	123.2	156.1	75.2	83.2	100.0	119.9	151.6
Non-manual women	KCHV	KCHW	KCHX	KCHY	KCHZ	KCIA	KCIB	KCIC	KCID	KCIE
1983	63.8	79.1	100.0	136.4	170.3	66.3	80.7	100.0	129.6	169.4
1984	65.0	79.5	100.0	135.8	171.9	67.8	79.4	100.0	129.6	165.2
1985	63.6	75.9	100.0	135.0	165.0	67.0	80.2	100.0	130.1	160.3
1986	61.8	76.5	100.0	139.8	163.2	64.7	79.4	100.0	132.4	165.9
1987	59.8	73.5	100.0	140.0	171.0	61.9	75.3	100.0	130.7	172.4
1988	58.5	72.2	100.0	145.0	179.6	62.8	74.5	100.0	131.9	174.5
1989	62.2	76.7	100.0	151.3	185.8	65.2	78.5	100.0	143.1	184.6
1990	58.7	75.2	100.0	149.5	180.0	61.8	76.5	100.0	146.6	190.4
1991	55.3	72.3	100.0	145.7	174.0	59.1	75.7	100.0	138.7	184.3

See footnotes on page 128.

Source: Department of Economic Development (Northern Ireland)

Employment

6.19 Average earnings by age group of full-time employees whose pay for the survey pay period was not affected by absence   Great Britain

New Earnings Survey April 1991

	\multicolumn{7}{c}{Gross weekly earnings}		Average weekly hours[1]		Average hourly earnings excluding overtime pay[1]
	Average		As percentage of the median			As a percentage of the median		Percentage earning under £160			
	Total	Overtime pay	Lowest decile	Lower quartile	Median	Upper quartile	Highest decile		Total	Normal basic	
	£	£	per cent	per cent	£	per cent	per cent				£
All males											
Under 18	109.9	5.8	66.2	80.2	100.8	126.5	161.1	89.3	40.1	38.5	267.6
18 to 20	163.4	12.3	66.2	80.4	151.0	125.8	157.7	56.9	40.7	38.4	392.6
21 to 24	228.7	19.9	63.9	78.7	212.1	126.6	155.6	21.0	41.5	38.4	541.2
25 to 29	286.1	23.0	61.6	77.6	260.7	128.8	164.9	9.8	41.6	38.3	680.2
30 to 39	340.8	24.0	59.1	75.7	304.0	131.7	173.9	5.7	41.4	38.1	816.8
40 to 49	368.2	23.5	57.8	74.1	322.2	133.3	181.7	4.9	41.4	38.1	877.1
50 to 59	329.5	22.3	59.8	75.4	281.5	136.7	188.7	7.8	41.6	38.2	779.7
60 to 64	273.6	19.3	62.5	78.0	234.3	132.6	184.4	15.2	41.6	38.5	638.7
All ages	314.2	22.1	56.1	73.8	273.8	136.2	184.0	11.5	41.4	38.2	745.2
Manual males											
Under 18	106.4	6.3	66.4	79.2	97.7	126.8	162.6	90.5	40.6	38.9	256.7
18 to 20	162.4	15.3	63.7	79.3	150.6	126.3	160.2	57.1	42.2	39.2	376.2
21 to 24	217.6	28.0	64.8	79.7	202.0	126.7	157.4	24.3	43.9	39.2	483.0
25 to 29	247.5	33.9	64.3	79.6	231.5	125.2	155.7	14.0	44.4	39.2	542.4
30 to 39	268.8	39.5	64.8	79.8	250.4	125.0	158.5	9.3	44.8	39.1	580.6
40 to 49	273.4	40.5	65.3	80.2	254.1	126.4	156.9	8.2	44.9	39.1	591.0
50 to 59	254.7	34.7	66.3	80.4	237.0	125.8	157.4	11.1	44.3	39.0	563.5
60 to 64	228.6	27.1	66.1	80.0	212.9	125.0	157.2	19.7	43.4	39.1	516.5
All ages	248.6	34.4	61.0	78.2	231.9	127.2	160.8	16.0	44.3	39.1	545.0
Non-manual males											
Under 18	117.5	4.7	67.0	81.5	107.1	130.3	158.2	86.7	38.9	37.7	293.2
18 to 20	164.8	8.5	68.9	82.1	151.6	125.1	153.4	56.6	38.8	37.4	415.3
21 to 24	239.6	12.0	64.2	78.4	221.3	126.5	154.0	17.7	39.1	37.5	602.9
25 to 29	319.5	13.5	60.3	78.1	290.9	127.5	164.5	6.2	39.1	37.4	810.7
30 to 39	394.6	12.5	59.3	77.9	353.7	128.4	171.7	2.9	38.6	37.2	1 018.2
40 to 49	439.6	10.6	59.3	78.1	384.5	130.9	181.2	2.5	38.4	37.2	1 129.2
50 to 59	405.4	9.7	54.7	74.0	352.5	135.2	186.9	4.4	38.5	37.3	1 036.7
60 to 64	336.7	8.5	58.3	74.7	281.4	141.0	193.9	8.9	38.9	37.7	834.3
All ages	371.9	11.3	52.4	72.2	330.1	132.5	181.2	7.5	38.7	37.3	945.8
All females											
Under 18	107.4	2.4	62.1	78.3	104.4	124.5	150.2	91.1	37.7	37.2	284.9
18 to 20	146.3	4.2	70.4	84.0	139.7	119.4	143.5	70.0	37.8	37.1	384.3
21 to 24	189.3	5.9	67.1	80.9	177.4	125.8	152.4	36.6	37.9	37.0	496.5
25 to 29	237.0	6.9	60.5	76.8	220.9	128.7	159.9	20.2	37.7	36.8	623.8
30 to 39	252.3	5.1	57.4	73.4	227.7	138.1	171.7	21.6	37.1	36.4	675.1
40 to 49	233.4	4.7	60.7	76.1	204.2	147.6	180.0	27.1	37.0	36.2	623.7
50 to 59	220.9	4.4	62.4	77.4	190.6	143.4	188.6	31.6	37.1	36.4	586.1
60 to 64	198.8	3.2	62.0	77.6	178.9	128.9	184.9	38.0	37.0	36.5	533.0
All ages	220.0	5.2	61.2	76.7	193.0	139.5	182.2	31.4	37.4	36.6	582.3
Manual females											
Under 18	99.5	3.1	54.9	78.9	97.1	125.5	147.9	95.0	39.4	38.6	252.1
18 to 20	131.9	5.7	68.6	81.2	126.2	121.3	149.5	81.0	39.7	38.5	328.0
21 to 24	155.6	8.5	70.3	82.8	142.8	124.6	159.0	64.0	40.1	38.5	383.1
25 to 29	170.7	10.0	67.3	80.2	157.9	127.4	160.2	51.2	40.2	38.3	413.6
30 to 39	165.8	9.2	66.0	80.6	152.0	128.6	166.1	55.5	39.9	38.2	408.5
40 to 49	162.4	9.5	68.2	81.4	150.2	126.0	157.5	56.6	39.8	37.9	403.2
50 to 59	156.5	7.4	69.6	82.2	146.2	123.6	156.0	61.0	39.1	37.7	397.2
60 to 64	152.3	6.0	68.0	82.1	146.9	120.7	146.0	62.5	38.6	37.5	394.2
All ages	157.4	8.4	67.4	81.0	145.8	126.3	159.5	60.9	39.7	38.1	391.0
Non-manual females											
Under 18	110.6	2.1	64.0	78.3	106.8	125.1	151.9	89.6	37.1	36.7	298.3
18 to 20	149.8	3.8	72.5	84.3	142.0	119.3	142.0	67.3	37.4	36.7	398.5
21 to 24	196.1	5.4	68.8	82.7	183.6	125.1	150.8	31.1	37.4	36.7	519.8
25 to 29	246.7	6.4	62.3	77.4	231.1	126.2	156.6	15.7	37.3	36.5	655.7
30 to 39	268.4	4.4	59.0	73.3	244.9	135.1	165.4	15.3	36.6	36.0	728.1
40 to 49	251.3	3.5	60.7	75.0	226.1	142.5	170.0	19.7	36.2	35.7	685.5
50 to 59	245.2	3.3	62.3	77.6	216.0	145.4	175.6	20.5	36.3	35.8	663.6
60 to 64	219.0	1.9	60.5	78.3	196.1	129.3	183.2	27.4	36.3	36.0	599.6
All ages	234.3	4.5	61.1	76.9	208.8	138.3	174.3	24.7	36.8	36.2	628.8

[1] The estimates given relate to employees for whom normal basic hours were reported.

Source: Department of Employment

Employment

6.20 Trade unions[1,2]
United Kingdom
At end of year

per cent

		1980	1981	1982	1983	1984	1985	1986	1987	1988	1989	1990
Number of trade unions	KCLB	438	414	408	394	375	370	335	330	315	309	287
Analysis by number of members:												
Under 100 members	KCLC	15.8	17.1	19.1	17.8	17.6	16.5	18.5	16.1	17.5	15.5	15.3
100 and under 500	KCLD	26.9	28.0	24.3	26.4	25.1	25.1	24.2	25.8	24.1	23.6	22.6
500 and under 1 000	KCLE	10.3	9.9	11.8	10.7	10.1	10.0	9.0	7.9	8.3	6.1	7.7
1 000 and under 2 500	KCLF	12.8	12.1	12.5	14.4	14.9	14.9	14.9	15.8	14.9	15.9	15.0
2 500 and under 5 000	KCLG	8.9	8.9	9.3	7.9	8.8	7.3	6.6	6.7	8.3	8.7	9.4
5 000 and under 10 000	KCLH	5.7	5.6	5.6	4.5	4.3	3.8	4.8	4.8	4.7	5.8	5.2
10 000 and under 15 000	KCLI	1.6	1.0	0.7	0.5	0.8	1.1	1.5	1.8	1.3	1.6	2.1
15 000 and under 25 000	KCLJ	4.8	3.6	4.4	5.1	4.0	3.0	3.0	3.3	3.5	3.9	3.1
25 000 and under 50 000	KCLK	4.3	4.1	3.7	3.8	5.1	6.2	7.5	7.3	7.6	7.8	8.7
50 000 and under 100 000	KCLL	3.2	3.4	3.2	3.3	3.5	2.4	2.1	2.1	2.5	2.3	2.4
100 000 and under 250 000	KCLM	3.4	3.4	2.7	3.0	3.5	3.8	4.5	3.9	4.1	4.2	4.9
250 000 and over	KCLN	2.3	2.9	2.7	2.5	2.4	2.7	2.7	3.3	3.2	3.2	3.1
Membership unknown[3]	KCLO	–	–	–	–	–	3.2	0.9	1.2	–	1.3	0.3
All sizes	KCLP	100	100	100	100	100	100	100	100	100	100	100
Membership[4] (Thousands)												
Analysis by size of union:												
Under 100 members	KCLQ	–	–	–	–	–	–	–	–	–	–	–
100 and under 500	KCLR	0.2	0.2	0.2	0.2	0.2	0.2	0.2	0.2	0.2	0.2	0.2
500 and under 1 000	KCLS	0.2	0.2	0.3	0.2	0.2	0.2	0.2	0.2	0.2	0.1	0.2
1 000 and under 2 500	KCLT	0.7	0.7	0.7	0.8	0.8	0.8	0.8	0.8	0.8	0.8	0.7
2 500 and under 5 000	KCLU	1.1	1.0	1.1	1.0	1.0	0.9	0.7	0.8	0.9	0.9	1.0
5 000 and under 10 000	KCLV	1.3	1.3	1.3	1.0	1.0	0.8	0.8	1.0	1.0	1.2	1.0
10 000 and under 15 000	KCLW	0.6	0.4	0.4	0.2	0.3	0.4	0.6	0.7	0.5	0.6	0.7
15 000 and under 25 000	KCLX	3.0	2.9	3.1	3.6	2.7	1.9	1.8	2.1	2.0	2.3	1.7
25 000 and under 50 000	KCLY	5.6	5.0	4.7	4.9	6.0	7.5	8.6	8.4	8.5	8.6	9.0
50 000 and under 100 000	KCLZ	7.9	7.9	8.4	8.6	8.9	6.1	5.2	5.3	5.5	4.9	4.9
100 000 and under 250 000	KCMA	19.4	17.9	16.1	18.6	22.3	22.8	25.2	20.3	20.2	20.0	22.4
250 000 and over	KCMB	59.9	62.2	63.7	60.9	56.5	58.4	55.6	60.3	60.1	60.4	58.2
All sizes	KCMC	100	100	100	100	100	100	100	100	100	100	100
Total	KCMD	12 947	12 106	11 593	11 236	10 994	10 821	10 539	10 475	10 376	10 158	9 947

1 The statistics relate to all organisations of employees with head offices in the United Kingdom.
2 Figures are confined to organisations which appear to satisfy the statutory definition of a trade union in Section 28 of the Trade Union and Labour Relations Act 1974.
3 There was 1 newly formed union in 1990 whose membership was not reported.
4 The figures include home and overseas memberships of contributory and non-contributory members, the figures may include some people who are self-employed, unemployed or retired. A small number of people who are members of more than one union are included more than once in the figures, but the effect on the aggregates is relatively insignificant.

Source: Department of Employment

7 Defence

This section includes figures on Defence expenditure, on the size and role of the Armed Forces and on related support activities.

Much of the material in this section can be found in *Defence Statistics 1992* (HMSO 1992).

Formation of the Armed Forces *(Table 7.1)*. This table shows the number of units which comprise the 'teeth' elements of the Armed Forces and excludes supporting units. Greater detail for the current year is given in Volume 1 of the *Statement on the Defence Estimates 1992* (CM. 1981).

Service personnel *(Tables 7.3 to 7.6 and 7.10)*. The Regular Forces consist entirely of volunteer members serving on a whole-time basis. The figures for females consist of all members of the Women's Services (ie WRNS and WRAF) and female members of the Nursing Services. Certain male members of the RAF Medical Branch were transferred to the Princess Mary's RAF Nursing Service on 1 April 1980 and certain members of the RN Medical specialisation were transferred to the Queen Alexandra's Royal Naval Nursing Service on 1 April 1983 as a result of reorganisations. They continue to be shown in the male figures in Table 7.3 and are now included in the Nursing Services figures in Table 7.10.

Locally Entered Personnel are recruited outside the United Kingdom for whole-time service in special formations with special conditions of service and normally restricted locations. The Brigade of Gurkhas is an example.

The Regular Forces are supported by Reserves and Auxiliary Forces. There are both regular and volunteer Reserves. Regular Reserves consist of former Service personnel with a Reserve liability. Volunteer Reserves are open to both former Service personnel and civilians. The call out liabilities of the various reserve forces differ in accordance with their roles.

All three Services run cadet forces for young people and the Combined Cadet Force, which is found in certain schools where education is continued to the age of 17 or above, may operate sections for any or all of the Services.

Deployment of Service personnel *(Table 7.6)*. The source from which the individual national totals are compiled is different from that used to obtain the total UK strength and consequently the figures for England, Wales, Scotland and Northern Ireland do not add up to the UK figure. Royal Navy and Royal Marines personnel on board ship are included in the UK figure if the ship was in home waters on the situation date or otherwise against the appropriate overseas area. The overseas figures include personnel who are on loan to countries in the areas shown.

Service married accommodation and Defence land holdings *(Table 7.7)*. Accommodation is provided for Service families in the United Kingdom and abroad, partly by building to approved standards and partly by renting accommodation. Permanent holdings in the United Kingdom include a small number of unfurnished hirings taken on from local authorities which are not recorded separately. Multiple hirings relate to accommodation built by private developers and leased by the Federal German Authorities and the Government of Gibraltar on behalf of British Forces.

The table also presents statistics of land and foreshore in the United Kingdom owned by the Ministry of Defence or over which it has limited rights under grants or licences. Land declared as surplus to Defence requirements is also included. At 1 April 1992 about 1214 hectares were awaiting disposal by the Property Services Agency.

Civilian personnel *(Table 7.8)*. This table gives an analysis of the number of civilians employed in the various management areas, *viz* Centre (those authorities not in the Service Departments, the Procurement Executive (PE) or the Royal Ordnance Factories (ROFs)), Royal Dockyards, Other Navy, Army, Royal Air Force, PE and ROFs. The attribution of civilian staff can change according to circumstances so that figures for successive years may not always be comparable.

Some civilians from the United Kingdom serve tours of duty overseas. There were 5 576 such civilians serving abroad on 1 April 1992. Other civilian staff are engaged overseas to work locally as circumstances demand.

Health *(Tables 7.9-7.11)*. The Services operate a number of hospitals in this country and in areas abroad where there is a significant British military presence. These hospitals take as patients members of all three Services and their dependants; in addition the hospitals in the United Kingdom take civilian patients under arrangements agreed with the National Health Service. Medical support is also supplied by Service medical staff at individual units, ships and stations.

Sickness, medical discharges and deaths of UK Service personnel *(Table 7.11)*. It should be noted that, whereas the Royal Air Force content is for all episodes of bedded sickness lasting two days or more terminating in the year, that for the Army covers only those cases admitted to medical units (including hospitals) for two days or more, and the Royal Navy episodes exclude less than seven days sickness on shore.

Search and rescue *(Table 7.12)*. This table covers incidents in which Rescue Co-ordinating Centres (RCCs) in the United Kingdom co-ordinated search and rescue (SAR) action in which elements of the Armed Forces were involved. The table also includes urgent medical incidents in which the Forces SAR facilities gave assistance (eg inter-hospital transfers).

Defence services and the civilian community *(Table 7.13)*. The Ministry of Defence helps the civil community in a variety of ways, for example by providing assistance in time of natural disasters or other emergencies and by undertaking community projects which are of training value to the Services. In some cases facilities established primarily for defence purposes also provide benefits to the general public. Overall figures are not available, but the table presents information on a number of these activities and facilities.

Service assistance may be provided during an industrial dispute at the request of the civil ministries in order to maintain services essential to the life of the community (eg maintenance of emergency fire services in 1977/78).

The Royal Navy Fishery Protection squadron operates within the UK fishery limits on behalf of Fishery departments, who pay some of the running costs of the squadron.

The Hydrographer of the Navy is the national authority responsible for hydrographic and oceanographic surveys and nautical charting. The Admiralty chart series comprises some 3 400 basic charts and 600 latticed versions covering the whole world.

Defence energy consumption *(Table 7.14)*. Consumption is expressed in terms of the System International (SI) unit of energy, the joule.

Defence

7.1 Formation of the Armed Forces
At 1 April[1]

Number

		Unit[1]	1982	1983	1984	1985	1986	1987	1988	1989	1990	1991	1992
Royal Navy[2]													
Submarines	KCGA	Vessels	22	21	22	24	26	26	24	26	24	24	20
Carriers and assault ships	KCGB	Vessels	3	4	4	4	4	3	3	4	4	3	3
Destroyers and frigates	KCGC	Vessels	49	55	52	46	47	46	42	39	44	42	43
Mine counter-measure	KCGE	Vessels	33	36	34	32	39	36	35	36	37	35	31
Patrol ships and craft	KCGF	Vessels	21	25	31	28	32	28	31	34	32	31	26
Fixed wing aircraft	KCGG	Squadrons	3	3	3	3	3	3	3	3	3	3	3
Helicopters	KCGH	Squadrons	15	13	12	14	14	14	14	14	13	13	13
Royal Marines	KCGI	Commandos	3	3	3	3	3	3	3	3	3	3	3
Army[3,4]													
Royal Armoured Corps	KCGJ	Regiments	19	19	19	19	19	19	19	19	19	19	19
Royal Artillery[5]	KCGK	Regiments	22	22	22	22	22	22	22	22	22	22	21
Royal Engineers[6]	KCGL	Regiments	11	12	12	13	13	13	13	13	13	13	13
Infantry[6]	KCGM	Battalions	57	56	56	56	56	55	55	55	55	55	55
Special Air Service	KCGN	Regiments	1	1	1	1	1	1	1	1	1	1	1
Army Air Corps[8]	KCGO	Regiments	6	4	4	4	4	4	4	4	4	4	5
Royal Air Force													
Strike/attack	KCGP	Squadrons	12	10	11	11	11	11	11	11	11	11	9
Offensive support	KCGQ	Squadrons	5	5	5	5	5	5	5	5	5	5	5
Air defence	KCGR	Squadrons	9	9	8	9	9	9	9	9	9	11	9
Maritime patrol	KCGS	Squadrons	4	4	4	4	4	4	4	4	4	4	4
Reconnaissance	KCGT	Squadrons	3	2	3	3	3	3	3	3	3	5	5
Airbourne early warning	KCGU	Squadrons	1	1	1	1	1	1	1	1	1	1	1
Transport[7]	KCGV	Squadrons	10	11	10	14	15	15	15	15	15	15	15
Tankers	KCGW	Squadrons	2	3	3	3	4	3	3	3	3	3	3
Search and rescue	KCGX	Squadrons	3	3	2	2	2	2	2	2	2	2	2
Surface to air missiles	KCGY	Squadrons	8	8	8	8	8	8	8	8	7	7	6
Ground defence	KCGZ	Squadrons	6	6	5	5	5	5	5	6	6	5	5

1 The number of personnel and the amount of equipment in each vessel, Regiment, etc, varies according to the role currently assigned.
2 Excludes vessels undergoing construction, major refit, conversion, or on stand-by, etc.
3 Front-line Squadrons in the NATO area.
4 Combat Arm major units only.
5 The 1992 figure excludes the Training Regiment.
6 Includes Gurkhas.
7 Includes helicopters. This also includes 3 helicopter squadrons deployed outside the NATO area not previously shown.
8 A fifth Army Air Corps regiment (9AAC) has begun formation and will be complete by 1991.

Source: Ministry of Defence

7.2 Defence expenditure[1,2]

£ million

		1980/81	1981/82	1982/83	1983/84	1984/85	1985/86	1986/87	1987/88	1988/89	1989/90	1990/91
Total expenditure at outturn prices[3]	KDAA	11 182	12 607	14 412	15 487	17 122	17 943	18 163	18 856	19 072	20 755	22 298
of which:												
Expenditure on personnel	KDAB	4 556	5 058	5 455	5 726	5 983	6 379	6 890	7 212	7 572	8 099	8 811
of the Armed Forces	KDAC	2 460	2 728	2 914	3 076	3 236	3 510	3 787	4 032	4 300	4 539	4 811
of the retired Armed Forces	KDAD	503	624	680	777	828	899	980	1 079	1 060	1 197	1 406
of civilian staff	KDAE	1 593	1 706	1 861	1 873	1 919	1 970	2 123	2 101	2 212	2 363	2 594
Expenditure on equipment	KDAF	4 885	5 638	6 297	6 939	7 838	8 193	7 885	8 270	8 038	8 536	8 838
Sea systems	KDAG	1 513	1 624	1 730	1 849	2 228	2 499	2 494	2 797	2 633	2 890	2 955
Land systems	KDAH	904	1 101	1 353	1 475	1 638	1 887	1 759	1 700	1 554	1 738	1 927
Air systems	KDAI	2 059	2 458	2 640	3 057	3 474	3 296	3 090	3 230	3 085	3 102	3 197
Other	KDAJ	410	456	574	558	498	511	542	543	766	806	759
Other expenditure	KDAK	1 741	1 910	2 659	2 822	3 302	3 370	3 387	3 374	3 462	4 120	4 649
Works, buildings and land	KDAL	623	664	832	1 067	1 271	1 413	1 498	1 453	1 411	1 900	2 067
Miscellaneous stores and services	KDAM	1 118	1 246	1 827	1 754	2 031	1 958	1 889	1 921	2 051	2 220	2 582
Total expenditure at constant (1990/91) prices[3]	KDAN	21 082	21 382	22 683	22 997	23 904	23 870	23 044	22 660	21 674	22 297	22 298

1 Expenditure as given in the annual Appropriation Accounts for the Defence votes, Class 1.
2 Including expenditure of government departments other than the Ministry of Defence in years when these contributed to the Defence budget.
3 Because of changes in the responsibilities of the Ministry of Defence, expenditures in successive years are not necessarily comparable.

Source: Ministry of Defence

Defence

7.3 Defence manpower strengths
At 1 April[1]

Thousands

		1981	1982	1983	1984	1985	1986	1987	1988	1989	1990	1991	1992
UK service personnel													
All services:													
Male	KCEB	316.8	311.9	305.2	309.7	309.8	306.5	303.4	300.7	295.2	288.2	279.2	273.8
Female	KCEC	16.9	15.7	15.4	16.2	16.4	16.0	16.4	16.2	16.5	17.5	18.8	19.6
Total	KCEA	333.8	327.6	320.6	325.9	326.2	322.5	319.8	316.9	311.6	305.7	298.1	293.4
Royal Naval Services:[2]													
Male	KCEE	70.0	69.0	67.8	67.4	66.7	64.4	63.2	62.2	61.2	59.6	57.9	57.5
Female	KCEF	4.1	4.0	3.9	3.9	3.7	3.4	3.4	3.3	3.5	3.6	4.2	4.6
Total	KCED	74.3	73.0	71.7	71.3	70.4	67.9	66.5	65.5	64.6	63.2	62.1	62.1
Army:													
Male	KCEJ	159.4	157.2	152.9	155.0	155.6	154.8	153.1	151.7	148.9	145.8	140.3	137.6
Female	KCEK	6.6	6.0	6.1	6.6	6.8	6.6	6.6	6.4	6.7	7.0	7.3	7.8
Total	KCEI	166.0	163.2	159.1	161.5	162.4	161.4	159.7	158.1	155.6	152.8	147.6	145.4
Royal Air Force:													
Male	KCEM	87.2	85.7	84.5	87.3	87.5	87.2	87.2	86.9	85.1	82.9	81.1	78.7
Female	KCEN	6.3	5.8	5.4	5.7	6.0	6.0	6.4	6.4	6.4	6.8	7.3	7.3
Total	KCEL	93.5	91.5	89.8	93.1	93.4	93.2	93.6	93.3	91.4	89.7	88.4	86.0
Personnel locally entered overseas:													
Total	KCEO	9.7	10.1	10.1	10.1	10.2	10.1	9.8	9.4	9.1	9.0	9.1	9.0
Regular Reserves:[1]													
Royal Naval Services[2]	KCEP	28.9	26.9	26.1	25.8	25.6	26.5	26.8	27.1	27.6	28.4	28.5	27.5
Army	KCES	137.5	140.2	138.3	143.2	150.2	153.9	160.4	167.7	175.3	183.4	187.7	188.6
Royal Air Force	KCET	30.1	29.3	28.9	29.0	29.8	31.5	33.7	35.4	37.5	40.1	42.5	44.8
Total	KCER	196.5	196.4	193.4	198.0	205.5	211.6	220.9	230.2	240.4	252.0	258.7	260.8
Volunteer Reserves and Auxillary Forces:													
Royal Naval Services[2]	KCEV	6.4	6.4	6.5	6.3	6.4	6.7	6.8	6.8	6.8	7.0	7.0	5.8
Territorial Army	KCEX	69.5	72.1	72.8	71.4	73.7	77.7	78.5	74.7	72.5	72.5	73.3	71.3
Ulster Defence Regiment	KCEY	7.5	7.1	7.1	6.8	6.4	6.6	6.5	6.4	6.3	6.2	6.1	6.0
Home Service Force	KCEZ	..	..	0.3	0.3	0.9	3.0	3.3	3.1	3.0	3.2	3.4	2.9
Royal Air Force	KCFA	0.6	0.6	0.8	1.1	1.2	1.4	1.6	1.8	1.7	1.7	1.8	2.2
Total[1]	KCEU	84.0	86.3	87.5	85.9	88.6	95.4	96.8	92.8	90.4	90.6	91.6	88.3
Cadet Forces:[1,3]													
Royal Navy	KCFC	31.1	28.7	29.4	28.4	28.4	28.0	27.5	27.1	26.5	26.2	27.0	27.0
Army	KCFD	75.1	74.1	74.5	73.8	72.1	70.9	71.2	69.3	65.9	65.7	64.6	64.6
Royal Air Force	KCFE	44.4	45.9	45.1	44.3	44.1	44.5	47.0	48.3	46.7	44.2	43.1	43.8
Total	KCFB	150.6	148.7	149.0	146.5	144.7	143.4	145.7	144.6	139.2	136.0	134.7	135.3

1 A few of the figures for reserves and cadets were collected at irregular intervals and do not necessarily refer to 1 April; they are the latest figures available at that date.
2 Royal Navy and Royal Marines figures have been combined under the Royal Naval Services heading.
3 Combined Cadet Force cadets are included under the relevant service.

Source: Ministry of Defence

7.4 Recruitment of UK Service personnel to each Service

Number

		1981/82	1982/83	1983/84	1984/85	1985/86	1986/87	1987/88	1988/89	1989/90	1990/91	1991/92
All Services:												
Male	KCJB	21 188	19 342	33 760	32 076	30 407	31 107	31 176	30 821	32 297	26 782	24 357
Female	KCJC	1 419	2 305	3 231	2 645	2 244	2 942	2 650	3 042	4 115	4 428	3 550
Total	KCJA	22 607	21 647	36 991	34 721	32 651	34 049	33 826	33 863	36 412	31 210	27 907
Royal Naval Services[1]**:**												
Male	KCJE	4 052	3 525	4 670	5 185	5 080	6 024	5 592	5 535	5 759	5 712	5 570
Female	KCJF	452	506	562	351	289	545	580	700	860	1 199	1 013
Total	KCJD	4 504	4 031	5 232	5 536	5 369	6 569	6 172	6 235	6 619	6 911	6 583
Army:												
Male	KCJJ	13 603	11 679	20 811	20 914	19 173	18 696	19 873	19 898	20 378	15 955	15 544
Female	KCJK	601	1 392	1 537	1 364	1 095	1 222	1 168	1 450	1 706	1 547	1 594
Total	KCJI	14 204	13 071	22 348	22 278	20 268	19 918	21 041	21 348	22 084	17 502	17 138
Royal Air Force:												
Male	KCJM	3 533	4 138	8 279	5 977	6 154	6 393	5 715	5 395	6 166	5 122	3 243
Female	KCJN	366	407	1 132	930	860	1 169	898	885	1 543	1 675	943
Total	KCJL	3 899	4 545	9 411	6 907	7 014	7 562	6 613	6 280	7 709	6 797	4 186

1 Royal Navy and Royal Marines figures have been combined under the Royal Naval Services heading.

Source: Ministry of Defence

Defence

7.5 Outflow of UK Service personnel from each Service

Number

		1981/82	1982/83	1983/84	1984/85	1985/86	1986/87	1987/88	1988/89	1989/90	1990/91	1991/92
All Services:												
Male	KDNA	26 799	26 108	29 468	32 095	33 881	34 173	34 034	36 536	39 461	36 017	30 057
Female	KDNB	2 652	2 549	2 458	2 459	2 640	2 788	2 904	2 742	3 106	3 062	2 748
Total	KDNC	29 451	28 657	31 926	34 554	36 521	36 961	36 938	39 278	42 567	39 079	32 805
Royal Naval Services[1]:												
Male	KDND	5 912	4 710	5 215	5 924	7 444	7 362	6 609	6 474	7 377	7 428	6 105
Female	KDNE	577	532	581	561	559	625	622	591	657	680	662
Total	KDNF	6 489	5 242	5 796	6 485	8 003	7 987	7 231	7 065	8 034	8 108	6 767
Army:												
Male	KDNI	15 878	15 960	18 854	20 286	19 999	20 460	21 380	22 823	23 760	21 582	18 304
Female	KDNJ	1 216	1 218	1 105	1 162	1 302	1 301	1 369	1 233	1 301	1 242	1 147
Total	KDNK	17 094	17 178	19 959	21 448	21 301	21 761	22 749	24 056	25 061	22 824	19 451
Royal Air Force:												
Male	KDNL	5 009	5 438	5 399	5 885	6 438	6 351	6 045	7 239	8 324	7 007	5 648
Female	KDNM	859	799	772	736	779	862	913	918	1 148	1 140	939
Total	KDNN	5 868	6 237	6 171	6 621	7 217	7 213	6 958	8 157	9 472	8 147	6 587

1 Royal Navy and Royal Marines figures have been combined under the Royal Naval Services heading.

Source: Ministry of Defence

7.6 Deployment of Service personnel
At 1 July

Thousands

		1981	1982	1983	1984	1985	1986	1987	1988	1989	1990	1991
UK Service personnel, Regular Forces:												
In United Kingdom	KDOB	245.0	215.2	228.8	230.4	229.6	228.3	228.1	226.2	220.2	215.9	207.9
England[1]	KDOC	207.7	195.9	195.1	194.5	193.3	191.7	190.9	189.8	183.3	179.6	173.3
Wales[1]	KDOD	6.3	6.1	6.1	6.2	6.3	6.3	6.1	5.8	5.4	5.3	5.2
Scotland[1]	KDOE	18.9	19.0	18.7	20.6	20.1	19.7	19.6	19.3	20.0	19.3	18.2
Northern Ireland[2]	KDOF	11.6	10.9	10.2	10.0	9.7	10.5	11.4	11.2	11.2	11.5	11.2
Overseas	KDOG	91.3	109.8	94.0	96.1	96.9	94.1	91.3	90.4	88.4	88.9	89.3
Federal Republic of Germany[3]	KDOH	70.4	69.8	67.0	66.7	67.3	66.7	66.8	65.6	63.9	63.2	69.7
Elsewhere in Continental Europe[4,7]	KDOI	6.1	6.2	6.1	7.2	7.7	6.3	6.9	6.9	7.0	6.8	–
Gibraltar	KDOJ	2.2	2.7	2.0	2.1	2.4	2.3	2.1	1.8	1.6	1.8	1.0
Cyprus	KDOL	4.9	4.8	4.9	4.8	4.7	4.9	4.6	4.5	4.8	4.8	5.2
Elsewhere in Mediterranean Near East and Gulf	KDOM	1.4	1.1	0.3	1.2	2.3	0.4	1.1	3.4	1.8	1.3	1.1
Hong Kong	KDON	2.5	2.5	2.4	2.5	2.4	2.4	2.3	2.3	2.1	2.1	2.3
Elsewhere in the Far East	KDOP	0.3	0.3	0.7	0.6	0.4	0.3	0.3	0.3	0.6	0.5	0.5
Other locations[1,5]	KDOQ	3.5	22.4	10.5	11.3	9.8	10.9	7.0	5.6	6.6	8.4	9.5
Total	KDOA	334.3	324.3	321.7	325.9	325.8	321.7	318.7	315.8	307.8	303.1	297.2
Locally entered service personnel:												
United Kingdom	KDOS	1.3	0.6	1.2	1.2	1.2	1.3	1.2	1.3	1.2	1.4	1.4
Gibraltar	KDOT	0.1	0.1	0.1	0.1	0.1	0.1	0.1	0.1	0.1	0.1	0.1
Hong Kong	KDOV	6.7	6.6	6.6	6.7	6.7	6.4	6.0	5.8	5.5	5.5	5.5
Brunei	KDOW	0.8	0.8	0.8	0.8	0.8	0.8	0.8	0.8	0.9	0.9	0.8
Nepal	KDOX	1.2	1.3	1.4	1.3	1.3	1.4	1.5	1.4	1.4	1.1	1.3
Other locations[6]	KDOY	–	0.6	–	–	–	–	–	–	–	–	–
Total	KDOK	10.0	9.9	10.0	10.1	10.1	10.0	9.6	9.4	9.0	8.9	9.1

1 From 1982 the England, Wales and Scotland national figures include personnel who were UK based but temporarily deployed in the South Atlantic. These have been included also in the Overseas numbers against 'Other locations'.
2 The figures for Northern Ireland include all personnel from other parts of the United Kingdom and the British Army of the Rhine who are serving on emergency tours of duty, but exclude the Ulster Defence Regiment.
3 Army personnel serving in Northern Ireland on emergency tours of duty but remaining under the command of the Commander-in-Chief British Army of the Rhine are included in these figures.
4 These figures include personnel stationed in Berlin and Sardinia.
5 These figures include Defence Attaches/Advisers and their staffs.
6 The 1982 figures comprise Gurkha troops serving in the Falkland Islands.
7 As from 1991 figures for Federal Republic of Germany and Elsewhere in Continental Europe are combined.

Source: Ministry of Defence

Defence

7.7 Service married accommodation and Defence land holdings

		1982	1983	1984	1985	1986	1987	1988	1989	1990	1991	1992
						Thousands						
Married accommodation[1]												
United Kingdom: total	KDPA	87.5	87.0	86.4	85.1	83.3	82.0	79.8	77.2	75.0	73.6	72.3
Permanent holdings	KDPB	87.2	86.6	86.1	84.8	83.1	81.9	79.8	77.2	75.0	73.6	72.3
Hirings	KDPC	0.3	0.3	0.3	0.3	0.2	0.1	–	–	–	–	–
Overseas: total	KDPD	46.0	46.0	46.0	47.5	50.1	50.5	47.0	45.2	46.7	48.9	..
Permanent holdings	KDPE	21.4	21.4	21.4	21.3	21.5	21.4	21.1	20.9	21.3	24.2	..
Hirings[2]	KDPK	24.5	24.6	24.6	26.2	28.6	29.1	25.9	24.3	25.4	24.7	..
						Thousand hectares						
Land holdings[3]												
United Kingdom												
Land: freehold	KDPF	217.8	215.9	215.0	211.1	210.9	210.3	211.1	212.5	212.1	213.8	214.4
leasehold	KDPG	11.9	11.9	11.6	11.4	10.9	10.9	10.8	10.8	10.5	11.0	11.0
Foreshore: freehold	KDPH	13.2	13.1	13.1	13.1	13.1	13.1	13.1	13.0	13.0	13.0	13.0
leasehold	KDPI	4.9	4.9	4.9	4.9	4.9	5.0	5.0	5.0	5.0	5.0	5.0
Rights[4]	KDPJ	36.7	36.7	36.0	36.0	36.2	36.2	99.9	101.1	103.4	121.3	120.7
Defence land (freehold and leasehold)												
Used for agricultural purposes	KDPL	109.1	109.7	110.0	109.1	107.6	105.5	105.4	109.6	110.8	109.9	109.3
Used for grazing only	KDPM	58.8	58.8	58.8	58.6	58.1	57.6	56.9	61.4	61.2	63.9	62.6
Full agricultural use	KDPN	50.3	50.9	51.2	50.5	49.5	47.9	48.5	48.2	49.6	46.0	46.7

1 From 1982 to 1983 at 15 January each year, from 1984 to 1986 at 15 April each year. Figures from 1987 onwards are taken as at 1 April each year.
2 Includes multiple hirings.
3 At 1 April each year.
4 The 1988 figure includes the renewal of two leases granting long-term rights when in previous years these were on a short-term basis and were not included.

Source: Ministry of Defence

7.8 Defence civilian manpower strengths
At 1 April

Thousands

		1982	1983	1984	1985	1986	1987	1988	1989	1990	1991	1992
Ministry of Defence civilians												
UK based[2]	KDQB	216.9	208.9	199.1	174.1	169.5	164.0	143.4	141.3	141.4	140.2	139.5
Non-industrial	KDQC	108.1	105.6	103.3	94.9	93.8	93.3	88.6	88.7	89.9	90.3	90.7
Industrial	KDQD	108.8	103.3	95.8	79.1	75.6	70.7	54.8	52.6	51.5	49.9	48.8
of which												
Centre[5]												
Non-industrial	KDQE	18.3	14.5	14.1	13.8	13.5	13.3	13.3	17.2	17.7	21.8	22.9
Industrial	KDQF	0.6	0.6	0.5	0.5	0.5	0.5	0.2	0.3	0.4	0.7	0.8
Royal Dockyards[3]												
Non-industrial	KDQG	8	7	6	6	6	5	–	–	–	–	–
Industrial	KDQH	22	21	18	17	16	15	–	–	–	–	–
Other Navy												
Non-industrial	KDQI	13.1	14.5	14.3	14.6	14.5	15.4	16.4	14.8	15.1	14.9	14.9
Industrial	KDQJ	19.0	18.4	17.2	17.1	16.4	15.8	17.5	17.1	16.4	15.8	15.2
Army												
Non-industrial	KDQK	23.9	24.2	23.6	22.9	23.0	22.7	22.6	21.9	22.1	21.4	21.2
Industrial	KDQL	26.3	25.2	24.0	23.3	22.6	20.8	19.1	17.8	17.7	17.0	17.0
Air Force												
Non-industrial	KDQM	13.4	13.5	13.4	13.2	12.9	12.7	12.7	12.2	12.4	10.2	10.7
Industrial	KDQN	10.7	10.1	9.5	8.7	8.4	8.1	7.8	7.8	8.0	7.7	7.7
Procurement Executive												
Non-industrial	KDQO	26.4	26.8	26.3	24.9	24.3	23.9	23.5	22.6	22.6	22.0	21.0
Industrial	KDQP	15.9	14.9	14.0	12.8	12.0	11.0	10.2	9.5	9.1	8.6	8.1
Royal Ordnance Factories[4]												
Non-industrial	KDQR	5.4	5.1	5.2	..	..	..	..	..	..	..	..
Industrial	KDQS	14.0	13.4	12.7	..	..	..	..	..	..	..	..
Locally engaged overseas	KDQA	34.8	33.8	33.4	32.4	32.2	32.1	31.8	31.2	30.9	29.1[6]	27.0
Non-industrial	KDQT	10.7	10.5	10.4	10.2	10.3	10.3	10.2	10.2	10.1	9.9[6]	9.7
Industrial	KDQU	24.1	23.3	23.0	22.2	22.0	21.8	21.6	21.1	20.8	19.2[6]	17.3
Total[1]	KFHT	251.7	242.7	232.5	206.5	201.7	196.1	175.1	172.5	172.3	169.3[6]	166.5

1 Two part-time employees are counted as one whole-time employee.
2 Including UK-based civilians serving overseas.
3 From 1985 these figures exclude Gibraltar but still include Portsmouth, which is now classified as a Fleet Maintenance Repair Organisation establishment. Following the contractorisation of the Devonport and Rosyth Docky on 6 April 1987, staff employed at Naval Bases are now included in the
4 The Royal Ordnance Factories changed to independant Companies Act status in January 1985. Staff employed at the factories are excluded from the MOD strengths from that date.
5 From 1989 the 'Centre' figure includes all MOD Police. From 1991 the from 'Air Force'), staff in the Chemical Defence Establishment (transferred from 'Procurement Executive'), and all personnel serving overseas in support of the services (other than in BAOR or RAF Germany).
6 Estimated figures.

Source: Ministry of Defence

Defence

7.9 Service hospitals

		1981	1982	1983	1984	1985	1986	1987	1988[4]	1989	1990	1991[5]
Average number of beds[1]												
United Kingdom	KDLA	2 286	2 195	2 113	1 956	1 986	1 959	1 846	1 765	1 661	1 441	1 264
Overseas	KDLB	1 269	1 252	1 261	1 218	1 184	1 117	1 029	985	985	825	815
In-patient admissions(thousands)												
United Kingdom:	KDLE	75.9	71.3	69.9	71.6	75.1	72.1	71.7	71.3	69.9	61.8	50.2
Service personnel	KDLF	28.6	27.0	26.9	26.9	27.9	26.3	25.8	25.1	24.6	22.2	20.7
Service dependants	KDLG	14.4	14.1	12.8	12.7	12.6	11.4	10.8	9.9	8.6	7.6	5.8
NHS/Other	KDLH	32.9	30.2	30.1	32.0	34.6	34.4	35.1	36.3	36.7	32.0	23.8
Overseas:	KDLI	42.3	42.7	43.6	43.5	41.7	40.6	39.2	38.4	35.3	31.4	27.0
UK Service personnel	KDLJ	12.7	13.6	14.3	14.5	13.8	13.6	12.9	12.3	11.1	9.8	7.9
Service dependants	KDLK	21.5	23.2	22.9	22.2	22.1	22.2	22.1	22.0	20.2	19.3	17.1
Others	KDLL	8.1	5.9	6.3	6.8	5.9	4.9	4.2	4.2	3.9	2.3	1.9
Average number of admissions per bed[2]												
United Kingdom	KDLM	33.1	32.5	33.1	36.6	37.8	36.8	38.3	41.3	42.8	43.7	40.7
Overseas	KDLN	33.4	34.1	34.5	35.7	35.3	36.4	38.1	39.1	36.0	38.4	33.6
Average days in hospital per patient												
United Kingdom	KDLO	7.1	6.9	6.8	6.4	6.0	5.9	5.6	5.4	5.1	5.0	5.0
Overseas	KDLP	6.4	6.1	5.8	5.6	5.2	4.9	4.6	4.5	4.4	4.0	4.1
Outpatient attendances (thousands)[3]												
United Kingdom:	KDLQ	401.4	399.7	369.4	381.6	373.7	373.8	359.6	374.7	371.5	362.1	281.3
Service personnel	KDLR	133.0	134.3	118.0	123.1	119.3	117.2	116.4	119.8	111.4	109.0	93.3
Service dependants	KDLS	67.9	65.1	58.5	54.3	48.7	46.2	41.1	39.4	38.4	37.1	30.7
NHS/Others	KDLT	200.5	200.2	192.8	204.3	205.7	210.3	202.1	215.5	221.7	216.1	157.4
Overseas:	KDLU	229.0	232.1	241.1	235.7	229.6	212.9	202.8	179.6	171.2	138.7	134.8
UK Service personnel	KDLV	65.5	68.7	73.4	68.0	64.4	59.6	56.5	50.2	50.8	51.4	49.8
Service dependants	KDLW	111.8	111.5	116.2	108.2	102.9	96.5	94.0	84.1	81.8	75.8	75.2
Others	KDLX	51.7	51.9	51.5	59.5	62.3	56.8	52.2	45.3	38.5	11.4	9.9

1 These relate to the numbers of available beds.
2 Based on the number of beds as defined above.
3 In addition 8 000 patients were seen at outlying clinics of the hospitals and some 14 000 day patients were treated in the UK and 4 000 overseas in 1991.
4 Changes to the Statistical package used in certain hospitals to produce figures from 1988 onwards, mean that these figures are not fully comparable with those for earlier years.
5 Provisional.

Source: Ministry of Defence

7.10 Strength of uniformed medical staff[1]
At 1 April

Number

		1982	1983	1984	1985	1986	1987	1988	1989	1990	1991	1992
Qualified doctors:												
Royal Navy	KDMA	295	285	289	283	291	289	283	279	275	267	263
Army	KDMB	493	507	515	539	549	560	570	547	501	649	530
Royal Air Force	KDMC	392	373	367	377	370	363	360	350	374	371	375
Total	KDMD	1 180	1 165	1 171	1 199	1 210	1 212	1 213	1 176	1 150	1 287	1 168
Qualified dentists:												
Royal Navy	KDME	101	101	92	92	80	81	80	81	83	77	75
Army	KDMF	182	197	197	198	197	200	201	200	197	194	183
Royal Air Force	KDMG	116	108	110	110	112	118	115	117	120	120	121
Total	KDMH	399	406	399	400	389	399	396	398	400	391	379
Support staff:[2]												
Royal Navy	KDMI	1 913	1 863	1 747	1 648	1 473	1 329	1 315	1 244	1 249	1 254	1 308
Army	KDMJ	4 688	4 859	5 089	5 121	4 912	4 856	4 716	4 696	4 706	4 941	4 297
Royal Air Force	KDMK	2 183	2 134	2 081	2 070	2 004	2 020	2 102	2 032	1 964	1 974	1 948
Total	KDML	8 784	8 856	8 917	8 839	8 389	8 205	8 133	7 972	7 919	8 169	7 553

1 Includes staff employed at units (including ships) and in hospitals.
2 Includes all members of the Nursing Services/Nursing Corps.

Source: Ministry of Defence

Defence

7.11 Sickness, medical discharges and deaths of UK Service personnel[1]

		ICD Codes[2]	1982	1983	1984	1985	1986	1987	1988	1989	1990	1991[3]
Average strength: (Thousands)		KDJA		325.0	322.4	326.3	325.5	322.2	319.1	315.8	309.3	303.7	297.9
Male		KDJB		309.5	306.6	309.8	309.0	305.8	302.8	299.6	292.6	285.8	279.3
Female		KDJC		15.5	15.8	16.5	16.5	16.4	16.3	16.2	16.7	17.9	18.6
Number of episodes of sickness[4]												
All causes		KDJD	001-999	51 676	51 001	52 034	49 224	47 035	44 452	42 818	40 945	36 739	36 063
Male		KDJE	and	47 453	46 845	47 592	47 972	43 143	40 785	39 299	37 352	33 204	32 256
Female		KDJF	V01-V82	4 223	4 156	4 442	4 252	3 892	3 667	3 519	3 593	3 535	3 807
All diseases		KDJG	001-799	38 759	39 402	41 126	38 558	36 928	35 127	33 945	32 719	29 045	27 921
Infective and parasitic diseases		KDJH	001-139	2 905	3 199	3 301	3 061	3 063	2 998	2 674	2 692	2 345	2 029
Neoplasms		KDJI	140-239	608	656	737	739	655	587	631	638	516	478
Endocrine, nutritional and metabolic		KDJJ	240-279	405	392	351	286	243	234	230	200	180	196
Diseases of the blood and blood forming organs		KDJK	280-289	90	88	89	69	73	62	63	43	57	52
Mental disorders		KDJL	290-319	1 105	1 165	1 027	1 078	1 040	994	965	1 018	1 007	949
Diseases of the nervous system and sense organs		KDJM	320-389	1 105	1 121	1 058	951	1 015	971	873	804	745	741
Diseases of the circulatory system		KDJN	390-459	1 509	1 654	1 613	1 461	1 405	1 278	1 145	1 122	1 025	1 080
Diseases of the respiratory system		KDJO	460-519	9 201	8 618	9 741	8 689	7 544	7 170	7 129	6 631	5 668	6 038
Diseases of the digestive system		KDJP	520-579	7 668	7 513	7 446	7 105	7 115	6 730	6 609	6 208	5 295	4 787
Diseases of the genito-urinary system		KDJQ	580-629	2 394	2 487	2 479	2 275	2 257	2 260	2 247	1 911	1 719	1 633
Complications of pregnancy, childbirth and the puerperium		KDJR	630-676	207	150	149	175	150	147	137	170	174	247
Diseases of the skin and subcutaneous tissue		KDJS	680-709	2 136	2 053	1 944	1 849	1 729	1 583	1 364	1 351	1 106	1 084
Diseases of the musculoskeletal system and connective tissue		KDJT	710-739	6 917	7 633	8 325	8 161	8 055	7 830	7 587	7 793	7 068	6 799
Congenital anomalies		KDJU	740-759	266	285	275	224	203	209	154	177	182	148
Symptoms and ill-defined conditions		KDJV	780-799	2 243	2 388	2 591	2 435	2 381	2 074	2 137	1 961	1 958	1 660
All injuries[5]		KDJW	800-999	10 631	9 500	9 006	8 761	8 606	7 976	7 697	7 270	6 811	7 427
Aircraft accident injuries		KDJX		121	139	92	120	99	94	93	106	91	81
Training and exercise injuries		KDJY		930	1 286	1 257	1 346	1 221	1 132	1 143	921	779	657
Road traffic accident injuries		KDJZ		1 680	1 331	1 149	1 098	929	897	849	914	776	887
Sports injuries		KDKA		1 777	1 722	1 679	1 602	1 717	1 516	1 538	1 399	1 391	1 581
Accidents due to falls or jumps		KDKB		1 707	1 705	1 679	1 699	1 544	1 474	1 308	1 184	1 169	1 190
Other injuries		KFHU		4 416	3 317	3 150	2 896	3 096	2 863	2 766	2 746	2 605	3 031
Supplementary classifications[6]		KDKC	V01-V82	2 286	2 099	1 902	1 905	1 501	1 349	1 176	956	883	715
Number of medical discharges												
All causes		KDKD	001-999	800	794	1 071	1 393	1 343	1 112	1 312	1 413	1 412	1 289
Male		KDKE		772	761	1 025	1 360	1 291	1 051	1 271	1 351	1 360	1 234
Female		KDKF		28	33	46	33	52	61	41	62	52	55
All diseases		KDKG	001-799	677	628	840	1 050	1 048	911	1 063	1 128	1 224	1 185
Mental disorders		KDKH	290-319	107	114	106	123	102	93	95	83	88	130
Diseases of the nervous system and sense organs		KDKI	320-389	152	160	177	169	147	140	125	118	117	122
Diseases of the musculoskeletal system		KDKJ	710-739	222	164	313	472	536	494	609	664	743	705
Other diseases		KDKK	001-799 nes	196	190	244	286	263	184	234	263	276	228
All injuries		KDKL	800-999	123	166	231	343	295	201	249	285	188	104
Number of deaths												
All causes		KDKM	001-999	596	349	332	314	295	296	316	349	317	308
Male		KDKN		592	345	325	309	292	294	310	342	311	308
Female		KDKO		4	4	7	5	3	2	6	7	6	–
All diseases		KDKP	001-799	119	129	120	112	118	105	110	95	106	88
Neoplasms		KDKQ	140-239	48	49	54	62	51	47	52	40	46	40
Heart and cerebrovascular diseases		KDKR	390-438	56	63	56	44	56	51	47	45	42	35
Other diseases		KDKS	001-799 nes	15	17	10	6	11	7	11	10	18	13
All injuries		KDKT	800-999	477	220	212	202	177	191	206	254	211	220
Road traffic accident injuries		KDKU		115	115	113	113	78	100	73	117	99	83
Other injuries		KDKV		362	105	99	89	99	91	133	137	112	137

1 Regular Service personnel only, includes all deaths whether occurring on or off duty.
2 Code numbers refer to the Ninth Revision (1975) of the *International Statistical Classification of Diseases, Injuries and Causes of Death*.
3 Figures for the latest year are provisional.
4 Based upon spells of bedded sickness lasting two days or more terminating during the year except for:-
a) the Army, where the coverage is for admissions to medical units for two days or more,
b) Royal Navy episodes exclude less than seven days sickness on shore.
5 Where an injury could be classified under more than one cause it is shown under the first listed cause.
6 Used where no classifiable diagnosis is reported or where the person is not sick, eg admissions for investigation, preventive measures or elective surgery.

Source: Ministry of Defence

Defence

7.12 Search and rescue operations at home

Number

		1979	1980	1981	1982	1983	1984	1985	1986	1987	1988	1989	1990	1991
Call outs[1]														
of helicopters	KCME	1 309	1 090	1 168	1 164	1 224	1 211	1 215	1 251	1 486	1 734	1 736	1 851	1 779
of other aircraft	KCMF	98	68	58	59	73	56	62	74	80	81	84	86	87
of marine craft[2]	KCMG	2	27	16	10	7	8	4	–	–	1	7	1	5
of mountain rescue teams[3]	KCMH	55	45	43	58	46	56	33	73	79	80	76	83	92
Persons rescued[4]**:total**	KCMI	986	859	859	898	969	1 061	883	811	950	1 234	1 275	1 866	1 458
by helicopters	KCMJ	974	837	840	834	948	1 028	869	797	929	1 194	1 241	1 418	1 423
by marine craft[2]	KCMK	–	1	–	1	3	2	–	–	–	–	–	–	–
by mountain rescue teams[3]	KCML	12	21	19	63	18	31	14	14	21	40	34	448	35
Incidents: total	KCMM	1 268	1 070	1 097	1 111	1 146	1 145	1 129	1 188	1 361	1 599	1 675	1 851	1 783

1 More than one element of the search and rescue services may be called out to a reported incident.
2 The RAF Marine craft unit was disbanded during 1986. Figures include HM Ships and Auxilary Vessels on permanent standby.
3 Royal Air Force only.
4 Figures for persons rescued relate only to number of persons who were actually removed (alive) from a hazard or who were assisted in an urgent medical incident.

Source: Ministry of Defence

7.13 Defence services and the civilian community

		1981	1982	1983	1984	1985	1986	1987	1988	1989	1990	1991
Military aid to civil ministries during industrial disputes (Manweeks of Service personnel deployed)[1]	KCMN	3	305	–	–	–	389	256	14 762	11 550	–	–
Fishery protection Vessels boarded[2]	KCMO	1 548	1 869	2 102	1 858	1 687	1 458	1 488	2 202	2 284	1 992	2 284
Hydrographic services												
New charts produced	KCMP	143	163	226	198	152	118	144	212	148	240	96
New editions of charts	KCMQ	300	372	277	280	266	274	293	323	231	190	276
Charts printed(millions)	KCMR	3.6	3.5	2.8	3.2	2.8	2.5	2.5	2.6	2.5	2.9	3.1

1 Data relates to financial years (1April-31 March) commencing in the year shown.
2 Boardings by RN Fishery Protection Squadron only.

*Sources: Ministry of Defence;
Ministry of Agriculture, Fisheries and Food;
Scottish Office Agriculture and Fisheries Department*

7.14 Defence energy consumption
Financial years

Petajoules[1]

			1981/82	1982/83	1983/84	1984/85	1985/86	1986/87	1987/88	1988/89	1989/90	1990/91
All fuels	KCMS		136.5	154.2	150.9	139.3	131.1	137.2	127.7	122.7	119.5	–
Royal Navy	KFHV	KHDI	40.8	54.6	52.2	42.1	36.6	39.9	33.1	34.0	31.7	..
Royal Dockyards[2]		KCMT				3.0	3.7	3.7	0.8	34.0	31.7	–
Army	KCMU		24.4	23.6	24.3	24.9	24.8	24.0	22.4	21.0	19.9	..
Royal Air Force	KCMV		56.9	63.0	60.5	59.8	59.0	63.7	65.3	61.3	62.0	..
Procurement Executive	KCMW		7.7	7.2	7.4	5.9	7.0	5.9	6.1	6.4	5.9	..
Royal Ordnance Factories[3]	KCMX		6.7	5.8	6.5	3.7	–	–	–	–	–	–
Operational fuels	KCMY		81.7	102.2	98.1	92.4	86.1	93.6	88.5	86.5	85.0	319.5
Aviation fuels	KCMZ		46.7	54.0	51.3	50.4	49.8	54.4	56.1	52.2	53.8	58.0
Diesel	KCNA		22.9	36.7	35.9	31.8	27.8	30.1	24.8	26.7	24.7	134.7
Petroleum	KCNB		3.6	3.8	3.7	3.9	3.7	3.7	3.1	2.9	2.6	95.0
Other liquid fuels	KCNC		8.5	7.7	7.2	6.3	4.8	5.4	4.5	4.7	3.9	31.8
Non-Operational fuels[4]	KCND		54.8	52.0	52.7	47.1	44.9	43.6	39.2	36.2	34.5	–
Furnace fuel oil[5]	KCNE		31.1	28.4	27.1	23.9	22.2	19.4	16.6	15.3	13.9	..
Other liquid fuels	KCNF		0.8	0.8	0.8	0.9	0.9	0.9	0.9	0.9	0.8	..
Electricity	KCNG		8.7	8.6	9.2	8.6	8.7	9.1	8.5	8.4	8.3	..
Gas	KCNH		8.4	8.8	9.9	9.5	9.7	11.1	10.2	9.3	9.6	..
Solid fuel	KCNI		5.8	5.4	5.7	4.2	3.4	3.1	3.0	2.3	1.9	..

1 Petajoules=10[15]joules.
2 The Royal Dockyards came under Commercial Management during 1987/88 and are therefore excluded in subsequent years.
3 Up to January 1985 when the ROFs became a Companies Act company.
4 Non-operational energy is that energy used for domestic purposes, space heating, lighting and the operation of plant and machinery; it does not include energy used for the propulsion of vehicles, weapons, aircraft or ships.
5 Other than that used by the Fleet.
6 Provisional.

Source: Ministry of Defence

8 Production

Censuses of Production *(Table 8.1)*
The Census of Production provides information about the structure of industry in the United Kingdom. The results meet a wide range of needs for government, economic analysts and the business community at large. In official statistics the censuses are an important source for the national accounts and input-output tables, but they also provide weights for the indices of production and producer prices. Census results also enable the United Kingdom to meet statistical requirements of the European Community.

For most industries, census forms are sent to around a quarter of businesses with an employment of between 20 and 49, and half of those with an employment of between 50 and 99. All larger businesses are sent census forms. In the 1984 and 1989 'benchmark' censuses, forms were sent to around half of businesses with an employment of 20 to 49, and to all larger businesses.

Census results are published in 110 separate industry monitors in the PA Business Monitor series and in a summary volume.

Electricity
The presentation of the electricity Tables (8.8 to 8.10) has been changed in this issue. This arises from the restructuring of the public electricity industry in Great Britian on 31 March 1990 in preparation for the privatisation of the industry. Wherever possible the new tables cover all generators and suppliers of electricity in the United Kingdom.

The relationship between generation, supply availability, and consumption is as follows:
Electricity generated
less electricity used on works _equals_ electricity supplied (gross)
less electricity used in pumping at pumped storage stations
equals electricity supplied (net) _plus_ imports (net of exports) of electricity
equals electricity available _less_ losses and statistical differences
equals electricity consumed.

In Table 8.10 all fuels are converted to the common unit of million tonnes of oil equivalent, ie the amounts of oil which would be needed to produce the output of electricity generated from those fuels.

Table 8.8 shows consumption by sector. Due to the change to the Standard Industrial Classification 1980, some of the data prior to 1984 have had to be estimated and it has not been possible to provide separate figures for fuel industries.

More detailed statistics on energy are given in the *Digest of United Kingdom Energy Statistics 1992*.

8.1 Censuses of production: summary table
Standard Industrial Classification Revised 1980

Estimates for all firms

	Gross output (production)[1]	Gross value added	Stocks and work in progress At end of year	Stocks and work in progress Change during year	Capital expenditure *less* disposals	Wages and salaries	Average number of persons employed[2]	Gross value added per person employed
	£ million						Thousands	£
Production and construction Divisions 1-5[3]								
1983	259 915	89 901	..	..	10 621	50 694	6 845	13 134
1984	284 381	91 906	..	..	12 453	52 140	6 786	13 544
1985	307 987	101 415	..	..	13 519	56 787	6 591	15 386
1986	311 772	107 141	..	-224	13 669	59 705	6 468	16 565
1987	345 812	117 216	..	..	14 797	..	6 448	18 177
1988	386 112	131 584	..	..	18 026	..	6 487	20 283
1989	421 674	144 135	..	..	21 000	..	6 494	22 195
1990	454 031	149 788	..	..	21 666	..	6 364	21 530
Production industries (Revised definition) Divisions 1-4[3]								
1983	227 083	78 727	44 736	2 077	9 955	41 134	5 654	13 924
1984	248 376	79 892	47 481	3 116	11 863	42 723	5 604	14 254
1985	268 824	89 322	48 017	1 010	12 933	46 494	5 466	16 341
1986	268 313	93 958	47 028	225	13 032	48 854	5 346	17 576
1987	297 798	102 748	49 501	2 113	14 019	52 040	5 309	19 354
1988	326 814	114 523	52 676	..	16 789	56 202	5 341	21 443
1989	355 406	123 709	55 391	..	19 578	61 594	5 334	23 194
1990	380 790	129 106	55 699	..	20 591	65 782	5 202	24 821
Manufacturing (Revised definition) Divisions 2-4								
1983	189 200	65 753	39 219	2 255	6 061	36 008	5 078	12 947
1984	209 656	71 092	42 069	3 203	7 589	38 516	5 059	14 052
1985	226 636	76 499	43 188	1 523	8 742	41 256	4 976	15 375
1986	232 499	80 955	42 979	515	8 705	43 426	4 878	16 595
1987	254 683	89 745	44 797	2 111	9 754	46 429	4 874	18 412
1988	283 434	99 934	48 338	3 459	12 170	50 664	4 932	20 261
1989	309 020	108 291	51 510	3 530	14 499	55 492	4 953	21 863
1990	319 295	111 051	51 546	376	14 308	59 712	4 840	22 945
Energy and water supply industries Division 1[3,4]								
1983	37 883	12 974	5 517	-178	3 894	5 126	575	22 552
1984	38 719	8 800	5 412	-87	4 274	4 207	545	16 134
1985	42 188	12 823	4 830	-513	4 191	5 238	490	26 142
1986	35 814	13 003	4 049	-740	4 327	5 428	468	27 799
1987	43 116	13 003	4 704	2	4 269	5 611	435	29 916
1988	43 380	14 589	4 338	281	4 620	5 539	409	35 704
1989	46 386	15 418	3 882	-132	5 080	6 102	380	40 508
1990	61 495	18 055	4 152	100	6 282	6 070	362	49 920

See footnotes on page 145.

Source: Central Statistical Office

Production

8.1 Censuses of production: summary table
(continued)
Standard Industrial Classification Revised 1980

	Gross output (production)[1]	Gross value added	Stocks and work in progress — At end of year	Stocks and work in progress — Change during year	Capital expenditure less disposals	Wages and salaries	Average number of persons employed[2]	Gross value added per person employed
	£ million	£ million	£ million	£ million	£ million	£ million	Thousands	£
Coal extraction, coke ovens and manufacture of solid fuels Classes 11 and 12								
1983	4 471	3 012	920	-86	611	1 902	241	12 498
1984	1 662	863	858	-54	339	925	222	3 892
1985	4 349	2 696	584	-277	559	1 816	176	15 280
1986	4 007	2 513	546	8	507	1 828	160	15 691
1987	3 859	2 266	468	-72	507	1 878	132	17 166
1988	3 924	2 375	557	89	401	1 649	112	21 207
1989	3 700	2 030	533	-24	347	1 724	90	22 556
1990	3 466	1 853	566	29	297	1 406	76	24 382
Extraction of mineral oil and natural gas Class 13[5]								
1983	18 603	16 268	..	-68	2 865	345	28	580 986
1984	22 517	19 580	..	-1	3 149	407	31	631 626
1985	22 515	19 030	..	104	2 817	468	29	656 224
1986	11 861	9 000	..	-89	2 579	..	23	391 322
1987	12 664	10 088	..	54	2 042	..	28	360 275
1988	9 957	7 147	..	-56	2 136	..	29	246 455
1989	10 224	7 123	..	28	2 705	..	31	229 835
1990	11 945	7 928	..	-90	2 534	..	37	214 270
Mineral oil processing Class 14								
1983	14 318	1 548	1 672	-128	199	212	19	79 989
1984	16 720	1 252	1 833	171	189	212	18	71 680
1985	15 721	1 312	1 577	-182	264	215	16	83 229
1986	9 080	1 337	994	-541	301	199	14	93 139
1987	16 328	1 349	996	-20	223	226	15	91 198
1988	15 173	1 609	738	-176	334	254	16	102 685
1989	16 528	1 960	791	222	303	268	15	131 910
1990	19 016	2 492	1 029	192	343	279	14	174 213
Other energy and water supply Classes 15 to 17[4]								
1983	19 094	8 415	2 925	36	3 084	3 012	315	26 722
1984	20 337	6 684	2 720	-205	3 746	3 070	306	21 828
1985	22 117	8 814	2 668	-54	3 368	3 206	298	29 550
1986	22 727	9 153	2 509	-208	3 518	3 401	293	31 215
1987	22 929	9 388	3 240	94	3 535	3 508	287	32 711
1988	24 282	10 605	3 043	368	3 885	3 046	282	37 607
1989	26 157	11 428	2 558	-330	4 430	4 109	276	41 390
1990	39 013	13 710	2 556	-121	5 642	4 384	270	50 778
Extraction of minerals and ores other than fuels; manufacture of metals, mineral products and chemicals Division 2								
1983	40 455	12 757	6 576	404	1 544	5 716	700	18 217
1984	44 579	13 927	7 025	610	1 744	5 931	682	20 430
1985	48 088	14 778	7 274	258	2 201	6 331	668	22 117
1986	46 618	15 700	7 068	-216	2 249	6 669	655	23 961
1987	51 645	18 427	7 505	470	2 680	7 226	653	28 223
1988	58 159	21 202	8 058	610	3 216	7 946	662	32 036
1989	63 288	22 068	8 679	563	3 907	8 788	676	32 641
1990	62 684	20 839	8 666	1	4 008	9 384	656	31 782
Extraction and preparation of metalliferous ores Class 21								
1983	25	15	2	-	2	10	1	12 365
1984	42	25	3	-	3	15	1	17 797
1985	37	18	7	4	4	16	2	12 193
1986	25	4	6	-	6	12	1	4 486
1987	19	-1	12	6	11	11	1	1 925
1988	3	2	1	..	..	2	-	10 454
1989	3	1	..	..	..	2	-	4 447
1990	-	-	-	-	-	-	-	-6 773
Metal manufacturing Class 22								
1983	10 281	2 532	2 006	179	256	1 460	178	14 259
1984	11 172	2 589	2 040	198	295	1 448	163	15 888
1985	12 066	2 810	2 055	-6	358	1 564	162	17 386
1986	11 134	2 956	2 008	-25	417	1 593	153	19 278
1987	12 368	3 539	2 055	120	461	1 622	142	24 848
1988	14 549	4 247	2 298	219	580	1 766	141	30 124
1989	15 600	4 236	2 302	-13	688	1 878	141	30 002
1990	14 685	3 638	2 086	-183	692	1 980	136	26 578

See footnotes on page 145

Source: Central Statistical Office

Production

8.1 Censuses of production: summary table
(continued)
Standard Industrial Classification Revised 1980

	Gross output (production)[1]	Gross value added	Stocks and work in progress – At end of year	Stocks and work in progress – Change during year	Capital expenditure *less* disposals	Wages and salaries	Average number of persons employed[2]	Gross value added per person employed
	£ million						Thousands	£
Extraction of minerals nes *Class 23*								
1983	731	403	49	-1	48	102	13	30 531
1984	629	334	38	4	36	93	11	29 840
1985	660	352	45	6	43	92	10	34 596
1986	659	343	41	-3	30	98	10	34 578
1987	670	350	43	3	43	102	9	37 191
1988	743	370	41	-2	70	111	10	39 028
1989	717	371	41	5	63	116	9	39 648
1990	717	385	52	12	66	126	9	42 803
Manufacture of non-metallic mineral products *Class 24*								
1983	7 719	3 176	1 020	-36	365	1 524	208	15 229
1984	8 156	3 414	1 112	94	484	1 597	206	16 558
1985	8 587	3 517	1 178	98	524	1 693	203	17 324
1986	9 021	3 848	1 170	-13	431	1 780	200	19 274
1987	10 013	4 364	1 185	10	601	1 964	202	21 583
1988	11 786	5 308	1 257	54	822	2 251	214	24 816
1989	12 936	5 650	1 455	190	1 028	2 526	220	25 719
1990	12 631	5 256	1 567	114	891	2 616	210	25 063
Chemical industry *Class 25*								
1983	20 960	6 454	3 396	257	853	2 499	288	22 442
1984	23 764	7 354	3 717	305	906	2 664	288	25 491
1985	25 869	7 842	3 881	164	1 237	2 847	281	27 918
1986	24 889	8 221	3 738	-171	1 318	3 061	281	29 298
1987	27 620	9 814	4 099	324	1 504	3 392	287	34 166
1988	30 153	10 869	4 357	344	1 712	3 681	287	37 862
1989	33 014	11 394	4 776	380	2 048	4 124	296	38 449
1990	33 601	11 120	4 838	42	2 271	4 506	290	38 265
Production of man-made fibres *Class 26*								
1983	739	178	103	4	19	122	12	14 558
1984	816	211	114	10	20	115	12	18 388
1985	869	239	109	-8	36	119	11	21 781
1986	889	329	105	-4	47	125	11	30 454
1987	956	362	112	6	59	135	11	33 113
1988	925	405	104	-6	32	136	10	39 752
1989	1 018	418	106	2	81	142	10	42 824
1990	1 048	439	123	17	88	155	9	46 606
Metal goods, engineering and vehicles industries *Division 3*								
1983	69 646	28 209	21 529	1 163	2 225	17 027	2 314	12 189
1984	76 582	30 359	22 898	1 570	2 919	18 082	2 261	13 429
1985	84 839	32 756	23 668	944	3 291	19 406	2 216	14 783
1986	87 583	34 104	23 855	879	3 183	20 242	2 156	15 821
1987	95 497	36 453	24 394	716	3 182	21 286	2 116	17 231
1988	108 319	41 058	26 144	1 775	4 092	23 199	2 131	19 269
1989	120 878	45 674	28 134	2 259	5 149	25 400	2 130	21 440
1990	126 974	47 571	27 960	-38	5 300	27 730	2 111	22 535
Manufacture of metal goods nes *Class 31*								
1983	8 808	3 562	1 462	69	222	2 221	344	10 367
1984	9 726	3 821	1 577	131	320	2 388	338	11 294
1985	10 123	4 034	1 565	36	332	2 455	324	12 463
1986	10 611	4 298	1 581	27	350	2 610	322	13 339
1987	11 331	4 560	1 653	100	407	2 750	316	14 428
1988	12 954	5 229	1 872	176	536	3 088	325	16 090
1989	14 340	5 776	1 962	139	644	3 450	335	17 265
1990	15 364	6 272	2 014	-45	629	3 816	338	18 524
Mechanical engineering *Class 32*								
1983	19 859	8 427	6 112	92	511	5 164	676	12 464
1984	21 132	8 823	6 316	523	637	5 338	647	13 642
1985	23 568	9 534	6 611	348	785	5 799	642	14 856
1986	23 541	9 651	5 886	-62	711	5 958	615	15 681
1987	24 351	9 966	5 710	51	696	5 973	586	16 995
1988	27 463	11 079	5 905	356	801	6 491	586	18 901
1989	31 186	12 622	6 277	456	1 029	7 170	590	21 401
1990	33 296	13 300	6 184	-100	1 136	7 902	588	22 596

See footnotes on page 145.

Source: Central Statistical Office

8.1 (continued) Censuses of production: summary table
Standard Industrial Classification Revised 1980

Production

	Gross output (production)[1]	Gross value added	Stocks and work in progress — At end of year	Stocks and work in progress — Change during year	Capital expenditure *less* disposals	Wages and salaries	Average number of persons employed[2]	Gross value added per person employed
	£ million	£ million	£ million	£ million	£ million	£ million	Thousands	£
Electrical and electronic engineering and manufacturing of office machinery and data processing equipment								
Classes 33 and 34								
1983	18 362	7 829	4 696	401	678	4 191	586	13 362
1984	22 050	9 080	5 451	578	969	4 729	604	15 037
1985	24 303	9 630	5 554	174	1 082	5 127	597	16 125
1986	24 729	9 914	5 676	135	950	5 389	590	16 795
1987	27 401	10 861	5 868	261	999	5 796	590	18 408
1988	31 379	12 434	6 411	369	1 288	6 372	599	20 758
1989	34 104	12 650	6 772	450	1 444	6 878	590	21 440
1990	35 254	12 750	6 810	51	1 300	7 236	566	22 526
Manufacture of motor vehicles and parts thereof								
Class 35								
1983	12 050	3 580	2 549	300	498	2 353	302	11 839
1984	12 641	3 807	2 584	66	596	2 467	288	13 218
1985	14 282	4 273	2 718	162	659	2 634	277	15 441
1986	15 140	4 657	2 907	173	677	2 688	261	17 844
1987	17 629	5 112	2 925	82	612	2 804	258	19 814
1988	20 882	5 564	3 363	409	925	3 180	265	20 967
1989	23 399	6 686	3 637	301	1 339	3 519	267	25 067
1990	23 660	6 331	3 880	180	1 522	3 826	268	23 663
Manufacture of other transport equipment								
Class 36								
1983	8 565	3 884	6 104	267	246	2,538	325	11,945
1984	8 849	3 819	6 332	208	305	2,574	304	12,562
1985	10 048	4 124	6 487	158	324	2,720	293	14,062
1986	10 889	4 401	7 055	599	387	2,871	284	15,485
1987	11 854	4 695	7 461	366	354	3,183	282	16,640
1988	12 245	5 218	7 688	347	402	3,192	268	19,449
1989	14 163	6 417	8 540	883	526	3,414	262	24,497
1990	15 552	7 291	8 143	-69	570	3,911	265	27,487
Instrument engineering								
Class 37								
1983	2 002	928	606	35	70	561	81	11,427
1984	2 183	1 009	638	65	92	586	80	12,652
1985	2 516	1 160	733	67	109	671	83	13,964
1986	2 674	1 183	750	7	109	726	82	14,350
1987	2 932	1 259	776	20	114	779	83	15,128
1988	3 396	1 533	906	118	140	875	87	17,685
1989	3 685	1 522	947	30	167	968	88	17,393
1990	3 847	1 627	928	-56	144	1,039	85	19,056
Other manufacturing industries								
Division 4								
1983	79 099	24 786	11 114	688	2 293	13 265	2 064	12 009
1984	88 496	26 806	12 146	1 022	2 926	14 503	2 117	12 663
1985	93 709	28 965	12 246	321	3 250	15 518	2 092	13 848
1986	98 298	31 151	12 056	-147	3 273	16 513	2 067	15 067
1987	107 540	34 865	12 897	926	3 892	17 917	2 106	16 556
1988	116 957	37 674	14 135	1 074	4 862	19 519	2 140	17 607
1989	124 854	40 548	14 696	708	5 442	21 305	2 147	18 889
1990	129 638	42 641	14 920	413	4 999	22 596	2 073	20 568
Food, drink and tobacco manufacturing industries								
Classes 41/42								
1983	40 085	9 493	4 885	264	1 075	3 968	603	15,742
1984	44 205	9 673	5 234	245	1 255	4 264	613	15 785
1985	45 336	10 175	5 084	28	1 340	4 455	591	17 207
1986	47 023	10 801	4 808	-384	1 275	4 735	582	18 572
1987	49 272	11 696	4 844	66	1 453	5 082	594	19 692
1988	52 004	12 134	5 190	267	1 660	5 406	592	20 483
1989	55 029	13 268	5 482	314	1 909	5 882	598	22 191
1990	58 298	14 390	5 867	407	2 076	6 364	591	24 347

See footnotes on page 145.

Source: Central Statistical Office

Production

8.1 (continued) Censuses of production: summary table
Standard Industrial Classification Revised 1980

	Gross output (production)[1]	Gross value added	Stocks and work in progress — At end of year	Stocks and work in progress — Change during year	Capital expenditure less disposals	Wages and salaries	Average number of persons employed[2]	Gross value added per person employed
	£ million						Thousands	£
Textile industry Class 43								
1983	5 439	1 978	1 046	80	140	1 210	235	8 421
1984	6 140	2 169	1 189	134	191	1 316	236	9 177
1985	6 648	2 342	1 238	94	228	1 392	230	10 186
1986	6 788	2 503	1 207	-4	265	1 504	229	10 929
1987	7 571	2 873	1 338	125	271	1 623	228	12 596
1988	7 930	2 980	1 448	139	353	1 709	225	13 234
1989	7 942	2 962	1 484	10	296	1 791	216	13 745
1990	7 648	2 941	1 338	-82	251	1 785	196	15 035
Footwear and clothing industries and manufacture of leather and leather goods Classes 44 and 45								
1983	5 501	2 200	1 089	69	116	1 386	320	6 883
1984	6,223	2,497	1 205	136	148	1 534	333	7 493
1985	6,940	2,759	1 340	116	168	1 675	341	8 058
1986	7,143	2,864	1 342	45	174	1 798	341	8 399
1987	7,800	3,104	1 509	198	194	1 904	341	9 103
1988	8,217	3,229	1 618	125	212	2 042	341	9 470
1989	8,321	3,288	1 565	-4	188	2 066	320	10 277
1990	8,499	3,448	1 620	82	192	2 104	298	11 570
Timber and wooden furniture industries Class 46								
1983	6 330	2 100	1 068	145	162	1 299	202	10 394
1984	6 294	2 025	1 054	69	196	1 298	193	10 514
1985	6 761	2 240	1 094	19	208	1 417	194	11 544
1986	7 112	2 393	1 119	51	197	1 513	193	12 428
1987	8 335	2 884	1 230	155	271	1 647	198	14 544
1988	9 783	3 339	1 405	137	351	1 925	213	15 705
1989	10 138	3 478	1 418	82	397	2 082	215	16 207
1990	10 295	3 459	1 383	1	260	2 186	207	16 715
Manufacture of paper and paper products; printing and publishing Class 47								
1983	14 096	6 074	1 692	98	496	3 700	447	13 598
1984	16 353	6 974	1 956	282	701	4 112	458	15 233
1985	18 174	7 659	1 964	18	845	4 461	455	16 832
1986	19 396	8 364	1 982	91	870	4 653	439	19 065
1987	21 914	9 327	2 156	169	1 070	5 051	446	20 908
1988	24 824	10 464	2 451	213	1 521	5 517	456	22 956
1989	27 389	11 469	2 589	199	1 771	6 142	469	24 454
1990	28 304	12 004	2 534	-46	1 398	6 582	462	25 983
Processing of rubber and plastics Class 48								
1983	6 183	2 417	903	24	267	1 393	200	12 063
1984	7 054	2 617	1 008	106	365	1 515	203	12 867
1985	7 535	2 894	1 042	41	388	1 617	200	14 492
1986	8 379	3 274	1 125	44	419	1 777	204	16 084
1987	9 869	3 876	1 280	135	549	2 011	214	18 075
1988	11 028	4214	1 362	124	651	2 250	225	18 729
1989	12 542	4704	1 494	64	763	2 578	237	19 867
1990	13 085	5026	1 555	46	710	2 794	234	21 451
Other manufacturing industries Class 49								
1983	1 465	524	430	8	36	310	58	9 122
1984	2 228	850	500	51	70	465	81	10 545
1985	2 315	895	485	4	73	500	80	11 165
1986	2 458	952	475	11	73	534	81	11 747
1987	2 778	1 106	540	78	86	597	84	13 223
1988	3 171	1 314	662	112	115	670	88	14 914
1989	3 492	1 378	666	43	119	763	93	14 906
1990	3 507	1 372	622	6	111	786	85	16 128

See footnotes on page 145.

Source: Central Statistical Office

8.1 (continued) Censuses of production: summary table
Standard Industrial Classification Revised 1980

Production

Estimates for all firms

	Gross output (production)[1]	Gross value added	Stocks and work in progress — At end of year	Stocks and work in progress — Change during year	Capital expenditure less disposals	Wages and salaries	Average number of persons employed[2]	Gross value added per person employed
	£ million						Thousands	£
Construction Division 5								
1983	32 831	11 174	..	..	666	9 561	1 191	9 384
1984	36 005	12 014	..	..	590	9 106	1 181	10 171
1985	39 164	12 094	..	..	587	10 293	1 125	10 749
1986	43 459	13 183	..	..	637	10 851	1 122	11 751
1987	48 013	14 168	..	..	779	11 948	1 140	12 696
1988	59 298	17 061	..	..	1 237	13 261	1 146	14 880
1989	66 268	20 426	..	..	1 422	13 018	1 160	17 605
1990	73 240	20 681	..	..	1 076	16 311	1 163	17 782

1 Figures for gross output include a substantial amount of duplication represented by the total value of partly manufactured goods sold by one industrial establishment to another. The extent of duplication varies from one census industry to another.
2 The figures include working proprietors but exclude outworkers.
3 Figures for mineral oil and natural gas not included.
4 Figures for stocks and work in progress exclude water undertakings and work in progress in the gas industry.
5 Figures for stocks and work in progress exclude goods on hand for sale.

Source: Central Statistical Office

Energy

8.2 Total inland energy consumption
Heat supplied basis

Million therms[1]

		1981	1982	1983	1984	1985	1986	1987	1988	1989	1990	1991
Inland energy consumption of primary fuels and equivalents	KLWA	78 740	77 315	77 673	77 352	81 050	83 269	84 037	84 702	84 902	85 710	88 049
Coal[2]	KLWB	28 926	26 978	27 229	19 348	25 734	27 790	28 472	27 625	26 749	26 666	26 455
Petroleum[3]	KLWC	28 117	28 189	27 046	33 924	29 167	28 711	27 953	29 661	30 232	30 955	31 009
Primary electricity[4]	KLWD	3 677	4 218	4 708	4 958	5 583	5 859	6 138	7 038	7 746	7 278	8 142
Natural gas[5]	KLWE	18 020	17 930	18 690	19 122	20 565	20 907	21 473	20 378	20 175	20 811	22 441
less Energy used by fuel producers and losses in conversion and distribution	KLWF	23 819	23 036	23 630	23 462	24 731	25 449	25 805	25 906	26 572	27 098	27 598
Total consumption by final users	KLWG	54 921	54 279	54 043	53 890	56 319	57 820	58 232	58 796	58 330	58 612	60 451
Analysed by type of fuel												
Coal (direct use)	KLWH	4 748	4 831	4 640	3 840	4 814	4 902	4 257	3 866	3 381	3 071	3 258
Coke and breeze	KLWI	2 039	1 850	1 945	1 983	2 118	1 933	2 121	2 225	2 107	1 958	1 841
Other solid fuel[6]	KLWJ	523	512	502	316	439	422	436	381	331	320	317
Coke oven gas	KLWK	264	240	252	213	305	309	326	306	295	289	272
Natural gas (direct use)[7]	KLWL	16 631	16 691	16 797	17 186	18 253	18 517	19 103	18 366	18 066	18 504	19 936
Electricity	KLWM	7 521	7 371	7 486	7 654	7 987	8 217	8 834	9 054	9 226	9 366	9 590
Pertroleum (direct use)	KLWN	23 191	22 772	22 412	22 691	22 397	23 519	23 155	24 954	24 924	25 104	25 235
Other fuels (direct use)[8]	KLWO	4	12	9	7	6	1	–	–	–	–	–
Analysed by class of consumer												
Agriculture	KLWP	557	558	566	550	564	565	544	536	502	504	514
Iron and steel industry	KLWQ	3 249	2 934	2 972	2 935	3 048	2 790	3 081	3 262	3 220	3 042	2 895
Other industries	KLWR	14 893	14 502	13 748	13 376	13 469	13 418	13 085	12 881	12 539	12 348	12 371
Railways[9]	KLWS	466	420	441	423	428	425	408	416	388	445	483
Road transport	KLWT	10 722	11 035	11 372	11 912	12 142	12 944	13 522	14 384	15 007	15 409	15 298
Water transport	KLWU	437	472	480	527	498	457	438	460	538	541	565
Air transport	KLWV	1 993	1 982	2 022	2 137	2 216	2 432	2 572	2 741	2 901	2 911	2 728
Domestic	KLWW	15 750	15 569	15 488	15 044	16 698	17 348	17 253	16 737	16 073	16 191	17 876
Public administration	KLWX	3 504	3 441	3 497	3 497	3 540	3 544	3 405	3 285	3 049	3 045	3 246
Miscellaneous[10]	KLWY	3 350	3 366	3 446	3 490	3 714	3 898	3 921	4 093	4 114	4 177	4 504

1 Estimates of the gross calorific values used for converting the statistics for the various fuels to them are given in the *Digest of United Kingdom Energy Statistics 1992.*
2 Including net trade and stock change in other solid fuels.
3 Refinery throughput of crude oil, *plus* net foreign trade and stock change in petroleum products. Liquid fuels derived from coal (which are included in coal consumption) and petroleum products not used as fuels (chemical feedstock, industrial and white spirits, lubricants, bitumen and wax) are excluded.
4 Primary electricity comprises produced electricity in the UK at nuclear, natural flow, hydro and wind stations, *plus* net imports of electricity. The figures represent the notional thermal input of fossil fuel that would have been needed to produce the same quantities of electricity at the efficiency of contemporary UK conventional steam power stations.
5 Natural gas includes both indigenous and imported natural gas and colliery methane piped to the surface and consumed at collieries or sold.
6 Including briquettes, ovoids, Phurnacite, Coalite, Rexco, etc.
7 Figures for Natural gas up to 1988 include Town gas. Data for consumption of Town gas in 1988 and previous years may be found in earlier editions of this publication.
8 Liquid fuels derived from coal.
9 Including fuel used at transport premises from 1990.
10 Including fuel used at transport premises prior to 1990.

Source: Department of Trade and Industry

Energy

8.3 Coal: supply and demand

Million tonnes

		1980	1981	1982	1983	1984	1985	1986	1987	1988	1989	1990	1991
Supply													
Production of deep-mined coal	KLXA	112.4	110.5	106.2	101.7	35.2	75.3	90.4	86.0	83.8	79.6	72.9	73.4
Production of opencast coal	KLXB	15.8	14.8	15.3	14.7	14.3	15.6	14.3	15.8	17.9	18.7	18.1	18.6
Total	KLXC	128.2	125.3	121.5	116.4	49.5	90.9	104.6	101.7	101.7	98.3	91.0	92.0
Recovered slurry, fines, etc	KLXD	1.9	2.2	3.3	2.8	1.6	3.3	3.5	2.8	2.4	2.8	3.4	4.2
Imports	KLXE	7.3	4.3	4.1	4.5	8.9	12.7	10.6	9.8	11.7	12.1	14.8	19.5
Total	KLXF	137.4	131.8	128.8	123.7	60.1	106.8	118.7	114.3	115.8	113.3	109.2	115.6
Change in colliery stocks	KLXG	5.3	4.3	0.2	1.2	−7.9	−5.3	0.3	−1.1	0.7	1.3	−0.9	2.8
Change in stocks at opencast sites	KLXH	2.4	0.5	−0.4	0.8	4.7	−6.3	−0.8	−1.5	0.5	1.5	−0.1	−0.8
Total supply	KLXI	129.7	127.0	128.9	121.7	63.2	118.3	119.2	116.9	114.6	110.6	108.1	117.6
Home consumption													
Electricity supply industry[1]	KLXJ	89.6	87.2	80.2	81.6	53.4	73.9	82.7	86.2	82.5	80.6	82.6	82.0
Coke ovens	KLXK	11.6	10.8	10.4	10.4	8.2	11.1	11.1	10.9	10.9	10.8	10.9	10.0
Low temperature carbonization plants	KLXL	1.9	1.3	1.2	1.2	1.1	1.4	1.0	1.0	0.8	0.8	0.8	0.8
Manufactured fuel plants	KLXM	1.1	1.1	1.1	0.9	0.2	0.8	1.0	1.0	1.2	0.9	0.8	0.7
Railways	KLXN	0.1	0.1	0.1	–	–	–	–	–	–	–	–	–
Collieries	KLXO	0.7	0.6	0.5	0.5	0.2	0.3	0.3	0.2	0.2	0.1	0.1	0.1
Industry:													
Iron and steel	KLXP	0.2	0.2	0.1	0.1	0.1	–	–	–	–	–	–	–
Other industries[2,3]	KLXQ	7.6	6.8	7.0	7.1	6.0	7.4	8.2	8.0	8.1	7.5	7.4	7.0
Domestic:													
House coal [3,4]	KLXR	5.5	5.2	5.2	4.8	4.1	5.3	5.6	4.7	4.3	3.6	2.8	3.5
Anthracite and dry steam coal [4,5,6]	KLXS	1.7	1.6	1.8	1.7	1.6	2.1	1.5	1.5	1.5	1.4	1.3	1.7
Miners' coal	KLXT	1.7	1.6	1.6	1.5	0.8	1.2	1.3	1.0	0.8	0.7	0.6	0.5
Public services	KLXU	1.5	1.4	1.4	1.4	1.3	1.3	1.3	1.2	1.0	0.9	0.9	0.8
Miscellaneous	KLXV	0.3	0.4	0.5	0.4	0.5	0.4	0.2	0.2	0.2	0.2	0.3	0.3
Total home consumption	KLXW	123.5	118.4	111.0	111.4	77.3	105.4	114.2	115.9	111.5	107.6	108.3	107.5
Overseas shipments and bunkers	KLXX	3.8	9.1	7.4	6.6	2.3	2.4	2.7	2.4	1.8	2.0	2.5	1.7
Total consumption and shipments	KLXY	127.3	127.5	118.4	118.0	79.6	107.8	116.9	118.2	113.3	109.6	110.8	109.2
Change in distributed stocks[7]	KLXZ	2.1	−0.2	10.3	3.5	−18.2	10.0	4.0	−2.8	1.7	0.4	−0.4	3.6
Balance[8]	KLYA	0.3	−0.3	0.2	–	1.9	0.5	−1.8	1.3	−0.4	0.6	−2.3	4.8
Stocks at end of year													
Distributed[7]	KLYB	20.4	20.1	30.4	34.0	15.8	25.8	29.8	27.1	28.8	29.2	28.7	32.3
At collieries	KLYC	13.1	17.4	17.7	18.9	11.0	5.7	6.0	4.9	5.6	6.9	6.0	8.8
At opencast sites	KLYD	4.2	4.7	4.3	5.1	9.8	3.5	2.7	1.2	1.7	3.2	3.0	2.2
Total stocks	KLYE	37.7	42.3	52.4	58.0	36.5	35.0	38.5	33.2	36.2	39.2	37.8	43.3

TIME SERIES. Figures relate to periods of 52 weeks.
For 1990, figures relate to 52 weeks estimate for period ended 29 December 1990.

1 Includes quantities used in the production of steam for sale.
2 Colliery and opencast disposals to industry.
3 From 1984 includes estimated proportions of steam coal imports.
4 Colliery and opencast disposals to merchants.
5 Including disposals of imported anthracite.
6 Anthracite is also consumed under other categories, including miners' coal and manufactured fuel plants.
7 Great Britain. Stock change excludes industrial and domestic stocks.
8 This is the balance between supply and consumption, shipments and changes in known distributed stocks.

Source: Department of Trade and Industry

Energy

8.4 Coal: production[1]
Great Britain
Years ended March

Million tonnes

		1981/82	1982/83	1983/84	1984[2]/85	1985[3]/86	1986/87	1987/88	1988/89	1989/90	1990/91	1991/92
Scottish	KCNJ	7.22	6.62	5.27	0.30	4.26	3.43	2.59	1.90	1.90	2.14	2.22
North East	KCNK	13.41	12.42	10.91	0.38	9.50	10.17	10.22	10.30	10.04	8.96	7.55
Selby[4]	KCNL	–	–	–	–	–	–	–	–	–	5.94	14.28
North Yorkshire[3]	KCNM KGSW	8.26	8.39	7.55	0.32	13.90	14.24	14.30	15.85	13.26	10.06	..
Barnsley[3]	KCNN	8.40	8.13	6.19	0.12							
Doncaster[3]	KCNO KGSX	7.12	6.78	5.82	0.01	12.48	12.49	11.55	13.23	10.87	8.58	13.38[7]
South Yorkshire[3]	KCNP	7.23	7.33	6.57	0.17							
North Derbyshire	KCNQ	8.48	8.15	6.29	1.44	6.21	6.04	10.57[5]	10.87[5]	10.66[5]	9.60[6]	..
North Nottingham[3]	KCNR KGSY	12.26	12.36	11.60	9.16	18.67	18.06	17.61	17.15	16.50	16.89	17.22
South Nottingham[3]	KCNS	8.54	8.25	6.97	5.59							
South Midlands and Kent	KCNT	8.64	8.17	6.65	4.98	6.74	6.14	0.35[6]	0.44[6]	0.14[6]	–	–
Western	KCNU	11.08	10.78	9.08	4.82	9.38	10.09	9.55	9.73	6.82	6.39	–
South Wales	KCNV	7.56	6.88	6.58	0.29	6.63	6.48	5.01	4.98	3.37	3.15	–
Midlands and Wales	KGEN	..	..	..	..	..	..	..	..	..	..	15.92[7]
Total - Saleable mined coal	KCNW	108.20	104.26	89.48	27.58	87.76	87.14	81.75	84.44	73.55	71.71	70.57

TIME SERIES. Figures relate to periods of 52 weeks. For 1989/90, figures relate to 52 weeks estimate for period ended 31 March 1990.

1 Collieries operated by the British Coal Corporation(B.C.C.). Excludes coal extracted in work on capital account (0.59 million tonnes in 1990/91).
2 Production was affected by a national overtime ban from 1st November 1983 and by wider industrial action from 12th March 1984.
3 With effect from 1985/86 the B.C.C. altered their regional structure and incorporated Barnsley into North Yorkshire Area, Doncaster into South Yorkshire Area and merged North and South Nottingham into Nottinghamshire Area. See also note 4.
4 Selby (previously part of North Yorkshire) became a separate B.C.C. Area with effect from 1990/91.
5 From 1987/88 figures relate to B.C.C.'s Central Area (previously North Derbyshire and South Midlands).
6 From 1987/88 figures relate to B.C.C.'s Kent Area only. Mining operations ceased on 29 July 1989. See also footnote above.
7 With effect from October 1991 the three Areas of Central, North Western and South Wales have been replaced by a single amalgamated Midland and Wales Area. North Yorkshire has ceased to operate as a separate area, its operation has been transferred to the Selby and South Yorkshire Areas.

Source: Department of Trade and Industry

8.5 Coal: average number of wage-earners on colliery books[1]
Great Britain
Years ended March

Thousands

		1981/82	1982/83	1983/84	1984/85	1985[2]/86	1986/87	1987/88	1988/89	1989/90	1990/91	1991/92
Scottish	KCNX	18.3	16.9	14.5	12.3	8.8	6.0	4.3	3.3	1.8	1.5	1.4
North East	KCNY	30.4	27.6	24.5	22.2	19.7	15.9	12.9	11.5	9.9	9.1	7.8
Selby[3]	KCNZ	–	–	–	–	–	–	–	–	–	3.6	7.5
North Yorkshire[2]	KCOA KGTU	14.8	14.4	13.6	12.7	22.8	19.0	16.5	12.9	11.1	8.5	..
Barnsley[2]	KCOB	15.1	15.0	14.3	13.6							
Doncaster[2]	KCOC KGTV	15.9	15.0	13.9	12.8	22.0	16.9	15.5	13.7	11.3	8.2	10.7[6]
South Yorkshire[2]	KCOD	16.3	15.5	14.7	13.7							
North Derbyshire	KCOE	12.0	11.8	11.1	10.1	9.7	8.2	12.7[4]	10.8[4]	10.7[4]	8.6[4]	..
North Nottingham[2]	KCOF KGTW	18.1	17.8	17.1	16.5	27.2	24.5	20.3	16.4	13.9	13.4	13.0
South Nottingham[2]	KCOG	15.3	14.8	13.7	11.7							
South Midlands and Kent	KCOH	16.1	15.2	13.6	12.6	11.4	9.3	0.8[5]	0.7[5]	0.3[5]	–	..
Western	KCOI	21.5	20.3	19.1	17.5	16.3	13.5	11.5	10.3	6.3	5.5	..
South Wales	KCOJ	24.8	23.4	21.5	19.7	16.7	12.1	9.9	7.4	4.5	2.5	..
Midlands and Wales	KGEY	..	..	..	..	..	..	..	..	..	..	12.0[6]
Total	KGTX	218.5	207.7	191.5	175.4	154.6	125.4	104.4	86.9	69.8	60.9	52.3

1 Collieries operated by the British Coal Corporation.
2 See footnote 3 to Table 8.4.
3 See footnote 4 to Table 8.4.
4 See footnote 5 to Table 8.4.
5 See footnote 6 to Table 8.4.
6 See footnote 7 to Table 8.4.

Source: Department of Trade and Industry

8.6 Coal: output per manshift[1]
Great Britain
Years ended March

Tonnes

			1981/82	1982/83	1983/84	1984/85	1985[2]/86	1986/87	1987/88	1988/89	1989/90	1990/91	1991/92
Total	KCOK		2.40	2.44	2.43	2.08	2.72	3.29	3.62	4.14	4.32	4.70	5.31
Scottish	KCOL		2.00	1.97	1.95	0.37	2.21	2.54	2.71	2.45	4.36	5.60	5.85
North East	KCOM		2.07	2.09	2.23	0.47	2.23	2.98	3.51	3.81	4.09	3.86	3.74
Selby[3]	KCON		–	–	–	–	–	–	–	–	–	6.81	7.48
North Yorkshire[2]	KCOO	KGSZ	2.80	3.01	3.13	1.29	3.04	3.89	4.45	5.26	5.01	4.66	..
Barnsley[2]	KCOP		2.71	2.64	2.36	0.51							
Doncaster[2]	KCOQ	KGTR	2.27	2.30	2.31	0.40	2.90	3.57	3.61	4.31	4.14	4.32	5.12[6]
South Yorkshire[2]	KCOR		2.22	2.35	2.47	0.50							
North Derbyshire	KCOS		3.33	3.30	2.90	2.13	3.04	3.48	3.81[4]	4.31[4]	4.09[4]	4.56[5]	..
North Nottingham[2]	KCOT	KGTS	3.17	3.25	3.35	3.11	3.21	3.45	3.89	4.35	4.69	4.94	5.26
South Nottingham[2]	KCOU		2.68	2.69	2.55	2.62							
South Midlands and Kent	KCOV		2.52	2.51	2.41	2.62	2.82	3.12	1.93[5]	2.90[5]	2.40[5]	..	..
Western	KCOW		2.45	2.53	2.44	2.09	2.74	3.36	3.58	3.91	4.34	4.57	..
South Wales	KCOX		1.47	1.47	1.57	0.39	1.87	2.47	2.30	2.88	3.04	5.00	..
Midlands and Wales	KGOM		..	..	..	..	..	..	..	..	..	..	5.15[6]

1 Collieries operated by the British Coal Corporation(B.C.C.).
2 See footnote 3 to Table 8.4.
3 See footnote 4 to Table 8.4.
4 See footnote 5 to Table 8.4.
5 See footnote 6 to Table 8.4.
6 See footnote 7 to Table 8.4.

Source: Department of Trade and Industry

Energy

8.7 Fuel input and gas output: gas sales
Public supply

		1981	1982	1983	1984	1985	1986	1987	1988	1989	1990	1991
Fuel input to gas industry		*million tonnes*										
Petroleum	KLZA	0.1	0.1	0.1	0.1	0.1	0.1	0.1	–	–	–	–
		million therms										
Petroleum gases[1]	KLZB	71	52	33	30	28	36	6	1	3	1	1
Natural gas	KLZC	–	–	–	–	–	–	–	–	–	–	–
Coke oven gas	KLZD	–	–	–	–	–	–	–	–	–	–	–
Total to gas works	KLZE	100	85	61	56	57	55	20	6	3	1	1
Natural gas for direct supply	KLZF	17 044	16 667	17 153	17 739	18 988	19 747	20 198	19 083	18 826	19 231	21 087
Total fuel input	KLZG	17 144	16 752	17 214	17 794	19 046	19 802	20 218	19 089	18 829	19 232	21 083
Fuel input to gas industry		*million tonnes of coal or coal equivalent*										
Petroleum	KLZH	0.1	0.1	0.1	0.1	0.1	0.1	0.1	–	–	–	–
Petroleum gases[1]	KLZI	0.2	0.2	0.1	0.1	0.1	0.1	–	–	–	–	–
Natural gas	KLZJ	–	–	–	–	–	–	–	–	–	–	–
Coke oven gas	KLZK	–	–	–	–	–	–	–	–	–	–	–
Total to gas works	KLZL	0.3	0.3	0.2	0.2	0.2	0.2	0.1	–	–	–	–
Natural gas for direct supply	KLZM	68.2	66.7	68.6	71.0	76.0	79.0	80.8	76.3	75.3	76.9	84.3
Total fuel input	KLZN	68.5	67.0	68.8	71.2	76.2	79.2	80.9	76.3	75.3	76.9	84.4
Gas output and sales		*million therms*										
Gas output:												
Town gas	KLZO	31	26	23	21	20	18	13	4	1	1	1
Natural gas supplied direct[2]	KLZP	17 108	16 719	17 186	17 764	19 017	19 775	20 205	19 083	18 826	19 231	21 087
Gross total available	KLZQ	17 139	16 745	17 209	17 785	19 038	19 793	20 218	19 087	18 827	19 232	21 088
Own use[3]	KLZR	139	126	–121	–129	–140	–152	–137	–120	–101	–81	–103
Statistical difference[4]	KLZS	–378	38	–243	–351	–531	–613	–708	–328	–377	–223	–691
Total sales	KLZT	16 622	16 657	16 845	17 305	18 367	18 496	19 373	18 639	18 349	18 928	20 294
Analysis of gas sales		*million therms*										
Fuel producers												
Power stations	BHIB	78	76	77	178	197	75	357	381	395	396	467
Coal extraction and manufacture of solid fuels[5]	KLZU	..	..	9	13	12	14	18	14	15	13	18
Coke ovens[5]	KLZV	..	..	10	10	11	3	1	1	2	3	2
Petroleum refineries[5]	KLZW	..	..	76	29	8	10	11	11	10	9	9
Nuclear fuel production[5]	KLZX	..	..	18	18	18	17	23	15	14	14	16
Production and distribution of other energy	KLZY	..	..	6	4	11	5	8	4	7	3	12
Total final producers	KLZZ	78	76	196	252	257	124	418	426	443	438	524
Final users:												
Iron and steel industry[6]	BHIC	409	365	390	449	449	419	465	446	467	461	404
Other industries[5]	KLYS	5 261	5 319	5 040	5 249	5 310	4 804	4 997	4 515	4 606	4 779[8]	4 519
Domestic	BHIE	8 764	8 719	8 871	8 933	9 684	10 242	10 500	10 255	9 914	10 250	11 395
Public administration	KLYT	966	1 003	1 100	1 095	1 184	1 286	1 326	1 242	1 188	1 204	1 365
Agriculture[7]	KLYU	..	..	11	13	20	24	29	30	32	34	35
Miscellaneous[7]	KLYV	1 144	1 175	1 237	1 314	1 463	1 597	1 636	1 725	1 699	1 760	2 050
Total final users	KLYW	16 544	16 581	16 649	17 053	18 110	18 372	18 953	18 213	17 906	18 488	19 768
Total sales	BHIA	16 622	16 657	16 845	17 305	18 367	18 496	19 373	18 639	18 349	18 928	20 294

Note: The breakdown of consumption by industrial users is made according to the 1980 Standard Industrial Classification, though only data from 1984 are available on this basis.

1 Butane, propane, ethane and refinery tail gases.
2 Including substitute natural gas.
3 Used in works, offices, showrooms, etc.
4 Supply greater than recorded demand (-).Includes losses in distribution.
5 Prior to 1984, included in Other industries under Final users.
6 Prior to 1984, as reported by the Iron and Steel Statistics Bureau.
7 Prior to 1984, included in Miscellaneous.
8 Includes 27 million therms by independent gas suppliers.

Source: Department of Trade and Industry

Energy

8.8 Electricity: generation, supply and consumption
United Kingdom

Gigawatt-hours[6]

		1981	1982	1983	1984	1985	1986	1987	1988	1989	1990	1991
Electricity generated												
Major generating companies[1]: total	KLUA	259 731	255 439	260 436	265 990	279 972	282 258	282 745	288 511	292 896	298 495	301 176
Coventional steam stations	KLUB	220 259	209 957	208 514	209 121	216 255	221 426	226 426	222 887	219 712	230 376	229 190
Nuclear stations	KLUC	34 043	40 001	45 776	49 498	56 354	54 005	50 282	58 867	66 740	61 306	66 329
Gas turbines and oil engines	KLUD	509	517	356	1 947	1 084	508	487	464	529	432	355
Hydro-electric stations:												
Natural flow	KLUE	3 917	3 884	3 892	3 368	3 447	4 098	3 474	4 171	4 002	4 393	3 777
Pumped storage	KLUF	1 003	1 080	1 897	2 055	2 831	2 221	2 075	2 121	1 910	1 982	1 523
Other (mainly wind)	KLUG	–	–	–	1	1	1	–	1	2	4	3
Other generators[2]: total	KLUH	17 971	17 344	17 037	16 553	17 659	18 813	19 367	19 593	20 929	20 483	20 956
Conventional staem stations[3]	KLUI	13 580	12 700	12 216	11 435	12 271	13 057	13 688	14 332	15 279	15 355	16 037
Nuclear stations	KLUJ	3 926	3 971	4 152	4 481	4 740	5 074	4 956	4 589	4 994	4 441	4 214
Hydro-electric stations (natural flow)	KLUK	465	673	669	637	648	682	723	672	657	687	706
All generating companies: total	KLUL	277 702	272 783	277 473	282 543	297 631	301 071	302 112	308 104	313 825	318 979	322 132
Conventional steam stations [3]	KLUM	233 839	222 657	220 730	220 556	228 526	234 483	240 114	237 219	234 991	245 732	245 227
Nuclear stations	KLUN	37 969	43 972	49 928	53 979	61 094	59 079	55 238	63 456	71 734	65 747	70 543
Gas turbines and oil engines	KLUO	509	517	356	1 947	1 084	508	487	464	529	432	355
Hydro-electric stations:												
Natural flow	KLUP	4 382	4 557	4 561	4 005	4 095	4 780	4 198	4 843	4 659	5 080	4 482
Pumped storage	KLUQ	1 003	1 080	1 897	2 055	2 831	2 221	2 075	2 121	1 910	1 982	1 523
Other (mainly wind)	KLUR	–	–	–	1	1	1	–	1	2	4	3
Electricity used on works: Total	KLUS	17 799	17 704	18 115	18 332	19 643	19 602	19 600	20 198	20 234	19 583	20 083
Major generating companies[1]	KLUT	16 429	16 380	16 794	17 011	18 235	18 105	18 041	18 694	18 610	17 891	18 420
Other generators [2]	KLUU	1 370	1 324	1 321	1 321	1 408	1 497	1 559	1 504	1 624	1 691	1 663
Electricity supplied (gross)												
Major generating companies[1]: total	KLUV	243 302	239 059	243 642	248 979	261 737	264 154	264 704	269 817	274 286	280 604	282 757
Conventional steam stations[4]	KLUW	208 589	198 822	197 600	200 240	205 906	209 977	214 836	211 502	208 675	218 957	217 947
Nuclear stations	KLUX	29 818	35 310	40 344	43 407	49 694	47 484	43 947	51 699	59 312	54 964	59 265
Gas turbines and oil engines[4]	KLUY	..	..	..	..	..	475	454	430	494	403	310
Hydro-electric stations:												
Natural flow	KLUZ	3 906	3 873	3 882	3 358	3 435	4 087	3 460	4 160	3 992	4 384	3 767
Pumped storage	KLVA	989	1 054	1 812	1 974	2 701	2 129	2 006	2 025	1 812	1 892	1 465
Other (mainly wind)	KLVB	–	–	–	–	–	1	–	1	2	3	3
Other generators[2]: total	KLVC	16 637	16 024	15 719	15 168	16 184	17 316	17 809	18 089	19 305	18 792	19 293
Conventional steam stations[3]	KLVD	12 801	11 943	11 486	10 685	11 467	12 278	12 831	13 478	14 362	14 409	15 095
Nuclear stations	KLVE	3 373	3 411	3 567	3 849	4 073	4 359	4 257	3 942	4 290	3 700	3 496
Hydro-electric stations (natural flow)	KLVF	463	670	666	634	645	679	720	669	654	684	702
All generating companies: total	KLVG	259 939	255 083	259 361	264 148	277 922	281 469	282 512	287 906	293 592	299 396	302 050
Conventional steam stations[3,4]	KLVH	221 390	210 765	209 086	210 925	217 373	222 255	227 667	224 980	223 037	233 366	233 042
Nuclear stations	KLVI	33 191	38 721	43 911	47 256	53 767	51 843	48 205	55 642	63 602	58 664	62 761
Gas turbines and oil engines[4]	KLVJ	..	..	..	..	..	475	454	430	494	403	310
Hydro-electric stations:												
Natural flow	KLVK	4 369	4 543	4 548	3 992	4 080	4 766	4 180	4 829	4 645	5 067	4 469
Pumped storage	KLVL	989	1 054	1 816	1 974	2 701	2 129	2 006	2 025	1 812	1 892	1 465
Other (mainly wind)	KLVM	–	–	–	–	–	1	–	1	2	3	3
Electricity used in pumping												
Major generating companies [1]	KLVN	1 196	1 272	2 337	2 613	3 494	2 993	2 804	2 888	2 572	2 626	2 109
Electricity supplied (net): Total	KLVO	258 743	253 811	257 024	261 535	274 427	278 476	279 708	285 018	291 019	296 770	299 942
Major generating companies [1]	KLVP	242 106	237 787	241 305	246 367	258 242	261 160	261 899	266 929	271 714	277 978	280 649
Other generators[2]	KLVQ	16 637	16 024	15 719	15 168	16 184	17 316	17 809	18 089	19 305	18 792	19 293
Net imports	KGEZ	–	–	–	–	–	4 256	11 636	12 830	12 631	11 943	16 407
Electricity available	KGIZ	258 743	253 811	257 024	261 535	274 427	282 732	291 344	297 848	303 650	308 713	316 349
Losses in transmission etc[5]	KGKW	20 410	20 662	21 371	21 070	22 637	22 914	22 958	23 343	24 251	24 293	25 508
Electricity consumption: Total [5]	KGKX	238 333	233 149	235 653	240 465	251 790	259 818	268 386	274 505	279 399	284 420	290 841
Fuel industries[5]	KGKY	..	..	..	8 297	9 236	9 505	9 492	9 163	9 001	9 986	9 794
Final users: total[5]	KGKZ	..	..	232 168	242 554	250 313	258 894	265 342	270 398	274 434	281 048
Industrial sector[5]	KGLZ	94 213	90 289	89 683	86 503	88 009	88 800	93 137	97 143	99 417	100 643	99 570
Domestic sector	KGMZ	84 440	82 790	82 950	83 898	88 228	91 826	93 254	92 362	92 270	93 793	98 098
Other sectors[5]	KGNZ	59 680	60 070	63 020	61 767	66 317	69 687	72 503	75 837	78 711	79 997	83 380

1 Generating companies corresponding to the old public sector supply system, ie National Power, PowerGen, Nuclear Electtric, National Grid Company, Scottish Power, Hydro-Electric, Scottish Nuclear, Northern Ireland Electricity, Midalnds Electricity and South Western Electricity.
2 Larger establishments in the industrial and transport sectors generating 1 Gigawatt-hour or more a year. The prototype reactors operated by the United Kingdom Atomic Energy Authority and by British Nuclear Fuels plc are included.
3 For other generators, conventional steam stations cover all types of station, including combined heat and power plants, other than nuclear and hydro-electric stations.
4 Prior to 1986 gas turbines and oil engines are included with conventional steam stations.
5 Until 1983 consumption by fuel industries is included with industrial sector consumption. The figures for consumption, and hence losses, in these years are subject to some estimation.
6 1 Gigawatt-hour equals 1 million Kilowatt hours.

Source: Department of Trade and Industry

Energy

8.9 Electricity: plant capacity and demand
United Kingdom

Megawatts end-March

		1987	1988	1989	1990	1991	1992
Major generating companies[1]: Total declared net capability	KGON	62 883	63 835	66 536	70 327	69 323	66 110
Conventional steam stations	KGOO	48 841	50 190	51 540	52 504	51 365	48 309
Nuclear stations	KGOP	6 479	6 519	7 598	10 373	10 733	10 733
Gas turbines and oil engines	KGOQ	3 476	3 041	3 313	3 356	3 130	2 968
Hydro-electric stations:							
Natural flow	KGOR	1 298	1 293	1 293	1 306	1 302	1 308
Pumped storage	KGOS	2 788	2 788	2 788	2 787	2 787	2 787
Other (mainly wind)	KGOT	1	4	4	2	6	5
Other generators[2]: total capacity of own generating plant[3]	KGOU	3 804	3 751	3 657	3 713	3 690	3 912
Conventional steam stations[4]	KGOV	3 012	2 959	2 864	2 921	2 988	3 208
Nuclear stations	KGOW	710	710	710	710	620	..
Hydro-electric stations (natural flow)	KGOX	82	82	82	82	82	..
All generating companies: total capacity[3]	KGOY	66 687	67 585	70 193	74 040	73 013	70 022
Conventional steam stations[4]	KGOZ	51 853	53 149	54 404	55 425	54 353	51 517
Nuclear stations	KGPM	7 189	7 229	8 308	11 083	11 353	11 353
Gas turbines and oil engines	KGPN	3 476	3 041	3 313	3 356	3 130	3 131
Hydro-electric stations:							
Natural flow	KGPO	1 380	1 375	1 375	1 388	1 384	1 392
Pumped storage	KGPP	2 788	2 788	2 788	2 787	2 787	2 787
Other (mainly wind)	KGPQ	1	4	4	2	6	5
Major generating companies[1]: simultaneous maximum load met [5]	KGPR	55 330	53 833	53 555	53 414	54 068	54 452
Major generating companies[1]: system load factor[6] (percentage)	KGQY	*55.9*	*58.7*	*60.2*	*62.5*	*62.2*	*63.1*

1 See note [1] to Table 8.8.
2 See note [2] to Table 8.8.
3 Capacity figures for other generators are as at end-December of the previous year.
4 For other generators, conventional steam stations cover all types of stations, including combined heat and power plants (electrical capacity only), other than nuclear and hydro-electric plants.
5 Maximum load in year to end of March.
6 The average hourly quantity of electricity available during the year ended March expressed as a percentage of the maximum demand.

Source: Department of Trade and Industry

8.10 Electricity : fuel used in generation
United Kingdom

Million tonnes of oil equivalent

		1981	1982	1983	1984	1985	1986	1987	1988	1989	1990	1991
Major generating companies[1]:												
Total all fuels	KGPS	64.9	63.1	63.5	64.4	67.4	68.4	69.9	70.7	71.4	72.7	73.3
Coal	FTAJ	51.3	47.1	47.9	31.4	43.5	48.6	50.7	48.5	47.4	48.6	48.2
Oil	FTAK	5.1	6.2	4.8	21.3	10.6	6.1	4.8	5.4	5.5	6.7	5.7
Gas[2]	KGPT	–	–	–	0.2	0.3	..	..	..	..	..	..
Nuclear	FTAL	7.2	8.5	9.6	10.4	11.9	11.4	10.6	12.4	14.2	13.2	14.2
Hydro (natural flow)	FTAM	1.2	1.2	1.2	1.1	1.0	1.3	1.1	1.3	1.2	1.3	1.2
Other fuels used by UK companies[2]	KGPU	0.1	0.1	–	–	–	–	–	–	–	–	–
Net imports	KGPV	–	–	–	–	–	1.0	2.8	3.1	3.0	2.9	3.9
Other generators[3]:												
Total all fuels	KGPW	1.3	1.3	1.4	1.5	1.5	1.6	1.5	1.5	1.6	5.3	5.5
Transport undertakings												
Gas	KGPX	0.2	0.2	0.2	0.2	0.2	0.2	0.2	0.2	0.2	0.2	0.2
Undertakings in industrial sector												
Coal	KGPY	–	–	–	–	–	–	1.0	1.1	1.1	1.2	1.2
Oil	KGPZ	–	–	–	–	–	–	1.1	1.2	1.2	1.3	1.3
Gas	KGQM	–	–	–	–	–	–	0.7	0.7	0.7	0.7	0.9
Nuclear	KGQN	0.9	0.9	1.0	1.1	1.1	1.2	1.1	1.1	1.2	1.0	0.9
Hydro (natural flow)	KGQO	0.2	0.2	0.2	0.2	0.2	0.2	0.2	0.2	0.2	0.2	0.2
Other fuels	KGQP	–	–	–	–	–	–	0.7	0.7	0.7	0.7	0.8
All generating companies[3]:												
Total fuels	KGQQ	66.1	64.4	64.9	65.8	68.9	70.0	74.9	75.8	76.8	77.9	78.8
Coal	KGQR	51.3	47.1	47.9	31.4	43.5	48.6	51.7	49.6	48.5	49.7	49.4
Oil	KGQS	5.1	6.2	4.8	21.3	10.6	6.1	5.9	6.5	6.8	7.9	7.1
Gas[2]	KGQT	0.2	0.2	0.2	0.4	0.5	0.2	0.8	0.9	0.9	0.9	1.1
Nuclear	KGQU	8.1	9.4	10.6	11.5	13.0	12.6	11.7	13.5	15.4	14.2	15.2
Hydro (natural flow)	KGQV	1.4	1.4	1.4	1.2	1.2	1.5	1.3	1.5	1.4	1.6	1.4
Other fuels used by UK companies[2]	KGQW	0.1	0.1	–	–	–	–	0.7	0.7	0.7	0.7	0.8
Net imports	KGQX	–	–	–	–	–	1.5	2.8	3.1	3.0	2.9	3.9

1 See note[1] to Table 8.8.
2 From 1990, gas used by major generating companies is included with other fuels for reasons of confidentiality.
3 See note[2] to Table 8.8. Prior to 1987 'other generators' covers only transport undertakings and industrial hydro and nuclear stations. For years 1987 to 1989 figures for fuel used by other generators are largely estimated.

Source: Department of Trade and Industry.

Energy

8.11 Indigenous production, refinery receipts, arrivals and shipments of oil[1]

Thousand tonnes

		1981	1982	1983	1984	1985	1986	1987	1988	1989	1990	1991
Total indigenous petroleum production[2]	KMBA	89 480	103 219	115 045	126 065	127 642	127 053	123 351	114 459	91 827	91 602	91 256
Crude petroleum[3]:												
Refinery receipts total	KMBB	76 616	76 705	76 344	78 450	78 653	79 666	80 363	83 925	88 840	59 735	92 523
Indigenous[4]	KMBC	37 769	40 294	44 815	45 304	43 231	38 780	38 794	40 582	39 585	37 754	35 932
Other[5]	KMBD	2 486	3 162	2 366	2 196	1 095	1 006	939	730	904	916	772
Net foreign arrivals[6]	KMBE	36 361	33 249	29 163	30 950	34 327	39 880	40 630	42 613	48 351	51 065	55 819
Foreign trade												
Arrivals[6]	KMBF	36 855	33 754	30 324	32 272	35 576	41 209	41 541	44 272	49 500	52 710	57 084
Shipments												
Indigenous	KMBG	51 149	60 195	67 397	77 271	79 335	83 341	80 043	69 965	49 130	54 022	52 378
Other[7]	KMBH	494	505	1 161	1 363	1 416	1 635	1 113	1 967	1 332	1 878	1 424
Petroleum products												
Foreign trade												
Arrivals[6]	KMBI	9 402	12 524	9 907	23 082	13 101	11 767	8 570	9 219	9 479	11 005	10 140
Shipments[6]	KMBJ	12 793	13 858	14 674	14 234	17 038	17 726	17 056	17 176	17 873	18 002	20 677
Net arrivals[6]	KMBK	−3 391	−1 061	−4 767	8 848	−3 937	−5 959	−8 486	−7 957	−8 394	−6 997	−10 537
Bunkers[8]	KMBL	2 073	2 583	2 019	2 248	2 118	2 091	1 668	1 831	2 396	2 538	2 486

1 The term indigenous is used in this table for convenience to include oil from the UK Continental Shelf as well as the small amounts produced on the mainland.
2 Crude oil *plus* condensates and petroleum gases derived at onshore treatment plants.
3 Includes process(partly refined) oils.
4 Includes condensate for distillation.
5 Mainly recycled products.
6 Foreign trade as recorded by the petroleum industry and may differ from figures published in *Overseas Trade Statistics*.
7 Re-exports of imported crude which may include some indigenous oil in blend.
8 International marine bunkers.

Source: Department of Trade and Industry

8.12 Throughput of crude and process oils and output of refined products from refineries[1]

Thousand tonnes

		1981	1982	1983	1984	1985	1986	1987	1988	1989	1990	1991
Throughput of crude and process oils	KMAU	78 287	77 130	76 876	79 117	78 431	80 155	80 449	85 662	87 699	88 692	92 001
less: Refinery fuel[2]:	KMAA	5 445	5 549	5 297	5 350	5 179	5 404	5 216	5 484	5 816	5 838	6 058
Losses	KMAB	836	834	652	579	348	662	577	340	491	568	467
Total output of refined products	KMAC	72 006	70 747	70 927	73 187	72 904	74 089	74 656	79 837	81 392	82 286	85 476
Gases:												
Butane and propane	KMAE	1 391	1 400	1 482	1 578	1 436	1 328	1 422	1 581	1 568	1 514	1 664
Other petroleum	KMAF	75	75	56	78	60	93	52	68	90	106	134
Naphtha and other feedstock	KMAG	3 406	3 492	3 550	3 206	2 883	2 652	2 014	1 856	2 073	2 139	2 515
Aviation spirit	KMAH	57	44	–	1	4	–	–	–	–	–	–
Wide-cut gasoline	KMAI	–	–	–	–	–	–	–	–	–	–	–
Motor spirit	KMAJ	17 140	19 134	21 053	22 236	22 254	23 360	24 680	26 409	27 237	26 724	27 793
Industrial and white spirit	KMAK	115	115	134	142	140	104	117	112	105	121	136
Kerosene:												
Aviation turbine fuel	KMAL	4 559	4 457	4 723	5 352	5 257	5 813	6 063	6 725	7 092	7 541	7 037
Burning oil	KMAM	1 904	1 851	1 770	2 066	2 307	2 147	2 270	2 289	2 344	2 309	2 446
Gas/diesel oil	KMAN	20 411	20 581	21 029	21 547	21 701	22 409	21 424	23 925	23 292	23 402	26 057
Fuel oil	KMAO	19 069	15 808	13 483	13 071	12 896	12 523	12 797	12 495	13 020	13 805	13 205
Lubricating oil	KMAP	1 063	990	936	1 108	1 188	909	886	970	1 050	974	973
Bitumen	KMAQ	1 735	1 862	1 798	1 795	1 764	1 887	2 056	2 296	2 393	2 454	2 302
Petroleum wax	KMAR	82	71	56	80	71	58	57	63	54	40	37
Petroleum coke	KMAS	505	492	499	506	517	514	517	541	564	586	555
Other products	KMAT	494	375	358	422	426	293	300	509	510	569	620

1 Crude and process oils comprise all feedstocks, other than distillation benzines, for treatment at refinery plants. Refinery production does not cover further treatment of finished products for special grade such as in distillation plant for the preparation of industrial spirits.
2 Comprising 2 791 thousand tonnes gases, 2 020 thousand tonnes fuel oil and 1 025 thousand tonnes other products in 1990.

Source: Department of Trade and Industry

Energy

8.13 Deliveries of petroleum products for inland consumption

Thousand tonnes

		1981	1982	1983	1984	1985	1986	1987	1988	1989	1990	1991
Total (including refinery fuel)	KMCA	71 701	72 795	69 761	86 785	74 960	74 631	72 917	77 801	78 844	79 781	80 564
Total (excluding refinery fuel)	KMCB	66 256	67 246	64 464	81 435	69 781	69 227	67 701	72 317	73 028	73 943	74 506
Gases:												
Butane and propane:												
For gas works	KMCC	34	39	35	41	41	44	41	35	33	37	42
Other uses	KMCD	1 116	1 312	1 522	1 438	997	1 014	1 090	1 052	1 045	1 009	1 172
Other gases												
For gas works	KMCE	137	97	63	58	50	66	8	–	–	–	–
Other uses	KMCF	5	154	307	313	45	57	55	59	49	48	63
Feedstock:												
For petroleum chemical plants	KMCG	4 492	4 165	4 513	4 695	5 032	5 652	5 537	5 942	5 816	5 115	5 935
Naphtha (LDF) for gasworks[1]	KMCH	74	71	56	52	51	46	30	10	–	–	–
Aviation spirit	KMCI	32	27	28	27	28	29	28	28	29	26	24
Wide-cut gasoline	KMCJ	2	3	2	2	1	–	1	–	–	–	–
Dealers:												
4 star	KMCK	15 041	15 656	16 107	16 990	17 361	18 621	19 506	20 599	18 325	15 586	13 793
3 star	KMCL	410	257	166	111	77	48	29	17	2	–	–
2 star	KMCM	2 286	2 483	2 431	2 331	2 188	2 052	1 877	1 669	321	–	–
Unleaded	KMCN	–	–	–	–	–	..	14	247	4 543	8 059	9 586
Commercial consumers:												
4 star	KMCO	719	616	621	561	552	535	578	548	582	472	360
3 star	KMCP	118	103	99	90	86	77	62	51	14	–	–
2 star	KMCQ	144	132	142	143	139	136	115	109	31	–	–
Unleaded	KMCR	–	–	–	–	–	..	4	11	105	197	282
Motor spirit: total	BHOD	18 718	19 247	19 566	20 226	20 403	21 470	22 184	23 249	23 924	24 312	24 021
Industrial and white spirits	KMCS	174	175	196	220	214	206	218	246	207	171	162
Kerosene:												
Aviation turbine fuel	BHOE	4 495	4 474	4 566	4 828	5 007	5 497	5 815	6 200	6 564	6 589	6 176
Burning oil	KMCT	1 906	1 745	1 663	1 710	1 870	2 020	2 034	1 992	1 937	2 058	2 383
Gas/diesel oil:												
Derv fuel	BHOI	5 549	5 731	6 183	6 755	7 106	7 866	8 469	9 370	10 118	10 652	10 694
Other	BHOJ	10 994	10 552	9 944	9 967	9 732	9 241	8 608	8 456	8 323	8 046	8 031
Fuel oil	BHOK	15 645	16 191	12 512	27 843	15 969	12 514	9 935	11 865	11 125	11 997	11 948
Lubricating oils	BHOL	837	827	818	818	816	803	828	849	839	822	759
Bitumen	BHOM	1 666	1 956	1 987	1 900	1 887	2 019	2 162	2 342	2 423	2 491	2 514
Petroleum wax	KMCU	64	56	57	59	58	60	59	67	77	55	49
Petroleum coke	KMCV	98	128	142	104	96	268	260	136	120	112	154
Miscellaneous products	KMCW	218	296	306	379	379	355	339	419	399	403	380

1 Including a small quantity supplied for use as fuel by other consumers.

Source: Department of Trade and Industry

Industrial materials

8.14 Iron and steel
Summary of steel supplies, deliveries and stocks

		1980[3]	1981	1982	1983	1984	1985	1986	1987	1988	1989	1990	1991
		\multicolumn{12}{c}{Finished product weight - thousand tonnes}
Supply, disposal and consumption													
UK producers' home deliveries	KLTA	8 224	9 175	8 790	8 757	9 036	8 917	8 337	9 197	10 780	10 907	9 711	7 951
Imports excl steelworks receipts	KLTB	3 977	2 738	2 988	2 760	2 691	2 924	3 409	3 595	4 228	4 424	4 446	4 509
Total deliveries to home market (a)	KLTC	12 201	11 913	11 978	11 517	11 727	11 841	11 745	12 792	15 007	15 331	14 157	12 009
Total exports (producers, consumers, merchants)	KLTD	2 553	3 718	3 281	3 812	3 843	4 562	4 922	6 057	6 168	6 180	6 550	7 444
Exports by UK producers	KLTE	2 165	3 514	3 045	3 502	3 527	4 156	4 804	5 815	5 902	5 973	6 370	7 082
Derived consumers and merchants exports (b)	KLTF	388	204	236	310	316	406	118	242	266	207	180	362
Net home disposals (a)-(b)	KLTG	11 813	11 541	11 542	11 207	11 411	11 435	11 628	12 549	14 742	15 124	13 977	12 098
Consumers and merchants stock change[1]	KLTH	−674	−713	−370	−300	170	−180	−310	100	30	220	−290	−400
Estimated home consumption	KLTI	12 487	12 164	11 912	11 507	11 241	11 615	11 938	12 449	14 712	14 904	14 267	12 498
Stocks													
Producers-ingots and semi-finished steel	KLTJ	1 196	1 243	1 056	1 072	1 130	1 629	1 121	1 198	1 311	1 182	1 245	1 035
-finished steel	KLTK	1 655	1 560	1 488	1 548	1 633	1 604	1 657	1 701	1 633	1 692	1 563	1 719
Consumers	KLTL	2 870	2 330	2 110	1 800	1 830	1 640	1 380	1 430	1 480	1 700	1 590	1 400
Merchants	KLTM	1 413	1 240	1 090	1 100	1 240	1 250	1 200	1 250	1 230	1 230	1 050	840
		\multicolumn{12}{c}{Crude steel equivalent - million tonnes}
Estimated home consumption													
Crude steel production[2]	KLTN	11.28	15.57	13.70	14.99	15.12	15.72	14.72	17.41	18.95	18.74	17.84	16.47
Producers stock change[1]	KLTO	−1.12	−0.06	−0.33	0.10	0.18	0.60	−0.69	0.20	0.06	−0.09	−0.08	−0.07
Re-useable material	KLTP	0.09	0.06	0.08	0.10	0.07	0.08	0.08	0.10	0.08	0.10	0.10	0.07
Total supply from home sources	KLTQ	12.49	15.69	14.11	14.99	15.01	15.20	15.49	17.31	18.97	18.93	18.02	16.61
Total imports[4]	KLTR	5.99	4.30	4.74	4.07	4.34	4.54	4.95	5.06	5.95	6.25	5.96	6.21
Total exports[4]	KLTS	3.31	4.83	4.45	4.73	4.80	5.62	6.01	7.26	7.39	7.49	7.66	8.72
Net home disposals	KLTT	15.17	15.16	14.70	14.33	14.55	14.12	14.43	15.11	17.53	17.69	16.32	14.10
Consumers and merchants stock change[1]	KLTU	−0.88	−0.93	−0.48	−0.38	0.22	−0.23	−0.39	0.13	0.04	0.29	−0.37	−0.50
Estimated home consumption	KLTV	16.05	16.09	15.18	14.71	14.33	14.35	14.82	14.98	17.49	17.40	16.69	14.60

1 TIME SERIES. The figures relate to periods of 52 weeks(53 weeks in 1981).

Note: Figures in the above table have been amended to reflect the Iron and Steel Statistics Bureau's revised definition of the iron and steel industry.

1 Increases in stock are shown as + and decreases in stock (ie deliveries from stock) as -.
2 Includes liquid steel for castings.
3 Statistics for 1980 were affected by the steel strike.
4 Based on HM Customs Statistics, reflecting total trade rather than producers trade.

Sources: Department of Trade and Industry;
Iron and Steel Statistics Bureau

Industrial materials

8.15 Iron and steel
Iron ore, manganese ore, pig iron and iron and steel scrap

Thousand tonnes

		1981	1982	1983	1984	1985	1986	1987	1988	1989	1990	1991
Iron ore												
Jurassic	KLOA	729	468	382	377	272	288	261	222	32	53	57
Hematite	KLOB	2	2	3	2	3	1	2	2	–	–	–
Production: total	KLOC	731	470	384	379	274	289	263	224	32	53	57
Home produced	KLOD	923	527	449	403	326	352	305	237	37	53	57
Imported	KLOE	12 854	11 125	12 756	13 273	14 812	13 991	17 330	19 233	18 563	17 935	17 833
Consumption: total	KLOF	13 777	11 652	13 205	13 676	15 138	14 343	17 635	19 470	18 600	17 988	17 890
Manganese ore												
Consumption	KLOG	259	188	262	252	291	309	292	307	339	340	383
Pig iron (and blast furnace ferro-alloys)												
Average number of furnaces in blast during period	KLOH	11	10	11	11	11	11	11	11	11	10	8
Production												
Steelmaking iron	KLOI	9 395	8 279	9 400	9 365	10 167	9 632	11 916	12 943	12 551	12 218	11 834
Foundry iron[1]	KLOJ	75	48	77	122	214	53	101	113	87	102	50
Speigeleisen and ferro-manganese	KLOK	84	61	83	75	77	100	92	107	143	143	178
In blast furnaces: total	KLOL	9 554	8 388	9 560	9 562	10 458	9 785	12 110	13 163	12 781	12 463	12 062
In steel works and steel foundries	KLOM	9 473	8 160	9 468	9 271	10 125	9 613	11 922	13 022	12 771	12 358	11 836
In iron foundries	KLON	178	152	182	190	160	141	139	145	143	..	..
Consumption of pig iron: total	KLOO	9 651	8 312	9 650	9 461	10 285	9 754	12 061	13 167	12 914	..	..
Pig iron stocks (end of period)	KLOP	94	202	112	106	157	110	98	95	85	..	..
Iron and steel scrap												
Steelworks and steel foundries												
Circulating scrap	KLOQ	4 146	3 772	3 849	3 558	2 942	2 816	2 652	2 846	2 817	2 489	2 332
Purchased receipts	KLOR	3 948	3 976	3 750	4 475	4 270	4 147	4 438	4 654	5 172	4 730	3 694
Consumption	KLOS	8 216	7 463	7 670	7 866	6 994	6 660	7 060	7 700	7 904	7 251	6 085
Stocks (end of period)	KLOT	618	742	467	439	438	552	582	382	467	430	365
Iron foundries												
Arisings	KLOU	773	701	697	626	549	453	407	418	453	693	..
Consumption	KLOV	2 093	2 035	1 891	1 698	1 402	1 166	1 143	1 166	1 145	..	..
Stocks (end of period)	KLOW	158	160	108	75	68	89	67	65	64	..	..

TIME SERIES. The figures relate to periods of 52 weeks (53 weeks in 1981).

Sources: Department of Trade and Industry; Iron and Steel Statistics Bureau

1 Includes Hematite Iron.

Industrial materials

8.16 Iron and steel
Number of furnaces and production of steel

Thousand tonnes

		1980[4]	1981	1982	1983	1984	1985	1986	1987	1988	1989	1990	1991
Steel furnaces (Number in existance at end of period)[1]													
Total	KLPA	399	400	353	321	310	297	283	268	259	229	214	209
Open hearth	KLPB	–	–	–	–	–	–	–	–	–	–	–	–
Oxygen converters	KLPC	16	14	14	14	14	14	14	14	14	14	14	14
Electric	KLPD	380	384	339	307	296	283	269	254	248	215	200	195
Stock and tropenas	KLPE	3	2	–	–	–	–	–	–	–	–	–	–
Production of crude steel (thousand tonnes)													
Total	KLPF	11 277	15 573	13 705	14 986	15 121	15 722	14 725	17 414	18 950	18 740	17 841	16 747
by process													
Open hearth	KLPG	–	–	–	–	–	–	–	–	–	–	–	–
Oxygen converters	KLPH	6 689	10 535	9 036	10 496	10 295	11 185	10 560	12 957	14 008	13 627	13 169	12 540
Electric	KLPI	4 579	5 038	4 669	4 490	4 826	4 537	4 165	4 457	4 942	5 113	4 672	3 934
Stock and tropenas	KLPJ	9	–	–	–	–	–	–	–	–	–	–	–
by cast method													
Cast to ingot	KLPK	7 845	10 306	8 020	7 754	7 015	6 863	5 573	5 896	5 361	3 469	2 692	2 201
Continuously cast	KLPL	3 059	4 959	5 341	6 986	7 858	8 620	8 903	11 293	13 356	15 031	14 909	14 085
Steel for castings	KLPM	373	308	344	247	248	239	249	225	233	240	240	189
by quality													
Non alloy steel	KLPN	10 041	14 088	12 500	13 887	13 890	14 502	13 587	16 149	17 610	17 371	16 641	15 496
Stainless and other alloy steel	KLPO	1 236	1 485	1 205	1 100	1 231	1 220	1 138	1 265	1 340	1 369	1 200	978
Production of finished steel products (all quantities)[2] (thousand tonnes)													
Rods and bars for reinforcement (in coil and lengths)	KLPP	709	711	675	814	846	916	879	914	1 168	1 219	1 241	1 151
Wire rods and other rods and bars in coil	KLPQ	1 004	1 169	1 011	1 040	1 125	1 136	1 149	1 273	1 349	1 417	1 407	1 272
Hot rolled bars in lengths	KLPR	1 082	1 020	913	795	834	836	781	836	950	1 115	1 210	1 083
Bright steel bars[3]	KLPS	353	331	300	292	347	319	307	315	342	340	318	257
Light sections other than rails	KLPT	268	246	175	177	175	236	283	272	335	326	325	324
Heavy and light rails and accessories	KLPU	176	219	209	260	227	226	172	237	395	2 540	2 583	2 297
Other heavy sections	KLPV KGQZ	1 336	1 856	1 621	1 712	1 594	1 770	1 836	2 060	2 100			
Hot rolled plates and sheets in coil and lengths	KLPW	3 863	6 181	5 506	6 080	6 357	6 135	6 166	7 106	7 853	7 982	7 947	7 132
Cold rolled plates and sheets in coil and lengths	KLPX	1 873	3 081	2 964	3 208	3 357	3 418	3 342	3 730	3 952	3 976	3 749	3 592
Hot rolled strip	KLPY	414	249	267	300	320	306	273	301	314	222	268	248
Cold rolled strip	KLPZ	306	297	287	286	315	300	302	329	394	388	357	286
Tinplate	KLQW	605	886	894	916	963	899	953	1 041	1 018	960	855	742
Other coated sheet	KLQX	556	838	921	1 027	1 111	1 135	1 153	1 373	1 603	1 568	1 657	1 647
Tubes and pipes[3]	KLQY	1 049	1 269	1 227	1 201	1 348	1 357	1 209	1 317	1 482	1 519	1 465	1 260
Forged bars[3]	KLQZ	15	19	23	12	17	20	13	15	17	16	16	7

TIME SERIES. The figures relate to periods of 52 weeks (53 weeks in 1981).

1 Includes steel furnaces at steel foundries.
2 Includes material for conversion into other products listed in the table.
3 Based on producers' deliveries.
4 Statistics for 1980 were affected by the steel strike.

Sources: Department of Trade and Industry; Iron and Steel Statistics Bureau

Industrial materials

8.17 Non-ferrous metals

Thousand tonnes

		1980	1981	1982	1983	1984	1985	1986	1987	1988	1989	1990	1991
Copper													
Production of refined copper:													
Primary	KLAA	68.3	59.8	63.2	67.5	69.5	63.9	62.4	54.0	49.3	48.6	47.0	16.6
Secondary	KLAB	93.0	76.3	71.0	76.8	67.4	61.6	63.2	68.3	74.7	70.4	74.6	53.5
Home consumption:													
Refined	KLAC	409.2	333.1	355.4	358.0	352.9	346.5	339.6	327.7	327.7	324.7	317.2	269.4
Scrap (metal content)	KLAD	121.2	128.0	128.4	109.6	132.5	131.5	135.3	137.7	132.1	129.7	126.3	118.5
Stocks (end of period)[1,2]	KLAE	82.0	62.0	69.3	75.8	43.4	37.6	31.6	11.7	12.2	14.5	11.7	9.3
Analysis of home consumption													
(refined and scrap):[3] total	KLAF	530.4	461.1	483.8	467.6	485.4	477.9	474.9	465.4	459.8	454.4	443.5	387.9
Wire[4]	KLAG	255.7	215.2	226.0	227.0	226.9	225.4	229.6	220.3	217.8	221.7	220.2	191.9
Rods, bars and sections	KLAH	65.7	56.3	58.8	58.9	67.9	64.6	61.4	62.5	57.3	55.5	54.4	52.7
Sheet, strip and plate	KLAI	80.1	63.4	69.2	59.9	67.7	66.9	62.4	62.5	66.3	59.2	54.4	37.1
Tubes	KLAJ	78.1	77.2	80.8	80.1	81.3	79.6	80.4	79.1	77.5	77.7	73.0	65.5
Castings and miscellaneous	KLAK	50.8	48.9	49.0	41.7	41.5	41.4	41.2	41.0	40.9	40.4	41.5	40.7
Zinc													
Slab zinc:													
Production	KLAL	86.7	81.7	79.3	87.7	85.6	74.3	85.9	81.4	76.0	79.8	93.3	100.7
Home consumption	KLAM	181.3	185.4	181.6	177.2	182.2	189.3	181.9	188.1	192.8	194.5	189.0	173.3
Stocks (end of period)	KLAN	19.7	16.1	16.0	19.3	15.9	15.5	15.3	14.0	13.2	13.9	12.0	11.1
Other zinc (metal content):													
Consumption	KLAO	62.3	56.1	57.8	54.4	54.0	53.3	53.4	52.6	51.7	49.6	52.4	50.1
Analysis of home consumption													
(slab and scrap): total	KLAP	243.6	241.5	239.3	231.6	236.2	242.6	235.3	240.7	244.4	244.1	241.3	223.7
Brass	KLAQ	66.7	56.8	59.3	56.6	61.8	58.3	55.1	55.8	54.1	51.1	51.5	47.2
Galvanized products	KLAR	69.1	80.1	83.5	86.6	90.5	90.5	87.2	95.8	101.4	104.3	100.5	86.8
Zinc sheet and strip	KLAS	19.1	15.9	14.1	8.6	5.7	5.8	4.6	4.0	4.1	4.0	3.6	3.6
Zinc alloy die castings	KLAT	37.7	40.1	37.5	39.7	34.9	43.2	44.8	44.0	43.5	43.1	44.4	45.4
Zinc oxide	KLAU	26.6	21.5	18.7	20.6	19.6	23.4	23.7	22.8	23.2	21.7	21.2	20.5
Other products	KLAV	24.4	27.2	26.1	19.6	23.8	21.4	20.1	18.3	18.2	19.8	20.2	20.2
Refined lead													
Production[5,6]	KLAW	324.8	333.4	306.2	322.2	338.4	327.2	328.6	347.0	373.8	350.0	329.4	300.6
Home consumption[6,7]													
Refined lead	KLAX	295.5	265.8	271.9	292.9	295.3	274.3	282.1	287.5	302.5	301.3	301.6	266.4
Scrap and remelted lead[6]	KLAY	10.0	8.2	9.9	14.3	19.8	29.0	27.0	36.6	37.0	35.0	32.5	33.9
Stocks (end of period)[8]													
Lead bullion	KLAZ	115.7	94.6	13.6	14.8	18.0	13.4	16.1	26.1	18.6	17.0	18.0	22.4
Refined soft lead at consumers	KLBA	19.7	21.3	25.7	28.1	28.2	29.5	28.3	24.4	26.7	25.7	22.3	21.6
In LME Warehouses (UK)	KLBB	19.0	39.5	53.7	60.3	34.8	27.5	18.5	2.8	..	11.0	12.1	..
Analysis of home consumption													
(refined and scrap): total	KLBC	305.5	274.0	281.8	307.1	315.4	303.6	309.1	324.1	339.4	336.4	334.0	300.2
Cables	KLBD	21.7	19.4	20.9	19.2	15.1	13.1	13.0	10.0	11.0	12.6	10.4	8.6
Batteries (excluding oxides)	KLBE	49.3	41.5	43.7	43.3	46.9	47.4	47.6	48.0	49.2	50.5	51.0	52.2
Oxides and compounds:													
Batteries	KLBF	49.3	37.7	45.0	44.4	43.9	49.6	46.7	49.0	51.4	51.7	52.8	54.4
Other uses[9]	KLBG	81.9	75.9	73.5	74.7	75.1	72.1	72.4	82.7	76.8	72.0	73.7	55.8
Sheets and pipes	KLBH	50.9	51.7	53.6	77.2	84.3	77.6	84.5	86.1	102.4	98.1	96.8	81.3
White lead	KLBI	0.9	0.7	0.7	0.5	0.4	0.4	..	..	..	..	..	..
Solder	KLBJ	9.7	9.6	9.0	8.4	7.7	7.9	7.6	7.4	9.0	9.1	8.0	7.7
Alloys	KLBK	11.9	7.1	7.9	11.2	10.9	11.2	11.5	13.6	13.5	13.4	14.0	12.2
Other uses	KLBL	29.9	30.4	27.6	28.3	31.1	27.0	26.0	27.3	26.1	28.3	27.5	28.1
Tin													
Tin ore (metal content):													
Production	KLBM	3.0	3.9	4.2	4.1	5.0	5.2	4.3	3.6	3.4	4.0	3.4	1.1
Tin metal[10]:	KLBN	..	..	..	..	..	..	..	..	..	..	..	..
Production[11]	KLBO	11.4	12.9	13.6	13.3	13.8	14.8	14.9	17.0	16.8	10.8	12.0	5.2
Home consumption[11]	KLBP	9.9	10.9	10.4	10.2	10.0	9.4	9.7	9.8	10.2	10.2	10.4	10.2
Exports and re-exports[12]	KLBQ	7.0	6.3	5.4	1.0	11.1	7.3	13.6	14.8	14.0	5.4	5.7	2.9
Stocks (end of period):													
Consumers	KLBR	1.1	1.1	0.9	0.9	1.0	1.0	1.0	1.0	1.0	1.0	1.0	1.0
Merchants and others	KLBS	..	..	..	..	..	..	..	..	..	..	..	..
Analysis of home consumption													
(excluding scrap): total	KLBT	9.9	10.9	10.4	10.2	10.0	9.4	9.7	9.8	10.2	10.2	10.4	10.2
Tinplate	KLBU	3.1	4.3	4.0	3.8	3.7	3.4	3.3	3.6	3.4	3.6	3.6	3.6
Alloys	KLBV	3.6	3.4	3.4	3.2	3.1	3.1	3.1	3.2	3.4	3.4	3.4	3.3
Solder	KLBW	0.9	1.0	0.8	0.9	0.8	0.8	0.9	0.9	1.0	1.0	1.0	1.0
Other uses	KLBX	2.3	2.2	2.2	2.2	2.4	2.1	2.5	2.1	2.3	2.2	2.4	2.3

See footnotes page 159.

Sources: Department of Trade and Industry; World Bureau of Metal Statistics

8.17 Non-ferrous metals
continued

Industrial materials

Thousand tonnes

		1980	1981	1982	1983	1984	1985	1986	1987	1988	1989	1990	1991
Primary aluminium[13]													
Production	KLBY	374.4	339.2	240.8	252.5	287.9	275.4	275.9	294.4	300.2	297.3	289.8	293.5[12]
Despatches to consumers	KLBZ	520.9	446.2	399.2	418.3	448.3	436.0	451.2	461.6	541.3	494.2	520.2	485.4
Secondary aluminium													
Production	KLCA	162.1	148.0	114.6	128.3	143.9	127.6	116.4	116.7	105.8	109.5	120.9	136.5
Despatches to consumers	KLCB	161.0	148.8	114.9	127.5	142.1	126.6	117.2	120.9	107.3	116.7	127.2	146.8
Exports	KLCC	..	59.2	40.0	37.7	42.1	40.7	42.2	36.7	45.0	66.7	65.1	70.7
Fabricated aluminium													
Total despatches[14]	KLCD	521.1	444.3	455.4	460.5	473.8	466.0	..	..	..	..	..	..
Rolled products[15]	KLCE	199.4	165.8	173.7	174.9	191.2	194.6	215.5	224.4	225.7	236.2	261.0	269.4
Extrusions and tubes[16]	KLCF	183.6	161.2	169.6	177.7	174.5	168.9	..	..	..	..	..	..
Wire products	KLCG	33.3	31.6	31.9	29.2	28.9	29.9	27.3	27.0	20.9	24.5	15.5	..
Castings	KLCH	101.9	83.3	78.3	77.0	77.5	72.6	73.3	74.8	..	..	..	..
Forging	KLCI	2.9	2.3	1.9	1.7	1.7	..	..	..	..	..	..	..
Foil products (Aluminium content)	KLCJ	40.4	37.8	..[19]	..[19]	..[19]	..[19]	..[19]	..	..	..	..	..
Magnesium and magnesium alloys													
Productions[17]	KLCK	2.8	1.9	1.8	..[19]	..[19]	..[19]	..[19]	..[19]	..[19]	..[19]	..	..
Consumption: total[18]	KLCL	5.4	4.1	4.1	..[19]	..[19]	..[19]	..[19]	..[19]	..[19]	..[19]	..	..
Refined nickel													
Production (including ferro-nickel)	KLCM	19.3	25.4	6.9	23.2	22.3	17.8	30.9	29.5	28.0	26.1	26.5	29.0

1 Unwrought copper (electrolytic, fire refined and blister).
2 Reported stocks of refined copper held by consumers and those held in London Metal Exchange (LME) warehouses in the United Kingdom.
3 Copper content.
4 Consumption for high-conductivity copper and cadmium copper wire represented by consumption of wire rods, production of which for export is also included.
5 Lead reclaimed from secondary and scrap material and lead refined from bullion and domestic ores.
6 From 1975, figures for production and consumption of refined lead include antimonial lead, and for scrap and remelted lead, exclude secondary antimonial lead.
7 Including toll transactions involving fabrication.
8 Excluding goverment stocks.
9 Includes values for White Lead wef 1986.
10 Including production from imported scrap and residues refined on toll.
11 Primary and secondary metal.
12 Including re-exports on toll transactions.
13 Including primary alloys.
14 Includes wrought, cast and forged products, and excludes foil products.
15 Includes foil stock and excludes foil products.
16 Excluding forging bars, wirebars, and almost two-thirds of despatches of hot rolled rod.
17 Primary and remelt alloys.
18 Despatches to consumers of primary metal, primary and remelt alloys.
19 Data no longer obtainable.

Sources: Department of Trade and Industry;
World Bureau of Metal Statistics;
Aluminium Federation

Industrial materials
8.18 Cotton, man-made fibres and wool

		Unit	1982	1983	1984	1985	1986	1987	1988	1989	1990	1991
Raw cotton[1]												
Imports	KLKC	Thousand	54	50	48	54	52	55	48	43	32	23
Home consumption: total	BKCA	tonnes	45	45	44	44	47	51	43	39	28	19
Stocks (end of period)	BKCB	"	5	5	4	4	3	4	4	3	1	1
Cotton waste												
Imports	KLKD	"	30.2	28.9	27.0	28.7	24.3	28.1	28.4	29.2	36.1	31.3
Cotton linters												
Imports	KLKE	"	37.8	24.8	31.7	38.4	23.1	23.6	13.6	18.0	13.7	16.1
Man-made fibres[2]												
Production: total	KLKF	"	333.6	389.3	383.3	330.2	288.0	276.7	280.1	272.5	273.2	267.3
Continuous filament yarn	KLKG	"	89.3	102.6	102.5	99.1	100.8	99.0	105.3	108.5	101.7	92.6
Staple fibre	KLKH	"	244.3	286.6	280.9	231.1	187.2	177.7	174.9	164.0	171.5	174.7
Cotton and man-made fibre yarn												
Production of single yarn:												
Cotton[3]	KLKI	"	42.3	40.9	38.0	38.6	39.8	41.8	35.4	28.4	22.5	12.5
Cotton mixture yarn	KLKJ	"	15.6	17.1	17.2	16.5	15.9	16.4	16.5	15.4	13.8	12.7
Spun man-made fibre yarn	KLKK	"	26.5	28.2	28.9	30.1	31.3	33.1	30.0	24.2	21.7	16.7
Cotton waste yarn[4]	KLKL	"	8.7	9.0	9.3	9.5	8.6	9.0	8.3	7.7	7.5	7.9
Other waste yarn	KLKM	"	1.7	2.1	2.6	3.8	3.9	4.1	3.9	3.2	2.0	1.7
Production of doubled yarn	KLKN	"	34.1	30.6	29.8	32.6	31.8	31.4	31.1	25.9	26.0	23.2
Spindle activity[5]:												
Single yarn spindles:												
total (ring equivalent)	KLKO	Millions	1.04	0.96	0.95	0.93	0.90	0.86	0.82	0.69	0.52	..
Doubling spindles	KLKP	"	0.12	0.11	0.10	0.09	0.09	0.08	0.08	0.08	0.07	..
Yarn consumed in cotton and man-made fibre weaving:												
Cotton and waste yarns	KLKQ	Thousand	35.8	36.2	39.0	39.5	37.0	37.0	31.4	30.3	27.8	23.9
Mixtures yarn[6]	KLKR	tonnes	15.4	16.7	15.1	15.9	17.2	15.9	17.2	15.6	15.3	13.6
Man-made fibres: total	KLKS	"	45.0	41.7	45.7	50.4	51.6	52.4	49.8	49.9	50.4	47.1
Continuous filament yarn	KLKT	"	35.0	31.9	35.0	37.5	38.2	37.2	34.5	35.3	34.4	31.8
Spun yarn	KLKU	"	10.0	9.8	10.7	12.9	13.4	15.2	15.3	14.6	16.0	15.3
Cotton and man-made fibre weaving												
Production of woven cloth:		Million linear										
Cotton	KLKV	metres	261	255	265	274	275	245	219	206	169	154
Man-made fibres	KLKW	"	204.8	176.0	182.7	206.6	217.7	214.7	212.5	217.4	216.3	193.3
Cotton/man-made fibre mixtures	KLKX	"	45.7	52.3	55.9	48.1	44.7	44.6	44.6	41.5	43.6	39.1
Loom activity												
Average number of looms running on cotton and man-made fibres	KLKY	Thousands	16.9	14.7	14.0	13.3	12.6	11.6	11.6	10.6	9.0	..
Wool												
Virgin wool (clean weight):		Million kilo-										
Production[7]	KLKZ	grammes	33	33	37	40	40	42	44	47	45	..
Imports	KLLA	"	71[7]	77	82	90	83	98	89	77	62	65
Exports[8]	KLLB	"	24[7]	26	28	28	31	34	34	33	27	26
Stocks at 31 August	KLLC	"	21	19	20	23	22	22	21	21	20	28
Consumption:												
Wool	KLLD	"	88.1	90.0	94.9	96.6	100.2	104.0	104.5	97.2	93.6	87.9
Hair	KLLE	"	5.9	6.6	7.2	7.9	7.5	8.3	7.0	6.5	5.9	5.6
Man-made fibres	KLLF	"	48.8	51.5	50.4	53.9	57.6	56.2	53.9	45.9	40.6	37.7
Other fibres[9]	KLLG	"	10.1	10.1	9.0	9.3	8.8	9.8	10.0	8.9	6.4	5.6
Tops												
Production: total	KLLH	"	66.5	70.3	76.0	81.8	83.6	83.1	80.0	69.1	60.5	61.9
Wool and hair	KLLI	"	37.3	38.5	42.9	44.5	43.8	43.8	42.8	38.7	34.2	36.0
Man-made fibres	KLLJ	"	29.2	31.8	33.2	37.3	39.8	39.3	37.2	30.4	26.3	25.9
Worsted yarns[10]:												
Production	KLLK	"	53.4	55.6	59.6	61.8	64.8	66.3	60.2	52.4	47.2	44.8
Semi-worsted yarns[10]:												
Production	KLLL	"	8.1	9.4	6.5	7.5	10.2	12.5	13.5	12.7	11.4	7.6
Woollen yarn[7]:												
Production	KLLM	"	53.4	56.2	60.5	64.3	72.9	76.7	78.3	74.9	72.7	66.1
Woven woollen and worsted fabrics[11]:		Million square										
Deliveries	KLLN	metres	100.3	94.0	90.7	90.9	93.1	90.3	89.0	85.4	79.0	72.0
Blankets:												
Deliveries	KLLO	"	9.4	8.3	9.3	8.9	6.9	6.7	7.2	7.0	7.3	6.2

TIME SERIES. Figures for consumption of raw cotton, and production and consumption of cotton and man-made fibre yarn are for periods of 52 weeks (53 weeks in 1980 and 1986).

1 From 1978 figures for consumption of raw cotton are for calendar months.
2 Figures are based on returns from producers (excluding waste) and include all man-made fibres in commercial production.
3 Excluding waste yarns.
4 Yarns wholly of cotton waste, cotton yarn spun on condenser system and mixture yarns of cotton and cotton waste.
5 Average of numbers running in last week of each month. Waste spinning spindles are excluded.
6 Figures prior to 1982 are not provided.
7 Estimated.
8 Including imported wool and wool from imported skins, scoured, etc in the United Kingdom.
9 Including noils, broken tops, wastes, mungo and shoddy.
10 Including all yarn spun on the worsted system.
11 Includes mixture and man-made fibre fabrics classified as wool or worsted, but excludes blankets.

*Sources: Department of Trade and Industry;
British man-made Fibres Federation;
Wool Industry Bureau of Statistics;
Textile Statistics Bureau*

Industrial materials

8.19 Packaging products of paper and board: manufacturers' sales[1]
United Kingdom

£ million

		1980	1981	1982	1983	1984	1985	1986	1987	1988	1989	1990	1991
Rigid boxes	KLJG	63.5	59.8	60.2	67.0	81.8	88.1	88.7	97.8	91.1	88.7	92.8	95.5
Cartons	KLJH	449.5	451.6	490.7	505.4	516.6	582.5	633.2	697.3	746.2	773.7	800.7	802.4
Fibreboard packing cases:													
Solid	KLJI	34.4	31.0	29.0	27.2	27.6	23.8	..	..	..	..	..	..
Corrugated	KLJJ	512.0	513.8	529.4	558.8	653.7	695.7	709.1	768.5	852.2	944.9	916.2	918.3
Paper bags	KLJK	58.1	55.8	57.1	49.1	49.8	53.7	53.0	53.8	54.6	53.2	54.7	..
Paper carrier bags	KLJL	2.8	2.3	3.6	6.8	7.2	6.7	6.4	8.2	8.1	5.6	7.5	..
Paper sacks	KLJM	116.0	114.7	121.0	119.7	112.5	120.2	108.3	113.4	111.9	108.9	110.9	..

1 From 1980 sales are by manufacturers employing 25 or more people, and by those employing 75 or more in the case of board products or 100 or more in the case of paper products.

Source: Department of Trade and Industry

8.20 Timber
United Kingdom

Thousand cubic metres

		1980	1981	1982	1983	1984	1985	1986	1987	1988	1989	1990	1991
Softwood													
Deliveries													
Imported	KLNA	6 131	5 649	6 237	6 895	6 650	6 441	7 010	..	..	..	..	..
Home grown[1,2]	KLNB	388	428	595	618	594	641	781	819	909	832	..	..
Stocks (end of period):													
Imported	KLNC	1 846	1 646	1 494	1 729	1 765	1 435	1 429	..	..	..	..	..
Total	KLND	6 519	6 077	6 832	7 513	7 244	7 082	7 788	..	..	..	..	..
Hardwood													
Deliveries													
Imported	KLNE	766	717	740	951	841	830	855	..	..	..	..	..
Home grown[1,2]	KLNF	108	85	74	78	47	63	89	63	59	59	..	..
Stocks (end of period):													
Imported	KLNG	228	223	232	272	271	249	241	..	..	..	..	..
Total	KLNH	874	802	814	1 029	888	893	944	..	..	..	..	..
Imported plywood													
Deliveries	KLNI	830	972	920	1 068	1 019	1 090	1 119	..	..	..	..	..
Stocks (end of period)	KLNJ	142	209	130	191	212	163	247	..	..	..	..	..
Mining timber													
Production:													
Sawn	KLNK	407.6	407.2	428.3	415.2	135.6	306.8	335.9	300.2	281.7	253.4	243.4	215.7
Round	KLNL	152.6	149.7	136.3	124.2	45.8	94.9	87.9	65.3	48.8	38.7	31.8	24.2
Total	KLNM	560.2	556.9	564.6	539.4	181.4[3]	401.7	423.8	365.5	330.5	292.1	275.2	239.9
Consumption:													
Sawn	KLNN	424.4	415.8	429.4	415.5	135.6	306.8	335.9	300.2	281.7	253.4	243.4	215.7
Round[4]	KLNO	214.6	198.1	175.9	149.6	48.2	101.0	94.2	68.9	48.8	38.7	31.8	24.2
Stocks(end of period):													
Sawn	KLNP	70.3	54.2	64.7	61.2	62.0	43.4	43.2	30.2	37.7	23.0	26.4	19.1
Round	KLNQ	45.2	96.1	62.6	39.9	27.7	21.0	18.0	10.5	10.4	7.0	4.9	3.2
Wood chipboard													
Production	KLNR	606.7	524.7	514.6	518.5	541.4	728.0	..	..	..	..	..	..
Stocks (end of period)	KLNS	55.4	24.1	45.5	39.4	38.5	47.8	..	..	..	..	..	..

TIME SERIES. Figures for wood chipboard relate to periods of 52 weeks (53 weeks in 1982).

1 Up to and including 1979 sales of home-grown timber and of plywood are by firms employing 25 or more people and from 1980 by firms employing 35 or more people.

2 Home-grown excludes mining timber and relates to sawn and planed only. Home-grown hardwood also excludes planed timber.
3 Reduction due to the miners' strike.
4 As from February 1988 imported materials no longer used for mining purposes.

Sources: Department of Trade and Industry;
Timber Trade Federation;
British Coal

Industrial materials

8.21 Synthetic rubber, carbon black and rubber products[1]
United Kingdom

	Unit	1980	1981	1982	1983	1984	1985	1986	1987	1988	1989	1990	1991
Synthetic rubber													
UK manufactures sales	Thousand tonnes												
Synthetic rubber: total KLMP		..	220.7	202.8	209.8	237.0	220.7	242.4	245.2	295.8	292.0	290.0	..
Solid KLMQ	"	..	139.6	139.0	145.3	165.9	162.4	182.8	178.5	204.4	214.0	205.0	..
Latex KLMR	"	..	81.1	63.8	64.5	71.1	58.3	59.6	66.7	91.4	78.0	85.0	..
Carbon black													
Production[2] KLMS	"	172.3	152.5	..[3]	..	..	..	..	..	..	..	..	..
Rubber products	£ million												
UK manufactures sales													
Rubber products: total KLMT		1 637.8	1 483.1	1 445.9	1 509.8	1 538.8	1 682.1	1 815.3	2 035.7	2 183.3	2 207.2	2 055.7	1 974.2
New tyres KLMU	"	650.9	588.3	574.5	608.7	609.0	662.4	742.3	865.1	930.3	1 022.6	987.2	977.3
Retreads KLMV	"	43.0	40.7	38.0	47.3	53.6	56.1	57.9	63.3	68.0	67.2	74.2	69.3
Tubes[4] KLMW	"	27.8	24.2	26.5	22.1	22.9	19.6	10.6	11.1	14.0	9.1	10.9	10.6
Belting KLMX	"	118.9	103.1	114.0	104.4	88.0	89.1	89.2	89.2	93.9	105.4	103.3	88.3
Hose / tubing KLMY	"	131.9	127.1	126.9	122.6	125.9	144.6	152.6	162.8	170.5	179.2	180.9	144.6
Other products KLMZ	"	665.6	599.7	566.0	604.7	639.4	710.3	762.7	844.2	906.6	823.7[5]	699.2	684.1

1 Figures prior to 1981 for synthetic rubber/carbon black and rubber products relate to establishments with minimum employment levels of 25 persons. From 1981 minimum employment levels for carbon black and rubber products are 75 and 100 respectively; except for those establishments producing new tyres and tubes whose minimum employment level is 300 persons. From 1990 the minimum employment level of rubber products is 150.

2 Including lamp and vegetable black; excluding acetylene and bone black.
3 Data no longer published.
4 Figures include Repair Kits/materials and moulded solid rubber tyres with or without metallic bondings.
5 From 1990 only BM 4811/12 and 4820 are used for Other products figures where previous years used additional sources. 1989 figures amended accordingly.

Source: Department of Trade and Industry

8.22 Fertilisers
Years ending 31 May[1]

Thousand tonnes

		1980	1981	1982	1983	1984	1985	1986	1987	1988	1989	1990	1991
Deliveries to UK agriculture													
N (nitrogen):- nutrient content													
Straight	KGRM	701.0	695.0	785.0	896.0	857.0	903.0	850.0	883.0	802.0	673.1	706.0	627.9
Compounds	KGRN	544.0	468.0	476.0	529.0	476.0	471.0	445.0	472.0	498.0	491.3	513.5	462.1
P_2O_5 (phosphate)	KGRO	394.0	372.0	379.0	407.0	395.0	404.0	367.0	355.0	354.0	334.0	332.9	278.4
K_2O (potash)	KGRP	425.0	386.0	407.0	467.0	465.0	477.0	454.0	446.0	444.0	429.0	443.2	365.3
Compounds - total weight	KGRQ	3 120.0	2 819.0	2 922.0	3 260.0	3 082.0	3 167.0	3 022.0	2 997.0	3 129.0	3 034.0	2 964.3	2 744.0

1 From 1990 the year ended is 30 June.

*Sources: Department of Trade and Industry;
Fertiliser Manufacturers Association*

8.23 Synthetic dyestuffs, colours, paint, varnish and allied products [1]

Industrial materials

		Unit	1980	1981[1]	1982	1983	1984	1985	1986	1987	1988	1989	1990	1991
Dyestuffs and pigments		Thousand tonnes												
Finished synthetic dyestuffs	KLMA	"	46.2	42.6	42.4	42.1	43.5	42.9	46.0[3]	51.3[3]	53.9[3]	56.0[3]	54.4[3]	58.5[3]
Synthetic organic pigments	KLMB	"	13.0	10.5	9.8	11.9	..[3]	..[3]	..[3]	..[3]	..[3]	..[3]	..[3]	..[3]
Inorganic pigment colours	KLMC	"	17.0	13.2[3]	11.9[3]	13.6[3]	12.8[3]	12.2[3]	11.1[3]	12.1[3]	12.9[3]	14.3[3]	14.4[3]	12.4[3]
Ochres and mineral colours	KLMD	"	16.0	..[3]	..[3]	..[3]	..[3]	..[3]	..[3]	..[3]	..[3]	..[3]	..[3]	..[3]
Titanium dioxide	KLME	"	186.7	169.6[3]	172.3[3]	194.9[3]	206.0[3]	219.1[3]	229.9[3]	255.6[3]	266.3[3]	261.0[3]	237.1[3]	..[3]
White lead	KLMF	"	0.4	..[3]	..[3]	..[3]	..[3]	..[3]	..[3]	..[3]	..[3]	..[3]	..[3]	..[3]
Paint, varnish and allied products														
Sales by larger establishments		Million litres												
All paints and varnishes: total	KLMG		596.0	523.0	533.1	541.5[4]	560.7	573.2	597.7	660.6	676.1	595.2	581.4	553.9
Emulsion paints	KLMH		173.4	158.2	171.5	178.2	186.4	202.3	210.7	235.0	240.6	218.0	208.4	210.1
Other aqueous paints	KLMI		23.7	33.9	38.0	39.3	41.4	45.1	47.1	60.7	51.8	54.1	51.4	44.6
Cellulose based varnishes, lacquers and clear solutions and pigmented cellulose paints	KLMJ		40.2	32.2	26.2	28.9	29.4	26.8	31.7	35.4	36.1	30.4	28.8	29.7
Varnishes, lacquers and stains (other than cellulose)	KLMK		8.9	9.2	9.4	10.0	9.6	10.1	11.1	9.8	10.5	6.0	6.8	3.7
Others[2]	KLML		349.8	289.5	287.9	285.0[4]	293.9	288.9	297.0	319.7	337.1	286.7	286.0[5]	267.4[5]
Manufactured thinners (solvent mixtures), removers and strippers	KLMM		66.3	60.2	57.0	61.0	63.4	61.1	63.4	63.3	66.5	57.1[7]	56.2[7]	51.1[7]
Mastics and putty	KLMN	Mn. kilogrammes	65.1	64.6	73.5	76.8	85.5	100.2	119.8	139.6	153.7	172.1	155.1[6]	173.1[6]

1 Figures relate to sales by manufacturers in the United Kingdom employing 25 or more persons and from 1981 those with a minimum employment of 50. From the first quarter 1990, minimum of employment base raised to 100, 1989 and 1990 figures revised accordingly.
2 Including oil and/or synthetic based non-aqueous products, marine paints, and bituminous paints. Figures prior to 1981 include paste fillers.
3 Data no longer published.
4 1983 is an estimated figure.
5 1990 excluding Marine paint and compositions, other paints, varnishes etc. in dry, liquid and paste forms.
6 1990 excluding putty.
7 Estimated.

Source: Department of Trade and Industry

Industrial materials

8.24 Inorganic chemicals

Thousand tonnes

		1980	1981	1982	1983	1984	1985	1986	1987	1988	1989	1990	1991
Materials used for the manufacture of sulphuric acid													
Zinc concentrates: Consumption	KLFO	242.6	188.7	210.2	238.1	243.6	237.3	242.8	220.7	195.6	216.8	255.6	241.3
Spent oxide: Consumption	KLFP	10.6	7.6	6.1	6.6	1.3	..	..	..	..	..	..	..
Stocks (end of period)	KLFQ	0.9	0.8	8.1	4.7	4.7	..	..	..	..	..	..	..
Sulphur: Consumption (for acid production)[1]	KLFR	1 064.1	911.9	805.7	824.2	828.1	784.9	719.1	657.9	700.0	660.0	594.6	547.8
Stocks (end of period)[1]	KLFS	48.7	50.5	36.7	32.1	45.8	31.0	18.8	21.1	22.3	18.4	13.7	14.5
Sulphuric acid[2]													
Production	KLFT	3 380.7	2 888.9	2 587.3	2 628.7	2 654.2	2 525.1	2 329.8	2 157.7[2]	2 257.5	2 148.1	1 996.1	1 852.4
Consumption[3]: total	KLFU	3 241.2	2 899.2	2 586.6	2 809.7	2 786.4	2 667.0	2 479.6	2 335.3	2 439.2	2 318.4	2 155.3	2 002.3
Fertilisers	KLFV	1 042.8	901.2	749.3	857.1	739.4	661.3	508.4	335.8	246.5	149.3	61.1	30.4
All other chemical uses[4]	KLFW	1 571.7	1 998.0	1 837.3	1 952.6	2 047.0	2 005.7	1 971.1	1 999.5	2 192.8	2 169.1	2 094.3	1 971.9
Metallurgy	KLFX	50.4	..	..	..	..	..	..	..	..	..	..	..
Other (incl. Textiles)	KLFY	576.3	..	..	..	..	..	..	..	..	..	..	..
Stocks (end of period)	KLFZ	145.0	151.2	122.3	113.0	118.8	106.9	91.5	72.7	76.9	86.7	94.0	72.1

1 Filter cake and boiler bottom are excluded.
2 As 100 per cent acid.
3 Including recovered and imported acid.
4 Figures from 1981 include Metallurgy and other (incl. Textiles).

Sources: Department of Trade and Industry;
National Sulphuric Acid Association

8.25 Organic chemicals: production [1]

Thousand tonnes[2]

		1980	1981	1982	1983	1984	1985	1986	1987	1988	1989	1990	1991
Ethylene[3]	KLCP	1 094.9	1 235.5	1 115.4	1 154.6	1 324.3	1 446.5	1 740.1	1 797.9	2 005.2	1 975.4	1 498.1	1 794.9
Propylene[3]	KLCQ	572.7	736.6	824.2	831.9	975.8	973.2	864.2	874.9	850.4	796.8	751.3	834.3
Butadiene[3]	KLCR	191.9	207.9	228.8	237.7	259.2	297.6	192.9	231.4	239.7	225.9	198.1	197.5
Benzene[4]	KLCS	825.5	751.9	569.5	725.9	754.7	834.9	852.8	911.6	872.8	1 024.9	702.0	869.7
Toluene[5]	KLCT	170.1	179.0	..[8]	..[8]	..[8]	164.8	..	..	..	..	..	..
Formaldehyde[6]	KLCU	123.9	113.0	107.2	97.8	103.6	123.7	103.2	113.5	111.6	79.7	42.8	59.6
Propyl alcohols	KLCV	61.4	..[9]	..	..	..	..	..	..	..	..	..	..
Acetone	KLCW	122.6	111.2	135.3	121.8	161.5	146.8	123.2	117.9	127.5	130.3	128.5	125.3
Phenol (synthetic)	KLCX	..	109.7	140.0	143.2	184.4	117.5	52.9	..	..	..	..	..
Phthalic anhydride	KLCY	46.3	61.1	73.0	..[9]	..	..	..	..	..	..	..	..
Ethyl alcohol[7] (Thousand hectolitres of alcohol)	KLCZ	1 810.6	1 839.4	2 071.5	2 398.1	3 043.3	2 509.5	2 538.0	2 980.1	2 968.1	2 886.9	3 061.8	2 959.3

1 Figures relate to total production ie 'captive use' is included.
2 Except for Ethyl alcohol which is measured in thousand hectolitres of alcohol.
3 Produced from oil base, other than for use as fuel.
4 Includes production obtained by dealkylation of toluene (excludes production from coal).
5 Includes that used for the production of benzene, but excludes production from coal.
6 Including paraformaldehyde (expressed as 100 per cent formaldehyde).
7 Industrial alcohol made from molasses and derived from other processes. The figures include a small quantity of beverage spirits produced by rectification of spirits distilled from molasses. In the financial year ended 31 March 1985 this amounted to about 13.21 thousand hectolitres of alcohol a month.
8 Figures supressed for disclosure reasons.
9 No longer published in the *Business Monitor* series.

Sources: Department of Trade and Industry;
HM Customs and Excise

Industrial materials

8.26 Production of synthetic resins[1]

Thousand tonnes

		1980	1981[2]	1982	1983	1984	1985	1986	1987	1988	1989	1990
All synthetic resins	KLHA	2 259.3	1 972.8[4]	1 664.4[4]	1 411.7[4]	1 559.2[4]	1 698.9[4]	1 080.9[4]	1 627.5[4]	1 609.1[4]	1 577.3[4]	1 310.5[4]
Products of condensation, poly-condensation and polyaddition	KLHB	729.9	673.3	617.0	466.5[4]	595.5[4]	608.0[4]	382.2[4]	653.0[4]	461.2[4]	411.0	264.6
Alkyds (including styrenated alkyds and unsaturated polyesters):												
Solid and liquid alkyd resins including solutions, emulsions and dispersions (net resin content including oil but excluding solvent)	KLHC	111.8	102.5	99.1	98.0	97.8	79.2	78.5	82.0	97.1	111.2	122.6
Unsaturated polyester resins (including reactive monomer, but excluding filler)	KLHD	48.4	51.0	48.6	50.2	52.1	55.0	58.7	66.7	80.0	81.1	61.5
Aminoplastics:												
Alkylated resin solutions (actual weight including solvent)												
Solid resins	KLHE	164.8	155.1	139.4	143.7	161.0	157.2	167.6	184.3	202.7	134.5	..
Other liquid resins and solutions (actual weight including solvent)												
Phenolics:												
Straight liquid resins, including aqueous solutions and dispersions (actual weight including water)	KLHF	15.9	17.1	17.3	18.5	15.7	15.6	14.5	14.5	16.3	14.7	16.2
Straight resins, solid or in organic soluton	KLHG KGRR	20.7	18.3	20.2	21.5	18.4	19.3	18.4	27.2	26.4	29.4	31.6
Modified resins, including those in solution	KLHH	4.6	4.1	3.8	3.6	4.6	4.1	..[5]				
Polyurethanes	KLHI	73.2	75.0	83.9	93.3	..[5]	..[5]	..[5]	..[5]	..[5]	..[5]	
Epoxide resins (net resin content excluding added non-reactive solvent and/or filler)	KLHJ	27.0	28.4	27.7	37.7	36.3	43.7	44.5	43.0	38.7	40.1	32.7
Other[3]	KLHK	263.5	222.0	177.0	..[5]	209.6	233.9	..[5]	235.3	..[5]	..[5]	..
Products of polymerisation and co-polymerisation	KLHL	1 323.4	1 207.7[4]	972.8[4]	884.8[4]	893.2[4]	1 019.5[4]	627.2[4]	907.0[4]	1 128.6[4]	1 145.8	1 045.9
Acrylics:												
Lattices, dispersions and solutions												
Moulding and extrusion compounds, cast sheet, cast rod and cast tube (based on methyl methacrylic monomer)	KLHM	58.7	50.3	63.7	59.3	67.8	69.0	75.8	102.6	114.6	122.2	124.0
Polyolefines:												
Polyethylene	KLHN	434.8	454.4	425.8	407.2	406.1	520.1	427.4	398.0	461.4	514.1	423.5
Polypropylene	KLHO	190.4	197.5	221.4	229.9	258.2	269.0	..[5]	277.7	307.6	353.0	349.5
Polyvinyl acetate, including solutions and dispersions (net resin content excluding plasticiser)	KLHP	93.9	94.8	92.8	91.6	100.2	103.2	117.4	128.7	130.5	154.6	146.4
Polyvinyl chloride (including lattices, solutions and dispersions)	KLHQ	349.7	314.8	..[5]	..[5]	..[5]	..[5]	..[5]	..[5]	..[5]	..[5]	..
Styrene polymers and co-polymers:												
Non-toughened straight polystyrene resins, moulding and extrusion compounds	KLHR	39.5	36.9	22.0	29.8	..[5]	..[5]	..[5]	..[5]	2.3	1.2	2.5
Toughened grades of resins, moulding and extrusion compounds	KLHS	67.0	59.0	61.2	67.0	60.9	58.2	..[5]	..[5]	63.8	..[5]	..
Other, including solutions, emulsions and dispersions, co-polymer resins and non-toughened co-polymer moulding and extrusion compounds but excluding styrene-butadiene co-polymers	KLHT	50.6	..[5]	..[5]	..[5]	..[5]	..[5]	..[5]	..[5]	..[5]	0.7	0.7
Other	KLHU	38.8	..[5]	85.9	..[5]	..[5]	..[5]	..[5]	..[5]	47.7	..	..
Cellulosics and other plastics and modified natural resins	KLHV	93.6	91.8	74.6	57.0[4]	70.5	71.4	71.5	67.5	..[5]	..[5]	..
Regenerated cellulose film	KLHW	78.8	76.7	62.6	57.0	54.6	55.0	52.9	49.3	..[5]	..[5]	..
Other cellulosics and other plastics and modified natural resins (including casein, alignates and resin ester gums)	KLHX	14.8	15.1	12.0	..[5]	15.9	16.4	18.6	18.2	19.3	20.5	..

1 Unless separately specified, all figures are in terms of net resin content and co-polymers are recorded against the heading for resins made from the major monomeric ingredient of the co-polymer.
2 From 1981 figures relate to establishments with a minimum employment level of 75. Previous figures were based on a minimum of 25 persons.
3 Includes production of polymers and co-polymers of polyamide and polyester by firms classified to man-made fibre industry.
4 Totals do not include suppressed figures.
5 Data suppressed for disclosure reasons.

Source: Department of Trade and Industry

Industrial materials

8.27 Minerals: production

Thousand tonnes

Great Britain

		1981	1982	1983	1984	1985	1986	1987	1988	1989	1990	1991
Limestone	KLEA	62 850	69 114	75 753	75 533	77 567	81 207	93 617	103 410	107 908	99 775	91 999
Sandstone	KLEB	9 611	10 803	12 199	12 529	10 870	11 337	13 804	16 031	16 748	14 952	12 928
Igneous rock	KLEC	25 323	29 987	30 733	29 969	31 720	34 038	39 529	44 636	46 809	49 542	46 008
Clay/shale	KLED	18 799	20 323	22 403	17 817	18 909	17 169	17 862	18 534	19 011	15 864	13 038
Industrial sand	KLEE	4 451	4 123	4 026	4 328	4 178	4 108	4 029	4 340	4 380	4 132	4 201
Chalk	KLEF	11 756	11 616	12 430	12 022	12 023	12 511	13 444	14 516	13 877	13 129	10 317
Fireclay	KLEG	992	850	689	757	831	940	900	1 057	1 052	892	867
Barium sulphate	KLEH	63.3	81.1	36.0	62.7	107.3	86.8	76.8	76.2	70.0	67.6	85.5
Calcium fluoride	KLEI	255.5	200.8	131.3	136.7	167.4	133.4	120.4	103.7	122.1	118.5	77.9
Copper	KLEJ	0.6	0.6	0.7	0.7	0.6	0.6	0.8	0.7	0.5	1.0	0.2
Lead	KLEK	7.0	4.0	3.8	2.4	4.0	0.6	0.7	1.2	2.2	1.4	0.2
Tin	KLEL	3.7	4.2	4.0	5.2	4.3	3.8	3.7	3.4	3.8	3.4	2.3
Zinc	KLEM	10.9	10.2	8.9	7.5	5.3	5.7	6.6	5.5	5.8	6.7	1.0
Iron ore: crude	KLEN	703	392	262	246	147	291	246	227	4	4	..
Iron ore: iron content	KLEO	162	85	57	53	31	77	56	50	2	2	..
Calcspar	KLEP	20	18	10	7	6	10	..	23	22	34	8
China clay (including ball clay)	KLEQ	3 508	3 358	3 346	3 607	3 762	3 780	4 054	4 352	4 190	4 042	3 744
Chert and flint	KLER	10	..	174	17	22	14	16	11	..	14	5
Fuller's earth	KLES	205	243	267	286	292	248	..	277	265	228	202
Lignite	KLET	..	..	1	2	5	7	6	18	4	5	3
Rock salt	KLEU	1 350	2 209	1 316	1 569	2 030	2 040	1 855	877	594	815	2 088
Salt from brine	KLEV	1 454	1 554	1 394	1 423	1 552	1 510	1 554	1 426	..	..	1 319
Salt in brine	KLEW	3 916	3 874	3 601	4 134	3 563	3 305	3 672	3 827	..	..	..
Anhydrite	KLEX	47	67	51	56	59	53	..	..	..	..	..
Dolomite	KLEY	13 936	13 727	14 983	14 228	14 953	15 851	17 037	19 861	21 271	20 674	19 454
Gypsum	KLEZ	2 897	2 674	2 916	3 082	3 130	3 363	..	..	..	..	..
Slate[1]	KLFA	350	785	494	157	158	242	322	708	590	359	360
Soapstone and talc	KLFB	18	19	16	19	20	12	12	14	15	15	11
Sand and gravel (land-won)	KLFC	77 951	79 287	88 002	87 092	87 813	90 215	95 409	110 516	110 504	98 993	85 479
Sand and gravel (marine dredged)	KLFD	11 501	11 919	12 797	12 582	13 792	15 284	16 220	19 638	20 728	17 179	12 439

1 Includes waste used for constructional fill, and powder and granules used in manufacturing.

Source: Central Statistical Office

Northern Ireland

		1980	1981	1982	1983	1984	1985	1986	1987	1988	1989	1990
Chalk	KLFE	317	..	..	..	..	..	..	..	..	..	..
Clay and shale	KLFF	..	..	..	..	..	..	397	409	..	..	..
Sand and gravel	KLFG	3 807	3 738	3 665	3 207	3 506	3 627	4 226	3 634	3 871	4 554	4 030
Basalt and igneous rock (other than granite)	KLFH	6 179	5 449	6 151	6 140	6 856	6 717	6 731	6 380	7 324	7 463	7 691
Limestone	KLFI	2 290	2 281	2 609	3 249	3 707	3 057	3 436	3 041	2 409	3 485	2 866
Grit and conglomerate	KLFJ	2 809	2 622	2 524	2 532	2 578	2 307	2 693	2 573	2 870	2 845	3 090
Diatomite	KLFK	..	..	..	..	..	..	..	..	..	..	..
Granite	KLFL	..	..	..	..	..	..	189	107	..	..	..
Sandstone	KLFM	..	..	..	..	..	..	..	..	..	..	..
Rock salt	KLFN	..	..	..	..	..	..	..	..	..	..	..

Source: Department of Economic Development (Northern Ireland)

Building and construction

8.28 Building materials and components: production[1]
Great Britain

		Unit	1980	1981	1982	1983	1984	1985	1986	1987	1988	1989	1990	1991
Building bricks (excluding refractory and glazed)	KLGA	Millions	4 562	3 725	3 517	3 806	4 012	4 100	3 971	4 222	4 682	4 654	3 802	3 212
Cement[2]	KLGB	Thousand tonnes	14 805	12 729	12 962	13 396	13 481	13 339	13 413	14 311	16 506	16 849	14 740	..
Building sand[3,4]	KLGC	"	18 005	15 675	17 044	19 151	18 187	18 346	20 423	20 620	23 415	23 290	20 948	18 573[11]
Concreting sand[4]	KLGD	"	26 699	25 427	25 242	26 720	28 172	28 694	30 347	32 823	39 174	41 223	37 213	29 456[11]
Gravel[4,5]	KLGE	"	51 454	48 351	48 920	54 929	53 316	54 564	54 729	58 185	67 566	66 718	58 010	46 907[11]
Crushed rock aggregates:[6]		Thousand tonnes												
used as roadstone (coated)	KLGF	"	14 366	13 179	17 739	18 562	17 424	18 188	19 239	22 599	28 860	23 733	26 430	..
roadstone (uncoated)	KLGG	"	42 896	35 949	35 259	38 522	36 660	41 168	44 185	50 784	54 187	66 015	61 742	..
fill and ballast	KLGH	"	31 619	31 049	37 129	40 416	42 234	42 426	45 227	53 411	59 989	59 689	54 640	..
concrete aggregate	KLGI	"	13 653	11 205	12 721	14 582	14 360	13 214	13 715	15 443	17 978	19 356	18 804	..
Ready mixed concrete[2]	KLGJ	Million m^3	22.4	19.9	20.7	21.5	20.8	21.6	21.5	24.4	28.8	29.6	26.8	22.0
Fibre cement products	KLGK	Thousand tonnes	352.2	265.6	261.7	239.5	255.5	252.6	217.4	205.4	251.0	220.7	234.7	133.7
Clay roofing tiles[2,7]	KLGL	Thousand m^2	1 698	1 635	1 632	2 206	2 051	2 143	2 587	3 019	3 459	3 756	2 912	2 191
Concrete roofing tiles	KLGM	"	28 813	23 345	25 551	33 243	34 685	27 870	30 843	34 707	38 818	35 878	31 510	26 359
Concrete building blocks:[2]														
dense aggregate	KLGN	"	21 014	18 911	23 918	29 186	31 907	30 431	33 483	36 548	44 404	45 564	39 297	32 456
lightweight aggregate	KLGO	"	23 779	20 896	23 395	25 544	24 378	21 867	27 515	31 121	33 530	31 041	23 768	18 581
aerated concrete	KLGP	"	22 027	15 758	16 372	20 912	25 358	22 147	26 156	29 328	32 095	31 394	28 089	23 594
Concrete pipes[2,7]	KLGQ	Thousand tonnes	692	648	694	744	701	571	630	533	700	717	737	722
Roofing slates[8]	KLGR	"	17.7	16.3	22.7	18.4	22.0	34.0	34.7	45.6	40.9	46.6	44.1	41.0
Slates (damp-proof course)[8]	KLGS	"	3 264	2 667	2 566	2 978	3 155	3 074	3 253	..[10]	..	..	..	..
Gypsum (excluding anhydrite)	KLGS	"												
Plaster	KLGT	"	960	775	764	855	912	876	912	..[10]	..	..	..	..
Plasterboard	KLGU	Thousand m^2	111 132	101 987	107 867	120 819	127 668	122 599	134 501	..[10]	..	..	..	..
Unglazed floorquarries[2,7]	KLGV	Thousand m^2	1 123	1 007	949	1 013	1 000	1 061	1 075	1 078	2 681[12]	1 180	1 070	1 037
Unglazed tiles[2,7]	KLGW	"	2 332	2 085	1 357	1 146	1 277	1 102	1 207	1 175	–[12]	1 521	1 349	1 371
Copper tubing[2,9]	KLGX	Thousand tonnes	69	68	72	74	..[10]	..	..	..	..	..	..	..

1 The figures are summaries of returns made by manufacturers and producers. They represent total production and not merely the quantities available for building purposes.
2 United Kingdom.
3 Including sand used in the production of sand lime bricks.
4 From 1979 figures represent volume sold, not production.
5 Figures include hoggin, concrete aggregate, other purposes (excluding fill) and fill.
6 From 1979 figures represent volume sold, not production.
7 Figues represent volume sold, not production.
8 From 1985 figures refer to slates used for architectural and cladding uses, roofing and damp-proof courses.
9 Figures relate to the production of copper tubes for all purposes including those used in the construction industry.
10 Series discontinued.
11 Provisional.
12 Unglazed floorquarries and unglazed tiles figures merged for 1988.

Sources: Department of the Environment;
World Bureau of Metal Statistics;
Central Statistical Office

Building and construction

8.29 Construction: value of output in Great Britain[1]

£ million

		1980	1981	1982	1983	1984	1985	1986	1987	1988	1989	1990	1991
All work: total	FGAY	22 052	21 547	22 540	24 343	26 203	27 850	30 123	34 581	40 546	46 174	48 467	43 709
New work: total	BLAB	13 055	12 354	12 629	13 396	14 192	14 921	16 286	19 066	23 420	27 315	28 354	24 967
New housing: total	KLQA	4 296	3 738	3 920	4 849	4 908	4 766	5 539	6 745	8 469	8 067	6 884	5 656
For public sector	BLAC	1 711	1 222	1 021	1 120	1 077	918	842	933	922	979	965	810
For private sector	BLAD	2 585	2 516	2 899	3 729	3 831	3 848	4 697	5 812	7 547	7 088	5 919	4 846
Other new work: total	KLQB	8 760	8 616	8 709	8 546	9 285	10 154	10 747	12 321	14 951	19 248	21 470	19 310
For public sector	BLAE	3 524	3 572	3 671	3 729	3 833	3 786	3 888	3 870	4 318	5 095	5 837	5 772
For private sector: total	KLQC	5 236	5 044	5 038	4 817	5 452	6 368	6 859	8 451	10 633	14 153	15 633	13 538
Industrial	BLAF	2 806	2 382	2 087	1 850	2 342	2 848	2 632	3 204	4 023	4 936	5 243	5 314
Commercial	BLAG	2 430	2 662	2 951	2 967	3 110	3 520	4 226	5 247	6 610	9 217	10 390	8 224
Repair and maintenance: total	BLAH	8 997	9 193	9 911	10 948	12 011	12 930	13 837	15 515	17 125	18 859	20 113	18 743
Housing: total[2]	KLQD	4 480	4 568	4 970	5 622	6 251	6 809	7 427	8 360	9 327	10 210	10 710	9 768
For public sector	BLBK	..	..	..	..	..	2 993	3 186	3 462	3 791	4 109	4 386	3 964
For private sector	BLBL	..	..	..	..	..	3 816	4 241	4 898	5 536	6 101	6 324	5 804
Public other work	BLAJ	2 920	3 026	3 285	3 548	3 746	3 800	3 768	4 042	4 251	4 635	5 044	4 807
Private other work	BLAK	1 597	1 599	1 656	1 777	2 014	2 321	2 642	3 112	3 547	4 014	4 360	4 168

1 Output by contractors, including unrecorded estimates by small firms and self-employed workers, and by the public sector's direct labour departments classified to construction in the Standard Industrial Classification, Revised 1980.
2 Separate figures for public and private sectors unavailable before 1985.

Source: Department of the Environment

8.30 Construction: value of new orders obtained by contractors[1] Great Britain

£ million

		1980	1981	1982	1983	1984	1985	1986	1987[3]	1988	1989	1990	1991
New work: total	FHAA	10 115	10 722	11 444	13 518	14 630	15 343	17 108	22 119	26 299	27 142	22 492	19 457
New housing: total	FGAU	2 702	2 685	3 912	5 063	4 877	5 290	6 193	7 344	8 776	7 369	5 539	5 427
From public sector	BLBC	753	672	984	985	876	734	772	903	882	872	683	875
From private sector[2]	BLBD	1 944	2 013	2 928	4 078	4 001	4 555	5 421	6 441	7 894	6 497	4 856	4 552
Other new work: total	BLBE	7 413	8 037	7 532	8 455	9 753	10 054	10 915	14 775	17 523	19 773	16 953	14 030
From public sector: total	BLBF	3 248	3 690	3 433	4 175	4 150	3 877	4 142	4 513	5 116	6 205	5 146	4 767
Gas, electricity, coalmining	KLDA	396	431	280	287	161	253	229	301	234	315	200	59
Railways and air transport	KLDB	173	275	82	136	222	195	348	204	138	379	195	252
Schools	KLDC	292	239	219	326	338	297	305	317	435	471	526	584
Universities	KLDD	38	42	32	34	31	45	59	52	66	140	146	150
Health	KLDE	320	478	467	444	619	491	430	492	712	824	665	578
Offices, factories, etc	KLDF	589	519	584	691	750	617	638	688	853	861	814	665
Roads	KLDG	562	781	770	799	849	802	853	894	1 029	1 181	1 351	1 386
Harbours and waterways	KLDH	97	95	95	122	100	109	132	233	134	108	129	133
Water	KLDI	67	129	110	128	117	104	160	155	153	175	13	16
Sewerage	KLDJ	227	211	221	304	256	257	268	251	313	285	164	202
Miscellaneous	KLDK	487	489	574	905	706	709	720	925	1 048	1 468	944	743
From private sector: total[2]	BLBG	4 165	4 347	4 099	4 280	5 603	6 176	6 773	10 262	12 407	13 568	11 807	9 263
Industrial: total	FGAS	1 803	1 554	1 327	1 543	2 203	2 149	1 993	3 660	3 128	3 377	3 736	3 452
Commercial: total	BLBI	2 362	2 793	2 772	2 737	3 400	4 028	4 781	6 602	9 279	10 191	8 071	5 811
Offices	KLDL	1 045	1 451	1 414	1 209	1 601	1 775	2 256	3 110	4 585	5 271	4 216	2 216
Shops	KLDM	536	531	521	549	702	1 022	1 102	1 616	2 048	2 086	1 344	1 222
Entertainment	KLDN	342	388	382	363	564	577	739	991	1 356	1 419	1 195	1 111
Garages	KLDO	125	98	134	166	171	133	190	228	375	405	365	261
Schools and colleges	KLDP	44	48	48	67	65	85	72	87	182	173	169	169
Miscellaneous	KLDQ	270	278	273	384	296	435	422	570	734	839	782	833

1 Classified to construction in the Standard Industrial Classification, Revised 1980.
2 Figures for private sector include work to be carried out by contractors on their own initiative for sale.
3 Orders for 1987 include the Channel Tunnel project in the private industrial sector.

Source: Department of the Environment

Engineering

8.31 Metal goods, engineering and vehicles industries
Estimated total sales of UK manufactured goods[1,2] Standard Industrial Classification 1980

£ million

		Activity heading	1981	1982	1983	1984	1985	1986	1987	1988	1989	1990[7]	1991[7]
Division 3													
Manufacture of metal goods not elsewhere specified[3]														
Class 31														
Forging, pressing and stamping	BJFB	3 120	885	935	1 014	1 158	1 167	1 209	1 311	1 364	1 434	1 214	917
Bolts, nuts, washers, rivets, springs and non-precision chains	BJFC	3 137	410	424	470	515	532	553	587	758	828	863	817
Heat and surface treatment of metals, (including sintering)	BJPU	3 138	273	339	372	446	515	495	561	584	658	651	642
Metal doors, windows, etc	BJFD	3 142	502	532	600	675	573	631	669	897	956	1 043	986
Hand tools and implements	BJFE	3 161	191	190	211	215	236	229	258	246	267	346	311
Cutlery, spoons, forks and similar tableware; razors	BJFF	3 162	80	81	89	101	109	105	104	153	180	228	301
Metal storage vessels (mainly non-industrial)	BJFG	3 163	68	71	77	64	63	71	77	93	115	129	112
Packaging products of metal	BJFH	3 164	1 108	1 202	1 311	1 462	1 539	1 600	1 660	1 913	1 976	2 236	2 122
Domestic heating and cooking appliances (non-electrical)	BJFI	3 165	242	251	279	291	319	350	366	411	400	433	419
Metal furniture and safes	BJFJ	3 166	356	370	413	457	483	539	571	795	870	968	917
Domestic utensils of metal	BJFK	3 167	171	166	176	183	192	216	199	263	220	228	201
Miscellaneous finished metal products	BJFL	3 169	1 632	1 859	2 000	2 199	2 363	2 509	2 838	3 474	3 829	4 033	4 044
Total	BJFA		5 918	6 420	7 012	7 766	8 095	8 507	9 201	10 365	11 075	11 720	11 146
Mechanical engineering[4]														
Class 32														
Fabricated constructional steelwork	BJFN	3 204	1 013	1 286	1 370	1 395	1 513	1 474	1 791	2 038	2 432	2 535	2 531
Boilers and process plant fabrications	BJFO	3 205	1 251	1 598	1 864	1 621	1 577	1 784	1 810	1 760	1 948	2 160	2 308
Agricultural machinery	BJFP	3 211	247	277	322	279	302	256	277	349	342	378	369
Wheeled tractors	BJFQ	3 212	914	882	916	1 016	982	894	1 033	1 166	1 109	1 183	865
Metal-working machine tools	BJFR	3 221	565	598	562	683	822	840	877	1 148	1 286	1 415	1 141
Engineers' small tools	BJFS	3 222	580	566	556	649	770	790	818	908	992	1 044	1 024
Textile machinery	BJFT	3 230	256	230	219	306	307	324	321	421	399	457	404
Food, drink and tobacco processing machinery; packaging and bottling machinery	BJFU	3 244	430	493	521	521	538	619	656	807	858	960	912
Chemical industry machinery; furnaces and kilns; gas, water and waste treatment plant	BJFV	3 245	357	388	397	395	439	478	497	578	580	682	696
Mining machinery	BJFW	3 251	599	720	630	507	631	788	678	753	832	780	712
Construction and earth moving equipment	BJFX	3 254	1 023	940	839	876	1 011	1 006	996	1 606	1 811	1 946	1 700
Mechanical lifting and handling equipment	BJFY	3 255	1 038	1 166	1 422	1 586	1 747	1 758	1 826	2 179	2 396	2 650	2 612
Precision chains and other mechanical power transmission equipment	BJFZ	3 261	508	474	472	552	648	684	780	993	1 037	1 128	1 071
Ball, needle and roller bearings	BJOA	3 262	214	210	195	206	229	254	272	481	522	566	514
Machinery for working wood, rubber, plastics, leather and making paper, glass, bricks and similar materials; laundry and dry cleaning machinery	BJOB	3 275	259	328	351	380	458	485	524	636	781	710	630
Printing, bookbinding and paper goods machinery	BJOC	3 276	351	363	364	433	580	639	680	909	924	952	815
Industrial (including marine) engines	BJOD	3 281	879	904	764	920	876	778	783	1 093	1 233	1 448	1 422
Compressors and fluid power equipment	BJOE	3 283	549	593	598	713	778	803	828	1 131	1 241	1 322	1 270
Refrigerating, space-heating, ventilating and air-conditioning equipment	BJOF	3 284	801	961	1 118	1 181	1 267	1 322	1 481	1 540	1 779	2 347	2 415
Scales, weighing machinery and portable power tools	BJOG	3 285	249	222	237	233	268	271	342	582	589	561	577
Miscellaneous industrial and commercial machinery	BJOH	3 286	539	608	630	650	767	854	1 040	1 172	1 261	1 264	1 257
Pumps	BJOI	3 287	394	409	384	409	474	473	477	682	813	892	911
Industrial valves	BJOJ	3 288	406	432	414	401	456	475	447	608	704	665	645
Miscellaneous mechanical marine and precision engineering	BJOK	3 289 3 289	777	749	1 158	1 538	1 553	1 508	1 512	2 102	2 461	3 032	2 871
Ordnance, small arms and ammunition	BJOL	3 290	622	742	847	835	806	788	828	1 157	1 123	1 170	1 022
Total	BJFM		14 821	16 139	17 154	18 285	19 799	20 346	21 574	26 798	29 453	32 247	30 691
Manufacture of office machinery and data processing equipment														
Class 33														
Office machinery	BJON	3 301	113	114	120	139	169	218	279	345	394	414	381
Electronic data processing equipment	BJOO	3 302	1 047	1 278	1 535	2 519	3 459	2 954	4 282	6 438	7 412	7 815	8 081
Total	BJOM		1 160	1 392	1 653	2 656	3 628	3 199	4 561	6 783	7 806	8 229	8 462

Note: More detailed information can be found in the PQ and PA series of Business Monitors for the activities listed above.

1 These figures represent the total sales of principal products of each activity excluding waste products and work done. Estimates of the sales of principal products of establishments falling below the employment threshold of the Quarterly and Annual Sales Inquiries are included.
2 The total may differ from the sum of its constituent parts due to rounding.
3 Excluding ferrous and non-ferrous metal foundries AH3111/2.
4 Excluding process engineering contractors AH3246.
5 Excluding electrical equipment installation AH3480.
6 Excluding shipbuilding and repairing AH3610.
7 Royalties and reproduction rights are excluded from sales for 1990 and 1991.

Source: Central Statistical Office

Engineering

8.31 Metal goods, engineering and vehicles industries
continued

Estimated total sales of UK manufactured goods[1,2] Standard Industrial Classification 1980

£ million

		Activity heading	1981	1982	1983	1984	1985	1986	1987	1988	1989	1990	1991
Electrical and electronic engineering[5] **Class 34**													
Insulated wires and cables	BJOQ	3 410	910	966	1 051	1 141	1 256	1 268	1 420	1 748	2 100	2 176	1 815
Basic electrical equipment	BJOR	3 420	1 949	2 186	2 193	2 342	2 367	2 743	2 656	3 243	3 590	4 176	4 422
Batteries and accumulators	BJOS	3 432	309	335	298	324	367	361	410	523	534	588	601
Alarms and signalling equipment	BJOT	3 433	188	184	237	246	301	338	402	474	581	680	742
Electrical equipment for motor vehicles, cycles and aircraft	BJOU	3 434	416	456	514	613	711	710	796	805	973	982	956
Miscellaneous electrical equipment for industrial use	BJOV	3 435	225	252	241	299	339	320	299	502	512	551	493
Telegraph and telephone apparatus and equipment	BJOW	3 441	1 128	1 275	1 418	1 475	1 668	1 753	1 674	2 279	2 577	2 395	2 354
Electrical instruments and control systems	BJOX	3 442	737	837	974	1 081	1 301	1 354	1 489	1 805	2 005	1 959	1 926
Radio and electronic capital goods	BJOY	3 443	1 760	1 962	2 311	2 633	2 853	2 961	3 153	3 724	3 835	3 804	3 882
Components other than active components, mainly for electronic equipment	BJOZ	3 444	664	754	831	1 064	1 128	1 154	1 229	1 441	1 583	1 829	1 758
Vinyl records and pre-recorded tapes	BJPA	3 452	130	129	148	194	236	304	394	492	512	493	513
Active components and electronic sub-assemblies	BJPB	3 453	655	676	868	1 092	1 139	1 150	1 167	2 133	2 217	2 220	2 106
Electronic consumer goods and miscellaneous equipment	BJPC	3 454	545	586	735	873	885	959	1 089	1 914	2 063	2 380	2 082
Domestic-type electric appliances	BJPD	3 460	915	920	1 083	1 140	1 208	1 327	1 540	1 966	1 938	1 803	1 815
Electric lamps and other electric lighting equipment	BJPE	3 470	524	559	635	700	726	798	877	1 065	1 244	1 307	1 128
Total	BJOP		11 055	12 077	13 537	15 017	16 485	17 500	18 595	24 113	26 265	27 341	26 593
Manufacture of motor vehicles and parts thereof **Class 35**													
Motor vehicles and their engines	BJPG	3 510	4 420	4 854	4 786	5 505	6 762	7 229	9 535	10 928	12 049	12 002	12 170
Motor vehicle bodies and vehicle parts	BJPH	3 521 and 3 530	3 051	3 179	3 509	3 705	3 858	4 078	4 433	4 431	4 906	5 249	5 317
Trailers, semi-trailers and caravans	BJPI	3 522/3	332	340	417	486	509	545	683	924	1 055	1 049	1 021
Total	BJPF		7 803	8 373	8 712	9 696	11 129	11 852	14 657	16 283	18 011	18 300	18 508
Manufacture of other transport equipment[6] **Class 36**													
Railway and tramway vehicles	BJPK	3 620	355	344	286	247	242	273	264	740	708	811	799
Aerospace equipment manufacturing, repairing and modification	BJPL	3 640	4 288	4 698	4 757	4 272	4 905	5 741	6 890	7 891	11 015	12 176	11 532
Baby carriages and wheelchairs	BJPM	3 650	45	57	62	77	88	87	99	92	100	127	131
Total	BJPJ		4 688	5 099	5 105	4 596	5 235	6 101	7 253	8 723	11 823	13 114	12 462
Instrument engineering **Class 37**													
Measuring, checking and precision instruments and apparatus	BJPO	3 710	817	928	1 088	1 239	1 433	1 507	1 569	1 685	1 841	1 925	1 909
Medical and surgical equipment and orthopaedic appliances	BJPP	3 720	243	293	307	341	355	370	406	645	705	864	903
Spectacles and unmounted lenses	BJPQ	3 731	98	95	117	140	143	124	127	221	196	226	282
Optical precision instruments	BJPR	3 732	91	107	140	148	166	180	182	338	331	356	294
Photographic and cinematographic equipment	BJPS	3 733	212	215	199	193	180	244	271	397	378	365	514
Clocks, watches and other timing devices	BJPT	3 740	97	134	111	117	100	92	89	90	89	111	123
Total	BJPN		1 558	1 772	1 962	2 178	2 377	2 517	2 644	3 375	3 540	3 848	4 025

See footnotes on page 169.

Source: Central Statistical Office

8.32 Volume index numbers of sales and orders for the engineering industries
United Kingdom

	Total			Home			Export		
	Orders on hand end of period	Net orders[1]	Sales	Orders on hand end of period	Net orders[1]	Sales	Orders on hand end of period	Net orders[1]	Sales
	1985 Average = 100	1985 Average monthly sales = 100		1985 Average = 100	1985 Average monthly sales = 100		1985 Average = 100	1985 Average monthly sales = 100	
Engineering industries combined SIC 1980 Class 32, 33, 34 and 37									
1986	99	99	100	97	99	99	98	99	100
1987	100	105	104	103	105	102	96	106	106
1988	107	119	115	109	115	112	104	125	120
1989	120	128	121	120	121	116	121	142	132
1990	113	120	124	110	112	117	117	136	138
1991	103	111	116	97	100	107	112	133	136
Percentage change 1991 on 1990[2]	*-9.0*	*-7.5*	*-6.5*	*-12.0*	*-11.0*	*-8.5*	*-4.5*	*-2.0*	*-1.5*
Mechanical engineering SIC 1980 Class 32									
1986	91	95	98	90	95	98	94	94	97
1987	96	100	98	99	102	98	89	96	98
1988	97	107	106	102	109	107	86	102	104
1989	105	114	110	106	112	110	104	118	109
1990	94	107	113	95	106	111	94	111	116
1991	80	94	101	81	92	99	80	97	104
Percentage change 1991 on 1990[2]	*-15.0*	*-12.0*	*-10.5*	*-14.5*	*-13.0*	*-11.0*	*-15.0*	*-12.5*	*-10.5*
Electrical and instrument engineering SIC 1980 Class 33, 34 and 37									
1986	101	103	101	102	102	100	100	104	103
1987	104	110	109	105	108	106	101	115	114
1988	116	128	122	115	121	116	116	145	135
1989	131	139	131	130	129	121	131	163	152
1990	127	130	133	123	118	121	133	159	158
1991	119	125	129	110	107	113	132	165	165
Percentage change 1991 on 1990[2]	*-6.5*	*-4.0*	*-3.0*	*-10.5*	*-9.5*	*-6.5*	*-1.0*	*+4.0*	*+4.5*

1 Net of cancellations.

2 The percentage changes have been rounded to the nearest half percentage point.

Source: Central Statistical Office

Ship building

8.33 Merchant shipbuilding[1]
United Kingdom

		1981	1982	1983	1984	1985	1986	1987	1988	1989	1990	1991
Total Gross new orders[2]												
Number	KLRA	72	57	45	90	58	61	37	41	42	35	21
Thousand gross tonnes[3,4]	KLRB	482	355	172	127	291	146	163	26	534	92	614
£ million	KLRC	383	313	279	224	330	280	277	84	430	216	..
For Overseas Registration												
Number	KLRD	26	21	12	3	8	28	10	1	13	14	6
Thousand gross tonnes[3,4]	KLRE	386	123	80	1	77	97	112	1	500	67	114
£ million	KLRF	251	151	82	6	59	102	78	–	301	–	242
Total Orders on hand[5]												
Number	KLRG	99	88	63	97	65	74	65	56	55	57	47
Thousand gross tonnes[3,4]	KLRH	1 117	990	562	301	387	426	305	265	698	657	1 163
£ million	KLRI	783	720	563	444	515	609	622	562	840	819	1 128
For Overseas Registration												
Number	KLRJ	26	35	24	10	8	31	31	18	19	25	22
Thousand gross tonnes[3,4]	KLRK	386	384	195	95	73	140	160	123	548	565	600
£ million	KLRL	271	339	194	85	64	135	144	102	340	445	576
Total Completions												
Number	KLRM	51	67	68	56	86	48	43	41	43	33	31
Thousand gross tonnes[3,4]	KLRN	217	453	540	411	225	106	247	31	106	134	110
£ million	KLRO	194	408	390	311	259	175	278	106	157	238	209
For Overseas Registration												
Number	KLRP	10	12	22	18	10	5	10	5	12	8	10
Thousand gross tonnes[3,4]	KLRQ	101	104	276	141	101	29	53	4	78	52	82
£ million	KLRR	57	57	200	128	81	30	47	10	63	..	..

1 Merchant registered ships of 100 gross tonnes and over built in the United Kingdom (including drilling ships but excluding floating platform drilling rigs).
2 Includes vessels which may have been cancelled at a late stage.
3 From 1984, tonnages conform to the 1969 IMO Convention on the tonnage measurement of ships. Earlier years relate to gross registered tonnes.
4 Tonnages are only accurately measured on completion: earlier figures are estimates.
5 Includes both vessels under construction and those not yet commenced.

Source: Department of Trade and Industry

8.34 Motor vehicle production
United Kingdom

Number

		1981	1982	1983	1984	1985	1986	1987	1988	1989	1990	1991
Motor vehicles												
SIC 1980, Group 351												
Passenger cars: total	KLSA	954 650	887 679	1 044 597	908 906	1 047 973	1 018 962	1 142 683	1 226 835	1 299 082	1 295 610	1 236 900
1 000 c.c. and under	KLSB	229 189	197 153	194 064	161 884	183 383	162 090	153 214	129 446	133 135	93 039	26 621
Over 1 000 c.c. but not over 1 600 c.c.	KLSC	526 498	547 676	723 289	637 868	694 876	665 093	718 046	764 289	716 784	809 219	830 530
Over 1 600 c.c. but not over 2 800 c.c.	KLSD	153 957	97 536	77 504	56 587	109 437	134 802	205 067	260 231	375 309	325 116	338 877
Over 2 800 c.c.	KLSE	45 006	45 314	49 740	52 567	60 277	56 977	66 356	72 869	73 854	68 236	40 872
Commercial vehicles: total	KLSF	229 555	268 798	244 514	224 825	265 973	228 685	246 728	317 343	326 590	270 346	217 141
Of which:												
Light commercial vehicles	KLSG	157 744	189 094	175 338	157 963	195 475	175 825	188 858	250 053	267 135	230 510	184 005
Trucks:												
Under 7.5 tonnes	KLSH	14 294	16 367	12 792	13 057	14 601	12 451	15 697	19 732	17 687	10 515	8 833
Over 7.5 tonnes	KLSI	41 152	43 469	34 850	31 945	33 716	22 718	22 834	24 887	21 083	13 674	11 766
Motive units for articulated vehicles	KLSJ	3 921	6 761	5 918	5 361	6 154	5 351	5 343	6 171	5 827	3 327	2 700
Buses, coaches and mini buses:												
Single deck buses	KLSK	9 903	11 518	13 870	14 811	14 842	11 180	13 397	15 836	14 140	11 782	9 426
Double deck buses	KLSL	2 541	1 589	1 746	1 688	1 185	1 160	599	664	718	538	411

TIME SERIES. Figures for motor vehicles relate to periods of 52 weeks (53 weeks in 1983 and 1988).

Source: Central Statistical Office

Drink and tobacco

8.35 Alcoholic drink
United Kingdom

			1981	1982	1983	1984	1985	1986	1987	1988	1989	1990	1991
Spirits[1]		Thousand hectolitres of alcohol											
Production	KMEA		3 251	3 021	2 898	2 986	3 124	2 966	3 136	3 568	4 211	4 676	4 476
Released for home consumption													
Imported:													
Rum	KMEB	"	80	73	73	75	77	78	81	90	88	..	..
Brandy	KMEC	"	64	66	69	70	77	79	82	90	85	..	..
Other	KMED	"	58	59	65	71	72	74	86	89	85	..	..
Home produced:													
Whisky (mature)[3]	KMEE	"	477	448	445	434	461	456	446	452	430	413	383
Gin	KMEF	"	130	124	137	133	139	131	128	135	124	..	..
Other	KMEG	"	136	122	127	129	148	151	161	179	187	..	..
Total[2]	KMEH	"	945	891	916	912	974	971	983	1 035	1 000	980	912
Beer[4]		Thousand hectolitres											
Production	KMEI		61 721	59 786	60 324	60 105	59 655	59 446	59 906	60 145	60 015	59 653	57 359
Released for home consumption													
Home produced	KMEJ	"	60 024	58 668	59 586	59 241	58 431	57 911	58 519	58 913	58 679	58 026	55 515
Imported	KMEK	"	2 293	2 252	2 646	2 841	3 076	3 302	3 454	4 350	4 533	5 067	5 329
Total	KMEL	"	62 317	60 920	62 232	62 082	61 507	61 213	61 973	63 263	63 212	63 093	60 844
Imported wine/wine of fresh grapes													
Released for home consumption													
Heavy	KMEM	"	1 191	1 074	1 079	1 022	861	559	489	451	406	378	357
Light	KMEN	"	2 941	3 132	3 512	4 152	4 525	5 061	5 474	5 680	5 871	5 893	5 980
Sparkling	KMEO	"	196	193	218	224	257	281	315	352	392	365	317
Total	KMEP	"	4 328	4 399	4 810	5 398	5 644	5 902	6 278	6 483	6 669	6 636	6 654
British wine/made-wine													
Released for home consumption	KMEQ	"	539	509	549	492	538	528	561	593	591	706	702
Cider and perry													
Released for home consumption	KMER	"	2 409	2 899	3 258	3 259	3 174	3 233	3 226	3 103	3 272	3 666	3 738

1 Potable spirits distilled.
2 Breakdown of minor spirits not available for 1990.
3 Before April 1983, the figures represent quantities of all mature home produced spirits.
4 From 1976 the figures take account of brewing at high gravity with the addition of some brewing liquor after fermentation.

Source: HM Customs and Excise

8.36 Tobacco products
United Kingdom

			1981	1982	1983	1984	1985	1986	1987	1988	1989	1990	1991
Released for home consumption													
Cigarettes:		Thousand million											
Home produced	KMFA	"	108.3	100.6	100.6	93.4	88.6	83.3	90.1	87.9	87.5	87.4	85.3
Imported	KMFB	"	1.5	1.8	2.0	6.4	11.1	11.7	12.2	9.4	10.3	10.3	10.3
Total	KMFC	"	109.8	102.3	102.6	99.9	99.7	95.0	102.3	97.3	95.9	97.8	95.6
Cigars:		Million kg.											
Home produced	KMFD	"	2.2	2.3	2.4	2.4	2.3	2.3	2.4	2.4	2.3	2.1	1.9
Imported	KMFE	"	0.7	0.4	0.2	0.2	0.2	0.2	0.2	0.2	0.2	0.2	0.1
Total	KMFF	"	2.9	2.7	2.7	2.5	2.5	2.5	2.6	2.6	2.4	2.3	2.0
Hand-rolling tobacco:													
Home produced	KMFG	"	6.2	6.2	5.9	5.4	5.1	4.8	4.8	4.5	4.3	4.1	4.1
Imported	KMFH	"	–	–	–	–	–	–	–	–	–	–	0.1
Total	KMFI	"	6.2	6.3	5.9	5.4	5.1	4.8	4.8	4.5	4.8	4.1	4.2
Other smoking and chewing tobacco:													
Home produced	KMFJ	"	3.5	3.3	3.1	3.0	2.9	2.7	2.6	2.5	2.2	2.1	2.0
Imported	KMFK	"	–	–	–	–	–	–	–	–	0.1	0.1	0.1
Total	KMFL	"	3.5	3.3	3.1	3.0	2.9	2.7	2.6	2.5	2.6	2.2	2.1

Source: HM Customs and Excise

9 Agriculture, fisheries and food

Agricultural censuses and surveys *(Tables 6.5, 9.3 and 9.5)*

The data in these tables vary between the different countries of the United Kingdom as follows.

The coverage from 1976 to 1979 includes all holdings in the United Kingdom with 40 standard man days or more (a standard man day (smd) represents 8 hours productive work by an adult male worker under average conditions). All holdings with less than 40 smd in Scotland are excluded but in England and Wales and Northern Ireland holdings with less than 40 smd are excluded only if they have less than 4 hectares of crops and grass and no regular whole-time worker.

From 1977 (Table 9.4 from 1980) figure for England and Wales relate to all known agricultural holdings including minor holdings. Data on minor holdings in Scotland and Northern Ireland are excluded but see footnote 2 to Table 9.4.

From 1981 the figures included for Northern Ireland relate to all holdings with one European size Unit (ESU) or more; or 6 hectares or more of total area; or one or more whole-time workers (excluding the owner). This revised threshold resulted in the deletion of 7000 holdings.

The estimated yields of sugar beet and hops (Table 9.4) are obtained from production figures supplied by British Sugar plc, and English Hops plc. In Great Britain potato yields are estimated in consultation with the Potato Marketing Board.

Average weekly earnings and hours of agricultural workers *(Tables 9.7 and 9.8)*

Data on the earnings and hours of agricultural workers have been collected since 1945 through a series of investigations known as the Wages and Employment Enquiry. From January 1991, a postal survey has replaced the Wages and Employment Enquiry for England and Wales. The survey is carried out monthly and analyses the earnings and hours of Agricultural workers from 200 holdings. The analysed results are published in quarterly press notices and annual reports. Summary tables of earnings and hours are also published by the Department of Employment, the Welsh Office Agricultural Department and the Department of Agriculture and Fisheries for Scotland. The survey also provides data used by the Agricultural Wages Board when considering wage claims and by the Ministry in estimating the cost of labour in agriculture for the Annual Review and similar purposes.

Fisheries *(Tables 9.13-9.15)*

Data relating to the weight and value of landings of fish in the United Kingdom (Table 9.13) is generally obtained from sales notes completed at fish market auctions.

Fishing fleet information (Tables 9.14 and 9.15) is obtained from vessel registers maintained by the Ministry of Agriculture, Fisheries and Food in England and Wales and the Department of Agriculture and Fisheries for Scotland.

Estimated food consumption by all households in Great Britain - National Food Survey *(Table 9.16)*

The Sample
In the course of a year the National Food Survey investigates the food budgets of about 7500 households throughout Great Britain. Fieldwork takes place in 52 local authority districts selected so as to be representative of Great Britain as a whole and, from the beginning of 1986, a proportion of the local authorities used are replaced for sampling purposes at the end of each calendar quarter and a description of the sampling methods used in the National Food and Sense Survey is given in the respective Annual Reports: for example, *Household Food Consumption and Expenditure 1990* (HMSO 1991).

Household
A group of persons living in the same dwelling and sharing common catering arrangements. The size of household is defined in terms of the number of persons who spend at least four nights in the household during the week of the Survey *and* also have at least one meal a day from the household food supply on at least four days. The head of the household and the housewife are regarded as persons in *all* cases.

Adult - A person aged 18 years or over.

Child - A person under 18 years of age.

Food purchased
Quantities of all foods purchased during the week for consumption in the home (but including *purchases* of milk at school). The Survey excludes food eaten outside the home (except packed meals prepared at home), chocolate and sugar confectionery, soft drinks, alcoholic drinks, vitamin preparations, and food obtained specifically for consumption by domestic pets. For a few minor miscellaneous items, expenditure is recorded, but not the quantity (eg artificial sweeteners, flavourings, colourings, etc).

Free food
Quantity of food entering the household without payment, for consumption during the Survey week. Milk supplied under the Milk in Schools Scheme is included although it does not actually enter the household. Food grown or produced by the household and stored in bulk is recorded only when it is withdrawn from store.

Consumption
Averaged over a sufficiently large number of households and a sufficiently long period, the average quantity of food purchased *plus* the quantity of 'free' food will equal the average consumption if there is no general change in the level of larder stocks.

Agriculture

9.1 Outputs, inputs and net product at current prices
Calendar years

£ million

		1981	1982	1983	1984	1985	1986	1987	1988	1989	1990	1991[18]
Output[1]												
Cereals												
Wheat	KFKA	855	1 137	1 115	1 461	1 409	1 368	1 264	1 155	1 368	1 417	1 546
Barley	KFKB	811	895	851	930	842	758	692	627	647	599	589
Oats	KFKC	25	28	28	26	28	31	29	31	31	34	35
Rye, mixed corn and triticale	KFKD	2	3	3	3	3	3	3	3	3	4	4
Other receipts[2]	KFKE	–	–	–	–	–	–	2	2	2	1	2
1. Total cereals	KFKF	1 693	2 062	1 996	2 420	2 281	2 159	1 990	1 818	2 052	2 055	2 176
Other crops												
Oilseed rape	KFKG	87	157	174	254	244	271	298	241	279	343	324
Sugar beet	KFKH	192	253	218	251	232	220	223	239	250	272	269
Hops	KFKI	25	29	28	27	16	12	13	13	14	14	18
Peas and beans for stockfeed	KFKJ	32	28	34	51	64	111	109	142	116	121	110
Hay and dried grass	KFKK	18	19	22	21	21	21	16	14	14	22	21
Grass and clover seed	KFKL	13	14	13	21	22	11	14	14	14	14	11
Linseed fodder and other minor crops[3]	KFKM	14	15	19	22	29	39	49	52	45	53	84
2. Total other crops	KFKN	380	514	507	647	627	684	721	714	732	840	836
Potatoes												
3. Total potatoes	KFKO	394	441	473	562	316	430	486	399	489	508	509
Horticulture												
Vegetables[4]	KFKP	607	621	729	814	804	808	959	985	1 028	1 088	1 030
Fruit[4]	KFKQ	187	213	230	242	232	256	243	255	284	298	299
Ornamentals	KFKR	189	205	217	232	251	280	320	389	446	495	503
Other[5]	KFKS	4	3	4	3	4	6	9	7	7	6	5
4. Total horticulture	KFKT	987	1 041	1 179	1 292	1 290	1 349	1 531	1 636	1 766	1 887	1 837
Livestock												
Finished cattle and calves	KFKU	1 661	1 738	1 899	2 049	2 044	1 902	2 069	1 976	2 100	1 973	2 035
Finished sheep and lambs	KFKV	538	598	653	733	766	792	815	903	968	993	1 076
Finished pigs	KFKW	849	909	898	979	946	927	930	881	1 023	1 014	952
Poultry	KFKX	518	607	629	676	696	753	789	805	824	881	878
Other livestock[6]	KFKY	87	91	92	94	104	107	120	125	136	146	150
Other receipts[7]	KFKZ	7	6	4	4	4	4	2	1	–	–	–
5. Total livestock	KFLA	3 660	3 949	4 175	4 535	4 560	4 485	4 725	4 691	5 051	5 007	5 091
Livestock products												
Milk	KFLB	2 097	2 382	2 489	2 331	2 394	2 505	2 433	2 561	2 727	2 802	2 751
Eggs	KFLC	512	498	451	503	461	397	447	397	397	478	439
Clip wool	KFLD	35	34	37	37	42	41	43	48	52	49	45
Other[8]	KFLE	20	21	32	25	23	26	26	29	42	39	45
6. Total livestock products	KFLF	2 664	2 935	3 009	2 896	2 920	2 969	2 950	3 035	3 218	3 368	3 280
Own account capital formation[9]												
Breeding livestock	KFLG	3	28	–7	–28	13	4	–29	33	40	31	–41
Other assets	KFLH	91	109	112	122	116	103	98	115	126	149	149
7. Total own account capital formation	KFLI	94	137	105	93	128	107	69	148	166	180	108
8. Total output	KHWU	9 872	11 078	11 443	12 444	12 121	12 183	12 472	12 441	13 475	13 845	13 836
Other direct receipts												
Set-aside	KFLK	–	–	–	–	–	–	–	–	10	19	27
Milk quota cuts	KFLL	–	–	–	–	–	–	11	57	74	65	60
Milk outgoers	KFLM	–	–	–	2	6	10	11	10	8	2	2
Other receipts	KFLN	52	51	55	42	37	54	23	29	38	44	54
9. Total other direct receipts	KFLO	52	51	55	44	43	64	44	96	130	134	143
10. Total receipts	KFLP	9 924	11 129	11 499	12 489	12 164	12 247	12 516	12 537	13 605	13 979	13 979
Value of physical increase in:												
Work-in-progress[10]	KFLQ	–15	47	–15	–17	–73	–33	–87	–36	–30	–48	–16
Output stocks[10]	KFLR	–74	–19	54	131	–171	–	–44	–8	–3	–8	3
11. Total value of physical increase	KFLS	–89	28	39	114	–244	–32	–131	–44	–93	–56	–13
12. Gross output	KFLT	9 834	11 157	11 537	12 602	11 920	12 214	12 384	12 493	13 512	13 923	13 966

See footnotes on page 177.

Agriculture

9.1 Outputs, inputs and net product at current prices
Calendar years
continued

£ million

		1981	1982	1983	1984	1985	1986	1987	1988	1989	1990	1991[18]
Intermediate Output[11]												
Feed	KFLU	564	728	813	767	678	719	566	575	553	478	586
Seed	KFLV	105	112	134	127	120	126	133	131	137	140	138
13. Total intermediate output	KFLW	668	840	947	894	798	845	699	706	689	618	723
14. Final output	KFLX	9 166	10 317	10 591	11 708	11 122	11 369	11 686	11 787	12 823	13 305	13 243
Inputs												
Expenditure (net of reclaimed VAT)												
Feedingstuffs: compounds	KFLY	1 650	1 870	2 066	1 932	1 789	1 800	1 722	1 833	1 919	2 029	2 071
straights	KFLZ	413	467	491	605	666	653	720	726	680	659	724
others	KFMA	96	138	144	130	83	174	172	172	149	160	162
15. Total feedingstuffs	KFMB	2 159	2 475	2 701	2 667	2 538	2 628	2 614	2 731	2 747	2 848	2 957
Seeds: cereals	KFMC	118	110	119	126	112	122	116	125	126	121	124
other	KFMD	105	127	165	143	143	145	166	155	165	177	169
16. Total seeds	KFME	223	237	284	269	255	268	282	280	291	298	293
Livestock: imported	KFMF	48	53	66	71	68	61	48	57	37	36	27
inter-farm expenses	KFMG	117	132	136	132	138	136	138	144	148	136	142
17. Total livestock (imported and inter-farm expenses)	KFMH	165	184	202	202	206	197	186	201	185	173	169
Fertilisers and lime: straights	KFMI	271	298	348	402	372	317	298	284	298	290	251
compounds	KFMJ	437	419	456	478	462	416	343	348	372	365	346
lime	KFMK	32	37	43	44	38	38	37	36	42	42	41
other	KFML	18	22	21	23	26	28	30	31	33	36	38
18. Total fertilisers and lime	KFMM	758	773	869	947	897	799	708	699	744	732	676
19. Pesticides	KFMN	187	265	306	320	351	349	360	440	482	463	444
Machinery: repairs	KFMO	336	370	398	427	475	515	544	578	605	646	699
fuel and oil	KFMP	335	386	428	431	474	350	292	258	266	300	321
licences	KFMQ	22	26	26	28	31	33	33	33	32	32	35
insurances	KFMR	39	40	40	42	44	51	60	70	72	73	81
other	KFMS	9	10	11	12	13	14	15	15	16	18	20
20. Total machinery	KCOY	741	832	905	940	1 037	963	944	955	992	1 069	1 156
Farm maintenance: occupier	KCOZ	148	169	177	195	203	209	233	238	253	281	295
landlord	KCPA	43	46	51	55	59	62	63	62	61	60	59
21. Total farm maintenance[12]	KCPB	190	215	229	251	262	271	295	300	313	340	354
Miscellaneous expenditure												
Veterinary expenses and medicines	KCPC	99	110	118	122	133	145	152	157	158	168	177
Power and fuel (mainly electricity)	KCPD	123	135	134	136	142	152	155	161	171	175	186
Containers	KCPE	76	87	94	102	106	106	116	123	130	134	128
Sundry equipment	KCPF	109	113	123	132	138	144	148	157	167	173	185
Other[12,13]	KCPG	283	313	336	357	394	422	451	477	528	488	586
22. Total miscellaneous expenditure	KCPH	690	759	804	848	914	970	1 022	1 076	1 154	1 137	1 261
23. Total expenditure	KCPI	5 113	5 740	6 300	6 443	6 459	6 443	6 411	6 681	6 907	7 061	7 310
Value of physical increase in stocks of:												
Purchased feed	KCPJ	33	8	−6	−29	18	41	−27	−23	−10	11	11
Fertilisers	KCPK	20	−10	−62	25	−32	36	−35	−72	14	4	−
24. Total value of physical increase in input stocks	KCPL	53	−2	−67	−4	−14	77	−62	−95	4	15	11
25. Gross input (23 − 24)	KCPM	5 060	5 742	6 367	6 446	6 473	6 366	6 473	6 776	6 903	7 046	7 299
26. Net input (25 − 13)	KCPN	4 392	4 902	5 420	5 553	5 676	5 521	5 774	6 070	6 214	6 428	6 575

See footnotes on page 177.

Agriculture

9.1 Outputs, inputs and net product at current prices (continued)
Calendar years

£ million

		1981	1982	1983	1984	1985	1986	1987	1988	1989	1990	1991[18]
27. Gross product (12-25) or (14-26)	KCPO	4 774	5 416	5 171	6 156	5 447	5 848	5 912	5 717	6 609	6 877	6 667
Depreciation												
Buildings and works: landlord[12]	KCPP	77	75	74	74	76	81	83	87	94	101	101
other	KCPQ	376	378	387	401	434	465	498	525	577	635	672
Plant, machinery and vehicles	KCPR	752	820	856	886	928	910	921	975	1 026	1 040	1 026
28. Total depreciation	KCPS	1 205	1 273	1 317	1 360	1 438	1 456	1 503	1 586	1 696	1 776	1 799
29. Net product (27-28)	KCPT	3 568	4 142	3 854	4 795	4 009	4 392	4 409	4 131	4 913	5 101	4 869
30. Interest[14]	KCPU	513	547	517	593	744	696	649	702	946	1 047	899
31. Net rent[12]	KCPV	88	104	125	141	153	158	161	154	142	130	128
32. Income from agriculture of total labour input (29-30-31)	KCPW	2 967	3 491	3 212	4 061	3 112	3 538	3 599	3 275	3 825	3 924	3 842
Hired labour[15]												
Wages and salaries	KCPX	995	1 078	1 160	1 193	1 293	1 275	1 283	1 330	1 376	1 490	1 543
Insurances	KCPY	125	128	126	124	118	103	102	106	112	120	125
Other	KCPZ	3	4	4	6	7	7	7	7	8	7	7
33. Total hired labour[15]	KCQA	1 123	1 211	1 290	1 323	1 418	1 385	1 392	1 443	1 496	1 618	1 674
34. Total income from farming (32-33)	KCQB	1 845	2 280	1 923	2 739	1 695	2 154	2 207	1 832	2 329	2 306	2 168
35. Total family, partners' and directors' labour[16]	KCQC	523	576	630	646	699	742	765	803	821	888	944
36. Farming income (34-35)[17]	KCQD	1 322	1 704	1 293	2 093	995	1 412	1 442	1 029	1 508	1 418	1 224

1 Output is net of VAT collected on the sale of non-edible products. Figures for total output include subsidies but not 'Other Direct Receipts'.
2 Payments to small scale cereal producers.
3 Root and fodder crop seed, straw, linseed, mustard and other minor crops.
4 Includes the value of the produce of gardens and allotments.
5 Seeds, hedgerow fruits and nuts.
6 Horses, breeding livestock exported, poultry for export, rabbits and game, knacker animals and other minor livestock.
7 Guidance premium for beef and sheepmeat.
8 Honey, goats' milk, exports of eggs for hatching and minor livestock products.
9 This comprises the cost of that part of investment in buildings and works which is physically undertaken by the farmer or farm labour and the value of the physical increase in breeding livestock.
10 Work-in-progress is livestock other than breeding stock. Output stocks comprise cereals, potatoes and some fruits.
11 Sales included in output but subsequently re-purchased and also included within output.
12 Landlords expenses are included within farm maintenance, miscellaneous expenditure and depreciation on buildings and works. Net rent is the rent paid on tenanted land less these landords' expenses and the benefit value of dwellings on that land.
13 Including fees, insurance, telephones and drainage, water and local authority rates (but see reference to farm cottages at [15] below).
14 Interest charges on loans for current farming purposes and buildings and works less interest on money held on short-term deposit.
15 Including employers' national insurance contributions, perquisites and other payments (including the payment by farmers of rates on farm cottages occupied by farm workers and of their community charge).
16 The estimate in respect of family workers, non-principal partners and directors (and their spouses) is calculated on the basis of the earnings of hired workers.
17 The return to farmers and their spouses for their labour, management skills and their own capital invested after providing for depreciation.
18 Forecast.

Source: Agricultural Departments

Agriculture

9.2 Outputs, inputs and net product at constant (1985) prices
United Kingdom - Calendar years

£ million

		1981[1]	1982[1]	1983	1984	1985	1986	1987	1988	1989	1990	1991[1,2]
Output[2]												
Cereals												
Wheat	KFNA	884	1 125	1 008	1 420	1 409	1 367	1 269	1 242	1 458	1 444	1 479
Barley	KFNB	719	732	636	877	842	746	695	639	642	580	572
Oats	KFNC	26	29	25	22	28	31	26	30	32	32	33
Rye, mixed corn and triticale	KFND	3	3	3	3	3	3	3	3	3	4	4
1. Total cereals	KFNE	1 649	1 890	1 671	2 321	2 281	2 146	1 993	1 914	2 136	2 060	2 087
Other crops												
Oilseed rape	KFNF	93	159	154	253	244	261	371	285	268	345	359
Sugar beet	KFNG	213	301	225	271	232	244	240	245	244	237	237
Hops	KFNH	22	25	21	19	16	13	13	12	12	11	14
Peas and beans for stockfeed	KFNI	35	29	33	49	64	88	96	157	119	129	117
Hay and dried grass	KFNJ	20	21	21	20	21	21	22	20	19	22	22
Grass and clover seed	KFNK	22	19	20	20	22	17	16	20	27	24	19
Linseed, fodder and other minor crops[3]	KFNL	17	17	17	20	29	39	35	45	42	56	98
2. Total other crops	KFNM	424	573	490	652	627	683	792	784	726	825	866
Potatoes												
3. Total potatoes	KFNN	313	282	284	277	316	293	279	285	282	276	277
Horticulture												
Vegetables[4]	KFNO	736	768	732	800	804	837	832	896	900	868	866
Fruit[4]	KFNP	216	234	238	250	232	226	224	208	251	227	211
Ornamentals	KFNQ	234	236	236	245	251	253	248	262	270	283	286
Other[5]	KFNR	6	5	5	3	4	5	9	7	7	6	5
4. Total horticulture	KFNS	1 194	1 244	1 210	1 298	1 290	1 321	1 312	1 373	1 427	1 384	1 367
Livestock												
Finished cattle and calves	KFNT	1 878	1 772	1 887	2 053	2 044	1 918	2 024	1 707	1 757	1 803	1 847
Finished sheep and lambs	KFNU	666	675	727	730	766	730	760	836	941	959	1 014
Finished pigs	KFNV	923	955	1 003	934	946	971	984	1 004	930	938	975
Poultry	KFNW	598	653	648	681	696	741	800	850	819	840	871
Other livestock[6]	KFNX	113	110	106	104	108	107	112	113	116	117	117
5. Total livestock	KFNY	4 177	4 173	4 370	4 501	4 560	4 467	4 680	4 509	4 562	4 657	4 824
Livestock products												
Milk	KFNZ	2 365	2 497	2 571	2 417	2 394	2 427	2 303	2 250	2 216	2 265	2 191
Eggs	KFOA	578	555	512	465	461	442	446	439	385	407	420
Clip wool	KFOB	40	39	42	40	42	43	46	50	54	54	54
Other[7]	KFOC	23	20	30	24	23	18	23	24	33	31	31
6. Total livestock products	KFOD	2 998	3 109	3 153	2 946	2 920	2 930	2 817	2 762	2 689	2 756	2 696
Own account capital formation[8]												
Breeding livestock	KFOE	4	28	−7	−29	13	5	−29	32	36	27	−34
Other assets	KFOF	126	139	129	133	116	100	91	101	101	118	118
7. Total own account capital formation	KFOG	129	166	122	104	128	105	63	133	138	145	84
8. Total output	KFOH	10 903	11 489	11 301	12 098	12 121	11 944	11 935	11 760	11 959	12 102	12 201
9. Total other direct receipts	KFOI	58	54	56	44	43	63	42	86	109	112	121
10. Total receipts	KFOJ	10 963	11 542	11 357	12 142	12 164	12 006	11 977	11 846	12 068	12 215	12 322
Value of physical increase in:												
Work in progress[9]	KFOK	−17	49	−16	−17	−73	−33	−90	−36	−28	−43	−14
Output stocks[9]	KFOL	−84	−20	63	156	−171	3	−43	−8	−6	−7	4
11. Total value of physical increase	KFOM	−101	−29	47	139	−244	−31	−134	−44	−84	−49	−10
12. Gross output	KFON	10 832	11 567	11 404	12 281	11 920	11 975	11 844	11 802	11 984	12 166	12 312

See footnotes on page 179.

Agriculture

9.2 Outputs, inputs and net product at constant (1985) prices
United Kingdom - Calendar years

continued

£ million

		1981[1]	1982[1]	1983	1984	1985	1986	1987	1988	1989	1990	1991[12]
Intermediate output[10]												
Feed	KFOO	501	607	619	727	678	715	576	594	572	462	564
Seed	KFOP	114	112	123	116	120	117	120	124	116	113	107
13. Total intermediate output	KFOQ	613	720	742	843	798	833	696	718	689	575	671
14. Final output (12 - 13)	KFOR	10 242	10 856	10 662	11 438	11 122	11 143	11 148	11 084	11 295	11 591	11 641
Inputs												
Expenditure (net of reclaimed VAT)												
Feedingstuffs	KFOS	2 442	2 646	2 691	2 548	2 538	2 692	2 633	2 622	2 536	2 580	2 640
Seeds	KFOT	242	239	262	246	255	250	256	264	248	240	228
Livestock (imported and inter-farm expenses)	KFOU	200	204	210	207	206	205	194	204	186	173	161
Fertilisers and lime	KFOV	867	848	903	958	897	908	890	845	916	887	836
Pesticides	KFOW	210	287	330	334	351	349	338	399	418	365	316
Machinery: repairs	KFOX	469	474	471	467	475	484	489	492	488	480	484
fuel and oil	KFOY	480	483	485	476	474	468	445	432	411	402	406
other	KFOZ	89	89	89	89	89	88	87	85	84	82	81
Total machinery	KFPA	1 039	1 046	1 046	1 031	1 037	1 041	1 020	1 009	983	964	972
Farm maintenance[11]	KFPB	258	268	263	269	262	258	267	267	260	271	270
Miscellaneous expenditure	KFPC	900	898	891	898	914	904	918	907	923	857	901
15. Total expenditure	KFPD	6 123	6 420	6 595	6 491	6 459	6 607	6 517	6 517	6 470	6 336	6 324
16. Total value of physical increase in input stocks	KFPE	56	−2	−58	−17	−14	93	−70	−103	9	16	10
17. Gross input (15 - 16)	KFPF	6 052	6 414	6 652	6 507	6 473	6 514	6 586	6 620	6 461	6 320	6 314
18. Net input (17 - 13)	KFPG	5 463	5 693	5 910	5 664	5 676	5 681	5 891	5 902	5 772	5 746	5 644
19. Gross product (12 - 17) or (14 - 18)	KFPH	4 741	5 105	4 752	5 774	5 447	5 461	5 257	5 182	5 523	5 845	5 998
20. Total depreciation[11]	KFPI	1 372	1 397	1 414	1 420	1 438	1 436	1 422	1 389	1 399	1 365	1 310
21. Net product (19 - 20)	KFPJ	3 365	3 696	3 338	4 354	4 009	4 026	3 835	3 794	4 124	4 480	4 688

1 For this year the required national accounts method of calculating totals and sub-totals means that they do not necessarily equate to the sum of the individual items within them.
2 Output is net of VAT collected on the sale of non-edible products. Figures for total output include subsidies but not 'Other direct receipts'.
3 Root and fodder crop seed, straw, linseed, mustard and other minor crops.
4 Includes the value of the produce of gardens and allotments.
5 Seeds, hedgerow fruits and nuts.
6 Horses, breeding livestock exported, poultry for export, rabbits and game, knacker animals and other minor livestock and the Guidance premium for beef and sheepmeat.
7 Honey, goats' milk, exports of eggs for hatching and minor livestock products.
8 This comprises the cost of that part of investment in buildings and works which is physically undertaken by the farmer or farm labour and the value of the physical increase in breeding livestock.
9 Work-in-progress is livestock other than breeding livestock. Output stocks comprise cereals, potatoes and some fruits.
10 Sales included in output but subsequently re-purchased and so reappearing as input.
11 Landlords' expenses are included within farm maintenance, miscellaneous expenditure and depreciation on buildings and works.
12 Forecast.

Source: Agricultural Departments

Agriculture

9.3 Agriculture-land use
United Kingdom
Area at the June census[1]

Thousand hectares

			1981	1982	1983	1984	1985	1986	1987	1988	1989	1990	1991
Cereals	KFDA		1 491	1 663	1 695	1 939	1 902	1 997	1 994	1 886	2 083	2 013	1 980
Wheat	KFDB		2 327	2 222	2 143	1 978	1 965	1 916	1 830	1 878	1 652	1 516	1 393
Oats	KFDB		2 327	2 222	2 143	1 978	1 965	1 916	1 830	1 878	1 652	1 516	1 393
Mixed corn	KFDD		11	10	8	8	7	7	6	5	5	4	4
Rye	KFDE		6	6	7	6	8	7	7	7	7	8	9
Potatoes													
Early crop	KFDF	KGRS	24	25	24	198	191	178	177	180	175	177	177
Main crop	KFDG		167	167	171								
Fodder crops													
Field Beans[2]	KFDH		45	40	34	32	45	60	91	154	129	139	131
Turnips and swedes[3]	KFDI		79	71	66	64	62	59	56	54	51	46	42
Fodder beet and mangolds[3]	KFDJ		5	5	5	8	12	13	13	12	11	12	13
Maize for threshing or stockfeeding	KFDK		18	16	15	16	20	23	24	24	25	34	44
Kale, cabbage, savoys, kohl rabi, Rape for stockfeeding	KFDL		49	43	40	39	37	33	30	28	25	24	25
Peas harvested dry[4]	KFDM		..	..	29	56	92	91	117	107	86	77	72
Other crops for stockfeeding	KFDN		26	31	25	22	20	20	15	14	10	9	10
Horitcultural crops[5]													
Orchards and small fruit	KFDO		62	60	58	56	55	53	53	52	51	50	48
Vegetables grown in the open:													
Brussels sprouts	KFDP		13	13	11	11	11	11	10	10	8	7	8
Cabbage (all kinds), kale, cauliflower and broccoli[6]	KFDQ		26	27	25	25	24	26	25	26	27	26	26
Carrots	KGRT	KGRU	14	14	13	14	14	14	13	15	15	15	16
Parsnips		KGRV		3	2	3	3	3	3	3	3	3	3
Turnips and swedes[7]	KFDS		3	3	..	..	..	..	..	..	..	..	..
Beetroot	KFDT		2	2	2	2	2	2	2	2	2	2	2
Onions, salad and dry bulb	KFDU		8	9	8	8	9	9	9	9	8	9	9
Beans (broad, runner and French)	KFDV		11	12	11	10	11	10	10	10	10	8	9
Green peas	KFDW		55	56	47	46	53	52	42	46	48	51	46
Peas, for harvesting dry[8]	KFDX		28	27	18	..	..	..	..	..	..	..	..
Celery	KFDY		1	1	1	1	1	1	1	1	1	1	1
Sweet corn	KFEA		..	..	1	1	1	1	1	1	1	1	2
Hardy nursery stock bulbs and other flowers grown in the open:													
Hardy nursery stock	KFEC		7	7	7	7	7	7	7	8	8	8	8
Bulbs	KFED		5	5	4	4	4	4	4	5	5	5	5
Other flowers	KFEE		1	1	1	1	1	1	1	1	1	1	1
Area under glass	KFEF		2	2	2	2	2	2	2	2	2	2	2
Other crops													
Sugar beet	KFEG		210	204	199	199	205	205	202	201	197	194	196
Rape grown for oilseed	KFEH		125	174	222	269	296	299	388	347	321	390	440
Hops[9]	KEEI		..	..	..	..	201	288	290	205	205	560	3 405
Other crops not for stockfeeding	KEEJ		..	..	..	..	928	1 050	1 264	1 564	5 095	10 820	27 500
Bare fallow	KEEK		..	..	..	..	861	897	649	393	350	365	530
Total tillage	KEEL						251	210	210	163	215	890	915
All grasses under five years old	KFEM		1 911	1 859	1 846	1 794	1 796	1 723	1 691	1 613	1 534	1 580	1 581
I arable	KFEN		6 982	6 986	6 970	6 990	7 061	7 011	7 004	6 924	6 736	6 657	6 601
All grass five years old and over	KFEO		5 103	5 097	5 107	5 105	5 019	5 077	5 112	5 161	5 251	5 263	5 267
Total crops and grass	KFEP		12 085	12 083	12 078	12 095	12 080	12 088	12 116	12 085	11 987	11 921	11 868
Rough grazings													
Sole rights	KEEQ		14 181	14 842	14 373	14 539	16 186	14 167	13 218	12 007	9 626	7 299	5 937
Common (estimated)	KEER		13 614	14 352	14 304	14 192	15 024	12 965	12 354	11 541	9 784	6 852	6 506
Woodland on agricultural holdings	KEES		9 860	10 857	13 455	12 985	13 627	11 791	16 370	18 369	21 637	21 723	..
ll other land on agricultural holdings	KFET		211	217	227	218	223	227	225	229	273	323	344
Total area of agricultural land	KFEV		24 089	24 088	24 088	24 088	24 085	24 086	24 086	24 086	24 086	24 086	24 086
Total area of the United Kingdom	KFEU		18 808	18 783	18 735	18 720	18 703	18 676	18 622	18 575	18 553	18 542	18 487

1 Figures include estimates for minor holdings not surveyed at the June census in England and Wales. See notes on page 174.
2 Prior to 1986 collected as 'Beans for stockfeeding' in England and Wales.
3 See footnote 5 to Table 9.4.
4 Includes 'Peas for harvesting dry for both human consumption and stockfeeding' from 1984 onwards.
5 Figures relate to land usage at 1 June and are not necessarily good indicators of production as for some crops more than one crop may be obtained in each season or a crop may overlap two seasons.
6 Excludes kale from 1983 which is included with 'Other vegetables'.
7 From 1983 included with 'Other vegetables'.
8 Following a change in definition in 1986 'Peas for harvesting dry for human consumption' is not included with 'Peas harvested dry for stockfeeding'. Data from 1984 reflect this change.
9 Collected as England only.

Source: Agricultural Departments

Agriculture

9.4 Estimated quantity of crops and grass harvested[1,2]
United Kingdom

Thousand tonnes

		1981	1982	1983	1984	1985	1986	1987	1988	1989	1990	1991	1992
Cereals													
Wheat	KFQA	8 707	10 317	10 802	14 969	12 046	13 911	11 940	11 751	14 033	14 033	14 363	..
Barley	KFQB	10 227	10 956	9 980	11 072	9 740	10 014	9 229	8 778	8 073	7 911	7 627	..
Oats	KFQC	619	575	466	517	614	503	454	548	529	530	523	..
Mixed corn for threshing	KFQD	44	39	35	35	31	29	26	22	18	17	15	..
Rye for threshing	KFQE	24	27	24	28	35	32	32	34	36	40	49	..
Maize for threshing[3]	KFQF	..[4]	..[4]	..[4]	..[4]	..[4]	..[4]	..	..	..	..	..	..
Potatoes													
Early crop[4,8]	KFQG	383	432	322	396	401	361	391	420	366	437	359	..
Main crop[4,8]	KFQH	5 732	6 498	5 527	6 982	6 462	6 051	6 306	6 470	5 884	6 037	5 906	..
Fodder crops													
Beans for stockfeeding	KFQI	125	120	105	125	155	230	294	–	..	..	..	..
Turnips, swedes[5]	KFQJ	4 795	4 575	3 655	3 960	3 300	3 855	3 451	3 325	2 720	..	..	..
Fodder beet and mangolds[5]	KFQK	320	370	295	570	815	845	782	735	600	..	..	..
Maize for threshing or stockfeeding[3]	KFQL	635	635	550	580	770	915	782	875	940	..	..	..
Rape for stockfeeding	KFQM	..	..	..	..	..	..	..	..	..	..	..	..
Kale, cabbage, savoys and kohl rabi	KFQN	2 195	1 985	1 660	1 805	1 555	1 380	1 320	735	600	..	..	..
Peas harvested dry for stockfeeding	KFQP	..	..	85	170	215	330	310	–	..	..	..	..
Other crops													
Sugar beet[6]	KFQQ	7 395	10 005	7 495	9 015	7 715	8 120	7 992	8 150	8 115	..	..	..
Rape grown for oilseed	KFQR	325	580	565	925	895	965	1 326	–	..	..	..	..
Hops	KFQS	9	10	9	8	6	5	5	5	5	5	..	..
Hay[7]													
From all grasses under five years old	KFQT	6 775	6 550	6 000	5 700	4 650	4 675	..	..	..	..	..	..
From all grasses five years old and over	KFQU	..	..	..	..	..	..	..	..	..	..	..	..
Horticultural crops													
Vegetables grown in the open													
Brussels sprouts	KFQW	197	223	154	169	152	168	173	165	134	102	105	..
Cabbage (including savoys and spring greens)	KFQX	546	610	518	670	683	688	698	743	704	659	655	..
Cauliflowers	KFQY	325	353	299	344	356	360	370	376	364	332	342	..
Carrots	KFQZ	711	725	555	572	600	635	549	675	587	573	641	..
Parsnips	KFRA	53	55	51	57	62	68	64	70	55	54	59	..
Turnips and swedes	KFRB	109	145	135	143	140	163	161	171	137	158	162	..
Beetroot	KFRC	97	105	94	115	114	95	104	105	97	93	99	..
Onions, Dry bulb	KFRD	232	231	175	238	268	247	298	299	223	235	231	..
Onions, Salad	KFRE	25	27	25	22	25	30	31	30	27	24	28	..
Leeks	KFRF	40	43	44	53	60	71	72	71	74	70	72	..
Broad beans	KFRG	17	19	17	21	19	14	13	15	15	16	24	..
Runner beans including French	KFRH	69	92	65	77	65	67	52	56	48	30	41	41
Peas, Green for market	KFRI	25	28	23	27	26	20	14	14	10	9	9	9
Peas, Green for processing	KFRJ	277	238	198	241	206	239	229	226	229	252	254	234
Celery	KFRK	50	51	46	57	53	65	53	58	56	49	54	54
Lettuce	KFRL	134	161	155	153	166	158	174	194	175	167	167	..
Rhubarb	KFRM	41	39	29	26	26	28	31	27	25	26	24	..
Protected crops													
Tomatoes	KFRN	125	121	121	129	125	131	123	130	152	139	141	..
Cucumbers	KFRO	54	56	61	68	71	76	81	99	101	105	133	..
Lettuce	KFRP	37	45	49	48	49	50	47	52	49	51	50	..
Fruit crops													
Total Dessert Apples	KFRQ	152	216	186	184	161	163	165	134	253	158	173	..
Total Culinary Apples	KFRR	80	147	126	163	145	139	123	134	185	152	157	..
Pears	KFRS	49	40	54	48	51	47	66	32	43	37	39	..
Plums	KFRT	16	34	36	34	24	33	36	23	11	8	25	..
Cherries	KFRU	3	7	3	5	5	4	4	2	3	2	2	..
Soft fruit	KFRV	105	109	124	114	111	109	107	104	96	94	101	..

1 UK gross production in calendar years; for horticultural crops and potatoes it is in crop years.
2 Except for sugar beet and hops, the production area for England and Wales is the area returned at the June census together with estimates for very small holdings (known as minor holdings). In Scotland and Northern Ireland the area returned at June is also the production area except that estimates for minor holdings are included in Scotland for potatoes and in Nothern Ireland for barley, oats and potatoes.
3 From 1979 maize for threshing is included with maize for stockfeeding.
4 Revised basis of calculation adopted which prevents direct comparison with post - 1980 figures and earlier years.
5 Before 1977 fodder beet was included with turnips and swedes for stockfeeding. In 1977, as a result of changes in the census categories, fodder beet was included with mangolds in England and Wales but continued to be included with turnips and swedes for stockfeeding in Scotland and Northern Ireland. Scotland collected fodder beet separately for the first time in 1986.
6 The production area for sugar beet is provided by British Sugar plc.
7 The production of hay in England and Wales is calculated from the area cut for hay and actually harvested and does not include the area mown for silage, drying or seed; the production of hay in Scotland and Northern Ireland is calculated from the area cut for hay only and does not include grass mown for silage or drying.
8 Potatoes for 1990 - Provisional figures only.

Source: Agricultural Departments

Agriculture

9.5 Cattle, sheep, pigs and poultry on agricultural holdings[1]
United Kingdom - At June each year

Thousands

		1981	1982	1983	1984	1985	1986	1987	1988	1989	1990	1991
Cattle and calves:												
Dairy herd	KFCT	3 191	3 250	3 333	3 281	3 150	3 138	3 042	2 911	2 865	2 847	2 770
Beef herd	KFCU	1 420	1 389	1 358	1 351	1 333	1 308	1 343	1 373	1 495	1 599	1 666
Heifers in calf (first calf)	KFCV	863	851	847	811	874	879	774	834	793	757	733
Bulls for service	KFCW	84	84	83	80	78	76	74	75	78	82	81
Other cattle:												
Two years old and over	KFCX	963	937	904	905	852	769	732	726	733	722	678
One year old and under two	KFCY	3 041	3 057	3 059	3 069	3 012	2 819	2 749	2 669	2 600	2 654	2 581
Six months old and under one year	KFCZ	1 876	1 890	1 924	1 949	1 905	1 876	1 844	1 702	1 775	1 746	1 695
Under six months old	KFSA	1 699	1 786	1 783	1 768	1 707	1 668	1 599	1 581	1 637	1 652	1 662
Total	KFSB	13 138	13 244	13 290	13 213	12 911	12 533	12 158	11 872	11 977	12 059	11 866
Sheep and lambs:												
Breeding ewes	KFSC	12 528	12 909	13 310	13 648	13 893	14 252	14 780	15 461	16 154	16 760	16 944
Rams for service	KFSD	358	366	383	393	406	419	437	461	491	500	503
Other sheep	KFSE	3 584	3 748	3 764	3 680	3 763	3 961	4 107	4 433	4 740	4 515	4 232
Lambs under one year old	KFSF	15 628	16 044	16 612	17 080	17 566	18 384	19 377	20 587	21 582	22 023	21 942
Total	KFSG	32 097	33 067	34 069	34 802	35 628	37 016	38 701	40 942	42 967	43 799	43 621
Pigs:												
Breeding herd	KFSH	836	864	856	800	828	824	820	804	757	769	786
Boars for service	KFSI	43	45	45	42	44	44	44	43	42	43	45
Gilts not yet in pig	KFSJ	87	89	82	77	80	79	81	73	74	85	89
Barren sows for fattening[2]	KFSK	11	12	15	12	12	12	11	12	10	10	10
Other pigs												
110 Kg and over[2]	KFSL	90	117	100	91	89	80	67	62	45	51	40
80 Kg and under 110 Kg	KFSM	638	630	605	599	589	603	615	621	613	620	652
50 Kg and under 80 Kg	KFSN	1 776	1 824	1 868	1 787	1 813	1 863	1 890	1 898	1 779	1 741	1 767
20 Kg and under 50 Kg	KFSO	2 227	2 281	2 362	2 198	2 260	2 270	2 253	2 263	2 131	2 109	2 143
Under 20 Kg	KFSP	2 119	2 163	2 241	2 082	2 151	2 163	2 160	2 204	2 058	2 022	2 065
Total	KFSQ	7 828	8 023	8 174	7 689	7 865	7 937	7 942	7 980	7 509	7 449	7 596
Poultry:												
Fowls:												
Growing pullets	KFSR	14 219	14 766	11 828	12 536	12 503	12 502	12 230	11 236	9 411	10 452	11 016
Laying flock	KFSS	44 473	44 792	41 127	40 573	39 538	38 096	38 498	37 389	33 957	33 468	33 273
Breeding flock	KFST	6 117	6 457	6 012	6 396	6 104	6 334	7 146	6 879	6 788	7 107	7 238
Table birds	KFSU	57 830	60 075	58 887	59 341	61 311	63 807	70 754	75 305	70 042	73 588	75 701
Total	KFSV	122 639	126 091	117 854	118 846	119 456	120 740	128 628	130 809	120 198	124 615	127 228
Ducks[3]	KFSW KGRW	1 333	1 443	1 566	1 530	1 654	1 747	1 757	1 836	2 101	2 216	2 191
Geese[3]	KFSX	148	157									
Turkeys	KFSY	8 167	7 672	8 198	7 134	7 864	..	..	..	..	..	..
Total	KFSZ	132 286	135 363	127 618	127 507	128 968	..	..	..	..	..	..

1 Figures from 1979 onwards include estimates for minor holdings not surveyed at the June census in England and Wales. See notes on page 173. Excludes Scotland except for years 1979, 1983 and 1984.
2 Barren sows for fattening in Northern Ireland are included with 'all other pigs weighing 110 Kg and over'.
3 Excludes data for Scotland 1978, 1980, 1981, 1982.

Source: Agricultural Departments

9.6 Forestry
End of period

Agriculture

Area - thousand hectares, Volume - million cubic metres

		1980/81	1981/82	1982/83	1983/84	1984/85	1985/86	1986/87	1987/88	1988/89	1989/90	1990/91	1991/92
		Years ending 31 March											
Forest area[1]													
United Kingdom	KUAA	2 121	2 142	2 233	2 258	2 277	2 301	2 328	2 368	2 364	2 400	2 410	2 425
Great Britain	KUAB	2 054	2 075	2 165[5]	2 189	2 207	2 230	2 256	2 285	2 291	2 327	2 336	2 350
Northern Ireland	KUAC	67	67	68	69	70	71	72	73	73	73	74	75
Forestry Commission (Great Britain)													
Productive woodland	KUAD	896	905	909	902	892	889	890	888	888	865[6]	859	855
Plantations and plantable land acquired during year[2]	KUAE	1.1	2.1	-3.0	-13.7	-15.3	-7.3	-3.7	-4.7	-2.5	-4.5	-0.8	-4.2
New planting[3]	KUAF	11.6	11.0	9.0	8.4	5.2	4.3	5.3	5.0	4.1	4.1	3.5	3.1
Replanting[3]	KUAG	5.0	5.5	5.8	6.7	6.0	7.3	8.0	8.1	8.5	7.9	7.7	8.3
Volume of timber removed[4]	KUAH	2.5	2.7	2.8	3.0	2.9	3.1	3.2	3.4	3.6	3.6	3.6	3.9
Total estates	KUAI	1 264	1 259	1 251	1 209	1 181	1 166	1 157	1 148	1 143	1 140	1 133	1 128
Private forestry (Great Britain)													
Productive woodland	KUAJ	873	886	1 084[5]	1 116	1 145	1 171	1 195	1 227	1 231	1 266	1 281	1 298
New planting[3]	KUAK	8.7	12.6	12.5	16.9	16.6	19.4	19.4	24.0	25.4	15.6	15.5	14.3
Replanting[3]	KUAL	3.3	3.5	3.2	3.2	3.2	4.6	4.6	5.0	4.9	6.3	7.1	7.9
Volume of timber removed[4]	KUAM	2.3	2.0	2.2	1.8	2.0	2.2	2.4	2.6	3.0	3.0	3.0	2.8

		1980	1981/82	1982/83	1983/84	1984/85	1985/86	1986/87	1987/88	1988/89	1989/90	1990/91	1991/92
State afforestation in Northern Ireland													
Land under plantation	KUAN	53.9	54.4	55.2	56.3	56.6	57.3	57.9	58.4	58.3	58.5	58.8	60.6
Plantable land acquired during year	KUAO	0.8	0.3	0.6	0.4	0.1	0.2	0.5	0.4	0.4	0.6	0.4	0.3
Total area planted during year[3]	KUAP	1.1	1.1	1.2	1.1	1.0	1.2	1.0	1.0	1.0	1.0	1.0	0.9
Total estates	KUAQ	71.5	71.9	72.5	73.2	73.3	73.5	73.9	74.1	74.3	74.6	74.8	75.1

1 Includes unproductive woodland.
2 Net area acquired.
3 Total area now shows areas of New planting (planting on ground not previously carrying forest) and areas of Replanting (replacing trees after felling).
4 Calendar year ending previous December.
5 The apparent increase in 1982/83 ia a result of data from the Census of Woodlands and Trees becoming available. The change is entirely in the private sector of the industry.
6 The apparent decrease in 1989/90 is mainly the result of re-classification of certain woodland types within the Forestry Commission.

Sources: Forestry Commission; Department of Agriculture (Northern Ireland)

9.7 Average weekly earnings[1] and hours of agricultural workers
Great Britain

		1980	1981	1982	1983	1984	1985	1986	1987	1988	1989	1990	1991
Men[2]													
Earnings	KCQE	86.26	96.52	106.87	117.02	123.11	134.67	141.32	148.61	154.62	167.33	187.28	207.03
Hours	KCQF	46.4	46.9	46.7	46.7	46.2	46.9	46.8	46.6	47.1	46.6	46.8	47.3
Youths[3]													
Earnings	KCQG	56.66	62.15	69.40	76.02	80.20	85.81	89.83	95.34	98.20	109.56	122.58	129.99
Hours	KCQH	44.8	44.9	45.0	45.5	44.7	44.8	45.5	45.9	44.8	45.1	46.4	45.1
Females													
Earnings	KCQI	65.53	70.35	80.36	87.70	93.47	102.06	107.77	121.78	124.82	137.45	153.70	157.15
Hours	KCQJ	42.1	41.7	42.9	42.6	41.7	42.7	42.6	42.6	42.8	43.5	43.3	42.6

1 Total earnings of hired regular whole-time workers, including payments-in-kind valued, where applicable, in accordance with Agricultural Wages Orders.
2 Aged 20 and over.
3 Aged under 20 years.

Source: Agricultural Departments

9.8 Distribution of regular whole-time hired men in agriculture by earnings band in Great Britain 1991

	General farm workers	Foremen and grieves	Dairy cowmen	All other stockmen	Tractor drivers	Horticultural workers	All Hired men
Less than £120.00	2.1	0.0	1.1	1.6	0.0	1.5	1.3
£120.00 - £149.99	13.0	0.0	0.0	4.4	7.8	35.2	10.1
£150.00 - £179.99	28.5	14.3	8.6	28.3	30.1	9.3	24.3
£180.00 - £209.99	27.9	20.2	13.5	24.4	18.6	24.3	23.0
£210.00 - £239.99	14.9	21.9	21.4	15.2	15.5	14.8	16.2
£240.00 - £269.99	7.0	15.4	19.6	12.4	12.0	8.9	10.5
£270.00 - £299.99	2.7	9.7	11.8	5.0	8.2	2.9	5.7
£300.00 and over	3.9	18.6	23.9	8.9	8.1	2.9	8.9
Average weekly earnings (£)	192.81	246.37	248.34	208.78	212.79	170.25	207.03

Source: Agricultural Departments

Agriculture

9.9 Sales for food of agricultural produce and livestock
United Kingdom

		Unit	1980	1981	1982	1983	1984	1985	1986	1987	1988	1989	1990	1991
Cereals:														
Wheat[1]	KCQK	Thousand tonnes	2 628	3 222	3 196	3 398	3 698	3 606	3 265	3 931	3 395	4 228	4 347	4 252
Barley	KCQL	"	3 530	5 142	4 316	4 399	5 584	4 486	5 656	4 791	4 560	5 026	3 791	3 849
Oats[2]	KCQM	"	121	139	136	116	125	145	162	161	196	239	222	209
Potatoes[3]	KCQN	"	5 146	5 123	4 855	4 934	4 868	5 241	5 197	4 980	5 067	5 027	4 996	5 011
Milk:														
For consumption as liquid milk	KCQO	"	7 196	7 082	7 001	6 978	6 958	6 898	6 851	6 812	6 792	6 793	6 780	6 745
For manufacture[4]	KCQP	"	7 986	7 992	8 928	9 449	8 472	8 350	8 597	7 806	7 429	7 146	7 403	6 901
Total	KCQQ	Million litres	15 182	15 084	15 943	16 442	15 446	15 263	15 460	14 630	14 234	13 985	14 197	13 664
Eggs in shell[5]	KCQR	Million dozens	1 104	1 054	1 036	981	935	912	886	884	876	770	813	841
Animals slaughtered:														
Cattle and calves:														
Cattle	KCQS	"	4 110	3 929	3 536	3 811	4 180	4 185	3 864	4 047	3 345	3 414	3 478	3 567
Calves	KCQT	"	145	120	94	117	133	101	79	66	35	28	46	50
Total	KCQU	Thousands	4 255	4 049	3 629	3 928	4 313	4 286	3 943	4 114	3 380	3 442	3 524	3 616
Sheep and lambs	KCQV	"	14 316	13 978	13 894	15 068	14 953	15 893	15 473	15 762	17 128	19 618	20 012	20 940
Pigs:														
For bacon:														
Used wholly	KCQW	"	2 042	1 811	1 786	1 866	1 788	1 720	1 726	2 156	2 034	1 966	1 903	14 082
Used in part	KCQX	"	4 046	4 053	3 686	3 966	4 040	4 095	4 087	3 592	3 494	3 449	3 281	..
Other uses	KCQY	"	8 208	8 673	9 230	9 717	8 791	9 164	9 454	9 721	9 872	8 767	8 694	..
Sows and boars	KCQZ	"	328	329	353	440	319	327	342	339	384	325	325	366
Total	KCRA	"	14 624	14 865	15 055	15 989	14 938	15 305	15 609	15 807	15 784	14 514	14 203	14 448
Poultry:[6] slaughtered	KCRB	Millions	441	442	473	460	484	502	521	554	588	542	566	588

TIME SERIES. The figures for cereals and for animals slaughtered relate to periods of 52 weeks (53 weeks in 1981 and 1987).

1 Flour millers' receipts of home-grown wheat.
2 Oatmeal millers' receipts of home-grown oats.
3 Human consumption of UK produced potatoes.
4 The totals of liquid consumption and milk used for manufacture may not add up to the total sales because of adjustments for waste in transit and exports.
5 Includes duck eggs.
6 Total fowls, ducks, geese and turkeys.

Source: Ministry of Agriculture, Fisheries and Food

9.10 Stocks of food and feedingstuffs[1]
United Kingdom
At end-December in each year

Thousand tonnes

		1980	1981	1982	1983	1984	1985	1986	1987	1988	1989	1990	1991
Wheat and flour (as wheat)	KCRC	1 164	927	813	909	931	1 021	1 254	1 055	918	918	860	647
Barley (GB only)	KCRD	1 151	1 157	1 003	971	1 118	975	1 154	1 202	1 127	1 043	1 120	864
Maize	KCRE	202	145	142	122	93	61	39	54	64	70	41	34
Oilcake and meal[2]	KCRF	119	83	170	158	168	205	202	214	190	148	152	..
Oilseeds and nuts (crude oil equivalent)	KCRG	23	23	27	29	23	37	39	36	26	24	28	21
Vegetable oil (as crude oil)	KCRI	81	64	79	63	63	71	75	95	86	85	109	89
Marine oil (as crude oil)	KCRJ	48	40	54	44	51	42	22	16	12	11	9	11
Butter[3]	KCRK	90	75	111	177	231	264	323	220	82	55	74	65
Imported meat and offal[4]	KCRL	50	34	60	110	131	182	144	136	110	85	139	212
Raw coffee[5]	KCRM	6	9	8	5	11	11	8	8	8	7	11	10
Tea[6]	KCRN	92	72	67	55	62	56	66	51	50	51	48	43
Sugar	KCRO	1 114	1 010	1 013	917	1 015	869	908	899	978	860	824	824
Chocolate and sugar confectionery[7]	KCRP	70.4	68.5	67.8	70.6	73.7	62.5	64.5	63.0	..	..	..	..

1 Recorded stocks, including stocks in bond or held by the main processors.
2 Excluding castor meal, cocoa cake and meal.
3 In addition to stocks in public cold stores surveyed by MAFF, closing stocks include all intervention stocks in private cold stores.
4 For meat and offals, from 1983 the figure represents imported and home-produced stocks.
5 Including manufacturers' stocks and additional public warehouses.
6 Including stocks held by primary wholesalers.
7 Manufacturers' stocks only.

Source: Ministry of Agriculture, Fisheries and Food

9.11 Processed food and animal feedingstuffs: production
United Kingdom

Thousand tonnes

		1981	1982	1983	1984	1985	1986	1987	1988	1989	1990	1991
Flour milling:												
Wheat milling: total	KFTA	4 753	4 616	4 478	5 044	4 749	4 830	4 919	5 112	5 032	4 875	4 790
Home produced	KFTB	3 178	3 172	3 256	3 948	3 614	3 082	3 825	3 356	4 161	4 273	4 180
Imported	KFTC	1 575	1 444	1 222	1 096	1 135	1 748	1 094	1 756	871	605	610
Flour produced	KFTD	3 596	3 504	3 426	3 608	3 647	3 702	3 874	3 973	3 928	3 879	3 846
Offals produced	KFTE	1 174	1 121	1 050	1 076	1 092	1 107	1 067	1 157	1 076	999	969
Oat milling:												
Oats milled by oatmeal millers	KFTF	144	138	144	144	148	157	161	183	221	230	211
Products of oat milling	KFTG	85	82	81	87	89	96	100	109	129	133	123
Seed crushing:												
Oilseeds and nuts processed	KFTH	1 724	1 706	1 342	1 188	1 213	1 272	1 526	1 870	1 725	1 877	1 720
Crude oil produced, including production of maize oil	KFTI	449	431	398	383	407	431	561	659	589	630	597
Oilcake and meal produced, excluding castor meal, cocoa cake and meal	KFTJ	1 241	1 240	945	790	841	823	923	1 162	1 077	1 193	1 077
Production of home-killed meat: total including meat subsequently canned	KFTK	2 188	2 107	2 264	2 318	2 353	2 260	2 366	2 220	2 215	2 277	2 352
Beef	KFTL	1 053	961	1 046	1 146	1 150	1 058	1 115	944	976	1 000	1 017
Veal	KFTM	5	5	6	6	5	4	3	2	1	2	2
Mutton and lamb	KFTN	263	264	287	288	303	289	296	322	366	370	386
Pork	KFTO	710	728	763	708	723	747	784	796	709	740	777
Offal	KFTP	157	149	161	170	171	162	168	156	162	165	170
Production of poultry meat[5]	KFTQ	747	813	805	847	869	919	989	1 050	993	1 025	1 063
Production of bacon and ham, including meat subsequently canned	KFTR	200	197	212	208	203	206	199	196	206	175	172
Production of milk products:												
Butter	KFTS	172	216	241	206	202	222	176	140	130	138	112
Cheese (including farmhouse)	KFTT	242	244	245	246	256	259	264	299	279	312	298
Condensed milk: includes skim concentrate and condensed milk used in manufacture of chocolate crumb	KFTU	219	225	194	184	181	174	180	183	207	204	198
Milk powder: excluding buttermilk and whey powder												
Full cream	KFTV	29	34	35	53	61	57	94	104	95	70	73
Skimmed	KFTW	251	296	302	223	241	268	194	137	133	166	133
Cream, fresh and sterilised; including farm cream[1]	KFTX	77	75	74	59	45	39	51	53	60	64	74
Sugar: production from home-grown sugar-beet (as refined sugar)	KFTY	1 092	1 418	1 062	1 314	1 210	1 318	1 226	1 304	1 267	1 241	1 220
Production of compound fats:												
Margarine and other table spreads[4]	KFTZ	398	399	387	382	378	460	464	469	489	475	465
Solid cooking fats	KFUA	153	157	153	115	108	104	107	104	121	121	115
Production of other processed foods:												
Jam and marmalade	KFUB	173	177	168	174	182	174	175	174	181	–	..
Syrup and treacle	KFUC	60	52	52	56	56	52	53	53	52	51	51
Canned vegetables[2]	KFUD	753	810	811	789	786	782	723	701	732[3]	–	–
Canned and bottled fruit[2]	KFUE	29	39	42	42	39	35	41	36	37	..	..
Soups, canned and powdered	KFUF	261	286	301	302	333	314	329	314	–	..	..
Canned meat	KFUG	95	86	93	98	98	86	93	86	118	91	147
Canned fish	KFUH	6	5	4	7	8	7	6	8	9	..	..
Biscuits, total disposals of home produced	KFUI	632	622	698	643	704	709	699	724	–	–	..
Breakfast cereals, other than oatmeal and oatmeal flakes	KFUJ	219	229	233	248	249	264	259	273	–	–	..
Glucose	KFUM	434	446	449	472	460	472	452	499	542	546	557
Production of soft drinks (million litres):												
Concentrated	KFUN	503	523	570	602	511	544	558	566	555	557	..
Unconcentrated	KFUO	2 231	2 458	2 642	2 690	2 899	3 417	3 713	3 628	4 112	4 316	..
Compound feedingstuffs: total	KFUP	10 943	11 855	12 234	10 743	10 420	11 187	10 625	10 729	11 115	11 363	11 361
Cattle food	KFUQ	4 538	5 012	5 456	4 382	4 116	4 486	3 826	3 780	3 947	3 909	3 781
Calf food	KFUR	436	478	504	422	401	402	352	345	347	324	278
Pig food	KFUS	2 169	2 317	2 292	2 099	2 142	2 186	2 189	2 180	2 158	2 276	2 360
Poultry food	KFUT	3 445	3 640	3 532	3 331	3 229	3 473	3 589	3 672	3 616	3 812	3 857
Other compounds	KFUU	355	408	450	509	532	640	670	753	1 045	1 042	1 088

TIME SERIES. The figures relate to periods of 52 weeks (53 weeks in 1981 and 1987) with the following exceptions which are on a calendar year basis: butter, cheese, cream, canned meat, soft drinks, condensed milk and milk powder, canned vegetables, canned and bottled fruit, jam and marmalade, and soups.

3 Provisional figures.
4 Table spreads are only included from 1986 onwards.
5 Total of fowl, ducks, geese and turkeys.

Source: Ministry of Agriculture, Fisheries and Food

1 Excludes cream made from the residual fat of low fat milk production.
2 From 1981 the method of collecting these figures has changed. They are therefore not comparable with previous years.

Food

9.12 Food and animal feedingstuffs: disposals

Thousand tonnes

		1980	1981	1982	1983	1984	1985	1986	1987	1988	1989	1990	1991
Flour	KFPU	3 706	3 041	3 547	3 492	3 626	3 640	3 591	3 887	3 866	3 858	3 831	3 801
Sugar (as refined sugar): total disposals	KFPV	2 278	2 215	2 341	2 258	2 287	2 249	2 257	2 297	2 316	2 354	2 332	2 297
For food in the United Kingdom[1]	KFPW	2 254	2 188	2 317	2 236	2 264	2 227	2 233	2 276	2 301	2 336	2 320	2 281
Syrup and treacle	KFPX	61	60	52	52	56	56	52	53	53	52	51	51
Meat and fish:													
Fresh and frozen meat and offal, including usage for canning:													
Beef and veal	KFPY	1 328	1 263	1 141	1 215	1 259	1 287	1 320	1 367	1 235	1 219	1 103	1 129
Mutton and lamb	KFPZ	469	432	457	472	449	466	447	455	465	506	518	512
Pork	KFVA	724	746	756	801	747	760	779	832	857	802	819	852
Offal	KFVB	277	275	270	277	283	284	262	262	249	247	232	224
Poultry-meat[7]	KFVC	780	786	838	855	911	936	1 001	1 057	1 130	1 102	1 147	1 183
Bacon and ham, including usage for canning	KFVD	512	505	482	483	474	467	465	457	451	466	441	429
Fresh, frozen and cured fish (landed weight, excluding shellfish, including usage for canning):													
Total disposals	KFVG	1 104	1 034	1 063	1 008	1 012	1 060	1 464	1 172	1 045	994[5]	716	816
For food in the United Kingdom	KFVH	715	703	706	607	694	712	711	791	717	677[5]	475	501
Dairy products:													
Butter	KFVI	398	400	382	368	309	324	328	399	375	267	236	224
Cheese	KFVJ	353	366	372	374	399	408	423	435	464	468	504	511
Condensed milk[2]	KFVK	225	214	232	201	187	198	187	188	191	213	218	212
Milk powder, excluding buttermilk and whey powder:													
Full cream	KFVM	30	30	35	38	54	71	71	103	106	98	76	74
Skimmed	KFVN	227	262	298	333	246	253	288	210	143	150	178	146
Eggs in shell[6]	KFVO	798	759	732	705	681	667	642	632	629	565	613	614
Oils (as crude oil):													
Vegetable oil	KFVP	891	883	936	990	933	1 032	1 195	1 412	1 555	1 501	1 674	1 700
Marine oil for the manufacture of margarine and compound fat	KFVQ	212	216	203	182	200	196	178	167	129	141	133	121
Potatoes: total disposals[3]	KFVR	5 728	6 205	5 825	5 935	5 642	6 374	6 176	5 987	6 165	6 125	5 916	5 876
For food in the United Kingdom[4]	KFVS	5 633	5 671	5 735	5 664	5 541	5 839	5 918	5 834	5 917	5 887	5 744	5 737
Other foods:													
Chocolate confectionery	KFVT	..	..	..	484	509	516	505	522	535	562	584	601
Sugar confectionery, excluding medicated	KFVU	..	..	..	319	336	350	345	361	362	360	372	371
Tea excluding re-exports	KFVV	184	178	174	168	177	161	161	158	164	162	145	152
Raw coffee	KFVW	76	89	91	98	106	104	105	113	103	98	104	101
Cocoa beans excluding re-exports	KFVX	66	86	88	77	90	91	87	95	101	115	125	148
Barley:													
For brewing and distilling and for food	KFVY	3 706	5 056	4 279	4 435	5 403	4 725	5 640	4 830	4 554	5 095	3 858	3 917
Maize (including maize meal): total disposals	KFVZ	2 868	2 315	2 123	1 819	1 595	1 451	1 482	1 475	1 330	1 405	1 658	1 511
Animal feed	KCRT	1 083	815	592	357	319	304	312	309	202	176	292	146
Oilcake and meal	KCRQ	2 380	2 505	2 837	2 889	2 695	2 892	3 059	3 007	3 163	3 174	3 570	3 407
Wheat milling offals	KCRR	1 298	1 258	1 270	1 194	1 156	1 221	1 229	1 213	1 292	1 169	1 133	1 063
Fish and meat meal for animal feed, figures relate to sales	KCRS	365	275	255	291	289	277	309	309	300	..	..	..

TIME SERIES. The figures relate to periods of 52 weeks (53 weeks in 1981 and 1987) with the following exceptions which are on a calendar year basis: fish and potatoes; condensed milk; milk powder; and butter.

1 Including sugar used in the manufacture of other foods subsequently exported. Excluding sugar in imported manufactured foods.
2 Includes skim concentrate and condensed milk used in the manufacture of chocolate crumb.
3 Disposals (excluding seed and chats) of home-grown and imported potatoes for human consumption, processing, export and sales for stockfeed through schemes for implementing the Agricultural Act, 1947.
4 Disposals of home-grown and imported potatoes for human consumption in the United Kingdom.
5 Provisional.
6 Includes duck eggs.
7 Total of fowls, ducks, geese and turkeys.

Sources: Central Statistical Office;
Ministry of Agriculture, Fisheries and Food

Fisheries

9.13 Landings of fish of British taking: landed weight and value
United Kingdom

		\multicolumn{6}{c}{Landed weight (Thousand tonnes)}		\multicolumn{6}{c}{Value (£ thousand)}
		1986	1987	1988	1989	1990	1991		1986	1987	1988	1989	1990	1991
Total all fish	KFAA	716.9	790.4	742.0	671.9	621.5	562.3	KGTT	361 680	435 162	402 893	394 346	430 503	396 469
Total wet fish	KFAB	629.3	679.3	645.5	580.5	528.4	477.7	KFFB	284 161	339 223	310 412	299 354	329 491	310 042
Demersal:														
Catfish	KFAD	1.5	1.6	1.6	1.8	1.7	1.7	KFFC	1 035	1 318	1 223	1 557	1 816	1 785
Cod	KFAE	76.5	93.4	77.7	68.2	60.4	51.8	KFFD	69 140	86 312	74 849	69 568	76 759	69 243
Dogfish	KFAF	11.6	13.6	13.0	11.3	110.8	9.9	KFFE	6 376	7 201	7 066	7 762	8 944	8 485
Haddock	KFAG	131.0	102.4	97.6	71.9	490.8	46.2	KFFF	79 019	78 079	68 708	61 918	59 369	52 915
Hake	KFAH	3.0	3.3	3.6	4.0	4.6	4.5	KFFG	4 549	5 540	6 389	7 699	11 610	11 931
Halibut	KFAI	0.1	0.1	0.1	0.1	0.1	0.2	KFFH	372	446	482	442	1 171	639
Lemon sole	KFAJ	5.0	5.3	5.4	5.0	5.7	5.7	KFFI	8 265	9 018	8 788	8 945	10 887	11 021
Plaice	KFAK	21.3	25.7	27.3	26.2	25.3	21.0	KFFJ	16 048	22 541	22 348	20 400	23 815	27 932
Redfish	KFAL	0.1	0.2	0.2	0.2	0.3	0.6	KFFK	56	62	71	101	189	425
Saithe (Coalfish)	KFAM	17.7	15.2	14.4	11.8	12.2	13.5	KFFL	6 361	7 077	5 657	4 868	5 834	7 869
Skate and ray	KFAN	6.9	8.6	8.4	7.4	7.3	6.7	KFFM	3 908	4 742	4 796	4 596	5 326	5 206
Sole	KFAO	3.2	3.1	3.0	2.9	3.1	2.4	KFFO	14 500	16 991	14 067	14 370	14 274	10 651
Turbot	KFAP	0.6	0.7	0.7	0.5	0.6	0.6	KFFP	2 607	3 612	3 690	3 014	3 481	3 275
Whiting	KFAQ	41.1	31.9	35.6	38.4	38.4	38.4	KFFQ	18 460	25 198	21 143	20 834	26 085	21 477
Livers[1]	KFAR	..	..	..	..	–	1.0	KFFR	..	..	..	..	..	..
Roes	KFAS	0.5	0.5	0.5	0.5	0.4	0.3	KFFS	348	499	473	457	446	213
Other demersal	KFAT	63.1	55.0	66.9	63.0	54.2	41.7	KFFT	25 660	35 690	37 198	41 861	48 193	49 139
Total	KFAU	383.2	381.3	366.0	313.2	374.3	345.8	KFFU	256 705	304 326	276 948	268 392	298 649	282 287
Pelagic:														
Herring	KFAV	106.1	100.3	93.2	99.4	98.8	92.4	KFFV	11 881	12 213	11 244	11 257	11 705	9 778
Mackerel[2]	KFAW	132.1	189.4	176.1	157.9	146.6	124.9	KFFW	14 766	21 484	20 791	18 702	18 043	16 424
Other pelagic	KFAX	7.9	8.3	10.2	10.0	8.7	14.6	KFFX	809	1 200	1 429	1 003	1 094	1 558
Total	KGST	246.1	298.0	279.5	267.3	254.0	231.9	KGSU	27 456	34 897	33 464	30 962	30 842	27 755
Total shell fish	KFAY	87.6	111.1	96.5	91.4	93.1	84.6	KFFY	77 519	95 939	92 481	94 992	101 012	86 427
Cockles	KFAZ	19.4	39.0	24.6	14.8	19.6	20.4	KFFZ	1 165	4 285	3 276	1 274	1 663	2 049
Crab	KFBA	12.6	13.5	15.2	14.1	16.0	9.2	KFGA	9 599	11 400	13 908	14 143	15 064	8 181
Lobster	KFBB	1.0	1.1	1.3	1.3	1.3	1.1	KFGB	7 680	9 346	10 163	10 650	11 115	8 618
Mussels	KFBC	6.3	4.9	6.9	9.0	6.6	6.3	KFGC	541	543	906	1 190	923	942
Nephrop (Norway lobster)	KFBD	25.4	24.2	27.8	27.0	25.4	25.1	KFGD	39 119	43 007	44 585	42 122	49 659	44 289
Oysters[3]	KFBE	0.6	0.1	0.1	0.1	0.2	0.3	KFGE	845	241	225	179	4 367	294
Shrimps[4]	KFBF	1.4	3.3	1.7	1.8	1.2	0.2	KFGF	1 254	2 346	1 785	2 627	1 959	217
Whelks	KFBG	2.0	2.7	2.0	1.2	0.8	1.6	KFGG	418	665	473	251	175	336
Other shell fish	KFBH	18.9	22.3	17.3	22.1	20.6	20.6	KFGH	16 898	24 106	17 165	22 556	16 087	21 501

1 Including the raw equivalent of any liver oils landed.
2 Includes transhipments of mackerel or herring ie caught by British boats but not actually landed at British ports. These quantities are transhipped to foreign vessels and are later recorded as exports.
3 The weight of oysters is calculated on the basis of one tonne being equal to 15,748 oysters in England & Wales.
4 From 1986, data for prawn is included.

Sources: Ministry of Agriculture, Fisheries and Food; Department of Agriculture and Fisheries for Scotland

Fisheries

9.14 Fishing fleet[1]
England and Wales
At 31 December in each year

Number

		1981	1982	1983	1984	1985	1986	1987	1988	1989	1990[3]	1991
By size:												
Under 40 ft.	KCRV	3 504	3 126	3 662	4 079	4 482	4 919	4 812	4 623	4 660	7 158	7 489
40 ft. - 79.9 ft.	KCRW	969	931	853	834	764	572	614	624	642	634	654
80 ft. - 109.9 ft.	KCRX	64	76	82	89	91	95	109	123	81	100	119
110 ft. - 139.9 ft.	KCRY	63	63	57	55	37	48	52	53	26	39	63
140 ft. +	KGSV	37	32	26	10	7	5	8	10	8	16	16
Total	KCRZ	4 637	4 228	4 680	5 067	5 381	5 639	5 595	5 433	5 417	7 947	8 341
By normal method of fishing:												
Trawlers	KCSB	1 750	1 759	1 757	1 686	1 285	1 561	1 708	1 711	1 664	1 241	1 289
Seine nets	KCSC	227	216	195	181	150	83	63	71	71	62	55
Lines	KCSD	794	469	499	629	534	802	750	656	629	132	635
Purse seine	KCSE	4	3	5	3	2	1	–	–	–	–	–
Other nets	KCSF	133	89	111	114	99	257	76	104	104	81	205
Other and unknown[2]	KCSG	1 729	1 692	2 113	2 454	3 311	2 935	2 998	2 891	2 949	6 431	6 157

1 Changes in the numbers of vessels (especially those under 40 ft.) are due partly to changes in the definitions used.
2 Includes shellfishing.
3 Prior to 1990 figures were the numbers of active vessels. From 1990 they are the numbers of registered vessels. At present the 1990 figures include UK registered vessels of unknown nationality (ie English, Welsh, Scottish or Northern Irish) and may therefore overstate the true position for England and Wales.

Source: Ministry of Agriculture, Fisheries and Food

9.15 Scottish fishing vessels
At 31 December in each year

Number

		1981	1982	1983	1984	1985	1986	1987	1988	1989	1990	1991
By size:												
Under 40 ft.	KCSH	1 288	1 189	1 191	1 184	1 216	1 216	1 275	1 342	1 443	1 515	1 437
40 ft. - 59.9 ft.	KCSI	530	514	496	469	461	435	440	441	430	409	396
80 ft. - 109.9 ft.	KCSK	51	40	38	35	32	33	38	35	35	38	42
110 ft. - 139.9 ft.	KCSL	24	22	20	20	21	22	26	27	28	28	32
140 ft. +	KCSM	–	–	2	3	7	12	15	18	20	17	17
Total	KCSN	2 370	2 233	2 214	2 180	2 198	2 183	2 263	2 334	2 424	2 368	2 375
By normal method of fishing:												
Demersal trawl	KCSO	339	315	291	244	253	235	253	288	280	279	270
Demersal pair trawl	KCSP	72	70	76	104	116	122	132	129	108	100	100
Industrial trawl	KCSQ	9	19	17	12	10	6	6	6	6	1	–
Lines	KCSS	208	147	112	94	83	70	69	63	61	53	44
Purse seine	KCST	43	45	42	44	45	47	47	46	46	47	40
Pelagic trawl	KCSU	35	34	26	23	20	12	7	6	14	13	14
Other nets[1]	KCSV	22	27	43	48	46	43	32	31	26	30	26
Nephrops trawl	KCSW	303	302	317	337	335	383	412	446	458	458	462
Other shellfishing[2]	KCSX	1 031	978	988	983	999	982	1 028	1 068	1 200	1 170	1 200

1 Gill and cod nets, drift and ring nets.
2 All shellfishing methods except nephrops trawl.

Source: The Scottish Office Agriculture and Fisheries Department

9.16 Estimated household food consumption by all households in Great Britain

Ounces per person per week

		1981	1982	1983	1984	1985	1986	1987	1988	1989	1990	1991
Liquid wholemilk[1] (pints)	KFYA	4.01	3.95	3.80	3.61	3.32	3.04	2.88	2.66	2.42	2.17	1.94
Other milk (pints or equivalent pints)	KFYB	0.42	0.43	0.49	0.67	0.79	1.08	1.19	1.35	1.50	1.65	1.80
Cheese	KFYC	3.89	3.80	4.01	3.84	3.91	4.16	4.09	4.13	4.07	4.00	4.11
Butter	KFYD	3.69	3.17	3.27	2.87	2.83	2.27	2.14	2.00	1.75	1.61	1.54
Margarine	KFYE	4.11	4.33	4.08	4.08	3.76	4.10	3.98	3.78	3.47	3.19	3.14
All other oils and fats (fl ozs for oils)	KFYF	3.26	3.48	3.33	3.34	3.47	4.12	3.92	4.07	4.25	4.20	4.07
Eggs (number)	KFYG	3.68	3.51	3.53	3.21	3.15	3.01	2.89	2.67	2.29	2.20	2.25
Preserves and honey	KFYH	2.08	1.99	2.05	1.95	1.87	1.98	1.88	1.85	1.76	1.69	1.79
Sugar	KFYI	11.08	10.31	9.84	9.15	8.41	8.04	7.48	6.94	6.46	6.03	5.88
Beef and veal	KFYJ	6.96	7.06	6.57	6.27	6.51	6.58	6.77	6.35	6.03	5.25	5.35
Mutton and Lamb	KFYK	4.25	3.59	3.87	3.32	3.27	3.01	2.65	2.78	2.99	2.91	3.02
Pork	KFYL	3.82	4.02	3.53	3.29	3.45	3.64	3.17	3.29	3.15	2.97	2.88
Bacon and ham, uncooked	KFYM	4.14	3.95	4.02	3.58	3.69	3.68	3.46	3.48	3.35	3.03	3.00
Bacon and ham, cooked (including canned)	KFYN	1.13	1.15	1.09	1.11	1.14	1.13	1.15	1.13	1.22	1.15	1.15
Poultry and cooked chicken	KFYO	7.30	6.85	6.99	7.24	6.90	7.30	8.14	8.09	7.76	7.95	7.63
Other cooked and canned meats	KFYP	2.42	2.51	2.65	2.45	2.60	2.59	2.45	2.62	2.48	2.18	2.11
Offals	KFYQ	1.04	0.97	0.84	0.83	0.79	0.74	0.69	0.63	0.55	0.51	0.47
Sausages, uncooked	KFYR	3.41	3.33	3.33	3.00	2.97	2.73	2.66	2.48	2.53	2.41	2.18
Other meat products	KFYS	4.81	5.19	5.18	5.44	5.42	5.67	5.84	5.72	5.89	5.78	6.14
Fish, fresh and processed	KFYT	2.81	2.75	2.81	2.64	2.53	2.66	2.62	2.60	2.60	2.41	2.29
Canned fish	KFYU	0.69	0.63	0.77	0.70	0.71	0.84	0.91	0.90	0.95	1.03	1.06
Fish and fish products, frozen	KFYV	1.42	1.65	1.55	1.56	1.67	1.64	1.57	1.56	1.66	1.65	1.53
Potatoes (excluding processed)	KFYX	41.87	41.11	39.88	39.82	40.96	38.76	37.68	36.43	35.59	35.17	33.81
Fresh green vegetables	KFYY	11.98	11.24	10.78	10.83	9.78	11.11	9.97	10.42	10.23	9.78	9.13
Other fresh vegetables	KFYZ	15.74	15.66	15.71	15.26	15.70	16.82	16.67	16.81	17.13	16.18	16.26
Frozen vegetables	KFZA	4.88	5.25	4.92	5.19	5.97	6.28	6.72	6.53	6.70	6.56	7.04
Canned beans	KFZB	4.12	4.16	4.45	4.45	4.43	4.79	4.59	4.64	4.44	4.37	4.35
Other canned vegetables	KFZC	5.23	5.17	5.08	4.76	5.37	5.41	4.86	4.88	4.53	4.33	4.45
Apples	KFZD	7.28	7.02	7.08	6.84	6.93	7.26	7.05	7.17	7.26	7.10	6.70
Bananas	KFZE	3.12	2.94	2.86	2.91	2.81	3.06	3.21	3.58	4.00	4.39	4.55
Oranges	KFZF	3.05	2.70	2.82	2.70	2.48	3.10	2.70	3.13	2.99	2.82	2.67
All other fresh fruit	KFZG	6.52	6.09	6.87	6.55	6.31	6.91	7.30	7.14	7.20	7.03	7.61
Canned fruit	KFZH	2.61	2.65	2.42	2.28	2.05	2.22	2.06	2.15	2.15	1.83	1.85
Dried fruit, nuts and fruit and nut products	KFZI	1.25	1.21	1.43	1.27	1.23	1.38	1.49	1.30	1.24	1.28	1.37
Fruit juices (fl oz)	KFZK	3.99	4.30	5.20	5.28	5.21	6.34	7.17	7.43	7.52	7.11	8.80
Flour	KFZL	5.96	5.28	4.97	4.34	4.05	4.14	3.93	3.59	3.28	3.19	2.84
Bread	KFZM	31.23	31.03	30.74	30.57	30.99	30.79	30.60	30.23	29.43	28.10	26.53
Buns, scones and teacakes	KFZN	0.96	1.02	0.97	0.98	1.01	1.05	1.09	1.11	1.15	1.19	1.37
Cakes and pastries	KFZO	2.81	2.74	2.62	2.58	2.48	2.55	2.61	2.56	2.45	2.47	2.78
Biscuits	KFZP	5.39	5.66	5.47	5.29	5.22	5.42	5.32	5.28	5.25	5.26	5.18
Breakfast cereals	KFZQ	3.53	3.54	3.83	4.13	4.04	4.38	4.42	4.47	4.45	4.47	4.72
Oatmeal and oat products	KFZR	0.46	0.37	0.45	0.42	0.49	0.55	0.49	0.63	0.55	0.52	0.69
Tea	KFZS	1.98	2.02	2.04	1.80	1.74	1.74	1.71	1.65	1.61	1.52	1.48
Instant coffee	KFZT	0.52	0.51	0.53	0.54	0.54	0.55	0.52	0.53	0.50	0.48	0.53
Canned soups	KCSY	2.81	2.66	2.69	2.68	2.70	2.54	2.81	2.78	2.71	2.41	2.45
Pickles and sauces	KCSZ	2.01	1.97	2.15	2.10	2.14	2.18	2.09	2.30	2.34	2.37	2.44

Note: Page 174 contains a description of the National Food Survey.
1 Including also school and welfare milk.

Source: Ministry of Agriculture, Fisheries and Food (National Food Survey)

10. Transport and Communications

10.1 Goods transport in Great Britain

		1981	1982	1983	1984	1985	1986	1987	1988	1989	1990	1991[1]
Road[2]	KCTA	93.5	94.5	95.9	100.4	103.2	105.4	113.3	130.2	137.8	136.3	130.0
Rail[3]	KCTB	17.5	15.9	17.1	12.7	15.3	16.6	17.3	18.2	17.3	15.8	15.2
Water:[4] Coastwise oil	KCTC	38.0	39.9	40.2	41.0	38.9	33.9	31.6	34.2	34.1	32.1	31.3
Water:[4] Other	KCTD	14.7	18.8	20.0	18.7	18.7	20.9	22.5	25.1	23.8	23.6	24.6
Pipelines[5]	KCTE	9.3	9.5	9.9	10.4	11.2	10.4	10.5	11.1	9.8	11.0[6]	11.1
Total tonne kilometres (thousand millions)	KCTF	173.0	178.6	183.1	183.2	187.3	187.2	195.2	218.8	222.8	218.8	212.2
Road[2]	KCTG	1 299	1 389	1 358	1 400	1 452	1 473	1 542	1 758	1 812	1 749	1 600
Rail[3]	KCTH	154	142	145	79	122	140	141	150	146	141	135
Water:[4] Coastwise oil	KCTI	52	54	53	53	50	46	43	47	46	44	44
Water:[4] Other	KCTJ	77	83	90	87	92	98	100	109	109	108	100
Pipelines[5]	KCTK	75	78	82	88	89	79	83	99	93	121[6]	105
Total (million tonnes)	KCTL	1 657	1 746	1 724	1 707	1 805	1 836	1 909	2 163	2 206	2 163	1 984

1 Water figures are provisional for 1991.
2 All road freight by goods vehicles (over 3.5 tonnes gross vehicle weight) and small commercial vehicles.
3 British Rail only. Traffic was affected by ASLEF industrial action in 1982 and by the miners' strike and associated action by BR staff in 1984 and 1985.
4 Oil comprises crude oil and all petroleum products. 'Coastwise' includes all sea traffic within the UK, Isle of Man and Channel Islands. 'Other' other means coastwise plus inland waterway traffic and one-port traffic (largely) crude oil direct from rigs).
5 Excluding movements of gases by pipelines.
6 The increase as compared to the corresponding figure for 1989 is believed to be largely due to changes in coverage.

Source: Department of Transport

10.2 Passenger transport in Great Britain: estimated passenger kilometres

Thousand million passenger kilometres

		1981	1982	1983	1984	1985	1986	1987	1988	1989	1990	1991[5]
Air[1]	KCTM	3	3	3	3	4	4	4	5	5	5	5
Rail[2]	KCTN	34	31	34	35	36	37	39	41	40	41	38
Road:												
Public service vehicles[3]	KCTP	49	48	48	48	49	47	47	46	47	46	45
Cars and vans [4,6,7]	KCTQ	396	408	413	434	443	467	501	536	581	591	590
Motor cycles[4,6]	KCTR	10	10	9	9	8	8	7	7	6	6	6
Pedal cycles	KCTS	5	6	6	6	6	5	6	5	5	5	5
Total	KCTT	497	506	513	535	546	568	604	640	684	694	689

1 Domestic scheduled and non-scheduled services, including Northen Ireland, Isle of Man and Channel Islands.
2 British Rail, London Regional Transport and Passenger Transport Executive railway systems. The basis of calculating London Regional Transport railways' passenger kilometres has been revised from passenger kilometres paid for to passenger kilometres travelled. During 1982, British Rail traffics were affected by industrial action which took place on 34 days.
3 Calculated from operators' returns of numbers of passengers carried, using estimates for average length of journey.
4 Based on statistics of vehicle mileage derived from the traffic counts and estimates of average numbers of persons per vehicle, derived from the National Travel surveys.
5 Provisional figures.
6 In 1991 the occupancy rates, estimated from the National Travel Survey were, 1.66 for cars and taxis and 1.09 for motor cycles.
7 Includes taxis.

Source: Department of Transport

10.3 Length of public roads in Great Britain
At 1 April in each year

Kilometres

		1981	1982	1983	1984	1985	1986	1987	1988	1989	1990	1991
Motorway[1]	KCTU	2 646	2 692	2 741	2 786	2 813	2 920	2 975	2 992	2 995	3 070	3 099
Trunk	KCTV	12 269	12 209	12 231	12 271	12 201	12 439	12 419	12 480	12 623	12 597	12 356
Principal	KCTW	34 656	34 700	34 819	34 753	34 800	34 868	34 987	34 939	35 039	35 149	35 629
Other[2]	KCTX	292 749	294 341	295 985	297 779	298 885	299 849	302 314	303 904	305 946	307 142	308 962
Total	KCTY	342 320	343 942	345 776	347 589	348 699	350 076	352 695	354 315	356 602	357 958	360 046

1 Including local authority motorways, the percentage of which is small, less than 5%.
2 Excluding unsurfaced roads and green lanes.

Source: Department of Transport

Road transport

10.4 Estimated traffic on all roads in Great Britain

Billion vehicle kilometres

		1981	1982	1983	1984	1985	1986	1987	1988	1989	1990	1991[1]
All motor vehicles	KCVZ	276.9	284.5	288.0	303.1	309.7	325.2	350.5	375.7	406.9	410.8	411.6
Cars and taxis[2]	KCWA	219.5	227.3	231.2	244.0	250.5	264.4	284.6	305.4	331.3	335.9	335.2
Two-wheeled motor vehicles	KCWB	8.9	9.2	8.3	8.1	7.4	7.1	6.7	6.0	5.9	5.6	5.4
Buses and coaches	KDZS	3.5	3.5	3.7	3.9	3.7	3.7	4.1	4.3	4.5	4.6	4.8
Light vans[3]	KDZT	23.4	23.2	23.2	24.5	25.2	26.5	29.0	32.0	35.4	35.7	37.2
Other goods vehicles	KDZU	21.7	21.2	21.7	22.6	23.0	23.6	26.1	27.9	29.8	29.1	29.0
Total goods vehicles	KDZV	45.1	44.4	44.9	47.1	48.2	50.1	55.1	59.9	65.2	64.8	66.2
Pedal cycles	KDZW	5.5	6.4	6.4	6.4	6.1	5.5	5.7	5.2	5.2	5.3	5.2

1 Provisional.
2 This category includes three-wheeled cars; excludes all vans whether licensed for private or for commercial use.
3 Not exceeding 30 cwt unladen weight.

Source: Department of Transport

10.5 Motor Vehicles Currently Licensed[1,2]
Great Britain

Thousands

		1981	1982	1983	1984	1985	1986	1987	1988	1989	1990	1991
Total	BMBI	19 347	19 762	20 209	20 765	21 157	21 699	22 152	23 302	24 196	24 673	24 511
Private cars[3]	BMBJ	14 943	15 303	15 543	16 055	16 453	16 981	17 421	18 432	19 248	19 742	19 737
Other vehicles[3]	BMBK	1 548	1 585	1 709	1 770	1 804	1 879	1 952	2 095	2 199	2 247	2 215
Private and light goods[3]	KCTZ	16 491	16 888	17 252	17 825	18 258	18 860	19 373	20 527	21 447	21 989	21 952
Up to 50c.c.	KCUA	472	489	474	449	423	389	352	312	280	248	207
Other	KCUB	899	881	816	776	725	676	626	600	595	585	543
Motor cycles, etc: total	BMBB	1 371	1 370	1 290	1 225	1 148	1 065	978	912	875	833	750
Public road passenger vehicles: total	BMBE	110	111	113	116	120	125	129	132	122	115	109
Buses, coaches, taxis, etc												
Not over 8 passengers	KCUC	40	43	46	49	53	57	58	59	49	42	38
Over 8 passengers	KCUD	70	68	68	67	67	68	71	73	73	73	71
Goods[4,5]	BMBD	488	477	496	497	486	484	484	503	505	482	449
Agricultural tractors, etc[6]	BMBC	365	371	376	375	374	371	374	383	384	376	346
Other licensed vehicles[7]	BMBF	95	91	86	82	77	72	68	83	77	71	65
Crown vehicles	KCUE	37	37	39	39	39	39	39	38	38	37	36
All other exempt vehicles	KCUF	390	417	582	631	656	681	706	722	747	770	804
Exempt from license duty: total[8]	BMBL	427	454	621	670	695	720	744	761	785	807	840

1 Since 1978, censuses have been taken annually on 31 December and are obtained from a full count of licensing records held at DVLA Swansea. Prior to this, figures were compiled from a combination of DVLA data and records held at Local Taxation offices.
2 Excludes vehicles officially registered by the Armed Forces.
3 Includes all vehicles used privately. Mostly consists of private cars and vans. However, from October 1990, goods vehicles less than 3500 kgs gross vehicle weight are now included in this category.
4 Mostly Goods vehicles over 3500 kgs gross vehicle weight but includes farmers' and showmen's vehicles that are less than 3500 kgs.
5 Includes agricultural vans and lorries, showmen's goods vehicles licensed to draw trailers.
6 Includes combine harvesters, mowing machines, digging machines, mobile cranes and works trucks.
7 Includes three wheelers, pedestrian controlled vehicles and showmen's haulage and recovery vehicles. New tax class introduced January 1988.
8 From 1980 includes electric vehicles which are now exempt from licence duty.

Source: Department of Transport

Road transport

10.6 New vehicle registrations by taxation class
Great Britain

Thousands

		1981	1982	1983	1984	1985	1986	1987	1988	1989	1990	1991
Total[1]	BMAX	2 030.3	2 103.9	2 307.5	2 238.9	2 309.3	2 333.7	2 473.9	2 723.5	2 828.9	2 438.4	1 921.5
Private and light goods [2]												
Private cars	BMAA	1 434.8	1 527.0	1 773.3	1 721.6	1 804.0	1 839.3	1 962.7	2 154.7	2 241.2	1 942.3	1 526.6
Other vehicles	BMAE	192.4	201.0	197.6	211.1	224.9	231.3	248.3	282.4	293.6	237.6	171.9
Total	KCUG	1 627.2	1 728.0	1 970.9	1 913.2	2 006.9	2 047.2	2 184.3	2 403.6	2 494.0	2 179.9	1 708.5
Motor cycles, etc												
Up to 50 cc	KCUH	94.8	94.0	67.4	55.4	48.3	37.5	29.7	24.7	22.9	18.6	12.9
Other	KCUI	177.10	137.60	107.10	89.80	77.50	68.90	61.10	65.40	74.40	75.90	63.60
Total	BMAD	271.9	231.6	174.5	145.2	125.8	106.4	90.8	90.1	97.3	94.4	76.5
Public road passenger vehicles												
Buses, coaches, taxis, etc												
Not over 8 seats	KCUJ	2.6	2.8	3.0	3.3	3.1	3.4	3.6	4.2	3.0	2.9	2.2
Over 8 seats	KCUK	4.9	4.3	4.3	3.9	3.7	5.5	5.1	5.0	5.0	4.5	3.0
Total	BMAG	7.5	7.1	7.3	7.2	6.8	8.9	8.7	9.2	8.0	7.4	5.2
Heavy general goods[2] and farmers'[3] goods vehicles: by weight	KCUL	56.3	58.8	64.9	69.1	74.2	74.9	82.2	96.9	105.6	72.3	28.6
Privately owned agricultural tractors and engines[4]	BMAH	32.6	38.9	42.1	40.1	40.1	34.8	37.7	45.6	42.5	34.2	26.1
Other licensed vehicles[5]	KCUM	3.4	3.9	3.8	3.3	3.0	3.0	2.6	8.5	2.8	2.2	1.7
Exempt from licence duty												
Crown vehicles	KCUN	4.6	4.6	5.0	5.1	5.8	5.3	4.6	4.1	4.4	4.0	3.2
All other exempt vehicles[1,6]	KCUO	26.8	31.1	39.1	55.7	46.7	53.2	63.0	66.0	74.2	72.2	72.6
Total	KCUP	31.4	35.7	44.1	60.8	52.5	58.5	67.5	70.1	78.6	76.2	75.8

1 Including personal and direct export vehicles.
2 For years up to 1990 retrospective counts within these new taxation classes have been estimated.
3 Owned by a farmer and available for hauling produce and requisites for his farm.
4 Agricultural tractors are excluded unless driven on public roads.
5 Includes three wheelers, pedestrian controlled vehicles, general haulage and showmen's tractors and recovery vehicles. New tax class introduced January 1988.
6 From 1980 includes electric vehicles which are now exempt from licence duty.

Source: Department of Transport

10.7 Driving tests
Great Britain - applications and results

Thousands

		1981	1982	1983	1984	1985	1986	1987	1988	1989	1990	1991
Applications received	KCUQ	1 837.3	1 891.6	1 917.0	1 955.7	1 935.2	1 968.7	1 990.4	2 170.2	2 117.9	2 048.8	1 805.5
Tests conducted	KCUR	2 031.3	2 005.3	1 892.3	1 784.1	1 841.8	1 945.6	1 981.0	2 001.9	1 939.3	1 992.8	1 803.9
Tests passed	KCUS	966.9	965.0	921.0	875.4	895.9	932.0	998.7	1 028.1	1 002.2	1 033.0	917.8
Percentage of passes	KCUT	48	48	49	49	49	48	50	51	52	52	51

Source: Department of Transport

Road transport

10.8 Vehicles with licences current[1]
Northern Ireland

Number

		1980	1981	1982	1983	1984	1985	1986	1987[3]	1988[4]	1989	1990	1991
Private cars, etc	KNKA	364 590	365 000	388 030	411 780	430 660	405 090	415 050	434 237	443 081	456 611	481 090	498 471
Cycles and tricycles	KNKB	14 720	14 550	15 500	14 790	15 700	12 360	10 820	8 946	8 957	9 460	10 167	9 684
Public road passenger vehicles: total	KNKC	2 270	2 510	2 210	2 200	2 780	2 460	2 450	3 258	3 333	2 962	2 786	2 887
Taxis up to 4 seats	KNKD	710	840	720	940	1 240	860	940	1 087	1 128	741	603	656
Buses, coaches, over 4 seats	KNKE	1 560	1 670	1 490	1 260	1 540	1 600	1 510	2 171	2 205	2 221	2 183	2 231
General (HGV) goods vehicles: total	KNKF	38 900	33 760	34 060	29 450	34 510	26 650	23 610	22 789	22 547	23 514	16 191	13 907
Unladen weight													
Not over 1525 kgs	KNKG	16 720	13 190	15 490	10 530	15 440	8 850	7 830	29 009	..	..	..	..
Over 1525 and not over 12000 kgs	KNKH	6 710	6 140	5 730	9 690	9 310	8 070	7 690	17 521	17 524	18 424	..	..
Over 12000 kgs	KNKI	10 740	10 510	11 660	7 740	8 230	7 960	6 880	7 318	..	..	..	..
Farmers goods vehicles[2]	KNKJ	4 620	3 770	1 090	1 440	1 430	1 630	1 090	5 101	4 858	4 948	4 962	4 994
Tractors for general haulage	KNKK	80	130	70	50	90	120	100	148	144	120	..	..
Tower wagons	KNKL	30	20	20	..	10	20	20	19	21	22	..	..
Agricultural tractors and engines, etc[4]	KNKM	9 580	7 660	9 150	9 870	9 840	8 370	7 310	6 806	7 640	7 965	8 021	7 199
Other	KNKN	..	..	..	..	..	..	..	..	..	..	513	403
Vehicles exempt from duty:total	KNKO	12 288	13 215	13 610	13 764	13 208	13 681	13 615	13 308	15 427	17 144		
Government owned	KNKP	7 978	9 395	9 390	9 604	10 258	11 071	11 115	4 458	5 021	5 142	5 211	5 120
Other:													
Ambulances	KNKQ	70	10	290	342	358	203	324	41	49	56	74	98
Fire engines	KNKR	60	110	140	40	50	80	50	14	210	234	162	250
Other exempt	KNKS	4 180	3 700	3 790	3 778	2 542	2 327	2 126	8 795	10 147	11 712	13 937	15 305
Total	KNKT	442 348	436 695	462 560	481 854	506 698	468 611	472 855	489 344	500 985	517 656	543 114	558 318

1 Licences current at any time during the quarter ended December.
2 Owned by a farmer and available for hauling produce and requisites for his farm.
3 Licences current at 31 March 1988.
4 Licences current at 31 December 1988.

Source: Department of the Environment for Northern Ireland

10.9 New vehicles registrations
Northern Ireland

Number

			1981	1982	1983	1984	1985	1986	1987	1988	1989	1990	1991
Private cars, etc	KNLA		44 427	54 793	64 493	68 627	66 629	60 591	62 480	66 153	67 112	68 918	63 739
Cycles and tricycles	KNLB		3 533	3 111	2 814	2 815	2 286	1 893	1 447	1 870	2 163	2 343	2 218
Public road passenger vehicles: total	KNLC		150	141	273	308	316	286	314	597	602		
Taxis	KNLD	KGTY	32	38	153	182	163	142	34	61	74	606[4]	620
Buses, coaches etc	KNLE		118	103	120	126	153	144	280	536	528		
Goods vehicles: total	KNLF		4 631	5 482	5 961	7 617	7 996	6 537	6 833	8 246	8 407	..	..
General haulage vehicles: total	KNLG		4 288	5 136	5 701	7 329	7 635	6 196	6 501	7 758	7 930	..	..
Unladen weight:													
Not over 1 1/2 tons	KNLH		2 561	3 225	3 466	4 782	4 898	3 698	3 829	3 847	3 813	4 301[5]	6 273
Over 1 1/2 tons and not over 3 tons[3]	KNLI		722	638	1 061	1 227	1 394	1 245	1 264	..	..	..	..
Over 3 tons	KNLJ		1 005	1 273	1 174	1 320	1 343	1 253	1 408	3 911	4 117	4 630[6]	2 619
Agricultural vans and lorries[1]	KNLK		339	343	249	271	336	340	322	476	466	..	..
Tractors for general haulage	KNLL		4	3	11	17	25	1	10	12	11	..	..
Agricultural tractors and engines, etc[2]	KNLM		1 158	1 324	1 894	2 139	2 511	1 565	1 394	1 731	1 805	1 610[7]	1 177
Vehicles exempt from duty: total	KNLN		1 000	1 145	1 232	1 256	1 209	1 243	1 233	1 940	2 236	..	..
Ambulances	KNLO	KGVE	34	10	13	51	3	9	10	–	9	332[8]	330
Fire engines	KNLP		7	8	1	8	10	–	3	2	–	..	..
Road construction vehicles	KNLQ		24	38	24	27	5	6	23	4	2	..	..
Other exempt	KNLR		935	1 089	1 194	1 170	1 191	1 228	1 197	1 934	2 225	2 181	2 006
Total	KNLS		54 899	65 996	76 667	82 762	80 947	72 115	73 701	80 537	82 325	84 921	78 982

1 Owned by a farmer and available for hauling produce and requisites for his farm.
2 Agricultural tractors are excluded unless driven on public roads.
3 Goods vehicles 1 1/2 - 3 tons from 1988.
4 From 1990 figure is for Hackneys.
5 From 1990 figure is for light goods.
6 From 1990 figure is for heavy goods.
7 From 1990 figure is for tractors only.
8 From 1990 figure is for crown vehicles.

Source: Department of the Environment for Northern Ireland

Road transport

10.10 Buses and Coaches[1]
Great Britain

		1980	1981	1982	1983	1984	1985/86	1986/87	1987/88	1988/89	1989/90	1990/91
Number of vehicles	KNAA	69.1	69.9	70.7	70.2	68.8	67.9	69.6	71.7	72.0	72.6	72.1
Single deck	KNAB	43.6	44.7	44.8	44.9	43.2	42.9	45.2	47.6	48.5	49.8	49.9
Double deck	KNAC	25.6	25.2	25.9	25.3	25.6	25.0	24.5	24.1	23.5	22.8	22.2
London Buses Ltd[2]	KNAD	6.2	5.9	6.2	5.6	5.7	5.20	5.10	5.90	5.10	5.00	5.20
Metropolitan PTCs[3]	KNAE	10.3	10.1	9.9	9.6	9.5	9.1	8.6	8.4	8.4	8.2	8.1
Municipal PTCs[3]	KNAF	5.7	5.5	5.3	5.3	5.3	5.2	5.1	5.4	5.6	5.5	5.5
National Bus Company[4,5]	KNAG	16.0	15.3	15.0	14.6	14.5	14.7	16.4	16.4	..	..	..
Scottish Bus Group[4]	KNAH	3.6	3.4	3.3	3.1	3.1	3.4	3.4	3.1	3.1	2.8	2.7
Independent operators[5]	KNAI	27.4	29.7	31.0	31.9	30.8	30.3	31.1	33.4	..	..	..
NBC and Independents	KGRX	..	..	..	..	..	..	..	..	49.8	51.0	50.6
Vehicle kilometres (millions)	KNAJ	3 280	3 227	3 206	3 280	3 314	3 323	3 413	3 664	3 735	3 847	3 838
London Buses Ltd[2]	KNAK	279	282	265	264	268	262	251	245	249	253	261
Metropolitan PTCs[3]	KNAL	510	487	485	482	486	488	458	485	485	486	476
Municipal PTCs[3]	KNAM	241	233	232	231	235	233	237	257	278	284	275
National Bus Company[4,5]	KNAN	1 026	973	972	969	981	979	1 042	1 047	..	..	..
Scottish Bus Group[4]	KNAO	203	206	200	202	201	210	210	204	207	209	195
Independant operators[5]	KNAP	1 020	1 048	1 051	1 131	1 142	1 152	1 214	1 425	..	..	..
NBC and Independents	KGRY	..	..	..	..	..	..	..	..	2 516	2 605	2 632
Passenger journeys (millions)	KNAQ	6 783	6 278	6 097	6 210	6 237	6 177	5 915	5 913	5 805	5 682	5 470
London Buses Ltd[2]	KNAR	1 183	1 081	1 043	1 089	1 163	1 147	1 122	1 167	1 140	1 090	1 068
Metropolitan PTCs[3]	KNAS	1 973	1 814	1 765	1 796	1 826	1 847	1 606	1 504	1 444	1 385	1 287
Municipal PTCs[3]	KNAT	952	886	854	854	837	802	777	728	721	681	634
National Bus Company[4,5]	KNAU	1 669	1 529	1 479	1 460	1 440	1 455	1 417	1 396	..	..	..
Scottish Bus Group[4]	KNAV	339	322	314	319	311	320	307	288	284	255	236
Independent operators[5]	KNAW	666	647	642	691	659	606	686	835	..	..	..
NBC and Independents	KGRZ	..	..	..	..	..	..	..	..	2 216	2 272	2 244
Passenger receipts (£million)	KNAX	1 637	1 745	1 908	2 024	2 085	2 219	2 269	2 389	2 514	2 724	2 853
London Buses Ltd[2]	KNAY	207	209	254	266	264	292	288	292	307	336	360
Metropolitan PTCs[3]	KNAZ	328	334	364	379	389	406	417	431	450	470	475
Municipal PTCs[3]	KNEW	160	173	181	196	210	220	220	228	239	255	268
National Bus Company[4,5]	KNEX	491	520	543	573	593	629	636	640	..	..	..
Scottish Bus Group[4]	KNEY	109	117	127	134	136	140	138	129	131	128	127
Independent operators[5]	KNEZ	342	393	437	476	494	532	570	668	..	..	..
NBC and Indepenents	KGSQ	..	..	..	..	..	..	..	..	1 387	1 534	1 622

1 Include trams.
2 1979-83 London Transport Executive; 1984 London Regional Transport; 1985 onwards London Buses Ltd.
3 Including ex-PTCs.
4 Including former NBC or SBG operators.
5 Following structural changes to the industry, data for 1988/89 onwards are not shown separately for ex-NBC and independent operators.

Source: Department of Transport

10.11 Indices of local (stage) bus service fares
Great Britain

1985 = 100

		1980	1981	1982	1983	1984	1985	1986/87	1987/88	1988/89	1989/90	1990/91
London Regional Transport[1]	KNEP	74.2	79.1	98.1	100.0	91.6	100.0	107.8	113.1	125.3	138.2	152.4
Metropolitan PTCs'[2]	KNEQ	81.3	88.4	97.4	99.4	98.5	100.0	124.4	135.4	143.3	154.2	168.7
Municipal PTCs'[2]	KNER	62.3	74.7	83.0	88.9	95.7	100.0	105.3	111.4	117.3	126.7	141.9
All PTCs'[2]	KNES	73.9	83.0	91.8	95.3	97.4	100.0	117.4	126.5	133.6	144.0	158.9
Other operators[3]	KNET	66.5	76.4	84.9	90.9	95.9	100.0	107.4	111.9	117.4	126.0	138.4
All operators	KNEU	68.1	76.7	88.7	93.7	95.8	100.0	110.9	117.2	124.3	134.3	147.8
Retail prices index[4]	KNEV	70.7	79.0	85.9	89.8	94.3	100.0	104.4	108.6	115.1	124.1	..

1 1979-83 London Transport Executive; 1984 London Regional Transport; 1985 onwards London Buses Ltd.
2 Formerly Passenger Transport Executives.
3 National Bus Company, Scottish Bus Group and private operators.
4 The published retail prices index has been rescaled to 1985 = 100 for comparability.

Source: Department of Transport.

Road transport

10.12 Road accidents, vehicles involved and casualties
Great Britain

Number

		1981	1982	1983	1984	1985	1986	1987	1988	1989	1990	1991
Road accidents	KKKA	248 276	255 980	242 876	253 183	245 645	247 854	239 063	246 994	260 759	258 441	235 798
Vehicles involved:												
Pedal cycles	KKKB	26 496	29 428	31 824	32 210	27 953	27 039	27 010	26 561	29 327	27 108	25 424
Motor vehicles	KKKC	390 736	401 460	377 289	396 735	389 473	397 671	387 521	404 571	429 237	427 625	391 769
Two-wheeled motor vehicles	KKKD	70 949	73 033	65 962	65 340	57 822	53 562	47 024	44 279	43 995	40 404	31 702
Cars and taxis	KKKE	265 531	275 507	261 714	279 954	278 517	290 560	287 636	303 693	325 213	330 181	308 007
Light goods vehicles[2]	KKKF	22 106	21 704	19 853	20 911	23 113	23 434	22 651	24 671	25 793	24 052	21 792
Heavy goods vehicles[3]	KKKG	14 554	14 688	13 504	14 197	14 452	14 773	15 107	16 376	17 894	16 524	15 235
Buses and coaches	KKKH	13 083	12 911	12 763	12 302	12 468	12 137	11 766	12 086	12 711	12 200	11 403
Other motor vehicles	KKKI	4 513	3 617	3 493	3 531	3 101	3 205	3 337	3 466	3 631	3 664	3 630
Vehicles involved per hundred million kilometres travelled:												
Pedal cycles	KKKL	486	460	499	504	462	495	471	508	563	517	435
All two- wheeled motor vehicles	KKKM	799	792	798	805	785	758	701	734	741	725	562
Cars and taxis	KKKN	121	121	113	115	111	110	101	99	98	98	94
Light goods vehicles[2]	KKKO	94	94	86	85	92	88	78	77	73	69	60
Heavy goods vehicles[3]	KKKP	69	71	62	63	63	63	58	59	60	57	54
Total casualties	KKKQ	324 840	334 296	308 584	324 314	317 524	321 451	311 473	322 305	341 592	341 141	311 269
Killed[4]:												
Total	KKKR	5 846	5 934	5 445	5 599	5 165	5 382	5 125	5 052	5 373	5 217	5 568
Pedestrians	KKKS	1 874	1 869	1 914	1 868	1 789	1 841	1 703	1 753	1 706	1 694	1 496
Pedal cycles	KKKT	310	294	323	345	286	271	280	227	294	256	242
All two-wheeled motor vehicles	KKKU	1 131	1 090	963	967	796	762	723	670	683	659	548
Cars and taxis	KKKV	2 287	2 443	2 019	2 179	2 061	2 231	2 206	2 142	2 426	2 371	2 053
Others	KKKW	244	238	226	240	233	277	213	260	264	237	229
Killed and seriously injured[5]:												
By age group[6]												
0-4	KKKY	1 286	1 345	1 403	1 435	1 429	1 289	1 277	1 339	1 342	1 363	1 272
5-9	KKKZ	3 909	3 717	3 586	3 740	3 579	3 254	3 219	3 122	3 094	3 217	2 658
10-14	KKLA	5 162	5 474	5 450	5 541	4 903	4 426	3 988	3 871	3 943	3 832	3 367
15-19	KKLB	21 848	21 413	18 456	18 484	16 582	15 591	13 752	12 866	12 616	11 595	8 749
20-24	KKLC	13 682	14 522	12 575	13 214	13 282	13 058	12 041	11 629	11 512	10 583	8 835
25-29	KKLD	6 466	6 964	6 072	6 549	6 647	6 916	6 854	7 026	7 404	7 240	6 449
30-39	KKLE	8 973	9 366	8 102	8 391	8 276	8 455	8 029	7 999	8 047	7 905	6 974
40-49	KKLF	6 161	6 250	5 441	5 765	5 911	5 698	5 915	5 892	5 873	5 737	5 135
50-59	KKLG	5 771	5 784	4 980	5 027	5 038	4 827	4 566	4 620	4 532	4 425	3 853
60 and over	KKLH	10 399	10 464	10 003	10 512	9 850	10 017	9 081	9 517	9 596	9 113	8 218
By type of road user:												
Child pedestrians[7]	KKLJ	6 547	6 695	6 640	6 823	6 663	5 992	5 472	5 471	5 437	5 545	4 790
Adult pedestrians	KKLK	11 817	12 169	12 139	12 638	12 576	12 880	11 978	12 207	11 859	11 597	10 032
Child pedal cyclists[7]	KKLL	2 096	2 058	2 287	2 269	1 704	1 396	1 458	1 322	1 370	1 295	1 200
Adult pedal cyclists	KKLM	3 393	3 893	4 109	4 326	3 910	3 814	3 638	3 526	3 730	3 270	2 945
Moped riders	KKLN	2 903	3 109	3 241	3 188	2 919	2 571	2 221	1 903	1 729	1 417	989
Motor scooter riders	KKLO	515	608	647	748	715	606	499	380	382	289	226
Motor scooter passengers	KCUU	62	106	95	100	93	66	71	46	44	24	20
Motor cycle riders	KCUV	16 398	16 296	14 260	14 109	12 838	11 819	9 989	9 364	9 414	8 576	6 600
Motor cycle passengers	KCUW	2 400	2 514	2 021	1 805	1 547	1 370	1 086	924	884	783	651
Car and taxi drivers	KCUX	19 149	19 460	15 472	16 530	16 722	17 132	17 167	17 576	17 834	17 403	15 629
Car and taxi passengers	KCUY	14 476	14 525	11 574	12 467	12 385	12 554	11 919	11 770	11 850	11 717	9 764
Users of buses and coaches	KCUZ	961	962	969	929	1 036	859	892	912	835	807	725
Users of goods vehicles	KCVA	2 891	2 797	2 283	2 354	2 454	2 552	2 637	2 485	2 673	2 399	2 122
Users of other vehicles	KCVB	308	312	278	313	254	263	229	255	247	251	229
All severities:												
Total	KCVC	324 840	334 296	308 584	324 314	317 524	321 451	311 473	322 305	341 592	341 141	311 269
Pedestrians	KCVD	60 750	61 419	61 674	63 474	61 390	60 875	57 453	58 843	60 080	60 230	53 992
Vehicle users	KCVE	264 090	272 877	246 910	260 840	256 134	260 576	254 020	263 462	281 512	280 911	257 277
Breath tests on car drivers involved in accidents:												
All drivers	KCVG	265 531	275 507	261 714	279 959	278 517	290 560	287 633	303 693	325 213	330 181	308 007
Tested	KCVH	32 640	34 472	33 769	35 192	36 655	49 559	52 760	60 798	81 771	91 661	90 116
Failed test[8]	KCVI	10 121	11 145	10 200	10 422	10 432	10 014	9 222	8 549	8 508	8 073	7 354

1 Accidents on public roads, involving injury, which are reported to the police.
2 1.5 tons unladen weight and under.
3 Over 1.5 tons unladen weight.
4 Died within 30 days of accident.
5 Hospital in-patients *plus* casualties with any fracture, internal injury, concussion, crushing, severe general shock, etc, *plus* deaths after 30 days.
6 These figures may not add up to total fatal and serious figures, due to the exclusion of road users whose age was not reported.
7 Age 0 - 14.
8 Positive result, or refused to provide a specimen.

Source: Department of Transport

Road transport

10.13 Road accident casualty rates: by type of road user and severity
Great Britain

Rate per 100 million vehicle kilometres

		1981	1982	1983	1984	1985	1986	1987	1988	1989	1990	1991[2]
Pedal cyclists:												
Killed	KNMA	5.7	4.6	5.1	5.4	4.7	5.0	4.9	4.7	5.7	4.9	4.1
Killed or seriously injured	KNMB	101	93	100	103	93	96	90	93	99	87	72
All severities	KNMC	465	440	480	485	446	479	457	494	552	501	424
Two-wheel motor vehicle riders:												
Killed	KNMD	11	10	10	11	10	10	10	10	11	11	9
Killed or seriously injured	KNME	223	217	220	222	224	213	189	193	195	184	139
All severities	KNMF	694	690	699	711	701	680	628	657	668	646	502
Car drivers:												
Killed	KNMG	0.6	0.6	0.5	0.5	0.5	0.5	0.5	0.4	0.5	0.4	0.4
Killed or seriously injured	KNMH	9	9	7	7	7	6	6	6	5	5	5
All severities	KNMI	37	37	32	33	34	34	32	33	33	34	33
Bus and coach drivers:												
Killed	KNMJ	0.1	0.1	0.1	0.1	–	–	–	0.1	–	0.1	–
Killed or seriously injured	KNMK	2	2	2	2	1	2	1	1	1	2	1
All severities	KNML	15	14	13	12	15	14	13	13	15	14	13
Light goods vehicle drivers:												
Killed	KNMM	0.4	0.3	0.3	0.3	0.3	0.3	0.3	0.3	0.3	0.2	0.2
Killed or seriously injured	KNMN	6	5	4	4	4	4	4	4	3	3	3
All severities	KNMO	24	23	19	19	21	22	20	20	19	18	16
Heavy goods vehicle drivers:												
Killed	KNMP	0.2	0.3	0.2	0.3	0.2	0.3	0.2	0.2	0.2	0.2	0.2
Killed or seriously injured	KNMQ	3	3	3	3	3	3	3	2	2	2	2
All severities	KNMR	11	12	11	12	12	12	11	11	11	11	11
All road users[1]:												
Killed	KNMS	2.1	2.0	1.8	1.8	1.6	1.6	1.4	1.4	1.3	1.3	1.1
Killed or seriously injured	KNMT	30	30	26	25	24	22	19	19	17	16	14
All severities	KNMU	115	115	105	105	101	97	87	89	84	82	76

1 Includes other road users and road user not reported.
2 Rate based on provisional traffic estimates.

Source: Department of Transport

10.14 Road goods transport: analysis by mode of working and by gross weight of vehicle[1,2]
Great Britain

		1981	1982	1983	1984	1985	1986	1987	1988	1989	1990	1991
Estimated tonne kilometres (Thousand million)												
Total	KNNB	90.2	91.1	92.3	96.6	99.1	101.1	108.6	124.8	132.1	130.6	124.6
Own account	KNNC	34.4	34.3	33.5	34.2	32.5	32.4	31.5	37.2	36.8	36.0	38.8
Public haulage	KNND	55.8	56.8	58.8	62.3	66.6	68.7	77.1	87.6	95.3	94.7	85.8
By gross weight of vehicle- (Billion tonne kilometres)												
Not over 25 tonnes	KNNF	27.1	29.0	27.9	28.0	26.4	25.6	25.8	30.1	30.6	29.2	28.0
Over 25 tonnes	KNNG	63.1	62.1	64.3	68.6	72.7	75.5	82.8	94.7	101.5	101.4	96.6
Estimated tonnes carried (Millions)												
Total	KNNI	1 225	1 310	1 280	1 319	1 367	1 386	1 450	1 653	1 704	1 645	1 505
Own account	KNNJ	591	651	616	642	619	618	600	696	684	667	643
Public haulage	KCVJ	635	659	664	678	748	769	850	957	1 020	978	862
By gross weight of vehicle- (Million tonnes)												
Not over 25 tonnes	KCVL	594	655	622	637	625	604	613	682	672	632	578
Over 25 tonnes	KCVM	632	655	658	682	743	783	838	971	1 033	1 013	927

1 Includes the small amount of work performed in Northern Ireland by British registered goods vehicles.
2 Excludes work done by small goods vehicles not exceeding 3.5 tonnes gross vehicle weight.

Source: Department of Transport

Rail transport

10.15 British Rail: assets and privately-owned freight vehicles operated at year end
Great Britain

		Unit	1981	1982	1983	1984	1985/86	1986/87	1987/88	1988/89	1989/90	1990/91	1991/92
Rolling stock													
Tractive units: total	KNCA	Number	7 947	7 690	7 374	7 153	7 101	7 032	6 768	6 636	6 487	6 425	..
Locomotives: total	KNCB	"	3 131	3 016	2 850	2 756	2 581	2 441	2 270	2 180	2 095	2 030	1 896
Diesel[1]	KNCC	"	2 864	2 750	2 603	2 512	2 338	2 201	2 040	1 920	1 835	1 752	1 634
Electric	KNCD	"	267	266	247	244	243	240	230	260	260	278	262
Power cars: total	KNCE	"	4 816	4 674	4 524	4 397	4 520	4 591	4 498	4 456	4 392	4 413	..
Advanced passenger train	KNCF	"	6	6	6	6	6	4	2	–	–	–	..
High speed train	KNCG	"	181	197	197	197	197	197	197	197	197	197	197
Diesel[2]	KNCH	"	1 836	1 734	1 641	1 616	1 787	1 851	1 790	1 836	1 668	1 751	..
Electric[3]	KNCI	"	2 793	2 737	2 680	2 578	2 530	2 539	2 509	2 423	2 527	2 539	..
Coaching vehicles: total	KNCJ	"	18 962	17 628	16 963	16 489	16 164	15 336	14 648	14 258	13 833	13 631	12 925
Passenger carriages: total	KNCK	"	16 166	15 400	14 807	14 362	14 062	13 677	13 013	12 924	12 514	12 451	11 825
Locomotive hauled	KNCL	"	5 070	4 468	4 059	3 865	3 582	3 276	2 891	2 595	2 465	2 372	2 114
Advanced passenger train	KNCM	"	30	30	30	30	30	30	6	–	–	–	..
High speed train	KNCN	"	664	709	709	713	722	712	712	712	718	728	728
Diesel multiple unit[4]	KNCO	"	3 096	2 917	2 703	2 627	2 744	2 625	2 382	2 361	2 134	2 131	2 074
Electric multiple unit[5]	KNCP	"	7 306	7 276	7 306	7 127	6 984	7 034	7 022	7 256	7 197	7 220	6 909
Non-passenger-carrying vehicles[6]	KNCQ	"	2 796	2 228	2 156	2 127	2 102	1 659	1 635	1 334	1 319	1 180	1 100
Seats or berths in passenger carriages	KNCR	Thousands	1 040	1 000	970	940	930	900	870	880	860	850	810
Freight wagons operated: total	KNCS	Thousands	105.6	87.9	70.4	61.7	54.4	48.4	44.2	40.2	37.7	36.1	34.4
Wagons owned by British Rail: total	KNCT	"	86.2	69.4	52.4	44.7	37.9	32.4	28.4	25.3	22.3	21.1	19.9
Air-braked wagons	KNCU	"	20.0	20.1	19.8	19.5	19.4	19.4	20.0	20.7	20.5	20.3	..
Vacuum-braked wagons	KNCV	"	50.1	40.2	28.3	21.9	15.6	10.8	7.6	4.2	1.6	0.6	..
Unbraked wagons	KNCW	"	16.1	9.1	4.3	3.3	2.9	2.2	0.8	0.4	0.2	0.2	..
Wagons owned by Freightliners Ltd	KNCX	"	2.1	2.1	2.1	2.0	2.0	1.9	1.7	1.6	1.5	1.4	1.3
Wagons owned by customers of British Rail	KNCY	"	17.2	16.4	15.9	15.0	14.5	14.1	14.1	13.3	13.9	13.6	13.2
Permanent way and stations													
Route open for traffic: total	KNCZ	Kilometers	17 431	17 229	16 964	16 879	16 752	16 670	16 633	16 599	16 587	16 584	16 558
Electrified	KNDA	"	3 729	3 753	3 750	3 798	3 809	4 154	4 207	4 376	4 546	4 912	4 886
Non electrified	KNDB	"	13 702	13 476	13 214	13 081	12 943	12 516	12 426	12 223	12 041	11 672	11 672
Route open for passenger traffic	KNDC	"	14 394	14 371	14 375	14 304	14 310	14 304	14 302	14 309	14 318	14 317	14 291
Track open for traffic: total	KNDD	"	42 760	42 012	41 302	40 000	39 448	38 053	37 911	37 868	37 849	37 810	..
Running lines	KNDE	"	34 705	34 289	33 778	33 312	33 027	32 728	32 665	32 628	32 623	32 604	..
Sidings	KNDF	"	8 055	7 723	7 524	6 688	6 421	5 325	5 246	5 240	5 226	5 206	..
Stations: total[7]	KNDG	Number	2 742	2 711	2 619	2 523	2 526	2 530	2 541	2 596	2 598	2 615	2 556
Passenger	KNDH	"	2 361	2 369	2 363	2 375	2 385	2 405	2 426	2 470	2 471	2 488	2 473
Parcel	KNDI	"	3	3	3	3	4	2	1	1	2	2	..
Freight	KNDJ	"	378	339	253	145	137	123	114	125	125	125	83

1 Includes shunting locomotives (416 in 1991/2)
2 Diesel multiple unit power cars including a small number of non-passenger-carrying power cars.
3 Electric multiple unit power cars including a small number of non-passenger-carrying power cars.
4 Includes Diesel multiple unit power cars also included under Tractive units-Power cars-Diesel.
5 Includes Electric multiple unit power cars also included under Tractive units-Power cars-Electric.
6 Includes Advanced Passenger Train and High Speed Train power cars; also includes non-passenger-carrying power cars which are also shown under Tractive units, Power cars); also includes brake vans.
7 Combined passenger and freight stations have been reclassified as single purpose stations over the period.

Source: Department of Transport

Rail transport

10.16 British Rail: passenger and freight receipts and traffic
Great Britain

			Units	1981	1982[1]	1983	1984[1]	1985[1]	1986	1987	1988	1989	1990	1991
Traffic receipts: total[2]	KNDK		£ million	1 646.3	1 494.9	1 763.0	1 633.8	1 882.4	2 065.5	2 209.1	2 524.6	2 627.5	2 838.4	2 831.6
Passenger: total[2,3]	KNDL		£ million	1 022.7	924.1	1 129.6	1 195.6	1 286.2	1 410.1	1 539.0	1 750.6	1 847.5	2 044.9	2 073.8
Full fares	KNDM	KGVF	"	419.1	358.0									
Reduced fares	KNDN		"	347.7	335.4	842.1	889.2	943.2	1 026.8	1 106.8	1 248.8	1 308.8	1 470.1	1 484.3
Season tickets	KNDO		"	255.9	230.7	287.6	305.9	339.5	383.3	432.2	501.8	538.7	574.8	589.5
Freight: total	KNDP		"	623.1	580.0	643.6	438.2	596.2	655.4	670.1	774.0	780.0	793.5	757.8
Coal and Coke	KNDQ		"	274.1	270.5	280.4	84.9	226.5	283.2	282.5	287.7	305.9	316.4	310.3
Iron and steel	KNDR		"	65.0	51.9	57.5	50.8	52.8	59.0	68.5	78.2	78.3	77.9	74.2
Other	KNDS		"	164.6	165.0	190.7	184.9	191.1	195.5	198.0	281.5	281.5	280.5	268.8
Merchandise by coaching train	KNDT		"	..	..	..	..	..	..	..	..	..	..	..
Postal parcels and letter mails by coaching train	KNDU		"	..	..	..	..	..	..	..	..	..	..	..
Traffic														
Passenger journeys: total[3]	KNDV		Million	718.5	630.1	693.7	702.4	697.4	699.1	710.5	766.1	743.5	778.9	731.4
Full fares	KNDW		"	184.4	159.0	..	..	..	..	..	..	..	..	..
Reduced fares	KNDX		"	211.6	202.9	..	..	..	..	..	..	..	..	..
Season tickets[4]	KNDY		"	322.5	268.2	307.3	307.7	323.1	317.2	311.7	363.2	357.5	373.8	353.4
Passenger kilometres: (estimated) total[3]	KNDZ		"	29 700	27 200	29 500	29 800	29 700	31 000	32 300	34 400	33 200	34 100	31 900
Full fares	KNEA	KNEN	"	10 100	8 300	21 800	21 800	21 600	21 900	22 600	23 300	22 500	23 300	21 900
Reduced fares	KNEB		"	11 400	11 600									
Season tickets[4]	KNEC		"	8 200	7 300	7 800	7 900	8 100	9 000	9 700	11 100	10 800	10 800	10 000
Freight traffic originating: total[5]	BMHA		Million tonnes	154.2	141.9	145.1	78.4	122.0	139.6	141.0	149.5	145.8	141.1	134.8
Coal and coke	BMHB		"	95.2	88.4	87.9	25.5	65.9	79.7	77.7	78.8	76.5	74.9	74.8
Iron and steel	BMHC		"	18.2	14.2	15.9	12.4	14.1	16.8	19.1	20.5	19.7	18.4	17.3
Other	BMHD		"	40.8	39.2	41.1	41.3	40.5	43.2	44.2	50.1	49.6	47.8	42.7
Merchandise by coaching train	KNEH		"	..	..	..	..	..	..	..	..	..	..	..
Postal parcels and letter mails by coaching train	KNEI		"	..	..	..	..	..	..	..	..	..	..	..
Tonne kilometres: (estimated) total[5,6]	KNEJ		Millions	17 505	15 880	17 144	12 700	15 300	16 600	17 300	18 200	17 300	15 800	15 200
Coal and coke	KNEK		"	6 544	5 741	5 875	1 600	4 100	5 100	4 700	4 600	4 800	5 000	5 000
All other freight train traffic	KNEL		"	10 961	10 139	11 269	11 100	11 300	11 500	12 600	13 600	12 500	10 800	10 200

1 British Rail traffic was affected by industrial action by ASLEF in 1982 and by the miners' strike and associated action by British Rail staff in 1984 and 1985.
2 Grants received by British Rail in respect of certain subsidised passenger services are not included in passenger receipts.
3 The receipts and passenger kilometres include an appropriate proportion in respect of through bookings with the railways of London Regional Transport and other administrations. Passenger journeys in respect of such through bookings are included. In 1985, 697 million journeys originated on British Rail only. Season ticket journeys include those in respect of West Midlands travel cards.
4 All season ticket journeys and passenger kilometres were calculated on a rate of 480 journeys per year per annual season ticket and 540 journeys for shorter period tickets. Return tickets have been counted as two journeys.
5 Excluding free-hauled traffic on freight trains.
6 Excluding freight carried by coaching trains.

Source: Department of Transport

Rail transport

10.17 British Rail: operations
Great Britain

		Unit	1981	1982[1]	1983	1984[1]	1985	1986/87	1987/88	1988/89	1989/90	1990/91	1991/92
Loaded train kilometres													
Coaching; total[2]	KNNL	Millions	336.2	298.0	325.4	323.9	327.7	327.7	340.6	351.8	355.2	363.0	362.2
High speed trains	KNNM	"	23.3	26.2	32.3	33.5	34.7	34.3	35.9	36.1	34.4	34.3	31.2
Diesel locomotives	KNNN	"	69.0	57.9	62.0	61.2	59.1	54.1	47.1	37.2	32.4	28.5	20.4
multiple units	KNNO	"	86.7	74.5	78.4	76.5	79.3	82.5	91.1	107.6	117.8	123.7	123.8
Electric locomotives	KNNP	"	30.9	26.4	27.2	28.2	30.0	30.1	32.9	32.7	33.1	34.3	40.9
multiple units	KNNQ	"	126.3	113.0	125.5	124.5	124.6	126.7	133.6	138.2	137.5	142.2	145.8
of which: Non-passenger[3]	KNNR	"	*13.7*	*11.5*	*14.5*	*14.8*	*16.2*	*16.0*	*15.5*	*12.4*	*11.7*	*9.5*	*8.5*
Freight total[4]	KNNS	"	48.9	43.4	45.4	38.7	36.8	50.0	50.4	51.8	49.5	48.0	44.5
Diesel locomotives	KNNT	"	41.6	37.0	38.5	31.7	30.2	43.9	44.5	45.6	43.7	43.0	40.1
Electric locomotives	KNNU	"	7.3	6.4	6.9	7.0	6.6	6.1	5.9	6.2	5.8	5.0	4.4

1 British Rail traffic was affected by industrial action by ASLEF in 1982 and by the miners strike in 1984.
2 Train kilometres worked by British Rail trains over all lines including certain London Regional Transport lines.
3 Non-passenger trains consist of vehicles for the conveyance of freight at coaching train rates.
4 Excludes free-hauled traffic on freight trains. From 1978, figures have been revised to reflect a change in the calculation of loaded train kilometres for "Merry-Go-Round" coal traffic to power stations. From 1986/87 figures include unladen freight trains.

Source: Department of Transport

10.18 London Underground: receipts, operations and assets

			Unit	1981	1982	1983	1984/85	1985/86	1986/87	1987/88	1988/89	1989/90	1990/91	1991/92
Receipts														
Passenger: total	KNOA		£ million	251.1	276.5	285.4	298.0	339.4	369.3	397.9	431.1	461.1	529.3	557.5
Ordinary	KNOB	KGSR	"	137.4	161.5	158.0	175.0	186.9	202.1	206.9	227.6	261.3	294.3	305.6
Reduced rate	KNOC		"	28.8	31.2	27.4								
Season tickets	KNOD		"	85.0	83.8	100.0	123.0	152.5	167.2	191.0	203.5	199.9	235.0	251.9
Traffic														
Passenger journeys: total	KNOE		Million	541	498	563	672	732	769	798	815	765	775	751
Ordinary	KNOF	KGSS	"	296	289	273	354	341	355	373	363	380	399	368
Reduced rate	KNOG		"	63	49	77								
Season tickets	KNOH		"	182	159	212	318	391	414	425	452	385	376	383
Passenger kilometres	KNOI		"	4 088	3 653	4 345	5 375	5 971	6 215	6 257	6 292	6 016	6 164	5 895
Operations														
Loaded train kilometres	KNOJ		Million	49	46	46	47	48	49	51	52	51	54	54
Place kilometres	KNOK		"	41 638	39 479	39 685	40 100	40 400	41 700	43 300	43 600	43 000	44 900	45 300
Rolling stock														
Railway cars	KNOL		Number	4 267	4 069	3 885	3 918	3 875	3 877	3 905	3 950	3 908	4 146	4 146
Seating capacity	KNOM		Thousand	165.7	169.0	165.0	167.7	166.2	166.2	167.2	169.8	171.6	171.6	166.9
Permanent way and stations														
Route kilometres open for traffic	KNON		Kilometres	388	388	388	388	388	394	394	394	394	394	394
Stations	KNOO		Number	247	247	247	247	247	248	248	248	247	248	248

Source: Department of Transport

Rail transport

10.19 Accidents on railways
Great Britain

Number

		1980	1981	1982	1983	1984	1985	1986	1987	1988	1989	1990	1991/92
Train accidents													
Number of accidents: total[1]	KNIA	930	1 014	998	1 255	1 359	1 240	1 171	1 165	1 330	1 434	1 283	960
Collisions	KNIB	290	280	250	315	300	282	266	290	296	329	290	187
Derailments	KNIC	138	148	173	220	230	229	192	193	231	192	183	144
Running into level crossing gates and other obstructions	KNID	286	353	284	363	471	440	451	391	486	510	473	340
Fires	KNIE	151	165	163	165	168	191	174	191	229	283	257	225
Miscellaneous	KNIF	65	68	128	192	190	98	88	101	88	120	80	64
Persons killed	KNIG	7	7	11	10	30	6	27	11	40	18	4	11
Passengers	KNIH	–	4	–	2	18	–	8	3	34	6	–	2
Railway staff	KNII	4	1	8	1	6	–	5	1	2	6	1	2
Others	KNIJ	3	2	3	7	6	6	14	7	4	6	3	7
Persons injured	KNIK	447	195	264	218	475	380	510	396	705	405	243	391
Passengers	KNIL	387	127	150	88	386	261	342	310	615	312	157	307
Railway staff	KNIM	45	34	92	93	68	88	137	65	68	71	73	65
Others	KNIN	15	34	22	37	21	31	31	21	22	22	13	19
Other accidents through movement of railway vehicles													
Persons killed	KNIO	52	58	40	53	41	55	41	57	53	41	75	73
Passengers	KNIP	25	31	18	25	21	31	24	36	34	25	37	53
Railway staff	KNIQ	20	21	17	24	14	16	8	11	11	8	19	9
Others	KNIR	7	6	5	4	6	8	9	10	8	8	19	11
Persons injured	KNIS	2 265	2 450	1 946	2 459	2 486	2 489	2 443	2 776	2 810	2 769	2 777	2 360
Passengers	KNIT	1 945	2 218	1 822	2 341	2 400	2 383	2 346	2 689	2 721	2 698	2 658	2 254
Railway staff	KNIU	309	219	121	97	73	96	80	84	85	63	116	104
Others	KNIV	11	13	3	21	13	10	17	3	4	8	3	2
Other accidents on railway premises													
Persons killed	KNIW	10	11	6	6	5	13	4	37	4	10	5	10
Passengers	KNIX	1	4	2	2	–	2	1	29	1	2	2	3
Railway staff	KNIY	8	5	2	3	5	9	3	4	3	4	2	6
Others	KNIZ	1	2	2	1	–	2	–	4	–	4	1	1
Persons injured	KNJA	8 138	7 379	6 490	6 590	6 267	6 295	6 528	6 614	7 351	7 628	6 978	6 900
Passengers	KNJB	2 977	2 657	2 571	3 381	3 473	3 518	3 577	3 650	4 035	4 429	3 647	..
Railway staff	KNJC	4 848	4 530	3 740	2 981	2 530	2 533	2 691	2 761	3 142	3 001	3 118	3 335
Others	KNJD	313	192	179	228	264	244	260	203	174	198	213	146
Trespassers and suicides													
Persons killed	KNJE	360	369	296	358	339	318	325	317	374	298	285	334
Persons injured	KNJF	141	127	141	153	128	128	120	101	129	92	123	92

1 The figures from 1982 onwards include accidents to non-passenger trains on non-passenger lines not previously reported.

Source: Department of Transport

Rail transport

10.20 Railways: permanent way and rolling stock
Northern Ireland
At end of year

Number

		1980	1981	1982	1983	1984	1985	1986	1987	1988	1989	1990	1991
Length of road open for traffic [1] (Km)	KNRA	332	332	332	332	332	332	332	332	332	332	332	332
Length of track open for traffic (Km)													
Total	KNRB	575	575	575	575	575	575	575	553	553	553	553	553
Running lines	KNRC	521	521	521	521	521	521	521	500	500	500	500	500
Sidings (as single track)	KNRD	53	53	53	53	53	53	53	53	53	53	53	53
Locomotives													
Diesel-electrics	KNRE	8	8	8	8	9	9	13	12	12	12	9	9
Passenger carrying vehicles													
Total	KNRF	113	114	115	105	106	108	112	112	115	115	115	115
Rail motor vehicles:													
Diesel-electric, etc	KNRG	35	35	35	30	30	28	31	31	31	30	30	30
Trailer carriages:													
Total locomotive hauled	KNRH	33	33	33	32	28	28	25	27	28	28	28	28
Ordinary coaches	KNRI	32	32	32	30	26	26	23	25	26	26	26	26
Restaurant cars	KNRJ	1	1	1	2	2	2	2	2	2	2	2	2
Rail car trailers	KNRK	45	46	47	43	48	52	56	56	56	56	56	56
Non-passenger carrying vehicles													
Post Office and luggage vans, etc	KNRL	27	27	27	20	9	6	–	–	–	–	–	–
Trucks and wagons owned													
Total	KNRM	139	123	119	111	21	20	17	17	17	17	17	17
Merchandise wagons:													
Open	KNRN	82	82	78	74	3	3	–	–	–	–	–	–
Covered	KNRO	6	6	6	6	–	–	–	–	–	–	–	–
Rail and timber trucks	KNRP	2	2	2	2	–	–	–	–	–	–	–	–
Brake vans	KNRQ	1	1	1	–	–	–	–	–	–	–	–	–
Special wagons	KNRR	48	32	32	29	18	17	17	17	17	17	17	17
Containers	KNRS	10	10	10	10	10	10	–	–	–	–	–	–
Rolling stock for maintenance and repair	KNRT	162	170	158	115	60	64	54	44	46	55	55	55

1 The total length of railroad open for traffic irrespective of the number of tracks comprising the road.

Source: Department of the Environment for Northern Ireland

10.21 Operating statistics of railways
Northern Ireland

		Unit	1980	1981	1982	1983	1984	1985	1986	1987	1988	1989	1990	1991
Maintenance of way and works														
Material used:														
Ballast	KNSA	Thousand m^2	28.4	25.7	19.8	15.0	17.0	19.8	17.7	25.5	28.3	33.0	25.0	22.5
Rails	KNSB	Thousand tonnes	1.02	1.38	1.70	1.06	1.86	1.95	2.20	0.73	1.72	1.60	0.91	1.68
Sleepers	KNSC	Thousands	13.30	16.50	21.10	13.70	21.10	24.00	17.00	17.00	23.20	18.00	19.00	23.20
Track renewed	KNSD	Km	9.00	12.50	16.09	9.60	16.09	16.90	5.00	15.30	17.20	9.70	8.80	10.40
Engine kilometres														
Total[1]	KNSE	Thousand Km	3 730.003	712.003	683.003	579.003	410.003	558.003	579.003	576.003	572.003	575.003	200.003	200.00
Train kilometres:														
Total	KNSF	"	3 200	3 105	3 102	3 392	3 405	3 411	3 401	3 398	3 394	3 391	3 844	3 410
Coaching	KNSG	"	3 065	3 001	3 086	3 373	3 402	3 407	3 396	3 394	3 391	3 393	3 840	3 406
Freight	KNSH	"	135	105	16[2]	19	3	4	4	4	4	4	4	4

1 Including shunting, assisting, light, departmental, maintenance and repair.
2 The reduction in mileage from 1982 is a result of changes in CIE/NIR freight contract.

Source: Department of the Environment for Northern Ireland.

Air transport

10.22 Main output[1] of UK airlines

		1981	1982	1983	1984	1985	1986	1987	1988	1989	1990	1991
All services: total	KNTA	13 087	11 848	12 011	13 155	13 408	14 306	15 853	17 225	18 923	20 377	20 166
Percentage growth on previous year	KNTB	-0.9	-9.5	1.4	9.5	1.9	6.7	10.8	8.7	9.9	7.7	-1.0
Scheduled services: total	KNTC	9 936	9 068	8 989	9 854	10 166	10 655	11 430	12 405	13 427	15 274	15 188
Percentage growth on previous year	KNTD	1.1	-8.7	-0.9	9.6	3.2	4.8	7.3	8.5	8.2	13.8	-0.6
Non-scheduled services: total	KNTE	3 151	2 780	3 022	3 301	3 242	3 651	4 423	4 820	5 496	5 103	4 978
Percentage growth on previous year	KNTF	-6.9	-11.8	8.7	9.2	-1.8	12.6	21.1	9.0	14.0	-7.2	-2.5

1 Available Tonne Kilometres (millions).

Source: Civil Aviation Authority

10.23 Air traffic between the United Kingdom and abroad[1]
Aircraft flights and passengers carried

Thousands

		1981	1982	1983	1984	1985	1986	1987	1988	1989	1990	1991
Flights												
United Kingdom airlines												
Scheduled services	KNUA	149.7	143.5	141.9	151.3	170.8	177.5	188.5	216.9	245.0	271.0	250.5
Non-scheduled services	KNUB	162.2	176.3	184.9	214.0	196.2	198.8	219.2	225.5	221.3	207.9	202.6
Overseas airlines[2]												
Scheduled services	KNUC	152.0	154.3	155.2	160.9	172.8	195.8	222.8	249.8	269.9	294.8	300.4
Non-scheduled services	KNUD	31.9	37.3	36.5	40.2	39.5	43.6	45.2	43.0	46.1	45.5	34.6
Total	KNUE	495.8	511.4	518.5	566.3	579.3	615.8	675.7	735.2	782.3	819.2	788.1
Passengers carried												
United Kingdom airlines												
Scheduled services	KNUF	13 559.0	12 214.7	12 140.0	13 174.2	14 854.3	15 082.9	17 473.8	19 237.6	21 863.2	25 316.8	23 271.6
Non-scheduled services	KNUG	12 128.9	13 216.6	14 661.9	16 643.7	15 529.0	12 929.7	22 250.5	23 062.1	22 558.8	19 679.1	19 715.2
Overseas airlines[2]												
Scheduled services	KNUH	15 398.8	15 520.5	16 065.6	17 623.0	18 815.6	19 409.5	22 441.5	25 029.3	26 517.8	28 224.4	26 719.4
Non-scheduled services	KNUI	2 645.4	3 180.1	3 417.4	3 713.9	3 663.8	4 186.0	4 412.8	4 086.5	4 325.6	4 187.9	3 078.8
Total	KNUJ	43 732.0	44 131.9	46 284.9	51 154.8	52 862.7	51 608.1	66 578.6	71 415.5	75 265.3	77 408.2	72 785.0

1 Excludes travel to and from the Channel Islands.
2 Includes airlines of overseas UK Territories.

Source: Civil Aviation Authority

10.24 UK airlines[1]
Operations and traffic on scheduled services: revenue traffic

Air transport

		Unit	1981	1982	1983	1984	1985	1986	1987	1988	1989	1990	1991
All services													
Aircraft stage flights:													
Number	KNFA	Number	410 115	414 167	431 615	447 336	470 989	475 263	499 764	546 386	606 505	617 477	568 122
Average length	KNFB	Kilometres	878	801	752	784	787	809	813	811	801	848	876
Aircraft-kilometres													
flown	KNFC	Millions	359.9	331.7	324.6	350.9	370.6	384.7	406.3	443.2	485.7	523.8	497.7
Passengers uplifted	KNFD	"	21.4	20.6	20.4	22.6	24.8	25.0	28.5	31.4	35.2	38.4	34.6
Seat-kilometres used	KNFE	"	52 209.6	46 404.3	43 887.4	48 235.3	51 436.9	51 400.9	59 887.2	63 868.1	70 196.0	79 579.6	74 615.4
Cargo and mail													
uplifted: total	KNFF	Tonnes	294 866	263 798	294 247	363 461	358 927	376 023	405 419	435 071	453 430	485 535	466 622
Tonne-kilometres													
used: total	KNFG	Millions	6 188.4	5 593.2	5 521.8	6 337.3	6 466.5	6 606.4	7 586.0	8 106.3	8 973.5	10 023.0	9 570.5
Passenger	KNFH	"	4 674.5	4 223.7	4 004.0	4 405.1	4 700.6	4 708.9	5 497.6	5 869.8	6 604.9	7 465.6	7 007.9
Cargo	KNFI	"	1 343.5	1 200.4	1 338.1	1 736.2	1 563.1	1 698.1	1 885.6	2 057.3	2 206.4	2 388.7	2 379.9
Mail	KNFJ	"	170.5	169.1	179.7	196.0	202.8	199.3	202.8	179.2	162.3	168.6	182.6
Domestic services													
Aircraft stage flights:													
Number	KNFK	Number	188 534	201 887	221 560	254 064	258 502	255 764	266 226	277 682	303 147	300 683	285 346
Average length	KNFL	Kilometres	282	279	274	265	268	278	276	279	281	288	301
Aircraft-kilometres													
flown	KNFM	Millions	53.1	56.2	60.7	67.3	69.3	71.1	73.6	77.4	85.2	86.5	86.0
Passengers uplifted	KNFN	"	6.6	7.1	7.2	8.3	9.0	9.1	10.1	11.2	12.2	12.7	11.6
Seat-kilometres used	KNFO	"	2 600.7	2 752.7	2 791.4	3 237.8	3 494.3	3 566.9	3 926.5	4 381.1	4 767.6	5 020.8	4 663.7
Cargo and mail													
uplifted: total	KNFP	Tonnes	35 212	37 993	39 739	45 529	46 337	47 550	50 783	48 794	46 660	45 818	37 739
Tonne-kilometres													
used: total	KNFQ	Millions	229.7	237.3	240.7	278.4	299.9	305.9	335.6	371.5	408.0	428.3	396.5
Passenger	KNFR	"	218.1	224.7	227.1	262.8	283.8	289.5	318.5	355.2	392.0	412.0	382.3
Cargo	KNFS	"	7.3	7.5	7.7	10.2	10.2	10.5	10.7	10.1	8.9	8.7	6.7
Mail	KNFT	"	4.3	5.2	5.9	5.4	6.0	5.9	6.4	6.3	7.1	7.6	7.4
International services													
Aircraft stage flights:													
Number	KNFU	Number	221 581	212 280	210 055	193 272	212 487	219 499	233 537	268 704	303 358	316 794	282 776
Average length	KNFV	Kilometres	1 385	1 298	1 256	1 467	1 418	1 428	1 425	1 361	1 320	1 381	1 456
Aircraft-kilometres													
flown	KNFW	Millions	306.8	275.5	263.9	283.6	301.3	313.5	332.8	365.8	400.5	437.4	411.7
Passengers uplifted	KNFX	"	14.8	13.5	13.2	14.3	15.8	15.9	18.5	20.2	22.9	25.7	22.9
Seat-kilometres used	KNFY	"	49 608.9	43 651.6	41 096.1	44 997.5	47 942.7	47 834.0	55 960.7	59 487.1	65 428.3	74 558.8	69 951.7
Cargo and Mail													
uplifted: total	KNFZ	Tonnes	259 654	225 806	254 507	317 932	312 589	328 473	354 636	386 277	406 770	439 717	428 883
Tonne-kilometres													
used: total	KNJW	Millions	5 958.7	5 355.9	5 281.1	6 058.9	6 166.6	6 300.4	7 250.4	7 734.8	8 565.6	9 594.7	9 174.0
Passenger	KNJX	"	4 456.3	3 998.9	3 776.9	4 142.3	4 416.8	4 419.4	5 179.1	5 514.6	6 212.9	7 053.6	6 625.6
Cargo	KNJY	"	1 336.2	1 193.0	1 330.4	1 726.0	1 552.9	1 687.6	1 875.0	2 047.2	2 197.4	2 380.1	2 373.2
Mail	KNJZ	"	166.2	164.0	173.8	190.7	196.9	193.4	196.3	172.9	155.2	161.1	175.2

1 Includes services of British Airways and other UK private companies (including operations performed by Cathay Pacific Airways on their scheduled service London-Hong Kong from May 1981 until December 1984).

Source: Civil Aviation Authority

Air transport
10.25 Non-scheduled services by UK airlines[1]

		Unit	1979	1980	1981	1982	1983	1984	1985	1986	1987	1988	1989[5]
All non-scheduled services[2,4] Total	KNGA	Tonne km available (millions)	3 909.8	3 383.4	3 151.3	2 780.0	3 022.2	3 301.1	3 242.1	3 650.8	4 423.3	4 820.2	5 496.2
Percentage of all UK services	KNGB		*30.7*	*25.6*	*24.1*	*23.5*	*25.2*	*25.1*	*24.2*	*25.5*	*27.9*	*28.0*	*28.3*
Inclusive tours[3] Total	KNGC	Tonne km available (millions)	1 546.4	1 813.2	1 950.1	2 180.1	2 371.8	2 635.6	2 477.6	3 100.0	3 786.9	4 012.4	4 167.0
Percentage of all UK services	KNGD		*12.1*	*13.7*	*14.9*	*18.4*	*19.7*	*20.0*	*18.5*	*21.7*	*23.9*	*23.3*	*22.0*
Other separate fare and advance booking charters[3] Total	KNGE	Tonne km available (millions)	352.3	344.9	335.9	184.5	240.4	291.1	327.7	264.9	308.4	403.0	651.7
Percentage of all UK services	KNGF		*2.8*	*2.6*	*2.6*	*1.6*	*2.0*	*2.2*	*2.4*	*1.9*	*1.9*	*2.3*	*3.4*
Other charters Total	KNGG	Tonne km available (millions)	2 011.1	1 225.3	864.8	415.4	410.0	374.3	436.8	285.9	328.0	404.8	671.2
Percentage of all UK services	KNGH		*15.8*	*9.3*	*6.6*	*3.5*	*3.4*	*2.8*	*3.3*	*2.0*	*2.1*	*2.4*	*3.6*
			\multicolumn{11}{c}{Load factors and distances}										
Inclusive tours[3] Seat-kilometres available (A)	KNGI	Millions	17 635	20 345	21 710	24 561	26 480	30 095	28 073	35 130	42 995	45 328	47 389
Seat-kilometres used (B)	KNGJ	"	14 921	17 117	18 516	20 775	22 731	25 855	24 996	32 091	38 700	40 830	41 942
(B) as a percentage of (A)	KNGK		*84.6*	*84.1*	*85.3*	*84.6*	*85.8*	*85.9*	*89.0*	*91.4*	*90.0*	*90.1*	*88.5*
Passengers uplifted	KNGL	Millions	8.750	9.663	10.156	11.902	13.038	14.616	13.631	17.374	20.723	21.251	20.459
Stage flights	KNGM	Number	80 441	86 298	87 689	104 700	108 173	116 404	102 674	121 747	140 143	139 478	138 968
Aircraft-kilometres flown	KNGN	Millions	130.8	147.1	154.3	178.5	181.9	197.0	177.6	213.1	248.9	255.1	263.1
Average distance per stage flight	KNGO	Kilometres	1 626.0	1 705.0	1 760.0	1 705.0	1 682.0	1 692.0	1 730.0	1 750.0	1 776.0	1 829.0	1 893.0
Average distance per passenger	KNGP	"	1 705	1 771	1 823	1 746	1 743	1 769	1 834	1 847	1 867	1 921	2 050
Other separate fare and advance booking charters[3] Seat-kilometres available (C)	KNGQ	Millions	3 732	3 729	3 715	2 104	2 526	3 203	3 684	2 978	3 461	4 122	6 814
Seat-kilometres used (D)	KNGR	"	2 872	2 943	3 071	1 759	2 189	2 789	3 090	2 507	2 882	3 476	6 010
(D) as a percentage of (C)	KNGS		*77.0*	*78.9*	*82.7*	*83.6*	*86.6*	*87.1*	*83.9*	*84.2*	*83.3*	*84.3*	*88.2*
Passengers uplifted	KNGT	"	1.069	1.161	1.457	0.685	0.677	0.825	1.018	0.728	0.907	1.211	1.383
Stage flights	KNGU	Number	10 933	12 655	13 058	6 353	5 914	7 938	8 687	6 036	7 602	10 914	11 668
Aircraft-kilometres flown	KNGV	Millions	20.8	21.8	22.8	12.1	13.9	15.8	17.0	13.5	15.6	20.4	27.6
Average distance per stage flight	KNGW	Kilometres	1 903	1 724	1 746	1 905	2 344	1 990	1 954	2 238	2 057	1 872	2 368
Average distance per passenger	KNGX	"	2 687	2 534	2 108	2 568	3 232	3 381	3 035	3 446	3 176	2 870	4 346

1 Includes services of the British Airways Board and other UK companies.
2 Excludes Air Taxi operations.
3 Inclusive tours performed under Class 4 licences are included with Other separate fare and advance booking charters.
4 Includes Class 5 operations.
5 Figures discontinued in 1990.

Source: Civil Aviation Authority

Air transport

10.26 Trends in major United Kingdom airlines
Operating costs and revenues 1980-1989

		1980	1981	1982	1983	1984	1985[1]	1986[1]	1987[2]	1988[4]	1989
All airlines											
Costs											
Comparison with 1980 (1980=100)											
Aircraft fuel and oil	KNHA	100.0	105.5	109.5	106.5	126.2	122.4	82.6	84.5	..	..
Crew salaries and expenses	KNHB	100.0	114.4	107.1	113.7	125.5	133.4	160.2	177.3	..	..
Aircraft depreciation and rental	KNHC	100.0	113.8	100.3	106.8	149.3	194.4	217.2	279.4	..	..
Other costs	KNHD	100.0	97.4	104.3	115.1	136.9	158.2	180.0	203.0	..	..
Total Operating costs	KNHE	100.0	101.5	105.7	112.1	134.1	149.0	153.7	172.8	..	..
Comparison with Total - Percentage distribution											
Aircraft fuel and oil	KNHF	28.2	29.3	29.2	26.8	26.5	23.2	15.1	13.8	..	..
Crew salaries and expenses	KNHG	5.0	5.7	5.1	5.1	4.7	4.5	5.3	5.2	..	..
Aircraft depreciation and rental	KNHH	5.9	6.6	5.6	5.6	6.5	7.7	8.3	9.5	..	..
Other costs	KNHI	60.9	58.4	60.1	62.5	62.2	64.6	71.3	71.5	..	..
Total Operating costs	KNHJ	100.0	100.0	100.0	100.0	100.0	100.0	100.0	100.0	..	..
Revenues											
Comparison with 1980 (1980=100)											
Scheduled services	KNHK	100.0	103.6	114.4	124.4	147.3	160.1	161.1	183.8	..	..
Non-scheduled services	KNHL	100.0	114.8	133.8	147.2	170.5	171.1	186.2	216.9	..	..
Incidental revenues	KNHM	100.0	86.7	79.7	97.1	120.3	206.4	196.3	218.1	..	..
Total Operating revenues	KNHN	100.0	105.3	117.4	128.1	151.1	163.0	166.4	190.5	..	..
Comparison with Total-Percentage distribution											
Scheduled services	KNHO	79.7	78.3	77.7	77.4	77.7	78.3	77.1	76.8	..	..
Non-scheduled services	KNHP	18.5	20.1	21.1	21.2	20.8	19.4	20.7	21.0	..	..
Incidental revenues	KNHQ	1.9	1.5	1.3	1.4	1.5	2.4	2.2	2.1	..	..
Total Operating revenues	KNHR	100.0	100.0	100.0	100.0	100.0	100.0	100.0	100.0	..	..

Revenues, expenses and profits of major United Kingdom airlines 1979-1989

		1980	1981	1982	1983	1984	1985[1]	1986[1]	1987[2]	1988[2,3]	1989	1990
Total Operating Revenues	KNHS	2 616.5	2 756.0	3 070.5	3 351.6	3 953.2	4 265.7	4 353.3	4 984.8	5 171.2	5 886.1	6 325.2
Total Operating Expenses	KNHT	2 690.0	2 730.2	2 842.5	3 015.3	3 606.2	4 007.0	4 135.1	4 647.5	4 739.6	5 436.9	6 153.7
Operating profit (or loss)	KNHU	−73.4	25.8	228.0	336.3	346.9	258.7	218.2	319.1	411.3	449.2	171.5
Non-operating items (net)	KNHV	−52.7	−131.7	−126.7	−103.4	−132.9	−38.4	−22.5	−13.0	−74.8	−59.2	−64.8
Profit (or loss) before tax	KNHW	−126.1	−105.9	101.3	232.9	214.0	220.3	195.7	306.0	344.4	390.1	106.8

1 Excludes Virgin Atlantic whose Financial Report covers 18 months.
2 Excludes British Air Ferries. Operating profit (or loss), net operating items (net) and profit (or loss) before tax include British Caledonian Airways for the months of January 1988 - March 1988.
3 Excludes British Island Airways.
4 Figures discontinued in 1988.

Source: Civil Aviation Authority

Air transport

10.27 United Kingdom airlines[1]
Accidents on scheduled fixed wing passenger-carrying services[2]

	Passenger casualties			Crew casualties		Thousand aircraft stage flights per fatal accident	Million aircraft-Kms. flown per fatal accident	Thousand passengers carried per passenger killed	Million passenger Kms. flown per passenger killed	Fatal accidents		Passengers killed per hundred million passenger-Kms.
	Number of fatal accidents	Killed	Seriously injured	Killed	Seriously injured					per 100,000 aircraft stage flights	per hundred million aircraft-Kms.	
1950-54	7	194	9	28	4	107.4	61.8	46.1	50.0	0.93	1.62	1.99
1955-59	7	123	28	29	8	158.3	92.1	155.2	158.5	0.63	1.09	0.63
1960-64	5	104	35	21	6	303.7	182.3	373.4	390.6	0.33	0.55	0.25
1965-69	6	273	2	32	2	282.7	194.9	222.2	255.2	0.35	0.52	0.39
1970-74	2	167	5	14	2	897.4	737.6	466.3	657.7	0.11	0.14	0.15
1975-79	1	54	6	9	-	1 797.2	1 481.6	1 697.0	3 240.0	0.06	0.07	0.03
1980-84	-	-	4	-	-							-
1985-89	2	47	-	1	-	1 220.0	1 014.5	3031.0	6 262.9	0.08	0.10	0.02
	KCVN	KCVO	KCVP	KCVQ	KCVR	KCVS	KCVT	KCVU	KCVV	KCVW	KCVX	KCVY
1986	..	..	..	..	..	..	..	..	..	..	..	..
1987	-	-	-	-	-	..	..	..	..	..	..	..
1988	-	-	-	-	-	..	..	..	..	..	..	..
1989	1	47	67	-	7	2 682.4	2 295.6	3 515.0	7 353.6	0.04	0.04	0.01
1990	-	-	-	-	-	..	..	..	..	..	..	..

1 Including services of UK Airways Corporations (reconstituted as the British Airways Board in 1973) and private companies.
2 Excluding accidents involving the deaths of third parties only.

Source: Civil Aviation Authority

10.28 Activity at civil aerodromes
United Kingdom

		1981	1982	1983	1984	1985	1986	1987	1988	1989	1990	1991
Movement of civil aircraft												
(thousands)	KNQA	2 103	2 113	2 238	2 363	2 354	2 439	2 614	2 868	3 137	3 255	2 947
Commercial: total	KNQB	1 028	1 072	1 243	1 179	1 205	1 238	1 312	1 402	1 487	1 547	1 481
Transport	KNQC	927	974	1 019	1 079	1 097	1 125	1 193	1 279	1 359	1 420	1 365
Other[1]	KNQD	101	98	224	100	108	113	118	123	128	127	115
Non-commercial[2]	KNQE	1 075	1 041	995	1 184	1 149	1 201	1 303	1 466	1 650	1 708	1 466
Passengers handled (thousands):												
total	KNQF	58 979	60 033	62 301	68 830	71 812	76 593	87 517	94 640	100 553	104 142	97 293
Terminal	KNQG	57 771	58 778	61 099	67 572	70 434	75 161	86 041	93 162	98 898	102 417	95 768
Transit	KNQH	1 208	1 255	1 202	1 258	1 377	1 432	1 476	1 479	1 655	1 725	1 525
Commercial freight handled[3]												
(tonnes): total	KNQI	723 709	692 693	725 897	860 629	850 268	881 202	975 879	1 088 151	1 148 457	1 193 050	1 119 973
Set down	KNQJ	341 932	320 604	332 162	3 882 923	377 127	419 275	485 468	572 426	592 139	625 131	595 886
Picked up	KNQK	381 777	372 088	393 737	472 335	473 140	461 927	490 412	515 725	556 318	567 919	524 087
Mail handled (tonnes): total	KNQL	106 497	118 406	124 080	136 640	145 770	153 467	155 199	153 308	162 504	172 164	170 472
Set down	KNQM	50 063	55 200	56 943	61 461	64 138	67 802	67 758	66 978	71 918	76 262	77 082
Picked up	KNQN	56 434	63 206	67 138	75 179	81 632	85 665	87 441	86 330	90 586	95 902	93 390

1 Local pleasure flights and non-transport charter flights for reward (for example: aerial survey work, crop dusting and delivery of empty aircraft).
2 Test and training flights, scheduled service positioning flights, private, aero-club and official flights, etc.
3 Figures include weight of vehicles carried on vehicle ferry services.

Source: Civil Aviation Authority

Sea transport

10.29 United Kingdom and Crown Dependency registered trading vessels of 500 gross tons and over[1]

Summary of tonnage by type End of year

		1980	1985	1986			1986	1991
Number					**Number**			
Passenger[3]	KNVA	102	83	79	Passenger[7]	KMTA	8	8
Cargo liners	KNVB	232	87	68	Container (FC)	KMTB	47	32
Tramps	KNVC	252	155	132	Other general cargo[6]	KMTC	128	99
Bulk carriers[2]	KNVD	190	73	50	Bulk carriers[4]	KMTD	73	32
Tankers	KNVE	427	242	169	Tankers	KMTE	165	124
Container (FC)	KNVF	72	53	47	Specialised carriers	KMTF	21	18
					Ro-ro[5]	KMTG	104	96
All vessels	KNVG	1 275	693	545	All vessels	KMTH	546	409
Thousand gross tons					**Thousand gross tons**			
Passenger[3]	KNVH	617	616	588	Passenger[7]	KMT I	259	271
Cargo liners	KNVI	1 992	728	564	Container (FC)	KMTJ	1 369	1 091
Tramps	KNVJ	554	335	244	Other general cargo[6]	KMTK	510	242
Bulk carriers[2]	KNVK	6 428	2 851	1 864	Bulk carriers[4]	KMTL	2 003	489
Tankers	KNVL	14 578	6 191	3 083	Tankers	KMTM	3 249	2 166
Container (FC)	KNVM	1 600	1 489	1 369	Specialised carriers	KMTN	95	99
					Ro-ro[5]	KMTO	561	604
All vessels	KNVN	25 769	12 208	7 711	All vessels	KMTP	8 046	4 963
Thousand deadweight tonnes					**Thousand deadweight tonnes**			
Passenger[3]	KNVO	182	162	156	Passenger[7]	KMTQ	47	49
Cargo liners	KNVP	2 669	1 002	748	Container (FC)	KMTR	1 298	1 019
Tramps	KNVQ	872	527	395	Other general cargo[6]	KMTS	749	349
Bulk carriers[2]	KNVR	11 306	5 072	3 321	Bulk carriers[4]	KMTT	3 569	825
Tankers	KMSY	26 437	10 378	5 499	Tankers	KMTU	5 908	3 875
Container (FC)	KMSZ	1 519	1 395	1 284	Specialised carriers	KMTV	122	81
					Ro-ro[5]	KMTW	380	279
All vessels	KMUU	42 985	18 894	11 402	All vessels	KMTX	12 073	6 477

1 In 1986 a new classification of ship types was introduced. This is based on ship descriptions used by Lloyd's Register of Shipping from which the Department of Transport has been taking figures data since 1986. Because of this change, figures for 1986 in Table 10.29 have been given on both bases.
2 Bulk carriers 10,000 deadweight tonnes and over or approximately 6,000 gross tons and over including combination - ore/oil and ore/bulk/oil-carriers.
3 All vessels with passenger certificates.
4 Bulk carriers (large and small) including combination -ore/oil and ore/bulk/oil-carriers.
5 Ro-ro passenger and cargo vessels.
6 General cargo roll-on/roll-off and lift-on/lift-off vessels, specialised dry cargo vessels and passenger ro-ro vessels.
7 Cruise liner and other passenger.

Source : Department of Transport

Sea transport

10.30 United Kingdom and Crown Dependency registered trading vessels of 100 gross tonnes and over[1]
Age distribution by type of vessel
End of year

Per cent

	1990								1991							
	Passenger[5]	Container (FC)	Specialised carriers	Other general cargo[4]	Bulk carriers[2]	Tankers	Ro-Ro[3]	All vessels	Passenger[5]	Container (FC)	Specialised carriers	Other general cargo[4]	Bulk carriers[2]	Tankers	Ro-Ro[3]	All vessels
Percentage of vessels in each age group																
Age (years)																
Under 5	19	8	9	7	10	2	13	8	15	6	10	7	3	3	15	8
5-9	15	8	36	17	46	14	9	17	26	9	29	18	56	9	10	16
10-14	8	33	23	16	26	27	25	22	4	38	29	15	25	26	20	21
15-19	15	33	18	14	18	23	29	21	15	31	19	13	13	24	28	20
20-24	8	18	0	22	0	17	13	12	7	16	5	13	3	19	11	13
25 and over	35	0	14	34	0	18	10	21	33	0	10	35	0	19	15	22
Total	100	100	100	100	100	100	100	100	100	100	100	100	100	100	100	100
No of vessels	26	39	22	229	39	154	120	629	27	32	21	215	32	156	124	607
Percentage of deadweight tonnage in each age group																
Age (years)																
Under 5	-	6	4	15	6	-	11	3	0	6	5	9	3	0	16	3
5-9	25	6	53	16	46	12	4	19	24	4	69	29	53	10	6	16
10-14	0	28	14	20	11	53	52	38	0	30	19	17	39	33	35	32
15-19	14	44	3	29	37	23	24	29	6	45	5	28	40	40	33	35
20-24	42	16	0	12	0	8	7	8	38	14	1	9	0	11	6	10
25 and over	18	0	27	8	0	3	2	3	30	0	1	8	-	5	4	4
Total	100	100	100	100	100	100	100	100	100	100	100	100	100	100	100	100
Total deadweight tonnes	50	1 212	111	428	1 425	4 006	285	7 518	50	1 019	83	399	825	3 882	282	6544

1 Steam and motor vessels only excluding miscellaneous craft.
2 Bulk carriers (large and small) including combination ore/oil and ore/bulk/oil carriers.
3 Ro-Ro passenger and cargo vessels.
4 Reefer vessels, general cargo/passenger vessels, and single and multi-deck general cargo vessels.
5 Cruise liner and other passenger.

Source: Department of Transport

Sea transport

10.31 United Kingdom and Crown Dependency registered trading vessels of 100 gross tons and over
Analysis by deadweight tonnage (dwt) and type of vessel

End of year — Per cent

	Tankers	Bulk carriers[2]	Specialised carriers	Container (FC)	Ro-Ro[3]	Other general cargo[4]	Passenger	All vessels
1990								
Percentage of vessels in each size group								
Under 10	66	21	91	15	97	94	96	78
10 and under 20	5	31	0	5	1	6	4	6
20 and under 50	14	36	9	77	3	0	0	11
50 and under 100	8	3	0	3	0	0	0	2
100 and under 250	3	10	0	0	0	0	0	1
250 and over	3	0	0	0	0	0	0	1
Total	100	100	100	100	100	100	100	100
Number of vessels	154	39	22	39	120	229	26	629
Percentage of deadweight tonnage in each size group								
Under 10	5	3	34	2	73	60	68	11
10 and under 20	3	12	0	3	5	40	32	7
20 and under 50	16	30	66	90	23	0	0	31
50 and under 100	22	5	0	5	0	0	0	13
100 and under 250	16	50	0	0	0	0	0	18
250 and over	38	0	0	0	0	0	0	20
Total	100	100	100	100	100	100	100	100
Total deadweight tonnes	4 006	1 425	111	1 212	285	428	50	7 518
1989								
Percentage of vessels in each size group								
Under 10	68	24	86	16	100	94	96	79
10 and under 20	5	24	5	2	0	6	4	5
20 and under 50	15	24	9	79	0	0	0	11
50 and under 100	7	2	0	2	0	0	0	2
100 and under 250	3	26	0	0	0	0	0	2
250 and over	3	0	0	0	0	0	0	-
Total	100	100	100	100	100	100	100	100
Number of vessels	168	42	22	43	120	262	24	670
Percentage of deadweight tonnage in each size group								
Under 10	5	3	30	2	100	57	64	10
10 and under 20	3	6	8	1	0	43	36	6
20 and under 50	19	14	61	92	0	0	0	28
50 and under 100	20	3	0	5	0	0	0	11
100 and under 250	16	74	0	0	0	0	0	27
250 and over	38	0	0	0	0	0	0	18
Total	100	100	100	100	100	100	100	100
Total deadweight tonnes	4 074	2 238	120	1 308	223	484	45	8 491

1 Steam and motor vessels only, excluding miscellaneous craft.
2 Bulk carriers (large and small) including combination-ore/oil and ore/bulk/oil-carriers.
3 Ro-Ro passenger and cargo vessels.
4 Reefer vessels, general cargo/passenger vessels, and single and multi-deck general cargo vessels.
5 Cruise liner and other passenger.

Source: Department of Transport

Sea transport

10.32 International seaborne trade of the United Kingdom:
Analysis by area of consignment and proportion carried by UK registered vessels

	Dry cargo 1990 Total (Million tonnes)	Dry cargo 1990 UK flag (Per cent)	Dry cargo 1991 Total (Million tonnes)	Dry cargo 1991 UK flag (Per cent)	Tanker cargo 1990 Total (Million tonnes)	Tanker cargo 1990 UK flag (Per cent)	Tanker cargo 1991 Total (Million tonnes)	Tanker cargo 1991 UK flag (Per cent)	All cargo 1990 Total (Million tonnes)	All cargo 1990 UK flag (Per cent)	All cargo 1991 Total (Million tonnes)	All cargo 1991 UK flag (Per cent)
Exports and re-exports												
Near and short sea:												
EC[1]	31.1	30	35.4	27	46.5	24	50.7	20	77.6	26	86.1	23
Scandinavia[2] and Baltic	6.4	7	4.5	13	4.8	21	4.9	10	11.1	13	9.4	12
Rest of Europe and Mediterranean	3.2	25	3.1	20	0.2	2	1.5	2	3.4	24	4.6	14
All[3]	40.7	26	43.0	25	51.5	24	57.1	19	92.2	25	100.1	22
Deep sea:												
Central and West Africa	0.4	7	0.6	41	-	0	-	4	0.4	6	0.7	39
South and East Africa	0.7	7	0.7	10	-	2	-	20	0.8	6	0.7	10
Gulf and Indian Ocean	2.3	9	2.2	8	0.3	14	0.2	12	2.6	9	2.4	8
Far East	3.5	13	3.9	14	0.1	24	0.1	3	3.7	13	4.0	14
Australasia	0.5	29	0.5	24	-	6	-	8	0.5	29	0.5	24
North America	2.7	10	2.2	11	22.3	3	16.4	4	25.0	4	18.7	5
Central and South America	0.4	16	0.5	12	-	1	0.2	0	0.4	14	0.7	9
West Indies	0.4	18	0.4	20	0.3	1	-	27	0.7	11	0.4	20
All	11.0	12	11.1	14	23.1	3	17.0	4	34.1	6	28.1	8
All trades	51.7	23	54.1	23	74.6	18	74.1	16	126.3	20	128.2	19
Imports												
Near and short sea:												
EC[1]	50.8	33	50.8	34	13.0	20	11.5	21	63.8	30	62.3	31
Scandinavia[2] and Baltic	15.7	10	13.8	7	23.7	6	25.6	5	39.4	8	39.4	6
Rest of Europe and Mediterranean	3.8	17	3.2	19	7.7	6	5.4	5	11.5	9	8.6	10
All[3]	70.3	27	67.9	28	44.4	10	42.4	9	114.7	20	110.3	21
Deep sea:												
Central and West Africa	1.6	13	1.6	13	2.1	10	2.4	1	3.6	11	4.0	5
South and East Africa	4.1	13	4.5	7	-	17	-	34	4.2	13	4.6	8
Gulf and Indian Ocean	1.4	13	1.1	19	11.4	8	12.1	5	12.8	9	13.1	6
Far East	3.4	13	3.5	17	0.6	9	0.5	2	4.0	13	4.1	15
Australasia	7.5	15	8.2	8	0.2	6	0.1	15	7.6	14	8.3	8
North America	16.5	21	16.3	12	0.4	1	0.7	28	16.9	21	16.9	13
Central and South America	6.5	19	6.3	19	1.7	2	2.0	1	8.2	16	8.3	15
West Indies	1.1	20	1.0	19	0.9	0	0.8	0	2.0	11	1.8	11
All	42.1	18	42.4	13	17.4	7	18.7	5	59.5	15	61.1	10
All trades	112.3	23	110.3	22	61.9	10	61.1	8	174.2	18	171.4	17

1 Figures for European Community (EC) relate to the eleven other member countries.
2 Excluding Denmark.
3 Total near and short sea imports for tanker cargo include imports from the Continental Shelf (foreign) not separately identified.

Sources: Department of Transport; HM Customs and Excise

10.33 International seaborne trade of the United Kingdom
Sea transport

Total and proportion carried by UK registered vessels

		Total seaborne trade								Percentage carried						
		1985	1986	1987	1988	1989	1990	1991		1985	1986	1987	1988	1989	1990	1991
Exports[1] *plus* Imports by sea																
Weight (million tonnes)																
All cargo	KMTY	286.1	298.4	297.9	289.0	287.3	300.5	299.6	KMUG	23.0	21.0	22.0	21.0	21.0	19.0	18.0
Dry bulk cargo	KMTZ	73.4	72.0	73.6	76.2	80.5	77.7	77.7	KMUH	26.0	22.0	24.0	22.0	23.0	22.0	21.0
Other dry cargo	KMUA	66.1	70.9	76.3	81.7	85.7	86.3	86.8	KMUI	31.0	27.0	27.0	24.0	25.0	24.0	23.0
Tanker cargo	KMUB	146.6	155.5	148.0	131.2	121.1	136.5	135.2	KMUJ	18.0	18.0	18.0	17.0	17.0	14.0	12.0
Value (£ hundred million)																
All cargo	KMUC	1 279.2	1 219.2	1 332.6	1 416.8	1 619.9	1 731.5	1 692.2	KMUK	36.0	37.0	37.0	32.0	35.0	34.0	35.0
Dry bulk cargo	KMUD	74.2	66.4	64.2	69.3	78.4	77.1	69.3	KMUL	22.0	19.0	19.0	16.0	17.0	16.0	16.0
Other dry cargo	KMUE	960.3	1 023.8	1 136.8	1 255.4	1 435.6	1 516.9	1 498.8	KMUM	42.0	40.0	40.0	34.0	38.0	37.0	37.0
Tanker cargo	KMUF	244.7	128.9	131.7	92.1	105.9	137.5	124.1	KMUN	19.0	19.0	18.0	18.0	18.0	15.0	14.0

1 Exports (including re-exports) plus imports.

*Sources: Department of Transport;
HM Customs and Excise*

Sea transport

10.34 International seaborne trade of the United Kingdom
Proportion of trade carried by the principal flags

Percentage

	Dry cargo				Tanker cargo				All cargo			
	1990		1991		1990		1991		1990		1991	
	Weight	Value	Weight	Value	Weight	Value	Weight	Value	Weight	Value	Weight	Value
Exports[1]												
United Kingdom	22.7	37.0	22.7	36.5	17.6	18.2	15.5	17.0	19.7	35.1	18.6	34.8
Bahamas	6.0	6.5	5.8	7.4	15.0	14.4	20.4	18.7	11.3	7.3	14.2	8.4
Liberia	1.9	1.0	1.6	0.8	22.4	21.8	16.2	15.0	14.0	3.1	10.0	2.0
Germany[2]	12.4	10.7	13.5	11.9	1.8	2.6	1.9	2.8	6.1	9.9	6.8	11.1
Greece	2.2	0.3	3.0	0.4	3.1	2.8	4.9	4.1	2.8	0.6	4.1	0.7
Panama	3.3	2.2	3.8	2.5	1.8	1.9	2.2	2.4	2.4	2.2	2.9	2.5
Other EC[3]	20.5	20.9	20.9	21.3	9.6	10.0	9.3	10.3	14.1	19.8	14.2	20.3
All other flags	31.0	21.4	28.7	19.2	28.7	28.3	29.6	29.7	29.6	22.0	29.2	20.2
All	100.0	100.0	100.0	100.0	100.0	100.0	100.0	100.0	100.0	100.0	100.0	100.0
Imports												
United Kingdom	23.3	34.9	21.8	36.1	9.5	10.8	7.9	9.2	18.4	33.4	16.9	34.5
Norway	7.4	2.2	6.4	2.1	24.5	25.4	26.9	28.0	13.5	3.7	13.7	3.7
Germany[2]	11.2	12.0	11.5	12.5	1.4	2.3	1.6	2.4	7.8	11.4	8.0	11.9
Liberia	2.2	0.6	2.0	0.6	13.4	11.7	12.3	10.5	6.2	1.3	5.6	1.2
Netherlands	6.0	5.7	6.2	5.8	0.8	1.5	0.8	1.5	4.2	5.5	4.3	5.5
Panama	3.8	2.7	3.0	2.6	3.3	3.6	2.7	3.0	3.6	2.7	2.9	2.6
Other EC[3]	13.4	17.4	13.5	15.8	15.8	14.9	14.6	14.3	14.3	17.2	13.9	15.7
All other flags	32.7	24.5	35.6	24.5	31.3	29.8	33.2	31.1	32.0	24.8	34.7	24.9
All	100.0	100.0	100.0	100.0	100.0	100.0	100.0	100.0	100.0	100.0	100.0	100.0

1 Including re-exports.
2 Germany (including West Germany and German Democratic Republic).
3 European Community.

Sources: Department of Transport; HM Customs and Excise

Sea transport

10.35 Seaport traffic of Great Britain
Analysis of all foreign and domestic[1] traffic by mode of appearance

Million gross tonnes[2]

		1980	1981	1982	1983	1984	1985	1986	1987	1988	1989	1990	1991
Foreign traffic													
Imports													
Bulk fuel traffic	KNPA	63.8	53.7	49.1	42.0	60.0	57.2	61.7	57.3	62.9	64.2	75.1	78.0
Other bulk traffic	KNPB	29.4	32.8	31.8	34.3	34.6	36.7	37.3	42.0	45.0	47.0	45.1	43.1
Container and roll-on traffic	KNPC	20.4	21.9	23.4	26.0	28.1	29.8	31.1	34.0	38.0	40.9	40.5	40.2
Semi-bulk traffic	KNPD	13.6	12.3	14.1	14.6	14.6	14.5	15.8	16.9	18.9	18.1	17.3	15.5
Conventional traffic	KNPE	4.0	3.0	2.3	2.3	2.3	1.7	1.5	1.6	1.6	1.2	1.8	1.3
All imports	KNPF	131.2	123.7	120.7	119.1	139.6	139.9	147.4	151.8	166.4	171.4	179.8	178.1
Exports													
Bulk fuel traffic	KNPG	79.9	86.9	92.0	96.0	97.3	103.1	101.9	100.2	91.1	72.9	80.3	84.7
Other bulk traffic	KNPH	14.7	16.2	15.3	16.3	18.7	17.7	21.1	20.4	18.5	19.5	19.0	19.6
Container and roll-on traffic	KNPI	16.7	16.5	17.1	18.6	20.3	21.3	22.1	23.9	26.5	29.4	30.8	32.4
Semi-bulk traffic	KNPJ	2.7	3.6	3.0	3.5	3.6	4.1	4.0	5.0	4.6	4.6	4.3	5.1
Conventional traffic	KNPK	3.3	2.7	2.9	2.1	1.8	1.6	1.2	1.2	1.0	0.7	1.1	0.9
All exports	KNPL	117.1	125.8	130.3	136.5	141.7	147.8	150.4	150.6	141.7	127.1	135.7	142.7
Domestic traffic[1]													
Bulk fuel traffic	KNPM	124.3	118.3	129.1	130.8	123.3	120.0	112.3	108.3	115.5	108.5	101.7	102.1
Other bulk traffic	KNPN	31.6	29.6	30.3	31.7	31.0	31.7	32.7	34.8	41.1	45.5	44.0	41.1
Container and roll-on traffic	KNPO	4.6	4.5	5.1	5.4	5.4	5.9	6.2	7.3	7.6	8.1	8.0	8.2
Semi-bulk traffic	KNPP	0.3	0.3	0.2	0.2	0.4	0.3	0.2	0.2	0.3	0.3	0.3	0.4
Conventional traffic	KNPQ	1.0	0.7	0.4	0.3	0.2	0.3	0.3	0.3	0.3	0.4	0.3	0.4
Non-oil traffic with UK offshore installations	KNPR	1.9	2.1	2.1	2.2	3.2	3.6	3.3	3.5	3.9	4.2	5.5	4.8
All domestic traffic	KNPS	163.7	155.6	167.3	170.5	163.6	167.7	154.9	154.4	168.8	166.9	159.8	157.0
Total foreign and domestic traffic	KNPT	412.0	405.1	418.4	426.1	444.8	449.4	452.7	456.8	476.9	465.4	475.3	477.8

1 Domestic traffic refers to traffic through the ports of Great Britain only, to all parts of the United Kingdom, Isle of Man and the Channel Islands. Traffic to and from offshore installations, landing of sea dredged aggregates and material shipped for dumping at sea are included.
2 Including crates and immediate packaging.

Note The mode of appearance classification was introduced by the Department of Transport and the British Ports Federation from 1982 onwards and corresponds with similar classifications used in other countries including the Statistical Office of the European Communities. It refers to the way cargoes are presented for loading/unloading at ports. Primarily, it distinguishes between bulk and break-bulk cargoes but the latter are further sub-divided into categories which are more meaningful to ports, shipping and inland transport from an operational point of view.

Source: Department of Transport

Passenger movement

10.36 United Kingdom international passenger movement by sea and air
Arrivals plus departures by country of embarkation or landing

Thousands

		1980	1981	1982	1983	1984	1985	1986	1987	1988	1989	1990	1991
All passenger movements													
By sea	KMUO	23 621	25 222	26 359	26 776	26 205	26 287	26 797	26 103	24 994	28 967	29 650	31 128
By air	KMUP	42 068	42 962	43 477	45 244	49 984	51 772	56 555	65 742	70 524	74 424	76 417	71 889
Irish Republic:													
By sea	KMUQ	2 502	2 422	2 621	2 761	2 875	2 866	2 628	2 581	2 434	2 737	2 773	2 037
By air	KMUR	1 861	1 806	1 726	1 645	1 714	1 807	2 107	2 721	3 521	4 091	4 436	3 948
Total	KMUS	4 363	4 228	4 347	4 406	4 589	4 673	4 735	5 302	5 955	6 828	7 209	5 985
European continent and Mediterranean Sea area[5]													
By sea: total	BMLA	20 892	22 603	23 628	23 856	23 172	23 240	24 025	23 358	22 399	26 071	26 876	27 849
Belgium	BMLB	5 192	4 716	4 678	4 415	4 609	4 410	3 793	3 328	3 230	3 444	3 587	3 510
France[6]	BMLC	12 622	14 734	15 746	16 141	15 353	15 646	16 867	16 826	15 977	19 247	20 103	21 248
Netherlands	BMLD	1 939	1 958	1 969	2 211	2 191	2 206	2 258	2 091	2 218	2 364	2 507	2 459
Other European Community[7]	KMUT	748	772	808	705	656	589	649	671	590	591	383	416
Other countries	BMLF	456	493	507	467	452	477	459	440	377	545	449	252
By air: total	BMLG	27 395	27 814	28 952	30 252	33 023	34 066	38 723	45 159	47 968	49 791	50 265	46 373
Belgium and Luxembourg	BMLI	808	757	748	832	931	980	987	1 112	1 221	1 309	1 408	1 351
Denmark	BMLJ	557	510	489	547	587	611	622	670	697	781	885	909
Germany	KMQN	3 136	3 948	2 998	3 006	3 384	3 644	3 820	4 347	4 492	4 800	5 591	5 115
France	BMLL	3 068	3 105	3 193	3 272	3 511	3 720	3 667	4 235	4 889	5 711	6 236	5 918
Italy	BMLQ	2 691	2 335	2 378	2 494	2 584	2 581	2 715	3 064	3 098	3 314	3 451	3 079
Netherlands	BMLS	1 902	1 813	1 845	1 815	1 983	2 211	2 311	2 660	2 899	3 073	3 292	3 162
Norway	BMLT	556	543	584	617	646	722	706	725	850	797	864	769
Portugal[1]	BMLU	701	849	963	1 068	1 216	1 537	1 915	2 133	2 024	1 981	2 053	2 193
Sweden	BMLW	449	450	433	453	503	512	566	644	754	841	940	835
Switzerland	BMLX	1 443	1 469	1 576	1 729	1 872	2 009	2 112	2 325	2 491	2 655	2 738	2 541
Greece	BMLO	1 840	2 095	2 123	2 007	2 249	2 875	3 350	3 979	3 795	3 528	3 577	3 459
Spain[2]	BMLV	5 592	6 332	7 624	8 293	9 218	7 708	10 291	11 919	11 738	11 110	8 916	8 406
Yugoslavia	BMLZ	414	492	477	480	581	812	899	1 069	1 047	1 052	1 144	257
Eastern Europe	KMRR	533	454	360	408	476	590	543	629	751	852	994	1 081
Middle East countries[4]	KMRS	1 528	1 490	1 513	1 556	1 563	1 596	1 609	1 638	1 622	1 716	1 716	1 619
Austria	BMLH	531	454	361	408	468	364	381	528	707	851	908	844
Other Western Europe[3]	KMRU	..	..	..	..	..	..	..	2 784	3 492	3 795	3 847	3 622
Rest of World													
By sea: total	BMMF	45.9	35.4	22.6	35.5	36.1	42.4	36.2	40.8	33.6	31.1	21.7	34.0
United States of America	BMMG	33.4	27.5	16.9	28.7	28.9	35.1	31.4	36.0	30.7	29.3	18.0	29.5
Canada	BMMH	2.5	1.9	1.4	1.7	1.1	1.1	1.5	2.4	–	–	–	–
Australia	BMMI	4.2	2.0	1.7	1.3	1.6	2.1	1.0	1.0	1.1	0.4	1.7	1.7
New Zealand	BMMJ	0.7	0.5	0.4	0.2	0.2	–	0.4	0.4	0.2	0.1	0.3	0.3
South Africa	BMMK	1.9	0.6	0.2	1.4	2.3	2.3	0.9	0.6	0.6	0.1	0.7	0.8
West Africa	BMML	0.6	0.4	0.2	0.2	0.2	0.1	0.2	0.2	0.3	0.1	0.3	0.5
British West Indies and Bermuda	BMMM	0.2	0.1	–	0.2	–	–	–	–	–	–	–	0.1
Other countries	BMMN	2.4	2.4	1.6	1.7	1.6	1.4	0.9	0.9	0.5	1.0	0.5	0.8
By air: total	BMMO	13 712	14 289	13 767	14 412	15 733	16 740	16 781	19 224	21 156	22 991	24 398	24 073
United States of America	BMNC	5 913	6 132	5 334	5 783	6 517	6 970	6 345	7 745	8 587	9 447	10 244	9 697
Canada	BMMQ	1 498	1 451	1 370	1 367	1 387	2 228	1 501	1 684	1 879	1 996	2 088	1 853
Australasia	BMMP	596	509	539	500	509	509	494	531	573	486	615	753
North Africa	KMRX	729	765	687	684	648	717	737	872	932	930	859	604
Rest of Africa	KMRY	1 163	1 257	1 277	1 268	1 231	1 303	1 254	1 184	1 249	1 321	1 445	1 542
South America	BMNB	133	123	100	83	82	95	106	122	150	192	249	285
Latin America and Caribbean	KMRZ	415	454	433	361	..	..	..	..	..	..	..	..
Indian sub-continent	KMRO	652	671	683	634	628	676	719	786	897	1 037	1 109	908
Japan	BMMY	235	253	264	264	303	337	356	459	549	699	822	820
Rest of Asia	KMRP	716	933	978	1 038	1 115	1 233	1 340	1 517	1 610	1 820	1 951	1 988
Pleasure cruises beginning and/or ending at United Kingdom seaports	KMRQ	180	162	86	124	121	137	107	125	127	129	153	172

1 Includes Azores and Madeira.
2 Includes Canary Islands.
3 Includes Cyprus, Faroes, Finland, Gibraltar, Iceland, Malta, Turkey, Indian Ocean Islands.
4 Includes Israel, Iran, Iraq, Jordan, Kuwait, Lebanon, Gulf States, Saudi Arabia, United Arab Emirates, Yemeni Arab Republic, Yemeni Peoples' Republic.
5 Includes North Africa and Middle East Mediterranean countries.
6 Includes hovercraft passengers.
7 Greece, Portugal and Spain have been included in this grouping from 1977 onwards even though they joined the EC in 1981 and 1986 respectively.

Sources: Department of Transport; Civil Aviation Authority

Communications

10.37 Postal services and television licences
Years ended 31 March[1]
United Kingdom

		Unit	1981	1982	1983	1984	1985	1986	1987	1988	1989[12]	1990	1991	1992
Letters and parcel post														
Letters, etc posted[2]	KMRA	Millions	10 072	9 985	10 255	10 665	11 439	11 721	12 535	13 568	13 741	15 293	15 902	..
of which:														
Registered and insured	KMRB	"	36.6	33.5	33.5	32.5	33.5	33.2	33.2	33.1	21.0	22.2	21.3	..
Airmail (Commonwealth and foreign)[3]	KMRC	"	436.8	393.0	378.0	379.3	417.8	383.1	377.7	427.2	403.0	444.0	467.7	..
Business reply and freepost items	KMRD	"	309.2	308.2	336.2	356.9	352.6	365.4	370.0	371.1	377.3	438.7	416.7	..
Parcels posted[4]	KMRE	"	168.8	179.6	189.6	194.9	202.5	186.5	192.2	197.1	..	..	..	..
of which:														
Registered and insured[5,13]	KMRF	"	4.2	3.8	3.6	3.8	3.9	3.7	3.5	3.2	0.4	0.3	0.4	..
Inward and transit parcels handled	KMRG	"	3.6	3.4	3.2	3.1	3.0	2.6	2.8	2.6	2.7	2.8	..	..
Postal orders														
Total issued[6]	KMRH	Thousands	121 636	87 154	68 605	63 511	58 553	56 466	54 779	49 984	43 882	42 281	39 644	39 867
Telegrams and telephones[11]														
Telegrams: total	KMRI	Thousands	13 662	11 521	7 694[10]	5 710	..	..	..	..	..	..	..	..
Inland	KMRJ	"	2 963	2 276	901[10]	..	..	..	..	..	..	..	..	..
Foreign (via Post Office system)[7]	KMRK	"	10 699	9 245	6 793	5 710	..	..	..	..	..	..	..	..
Telex connections	KMRL	Number	89 930	92 378	92 622	95 115	..	..	..	..	..	..	..	..
Telephone calls (Inland): total	KMRM	Millions	20 175	20 806	21 403	22 686	..	..	..	..	..	..	..	..
Local	KMRN	"	16 840	17 360	17 800	18 750	..	..	..	..	..	..	..	..
Trunk	KMQA	"	3 335	3 446	3 603	3 936	..	..	..	..	..	..	..	..
Telephone calls (international): total	KMQB	Thousands	116 533	132 255	148 478	172 746	..	..	..	..	..	..	..	..
Continental	KMQC	"	79 467	86 352	93 109	104 065	..	..	..	..	..	..	..	..
Intercontinental	KMQD	"	36 971	45 806	55 265	68 574	..	..	..	..	..	..	..	..
Maritime	KMQE	"	95	97	104	107	..	..	..	..	..	..	..	..
Telephone stations[8]: total	KMQF	Thousands	27 870	28 450	28 882	29 336	..	..	..	..	..	..	..	..
Public call offices	KMQG	"	77	77	77	77	..	..	..	..	..	..	..	..
Private stations	KMQH	"	27 793	28 373	28 805	29 259	..	..	..	..	..	..	..	..
Telephone exchanges[9]: total	KMQI	Number	6 338	6 318	6 296	..	..	..	..	..	..	..	..	..
Automatic	KMQJ	"	6 338	6 318	6 296	..	..	..	..	..	..	..	..	..
Manual	KMQK	"	..	..	..	..	..	..	..	..	..	..	..	..
Television licences														
in force on 31 March	KMQL	Thousands	18 667	18 554	18 494	18 632	18 716	18 705	18 953	19 354	19 396	19 645	19 546	19 631
of which:														
Colour	KMQM	"	13 780	14 261	14 699	15 370	15 819	16 025	16 539	17 134	17 469	17 964	18 111	18 426

1 Years ended 31 March for letter and parcel post, postal orders and telegrams sent. For all other items figures relate to 31 March in each year.
2 Including printed papers, newspapers, postcards and sample packets.
3 Including letters without special charge for air transport.
4 Includes Irish Republic inward traffic.
5 Includes compensation fee parcels.
6 Excluding those issued on HM ships, in many British possessions and in other places abroad. For 1980,1981,1984,1986,1987,1988,1989,1990,1991 and 1992 includes Overseas and Army.
7 Excluding those sent abroad via the private cable companies system.
8 A station is a telephone provided for the use of a customer or renter.
9 Excluding auto-manual and trunk exchanges.
10 Inland telegram service ceased from 1 October 1982, 1983 figures are therefore not comparable with earlier years.
11 Any enquiries should be referred to: British Telecom plc, 81 Newgate Street, London EC1A 7AJ.
12 Industrial Action during year.
13 Registered Service to Irish Republic ceased in 1989.

Sources: Subscription Services Limited; Post Office

11 Distributive Trades, Research and Development

Annual retailing inquiries *(Table 11.1)*

The retailing inquiry covers businesses which operate in Great Britain and are engaged in retail distribution. It is undertaken on a sample basis from a register of businesses which the Central Statistical Office (CSO) maintains largely from information obtained by Customs and Excise in the administration of Value Added Tax (VAT). The inquiry is addressed to businesses classified to the retail headings in the VAT trade classification (other than opticians) and also businesses outside retailing which are believed to undertake retailing activity. The inquiry does not cover those businesses that are not registered for VAT.

The 1990 inquiry was a 'benchmark', that is, it collected more detailed information from a larger number of businesses (20 000). Commodity sales information, for example, was collected across 41 headings from most businesses and across 68 headings from the very largest. This compares with the 1989 'intermediate' inquiry, which was directed to 12 000 businesses and asked for limited commodity detail (16 headings), and the 1988 'enhanced intermediate' inquiry which also had a sample size of 12 000 but asked for commodity sales data against 41 headings from all businesses. Since the commodity sales information is used to classify businesses according to a 'kind of business' (kob) classification, which is consistent with the Standard Industrial Classification 1980, the level of published aggregates for 1989 is correspondingly reduced to seven 'broad kobs', for example "food retailers".

A review of the retailing inquiry, published in 1986, resulted in changes which were introduced.

The same review resulted in other changes which were introduced with effect from the 1986 inquiry. The main change concerned the collection of information in the survey, which is now directed much more towards retail businesses. In this context retail businesses are defined as those businesses whose main activity is retailing, as opposed to non-retail businesses which here are those only engaged in retailing as a subsidiary activity. Previously in each full inquiry, the complete range of information relating only to the retailing activity of the business (eg stocks for retail trading) was collected from both retail and non-retail businesses. From the 1986 inquiry, retail businesses have been asked to provide the complete range of information but relating to their total and not their retail activity. Non-retail businesses have been asked to provide only retail turnover and employment, instead of the complete range of information on their retailing activity. Table 11.1 only includes figures for retail businesses. It should be noted that the figures for 1989 shown in Table 11.1 are only the provisional results of the retailing inquiry. Final figures will appear in Business Monitor SDA 25.

Retail trade: Index numbers of value and volume *(Table 11.2)*

The retail sales index is based on monthly returns provided voluntarily by a panel of contributors. In its calculation, receipts under the National Health Service are excluded.

The retail sales index has been adjusted to reflect the results of the 1988 retailing inquiry. The effect is to reduce previously published estimates of growth over the period 1986 to 1988 by about two thirds of one per cent a year and by a third of one per cent a year since 1988. A similar routine procedure has been carried out previously every two years.

Motor Trades and Catering Inquiries *(Tables 11.3 and 11.4)*

The motor trades and catering inquiries are conducted on a sample basis from the CSO's VAT-based register of businesses. In general the inquiries are addressed solely to businesses classified to these trades, in that businesses who may be engaged in the catering or motor trades as a subsidiary activity are excluded. (An exception is that the catering inquiry includes certain large groups of managed public houses owned by breweries.) The results generally relate to the total activity of all businesses registered for VAT, including those with a VAT turnover beneath the mandatory registration threshold.

Research and Development

Research and development (R & D) in the United Kingdom is financed and carried out mainly by the Government, industry, universities and further education institutions, and various non-profit-making bodies. Until 1981, large scale surveys of industrial R & D were held every third year, but there is now a four-year-cycle, with a large scale (benchmark) survey every fourth year, and smaller-scale (sample) inquiries in the other three years. The latest benchmark survey related to 1990. Surveys of government expenditure and employment on R & D are carried out every year. Information from these surveys is used to build up the total expenditure on R & D in the United Kingdom, which in 1987 was £9.4 billion and in 1990, £12.1 billion.

In line with international recommendations, research and experimental development is defined for statistical purposes as 'creative work undertaken on a systematic basis in order to increase the stock of knowledge, including knowledge of man, culture and society, and the use of this stock of knowledge to devise new applications'.

Definitions of the sectors surveyed and notes on the survey procedures employed are given in an article which appeared in *Economic Trends* (HMSO) August 1992.

For the 1990 inquiry, industrial firms were asked to provide figures relating to the calendar year 1990, or the business year ending on a date between 6 April 1990 and 5 April 1991.

Returns from government departments relate to financial years ended 31 March. Further details of trends in Government R & D expenditure are given in *Economic Trends*, and the *Annual Review of Government Funded R & D*.

Table 11.5

This table covers both R & D in the natural and medical sciences and engineering, and R & D in the social sciences and humanities. The totals of both sections of the table are the amounts of R & D performed in the United Kingdom and exclude R & D performed abroad which is financed from within this country. No surveys of R & D performed by local authorities have been carried out since 1972, but estimates of local authorities' expenditure in these years have been included in the Government sector figures.

Tables 11.6 and 11.7

Central government expenditure on R & D, including that of research councils, is surveyed annually and covers R & D in the social sciences as well as R & D in the natural sciences. The borderline between research and other related activities, such as information services and general purpose data collection, is difficult to define, especially for the social sciences.

Table 11.6, as distinct from Table 11.5, includes money spent by the government to finance R & D work performed overseas. It shows the gross expenditure of government on R & D: 'gross' in that any receipts used to finance the expenditure are not deducted. Money spent on R & D work done by government itself (intra-mural expenditure) is distinguished from money passed to other sectors to fund R & D work (extra-mural expenditure).

Table 11.7 relates to net government expenditure on R & D, that is, gross expenditure *less* receipts allocated directly towards financing the expenditure. The table shows total expenditure broken down according to the Statistical Office of the European Community' objectives classification of budgeted expenditure on R & D.

continued on page 219

11.1 Retail trades by form of organisation and kind of business
Standard Industrial Classification 1980
Great Britain

	1988[2]				1989[3]				1990[4]			
	Businesses	Outlets	Persons engaged	Retail turnover (inclusive of VAT)	Businesses	Outlets	Persons engaged	Retail turnover (inclusive of VAT)	Businesses	Outlets	Persons engaged	Retail turnover (inclusive of VAT)
	Number	Number	Thousand	£ million	Number	Number	Thousand	£ million	Number	Number	Thousand	£ million
Total retail trade	237 832	338 248	2 347	110 564	242 356	350 015	2 463	118 842	242 194	349 847	2 476	126 879
Single outlet retailers[1]	212 711	212 711	754	30 924	215 736	215 736	837	32 644	215 793	215 793	828	34 533
Small multiple retailers[1]	24 286	61 637	298	12 737	25 726	67 760	318	13 935	25 492	65 802	325	14 723
Large multiple retailers[1]	835	63 900	1 294	66 903	894	66 520	1 307	72 263	903	68 252	1 323	77 624
of which												
Co-operative societies accounted for	*83*	*4 270*	*102*	*4 441*	*79*	*4 207*	*104*	*4 725*	*77*	*4 085*	*99*	*4 797*
Food retailers	67 755	87 758	809	38 311	67 849	90 075	845	41 743	65 800	86 843	857	46 404
Large grocery retailers	69	8 328	504	27 935					78	8 097	527	35 196
Other grocery retailers	24 821	26 992	106	4 123					21 287	23 453	109	4 400
Dairymen	9 949	11 264	43	1 615					11 175	12 549	47	1 674
Butchers, poulterers	14 295	18 215	68	2 586					13 383	17 300	72	2 737
Fishmongers	2 500	2 802	7	228					2 408	2 937	8	251
Greengrocers, fruiterers	11 665	14 263	52	1 333					12 156	14 708	58	1 500
Bread and flour confectioners	4 456	5 895	29	492					5 312	6 799	37	645
Drink, confectionery and tobacco retailers	48 893	60 877	259	11 180	48 744	61 641	328	11 885	48 349	60 557	290	12 713
Retailers of confectionery, tobacco and newsagents	42 795	50 733	219	8 644					42 891	50 759	243	9 885
Off-licences	6 098	10 144	40	2 516					5 457	9 798	42	2 829
Clothing, footwear and leather goods retailers	30 170	57 768	298	11 068	31 429	58 538	304	11 830	31 621	61 115	307	12 172
Men's and boys' wear retailers	3 938	8 005	37	1 933					3 994	8 298	40	2 115
Women's, girls', children's and infants' wear retailers	15 811	26 758	113	4 040					17 047	28 010	124	4 854
General clothing businesses	5 230	9 079	58	2 486					5 116	9 727	50	2 140
Footwear retailers	3 934	12 066	82	2 337					4 306	13 262	85	2 806
Leather and travel goods retailers	1 258	1 861	8	272					1 157	1 819	8	257
Household goods retailers	45 678	63 795	319	18 827	48 735	69 599	319	19 372	49 744	67 213	314	19 438
Household textiles retailers	3 721	5 074	21	722					4 379	6 095	23	894
Carpet retailers	4 570	5 691	20	1 331					4 836	5 908	23	1 466
Furniture retailers	10 956	14 743	72	4 691					12 419	15 437	61	4 816
Electrical, gas and music goods retailers	11 485	18 622	94	6 791					12 286	19 812	94	6 996
Hardware, china and fancy goods retailers	9 147	11 485	47	1 658					9 851	12 139	49	1 761
Do-it-yourself retailers	5 799	8 180	64	3 634					5 073	7 822	65	3 505
Other non-food retailers	39 604	52 944	237	10 051	39 156	52 543	248	11 014	41 355	56 690	273	12 352
Chemists	8 590	13 294	80	3 781					7 942	12 403	85	4 431
Newsagents and stationers	3 353	4 766	23	768					3 560	5 533	29	1 007
Booksellers	2 271	3 096	16	694					2 273	3 443	18	848
Photographic goods retailers	506	861	4	250					587	995	5	396
Jewellers	5 102	7 985	36	1 694					4 866	7 933	39	1 922
Toys, hobby, cycle and sports goods retailers	8 324	9 804	32	1 446					8 943	10 554	37	1 192
Florists, nurserymen and seedsmen	6 718	7 854	34	1 043					7 408	8 837	40	1 192
Non-food retailers (nes)	4 741	5 285	13	374					5 775	6 992	21	682
Mixed retail businesses	3 528	9 402	387	19 835	4 149	11 542	383	21 231	3 309	12 208	400	22 472
Large mixed businesses	44	5 200	329	15 524					50	6 140	336	17 699
Other mixed businesses	3 438	4 090	27	866					3 215	5 567	32	1 075
General mail order houses	45	112	31	3 444					43	500	32	3 693
Hire and repair businesses	2 204	5 703	38	1 292	2 294	6 079	35	1 268	2 015	6 220	34	1 928
Television hire businesses	958	3 461	28	1 114					789	3 060	25	1 138
Other hire or repair	1 246	2 242	10	179					1 227	3 160	9	190

1 The terms 'single outlet retailers', 'small multiple retailers' and 'large multiple retailers' are used in the table to denote retail businesses with 1, 2-9 and 10 or more retail outlets respectively.
2 The 1988 retailing inquiry was the first 'enhanced intermediate' inquiry. It collected commodity sales across 41 headings from 12 000 businesses.
3 The 1989 retailing inquiry was the second of the new style of 'intermediate' inquiries.
4 Provisional figures. The 1990 retailing inquiry was a benchmark.

Source: Central Statistical Office

Retailing

11.2 Retail trade: Index numbers of value and volume of sales[1]

	Weekly average 1985=100					Sales in 1985 £m	Weekly average 1985=100					
	1980	1981	1982	1983	1984		1986	1987	1988	1989	1990	1991
Value												
All kinds of business: all retailers total	66.3	71.8	77.6	84.8	91.7	87 920	109	117	129	137	146	154
Small retailers	75	79	84	88	94	29 294	106	113	123	130	137	140
Large retailers	62	68	75	83	90	58 626	110	120	132	141	151	160
Food retailers total	68.1	74.7	80.9	86.8	93.3	32 986	107	114	123	134	147	158
Small retailers	87	91	95	95	98	8 601	103	105	108	114	118	119
Large retailers	62	69	76	84	92	24 385	108	117	128	141	157	171
Grocery retailers including co-operative societies	65	73	79	85	92	25 895	108	115	126	139	155	168
Dairymen	81	89	94	98	100	1 843	100	116	132	140	145	147
Butchers	81	85	89	93	99	2 749	100	98	97	101	100	98
Fishmongers	73	79	83	86	89	210	119	114	112	118	125	122
Greengrocers and fruiterers	67	74	81	89	100	1 285	105	107	107	114	118	118
Bread and flour confectioners	77	78	78	84	94	1 004	116	117	118	123	131	134
Clothing and footwear retailers: total	63	65	69	79	88	8 677	112	121	130	135	141	142
Small retailers	74	73	76	84	91	3 510	107	112	120	125	131	133
Large retailers	56	60	65	75	85	5 167	115	127	136	142	148	148
Men's and boys' wear retailers	78	77	81	87	93	1 267	108	130	153	156	157	148
Women's, girls', children's and infants' wear retailers; general clothing businesses; leather and travel goods retailers	61	62	66	75	85	5 323	115	122	130	137	144	147
Footwear retailers	60	63	70	80	90	2 087	108	113	114	118	124	126
Household goods retailers (including hire and repair businesses): total	63	67	72	82	90	14 717	113	126	143	150	154	162
Small retailers	73	77	80	86	93	6 586	109	120	138	145	150	154
Large retailers	55	59	66	79	87	8 131	116	130	148	154	157	169
Furniture, carpets and household textiles retailers	69	72	76	84	89	4 902	112	124	144	147	146	151
Electrical and music goods retailers, gas showrooms, electricity showrooms	56	60	67	83	93	5 011	110	125	143	144	146	151
Hardware, china and fancy goods retailers	89	90	89	89	90	1 194	113	130	150	162	176	184
DIY retailers	47	55	60	71	83	2 357	122	137	161	182	198	220
Television and other hire and repair businesses	75	82	88	92	92	1 253	114	112	107	108	113	121
Other non-food retailers (including off licences, confectioners, tobacconists and newsagents): total	64	72	79	85	92	15 675	107	117	131	142	153	159
Small retailers	67	73	80	85	92	10 055	107	115	128	138	148	153
Large retailers	61	70	77	84	91	5 620	108	121	136	149	161	169
Retailers of confectionery, tobacco and newspapers	65	75	82	86	92	7 161	108	113	124	131	143	153
Off licences	64	72	77	83	92	2 287	107	115	122	128	136	143
Booksellers, stationers and specialist newsagents	60	67	75	87	95	1 208	105	119	137	153	166	170
Chemists	54	63	72	78	86	1 445	111	123	143	159	168	178
Jewellers	68	72	78	86	94	1 246	106	120	138	162	171	162
Toys, hobby and sports goods, and cycle retailers	76	75	77	86	95	1 054	106	126	144	157	172	170
All other non-food retailers	62	69	76	83	89	1 274	108	123	149	164	173	175
Mixed retail businesses: total	68.9	73.1	79.2	85.8	91.5	15 865	108	116	125	130	135	138
Mixed businesses with turnover exceeding £11 million in 1986	66	72	78	86	91	11 965	109	118	129	135	141	144
Other mixed businesses	71	74	82	88	92	928	109	100	97	106	116	122
General mail order houses	78	77	81	86	92	2 972	106	114	116	116	117	120
Volume												
All retailers	85.8	85.9	87.6	92.0	95.5	87 920	105	111	118	120	120	120
Food retailers	90.3	91.0	91.7	94.8	96.6	32 986	103.4	107	112	115	117	119
Clothing and footwear retailers	77	75	77	85	92	8 677	109	115	120	120	119	117
Household goods retailers	73	74	77	86	93	14 717	111	122	136	138	137	137
Other non-food retailers	96	95	95	96	99	15 675	102	107	115	120	121	116
Mixed retail businesses	86	87	90	93	96	15 865	105	110.6	114	113	112	110

1 Please see notes on page 216.

Source: Central Statistical Office

Retail trades

11.3 Motor trades
Great Britain

£m exclusive of VAT

6148, 6510, 6520 and 6710 SIC 1980	Number of businesses	Turnover	Stocks Beginning of year	Stocks End of year	Capital expenditure New building work	Capital expenditure Vehicles	Capital expenditure Plant and machinery	Capital expenditure Net capital expenditure	Capital expenditure Land and existing buildings
Total motor trades									
1983	68 573	36 556	3 398	3 833	78	99	124	301	28
1984	69 156	39 448	3 723	3 941	97	148	141	387	42
1985	67 704	40 195	3 831	4 117	109	142	136	387	44
1986	68 109	46 793	4 136	4 655	155	128	148	431	96
1987	69 660	54 206	4 653	5 354	158	163	200	520	114
1988	69 628	64 474	5 260	6 301	204	168	229	601	202
1989	74 225	73 630	6 385	7 283	279	172	285	736	193
1990	76 733	73 999	6 981	7 376	281	142	281	704	190
Distribution, repair and service of motor vehicles (including caravans, tyres, motor accessories and spares)									
1983	60 749	31 057	3 226	3 644	68	87	111	266	28
1984	61,043	33,425	3,544	3 745	85	143	127	355	33
1985	59,764	33,647	3,628	3896	92	130	123	345	34
1986	60,046	39,983	3,923	4 444	133	117	130	381	81
1987	61,640	47,187	4,441	5 128	132	149	177	458	92
1988	61,931	56,853	5,037	6 049	181	151	196	528	169
1989	66,573	65,361	6,147	6 998	243	149	250	642	147
1990	68,896	64,724	6,697	7 062	216	125	243	584	152
Petrol filling stations									
1983	7,824	5,500	172	188	10	12	14	35	-1
1984	8,113	6,023	179	195	12	5	14	31	9
1985	7,941	6,548	203	221	17	12	13	42	10
1986	8,063	6,810	213	211	22	11	17	50	16
1987	8,021	7,019	212	226	25	14	24	63	21
1988	7,697	7,621	222	252	23	17	33	73	33
1989	7,652	8,269	238	285	36	23	35	94	46
1990	7,837	9,275	284	314	65	17	38	120	38

Motor trades: commodity analysis of 1983-1990 sales
Great Britain

£m exclusive of VAT

		Turnover	of which Motor trades turnover	Retail sales New cars	Retail sales Other new motor vehicles and motor cycles	Sales to other dealers New cars	Sales to other dealers Other new motor vehicles and motor cycles	Used motor vehicles and motor cycles	Petrol and oil	Other sales and receipts
Total motor trades	1983	36 556	*36 268*	7 670	1 582	3 784	709	6 185	7 461	8 876
	1984	39 448	*38 912*	7 927	1 663	3 947	773	7 329	7 883	9 390
	1985	42 196	*41 578*	8 371	1 786	4 159	779	7 812	8 218	10 453
	1986	46 793	*46 211*	9 862	1 929	4 923	847	9 418	8 113	11 119
	1987	54 206	*53 478*	11 263	2 325	6 065	940	11 626	8 332	12 928
	1988	64 474	*63 700*	13 115	2 822	8 796	1 229	13 913	8 436	15 390
	1989	73 630	*72 740*	14 958	3 080	10 275	1 636	16 335	9 251	17 205
	1990	73 999	*72 659*	13 642	2 518	10 233	1 248	15 819	10 201	18 998
Distribution, repair and servicing of motor vehicles (including caravans, tyres, motor accessories and spares)	1983	31 057	*30 849*	7 536	1 577	3 772	709	6 027	2 725	8 502
	1984	33 425	*33 045*	7 764	1 649	3 932	773	7 179	2 731	9 018
	1985	35 647	*35 206*	8 187	1 779	4 149	779	7 577	2 728	10 007
	1986	39 983	*39 677*	9 658	1 912	4 893	847	9 190	2 500	10 677
	1987	47 187	*46 745*	11 049	2 310	6 053	940	11 380	2 581	12 432
	1988	56 853	*56 476*	12 908	2 798	8 787	1 229	13 668	2 244	14 842
	1989	65 361	*64 921*	14 774	3 071	10 268	1 636	16 051	2 431	16 690
	1990	64 724	*64 015*	13 463	2 515	10 229	1 248	15 534	2 560	18 466
Petrol filling stations	1983	5 500	*5 419*	134	5	12	-	158	4 736	374
	1984	6 023	*5 867*	163	13	15	-	150	5 152	373
	1985	6 548	*6 372*	185	8	10	-	235	5 489	446
	1986	6 810	*6 534*	204	17	30	-	228	5 613	442
	1987	7 019	*6 733*	214	15	11	-	245	5 751	496
	1988	7 621	*7 224*	207	23	9	-	245	6 191	548
	1989	8 269	*7 819*	184	9	7	-	284	6 820	515
	1990	9 275	*8 644*	179	3	4	-	285	7 641	532

Continued from page 216

Source: Central Statistical Office

Tables 11.8 and 11.9

Table 11.8 shows expenditure at current, and constant 1985 prices, for the period 1985 to 1990 for R & D performed in the United Kingdom by industry, analysed by major product group. Table 11.9 shows the sources of funds for R & D within industry in the United Kingdom for the period 1985 to 1990. Note that the figures for 1985 exclude the United Kingdom Atomic Energy Authority which became a public corporation in April 1986. From 1989 the data were collected giving the breakdown by civil and defence purposes. More details are given in CSO Bulletin 14/92 *Industrial Research and Development 1990.*

Catering

11.4 Catering and allied trades 1981 - 1990
Great Britain

£m exclusive of VAT

	Year	No. of businesses	Turnover (inclusive of VAT)	Stocks Beginning of year	Stocks End of year	New building work	Land and existing buildings	Vehicles	Plant and machinery	Net capital expenditure
Total catering and allied trades	1982	113 333	14 926	487	501	337	74	43	262	716
	1983	114 563	15 871	494	517	330	45	46	314	734
	1984	117 715	17 284	513	542	374	145	36	346	902
	1985	117 788	19 271	529	580	454	232	47	425	1 157
	1986	119 889	20 971	571	610	610	405	48	531	1 594
	1987	121 050	23 111	600	659	834	757	57	499	2 146
	1988	122 281	25 406	609	675	1 029	520	74	686	2 309
	1989	124 313	27 760	647	702	1 177	700	104	726	2 707
	1990	124 900	30 672	703	770	1 161	637	95	699	2 593
Hotels and other residential establishments	1982	13 385	2 880	72	74	83	31	9	61	184
	1983	12 902	2 986	73	76	83	18	6	72	179
	1984	12 934	3 374	75	79	112	56	4	96	268
	1985	12 767	4 050	79	88	168	89	10	141	408
	1986	12 855	4 279	83	94	225	187	11	187	610
	1987	12 960	4 781	92	102	388	427	12	204	1,031
	1988	13 648	5 514	94	103	494	236	20	163	913
	1989	13 979	5 892	95	106	507	273	21	250	1,050
	1990	14 444	6 370	103	113	679	296	18	238	1,231
Holiday camps, camping and holiday caravan sites	1982	1 542	390	15	14	21	2	2	11	37
	1983	1 620	418	18	18	11	6	2	15	34
	1984	1 605	456	20	20	14	5	1	20	41
	1985	1 562	503	21	20	17	16	4	24	61
	1986	1 621	567	21	24	16	12	3	28	59
	1987	1 615	590	25	26	43	73	3	37	156
	1988	1 636	696	22	26	62	18	2	40	122
	1989	1 889	843	27	34	77	28	3	44	152
	1990	2 027	939	41	44	32	49	4	41	125
Restaurants, cafes, snack bars, etc selling food for consumption on the premises ony	1982	11 817	1 639	48	50	27	3	4	31	65
	1983	12 119	1 742	47	52	23	..[2]	5	41	..[2]
	1984	12 692	1 900	50	56	28	14	7	40	90
	1985	13 362	2 194	55	62	41	23	6	37	107
	1986	14 348	2 260	59	62	48	28	4	40	120
	1987	15 184	3 064	81	95	100	48	10	68	225
	1988	16 308	3 192	75	88	93	66	10	160	328
	1989	17 327	3 588	87	95	95	44	17	104	260
	1990	17 842	3 906	98	98	134	47	15	93	289
Fish and chip shops, sandwich and snack bars and other establishments selling food partly or wholly for consumption off the premises	1982	26 256	1 497	24	26	34	5	4	36	78
	1983	27 049	1 664	24	27	45	..[2]	5	38	..[2]
	1984	29 205	1 869	29	32	14	5	5	41	65
	1985	28 274	2 063	30	34	20	14	9	47	90
	1986	28 436	2 435	35	36	59	37	7	49	152
	1987	28 686	2 826	37	41	21	19	7	65	111
	1988	29 124	3 377	42	45	61	50	12	81	204
	1989	29 928	3 682	40	47	115	82	22	89	308
	1990	30 921	4 162	44	53	44	46	16	92	198
Public houses[1]	1982	41 457	6 002	229	238	134	15	18	102	269
	1983	41 868	6 424	232	242	142	30	24	125	321
	1984	42 010	6 888	233	249	156	47	16	114	333
	1985	42 294	7 336	238	263	165	70	17	145	397
	1986	42 901	8 043	258	273	213	126	19	191	549
	1987	42 873	8 274	249	277	250	171	19	93	534
	1988	42 077	8 716	261	290	270	139	22	199	629
	1989	41 339	9 712	275	293	338	235	33	203	808
	1990	40 155	10 648	300	329	223	157	31	177	588
Clubs (excluding sports clubs and gaming clubs)	1982	17 568	1 776	89	89	34	16	4	13	67
	1983	17 636	1 847	88	87	22	12	1	15	50
	1984	17 786	1 948	92	91	46	18	-	28	93
	1985	17 963	2 128	90	94	41	18	-2	23	80
	1986	18 002	2 203	97	101	46	13	-1	26	84
	1987	17 821	2 288	96	97	30	13	1	21	64
	1988	17 295	2 387	95	97	43	11	3	30	87
	1989	17 342	2 401	96	96	38	32	2	23	95
	1990	16 806	2 587	94	104	46	34	2	37	118
Catering contractors	1982	1 308	743	10	10	3	1	3	8	15
	1983	1 367	790	12	15	3	-	3	9	15
	1984	1 483	849	14	15	2	1	3	7	13
	1985	1 566	998	16	20	1	1	3	7	12
	1986	1 727	1 183	18	20	3	2	4	10	19
	1987	1 912	1 288	20	22	2	6	6	11	25
	1988	2 193	1 525	20	26	6	1	6	14	27
	1989	2 509	1 642	27	30	6	6	8	14	34
	1990	2 704	2 059	24	30	3	9	9	21	43

1 The figures include, besides those businesses registered as public houses, brewers known to operate managed public houses. These businesses account for about one-third of the total activity of public houses.

2 Figures suppressed for disclosure reasons.

Source: Central Statistical Office

Research and development

11.5 Cost of research and development: analysis by sector

Work performed within each sector

	1987[1]		1988[1]		1989[1]		1990	
	£ million	Per cent	£ million	Per cent	£ million	Per cent	£ million	Per cent
Sector carrying out the work								
Government	1 360.0	14.4	1 481.6	14.3	1 674.9	14.7	1 701.7	14.0
Higher Education Institutes	1 402.8	14.8	1 514.9	14.7	1 621.9	14.2	1 790.0	14.7
Industry[2]	6 335.2	67.1	6 921.6	67.0	7 649.8	66.9	8 082.4	66.6
Other	350.0	3.7	410.0	4.0	482.0	4.2	562.4	4.6
Total	9 448.0	100.0	10 328.1	100.0	11 428.6	100.0	12 136.5	100.0

Finance provided by each sector

	1987[1]		1988[1]		1989[1]		1990	
	£ million	Per cent	£ million	Per cent	£ million	Per cent	£ million	Per cent
Government	3 695.0	39.1	3 755.7	36.4	4 163.0	36.4	4 348.3	35.8
Higher Education Institutes	65.0	0.7	77.0	0.7	80.9	0.7	84.3	0.7
Industry[2]	4 650.4	49.2	5 337.5	51.7	5 794.6	50.7	6 000.0	49.4
Other	1 037.6	11.0	1 157.9	11.2	1 390.1	12.2	1 703.9	14.0
Total	9 448.0	100.0	10 328.1	100.0	11 428.6	100.0	12 136.5	100.0

1 Data for 1987, 1988 and 1989 have been revised.
2 Including research associations and public corporations.

Source: Central Statistical Office

Research and development

11.6 Gross central government expenditure on research and development

£ million

	1986-87		1987-88		1988-89		1989-90[1]		1990-91	
	Intra-mural	Extra-mural	Intra-mural	Extra-mural	Intra-mural	Extra-mural	Intra-mural	Extra-mural	Intra-mural	Extra-mural
Defence	728.3	1 404.2	756.3	1 371.5	810.5	1 293.3	938.8	1 325.4	900.9	1 388.3
Research councils	366.0	306.3	380.8	351.6	409.2	362.8	474.1	409.1	497.3	465.3
Higher Education Institutes	-	720.0	-	760.0	-	830.4	-	829.8	-	863.2
Other programmes	203.2	829.6	214.9	904.1	250.0	739.9	252.0	752.7	293.7	800.8
Total	1 372.0	3 400.1	1 352.0	3 244.3	1 469.6	3 226.4	1 665.0	3 317.0	1 691.9	3 517.6
	4 557.6		4 596.3		4 696.1		4 982.0		5 209.5	

1 Data for 1989-90 have been revised.

Source: Central Statistical Office

Research and Development

11.7 Net central government expenditure on research and development, using European Community objectives for R&D expenditure

£ million

	1984-85	1985-86	1986-87	1987-88	1988-89	1989-90[1]	1990-91	1991-92[2]
Exploration and exploitation of the earth	73.9	77.1	79.4	85.2	95.5	119.9	138.8	125.3
Infrastructure and general planning of land-use	60.3	54.1	65.5	66.8	66.8	71.6	74.1	86.2
Control of environmental pollution	51.6	53.3	48.7	56.1	58.2	53.0	70.2	85.1
Protection and promotion of human health	158.1	163.0	190.0	203.9	217.7	257.9	286.9	301.0
Production, distribution and rational utilization of energy	207.8	204.9	187.6	170.4	177.3	157.7	141.7	120.4
Agricultural production and technology	205.5	203.5	198.1	196.1	206.3	194.9	198.3	204.0
Industrial production and technology	288.0	435.3	443.6	411.8	394.8	451.6	475.0	404.8
Social structures and relationships	43.9	55.8	62.3	70.5	95.5	100.4	111.7	116.9
Exploration and exploitation of space	80.8	127.9	123.9	129.8	146.4	145.1	154.2	165.1
Research financed from General University Funds	630.0	669.0	720.0	795.6	830.4	829.8	863.2	960.4
Non-oriented research	281.0	183.8	192.8	209.3	215.9	222.9	254.9	245.5
Other civil research	11.4	12.4	14.2	13.6	13.8	11.9	11.0	13.0
Defence	1 961.6	2 110.8	2 040.9	2 009.1	1 984.9	2 153.5	2 183.0	2 246.2
Total	4 054.2	4 351.0	4 367.1	4 418.0	4 503.6	4 770.2	4 962.9	5 073.9

1 See note 1 at table 11.6.
2 Provisional.

Source: Central Statistical Office

11.8 Intra-mural expenditure on Industrial research and development, 1985 to 1990
At current prices

£ million

	1985[1]	1989[2] Total	1989[2] Civil	1989[2] Defence	1990 Total	1990 Civil	1990 Defence
All product groups	5 121.6	7 649.8	5 923.3	1 726.5	8 082.4	6 279.4	1 803.0
All products of manufacturing industry	4 673.2	6 511.5	4 871.9	1 639.6	6 929.3	5 222.2	1 707.2
Chemical industries	941.9	1 691.4	1 672.9	18.5	1 923.1	1 909.5	13.6
Mechanical engineering	262.6	265.3	175.2	90.1	232.9	143.0	89.9
Electronics[3]	1 758.6	2 253.0	1 538.5	714.5	2 327.3	1 649.2	678.2
Other electrical engineering	125.6	113.6	108.3	5.3	148.1	139.9	8.3
Aerospace	818.0	1 090.1	335.2	754.9	1 212.2	355.4	856.8
Motor vehicles	371.6	484.3	475.9	8.4	501.3	484.9	16.4
Other manufactured products	394.9	613.8	565.9	47.9	584.3	540.3	44.0
Non-manufactured products	448.4	1 138.3	1 051.4	86.9	1 153.1	1 057.3	95.8

For footnotes see page 219.

Source: Central Statistical Office

Research and development

11.8 Intra-mural expenditure on industrial research and development, 1985 to 1990
At 1985 prices
(continued)

£ million

	1985[1]	1989[2] Total	1989[2] Civil	1989[2] Defence	1990 Total	1990 Civil	1990 Defence
All product groups	5 121.6	6 184.2	4 788.4	1 395.7	6 118.4	4 753.5	1364.9
All products of manufacturing industry	4 673.2	5 263.9	3 938.5	1 325.5	5 245.4	3 953.2	1 292.3
Chemicals industries	941.9	1 367.3	1 352.4	15.0	1 455.8	1 445.5	10.3
Mechanical engineering	262.6	214.5	141.6	72.8	176.3	108.3	68.1
Electronics[3]	1 758.6	1 821.3	1 243.7	577.6	1 761.8	1 248.4	513.4
Other electrical engineering	125.6	91.8	87.6	4.3	112.1	105.9	6.3
Aerospace	818.0	881.2	271.0	610.3	917.6	269.1	648.6
Motor vehicles	371.6	391.5	384.7	6.8	379.4	367.0	12.4
Other manufactured products	394.9	496.2	457.5	38.7	442.3	409.0	33.3
Non-manufactured products	448.4	920.2	850.0	70.3	872.9	800.3	72.6

1 Figures for 1985 exclude UKAEA which became a public corporation in April 1986.
2 Data for 1989 have been revised.
3 Including office machinery and electronic data processing equipment.

Source: Central Statistical Office

11.9 Sources of funds for R & D within industry in the United Kingdom, 1985 to 1990

£ million

	1985	1989 Total	1989 Civil	1989 Defence	1990 Total	1990 Civil	1990 Defence
Funds for industry's R & D (£m)							
Total	5 121.6	7 649.8	5 923.3	1 726.5	8 082.4	6279.4	1 803.0
Government funds	1 175.5	1 312.1	305.5	1 006.6	1 352.2	364.6	987.5
Overseas funds	569.0	1 023.2	739.3	283.9	1 252.5	858.7	393.8
Mainly own funds	3 377.1	5 314.5	4 878.5	436.0	5 477.7	5 056.1	421.6
Per cent of total	100	100	100	100	100	100	100
Government funds	23	17	5	58	17	6	55
Overseas funds	11	13	12	16	15	14	22
Mainly own funds	66	69	82	26	68	81	23

See notes 1 and 2 at table 11.8.

Source: Central Statistical Office

12 External Trade

The tables covering external trade have been compiled from the annual and monthly *Overseas Trade Statistics of the United Kingdom* published by HMSO as Business Monitor MA20 and MM20. United Kingdom is defined as Great Britain, Northern Ireland, the Isle of Man, the Channel Islands and the Continental Shelf (United Kingdom part). Commodities are grouped according to the Standard International Trade Classification (Revision 3) or SITC (R3) which replaced SITC (R2) from 1 January 1988. The statistics in Table 12.1 are on a balance of payments basis; all other statistics in this section are on an *Overseas Trade Statistics* basis. For more detailed figures, notes and definitions relating to external trade, reference should be made to these volumes and also to the annual publication *United Kingdom Balance of Payments* (the CSO Pink Book) and *Monthly Digest of Statistics, Supplement of Definitions and Explanatory Notes*.

Changes in the coverage of the overseas trade statistics are made from time to time but as far as possible figures in these tables have been adjusted to the current basis. For latest data reference should be made to the *Monthly Review of External Trade Statistics*, available from the Central Statistical Office.

The value of UK trade with selected areas, analysed by commodity divisions, is obtainable from the annual edition of the *Overseas Trade Statistics of the United Kingdom*.

Import penetration and export sales ratios *(Table 12.2)*

The ratios were first introduced in the August 1977 edition of *Economic Trends* in an article 'The Home and Export Performance of United Kingdom Industries'. The article described the conceptual and methodological problems involved in measuring such variables as import penetration. The industries are currently grouped according to the 1980 Standard Industrial Classification. The latest ratios for the full detail within manufacturing (over 200 activity headings) are shown in Business Monitor MQ12, *'Import Penetration and Export Sales Ratios for Manufacturing Industry'*.

12.1 Visible trade of the United Kingdom
On a balance of payments basis[1]

		1980	1981	1982	1983	1984	1985	1986	1987	1988	1989	1990	1991
Value(£ million)													
Exports	CGJP	47 149	50 668	55 331	60 700	70 265	77 991	72 627	79 153	80 346	92 154	101 718	103 413
Imports(fob)	CGGL	45 792	47 416	53 421	62 237	75 601	81 336	82 186	90 735	101 826	116 837	120 527	113 703
Visible balance	HCHL	1 357	3 251	1 911	−1 537	−5 336	−3 345	−9 559	−11 582	−21 480	−24 683	−18 809	−10 290
Unit value index numbers													
1985=100													
Exports (fob)	CGTO	69.9	76.2	81.4	88.0	95.0	100.0	90.1	93.5	93.4	100.8	106.2	106.4
Imports (fob)	CGTP	67.8	73.7	79.9	87.4	95.3	100.0	95.4	98.0	96.9	104.1	108.0	108.4
Terms of trade[2]	CGTQ	103.1	103.4	101.9	100.8	99.7	100.0	94.4	95.4	96.4	96.8	98.3	98.2
Volume index numbers													
1985=100													
Exports	CGTR	84.1	83.3	85.6	87.6	94.8	100.0	104.2	109.7	111.6	116.6	124.2	126.3
Imports	CGTS	79.0	75.8	80.1	87.0	96.9	100.0	107.4	115.3	130.1	140.5	142.1	138.1

1 Statistics of visible trade on a balance of payments basis are obtained by making certain adjustments in respect of valuation and coverage to the statistics recorded in the *Overseas Trade Statistics*. These adjustments are described in detail in *United Kingdom Balance of Payments 1991 Edition*.

2 Export unit value index as a percentage of the import unit value index.

Source: Central Statistical Office

External trade

12.2 Import penetration and export sales ratios for products of manufacturing industry
United Kingdom

		1980 SIC Class	1977	1978	1979	1980	1981	1982	1983	1984	1985	1986	1987	1988	1989[2,3]
Ratio 1 Imports/Home demand															
Div 2-4 Manufacturing industries[1]	BYAA	21-49	25.1	26.0	26.9	26.2	27.8	29.0	31.1	33.4	34.3	34.3	35.2	35.6	36.7
Class:															
Metals	KMKJ	21-22	32	31	32	33	30	33	36	43	45	..	..	..	..
Other minerals and mineral products	KMKK	23-24	12	12	13	12	12	12	13	15	15	15	18	18	17
Chemicals and man-made fibres	KMKL	25-26	27	28	30	29	31	34	36	39	41	41	43	42	42
Metal goods nes	BYAJ	31	9	10	10	11	11	12	13	14	16	16	18	17	18
Mechanical engineering	BYAK	32	30	32	29	29	32	32	32	34	36	37	38	39	40
Office machinery and data processing equipment	BYAL	33	84	92	92	96	96	105	106	105	100	100	93	91	95
Electrical and electronic engineering	BYAM	34	30	31	31	31	36	39	42	44	47	47	49	50	52
Motor vehicles and their parts	BYAN	35	35	35	41	39	42	47	52	51	50	51	48	50	51
Other transport equipment	BYAO	36	45	41	38	38	41	39	42	51	45	45	42	45	49
Instrument engineering	BYAP	37	51	52	53	52	58	56	55	57	57	56	58	58	60
Food, drink and tobacco	BYAR	41-42	17	18	18	16	16	16	17	18	18	18	18	18	18
Textile industry	BYAS	43	27	31	33	34	39	39	41	44	44	45	47	48	48
Leather and leather goods	BYAT	44	32	34	40	40	42	42	44	44	49	46	49	49	52
Clothing and footwear	BYAU	45	25	26	29	29	33	33	33	36	35	36	39	39	40
Timber and wooden furniture	BYAV	46	28	27	29	27	29	29	32	32	30	31	31	30	30
Paper, printing and publishing	BYAW	47	21	19	19	19	20	19	20	21	21	21	22	21	22
Rubber and plastics processing	BYAX	48	17	18	18	18	21	22	24	25	26	27	28	26	26
Other manufacturing industries	BYAY	49	34	35	36	41	48	38	38	39	38	39	46	44	45
Ratio 2 Imports/Home demand and Exports															
Div 2-4 Manufacturing industries[1]	BYBA	21-49	19.9	20.6	21.6	20.7	21.8	22.9	24.9	26.4	26.7	26.9	27.5	28.1	28.8
Class:															
Metals	KMLC	21-22	27	26	27	29	26	27	30	34	35	..	..	..	..
Other minerals and mineral products	KMLD	23-24	10	10	11	10	10	11	12	13	13	13	15	15	15
Chemicals and man-made fibres	KMLE	25-26	19	20	21	20	22	23	25	26	26	27	28	28	28
Metal goods nes	BYBJ	31	8	9	9	10	10	11	12	13	14	14	16	15	16
Mechanical engineering	BYBK	32	19	21	19	19	20	20	22	24	24	25	26	28	28
Office machinery and data processing equipment	BYBL	33	51	54	53	52	57	61	63	60	54	56	52	51	53
Electrical and electronic engineering	BYBM	34	21	22	23	23	27	29	31	32	33	33	35	36	37
Motor vehicles and their parts	BYBN	35	23	25	31	28	30	35	40	39	39	41	38	41	41
Other transport equipment	BYBO	36	30	27	26	26	25	24	25	28	27	26	24	27	28
Instrument engineering	BYBP	37	34	35	35	33	36	35	38	39	40	40	40	40	41
Food, drink and tobacco	BYBR	41-42	16	16	16	14	15	15	15	17	17	17	17	16	16
Textile industry	BYBS	43	21	25	26	26	30	31	33	35	35	36	38	38	39
Leather and leather goods	BYBT	44	25	27	32	31	34	33	34	34	37	36	37	37	39
Clothing and footwear	BYBU	45	21	22	25	25	28	29	29	32	31	31	33	34	35
Timber and wooden furniture	BYBV	46	26	26	27	26	27	28	31	31	29	30	30	29	29
Paper, printing and publishing	BYBW	47	19	17	18	17	18	18	18	20	19	19	20	20	20
Rubber and plastics processing	BYBX	48	14	14	15	14	17	18	20	21	22	22	23	22	22
Other manufacturing industries	BYBY	49	25	25	27	31	36	31	31	32	31	31	36	35	36

1 Certain sectors are excluded since they are inappropriate for this analysis. They are the following activity headings: 2396 (pt) unworked precious stones, 2436 ready-mixed concrete, 3138 heat and surface treatment of metals, 3246 process engineering contractors, 3480 electrical equipment installation, 4121 slaughterhouses, 4370 textile finishing, 4560 fur goods, 4672 shop and office fitting, 4820 retreading and specialist repairing of rubber tyres, 4910 jewellery and coins, 4930 photographic and cinematographic processing laboratories.

2 12 months ending June 1989.
3 1990 figures not available. As a result of recommendations made in the 1989 review of Department of Trade and Industry statistics, quarterly sales data for most manufacturing industries, which are used in the calculation of this ratio, are no longer collected. Data since 1989 are therefore not available.

Source: Department of Trade and Industry

External trade

12.2 Import penetration and export sales ratios for products of manufacturing industry
United Kingdom *continued*

		1980 SIC Class	1978	1979	1980	1981	1982	1983	1984	1985	1986	1987	1988	1989[2,3]
Ratio 3 Exports/ Manufacturers' sales														
Div 2-4 Manufacturing industries[1]	BYCA	21-49	26.1	25.1	26.5	27.3	27.2	26.6	28.4	30.2	29.4	30.3	29.2	30.0
Class:														
Metals	KMLV	21-22	22	23	21	23	23	25	32	35	..	..	..	..
Other minerals and mineral products	KMLW	23-24	16	15	16	15	14	14	14	15	15	16	16	18
Chemicals and man-made fibres	KMLX	25-26	36	36	38	39	41	42	45	48	48	47	47	47
Metal goods nes	BYCJ	31	13	12	14	14	14	12	13	14	13	13	13	13
Mechanical engineering	BYCK	32	44	42	45	47	45	40	42	43	42	42	39	39
Office machinery and data processing equipment	BYCL	33	90	90	96	94	108	110	107	100	100	91	90	93
Electrical and electronic engineering	BYCM	34	37	33	34	36	38	37	39	43	43	43	44	46
Motor vehicles and their parts	BYCN	35	38	36	38	41	38	37	37	37	34	34	32	33
Other transport equipment	BYCO	36	45	43	42	50	53	55	63	55	59	57	55	60
Instrument engineering	BYCP	37	51	53	55	59	57	51	52	50	48	52	53	54
Food, drink and tobacco	BYCR	41-42	11	10	10	10	11	10	10	11	11	12	11	12
Textile industry	BYCS	43	27	27	30	30	29	28	30	31	30	32	32	32
Leather and leather goods	BYCT	44	26	29	32	30	33	33	35	38	36	40	38	41
Clothing and footwear	BYCU	45	18	18	19	20	18	18	18	19	18	21	19	19
Timber and wooden furniture	BYCV	46	7	6	7	6	6	6	6	6	5	5	4	4
Paper, printing and publishing	BYCW	47	11	10	10	10	10	10	10	11	11	11	10	10
Rubber and plastics processing	BYCX	48	21	20	23	24	22	22	22	22	21	22	20	20
Other manufacturing industries	BYCY	49	38	36	36	38	28	28	28	28	28	34	31	30
Ration 4 Exports/ Manufacturers' sales and Imports														
Div 2-4 Manufacturing industries[1]	BYDA	21-49	20.7	19.7	21.0	21.4	21.0	20.0	20.9	22.1	21.5	21.8	21.0	21.3
Class:														
Metals	KMJP	21-22	16	17	15	17	17	18	21	23	..	..	..	..
Other minerals and mineral products	KMJQ	23-24	15	14	14	13	12	12	12	13	13	14	14	14
Chemicals and man-made fibres	KMJR	25-26	29	28	31	31	31	32	33	35	35	34	34	34
Metal goods nes	BYDJ	31	12	11	13	12	12	11	11	12	11	11	11	11
Mechanical engineering	BYDK	32	35	33	36	38	36	31	32	33	32	31	28	28
Office machinery and data processing equipment	BYDL	33	42	42	45	40	42	41	43	46	44	43	44	44
Electrical and electronic engineering	BYDM	34	28	26	27	27	27	26	26	29	28	28	28	29
Motor vehicles and their parts	BYDN	35	28	25	28	29	25	22	23	22	20	21	19	20
Other transport and equipment	BYDO	36	33	32	31	38	40	41	45	40	44	43	40	43
Instrument engineering	BYDP	37	33	34	37	38	37	32	31	30	29	32	32	32
Food, drink and tobacco	BYDR	41-42	9	9	9	9	9	9	9	9	9	10	9	10
Textile industry	BYDS	43	20	20	22	21	20	19	19	20	19	20	19	20
Leather and leather goods	BYDT	44	19	20	22	20	22	22	23	24	23	25	24	25
Clothing and footwear	BYDU	45	14	14	14	14	13	12	13	13	13	14	13	12
Timber and wooden furniture	BYDV	46	5	4	5	4	5	4	4	4	4	3	3	3
Paper, printing and publishing	BYDW	47	9	8	9	8	8	8	8	9	9	9	8	8
Rubber and plastics processing	BYDX	48	18	17	19	20	18	17	17	17	17	17	15	15
Other manufacturing industries	BYDY	49	28	26	25	25	20	19	19	20	19	21	20	19

1 Certain sectors are excluded since they are inappropriate for this analysis. They are the following activity headings: 2396 (pt) unworked precious stones, 2436 ready-mixed concrete, 3138 heat and surface treatment of metals, 3246 process engineering contractors, 3480 electrical equipment installation, 4121 slaughterhouses, 4370 textile finishing, 4560 fur goods, 4672 shop and office fitting, 4820 retreading and specialist repairing of rubber tyres, 4910 jewellery and coins, 4930 photographic and cinematographic processing laboratories.
2 12 months ending June 1989.
3 1990 figures not available. As a result of the recommendations made in the 1989 review of Department of Trade and Industry statistics, quarterly sales data for most manufacturing industries, which are used in the calculation of this ratio, are no longer collected. Data since 1989 are therefore not available.

Source: Department of Trade and Industry

External trade

12.3 Value of United Kingdom exports (fob)[1]
Analysis by sections and divisions

£ million

		1982	1983	1984	1985	1986	1987	1988	1989	1990	1991[2]
Total UK exports	BQTR	55 557.8	60 684.3	70 488.3	78 391.8	72 987.7	79 848.7	81 654.9	93 770.9	103 692.4	104 877.0
0. Food and live animals chiefly for food	BQRA	2 508.3	2 754.6	3 114.8	3 252.4	3 745.8	3 738.5	3 458.2	4 228.8	4 341.9	4 715.8
00. Live animals chiefly for food	BQRB	179.1	187.4	191.0	262.0	299.9	333.1	254.8	265.7	258.0	288.4
01. Meat and meat preparations	BQRC	347.5	495.7	491.1	497.4	521.9	625.9	590.4	699.6	610.3	672.6
02. Dairy products and birds' eggs	BQRD	325.6	308.1	246.6	281.3	331.5	318.8	389.1	501.8	458.2	451.9
03. Fish, crustaceans and molluscs, and preparations thereof	BQRE	162.3	203.2	224.4	260.3	328.9	407.2	384.4	450.0	505.3	574.4
04. Cereals and cereal preparations	BQRF	773.9	740.9	992.7	833.0	1 177.5	813.8	674.8	951.6	1 061.6	1 102.8
05. Vegetables and fruit	BQRG	154.0	163.2	190.8	205.3	251.7	300.3	222.3	281.2	263.7	298.5
06. Sugar, sugar preparations and honey	BQRH	121.1	145.1	165.7	220.8	170.4	219.6	196.2	228.2	240.4	247.5
07. Coffee, tea, cocoa, spices and manufactures thereof	BQRI	252.2	291.4	363.4	390.8	364.0	377.8	362.8	387.7	438.7	465.2
08. Feedingstuff for animals (not including unmilled cereals)	BQRJ	69.0	78.9	96.8	121.8	139.3	155.8	176.4	228.7	238.9	302.6
09. Miscellaneous edible products and preparations	BQRK	123.8	140.8	152.3	179.7	160.6	186.1	207.1	234.2	266.8	311.7
1. Beverages and tobacco	BQRL	1 451.5	1 486.2	1 577.9	1 719.1	1 737.9	1 860.3	2 075.4	2 326.3	2 770.2	3 031.8
11. Beverages	BQRM	1 060.1	1 051.2	1 157.0	1 253.7	1 331.6	1 410.5	1 575.4	1 802.2	2 112.8	2 251.7
12. Tobacco and tobacco manufactures	BQRN	391.4	435.0	420.9	465.4	406.3	449.8	500.0	524.1	657.5	780.3
2. Crude materials, inedible, except fuels	BQRO	1 293.7	1 527.7	1 898.1	2 032.1	1 940.9	1 980.0	2 031.6	2 264.6	2 162.5	1 919.7
21. Hides, skins and furskins, raw	BQRP	180.5	200.2	280.3	288.5	260.2	311.5	254.8	253.9	188.8	135.1
22. Oil seeds and oleaginous fruit	BQRQ	7.9	37.8	54.0	90.4	155.5	86.2	41.7	37.2	67.3	52.6
23. Crude rubber (including synthetic and reclaimed)	BQRR	122.8	141.7	166.9	173.9	183.0	180.0	193.0	211.6	221.9	198.1
24. Cork and wood	BQRS	28.6	24.1	25.5	25.7	22.9	28.7	26.2	27.8	27.7	27.9
25. Pulp and waste paper	BQRT	11.6	15.8	27.2	24.7	25.0	33.9	46.4	51.6	53.1	38.8
26. Textile fibres (other than wool tops) and their wastes (not manufactured into yarn or fabric)	BQRU	314.2	375.1	427.9	419.4	373.0	447.8	439.5	496.1	494.5	466.2
27. Crude fertilisers and crude minerals (excluding coal, petroleum and precious stones)	BQRV	224.2	223.8	249.1	269.2	271.9	340.6	339.3	368.9	369.9	365.5
28. Metalliferous ores and metal scrap	BQRW	346.6	444.2	591.4	645.8	538.9	451.6	593.0	712.4	633.5	526.9
29. Crude animal and vegetable materials	BQRX	57.3	64.9	75.6	94.3	110.4	99.7	97.6	103.1	105.9	108.5
3. Mineral fuels, lubricants and related materials	BQRY	11 237.1	13 102.7	15 308.4	16 795.5	8 671.9	8 747.4	5 817.8	6 174.9	7 868.7	7 169.0
33. Petroleum, petroleum products and related materials	BQRZ	10 685.7	12 501.2	14 851.8	16 133.9	8 207.9	8 444.3	5 575.9	5 918.6	7 544.6	6 814.1
32, 34 and 35. Coal, coke, gas and electric current	BQSA	551.4	601.5	456.6	661.6	464.0	303.1	241.9	256.3	324.1	355.0
4. Animal and vegetable oils, fats and waxes	BQSB	46.5	59.1	91.0	95.9	105.3	263.9	88.7	83.6	87.7	95.9
5. Chemicals and related products	BQSC	6 119.3	6 933.0	8 216.8	9 411.7	9 676.8	10 540.0	11 331.2	12 349.6	13 181.6	13 788.6
51. Organic chemicals	BQSD	1 592.3	1 930.2	2 381.7	2 742.8	2 571.0	2 830.5	3 138.3	3 373.3	3 351.6	3 468.4
52. Inorganic chemicals	BQSE	694.9	699.6	811.1	979.6	1 123.3	1 099.6	1 105.6	1 021.5	951.6	1 000.6
53. Dyeing, tanning and colouring materials	BQSF	464.1	568.8	633.3	692.0	763.2	885.3	938.7	1 063.3	1 193.5	1 216.4
54. Medicinal and pharmaceutical products	BQSG	978.0	1 073.4	1 222.4	1 427.0	1 532.7	1 620.7	1 734.4	2 016.3	2 257.5	2 556.1
55. Essential oils and perfume materials; toilet, polishing and cleansing materials	BQSH	525.1	574.5	690.5	767.9	807.7	886.4	943.2	1 003.4	1 161.9	1 298.4
56. Fertilisers, manufactured	BQSI	..	..	..	..	..	85.4	90.0	105.8	110.3	103.2
57. Explosives and pyrotechnic products (Rev 3) Plastics in primary forms	BQSJ	36.8	40.1	47.6	45.7	42.8	834.0	1 113.9	1 245.3	1 342.4	1 332.9
58. Artificial resins and plastic materials, and cellulose esters and ethers (Rev 3) Plastics in non-primary forms	BQSK	875.3	980.5	1 179.8	1 330.7	1 401.1	715.0	616.1	686.2	781.7	786.9
59. Chemical materials and products, not elsewhere specified (Rev 3) Chemical materials	BQSL	904.1	996.4	1 186.0	1 351.3	1 367.5	1 583.1	1 651.0	1 834.5	2 031.1	2 025.7

Note: The statistics are on an overseas trade statistics basis (see footnote 1 to Table 12.1).

2 Provisional.

Source: Department of Trade and Industry

1 The numbers on the left hand side of the table refer to the Section and Division code numbers of the *Standard International Trade Classification, (Revision 3)* which came into effect from 1 January 1988. The broad structure of SITC(R3) follows that of SITC(R2) but one major change should be noted: Explosives and pyrotechnic products: Div. 57 in SITC (R2) forms part of Div. 59 in SITC(R3). Div. 58 in SITC (R2) has been split into Div. 57 and 58 in SITC (R3).

External trade

12.3 Value of United Kingdom exports (fob)[1]
Analysis by sections and divisions
continued

£ million

		1982	1983	1984	1985	1986	1987	1988	1989	1990	1991[2]
6. Manufactured goods classified chiefly by material	BQSM	7 940.5	9 016.4	10 010.6	10 430.2	10 977.8	11 751.2	12 714.5	14 517.2	15 821.6	15 581.1
61. Leather, leather manufactures, nes, and dressed furskins	BQSN	202.1	233.3	312.5	295.2	321.5	360.3	311.4	326.5	311.8	258.0
62. Rubber manufactures, nes	BQSO	417.9	451.6	481.8	554.4	611.8	678.0	715.4	801.6	872.8	887.9
63. Cork and wood manufactures (excluding furniture)	BQSP	83.2	85.5	104.6	84.1	77.2	84.7	82.7	91.0	114.2	116.4
64. Paper, paperboard, and articles of paper pulp, of paper or of paperboard	BQSQ	503.1	543.1	678.6	767.6	824.3	964.4	1 093.7	1 246.1	1 539.4	1 623.8
65. Textile yarn, fabrics, made-up articles, nes, and related products	BQSR	1 192.0	1 285.0	1 484.8	1 709.1	1 711.5	1 833.8	1 934.9	2 204.7	2 447.0	2 349.0
66. Non-metallic mineral manufactures, nes	BQSS	1 609.9	1 995.5	2 298.7	2 164.5	2 549.3	2 654.3	2 974.0	3 199.9	3 191.3	3 177.1
67. Iron and steel	BQST	1 291.8	1 330.7	1 528.9	1 856.2	1 866.5	2 153.4	2 392.0	2 893.8	3 036.0	3 011.3
68. Non-ferrous metals	BQSU	1 244.7	1 766.6	1 656.7	1 379.6	1 551.3	1 505.0	1 650.8	1 966.9	2 193.6	1 975.2
69. Manufactures of metal, nes	BQSV	1 395.6	1 325.1	1 464.1	1 619.6	1 464.5	1 517.4	1 560.0	1 786.6	2 115.6	2 182.4
7. Machinery and transport equipment	BQSW	18 100.9	18 324.8	21 520.5	24 667.5	25 351.2	28 818.4	32 101.5	37 797.7	41 850.6	43 627.1
71. Power generating machinery and equipment	BQSX	2 809.1	2 472.7	2 709.0	3 061.3	3 251.1	3 241.5	3 884.8	4 738.9	5 250.7	5 073.1
72. Machinery specialised for particular industries	BQSY	2 601.3	2 335.0	2 676.8	3 077.6	3 101.1	3 348.7	3 288.6	3 773.0	4 234.1	3 922.1
73. Metalworking machinery	BQSZ	522.4	416.2	503.8	521.1	581.2	692.3	780.3	748.8	912.5	812.5
74. General industrial machinery and equipment, nes, and machine parts nes	BQTA	2 411.8	2 334.2	2 577.1	2 937.5	3 037.2	3 066.7	3 577.7	4 037.2	4 545.7	4 520.6
75. Office machines and automatic data processing equipment	BQTB	1 599.5	2 048.8	3 046.6	3 746.7	3 561.9	4 483.2	5 299.4	6 115.9	6 341.7	6 590.9
76. Telecommunications, sound recording and reproducing apparatus and equipment	BQTC	897.2	991.6	1 117.0	1 295.1	1 401.6	1 567.6	1 759.0	2 222.6	2 685.5	2 942.8
77. Electrical machinery, apparatus and appliances, nes, and electrical parts thereof (including non-electrical counterparts, nes, of electrical household type equipment)	BQTD	2 117.0	2 292.3	2 805.3	3 380.1	3 382.6	3 782.7	4 343.5	5 049.9	5 648.2	5 709.7
78. Road vehicles (including air cushion vehicles)	BQTE	3 109.0	3 092.2	3 318.8	3 910.6	3 953.5	4 876.8	4 992.8	6 071.2	7 296.5	8 555.4
79. Other transport equipment	BQTF	2 033.5	2 341.9	2 766.1	2 737.4	3 080.9	3 758.9	4 175.5	5 040.1	4 935.7	5 500.2
8. Miscellaneous manufactured articles	BQTG	5 151.8	5 813.0	6 955.0	7 996.8	8 574.7	9 895.1	10 070.8	11 772.6	13 349.0	13 140.4
81. Sanitary, plumbing, heating and lighting fixtures and fittings, nes	BQTH	107.0	108.4	118.9	135.0	126.3	177.3	199.4	222.3	260.3	267.3
82. Furniture and parts thereof	BQTI	240.9	257.9	282.0	357.7	356.3	373.8	377.6	460.8	533.2	564.2
83. Travel goods, handbags and similar containers	BQTJ	19.1	19.3	22.4	29.4	30.6	34.8	43.9	56.3	69.9	72.4
84. Articles of apparel and clothing accessories	BQTK	840.0	865.2	996.3	1 171.7	1 228.2	1 428.4	1 414.3	1 444.8	1 699.4	1 920.1
85. Footwear	BQTL	114.9	123.4	142.7	159.2	167.2	198.4	210.4	227.6	274.4	314.8
87. Professional, scientific and controlling instruments and apparatus, nes	BQTM	1 255.4	1 472.1	1 777.6	2 151.7	2 283.7	2 348.4	2 531.6	2 793.0	2 945.2	2 992.7
88. Photographic apparatus, equipment and supplies and optical goods, nes, watches and clocks	BQTN	551.9	573.4	573.4	694.2	817.3	977.3	1 004.1	1 134.6	1 167.0	1 266.1
89. Miscellaneous manufactured articles, nes	BQTO	2 022.7	2 393.4	2 920.8	3 174.9	3 539.2	4 356.5	4 289.5	5 433.1	6 399.5	5 742.9
5 - 8. Manufactured goods	BQTP	37 312.6	40 087.2	46 703.0	52 506.1	54 580.5	61 004.7	66 218.1	76 437.1	84 202.8	86 137.2
9. Commodities and transactions not classified elsewhere	BQTQ	1 708.2	1 666.9	1 795.3	1 990.7	2 205.5	2 254.0	1 965.1	2 255.6	2 258.5	1 807.6

Note: The statistics are on a overseas trade statistics basis (see footnote 1 to Table 12.1).   2 Provisional.

Source: Department of Trade and Industry

1 The numbers on the left hand side of the table refer to the Section and Division code numbers of the *Standard International Trade Classification (Revision 3).* which came into effect from 1 January 1988
(See the full note on page 230.)

External trade

12.4 Value of United Kingdom imports (cif)[1]
Analysis by sections and divisions

£ million

		1982	1983	1984	1985	1986	1987	1988	1989	1990	1991[2]
Total UK imports	BQWR	56 978.2	66 101.1	78 967.4	85 027.0	86 175.5	94 026.2	106 571.2	121 699.2	126 086.1	118 786.0
0. Food and live animals chiefly for food	BQUA	6 414.1	6 907.2	7 820.4	8 106.5	8 718.6	8 702.3	9 093.4	9 760.6	10 408.7	10 389.3
00. Live animals chiefly for food	BQUB	133.1	170.3	196.8	238.3	293.4	240.6	287.1	286.5	290.7	203.3
01. Meat and meat preparations	BQUC	1 370.9	1 313.4	1 342.2	1 400.9	1 465.3	1 562.2	1 646.2	1 826.9	1 887.8	1 845.0
02. Dairy products and birds' eggs	BQUD	567.9	629.2	604.6	606.3	653.2	663.4	761.2	786.4	913.7	871.0
03. Fish, crustaceans and molluscs, and preparations thereof	BQUE	404.2	505.2	537.8	600.4	747.8	759.1	785.8	884.6	968.9	978.5
04. Cereals and cereal preparations	BQUF	549.9	593.5	629.0	713.2	769.3	742.7	751.2	722.2	785.1	818.5
05. Vegetables and fruit	BQUG	1 608.3	1 718.5	1 930.3	2 037.1	2 184.4	2 414.4	2 458.9	2 725.8	2 964.5	3 002.6
06. Sugar, sugar preparations and honey	BQUH	429.5	443.2	524.3	508.1	530.3	542.9	575.7	603.6	639.2	681.2
07. Coffee, tea, cocoa, spices and manufactures thereof	BQUI	722.4	799.9	1 291.4	1 205.7	1 220.6	992.5	946.0	941.4	904.4	869.7
08. Feedingstuff for animals (not including unmilled cereals)	BQUJ	446.6	523.6	501.5	487.4	527.3	505.5	557.7	582.2	624.6	619.1
09. Miscellaneous edible products and preparations	BQUK	181.1	210.4	262.6	309.0	326.9	278.9	323.7	401.0	429.9	500.4
1. Beverages and tobacco	BQUL	836.7	962.0	1 112.5	1 230.8	1 346.7	1 428.7	1 521.4	1 667.4	1 907.1	1 936.1
11. Beverages	BQUM	517.5	617.4	705.5	843.6	1 007.9	1 100.9	1 196.1	1 321.9	1 529.7	1 464.8
12. Tobacco and tobacco manufactures	BQUN	319.2	344.6	407.1	387.2	338.7	327.9	325.3	345.4	377.4	471.3
2. Crude materials, inedible, except fuels	BQUO	3 612.9	4 416.1	4 884.9	4 856.8	4 622.4	5 230.8	5 612.2	6 105.7	5 721.1	4 678.3
21. Hides, skins and furskins, raw	BQUP	189.5	184.9	235.3	238.9	216.4	264.1	194.2	149.2	100.5	68.8
22. Oil seeds and oleaginous fruit	BQUQ	259.6	268.6	234.8	238.8	271.3	255.0	227.5	238.9	273.0	224.0
23. Crude rubber (including synthetic and reclaimed)	BQUR	182.9	197.4	223.5	228.3	203.5	227.1	236.3	250.1	244.9	223.6
24. Cork and wood	BQUS	673.8	937.8	1 009.3	895.3	1 000.3	1 220.7	1 355.5	1 429.0	1 409.9	1 043.7
25. Pulp and waste paper	BQUT	412.0	428.0	611.7	505.9	523.3	657.2	723.5	896.7	777.2	608.0
26. Textile fibres (other than wool tops) and their wastes (not manufactured into yarn or fabric)	BQUU	410.8	475.9	596.7	662.8	546.9	658.2	687.9	681.2	548.9	452.6
27. Crude fertilisers and crude minerals (excluding coal, petroleum and precious stones)	BQUV	263.5	285.8	312.6	354.1	317.1	286.6	353.6	368.0	344.7	284.8
28. Metalliferous ores and metal scrap	BQUW	977.5	1 357.8	1 343.8	1 371.8	1 139.5	1 223.1	1 369.0	1 574.3	1 479.2	1 232.7
29. Crude animal and vegetable materials	BQUX	243.4	279.7	317.3	361.0	404.1	438.6	464.7	518.1	542.7	540.1
3. Mineral fuels, lubricants and related materials	BQUY	7 408.6	7 076.3	10 333.8	10 663.6	6 400.4	6 099.0	5 037.8	6 239.5	7 864.5	7 510.7
33. Petroleum, petroleum products and related materials	BQUZ	6 276.9	5 743.3	8 219.8	8 316.2	4 461.3	4 475.3	3 484.8	4 674.4	6 285.1	5 773.6
32, 34 and 35. Coal, coke, gas and electric current	BQVA	1 131.6	1 333.1	2 114.0	2 347.4	1 939.1	1 623.7	1 553.0	1 565.1	1 579.4	1 737.1
4. Animal and vegetable oils, fats and waxes	BQVB	317.0	358.8	533.2	531.5	365.1	458.2	372.2	384.9	377.3	387.5
5. Chemicals and related products	BQVC	4 179.1	5 118.9	6 322.1	6 900.8	7 345.3	8 346.8	9 313.8	10 438.0	10 834.0	10 978.6
51. Organic chemicals	BQVD	1 171.9	1 456.3	1 874.4	1 893.8	1 830.7	2 087.3	2 352.6	2 630.6	2 593.4	2 618.4
52. Inorganic chemicals	BQVE	539.3	560.8	709.8	897.0	951.4	924.8	910.7	1 005.3	1 000.1	1 033.5
53. Dyeing, tanning and colouring materials	BQVF	198.0	235.1	269.7	310.9	396.5	469.3	543.5	612.6	651.3	620.9
54. Medicinal and pharmaceutical products	BQVG	374.6	470.2	542.3	590.4	679.7	786.3	877.1	1 061.6	1 157.8	1 371.2
55. Essential oils and perfume materials; toilet, polishing and cleansing materials	BQVH	242.2	305.3	377.1	443.3	480.3	554.5	615.1	681.8	756.1	798.1
56. Fertilisers manufactured	BQVI	127.1	171.7	219.4	217.3	213.2	210.6	204.1	271.2	285.6	283.0
57. Explosives and pyrotechnic products (Rev 3) Plastics in primary forms	BQVJ	10.9	14.1	19.0	20.0	22.0	1 474.4	1 935.0	2 059.5	2 212.6	2 053.1
58. Artificial resins and plastic materials, and cellulose esters and ethers (Rev 3) Plastics in non-primary forms	BQVK	1 017.7	1 323.5	1 609.4	1 763.5	1 985.2	919.6	910.8	996.2	1 015.0	976.6
59. Chemical materials and products, not elsewhere specified (Rev 3) Chemical materials	BQVL	497.4	581.9	700.8	764.6	786.4	920.0	964.9	1 119.2	1 162.1	1 223.7

See *Note* and footnotes on page 230.   2 Provisional.   *Source: Department of Trade and Industry*

External trade

12.4 Value of United Kingdom imports (cif)[1]
Analysis by sections and divisions continued

£ million

		1982	1983	1984	1985	1986	1987	1988	1989	1990	1991[2]
6. Manufactured goods classified chiefly by material	BQVM	9 852.5	11 846.6	13 447.4	14 342.3	15 328.1	16 827.7	19 673.3	21 739.8	21 902.4	20 519.9
61. Leather, leather manufactures, nes, and dressed furskins	BQVN	154.6	183.9	245.1	250.3	247.9	268.0	245.3	242.7	240.8	185.9
62. Rubber manufactures, nes	BQVO	326.2	419.6	457.1	527.4	589.2	682.4	799.1	827.0	880.4	872.2
63. Cork and wood manufactures (excluding furniture)	BQVP	460.0	605.0	652.0	665.0	720.0	824.9	964.9	966.9	949.3	821.2
64. Paper, paperboard, and articles of paper pulp, of paper or of paperboard	BQVQ	1 675.1	1 905.8	2 280.4	2 532.0	2 702.8	3 165.4	3 621.6	4 014.5	4 014.3	3 868.4
65. Textile yarn, fabrics, made-up articles, nes, and related products	BQVR	1 927.6	2 320.2	2 705.4	3 032.0	3 162.4	3 471.5	3 635.5	3 769.6	3 936.1	3 738.0
66. Non-metallic mineral manufactures, nes	BQVS	1 520.3	2 085.4	2 269.3	2 242.6	2 661.7	2 747.4	3 385.4	3 566.0	3 601.9	3 332.9
67. Iron and steel	BQVT	1 367.3	1 260.3	1 487.2	1 715.5	1 796.2	1 868.4	2 369.0	2 802.4	2 683.4	2 620.2
68. Non-ferrous metals	BQVU	1 495.7	1 985.0	1 996.2	1 903.4	1 835.7	1 946.3	2 506.0	3 069.0	3 003.3	2 557.9
69. Manufactures of metal, nes	BQVV	949.5	1 107.8	1 384.4	1 507.2	1 644.5	1 853.5	2 146.6	2 481.6	2 592.9	2 523.1
Machinery and transport equipment	BQVW	16 464.2	20 260.7	23 781.7	26 937.5	28 765.7	32 834.1	40 103.2	46 794.8	47 160.9	43 101.6
71. Power generating machinery and equipment	BQVX	1 482.7	1 568.7	1 782.4	1 997.5	2 237.3	2 513.3	3 046.6	3 485.1	3 518.4	3 345.5
72. Machinery specialised for particular industries	BQVY	1 485.9	1 735.6	2 078.6	2 327.3	2 362.7	2 895.6	3 477.7	3 854.0	3 521.9	3 005.6
73. Metalworking machinery	BQVZ	380.6	342.3	432.7	525.1	645.7	570.0	804.3	948.5	993.4	860.7
74. General industrial machinery and equipment, nes, and machine parts nes	BQWA	1 634.4	1 845.2	2 249.9	2 603.9	2 757.2	3 013.2	3 544.7	4 168.2	4 359.8	4 202.8
75. Office machines and automatic data processing equipment	BQWB	2 121.9	3 017.5	4 102.7	4 510.0	4 542.1	5 431.1	6 289.6	7 558.3	7 715.0	7 586.5
76. Telecommunications and sound recording and reproducing apparatus and equipment	BQWC	1 586.2	1 915.9	1 848.3	2 130.6	2 401.6	2 800.8	3 199.6	3 692.1	3 486.8	3 351.2
77. Electrical machinery, apparatus and appliances, nes, and electrical parts thereof (including non-electrical counterparts, nes, of electrical household type equipment)	BQWD	2 179.1	2 805.8	3 846.7	4 276.9	4 445.9	5 034.0	5 821.7	6 680.3	6 921.9	7 078.4
78. Road vehicles (including air cushion vehicles)	BQWE	4 489.6	5 753.8	5 957.6	6 800.6	7 938.8	8 809.7	11 255.5	13 003.4	12 594.2	10 227.2
79. Other transport equipment	BQWF	1 103.8	1 275.9	1 482.9	1 765.6	1 434.5	1 766.4	2 663.5	3 404.9	4 049.5	3 443.7
8. Miscellaneous manufactured articles	BQWG	6 618.4	7 710.4	9 459.5	10 131.6	11 386.1	12 956.6	14 430.8	17 056.4	18 252.5	17 559.3
81. Sanitary, plumbing, heating and lighting fixtures and fittings, nes	BQWH	103.5	126.7	151.2	177.2	216.6	298.1	336.2	371.7	394.5	368.3
82. Furniture and parts	BQWI	400.1	490.4	591.6	662.8	776.0	870.0	988.7	1 099.6	1 112.0	1 004.7
83. Travel goods, handbags and similar containers	BQWJ	108.6	131.1	161.9	174.9	199.9	230.9	251.5	293.0	309.1	285.1
84. Articles of apparel and clothing accessories	BQWK	1 500.0	1 601.3	2 011.7	2 090.1	2 386.1	2 773.7	3 111.4	3 542.2	3 904.1	4 128.5
85. Footwear	BQWL	468.3	542.0	642.0	671.1	734.4	828.7	907.8	973.1	1 168.9	1 169.0
87. Professional, scientific and controlling instruments and apparatus, nes	BQWM	1 052.1	1 301.3	1 593.8	1 761.5	1 790.0	1 912.6	2 025.0	2 377.3	2 482.1	2 525.1
88. Photographic apparatus, equipment and supplies and optical goods, nes, watches and clocks	BQWN	761.0	862.2	1 068.7	1 173.0	1 285.6	1 358.9	1 467.0	1 615.6	1 591.5	1 565.5
89. Miscellaneous manufactured articles, nes	BQWO	2 224.9	2 655.5	3 238.7	3 420.9	3 997.5	4 683.9	5 343.2	6 784.0	7 290.3	6 513.3
5 - 8. Manufactured goods	BQWP	37 114.2	44 936.5	53 010.7	58 312.2	62 825.3	70 965.2	83 521.1	96 029.0	98 149.8	92 159.4
9. Commodities and transactions not classified elsewhere	BQWQ	1 274.8	1 444.3	1 271.8	1 325.7	1 897.0	1 142.0	1 413.1	1 512.0	1 657.6	1 724.7

Note The statistics are on an overseas statistics basis (see footnote 1 to Table 12.1).

2 Provisional.

Source: Department of Trade and Industry

1 The numbers on the left hand side of the table refer to the Section and Division code numbers of the *Standard International Trade Classification (Revision 3)* which came into effect from 1 January 1988. The broad structure of SITC(R3) follows that of SITC(R2) but *one major* change should be noted: explosives and pyrotechnic products: Div. 57 SITC(R2) forms part of Div. 59 in SITC (R3). Div. 58 in SITC (R2) has been split into Div. 57 and 58 in SITC (R3).

External trade

12.5 Value of United Kingdom exports (fob)
Analysis by destination

£ million

		1982	1983	1984	1985	1986	1987	1988	1989	1990	1991[2]
Total trade	BQXA	55 557.8	60 684.3	70 488.3	78 391.8	72 987.7	79 848.7	81 654.9	93 770.9	103 692.4	104 877.0
European Community[3]											
Total	BQXB	23 123.6	26 508.8	31 506.7	36 233.8	34 996.3	39 414.9	40 937.5	47 140.2	55 024.7	..
France	BQXC	4 491.8	5 650.8	6 996.3	7 771.4	6 210.5	7 781.4	8 271.5	9 542.5	10 894.5	11 596.7
Belgium and Luxembourg	BQXD	2 309.6	2 574.5	3 051.9	3 347.7	3 832.9	3 857.4	4 251.8	4 889.3	5 649.4	5 873.3
Netherlands	BQXE	4 642.8	5 441.1	6 127.0	7 344.8	5 441.7	5 855.8	5 584.3	6 671.4	7 561.3	8 257.7
Germany[4]	BQXF	5 412.5	6 068.7	7 484.2	8 966.1	8 549.1	9 404.2	9 525.7	11 110.6	13 169.4	..
Italy	BQXG	2 024.3	2 279.1	2 903.5	3 466.2	3 463.5	4 145.7	4 106.1	4 630.6	5 553.0	6 140.2
Irish Republic	BQXH	2 889.4	3 055.3	3 393.8	3 631.1	3 553.5	3 831.6	4 056.9	4 716.4	5 313.0	5 295.3
Denmark	BQXI	1 098.2	1 159.2	1 195.5	1 371.1	1 211.6	1 230.0	1 171.2	1 209.2	1 419.3	1 408.6
Greece	BQXJ	255.1	280.2	354.3	335.4	356.0	444.5	468.0	571.4	682.9	667.9
Spain	BQXL	871.4	1 128.4	1 234.3	1 552.6	1 905.5	2 164.3	2 691.5	3 138.0	3 620.9	4 279.2
Portugal	BQXK	428.5	397.0	386.4	439.6	472.1	699.9	810.5	915.7	1 031.8	1 085.1
Other Western Europe[3]											
Total	BQXM	6 680.9	7 506.2	8 752.9	9 430.6	6 961.1	7 621.3	7 411.2	8 120.2	9 299.5	..
Norway	BQXN	933.9	829.1	972.9	1 140.7	1 147.6	1 220.7	1 053.5	1 057.2	1 292.0	1 357.7
Sweden	BQXO	1 935.6	2 387.7	2 893.9	3 025.3	2 307.8	2 322.2	2 195.0	2 431.9	2 712.3	2 471.2
Finland	BQXP	513.3	539.7	699.5	705.4	664.1	797.2	825.0	932.2	1 041.7	845.8
Switzerland	BQXQ	1 195.7	1 385.8	1 549.5	1 306.6	1 575.2	1 835.8	1 854.8	2 246.3	2 358.9	2 104.7
Austria	BQXR	250.8	273.8	320.9	381.0	403.0	463.2	510.0	598.1	705.8	766.8
Turkey	BQXT	218.1	243.8	331.4	459.8	433.3	513.5	477.7	434.6	614.0	730.1
Other countries	BQXU	174.8	173.1	200.3	242.1	241.7	261.7	292.2	288.9	584.0	361.7
North America											
Total	BQXV	8 353.3	9 495.8	11 416.3	13 331.5	12 118.5	12 992.4	12 794.5	14 436.7	14 945.5	13 124.5
Canada	BQXW	852.1	973.8	1 183.6	1 693.6	1 698.2	1 938.2	2 038.5	2 168.2	1 906.4	1 700.6
United States	BQXX	7 474.8	8 485.8	10 159.2	11 519.4	10 369.9	11 013.4	10 715.5	12 185.4	12 966.8	11 340.7
Other countries[1]	BQXY	26.4	36.3	73.4	118.6	50.4	40.7	40.5	83.1	72.3	83.2
Other OECD countries											
Total	BQXZ	3 235.4	3 136.7	3 687.9	3 791.1	3 614.0	4 045.7	4 495.2	5 408.6	5 830.0	..
Japan	BQYB	680.9	799.2	926.6	1 012.3	1 193.7	1 495.1	1 742.7	2 307.3	2 631.3	2 260.0
Australia	BQYC	1 041.5	940.6	1 189.0	1 373.0	1 227.7	1 223.7	1 377.5	1 711.2	1 632.9	1 355.7
New Zealand	BQYD	322.3	286.1	368.3	396.6	343.2	378.4	300.0	399.3	439.6	260.1
Oil exporting countries											
Total	BQYE	6 445.1	6 127.9	5 806.3	5 952.1	5 498.8	5 222.6	5 020.5	5 832.4	5 576.6	5 783.0
Algeria	BQYF	199.2	233.9	272.4	176.6	129.6	73.1	86.6	74.4	73.8	55.7
Libya	BQYG	261.0	274.1	246.5	237.2	263.8	220.6	236.0	239.2	244.8	255.7
Nigeria	BQYH	1 225.8	800.3	768.8	961.0	565.4	481.6	390.5	388.8	499.8	544.6
Gabon	BQYI	14.2	18.8	20.5	30.7	16.6	12.0	18.8	14.9	17.6	30.6
Saudi Arabia	BQYJ	1 361.5	1 480.2	1 386.7	1 249.0	1 508.2	1 978.4	1 713.5	2 432.9	2 011.4	2 254.7
Kuwait	BQYK	333.1	333.5	301.5	347.9	300.6	225.2	237.5	228.7	181.5	178.4
Bahrain	BQYL	152.0	150.3	138.7	161.5	131.0	125.2	138.1	138.4	127.3	147.5
Qatar	BQYM	245.4	216.5	133.8	142.1	112.1	105.1	88.9	89.3	98.5	109.2
Abu Dhabi	BQYN	272.9	219.3	215.9	246.7	168.1	150.0	128.8	155.4	170.2	220.1
Dubai	BQYO	253.9	313.3	298.8	345.3	379.5	306.8	306.7	370.8	444.0	476.2
Sharjah, etc	BQYP	32.1	25.5	27.0	29.3	34.2	22.2	27.8	45.2	50.5	60.8
Oman	BQYQ	265.2	449.1	390.4	489.9	399.6	249.9	344.9	299.0	272.1	237.9
Iraq	BQYR	873.7	399.9	343.1	444.7	443.8	271.7	411.8	451.0	293.4	12.0
Iran	BQYS	333.6	630.7	703.4	525.6	399.4	307.9	247.8	257.1	384.2	512.1
Brunei	BQYT	41.8	106.5	122.7	71.5	154.1	204.3	171.6	264.4	224.6	215.2
Indonesia	BQYU	212.1	193.6	186.7	175.3	196.5	236.0	203.3	183.9	198.0	198.0
Trinidad and Tobago	BQYV	158.4	149.0	113.5	93.9	79.0	57.0	39.9	44.9	49.9	62.5
Venezuela	BQYW	148.6	88.3	101.5	165.3	170.1	157.8	177.8	124.7	204.9	166.7
Ecuador	BQYX	60.8	35.0	34.3	58.6	47.1	37.9	50.4	29.4	30.2	45.2

1 Greenland, Puerto Rico and St. Pierre and Miquelon.
2 Provisional.
3 With effect from 1 January 1986 European Community figure includes Portugal and Spain, Rest of Western Europe excludes both countries.
4 See page 232 (footnote No 4) for New Countries, grouping and definitions.

Source: Department of Trade and Industry

External trade

12.5 Value of United Kingdom exports (fob)
Analysis by destination
continued

£ million

		1982	1983	1984	1985	1986	1987	1988	1989	1990	1991[3]
Other countries											
Total	BQYY	6 607.8	6 664.6	7 550.1	7 923.5	7 647.6	8 514.4	8 616.4	9 720.9	10 606.5	..
Egypt	BQYZ	338.8	370.9	427.7	470.5	371.0	342.3	289.3	296.3	298.3	282.9
Ghana	BQZA	66.7	82.2	82.9	116.9	113.2	138.1	126.0	121.1	162.1	170.2
Kenya	BQZB	153.7	111.4	176.1	160.6	170.7	199.0	202.1	208.5	243.1	206.9
Tanzania	BQZC	71.9	62.1	60.4	88.6	62.9	91.9	88.7	93.0	84.7	72.8
Zambia	BQZD	61.2	55.5	66.7	85.9	77.9	75.2	85.8	119.1	92.8	62.7
South Africa	BQYA	1 191.0	1 111.0	1 204.0	1 009.0	849.0	948.6	1 074.9	1 038.6	1 113.6	1 023.6
Cyprus	BQZE	111.8	127.9	146.8	151.2	140.5	141.1	159.8	173.1	204.9	209.9
Lebanon	BQZF	67.6	81.4	76.2	52.8	55.9	40.7	55.6	48.5	53.3	87.8
Israel	BQZG	264.1	354.6	393.0	434.5	462.4	523.6	491.0	502.4	567.7	531.5
Pakistan	BQZH	199.1	191.9	282.5	255.4	227.0	253.0	263.2	233.5	251.8	272.0
India	BQZI	805.0	805.2	780.7	895.1	941.2	1 090.1	1 112.7	1 383.7	1 264.2	1 017.4
Thailand	BQZJ	104.8	132.3	149.7	157.7	158.2	206.6	279.8	427.5	416.6	463.5
Malaysia	BQZK	210.6	248.3	283.1	281.7	226.9	258.0	310.4	441.5	550.7	582.3
Singapore	BQZL	406.0	469.4	556.5	612.9	547.4	602.6	632.5	773.9	1 040.7	1 018.4
Taiwan	BQZM	125.2	128.4	150.6	164.8	192.5	292.3	355.7	407.4	430.6	519.8
Hong Kong	BQZN	730.7	727.3	897.4	949.2	961.0	1 013.0	1 030.8	1 111.5	1 238.0	1 387.4
South Korea	BQZO	167.7	169.0	219.6	247.8	288.4	427.2	450.8	494.1	620.7	786.1
Philippines	BQZP	97.7	102.9	92.0	94.4	79.8	113.8	124.0	137.0	158.0	146.6
Jamaica	BQZQ	55.9	116.2	48.1	44.3	43.4	54.6	48.9	61.4	58.7	54.7
Mexico	BQZR	162.9	95.7	150.2	203.4	162.3	198.9	190.0	205.2	263.0	276.1
Chile	BQZS	56.9	43.5	75.0	73.9	67.5	105.8	80.9	96.0	130.4	107.4
Brazil	BQZT	158.4	158.4	238.7	211.5	299.8	347.9	304.8	338.9	320.5	339.4
Argentina	BQZU	37.3	4.5	5.2	3.8	10.1	10.3	13.0	13.6	36.0	69.7
Other countries	BQZV	2 153.4	2 025.6	2 190.9	2 166.5	1 987.6	1 988.4	1 920.8	2 035.0	2 083.6	..
Eastern Europe and the former USSR[4]											
Total	BQZW	974.2	1 113.3	1 629.6	1 587.2	1 710.3	1 538.7	1 612.4	1 786.3	1 752.8	..
Former USSR	BQZX	356.1	445.4	734.8	536.5	542.5	491.6	511.9	681.4	606.6	354.7
Poland	BQZZ	133.2	151.7	170.0	184.2	167.1	181.5	175.7	196.4	221.7	347.6
Czechoslovakia	BRAA	70.1	69.5	78.1	100.5	108.8	114.1	130.4	131.4	133.1	129.4
Romania	BRAB	115.2	82.2	71.6	78.5	82.0	55.6	50.1	38.1	85.9	58.7
Yugoslavia	BQXS	158.8	147.8	163.9	177.5	188.4	206.9	203.1	219.9	261.0	193.9
Other countries[1]	BRAC	235.9	303.5	483.0	623.8	727.9	614.4	633.0	632.2	649.2	..
Low value trade[2]	BRAD	137.5	131.0	138.5	141.9	441.1	498.7	767.1	893.7	850.1	777.5

1 Hungary, Albania, Bulgaria.
2 Currently items valued at less than £600 have not been allocated to specific countries and areas (threshold was £200 prior to 1 January 1986; raised to £475 at 1 January 1986 and £600 at 1 January 1988).
3 Provisional.
4 From January 1991 back data has been recalculated to take into account changes in country grouping and country definitions. Changes are:
(a) FR Germany and GDR became Germany.
(b) Rest of Western Europe becomes Other Western Europe and Yugoslavia is excluded.
(c) Other Developing Countries now becomes Other Countries and includes South Africa.
(d) Centrally Planned Economies changed to Eastern Europe and the Soviet Union and GDR is replaced by Yugoslavia.

Source: Department of Trade and Industry

External trade

12.6 Value of United Kingdom imports (cif)
Analysis by source

£ million

		1982	1983	1984	1985	1986	1987	1988	1989	1990	1991[2]
Total trade	BGAA	56 978.2	66 101.1	78 967.4	85 027.0	86 175.5	94 026.2	106 571.2	121 699.2	126 086.1	118 786.0
European Community[3]											
Total	BGAB	25 269.0	30 104.1	35 159.3	39 004.8	44 576.8	49 555.4	55 807.0	63 495.0	65 855.5	..
France	BGAC	4 266.9	5 042.2	5 885.7	6 635.8	7 387.1	8 381.5	9 398.7	10 842.4	11 872.3	11 075.4
Belgium and Luxembourg	BGAD	2 857.5	3 129.0	3 688.1	4 015.2	4 084.3	4 361.9	4 959.4	5 699.7	5 732.0	5 472.5
Netherlands	BGAE	4 512.0	5 103.8	6 115.2	6 553.2	6 623.0	7 148.4	8 281.6	9 617.8	10 483.2	9 969.0
Germany[4]	BGAF	7 405.9	9 665.7	11 088.1	12 655.3	14 137.8	15 783.0	17 674.9	20 005.3	19 907.1	..
Italy	BGAG	1 415.8	1 610.9	1 560.5	1 824.1	4 666.1	5 216.6	5 817.3	6 707.4	6 732.8	6 378.7
Irish Republic	BGAH	2 003.4	2 289.4	2 635.1	2 817.2	3 054.0	3 488.2	3 879.6	4 279.5	4 497.4	4 416.3
Denmark	BGAI	1 335.3	1 512.4	1 659.2	1 714.8	1 756.8	1 873.4	2 028.2	2 236.5	2 278.5	2 226.7
Greece	BGAJ	151.3	164.9	278.9	320.1	309.1	355.3	357.0	395.1	400.5	377.8
Spain	BGAL	941.0	1 110.2	1 603.7	1 773.4	1 790.2	2 099.0	2 482.3	2 813.2	2 870.7	2 627.7
Portugal	BGAK	379.9	475.6	644.8	695.7	768.4	848.0	928.0	1 041.3	1 176.2	1 043.3
Other Western Europe[3]											
Total	BGAM	8 390.4	10 457.4	13 432.3	14 571.5	11 886.8	12 883.5	14 028.5	15 348.5	15 905.9	..
Norway	BGAN	2 019.2	2 833.8	3 999.4	4 444.3	3 253.7	3 290.3	3 079.0	3 637.1	4 132.8	4 162.5
Sweden	BGAO	1 672.9	2 053.5	2 416.8	2 467.4	2 760.4	2 952.3	3 366.7	3 747.5	3 594.5	3 141.6
Finland	BGAP	921.8	996.0	1 248.2	1 324.0	1 346.0	1 551.7	1 813.2	1 893.1	1 775.7	1 522.3
Switzerland	BGAQ	1 664.5	2 153.2	2 490.1	2 370.9	3 020.1	3 299.4	3 921.9	4 134.2	4 247.9	3 754.2
Austria	BGAR	402.4	438.3	529.5	630.2	705.3	782.0	874.5	934.0	957.8	916.1
Turkey	BGAT	207.8	184.9	237.2	538.5	406.6	579.4	509.6	533.7	550.8	401.9
Other countries	BGAU	128.8	128.2	154.3	205.0	249.5	253.3	266.3	274.8	538.9	316.0
North America											
Total	BGAV	8 095.0	9 082.9	11 067.4	11 709.1	10 028.3	10 781.0	12 903.1	15 929.3	16 694.7	15 730.4
Canada	BGAW	1 436.2	1 523.3	1 618.1	1 653.0	1 470.4	1 569.2	2 041.9	2 286.4	2 207.7	1 923.1
United States	BGAX	6 624.1	7 497.2	9 367.7	9 925.5	8 471.5	9 134.5	10 767.7	13 521.3	14 352.7	13 692.5
Other countries[1]	BGAY	34.7	62.5	81.7	130.6	86.4	77.3	93.5	121.6	134.3	114.8
Other OECD countries											
Total	BGAZ	4 436.1	5 170.4	5 620.5	6 379.3	6 865.4	7 282.9	8 516.7	9 294.8	9 362.8	..
Japan	BGBB	2 658.8	3 355.4	3 771.9	4 115.5	4 936.9	5 464.0	6 531.1	7 103.7	6 761.3	6 753.5
Australia	BGBC	492.7	564.1	640.1	741.0	643.2	673.5	741.9	864.9	1 020.7	870.8
New Zealand	BGBD	538.9	486.4	482.9	533.0	455.7	487.3	442.7	436.8	483.6	391.6
Oil exporting countries											
Total	BGBE	3 453.4	2 832.7	2 934.2	2 814.7	2 103.0	1 699.7	2 084.9	2 312.7	2 974.2	2 794.4
Algeria	BGBF	176.3	157.7	274.1	262.1	140.9	172.9	159.7	177.5	260.0	194.9
Libya	BGBG	342.5	223.6	164.8	311.8	136.4	133.6	109.9	104.5	151.6	121.2
Nigeria	BGBH	356.8	388.0	434.6	663.0	329.0	159.4	128.0	129.4	297.4	249.5
Gabon	BGBI	27.6	66.1	67.5	48.3	36.6	5.4	5.1	2.4	1.8	3.2
Saudi Arabia	BGBJ	1 447.8	897.7	545.6	496.3	659.6	383.1	614.2	502.3	794.6	963.4
Kuwait	BGBK	104.7	67.3	141.5	161.5	62.7	81.5	72.3	150.4	109.0	29.8
Bahrain	BGBL	35.5	36.8	28.2	45.1	19.0	60.7	75.8	61.0	48.5	39.1
Qatar	BGBM	34.0	10.1	28.2	32.6	29.6	13.8	3.9	4.3	7.0	5.5
Abu Dhabi	BGBN	184.3	59.0	21.9	25.2	14.6	13.8	25.6	87.2	76.4	109.0
Dubai	BGBO	57.5	211.6	60.6	44.4	56.2	77.3	55.8	63.4	95.5	97.1
Sharjah, etc	BGBP	25.2	48.6	4.7	27.3	3.3	4.0	2.9	14.4	9.6	25.8
Oman	BGBQ	46.4	90.6	80.9	68.4	85.5	49.5	146.7	84.0	89.4	73.6
Iraq	BGBR	79.6	30.3	69.0	44.1	66.1	33.9	43.4	55.2	101.6	2.5
Iran	BGBS	225.9	100.6	368.6	63.3	100.3	187.6	140.2	250.5	279.1	158.4
Brunei	BGBT	2.4	27.2	27.3	23.3	71.6	34.1	142.5	185.2	158.5	147.7
Indonesia	BGBU	90.7	169.4	181.5	156.5	141.2	144.8	233.7	273.1	327.9	415.2
Trinidad and Tobago	BGBV	65.1	52.7	164.7	83.7	41.8	38.6	35.7	37.4	45.1	41.7
Venezuela	BGBW	141.9	184.4	257.5	238.9	97.4	91.7	76.6	111.1	101.7	100.5
Ecuador	BGBX	9.3	11.0	13.0	19.0	11.3	14.0	13.1	19.3	19.6	16.3

1 Greenland, Puerto Rico and St. Pierre and Miquelon.
2 Provisional.

3 With effect from 1 January 1986 European Community figure includes Portugal and Spain, Rest of Western Europe figure excludes both countries.
4 See page 234 (footnote No 4) for New Countries, grouping and definitions.

Source: Department of Trade and Industry

External trade

12.6 Value of United Kingdom imports (cif)
Analysis by source
continued

£ million

		1982	1983	1984	1985	1986	1987	1988	1989	1990	1991[3]
Other countries											
Total	BGBY	5 895.8	6 798.4	8 579.3	8 512.0	8 439.8	9 284.5	10 515.4	12 138.8	12 217.0	..
Egypt	BGBZ	412.8	79.8	179.9	162.0	87.7	127.3	164.4	212.7	145.3	136.4
Ghana	BGCA	78.4	58.1	61.5	99.4	103.5	113.9	106.3	92.2	105.1	77.3
Kenya	BGCB	104.3	128.5	203.1	185.6	163.7	129.2	147.2	154.3	149.5	142.0
Tanzania	BGCC	19.5	46.5	42.2	46.6	40.3	26.4	27.0	22.6	25.6	20.9
Zambia	BGCD	40.0	50.2	48.1	27.9	27.3	30.3	24.8	21.6	19.3	22.5
South Africa	BGBA	745.7	764.5	725.6	989.8	829.6	658.2	800.9	884.7	1 079.5	954.8
Cyprus	BGCE	89.9	87.4	94.3	93.7	124.1	118.2	121.9	145.0	152.9	141.1
Lebanon	BGCF	24.2	11.5	6.9	7.9	9.8	9.5	14.2	11.1	6.2	8.5
Israel	BGCG	276.1	313.7	392.7	404.0	385.2	437.0	459.8	479.7	506.1	455.7
Pakistan	BGCH	81.5	80.3	93.1	119.9	131.3	167.3	175.3	208.3	236.4	261.2
India	BGCI	378.7	366.8	571.0	434.5	440.6	536.5	566.0	701.6	799.4	777.0
Thailand	BGCJ	76.5	87.8	112.4	131.8	182.7	239.4	321.8	443.1	484.3	625.4
Malaysia	BGCK	185.2	222.5	319.5	383.9	349.9	397.1	525.0	675.6	775.5	930.0
Singapore	BGCL	245.5	403.1	488.4	441.3	463.0	473.8	579.6	902.9	1 021.1	1 134.3
Taiwan	BGCM	335.3	458.1	585.2	582.6	705.6	1 006.7	1 152.7	1 351.6	1 211.8	1 271.9
Hong Kong	BGCN	870.8	1 177.3	1 266.2	1 175.6	1 537.0	1 531.6	1 791.6	2 048.6	1 972.1	2 147.6
South Korea	BGCO	321.6	440.3	444.1	480.4	660.9	935.9	1 150.9	1 164.5	963.8	924.6
Philippines	BGCP	127.0	160.7	199.7	180.0	182.8	202.7	223.6	233.1	220.7	229.9
Jamaica	BGCQ	92.8	94.0	77.9	89.7	84.5	85.7	87.9	95.5	136.5	123.8
Mexico	BGCR	106.1	161.0	175.4	236.8	116.1	244.7	144.9	165.3	172.1	147.3
Chile	BGCS	111.2	107.6	108.4	134.7	127.9	112.8	179.6	193.3	222.5	177.9
Brazil	BGCT	443.9	560.2	637.8	610.9	552.1	636.7	739.8	817.5	719.8	766.1
Argentina	BGCU	58.3	0.2	–	2.0	28.6	64.6	66.1	99.0	144.2	135.6
Other countries	BGCV	1 416.2	1 702.8	2 470.6	2 480.6	1 935.2	1 657.3	1 744.8	1 902.0	2 025.1	..
Eastern Europe and the former USSR[4]											
Total	BGCW	1 327.2	1 535.1	2 042.7	1 893.2	1 863.9	2 097.5	2 031.4	2 280.6	2 323.4	..
Former USSR	BGCX	645.4	729.9	855.3	726.5	702.1	875.4	725.2	833.6	917.7	901.2
Poland	BGCZ	151.9	177.1	266.7	321.7	308.6	303.5	328.3	333.7	367.6	314.0
Czechoslovakia	BGDA	82.0	101.4	117.5	120.0	126.1	141.5	148.0	156.7	136.1	131.4
Romania	BGDB	51.5	58.9	226.1	99.2	86.7	92.5	100.9	117.7	61.2	58.5
Yugoslavia	BGAS	52.1	84.0	108.4	122.2	145.1	175.2	197.3	202.4	189.4	147.9
Other countries[1]	BGDC	262.5	300.2	278.9	421.6	444.9	504.3	576.0	674.0	722.9	..
Low value trade[2]	BGDD	111.3	119.3	131.7	142.5	411.7	441.8	684.3	731.4	778.1	743.3

1 Hungary, Albania, Bulgaria.
2 Currently items valued at less than £600 have not been allocated to specific countries and areas (threshold was £200 prior to 1 January 1986; raised to £475 at 1 January 1986 and £600 at 1 January 1988).
3 Provisional.
4 From January 1991 back data has been recalculated to take into account changes in country grouping and country definitions. Changes are:
(a) FR Germany and GDR became Germany.
(b) Rest of Western Europe becomes Other Western Europe and Yugoslavia is excluded.
(c) Other Developing Countries now becomes Other Countries and includes South Africa.
(d) Centrally Planned Economies changed to Eastern Europe and the Soviet Union and GDR is replaced by Yugoslavia.

Source: Department of Trade and Industry

13 Balance of Payments

Tables 13.1, 13.2 and 13.3 in this section are derived from *United Kingdom Balance of Payments 1991 Edition* - the CSO Pink Book and Tables 13.4 and 13.5 are based on the annual publication *British Aid Statistics*, the latest edition of which covers the period 1985 to 1989.

The following general notes and footnotes to the tables provide brief definitions and explanations of the figures and terms used. Further notes are included in the publications named above. As far as possible transactions have been included in the balance of payments at the rate of exchange at which the transactions took place.

CURRENT ACCOUNT

In principle, transactions are recorded when the ownership of goods or assets changes and when services are rendered.

Visible trade

The *Overseas Trade Statistics of the United Kingdom* are the basis of the balance of payments figures, with certain adjustments in respect of valuation and coverage.

Invisibles: Services

General government covers all UK government current expenditure and receipts not appropriate to other items in the current account.

Transport - sea transport covers both dry and wet cargo transactions of UK operators with overseas residents, and of overseas operators with UK residents. The figures relate to freight, charter hire, port disbursements and passage money.

Transport - civil aviation covers overseas transactions of British airlines, and the transactions of overseas airlines with UK residents. Figures relate to passenger fares, freight, charter hire and airport disbursements.

Travel covers personal expenditure by overseas residents in the United Kingdom and by UK residents in overseas countries.

Financial and other services comprises the earnings, net of expenses, of UK financial and allied institutions for services and all services transactions not included elsewhere.

Invisibles: Interest, profits and dividends

Includes all interest, profits and dividends accruing to UK residents from non-residents or payable overseas by UK residents (after deduction of local taxes and depreciation) and includes profits retained for re-investment.

Invisibles: Transfers

General government transfers includes principally grants to overseas countries and contributions and subscriptions to and grants from international organisations (including European Community institutions).

Private transfers. Value of private assets passing from non-resident to resident ownership or *vice versa* without a *quid pro quo* including transfers of assets by migrants other than their personal or household belongings.

TRANSACTIONS IN EXTERNAL ASSETS AND LIABILITIES

Overseas investment by and in the United Kingdom

Direct investment
Comprises mainly net investment by overseas companies in their UK affiliates, including the re-investment of retained profits, and by United Kingdom companies in their overseas branches, subsidiaries and associates. Government departments are excluded but public corporations' outward investment is included.

Also included are identified transactions in real estate; and outward investment includes transactions in non-bank financial institutions' loans and mortgages.

Portfolio investment
UK portfolio investment overseas consists of purchases (net of sales) of overseas government, municipal and company securities. *Overseas investment in the United Kingdom* comprises net investment by overseas residents in:
   UK company securities, including securities issued abroad;
   British government stocks;
   British government foreign currency bonds and notes; and local authorities' and public corporations' securities.

Net foreign currency transactions of UK banks

This item consists of changes in deposits of foreign currencies made with UK resident banks by non-residents and loans by the banks in those currencies to non-residents.

Net sterling transactions of UK banks

This item consists of sterling advances and overdrafts (net of repayments) provided to overseas residents (including banks abroad) by UK banks, sterling commercial bills discounted, acceptances, and sterling borrowing and deposit liabilities abroad.

Deposits with and lending to banks abroad by UK non-bank private sector

This item consists of UK residents' deposits with banks in the International Monetary Fund (IMF) reporting area supplemented by fiduciary accounts with Swiss banks and deposits with branches of US banks in Panama.

Borrowing from banks abroad

Covers predominately borrowing from commercial banks in the IMF reporting area, the European Investment Bank and the United States Export-Import Bank.

Official reserves

Consists of the sterling equivalent, at current rates of exchange, of drawings on or additions to the gold, convertible currencies and special drawing rights held in the reserves and of changes in the reserve position with the IMF.

Other external assets

Includes lending and identified trade credit (advance and progress payments on imports and until end-1982 export credit) between unrelated companies, inter-government loans by the United Kingdom; subscriptions to international lending bodies; and short-term assets.

Other external liabilities

Includes borrowing and identified trade credit (advance on progress payments on exports and import credit) between unrelated companies, inter-government loans to the United Kingdom, transactions with the IMF and overseas banks by general government; overseas holdings of Treasury bills and non-interest-bearing notes; and short-term liabilities.

Allocation of special drawing rights

The distribution of reserve assets created by the IMF.

Balancing item

Represents the net total of errors and omissions in other items in the current and capital accounts.

LEVELS OF UK EXTERNAL ASSETS AND LIABILITIES
(Table 13.3)

The figures in this table show the levels of the stocks of identified external financial assets and liabilities at the end of each calendar year. Changes in these levels reflect not only the capital transactions during the year but also, in many instances, revaluations and other changes. In particular some items may be valued in foreign currency terms and most investments are recorded at either book or market values; in such instances revaluations will usually occur regardless of whether transactions take place.

Because of the very varied data sources used to derive the estimates there are many inconsistencies in the figures resulting particularly from different methods of valuation, which wherever possible, are at market value. The balance between the estimates of identified external assets and liabilities has always been an imperfect measure of the UK's debtor/creditor position with the rest of the world and the persistence of a substantial positive balancing item in the balance of payments accounts in recent years has undoubtedly increased the uncertainty of the estimates. To the extent that the balancing item reflects unrecorded or misrecorded capital transactions, the external balance sheet will tend to fail to capture the corresponding levels of assets and liabilities concerned.

Identified assets include direct and portfolio investment overseas by UK residents, lending to overseas residents by UK banks, deposits and lending overseas by other UK residents and the official reserves. Identified liabilities include overseas residents' direct and portfolio investment in the United Kingdom, borrowing, etc from overseas residents by UK banks and borrowing from overseas by other UK residents.

General government comprises UK central government and local authorities.

For a more detailed explanation and analysis of the figures see Section 8 of the 1991 Pink Book.

OVERSEAS AID
(Tables 13.4 and 13.5)

The UK aid programme is administered by the Overseas Development Administration (ODA) to promote the economic development of developing countries. It is managed within financial years, the money being voted annually by Parliament. However the statistics relating to the programme are published for the calendar year as this basis is used both for international aid comparisons and for national purposes such as the balance of payments. Fluctuations may thus occur in the calendar year figures which are not reflected in the financial year figures. This has been particularly true in the case of India, the largest bilateral recipient, whose aid receipts in 1976, 1979 and 1981 were abnormally high, while its receipts in 1980 and 1982 were abnormally low.

Aid flows can be measured before (gross) or after (net) deduction of repayments of principal on past loans. These tables show only the gross figures.

Aid is provided in two main ways: *bilateral*, that is directly to governments of developing countries or to institutions in the United Kingdom for work on behalf of such countries, or *multilateral*, that is to international institutions for their economic development programmes. Table 13.4 shows the three main groups of multilateral agencies, the International Development Association being the largest in the World Bank Group.

Bilateral aid takes various forms. *Project aid* is finance for the establishment of new, or expansion of existing, production and infrastructure facilities. The bulk is provided by the ODA, either from country programmes or from the Aid and Trade Provision (a special allocation to soften the terms of credits to developing countries by mixing aid funds with private export credits). The Commonwealth Development Corporation invests in productive public or private sector projects in developing countries. *Non-project aid* includes programme aid (for import finance not related to specific projects), debt relief, budgetary aid, food aid and disaster relief. *Technical co-operation* is used to provide experts to work overseas, training for developing country nationals, consultancies, small items of equipment, to fund research and development in the United Kingdom of benefit to developing countries and support to voluntary organisations. Most of the aid not allocable by country in Table 13.5 is for technical co-operation provided through organisations in the United Kingdom.

Fuller statistics of Britain's aid effort are published annually in *British Aid Statistics* (obtainable from the Library, ODA, Abercrombie House, East Kilbride, Glasgow G75 8EA). International comparisons are available in the OECD Development Assistance Committee's annual report. The latest is *1991 Report: Development co-operation* (available from HMSO).

Balance of payments

13.1 Balance of Payments of the United Kingdom

£ million

		1981	1982	1983	1984	1985	1986	1987	1988	1989	1990	1991
Current account												
Visible trade												
Exports (fob)	CGJP	50 668	55 331	60 700	70 265	77 991	72 627	79 153	80 346	92 154	101 718	103 413
Imports (fob)	CGGL	47 416	53 421	62 237	75 601	81 336	82 186	90 735	101 826	116 837	120 527	113 703
Visible balance	HCHL	3 251	1 911	−1 537	−5 336	−3 345	−9 559	−11 582	−21 480	−24 683	−18 809	−10 290
Invisibles												
Credits	CGKR	57 085	65 162	65 569	77 251	80 022	77 255	79 826	87 739	107 778	115 150	116 164
Debits	CGHT	53 589	62 423	60 267	70 117	73 887	67 630	72 726	82 438	104 821	113 370	112 195
Invisibles balance	CGIK	3 496	2 741	5 302	7 134	6 136	9 625	7 099	5 302	2 956	1 778	3 969
of which:												
Services balance	CGIN	*3 792*	*3 022*	*4 064*	*4 519*	*6 687*	*6 808*	*6 745*	*4 397*	*4 039*	*4 581*	*4 990*
Interest, profits and dividends balance	CGOA	*1 251*	*1 460*	*2 831*	*4 345*	*2 560*	*4 974*	*3 754*	*4 423*	*3 495*	*2 094*	*328*
Transfers balance	CGIO	*−1 547*	*−1 741*	*−1 593*	*−1 730*	*−3 111*	*−2 157*	*−3 400*	*−3 518*	*−4 578*	*−4 897*	*−1 349*
Current balance	AIMG	6 748	4 649	3 765	1 798	2 790	66	−4 482	−16 179	−21 726	−17 029	−6 321
Transactions in external assets and liabilities[1]												
Investment overseas by UK residents												
Direct	HHBV	−6 005	−4 091	−5 417	−6 036	−8 449	−11 678	−19 239	−20 944	−21 515	−9 553	−10 261
Portfolio	CGOS	−4 467	−7 565	−7 350	−9 753	−16 754	−22 277	5 163	−11 239	−35 486	−15 844	−30 908
Total UK investment overseas	AINC	−10 474	−11 656	−12 768	−15 789	−25 203	−33 955	−14 076	−32 183	−57 001	−25 397	−41 169
Investment in the United Kingdom by overseas residents												
Direct	HHBU	2 932	3 027	3 386	−181	4 506	5 837	9 449	12 006	18 567	18 634	12 045
Portfolio	HEYR	257	−11	1 701	1 288	9 773	12 181	19 535	15 564	14 603	5 276	16 627
Total overseas investment in the UK	HCAM	3 189	3 016	5 087	1 107	14 279	18 018	28 984	27 570	33 170	23 910	28 672
Foreign currency lending abroad by UK banks[2]	HEZZ	−36 900	−16 520	−16 165	−9 427	−20 209	−47 876	−45 867	−15 064	−25 689	−37 440	27 394
Foreign currency borrowing abroad by UK banks[2]	HCAF	36 763	19 942	17 199	17 984	24 894	61 366	43 566	20 447	32 338	34 992	−14 802
Net foreign currency transactions of UK banks	HCAG	−137	3 422	1 034	8 557	4 685	13 490	−2 301	5 383	6 649	−2 448	12 592
Sterling lending abroad by UK banks	HCAD	−3 019	−4 046	−2 278	−4 932	−1 815	−5 871	−4 633	−4 626	−2 923	−3 800	4 837
Sterling borrowing and deposit liabilities abroad of UK banks	HEPD	2 497	4 479	4 094	6 155	4 148	5 502	8 867	13 641	12 401	12 620	−9 222
Net sterling transactions of UK banks	HCAH	−522	433	1 816	1 223	2 333	−369	4 234	9 015	9 478	8 820	−4 385
Deposits with and lending to banks abroad by the UK non-bank private sector	HESZ	−1 864	−598	863	−3 213	−1 305	−3 094	−4 914	−4 025	−9 334	−8 280	−3 580
Borrowing from banks abroad by												
UK non-bank private sector	HCAN	1 042	985	73	−2 215	2 618	3 816	2 075	3 973	8 017	10 006	13 032
Public corporations	HETH	−178	−36	−35	−47	64	−31	−166	−253	−1 726	−127	−49
General government	HCAP	−192	58	78	49	87	100	104	−10	529	−363	−65
Official reserves (additions to -, drawings on +)	AIPA	2 419	1 421	607	908	−1 758	−2 891	−12 012	−2 761	5 440	−79	−2 662
Other external assets of UK non-bank private sector and												
Public corporations	HETE	−1 026	126	−161	1 280	527	1 644	93	1 070	1 468	−3 479	−4 707
General government	HEUJ	93	−161	−478	−743	−730	−509	−796	−887	−873	−1 025	−894
Other external liabilities of UK non-bank private sector and												
Public corporations	HETQ	224	119	−15	558	732	569	1 382	1 664	21 191	8 272	10 710
General government	HCAR	−14	351	−661	−89	−64	77	1 725	842	2 252	1 281	−2 246
Net transactions in assets and liabilities	HEQU	−7 436	−2 519	−4 562	−8 414	−3 733	−3 134	4 334	9 396	19 259	11 091	5 249
Allocation of special drawing rights	HBUN	158	–	–	–	–	–	–	–	–	–	–
Balancing item	AASA	530	−2 130	797	6 616	943	3 068	148	6 783	2 467	5 938	1 072

1 Assets: increase-/decrease+. Liabilities: increase+/decrease-.   2 See notes on page 235.

Source: Central Statistical Office

Balance of payments
13.2 Current account

£ million

		1981	1982	1983	1984	1985	1986	1987	1988	1989	1990	1991
Credits												
Exports (f.o.b.)	CGJP	50 668	55 331	60 700	70 265	77 991	72 627	79 153	80 346	92 154	101 718	103 413
Services:												
General government	CGJR	401	404	470	474	483	511	521	550	445	425	412
Private sector and public corporations												
Sea transport	CGJW	3 731	3 215	3 043	3 244	3 211	3 216	3 282	3 522	3 848	3 732	3 658
Civil aviation	CGJO	2 359	2 471	2 665	2 931	3 078	2 786	3 159	3 192	3 758	4 358	3 927
Travel	CGKA	2 970	3 188	4 003	4 614	5 442	5 553	6 260	6 184	6 945	7 785	7 165
Financial and other services	HHDE	7 303	8 085	9 175	10 324	12 003	13 626	14 656	13 911	14 899	15 482	16 540
Interest, profits and dividends												
General government	CGNR	971	979	765	818	735	765	931	1 456	1 949	1 812	1 763
Private sector and public corporations	CGNT	36 559	43 419	41 685	50 803	51 535	46 928	47 067	55 092	72 040	77 525	75 906
Transfers												
General government	HDKD	1 675	2 154	2 235	2 392	1 760	2 138	2 282	2 115	2 143	2 231	4 894
Private sector	CGJV	1 117	1 248	1 528	1 652	1 775	1 732	1 666	1 715	1 750	1 800	1 900
Total invisibles	CGJY	57 085	65 162	65 569	77 251	80 022	77 255	79 826	87 739	107 778	115 150	116 164
Total credits	CGPZ	107 753	120 493	126 269	147 516	158 013	149 882	158 979	168 085	199 932	216 868	219 577
Debits												
Imports (f.o.b.)	CGGL	47 416	53 421	62 237	75 601	81 336	82 186	90 735	101 826	116 837	120 527	113 703
Services:												
General government	CGGI	1 264	1 754	1 522	1 655	1 781	1 920	2 141	2 351	2 699	2 784	2 808
Private sector and public corporations												
Sea transport	CGGW	3 818	3 589	3 665	3 600	3 508	3 302	3 310	3 499	3 754	3 743	3 643
Civil aviation	CGGG	2 005	2 184	2 363	2 676	2 877	3 194	3 775	4 203	4 397	4 769	4 397
Travel	CGHA	3 272	3 640	4 090	4 663	4 871	6 083	7 280	8 216	9 357	9 916	9 825
Financial and other services	HBVH	2 613	3 174	3 652	4 474	4 493	4 385	4 627	4 693	5 649	5 989	6 039
Interest, profits and dividends												
General government	HERS	940	1 090	1 188	1 342	1 494	1 677	2 046	2 323	2 510	2 237	1 897
Private sector and public corporations	HHII	35 338	41 847	38 429	45 934	48 216	41 042	42 199	49 804	67 984	75 004	75 443
Transfers												
General government	CGGJ	3 282	3 943	4 165	4 491	5 187	4 371	5 559	5 363	6 421	6 828	5 943
Private sector	CGGV	1 057	1 200	1 191	1 283	1 459	1 656	1 789	1 985	2 050	2 100	2 200
Total invisibles	CGGY	53 589	62 423	60 267	70 117	73 887	67 630	72 726	82 438	104 821	113 370	112 195
Total debits	CGQB	101 005	115 844	122 504	145 718	155 223	149 816	163 461	184 264	221 658	233 897	225 898
Balances												
Visible balance	HCHL	3 251	1 911	−1 537	−5 336	−3 345	−9 559	−11 582	−21 480	−24 683	−18 809	−10 290
Services:												
General government	CGIG	−863	−1 350	−1 052	−1 181	−1 298	−1 409	−1 620	−1 801	−2 254	−2 359	−2 396
Private sector and public corporations												
Sea transport	HBTO	−87	−374	−622	−356	−297	−86	−28	23	94	−11	15
Civil aviation	HDJA	354	287	302	255	201	−408	−616	−1 011	−639	−411	−470
Travel	HBYE	−302	−452	−87	−49	571	−530	−1 020	−2 032	−2 412	−2 131	−2 660
Financial and other services	HHCW	4 690	4 911	5 523	5 850	7 510	9 241	10 029	9 218	9 250	9 493	10 501
Interest, profits and dividends												
General government	HERV	30	−112	−424	−525	−758	−912	−1 115	−866	−561	−425	−134
Private sector and public corporations	CGQD	1 221	1 571	3 255	4 870	3 318	5 886	4 868	5 291	4 056	2 521	463
Transfers												
General government	HDKH	−1 607	−1 789	−1 930	−2 099	−3 427	−2 233	−3 277	−3 248	−4 278	−4 597	−1 049
Private sector	CGIM	60	48	337	369	316	76	−123	−270	−300	−300	−300
Invisibles balance	CGIK	3 496	2 741	5 302	7 134	6 136	9 625	7 099	5 302	2 956	1 778	3 969
of which: private sector and public corporations: services and IPD	HBZC	*5 876*	*5 943*	*8 371*	*10 570*	*11 303*	*14 103*	*13 233*	*11 489*	*10 349*	*9 461*	*7 849*
Current balance	AIMG	6 748	4 649	3 765	1 798	2 790	66	−4 482	−16 179	−21 726	−17 029	−6 321

Source: Central Statistical Office

Balance of payments/Overseas aid

13.3 Levels of UK external assets and liabilities[1]: by sector
End of period

£ million

		1981	1982	1983	1984	1985	1986	1987	1988	1989	1990	1991
Assets												
General government	HCDP	17 109	19 214	19 555	21 267	21 630	26 427	35 696	38 004	36 008	33 550	38 252
Public corporations	HEUZ	660	867	947	1 234	827	926	828	726	786	838	881
Private sector	HCAJ	312 587	396 002	465 955	600 999	570 756	693 230	658 949	737 294	923 019	866 472	911 245
Total	HCAK	330 356	416 082	486 456	623 500	593 213	720 583	695 474	776 024	959 813	900 860	950 378
Liabilities												
General government	HEVH	9 598	12 181	12 616	13 651	16 306	19 824	24 754	26 462	28 012	23 181	29 283
Public corporations	HEVI	3 876	4 197	4 532	4 767	3 990	4 114	3 090	2 751	793	706	629
Private sector	HEVJ	284 239	356 214	413 743	525 622	500 878	597 265	602 764	673 094	866 420	877 381	904 397
Total	HCAL	297 713	372 592	430 892	544 040	521 173	621 203	630 608	702 307	895 225	901 267	934 309
Net												
General government	HEVL	7 511	7 032	6 938	7 616	5 324	6 603	10 942	11 542	7 996	10 369	8 969
Public corporations	HEVM	–3 216	–3 330	–3 586	–3 533	–3 163	–3 188	–2 261	–2 025	–7	132	252
Private sector	HEVN	28 348	39 788	52 212	75 377	69 878	95 965	56 186	64 200	56 599	–10 909	6 848
Total	HEVO	32 643	43 490	55 565	79 460	72 039	99 380	64 866	73 717	64 588	–407	16 069

1 Because of the many inconsistencies in valuing the component series, and the omission of certain assets and liabilities which are unidentifiable, these estimates are not an exact measure of the UK's external debtor/ creditor position.

Source: Central Statistical Office

13.4 United Kingdom public expenditure on overseas aid
Gross aid-analysis by major components[1]

£ million

		1981	1982	1983	1984	1985	1986	1987	1988	1989	1990	1991
Total public expenditure on overseas aid	KGXG	1 183.6	1 085.3	1 174.3	1 315.6	1 324.4	1 350.2	1 295.3	1 666.7	1 793.3	1 725.2	2 081.9
Bilateral: total	KGXH	837.3	673.9	693.5	784.2	830.4	840.5	772.4	1 009.9	1 118.8	1 042.4	1 270.3
Project aid: total	KGXI	425.1	308.0	325.6	399.8	359.3	391.1	250.4	328.8	391.7	384.6	427.0
Overseas Development Administration excluding ATP	KGXJ	323.8	194.2	236.9	239.8	238.1	249.2	158.4	160.8	189.7	173.5	154.3
Aid and Trade Provision(ATP)	KGXK	33.3	62.6	32.6	51.5	42.4	78.2	29.2	56.4	51.0	74.2	113.0
Commonwealth Development Corporation	KGXL	68.0	51.1	56.0	108.4	78.7	63.7	62.9	111.6	151.0	136.8	159.7
Non-project aid	KGXM	163.9	121.5	103.7	109.9	157.0	120.0	145.7	220.0	253.9	149.8	255.3
Technical co-operation	KGXN	216.4	211.4	231.2	239.5	278.1	293.4	331.3	414.2	423.7	452.0	530.3
Administrative costs	KGXO	32.0	33.0	33.0	35.0	36.0	36.0	45.0	46.9	49.6	56.0	57.7
Multilateral: total	KGXP	346.3	411.5	480.8	531.3	494.0	509.6	522.9	656.8	674.5	682.8	811.6
European Community	KGXQ	158.1	173.8	188.7	225.6	234.1	223.3	222.0	273.7	305.1	332.7	421.0
World Bank Group	KGXR	115.5	153.7	205.5	197.4	128.1	153.7	157.3	228.8	202.9	183.5	203.4
UN Agencies	KGXS	48.6	58.0	57.3	65.8	83.9	81.2	99.6	108.4	118.8	113.4	133.8
Other multilateral	KGXT	24.1	25.9	29.3	42.6	47.9	51.5	43.9	45.8	47.7	53.2	53.3

1 See introductory notes on pages 235 - 236.

Source: Overseas Development Administration

Overseas aid

13.5 United Kingdom public expenditure on overseas aid
Gross bilateral aid-analysis by main recipient countries[1]

£ million

		1981	1982	1983	1984	1985	1986	1987	1988	1989	1990	1991
Total bilateral aid	KGXU	837.3	673.9	693.5	784.2	830.4	840.5	772.4	1 009.9	1 118.8	1 042.4	1 270.3
Africa: total	KGXV	299.7	247.2	236.8	268.0	315.5	285.4	307.7	427.3	514.1	389.1	521.3
Botswana	KGXW	10.2	7.6	13.3	16.0	8.7	12.3	12.2	8.0	7.8	8.3	12.2
Ethiopia	KGXX	0.6	5.6	3.4	7.0	28.1	9.6	9.3	18.5	11.7	20.0	21.8
Gambia	KGXY	2.3	2.5	2.4	3.6	3.6	9.9	7.0	6.4	5.0	7.3	5.3
Ghana	KGXZ	7.5	7.0	6.7	3.8	11.7	19.5	20.2	33.0	50.2	19.9	43.2
Ivory Coast	KGZE	2.6	1.3	1.8	1.6	2.6	7.4	4.5	7.2	8.8	10.6	6.9
Kenya	KGZF	39.7	37.5	31.9	38.3	34.4	33.8	28.5	49.8	53.9	44.4	49.5
Lesotho	KGZG	6.4	4.3	4.7	5.2	2.4	3.8	3.9	4.9	6.0	5.8	7.1
Malawi	KGZH	16.0	17.0	14.6	13.0	22.2	15.3	24.9	46.6	43.1	37.2	37.0
Mozambique	KGZI	5.4	1.9	1.8	4.2	8.4	7.4	23.8	30.1	22.4	25.4	22.6
Nigeria	KGZJ	4.2	4.9	5.5	5.6	6.2	5.6	6.6	8.2	63.0	14.0	38.6
South Africa	KGZK	–	–	–	–	0.7	0.8	1.6	4.2	4.9	6.3	8.6
St Helena and Depend	KGZL	4.1	5.8	6.5	7.5	9.4	9.2	12.2	15.2	28.7	13.1	8.4
Sudan	KGZM	32.7	39.4	32.2	27.4	42.3	26.0	20.4	26.0	31.4	21.4	27.4
Tanzania	KGZN	30.0	27.3	30.4	33.0	18.0	12.7	28.8	34.2	38.1	23.2	40.3
Uganda	KGZO	15.1	10.6	6.1	7.1	9.2	8.6	12.2	29.0	28.4	24.0	31.5
Zambia	KGZP	24.1	14.2	15.5	32.9	25.6	35.4	25.3	17.0	19.7	24.5	41.8
Zimbabwe	KGZQ	50.0	21.5	19.5	15.1	23.6	12.5	12.5	24.0	21.4	20.7	53.4
Other Countries	KGZR	48.7	38.7	40.6	46.8	58.5	55.7	53.7	64.8	69.5	62.9	65.7
America: Total	KGZS	49.0	92.2	67.9	58.4	70.3	58.0	58.8	69.8	91.3	93.3	110.2
Antigua and Barbuda	KGZT	0.9	0.5	0.4	0.4	0.5	0.8	1.0	1.2	0.8	1.0	2.2
Belize	KGZU	4.8	2.9	6.1	6.0	5.7	3.2	2.1	3.1	3.8	5.5	4.4
Bolivia	KGZV	1.1	1.0	1.2	1.2	1.4	2.0	1.7	3.1	4.0	4.1	4.5
Brazil	KGZW	0.6	10.0	5.6	7.8	4.0	0.9	0.8	1.4	2.4	1.4	3.7
Colombia	KGZX	0.8	0.6	0.6	0.5	0.8	1.0	0.8	1.8	2.0	2.0	5.3
Costa Rica	KGZY	0.6	0.5	1.8	1.7	12.7	10.0	2.8	1.6	5.8	4.9	8.2
Falkland Islands	KGZZ	1.1	4.0	9.1	6.0	10.7	10.3	8.2	4.3	3.7	1.0	1.8
Grenada	KHAR	0.1	0.1	0.1	0.7	1.5	0.8	0.7	1.2	1.4	1.1	2.8
Guyana	KHAS	2.5	1.7	1.6	0.4	0.4	0.5	0.6	0.6	6.6	15.3	6.2
Jamaica	KHAT	8.7	8.9	8.9	15.2	8.0	3.8	13.5	20.0	20.3	14.8	28.2
Montserrat	KHAU	1.1	1.8	1.0	1.3	1.2	2.0	1.3	2.3	4.0	4.3	4.6
Turks and Caicos	KHAV	3.4	5.7	4.2	3.9	3.6	5.4	5.4	4.2	5.2	4.9	8.9
Other Countries	KHAW	23.5	54.5	27.3	13.3	19.8	17.5	19.9	25.0	31.4	33.1	29.4
Asia: Total	KHAX	317.4	182.2	244.8	306.2	255.1	315.4	212.8	304.5	314.7	330.6	378.4
Bangladesh	KHAY	33.4	23.5	24.7	35.7	41.2	38.3	31.6	44.9	54.8	55.8	56.4
China	KHAZ	0.1	0.1	0.2	0.6	1.2	2.2	4.0	28.9	17.0	18.7	20.5
India	KHBK	168.6	54.2	127.6	146.5	106.5	143.5	78.5	101.1	99.5	87.8	114.0
Indonesia	KHBL	15.4	17.2	12.4	28.3	33.6	8.9	12.2	17.3	20.8	22.7	34.5
Jordan	KHBM	7.1	3.3	2.7	6.1	2.3	5.6	4.8	4.0	5.1	10.4	3.1
Malaysia	KHBN	10.1	6.4	3.9	5.0	7.5	55.5	9.8	10.7	8.7	21.1	21.2
Nepal	KHBO	8.0	9.6	7.4	8.6	9.7	9.9	10.0	11.0	17.3	15.2	19.1
Pakistan	KHBP	24.6	18.7	16.6	18.0	16.6	20.7	22.5	24.3	31.1	47.6	37.1
Philippines	KHBQ	3.3	1.2	3.7	3.8	1.8	0.2	0.3	1.0	11.9	10.9	8.2
Sri Lanka	KHBR	26.3	33.3	29.5	26.2	17.3	16.0	18.7	22.0	23.6	17.1	13.6
Thailand	KHBS	7.8	4.0	5.6	20.0	7.4	4.2	5.4	23.1	10.3	10.8	3.7
Yemen	KHBT	4.4	3.7	4.6	4.1	4.1	4.7	6.3	7.6	6.5	5.5	5.3
Other Countries	KHBU	8.4	6.9	6.0	3.4	5.9	5.6	8.8	8.4	8.2	6.9	41.6
Europe: Total	KHBV	37.3	19.6	8.8	9.6	33.5	19.4	13.1	12.5	4.9	4.5	16.9
Cyprus	KHBW	0.9	0.6	0.4	0.4	0.6	0.4	0.9	0.8	0.7	1.2	0.7
Gibraltar	KHBX	4.0	1.9	2.4	8.2	22.5	14.3	9.0	9.2	0.4	0.4	1.5
Turkey	KHBY	32.1	16.9	5.4	0.4	10.3	4.7	3.0	2.5	3.7	2.8	14.1
Other Countries	KHBZ	0.3	0.2	0.7	0.7	0.2	0.1	0.1	0.1	0.2	0.1	0.6
Oceania: Total	KHCK	33.0	31.6	24.7	27.3	22.2	26.1	28.8	35.7	30.7	28.3	29.3
Fiji	KHCL	7.0	8.7	4.0	4.7	4.0	7.1	2.0	1.5	4.6	4.4	2.4
Kiribati	KHCM	4.7	5.3	5.9	3.9	3.5	2.9	2.3	1.9	1.7	1.7	1.8
Papua New Guinea	KHCN	7.0	3.8	0.1	–	2.3	4.9	6.6	14.6	11.5	9.0	10.7
Solomon Islands	KHCO	7.3	6.3	6.8	7.3	4.1	3.7	4.2	5.3	5.6	5.3	6.9
Vanuatu	KHCP	4.6	4.3	5.9	8.1	6.0	5.4	5.5	5.5	5.8	6.1	5.4
Other Countries	KHCQ	2.4	3.1	2.0	3.2	2.3	2.0	8.1	7.0	1.6	1.8	2.0
World Unallocated	KHCR	68.9	68.1	77.5	79.8	97.8	100.1	106.2	113.2	113.5	140.5	156.5
Administrative costs	KHCS	32.0	33.0	33.0	35.0	36.0	36.0	45.0	46.9	49.6	56.0	57.7

1 See introductory notes on pages 235 - 236.

Source: Overseas Developement Administration

14 National Income and Expenditure

The tables which follow are taken from those in *United Kingdom National Accounts 1992 Edition*, (the *CSO Blue Book*) published by Her Majesty's Stationery Office (September 1992). Some of the figures are provisional and may have to be revised later; this applies particularly to the figures for 1990 and 1991. The 1983 and earlier editions were called *National Income and Expenditure*.

The *Blue Book* contains a brief introduction to the UK system of national accounts outlining some of the main concepts and principles of measurement used. This shows how the aggregate figures describing the whole economy are related to one another and to figures in the sector accounts. A more detailed description of the statistics, together with a detailed description of the sources, methods and definitions used in making the estimates, is given in *United Kingdom National Accounts: Sources and Methods Third Edition* (HMSO 1985). Further information on the structure and inter-relationships of the tables in the national accounts is given in *The National Accounts - A short guide* (HMSO 1981).

In the tables in this section, analyses by industry are based, as far as possible, on the Standard Industrial Classification 1980. The first aggregate measured in these tables is the **Gross domestic product** (GDP).

This is a concept of the value of the total economic activity taking place in UK territory. It can be viewed as incomes earned, as expenditures incurred, or as production. Adding net property income from abroad produces **Gross national product** (GNP). This is a concept of the value of all incomes earned by UK residents. **National income**, or Net national product, is GNP net of depreciation (that is, after deducting what is required to keep real capital intact).

The level of GDP is derived from the levels of the two broadly independent analyses of GDP based on income and expenditure. Account is taken also of the changes in volume of value added derived from the output analysis of GDP, which is compiled only in index number format. Such measures as GNP, National income, and Gross national disposable income (GNDI), can then be derived from GDP.

Gross national product *(Table 14.1)*. The upper half of this table shows the various money flows which generate the gross domestic product and the gross national product. These include expenditure by UK final buyers - that is, expenditure on goods and services other than for use in current production and resale - and expenditure on British exports by overseas purchasers. The sum of these two items overstates the amount of income generated in the United Kingdom by the value of imports of goods and services; this item is therefore subtracted to produce gross domestic product at market prices. Deducting taxes on expenditure and adding subsidies produces the total of the expenditure-based components at factor cost, which is equivalent to the sum of the incomes of the factors of production before deduction of depreciation (capital consumption).

The lower half of the table shows the contribution to the gross national product of the different factors of production. The profit items in the table—income from self-employment, trading profits of companies, trading surpluses of public co-porations and of other public enterprises—are shown before any deduction for depreciation and before providing for stock appreciation. (Stock appreciation is the change in value of stocks due to the change, if any, in the prices at which stocks are valued in the reckoning of profits.) This element of stock appreciation is deducted in reckoning the total of the gross national product.

Personal income and expenditure *(Table 14.2)*. 'Persons' are here defined as including unincorporated businesses and private non-profit-making bodies serving persons. Income is shown gross before providing for depreciation or stock appreciation. Employers' national insurance contributions (but not the surcharge) are treated as employee income taxed at source and therefore appear under both income and expenditure. Personal income also includes employers' contributions to pension funds. Personal saving before providing for depreciation or stock appreciation is estimated as a residual and is subject to a wide margin of error.

Corporate sector appropriation account *(Table 14.3)*. This table covers companies and public corporations. Trading profits earned in the United Kingdom are shown both before and after providing for stock appreciation but before deduction of depreciation allowances. Profits from operations outside the United Kingdom are included under income earned abroad. Dividends paid by one company to another are excluded both from dividends and from non-trading income.

Current account of general government *(Table 14.4)*. This table is a consolidation of central government and local authorities' transactions on current account.

Summary capital account *(Table 14.5)*. This table brings together the saving and investment of the several sectors of the economy and shows the total investment at home and overseas.

The index of output of the production industries *(Table 14.6)* (index of production), which accounts for 34$\frac{1}{2}$ per cent of gross domestic product shown in the same table, provides a general measure of changes in the volume of industrial production in the United Kingdom. Production industries comprise Division 1, energy and water supply (coal mining, oil and gas extraction, production of other fuels and water) and Divisions 2 to 4, manufacturing. The index of production is prepared by the Central Statistical Office in collaboration with the statistics divisions of other government departments and is published monthly, approximately six weeks after the end of the month to which it relates. The indices are calculated currently with 1985 as the base year, with the volume of production in other periods expressed as a percentage of the average monthly production in 1985. Annual series for broad industry groups from 1948, and quarterly series from 1952, are published in *Economic Trends Annual Supplement* (HMSO) and for more recent periods, along with monthly data, in *Economic Trends* (HMSO). More detailed monthly index of production series are published in the *Monthly Digest of Statistics* (HMSO).

The index of production is a weighted average of around 280 indicators, each representing the 'value added' by an individual industry or part of an industry as its contribution to total output of the United Kingdom. The weight given to each industry is proportional to its contribution to gross domestic product at factor cost in 1985; that is to say, the value the industry adds to its purchased materials, fuels and services. This is equal to the sum of income from employment *plus* profits after the deduction of stock appreciation. The weights are derived from the Annual Census of Production for that year, constrained to the aggregates shown in Table 2.1 of *United Kingdom National Accounts 1992 Edition* (HMSO). The weights shown in the table are those used in the compilation of the index from 1983 onwards. The 1985-based data were linked to the figures for earlier years on the basis of the annual figures for 1983 (see notes on rebasing below).

The gross output (that is, the total production) of an industry is the most frequently used proxy indicator for assessing change in value added, since the latter is difficult to measure in the short-term. In some cases the volume of production can be measured and such indicators make up about two-fifths of the index of production. About three-fifths of the index of production is derived from the volume of sales or deliveries or their value deflated by the relevant producer prices indices: however, adjustments for changes to stocks and work done in the industries represented by these indicators are made at a more aggregate level. A very small proportion of the index of production is derived from work done or input of labour or materials indicators. For further notes on the general method of constructing the index on the 1985 base see Industry Statistics: Occasional Paper No 22 *Series and weights used in the index of output of the production industries - 1985 base* (CSO 1989), which is obtainable from the IOP Branch, Central Statistical Office, Cardiff Road, Newport, Gwent NP9 1XG, price £10.00 (cheques payable to Central Statistical Office).

The index of production along with the national accounts is rebased at five-yearly intervals. Regular rebasing is required because the rate of growth in relative prices of net output of the various sectors may vary over time. In addition, the relative importance of each sector may change because of advances of technology, or variations in the pattern of demand for its goods. Index numbers for 1983 onwards were recalculated when the index was rebased onto 1985 = 100 in August 1988. The index numbers up to 1983 (on a 1980

= 100 base) were linked to the later figures by a simple rescaling of series, using the two sets of index numbers for 1983. An article describing the effect of rebasing for 1989 appeared in *Economic Trends* in February 1989.

Industrial classification. The industrial analysis of the index of production is in conformity with the *Standard Industrial Classification Revised 1980* (HMSO) to which reference should be made for the details of the composition of each industrial group.

Market sector classification. These groupings combine the output of industries which meet broadly similar categories of demand: consumer goods, investment goods and intermediate goods (materials and fuels). Because the index of production measures the output of an industry and not of commodities, each market sector group will include some output from the other sector. The industrial composition of the market sectors on the 1985 base is set out in Industry Statistics: Occasional Paper No 22 (see above).

Gross domestic product by industry *(Table 14.7)*. This table shows the contribution of each industry to the gross domestic product, measured as the sum of incomes, before providing for depreciation, arising in the industry. This is also equal to the 'value added' by the industry, that is, the excess of the value of its current output over the value of goods and services purchased from outside the industry and used in production.

Expenditure and output at constant prices *(Tables 14.6 and 14.8)*. These tables contain two virtually independent estimates of the gross domestic product of the United Kingdom at 1985 prices. The estimates in Table 14.6 are based on the index of industrial production and other statistics relating to the volume of output; those in Table 14.8 have been derived by revaluing estimates of final expenditure on goods and services at average 1985 prices. With full and accurate information the two methods would in theory lead to the same result. In practice, because there are numerous imperfections and gaps in the data, the two methods produce different results. Table 14.8 is expressed in £ million at 1985 prices, whereas Table 14.6 is expressed in index form, taking 1985 = 100. For a general account of the methods of compiling the output index numbers, see *United Kingdom National Accounts: Sources and Methods Third Edition*. Detailed notes on the construction of the output index are available in Occasional Paper 1/92 *Series and weights used in the output-based estimate of GDP at constant factor cost (1985 prices)*, which is obtainable from CSO Library, Cardiff Road, Newport, Gwent NP9 1XG, price £2.50 (cheques payable to Central Statistical Office).

Consumers' expenditure at current and constant prices *(Table 14.9)*. Consumers' expenditure is a major component of final expenditure contributing to gross domestic product at current prices *(Table 14.1)* and at constant prices *(Table 14.8)*.

Consumers' expenditure consists of personal expenditure on goods and services for current use. It is now classified in two ways, first in certain commodity groups which are also available on a quarterly basis in the *Monthly Digest of Statistics* and secondly (in more detail) according to purpose. It includes the value of income-in-kind; imputed rent of owner-occupied dwellings; and final expenditure by private non-profit-making bodies serving persons. It excludes business expenditure allowed as deductions in computing income for tax purposes of both employed and self-employed persons.

It includes expenditure on durable goods, for instance motor cars, which from the point of view of the individual might more appropriately be treated as capital expenditure. The only exceptions are the purchase of land and dwellings and costs incurred in connection with the transfer of their ownership and expenditure on major improvements by occupiers, which are treated as personal capital expenditure.

The estimates of consumers' expenditure include purchases of second-hand as well as new goods, *less* the proceeds of sales of used goods.

National accounts aggregates, *(Table 14.12)* gives two different kinds of information. The first part deals with National disposable income, which measures the total disposable income of the country's residents, that is, the command they have over resources. The second part gives volume indices at 1985 prices for the main estimates of total UK economic activity, and for the expenditure components.

Value of physical increase in stocks and work in progress *(Table 14.13)*. This table gives a broad analysis by industry, and, for manufacturing industry, by asset, of the physical increase in stocks and work in progress. For most industries, the physical increase at current prices equals the change in the book value of stocks *less* stock appreciation.

Gross domestic fixed capital formation *(Table 14.14)*. Fixed capital formation comprises expenditure on the replacement of, and additions to, the stock of fixed capital assets located in the United Kingdom, including all ships and aircraft of UK ownership.

Gross capital stock *(Table 14.15)*. The table shows estimates of the value of the reproducible capital assets (buildings, plant and machinery, vehicles, ships and aircraft) owned by various industry groups, without allowance for depreciation during the expended proportions of asset lives. The estimates are expressed at 1985 replacement cost. Leased assets are included on a 'user' basis. A rough analysis of these assets, which still constitute only a small proportion of total gross capital stock, appears in *United Kingdom National Accounts 1992 Edition*.

National Income

14.1 National product: by category of expenditure and factor incomes

£ million

		1981	1982	1983	1984	1985	1986	1987	1988	1989	1990	1991
Categories of expenditure at current market prices												
Consumers' expenditure[1]	AIIK	155 412	170 650	187 028	200 261	218 947	243 030	267 523	302 057	330 532	350 411	367 853
General government final consumption	AAXI	55 374	60 363	65 787	69 760	73 805	79 381	85 349	91 729	99 029	109 878	121 899
of which: Central Government	ACHC	33 879	37 000	40 654	43 142	45 879	48 801	52 040	55 610	60 527	67 052	74 442
Local authorities	CSBA	21 495	23 363	25 133	26 618	27 926	30 580	33 309	36 119	38 502	42 826	47 457
Gross domestic fixed capital formation	DFDC	41 304	44 824	48 615	54 967	60 353	64 514	74 077	89 857	103 262	106 028	95 442
Value of physical increase in stocks and work in progress	DHBF	−2 768	−1 188	1 465	1 296	821	716	1 388	4 782	3 138	−1 462	−5 303
Total domestic expenditure[1]	CTGQ	249 322	274 649	302 895	326 284	353 926	387 641	428 337	488 425	535 961	564 855	579 891
Exports of goods and services	DJAD	67 432	72 694	80 056	91 852	102 208	98 319	107 031	107 705	122 049	133 500	135 115
of which: Goods	CGJP	50 668	55 331	60 700	70 265	77 991	72 627	79 153	80 346	92 154	101 718	103 413
Services	CGJZ	16 764	17 363	19 356	21 587	24 217	25 692	27 878	27 359	29 895	31 782	31 702
Total final expenditure[1]	DJAK	316 754	347 343	382 951	418 136	456 134	485 960	535 368	596 130	658 010	698 355	715 006
less Imports of goods and services[2]	−DJAG	−60 388	−67 762	−77 529	−92 669	−98 866	−101 070	−111 868	−124 788	−142 693	−147 728	−140 415
of which: Goods	−CGGL	−47 416	−53 421	−62 237	−75 601	−81 336	−82 186	−90 735	−101 826	−116 837	−120 527	−113 703
Services	−CGGZ	−12 972	−14 341	−15 292	−17 068	−17 530	−18 884	−21 133	−22 962	−25 856	−27 201	−26 712
Statistical discrepancy (expenditure adjustment)[3]	GIXM	−1 515	−694	−1 108	330	–	–	–	–	–	−277	−445
Gross domestic product[1,4]	CAOB	254 851	278 887	304 314	325 797	357 268	384 890	423 500	471 342	515 317	550 350	574 146
Net property income from abroad	CGOA	1 251	1 460	2 831	4 345	2 560	4 974	3 754	4 423	3 495	2 094	328
Gross national product[1,4]	GIBF	256 102	280 347	307 145	330 142	359 828	389 864	427 254	475 765	518 812	552 444	574 474
Factor cost adjustment:												
Taxes on expenditure	AAXC	42 465	46 467	49 500	52 576	56 592	62 947	69 074	76 133	79 963	76 967	83 023
Subsidies	AAXJ	6 369	5 811	6 269	7 537	7 225	6 187	6 173	5 918	5 782	6 069	5 878
Factor cost adjustment (taxes *less* subsidies)	CTGV	36 096	40 656	43 231	45 039	49 367	56 760	62 901	70 215	74 181	70 898	77 145
Factor incomes												
Income from employment	DJAO	149 737	158 838	169 847	181 406	196 858	212 374	229 836	255 625	282 919	311 745	329 808
Income from self employment[5]	CFAN	19 980	22 140	24 750	27 909	30 404	35 104	40 122	47 612	54 093	59 971	57 507
Gross trading profits of companies[5,6]	CIAC	27 341	31 176	39 528	43 906	51 287	47 312	59 177	63 375	67 142	65 588	60 674
Gross trading surplus of public corporations[5]	ADRD	7 974	9 502	10 004	8 381	7 120	8 059	6 802	7 354	6 418	4 342	3 119
Gross trading surplus of general government enterprises[5]	DJAQ	236	216	50	−117	265	155	−75	−32	199	12	119
Rent[6]	DIDS	16 366	17 700	18 857	19 816	21 875	23 848	26 155	29 904	33 795	39 363	44 092
Imputed charge for consumption of non-trading capital	DIDT	2 351	2 426	2 498	2 619	2 830	3 068	3 307	3 634	4 005	4 391	4 490
Total domestic income[5]	DJAU	223 985	241 998	265 534	283 920	310 639	329 920	365 324	407 472	448 571	485 412	499 809
less Stock appreciation	−DJAT	−5 974	−4 276	−4 204	−4 513	−2 738	−1 790	−4 725	−6 345	−7 435	−6 288	−2 825
Statistical discrepancy (income adjustment)[3]	GIXQ	744	509	−247	1 351	–	–	–	–	–	328	17
Gross domestic product at factor cost	CAOM	218 755	238 231	261 083	280 758	307 901	328 130	360 599	401 127	441 136	479 452	497 001
Net property income from abroad	CGOA	1 251	1 460	2 831	4 345	2 560	4 974	3 754	4 423	3 495	2 094	328
Gross national product	GIBD	220 006	239 691	263 914	285 103	310 461	333 104	364 353	405 550	444 631	481 546	497 329
less Capital consumption	−EXCH	−31 641	−33 653	−36 150	−38 758	−41 883	−45 084	−48 149	−52 596	−56 632	−61 126	−63 968
Net national product at factor cost "National income"	GIBE	188 365	206 038	227 764	246 345	268 578	288 020	316 204	352 954	387 999	420 420	433 361

1 This series is affected by the abolition of domestic rates and the introduction of the community charge.
2 Excluding taxes on expenditure levied on imports.
3 The Statistical discrepancies (expenditure adjustment and income adjustment) are each part of the Residual error.
4 Including taxes on expenditure levied on imports.
5 Before providing for depreciation and stock appreciation.
6 Including financial institutions.

Source: Central Statistical Office

National Income

14.2 Personal sector: income and expenditure account

£ million

		1981	1982	1983	1984	1985	1986	1987	1988	1989	1990	1991
Income before tax												
Income from employment:												
Wages and salaries	CFAJ	125 348	133 557	142 616	152 779	166 774	180 748	196 320	219 416	244 029	270 089	284 281
Pay in cash and kind of HM Forces	CFAK	2 689	2 905	3 121	3 288	3 590	3 833	4 093	4 337	4 539	4 814	5 460
Total	AIJA	128 037	136 462	145 737	156 067	170 364	184 581	200 413	223 753	248 568	274 903	289 741
Employers' contributions:												
Social security	CEAN	8 814	9 344	10 536	11 269	12 245	13 540	14 878	16 817	17 912	20 076	21 362
Other	CFAL	12 886	13 032	13 574	14 070	14 249	14 253	14 545	15 055	16 439	16 766	18 705
Total income from employment	DJAO	149 737	158 838	169 847	181 406	196 858	212 374	229 836	255 625	282 919	311 745	329 808
Income from self-employment:												
After deducting stock appreciation	CEAP	19 354	21 778	24 200	27 584	29 929	34 938	39 632	46 853	53 284	59 288	57 136
Stock appreciation	DDAD	626	362	550	325	475	166	490	759	809	683	371
Total[1]	CFAN	19 980	22 140	24 750	27 909	30 404	35 104	40 122	47 612	54 093	59 971	57 507
Rent, dividends and net interest:												
Receipts by life assurance & pension schemes	CFBH	8 762	10 505	11 785	12 574	14 890	16 987	18 732	23 486	28 459	30 833	30 609
Imputed rent of owner-occupied dwellings	CDDF	9 114	10 160	11 264	11 863	12 880	13 993	15 280	17 272	19 633	23 251	26 995
Other receipts, net	CFBJ	3 402	3 149	2 768	4 511	4 289	2 899	2 457	2 092	−912	−1 007	−730
Total	CFAM	21 278	23 814	25 817	28 948	32 059	33 879	36 469	42 850	47 180	53 077	56 874
Social security benefits and other current grants from general government	AIIE	31 242	36 584	39 856	43 020	46 813	50 984	52 494	54 087	56 793	62 002	71 767
Current transfers from overseas	CGJV	1 117	1 248	1 528	1 652	1 775	1 732	1 666	1 715	1 750	1 800	1 900
Current transfers to charities from companies	CIBA	62	69	86	105	119	145	160	200	284	299	288
Imputed charge for capital consumption of private non-profit making bodies	CFBM	403	409	417	432	458	485	503	524	557	585	600
Total personal income[1]	AIIA	223 819	243 102	262 301	283 472	308 486	334 703	361 250	402 613	443 576	489 479	518 744
Deductions from income												
UK taxes on income	AIIG	28 949	31 366	33 180	34 736	37 774	40 805	43 386	48 272	53 579	61 520	63 749
Social security contributions	AIIH	15 916	18 095	20 780	22 322	24 210	26 165	28 642	32 106	32 902	34 651	36 643
Current transfers abroad	CGGV	1 057	1 200	1 191	1 283	1 459	1 656	1 789	1 985	2 050	2 100	2 200
Community charge	ADBH	–	–	–	–	–	–	–	–	586	8 629	8 162
Miscellaneous current transfers	CIJR	177	187	222	215	225	253	339	362	391	469	344
Personal disposable income[2]	AIIJ	177 720	192 254	206 928	224 916	244 818	265 824	287 094	319 888	354 068	382 110	407 646
Expenditure												
Consumers' expenditure	AIIK	155 412	170 650	187 028	200 261	218 947	243 030	267 523	302 057	330 532	350 411	367 853
Balance: saving[2]	AAAU	22 308	21 604	19 900	24 655	25 871	22 794	19 571	17 831	23 536	31 699	39 793
Total	AIIJ	177 720	192 254	206 928	224 916	244 818	265 824	287 094	319 888	354 068	382 110	407 646
Memorandum items												
Saving ratio (per cent)[3]	AIIM	12.6	11.2	9.6	11.0	10.6	8.6	6.8	5.6	6.6	8.3	9.8
Real personal disposable income[4]:												
At 1985 prices	CFAG	224 147	223 044	228 950	236 931	244 818	254 849	263 807	279 686	292 350	299 598	298 136
1985=100	CFAD	91.6	91.1	93.5	96.8	100.0	104.1	107.8	114.2	119.4	122.4	121.8

1 Before providing for depreciation and stock appreciation.
2 Before providing for depreciation, stock appreciation and additions to tax reserves.
3 Saving as a percentage of personal disposable income.
4 Personal disposable income revalued by the implied consumers' expenditure deflator (1985=100).

Source: Central Statistical Office

National Income

14.3 Corporate sector appropriation account[1]

£ million

		1981	1982	1983	1984	1985	1986	1987	1988	1989	1990	1991
Income												
Income arising in the United Kingdom:													
Gross trading profits and trading surplus:													
After deducting stock appreciation	GIBY	29 967	36 764	45 878	48 099	56 144	53 747	61 744	65 143	66 934	64 325	61 339
Stock appreciation	GIBZ	5 348	3 914	3 654	4 188	2 263	1 624	4 235	5 586	6 626	5 605	2 454
Total[2]	GICA	35 315	40 678	49 532	52 287	58 407	55 371	65 979	70 729	73 560	69 930	63 793
Rent and non-trading income	GICB	18 877	20 644	20 783	23 582	29 794	31 756	34 539	39 110	53 291	62 703	60 389
Total	GICC	54 192	61 322	70 315	75 869	88 201	87 127	100 518	109 839	126 851	132 633	124 182
Income from abroad[3,4]	GICD	8 963	9 234	11 163	13 991	14 863	15 075	17 542	21 424	26 610	28 123	25 576
Total income	GICE	63 155	70 556	81 478	89 860	103 064	102 202	118 060	131 263	153 461	160 756	149 758
Allocation of income													
Dividends and interest payments[5]	GICF	20 517	22 899	22 791	26 195	33 738	35 241	39 152	47 150	66 700	80 651	78 918
Current transfers to charities and central government from companies	EAEI	62	69	86	107	123	158	184	232	324	334	314
Profits due abroad, net of UK tax[3]	CIBU	4 695	4 659	5 258	6 271	7 563	5 285	7 014	8 611	9 157	6 901	5 721
UK taxes on income	GICI	8 564	10 489	12 028	14 121	16 556	14 543	15 822	18 041	22 192	21 497	17 735
Royalties and licence fees on oil and gas production	GICJ	1 362	1 600	1 887	2 459	2 366	941	1 151	823	556	654	581
Balance: undistributed income after taxation[6]	GICK	27 955	30 840	39 428	40 707	42 718	46 034	54 737	56 406	54 532	50 719	46 489
Total	GICE	63 155	70 556	81 478	89 860	103 064	102 202	118 060	131 263	153 461	160 756	149 758

1 The sum of two subsectors, namely public corporations plus companies and financial institutions. Flows between the two constituent subsectors are not netted out.
2 Before providing for depreciation and stock appreciation.
3 After deducting depreciation allowances but before providing for stock appreciation.
4 Includes net receipts of interest by UK banks and other financial institutions on their foreign currency lending to and borrowing from overseas residents.
5 Excludes dividends and debenture interest payments by UK subsidiaries to their overseas parents.
6 Before providing for depreciation, stock appreciation and additions to dividend and tax reserves.

Source: Central Statistical Office

14.4 General government: summary account

£ million

		1981	1982	1983	1984	1985	1986	1987	1988	1989	1990	1991
Current receipts													
Taxes on income	ACGB	36 134	40 282	43 344	46 655	51 643	52 239	55 702	61 861	70 400	77 021	75 105
Taxes on expenditure	AAXC	42 465	46 467	49 500	52 576	56 592	62 947	69 074	76 133	79 963	76 967	83 023
Social security contributions	AIIH	15 916	18 095	20 780	22 322	24 210	26 165	28 642	32 106	32 902	34 651	36 643
Community charge	ADBH	–	–	–	–	–	–	–	–	586	8 629	8 162
Gross trading surplus[1]	DJAQ	236	216	50	−117	265	155	−75	−32	199	12	119
Rent, etc.[2]	CTGA	4 715	4 857	4 836	5 373	5 510	4 101	4 347	4 117	3 902	4 179	4 302
Interest and dividends, etc.	ATAC	4 456	5 292	5 097	5 167	6 277	5 844	5 839	6 116	7 035	6 372	5 975
Miscellaneous current transfers	ACGX	177	187	222	217	229	266	363	394	431	504	370
Imputed charge for consumption of non-trading capital	AAXG	1 948	2 017	2 081	2 187	2 372	2 583	2 804	3 110	3 448	3 806	3 890
Total	AAXA	106 047	117 413	125 910	134 380	147 098	154 300	166 696	183 805	198 866	212 141	217 589
Current expenditure													
Current expenditure on goods and services	CTGD	53 426	58 346	63 706	67 573	71 433	76 798	82 545	88 619	95 581	106 072	118 009
Non-trading capital consumption	AAXG	1 948	2 017	2 081	2 187	2 372	2 583	2 804	3 110	3 448	3 806	3 890
Subsidies	AAXJ	6 369	5 811	6 269	7 537	7 225	6 187	6 173	5 918	5 782	6 069	5 878
Current grants to personal sector	AIIE	31 242	36 584	39 856	43 020	46 813	50 984	52 494	54 087	56 793	62 002	71 767
Current grants paid abroad (net)	−HDKH	1 607	1 789	1 930	2 099	3 427	2 233	3 277	3 248	4 278	4 597	1 049
Debt interest	AAXL	12 719	13 952	14 208	15 773	17 715	17 257	18 003	18 255	18 943	18 793	17 097
Total current expenditure	AAXH	107 311	118 499	128 050	138 189	148 985	156 042	165 296	173 237	184 825	201 339	217 690
Balance: current surplus[1]	AAXM	−1 264	−1 086	−2 140	−3 809	−1 887	−1 742	1 400	10 568	14 041	10 802	−101
Total	AAXA	106 047	117 413	125 910	134 380	147 098	154 300	166 696	183 805	198 866	212 141	217 589

1 Before providing for depreciation.
2 Includes royalties and licence fees on oil and gas production.

Source: Central Statistical Office

National Income

14.5 Summary capital account[1]

£ million

		1981	1982	1983	1984	1985	1986	1987	1988	1989	1990	1991
Receipts												
Saving[2]												
Personal sector	AAAU	22 308	21 604	19 900	24 655	25 871	22 794	19 571	17 831	23 536	31 699	39 793
Industrial & commercial companies	AAAQ	20 001	21 757	26 725	31 844	33 488	33 582	42 395	45 559	39 372	39 467	36 565
Financial companies and institutions	AAAM	2 393	2 476	5 188	2 614	3 837	6 337	7 209	4 817	9 868	7 616	7 527
Public corporations	AAAI	5 561	6 607	7 515	6 249	5 393	6 115	5 133	6 030	5 292	3 636	2 397
Central government	AAAA	−3 865	−4 177	−4 457	−5 873	−3 691	−3 952	−1 057	8 988	12 445	6 319	−2 241
Local authorities	AAAE	2 601	3 091	2 317	2 064	1 804	2 210	2 457	1 580	1 596	4 483	2 140
Total saving	GIGV	48 999	51 358	57 188	61 553	66 702	67 086	75 708	84 805	92 109	93 220	86 181
Capital transfers (net receipts):												
Personal sector	AAAV	88	367	1 019	1 266	422	−150	−268	−1 246	−759	−175	1 328
Industrial & commercial companies	AAAR	557	491	322	217	112	−45	−284	122	−525	−479	−392
Financial companies and institutions	AAAN	−315	−148	−61	−64	−118	−196	−190	−141	−151	−100	−100
Public corporations[3]	AAAJ	532	473	602	568	634	456	714	805	1 305	5 818	2 391
Central government[3]	AAAB	−904	−1 009	−1 107	−1 373	−1 080	−588	−400	62	−1 383	−6 239	−4 810
Local authorities	AAAF	42	−174	−775	−614	30	523	428	398	1 513	1 175	1 583
Total transfers[4]	AAAZ	–	–	–	–	–	–	–	–	–	–	–
Residual error[5]	DJAS	2 259	1 203	861	1 021	–	–	–	–	–	605	462
Total	GIHN	51 258	52 561	58 049	62 574	66 702	67 086	75 708	84 805	92 109	93 825	86 643
Expenditure												
Gross domestic fixed capital formation:												
Personal sector[6]	AAAW	9 840	12 046	13 927	14 784	15 661	18 191	21 756	28 745	27 993	26 758	23 479
Industrial & commercial companies	AAAS	16 434	17 329	17 704	22 304	28 558	29 492	36 006	43 499	52 347	54 863	49 683
Financial companies and institutions	AAAO	3 434	3 698	3 050	3 719	3 331	3 774	4 129	6 488	7 827	6 763	6 179
Public corporations	AAAK	6 924	7 314	8 065	7 441	5 931	5 548	4 609	4 619	5 513	4 985	3 928
Central government	AAAC	1 868	2 230	2 497	2 728	3 126	3 351	3 358	3 709	4 951	6 415	7 042
Local authorities	AAAG	2 804	2 207	3 372	3 991	3 746	4 158	4 219	2 797	4 631	6 244	5 131
Total	DFDC	41 304	44 824	48 615	54 967	60 353	64 514	74 077	89 857	103 262	106 028	95 442
Increase in book value of stocks and work in progress[7]:												
Personal sector	AAAX	415	420	698	513	430	521	807	1 358	1 238	767	78
Industrial & commercial companies	AAAT	2 531	1 845	4 316	5 370	2 575	2 573	5 926	9 833	9 207	4 060	−2 795
Financial companies and institutions	AAAP	9	4	38	24	–	–	–	–	–	–	–
Public corporations	AAAL	344	664	371	−378	104	−351	−122	258	291	−157	88
Central government	AAAD	−93	155	246	280	450	−237	−498	−322	−163	156	151
Total	DHHY	3 206	3 088	5 669	5 809	3 559	2 506	6 113	11 127	10 573	4 826	−2 478
Net investment abroad[8]	−AABI	6 748	4 649	3 765	1 798	2 790	66	−4 482	−16 179	−21 726	−17 029	−6 321
Total investment	GIHN	51 258	52 561	58 049	62 574	66 702	67 086	75 708	84 805	92 109	93 825	86 643
Financial surplus or deficit												
Personal sector	AABH	12 141	9 505	6 294	10 624	10 202	3 932	−3 260	−13 518	−6 454	3 999	17 564
Industrial & commercial companies	AABG	1 593	3 074	5 027	4 387	2 467	1 472	179	−7 651	−22 707	−19 935	−10 715
Financial companies and institutions	AABF	−1 365	−1 374	2 039	−1 193	388	2 367	2 890	−1 812	1 890	753	1 248
Public corporations	AABD	−1 175	−898	−319	−246	−8	1 374	1 360	1 958	793	4 626	772
Central government	AABA	−6 544	−7 571	−8 307	−10 254	−8 347	−7 654	−4 317	5 663	6 274	−6 491	−14 244
Local authorities	AABB	−161	710	−1 830	−2 541	−1 912	−1 425	−1 334	−819	−1 522	−586	−1 408
Total	GIHZ	4 489	3 446	2 904	777	2 790	66	−4 482	−16 179	−21 726	−17 634	−6 783
Net investment abroad[8]	−AABI	6 748	4 649	3 765	1 798	2 790	66	−4 482	−16 179	−21 726	−17 029	−6 321
less Residual error[5]	−DJAS	−2 259	−1 203	−861	−1 021	–	–	–	–	–	−605	−462

1 Figures for companies and public corporations are affected by privatisation.
2 Before providing for depreciation, stock appreciation and additions to dividend and tax reserves.
3 Excluding financial transactions on writing-off debt.
4 "Total capital transfers for the domestic sectors" equals capital transfers paid abroad.
5 Residual error is the difference between the totals of the expenditure and income components of Gross domestic product.
6 Gross and net fixed capital formation by the personal sector excludes that by Life assurance and pension funds: this is included with that of Financial companies and institutions.
7 Equal to stock appreciation plus value of physical increase in stocks and work in progress.
8 Net investment abroad is equal, but opposite in sign, to the Overseas sector's financial surplus or deficit.

Source: Central Statistical Office

National Income

14.6 Gross domestic product at constant factor cost: by industry of output

1985 = 100

	Weight per 1000[1] 1985		1981	1982	1983	1984	1985	1986	1987	1988	1989	1990	1991
Agriculture, forestry and fishing	19	CKAP	85.2	92.3	87.3	105.5	100.0	100.1	97.0	95.5	101.0	106.3	109.1
Production:													
Energy and water supply:													
Coal and coke	12	DVIO	136.2	130.4	125.2	55.9	100.0	114.2	110.8	110.0	105.8	97.4	99.5
Extraction of mineral oil and natural gas	62	DVIP	73.0	83.2	91.1	97.4	100.0	101.2	98.6	90.1	73.4	73.4	75.0
Mineral oil processing	4	DVIQ	94.5	94.2	96.7	99.6	100.0	100.9	102.1	109.4	112.0	111.2	115.3
Other energy and water supply	28	DVIR	94.6	93.9	97.2	82.4	100.0	109.9	112.9	113.8	115.0	116.1	124.4
Total energy and water supply	106	DVIN	86.5	91.6	96.8	88.8	100.0	105.0	103.9	99.3	89.6	88.9	92.4
Manufacturing:													
Metals	9	DVIT	95.4	92.8	94.2	92.9	100.0	100.3	108.6	122.3	124.7	121.2	110.2
Other minerals and mineral products	12	DVIU	91.8	93.7	96.8	100.4	100.0	101.3	106.8	117.3	120.1	113.4	103.0
Chemicals	24	DVIW	83.7	84.3	90.6	96.4	100.0	101.7	109.0	114.4	119.5	118.3	121.5
Man-made fibres	1	DVIX	109.4	87.5	100.6	104.9	100.0	103.6	109.9	107.8	114.5	117.2	120.0
Metal goods nes	13	DVIZ	93.5	94.1	96.5	104.4	100.0	99.4	103.4	111.5	113.5	110.8	99.6
Mechanical engineering	29	DVJA	96.7	98.1	94.3	96.0	100.0	96.5	96.8	105.3	109.7	112.4	100.2
Electrical and instrument engineering	34	DVJB	73.0	76.4	84.4	94.1	100.0	100.6	106.3	117.9	126.2	124.9	121.9
Motor vehicles and parts	13	DVJC	94.0	90.8	95.2	93.5	100.0	96.9	103.9	119.1	125.4	121.7	110.8
Other transport equipment including aerospace	13	DVJD	113.4	110.5	104.0	99.5	100.0	111.9	112.6	107.8	127.8	129.6	119.0
Food	23	DVJF	94.3	97.6	98.7	99.6	100.0	101.3	103.2	105.2	105.2	105.6	106.0
Drink and tobacco	8	DVJG	103.3	100.7	101.7	102.7	100.0	99.6	103.3	103.6	107.0	108.6	106.8
Textiles	7	DVJI	93.6	91.3	93.4	96.2	100.0	100.2	104.6	101.8	97.0	92.0	85.3
Clothing, footwear and leather	9	DVJJ	88.4	87.6	91.9	95.9	100.0	101.0	103.0	102.1	99.4	99.1	89.2
Paper, printing and publishing	24	DVJL	96.1	92.8	93.4	97.8	100.0	104.2	114.4	125.2	131.9	133.9	128.5
All other manufacturing (including timber, furniture, rubber and plastics)	19	DVJM	89.4	88.2	93.8	99.1	100.0	105.0	115.7	128.5	132.6	132.2	123.0
Total manufacturing	238	DVIS	91.0	91.2	93.8	97.4	100.0	101.3	106.6	114.1	119.0	118.4	112.2
Total production	344	DVIM	89.6	91.4	94.7	94.8	100.0	102.4	105.7	109.5	109.9	109.3	106.1
Construction	59	DVJO	82.9	89.4	95.1	99.6	100.0	104.1	112.9	125.6	133.0	134.3	122.6
Service industries:													
Distribution, hotels and catering; repairs	134	CKAQ	86.0	87.6	91.5	96.0	100.0	105.5	112.5	120.1	123.3	122.2	118.3
Transport and communication:													
Transport	43	CKBU	93.2	90.1	92.1	95.2	100.0	102.2	112.1	118.9	124.1	124.7	118.7
Communication	27	CKBM	84.8	87.4	90.8	97.6	100.0	107.6	113.2	120.3	127.8	133.7	132.3
Total transport and communication	70	CKAR	89.9	89.0	91.6	96.1	100.0	104.3	112.5	119.4	125.6	128.1	123.9
Banking, finance, insurance, business services and leasing	155	CKBV	76	81	87	94	100	111	122	132	138	141	138
Ownership of dwellings	59	CKBW	96	97	98	99	100	100	100	101	101	102	104
Public administration, national defence and compulsory social security	71	CKBX	102	100	100	100	100	100	100	99	98	100	101
Education and health services	85	CKCB	96	97	99	99	100	101	104	107	108	108	108
Other services[2]	59	CKCC	86	86	89	95	100	105	113	118	120	121	117
Adjustment for financial services	55	CKCA	76	81	88	94	100	114	127	136	140	143	138
Total services	578	CKCE	89.2	90.5	93.4	97.0	100.0	104.1	109.6	114.8	117.8	119.1	117.1
Gross domestic product		DJDD	89.3	90.9	94.2	96.1	100.0	103.8	108.6	113.5	115.8	116.6	113.8

1 The weights are proportional to the distribution of net output in 1985 and are used to combine the indices from 1983 onwards. For the method of calculation in earlier years see paragraph 5.19 of *United Kingdom National Accounts: Sources and Methods,* Third edition.

2 Comprising classes 92, 94, 96-99 and 00 of the Standard Industrial Classification Revised 1980.

Source: Central Statistical Office

National Income

14.6 Gross domestic product at constant factor cost: by industry of output (continued)

1985=100

	Weights per 1000[1] 1985		1981	1982	1983	1984	1985	1986	1987	1988	1989	1990	1991
Consumer goods industries:													
Cars, etc.	21	DVJQ	96.9	87.9	100.2	96.0	100.0	95.0	103.7	118.1	125.3	119.0	105.4
Other durables	26	DVJR	89.2	88.5	91.9	96.2	100.0	103.2	108.3	120.3	119.2	115.2	107.5
Clothing and footwear, etc.	27	DVJS	89.3	88.4	91.8	96.1	100.0	100.2	101.2	98.8	95.4	93.5	85.6
Food, drink and tobacco[2]	84	DVJT	97.0	98.1	99.2	100.5	100.0	100.6	103.4	104.5	105.8	106.4	106.3
Other	85	DVJU	90.4	89.3	92.6	97.3	100.0	102.9	111.1	119.7	125.4	126.7	122.1
Total	243	DVJP	93.0	92.5	95.3	98.1	100.0	101.2	106.4	112.0	114.6	114.0	109.5
Investment goods industries:													
Electrical	59	DVJW	70.1	74.3	82.7	93.3	100.0	98.4	103.5	115.9	125.9	124.2	125.5
Transport	56	DVJX	103.0	101.4	98.8	96.8	100.0	107.0	109.5	111.9	126.4	127.4	117.0
Other	80	DVJY	96.5	96.8	93.7	95.5	100.0	97.7	98.0	107.0	112.2	114.9	104.6
Total	195	DVJV	90.3	91.3	91.8	95.2	100.0	100.6	103.0	111.1	120.5	121.3	114.5
Intermediate goods industries:													
Fuels	299	DVKA	86.0	90.9	96.8	88.5	100.0	105.1	104.0	99.2	89.1	88.4	92.0
Materials	263	DVKB	89.5	89.8	94.0	98.5	100.0	102.0	109.2	117.7	121.3	119.6	112.6
Total	562	DVJZ	87.7	90.5	95.5	93.2	100.0	103.6	106.4	107.9	104.2	103.0	101.7

1 These sum to the total of 1000 for the production industries.

2 This does not include certain activities classified to intermediate goods industries: materials.

Source: Central Statistical Office

14.7 Gross domestic product by industry[1]

£ million

		1981	1982	1983	1984	1985	1986	1987	1988	1989	1990	1991
Agriculture, forestry and fishing	CAIY	4 839	5 508	5 346	6 456	5 941	6 565	6 918	7 008	8 139	8 753	8 772
Energy and water supply[2]	CAIZ	23 521	26 127	30 100	29 662	32 966	24 386	25 266	23 122	23 771	25 456	28 273
Manufacturing	CAJA	54 826	59 472	62 151	65 975	72 538	77 638	82 868	92 368	99 702	105 808	104 283
Construction	CAJB	13 027	14 100	15 733	17 183	18 399	20 718	24 083	28 988	32 084	35 616	33 686
Distribution; hotels and catering; repairs	CAJC	27 469	30 356	33 409	36 743	41 376	46 435	50 557	58 510	64 651	71 865	73 024
Transport and communication	GIYX	16 182	17 481	18 530	20 433	21 799	23 601	25 968	28 465	31 073	33 487	34 755
Banking, finance, insurance, business services and leasing	CAJF	25 013	28 722	34 608	36 726	43 816	51 611	59 511	67 351	82 776	87 151	88 179
Ownership of dwellings	CAJG	13 895	15 044	15 945	16 776	18 172	19 490	20 988	23 180	25 915	30 254	34 839
Public administration, national defence and compulsory social security	CAJH	16 287	17 418	18 875	20 251	21 463	23 062	24 972	27 103	28 447	31 647	34 786
Education and health services	CAJI	20 618	21 297	23 337	24 719	26 627	30 030	33 179	37 555	41 156	44 815	49 643
Other services[2]	CAJJ	12 039	13 344	15 189	16 973	18 629	20 627	23 286	26 836	29 474	30 431	33 915
Total		227 716	248 869	273 223	291 897	321 726	344 163	377 596	420 486	467 188	505 283	524 155
less Adjustment for financial services	GIJI	9 705	11 147	11 893	12 490	13 825	16 033	16 997	19 359	26 052	26 159	27 171
Statistical discrepancy (income adjustment)	GIXQ	744	509	−247	1 351	–	–	–	–	–	328	17
Gross domestic product	CAOM	218 755	238 231	261 083	280 758	307 901	328 130	360 599	401 127	441 136	479 452	497 001

1 The contribution of each industry to the gross domestic product before providing for depreciation but after providing for stock appreciation.

2 Comprising classes 92, 94, 96 and 00 of the Standard Industrial Classification, Revised 1980.

Source: Central Statistical Office

National Income

14.8 Gross national product by category of expenditure at 1985 prices[1]

£ million at 1985 prices

		1981	1982	1983	1984	1985	1986	1987	1988	1989	1990	1991
At 1985 market prices												
Consumers' expenditure	CCBH	196 011	197 980	206 932	210 959	218 947	232 996	245 823	264 096	272 917	274 744	269 033
General government final consumption	DJCZ	71 086	71 672	73 089	73 792	73 805	75 106	76 034	76 486	77 184	79 689	81 933
of which: Central Government	DJDK	44 108	44 421	45 281	45 741	45 879	46 684	46 753	46 942	47 365	48 627	49 819
Local authorities	DJDL	26 976	27 228	27 808	28 051	27 926	28 422	29 281	29 544	29 819	31 062	32 114
Gross domestic fixed capital formation	DFDM	48 298	50 915	53 476	58 034	60 353	61 813	67 753	77 395	82 997	80 464	72 462
Value of physical increase in stocks and work in progress	DHBK	−3 200	−1 281	1 357	1 084	821	737	1 158	4 010	2 657	−1 110	−3 507
Total domestic expenditure	DIEL	311 634	319 028	334 854	343 869	353 926	370 652	390 768	421 987	435 755	433 787	419 921
Exports of goods and services	DJCV	88 064	88 798	90 589	96 525	102 208	107 052	113 094	112 989	117 256	123 049	123 386
of which: Goods	CGTG	64 956	66 789	68 344	73 887	77 991	81 289	85 516	87 027	90 950	96 877	98 496
Services	CGTH	23 213	22 017	22 245	22 638	24 217	25 763	27 578	25 962	26 306	26 172	24 890
Total final expenditure	DJDA	399 644	407 791	425 443	440 394	456 134	477 704	503 862	534 976	553 011	556 836	543 307
less Imports of goods and services[2]	−DJCY	−78 522	−82 348	−87 709	−96 394	−98 866	−105 662	−113 916	−127 845	−137 281	−138 720	−134 428
of which: Goods	−CGTC	−61 531	−64 983	−70 789	−78 839	−81 336	−87 326	−93 782	−105 871	−114 277	−115 628	−112 365
Services	−CGTD	−16 996	−17 369	−16 920	−17 555	−17 530	−18 336	−20 134	−21 974	−23 004	−23 092	−22 063
Statistical discrepancy[3] (expenditure adjustment)	GIXS	−1 904	−815	−1 231	348	−	−	−	−	−	−207	−314
Gross domestic product[4]	CAOO	319 193	324 622	336 503	344 348	357 268	372 042	389 946	407 131	415 730	417 909	408 565
Net property income from abroad	DIEQ	1 627	1 774	3 203	4 520	2 560	5 200	3 823	4 531	3 362	1 966	314
Gross national product (average estimate)[4]	GIXX	320 826	326 402	339 706	348 868	359 828	377 242	393 769	411 662	419 092	419 875	408 879
At 1985 factor cost												
Gross domestic product at market prices	CAOO	319 193	324 622	336 503	344 348	357 268	372 042	389 946	407 131	415 730	417 909	408 565
less Factor cost adjustment[5]	−DJCU	−44 246	−44 895	−46 355	−48 347	−49 367	−52 312	−55 539	−57 727	−59 032	−58 929	−58 262
Gross domestic product at factor cost	CAOP	274 964	279 738	290 148	296 001	307 901	319 730	334 407	349 404	356 698	358 980	350 303
Net property income from abroad	DIEQ	1 627	1 774	3 203	4 520	2 560	5 200	3 823	4 531	3 362	1 966	314
Gross national product at factor cost	GIXY	276 608	281 528	293 351	300 521	310 461	324 930	338 230	353 935	360 060	360 946	350 617
less Capital consumption	−EXDI	−37 625	−38 744	−39 872	−40 916	−41 883	−42 552	−43 290	−44 383	−44 531	−45 470	−47 211
Net national product at factor cost "National income"	GIXZ	238 981	242 749	253 479	259 605	268 578	282 378	294 940	309 552	315 529	315 476	303 406

1 For the years before 1983, totals differ from the sum of their components.
2 Excluding taxes on expenditure levied on imports.
3 The difference between Gross domestic product and the total of its expenditure components at 1985 prices.
4 Including taxes on expenditure levied on imports.
5 This represents taxes on expenditure *less* subsidies valued at constant rates.

Source: Central Statistical Office

National Income

14.9 Consumers' expenditure at current market prices: classified by function

£ million

		1981	1982	1983	1984	1985	1986	1987	1988	1989	1990	1991
Food (household expenditure):												
Bread	CCXU	1 341	1 381	1 422	1 466	1 542	1 684	1 739	1 875	1 938	1 967	1 967
Cakes and biscuits	CCXV	1 146	1 225	1 305	1 350	1 420	1 489	1 592	1 716	1 831	1 978	2 085
Other cereals	CCXW	939	992	1 041	1 137	1 203	1 369	1 495	1 645	1 820	2 018	2 282
Meat and bacon	CDCJ	6 851	7 466	7 469	7 554	7 898	8 084	8 452	8 797	9 508	9 832	9 941
Fish	CDCK	782	821	921	946	1 055	1 179	1 229	1 372	1 519	1 594	1 671
Milk, cheese and eggs	CDCL	3 799	3 993	4 135	4 229	4 385	4 519	4 737	4 956	5 211	5 505	5 805
Oils and fats	CDCM	949	955	962	1 003	1 041	1 011	948	985	1 030	1 035	1 043
Fruit	CDCN	1 337	1 381	1 575	1 572	1 666	1 897	2 029	2 182	2 329	2 710	2 931
Potatoes	CDCO	897	1 052	1 186	1 356	1 211	1 349	1 553	1 539	1 714	1 889	2 045
Vegetables	CDCP	1 779	1 811	2 061	2 146	2 328	2 560	2 753	3 023	3 229	3 497	3 807
Sugar	CDCQ	357	362	374	358	331	315	317	325	317	320	333
Confectionery	CCIH	1 953	2 129	2 242	2 460	2 691	2 790	2 956	3 177	3 326	3 548	3 824
Coffee, tea and cocoa	CDCU	762	771	920	1 085	1 179	1 217	1 190	1 207	1 233	1 239	1 315
Soft drinks	CDCV	1 202	1 254	1 460	1 580	1 697	1 962	2 222	2 499	2 838	3 202	3 345
Other manufactured food	CDCW	852	897	988	1 032	1 010	1 136	1 217	1 289	1 421	1 535	1 659
Total	CCDW	24 946	26 490	28 061	29 274	30 657	32 561	34 429	36 587	39 264	41 869	44 053
Alcoholic drink:												
Beer	CCDX	5 971	6 450	7 138	7 734	8 416	8 902	9 398	10 039	10 677	11 745	12 775
Spirits	CDCX	2 908	3 003	3 265	3 471	3 831	3 947	4 152	4 564	4 632	5 013	5 354
Wine, cider and perry	CDCY	2 273	2 550	2 867	3 111	3 404	3 555	3 901	4 151	4 500	4 980	5 426
Total	CDCZ	11 152	12 003	13 270	14 316	15 651	16 404	17 451	18 754	19 809	21 738	23 555
Tobacco:												
Cigarettes	CDDA	4 762	5 048	5 352	5 739	6 112	6 552	6 729	7 001	7 223	7 702	8 661
Other	CDDB	753	833	857	883	894	919	924	944	952	981	1 085
Total	CCDZ	5 515	5 881	6 209	6 622	7 006	7 471	7 653	7 945	8 175	8 683	9 746
Clothing and footwear:												
Men's and boys' wear	CDDC	2 751	2 933	3 274	3 605	4 108	4 692	4 950	5 324	5 477	5 629	5 493
Women's, girls' and infants' wear	CDDD	5 562	5 924	6 550	7 051	8 024	8 971	9 649	10 500	11 066	11 567	11 816
Footwear	CCEB	1 842	2 068	2 296	2 512	2 780	2 998	3 085	3 210	3 400	3 679	3 725
Total	CDDE	10 155	10 925	12 120	13 168	14 912	16 661	17 684	19 034	19 943	20 875	21 034
Housing:												
Rents, rates and water charges:												
Imputed rent of owner-occupied dwellings	CDDF	9 114	10 160	11 264	11 863	12 880	13 993	15 280	17 272	19 633	23 251	26 995
Other rents	CDDG	4 998	5 989	6 454	6 663	7 154	7 670	8 231	8 664	9 399	10 719	12 251
Rates, sewerage and water charges[1]	CDDH	5 446	6 409	6 339	6 688	7 348	8 324	9 236	10 486	11 207	4 925	3 312
Maintenance, etc by occupiers:												
Do-it-yourself goods	CDDI	1 800	1 927	2 230	2 459	2 822	3 363	3 626	4 109	4 371	4 303	4 598
Contractors' charges and insurance	CDDJ	1 335	1 573	1 758	1 930	2 395	2 823	3 427	4 019	4 319	4 395	4 458
Total	CDDK	22 693	26 058	28 045	29 603	32 599	36 173	39 800	44 550	48 929	47 593	51 614
Fuel and power:												
Electricity	CDDL	3 973	4 264	4 450	4 564	4 910	5 180	5 210	5 412	5 878	6 280	7 260
Gas	CDDM	2 458	3 063	3 530	3 664	4 034	4 382	4 467	4 562	4 454	4 892	5 777
Coal and coke	CDDN	789	829	838	759	1 016	892	812	806	736	657	707
Other	CDDO	507	540	530	505	600	431	416	335	391	492	528
Total	CDDP	7 727	8 696	9 348	9 492	10 560	10 885	10 905	11 115	11 459	12 321	14 272
Household goods and services:												
Furniture, pictures, etc.	CDDQ	2 420	2 522	2 677	2 697	2 847	3 065	3 435	4 195	4 368	4 212	4 316
Carpets and other floor coverings	CDDR	1 068	1 093	1 206	1 274	1 346	1 449	1 624	1 985	2 066	1 993	2 044
Major appliances	CDDS	2 128	2 356	2 778	2 947	3 180	3 584	4 000	4 380	4 687	4 907	5 135
Textiles and soft furnishings	CDDT	1 145	1 142	1 202	1 227	1 414	1 624	1 777	1 977	2 055	2 085	2 191
Hardware	CDDU	1 325	1 383	1 481	1 639	1 882	2 243	2 420	2 743	2 919	2 874	3 073
Cleaning materials; matches	CDDV	886	970	1 050	1 142	1 243	1 317	1 402	1 571	1 799	1 903	2 049
Household and domestic services	CDDW	1 550	1 638	1 737	1 935	2 196	2 483	2 915	3 261	3 711	3 933	3 988
Total	CDDX	10 522	11 104	12 131	12 861	14 108	15 765	17 573	20 112	21 605	21 907	22 796

[1] Rates, sewerage and water charges are affected by the introduction of the community charge in Scotland from April 1989 and in England and Wales from April 1990. The community charge is not classified as a tax on expenditure and is not therefore part of consumers' expenditure.

Source: Central Statistical Office

National Income

14.9 Consumers' expenditure at current market prices: classified by function
continued

£ million

		1981	1982	1983	1984	1985	1986	1987	1988	1989	1990	1991
Transport and communication:												
Cars, motorcycles and other vehicles	CCDT	6 557	7 407	9 112	8 978	9 853	11 485	13 429	17 384	19 926	18 877	16 426
Petrol and oil	CDDY	5 695	6 331	6 872	7 481	8 018	7 358	7 773	8 228	9 059	10 172	10 793
Vehicle excise duty	CDDZ	840	1 022	1 184	1 289	1 482	1 566	1 612	1 693	1 793	1 837	1 879
Other running costs of vehicles	CDEA	4 755	5 055	5 424	6 103	7 142	8 295	9 671	10 992	11 914	13 641	14 038
Rail travel	CDEB	1 123	1 093	1 287	1 348	1 474	1 622	1 770	1 987	2 105	2 359	2 383
Buses and coaches	CDEC	1 572	1 697	1 789	1 833	1 971	1 952	2 048	2 181	2 341	2 469	2 606
Air travel	CDED	2 059	2 324	2 498	2 688	2 784	3 179	3 692	4 097	4 272	4 543	4 779
Other travel	CDEE	815	797	939	1 063	1 252	1 541	1 886	2 224	2 404	2 552	2 842
Postal services	CDEF	379	423	445	474	488	518	558	547	629	714	781
Telecommunications	CDEG	2 413	2 678	2 846	3 108	3 495	3 979	4 313	4 761	5 070	5 568	6 052
Total	CDEH	26 208	28 827	32 396	34 365	37 959	41 495	46 752	54 094	59 513	62 732	62 579
Recreation, entertainment and education:												
Radio, television and other durable goods	CDEI	1 769	2 061	2 477	2 742	2 940	3 253	3 750	4 232	4 296	4 257	4 347
Television and video hire charges, licence fees and repairs	CDEJ	1 732	2 034	2 305	2 353	2 550	2 817	2 725	2 958	3 162	3 234	3 363
Sports goods, toys, games and camping equipment	CDEK	1 339	1 454	1 638	1 833	2 053	2 329	2 572	2 797	3 156	3 560	3 557
Other recreational goods	CDEL	2 441	2 656	2 802	3 061	3 418	3 847	4 442	5 086	5 865	6 454	6 668
Betting and gaming	CDEM	1 626	1 776	1 842	1 972	2 120	2 253	2 492	2 646	2 881	3 108	3 134
Other recreational and entertainment services	CDEN	1 778	1 761	1 905	2 117	2 347	2 767	3 089	3 786	4 317	4 915	5 033
Books	CDEO	531	556	620	645	755	887	1 004	1 141	1 247	1 414	1 502
Newspapers and magazines	CDEP	1 686	1 907	1 967	2 118	2 309	2 426	2 638	2 793	3 025	3 261	3 303
Education	CDEQ	1 337	1 442	1 432	1 524	1 638	1 785	1 959	2 185	2 620	3 255	4 008
Total	CDER	14 239	15 647	16 988	18 365	20 130	22 364	24 671	27 624	30 569	33 458	34 915
Other goods and services:												
Pharmaceutical products and medical equipment	CDES	689	787	904	1 080	1 190	1 365	1 377	1 587	1 769	1 891	2 030
National health service payments and other medical expenses	CDET	857	1 055	1 214	1 259	1 427	1 652	1 877	2 106	2 443	2 856	3 403
Toilet articles; perfumery	CDEU	1 567	1 803	1 979	2 240	2 488	2 876	3 279	3 835	4 280	4 623	4 973
Hairdressing and beauty care	CDEV	860	910	1 021	1 153	1 300	1 425	1 596	1 733	1 839	1 979	2 130
Jewellery, silverware, watches and clocks	CDEW	1 094	1 169	1 281	1 398	1 502	1 632	1 853	2 060	2 374	2 363	2 226
Other goods	CDEX	1 300	1 458	1 610	1 795	1 978	2 201	2 503	3 019	3 528	3 910	4 169
Catering (meals and accommodation)	CDEY	8 820	9 461	10 928	12 509	13 875	16 195	18 307	22 942	26 027	29 398	31 049
Administrative costs of life assurance and pension schemes	CDEZ	2 092	2 475	2 935	3 407	3 806	4 884	6 277	8 389	9 365	10 846	11 803
Other services	CDFA	2 088	2 516	3 230	3 727	4 286	5 605	7 076	7 919	9 422	10 302	9 219
Total	CDFB	19 367	21 634	25 102	28 568	31 852	37 835	44 145	53 590	61 047	68 168	71 002
Total household and tourist expenditure in the United Kingdom	CDFC	152 524	167 265	183 670	196 634	215 434	237 614	261 063	293 405	320 313	339 344	355 566
less Expenditure by foreign tourists, etc in the United Kingdom	CDFD	–3 513	–3 792	–4 661	–5 336	–6 276	–6 455	–7 217	–7 172	–8 026	–8 878	–8 207
Household expenditure abroad	CDFE	3 131	3 483	3 855	4 275	4 440	5 651	6 702	7 605	8 668	9 052	8 978
Total household expenditure on goods and services	CDFF	152 142	166 956	182 864	195 573	213 598	236 810	260 548	293 838	320 955	339 518	356 337
Final expenditure by private non-profit making bodies	CDFG	3 270	3 694	4 164	4 688	5 349	6 220	6 975	8 219	9 577	10 893	11 516
Total consumers' expenditure	AIIK	155 412	170 650	187 028	200 261	218 947	243 030	267 523	302 057	330 532	350 411	367 853

Source: Central Statistical Office

National Income

14.10 Consumers' expenditure at 1985 market prices: classified by function [1]

£ million at 1985 prices

		1981	1982	1983	1984	1985	1986	1987	1988	1989	1990	1991
Food (household expenditure):												
Bread	CCXX	1 512	1 497	1 494	1 507	1 542	1 551	1 529	1 563	1 527	1 461	1 357
Cakes and biscuits	CCXY	1 405	1 441	1 455	1 426	1 420	1 457	1 496	1 575	1 576	1 578	1 546
Other cereals	CCXZ	1 198	1 171	1 189	1 218	1 203	1 312	1 377	1 450	1 513	1 564	1 645
Meat and bacon	CCFG	8 354	8 472	8 079	7 791	7 898	7 974	8 152	8 294	8 395	7 988	7 981
Fish	CCFH	1 023	1 024	1 057	1 034	1 055	1 092	1 039	1 138	1 229	1 166	1 144
Milk, cheese and eggs	CCFI	4 527	4 455	4 522	4 433	4 385	4 365	4 380	4 372	4 312	4 247	4 279
Oils and fats	CCFJ	1 139	1 095	1 103	1 051	1 041	1 056	1 044	1 037	1 017	965	933
Fruit	CCFK	1 800	1 705	1 798	1 696	1 666	1 871	2 028	2 106	2 249	2 324	2 265
Potatoes	CCFL	1 015	1 037	1 115	1 111	1 211	1 113	1 179	1 172	1 189	1 211	1 235
Vegetables	CCFM	2 111	2 053	2 270	2 229	2 328	2 574	2 611	2 793	2 881	2 888	3 046
Sugar	CCFN	434	403	384	359	331	314	303	290	266	248	239
Confectionery	CCIJ	2 343	2 488	2 535	2 633	2 691	2 597	2 683	2 809	2 842	2 928	2 952
Coffee, tea and cocoa	CCFP	1 237	1 222	1 270	1 200	1 179	1 190	1 177	1 187	1 156	1 111	1 126
Soft drinks	CCFQ	1 268	1 346	1 545	1 608	1 697	1 969	2 171	2 164	2 353	2 431	2 441
Other manufactured food	CCFR	921	921	985	980	1 010	1 106	1 155	1 175	1 227	1 227	1 220
Total	CCBM	30 217	30 299	30 801	30 276	30 657	31 541	32 324	33 125	33 732	33 337	33 409
Alcoholic drink:												
Beer	CCBN	8 561	8 261	8 412	8 447	8 416	8 406	8 483	8 540	8 532	8 515	8 211
Spirits	CCFS	3 693	3 503	3 597	3 641	3 831	3 815	3 880	4 098	3 961	3 902	3 681
Wine, cider and perry	CCFT	2 692	2 780	3 050	3 275	3 404	3 478	3 661	3 763	3 884	3 942	3 935
Total	CCFU	14 875	14 503	15 059	15 363	15 651	15 699	16 024	16 401	16 377	16 359	15 827
Tobacco:												
Cigarettes	CCFV	7 109	6 525	6 480	6 259	6 112	5 940	5 902	5 935	5 953	5 942	5 831
Other	CCFW	1 059	1 014	976	942	894	873	861	845	827	772	738
Total	CCBP	8 167	7 541	7 456	7 201	7 006	6 813	6 763	6 780	6 780	6 714	6 569
Clothing and footwear:												
Men's and boys' wear	CCFX	3 035	3 202	3 456	3 793	4 108	4 578	4 718	4 868	4 751	4 661	4 349
Women's, girls' and infants' wear	CCFY	6 564	6 669	7 096	7 328	8 024	8 749	9 313	9 849	9 889	9 966	10 061
Footwear	CCBR	2 195	2 358	2 519	2 646	2 780	2 893	2 902	2 904	2 926	2 989	2 895
Total	FCCB	11 788	12 227	13 071	13 767	14 912	16 220	16 933	17 621	17 566	17 616	17 305
Housing:												
Rents, rates and water charges:												
Imputed rent of owner-occupied dwellings	CCFZ	11 490	11 899	12 400	12 646	12 880	13 198	13 529	14 019	14 442	14 853	15 216
Other rents	CCGA	7 377	7 201	7 140	7 131	7 154	7 128	7 080	6 859	6 720	6 611	6 552
Rates, sewerage and water charges	CCGB	6 998	7 093	7 167	7 256	7 348	7 445	7 546	7 655	7 766	7 878	7 992
Maintenance, etc by occupiers:												
Do-it-yourself goods	CCGC	2 240	2 234	2 468	2 597	2 822	3 211	3 365	3 650	3 693	3 372	3 263
Contractors' charges and insurance	CCGD	1 807	1 886	1 969	2 029	2 395	2 673	3 236	3 517	3 529	3 477	3 111
Total	CCGE	29 756	30 229	31 144	31 659	32 599	33 655	34 756	35 700	36 150	36 191	36 134
Fuel and power:												
Electricity	CCGF	4 728	4 618	4 628	4 709	4 910	5 066	5 118	5 047	5 106	5 052	5 316
Gas	CCGG	3 704	3 712	3 788	3 809	4 034	4 286	4 404	4 499	4 195	4 324	4 762
Coal and coke	CCGH	1 042	1 023	955	794	1 016	860	782	765	688	596	633
Other	CCGI	754	685	545	539	600	586	626	557	575	601	667
Total	CCGJ	10 246	10 047	9 916	9 851	10 560	10 798	10 930	10 868	10 564	10 573	11 378
Household goods and services:												
Furniture, pictures, etc.	CCGK	2 797	2 827	2 912	2 787	2 847	2 945	3 218	3 794	3 773	3 445	3 327
Carpets and other floor coverings	CCGL	1 234	1 224	1 310	1 319	1 346	1 391	1 518	1 787	1 778	1 621	1 566
Major appliances	CCGM	2 341	2 501	2 859	3 021	3 180	3 564	3 976	4 161	4 412	4 528	4 532
Textiles and soft furnishings	CCGN	1 256	1 266	1 326	1 310	1 414	1 564	1 684	1 827	1 829	1 803	1 858
Hardware	CCGO	1 650	1 604	1 639	1 732	1 882	2 139	2 242	2 431	2 460	2 245	2 171
Cleaning materials; matches	CCGP	1 137	1 162	1 180	1 212	1 243	1 289	1 333	1 415	1 521	1 477	1 400
Household and domestic services	CCGQ	2 028	1 972	1 952	2 058	2 196	2 344	2 591	2 724	2 871	2 790	2 605
Total	CCGR	12 389	12 525	13 178	13 439	14 108	15 236	16 562	18 139	18 644	17 909	17 459

1 For the years before 1983, totals differ from the sum of their components.

Source: Central Statistical Office

National Income

14.10 Consumers' expenditure at 1985 market prices: classified by function [1]
continued

£ million at 1985 prices

		1981	1982	1983	1984	1985	1986	1987	1988	1989	1990	1991
Transport and communication:												
Cars, motorcycles and other vehicles	CCBJ	7 754	8 005	9 965	9 362	9 853	10 735	11 241	12 907	14 011	13 060	10 657
Petrol and oil	CCGS	7 096	7 369	7 504	7 904	8 018	8 501	8 837	9 484	9 793	10 043	9 953
Vehicle excise duty	CCGT	1 190	1 274	1 367	1 409	1 482	1 525	1 571	1 646	1 741	1 785	1 817
Other running costs of vehicles	CCGU	5 735	5 770	5 962	6 401	7 142	7 921	8 748	9 328	9 606	10 155	9 552
Rail travel	CCGV	1 344	1 257	1 402	1 452	1 474	1 545	1 605	1 686	1 625	1 676	1 571
Buses and coaches	CCGW	2 020	1 935	1 926	1 919	1 971	1 839	1 834	1 849	1 845	1 787	1 719
Air travel	CCGX	2 404	2 496	2 456	2 670	2 784	3 213	3 804	4 282	4 600	4 661	4 529
Other travel	CCGY	1 063	981	1 063	1 132	1 252	1 488	1 752	1 933	1 966	1 954	2 031
Postal services	CCGZ	469	487	486	504	488	519	535	509	556	586	572
Telecommunications	CCHA	2 931	2 921	3 133	3 311	3 495	3 777	4 007	4 385	4 616	4 792	4 801
Total	CCHB	31 787	32 282	35 264	36 064	37 959	41 063	43 934	48 009	50 359	50 499	47 202
Recreation, entertainment and education:												
Radio, television and other durable goods	CCHC	1 668	1 975	2 402	2 772	2 940	3 465	4 126	4 839	4 978	4 910	5 126
Television and video hire charges, licence fees and repairs	CCHD	1 995	2 122	2 448	2 528	2 550	2 728	2 589	2 711	2 750	2 667	2 606
Sports goods, toys, games and camping equipment	CCHE	1 510	1 576	1 712	1 888	2 053	2 250	2 383	2 539	2 777	3 012	2 897
Other recreational goods	CCHF	2 917	3 058	3 105	3 183	3 418	3 717	4 258	4 822	5 391	5 683	5 493
Betting and gaming	CCHG	2 102	2 078	2 050	2 098	2 120	2 169	2 296	2 318	2 341	2 310	2 196
Other recreational and entertainment services	CCHH	2 351	2 146	2 137	2 237	2 347	2 472	2 632	2 917	3 047	3 143	2 847
Books	CCHI	909	846	788	717	754	864	896	971	976	1 033	1 023
Newspapers and magazines	CCHJ	2 451	2 347	2 269	2 317	2 310	2 340	2 390	2 354	2 390	2 388	2 288
Education	CCHK	1 883	1 740	1 636	1 623	1 638	1 640	1 652	1 671	1 851	2 109	2 409
Total	CCHL	17 225	17 595	18 547	19 363	20 130	21 645	23 222	25 142	26 501	27 255	26 885
Other goods and services:												
Pharmaceutical products and medical equipment	CCHM	917	953	1 021	1 151	1 190	1 285	1 242	1 356	1 406	1 392	1 371
National health service payments and other medical expenses	CCHN	1 103	1 237	1 349	1 327	1 427	1 602	1 717	1 808	1 958	2 143	2 381
Toilet articles; perfumery	CCHO	2 054	2 176	2 269	2 434	2 488	2 744	3 030	3 393	3 555	3 532	3 500
Hairdressing and beauty care	CCHP	1 169	1 120	1 171	1 236	1 300	1 339	1 408	1 420	1 395	1 376	1 339
Jewellery, silverware, watches and clocks	CCHQ	1 367	1 499	1 392	1 495	1 502	1 582	1 758	1 950	2 229	2 188	2 028
Other goods	CCHR	1 839	1 908	1 947	1 952	1 978	2 083	2 286	2 617	2 934	3 086	3 098
Catering (meals and accommodation)	CCHS	12 261	12 002	12 710	13 309	13 875	15 208	16 089	18 674	19 914	20 742	20 028
Administrative costs of life assurance and pension schemes	CCHT	2 630	2 864	3 245	3 584	3 806	4 519	5 355	6 748	6 993	7 493	7 790
Other services	CCHU	3 095	3 275	3 765	3 915	4 286	5 112	5 763	6 434	7 070	7 440	6 193
Total	CCHV	26 425	27 080	28 869	30 403	31 852	35 474	38 648	44 400	47 454	49 392	47 728
Total household and tourist expenditure in the United Kingdom	CCHW	192 358	194 071	203 305	207 386	215 434	228 144	240 096	256 185	264 127	265 845	259 896
less Expenditure by foreign tourists, etc in the United Kingdom	CCHX	−4 646	−4 602	−5 323	−5 722	−6 276	−6 053	−6 381	−5 886	−6 127	−6 227	−5 385
Household expenditure abroad	CCHY	4 277	4 267	4 344	4 354	4 440	5 064	5 836	6 744	7 109	6 862	6 523
Total household expenditure on goods and services	CCHZ	191 952	193 697	202 326	206 018	213 598	227 155	239 551	257 043	265 109	266 480	261 034
Final expenditure by private non-profit making bodies	CCIA	4 060	4 283	4 606	4 941	5 349	5 841	6 272	7 053	7 808	8 264	7 999
Total consumers' expenditure	CCBH	196 011	197 980	206 932	210 959	218 947	232 996	245 823	264 096	272 917	274 744	269 033

[1] See footnote on previous page.

Source: Central Statistical Office

National Income

14.11 Consumers' expenditure at current market prices: classified by commodity

£ million

		1981	1982	1983	1984	1985	1986	1987	1988	1989	1990	1991
Durable goods:												
Cars, motorcycles and other vehicles	CCDT	6 557	7 407	9 112	8 978	9 853	11 485	13 429	17 384	19 926	18 877	16 426
Furniture and floor coverings	CCDU	3 488	3 615	3 883	3 971	4 193	4 514	5 059	6 180	6 434	6 205	6 360
Other durable goods	CCDV	3 897	4 417	5 255	5 689	6 120	6 837	7 750	8 612	8 983	9 164	9 482
Total	AIIL	13 942	15 439	18 250	18 638	20 166	22 836	26 238	32 176	35 343	34 246	32 268
Other goods:												
Food (household expenditure)	CCDW	24 946	26 490	28 061	29 274	30 657	32 561	34 429	36 587	39 264	41 869	44 053
Beer	CCDX	5 971	6 450	7 138	7 734	8 416	8 902	9 398	10 039	10 677	11 745	12 775
Other alcoholic drink	CCDY	5 181	5 553	6 132	6 582	7 235	7 502	8 053	8 715	9 132	9 993	10 780
Tobacco	CCDZ	5 515	5 881	6 209	6 622	7 006	7 471	7 653	7 945	8 175	8 683	9 746
Clothing other than footwear	CCEA	8 313	8 857	9 824	10 656	12 132	13 663	14 599	15 824	16 543	17 196	17 309
Footwear	CCEB	1 842	2 068	2 296	2 512	2 780	2 998	3 085	3 210	3 400	3 679	3 725
Energy products	CCEC	13 422	15 027	16 220	16 973	18 578	18 243	18 678	19 343	20 518	22 493	25 065
Other goods	CCED	15 803	17 212	18 764	20 637	23 054	26 110	28 893	32 718	36 388	38 641	40 339
Services:												
Rents, rates and water charges[1]	CCEE	19 558	22 558	24 057	25 214	27 382	29 987	32 747	36 422	40 239	38 895	42 558
Other services[2]	CCEF	40 919	45 115	50 077	55 419	61 541	72 757	83 750	99 078	110 853	122 971	129 235
Total consumers' expenditure	AIIK	155 412	170 650	187 028	200 261	218 947	243 030	267 523	302 057	330 532	350 411	367 853

1 See footnote on page 244.

2 Including the adjustments for international travel, etc and final expenditure by private non-profit-making bodies serving persons.

Source: Central Statistical Office

14.12 Consumers' expenditure at 1985 market prices: classified by commodity[1]

£ million at 1985 prices

		1981	1982	1983	1984	1985	1986	1987	1988	1989	1990	1991
Durable goods:												
Cars, motorcycles and other vehicles	CCBJ	7 754	8 005	9 965	9 362	9 853	10 735	11 241	12 907	14 011	13 060	10 657
Furniture and floor coverings	CCBK	4 031	4 051	4 222	4 106	4 193	4 336	4 736	5 581	5 551	5 066	4 893
Other durable goods	CCBL	3 973	4 461	5 261	5 793	6 120	7 029	8 102	9 000	9 390	9 438	9 658
Total	CCBI	15 707	16 504	19 448	19 261	20 166	22 100	24 079	27 488	28 952	27 564	25 208
Other goods:												
Food (household expenditure)	CCBM	30 217	30 299	30 801	30 276	30 657	31 541	32 324	33 125	33 732	33 337	33 409
Beer	CCBN	8 561	8 261	8 412	8 447	8 416	8 406	8 483	8 540	8 532	8 515	8 211
Other alcoholic drink	CCBO	6 363	6 273	6 647	6 916	7 235	7 293	7 541	7 861	7 845	7 844	7 616
Tobacco	CCBP	8 167	7 541	7 456	7 201	7 006	6 813	6 763	6 780	6 780	6 714	6 569
Clothing other than footwear	CCBQ	9 593	9 869	10 552	11 121	12 132	13 327	14 031	14 717	14 640	14 627	14 410
Footwear	CCBR	2 195	2 358	2 519	2 646	2 780	2 893	2 902	2 904	2 926	2 989	2 895
Energy products	CCBS	17 319	17 410	17 420	17 755	18 578	19 299	19 767	20 352	20 357	20 616	21 331
Other goods	CCCK	20 128	20 586	21 116	21 988	23 054	25 068	26 867	29 325	31 161	31 211	30 390
Services:												
Rents, rates and water charges	CCCL	25 728	26 134	26 707	27 033	27 382	27 771	28 155	28 533	28 928	29 342	29 760
Other services[2]	CCBV	53 164	53 476	55 854	58 315	61 541	68 485	74 911	84 471	89 064	91 985	89 234
Total consumers' expenditure	CCBH	196 011	197 980	206 932	210 959	218 947	232 996	245 823	264 096	272 917	274 744	269 033

1 For the years before 1983, totals differ from the sum of their components.

2 Including the adjustments for international travel, etc. and final expenditure by private non-profit-making bodies serving persons.

Source: Central Statistical Office

National Income

14.13 National accounts aggregates: national disposable income and volume indices

		1981	1982	1983	1984	1985	1986	1987	1988	1989	1990	1991
National disposable income (£ million)												
Gross national disposable income at current market prices[1]	GIBG	254 555	278 606	305 552	328 412	356 717	387 707	423 854	472 247	514 234	547 547	573 125
Real national disposable income at 1985 market prices	GIGS	318 462	323 855	337 882	346 087	356 717	370 721	386 203	405 413	414 852	417 587	413 556
Volume indices at 1985 prices (1985=100)												
At market prices												
Gross domestic product	FNAO	89.4	90.9	94.2	96.4	100.0	104.1	109.1	114.0	116.4	117.0	114.4
Gross national product	GIBJ	89.2	90.7	94.4	97.0	100.0	104.8	109.4	114.4	116.5	116.7	113.6
Gross national disposable income ("RNDI")	DJCR	89.3	90.8	94.7	97.0	100.0	103.9	108.3	113.7	116.3	117.1	115.9
At factor cost												
Gross domestic product	DJDD	89.3	90.9	94.2	96.1	100.0	103.8	108.6	113.5	115.8	116.6	113.8
Gross national product	GIBH	89.1	90.7	94.5	96.8	100.0	104.7	108.9	114.0	116.0	116.3	112.9
Net national product ("National income")	GIBI	89.0	90.4	94.4	96.7	100.0	105.1	109.8	115.3	117.5	117.5	113.0
Categories of expenditure:												
At market prices												
Consumers' expenditure	GIBK	89.5	90.4	94.5	96.4	100.0	106.4	112.3	120.6	124.6	125.5	122.9
General government final consumption	GIBL	96.3	97.1	99.0	100.0	100.0	101.8	103.0	103.6	104.6	108.0	111.0
of which: Central Government	GIBM	96.1	96.8	98.7	99.7	100.0	101.8	101.9	102.3	103.2	106.0	108.6
Local authorities	GIBN	96.6	97.5	99.6	100.4	100.0	101.8	104.9	105.8	106.8	111.2	115.0
Gross domestic fixed capital formation	GIBO	80.0	84.4	88.6	96.2	100.0	102.4	112.3	128.2	137.5	133.3	120.1
Total domestic expenditure	GIBP	88.1	90.1	94.6	97.2	100.0	104.7	110.4	119.2	123.1	122.6	118.6
Exports of goods and services	HHCX	86.2	86.9	88.6	94.4	100.0	104.7	110.7	110.6	114.7	120.4	120.7
of which: Goods	CGTR	83.3	85.6	87.6	94.7	100.0	104.2	109.7	111.6	116.6	124.2	126.3
Services	CGSI	95.9	90.9	91.9	93.5	100.0	106.4	113.9	107.3	108.7	108.1	102.8
Total final expenditure	GIBT	87.6	89.4	93.3	96.5	100.0	104.7	110.5	117.3	121.2	122.1	119.1
Imports of goods and services	HHCY	79.4	83.3	88.7	97.5	100.0	106.9	115.2	129.3	138.8	140.3	136.0
of which: Goods	CGTS	75.6	79.9	87.0	96.9	100.0	107.4	115.3	130.1	140.5	142.1	138.1
Services	CGSP	97.0	99.1	96.5	100.1	100.0	104.6	114.9	125.3	131.1	131.6	125.8
Factor cost adjustment	GIBX	89.6	90.9	93.9	97.9	100.0	106.0	112.5	116.9	119.6	119.4	118.0

1 This series is affected by the abolition of domestic rates and the introduction of the community charge.

Source: Central Statistical Office

National Income

14.14 Value of physical increase in stocks and work in progress

£ million

		1981	1982	1983	1984	1985	1986	1987	1988	1989	1990	1991
At current prices												
Energy and water supply		−446	−15	199	−661	9	−282	−185	−19	310	−495	175
Manufacturing[1]	DHBA	−1 565	−1 291	129	1 010	−443	−419	−262	979	−134	−1 953	−3 920
Materials and fuels	DHCO	−1 033	−543	−259	323	139	−117	112	335	−31	−215	−1 040
Work in progress	DHDE	−42	−561	386	352	−667	−127	−252	164	−628	−1 674	−1 300
Finished goods	DHCT	−491	−187	1	335	86	−176	−123	480	524	−64	−1 580
Retail distribution	DHFZ	−20	9	144	512	403	927	1 120	1 348	657	124	−901
Wholesale distribution	DHFY	−607	14	267	1	−122	351	636	1 196	1 040	−426	−884
Other industries		−130	95	726	434	974	139	79	1 278	1 265	1 288	227
Total	DHBF	−2 768	−1 188	1 465	1 296	821	716	1 388	4 782	3 138	−1 462	−5 303
Revalued at 1985 prices												
Energy and water supply		−566	68	41	−985	9	−216	−210	−108	252	−506	250
Manufacturing[1]	DHBH	−1 989	−1 461	135	1 057	−443	−403	−221	887	−22	−1 495	−2 782
Materials and fuel	DHCU	−1 260	−618	−293	323	139	−106	103	315	−31	−195	−841
Work in progress	DHCW	−66	−651	423	381	−667	−123	−220	145	−439	−1 181	−929
Finished goods	DHCX	−606	−196	3	354	86	−174	−108	427	448	−119	−1 011
Retail distribution	DHKH	−18	27	147	540	403	906	1 039	1 142	553	111	−683
Wholesale distribution	DHKG	−730	94	274	24	−122	371	578	1 030	907	−360	−650
Other industries		−81	50	760	448	974	79	−28	1 059	967	1 140	358
Total	DHBK	−3 200	−1 281	1 357	1 084	821	737	1 158	4 010	2 657	−1 110	−3 507

1 Differences between totals and the sum of constituent parts of manufacturing at 1985 prices for 1983 onwards and for all current prices are due to rounding. Differences between totals and components at 1985 prices before 1983 arise from the method of rebasing these years on to 1985 prices.

Source: Central Statistical Office

National Income

14.15 Gross domestic fixed capital formation

£ million

		1981	1982	1983	1984	1985	1986	1987	1988	1989	1990	1991
At current prices												
By type of asset												
Buses and coaches	DFKA	153	132	153	117	122	125	166	199	179	164	150
Other road vehicles	DFKB	2 971	3 710	3 676	4 302	4 970	5 329	6 754	7 677	8 603	8 016	6 552
Railway rolling stock	DFKC	136	123	101	75	106	95	126	187	242	377	367
Ships	GGBU	221	326	284	502	332	162	239	116	122	234	506
Aircraft	GGBV	365	–6	316	668	909	511	520	670	1 178	1 178	877
Plant and machinery[1]	DFCX	15 067	16 296	17 935	20 266	23 870	24 690	27 073	31 504	36 382	37 162	33 816
Dwellings	DFDK	8 138	8 920	10 447	11 718	11 854	13 622	15 274	19 354	20 986	19 906	16 645
Other new buildings and works	DFJL	12 471	13 386	13 306	14 646	15 218	16 514	19 874	24 694	31 189	34 736	32 366
By industry group												
Agriculture, forestry and fishing[1]	DFKI	1 040	1 299	1 429	1 464	1 181	1 196	1 265	1 420	1 485	1 368	1 199
Extraction of mineral oil and natural gas	DFDE	2 892	3 021	2 901	3 151	2 819	2 577	2 047	2 206	2 709	3 567	5 116
All other energy and water supply	DFEK	3 692	3 808	4 136	3 619	3 974	4 225	4 200	4 576	5 253	6 057	6 799
Manufacturing	DFDD	6 154	6 417	6 714	8 321	10 118	9 731	10 814	12 281	14 281	14 328	12 678
Construction	DFKK	464	583	626	573	626	609	763	1 142	1 111	965	..
Distribution, hotels and catering; repairs	DFDJ	3 453	3 880	4 033	4 929	5 739	6 269	7 687	9 456	9 468	8 951	..
Transport and communication	DFDI	3 656	3 522	4 100	5 142	5 867	5 674	6 840	8 152	9 601	9 154	..
Banking, finance, insurance business services and leasing	DFEL	4 673	5 160	5 262	6 023	7 133	8 206	11 537	15 162	20 199	21 357	..
Other services[4]	DFKP	5 360	6 277	6 570	7 354	8 070	8 939	9 599	10 652	13 788	16 120	15 391
Dwellings	DFDK	8 138	8 920	10 447	11 718	11 854	13 622	15 274	19 354	20 986	19 906	16 645
Transfer costs of land and buildings	DFBH	1 782	1 937	2 397	2 673	2 972	3 466	4 051	5 456	4 381	4 255	4 163
Total	DFDC	41 304	44 824	48 615	54 967	60 353	64 514	74 077	89 857	103 262	106 028	95 442

		1981	1982	1983	1984	1985	1986	1987	1988	1989	1990	1991
At 1985 prices[2]												
By type of asset												
Buses and coaches	DFKF	190	155	183	125	122	117	144	168	141	121	121
Other road vehicles	DFKG	3 808	4 338	4 223	4 659	4 970	4 922	5 725	6 115	6 415	5 534	4 208
Railway rolling stock, ships and aircraft	DFKH	901	530	771	1 317	1 347	730	779	830	1 221	1 367	1 355
Plant and machinery[1]	DFCY	18 269	18 478	19 401	21 227	23 870	24 250	25 943	29 855	33 591	32 739	29 361
Dwellings	DFDV	10 247	10 899	12 247	12 550	11 854	12 901	13 475	15 548	15 296	13 594	11 020
Other new buildings and works	DFKE	12 527	13 815	13 878	15 181	15 218	15 825	18 400	21 283	23 745	24 772	24 149
By industry group												
Agriculture, forestry and fishing[1]	DFKR	1 148	1 402	1 511	1 507	1 181	1 156	1 196	1 251	1 211	1 049	924
Extraction of mineral oil and natural gas	DFDO	3 196	3 283	3 086	3 260	2 819	2 486	1 928	1 941	2 165	2 713	4 027
All other energy and water supply	DFEN	4 276	4 253	4 435	3 779	3 974	4 105	3 975	4 096	4 348	4 700	5 244
Manufacturing	DFDN	7 672	7 482	7 410	8 823	10 118	9 423	10 048	11 198	12 395	11 759	10 347
Construction	DFKT	567	653	691	609	626	582	687	998	908	736	458
Distribution, hotels and catering; repairs	DFDU	4 024	4 351	4 427	5 237	5 739	5 956	6 995	8 360	7 812	6 998	6 938
Transport and communication	DFDT	4 338	3 993	4 524	5 423	5 867	5 478	6 281	7 228	8 128	7 430	7 321
Banking, finance, insurance business services and leasing	DFEO	4 756	5 239	5 417	6 203	7 133	7 985	10 819	13 822	17 275	17 216	12 261
Other services[4]	DFKY	5 744	6 685	6 955	7 668	8 070	8 673	9 062	9 357	10 871	11 932	11 674
Dwellings	DFDV	10 247	10 899	12 247	12 550	11 854	12 901	13 475	15 548	15 296	13 594	11 020
Transfer costs of land and buildings	DFDW	2 295	2 521	2 773	2 975	2 972	3 068	3 287	3 596	2 588	2 337	2 248
Total	DFDM	48 298	50 915	53 476	58 034	60 353	61 813	67 753	77 395	82 997	80 464	72 462

1 Including changes in the stock of breeding animals.
2 For the years before 1983, totals differ from the sum of their components due to the method of rebasing used. See Methodological notes in the *United Kingdom National Accounts, 1992* edition.
3 For explanation of unavailability of estimates for the year 1991 see Methodological notes in the *United Kingdom National Accounts, 1992* edition.
4 Comprising classes 91-99 of the Standard Industrial Classification Revised 1980.

Source: Central Statistical Office

14.16 Gross capital stock by industry at 1985 replacement cost[1]

£ billion at 1985 prices

		1981	1982	1983	1984	1985	1986	1987	1988	1989	1990	1991
Agriculture, forestry and fishing	EXED	29.3	29.6	29.9	30.2	30.2	30.1	30.1	30.2	30.2	30.1	28.5
Extraction of mineral oil and natural gas	EXEE	26.6	28.9	30.8	32.8	34.3	35.3	35.7	35.8	36.1	36.8	38.8
All other energy and water supply	EXEF	143.6	145.1	146.8	147.7	148.8	149.7	149.8	149.9	150.1	150.7	151.9
Manufacturing	EXEG	255.2	257.2	258.9	261.4	264.9	267.4	270.1	273.5	277.9	281.8	283.8
Construction	EXEH	15.6	15.8	15.9	15.8	15.9	15.9	15.9	16.3	16.6	16.8	..
Distribution, hotels and catering; repairs	EXEI	75.8	78.7	81.6	85.2	89.3	93.4	98.5	104.9	110.6	115.6	..
Transport	EXEJ	81.9	79.2	77.0	76.0	75.7	72.1	70.9	70.7	70.7	70.4	..
Communication	EXEK	38.0	39.1	40.2	41.5	42.4	43.9	45.9	47.9	50.2	51.9	..
Banking, finance, insurance, business, services and leasing	EXEL	75.7	80.3	84.9	90.1	96.0	102.7	111.9	123.8	138.8	153.8	..
Other services[2]	EXEM	202.3	207.6	213.1	219.3	225.8	232.8	240.1	247.5	256.5	266.6	..
Dwellings	EXEO	459.7	469.4	480.2	490.7	501.0	512.3	524.2	538.0	551.6	563.3	572.5
Total[3]	EXEP	1 403.6	1 430.8	1 459.4	1 490.8	1 524.2	1 555.9	1 593.2	1 638.5	1 689.3	1 737.6	1 777.7

1 For an account of the principles of valuation, see paragraphs 12.104-124 of *United Kingdom National Accounts: Sources and Methods*, Third edition. Figures relate to end of year. Assets are classified to industry on the basis of ownership, not use.

2 Comprising classes 91-99 of the Standard Industrial Classification Revised 1980.
3 Differences between totals and sums of components are due to rounding.

Source: Central Statistical Office

15 Personal Income, Expenditure and Wealth

Family Expenditure Survey *(Tables 15.3-15.5)*

The Family Expenditure Survey introduced in 1957, covers all types of private households in the United Kingdom. It is a continuous enquiry in which a total set sample of about 13 000 addresses is selected annually, from which an effective sample of some 10 400 households is obtained, of which about 70 per cent co-operate. The main purpose of the survey is to provide a source of the weighting pattern for the Index of Retail Prices and so it is primarily concerned with household expenditure on a wide range of goods and services. However, it does have several other important uses.

The income information the survey collects is basically to enable households to be classified into income groups and although most of the income information obtained is on a current basis, incomes from investment and self-employment are estimated over a twelve-month period. As income and expenditure figures relate to different periods, the difference between expenditure and income as measured in the survey should not be regarded as savings or dis-savings.

Although the survey is primarily concerned with the expenditure of private households, much additional information is collected about the characteristics of co-operating households. Consequently the survey provides a unique fund of important economic and social data.

Like all surveys based on a sample of the population, its results are subject to sampling error, and to some bias due to non-response. The sampling error is smallest in relation to the average expenditure of large groups of households or items purchased frequently when expenditure does not vary greatly between households. Conversely, it is largest in relation to small groups of households, and for items purchased infrequently for which expenditure varies considerably between households. However, comparison of the survey results over successive years justifies confidence in their reliability.

The results of the survey are published in an annual report, the latest being *Family Spending 1990* (HMSO). This includes a list of definitions used in the survey, items on which information is collected and a brief account of the field-work procedure.

15.1 Average incomes of households before and after taxes and benefits[1], 1989
United Kingdom

	Retired households[2]		Non-retired households								
	1 adult	2 or more adults	1 adult	2 adults	3 or more adults	1 adult with children[3]	2 adults with 1 child[3]	2 adults with children[3]	2 adults with 3 or more children[3]	3 or more adults with children[3]	All households
Number of households in the sample	1008	918	828	1578	633	313	620	793	347	372	7410
Average per household (£ per year)											
Original income	1870	4960	9080	17980	23130	3820	16560	19210	16740	20600	13110
Standard error[4]	130	240	280	350	520	400	470	510	820	670	160
Disposable income	3920	7690	7740	14810	19570	6270	14260	16410	15460	18410	12040
Standard error[4]	90	170	190	250	380	300	370	430	620	460	110
Post-tax income	3220	6090	6180	11920	15280	4880	11450	13360	12340	14380	9620
Standard error[4]	80	150	180	230	340	280	350	410	590	410	100

1 Original income is the total income in cash and kind of the household before the deduction of taxes or the addition of state benefits. The addition of cash benefits (retirement pensions, child benefit, etc) and the deduction of income tax, domestic rates and employees' national insurance contributions give disposable income. By further allowing for taxes paid on goods and services purchased, such as VAT, an estimate of 'post-tax' income is derived. These income figures are derived from estimates made by the Central Statistical Office, based largely on information from the Family Expenditure Survey, and published each year in *Economic Trends*.
2 A retired household is defined as one where the combined income of retired members amounts to at least half the total gross income of the household, where a retired person is defined as anyone who describes themselves as 'retired' or anyone over the minimum NI pension age describing themselves as 'unoccupied' or 'sick or injured but not intending to seek work'.
3 Children are defined as persons aged under 16 or aged between 16 and 18, unmarried and receiving non-advanced further education.
4 Standard error is a measure of the reliability of the average (or mean). It can be used when making inferences about the mean incomes of households in the whole country eg it is likely that disposible income for 1 adult retired households in the country as a whole is in the range £3 920 +/- (1.96 * £90) or £3 744 to £4 096 per year. The formula used to calculate the standard errors assumes that the co-operating households in the Family Expenditure Survey (FES) formed a simple random sample. The actual sample design of the FES is much more complicated.

Source: Central Statistical Office

Personal Incomes

15.2 Distribution of total incomes before and after tax
Years ended 5 April

Lower limit of range of income	1986/87 Annual Survey				Lower limit of range of income	1987/88 Annual Survey			
	Thousands	£ million				Thousands	£ million		
	Number of incomes	Total income before tax	Tax[5]	Total income after tax		Number of incomes	Total income before tax	Tax[5]	Total income after tax
All incomes[1,2,3,4]	22 200	241 000	42 800	198 000	All incomes[1,2,3,4]	22 500	261 000	45 300	216 000
Income before tax £					**Income before tax £**				
2 330	250	603	2	601	2 420	149	366	0	365
2 500	911	2 490	56	2 440	2 500	954	2 620	38	2 590
3 000	910	2 940	156	2 790	3 000	932	3 030	126	2 900
3 500	842	3 150	215	2 940	3 500	801	3 000	170	2 830
4 000	1 050	4 470	355	4 120	4 000	867	3 690	264	3 430
4 500	916	4 340	419	3 920	4 500	889	4 210	364	3 850
5 000	1 010	5 300	611	4 690	5 000	862	4 530	456	4 070
5 500	889	5 110	593	4 520	5 500	757	4 350	485	3 870
6 000	1 740	11 300	1 470	9 820	6 000	1 830	11 900	1 410	10 400
7 000	1 510	11 300	1 590	9 730	7 000	1 470	11 000	1 430	9 620
8 000	2 890	25 900	3 940	22 000	8 000	2 910	26 100	3 750	22 300
10 000	2 450	26 800	4 260	22 500	10 000	2 080	22 800	3 440	19 300
12 000	2 510	33 600	5 470	28 200	12 000	2 740	36 800	5 700	31 100
15 000	2 300	39 600	7 020	32 500	15 000	2 660	45 500	7 490	38 000
20 000	1 420	33 000	6 930	26 900	20 000	1 760	41 800	7 890	34 000
30 000	489	18 000	4 900	13 100	30 000	639	23 500	5 910	17 600
50 000	119	7 760	2 870	4 890	50 000	166	10 700	3 770	6 920
100 000 and over	25	4 110	1 990	2 120	100 000 and over	33	5 440	2 580	2 860
Income after tax £					**Income after tax £**				
2 330	291	706	5	701	2 420	166	408	1	407
2 500	1 230	3 510	134	3 370	2 500	1 170	3 290	78	3 220
3 000	1 050	3 660	257	3 400	3 000	1 080	3 700	200	3 500
3 500	1 150	4 750	446	4 310	3 500	1 030	4 210	336	3 870
4 000	1 400	6 660	712	5 950	4 000	1 110	5 200	487	4 710
4 500	1 110	5 990	731	5 260	4 500	1 090	5 770	623	5 150
5 000	1 150	6 920	912	6 010	5 000	1 050	6 270	764	5 510
5 500	1 100	7 260	951	6 300	5 500	1 080	7 080	891	6 180
6 000	2 000	15 300	2 270	13 000	6 000	1 990	14 900	1 990	13 000
7 000	1 700	15 100	2 330	12 800	7 000	1 820	15 900	2 290	13 600
8 000	3 070	32 500	5 060	27 400	8 000	2 750	28 900	4 300	24 500
10 000	2 190	28 500	4 530	24 000	10 000	2 270	29 400	4 510	24 900
12 000	2 170	35 000	5 960	29 000	12 000	2 500	39 600	6 230	33 400
15 000	1 580	33 400	6 350	27 000	15 000	1 930	39 900	7 000	32 900
20 000	824	25 600	6 240	19 400	20 000	1 120	33 700	7 440	26 300
30 000	192	10 500	3 520	6 940	30 000	298	15 500	4 830	10 700
50 000	33	3 770	1 630	2 140	50 000	51	5 580	2 330	3 260
100 000 and over	5	1 570	796	772	100 000 and over	7	1 950	976	973

1 The distributions cover only incomes as computed for tax purposes and above a level which for each year corresponds approximately to the single person's allowance. Incomes below these levels are not shown because the information about them is incomplete.

2 All figures have been independently rounded.

3 Investment income not known to local tax offices was not covered in previous years but is estimated in these tables. The missing investment income was distributed in a manner consistent with information from the Family Expenditure Survey and the National Accounts, to individuals where there is no investment income already reported by the tax office.

4 Total income was previously measured net of employees' superannuation contributions. These contributions are now estimated and included in total income. They have been distributed among earners in the Survey of Personal Incomes sample by a method consistent with information about the number of employees who are contracted in or out of the State Earnings Related Pension Scheme and the proportion of their earnings contributed.

5 Estimates of tax liability allow for interest relief at source at basic rate (eg MIRAS) as well as relief at higher rates.

Personal Incomes

15.2 (continued) Distribution of total incomes before and after tax
Years ended 5 April

Lower limit of range of income	1988/89 Annual Survey Thousands Number of incomes	£ million Total income before tax	Tax[5]	Total income after tax	Lower limit of range of income	1989/90 Annual Survey Thousands Number of incomes	£ million Total income before tax	Tax[5]	Total income after tax
All incomes[1,2,3,4]	23 100	296 000	46 500	249 000	All incomes[1,2,3,4]	23 500	333 000	53 400	280 000
Income before tax £					**Income before tax £**				
2 605	557	1 560	10	1 550	2 785	292	843	2	841
3 000	928	3 000	81	2 910	3 000	751	2 440	40	2 400
3 500	891	3 330	140	3 190	3 500	777	2 900	108	2 800
4 000	716	3 030	158	2 880	4 000	745	3 160	160	3 000
4 500	834	3 950	290	3 660	4 500	723	3 440	222	3 220
5 000	737	3 860	341	3 510	5 000	715	3 740	238	3 500
5 500	818	4 700	410	4 290	5 500	709	4 070	351	3 720
6 000	1 720	11 100	1 090	10 000	6 000	1 530	9 900	983	8 920
7 000	1 410	10 500	1 140	9 380	7 000	1 530	11 400	1 300	10 100
8 000	2 940	26 400	3 320	23 100	8 000	2 760	24 800	3 060	21 700
10 000	2 390	26 200	3 500	22 700	10 000	2 380	26 100	3 260	22 800
12 000	2 830	37 900	5 210	32 700	12 000	2 920	39 200	5 300	33 900
15 000	2 940	50 500	7 380	43 100	15 000	3 360	57 900	8 040	49 900
20 000	2 210	52 900	8 820	44 100	20 000	2 720	65 000	10 900	54 100
30 000	857	31 400	6 800	24 600	30 000	1 160	43 000	8 920	34 000
50 000	232	15 300	4 320	11 000	50 000	331	21 400	5 860	15 600
100 000 and over	55	9 930	3 440	6 490	100 000 and over	78	13 800	4 710	9 050
Income after tax £					**Income after tax £**				
2 605	677	1 930	24	1 900					
					2 785	334	971	5	966
3 000	1 130	3 810	138	3 680	3 000	923	3 090	81	3 010
3 500	935	3 700	207	3 500	3 500	910	3 580	176	3 410
4 000	1 040	4 810	369	4 440	4 000	896	4 090	278	3 810
4 500	854	4 430	386	4 050	4 500	843	4 370	358	4 020
5 000	1 110	6 510	695	5 820	5 000	965	5 570	496	5 070
5 500	962	6 170	644	5 520	5 500	949	6 110	651	5 460
6 000	1 890	13 800	1 530	12 300	6 000	1 880	13 900	1 620	12 200
7 000	1 810	15 600	1 970	13 600	7 000	1 720	14 800	1 860	12 900
8 000	3 000	30 900	4 070	26 800	8 000	2 910	30 000	3 850	26 100
10 000	2 650	31 000	4 190	26 800	10 000	2 540	32 100	4 260	27 800
12 000	2 678	41 500	5 790	35 700	12 000	2 810	43 700	5 860	37 900
15 000	2 410	48 900	7 460	41 500	15 000	3 060	61 800	9 290	52 600
20 000	1 570	45 900	8 640	37 200	20 000	1 880	54 700	9 920	44 800
30 000	424	20 600	5 120	15 500	30 000	679	32 500	7 710	24 700
50 000	105	9 730	3 000	6 730	50 000	146	13 500	4 040	9 450
100 000 and over	24	6 330	2 250	4 080	100 000 and over	32	8 390	2 980	5 410

Footnotes on page 257.

Source: Board of Inland Revenue

Income

15.3 Sources of household income[1]
United Kingdom

		1980	1981	1982	1983	1984	1985	1986	1987	1988	1989	1990	1991
Number of households supplying data[2]	KPDA	6 944	7 525	7 428	6 973	7 081	7 012	7 178	7 396	7 265	7 410	7 046	7 056
Average weekly household income[3] by source (£)													
Wages and salaries	KPCB	104.78	114.22	118.50	121.56	131.00	141.26	150.32	162.70	176.78	189.36	212.54	222.04
Self-employment	KPCC	8.16	10.24	10.59	12.26	12.07	14.65	17.96	21.53	29.59	28.51	32.09	29.73
Investments	KPCD	4.49	6.35	6.94	6.77	7.07	8.42	9.78	12.44	13.26	13.98	18.95	23.65
Annuities and pensions (other than social security benefits)	KPCE	3.79	5.20	5.26	7.39	7.72	9.58	10.14	11.87	13.78	14.43	15.51	17.31
Social security benefits[3]	KPCF	17.60	21.87	24.58	28.03	27.45	28.90	30.30	31.09	31.58	32.65	35.34	40.14
Imputed income from owner/rent-free occupancy[4]	KPCG	6.75	7.79	8.57	9.70	10.23	11.86	12.57	12.95	15.83	16.56	18.59	24.48
Other sources[5]	KPCH	1.61	1.93	2.24	2.15	1.84	2.21	2.61	3.72	3.04	4.46	4.53	5.30
Total	KPCI	147.18	167.60	176.67	187.86	197.37	216.86	233.68	256.31	283.86	299.95	337.55	362.65
Sources of household income as a percentage of total household income[3] (per cent)													
Wages and salaries	KPCJ	71.2	68.1	67.1	64.7	66.4	65.1	64.3	63.5	62.3	62.3	63.0	61.2
Self-employment	KPCK	5.5	6.1	6.0	6.5	6.1	6.8	7.7	8.4	10.4	9.4	9.5	8.2
Investments	KPCL	3.0	3.8	3.9	3.6	3.6	3.9	4.2	4.9	4.7	4.6	5.6	6.5
Annuities and pensions (other than social security benefits)	KPCM	2.6	3.1	3.0	3.9	3.9	4.4	4.3	4.6	4.9	4.7	4.6	4.8
Social security benefits[3]	KPCN	12.0	13.1	13.9	14.9	13.9	13.3	13.0	12.1	11.1	10.7	10.5	11.1
Imputed income from owner/rent-free occupancy[4]	KPCO	4.6	4.6	4.8	5.2	5.2	5.5	5.4	5.1	5.6	5.5	5.5	6.8
Other sources[5]	KPCP	1.1	1.2	1.3	1.2	0.9	1.0	1.1	1.5	1.1	1.5	1.3	1.5
Total	KPCQ	100.0	100.0	100.0	100.0	100.0	100.0	100.0	100.0	100.0	100.0	100.0	100.0

1 Information derived from the Family Expenditure Survey (FES).
2 In 1983 data was not collected for a few weeks at the time of the General Elections.
3 Because of the introduction of the Housing Benefit Scheme figures for 1983 and 1984 are not on a comparable basis, nor are those for 1983 consistent with earlier years.
4 Imputed income is the weekly equivalent of the rateable value: this is adjusted to allow for general increases in rents since date of valuation, and is included in income of households living rent-free. From 1976 the method of calculating this adjustment is changed. 1985 assessments of rateable values in Scotland were used from 1 April 1985 in the calculation of imputed income and housing expenditure of owner-occupiers and those living rent-free (1987 FES Report definitions 14(h),(g)).
5 From 1982 'Other sources' includes very small amounts of income previously classified under self-employment.

Source: Central Statistical Office

15.4 Availability in households of certain durable goods[1]
United Kingdom

		1980	1981	1982	1983	1984	1985	1986	1987	1988	1989	1990	1991
Number of households supplying data[2]	KPDA	6 944	7 525	7 428	6 973	7 081	7 012	7 178	7 396	7 265	7 410	7 046	7 056
		Percentage											
Car	KPDB	60.3	61.8	61.4	62.1	61.3	62.8	62.4	63.4	66.0	66.1	66.8	67.8
One	KPDC	45.0	46.3	46.6	45.4	44.8	45.2	44.3	44.8	45.0	44.5	43.9	44.7
Two	KPDD	13.1	13.4	12.7	14.4	13.5	14.6	14.9	15.5	17.5	18.0	19.1	18.9
Three or more	KPDE	2.2	2.1	2.0	2.3	3.0	2.9	3.2	3.1	3.6	3.6	3.8	4.1
Central heating, full or partial	KPDF	59.1	60.5	62.8	63.9	66.4	69.0	70.1	74.4	76.5	77.5	79.3	80.5
Washing machine	KPDG	78.7	80.7	81.1	81.3	81.9	83.0	82.9	84.6	84.6	85.7	86.3	87.2
Refrigerator or Fridge/Freezer	KPDH	..	..	..	..	..	97.6	96.9	97.6	98.0	98.0	98.1	98.2
Freezer or Fridge/Freezer	KPDI	..	..	..	..	..	67.3	69.2	72.6	75.2	78.5	80.1	81.7
Refrigerator	KPDJ	94.8	96.1	96.4	97.0	97.2	–	–	–	–	–	–	–
Television	KPDK	96.9	96.6	96.8	96.9	97.2	97.6	97.1	97.9	98.0	98.0	98.1	97.9
Telephone	KPDL	71.6	75.8	75.7	77.3	78.3	80.5	80.9	82.5	84.7	86.2	87.4	88.0
Home computer	KPDM	..	..	..	..	..	12.6	15.1	16.6	16.9	16.6	16.8	18.1
Video recorder	KPDN	..	..	..	..	..	30.1	36.3	43.5	50.2	56.6	61.2	64.6

1 Information derived from Family Expenditure Survey.
2 In 1983 data was not collected for a few weeks at the time of the General Elections.

Source: Central Statistical Office

Expenditure

15.5 Households and their expenditure[1]
United Kingdom

		1980	1981	1982	1983	1984	1985	1986	1987	1988	1989	1990	1991
Number of households													
supplying data[2]	KPDA	6 944	7 525	7 428	6 973	7 081	7 012	7 178	7 396	7 265	7 410	7 046	7 056
Total number of persons	KPEA	18 844	20 535	20 022	18 532	18 557	18 206	18 330	18 735	18 280	18 590	17 437	17 089
Total number of adults[3]	KPEB	13 408	14 685	14 386	13 401	13 618	13 401	13 554	13 902	13 640	13 850	12 939	12 934
Household percentage distribution by tenure													
Rented unfurnished	KPED	40.9	41.6	39.0	35.8	35.4	34.9	33.9	32.5	30.3	30.3	29.2	27.7
Rented furnished	KPEE	2.6	2.5	2.7	2.9	2.7	2.5	3.0	3.3	2.8	3.0	3.4	3.3
Rent-free	KPEF	2.2	2.2	2.0	2.2	1.8	2.1	2.0	2.1	1.7	1.4	1.3	2.0
Owner-occupied	KPEG	54.3	53.7	56.3	59.2	60.1	60.5	61.1	62.2	65.1	65.3	66.1	67.0
Average number of persons per household													
All persons	KPEH	2.714	2.729	2.695	2.658	2.621	2.596	2.554	2.533	2.516	2.509	2.475	2.422
Males	KPEI	1.307	1.329	1.317	1.289	1.266	1.258	1.236	1.223	1.229	1.217	1.193	1.169
Females	KPEJ	1.407	1.400	1.378	1.369	1.355	1.339	1.317	1.310	1.288	1.292	1.281	1.253
Adults[3]	KPEK	1.931	1.951	1.937	1.922	1.923	1.911	1.888	1.880	1.877	1.869	1.836	1.833
Persons under 65	KPEL	1.563	1.585	1.584	1.562	1.572	1.552	1.526	1.512	1.504	1.500	1.459	1.455
Persons 65 and over	KPEM	0.368	0.366	0.353	0.360	0.351	0.359	0.362	0.368	0.374	0.369	0.378	0.378
Children[3]	KPEN	0.783	0.777	0.759	0.736	0.698	0.685	0.665	0.653	0.639	0.640	0.638	0.589
Children under 2	KPEO	0.076	0.078	0.081	0.080	0.068	0.077	0.073	0.078	0.073	0.084	0.075	0.077
Children 2 and under 5	KPEP	0.116	0.109	0.119	0.123	0.114	0.114	0.118	0.118	0.111	0.117	0.119	0.112
Children 5 and under 18	KPEQ	0.591	0.591	0.559	0.533	0.516	0.495	0.474	0.457	0.455	0.439	0.444	0.400
Persons economically active[4]	KPER	1.357	1.363	1.221	1.172	1.179	1.164	1.160	1.161	1.168	1.167	1.195	1.171
Persons not economically active[4]	KPES	1.356	1.366	1.474	1.485	1.442	1.433	1.394	1.372	1.348	1.342	1.280	1.251
Men 65 and over, women 60 and over	KPET	0.386	0.396	0.383	0.403	0.399	0.407	0.403	0.408	0.406	0.401	0.405	0.408
Others	KPEU	0.971	0.970	1.092	1.082	1.043	1.026	0.991	0.965	0.942	0.940	0.875	0.843
Average weekly household expenditure on commodities and services (£)[7]													
Housing[5,8]	KPEV	16.56	19.76	22.29	23.99	24.06	26.63	29.92	30.42	35.81	38.44	44.42	50.24
Fuel, light and power	KPEW	6.15	7.46	8.35	9.22	9.42	9.95	10.43	10.55	10.48	10.58	11.11	12.25
Food	KPEX	25.15	27.20	28.19	29.56	31.43	32.70	34.97	35.79	38.28	41.67	44.81	46.13
Alcoholic drink	KPEY	5.34	6.06	6.13	6.91	7.25	7.95	8.21	8.70	9.19	9.53	10.01	10.83
Tobacco	KPEZ	3.32	3.74	3.85	4.21	4.37	4.42	4.55	4.67	4.45	4.77	4.82	5.15
Clothing and footwear	KCWC	8.99	9.23	9.69	10.00	11.10	11.92	13.46	13.32	14.52	15.25	16.03	15.80
Durable household goods	KCWD	7.70	9.40	9.65	10.26	11.57	11.61	13.83	–	–	–	–	–
Other goods	KCWE	8.75	9.45	10.06	10.81	11.89	12.59	13.87	–	–	–	–	–
Transport and vehicles	KCWF	16.15	18.70	19.79	20.96	22.77	24.56	25.43	–	–	–	–	–
Services	KCWG	11.96	13.84	15.37	16.09	17.41	19.48	22.67	–	–	–	–	–
Household goods[8]	KCWH	–	–	–	–	–	–	13.67	13.48	15.01	19.17	20.00	20.13
Household services[8]	KCWI	–	–	–	–	–	–	8.50	8.23	9.80	9.73	12.28	13.00
Personal goods and services	KCWJ	–	–	–	–	–	–	6.48	7.02	8.13	8.48	9.47	9.97
Motoring expenditure	KCWK	–	–	–	–	–	–	21.22	23.80	25.31	30.42	33.83	34.12
Fares and other travel costs	KCWL	–	–	–	–	–	–	4.21	4.60	4.88	5.35	6.19	5.58
Leisure goods	KCWM	–	–	–	–	–	–	8.54	9.03	9.65	10.97	11.28	12.06
Leisure services[8]	KCWN	–	–	–	–	–	–	13.18	18.11	18.13	19.02	21.54	22.20
Miscellaneous[6]	KCWO	0.53	0.58	0.53	0.58	0.64	0.68	0.74	0.88	0.78	0.93	1.37	1.59
Total	KCWP	110.60	125.41	133.92	142.59	151.92	162.50	178.10	188.62	204.41	224.32	247.16	259.04
Expenditure on commodity or service as a percentage of total expenditure (per cent)[7]													
Housing[5,8]	KPFH	15.0	15.8	16.6	16.8	15.8	16.4	16.8	16.1	17.5	17.1	18.0	19.4
Fuel, light and power	KPFI	5.6	5.9	6.2	6.5	6.2	6.1	5.9	5.6	5.1	4.7	4.5	4.7
Food	KPFJ	22.7	21.7	21.1	20.7	20.7	20.1	19.6	19.0	18.7	18.6	18.1	17.8
Alcoholic drink	KPFK	4.8	4.8	4.6	4.8	4.8	4.9	4.6	4.6	4.5	4.2	4.1	4.2
Tobacco	KPFL	3.0	3.0	2.9	3.0	2.9	2.7	2.6	2.5	2.2	2.1	2.0	2.0
Clothing and footwear	KPFM	8.1	7.4	7.2	7.0	7.3	7.3	7.5	7.1	7.1	6.8	6.5	6.1
Durable household goods	KPFN	7.0	7.5	7.2	7.2	7.6	7.2	7.8	–	–	–	–	–
Other goods	KPFO	7.9	7.5	7.5	7.6	7.9	7.8	7.8	–	–	–	–	–
Transport and vehicles	KPFP	14.6	14.9	14.8	14.7	15.0	15.1	14.3	–	–	–	–	–
Services	KPFQ	10.8	11.0	11.5	11.3	11.5	12.0	12.7	–	–	–	–	–
Household goods[8]	KCWQ	–	–	–	–	–	–	7.7	7.1	7.3	8.5	8.1	7.8
Household services[8]	KCWR	–	–	–	–	–	–	4.8	4.4	4.8	4.3	5.0	5.0
Personal goods and services	KCWS	–	–	–	–	–	–	3.6	3.7	4.0	3.8	3.8	3.8
Motoring expenditure	KCWT	–	–	–	–	–	–	11.9	12.6	12.4	13.6	13.7	13.2
Fares and other travel costs	KCWU	–	–	–	–	–	–	2.4	2.4	2.4	2.4	2.5	2.2
Leisure goods	KCWV	–	–	–	–	–	–	4.8	4.8	4.7	4.9	4.6	4.7
Leisure services[8]	KCWW	–	–	–	–	–	–	7.4	9.6	8.9	8.5	8.7	8.6
Miscellaneous[6]	KPFR	0.5	0.5	0.4	0.4	0.4	0.4	0.4	0.5	0.4	0.4	0.6	0.6
Total	KPFS	100.0	100.0	100.0	100.0	100.0	100.0	100.0	100.0	100.0	100.0	100.0	100.0

1 Information derived from the Family Expenditure Survey (FES).
2 In 1979 and 1983 data were not collected for a few weeks at the time of the General Elections.
3 Adults and children are:
Adults = all persons 18 and over and married persons under 18.
Children = all unmarried persons under 18.
4 Definitions of economic activity changed in 1982 and 1990: see Family Expenditure Survey Report for 1982 and Family Spending 1990 for details.
5 Excludes mortgage payments but includes imputed expenditure from owner-occupancy and from rent-free occupancy. Imputed expenditure is the weekly equivalent of the rateable value which is adjusted to allow for general increases in rents since date of valuation. From 1976 the method of calculating this adjustment is changed. Because of the introduction of the Housing Benefit Scheme, figures for expenditure on housing for 1983 and 1984 are not on a comparable basis. Nor are those for 1983 consistent with earlier years. 1985 assessments of rateable values in Scotland were used from 1 April 1985 in the calculation of imputed income and housing expenditure of owner-occupiers and those living rent-free (1987 FES Report definitions 14(h),(g)).
6 Miscellaneous expenditure was greater before 1980 when changes in classifying credit card expenditure was introduced.
7 The commodity/service groupings used to categorise FES expenditure have been revised to align with the categories recommended for the Retail Price Index (RPI) by the RPI Advisory Committee. The 11 commodity groups have been extended to 14. Both old and new versions are shown for 1986.
8 Expenditure on certain items was recorded on a retrospective basis from 1989 and 1990.

Source: Central Statistical Office

16 Home Finance

Public sector

In Table 16.1 the term public sector describes the consolidation of central government, local authorities and public corporations. The table sets out the relationship between the public sector financial surplus or deficit and the public sector borrowing requirement, (PSBR). A financial surplus or deficit represents the extent to which a sector's gross savings - that is, the balance of receipts and expenditure on current transactions - *plus* net capital transfers are more than sufficient or insufficient to finance the sector's expenditure on physical assets.

In recent years the public sector has usually been in deficit and has had to borrow. The surplus or deficit is not a complete indication of the borrowing requirement because it does not take into account lending to the private sector and overseas and other non-borrowing financial transactions. The borrowing requirement equals the financial surplus or deficit *plus* the net increase or decrease in these financial assets. A revised definition of the PSBR was announced by the Chancellor of the Exchequer on 10 February 1984. Under this definition changes in public sector bank deposits and holdings of other liquid assets are regarded as financing the PSBR rather than contributing to it.

Details of public sector borrowing and the contributions to the PSBR are given in Table 16.2. The PSBR indicates the extent to which the public sector borrows from other sectors of the economy and overseas to finance the balance of expenditure and receipts arising from its various activities. A considerable part of the central government borrowing requirement is needed to finance central government on-lending to local authorities and public corporations. Their additional 'contributions' to the PSBR are therefore equal to their borrowing requirements *less* their direct borrowing from central government.

General government borrowing requirement (GGBR) is the sum of the borrowing requirements of central government and local authorities *less* direct borrowing by local authorities from central government. The PSBR is the GGBR *plus* public corporations borrowing requirement *less* their direct borrowing from central government.

The borrowing requirements are measured from the financing items rather than as the difference between receipts and payments because for local authorities and public corporations, this information comes to hand more quickly and is regarded as more reliable.

Rateable values *(Table 16.12)*

Major changes to local authority finance in England and Wales took effect from 1 April 1990. These included the abolition of domestic rating - replaced by the community charge, the revaluation of all non-domestic properties, and the introduction of the Uniform Business Rate. As a result the analysis presented here for 1990 differs substantially from that shown for earlier years. Rateable values in 1990 are about eight times those for 1989, on average, but there are wide variations about this average both for individual properties and for classes of property. Also in 1990, a new classification scheme was introduced. While the new classifications have been matched as far as possible to those used in earlier years there are differences in coverage. Further differences are caused by legislative changes which have changed the treatment of certain types of property. Comparisons between 1990 and earlier years should therefore be made with caution.

Central government

The central government embraces all bodies for whose activities a Minister of the Crown, or other responsible person, is accountable to Parliament. It includes, in addition to the ordinary government departments, a number of bodies administering public policy but without the substantial degree of financial independence which characterises the public corporations; it also includes certain extra-budgetary funds and accounts controlled by departments.

The government's financial transactions are handled through a number of statutory funds, or accounts. The most important of these is the Consolidated Fund which is the government's main account with the Bank of England. Up to 31 March 1968 the Consolidated Fund was virtually synonymous with the term 'Exchequer' which was then the government's central cash account. From 1 April 1968 the National Loans Fund, with a separate account at the Bank of England, was set up by the National Loans Act, 1968. The general effect of this Act was to remove from the Consolidated Fund most of the government's domestic lending and the whole of the government's borrowing transactions and to provide for them to be brought to account in the National Loans Fund.

Revenue from taxation and miscellaneous receipts, including interest and dividends on loans made from Votes, continue to be paid into the Consolidated Fund. After meeting the ordinary expenditure on Supply Services and the Consolidated Fund Standing Services, the surplus or deficit of the Consolidated Fund (Table 16.4), is payable into or met by the National Loans Fund.

Table 16.4 also provides a summary of the transactions of the National Loans Fund. The service of the National Debt, previously borne by the Consolidated Fund, is now met from the National Loans Fund which receives (a) interest payable on loans to the nationalised industries, local authorities and other bodies, whether the loans were made before or after 1 April 1968 and (b) the profits of the Issue Department of the Bank of England, mainly derived from interest on government securities, which were formerly paid into the Exchange Equalisation Account. The net cost of servicing the National Debt after applying these interest receipts and similar items is a charge on the Consolidated Fund as part of the standing services. Details of National Loans Fund loans outstanding are shown in Table 16.7.

Details of borrowing and repayments of debt, other than loans from the National Loans Fund, are shown in Table 16.6.

Home finance

16.1 Public sector financial account

£ million

		1980/81	1981/82	1982/83	1983/84	1984/85	1985/86	1986/87	1987/88	1988/89	1989/90	1990/91	1991/92
Financial Surplus or deficit													
Public sector total	AABE	−11 759	−5 493	−8 656	−11 586	−13 633	−8 149	−8 164	−1 382	8 872	2 740	−4 197	−19 640
Transactions in financial liabilities													
Total	AAZC	14 695	9 248	10 594	12 276	13 675	6 686	5 037	−1 582	−10 300	−4 778	1 808	14 149
Public sector borrowing requirement: total	ABEN	12 519	8 631	8 904	9 678	10 134	5 622	3 559	−3 406	−14 657	−7 932	−457	13 728
Contributions by:-													
Central Government	ABEA	12 732	7 597	12 734	12 178	10 164	10 962	10 452	837	−7 119	−5 630	−2 465	12 928
Local authorities	AAZK	819	956	−2 701	−2 264	−909	−4 078	−5 574	−2 737	−4 602	−941	1 971	1 050
Public corporations	AAZL	−1 032	78	−1 129	−236	879	−1 262	−1 319	−1 506	−2 936	−1 361	37	−250
Other financial liabilities	AAZD	2 084	566	1 575	2 513	3 541	1 064	1 478	1 824	4 357	3 154	2 342	331
Transactions in financial assets													
Total	AAZH	2 891	4 050	1 679	859	73	−1 824	−4 031	−3 847	−4 484	−1 296	−3 633	−6 033
Net lending, etc to private sector and overseas													
Central government	AAZN	1 438	545	522	−937	−1 735	−2 641	−3 599	−5 109	−6 136	−3 602	−5 435	−8 144
Local authorities	AQYD	300	504	352	−233	−301	−393	−366	−132	−126	−47	−160	−292
Public corporations	AAZG	−1 102	245	79	65	−42	−41	88	−182	−98	121	−30	59
Other financial assets	AAZJ	2 257	2 757	729	1 966	2 151	1 251	−154	1 576	1 876	2 232	1 992	2 387
Total financial transactions	AAHD	−11 804	−5 198	−8 915	−11 417	−13 602	−8 510	−9 068	−2 265	5 816	3 482	−5 518	−20 133
Balancing item	AAHE	107	−354	253	82	−31	361	904	883	3 056	−742	1 321	493

Source: Central Statistical Office

16.2 Public sector borrowing and contributions to the public sector borrowing requirement

£ million

		1980/81	1981/82	1982/83	1983/84	1984/85	1985/86	1986/87	1987/88	1988/89	1989/90	1990/91	1991/92
Central government borrowing requirement	ABEA	12 732	7 597	12 734	12 178	10 164	10 962	10 452	837	−7 119	−5 630	−2 465	12 928
of which: own account	ABEB	9 391	6 560	7 742	7 998	6 533	4 261	4 663	−3 284	−13 044	−5 369	−2 922	11 738
Local authorities													
Direct borrowing from central government[1]	ABEC	1 301	−1 180	2 784	3 473	3 296	5 752	5 723	4 092	4 941	2 262	1 472	639
Net borrowing from other sources	ABEF	853	1 109	−2 828	−2 259	−874	−4 070	−5 571	−2 708	−4 554	−978	1 929	1 072
less Transactions in other public sector debt:													
Central government	ABEE	7	11	5	23	9	3	−	30	11	32	−32	19
Public corporations	AAEJ	27	142	−132	−18	26	5	3	−1	37	−69	−10	3
Borrowing requirement	ABEG	2 120	−224	83	1 209	2 387	1 674	149	1 355	339	1 321	3 443	1 689
General government borrowing requirement	ABEH	13 551	8 553	10 033	9 914	9 255	6 884	4 878	−1 900	−11 721	−6 571	−494	13 978
Public corporations:													
Direct borrowing from central government[1]	ABEI	2 040	2 217	2 208	707	335	949	66	29	984	−2 523	−1 015	551
Net borrowing from other sources	ABES	−715	381	−926	323	620	−978	−1 668	−978	−2 516	−1 742	−168	−499
less Transactions in other public sector debt:													
Central government	ABEK	165	339	155	482	−171	180	−124	472	428	−239	−219	−232
Local authorities	ABEL	152	−36	48	77	−88	104	−225	56	−8	−142	14	−17
Borrowing requirement	ABEM	1 008	2 295	1 079	471	1 214	−313	−1 253	−1 477	−1 952	−3 884	−978	301
Public sector borrowing requirement	ABEN	12 519	8 631	8 904	9 678	10 134	5 622	3 559	−3 406	−14 657	−7 932	−457	13 728
PSBR excluding privatisation proceeds	ABII	..	..	..	..	12 184	8 328	8 017	1 734	−7 588	−3 713	4 888	21 651

1 Excluding market transactions of central government in public sector debt; these transactions are included in 'Net borrowing from other sources.'

Source: Central Statistical Office

Home finance

16.3 Debt of the public sector: nominal amount outstanding[1]
At 31 March in each year

£ million

		1980	1981	1982	1983	1984	1985	1986	1987	1988	1989	1990	1991
Central government													
National debt													
Sterling debt[1]	ABSY	91 620	110 177	116 254	125 550	140 553	155 343	167 730	179 909	192 716	192 051	185 870	190 209
Foreign currency debt	AKRB	3 949	3 083	2 360	2 601	2 555	2 909	3 861	5 915	4 724	5 272	6 675	8 270
less Official holdings[2,3]	RZVX	17 448	18 277	14 506	13 938	12 201	11 568	13 159	16 483	19 364	30 146	32 293	34 646
equals Market holdings[4]	ABSZ	78 121	94 983	104 108	114 213	130 907	146 684	158 432	169 341	178 076	167 177	160 031	163 452
Other liabilities:													
Net indebtedness to Banking department	AKRE	599	650	725	676	474	–	–	319	583	969	1 451	1 245
Deposits with NSB ordinary account	AKRF	1 821	1 740	1 703	1 735	1 758	1 734	1 686	1 668	1 657	1 632	1 555	1 474
Deposits with TSB ordinary department	AKRG	..	..	..	..	..	..	..	..	..	..	..	..
Liability to Trustee Savings banks	AKRH	1 266	1 116	937	745	638	318	105	–	–	–	–	–
Accrued interest, etc on national savings	AKRI	1 429	1 953	2 493	3 002	3 795	4 629	5 229	5 754	6 109	5 440	4 647	4 311
Notes and coin in circulation	AKRJ	10 667	11 204	11 386	12 590	12 895	13 794	14 539	14 232	16 105	16 907	17 678	18 720
Northern Ireland government debt	AKRK	179	201	238	249	280	235	255	231	168	165	172	176
Public corporations' balances with the PMG	ALKA	74	55	134	149	150	134	72	53	79	77	44	41
Total held by other sectors[4]	AKRP	94 156	111 902	121 724	133 359	150 897	167 528	180 318	191 598	202 777	192 367	185 578	189 419
of which:													
Local authorities	AKRQ	51	56	61	74	86	96	96	98	120	147	181	149
Public corporations	AKRR	880	1 140	1 232	1 347	1 850	1 561	1 740	1 181	1 669	2 088	1 883	1 619
Domestic private sector[4]	AKRS	82 780	98 605	108 141	119 446	133 693	149 715	159 871	168 311	176 824	162 618	156 274	159 019
Overseas	AKRT	10 445	12 101	12 290	12 492	15 268	16 156	18 611	22 008	24 164	27 514	27 240	28 632
Local authorities													
Sterling debt	AKRW	33 880	36 190	36 103	36 314	37 806	40 517	42 814	45 229	48 036	51 136	51 929	54 148
Foreign currency debt	AKRX	233	192	222	359	444	504	614	719	768	742	733	642
Total held by other sectors	AKRY	34 113	36 382	36 325	36 673	38 250	41 021	43 428	45 948	48 804	51 878	52 662	54 790
of which:													
Central government	AKRZ	15 577	16 711	15 769	18 207	21 391	24 618	30 043	35 932	39 936	44 695	47 383	48 946
Public corporations	AKSA	231	262	284	331	403	319	359	198	254	246	102	116
Domestic private sector	AKSB	17 882	18 959	19 780	17 492	15 768	15 362	12 188	9 077	7 635	5 982	4 239	4 883
Overseas	AKSC	423	450	492	643	688	722	838	741	979	955	938	845
Public corporations													
Sterling debt	AKSD	25 504	27 120	26 841	27 139	27 842	26 061	25 574	23 180	23 397	19 580	13 340	13 252
Foreign currency debt	AKSE	4 523	4 158	4 762	5 291	5 609	5 498	5 149	4 548	3 001	2 276	1 421	1 160
Total held by other sectors	AKSF	30 027	31 278	31 603	32 430	33 451	31 559	30 723	27 728	26 398	21 856	14 761	14 412
of which:													
Central government	AKSG	22 902	24 689	23 676	24 834	25 551	22 796	23 838	22 069	22 182	18 598	12 787	12 809
Local authorities	AKSZ	1 369	1 369	1 469	1 172	1 108	1 006	804	454	291	247	36	26
Domestic private sector	AKSH	1 655	1 512	2 505	2 306	2 332	3 704	2 218	1 713	1 026	769	564	468
Overseas	AKSI	4 101	3 708	3 953	4 118	4 460	4 053	3 863	3 492	2 899	2 242	1 374	1 109
Public sector debt held outside the public sector													
Total	AKSJ	117 286	135 335	147 161	156 497	172 209	189 712	197 589	205 342	213 527	200 080	190 629	194 956
Sterling debt held by:													
Domestic private sector	AKSK	99 765	117 248	129 347	137 857	150 442	167 168	171 560	174 973	182 642	168 519	160 055	163 454
Overseas	AKSL	8 816	10 654	10 470	10 389	13 159	13 633	16 405	19 187	22 392	23 271	21 966	21 811
Foreign currency debt held by:													
Domestic private sector	AKSM	2 552	1 828	1 079	1 387	1 351	1 613	2 717	4 128	2 843	850	1 022	916
Overseas	AKSN	6 153	5 605	6 265	6 864	7 257	7 298	6 907	7 054	5 650	7 440	7 586	8 775
Debt excluded from PSBR financing[5]													
Central government[6]	ABSX	702	580	421	300	369	503	497	537	636	764	843	944

See footnotes on page 267.

Source: Central Statistical Office

16.3 Debt of the public sector: nominal amount outstanding[1]
continued
At 31 March in each year

£ million

		1980	1981	1982	1983	1984	1985	1986	1987	1988	1989	1990	1991
Contingent liabilities of central government													
Export credit guarantees	AKSO	24 337	25 585	30 838	50 901	42 790	42 298	38 389	37 213	36 128	36 552	34 089	33 851
Assistance to industry, guaranteed loans	AKSP	1 492	1 652	2 116	1 917	2 140	2 536	2 053	1 801	1 788	1 947	2 490	2 395
Overseas Development, guaranteed loans	AKSQ	25	54	53	61	56	66	40	32	5	5	4	4
National heritage acts, guaranteed loans	AROY	–	–	–	–	–	139	209	301	881	1 172	1 560	1 975
Other identified	AKSR	64	65	65	65	63	63	63	64	65	23	19	21
Total	AKSS	25 918	27 356	33 072	52 944	45 049	45 102	40 754	39 411	38 867	39 699	38 162	38 246
Percentage of total debt held outside public sector	AKST	74.1	75.4	77.6	77.3	77.4	79.0	77.6	77.4	76.8	75.2	75.3	75.4
Debt held outside sector as a percentage of GDP[7]	AKSU	52.1	54.4	53.9	52.6	53.8	54.5	52.6	50.1	46.9	39.8	35.1	34.3
Debt held overseas as a percentage of debt held outside public sector	AKSV	12.8	12.0	11.4	11.0	11.9	11.0	11.8	12.8	13.1	15.3	15.5	15.7
Debt held overseas as a percentage of GDP[7]	AKSW	6.7	6.5	6.1	5.8	6.4	6.0	6.2	6.4	6.2	6.1	5.4	5.4
Foreign currency debt as a percentage of debt held outside public sector	AKSX	7.4	5.5	5.0	5.3	5.0	4.7	4.9	5.4	4.0	4.1	4.5	5.0

1 Includes British government guaranteed stocks of nationalised industries.
2 At 31 March 1989 comprised:
    British government stocks   17005
    NILO stocks   550
    Treasury bills   2545
    Ways and means advances   12128
    Debt to Bank of England Issue Department   11
    ECU treasury bills   220
3 Excludes gifts held temporarily by the Issue Department under purchases and resale agreements with the monetary sector.
4 Includes gifts held temporarily by the Issue Department under purchases and resale agreements with the monetary sector.
5 Not included in the main body of the table, which is confined to liabilities which finance the public sector borrowing requirement.
6 Comprises liability to Post Office Superannuation Fund and court funds.
7 GDP (average measure) at current market prices for the twelve months centred on 31 March.

Source: Central Statistical Office

Home finance

16.4 Consolidated Fund: revenue and expenditure
Years ended 31 March

£ million

		1981/82	1982/83	1983/84	1984/85	1985/86	1986/87	1987/88	1988/89	1989/90	1990/91	1991/92
Revenue												
Inland Revenue	KCWZ	40 318.3	43 793.7	45 926.0	50 350.1	55 438.1	57 114.9	64 508.5	68 812.7	76 674.3	82 320.7	79 509.6
Customs and Excise	KCXA	25 247.8	27 895.5	31 434.3	35 502.2	37 397.9	41 094.0	44 737.5	49 565.3	52 190.2	55 336.9	61 826.9
Motor vehicle duties	KCXB	1 640.2	1 823.4	2 036.1	2 219.4	2 432.3	2 576.3	2 644.7	2 810.8	2 920.0	2 971.4	2 945.3
Selective employment tax and national insurance surcharge[1]	KCXC	3 596.3	2 831.3	1 670.5	924.1	34.7	1.0	–	1.5	0.6	0.5	–
Miscellaneous receipts	KCXE	5 952.4	6 927.5	7 297.0	9 250.9	10 828.8	10 424.7	11 078.0	12 402.5	13 136.5	21 736.6	27 193.0
Total revenue	KCXF	76 755.0	83 271.4	88 363.9	98 246.7	106 131.8	111 210.9	122 968.7	133 592.8	144 921.6	162 366.1	171 474.8
Expenditure												
Supply services	KCXG	74 090.8	80 456.4	86 749.3	93 412.1	97 961.7	102 358.7	104 875.5	110 713.9	122 548.8	145 763.1	168 702.6
Debt interest[2]	KCXH	6 503.5	5 392.7	6 485.1	7 520.1	7 567.5	8 893.4	9 598.5	10 827.7	11 343.3	10 229.2	8 942.6
Payments to Northern Ireland	KCXI	1 475.2	1 607.1	1 603.0	1 647.5	1 808.2	2 030.8	2 218.7	2 383.3	2 683.1	2 927.7	2 944.9
Payments to the European Community, etc	KCXJ	2 642.0	2 804.6	2 618.4	2 915.9	2 587.4	3 327.3	3 789.3	3 899.5	4 537.7	4 806.1	3 323.3
Other expenditure[3]	KCXL	73.9	210.0	–4.8	121.4	201.8	–149.7	79.0	177.8	380.7	503.7	276.3
Total expenditure	KCXM	84 785.5	90 470.8	97 451.0	105 617.0	110 126.6	116 460.5	120 561.0	128 002.2	141 493.6	164 229.8	184 189.7
Deficit met from the National Loans fund	KCXN	8 030.5	7 199.4	9 087.1	7 370.3	3 994.8	5 249.6	–2 407.7	–5 590.6	–3 428.0	1 863.7	12 714.9

National Loans Fund: summary of receipts and payments (£ million)

		1981/82	1982/83	1983/84	1984/85	1985/86	1986/87	1987/88	1988/89	1989/90	1990/91	1991/92
Receipts												
Interest on loans, and profits of Issue Department of the Bank of England	KCXO	4 702.1	5 430.9	5 347.4	5 405.0	6 645.0	6 721.1	6 807.0	7 411.1	7 523.4	7 676.3	7 747.7
Service of the National Debt-balance met from the Consolidated Fund	KCXP	6 503.5	5 392.7	6 485.1	7 520.1	7 567.5	8 893.4	9 598.5	10 827.7	11 335.5	10 229.3	8 942.6
Total	KCXQ	11 205.6	10 823.6	11 832.5	12 925.1	14 212.5	15 614.5	16 405.5	18 238.8	18 858.9	17 905.6	16 690.3
Exchange Equalisation Account-sterling capital[4]	KCXR	3 600.0	2 800.0	600.0	1 000.0	–2 300.0	–3 650.0	–10 250.0	–	6 175.0	–1 050.0	300.0
Net borrowing[5]	KCXS	4 833.6	7 906.9	13 372.7	13 964.8	9 008.1	13 279.7	12 071.8	–	–	3 684.7	12 112.0
International Monetary Fund-maintenance of sterling holdings	KCXT	44.4	–	–	–	–	151.3	–	234.7	–	–	59.8
Reduction of National Debt Commissioners Liability in respect of the National Savings Bank Investment Account	KCXU	315.5	1 215.9	46.9	19.5	14.1	–	–	–	–	–	–
Change in balances and other items	KCXV	–	2.0	–8.1	–4 929.2	3 840.9	1 096.4	–	–	–	–	–
Total	KCXW	19 999.1	22 748.4	25 844.0	22 980.2	24 775.6	26 491.9	18 227.3	18 473.5	25 033.9	20 540.3	29 162.1
Payments												
Service of the National Debt:												
Interest	KCXX	11 075.5	10 687.3	11 692.2	12 773.2	14 046.4	15 441.1	16 232.9	18 065.8	18 679.9	17 730.6	16 515.7
Management and expenses	KCXY	130.1	136.3	140.3	151.9	166.1	173.4	172.6	173.0	179.0	175.0	174.6
Total	KCXZ	11 205.6	10 823.6	11 832.5	12 925.1	14 212.5	15 614.5	16 405.5	18 238.8	18 858.9	17 905.6	16 690.3
Consolidated Fund deficit met from the National Loans Fund	KCYA	8 030.5	7 199.4	9 087.1	7 370.3	3 994.8	5 249.6	–2 407.7	–5 590.6	–3 435.7	1 863.7	12 714.9
Net repayment[5]	KCYB	–	–	–	–	–	–	–	1 846.8	7 923.3	–	–
Net lending	KCYC	763.0	4 463.8	3 413.3	2 501.1	6 378.6	5 627.8	4 132.0	3 978.5	1 538.3	623.9	–243.1
International Monetary Fund-maintenance of value of sterling holding	KCYD	–	261.6	188.5	183.7	189.7	–	97.5	–	149.1	147.1	–
International Monetary Fund-additional subscription	KCYE	–	–	1 322.6	–	–	–	–	–	–	–	–
Total	KCYF	19 999.1	22 748.4	25 844.0	22 980.2	24 775.6	26 491.9	18 227.3	18 473.5	25 033.9	20 540.3	29 162.1

1 Actual receipts in the year are shown gross, and payments of refunds and premiums are included in expenditure on supply services, national insurance surcharge from April 1977.
2 Payment to National Loans Fund representing its payments for the service of the National Debt *less* its receipts of interest on loans outstanding, etc.
3 Includes net issues to Contingencies Fund.
4 Minus sign indicates a net issue.
5 See Table 16.6.

Source: HM Treasury

Home finance

16.5 Central government borrowing requirement[1]
United Kingdom
Years ended 31 March

£ million

		1980/81	1981/82	1982/83	1983/84	1984/85	1985/86	1986/87	1987/88	1988/89	1989/90	1990/91	1991/92
National Loans Fund:													
Net lending	ACAW	3 557	746	4 464	3 412	2 501	6 378	5 628	4 132	3 979	1 537	627	−242
less Surplus from Consolidated Fund[2]	ACAP	−9 957	−8 049	−7 200	−9 086	−7 370	−3 995	−5 325	2 275	5 591	3 428	−1 658	−12 872
Other items	ACAX	13 514	8 794	11 664	12 498	9 871	10 373	10 953	1 856	−1 612	−1 890	2 259	12 630
Borrowing required													
Surplus of National Insurance Funds[2]	ACAY	−25	−604	−216	520	203	396	410	1 385	3 162	31	306	−3 121
Departmental balances and miscellaneous	ACAZ	840	1 818	−821	−166	−537	−1 000	84	−426	2 247	3 659	4 421	2 776
Northern Ireland central government debt	ACBA	33	17	33	34	−41	−15	−7	−60	−98	−50	2	−47
Central government borrowing requirement	ABEA	12 732	7 597	12 734	12 178	10 164	10 962	10 452	837	−7 119	−5 630	−2 465	12 928
Borrowing requirement analysed by investment													
Liabilities													
Notes and coin	AACB	−552	−189	−1 206	−324	−900	−744	290	−1 873	−802	−771	−1 053	1 069
Marketable debt:													
Treasury bills[3]	AACC	1 025	111	−195	−126	185	−124	−670	−789	−460	−5 748	−1 028	1 682
British government securities	AACD	−13 107	−5 959	−5 140	−11 677	−10 223	−5 675	−6 138	−7 073	13 328	15 792	2 956	−11 999
Non-marketable debt:													
National savings	AACE	−2 140	−4 321	−3 028	−3 258	−3 115	−2 134	−3 275	−2 281	−624	1 720	−1 390	−3 133
Tax instruments[4]	AACF	−490	−558	−1 035	235	−771	−376	682	22	635	−268	−151	−22
Other	AADP	68	99	173	−300	498	201	440	−323	29	−436	352	152
Net indebtedness to Bank of England, Banking Department	AACG	−50	−55	69	143	4 855	−3 803	−805	−230	−371	−443	190	−36
Northern Ireland central government debt[5]	AACH	−28	−17	−33	−34	40	15	7	12	3	16	−4	27
Exchange cover scheme: payment of claims	AACI	−59	−21	94	79	356	168	229	−64	−136	20	31	15
Government foreign currency debt	AACL	762	1 384	276	−	−75	−1 569	−2 684	272	−67	−882	−1 885	−694
Other government overseas financing	AACM	−100	75	87	100	105	86	86	69	73	83	73	75
Assets													
Overseas official financing:													
Net change in official reserves[6]	AIPA	−153	2 749	2 062	32	921	−2 428	−3 834	−11 142	−1 606	5 066	−2 354	..
Public sector debt and commercial bills[6] and government guaranteed stock	ACMO	1 667	4 505	−658	2 934	−118	568	−2 519	268	−6 296	1 580	1 811	−1 262
Bank deposits	AADM	119	98	−76	82	−80	−3	71	11	201	18	210	361

1 This is equal to National Loans Fund borrowing and special transactions (net) *less* receipts from other central government funds, etc.
2 A negative item represents a surplus, a positive item a deficit.
3 Excluding bills held as the stirling counterpart of assistance from overseas central banks, which are part of Overseas official financing.
4 Includes tax reserve certificates, tax deposit accounts, and certificates of tax deposit from October 1975.
5 Excluding foreign currency borrowed under the exchange cover scheme which is included in Overseas official financing: net official financing.
6 Market transactions by the Issue department, Bank of England and by the National Debt Commissioners.

Sources: HM Treasury; Central Statistical Office

Home finance

16.6 Borrowing and repayment of debt
Years ended 31 March

£ million

		1981/82	1982/83	1983/84	1984/85	1985/86	1986/87	1987/88	1988/89	1989/90	1990/91	1991/92
Borrowing												
Marketable securities: new issues	KQGA	10 997.6	10 704.6	15 888.4	16 057.3	11 897.6	15 182.7	16 735.6	4 045.6	–	3 269.3	15 920.7
National savings securities:												
National savings certificates	KQGB	4 116.2	2 077.8	1 631.4	2 208.1	961.8	1 303.7	395.5	2 139.4	1 256.2	2 658.1	3 549.1
Capital bonds	KQGC	–	–	–	–	–	–	–	190.1	288.0	188.7	282.1
Income bonds	KQGD	–	878.1	1 115.4	1 073.0	1 209.9	2 206.0	2 109.9	1 741.9	1 482.9	1 629.1	1 329.1
Deposit bonds	KQGE	–	–	106.3	137.1	130.2	236.0	230.2	143.7	2.4	–	–
British savings bonds	KQGF	–	–	–	–	–	–	–	–	–	–	–
Premium savings bonds	KQGG	144.5	179.8	186.9	207.9	186.4	211.7	290.3	320.0	256.5	185.9	246.5
Save As You earn	KQGH	136.7	138.0	123.9	116.9	91.5	66.5	62.0	66.9	76.4	88.2	94.3
Yearly plan	KQGI	–	–	–	28.6	106.0	126.1	132.3	114.2	88.8	71.0	87.0
National savings stamps and gift tokens	KQGJ	1.2	1.2	1.2	1.2	1.2	3.2	3.0	2.8	0.5	11.4	–
National Savings Banks deposits	KQGK	1 096.7	1 413.8	1 506.5	1 261.0	1 225.5	1 408.3	1 811.1	1 596.7	1 434.7	1 491.2	1 215.1
Childrens Bonus Bonds	KGVO	–	–	–	–	–	–	–	–	–	–	127.0
Certificate of tax deposit	KQGL	2 777.5	2 499.9	2 359.9	4 523.2	4 413.0	3 339.6	2 060.8	891.1	1 065.9	1 343.1	1 137.7
Nationalised industries', etc temporary deposits	KQGM	–	–	2 894.0	4 297.0	8 319.0	7 076.0	11 087.0	12 708.0	29 728.0	25 855.0	20 709.0
British Gas corporation deposits	KQGN	–	–	–	–	–	–	–	–	–	–	–
Sterling Treasury bills (net receipt)	KQGO	–	8.2	160.2	–	358.8	358.7	1 122.0	588.4	7 282.5	–	–
ECU Treasury bills (net receipt)	KQGP	–	–	–	–	–	–	–	1 562.1	625.3	429.2	–
ECU Treasury notes (net receipt)	KGGL	–	–	–	–	–	–	–	–	–	–	1 066.4
Ways and means (net receipt)	KQGQ	–	658.7	–	555.6	–	3 319.2	1 214.7	2 329.6	1 753.9	4 107.5	2 530.5
Other debt : payable in sterling :												
Interest free notes	KQGR	–	–	1 312.1	313.8	368.2	259.2	373.0	142.2	323.6	319.1	161.2
Other debt : payable in external currencies	KHCY	–	261.5	–	236.7	1 743.0	2 720.7	–	–	588.1	1 939.8	40.0
Total receipts	KHCZ	19 270.4	18 821.6	27 286.2	31 017.4	31 012.1	37 817.6	37 627.4	28 582.7	46 253.7	43 586.6	48 495.7
Repayment of debt												
Marketable securities : redemptions	KQGS	6 119.3	6 266.0	4 600.1	4 666.8	6 097.7	9 299.1	8 295.3	8 537.0	17 068.4	6 806.0	7 841.5
Statutory sinking funds	KQGT	4.0	3.8	3.6	3.4	3.2	3.1	3.0	2.8	2.8	2.7	2.5
Terminable annuities:												
National Debt Commissioners	KQGU	–	–	–	–	–	–	–	–	–	–	–
National savings securities												
National savings certificates	KQGV	922.1	1 331.6	1 144.3	1 298.5	1 220.7	1 495.9	1 483.8	2 514.3	2 879.1	2 187.4	1 653.6
Capital bonds	KQGW	–	–	–	–	–	–	–	–	5.9	23.5	14.6
Income bonds	KQGX	–	1.8	60.1	233.0	305.7	382.2	626.6	940.3	1 094.9	831.3	729.0
Deposit bonds	KQGY	–	–	–	16.6	43.6	66.2	105.3	135.3	202.5	138.4	86.8
Yearly Plan	KQGZ	–	–	–	–	2.2	8.4	10.9	17.0	81.8	127.5	107.1
British savings bonds	KQHA	153.4	90.3	99.2	82.1	18.7	0.7	2.9	–	–	–	–
Premium savings bonds	KQHB	102.3	100.0	102.6	110.1	117.0	125.8	130.9	134.0	185.7	194.0	154.3
Save as you earn	KQHC	67.7	184.2	110.0	117.6	159.1	130.0	86.9	94.1	87.9	89.6	103.6
National savings stamps and gift tokens	KQHD	1.2	1.2	1.2	1.2	1.2	2.5	2.8	2.3	0.1	11.1	–
National Savings Bank deposits (repayments)	KQHE	722.0	874.3	1 127.8	1 367.4	1 315.2	1 344.2	1 509.5	1 858.4	2 056.6	1 775.3	1 796.1
Childrens Bonus Bonds	KGVQ	–	–	–	–	–	–	–	–	–	–	0.1
Certificates of tax deposit	KQHF	2 219.7	1 465.0	2 595.2	3 802.2	3 987.3	4 022.0	2 082.1	1 526.3	797.1	1 192.3	1 116.5
Tax reserve certificates	KQHG	0.1	0.2	0.1	–	–	–	–	–	–	0.1	0.1
Nationalised industries', etc temporary deposits	KQHH	–	–	2 489.0	4 554.0	8 187.0	6 987.0	10 776.0	12 770.0	29 314.0	25 833.0	21 186.0
British Gas Corporation (Repayment of Deposits)	KQHI	–	–	–	–	–	300.0	–	–	–	–	–
Treasury bills (net repayment)	KQHJ	80.8	–	–	291.9	–	–	–	–	–	140.3	1 191.0
Ways and means (net repayment)	KQHK	2 393.7	–	1 394.5	–	226.6	–	–	–	–	–	–
Other debt: payable in sterling :												
Interest free notes	KQHL	341.8	394.8	89.0	61.1	39.4	205.6	97.2	330.0	170.8	169.6	268.3
Other	KQHM	0.1	–	0.1	0.1	0.1	0.1	0.1	0.1	0.1	0.1	0.1
Other debt : payable in external currencies	KQHN	1 308.6	201.5	96.7	446.6	279.3	165.1	342.3	1 567.6	229.3	379.7	132.5
Total payments	KQHO	14 436.8	10 914.7	13 913.5	17 052.6	22 004.0	24 537.9	25 555.6	30 429.5	54 177.0	39 901.9	36 383.7
Net borrowing	KQHP	4 833.6	7 906.9	13 372.7	13 964.8	9 008.1	13 279.7	12 071.8	–	–	3 684.7	12 112.0
Net repayment	KHDD	–	–	–	–	–	–	–	1 846.8	7 923.3	–	–

Source: HM Treasury

Home finance

16.7 Consolidated Fund and National Loans Fund: assets and liabilities
At 31 March in each year

£ million

		1982	1983	1984	1985	1986	1987	1988	1989	1990	1991
Consolidated Fund											
Total estimated assets	KQIA	7 562.3	7 239.1	7 924.8	8 719.4	9 477.1	9 879.8	9 918.3	8 654.9	6 820.0	7 350.6
Subscriptions and contributions to international financial organisations	KQIB	1 063.4	1 248.3	1 491.9	1 715.6	1 899.7	2 176.3	2 378.0	2 619.8	2 866.1	3 083.5
International Bank for Reconstruction and Development	KQIC	117.7	119.8	150.2	157.3	180.0	197.7	193.2	202.8	215.7	224.8
International Finance Corporation	KQID	21.3	25.6	26.3	30.8	25.6	31.2	29.8	37.0	41.6	39.3
International Development Association	KQIE	713.4	871.1	1 046.4	1 199.2	1 312.1	1 475.2	1 629.4	1 811.9	1 979.5	2 127.3
African Development Fund	KQIF	7.8	9.8	14.4	25.1	30.3	40.5	52.1	59.0	65.9	80.8
Asian Development Bank	KQIG	40.9	45.4	53.4	66.2	81.7	92.2	105.0	123.2	142.3	155.8
Caribbean Development Bank	KQIH	12.1	12.3	12.7	12.9	13.1	15.3	17.8	19.5	20.9	24.6
European Investment Bank	KQII	115.2	120.6	136.5	157.6	175.0	227.5	242.6	249.4	277.7	303.2
Inter-American Development Bank	KQIJ	30.1	36.1	41.5	50.8	62.0	73.5	82.1	85.2	87.5	89.9
International Fund for Agricultural Development	KQIK	4.8	7.6	10.5	15.7	19.9	23.2	26.0	28.7	31.8	34.7
Multilateral Investment Guarantee Agency	KQIL	–	–	–	–	–	–	–	3.1	3.2	3.0
Amounts due from overseas governments	KQIM	98.7	84.1	81.6	79.1	29.2	26.6	6.5	3.9	1.3	–
War of 1939-45	KQIN	64.3	64.5	64.6	64.8	17.4	17.5	–	–	–	–
Other	KQIO	34.4	19.6	17.0	14.4	11.8	9.1	6.5	3.9	1.3	–
Loans from Votes	KQIP	2 558.6	2 050.0	1 953.1	1 942.1	1 794.9	1 845.3	1 816.2	3 850.4	2 257.1	2 420.3
Issues of public divided capital:	KQIQ	3 513.5	3 369.2	4 053.5	4 532.6	5 134.0	5 388.9	5 502.3	1 641.7	1 629.0	1 617.9
British Airways Board	KQIR	180.0	180.0	180.0	–	–	–	–	–	–	–
British Steel Corporation	KQIS	2 618.0	2 361.0	2 757.0	3 424.0	3 980.0	3 980.0	3 980.0	–	–	–
Royal Ordnance Factories	KQIT	35.0	35.0	35.0	–	–	–	–	–	–	–
National Enterprise Board	KQIU	187.7	224.2	232.0	64.0	32.0	–	–	–	–	–
Royal Mint	KQIV	7.0	7.0	7.0	7.0	7.0	7.0	7.0	7.0	7.0	7.0
Post Office	KQIW	22.0	22.0	22.0	22.0	22.0	22.0	22.0	22.0	22.0	–
Scottish Development Agency	KQIX	6.8	11.4	15.2	16.3	17.1	19.2	21.5	21.5	7.9	–
Welsh Development Agency	KQIY	4.0	5.6	7.4	12.4	14.0	14.3	17.2	18.6	15.5	15.5
British Aerospace	KQIZ	–	–	–	–	–	–	–	–	–	–
British Shipbuilders	KQJA	453.0	523.0	797.9	986.9	1 061.9	1 346.4	1 454.6	1 572.6	1 576.6	1 595.4
Contingencies Fund - capital	KQJB	186.0	346.0	277.0	337.0	482.0	222.0	202.0	307.0	0.6	0.9
Balance on revenue accounts	KQJC	142.2	141.6	67.7	112.9	137.1	220.7	13.3	232.1	66.3	227.9
Total liabilities	KQJD	78 512.9	86 580.4	96 534.7	108 238.6	113 431.4	121 862.8	121 344.1	118 005.6	123 397.0	128 386.2
Liability to balance National Loans Fund	KQJE	77 187.7	84 742.1	94 623.3	106 084.0	111 448.6	119 976.2	118 778.5	115 545.2	121 170.9	125 807.1
Payment from Votes:	KQJF	72.8	72.4	71.9	71.9	70.8	70.3	69.7	69.0	68.3	67.6
Married quarters for Armed Forces	KQJG	72.8	72.4	71.9	71.9	70.8	70.3	69.7	69.0	68.3	67.6
Liability to Post Office Superannuation Fund	KQJH	33.3	–	–	–	–	–	–	–	–	–
Post-war credits outstanding and interest due - estimated	KQJI	62.0	62.0	47.0	46.9	46.8	46.7	46.4	46.3	46.2	46.1
Revenue paid over in advance of collection	KQJJ	11.8	29.8	85.4	69.1	39.7	–	74.2	10.3	0.5	–
Inland Revenue	KQJK	–	–	85.0	23.0	–	–	51.2	–	–	–
Customs and Excise	KQJL	–	–	–	–	0.8	–	23.0	–	0.5	–
Broadcast receiving licences	KQJM	3.5	4.8	–	–	–	–	–	–	–	–
Vehicle Excise Duty	KQJN	7.9	–	–	–	–	–	–	10.3	–	–
National insurance surcharge - Great Britain	KQJO	–	24.3	–	46.1	38.9	–	–	–	–	–
National insurance surcharge - Northern Ireland	KQJP	0.4	0.7	0.4	–	–	–	–	–	–	–

Source: HM Treasury

Home finance

16.7 Consolidated Fund and National Loans Fund: assets and liabilities
At 31 March in each year
continued

£ million

		1982	1983	1984	1985	1986	1987	1988	1989	1990	1991
Consolidated Fund (*continued*)											
Promissory notes issued by											
Minister of Overseas Development	KQJQ	1 145.3	1 674.1	1 707.1	1 966.7	1 825.5	1 769.6	2 375.3	2 334.8	2 111.1	2 465.1
International Development Association	KQJR	680.9	709.3	673.0	610.0	629.9	630.3	475.3	642.7	650.0	705.3
African Development Fund	KQJS	23.2	29.3	34.9	34.5	41.9	44.1	45.1	57.4	71.2	77.1
Asian Development Bank	KQJT	3.5	3.5	3.5	3.5	3.5	3.5	4.2	2.8	2.1	1.4
Asian Development Fund	KQJU	57.5	67.8	79.0	85.4	89.0	87.5	99.8	109.8	119.9	108.7
Caribbean Development Bank	KQJV	0.3	0.5	0.8	1.0	0.8	0.7	0.3	–	–	–
European Community/International Development Association Special Action Account	KQJW	24.5	7.2	–	–	–	–	–	–	–	–
European Investment Bank	KQJX	87.9	86.1	70.6	51.7	149.1	147.8	117.7	96.0	86.6	61.2
Inter-American Development Bank	KQJY	3.8	6.7	7.9	8.8	7.7	5.5	3.9	2.8	1.6	1.7
Fund for special operations	KQJZ	32.6	47.8	49.4	48.4	38.5	30.5	24.5	24.2	23.4	22.5
International Fund for Agricultural Development	KQKA	13.2	14.7	16.1	15.3	11.0	17.8	21.1	18.5	15.3	16.2
International Bank for Reconstruction and Development	KQKB	–	–	27.6	25.8	20.2	–	–	58.9	48.2	34.2
Special Development Fund	KQKC	–	–	–	–	1.7	1.7	6.6	6.2	9.5	8.1
Other contributions and instalments due in respect of international subscriptions, etc	KQYX	217.9	701.2	744.3	1 082.3	832.2	800.2	1 576.8	1 315.5	1 083.3	1 429.0
National Loans Fund											
Total assets	KQKD	118 390.4	127 927.3	142 885.2	158 028.5	171 367.2	185 814.3	197 430.4	197 319.8	192 981.4	198 703.4
Total National Loans Fund loans outstanding	KQKE	35 023.4	39 411.0	42 794.7	42 503.8	48 861.2	52 804.9	56 936.8	60 915.3	56 154.1	56 777.9
Loans to nationalised industries:											
Post Office	KQKF	190.6	178.6	174.4	172.3	170.1	170.1	170.1	–	–	–
British Coal	KQKG	2 588.9	2 989.1	3 407.8	3 531.8	3 243.1	3 276.5	3 374.3	1 908.6	1 145.9	387.4
Electricity Council	KQKH	3 963.7	3 988.3	3 276.3	2 578.5	3 275.4	2 617.5	1 698.5	1 335.4	–	–
North of Scotland Hydro-Electric Board	KQKI	369.6	419.1	393.8	373.7	339.5	329.7	394.9	416.7	–	–
Scottish Hydro-Electric	KQKJ	–	–	–	–	–	–	–	–	527.8	534.9
South of Scotland Electricity Board	KQKK	670.5	739.7	843.6	768.1	732.4	638.4	881.0	1 189.1	–	–
Scottish Power	KQKL	–	–	–	–	–	–	–	–	548.8	508.6
Scottish Nuclear Ltd	KQKM	–	–	–	–	–	–	–	–	205.0	203.2
British Gas Corporation	KQKN	–	40.0	–	–	–	–	–	–	–	–
British Steel Corporation	KQKO	–	–	–	–	–	–	–	–	–	–
British Airways Board	KQKP	41.3	42.4	–	–	–	–	–	–	–	–
Civil Aviation Authority	KQKQ	73.8	73.8	69.3	59.5	78.7	78.0	69.4	93.2	146.9	216.3
British Airports Authority	KQKR	62.3	57.6	52.9	48.2	43.5	–	–	–	–	–
British Railways Board	KQKS	471.4	449.2	427.6	406.3	437.0	365.9	254.4	233.0	202.8	938.5
British Transport Docks Board	KQKT	81.3	–	–	–	–	–	–	–	–	–
British Waterways Board	KQKU	19.6	21.3	22.3	23.0	23.3	24.6	25.0	24.2	22.8	21.6
National Freight Corporation	KQKV	–	–	–	–	–	–	–	–	–	–
National Bus Company	KQKW	161.0	151.2	143.3	128.3	96.4	79.4	23.0	–	–	–
Scottish Transport Group	KQKX	12.8	10.8	0.8	–	–	–	–	–	–	–
British National Oil Corporation	KQKY	–	1.7	–	–	–	–	–	–	–	–
British Aerospace	KQKZ	28.6	–	–	–	–	–	–	–	–	–
British Shipbuilders	KQLA	–	–	–	17.8	–	–	–	–	–	–
British Telecommunications	KQLB	3 056.1	2 943.7	2 789.9	–	–	–	–	–	–	–
Regional Water Authorities	KQLC	2 224.5	2 680.4	2 959.9	2 829.9	2 709.5	3 103.6	3 858.6	4 526.1	–	–
Loans to other public corporations:											
New Towns - Development Corporations and Commission	KQLD	3 940.9	4 271.5	4 453.8	4 653.3	4 742.3	3 057.3	2 975.0	2 731.6	2 481.0	1 714.6
Scottish Special Housing Association	KQLE	451.3	476.7	503.4	533.3	558.1	571.5	606.7	596.2	–	–
Scottish Homes	KQLF	–	–	–	–	–	–	–	–	796.1	786.4
Housing Corporation	KQLG	1 104.0	1 620.8	1 591.7	1 414.4	1 619.0	1 680.2	1 756.2	1 967.8	–	–
Housing Corporation (England)	KQLH	–	–	–	–	–	–	–	–	1 744.1	1 611.3
Housing for Wales	KQLI	–	–	–	–	–	–	–	–	139.9	125.8
Covent Garden Market Authority	KQLJ	23.1	21.1	19.7	18.9	18.3	17.6	2.0	1.0	0.4	–
National Enterprise Board	KQLK	3.3	1.4	2.0	–	–	–	–	–	–	–
Land Authority for Wales	KQLL	7.5	8.6	7.3	7.2	8.0	7.0	7.5	6.1	7.6	6.8
Scottish Development Agency	KQLM	6.5	8.7	9.7	9.6	9.5	8.7	6.7	6.3	5.7	5.4
Welsh Development Agency	KQLN	5.7	5.1	4.6	4.2	4.5	4.9	3.5	2.5	2.8	2.4
Development Board for Rural Wales	KQLO	20.7	25.2	29.3	34.6	41.0	8.3	8.3	8.8	8.8	8.8
Royal Mint	KQLP	4.6	3.7	2.7	1.6	0.9	0.7	0.5	0.3	0.1	–
Royal Ordnance Factories	KQLQ	10.5	6.3	2.1	–	–	–	–	–	–	–
The Crown Suppliers	KQLR	16.5	15.7	12.0	20.0	20.3	23.7	23.7	23.7	23.7	–
Crown Agents	KQLS	20.8	20.3	19.8	19.1	18.3	17.4	16.6	2.9	2.8	2.5
Her Majesty's Stationery Office	KQLT	75.9	69.8	63.0	56.3	49.6	41.2	34.4	27.7	22.6	16.8
Urban Development Corporations	KQLU	0.7	1.0	0.6	0.4	1.0	1.1	0.8	0.9	0.8	0.4
Harbour Authorities	KQLV	167.0	158.9	120.5	112.5	80.7	69.9	60.4	52.4	42.3	36.3
Commonwealth Development Corporation	KQLW	–	–	15.0	29.7	35.1	28.5	–	–	–	–
UK Atomic Energy Authority	KQLX	–	–	–	–	–	85.0	79.0	68.0	64.0	106.7

Source: HM Treasury

Home finance

16.7 Consolidated Fund and National Loans Fund: assets and liabilities
At 31 March in each year
continued

£ million

		1982	1983	1984	1985	1986	1987	1988	1989	1990	1991
National Loans Fund (*continued*)											
Loans to local authorities	KQLY	14 126.6	16 866.6	20 294.3	23 612.8	29 374.3	35 305.1	39 368.4	44 333.0	46 567.0	48 087.1
Loans to private sector:											
Shipbuilding Industry Board	KQLZ	3.5	2.2	2.2	–	–	–	–	–	–	–
Shipowners (Ship credit scheme)	KGVR	–	–	–	–	–	–	–	–	–	–
Housing associations	KGVS	23.3	21.2	20.0	19.4	18.9	18.5	17.8	16.5	15.8	14.9
Building societies	KGVT	–	–	–	–	–	–	–	–	–	–
British Nuclear Fuels Ltd	KGVU	7.6	7.1	6.5	5.9	5.1	4.3	3.4	2.4	1.3	–
British Aerospace plc	KGVV	–	24.6	20.6	16.6	12.6	8.6	5.5	3.3	1.1	–
Loans within central government:											
Northern Ireland Exchequer	KGVW	653.8	707.7	798.5	924.7	1 024.1	1 091.4	1 141.4	1 268.6	1 357.6	1 373.1
Married quarters for armed forces	KGVX	72.8	72.4	71.9	71.9	70.8	70.3	69.7	69.0	68.3	67.6
Redundancy Fund	KGVY	260.8	207.5	161.6	–	–	–	–	–	–	–
Other assets:											
Exchange Equalisation Account - capital	KGVZ	1 600.0	–	–	–	2 300.0	5 950.0	16 200.0	16 200.0	10 025.0	11 075.0
Subscriptions and contributions to international financial organisations:											
International Monetary Fund	KGXE	2 539.1	2 800.7	4 311.8	4 495.5	4 685.3	4 533.9	4 631.4	4 396.8	4 904.6	4 785.5
Borrowing included in national debt but not brought to account by 31 March	KGXF	755.2	893.1	1 113.7	–6.1	2 975.6	2 549.3	883.7	262.6	726.7	257.8
National Debt Commissioners' liability in respect of the National Savings Banks Investment Fund	KCYG	1 285.6	80.5	33.6	14.1	–	–	–	–	–	–
Other	KCYH	2.0	–	8.1	4 937.2	1 096.4	–	–	–	–	–
Consolidated Fund liability	KCYI	77 185.1	84 742.1	94 623.3	106 084.0	111 448.6	119 976.2	118 778.5	115 545.1	121 170.9	125 807.1
Total liabilities											
National Loans Fund - national debt outstanding	KCYJ	118 390.4	127 927.3	142 885.2	158 028.5	171 367.2	185 814.3	197 430.4	197 319.8	192 981.4	198 703.4

Source: HM Treasury

16.8 British government and government guaranteed marketable securities[1]
Nominal values of official and other holdings by maturity[2]
At 31 March in each year

£ million

		1982	1983	1984	1985	1986	1987	1988	1989	1990	1991	1992
Total holdings	KQMO	91 150	96 414	108 589	120 057	130 073	136 519	144 103	139 475	125 017	122 436	135 700
Up to 5 years	KQMP	25 470	27 635	34 513	41 753	43 666	40 678	41 480	41 242	36 523	34 933	40 741
Over 5 and up to 15 years	KQMQ	34 297	36 490	46 892	47 648	50 701	56 289	64 534	61 577	53 395	56 309	62 839
Over 15 years (including undated)	KQMR	31 383	32 289	27 184	30 656	35 706	39 552	38 091	36 656	35 099	31 194	32 120
Official holdings:												
Total	KQMS	9 616	8 739	7 994	6 861	8 312	8 579	9 564	17 266	17 005	15 441	12 408
Up to 5 years	KQMT	3 106	3 520	2 749	2 483	4 285	3 982	3 771	6 343	5 308	4 981	4 477
Over 5 and up to 15 years	KQMU	5 213	3 670	4 296	3 550	3 061	3 324	4 527	6 604	6 866	7 263	6 034
Over 15 years (including undated)	KQMV	1 275	1 524	921	797	935	1 273	1 246	4 319	4 830	3 197	1 897
Market holdings:												
Total	KQMW	81 534	87 675	100 595	113 196	121 761	127 940	134 559	122 209	108 012	106 995	123 292
Up to 5 years	KQMX	22 364	24 115	31 764	39 270	39 381	36 696	37 709	34 899	31 215	29 952	36 264
Over 5 and upto 15 years	KQMY	29 084	32 820	42 596	44 098	47 642	52 965	60 006	54 973	46 529	49 046	56 805
Over 15 years (including undated)	KQMZ	30 108	30 765	26 263	29 859	34 771	38 279	36 844	32 337	30 269	27 998	30 223

1 The government guaranteed securities of nationalised industries only. A relatively small amount of other government gauranteed securities is excluded.

2 Securities with optional redemption dates are classified according to the final redemption date.

Source: Bank of England

Home finance

16.9 National savings
Year ended 31 March

£ million

		1981/82	1982/83	1983/84	1984/85	1985/86	1986[8]/87	1987/88	1988/89	1989/90	1990/91	1991/92
Department for National Savings												
Receipts												
Total[1]	KQNA	5 898.4	5 211.8	5 302.5	5 701.2	4 517.3	6 521.8	6 069.7	6 995.0	5 559.7	6 406.5	7 702.3
Capital Bonds	KQNB	–	–	–	–	–	–	–	199.5	284.0	185.6	338.3
National savings certificates:												
Fixed interest	KQNC	2 054.8	1 380.9	1 451.0	2 107.8	731.0	1 309.6	457.8	1 383.1	632.6	696.7	2 119.6
Index-linked	KQND	1 990.3	638.3	186.3	106.5	217.7	171.1	253.7	785.2	634.6	1 503.2	1 500.8
Yearly plan	KQNE	–	–	–	27.7	106.9	126.9	128.8	115.8	86.9	71.8	86.9
Save as you earn:												
Fixed interest (1st, 2nd and 4th issues)	KQNF	4.7	11.5	18.0	23.7	34.4	42.0	52.6	63.3	76.2	83.2	94.1
Index-linked (3rd issue)	KQNG	131.3	123.8	106.6	90.2	56.4	23.8	8.8	2.9	0.2	–	–
Income bonds	KQNH	–	893.1	1 126.4	1 081.1	1 201.5	2 202.3	2 102.2	1 729.7	1 512.1	1 605.6	1 355.9
Investment account[2]	KQNI	992.5	1 346.3	1 447.9	1 255.8	1 204.2	1 517.4	1 886.9	1 629.6	1 491.5	1 515.7	1 247.7
Premium savings bonds	KQNJ	148.5	178.1	190.2	204.3	184.9	216.9	298.0	313.5	249.4	185.7	257.5
Ordinary account	KQNK	576.3	639.8	667.8	667.0	645.1	645.2	649.7	637.6	592.2	559.0	566.0
Childrens bonus bonds	KHCU											135.5
Deposit bonds	KQNL	–	–	108.3	137.1	130.3	247.2	225.8	134.8	–	–	–
Indexed-income bonds	KQNM	–	–	–	–	4.9	19.4	6.4	–	–	–	–
British savings bonds	KQNN	–	–	–	–	–	–	–	–	–	–	–
Repayments												
Total[1]	KQNO	3 012.1	3 698.2	3 777.5	4 649.3	4 718.2	5 341.2	6 044.9	8 488.0	9 432.0	7 339.8	6 495.7
Capital bonds	KQNP	–	–	–	–	–	–	–	–	5.0	23.6	14.9
National savings certificates:												
Fixed interest - Principal	KQNQ	772.6	513.8	453.3	776.6	713.7	971.7	1 296.9	2 117.3	2 498.2	1 455.3	1 193.4
- Accrued interest	KQNR	305.2	201.1	210.6	341.1	371.3	563.7	842.5	1 578.5	1 642.6	991.0	738.7
Index-linked - Principal	KQNS	208.0	821.2	672.6	527.6	521.8	618.6	369.4	409.4	394.4	412.9	418.8
- Accrued interest/index-linking, bonuses and supplements	KQNT	89.1	276.5	199.7	216.9	283.4	350.6	246.7	329.0	370.6	403.3	396.6
Yearly plan:												
Principal	KQNU	–	–	–	0.1	3.3	7.6	10.8	16.6	82.4	124.2	106.5
Interest	KQNV	–	–	–	–	–	0.2	0.5	1.3	23.6	43.2	40.9
Save as you earn:												
Fixed interest - Principal	KQNW	8.8	1.7	1.5	4.7	7.5	26.5	20.8	38.3	40.9	59.3	74.4
- Accrued interest	KQNX	4.0	0.5	0.1	0.6	1.3	6.6	4.5	10.8	9.7	13.3	16.0
Index-linked - Principal	KQNY	50.8	157.5	118.1	120.3	155.4	99.5	65.7	51.3	45.0	24.2	29.4
- Accrued interest/index-linking	KQNZ	18.0	87.2	54.4	49.7	51.2	33.4	27.4	28.5	33.7	27.1	38.5
Income bonds	KQOA	–	1.8	60.7	243.2	311.6	381.9	621.6	943.0	1 091.2	824.2	719.9
Investment account[2]	KQOB	670.8	770.3	1 085.4	1 391.1	1 343.8	1 349.0	1 560.2	1 957.3	2 074.3	1 904.0	1 803.9
Premium savings bonds	KQOC	103.9	98.6	102.2	110.5	119.6	124.2	131.1	133.5	186.4	193.4	153.7
Ordinary account	KQOD	695.6	678.2	722.8	770.1	772.1	741.8	737.5	727.8	733.2	700.9	663.7
Childrens bonus bonds	KHCV	–	–	–	–	–	–	–	–	–	–	0.1
Deposit bonds	KQOE	–	–	0.1	17.3	44.3	63.2	104.0	142.4	197.6	137.7	85.3
Indexed-income bonds	KQOF	–	–	–	–	–	1.3	4.1	3.0	3.2	2.2	1.0
British savings bonds:												
Before maturity	KQOG	32.9	16.0	6.3	2.0	–	–	–	–	–	–	–
On maturity	KQOH	102.4	73.8	89.7	77.5	17.9	1.4	1.2	–	–	–	–

1 Excludes Ulster Savings Certificates.
2 Investment Account contributes to the funding of PSBR/CGBR from January 1981.
3 Including National Savings stamps and gift tokens and securities on the National Savings register, which (except for British savings bonds) do not appear in the first part of the table.
4 Nominal value held in National Savings section.
5 Including accrued interest to date.
6 From September 1979 excludes £7.7 million deemed to be outstanding National Savings stamps written off on 15 August 1979.
7 Nominal value held (until 1979) in Trustee savings banks section.
8 From 1 April 1986 onwards the data series have been revised. The revisions, notably those for the estimates of accrued interest, coincided with the adoption of an improved transaction accounting system for National Savings.

Source: Department for National Savings

Home finance

16.9 National savings
Year ended 31 March — continued

£ million

		1981/82	1982/83	1983/84	1984/85	1985/86	1986[8]/87	1987/88	1988/89	1989/90	1990/91	1991/92
TSB not included above (contd.)												
Repayments												
Save as you earn:												
Fixed interest - Principal	KQOI	10.1	2.1	–	–	–	–	–	–	–	–	–
- Accrued interest	KQOJ	4.6	0.4	–	–	–	–	–	–	–	–	–
Ordinary department	KQOK	–	–	–	–	–	–	–	–	–	–	–
British savings bonds:												
Before maturity	KQOL	0.1	–	–	–	–	–	–	–	–	–	–
On maturity	KQOM	12.2	–	–	–	–	–	–	–	–	–	–
Total	KQON	27.0	2.5	–	–	–	–	–	–	–	–	–
Department for National savings												
Interest accruing												
Capital bonds	KQOO	–	–	–	–	–	–	–	–	12.2	42.0	76.8
National savings certificates:												
Fixed interest	KQOP	483.2	648.1	815.3	1 000.4	1 137.8	1 095.3	1 124.9	810.0	675.0	525.7	443.3
Index-linking (including bonuses and supplements)	KQOQ	401.9	332.1	364.1	361.3	389.3	314.4	267.5	365.8	422.0	477.0	351.7
Yearly plan	KQOR	–	–	–	–	3.9	12.0	23.2	33.1	46.0	43.3	39.1
Save as you earn:												
Fixed interest (1st, 2nd and 4th issues)	KQOS	2.0	0.8	1.9	3.7	5.5	8.7	9.3	11.5	13.6	14.4	18.3
Index-linked (3rd issue)	KQOT	41.9	93.0	52.4	46.1	44.1	28.3	31.2	33.7	26.3	21.1	8.8
Investment account[2]	KQOU	353.1	380.2	438.6	509.7	608.1	640.0	655.1	700.8	831.2	1 007.8	864.4
Ordinary account	KQOV	81.2	70.5	78.6	79.6	78.8	78.7	77.0	65.2	64.0	60.9	58.2
Childrens bonus bonds	KHCW	–	–	–	–	–	–	–	–	–	–	–
Deposit bonds	KQOW	–	–	1.5	17.8	37.8	49.7	73.7	87.0	97.4	95.4	77.9
Total[1]	KQOX	1 363.3	1 524.7	1 752.4	2 018.6	2 305.3	2 227.1	2 261.9	2 107.1	2 187.7	2 287.6	1 938.5
Amounts remaining invested												
Capital bonds[5]	KQOY	–	–	–	–	–	–	–	199.5	490.7	694.7	1 094.9
National savings certificates												
Fixed interest - Principal	KQOZ	5 832.8	6 699.9	7 697.6	9 028.8	9 046.1	9 318.1	8 479.0	7 744.8	5 879.2	5 120.6	6 046.8
- Accrued interest	KQPA	1 367.9	1 814.9	2 419.6	3 078.9	3 845.4	4 112.4	4 394.8	3 626.3	2 658.7	2 193.4	1 898.0
Index-linked - Principal	KQPB	4 236.5	4 053.6	3 567.3	3 146.2	2 842.1	2 422.9	2 307.2	2 683.0	2 923.2	4 013.5	5 095.5
- Bonuses and supplements/index-linking	KQPC	895.9	951.5	1 115.9	1 260.3	1 366.2	1 317.4	1 338.2	1 375.0	1 426.4	1 500.1	1 455.2
Yearly plan:												
Capital	KQPD	–	–	–	27.6	133.9	258.5	380.7	483.4	491.1	441.1	423.9
Interest	KQPE	–	–	–	–	1.2	9.4	27.9	56.2	75.4	73.1	68.9
Save as you earn:												
Fixed interest - Principal	KQPF	6.3	16.1	32.6	51.6	78.5	92.8	124.6	149.6	184.9	208.8	228.5
- Accrued interest	KQPG	0.6	0.9	2.7	5.8	10.0	12.0	16.8	17.5	21.4	22.5	24.8
Index-linked - Principal	KQPH	521.4	487.7	476.2	446.1	347.1	266.3	209.4	161.0	116.2	92.0	62.6
- Accrued interest/index-linking	KQPI	126.2	132.0	130.0	126.4	119.3	112.4	116.2	121.4	114.0	108.0	78.3
Stock on the National savings register (DNS only)[4]	KQPJ	842.1	812.5	818.1	891.7	872.3	836.0	811.2	846.4	868.4	963.1	1 026.2
Income bonds	KQPK	–	891.3	1 957.0	2 794.9	3 684.8	5 494.6	6 974.2	7 760.9	8 181.8	8 963.2	9 599.2
Investment account[5]	KQPL	2 995.1	3 951.3	4 752.4	5 126.8	5 595.3	6 403.7	7 385.5	7 758.6	8 007.0	8 626.5	8 934.7
Premium savings bonds	KQPM	1 506.2	1 585.7	1 673.7	1 767.5	1 832.8	1 924.1	2 091.0	2 271.0	2 334.0	2 326.3	2 430.1
Ordinary account[5]	KQPN	1 702.0	1 734.1	1 757.7	1 734.2	1 686.0	1 668.1	1 657.3	1 632.3	1 555.3	1 474.3	1 434.8
Childrens bonus bonds[5]	KHCX	–	–	–	–	–	–	–	–	–	–	135.4
Deposit bonds[5]	KQPO	–	–	109.7	247.3	371.1	605.0	800.5	879.9	779.7	737.4	730.0
Indexed-income bonds	KQPP	–	–	–	–	4.9	23.0	25.3	22.3	19.1	16.9	15.9
British saving bonds	KQPQ	285.8	196.0	100.0	20.5	2.6	1.2	–	–	–	–	–
National savings stamps and gift tokens[6]	KQPR	1.2	1.3	1.3	1.3	1.3	1.8	2.1	2.4	2.1	1.9	1.8
Total administered by DNS[3]	KQPS	20 320.0	23 328.8	26 611.8	29 755.9	31 840.9	34 879.7	37 141.9	37 791.5	36 128.6	37 577.4	40 785.5
Trustee savings bank												
Interest accruing												
Save as you earn:												
Fixed interest (1st and 2nd issues only)	KQPT	1.8	0.2	–	–	–	–	–	–	–	–	–
Total	KQPU	1.8	0.2	–	–	–	–	–	–	–	–	–
Amounts remaining invested												
Save as you earn:												
Fixed interest - Principal	KQPV	2.1	–	–	–	–	–	–	–	–	–	–
- Interest	KQPW	0.2	–	–	–	–	–	–	–	–	–	–
British savings bonds	KQPX	–	–	–	–	–	–	–	–	–	–	–
TSB stock register[7]	KQPY	–	–	–	–	–	–	–	–	–	–	–
Total Trustee savings bank	KQPZ	2.3	–	–	–	–	–	–	–	–	–	–

See footnotes on page 274.

Source: Department for National Savings

Home finance

16.10 Income tax: allowances and reliefs

	1982/83	1983/84	1984/85	1985/86	1986/87	1987/88	1988/89	1989/90	1990/91	1991/92	1992/93
Personal allowances											
Personal allowance	£1 565	£1 785	£2 005	£2 205	£2 335	£2 425	£2 605	£2 785	£3 005	£3 295	£3 445
Married man's allowance[1]	£2 445	£2 795	£3 155	£3 455	£3 655	£3 795	£4 095	£4 375	-	-	-
Married couple's allowance[2]	-	-	-	-	-	-	-	-	£1 720	£1 720	£1 720
Wife's earned income allowance[3]	£1 565	£1 785	£2 055	£2 205	£2 335	£2 425	£2 605	£2 785	-	-	-
Age allowance[4]:											
Married (either partner over 65 but neither partner over 75)	£3 295	£3 755	£3 955	£4 255	£4 505	£4 675[4]	£5 035[4]	£5 385	-	-	-
Married couple's allowance[2] (either partner over 65 but neither partner over 75)	-	-	-	-	-	-	-	-	£2 145	£2 355	£2 465
Married (either partner over 75)	£3 295	£3 755	£3 955	£4 255	£4 505	£4 845[4]	£5 205[4]	£5 565	-	-	-
Married couple's allowance[2] (either partner over 75)	-	-	-	-	-	-	-	-	£2 185	£2 395	£2 505
Personal (over 65 but under 75)	£2 070	£2 360	£2 490	£2 690	£2 850	£2 960	£3 180	£3 400	£3 670	£4 020	£4 200
Personal (over 75)	£2 070	£2 360	£2 490	£2 690	£2 850	£3 070	£3 310	£3 540	£3 820	£4 180	£4 370
Income limit	£6 700	£7 600	£8 100	£8 800	£9 400	£9 800	£10 600	£11 400	£12 300	£13 500	£14 200
Marginal fraction	2/3	2/3	2/3	2/3	2/3	2/3	2/3	1/2	1/2	1/2	1/2
Additional personal allowance[5]	£880	£1 010	£1 150	£1 250	£1 320	£1 370	£1 490	£1 590	£1 720	£1 720	£1 720
Widow's bereavement allowance[6]	£880	£1 010	£1 150	£1 250	£1 320	£1 370	£1 490	£1 590	£1 720	£1 720	£1 720
Dependent relative allowance[7]:											
Maintained by single woman	£145	£145	£145	£145	£145	£145	-	-	-	-	-
Other cases	£100	£100	£100	£100	£100	£100					
Limit of relative's income	£1 601	£1 708	£1 804	£1 901	£1 901	£1 901	-	-	-	-	-
Daughter's or son's services allowance[8]	£55	£55	£55	£55	£55	£55	-	-	-	-	-
Housekeeper allowance[9]	£100	£100	£100	£100	£100	£100	-	-	-	-	-
Blind person's allowance[10]	£360	£360	£360	£360	£360	£540	£540	£540	£1 080	£1 080	£1 080
Life assurance relief[11]											
(Percentage of gross premium)	15.0	15.0	15.0 or Nil	15.0 or Nil	15.0 or Nil	15.0 or Nil	15.0 or Nil	15.0 or Nil	15.0 or Nil	15.0 or Nil	15.0 or Nil

1 The married man's allowance was that for a full year, payable instead of the personal allowance. In the year of marriage the allowance is reduced by one twelfth of the difference between the married and single personal allowances for each complete month (beginning on the sixth day of each calender month) prior to the date of marriage.

2 Following the introduction of Independent Taxation from 1990-91 the married couple's allowance was introduced. It is payable in addition to the personal allowance. The married couple's allowance will initially be set against the husband's income. If there is any surplus this will be transferred to the wife. There will continue to be higher allowances for elderly taxpayers aged 65 to 74 or 75 and over.

3 The wife's earned income allowance has as its maximum value the amount shown. Where the earned income was less, the allowance is reduced to the actual amount of earned income. From 1990-91, under Independent Taxation, the allowance is abolished and wives obtain a personal allowance.

4 The age allowance replaces the single or married allowances, provided the taxpayer's income is below the limit shown. For incomes in excess of the limit, the allowance is reduced by £2 for each additional £3 of income until the ordinary single or married allowance is reached. From 1989-90 the allowance was reduced by £1 for each additional £2 of income. The relief was due where the taxpayer (or, prior to 1990-91, wife living with him) was aged 65 or over in the year of assessment. For 1989-90, 1990-91 and 1991-92 the increased level of relief is available to those aged 75 and over. The married age allowances were abolished in 1990-91, under Independent Taxation and replaced by age-related married couples allowances.

5 The additional personal allowance may be claimed by a single parent (or by a married amn if his wife is totally incapacitated) who maintains a resident child at his or her own expense.

6 Widow's bereavement allowance is due to a widow in the year of her husband's death and in the following year provided the widow has not remarried before the beginning of that year.

7 The dependent relative allowance was due to a taxpayer who maintained, wholly or partially, either (a) and aged or infirm relative, or (b) his or his wife's seperated, divorced or widowed mother. The relative's income had to be below the limits shown in order for the full allowances to be given (the limit was equal to the basic National Insurance Retirement Pension). The allowance was reduced by the excess of the relative's income over the income limit.

8 The daughter's or son's services allowance could be claimed by an aged or infirm taxpayer who maintained a daughter or son (before 1978-79 a daughter only) on whose services the taxpayer or his wife were dependent.

9 The housekeeper allowance could be claimed by a widow or widower who had a resident housekeeper (before 1978-79 a female housekeeper only). For 1978-79 and earlier years this allowance could also be claimed by an unmarried person who maintained a resident relative (before 1978-79 a female relative only) to look after a brother or sister for whom child allowance was given.

10 The blind person's allowance is due to a registered blind taxpayer and up to 1980-81 was reduced by the amount of any tax-free blindness disability pension which was receivable. Prior to 1990-91 where both spouses were blind the married man received two blind person's allowance.

11 Relief on life assurance premiums is given by deduction from the premium payable. From 1984-85, it is confined to policies made before 14 March 1984.

Source: Board of Inland Revenue

Home finance

16.11 Rates of Income tax

	1983/84		1984/85		1985/86		1986/87		1987/88	
	Slice of taxable income £	Rate per cent	Slice of taxable income £	Rate per cent	Slice of taxable income £	Rate per cent	Slice of taxable income £	Rate per cent	Slice of taxable income £	Rate per cent
Lower rate	-	-	-	-	-	-	-	-	-	-
Basic rate	1-14 600	30	1-15 400	30	1-16 200	30	1-17 200	29	1-17 900	27
Higher rates	14 601-17 200	40	15 401-18 200	40	16 201-19 200	40	17 201-20 200	40	17 901-20 400	40
	17 201-21 800	45	18 201-23 100	45	19 201-24 400	45	20 201-25 400	45	20 401-25 400	45
	21 801-28 900	50	23 101-30 600	50	24 401-32 300	50	25 401-33 300	50	25 401-33 300	50
	28 901-36 000	55	30 601-38 100	55	32 301-40 200	55	33 301-41 200	55	33 301-41 200	55
	over 36 000	60	over 38 100	60	over 40 200	60	over 41 200	60	over 41 200	60
Investment Income surcharge[1]	Slice of net investment income £	Rate per cent	Slice of net investment income £	Rate per cent	Slice of net investment income £	Rate per cent	Slice of net investment income £	Rate per cent	Slice of net investment income £	Rate per cent
Non-aged persons	1-7 100	-	-	-	-	-	-	-	-	-
Exempt slice	over 7 100	15								
Aged persons	1-7 100	-								
Exempt slice	over 7 100	15								

	1988/89		1989/90		1990/91		1991/92		1992/93	
	Slice of taxable income £	Rate per cent	Slice of taxable income £	Rate per cent	Slice of taxable income £	Rate per cent	Slice of taxalbe income £	Rate per cent	Slice of taxable income £	Rate per cent
Lower rate	-	-	-	-	-	-	-	-	1-2 000	20
Basic rate	1-19 300	25	1-20 700	25	1-20 700	25	1-23 700	25	2 001-23 700	25
Higher rate	over 19 300	40	over 20 700	40	over 20 700	40	over 23 700	40	over 23 700	40

1 Investment income surcharge was chargeable in addition to any basic or higher rates of tax where an individual's investment income exceeded the limits shown. It was abolished from 1984/85 onwards.

Source: Board of Inland Revenue

Home finance

16.12 Rateable values
England and Wales
At April in each year

		1981	1982	1983	1984	1985	1986	1987	1988	1989	1990[2]	1991[2]
Number of properties (Thousands)												
Total-all classes	KMIH	22 291.1	22 463.1	22 621.6	22 827.7	23 032.3	23 243.4	23 456.1	23 667.8	23 915.7	1 684.7	1 708.5
Domestic: total	KMII	18 578.4	18 736.7	18 873.8	19 055.6	19 238.3	19 429.1	19 621.2	19 817.8	20 057.5	–	–
Houses and flats with rateable values:												
Not over £75	KMIJ	1 323.5	1 291.5	1 267.8	1 249.6	1 234.1						
Over £75 but not over £100	KMIK KHDG	1 286.2	1 285.5	1 288.3	1 292.2	1 295.8	19 102.6[1]	19 301.9[1]	19 503.2[1]	19 747.8[1]	–	–
Over £100	KMIL	15 618.1	15 814.3	15 976.6	16 177.4	16 376.3						
Agricultural dwelling-houses, etc	KMIM	350.6	345.3	341.2	336.4	332.0	326.5	319.4	314.6	309.6		
Commercial: total	KMIN	3 092.3	3 102.9	3 120.7	3 138.2	3 156.0	3 171.8	3 187.0	3 200.2	3 210.1	1 190.2	1 210.7
Shops and cafes	KMIO	570.1	567.2	566.2	566.5	567.3	567.9	569.0	569.2	569.0	575.6	571.8
Offices	KMIP	177.3	179.7	182.9	186.6	191.3	197.1	202.9	209.0	214.2	222.8	233.6
Other	KMIQ	2 344.9	2 355.9	2 371.7	2 385.1	2 397.4	2 406.8	2 415.3	2 421.9	2 426.9	391.9	405.3
On-licensed premises: total	KMIR	54.9	54.8	54.8	55.1	54.9	54.8	54.9	54.8	54.8	55.3	55.2
Entertainment and recreational: total	KMIS	74.7	75.3	76.1	76.8	77.3	77.8	78.2	78.6	78.7	94.8	94.7
Cinemas	KMIT	1.1	1.0	1.0	1.0	0.9	0.8	0.8	0.7	0.7	0.6	0.6
Theatres and music-halls	KMIU	0.4	0.4	0.4	0.4	0.5	0.5	0.5	0.5	0.5	0.5	0.5
Other	KMIV	73.2	73.9	74.7	75.4	75.9	76.5	77.0	77.4	77.5	93.7	93.6
Public utility: total	KMIW	38.8	38.5	38.6	38.5	38.7	38.6	38.5	38.3	38.1	15.3	15.2
Educational and cultural: total	KMIX	42.2	42.1	41.8	41.6	41.3	41.0	40.8	40.5	40.3	41.6	42.1
Miscellaneous: total	KMIY	302.9	304.9	306.6	311.2	313.6	316.7	320.9	322.9	322.6	53.3	53.1
Industrial: total	KMIZ	106.9	107.9	109.1	110.7	112.3	113.6	114.7	114.8	113.7	234.2	237.4
Value of assessments (£ million)												
Total-all classes	KMHA	7 441.5	7 552.6	7 641.4	7 730.7	7 822.2	7 915.1	8 025.2	8 121.0	8 230.7	32 915.8	34 213.5
Domestic: total	KMHB	3 630.7	3 678.2	3 719.2	3 766.6	3 814.5	3 864.6	3 916.4	3 969.1	4 031.9	–	–
Houses and flats with rateable values:												
Not over £75	KMHC	75.4	73.8	72.7	71.8	71.0						
Over £75 but not over £100	KMHD KHDH	113.7	113.8	114.0	114.4	114.7	3 793.2[1]	3 845.3[1]	3 899.7[1]	3 963.4[1]	–	–
Over £100	KMHE	3 367.5	3 417.4	3 459.7	3 507.9	3 557.0						
Agricultural dwelling-houses, etc	KMHF	74.1	73.3	72.8	72.5	71.9	71.4	71.1	69.7	68.5	–	–
Commercial: total	KMHG	1 792.8	1 847.6	1 897.3	1 946.2	1 988.8	2 037.5	2 078.7	2 120.6	2 166.4	19 565.8	20 659.3
Shops and cafes	KMHH	607.4	615.2	621.1	628.1	634.1	638.5	644.6	648.6	655.6	7 228.7	7 382.3
Offices	KMHI	637.2	660.3	681.7	702.8	722.1	748.1	768.0	789.9	814.7	6 787.2	7 544.8
Other	KMHJ	548.2	572.1	594.5	615.3	632.6	650.9	666.0	682.1	696.1	5 549.9	5 732.2
On-licensed premises: total	KMHK	65.1	65.8	65.5	64.4	63.8	63.9	64.5	65.0	65.8	679.3	691.3
Entertainment and recreational: total	KMHL	77.3	79.4	81.3	83.6	85.0	86.4	88.2	89.5	91.0	950.5	993.5
Cinemas	KMHM	3.9	3.8	3.8	3.6	3.4	3.3	3.1	3.0	2.8	18.3	21.4
Theatres and music-halls	KMHN	1.8	1.9	1.9	2.1	2.1	2.1	2.1	2.1	2.1	20.7	21.3
Other	KMHO	71.6	73.7	75.6	77.9	79.5	81.0	82.9	84.4	86.1	911.5	950.9
Public utility: total	KMHP	407.7	406.1	406.7	407.6	412.6	409.8	423.1	428.3	435.0	3 485.4	3 493.2
Educational and cultural: total	KMHQ	244.3	244.6	243.9	242.0	240.4	239.2	237.9	236.3	234.9	1 980.8	1 993.8
Miscellaneous: total	KMHR	436.4	444.2	450.0	455.4	462.3	468.9	478.2	480.1	479.5	806.3	823.3
Industrial: total	KMHS	787.2	786.8	777.5	764.8	754.7	744.8	738.8	732.1	726.1	5 447.8	5 559.3

1 The detailed breakdown of the various rateable value bands for houses and flats is not available after 1985.
2 See introduction to this chapter on page 264.

Source: Board of Inland Revenue

Home finance

16.13 Local authorities: gross loan debt outstanding[1]
At 31 March in each year

£ million

		1982	1983	1984	1985	1986	1987	1988	1989	1990	1991
United Kingdom											
Total debt[2]	KQBR	41 806	44 387	47 546	49 343	49 972	53 412	53 484	..	..	..
Public Works Loan Board	KQBS	14 111	16 846	20 250	23 527	29 288	35 252	39 356	44 324	46 499	48 001
Northern Ireland Consolidated Fund[2]	KQBT	225	215	204	199	198	195	190	197	208	239
Other debt	KQBU	27 470	27 326	27 080	25 579	20 490	17 972	13 945	..	..	..
England and Wales											
Total debt	KQBV	35 862	38 116	40 816	42 266	42 540	45 548	45 176	50 091	51 689	49 914
of which Public Works Loan Board	KQBW	*12 129*	*14 331*	*17 310*	*20 141*	*24 887*	*29 901*	*33 379*	*37 563*	*39 969*	*41 025*
Scotland											
Total debt	KQBX	5 878	6 204	6 659	7 003	7 357	7 782	8 224	8 650	8 192	4 005
of which Public Works Loan Board	KQBY	*1 982*	*2 515*	*2 940*	*3 386*	*4 401*	*5 351*	*5 977*	*6 761*	*6 530*	*6 976*
Northern Ireland											
Total debt[2]	KQBZ	66	67	71	74	75	82	84	93	101	123

1 The sums shown exclude inter-authority loans and debt transfers, and temporary loans and overdrafts obtained for the purpose of providing for current expenses. No deduction has been made in respect of sums held in sinking funds for the repayment of debt.
2 The Northern Ireland Loans Fund was abolished on 1 April 1983 and it's functions transferred to the Northern Ireland Consolidated Fund.

Sources: Department of the Environment (1981 to 1990);
Scottish Office, Central Statistics Unit;
Public Works Loan Board;
Department of the Environment for Northern Ireland;
Welsh Office (1981 to 1990);
Chartered Institute of Public Finance and Accountancy (England and Wales, 1991)

16.14 Expenditure and income of local authorities: summary
Years ended 31 March

£ million

		1981/82	1982/83	1983/84	1984/85	1985/86	1986/87	1987/88	1988/89	1989/90	1990/91
United Kingdom											
Total expenditure:[1]											
Capital	KQEO	5 635.7	6 899.5	7 876.6	8 093.9	7 361.9	7 603.5	7 828.1	8 895.4	11 761.3	8 863.8
Other	KQEP	37 477.8	40 509.2	43 272.9	45 481.9	47 339.7	50 289.0	54 645.6	59 328.1	64 281.8	76 495.4
Total income	KQEQ	44 120.0	47 901.8	50 442.7	52 355.7	54 779.4	56 251.2	59 827.3	65 476.2	70 197.3	–
England and Wales											
Total expenditure:[1]											
Capital[2]	KQER	4 903.3	6 111.8	6 918.0	7 228.7	6 437.1	6 666.3	6 717.7[5]	7 719.3[6,5]	10 463.2[5]	7 576.7[7]
Other[3]	KQES	33 441.0	36 142.3	38 573.3	40 544.5	42 138.3	44 783.4	48 756.9	52 962.8	57 309.2	68 872.1
Total income[4]	KQET	39 311.2	42 617.6	44 718.7	46 602.7	48 581.4	49 873.3	52 734.6	57 873.7	61 731.8	66 190.8
Scotland											
Total expenditure:[1]											
Capital	KQEU	707.3	763.6	929.4	840.0	891.5	912.2	1 079.4	1 142.1	1 262.1	1 249.7
Other	KQEV	3 926.2	4 245.0	4 566.5	4 794.1	5 048.2	5 352.0	5 721.8	6 198.0	6 793.2	7 429.8
Total income	KQEW	4 672.6	5 133.1	5 558.7	5 581.8	6 046.4	6 235.1	6 922.5	7 438.3	8 288.7	–
Northern Ireland											
Total expenditure:[1]											
Capital	KQEX	25.1	24.1	29.2	25.2	33.3	25.0	31.0	34.0	36.0	37.4
Other	KQEY	110.6	121.9	133.1	143.3	153.2	154.1	166.9	167.3	179.4	193.5
Total income	KQEZ	136.2	151.1	165.3	168.8	151.6	142.8	170.2	164.2	176.8	187.5

1 'Capital' and 'Other' figures cannot be added to give a 'Total' figure because of double counting of loan charges, which are scored as both 'Capital' and 'Other' expenditure.
2 From Table 16.16.
3 From Table 16.15. Includes loan charges. Includes capital resources set aside to redeem debt for England and Wales for 1987/88 to 1989/90 and for England only for 1990/91.
4 From Table 16.18.
5 Includes leasing acquisitions. Excludes sums repaid to lenders or transferred to sinking funds out of unexpected balances of loans and other capital receipts.
6 From 1988/89 includes acquisition of share or loan capital.
7 New Capital System introduced. Includes credit cover required for credit arrangements (including those that are leases). Also includes expenditure treated as capital expenditure under direction.

Sources: Department of the Environment;
Scottish Office, Central Statistics Unit;
Department of the Environment for Northern Ireland;
Welsh Office

Home finance

16.15 Revenue account: gross expenditure of local authorities[1]
England and Wales
Years ended 31 March

£ million

		1980/81	1981/82	1982/83	1983/84	1984/85	1985/86	1986/87	1987/88	1988/89	1989/90	1990/91
Education including school catering services	KQRA	10 959.0	12 067.9	12 694.3	13 315.7	13 847.4	14 543.3	15 830.2	17 167.6	18 651.5	19 336.6	21 174.9
Libraries, museums and art galleries	KQRB	348.9	383.7	418.8	449.8	477.0	511.7	546.9	584.5	642.3	711.8	782.7
Local authority port health	KQRC	3.4	3.8	4.0	4.1	4.3	4.5	4.3	4.2	4.2	4.9	6.0
Personal social services	KQRD	2 155.5	2 387.8	2 609.4	2 805.8	2 975.7	3 179.7	3 473.3	3 879.1	4 327.6	4 866.1	5 450.0
Sheltered employment and workshops	KQRE	27.6	30.1	34.5	39.6	44.3	47.8	52.0	57.3	60.4	66.0	79.7
Police, including school crossing patrols	KQRF	1 979.5	2 343.5	2 600.2	2 852.1	3 336.8	3 269.2	3 653.6	3 687.5	4 023.0	4 425.2	4 993.7
Fire service	KQRG	451.3	515.1	573.5	624.4	677.4	730.9	783.0	858.1	936.5	1 049.1	1 163.5
Administration of justice	KQRH	233.6	269.5	295.8	319.8	344.0	372.3	408.6	435.0	496.1	577.7	664.5
Refuse collection and disposal	KQRI	632.2	667.9	704.9	718.8	739.5	793.0	815.2	882.3	948.5	993.9	1 077.9
Agriculture and fisheries	KQRJ	100.0	123.4	132.7	144.9	153.1	150.3	186.8	198.4	207.7	208.1	88.1
Local transport	KQRK	2 086.9	2 353.5	2 574.8	2 679.8	2 766.6	2 690.1	2 789.0	2 860.3	2 988.7	3 299.6	3 817.0
Parks and open spaces[2]	KQRL	770.0	832.8	935.2	1 019.3	1 105.1	1 219.4	1 292.1	1 407.7	1 548.1	1 683.9	1 954.0
Environmental health[2]	KQRM	332.6	353.1	383.2	407.3	425.8	444.9	477.7	832.1	566.4	642.5	775.5
Cemeteries and crematoria	KQRN	62.4	67.7	73.3	77.8	80.8	85.0	90.4	151.2	102.6	114.5	120.5
Town and country planning	KQRO	494.6	537.1	573.6	650.0	683.8	736.8	712.3	778.0	881.0	1 002.5	1 121.9
Housing to which the Housing revenue Account relates	KQRP	4 564.0	4 840.5	5 087.1	5 197.4	5 472.8	5 921.9	5 943.7	5 985.6	6 564.0	7 252.4	6 927.8
Other housing	KQRQ	933.6	904.6	926.5	1 422.3	1 832.7	1 923.0	2 429.0	2 481.3	2 557.7	2 950.7	3 115.1
Trading services: Passenger transport[3]	KQRR	162.4	172.8	182.6	194.0	201.8	207.8	..	..	..	..	..
Harbours, docks and piers	KQRS	47.4	51.8	51.9	52.2	45.9	47.6	49.1	50.9	55.2	60.0	52.4
Other trading services	KQRT	503.7	570.8	658.2	744.6	773.0	905.9	804.3	814.1	875.0	921.2	1 049.3
Other services	KQRU	679.4	816.1	900.7	1 047.6	1 135.8	1 309.8	1 339.9	1 435.0	1 585.6	1 886.8	2 863.3
Expenditure on general administration and all other expenditure and transfers[4]	KQRV	2 809.5	3 147.6	3 727.1	3 806.2	3 420.9	3 043.6	3 102.1	3 720.5	4 253.1	4 837.8	5 400.4
Total	KMHU	30 337.5	33 441.0	36 142.3	38 573.3	40 544.5	42 138.4	44 783.4	48 270.6	52 275.6	56 821.4	62 678.0
Total loan charges[5] included in expenditure above	KQRW	5 132.1	5 360.5	5 281.6	5 038.2	5 031.8	5 331.3	5 533.4	5 817.4	6 445.7	6 787.9	5 406.2
Allocated to: Rate fund services[6]	KQRX	2 132.8	2 257.0	2 178.1	1 997.3	2 201.9	1 962.9	2 550.7	2 644.2	3 020.3	3 252.5	3 515.4
Housing revenue	KQRY	2 876.5	2 953.7	2 911.3	2 859.4	2 632.7	3 168.9	2 789.5	2 980.4	3 173.0	3 325.2	1 700.3
Trading services	KQRZ	122.7	149.7	192.3	181.4	197.2	199.4	193.2	192.7	252.5	210.2	190.5
Capital resources set aside to redeem debt[7]	KMHT	425.9	587.9	669.5	588.4	499.8	373.4	348.8	486.3	687.2	487.8	6 194.1[8]

1 Expenditure on employees, running expenses, debt redemption, interest repayments, Revenue contributions to Capital outlay (to 1989/90) and Capital Expenditure charged to the Revenue Account (1990/91), for all revenue accounts. Expenditure of superannuation and statutory special funds is not included.
2 Baths and laundries are included with parks and open spaces; swimming baths are included with parks and open spaces; and other public baths and public laundries are included with environmental health.
3 Due to deregulation of Passenger Transport Services this information has not been supplied since 1985/86.
4 Rate fund/General fund contributions to the Housing Revenue Account are included.
5 Debt redemption and interest payments (including internal payments up to and including 1989/90).
6 General fund services excluding Housing Revenue Account, Trading services and DLOs/DSOs for 1990/91.
7 Included in Table 16.16 for 1980/81 to 1986/87.
8 England only for 1990/91. Includes reserved part of capital receipts set aside at 1 April 1990 on the introduction of the new capital system. Also includes reserved part of in-year capital receipts and voluntary set aside of capital receipts.

Sources: Department of the Environment;
Welsh Office

Home finance

16.16 Capital account expenditure of local authorities[1]
England and Wales
Years ended 31 March

£ million

		1981/82	1982/83	1983/84	1984/85	1985/86	1986/87	1987[8]/88	1988[8]/89	1989[8]/90	1990[10]/91
Education	KQSB	431.2	474.2	486.2	538.9	569.8	604.6	612.9	787.6	901.7	864.3
Libraries, museums and art galleries	KQSC	20.5	29.2	41.0	56.2	50.5	44.1	50.6	60.4	97.7	68.7
Local authority port health	KQSD	–	–	0.2	0.1	–	–	–	–	0.1	0.4
Personal social services	KQSE	99.8	104.0	111.0	122.3	124.9	133.5	146.8	175.2	220.0	179.2
Sheltered employment and workshops	KQSF	1.4	2.7	2.0	2.0	2.8	3.6	2.4	2.6	2.3	1.8
Police	KQSG	58.9	80.5	94.9	99.8	108.2	110.9	110.3	131.5	197.1	164.9
Fire service	KQSH	21.4	32.2	38.0	36.9	34.7	29.8	53.3	55.1	71.4	52.8
Administration of justice	KQSI	9.1	9.9	14.9	18.6	19.2	28.5	42.8	55.3	62.4	65.2
Refuse collection and disposal	KQSJ	55.2	64.2	63.0	60.7	53.1	55.4	96.9	99.5	111.4	80.1
Agriculture and fisheries	KQSK	116.2	112.1	61.7	40.2	44.8	49.8	39.3	46.2	54.6	55.1
Local transport	KQSL	606.7	700.8	794.3	830.0	757.3	740.5	820.7	993.0	1 167.2	1 028.5
Sport and recreation[2]	KHDJ	–	–	–	–	–	–	184.3	222.2	367.2	308.7
Parks and open spaces[2]	KQSM	140.9	202.9	243.8	274.3	223.7	250.7	66.6	81.2	95.2	80.6
Environmental health[3]	KQSN	14.4	25.0	19.1	18.3	18.1	21.8	32.3	39.9	54.0	39.1
Town and country planning[4]	KHDK	199.9	298.0	324.1	359.6	391.2	372.3	175.6	216.3	302.6	218.2
Derelict land reclamation[4]	KHDL	–	–	–	–	–	–	84.9	83.0	82.7	79.0
Urban programme[5]	KHDM	–	–	–	–	–	–	207.6	204.5	221.8	209.0
Housing to which the HRA relates	KQSQ	1 707.6	2 106.9	2 251.9	2 537.7	2 268.9	2 301.6	2 511.2	2 823.3	4 214.6	2 541.8
Other housing	KQSR	942.1	1 201.4	1 736.3	1 519.0	1 071.8	1 055.7	815.7	780.8	1 014.8	833.3
Trading services:											
Passenger transport[6]	KQSS	15.4	12.0	12.3	7.9	8.9	25.4	..	..	..	..
Harbours, docks and piers	KQST	12.3	12.0	10.6	8.3	13.9	10.3	204.5	225.5	332.9	230.0
Other trading services	KQSU	225.3	268.2	280.2	291.5	282.0	208.4	–	–	–	–
General administration	KQSW	135.9	249.2	188.2	240.0	250.3	318.0	347.6	442.8	624.8	331.3
Community charge preparation	KNDN	–	–	–	–	–	–	–	30.5	74.0	11.1
Other services	KHDO	89.1	126.3	144.4	291.5	142.7	301.5	111.6	163.1[9]	193.0[9]	85.7[9]
Current expenditure charged to capital[7]	KHDP	–	–	–	–	–	–	–	–	–	48.1
Total	KQSA	4 903.3	6 111.8	6 918.0	7 228.7	6 437.1	6 666.3	6 717.7	7 719.3	10 463.2	7 576.7

1 Expenditure met out of loans, government grants for capital works, sales of property etc. For 1980/81 to 1986/87 includes sums repaid to lenders or transferred to sinking funds out of unexpected balances of loans and other capital receipts. From 1987/88 such sums are excluded.
2 For 1980/81 to 1986/87 'Sport and recreation' is included in 'Parks and open spaces'.
3 Includes cemeteries and crematoria.
4 For 1980/81 to 1986/87 'Derelict land reclamation' is included in 'Town and country planning'.
5 For 1980/81 to 1986/87 service expenditure includes urban programme.
6 From 1986/87 grants and advances to Public Transport Companies are included.
7 Current expenditure treated as capital expenditure under direction.
8 Includes leasing acquisitions. Excludes sums repaid to lenders or transferred to sinking funds out of unexpected balances of loans and other capital receipts. Service expenditure is net of urban programme.
9 Includes acquisition of share or loan capital.
10 New Capital System introduced. Includes credit cover for credit arrangements (including those that are leases).

Sources: Department of the Environment; Welsh Office

16.17 Water industry expenditure[1,2,3,4]
England and Wales

£ million

		1989/90	1990/91
Operating expenditure			
Water supply	KQQX	1 629.1	1 853.4
Sewerage	KQQY	414.1	478.3
Sewage treatment and disposal	KQQZ	657.7	931.8
Capital expenditure			
Water supply	KQSX	632.9	986.4
Sewerage	KQSY	269.3	475.8
Sewage treatment and disposal	KQSZ	470.9	759.2

1 Data is taken from the annual and regulatory accounts of the water and sewerage companies and water companies of England and Wales.
2 Figures are given based on current cost rather than historical cost accounting principles.
3 The elements which make up operating expenditure are as follows:
Manpower costs
Other costs of employment
Power
Local Authority rates
Water charges
Local Authority sewerage agencies
Materials and consumables
Hired and contracted services
Charge for bad and doubtful debts
Depreciation
Infrastructure renewals expenditure
Infrastructure renewals accrual
Exceptional items
Other operating costs.
4 Capital Expenditure is the addition to tangible fixed assets, and is given net of grants and other contributions.

Source: Ofwat

Home finance

16.18 Income of local authorities: classified according to source[1]
England and Wales
Years ended 31 March

£ million

		1980/81	1981/82	1982/83	1983/84	1984/85	1985/86	1986/87	1987/88	1988/89	1989/90	1990/91
Capital income: total	KQAO	5 555.8	5 488.8	7 306.6	7 708.1	7 361.0	7 007.9	7 559.3	8 061.5	9 971.1	10 113.0	7 725.3
Loans	KQAS	3 050.5	2 668.9	3 572.6	3 806.3	3 632.2	3 206.9	3 061.9	3 237.8	3 240.5	3 215.9	3 067.5
Government grants	KQAT	524.8	508.9	456.8	424.1	374.3	401.8	372.8	333.8	304.4	482.9	1 024.2
Sales and other sources	KQAU	1 980.4	2 311.0	3 277.2	3 477.6	3 354.5	3 399.2	4 124.6	4 489.9	6 426.2	6 414.1	3 635.0
Revenue income: total[2]	KQAV	30 360.1	33 822.4	35 311.0	37 010.7	39 241.7	38 090.4	42 314.0	44 673.2	47 902.6	51 618.8	58 465.5
Rates and community charges[3]	KQAW	7 845.5	9 450.9	10 693.9	10 907.7	11 793.0	13 768.2	14 821.2	15 786.6	17 736.2	18 943.4	21 704.4
Government grants	KQAX	13 784.4	13 998.7	14 246.5	16 106.4	17 165.4	16 385.5	18 831.6	19 614.0	20 322.4	21 379.3	24 163.0
Other income including rents, tolls, fees and interest	KQAY	8 730.1	10 372.8	10 370.6	9 996.6	10 283.4	7 936.8	8 661.2	9 272.7	9 843.9	11 296.0	12 598.1
Total income	KQAZ	35 915.8	39 311.2	42 617.6	44 718.7	46 602.2	45 098.3	49 873.3	52 734.7	57 873.7	61 731.8	66 190.8

1 Excluding superannuation and statutory special funds.
2 Adjusted to eliminate double counting of general administration costs recharged to other services and receipts from other local education authorities.
3 Comprises domestic and non-domestic rates up to and including 1989/90 and community charges (net of rebates) and non-domestic rates for 1990/91.

Sources: *Department of the Environment;*
Welsh Office

Home finance

16.19 Income of local authorities from government grants including capital grants.
England and Wales
Years ended 31 March

£ million

		1980/81	1981/82	1982/83	1983/84	1984/85	1985/86	1986/87	1987[1]/88	1988[1,2]/89	1989[1,2]/90	1990[3]/91
Allocated to specific services: Education	KQQA	665.3	769.8	694.0	752.1	783.1	775.4	1 000.6	1 140.8	1 280.9	1 468.8	1 948.1
Libraries, museums and art galleries	KQQB	1.9	2.7	2.9	3.4	3.7	4.3	5.0	4.8	5.2	6.5	4.7
Personal social services[4]	KQQC	27.4	29.2	33.8	40.8	40.6	37.6	46.0	52.8	48.5	62.5	71.1
Sheltered employment and workshops[1]	KQQD	6.8	7.7	9.3	8.8	11.2	12.7	13.8	12.3	12.7	13.4	15.8
Police including school crossing patrols[2]	KQQE	860.0	1 033.6	1 130.1	1 227.9	1 504.5	1 400.2	1 598.6	1 691.8	1 863.2	2 097.9	2 367.3
Fire service[2]	KQQF	–	0.1	0.1	0.1	0.2	0.1	0.4	0.5	0.6	0.7	0.9
Administration of justice[2]	KQQG	172.9	197.0	216.1	228.7	249.2	270.5	271.4	322.8	357.4	448.4	485.5
Refuse collection and disposal[1]	KQQH	0.6	0.8	0.6	0.5	0.5	2.2	0.4	0.3	0.3	0.2	0.2
Agriculture and fisheries	KQQI	65.0	73.6	66.1	14.2	10.7	15.4	17.5	13.5	15.4	18.8	0.5
Local transport[5]	KQQJ	458.8	436.3	515.4	468.5	328.0	227.0	133.4	151.7	153.3	167.5	6.9
Parks and open spaces[1,6]	KQQK	22.2	24.0	27.1	29.8	33.0	41.1	47.6	36.5	39.1	37.1	38.4
Environmental health[1,6]	KQQL	4.3	2.8	3.3	3.0	3.6	2.7	3.0	1.7	1.7	2.4	2.9
Cemeteries and crematoria[1]	KQQM	0.1	–	0.1	0.1	0.1	–	–	–	0.1	0.1	0.1
Town and country planning[1]	KQQN	43.3	43.4	68.8	91.8	112.9	132.1	120.5	48.5	54.1	57.5	60.3
Housing to which the Housing Revenue Account relates[7]	KQQO	1 868.0	1 273.4	1 058.4	2 000.9	2 105.5	2 057.4	2 528.4	2 491.0	2 772.9	3 057.2	3 582.5
Other housing	KQQP	483.5	461.6	520.5	1 042.0	1 427.6	1 630.4	1 661.2	1 819.3	1 753.6	2 055.9	2 347.5
Trading services: Passenger transport[1,8]	KQQQ	8.3	7.4	4.1	4.4	3.9	9.8	..	..	..	..	..
Harbours, docks and piers[9]	KQQR	0.8	0.3	0.2	1.2	0.1	0.2	0.7	0.1	0.1	–	–
Other trading services[9]	KQQS	16.7	24.3	37.1	25.1	21.6	20.3	18.1	20.4	17.7	23.1	10.8
Other services[1]	KQQT	31.1	39.9	48.5	76.7	68.2	57.5	86.3	263.7	257.9	365.2	233.2
Not allocated to specific services: Local Government Acts grants[10]	KQQU	9 571.6	10 079.1	10 265.9	10 853.7	10 830.9	10 088.9	11 677.7	11 874.3	11 986.5	11 967.0	12 946.2
Local taxation licence duties	KQQV	0.5	0.6	0.8	0.9	1.0	1.0	1.0	0.9	5.7	12.1	40.1
Capital grants[3]	KHWO	..	..	..	..	..	..	..	..	..	..	1 024.2
Total	KQQW	14 309.2	14 507.6	14 703.3	16 875.6	17 539.7	16 787.2	19 231.9	19 947.8	20 626.9	21 862.3	25 187.2

1 For each of 1987/88, 1988/89 and 1989/90, the capital account data supplied for each of these services is grouped as one total (of 84.4, 79.1 and 94.9 respectively) in the 'Other services' row total.
2 For each of 1987/88, 1988/89 and 1989/90, the capital account data for police including school crossing patrols, fire service and administration of justice has been grouped as one total (of 1.8, 2.2 and 44.1 respectively) in the 'Administration of justice' row. This total also includes civil defence.
3 Figures for capital grants cannot be broken down by service for 1990/91. Instead, a single capital grants figure is given, so that the 1990/91 total is comparable with earlier years.
4 Includes Local authority port health.
5 Includes Public Transport Companies.
6 Baths and laundries are included with parks and open spaces; swimming baths are included with parks and open spaces; and other public baths and public laundries are included with environmental health.
7 Includes the rent rebate subsidy.
8 Due to deregulation of Passenger Transport Services this information has not been supplied since 1985/86.
9 For each of 1987/88, 1988/89 and 1989/90, the capital account data for 'Harbours, docks and piers' and 'Other trading services' is grouped as one total (8.1, 5.0 and 12.1 respectively) in the 'Other trading services' row total.
10 Up to and including 1989/90, comprises Rate Support Grant and Rate Rebate Grant. For 1990/91, comprises Revenue Support Grant, Community Charge Benefit Grant, Transitional Relief Grant and special grants to ease the transition into the community charge system.

Sources: Department of the Environment; Welsh Office

Home finance

16.20 Expenditure of local authorities
Scotland
Year ended 31 March

£ thousand

Out of revenue [1,8]

		1980/81	1981/82	1982/83	1983/84	1984/85	1985/86	1986/87	1987/88	1988/89	1989/90	1990/91
Total	KQTA	3 536 791	3 926 170	4 245 006	4 566 462	4 794 090	5 048 188	5 351 981	5 721 849	6 198 024	6 793 189	7 429 771
General Fund Services	KQTB	2 799 715	3 131 773	3 389 883	3 580 249	3 744 950	3 862 915	4 097 987	4 380 607	4 771 959	5 212 273	5 650 719
Education[2]	KQTC	1 190 993	1 331 560	1 423 903	1 487 339	1 535 138	1 588 425	1 691 333	1 817 823	1 977 117	2 174 652	2 390 134
Libraries, museums and galleries	KQTD	40 263	45 639	49 423	53 745	57 390	61 907	64 161	69 410	74 991	83 712	103 489
Social work[2]	KQTE	249 554	277 681	299 742	319 029	338 848	369 017	383 840	433 590	483 888	559 013	668 792
Law, order and protective services[2]	KQTF	254 283	294 266	325 742	359 383	388 309	402 458	437 168	480 487	514 793	580 977	653 197
Roads[3]	KQTG	299 278	320 862	359 423	368 793	385 018	404 427	425 932	439 473	467 912	506 562	561 522
Environmental services[4]	KQTH	228 933	237 974	250 059	261 484	274 190	289 276	297 278	317 334	336 953	221 857	264 507
Planning	KQTI	58 948	60 008	64 592	71 706	72 907	79 500	92 444	111 731	127 816	125 298	162 566
Leisure and recreation	KQTJ	133 956	146 218	157 651	167 269	173 643	182 057	195 626	217 527	237 221	276 331	338 532
Central administration[9]	KQTK	143 634	163 741	161 549	172 563	170 818	178 696	207 347	205 176	226 432	305 743	–
Other services[2,4]	KQTL	79 123	103 451	124 774	131 925	142 681	152 215	160 991	170 891	219 355	258 196	383 221
Other general fund expenditure[5]	KQTM	120 750	150 373	173 025	187 013	206 008	154 937	141 867	117 165	105 481	119 932	124 759
Housing	KQTN	689 972	745 431	819 026	941 484	1 025 160	1 098 802	1 166 619	1 257 988	1 325 226	1 330 796	1 473 950
Trading services	KQTO	167 854	199 339	209 122	231 742	229 988	241 408	229 242	200 419	206 320	370 052	429 861
Water supply	KQTP	101 395	111 995	119 561	122 508	127 685	134 660	135 237	142 223	151 002	168 347	188 478
Sewerage[6]	KQTQ	–	–	–	–	–	–	–	–	–	154 436	176 449
Passenger transport	KQTR	36 682	36 836	39 703	43 488	45 876	47 017	27 833	149	188	263	560
Ferries	KQTS	2 090	2 283	2 485	2 890	3 037	3 542	3 594	3 577	4 158	5 358	6 596
Harbours, docks and piers	KQTT	15 281	33 297	31 225	37 332	41 291	43 433	47 689	38 879	36 967	25 757	23 428
Airports	KQTU	1 216	1 364	1 632	1 793	1 543	1 366	1 315	951	1 142	–	–
Road bridges	KQTV	3 275	5 672	4 321	4 873	4 819	5 057	5 179	7 378	8 459	7 942	9 277
Slaughterhouses	KQTW	4 152	3 937	4 659	10 608	4 068	3 789	4 438	3 169	3 121	3 366	2 737
Markets	KQTX	1 213	1 630	1 822	1 777	1 717	1 744	1 878	2 193	2 184	–	–
Other trading services	KQTY	2 550	2 325	3 714	6 473	–48	800	2 079	1 900	–901	4 583	22 336
Loan charges (included above) : total	KQTZ	846 434	895 196	935 023	940 254	1 011 951	1 093 108	1 105 995	1 132 636	1 215 398	1 199 706	1 267 466
Allocated to :												
General Fund services	KMHV	349 889	365 594	388 838	393 532	423 245	466 597	478 185	502 383	538 518	538 693	567 143
Housing	KMHW	445 701	467 086	478 552	470 701	513 030	544 053	541 880	558 172	602 914	504 201	530 566
Trading services	KMHX	50 844	62 516	67 633	76 021	75 676	82 458	85 930	72 081	73 966	156 812	169 757

On capital works [7,8]

		1980/81	1981/82	1982/83	1983/84	1984/85	1985/86	1986/87	1987/88	1988/89	1989/90	1990/91
Total	KQUA	660 868	707 305	763 625	929 438	839 994	891 479	912 229	1 079 366	1 142 074	1 262 076	1 249 744
General Fund Services	KQUB	293 966	320 396	336 346	358 684	360 236	402 025	401 338	424 624	450 701	617 013	589 921
Education[2]	KQUC	58 857	66 545	60 827	55 282	53 274	58 612	54 226	60 201	72 144	81 643	75 166
Libraries, museums and galleries	KQUD	8 927	10 513	8 427	4 894	4 330	4 834	4 518	3 555	6 031	5 389	7 223
Social work[2]	KQUE	12 244	13 314	14 397	18 959	22 471	21 827	18 028	18 846	23 448	24 801	25 797
Law, order and protective services[2]	KQUF	12 795	10 541	12 956	15 485	15 723	20 324	21 286	27 121	27 257	29 789	23 378
Roads	KQUG	78 479	96 348	107 328	112 128	111 310	134 684	144 324	127 768	125 870	167 797	159 467
Environmental services[4]	KQUH	61 024	61 329	55 326	64 576	64 637	64 285	68 858	67 476	70 541	15 708	12 738
Planning	KQUI	23 761	21 718	29 661	29 687	24 528	32 873	26 762	34 600	30 076	30 897	55 899
Leisure and recreation	KQUJ	19 766	19 237	20 304	25 433	22 748	28 188	26 104	29 032	33 714	55 885	43 872
Administrative buildings & equipment[10]	KQUK	10 539	10 111	16 919	16 374	23 088	21 346	22 788	39 239	42 919	22 857	32 251
Other services[2,4]	KQUL	7 574	10 740	10 201	15 866	18 127	15 052	14 444	16 786	18 701	182 247	154 130
Housing	KQUM	311 010	329 276	373 464	519 266	431 703	439 843	461 099	603 511	629 816	501 082	504 378
Trading Services	KQUN	55 892	57 683	53 815	51 488	48 055	49 611	49 792	51 231	61 557	143 981	155 445
Water supply	KQUO	35 757	37 664	38 492	39 422	37 412	38 352	41 583	42 989	51 470	61 991	63 872
Sewerage[6]	KQUP	–	–	–	–	–	–	–	–	–	65 417	77 096
Passenger transport	KQUQ	4 700	5 264	5 575	5 636	4 489	1 160	1 414	–	24	–	–
Ferries	KQUR	843	1 925	879	745	1 999	1 841	639	564	1 573	3 422	846
Harbours, docks and piers	KQUS	10 173	7 730	6 404	3 334	2 159	6 701	3 917	4 155	5 703	3 281	8 458
Airports	KQUT	268	123	161	314	455	193	123	86	262	–	–
Road bridges	KQUU	371	1 929	398	878	478	962	1 633	998	1 440	2 276	237
Slaughterhouses	KQUV	3 725	2 587	426	380	342	127	17	85	67	170	73
Markets	KQUW	7	–	117	81	216	2	171	171	313	–	–
Other trading services	KMHY	48	411	1 363	698	505	273	295	2 183	705	7 424	4 863

1 Gross expenditure less inter-authority and inter-account transfers.
2 From 1989/90 Education includes careers service (previously Other Services); Social work includes sheltered employment (previously Other Services); Other series includes district courts (previously Law, order and protective services), public analyst (previously Environmental services) and Housing loans and grants (previously Housing).
3 Including general fund support for transport (LA and NON-LA).
4 in 1978/79, 1979/80, 1980/81 and 1989/90 onwards burial grounds and crematoria are included amongst Environmental services. From 1981/82 to 1988/89 (inclusive) they were included amongst Other services.
5 General fund contributions to Housing and Trading services (excluding transport), and therefore included in the expenditure figures for these services.
6 From 1989/90 onwards Sewerage is shown as a trading service (previously included in Environmental services).
7 Expenditure out of loans, government grants and other capital receipts.
8 Revenue contributions to capital are included as expenditure in both the revenue and capital tables above. See Table 16.21 for the amount of such contributions.
9 From 1990/91 Central Administration expenditure is included in the relevant service expenditure.
10 Prior to 1990-91 was called Central Administration.

Source: Scottish Office, Central Statistics Unit

Home finance

16.21 Income of local authorities: classified according to source
Scotland
Year ended 31 March
£thousand

		1981/82	1982/83	1983/84	1984/85	1985/86	1986/87	1987/88	1988/89	1989/90	1990/91
Revenue account											
Rates[1,2,3]	KQXA	1 255 542	1 440 682	1 377 275	1 420 354	1 609 148	1 717 558	1 942 864	2 050 666	1 265 922	1 229 972
Community charges	KQXB	–	–	–	–	–	–	–	–	867 519	890 645
Government grants											
RSG[4]:	KQXC	–	–	–	–	–	–	–	–	2 346 281	2 495 840
Needs element	KQXD	1 376 300	1 416 600	1 493 150	1 442 300	1 391 300	1 380 800	1 509 400	1 690 000	..	..
Resources element	KQXE	152 900	202 400	210 800	215 000	205 900	184 200	196 200	215 800	–	–
Domestic element	KQXF	14 100	14 100	14 300	14 400	102 900	91 300	90 800	91 900	–	–
Rate rebate grant[2]	KQXG	52 790	75 771	145 550	160 820	223 129	220 527	248 045	189 632	24 164	30 941
Community charge rebate grants	KQXH	–	–	–	–	–	–	–	–	187 182	192 378
Other grants and subsidies[5]	KQXI	378 655	372 091	471 892	518 950	582 653	631 343	750 741	796 789	808 535	882 296
Sales	KQXJ	46 428	43 980	41 931	44 185	42 190	49 327	60 769	55 881	49 439	50 001
Fees and charges[6]	KQXK	215 817	230 355	255 272	768 420	823 112	882 645	936 928	1 070 254	1 185 303	1 288 728
Other income[5,6]	KQXL	469 548	571 607	617 713	155 742	173 616	163 297	110 219	126 990	123 212	132 009
Changes in revenue balances	KHYJ	..	..	..	..	..	..	..	..	..	–548
Capital account											
Sale of fixed assets	KQXM	74 758	124 259	144 213	137 269	130 653	133 791	190 363	295 736	446 097	416 838
Loans	KQXN	574 587	560 420	693 851	608 797	656 826	694 587	790 368	774 490	682 767	..
Government grants	KQXO	32 814	32 139	35 518	37 236	36 437	47 577	44 974	25 134	..	..
Revenue contributions to capital	KQXP	11 505	13 062	17 407	9 314	6 527	10 726	18 665	14 391	11 812	48 997
Transfer from special funds	KMHZ	1 094	1 319	3 442	945	1 473	1 881	6 184	1 904	1 513	2 196
Other receipts	KMGV	15 793	34 325	36 351	48 078	60 577	25 560	26 004	38 715	23 156	24 649
Total income	KMGW	4 672 631	5 133 110	5 558 665	5 581 810	6 046 441	6 235 119	6 922 524	7 438 282	..	..

1 Excluding government grants towards rate rebates and domestic element of rate support grant (RSG). Including domestic water rate receipts.
2 Until 1982/83, certificated rate rebates paid in respect of supplementary benefit recipients were included with rate income. From 1983/84 onwards, they are included as part of rate rebate grant.
3 From 1989/90 rates refer to non-domestic rates only.
4 From 1989/90 onwards, RSG is not broken down into the three elements.
5 Until 1986/87, government grants not specific to service eg grants towards job creation, were included under other income. From 1987/88, these are included under other grants and subsidies.
6 Prior to 1984/85 rents are treated as other income. From 1984/85 onwards rents are included with fees and charges.

Source: Scottish Office

16.22 Income of local authorities from government grants[1]
Scotland
Year ended 31 March
£ thousand

		1981/82	1982/83	1983/84	1984/85	1985/86	1986/87	1987/88	1988/89	1989/90	1990/91
General fund services[2]	KQYA	153 336	167 318	182 062	190 594	202 313	223 462	278 888	274 707	295 169	339 619
Education	KQYB	2 564	3 549	3 208	4 170	4 365	5 235	13 323	15 801	11 510	17 809
Libraries, museums and galleries	KQYC	2 827	2 030	39	150	286	94	233	664	57	80
Social work	KQYD	1 553	2 265	2 295	2 968	3 427	2 166	3 228	4 434	8 311	10 561
Law, order and protective services	KQYE	105 695	117 032	125 194	137 232	140 796	155 876	173 228	185 772	211 304	235 477
Roads	KQYF	8 735	13 349	18 302	11 200	17 261	27 169	30 178	12 641	4 127	4 580
Environmental services	KQYG	9 174	6 213	6 270	6 233	6 615	5 370	5 615	4 491	150	50
Planning	KQYH	7 215	7 305	7 323	8 223	7 173	2 859	4 555	770	4 144	971
Leisure and recreation	KQYI	1 538	1 682	1 025	582	1 321	769	2 950	2 606	1 522	1 739
Central administration[3]	KQYJ	–	42	10	28	15	107	357	1 344	867	–
Other services	KQYK	14 035	13 851	18 396	19 808	21 054	23 817	45 221	46 184	53 177	68 352
Housing	KQYL	248 456	227 874	317 241	360 162	408 637	444 131	506 342	537 496	510 201	538 042
Trading services	KQYM	9 677	9 038	8 107	7 812	8 140	11 327	10 485	9 720	3 165	4 024
Water supply	KQYN	6 636	5 602	5 714	6 336	4 981	7 737	8 001	7 363	3 132	3 998
Ferries	KQYO	450	10	264	690	953	597	213	213	–	–
Other trading services	KQYP	2 591	3 426	2 129	786	2 206	2 993	2 271	2 144	33	26
Capital grants[4,5]	KQYQ	–	–	–	–	–	–	–	–	..	..
General fund services	KQYR	–	–	–	–	–	–	–	–	..	..
Other services	KMGX	–	–	–	–	–	–	–	–	..	..
Grants not allocated to specific services[6]	KMGY	1 596 090	1 708 871	1 863 800	1 832 520	1 923 229	1 876 827	2 044 445	2 187 332	2 557 627	2 719 159
Total	KMGZ	2 007 559	2 113 101	2 371 210	2 391 088	2 542 319	2 555 747	2 840 160	3 009 255	..	3 600 844

1 Including grants for capital works.
2 Until 1986/87, excludes government grants not specific to services, eg grants towards job creation. From 1987/88 includes such grants.
3 From 1990/91 Central Administration income is included in the relevant service income.
4 From 1989/90 service breakdown no longer includes capital grants.
5 From 1990-91, the total income from government grants does not include capital grants.
6 Revenue support grant and rate and community charge rebate grants.

Source: Scottish Office

Home finance

16.23 Expenditure of local authorities
Northern Ireland
Years ended 31 March

£ thousand

Out of revenue and special funds

		1980/81	1981/82	1982/83	1983/84	1984/85	1985/86	1986/87	1987/88	1988/89	1989/90	1990/91
Total	KQVA	96 828	110 557	121 856	133 056	143 346	153 223	154 142	166 911	167 303	179 404	193 450
Libraries, museums and art galleries	KQVB	113	218	271	321	493	485	517	678	683	3 606	3 881
Environmental health services:												
Refuse collection and disposal	KQVC	14 932	15 871	17 986	19 463	20 360	21 854	22 733	25 599	26 418	26 366	29 363
Public baths	KQVD	3 762	3 957	4 630	3 980	3 705	3 503	3 649	3 145	3 105	1 457	1 571
Parks, recreation grounds, etc	KQVE	20 834	25 274	30 338	35 397	40 059	45 336	49 491	56 478	59 871	63 284	68 593
Other sanitary services	KQVF	10 467	11 619	12 980	14 053	15 389	16 834	18 210	19 758	21 543	24 990	24 237
Housing (grants and small dwellings acquisition)[1]	KQVG	1 466	1 369	1 345	1 825	1 593	1 498	1 354	1 265	1 092	1 008	1 130
Trading services:												
Gas supply	KQVH	23 061	25 337	25 773	25 338	26 105	24 613	18 896	15 529	6 631	7 997	3 472
Cemeteries	KQVI	2 065	2 418	2 508	2 622	2 816	3 089	3 221	3 674	3 846	4 335	4 492
Other trading services (including markets, fairs and harbours)	KQVJ	3 681	4 047	4 313	5 024	5 570	6 051	5 589	5 242	5 348	6 491	7 340
Miscellaneous	KQVK	16 447	20 447	21 712	25 033	27 256	29 960	30 482	35 543	38 768	39 870	49 371
Total loan charges	KQVL	9 068	10 236	11 538	11 257	12 111	13 836	12 484	12 583	13 588	18 154	19 430
Loan charges included in terms of expenditure above:												
Allocated to rate fund services	KQVM	4 963	6 113	7 071	7 484	8 749	10 628	9 869	10 001	11 221	13 216	15 155
Allocated to trading services	KQVN	3 401	3 437	3 717	2 519	2 335	2 280	1 825	1 820	1 969	4 513	3 904
Not allocated	KQVO	704.0	686.0	750.0	1 254.0	1 027.0	928.0	790.0	762.0	398.0	425.0	371.0

On capital works[1]

		1980/81	1981/82	1982/83	1983/84	1984/85	1985/86	1986/87	1987/88	1988/89	1989/90	1990/91
Total	KQVP	24 079	25 078	24 073	29 192	25 176	33 102	24 226	28 958	33 943	34 955	37 800
Libraries, museums and art galleries	KQVQ	94	120	65	88	232	585	411	129	343	683	997
Environmental health services:												
Refuse collection and disposal	KQVR	1 337	1 964	2 170	2 801	1 231	1 954	1 490	3 551	5 107	3 917	7 254
Public baths	KQVS	1 205	811	454	1 249	596	556	359	75	271	73	189
Parks, recreation grounds, etc	KQVT	11 675	11 395	11 985	16 155	16 103	21 443	15 406	8 986	8 951	14 343	18 654
Other sanitary services	KQVU	554	742	719	829	739	766	499	891	1 333	1 666	1 844
Housing (including small dwellings acquisition)[1]	KQVV	965	639	211	484	262	242	264	438	104	84	254
Trading services:												
Gas supply	KQVW	421	282	648	646	391	214	4	112	86	22	–
Cemeteries	KQVX	139	280	103	343	470	402	388	645	1 161	597	795
Other trading services (including markets, fairs and harbours)	KQVY	3 215	3 113	2 679	2 864	1 403	2 204	1 506	2 520	4 125	4 493	2 762
Miscellaneous	KQVZ	4 474	5 732	5 041	3 733	3 749	4 736	3 907	11 835	12 462	9 077	5 051

1 Expenditure met out of loans, government grants for capital works, sales of property and other capital receipts.

Source: Department of the Environment for Northern Ireland

Home finance

16.24 Income of local authorities: classified according to source
Northern Ireland, Years ended 31 March

£ thousand

		1980/81	1981/82	1982/83	1983/84	1984/85	1985/86	1986/87	1987/88	1988/89	1989/90	1990/91
Total income	KQWA	120 114	136 219	151 064	165 348	168 786	190 145	179 700	203 851	201 189	216 779	234 037
Capital receipts: total	KQWB	19 420	21 676	23 502	23 274	22 114	29 701	23 656	27 308	26 421	30 127	33 860
Loans	KQWC	9 616	9 533	8 296	7 854	8 028	11 724	11 124	8 815	11 012	15 557	20 417
Government grants	KQWD	6 778	7 604	9 878	9 022	8 854	11 073	6 407	7 534	4 366	5 638	5 607
Other sources	KQWE	3 026	4 539	5 328	6 398	5 232	6 904	6 125	10 959	11 043	8 932	7 836
Other income: total	KQWF	61 513	73 019	83 684	95 758	98 374	103 047	112 368	130 110	130 646	135 587	145 168
Rates	KQWG	45 579	54 261	60 924	67 382	68 353	71 453	79 882	96 475	97 564	101 883	108 829
Government grants	KQWH	15 196	18 045	17 844	22 445	28 993	30 711	31 499	32 950	32 541	33 311	36 005
Housing[1] Grants and small dwellings acquisition	KQWI	738	713	729	1 237	1 028	883	987	685	541	393	334
Miscellaneous income	KQWJ	7 963	9 415	11 306	12 501	15 228	17 521	18 652	21 871	26 454	30 515	36 903
Trading services												
Total (capital and revenue)	KQWK	31 218	32 109	32 572	33 815	33 070	39 876	25 024	24 562	17 668	20 550	18 106
Gas: total	KQWL	24 342	24 666	26 056	25 016	25 604	31 840	18 110	16 564	7 954	7 599	6 362
Loans	KQWM	272	308	392	56	9	150	4	9	–	–	–
Government grants	KQWN	9 712	8 887	10 916	11 118	11 419	17 537	6 358	9 954	2 216	5 742	4 883
Miscellaneous	KQWO	14 358	15 471	14 748	13 842	14 176	14 153	11 756	6 601	5 738	1 857	1 479
Cemeteries: total	KQWP	507	830	637	919	1 049	1 046	1 023	1 507	1 833	2 122	2 427
Loans	KQWQ	78	170	20	294	150	173	284	497	904	866	1 216
Government grants	KQWR	–	4	15	85	50	42	33	16	11	99	116
Miscellaneous	KQWS	429	656	602	540	849	831	706	994	918	1 157	1 095
Other trading: total	KQWT	6 369	6 613	5 879	7 880	6 417	6 990	5 891	6 491	7 881	10 829	9 317
Loans	KQWU	1 700	1 522	824	948	307	598	343	674	2 739	4 662	4 670
Government grants	KQWV	1 346	1 551	1 453	1 970	755	189	257	916	1 330	1 857	23
Miscellaneous	KQWW	3 323	3 540	3 602	4 962	5 355	6 203	5 291	4 901	3 812	4 310	4 624

1 Including annuity repayments made by borrowers under the Small Dwellings Acquisition scheme.

Source: Department of the Environment for Northern Ireland

16.25 Income of local authorities from government grants[1]: classified according to services
Northern Ireland, Years ended 31 March

£ thousand

		1980/81	1981/82	1982/83	1983/84	1984/85	1985/86	1986/87	1987/88	1988/89	1989/90	1990/91
Total	KQXV	33 032	36 091	44 293	49 334	50 071	59 552	44 554	51 372	40 464	46 648	46 634
Allocated to specific services:												
Environmental health services	KQXW	8 118	8 951	12 190	11 838	11 820	14 123	9 225	6 537	6 500	7 596	8 355
Housing	KQXX	438	318	16	–	–	–	–	–	–	–	–
Other services	KQXY	12 329	12 420	14 072	15 051	14 013	19 670	8 536	16 015	4 958	9 017	6 012
Not allocated to specific services[2]	KQXZ	12 147	14 402	18 015	22 445	24 238	25 759	26 793	28 820	29 006	30 035	32 267

1 Including grants for capital works.

2 Assistance to local authorities under various Local Government Acts.

Source: Department of the Environment for Northern Ireland

287

17 Banking, Insurance, etc

Public sector borrowing requirement
Table 17.7

Net non-deposit sterling liabilities
This comprises changes in the sterling component of capital and internal funds and reserves of all monetary sector institutions, *less* their sterling investments in UK banks and other non-financial sterling assets, together with residual errors arising from the exclusion of sterling transactions between institutions within the sector. This item replaces 'Net non-deposit liabilities' which comprised changes in both sterling and foreign currency items. Total net non-deposit liabilities (in sterling and foreign currency) are shown in Table 17.4

External and foreign currency counterparts
This now includes changes in the foreign currency component of capital, internal funds and reserves of all monetary sector institutions, *less* their foreign currency investments in UK banks and other non-financial assets in currencies other than sterling: these items were formerly included in 'Net non-deposit liabilities'. Changes in these items are calculated in transactions terms, that is after an adjustment has been made for the estimated effect of changes in the sterling value of foreign currencies.

17.1 Bank of England

£ million

		1980 Dec	1981 Dec	1982 Dec	1983 Dec	1984 Dec	1985 Dec	1986 Dec	1987 Dec	1988 Dec	1989 Dec	1990 Dec	1991 Dec
Issue Department													
Liabilities:													
Notes in circulation	AEFA	10 611	11 001	11 271	12 152	12 610	12 612	14 119	14 654	16 071	16 849	17 283	17 466
Notes in Banking Department	AEFB	14	24	4	8	10	8	11	6	9	11	7	4
Assets:													
Government securities[1]	AEFC	8 430	6 329	3 217	4 699	1 888	938	2 718	9 783	10 339	13 946	14 672	11 791
Other securities	AEFD	2 195	4 696	8 058	7 461	10 732	11 682	11 412	4 877	5 741	2 914	2 618	5 679
Banking Department													
Liabilities:													
Total[2]	AEFE	1 162	2 039	2 754	2 356	2 595	2 328	2 606	3 059	3 203	5 398	8 613	5 825
Public deposits[3]	AEFF	33	40	41	44	99	83	86	100	94	69	44	104
Special deposits[4]	AEFG	–	–	–	–	–	–	–	–	–	..	..	..
Bankers' deposits[5]	AEFH	487	482	647	650	787	848	932	1 064	1 310	1 750	1 842	1 813
Reserves and other accounts	AEFI	627	1 503	2 051	1 647	1 694	1 382	1 574	1 880	1 784	3 565	6 713	3 894
Assets:													
Total	KCYT	1 162	2 039	2 754	2 356	2 595	2 328	2 618	3 053	3 385	5 870	7 080	6 196
Government securities	AEFJ	447	433	456	383	460	579	474	559	882	1 354	1 432	1 346
Advances and other accounts	AEFK	175	1 026	1 283	947	894	719	701	1 064	661	726	2 146	2 443
Premises, equipment and other securities	AEFL	526	556	1 011	1 018	1 231	1 022	1 420	1 430	1 651	3 307	5 030	2 031
Notes and coin	AEFM	15	24	4	8	10	8	11	6	9	11	7	5

1 Including the historic liability of the Treasury of £11 million.
2 The only liability not shown separately is the Bank's capital (held by the Treasury) which has been constant at £14.6 million.
3 Excluding local authorities' and public corporations' deposits which are included under Reserves and other accounts.
4 Deposits called from institutions are not at their free disposal. Until 19 August 1981, all banks and finance houses which observed the common ratio were liable for calls to lodge special deposits. With effect from 20 August 1981 only reporting institutions with eligible liabilities of £10 million or more are liable for special deposit calls. This item also includes deposits under the supplementary special deposits scheme which was in force on three occasions before 1980.
5 Up to 19 August 1981 these constituted the current accounts held at the Bank by the banks and discount houses. From the introduction of new arrangements for monetary control on 20 August, they consist of operational deposits held mainly by the clearing banks and non-operational cash ratio deposits for which institutions authorised under the Banking Act are liable.

Source: Bank of England

17.2 Value of inter-bank clearings[1]

£ billion

		1980	1981	1982	1983	1984	1985	1986	1987	1988	1989	1990
Bulk paper clearings												
Cheque (formerly general)	KCYY	406	432	479	548	622	680	766	860	953	1 030	1 089
Credit (formerly credit clearing)	KCYZ	52	61	63	68	69	73	80	92	103	107	109
High-value clearings												
Town	KCZA	4 051	4 404	5 292	6 258	6 922	7 464	8 173	8 325	7 693	6 754	4 776
CHAPS	KCZB	–	–	–	–	741	2 356	4 144	7 332	11 289	14 733	18 880
Electronic clearing	KCZC	91	104	130	154	190	253	301	356	423	526	668

1 Excludes inter-branch clearings and clearings in Scotland and Northern Ireland.

Source: Association of Payment Clearing Services (APACS)

Banking

17.3 UK Banks: liabilities and assets outstanding[1]
End-year

£ million

		1981[2]	1982	1983	1984	1985	1986	1987	1988	1989	1990	1991
Liabilities												
Total	AEAA	332 039	411 602	480 369	604 477	589 880	704 158	728 478	816 791	1 014 321	1 031 240	999 313
Public sector deposits												
Sterling	AEAJ	2 063	3 159	3 220	3 987	5 067	6 668	7 786	10 097	9 967	8 603	6 041
Other currencies[3]	AEAP	202	282	308	431	287	306	304	191	193	224	237
Private sector deposits												
Sterling	AEAS	73 825	80 892	90 443	100 414	114 905	138 626	171 870	207 978	278 857	310 477	321 617
Other currencies[3]	AGAK	9 849	12 717	16 376	20 947	20 144	29 051	31 519	34 988	48 463	53 033	37 393
Overseas sector deposits												
Sterling	AEBD	14 413	18 892	23 369	29 661	33 923	39 731	48 218	61 939	73 415	85 841	75 084
Other currencies	AEBG	217 904	279 510	327 338	423 955	382 072	453 474	425 456	448 771	534 707	502 881	487 200
Non-deposit liabilites (net)	AEBJ	13 783	16 150	19 315	25 082	33 482	36 303	43 325	52 827	68 718	70 181	71 742
Assets												
Total	AEAA	332 039	411 602	480 369	604 477	589 880	704 158	728 478	816 791	1 014 321	1 031 240	999 313
Lending to public sector												
Sterling	AEBP	22 650	20 322	18 389	19 299	17 274	16 242	15 984	14 711	14 735	14 651	14 480
Other currencies	AECB	1 000	1 170	1 399	2 011	1 938	1 860	1 037	442	449	447	441
Lending to private sector												
Sterling	AECE	68 322	82 910	97 521	112 206	131 888	161 764	204 007	260 865	352 820	398 388	405 697
Other currencies	AECK	15 616	20 038	24 735	38 028	35 505	44 611	46 829	56 733	80 252	72 626	62 055
Lending to overseas sector												
Sterling	AECP	11 196	14 339	17 257	23 108	25 653	31 396	37 172	41 466	44 796	47 947	41 930
Other currencies	AECS	213 255	272 823	321 068	409 825	377 622	448 285	423 449	442 574	521 269	497 181	474 710

1 At end-1981, in the quarterly series, the old banking sector was replaced by the monetary sector. The UK monetary sector comprised the UK offices of institutions either recognised as banks or licensed to take deposits under the Banking Act 1979, together with Girobank, the Banking Department of the Bank of England, and those institutions (including branches of mainland banks) in the Channel Islands and the Isle of Man which have opted to participate in the new monetary control arrangements introduced in August 1981. In 1989, the term 'monetary sector' was replaced with UK banks - the definition of these institutions that make up the new group, however remains the same. Inter-bank items are excluded and adjustments made to allow for transit items. Figures for other currencies are affected by changes in exchange rates.

2 The introduction of the monetary sector at end-1981 added about £9 850 to total assets and liabilities.

3 Before the introduction of new statistical returns during 1975 all UK residents deposits in foreign currency were allocated to the private sector.

Source: Bank of England

17.4 Banks: summary of monthly reporting institutions

£ million

		Second Wednesday in Dec				End Dec						
		1981[1]	1982[1]	1983[2,3]	1984	1985	1986	1987	1988	1989[4]	1990[5]	1991
Liabilities												
Notes outstanding	ATFA	625	716	836	917	995	1 145	1 266	1 407	1 560	1 678	1 840
Sterling deposits: total	ATFB	109 906	134 649	156 794	180 119	208 572	253 557	304 220	369 418	470 124	528 604	511 636
Sight deposits												
UK banks	ATFC	3 458	5 887	7 637	7 789	9 746	11 298	9 306	9 648	12 928	12 893	10 229
UK public sector	ATFD	823	992	1 118	1 078	1 244	1 927	2 314	2 913	3 049	3 697	2 953
UK private sector	ATFE	23 023	26 662	32 532	39 318	48 471	63 604	79 726	91 779	127 698	138 310	144 516
Overseas	ATFF	3 137	3 748	4 699	5 392	6 770	..	..	..	..	..	..
Time deposits												
UK banks	ATFG	20 728	28 542	28 358	35 450	40 540	45 838	52 588	63 322	76 888	84 736	72 344
UK public sector	ATFH	460	1 119	1 245	1 237	1 790	2 718	4 167	6 704	6 671	4 699	2 885
UK private sector	ATFI	41 124	44 796	53 843	55 735	61 491	70 081	79 988	98 040	130 547	148 934	154 223
Overseas	ATFJ	10 458	14 377	17 570	22 890	25 703	..	..	..	..	..	..
CDs etc	ATFK	6 695	8 525	9 792	11 230	12 818	19 829	29 682	37 700	42 767	53 225	52 307
Other currency deposits: total	ATFN	288 379	376 259	439 301	534 136	499 530	591 173	543 860	568 204	666 667	637 509	608 685
Sight and time deposits												
UK banks	ATFO	64 614	84 887	87 389	98 692	92 656	101 033	85 675	83 549	79 675	75 833	76 901
Other United Kingdom	ATFP	9 663	12 081	15 483	19 041	19 019	27 889	30 263	33 086	45 512	50 397	34 135
Overseas	ATFQ	173 678	221 993	265 972	336 754	323 730	384 878	356 647	373 747	457 569	440 307	432 000
CDs etc	ATFR	40 424	57 299	70 457	79 648	64 125	77 373	71 276	77 822	83 911	70 973	65 648

1 The table aggregates the balance sheets of the banks within the UK which report on a monthly basis, other than members of the London Discount Market Association(LDMA), the Trustee savings banks and the Banking Department of the Bank of England. For a description of the background of the reporting population see the December 1981 *Bank of England Quarterly Bulletin*, page 531.

2 From 1983, the Trustee savings banks and the Banking Department of the Bank of England are included.

3 From 1983 market loans to UK public corporations and the UK private sector are included as advances.

4 From 1989, Abbey National's data have been included.

5 From 1990 sterling commercial paper has been included.

Source: Bank of England

Banking

17.4 Banks: summary of monthly reporting institutions
continued

£ million

		Second Wednesday in Dec				End Dec						
		1981[1]	1982[1]	1983[2,3]	1984	1985	1986	1987	1988	1989[4]	1990[5]	1991
Sterling and other currencies												
Items in suspense and transmission	KDAX	6 140	6 107	7 198	10 702	10 738	12 107	14 200	13 994	15 042	16 899	16 986
Capital and other funds	KDAY	19 056	22 343	27 425	33 749	41 916	49 151	54 859	64 404	80 273	81 741	84 610
Total liabilities/assets	ATFU	424 105	540 074	631 554	759 622	761 751	907 133	918 404	1 017 428	1 233 666	1 266 430	1 223 757
of which Sterling Liabilities	ATFV	*131 270*	*158 561*	*185 575*	*213 369*	*242 912*	*295 802*	*352 826*	*425 689*	*537 193*	*604 222*	*590 738*
Sterling Assets	ATFW	*131 257*	*159 595*	*185 673*	*215 322*	*242 348*	*296 703*	*353 493*	*426 871*	*541 933*	*609 785*	*597 389*
Sterling assets: notes and coin	ATFY	1 612	1 586	1 938	2 006	2 313	2 608	2 994	3 405	3 890	3 956	3 920
Balances with Bank of England:												
Cash ratio deposits	KDDI	321	434	497	577	667	732	906	1 124	1 477	1 690	1 576
Special deposits	KDDJ	–	–	–	–	–	–	–	–	–	–	–
Other	ATGA	159	209	147	187	83	281	159	154	164	3	27
Market loans[3]												
Discount houses-secured	ATGB	4 317	4 685	5 764	6 070	6 367	6 823	7 947	7 992	10 077	10 466	8 577
Discount houses-unsecured	ATGC	21	20	37	45	47	53	50	75	139	260	162
Other UK banks	ATGD	21 658	30 695	32 830	39 099	45 517	54 863	58 388	68 317	83 198	91 047	77 568
UK bank CDs	ATHJ	4 094	4 573	4 980	5 847	6 210	7 735	10 409	12 609	14 423	20 271	19 661
Building society CDs and time deposits	ATHK	–	–	365	775	766	1 401	1 407	1 660	2 114	3 357	3 673
UK local authorities	ATGE	5 386	5 172	5 085	4 824	3 565	2 514	1 780	1 452	856	625	520
UK public corporations	KDDR	320	61	–	–	–	–	–	–	–	–	–
UK private sector	KDDS	1 129	1 160	–	–	–	–	–	–	–	–	–
Overseas	ATGF	4 060	4 441	4 634	6 837	8 891	14 019	19 199	24 248	25 575	28 707	23 978
Bills:												
Treasury bills	ATGG	707	313	333	286	300	291	776	1 632	1 898	3 242	4 045
Eligible local authority	ATGH	278	226	351	413	581	462	433	388	67	36	21
Eligible bank bills	ATGI	1 389	1 335	2 286	2 848	2 806	4 079	5 741	6 856	9 895	10 628	8 687
Other	ATGJ	278	253	258	275	297	428	665	566	762	502	393
Advances: total	ATGK	66 772	83 905	100 067	114 369	131 994	158 983	197 630	251 171	334 827	376 150	382 072
UK public sector	ATGL	3 053	3 033	2 613	2 616	2 067	1 366	1 670	1 907	1 761	1 701	1 788
UK private sector	ATGM	58 266	73 126	87 475	100 723	117 658	144 792	182 813	235 742	318 114	359 586	366 459
Overseas	ATGN	5 453	7 746	9 979	11 031	12 269	12 826	13 147	13 522	14 952	14 863	13 825
Banking Dept. lending to central government (net)	ATHL	..	..	387	461	574	..	3 468	8 196	14 118	16 440	15 866
Investments:												
British government stocks												
Up to 1 year	ATGO	505	567	..	..	..	..	..	..	..	..	..
Over 1 year and up to 5	KDFP	2 355	2 469	–	–	–	–	–	–	–	–	–
Over 5 years and undated	KDFQ	1 287	1 196	6 618	6 696	7 171	8 618	7 702	5 371	5 190	4 201	3 873
Other												
Public sector	ATGP	520	361	366	442	425	..	..	..	..	..	..
Other	KDFS	3 229	3 797	5 264	7 688	7 573	11 512	13 402	14 308	18 969	21 556	26 401
Sterling												
Miscellaneous assets												
Items in suspense and collections	ATGR	6 143	7 023	7 373	8 879	8 870	12 614	13 967	14 583	15 383	18 070	17 356
Assets leased	ATGS	1 292	1 076	1 195	1 302	1 426	1 432	1 278	1 065	943	995	782
Other	ATGT	3 424	4 038	4 898	5 396	5 904	6 325	7 339	8 731	10 506	12 045	12 346
Other currency												
Items in suspense and collections	ATGU	1 829	1 782	2 172	3 567	5 086	3 564	4 179	4 042	5 049	3 753	4 557
Assets leased	ATGV	12	20	17	16	10	10	1	–	–	–	–
Other	ATGW	1 405	3 265	2 613	1 930	1 589	2 414	2 732	2 163	2 538	1 510	1 369
Other currency assets												
Market loans and advances:												
Total	ATGX	283 400	365 773	426 195	513 290	478 474	558 587	520 210	544 209	635 008	598 889	556 214
of which Advances	ATGY	*68 849*	*91 389*	*109 186*	*134 784*	*120 287*	*128 030*	*118 295*	*129 411*	*165 569*	*152 556*	*139 110*
UK banks	ATGZ	61 325	80 013	83 714	95 010	89 171	97 225	78 827	78 139	75 596	72 229	72 961
UK bank CDs	ATHM	5 407	7 200	10 615	11 621	11 610	12 999	9 252	7 392	8 220	10 161	11 081
UK public sector	ATHA	902	1 028	1 376	1 864	1 632	1 526	925	70	50	39	28
UK private sector	ATHB	15 287	19 946	24 187	35 762	33 837	42 878	45 238	54 815	77 923	70 419	59 592
Overseas	ATHC	200 480	257 585	306 304	369 033	342 225	403 959	385 968	403 793	473 219	446 041	412 552
Bills	ATHD	822	1 070	1 242	1 562	1 717	3 143	2 399	3 837	4 556	5 562	7 835
Investments: total	ATHE	5 380	8 570	13 642	23 935	32 527	42 711	35 390	36 306	44 581	46 931	56 391
United Kingdom	KDHW	315	308	436	617	1 949	3 923	2 677	2 397	2 300	2 369	2 451
Overseas	ATHG	5 065	8 262	13 205	23 318	30 578	38 788	32 712	33 909	42 281	44 562	53 940
Acceptances												
Sterling	ATHH	7 921	12 198	13 385	16 335	18 251	20 926	18 303	18 743	20 643	20 286	19 081
Other currencies	ATHI	827	1 261	1 524	2 718	2 987	3 308	3 172	3 514	4 529	4 824	5 474

See footnotes on page 289.

Source: Bank of England

Banking

17.5 Analysis of bank lending to UK residents [1]
Amounts outstanding

£ million

		Third Wednesday in Nov			End Nov				
		1984	1985	1986	1987	1988	1989[2]	1990	1991
Total to UK residents	AFTA	150 793	168 280	203 069	242 899	304 996	413 663	451 611	476 664
Loans and advances	AFNA	139 315	154 919	189 671	230 752	289 518	395 971	433 619	459 585
of which in sterling	AFNB	*103 027*	*119 819*	*144 492*	*181 771*	*236 679*	*317 233*	*363 395*	*376 038*
Acceptances	KROC	11 478	13 361	13 398	12 147	15 478	17 692	17 992	17 075
of which in sterling	KROD	*10 579*	*12 407*	*12 768*	*11 706*	*15 016*	*17 062*	*17 545*	*16 735*
Agriculture, forestry and fishing									
Total	AFTV	5 495	5 878	6 088	6 080	6 530	6 836	7 118	7 124
of which in sterling	KROE	*5 469*	*5 859*	*6 048*	*6 041*	*6 461*	*6 697*	*6 990*	*7 018*
Energy and water supply									
Total	KROF	6 314	4 888	4 421	4 197	3 983	4 682	4 997	6 715
of which in sterling	KROG	*3 020*	*2 107*	*1 416*	*1 804*	*1 960*	*2 174*	*2 913*	*3 711*
Oil and extraction of natural gas	AFTW	3 996	3 072	2 723	2 731	3 161	3 797	3 792	5 224
Other energy industries	KROH	2 168	1 310	1 090	988	723	701	1 027	1 285
Water supply	KROI	150	506	608	478	99	185	178	235
Manufacturing industry									
Total	AFTG	26 390	27 433	29 648	29 900	40 688	51 175	54 291	51 588
of which in sterling	KROJ	*20 810*	*22 353*	*23 289*	*23 396*	*31 204*	*35 280*	*39 136*	*37 391*
Extraction of minerals and ores	KROK	770	805	644	650	719	1 252	1 019	1 410
Metal manufacturing	AFTI	1 660	1 268	1 106	1 118	1 456	1 803	2 123	1 816
Mineral products	KROL	926	960	1 072	930	1 100	1 471	1 922	1 932
Chemical industry	AFTJ	2 010	2 016	2 124	2 074	2 107	3 003	3 334	2 978
Mechanical engineering	AFTK	1 837	2 162	2 158	2 136	2 603	3 404	3 751	3 463
Electrical engineering	AFTL	3 071	3 628	3 548	3 460	4 604	5 916	5 586	5 733
Motor vehicles	AFTM	1 120	1 352	1 742	952	1 274	1 480	1 797	1 775
Other transport equipment	AFTN	1 569	1 474	1 515	1 444	1 585	1 390	1 604	1 678
Other engineering and metal goods	AFTO	2 009	1 989	1 982	1 811	2 527	3 263	3 299	2 966
Food, drink and tobacco	AFTP	4 810	4 595	6 029	6 039	9 328	9 542	10 796	10 350
Textiles, leather, clothing and footwear	AFTQ	1 546	1 796	1 720	2 041	2 500	3 347	3 220	3 056
Other manufacturing	AFTR	5 062	5 388	6 009	7 246	10 885	15 304	15 841	14 431
Construction									
Total	AFTY	4 609	5 074	5 675	7 203	10 751	15 135	17 335	16 414
of which in sterling	KROM	*4 243*	*4 614*	*5 253*	*6 677*	*9 841*	*13 682*	*15 729*	*14 452*
Garages, distribution, hotels and catering									
Total	KRON	19 746	22 388	24 362	27 525	32 832	42 010	44 648	45 106
of which in sterling	KROO	*14 792*	*17 057*	*18 572*	*20 812*	*25 388*	*32 320*	*36 710*	*36 689*
Retail motor trades	AFUB	2 006	2 246	2 486	2 794	3 172	4 302	4 869	5 168
Other retail distribution	AFUC	5 715	6 621	7 215	8 365	10 118	13 832	14 602	13 510
Wholesale distribution	AFUA	8 946	9 973	10 600	10 654	12 358	14 016	13 258	13 687
Hotels and catering	AFUD	3 079	3 548	4 060	5 712	7 184	9 859	11 919	12 709
Transport									
Total	KROP	3 571	3 509	3 559	3 402	4 221	5 298	6 758	7 110
of which in sterling	KROQ	*2 127*	*2 356*	*2 396*	*3 144*	*2 953*	*3 884*	*5 035*	*5 247*
Air transport	KROR	760	502	456	418	548	1 010	1 535	1 854
Other transport	KROS	2 811	3 007	3 103	2 984	3 673	4 289	5 223	5 257
Postal services and telecommunications									
Total	KROT	283	339	304	441	997	1 455	809	914
of which in sterling	KROU	*133*	*177*	*162*	*252*	*681*	*1 135*	*589*	*774*
Financial									
Total	KROV	31 644	32 574	55 504	69 532	80 754	103 654	111 396	130 287
of which in sterling	KROW	*13 822*	*18 072*	*30 032*	*41 175*	*53 698*	*63 970*	*76 554*	*82 618*
Building societies	AFUP	1 420	2 064	3 362	4 015	6 759	6 317	7 704	9 725
Investments and unit trusts	AFUQ	2 369	3 462	3 725	6 483	6 777	7 928	5 387	6 759
Insurance companies and pension funds	AFUR	2 248	2 370	2 906	3 928	3 336	4 356	4 257	3 723
Leasing companies	AFUS	4 508	6 660	7 799	10 181	11 283	16 003	22 125	24 644
Other financial	AFUT	21 099	18 018	25 050	30 137	37 361	48 830	49 768	49 884
Securities dealers, stockbrokers, jobbers,etc[3]	AFUU	..	..	13 706	62 536	57 670	73 627	84 336	120 345
Business and other services									
Total	KROY	18 694	25 094	25 185	31 764	46 119	66 489	77 028	77 755
of which in sterling	KROZ	*15 233*	*18 644*	*21 905*	*28 667*	*41 646*	*58 849*	*70 726*	*71 862*
Central and local government	AFUI	2 108	2 144	1 380	1 300	1 554	1 952	1 768	2 038
Property companies	AFUJ	5 420	7 109	9 349	13 360	21 348	31 963	38 996	39 674
Hiring of movables	KRPA	687	771	918	1 064	1 070	1 740	1 706	1 427
Other services	KRPB	10 479	15 070	13 538	16 040	22 146	30 834	34 557	34 620
Persons									
Total (loans and advances only)	AFOX	34 048	41 102	48 323	62 854	78 120	116 929	127 232	133 656
of which in sterling	KRPC	*33 956*	*40 991*	*48 145*	*62 629*	*77 879*	*116 306*	*126 560*	*133 008*
Bridging finance for house purchase	KRPD AFOY	828	832[4]	25 296	34 861	44 596	78 289	85 539	90 193
Other house purchase	KRPE	16 092	20 167						
Other advances to persons	AFOZ	17 128	20 103	23 027	27 994	33 525	38 639	41 692	43 463

1 This is a series of statistics based on the Standard Industrial Classification 1980 and comprises loans, advances and acceptances by all monthly reporting institutions other than members of the London Discount Market Association(LDMA).The table includes lending under the Department of Trade and Industry special scheme for domestic shipbuilding, secured money placed with Stock Exchange money brokers and gilt-edged market makers, time deposits placed with and certificates of deposit issued by building societies.

2 From 1989, Abbey National's data have been included.

3 From end November 1986 lending to securities dealers, stockbrokers and stock jobbers (including money placed with the Stock Exchange money brokers and gilt-edged market makers) is shown separately within the Financial sector. Such lending was previously included in the Other services line of Business and other services.

4 Now published as House Purchase.

Source: Bank of England

Banking

17.6 Discount houses[1,2]
December

£ million

		1981	1982	1983	1984	1985	1986	1987	1988	1989	1990	1991
Assets												
Total	ATKE	5 084	5 459	6 953	8 096	8 713	9 539	11 608	12 027	15 276	15 193	11 857
Treasury bills	ATJN	99	70	31	222	50	240	261	647	940	415	158
Other bills[3]:												
Sterling	KDIC	2 892	2 394	3 577	3 589	3 474	4 073	5 351	4 205	6 006	5 384	3 851
Other currencies	ATKC	34	24	13	77	135	30	25	51	45	80	13
British government securities	ATJW	742	555	364	401	292	21	33	8	4	13	61
UK banks CDs:												
Sterling	ATJS	642	1 468	2 044	2 179	2 729	3 022	3 705	4 304	4 338	5 753	5 408
Other currencies	ATKB	22	9	10	4	57	124	38	33	137	138	134
Building Society CDs and time deposits	KDIH	–	–	280	522	550	348	747	897	1 270	1 768	978
Local authority securities	ATJX	243	216	154	127	37	13	2	–	–	–	–
Other assets[4]:												
Sterling	KDIJ	212	574	410	673	1 241	1 501	1 328	1 745	2 316	1 399	1 138
Other currencies	KDIK	22	9	10	4	57	168	119	137	219	244	116
Borrowed funds[5]												
Total	KDIL	4 926	5 286	6 738	7 818	8 457	9 246	11 312	11 727	14 926	14 911	11 604
Bank of England, banking department	ATJD	20	–	55	48	80	–	45	35	113	43	–
Other UK banks:												
Sterling	ATJE	4 360	4 733	5 838	6 124	6 409	6 983	8 064	8 182	10 192	10 861	8 871
Other currencies	ATJI	157	136	49	293	121	129	59	68	145	92	66
Other sources:												
Sterling	KDIP	327	391	774	1 263	1 632	1 988	3 019	3 294	4 219	3 559	2 472
Other currencies	KDIQ	62	26	21	90	215	146	125	148	258	357	196

1 Comprises money market dealing counterparties of the Bank of England which are authorised under the Banking Act.
2 Securities, etc, are generally reported at the value standing in the reporting institutions books.
3 Including local authority and public corporation bills.
4 Including funds lent to UK banks and in the local authority market.
5 Excluding capital and reserves.

Source: Bank of England

17.7 Public sector borrowing requirement and other counterparts to changes in money stock during the year

£ million

		1981	1982	1983	1984	1985	1986	1987	1988	1989	1990	1991
Public sector borrowing requirement (surplus-)	ABEN	10 507	4 868	11 574	10 300	7 445	2 499	−1 434	−11 868	−9 276	−2 120	7 681
Sales(-) of public sector debt to UK private sector (other than banks and building societies)	KHGZ	−10 576	−9 289	−9 807	−10 247	−8 086	−5 969	−4 113	3 840	12 821	−1 676	−5 322
Sterling lending to the private sector[1]	AVBS	17 715	25 665	23 035	30 314	34 028	47 644	54 109	83 077	88 926	71 214	36 786
External and foreign currency finance of the public sector	KHJP	−957	−1 323	−1 569	−1 616	−3 142	−2 021	7 084	3 225	−3 476	4 478	−3 935
External and foreign currency transactions of UK banks and building societies[2,3]	AVBW	906	−1 595	−725	−2 019	519	−865	−5 046	−11 962	−14 647	−11 044	1 563
Net non-deposit liabilities (increase-)[3]	AVBX	−1 637	−1 797	−2 423	−3 321	−4 893	−6 202	−8 818	−13 642	−10 067	−9 581	−7 346
Money stock (M4)	AUZI	15 953	16 539	19 698	23 232	25 874	35 088	41 817	52 670	64 263	51 273	29 438

1 Bank and building society lending, plus holdings of commercial bills by the Issue Department of the Bank of England.
2 Including sterling lending to overseas sector.
3 With effect from the third quarter 1975 the external and foreign currency transactions of UK banks and building societies include net non-deposit currency liabilities. From this date 'Net non-deposit liabilities' comprise sterling components only. See note on page 288.

Source: Bank of England

Banking

17.8 Money stock and liquidity

£ million

		1981	1982	1983	1984	1985	1986	1987	1988	1989	1990	1991
Amounts outstanding at end-year												
Notes and coin in circulation with the M4 private sector	VQKT	10 148	10 557	11 150	11 469	11 966	12 696	13 405	14 447	15 359	15 256	15 716
UK private sector sterling non-interest bearing sight deposits[2,3]	AUYA	17 781	19 438	21 624	23 921	24 339	28 089	31 427	35 544	32 020	30 097	30 200
Money stock (M2)	AUYC	27 929	107 217	118 949	132 972	145 701	167 120	185 468	214 968	236 257	255 202	278 272
Money stock M4	AUYM	138 363	154 953	175 367	199 004	224 899	261 400	303 662	356 420	423 405	474 293	501 845
Changes during the year[4]												
Notes and coin in circulation with the M4 private sector[1]	VQLU	610	409	618	319	497	743	709	1 042	901	−103	460
UK private sector sterling non-interest bearing sight deposits[2,3]	AUZA	823	1 655	2 167	2 195	418	3 506	3 333	4 243	−3 734	−1 911	−708
Money stock (M2)	AUZE	1 433	4 595	11 172	15 271	12 493	21 084	17 589	31 229	21 330	18 816	23 083
Money stock M4	AUZI	15 953	16 539	19 698	23 232	25 874	35 088	41 817	52 670	64 263	51 273	29 438

1 The estimates of levels of coin in circulation include allowance for wastage, hoarding, etc.
2 Deposits are confined to those with institutions included in the United Kingdom monetary sector (See Table 17.3).
3 After deducting 60 per cent of transit terms.
4 As far as possible the changes exclude the effect of changes in the number of contributors to the series, and also of the introduction of new statistical returns in 1975.

Source: Bank of England

17.9 Money and bill rates
London clearing banks' base rates[1]
Percentage rates operative between dates shown

Rate

Date of change	Per cent	Date of change	Per cent	Date of change	Per cent
1982 Jan 22	14.00	1985 Jan 11	10.50	1988 Feb 2	9.00
Feb 25	13.50	Jan 14	12.00	Mar 17	8.50
Mar 12	13.00	Jan 28	14.00	Apr 11	8.00
Jun 8	12.50	Mar 20	13.50-14.00	May 18	7.50
Jul 13	12.00	Mar 21	13.50	Jun 3	8.00
Aug 2	11.50	Mar 29	13.00-13.50	Jun 6	8.00-8.50
Aug 18	11.00	Apr 2	13.00-13.25	Jun 7	8.50
Aug 31	10.50	Apr 12	12.75-13.00	Jun 22	9.00
Oct 7	10.00	Apr 19	12.50-12.75	Jun 29	9.50
Oct 14	9.50	Jun 12	12.50	Jul 5	10.00
Nov 4	9.00	Jul 15	12.00-12.50	Jul 19	10.50
Nov 26	10.00-10.25	Jul 16	12.00	Aug 8	10.50-11.00
		Jul 29	11.50-12.00	Aug 9	11.00
1983 Jan 12	11.00	Jul 30	11.50	Aug 25	11.00-12.00
Mar 15	10.50			Aug 26	12.00
Apr 15	10.00	1986 Jan 9	12.50	Nov 25	13.00
Jun 15	9.50	Mar 19	11.50		
Oct 4	9.00	Apr 8	11.00-11.50	1989 May 24	14.00
		Apr 9	11.00	Oct 5	15.00
1984 Mar 7	8.75-9.00	Apr 21	10.50		
Mar 15	8.50-8.75	May 27	10.00	1990 Oct 8	14.00
May 10	9.00-9.25	Oct 10	11.00		
Jun 27	9.25			1991 Feb 13	13.50
Jul 9	10.00	1987 Mar 10	10.50	Feb 27	13.00
Jul 12	12.00	Mar 19	10.00	Mar 22	12.50
Aug 9	11.50	Apr 29	9.50	Apr 12	12.00
Aug 10	11.00	May 11	9.00	May 24	11.50
Aug 20	10.50	Aug 7	10.00	Jul 12	11.00
Nov 7	10.00	Oct 26	9.50	Sep 4	10.50
Nov 20	9.75-10.00	Nov 5	9.00		
Nov 23	9.50-9.75	Dec 4	8.50	1992 May 5	10.00

1 See footnote 1 on page 294.

Source: Bank of England

Banking

17.9 Money and bill rates
London clearing banks' base rates[1]
(continued)
Percentage rates operative between dates shown

Rate per cent

	1982[1]	1983	1984	1985	1986	1987	1988	1989	1990	1991	1992
Treasury bills:[2] KDMM											
January	14.205	10.593	8.868	10.550	11.977	10.524	8.374	12.450	14.490	13.000	9.950
February	13.564	10.739	8.854	12.691	12.017	10.290	8.785	12.390	14.450	12.390	9.780
March	12.489	10.465	8.433	12.935	11.055	9.346	8.273	12.410	14.580	11.640	10.100
April	12.864	9.841	8.375	11.925	9.993	9.430	7.737	12.510	14.590	11.250	9.970
May	12.633	9.696	8.815	11.935	9.704	8.456	7.543	12.540	14.500	10.840	9.420
June	12.227	9.471	8.863	11.889	9.318	8.540	8.882	13.590	14.380	10.720	9.420
July	11.580	9.367	10.974	11.385	9.452	8.837	10.051	13.290	14.320	10.520	..
August	10.335	9.342	10.213	10.962	9.392	9.788	11.132	13.320	14.310	10.200	..
September	9.909	9.157	10.020	11.060	9.605	9.693	11.528	13.440	14.260	9.660	..
October	9.140	8.841	9.850	11.052	10.252	9.448	11.542	14.460	13.370	9.860	..
November	8.937	8.842	9.225	11.107	10.632	8.433	12.070	14.450	12.920	9.980	..
December	9.897	8.870	9.103	11.153	10.659	8.186	12.532	14.500	12.960	10.100	..
Three-months bank bills:[3] KDMY											
January	14.35	10.69	9.05	11.23	12.14	11.00	8.42	12.62	14.51	13.37	10.08
February	13.66	10.84	9.00	13.00	12.10	10.60	8.88	12.52	14.53	12.61	9.86
March	12.66	10.53	8.32	13.14	11.26	9.55	8.52	12.55	14.67	11.77	10.18
April	12.92	9.85	8.00	12.00	10.27	9.70	7.89	12.63	14.63	11.44	10.18
May	12.67	9.85	8.95	12.00	9.90	8.68	7.69	12.64	14.55	11.07	9.53
June	12.36	9.48	9.05	12.00	9.38	8.82	8.65	13.62	14.42	10.77	9.51
July	11.68	9.42	11.09	11.48	9.78	9.00	10.15	13.41	14.36	10.62	..
August	10.53	9.20	10.42	11.00	9.60	9.80	10.88	13.40	14.37	10.40	..
September	10.09	9.07	10.03	11.00	9.95	9.55	11.70	13.54	14.34	9.84	..
October	9.31	8.95	10.00	11.00	10.65	9.73	11.62	14.43	13.49	10.01	..
November	8.89	9.00	9.18	11.00	11.05	8.81	11.81	14.55	13.12	10.10	..
December	10.09	9.00	9.00	11.00	11.00	8.18	12.62	14.58	13.19	10.22	..
Three-months inter-bank deposits:[4,5] KDNY											
January	15.13	11.20	9.45	11.68	12.83	11.05	8.97	13.14	15.16	13.97	10.65
February	14.48	11.31	9.38	13.76	12.66	10.86	9.27	13.07	15.11	13.25	10.37
March	13.57	10.94	8.95	13.63	11.72	9.97	8.89	13.05	15.29	12.40	10.62
April	13.77	10.27	8.88	12.76	10.48	9.80	8.30	13.13	15.21	11.95	10.62
May	13.35	10.27	9.40	12.66	10.22	8.82	8.03	13.14	15.15	11.53	10.06
June	13.00	9.93	9.45	12.44	9.78	8.90	8.93	14.15	14.97	11.24	9.98
July	12.37	9.89	11.51	12.04	9.96	9.21	10.55	13.92	14.95	11.09	..
August	11.11	9.87	11.07	11.50	9.84	10.04	11.39	13.85	15.00	10.89	..
September	10.89	9.69	10.83	11.55	10.12	10.16	12.15	14.02	14.91	10.29	..
October	9.79	9.38	10.67	11.55	11.04	9.98	12.04	15.02	14.03	10.40	..
November	9.39	9.30	9.93	11.57	11.17	8.95	12.31	15.11	13.64	10.48	..
December	10.62	9.42	9.82	11.76	11.36	8.77	13.13	15.12	13.81	10.79	..
Three-months local authority deposits:[4,6] KDPX											
January	15.15	11.20	9.24	11.59	12.86	11.00	8.88	13.05	15.01	13.94	10.61
February	14.43	11.10	9.00	13.80	12.65	10.95	9.18	12.95	15.02	13.23	10.34
March	13.54	11.00	9.00	13.67	11.68	10.14	8.85	12.94	15.20	12.42	10.57
April	13.75	10.11	9.00	12.70	10.27	9.90	8.24	13.04	15.20	11.89	10.59
May	13.33	10.00	9.33	13.00	10.00	9.00	8.00	13.13	15.11	11.50	10.02
June	12.99	10.00	9.29	12.20	10.00	9.00	8.84	14.08	14.94	11.21	9.94
July	12.40	10.00	11.45	12.04	10.00	9.00	10.43	13.87	14.90	11.05	..
August	11.11	10.00	11.14	11.38	10.00	9.85	11.29	13.75	14.94	10.89	..
September	10.83	9.91	11.00	11.62	10.09	10.00	12.09	13.92	14.92	10.32	..
October	9.82	9.05	10.91	11.57	11.04	9.82	11.95	14.94	14.02	10.45	..
November	9.32	9.00	10.00	11.76	11.00	9.00	12.23	15.01	13.65	10.44	..
December	10.54	9.10	10.00	12.00	11.00	8.95	13.08	15.05	13.77	10.75	..

1 Each bank has a single base rate, which may sometimes differ from those of other banks. The rates of interest charged by the London clearing banks for their advances to customers and their discounting of trade bills are, in general, linked to their own individually declared base rates. The rates charged for advances depend on the nature and status of the customer; most lending is between 1 per cent and 5 per cent higher than base rate. Some lending is related to market rates instead of base rates.

2 Weighted averages of discount rates at the weekly allotments of 91 day bills.
3 The mean of the discount market's buying rates (discount rates per cent per annum). Averages of working days.
4 Figures are averages of working days.
5 The mean of the lowest bid and highest offer rates over the day. The yield on a three-month sterling certificate of deposit is usually close to that for a three-months inter-bank deposit.
6 For a minimum term of three months and thereafter at 7 days notice. The mean of the daily range. From June 1982 the rates are for 10.30am.

Source: Bank of England

Capital markets

17.10 Security yields and prices

		1980	1981	1982	1983	1984	1985	1986	1987	1988	1989	1990	1991	1992
British government securities														
Short dated (5 years)[1]	KDRE	13.84	14.65	12.79	11.19	11.29	11.13	10.01	9.37	9.66	10.73	12.07	10.18	..
Medium dated (10 years)[1]	KDRF	13.91	14.88	13.08	11.27	11.27	11.06	10.05	9.57	9.67	10.19	11.80	10.11	..
Long dated (20 years)[1]	KDRG	13.79	14.74	12.88	10.80	10.69	10.62	9.87	9.47	9.36	9.58	11.08	9.92	..
2.5 per cent Consols[2]:														
Average net price	KDRH	21.10	19.30	21.40	24.50	24.70	24.80	26.40	27.70	27.40	27.10	23.10	25.06	..
Average flat yield	KDRI	11.88	13.01	11.90	10.24	10.16	10.11	9.47	9.31	9.12	9.23	10.84	9.98	..
January		11.41	12.12	13.72	10.73	9.83	10.26	10.14	9.82	9.33	9.05	10.00	10.24	9.56
February		11.76	12.05	13.01	10.87	9.93	10.44	9.92	9.64	9.23	8.77	10.43	9.98	9.42
March		12.62	12.02	12.41	10.34	9.83	10.30	9.10	9.07	8.93	8.56	11.18	10.05	9.73
April		12.35	12.11	12.92	10.09	9.93	10.14	8.54	9.04	8.96	8.91	11.52	10.04	9.57
May		12.18	12.70	12.66	10.19	10.29	10.38	8.64	8.80	9.06	9.12	11.10	10.16	9.23
June		11.98	12.96	12.48	9.83	10.48	10.28	8.73	8.85	9.12	9.42	10.65	10.33	9.21
July		11.55	13.44	12.22	10.24	10.88	10.04	9.01	9.12	9.28	9.27	10.78	10.13	..
August		11.80	13.46	11.64	10.42	10.42	9.90	9.18	9.67	9.16	9.16	11.14	9.83	..
September		11.64	13.72	10.87	10.18	10.27	9.92	9.63	9.77	9.27	9.39	11.12	9.67	..
October		11.55	14.16	10.29	10.09	10.17	9.88	10.16	9.70	9.03	9.55	10.94	9.78	..
November		11.54	13.53	9.92	9.97	9.88	9.92	10.36	8.89	9.00	9.77	10.81	9.83	..
December		11.94	13.63	10.65	9.90	9.94	9.89	10.28	9.31	9.10	9.80	10.41	9.74	..

1 Par yields derived from yield-maturity curves fitted mathematically. The figures are averages of Wednesday yields until 1979. From 1980 the average is of all observations (usually 3 per week); from January 1982 figures are the average of working days. The method of calculation is described in the *Bank of England Quarterly Bulletin*, February 1990.

2 Averages of working days based, up to and including March 1982, on the mean of the middle opening and middle closing prices each day; thereafter the figures are based on closing prices only. Gross accrued interest is excluded; tax is ignored.

Sources: *Bank of England;*
Institute of Actuaries;
Faculty of Actuaries;
Financial Times

Capital markets

17.11 Securities quoted on the Stock Exchange[1]
At last working day in March

£ million

		1982	1983	1984	1985	1986	1987	1988	1989	1990	1991	1992
Total of all securities at market values	KDRV	455 995	688 493	832 098	1 107 548	1 247 580	1 547 845	1 427 397	1 861 091	2 106 146	2 195 213	2 054 926
British government and government guaranteed stocks[2]												
Nominal values	KDRW	91 106	96 039	107 932	118 115	128 850	138 777	142 857	133 780	117 857	118 702	130 143
Market values	KDRX	81 087	97 001	111 060	117 616	138 417	147 550	151 207	137 195	109 431	121 183	132 806
Other securities at market values:												
Irish government stocks	KDRY	2 457	4 732	5 013	5 891	8 398	9 727	11 026	10 730	11 834	11 878	13 359
Corporation stocks, public boards, etc	KDRZ	2 425	2 364	2 237	1 629	1 149	912	644	763	309	276	246
Dominion and foreign government and corporation stocks	KDSA	20 071	35 976	42 802	75 121	83 656	104 460	102 703	142 501	123 575	138 957	138 977
Company securities												
Total	KDSB	349 955	548 420	670 986	907 302	1 015 960	1 285 196	1 161 817	1 569 902	1 860 997	1 922 919	1 769 539
Loan capital	KDSC	4 905	6 320	8 256	8 680	9 004	12 013	11 820	13 621	16 788	14 129	15 164
Preference and preferred capital	KDSD	1 860	3 070	6 416	5 510	8 259	22 438	26 887	35 459	39 859	32 918	26 822
Ordinary and deferred capital[3]	KDSE	343 190	539 030	656 314	893 112	998 697	1 250 745	1 123 110	1 520 822	1 804 351	1 875 872	1 727 553

1 The stock exchanges of the United Kingdom and the Republic of Ireland form one exchange (The Stock Exchange).
2 Excluding marketable unlisted securities; including all outstanding amounts of 4 per cent Victory Bonds and 4 per cent Funding Loan, 1960-90 (that is, amounts for death duties and held by the National Debt Commissioners are included).
3 From 1978 shares of no par value are no longer distinguished separately.

Source: Council of The Stock Exchange

Footnotes to Table 17.12

1 The estimates relate to new money raised on the main stock market by issues of ordinary, preference and loan capital (public issues, offers for sale, issues by tender, placings, and issues to shareholders and employees) by listed public companies and local authorities in the United Kingdom; and by overseas borrowers split between central government, state and local governments and companies. The estimates include UK local authority negotiable bonds (of not less than one year) issued to or through the agency of banks, discount houses, issuing houses or brokers. Mortgages, bank advances and any other loans redeemable in less than twelve months are excluded; so also are loans from UK government funds (including the former Industrial Reorganisation Corporation and the National Enterprise Board) but not government subscriptions to company issues made *pari passu* with the market. Issues to shareholders are included only if the sole or principal share register is maintained in the United Kingdom. Estimates of issues are based on the prices at which securities are offered to the market. Subscriptions are recorded under the periods in which they are due to be paid. Redemptions relate to fixed interest securities of the kinds included as issues; conversion issues in lieu of cash repayment are included in the gross figures of both issues and redemptions. These figures include issues of debentures and loan stock carrying the right of conversion into, or subscription to, equity capital. Estimates for these issues *less* redemptions are: 1977 -5; 1978 -21; 1979 23; 1980 178; 1981 194; 1982 8; 1983 47; 1984 101; 1985 320.

The division between United Kingdom and overseas company borrowers is determined by the location of the registered office. The industrial classification of companies is according to the primary occupation of the borrowing company or group and is based up to 1982 on the former Standard Industrial Classification 1968 and from 1983 on the Revised Standard Industrial Classification 1980.
2 The estimates exclude issues on the unlisted securities market which was launched by the Stock Exchange in November 1980. These issues are mainly of ordinary shares by industrial and commercial companies. Estimates of new money raised are: 1980 88; 1981 54; 1982 87; 1983 164; 1984 159; 1985 181; 1986 320; 1987 967; 1988 632; 1989 767; 1990 364; 1991 261
3 Overseas companies including public corporations.
4 Other' includes special finance agencies (listed public companies engaged in the provision of medium and long-term finance to industry eg ICFC) and those finance houses and other consumer credit grantors not included under banks and building societies.

Source: Bank of England

Capital markets

17.12 Capital issues and redemptions in the United Kingdom[1,2]

£ million

		1981	1982		1983	1984	1985	1986	1987	1988	1989	1990	1991
Total issues and redemptions													
Gross issues	KDSF	3 311	2 907	KDSF	4 675	3 562	6 238	10 053	17 133	8 090	11 013	5 381	12 388
Gross redemptions	KDSG	1 341	1 351	KDSG	1 347	1 224	1 063	998	1 747	1 028	3 150	2 479	1 334
Issues *less* redemptions: total	KDSH	1 970	1 556	KDSH	3 328	2 338	5 175	9 055	15 386	7 062	7 863	2 901	11 054
Loan capital	KDSI	67	582	KDSI	980	874	527	1 185	−179	945	3 331	−278	−229
Preference shares	KDSJ	68	9	KDSJ	59	42	414	66	658	964	898	421	818
Ordinary shares	KDSK	1 835	965	KDSK	2 289	1 422	4 234	7 804	14 907	5 153	3 634	2 758	10 465
United Kingdom borrowers: total	KDSL	1 675	993	KDSL	2 746	1 463	4 500	8 519	15 201	6 659	6 816	2 674	11 068
Local authorities	KDSM	−157	−174	KDSM	−66	−258	−566	−202	−175	−34	−11	−35	−3
Listed public companies: total	KDSN	1 832	1 167	KDSN	812	1 721	5 066	8 721	15 376	6 693	6 827	2 709	11 071
Overseas borrowers: total	KDSO	295	563	KDSO	582	875	675	535	185	403	1 047	227	−15
Central government	KDSP	124	201	KDSP	246	351	250	164	−3	90	–	–	–
State, local government	KDSQ	6	85	KDSQ	−13	106	–	–	–	–	–	150	–
Companies[3]	KHDR	165	277	KHDR	349	418	425	371	188	313	1 047	77	−15
United Kingdom listed public companies													
All companies: total	KDSR	1 832	1 167	KDSR	2 812	1 721	5 066	8 721	15 376	6 693	6 827	2 709	11 071
Loan capital	KDSS	−72	195	KDSS	565	281	441	906	–	795	2 645	−71	−200
Preference shares	KDST	68	8	KDST	59	42	414	66	704	744	898	421	818
Ordinary shares	KDSU	1 836	964	KDSU	2 188	1 398	4 211	7 751	14 717	5 154	3 284	2 758	10 455
Financial companies: total	KDSV	123	296	KDSV	684	498	1 016	2 924	2 321	1 733	2 287	222	1 290
Loan capital	KDSW	−83	278										
Preference shares	KDSX	−8	–										
Ordinary shares	KDSY	214	18	KDSY	465	405	958	2 401	2 011	1 281	1 609	558	1 029
Other companies: total	KDSZ	1 709	871	KDSZ	2 128	1 223	4 050	5 798	13 055	4 960	4 540	2 486	9 783
Loan capital	KDTA	11	−83	KDTA	346	207	388	473	−300	623	2 191	−36	−113
Preference shares	KDTB	76	8	KDTB	59	23	409	−25	649	464	674	322	470
Ordinary shares	KDTC	1 622	946	KDTC	1 723	993	3 253	5 350	12 706	3 873	1 675	2 220	9 426
United Kingdom listed public companies													
Financial companies: total	KDTD	123	296	KDTD	684	498	1 016	2 924	2 321	1 733	2 287	222	1 290
Banks and building societies	KDTE	–	298	KDTE	549	278	729	743	829	458	21	−203	319
Insurance companies	KDTF	198	2	KDTF	5	−7	7	606	−2	–	–	71	124
Investment trust companies	KDTG	9	18	KDTG	92	135	157	374	325	143	1 110	373	689
Other[4]	KDTH	−84	−22	KDTH	38	92	123	1 201	1 169	1 132	1 156	−20	158
Other companies: total	KDTI	1 709	871	KDTI	2 128	1 223	4 050	5 798	13 055	4 960	4 540	2 486	9 783
Manufacturing industries: total	KDTJ	632	407	KDTJ	1 386	498	2 365	2 625	5 281	2 305	2 599	1 413	3 620
Food, drink and tobacco	KDTK	50	102										
Chemicals and allied industries	KDTL	85	111										
Metal manufacture	KDTM	−1	1										
Engineering, shipbuilding and electrical goods	KDTN	302	194										
Vehicles	KDTO	97	−2										
Textiles	KDTP	1	4										
Clothing and footwear	KDTQ	1	−5										
Paper, printing and publishing	KDTR	4	–										
Other	KDTS	93	2										
Public utilities, transport and communication	KDTT	83	6										
Distributive trades	KDTU	50	15										
Property companies	KDTV	97	258										
Rest	KDTW	847	185										
Minerals and metal manufacture				KDTX	253	29	221	301	286	97	498	108	493
Chemicals and allied industries				KDTY	314	−3	308	541	98	196	−113	545	178
Metal goods, engineering and vehicles				KDTZ	157	33	329	177	1 615	415	401	576	558
Electrical and electronic engineering				KDUA	200	156	355	158	514	63	66	270	234
Food, drink and tobacco				KDUC	200	105	183	557	289	748	1 110	−808	818
Other manufacturing				KDUD	262	178	969	891	2 479	786	637	721	1 340
Energy				KDUE	192	57	158	151	933	570	−1 416	−166	−267
Water				KDUF	30	2	34	49	46	16	−19	−75	3
Construction				KDUG	53	7	112	513	445	268	129	−10	783
Distribution, hotels and repairs				KDUH	172	107	597	748	2 740	378	877	435	2 970
Transport and communications				KDUI	9	26	177	−129	−250	5	284	179	630
Property companies				KDUJ	78	232	344	705	1 649	457	984	107	779
Services, agriculture, forestry and fishing				KDUK	208	294	263	1 136	2 211	1 242	1 102	605	1 264

See footnotes 1 - 4 on page 296.

Source: *Bank of England*

Other financial institutions

17.13 Building societies[1]
Great Britain (until 1985), United Kingdom (from 1986)

Number and balance sheets

		1982	1983	1984	1985	1986[2]	1987	1988	1989	1990	1991
Societies on register (number)	KRNA	227	206	190	167	151	138	130	126	117	110
Share investors (thousands)	KRNB	36 607	37 711	39 380	39 996	40 560	41 967	43 816	36 805	36 948	37 925
Depositors (thousands)	KRNC	1 094	1 200	1 550	2 149	2 850	3 648	4 306	4 490	4 299	4 698
Borrowers (thousands)	KRND	5 645	5 928	6 315	6 657	7 023	7 182	7 369	6 699	6 724	6 998
Liabilities (£ million):											
Shares	KRNE	64 968.0	75 197.3	88 087.0	102 331.8	115 550.8	129 954.3	149 791.1	143 359.3	160 538.2	177 519.4
Deposits and loans	KRNF	3 531.6	5 601.4	8 425.6	10 751.5	16 862.2	20 571.8	26 528.5	30 532.5	40 695.5	49 516.6
Taxation and other	KRNG	1 729.6	1 583.1	2 067.1	2 767.5	2 250.4	2 569.1	2 953.4	3 071.6	3 768.8	3 093.9
General reserves	KRNH	2 803.3	3 487.0	4 109.1	4 912.6	5 939.0	7 001.7	8 466.0	8 680.7	10 206.1	11 430.4
Subordinate debt	KRNI	–	–	–	–	–	–	1 105.1	1 368.0	1 639.7	2 419.4
Assets (£ million): total	KRNJ	73 032.5	85 868.8	102 688.8	120 763.4	140 602.5	160 096.9	188 844.2	187 012.1	216 848.3	243 979.7
Mortgages	KRNK	56 695.7	67 473.5	81 881.9	96 764.5	115 669.4	130 870.4	153 015.4	151 491.7	175 745.4	196 945.6
Investments	KRNL KHVZ	12 430.4	13 641.1	15 746.8	16 177.4	16 353.9	17 689.6	20 964.9	30 932.2	35 050.9	39 513.6
Cash	KRNM	2 925.2	3 676.3	3 861.2	6 507.4	7 105.0	9 590.4	11 748.1			
Other	KRNN	981.2	1 077.9	1 198.9	1 314.1	1 474.2	1 946.4	3 115.7	4 588.2	6 052.0	7 520.5

Current transactions : (£ million)

		1982	1983	1984	1985	1986[2]	1987	1988	1989	1990[5]	1991[5]
Shares:											
Received	KRNO	32 434.8	40 204.5	54 251.7	76 151.5	83 866.9	97 503.5	111 716.9	97 386.2	..	..
Interest thereon	KRNP	5 298.6	5 095.6	6 318.8	8 269.5	8 498.5	9 141.7	9 852.6	11 775.6	..	..
Withdrawn (including interest)	KRNQ	28 218.0	34 813.3	47 759.0	70 444.9	79 262.9	92 024.6	100 991.8	87 744.1	..	..
Deposits:											
Received	KRNR	2 029.3	4 801.4	11 244.2	17 924.9	28 100.8	38 325.7	58 637.2	62 271.1	..	..
Interest thereon	KRNS	273.2	327.4	581.5	853.7	1 263.7	1 683.7	2 170.0	2 887.8	..	..
Withdrawn (including interest)	KRNT	1 389.2	3 001.2	8 966.1	16 244.5	23 239.2	35 957.5	54 924.7	54 149.8	..	..
Mortgages:											
Advances	KRNU	15 036.4	19 346.5	23 770.9	26 530.8	35 913.2	36 034.0	47 374.9	42 032.2	43 081.0	42 948.0
Repayments of principal	KRNV	7 214.0	8 316.8	9 345.2	11 650.8	16 976.3	19 864.6	25 002.8	37 862.3	..	..
Interest[3]	KRNW	7 030.7	6 845.9	8 843.5	12 027.6	12 820.0	14 306.7	15 965.1	18 395.5	..	..
Management expenses	KRNX	874.6	1 002.2	1 109.9	1 264.9	1 437.4	1 668.0	2 074.7	2 093.2	2 363.0	2 581.0
Percentage rate of interest[4]											
Paid on shares	KRNY	8.80	7.27	7.74	8.69	7.80	7.45	7.04	8.03	..	..
Paid on deposits	KRNZ	9.12	7.24	8.30	8.92	9.15	9.00	9.21	10.12	..	..
Received on mortgage advances	KDUL	13.32	11.03	11.84	13.47	12.07	11.61	11.25	12.21	..	..

1 The figures for each year relate to accounting years ending on dates between 1 February of that year and 31 January of the following year.
2 1988 and subsequent years include Northern Ireland societies, responsibility for which was acquired under the Building Societies Act 1986.
3 Includes amounts recoverable from HM Government under Option Mortgage Scheme and MIRAS (Mortgage interest relief at source).
4 Based on the mean of the amounts outstanding at the end of the previous and the current year.
5 Apart from Mortgage Advances and Management expenses no new data is available for 1990 and 1991. This is due to procedure changes.

Source: Building Societies Commission

Other financial institutions

17.14 Consumer credit

£ million

			1981	*1981*	1982	1983	1984	1985	1986	1987	1988	1989	1990	1991
Broader coverage:														
Total amount outstanding	AILA		13 986	15 450[10]	15 905	18 810	22 229	26 049	30 150	36 174	42 544	48 404	52 579	53 617
Total net lending[1]	-AIKL		2 473		2 634	3 287	3 097	3 820	4 378	6 242	6 745	6 551	4 399	2 208
Retailers[2]	AAPP		31		146	139	119	210	95	248	190	5	64	60
Building societies' class 3 loans[3]	ALPY		–		–	–	–	–	–	70	214	303	223	–45
Banks														
Credit cards	AIKN	VTFY	2 050		2 344	2 593	382	808	948	797	675	540	1 761	774
Loans on personal accounts[4]		VTGA				2 222	2 129	2 443	4 363	5 227	5 000	1 978	1 707	
Insurance companies[5]	-AIKQ		28		19	40	12	62	69	17	86	97	114	127
Non-bank credit companies	-AGSJ		272		125	525	362	611	823	746	352	607	254	–417
Narrower coverage[6]														
Total amount outstanding	RLWE		6 247		7 646	9 669	11 674	14 534	16 781	20 589	24 226	27 057	30 255	30 624
Total net lending[7]	RLWF		916		1 399	2 023	2 005	2 860	2 247	3 837	3 913	3 165	3 683	1 060
Total new credit card advanced[8]	RLBY		6 872		8 678	10 866	13 135	16 672	23 192	29 528	36 306	41 506	46 145	47 112

1 Net lending series. This table now includes figures for "net lending" rather than simple changes in amounts outstanding. The latter were distorted by revaluations of the debt, for example those resulting from amounts written off during the period. The net lending series is now adjusted to remove distortions caused by the revaluations.
2 Self-financed credit advanced by clothing retailers, household goods retailers, mixed business retailers (other than co-operative societies) and general mail order houses.
3 Class 3 loans advanced under the terms of the Building Societies' Act 1986
4 Excludes loans for house purchase and bridging finance.
5 Prior to 1985 includes only policy loans.
6 Covers finance houses and other specialist credit grantors, bank credit cards (operated under the VISA and Mastercard systems), and unsecured loans by building societies (since the end of 1986).
7 Before 1987, net lending equals changes in amounts outstanding.
8 A high proportion of credit advanced in certain types of agreement, notably on credit cards, is repaid within a month. This reflects use of such agreements as a method of payment rather than a way of obtaining credit.
9 Includes net lending for Trustee Savings Bank.
10 Up to 1981, includes consumer credit companies recognised at bank. From 1982 includes consumer credit companies licensed to take deposits.

Source: Central Statistical Office

17.15 Finance houses and other credit companies in Great Britain: assets and liabilities
End-year

£ million

		1981[1]	*1981*	1982	1983	1984	1985	1986	1987	1988	1989	1990	1991
Assets													
Cash in hand and balances with UK monetary sector[2]	AGRB	204	49	30	43	54	58	60	78	214	212	250	240
Amounts outstanding on loans and advances:													
On agreements block discounted by retailers and financial institutions	AGRI	38	3	3	3	3	3	1	1	1	1	–	–
On finance leases[3]	AGRP	..		..	..	..	458	575	648	889	1 011	1 254	1 363
On other loans and advances[4]:													
to individuals (including unincorporated businesses)	AGRJ	3 039		1 317	1 842	2 204	2 815	3 561	4 307	4 619	5 226	5 480	5 507
To UK industrial and commercial companies	AGRL	1 537	464	597	862	891	1 041	897	1 042	1 341	1 547	1 770	1 454
Other current assets:													
Certificates of deposit	AGRC	17	7	8	6	6	7	6	5	6	3	3	1
Other	AGRD	81	48	83	115	143	146	255	362	512	660	807	606
Real assets:													
For own use	AGRE	29		34	25	24	40	53	62	70	78	71	72
For leasing under operating leases, hiring or renting out[3]	AGRF	391		503	496	494	30	26	36	100	135	159	171
Company and government securities	AGRN	104	30	25	25	24	30	33	33	33	33	3	10
Other assets	AGRO	117	30	20	18	15	20	42	76	82	43	35	71
Total	AGRA	6 295	2 234	2 620	3 435	3 858	4 648	5 509	6 650	7 867	8 949	9 832	9 495
Liabilities													
Borrowing (including deposits by and borrowing from other group companies)													
Commercial bills	AGRQ	944	339	452	557	658	772	750	682	587	802	828	502
Short-term borrowing from UK monetary sector (excl. deposits)	AGRR	415	845	900	1 197	1 364	1 646	1 833	2 647	3 601	4 437	4 882	4 760
Deposits and medium and long-term borrowing from UK monetary sector	AGRS	1 465	279	374	609	667	937	1 272	1 634	1 498	1 513	2 128	2 151
Borrowing from other UK financial institutions	AGRT	888	33	25	28	28	33	36	143	180	218	117	70
Other borrowing:													
UK	AGRU	890	99	113	190	209	170	345	231	235	215	225	223
Overseas	AGRV	165	21	22	21	22	26	27	27	23	21	25	35
Other current liabilities	AGRW	295	135	132	174	190	252	334	288	751	757	463	398
Issued capital	AGRX	585	111	106	106	108	106	109	112	134	138	171	325
Reserves and provisions	AGRY	648	372	496	553	612	706	803	886	858	848	993	1 031
Total	AGRA	6 295	2 234	2 620	3 435	3 858	4 648	5 509	6 650	7 867	8 949	9 832	9 495

1 Many companies included in these statistics became part of the new monetary sector at end-1981. See Table 17.3. The new coverage excludes such companies with the 1981 figures showing the position immediately after the transfer.
2 Data up to end-1981 were collected on a different return and in some cases have been estimated.
3 Prior to 1986, amounts outstanding on finance leases are included with real assets for leasing, hiring or renting out.
4 Net of unearned credit charges.

Source: Central Statistical Office

Other financial institutions

17.16 End-year assets and liabilities of investment trust companies, unit trusts and property unit trusts [1]

£ million

		1981	1982	1983	1984	1985	1986	1987	1988	1989	1990	1991
Investment trust companies												
Short-term assets and liabilities (net):	CBPL	283	249	154	487	346	438	1 461	619	1 217	1 227	908
Cash and UK ban deposits	AHAG	210	186	273	396	401	455	1 296	574	883	1 010	790
Other short-term assets	CBPN	221	269	244	475	684	575	618	403	751	501	544
Short-term liabilities	-CBPS	-148	-206	-363	-384	-739	-592	-453	-358	-417	-284	-426
Medium and long-term liabilites and capital:	-CBPO	-9 188	-10 241	-13 419	-15 722	-17 325	-21 055	-20 445	-19 834	-24 386	-20 250	-23 313
Issued share and loan capital	-CBPQ	-2 211	-2 087	-2 258	-2 325	-2 558	-3 237	-4 042	-4 335	-4 692	-5 193	-5 100
Foreign currency borrowing	-CBPR	-228	-361	-538	-449	-557	-406	-610	-427	-342	-318	-344
Other borrowing	-CBQA	-69	-88	-100	-102	-85	-178	-344	-306	-316	-265	-316
Reserves and provisions. etc.	-AHBC	-6 680	-7 705	-10 523	-12 846	-14 125	-17 234	-15 449	-14 766	-19 036	-14 474	-17 553
Investments:	CBPM	8 904	10 051	13 371	15 312	17 040	20 692	19 066	19 298	23 251	19 108	22 497
British government securities	AHBF	183	199	310	300	438	311	595	360	177	326	417
UK company securities:												
Loan capital and preference shares	CBGZ	136	129	172	128	262	378	494	878	903	687	722
Ordinary and deferred shares	CBGY	4 673	4 604	5 306	6 074	7 603	8 957	9 144	8 817	11 121	9 878	10 687
Overseas company securities:												
Loan capital and preference shares	CBHA	203	344	396	416	478	725	476	581	454	257	358
Ordinary and defeered shares	AHCC	3 514	4 256	6 570	7 563	7 368	9 356	7 482	8 116	10 259	7 392	9 146
Other investments	CBPT	195	519	617	831	891	965	875	546	337	568	1 167
Unit trusts												
Short-term assets and liabilities:	CBPU	254	348	569	901	1 179	1 392	2 996	1 682	2 286	2 457	1 982
Cash and UK bank deposits	AGYE	210	189	475	651	1 141	1 115	3 325	1 630	2 174	2 158	1 785
Other short-term assets	CBPW	90	204	205	420	462	792	662	469	513	759	643
Short-term liabilities	-CBPX	-46	-45	-111	-170	-424	-515	-991	-417	-401	-460	-446
Foreign currency borrowing	-AGYK	-3	-58	-123	-128	-475	-190	-685	-9	-70	-34	-38
Investments	CBPZ	5 369	7 309	10 843	13 997	18 433	30 309	33 024	39 592	55 783	41 609	50 525
British government securities	CBHT	175	322	415	566	512	538	663	480	393	411	480
UK company securities:												
Loan capital and preference shares	CBHU	106	154	225	283	505	961	1 518	1 610	1 779	1 337	1 530
Ordinary and deferred shares	RLIB	3 566	4 457	5 954	8 201	10 884	16 424	20 510	23 123	30 324	25 530	29 526
Overseas company securities:												
Loan capital and preference shares	CBHV	31	49	58	109	249	424	398	535	476	347	515
Ordinary and deferred shares	RLIC	1 454	2 229	4 091	4 689	6 179	11 747	9 720	13 640	22 528	13 791	18 072
Other assets	CBQE	37	98	100	149	104	215	215	204	283	193	402
Property unit trusts												
Short-term assets and liabilites (net)	AGVC	158	146	180	147	67	85	49	71	78	136	37
Property	CBQG	1 271	1 321	1 426	1 364	928	987	672	857	1 020	948	540
Other assets	AGVL	259	216	333	439	341	200	186	196	26	21	–
Long-term borrowing	-AGVM	-69	-67	-77	-81	-40	-29	-16	–	-6	-6	-4

Note: Assets are shown as positive: liabilities as negative.

Source: Central Statistical Office

1 Investments are at market value.

17.17 Self-administered pension funds: market value of assets
United Kingdom

£ million, end-year

		1980	1981	1982	1983	1984	1985	1986	1987	1988	1989	1990
Total pension funds[1]												
Total net assets	AHVA	55 791	65 682	86 907	111 375	139 290	168 059	211 220	227 551	267 446	338 950	302 670
Short-term assets	RYIQ	2 571	2 694	3 190	4 809	7 012	7 728	10 359	14 963	18 156	22 438	24 759
British government securities	AHVK	12 011	13 022	18 984	22 631	25 608	29 648	32 511	34 022	34 814	31 894	27 940
UK local authority long-term debt	AHVO	198	156	160	181	163	149	153	181	184	102	32
Overseas government securities	AHVT	102	120	422	518	772	1 203	1 313	1 367	1 968	4 187	5 442
UK company securities	RKPF	26 005	30 129	39 257	50 990	68 263	86 005	111 169	124 334	134 556	168 993	152 496
Overseas company securities	RKPJ	4 325	6 321	9 742	15 566	18 483	22 998	33 076	27 937	42 028	63 570	48 995
Loans and mortgages	RKPK	402	450	480	493	524	459	383	244	300	288	258
UK land, property and ground rent	AHWA	8 305	9 782	10 654	11 293	12 796	13 853	15 311	18 068	23 666	26 959	26 363
Overseas land, property and ground rent[2]	RYHU	–	–	996	1 300	2 022	1 666	1 728	1 728	1 835	1 880	1 006
Property unit trusts	AHVW	1 441	1 678	2 076	2 308	2 582	2 661	2 351	1 772	2 500	2 089	1 656
Other assets	RKPL	1 240	2 141	1 849	2 574	3 401	4 494	6 086	6 420	10 283	19 215	17 574
Long-term borrowing	AHVJ	365	447	451	525	1 114	1 250	1 126	1 122	346	303	220
Short-term liabilities	RYIV	444	364	452	763	1 222	1 555	2 094	2 363	2 498	2 362	3 631

1 These figures cover funded schemes only and therefore exclude the main superannuation arrangements in the central government sector.
2 Prior to 1982 figures are included with 'Other assets'.

Source: Central Statistical Office

Other financial institutions

17.18 Insurance companies: balance sheet
Market values

£ million, end year

		1985	1986	1987	1988	1989	1990	1991
		\multicolumn{7}{c}{Long-term insurance companies}							
Assets								
Total current assets (gross)	RYEW	4 198	5 369	7 767	8 793	10 418	15 749	14 914
Agents' and reinsurance balances (net)[1]	AHNY	214	303	306	382	..	..	..
Other debtors[2]	RKPN	1 375	1 941	2 204	2 865	4 053	3 997	..
British government securities	AHNJ	30 456	31 448	34 690	34 298	32 530	31 137	..
UK local authority securities etc	AHNN	656	995	791	745	832	820	..
UK company securities[3]	RKPO	55 315	74 516	81 333	93 988	124 790	114 482	..
Overseas company securities	RKPP	12 278	16 319	13 264	16 279	26 106	20 067	..
Overseas government securities	AHNS	1 803	2 142	2 093	2 619	3 231	4 935	..
Loans and mortgages	RKPQ	4 342	4 806	5 629	6 152	6 619	7 303	..
UK land, property and ground rent	AHNX	20 162	21 993	26 979	33 737	38 854	34 828	..
Overseas land, property and ground rent[4]	RGCP	304	311	278	289	279	236	..
Other investments[4]	RKPR	304	350	378	719	1 162	844	..
Total	RFXN	131 358	160 190	175 406	200 484	248 874	234 398	..
Net value of direct investment in:								
Non-insurance subsidiaries and associate companies in the United Kingdom	RYET	..	1 037	989	1 284	2 838	3 175	..
UK associate and subsidiary insurance companies and insurance holding companies	RYEU	..	804	909	876	65	85	..
Overseas subsidiaries and associates	RYEV	..	441	415	419	493	350	..
Total assets	RKBI	..	162 472	177 719	203 063	252 270	238 008	..
Liabilities								
Borrowing:								
Borrowing from UK banks	RGDF	1 184	1 519	2 050	2 178	2 332	2 467	..
Other UK borrowing	RGDE	104	167	507	758	1 487	954	..
Borrowing from overseas	RGDD	276	194	138	78	96	163	..
Long-term business:								
Funds	RKDC	..	118 884	134 109	154 722	186 367	197 686	..
Claims admitted but not paid	RKBM	..	572	609	664	795	841	..
Provision for taxation net of amounts receivable:								
UK authorities	RYPI	..	554	123	−183	−36	−585	..
Overseas authorities	RYPJ	..	21	14	8	1	−24	..
Provision for recommended dividends	RYPK	..	92	109	54	119	116	..
Other creditors and liabilities	RYPL	..	1 374	1 409	1 796	2 030	2 603	..
Excess of assets over above liabilities:								
Excess of value of assets over liabilities in respect of long-term funds	RKBR	..	38 531	38 057	42 448	58 206	32 978	..
Minority interests in UK subsidiary companies	RKTI	..	–	–	–	3	–	..
Shareholders' capital and reserves in respect of general business	RKBS	..	187	222	128	261	266	..
Other reserves including profit and loss account balances	RKBT	..	377	373	411	612	543	..
Total liabilities	RKBI	..	162 472	177 719	203 063	252 270	238 008	..

See footnotes on page 302.

Source: Central Statistical Office

Other financial institutions

17.18 Insurance companies: balance sheet
Market values
continued

£ million, end year

		1985	1986	1987	1988	1989	1990	1991
		\multicolumn{7}{c}{Other than long-term insurance companies}
Assets								
Total current assets (gross)	RYME	2 554	3 767	4 261	5 244	5 768	5 866	5 196
Agents' and reinsurance balances (net)[1]	AHMX	2 726	3 025	3 158	3 631	..	..	..
Other debtors[2]	RKPS	3 382	3 511	3 704	4 887	6 131	7 086	..
British government securities	AHMJ	4 860	5 853	6 704	6 546	5 864	5 464	..
UK local authority securities etc	AHMN	55	39	42	42	53	22	..
UK company securities[3]	RKPT	5 931	7 176	7 477	8 582	11 267	10 065	..
Overseas company securities	RKPU	2 210	3 022	2 380	2 976	4 495	3 233	..
Overseas government securities	AHMS	1 575	2 334	2 127	2 376	2 714	2 712	..
Loans and mortgages	RKPV	412	667	925	1 152	1 473	1 870	..
UK land, property and ground rent	AHMW	1 616	1 795	2 013	2 681	3 435	3 288	..
Overseas land, property and ground rent[4]	RYNK	99	41	35	49	61	79	..
Other investments[4]	RKPW	185	251	319	466	573	676	..
Total	RKAL	22 959	28 456	29 987	35 001	41 834	40 361	..
Net value of direct investment in:								
Non-insurance subsidiaries and associate companies in the United Kingdom	RYNR	..	1 087	1 100	1 098	1 510	1 418	..
UK associate and subsidiary insurance companies and insurance holding companies	RYNS	..	601	825	1 091	1 065	1 153	..
Overseas subsidiaries and associates	RYNT	..	6 466	6 020	7 688	8 969	6 823	..
Total assets	RKBY	..	36 610	37 932	44 878	53 378	49 755	..
Liabilities								
Borrowing:								
Borrowing from UK banks	RYMB	−557	747	892	755	956	1 054	969
Other UK borrowing	RYMC	−222	280	395	802	956	852	1 491
Borrowing from overseas	RYMD	−158	472	556	1 058	1 112	1 086	1 134
General business technical reserves	RKCT	..	17 351	19 273	22 082	25 754	29 139	..
Long-term business:								
Funds	RKTF	..	−	−	18	8	−	..
Claims admitted but not paid	RKTK	..	−	−	−	244	195	..
Provision for taxation net of amounts receivable:								
UK authorities	RYPO	..	176	175	451	525	−14	..
Overseas authorities	RYPP	..	24	17	17	11	12	..
Provision for recommended dividends	RYPQ	..	503	545	836	897	951	..
Other creditors and liabilities	RYPR	..	712	822	843	1 064	1 598	..
Excess of assets over above liabilities:								
Excess of value of assets over liabilities in respect of long-term funds	RKCG	..	−	−	76	29	61	..
Minority interests in UK subsidiary companies	RKCH	..	3	10	3	4	4	..
Shareholders' capital and reserves in respect of general business	RKCI	..	14 568	13 413	16 177	19 721	13 349	..
Other reserves including profit and loss account balances	RKCJ	..	1 774	1 835	1 759	2 095	1 471	..
Total liabilities	RKBY	..	36 610	37 932	44 878	53 378	49 755	..

1 Up to 1983, agents' and reinsurance balances are shown gross of amounts payable by insurance companies.
2 Including outstanding interest, dividends and rents (net) which, up to 1983 are shown gross of amounts payable by insurance companies. Amounts receivable from Inland Revenue are included up to 1983.
3 Including authorised unit trust units.
4 Prior to 1985 figures are included with 'Other investments'.

Source: Central Statistical Office

Other financial institutions

17.19 Industrial and provident societies[1]
Great Britain

		1980	1981	1982	1983	1984	1985	1986	1987	1988	1989	1990
Number of societies	KRFQ	9 664	9 736	9 601	9 662	9 799	9 940	10 207	10 486	10 871	11 243	11 329
Number of members (thousands)	KRFR	13 558	13 547	12 961	12 460	11 948	11 267	11 883	11 232	12 006	12 131	10 830
Assets (£ thousands)	KRFS	7 456 987	8 837 347	10 400 488	11 761 990	13 330 091	14 937 025	15 645 308	18 660 066	19 811 840	22 677 304	27 007 352

[1] The annual returns from which these figures are derived are mainly made up to dates varying between September of the year shown and January of the following year.

Source: Registry of Friendly Societies

17.20 Co-operative trading societies[1]
Great Britain

		1980	1981	1982	1983	1984	1985	1986	1987	1988	1989	1990
Number of societies												
General trading societies:												
Retail societies	KREA	270	251	243	237	229	217	213	203	200	210	195
Principal wholesale societies[2]	KREB	2	2	2	2	2	2	2	2	2	2	2
Other wholesale and productive societies	KREC	148	163	187	203	219	225	232	243	244	219	200
Agricultural and fishing trading societies	KRED	541	550	584	597	611	623	636	641	646	626	703
Number of members (thousands)												
General trading societies:												
Retail societies	KREE	9 752.9	9 426.4	8 849.4	8 359.3	7 857.1	7 186.1	7 805.4	7 429.0	7 646.0	7 588.0	7 750.0
Principal wholesale societies[2]	KREF	0.3	0.3	0.3	0.3	0.3	0.2	0.2	0.2	0.2	0.2	0.2
Other wholesale and productive societies	KREG	153.1	43.9	44.3	45.9	50.9	53.7	52.7	53.0	52.6	54.0	58.0
Agricultural and fishing trading societies	KREH	312.2	309.4	304.3	305.9	305.9	300.8	294.6	294.6[5]	286.0	277.0	307.7
Sales (£ million)												
General trading societies:												
Retail societies[3]	KREI	3 446.9	3 644.3	3 771.2	3 913.7	4 125.6	3 994.7	3 989.4	4 408.9	4 070.4	4 406.3	4 973.7
Principal wholesale societies[2]	KREJ	1 755.6	1 833.9	1 933.6	2 080.6	2 087.0	2 248.7	2 308.7	2 308.7	2 485.5	2 663.3	2 985.5
Other wholesale and productive societies	KREK	407.0	432.6	512.8	561.9	609.7	694.9	687.9	853.5[5]	828.6	367.7	1 005.9
Agricultural and fishing trading societies	KREL	1 228.7	1 365.3	1 541.9	1 596.6	1 700.7	1 697.6	1 683.3	1 670.5	1 760.0	1 704.0	1 725.6
Share and loan capital[4] (£ thousand)												
General trading societies:												
Retail societies	KREM	630 210	658 657	680 818	654 553	676 951	638 742	695 144	756 917	869 849	1 045 177	1 171 029
Principal wholesale societies[2]	KREN	250 084	269 645	301 194	313 668	292 194	301 294	299 127	299 127[5]	384 642	434 492	435 393
Other wholesale and productive societies	KREO	53 784	56 186	57 924	62 377	67 863	71 151	69 540	105 030	44 200	49 948	53 407
Agricultural and fishing trading societies	KREP	130 938	154 999	161 590	186 614	188 028	190 541	198 501	206 441	137 812[6]	194 009	202 560

[1] These societies are registered under the Industrial and Provident Societies Acts and are included in Table 17.19. See also footnote 1 to that table.
[2] Co-operative Wholesale Society Ltd., Scottish Co-operative Society Ltd., and Co-operative Tea Society Ltd. During 1973 the businesses of the last two mentioned societies were transferred to the Co-operative Wholesale Society Ltd. Only in respect of the Scottish Co-operative Society Ltd. has the registration been cancelled.
[3] These figures include the sale of goods purchased from the wholesale societies which are also included in the sales of those societies in this table.
[4] Including net balance disposable and reserves but excluding loans from non-members.
[5] 1986 figure.
[6] Share capital only.

Source: Registry of Friendly Societies

Other financial Institutions

17.21 Collecting societies
Great Britain

£ thousand

		1980	1981	1982	1983	1984	1985	1986	1987	1988	1989	1990
Income: total	KRIA	218 639	251 204	266 778	293 096	355 638	341 834	379 674	410 927	406 888	579 133	603 413
Premiums	KRIB	129 242	138 529	151 193	164 353	173 476	177 466	186 838	195 417	204 505	219 915	238 156
Interest	KRIC	88 188	99 263	113 971	124 373	142 087	158 191	173 618	185 474	194 821	226 576	243 220
Miscellaneous[1]	KRID	1 209	13 412	1 614	4 370	40 076	6 178	19 218	30 036	7 262	132 642	122 037
Expenditure: total	KRIE	135 051	147 430	172 724	190 483	196 417	208 377	235 503	270 370	287 576	313 787	206 928
Claims	KRIF	57 111	55 343	57 956	65 971	70 931	78 187	94 073	107 876	124 091	151 199	167 568
Cash bonuses	KRIG	1 045	1 052	1 383	1 126	1 156	1 143	1 039	..	..	..	..
Surrenders	KRIH	15 848	23 828	29 602	35 918	39 166	42 469	43 636	40 863	35 486	33 420	33 079
Expenses of management	KRII	57 784	64 676	72 496	74 288	77 688	79 058	86 074	93 202	95 292	106 669	119 444
Miscellaneous	KRIJ	3 263	2 532	11 287	13 179	7 476	7 519	10 681	28 181	31 561	24 389	45 840
Funds at end of year	KRIK	877 246	980 971	1 075 063	1 177 384	1 336 582	1 470 102	1 613 759	1 754 332	1 877 156	2 449 366	2 627 787

1 Including accrued interest.

*Sources: Office of the Industrial Assurance Commissioner;
Registry of Friendly Societies*

17.22 Friendly societies[1]
Great Britain

		1980	1981	1982	1983	1984	1985	1986	1987	1988	1989	1990
Number of societies, orders and branches[2]	KRFA	4 242	4 069	3 927	3 814	3 659	3 478	3 350	3 193	2 958	2 958	1 887
Number of members[2] (Thousands) total	KRFB	3 596	3 431	3 349	3 246	3 213	3 095	2 927	2 753	3 055	2 754	2 844
Orders and branches	KRFC	2 987	2 830	2 766	2 687	2 673	2 581	2 491	2 501	2 633	2 754	1 480
Societies without branches	KRFD	608	601	583	560	540	514	486	452	422	–	407
Benefits paid (£ thousand)												
Sickness pay: total	KRFE	6 578	7 109	7 982	7 639	8 396	9 280	10 671	11 526	12 029	13 867	14 514
Societies without branches	KRFF	5 747	6 290	7 193	6 841	7 660	8 558	9 995	10 841	11 335	13 368	14 006
Orders and branches	KRFG	831	819	789	798	736	722	676	685	694	499	508
Sums at death: total	KRFH	4 039	4 364	4 982	5 321	5 726	6 932	6 984	9 256	8 755	11 388	12 646
Societies without branches	KRFI	3 700	4 034	4 610	4 903	5 371	6 526	6 592	8 852	8 152	10 801	11 498
Orders and branches	KRFJ	339	330	372	418	355	406	392	404	603	587	1 148
Other benefits: total	KRFK	373 848	48 320	48 364	54 503	62 468	76 810	100 857	101 137	128 760	153 363	172 492
Societies without branches	KRFL	35 205	45 532	44 971	50 966	58 768	72 840	96 712	96 892	123 707	148 524	168 682
Orders and branches	KRFM	2 179	2 788	3 393	3 537	3 700	3 970	4 145	4 245	5 004	4 839	3 807[3]
Total funds[2] (£ thousand)	KRFN	545 915	613 817	719 040	851 790	1 023 990	1 227 190	1 233 799	1 657 264	2 016 988	2 217 346	2 245 123

1 Excluding collecting societies.
2 At end of year.

3 Due to changes in calculations figure is not directly comparable to previous years.

Source: Registry of Friendly Societies

Insurance

17.23 Life assurance[1]
Industrial business
Great Britain

£ thousand

		1981	1982	1983	1984	1985	1986	1987	1988	1989	1990
Companies established in Great Britain											
Income: total	KRDA	1 430 365	1 685 658	1 812 348	2 138 229	2 199 242	2 314 009	2 490 070	2 571 831	3 324 420	3 012 134
Premiums	KRDB	841 217	902 175	972 028	1 076 709	1 084 091	1 132 260	1 183 331	1 231 123	1 234 569	1 250 339
Interest, etc (gross)	KRDC	484 959	564 385	592 598	667 168	730 495	795 900	829 293	905 266	1 031 828	1 075 518
Miscellaneous	KRDD	104 189	219 098	247 722	394 352	384 656	385 849	477 446	457 462	1 058 023	68 627
Expenditure: total	KRDE	961 773	1 119 894	1 228 631	1 403 906	1 562 315	1 711 128	1 826 814	2 004 055	2 367 226	2 601 359
Claims paid and outstanding	KRDF	364 321	424 544	480 377	568 452	676 695	748 272	855 680	1 046 386	1 265 658	1 515 000
Surrenders	KRDG	189 519	243 322	256 393	288 729	314 143	338 248	334 101	285 307	307 928	230 316
Expenses of management	KRDH	339 157	357 047	378 058	407 967	425 031	448 848	469 562	484 068	513 713	552 992
Shareholders' surplus	KRDI	20 829	25 140	30 245	45 797	45 150	49 091	53 064	60 330	95 953	98 807
Miscellaneous (including income tax)	KRDJ	47 946	69 842	83 557	92 961	101 296	126 669	114 407	127 499	183 974	204 244
Industrial assurance funds at end of year	KRDK	4 400 480	4 969 117	5 552 834	6 287 156	6 924 083	7 527 524	8 190 872	8 831 983	9 786 306	10 147 633

1 The 'year' is, for each company included, its accounting year which ended between 1 September of the year shown and 31 August of the following year.

Source: Office of the Industrial Assurance Commissioner

17.24 Returns of industrial assurances taken up and discontinued
Great Britain

Thousands

		1981	1982	1983	1984	1985	1986	1987	1988	1989	1990
Industrial assurance companies[1]											
Paying:											
Assurances taken up during year	KRCA	3 314	3 330	3 203	3 375	3 235	3 019	2 876	2 157	2 040	1 957
Assurances discontinued during year:											
Claims on death	KHDS	696	688	656	628	612	583	541	526	444	472
Claims on maturity	KRCB	1 017	1 054	1 076	1 192	1 168	1 076	1 035	1 024	1 099	1 093
Surrender for cash	KRCC	2 051	2 217	2 084	2 044	1 940	1 858	1 695	1 335	1 170	1 077
Conversion to free policies											
For full sums assured	KRCD	462	421	450	424	455	528	399	370	1 650	333[3]
For reduced sums assured	KRCE	293	296	274	257	237	210	216	202	203	150
Forfeiture without grant of free policy or cash surrender value	KRCF	536	536	514	536	564	735	487	427	318	1 359[3]
Assurances in force at end of year	KRCH	41 772	39 888	38 040	37 119	35 376	33 401	31 899	30 134	27 036	25 485
Free:											
Assurances converted to free policies during year	KRCI	755	717	725	676	691	731	608	571	1 789	483
Assurances discontinued during year:											
Claims on death	KRCJ	521	519	512	502	513	515	483	490	491	514
Claims on maturity	KRCK	84	86	91	97	100	96	101	95	89	98
Surrender for cash	KRCL	192	193	197	183	201	178	179	161	167	164
Assurances in force at end of year	KRCM	15 135	15 055	14 987	14 881	14 758	14 700	14 545	14 383	17 252	15 112
Collecting societies[2]											
Paying:											
Assurances taken up during year	KRCN	463	440	417	370	356	343	336	275	259	249
Assurances discontinued during year:											
Claims on death	KRCO	206	211	199	183	182	172	157	173	154	152
Claims on maturity	KRCP	117	127	129	118	107	118	121	122	137	133
Surrender for cash	KRCQ	491	500	500	462	431	382	322	263	222	203
Conversion to free policies:											
For full sums assured	KRCR	171	165	161	154	149	136	121	120	124	129
For reduced sums assured	KRCS	93	80	77	69	64	66	53	63	56	50
Forfeiture without grant of free policy or cash surrender value	KRCT	69	65	61	64	66	64	65	68	49	39
Assurances in force at end of year	KRCU	11 847	11 137	10 419	9 741	9 108	8 519	8 011	7 377	6 900	6 642
Free:											
Assurances converted to free policies during year	KRCV	264	245	239	222	212	201	174	182	201	178
Assurances discontinued during year:											
Claims on death	KRCW	216	423	228	220	222	219	206	200	178	198
Claims on maturity	KRCX	3	52	10	16	30	7	17	4	16	19
Surrender for cash	KRCY	61	53	50	47	45	43	36	32	31	37
Assurances in force at end of year	KRCZ	7 935	7 653	7 595	7 535	7 452	7 381	7 296	7 238	7 196	7 117

1 Industrial assurance companies incorporated in Great Britain.
2 Collecting societies registered in Great Britain.
3 Due to changes in calculations, figures are not directly comparable with previous years.

Source: Office of the Industrial Assurance Commissioner

Companies

17.25 Acquisitions and mergers of UK companies
Analysis of expenditure by industry group of acquiring company

		Expenditure (£ million)[1]								Number of companies acquired						
		1985	1986	1987	1988	1989	1990	1991		1985	1986	1987	1988	1989	1990	1991
Industrial and commercial companies[2]																
Manufacturing industries:																
Food	KRDY	277	388	578	3 014	599	265	1 127	KHDT	24	61	72	59	37	38	31
Drink	KRDZ	473	4 164	310	319	131	19	194	KREZ	14	9	11	20	8	3	14
Tobacco	KRJA	662	–	–	–	–	160	–	KRKA	1	–	–	–	–	1	–
Chemicals and man-made fibres	KRJB	167	77	268	162	1 466	255	71	KRKB	17	18	32	31	39	14	14
Mineral and ore extraction	KRJC	62	19	8	330	112	9	116	KRKC	1	2	6	10	13	7	2
Metals	KRJD	52	62	384	165	424	179	62	KRKD	3	25	42	33	44	12	7
Mechanical and instrument engineering	KRJE	104	549	906	1 268	823	817	655	KRKE	36	65	144	148	115	84	52
Electrical and electronic engineering office machinery, etc	KRJF	158	186	1 154	838	2 452	238	1 949	KRKF	40	64	87	69	97	62	39
Shipbuilding and vehicles	KRJG	4	145	311	561	2 461	16	4	KRKG	2	6	25	19	25	6	3
Metal goods nes	KRJH	95	294	211	231	502	102	60	KRKH	31	31	52	38	35	17	18
Textiles	KRJI	249	909	100	45	38	117	203	KRKI	14	22	28	21	11	34	8
Leather, footwear and clothing	KRJJ	45	42	174	290	123	60	31	KRKJ	8	11	40	38	36	17	9
Non-metallic mineral products	KRJK	98	91	238	684	41	222	13	KRKK	9	12	19	23	20	17	4
Timber and furniture	KRJL	4	41	891	108	892	80	45	KRKL	3	11	31	30	24	16	12
Paper, printing and publishing	KRJM	635	848	1 146	1 534	1 437	584	170	KRKM	35	65	97	90	65	46	20
Other manufacturing	KRJN	84	96	152	352	283	101	125	KRKN	6	31	51	48	71	33	10
Mixed activity (mainly manufacturing)	KRJO	85	2 723	516	601	3 225	60	2 091	KRKO	7	15	14	15	10	7	10
Total manufacturing	KRJP	3 256	10 634	7 347	10 502	15 009	3 284	6 916	KRKP	251	448	751	692	650	414	255
Agriculture, forestry and fishing	KRJQ	4	–	2	4	6	4	3	KRKQ	2	1	1	4	4	4	2
Energy industries	KRJR	185	99	114	3 588	1 025	285	1 336	KRKR	14	8	15	33	20	7	9
Construction	KRJS	94	602	558	573	617	111	320	KRKS	9	31	78	93	62	32	18
Wholesaling (excluding petroleum)	KRJT	59	306	793	1 088	2 646	883	207	KRKT	29	82	189	170	139	64	40
Retailing	KRJU	2 016	1 750	2 468	3 031	1 012	285	143	KRKU	40	65	117	98	75	30	25
Hotels and catering	KRJV	13	40	185	29	705	351	–	KRKV	7	11	15	8	6	3	–
Transport and communication	KRJW	33	127	290	978	108	74	444	KRKW	12	32	55	35	19	17	19
Real estate	KRJX	293	292	1 824	551	1 151	722	142	KRKX	25	31	83	64	29	18	5
Services	KRJY	403	709	858	1 405	4 279	1 226	992	KRKY	64	113	194	274	302	181	123
Mixed activities (mainly non-manufacturing)	KRJZ	735	795	2 050	990	464	779	71	KRKZ	21	19	30	24	25	9	4
Total all industrial and commercial companies	KHYI	7 090	15 362	16 485	22 741	27 054	8 004	10 574	AIHA	474	841	1 528	1 495	1 331	779	500

1 A merger (which takes place when two companies combine to form a new company) is reckoned as the acquisition of the smaller company by the larger and is valued at the market value of the smaller company's share in the newly formed company.

2 This analysis is no longer compiled. The figures shown are as published in February 1992 and do not take account of subsequent revisions to the totals.

Source: Central Statistical Office

17.26 Income and finance of large companies [1,2]

Companies

£ million

		Balance sheet summary		
		1988	1989	1990
Balance sheet at end of accounting 'year' [3]				
Estimated number of companies	KHDW	*1 979*	*1 905*	*1 896*
Fixed assets:				
Net tangible assets	KRAA	238 486	290 791	319 778
Intangible assets	KRAB	21 667	32 233	36 130
Investments [6]	KRAC	29 575	37 004	50 153
Total net fixed assets	KRAD	289 728	360 028	406 061
Current assets and investments:				
Stocks and work-in-progress	KRAE	86 184	97 746	96 205
Total debtors and Government grants receivable	KRAF	112 317	127 015	133 782
Investments	KRAG	12 557	11 714	17 396
Cash at bank and in hand	KRAH	36 301	42 577	45 969
Total current assets and investments	KRAI	247 359	279 052	293 353
Current liabilities:				
Total creditors and accruals falling due within one year	KRAJ	150 829	177 605	185 598
Dividends and interest due	KRAK	8 826	10 180	11 118
Current taxation [7]	KRAL	23 959	25 519	24 899
Total current liabilities	KRAM	183 614	213 304	221 685
Net current assets	KRAN	63 745	65 748	71 667
Total net assets	KRAO	353 474	425 775	477 728
Financed by:				
Shareholders' interest	KRAP	239 834	274 459	291 939
Minority shareholders' interest	KRAQ	8 639	11 220	12 948
Provisions [8]	KRAR	20 955	26 665	46 810
Total creditors and accruals falling due after more than one year	KRAS	84 046	113 431	126 031

		Income and appropriation account		
		1988[4]	1989[4]	1990[5]
Accounts for 'year' [3]				
Estimated number of companies	KHDX	*1 979*	*1 905*	*1 896*
Income from trading and other activities:				
Gross trading profit [9]	KRAT	76 341	87 090	86 578
Total income	KRAU	84 453	98 034	97 921
Less:				
Interest on bank and short-term loans	KRAV	9 073	13 771	17 314
Gross income	KRAW	75 379	84 263	80 607
Appropriation of gross income:				
Depreciation and amounts written-off	KRAX	18 228	20 778	23 478
Taxation	KRAY	16 251	18 077	17 895
Dividends	KRAZ	15 277	17 494	18 455
Interest on long-term loans	KRBA	2 033	2 975	2 695
Minority shareholders' interest	KRBB	1 197	1 472	1 776
Retained income	KRBC	22 394	23 467	16 309
Total appropriation of gross income	KRBD	75 379	84 263	80 607

See note and footnotes on page 308.

Source: Central Statistical Office

Companies

17.26 Income and finance of large companies [1,2] *(continued)*

£ million

Sources and use of funds

		1988[4]	1989[4]	1990[5]
Accounts for 'year'[3]				
Estimated number of companies	KHDY	*1 979*	*1 905*	*1 896*
Receipts from issues of share and loan capital	KRBE	21 228	25 755	23 185
Increase in amount owing to banks, short-term lenders and creditors	KRBF	34 031	51 636	8 474
Gross income	KRBG	75 379	84 263	80 607
Other sources (including exchange differences)	KRBH	769	2 597	–6 461
Total sources of funds	KRBI	131 408	164 252	105 805
Payments out of income	KRBJ	29 379	34 910	39 200
Expenditure on fixed assets, etc	KRBK	71 605	92 022	65 239
Increase in current assets and investments	KRBL	30 424	37 319	1 367
Total uses of funds	KRBM	131 408	164 252	105 805

Supplementary information

		1988[4]	1989[4]	1990[5]
Accounts for 'year'[3]				
Estimated number of companies	KHDZ	*1 979*	*1 905*	*1 896*
Total Assets[10]	KRBN	315 439	377 983	433 936
Turnover (where reported)[11]	KRBO	600 497	688 945	727 692
Ratio of Pre-interest rate of return to average net assets (per cent)[12]	KRBP	20.1	19.6	16.6
Ratio of gross trading profit to turnover (per cent)	KRBQ	12.7	12.6	11.8
Ratio of borrowed funds to shareholders interest[13]	KRBR	42.8	50.3	51.0
Estimated number of overseas owned companies	KRBS	315	338	..

Note: All figures in this table are derived from an analysis of published accounts of a sample of GB-registered industrial and commercial companies rebased on accounting year 1990. Full details appeared in the 22nd and 23rd issues of Business Monitor MA3 '*Company Finance*' (HMSO September 1991 and March 1992). Following a decision by CSO Directors no further figures will be compiled for this series.

1 Listed and unlisted companies registered in Great Britain excluding companies whose main activity is insurance, banking or finance. The figures relate to limited companies only and are based on the consolidated annual accounts of independent companies registered in Great Britain. Please note that revisions made in the format of analysis to accord with the Companies Act, 1985, mean that some balance sheet items cannot be compared directly with their predecessors in previous editions of Annual Abstract of Statistics.
2 There may be a slight discrepancy between a total and the sum of its constituent items due to rounding.
3 The figures for a particular year relate to companies' accounting years ending between 1 April of the year shown and 31 March of the following year. 75 per cent of the larger companies have accounting periods ending in the fourth quarter of the calendar year or in the first quarter of the following year.
4 Revised figures.
5 Provisional
6 Includes shares in and loans to Group and Related companies, other investments other than loans, other loans and own shares.
7 Includes all corporation tax, irrespective of the date on which it is payable, but is net of advance corporation tax recoverable.
8 Includes pensions and similar obligations, deferred taxation and other taxation and provisions.
9 Relates to the position after charging directors' fees and emoluments, pensions to past directors, superannuation payments, compensation for loss of office, auditors' fees and any exceptional expenditure (eg on reorganisation or closure) but excluding any profit or loss on disposal of assets and before allowing for depreciation provisions, all interest on loans, and hire charges for plant and machinery.
10 Defined as total net fixed assets plus current assets.
11 Excludes VAT but includes excise duties.
12 Pre-interest return is gross trading profit plus other revenue income and non-tax prior year adjustments less depreciation.
13 Borrowed funds and long-term loans, short-term loans, bank loans and overdrafts. Shareholders interest includes minority interest.

Source: Central Statistical Office

Insolvency

17.27 Individual insolvencies

Number

		1981	1982	1983	1984	1985	1986	1987	1988	1989	1990	1991
England and Wales												
Bankruptcies[1,2]	AIHW	5 075	5 654	6 981	8 178	6 730	7 093	6 994	7 717	8 138	12 058	22 632
Individual voluntary arrangements	AIHI	–	–	–	–	–	–	404	779	1 224	1 927	3 002
Deeds of arrangement	AIHO	76	46	51	51	48	62	29	11	3	2	6
Total	AIHK	5 151	5 700	7 032	8 229	6 778	7 155	7 427	8 507	9 365	13 987	25 640
Scotland												
Sequestrations[4]	KRHA	181	213	282	292	298	437	818	1 401	2 301	4 350	7 665
Northern Ireland												
Bankruptcies[5,6]	KRHB	70	78	103	114	150	193	134	164	238	286	344
Deeds of arrangement	KRHC	–	–	–	–	–	–	–	–	–	–	24
Total	KRHD	70	78	103	114	150	193	134	164	238	286	368

1 Comprises receiving and administration orders under the Bankruptcy Act 1914 and bankruptcy orders under the Insolvency Act 1986.
2 Orders later consolidated or rescinded are included in these figures.
3 Introduced under the Insolvency Act 1986.
4 Sequestrations awarded but not brought into operation are included in these figures.
5 Comprises bankruptcy adjudication orders, arrangement protection orders and orders for the administration of estates of deceased insolvents.
6 Orders later set aside or dismissed are included in these figures.

Source: Department of Trade and Industry

17.28 Company insolvencies

Number

		1981	1982	1983	1984	1985	1986	1987	1988	1989	1990	1991
England and Wales												
Compulsory liquidations	AIHR	2 771	3 745	4 807	5 260	5 761	5 204	4 116	3 667	4 020	5 977	8 368
Creditors' voluntary liquidations	AIHS	5 825	8 322	8 599	8 461	9 137	9 201	7 323	5 760	6 436	9 074	13 459
Total	AIHQ	8 596	12 067	13 406	13 721	14 898	14 405	11 439	9 427	10 456	15 051	21 827
Scotland												
Compulsory liquidations	KRGA	158	177	263	272	306	299	253	228	229	251	304
Creditors' voluntary liquidations	KRGB	280	326	258	251	231	212	203	168	199	219	312
Total	KRGC	438	503	521	523	537	511	456	396	438	470	616
Northern Ireland												
Compulsory liquidations	KRGD	16	10	15	19	36	56	59	58	69	70	106
Creditors' voluntary liquidations	KRGE	83	111	96	64	75	108	91	68	56	62	73
Total	KRGF	99	121	111	83	111	164	150	126	125	132	179

Source: Department of Trade and Industry

Insolvency

17.29 Industry analysis: bankruptcies and deeds of arrangement[1]
England and Wales

Number

		1987	1988	1989	1990	1991
Industry						
Self-employed						
Agriculture and horticulture	KRFY	172	162	142	198	266
Manufacturing:						
Food, drink and tobacco	KRFZ	17	25	9	31	48
Chemicals	KRLA	2	3	3	4	12
Metals and engineering	KRLB	147	158	180	240	424
Textiles and clothing	KRLC	63	73	77	63	152
Timber and furniture	KRLD	83	94	62	116	233
Paper, printing and publishing	KRLE	39	60	39	80	143
Other	KRLF	35	30	38	67	120
Total	KRLG	386	443	408	601	1 132
Construction and transport:						
Construction	KRLH	1 123	1 590	1 652	2 348	3 812
Transport and communication	KRLI	464	527	601	953	1 620
Total	KHGP	1 587	2 117	2 253	3 301	5 432
Wholesaling:						
Food, drink and tobacco	KRLJ	45	53	42	57	68
Motor vehicles	KRLK	–	6	4	8	21
Other	KRLL	61	69	67	81	122
Total	KHGQ	106	128	113	146	211
Retailing:						
Food, drink and tobacco	KRLM	468	447	401	595	895
Motor vehicles and filling stations	KRLN	138	163	131	155	362
Other	KRLO	620	459	491	807	1 442
Total	KHGR	1 226	1 069	1 023	1 557	2 699
Services:						
Financial institutions	KRLP	99	86	95	143	247
Business services	KRLQ	486	325	386	622	1 284
Hotels and catering	KRLR	594	625	719	867	1 481
Total	KHGS	1 179	1 036	1 200	1 672	3 012
Other	KHGT	462	646	724	1 014	1 857
Total: self-employed	KRLT	5 118	5 601	5 863	8 489	14 609
Other individuals						
Employees	KRLU	591	686	856	1 172	1 639
No occupation and unemployed	KRLV	597	652	698	1 107	2 811
Directors and promoters of companies	KRLW	441	345	305	427	667
Occupation unknown	KRLX	276	444	419	865	2 906
Total: other individuals	KRLY	1 905	2 127	2 278	3 571	8 023
Total bankruptcies and deeds of arrangements[1]	KRLZ	7 023	7 728	8 141	12 060	22 632

1 From January 1991 Industrial Analysis excludes Deeds of Arrangement.

Source: Department of Trade and Industry

17.30 Industry analysis: company insolvencies[1]
England and Wales

Number

		1987	1988	1989	1990	1991
Industry						
Agriculture and horticulture	KRMA	126	73	78	111	135
Manufacturing:						
Food, drink and tobacco	KRMB	140	88	105	109	171
Chemicals	KRMC	97	75	85	97	134
Metals and engineering	KRMD	1 035	708	697	972	1 344
Textiles and clothing	KRME	1 041	811	959	921	1 052
Timber and furniture	KRMF	378	242	302	391	527
Paper, printing and publishing	KRMG	380	326	425	552	856
Other	KRMH	557	480	468	792	939
Total	KRMI	3 628	2 730	3 041	3 834	5 023
Construction and transport						
Construction	KRMJ	1 490	1 471	1 638	2 445	3 373
Transport and communication	KRMK	657	548	589	932	1 246
Total	KHGU	2 147	2 019	2 227	3 377	4 619
Wholesaling:						
Food, drink and tobacco	KRML	238	125	162	235	287
Motor vehicles	KRMM	134	91	69	107	152
Other	KRMN	511	487	428	724	841
Total	KHGV	883	703	659	1 066	1 280
Retailing:						
Food, drink and tobacco	KRMO	216	170	165	244	291
Motor vehicles and filling stations	KRMP	173	121	136	174	245
Other	KRMQ	1 047	795	738	1 181	1 578
Total	KHGW	1 436	1 086	1 039	1 599	2 114
Services:						
Financial institutions	KRMR	212	159	167	303	394
Business services	KRMS	781	843	952	1 558	2 396
Hotels and catering	KRMT	380	359	371	489	748
Total	AIHQ	11 439	9 427	10 456	15 051	21 827
Other	KHGX	1 846	1 455	1 922	2 714	5 118
Total company insolvencies	KHGY	11 439	9 427	10 456	15 051	21 827

1 Including partnerships.

Source: Department of Trade and Industry

18 Prices

Producer price index numbers *(Tables 18.1-18.5)*

The producer price indices were published for the first time in August 1983, replacing the former wholesale price indices. Full details of the differences between the two indices were given in an article published in *British business*, 15 April 1983.

The producer price indices are calculated using the same general methodology as that used by the wholesale price indices. A comprehensive guide to the collection and calculation of the wholesale price indices entitled *Wholesale price index: principles and procedures* is published by the Government Statistical Service.

The index numbers in Tables 18.1, 18.2 and 18.3 are constructed on a net sector basis. That is to say, they are intended to measure only transactions between the sector concerned and other sectors: within sector transactions are excluded. Index numbers for the whole of manufacturing are thus not weighted averages of sector index numbers.

All the index numbers are compiled exclusive of value-added tax. Excise duties on cigarettes, manufactured tobacco and alcoholic liquor are included as is the duty on hydrocarbon oils.

The indices relate to the average prices for a year.

Purchasing power of the pound *(Table 18.6)*

Changes in the internal purchasing power of a currency may be defined as the 'inverse' of changes in the levels of prices; when prices go up, the amount which can be purchased with a given sum of money goes down. Movements in the internal purchasing power of the pound are based on the consumers' expenditure deflator (CED) prior to 1962 and on the General index of retail prices (RPI) from January 1962 onwards. The CED shows the movement in prices implied by the national accounts estimates of consumers' expenditure valued at current and at constant prices, whilst the RPI is constructed directly by weighting together monthly movements in prices according to a given pattern of household expenditure derived from the Family Expenditure Survey. If the purchasing power of the pound is taken to be 100p in a particular month (quarter, year), the comparable purchasing power in a subsequent month (quarter, year) is

$$100 \times \frac{\text{earlier period price index}}{\text{later period price index}}, \text{ where the price index used is the CED}$$

for years 1946-1961 and the RPI for periods after 1961.

A long series on the purchasing power of the pound back to 1914, the latest information and a detailed explanation of the estimation of changes in the purchasing power of the pound are given in 'The Internal Purchasing Power of the Pound', a leaflet obtainable from the Press Office, Room 65c/3, Central Statistical Office, Government Offices, Great George Street London, SW1P 3AQ.

Index of retail prices *(Table 18.7)*

The retail prices index measures the change from month to month in the average level of prices of goods and services purchased by most households in the United Kingdom. The expenditure pattern on which the index is based is revised each year using information from the Family Expenditure Survey. The expenditure of certain higher income households and households of retired people dependent mainly on social security benefits is excluded.

The index covers a large and representative selection of more than 600 separate goods and services, for which price movements are regularly measured in 180 towns throughout the country. Around 150 000 separate price quotations are used in compiling the index.

The index of retail prices replaced the interim index from January 1956 (indices of the interim index of retail prices for the period 1952 to January 1956 were last published in *Annual Abstract of Statistics* No 103, 1965). A new set of weights was introduced, based on expenditure in 1953-54, valued at January 1956 prices. Between January 1962 and 1974 the weights have been revised each January on the basis of expenditure in the three years ended in the previous June, valued at prices obtaining at the date of revision. From 1975 the weights have been revised on expenditure for the latest available year.

Following the recommendations of the Retail Prices Index Advisory Committee, the index has been re-referenced to make January 13, 1987 = 100. Calculations of price changes which involve periods spanning the new reference date are made as follows:

$$\% \text{ change} = \frac{\text{Index for later month (Jan 1987 = 100)} \times \text{Index for Jan 1987 (Jan 1974 = 100)}}{\text{Index for earlier month (Jan 1974 = 100)}} - 100$$

Tax and price index (TPI) *(Table 18.8)*

The purpose and methodology of the TPI were described in an article in the August 1979 issue (No 310) of *Economic Trends* (HMSO). The TPI measures the change in *gross* taxable income needed for taxpayers to maintain their purchasing power, allowing for changes in retail prices. The TPI thus takes account of the changes to direct taxes (and employees' National Insurance contributions) facing a representative cross-section of taxpayers as well as changes in the retail prices index (RPI).

When direct taxation or employees' National Insurance contributions change the TPI will rise by less than or more than the RPI according to the type of changes made. Between Budgets the monthly increase in the TPI is normally slightly larger than that in the RPI, since all the extra income needed to offset any rise in retail prices is fully taxed.

Index numbers of agricultural prices *(Tables 18.9 and 18.10)*

The indices of agricultural prices for the United Kingdom are based on the calendar year 1985 and designed to provide an indication of movements in the purchase prices of the means of agricultural production and of the prices received by producers for their agricultural products. The methodology is comparable with that used for the other member states of the European Community and enables the compilation of indices for the Twelve, which appear in the Communities Eurostat series of publications.

Prices

18.1 Producer price index numbers of materials and fuel purchased
United Kingdom
Annual averages

1985=100

		1980 SIC [1] Division, class or group	1986	1987	1988	1989	1990	1991
Materials and fuel purchased by manufacturing industry	PFYL	2 to 4	92.4	95.3	98.4	104.0	103.8	102.6
Materials	PFYM		93.6	97.4	101.5	107.5	106.6	104.9
Fuel	PFYN		87.2	85.5	84.3	88.9[2]	91.3	92.7
Materials and fuel purchased by manufaturing industry -seasonally adjusted	PFYP		92.3	95.3	98.4	104.0	103.8	102.6
Materials and fuel purchased by manufacturing industry other than the food, drink and tobacco manufacturing industries	PFYQ	2 to 4 excl. 41/42	89.5	94.0	98.4	103.7	102.8	100.5
Materials	PFYR		90.1	96.5	102.6	108.2	106.4	102.9
Fuel	PAJF		87.7	86.0	84.9	89.4	91.8	93.2
Materials and fuel purchased by the food, drink and tobacco manufacturing industries	PFZI	41/42	98.8	99.5	100.9	107.1	109.2	110.9
Materials and fuel purchased by selected broad sectors of industry								
Metal manufacturing	PFYW	22	95.3	99.2	110.3	116.3	111.8	110.9
Extraction of minerals not elsewhere specified	PFYX	23	89.2	91.4	91.7	97.4	103.0	106.8
Non-metallic mineral products	PFYY	24	95.2	98.0	101.2	105.8	110.6	113.4
Chemical industry	PFYZ	25	82.9	86.8	85.7	90.2	95.2	96.4
Man-made fibres	PFZA	26	91.2	97.8	100.6	103.6	105.4	104.1
Metal goods, engineering and vehicles industries	PFYS	3	98.4	101.6	110.0	116.3	114.9	114.2
Metal goods not elsewhere specified	PFZB	31	97.9	101.0	111.4	117.5	114.2	112.3
Mechanical engineering	PFZC	32	101.4	104.4	111.6	118.9	122.5	126.3
Electrical and electronic engineering	PFZE	34	99.4	104.1	113.0	119.4	120.3	120.8
Motor vehicles and parts	PFZF	35	102.3	106.8	113.0	119.5	124.2	128.6
Other transport equipment	PFZG	36	101.6	105.1	112.1	118.3	123.2	128.2
Instrument engineering	PFZH	37	101.7	105.8	112.6	119.0	123.9	128.2
Food manufacturing industries	PFZJ	411 to 423	99.1	99.5	101.0	107.5	109.2	110.8
Materials	PFZK		99.9	100.4	102.0	108.6	110.3	111.8
Fuel	PFZL		84.4	83.3	81.2	85.9[2]	89.1	90.2
Textile industry	PFZM	43	97.4	103.2	107.9	115.0	112.8	109.1
Footwear and clothing industries	PFZO	45	100.0	104.5	106.9	109.8	113.6	115.6
Timber and wooden furniture industries	PFZP	46	99.6	105.5	109.4	116.9	126.6	128.3
Paper and paper products; printing and publishing	PFZQ	47	100.1	108.1	113.5	120.1	123.2	121.8
Processing of rubber and plastics	PFZR	48	98.2	104.8	111.1	117.7	113.9	112.3
Other manufacturing industries	PFZS	49	98.6	104.9	109.4	114.7	115.7	115.7
Construction materials	PFYT	5	103.6	109.3	115.4	123.4	129.6	133.6
Housebuilding materials	PFYU	Part of 5	103.8	110.1	116.2	124.1	130.2	134.0

1 Division, class or group.
2 Revised.

Source: Central Statistical Office

18.2 Producer price index numbers of output (home sales)
United Kingdom
Annual averages

1985=100

		1980 SIC [1]	1986	1987	1988	1989	1990	1991
Output of manufactured products	PGWS	2 to 4	104.3	108.3	113.2	119.0	126.0	133.0
Products of manufacturing industries other than the food, drink and tobacco manufacturing industries	PAJX	2 to 4 excl. 41/42	104.1	108.6	113.8	120.0	127.2	133.6
Products of the food, drink and tobacco manufacturing industries	PGXF	41/42	104.4	107.5	111.5	116.6	123.0	131.3
Output of selected broad sectors of industry								
Metal manufacturing	PAJZ	22	98.7	101.3	109.8	118.2	117.5	114.8
Extraction of minerals not elsewhere specified	PGWY	23	105.8	109.8	115.2	123.0	130.4	131.8
Non-metallic mineral products	PGWZ	24	103.4	108.9	114.4	121.8	129.8	136.0
Chemical industry	PAKA	25	101.7	105.8	111.5	116.4	121.7	126.5
Man-made fibres	PGXA	26	104.7	105.7	106.9	107.9	112.1	115.2
Metal goods, engineering and vehicles industries	PAJY	3	104.3	108.6	113.7	120.0	127.3[2]	134.3
Metal goods not elsewhere specified	PGXB	31	103.9	107.9	114.0	121.6	128.2	135.4
Mechanical engineering	PAKB	32	104.4	109.0	114.8	122.7	132.1[2]	140.3
Office machinery and data processing equipment	KHWP	33	..	92.1	90.6	89.6	92.0	85.2
Electrical and electronic engineering	PAKC	34	104.2	108.2	111.9	116.0	121.9	128.2
Motor vehicles and parts	PGXD	35	106.5	114.3	122.7	131.6	140.8	149.7
Instrument engineering	PAKD	37	105.0	109.3	114.3	121.4	129.3	138.4
Food manufacturing industries	PAKE	411 to 423	102.8	105.5	109.5	114.9	119.8	125.2
Drink and tobacco manufacturing industries	PGXH	424 to 429	..	..	..	..	129.1	142.8
Textile industry	PGXI	43	104.5	109.4	115.2	120.5	126.3	131.2
Footwear and clothing industries	PGXK	45	104.7	108.3	113.5	118.3	123.6	129.8
Timber and wooden furniture industries	PAKF	46	104.1	110.6	115.8	121.5	130.8	135.2
Paper and paper products: printing and publishing	PAKG	47	103.7	109.3	113.6	119.8	127.2	133.3
Processing of rubber and plastics	PGXL	48	104.4	108.8	114.4	119.6	125.7	133.1
Other manufacturing industries	PGXM	49	105.7	111.5	115.6	120.8	130.9	139.4

See footnotes to Table 18.1.

Source: Central Statistical Office

Prices

18.3 Price index numbers of materials and fuel purchased by detailed sectors of industry

United Kingdom Annual averages

1985 = 100

		1980 SIC[1]	1986	1987	1988	1989	1990	1991
Extraction and preparation of metalliferous ores		21						
Extraction and preparation of metalliferous ores	PGAE		102.0	104.6	109.3	116.6	122.4	130.3
Metal manufacturing		22						
Iron and steel industry	PGAG		93.0	94.0	100.1	107.6	105.8	105.0
Steel tubes	PGAI		99.3	100.2	107.6	114.3	112.8	113.2
Drawing and manufacture of steel wire and steel wire products	PGAK		98.2	99.9	108.4	115.6	112.6	111.8
Other drawing, cold rolling and cold forming of steel	PGAM		99.2	100.8	109.4	116.1	113.1	112.0
Aluminium and aluminium alloys	PGAO		98.7	107.6	136.4	125.4	112.5	105.2
Copper, brass and other copper alloys	PGAQ		89.9	98.5	119.1	137.1	125.6	116.9
Other non-ferrous metals and their alloys	PGAS		96.3	100.1	107.1	118.0	117.6	116.9
Extraction of minerals not elsewhere specified		23						
Extraction of stone, clay, sand and gravel	PGAU		83.5	86.1	84.6	89.5	96.1	99.9
Salt extraction and refining	PGAW		95.2	97.0	99.1	102.7	107.1	110.2
Extractions of other minerals not elsewhere specified	PGAY		91.1	92.7	93.6	100.3[2]	106.4	110.6
Non-metallic mineral products		24						
Structural clay products	PGBA		92.0	92.8	93.3	98.5[2]	104.3	105.7
Cement, lime and plaster	PGBC		100.1	101.1	104.3	109.0[2]	112.6	114.1
Ready mixed concrete	PGBE		102.9	104.9	109.4	118.7	126.1	128.1
Other building products of concrete, cement or plaster	PGBG		99.6	102.2	105.9	113.7[2]	120.2	122.8
Asbestos goods	PGBI		95.2	98.1	101.7	106.7	108.6	110.1
Working of stone and other non-metallic minerals not elsewhere specified	PGBK		87.6	91.1	95.4	96.6[2]	100.5	107.3
Abrasive products	PGBM		99.1	101.4	103.9	109.5	112.6	115.3
Flat glass	PGBO		94.0	96.5	99.0	102.5	106.8	110.0
Glass containers	PGBQ		93.4	95.9	96.3	99.7	105.5	109.8
Other glass products	PGBS		99.4	104.4	108.4	111.9	115.9	118.9
Refractory goods	PGBU		97.9	101.0	102.4	110.9	117.5	121.1
Ceramic goods	PGBW		99.6	102.5	105.0	109.7	113.9	115.1
Chemical industry		25						
Inorganic chemicals except industrial gases	PGBY		87.1	90.6	89.3	93.1	95.9	95.4
Basic organic chemicals except specialised pharmaceutical chemicals	PGCA		69.9	74.4	70.0	76.4	84.0	84.1
Fertilisers	PGCC		81.5	84.5	83.7	91.3	98.9	101.2
Synthetic resins and plastics materials	PGCE		75.6	81.2	79.8	85.2	91.6	91.1
Synthetic rubber	PGCG		91.9	97.6	100.2	102.2	104.8	105.9
Dyestuffs and pigments	PGCI		91.9	97.1	100.6	104.0	106.6	106.9
Paints varnishes and painters' fillings	PGCK		97.8	103.6	109.1	112.9	116.3	115.9
Printing ink	PGCM		97.5	103.2	108.6	114.5[2]	119.4	118.8
Formulated adhesives and sealants	PGCO		93.2	98.3	100.8	102.7	104.7	105.1
Chemical treatments of oils and fats	PGCQ		68.8	67.0	73.6	75.2	73.1	75.0
Essential oils and flavouring materials	PGCS		91.9	99.1	106.2	110.8	109.8	106.7
Explosives	PGCU		95.8	99.6	104.0	108.2	112.1	114.1
Miscellaneous chemical products for industrial use	PGCW		92.0	97.0	101.0	103.8	105.6	106.3
Formulated pesticides	PGCY		91.0	97.5	100.2	101.8	105.0	105.6
Adhesive film, cloth and foil	PGDA		101.1	107.7	112.4	115.1	119.4	120.9
Pharmaceutical products	PGDC		97.8	102.1	103.4	104.1	107.6	110.1
Soap and synthetic detergents	PGDE		92.5	95.5	100.1	103.6	106.3	109.7
Perfumes, cosmetics and toilet preparations	PGDG		98.7	102.5	106.5	110.4	115.2	119.1
Photographic materials and chemicals	PGDI		98.8	105.5	109.7	114.4	118.0	118.2
Chemical products not elsewhere specified	PGDK		99.9	104.4	109.6	114.7	118.5	120.6
Man-made fibres		26						
Man-made fibres	PGDM		91.3	98.1	101.0	104.0	105.7	104.4
Metal goods not elsewhere specified		31						
Ferrous metal foundries	PGDO		94.8	96.6	105.4	112.5	112.2	109.3
Non-ferrous metal foundries	PGDQ		95.9	100.2	116.0	118.7	109.2	102.2
Forging, pressing and stamping	PGDS		96.7	99.3	109.0	115.9	112.2	110.1
Bolts, nuts, washers, rivets, springs and non-precision chains	PGDU		99.0	102.0	110.2	118.2	118.1	118.6
Heat and surface treatment of metals, including sintering	PGDW		98.2	100.7	108.1	113.9	112.4	111.9
Metal doors, windows etc	PGDY		101.2	106.2	116.9	120.7	119.5	118.4
Hand tools and implements	PGEA		100.7	103.3	109.2	115.8	119.0	121.2
Cutlery, spoons, forks and similar tableware; razors etc	PGEC		99.8	103.7	111.7	118.2	119.2	119.4
Metal storage vessels (mainly non-industrial)	PGEE		93.7	99.9	119.2	131.5	121.2	113.6
Packaging products of metal	PGEG		99.2	101.7	112.3	116.8	112.1	112.0
Domestic heating and cooking appliances (non-electrical)	PGEI		101.6	105.7	113.3	120.6	123.3	126.2
Metal furniture and safes	PGEK		101.1	104.1	110.7	117.6	120.0	121.8
Domestic and similar utensils of metal	PGEM		99.0	102.6	111.1	116.6	116.6	116.5
Finished metal products not elsewhere specified	PGEO		98.5	102.2	113.1	121.1	118.7	117.2

1 Class number
2 Revised

Source: Central Statistical Office

Prices

18.3 continued Price index numbers of materials and fuel purchased by detailed sectors of industry
United Kingdom Annual averages

1985 = 100

		1980 SIC[1]	1987	1988	1989	1990	1991
Mechanical engineering		32					
Fabricated contructional steelwork	PGEQ		101.1	111.0	119.2	115.0	114.5
Boilers and process plant fabrications	PGES		104.0	112.3	118.9	123.0	126.4
Agricultural machinery	PGEU		104.8	110.7	117.8	122.7	127.5
Wheeled tractors	PGEW		108.0	113.9	120.7	128.2	135.4
Metal working machine tools	PGEY		106.0	112.6	120.3	127.6	133.9
Engineers' small tools	PGFA		100.7	106.9	113.7	114.2	115.8
Textile machinery	PGFC		105.5	111.8	119.3	124.9	129.6
Food, drink, and tobacco processing machinery; packing and bottling machinery	PGFE		105.6	112.4	119.9	125.7	130.7
Chemical industry machinery; furnaces and kilns; gas, water and waste treatment plant	PGFG		106.5	112.9	120.7	127.2	133.3
Mining machinery	PGFK		105.2	111.6	119.7	124.5	129.6
Construction and earth moving equipment	PGFM		106.9	113.4	120.9	127.7	134.7
Mechanical lifting and handling equipment	PGFO		105.9	112.6	120.3	126.7	132.7
Precision chains and other mechanical power transmission equipment	PGFQ		104.0	110.8	117.8	122.2	126.4
Ball, needle and roller bearings	PGFS		103.2	110.8	118.1	121.7	124.7
Machinery for working wood, rubber, plastics, leather and making paper, glass, bricks and similar materials; laundry and dry cleaning machinery	PGFU		106.6	112.9	120.6	127.5	133.9
Printing, bookbinding and paper goods machinery	PGFW		104.6	115.3	119.1	118.6	118.8
Internal combustion engines, (except for road vehicles, wheeled tractors primarily for agricultural purposes and aircraft) and other prime movers	PGFY		106.3	112.4	120.1	127.7	134.6
Compressors and fluid power equipment	PGGA		105.5	113.1	120.6	124.6	129.0
Refrigerating machinery, space heating, ventilating and air-conditioning equipment	PGGC		105.0	112.6	119.6	122.9	126.0
Scales, weighing machinery conditioning equipment and portable power tools	PGGE		106.1	112.4	119.5	125.7	131.2
Other industrial and commercial machinery	PGGG		106.6	112.9	120.4	127.2	133.6
Pumps	PGGI		106.1	113.0	121.0	127.4	133.7
Industrial valves	PGGK		104.4	112.4	120.4	124.0	127.6
Mechanical, marine and precision engineering not elsewhere specified	PGGM		104.0	111.3	118.6[2]	120.8	123.7
Ordnance, small arms and ammunition	PGGO		106.1	113.5	120.4	126.1	133.0
Office machinery and data processing equipment		33					
Office machinery	PGGQ		106.4	113.3	119.7	126.0	131.1
Electrical and electronic engineering		34					
Insulated wire and cables	PGGU		101.2	116.8	122.9	116.6	109.8
Basic electrical equipment	PGGW		104.5	112.3	119.7	122.8	126.3
Batteries and accumulators	PGGY		102.3	112.7	118.3	116.0	113.5
Alarms and signalling equipment	PGHA		103.7	109.1	114.8	120.7	124.9
Electrical equipment for motor vehicles, cycles and aircraft	PGHC		104.3	110.6	117.1	121.6	125.3
Electrical equipment for industrial uses not elsewhere specified	PGHE		101.3	107.4	114.3	118.6	121.7
Telegraph and telephone apparatus and equipment	PGHG		101.0	106.1	110.4	115.9	119.8
Electrical instruments and control systems	PGHI		104.0	109.5	115.5	121.7	126.7
Radio and electronic capital goods	PGHK		103.6	108.1	112.8	119.5	124.0
Components other than active components, mainly for electronic equipment	PGHM		102.0	109.0	113.4	114.0	114.4
Gramophone records and pre-recorded tapes	PGHO		101.0	105.0	108.0	107.9	106.1
Active components and electronic sub-assemblies	PGHQ		105.9	112.2	118.4	123.5	127.1
Electronic consumer goods and other electronic equipment not elsewhere specified	PGHS		101.4	106.0	110.2	116.7	120.2
Domestic-type electric appliances	PGHU		105.4	112.3	118.6	122.6	126.4
Electric lamps and other electric lighting equipment	PGHW		105.8	114.2	120.3	123.3	125.6
Motor vehicles and parts		35					
Motor vehicles and their engines	PGHY		108.4	114.8	121.5	127.2	133.2
Motor vehicle bodies	PGIA		105.7	113.1	118.7	121.5	123.9
Trailers and semi-trailers	PGIC		105.7	113.1	120.5	125.1	128.8
Caravans	PGIE		106.7	114.0	119.1	123.3	124.1
Motor vehicle parts	PGIG		103.7	110.8	117.5	119.8	122.4
Other transport equipment		36					
Shipbuilding and repairing	PGII		105.8	111.6	118.4[2]	124.6	130.9
Railway and tramway vehicles	PGIK		105.9	111.8	118.5	125.3	132.2
Pedal cycles and parts	PGIO		103.6	110.5	116.4	118.8	120.7
Aerospace equipment manufacturing and repairing	PGIQ		104.0	112.1	118.8[2]	123.4	127.6
Other vehicles	PGIS		106.8	115.6	120.0	123.0	126.2

1 Class number.
2 Revised.

Source: Central Statistical Office

18.3 Price index numbers of materials and fuel purchased by detailed sectors of industry
United Kingdom Annual averages

1985 = 100

		1980 SIC[1]	1987	1988	1989	1990	1991
Instrument engineering		37					
Measuring, checking and precision instruments and apparatus	PGIU		105.9	112.3	118.9	124.7	129.9
Medical and surgical equipment and orthopaedic appliances	PGIW		105.6	112.6	117.4	119.3	120.7
Spectacles and unmounted lenses	PGIY		107.2	113.4	119.2	125.0	129.4
Optical precision instruments	PGJA		106.0	112.1	119.1	126.2	132.7
Photographic and cinematograhic equipment	PGJC		104.9	113.5	119.9	122.0	123.5
Clocks, watches and other timing devices	PGJE		105.4	112.4	119.4	126.0	131.1
Food, drink and tobacco manufacturing industries		41/42					
Margarine and compound cooking fats	PGJG		69.7	78.1	79.0	75.8	79.9
Processing organic oils and fats (other than crude animal fat production)	PGJI		69.9	75.2	77.9	73.4	74.2
Bacon curing and meat processing	PGJL		101.5	101.0	112.2	112.3	107.7
Poultry slaughter and processing	PGJN		97.9	97.7	103.1	110.0	107.4
Preparation of milk and milk products	PGJQ		104.1	110.1	121.1	123.7	127.4
Processing of fruit and vegetables	PGJS		112.1	109.4	120.7	133.2	130.1
Fish processing	PGJU		117.7	119.1	122.4	136.2	140.1
Grain milling	PGJW		101.4	97.2	94.7	97.4	106.1
Starch	PGJY		105.5	104.0	103.2	106.7	112.6
Bread and flour confectionery	PGKA		106.7	110.6	112.2	116.5	121.8
Biscuits and crispbread	PGKC		95.3	99.1	101.2	105.0	111.1
Sugar and sugar by-products	PGKE		98.0	98.7	101.9	107.3	112.7
Ice cream	PGKG		100.0	107.1	113.8	116.6	122.5
Cocoa, chocolate and sugar confectionery	PGKI		87.5	84.1	85.1	85.9	88.7
Compound animal feeds	PGKK		96.6	96.4	100.1	100.2	103.4
Pet foods and non-compound animal feeds	PGKM		104.5	107.7	113.3	116.8	118.6
Miscellaneous foods	PGKO		90.8	90.4	94.8	94.6	96.2
Spirit distilling and compounding	PGKQ		100.1	100.9	103.8	109.3	114.9
Brewing and malting	PGKW		99.7	100.0	103.8	106.2	111.3
Tobacco industry	PGLC		96.8	93.6	99.9	104.8	108.3
Textile industry		43					
Woollen and worsted industry	PGLE		103.2	114.0	128.2	113.4	101.4
Spinning and doubling on the cotton system	PGLG		96.7	95.4	102.4	103.8	102.0
Weaving of cotton, silk and man-made fibres	PGLI		108.4	110.7	114.5	118.8	118.6
Throwing, texturing etc of continuous filament yarn	PGLK		107.8	111.0	113.9	118.3	118.4
Spinning and weaving of flax, hemp and ramie	PGLM		95.3	91.5	100.9	104.0	101.5
Jute and polypropylene yarns and fabrics	PGLO		100.5	103.1	105.8	107.0	105.7
Hosiery and other weft knitted goods and fabrics	PGLQ		106.8	111.1	115.3	118.0	118.3
Warp knitted fabrics	PGLS		104.4	107.8	112.4	116.3	116.6
Textile finishing	PGLU		101.4	104.4	109.2	113.8	114.2
Pile carpets, carpeting and rugs	PGLW		104.5	109.9	111.7	109.6	107.7
Other carpets, carpeting, rugs and matting	PGLY		100.4	102.6	105.2	106.3	106.2
Lace	PGMA		106.7	107.6	111.1	115.3	116.1
Rope, twine and nets	PGMC		104.4	109.2	112.1	114.7	114.1
Narrow fabrics	PGME		104.9	107.0	110.9	114.8	116.2
Other miscellaneous textiles	PGMG		100.3	101.8	103.8	104.6	105.0
Leather and leather goods		44					
Leather (tanning and dressing) and fellmongery	PGMI		110.2	116.8	120.2	113.1	85.7
Leather goods	PGMK		109.8	115.9	118.6	125.0	126.0
Footwear and clothing industries		45					
Footwear	PGMM		102.5	107.4	110.0	117.2	116.7
Weatherproof outerwear	PGMO		105.1	106.8	109.7	112.7	114.9
Men's and boys' tailored outerwear	PGMQ		104.0	107.6	111.1	112.9	114.3
Women's and girls' tailored outerwear	PGMS		104.8	108.3	111.7	114.0	115.4
Work clothing and men's and boys' jeans	PGMU		105.1	105.1	107.7	110.9	113.1
Men's and boys' shirts, underwear and nightwear	PGMW		105.0	105.8	108.5	111.9	114.5
Women's and girls' light outerwear, lingerie and infants' wear	PGMY		105.7	107.6	110.4	114.4	117.9
Hats, caps and millinery	PGNA		105.8	108.1	112.2	116.3	117.5
Gloves	PGNC		108.5	111.5	115.4	119.8	118.6
Other dress industries	PGNE		106.0	108.5	111.8	116.3	120.3
Soft furnishings	PGNG		104.7	104.6	106.7	109.6	111.9
Canvas goods, sacks and other made-up textiles	PGNI		104.0	104.9	106.8	108.9	110.9
Household textiles	PGNK		104.0	104.5	107.6	110.4	111.7
Fur goods	PGNM		100.3	103.0	110.4	113.6	109.1

1 Class number
2 Revised

Source: Central Statistical Office

Prices

18.3 (continued) Price index numbers of materials and fuel purchased by detailed sectors of industry
United Kingdom Annual averages
1985 = 100

		1980 SIC[1]	1987	1988	1989	1990	1991
Timber and wooden furniture industries		46					
Sawmilling, planing etc of wood	PGNO		104.4	107.3	117.7	133.5	133.4
Manufacture of semi-finished wood products and further processing and treatment of wood	PGNQ		105.0	109.8	115.0	123.8	121.6
Builders' carpentry and joinery	PGNS		106.9	111.7	118.9	129.9	127.5
Wooden containers	PGNU		106.2	110.4	118.0	129.5	127.0
Other wooden articles (except furniture)	PGNW		105.3	110.0	117.6	127.4	125.9
Brushes and brooms	PGNY		104.3	107.9	114.1	118.2	119.6
Articles of cork and basketware, wickerwork and other plaiting materials	PGOA		106.4	108.9	117.5	129.4	132.9
Wooden and upholstered furniture	PGOC		106.9	110.5	116.2	124.2	125.0
Shop and office fittings	PGOE		107.1	114.5	120.6	125.5	127.1
Paper and paper products; printing and publishing		47					
Pulp, paper and board	PGOG		101.6	106.5	116.5	115.0	105.4
Wall coverings	PGOI		107.2	112.7	116.8	120.1	119.2
Household and personal hygiene products of paper	PGOK		107.2	111.6	121.5	121.6	113.3
Stationery	PGOM		108.5	113.3	119.0	123.4	124.3
Packaging products of paper and pulp	PGOO		109.0	114.1	119.4	124.1	125.2
Packaging products of board	PGOQ		109.0	113.7	119.8	125.2	126.9
Other paper and board products	PGOS		107.3	111.7	118.2	121.6	120.9
Printing and publishing of newspapers	PGOU		111.3	120.8	122.2	126.6	128.6
Printing and publishing of periodicals	PGOW		109.1	115.3	120.3	125.0	127.4
Printing and publishing of books	PGOY		108.1	112.2	116.7	121.2	124.7
Other printing and publishing	PGPA		109.2	115.7	120.2	124.8	126.8
Processing of rubber and plastics		48					
Rubber tyres and inner tubes	PGPC		100.3	106.0	103.0	104.2	103.3
Other rubber products	PGPE		102.2	105.6	106.9	110.6	110.9
Retreading and specialist repairing of rubber tyres	PGPG		97.7	136.6	97.2	92.9	92.3
Plastic coated textile fabric	PGPI		102.9	105.5	107.0	110.4	110.6
Plastics semi-manufactures	PGPK		104.7	110.2	111.7	113.9	112.0
Plastics floorcoverings	PGPM		106.0	112.1	113.7	115.6	113.3
Plastics building products	PGPO		107.3	113.6	115.0	118.0	117.1
Plastics packaging products	PGPQ		108.7	115.4	116.5	119.1	117.6
Plastics products not elsewhere specified	PGPS		107.2	114.0	116.3	118.8	117.8
Other manufacturing industries		49					
Jewellery	PGPU		99.1	100.7	106.1	96.5	89.0
Musical instruments	PGPW		104.8	114.9	119.0	118.8	115.2
Toys and games	PGPZ		108.2	114.0	119.7	125.0	129.6
Sports goods	PGQB		105.3	112.3	117.5	122.0	123.8
Miscellaneous stationers' goods	PGQD		107.4	112.9	118.2	123.5	125.3
Other manufactures not elsewhere specified	PGQF		107.4	113.5	117.9	121.8	123.5

1 Class number.
2 Revised.

Source: Central Statistical Office

Prices

18.4 Producer price index numbers of products manufactured in the United Kingdom (home sales)
Annual averages

1985 = 100

		1980 SIC[1]	1986	1987	1988	1989	1990	1991
Energy and water supply industries		1						
Coal mining	PAAB	1113	101.3	100.7	104.5	104.5	106.1	108.1
Coke ovens		1200						
Foundry coke	PALR		101.6	101.6	101.6	102.8	108.7	116.3
Mineral oil refining (including duty)		1401						
Petroleum products (including duty)	PAAM		79.6	79.6	76.6	83.0	93.0	97.4
Motor spirit (including duty)	PAAG		86.6	87.2	87.0	93.4	103.8	110.2
Kerosene (including duty)	PALX		80.5	79.6	78.6	83.8	96.8	104.3
Gas oil/derv (including duty)	PALY		75.0	72.0	66.4	74.2	84.7	87.5
Gas oil fuel (including duty)	PAAH		64.0	60.3	50.2	60.2	71.7	69.9
Derv (including duty)	PAAI		84.9	82.4	80.8	86.6	96.2	103.0
Fuel oil (including duty)	PALU		55.3	60.8	46.9	51.2	57.4	51.7
Light fuel oil (including duty)[2]	PAAJ		71.4	80.8	84.4	103.9	99.4	96.5
Medium fuel oil (including duty)[2]	PAAE		70.3	78.0	77.0	83.5	84.0	85.3
Heavy fuel oil (including duty)	PAAK		52.8	58.0	41.8	45.6	52.8	46.0
Petroleum bitumen[2]	PALV		75.0	80.3	88.9	80.4	80.1	95.7
Other treatment of petroleum products (excluding petrochemical manufacture)		1402						
Insulating oil	KHJQ		..	..	..	92.4	100.2	110.3
Lubricating oils and greases	PAAN		95.4	95.2	92.5	95.9	108.6	122.3
Water supply industry		1700						
Water for industrial use[3]	PAAR		107.7	114.8	122.6	134.1	153.0	179.2
Metal manufacturing		22						
Iron and steel	PAAS	2210	101.1	102.1	106.8	111.3	113.4	113.9
Foundry pig iron	PAMD		97.3	97.3	97.3	97.3	97.3	97.3
Ordinary steel	PAME		101.8	102.3	106.2	109.9	112.6	112.1
Billets	PAMG		100.0 B	100.0 B	100.0 B	107.2 B	108.6	108.6
Finished rolled products	PAMH		102.5	103.0	107.7	112.1	114.1	112.5
Rails and accessories	PAAT		103.8	108.2	109.2	113.2	118.9	124.8
Sheet piling	PAMI		103.2	109.0	114.0	115.3	118.7	123.5
Heavy sections	PAMJ		103.2	103.7	106.0	111.6	116.6	116.7
Wide flats - finished rolled products	PAMP		102.5	103.0	107.7	110.7	115.5	116.5
Hot rolled narrow strip (less than 600 mm)	PAMQ		105.7	109.3	115.2	119.6	124.3	125.5
Hot rolled coil, plate and sheet	PAMR		102.8	105.1	110.3	115.4	119.4	120.1
3 mm thick and over	PAMS		103.2	105.4	110.6	116.0	120.1	120.8
Less than 3 mm thick	PAMT		101.6	103.8	109.4	113.0	116.3	117.0
Cold rolled sheets	PAMU		102.3	103.5	111.0	113.9	117.2	118.0
Reversing mill plate	PAMV		102.5	103.0	107.7	109.0	112.3	111.3
Ordinary steel end proucts	PAMW		99.8	100.8	103.0	105.2	110.3	113.0
Tinplate	PAMX		99.6	100.7	104.2	106.5	109.6	114.1
Black plate	PAMY		102.4	104.7	108.5	110.9	114.6	119.9
Zinc coated, lead coated and other coated sheet	PAMZ		100.0	100.0	100.0	102.0	108.7	108.9
Electrical sheet (including hot rolled electrical strip)	PANA		100.0	106.6	111.9	115.2	126.4	129.5
Grain non-orientated	PANB		100.0	107.1	112.6	115.9	126.8	129.6
Grain orientated	PANC		100.0	105.5	110.4	113.6	125.6	129.5
Special steels	PAND		97.9	101.2	110.4	119.0	118.0	124.1
Semis for direct use	PANF		100.6	103.5	108.4	112.2	117.4	125.8
Other alloy special steel	PANG		100.8	102.6	104.0	111.4	112.6	118.8
Semis for direct use	PANH		101.2	103.1	104.9	116.3	117.0	124.4
Finished flat products	PANI		102.2	102.7	107.3	112.8	120.1	121.1
Plate 3 mm and over	PANJ		102.2	102.7	107.3	112.8	120.1	121.1
Merchant bars, sections and other products	PANL		100.4	103.3	104.0	110.7	110.9	117.6
Stainless and heat resisting steels	PANM		91.3	97.0	122.0	136.2	127.0	131.2
Semis for direct use	PANN		96.0	97.8	121.6	145.4	121.4	123.9
Plate 3 mm and over	PANP		90.4	102.6	122.2	133.5	119.9	128.3
Finished flat products - Sheet and strip	PANQ		90.4	102.6	122.2	134.7	131.7	136.7
Other finished products - Bars and rods in coils	PANS		91.3	97.0	122.0	136.4	116.3	113.2
Steel for reinforcement; cut; bent and delivered	PANX		98.3	93.5	105.6	119.0	..	118.0
Light re-rolled bars and sections	PANY		99.8	94.2	101.7	112.1	109.9	103.4
Steel tubes	PAAU	2220	103.6	109.2	117.8	124.3	131.4	132.4
Drawing and manufacture of steel wire and steel wire products	PAAV	2234	103.3	106.0	109.4	118.0	123.1	125.2
Single drawn wire of iron and steel whether covered or not (excluding insulated electric wire)	PAOJ		104.7	108.5	111.1	117.7	122.4	126.8
Single drawn wire of iron and steel whether covered or not (excluding insulated electric wire) of high carbon steel	PAOL		106.0	109.6	110.0	112.4	115.6	117.8
Iron and steel barbed wire ropes (excluding insulated electric wire and cables)	KHJR		..	..	..	..	..	126.9
Woven wire cloth, gauze, fabric etc of iron and steel (excluding netting, fencing and similar iron and steel manufactures and fabric reinforcements of concrete) in squares or rectangular mesh	PAOR		105.2	109.9	116.7	132.8	143.4	153.7
Stainless steel	PAOS		108.2	114.6	124.3	136.2	147.4	160.6
Other than stainless steel	PAOT		103.6	107.6	112.9	130.9	141.3	150.2
Wire nails, tacks and staples (including insulated staples) of iron and steel	PAOV		..	..	..	..	119.5	107.8
Fabric reinforcement manufacture to BS 4483 and rods and bars cut and/or bent, sold for use as concrete reinforcements to BS 4449 or BS 4461	PAOW		101.2	103.3	111.2	121.2	122.3	..

1 Division, class or activity heading.
2 This index is based on list prices rather than prices actually charged.
3 This index is based on volumetric charges and does not reflect fixed or standing charges.

Source: Central Statistical Office

Prices

18.4 Producer price index numbers of products manufactured in the United Kingdom (home sales)
continued — Annual averages

1985 = 100

		1980 SIC[1]	1986	1987	1988	1989	1990	1991
Metal manufacturing (*continued*)								
Other drawing, cold rolling and cold forming of steel	PAAW	2235	101.8	102.2	107.0	111.5 B	117.7 B	121.5 B
Other drawing, cold rolling and cold forming of non-alloy steel	PAOZ		102.5	102.7	108.1	112.9 B	119.3 B	123.1 B
Over 0.25% carbon	PAPD		107.2	111.3	115.8	121.6	127.5	129.0
Other drawing, cold rolling and cold forming of other alloy steels	PAOZ		102.5	102.7	108.1	112.9 B	119.3 B	123.1 B
Bright bars	PAPA		..	..	..	..	..	..
Aluminium and aluminium alloys		2245						
Plate, sheet, strip circles and blanks	PAPJ		94.5	97.8	106.6	119.2	114.5	106.6
Strip	PAPK		95.4	101.2	109.4	123.0	119.2	112.5
Plate, sheet, blanks and circles	PAPL		93.7	94.5	103.9	115.3	109.9	100.0
Extrusions and tubes (bars, rods, sections etc)	PAPM		99.3	100.1	114.1	125.4	117.2	107.0
Copper, brass and other copper alloys		2246						
Primary and secondary copper and copper based alloys unwrought	PAPR		86.4	78.3	86.2	110.6	116.9	106.0
Brass and other copper alloys, unwrought (ie alloys in which copper is the largest constituent by weight, excl. cadmium copper)	PAPS		86.4	78.3	86.2	110.6	116.9	106.0
Copper rods	PAPW		86.8	97.2	128.8	152.6	134.0	121.3
Copper tubes	PAPX		99.2	112.5	131.7	139.5	148.4	139.0
Wire and wire manufactures of copper, brass and other copper alloys (incl. nickel silver and cupro-nickel but excl. all other nickel alloys)	PAQD		90.2	99.2	125.2	144.0	129.6	118.6
Single drawn wire, uninsulated of copper (including cadmium copper)	PAQF		89.6	98.8	126.0	145.0	129.1	117.6
Copper, brass and other copper alloy scrap	PAQI		82.3	89.0	119.0	150.9	136.2	118.0
Other non-ferrous metals and their alloys		2247						
Titanium	PAQQ		90.2	88.5	95.2	105.5	..	..
Extraction of minerals not elsewhere specified		23						
Extraction of stone, clay, sand and gravel unprocessed before sale	PABA	2310	106.2	110.5	116.9	126.2	133.4	128.6
Sand, gravel and pebbles (excluding sand for foundry purposes, glassmaking or other industrial uses)	PARE		105.4	110.2	117.9	128.2	136.8	131.4
Sand and gravel delivered	PARF		105.6	110.2	117.7	127.7	131.9	131.6
Salt extraction and refining	PABB	2330	106.3	108.2	112.0	117.4	125.1	138.2
Rock salt	PABC		108.1	111.8	122.6	127.8	137.2	156.2
White salt	PARG		105.6	106.6	107.3	112.9	119.8	130.3
Non-metallic mineral products		24						
Structural clay products	PABE	2410	105.4	115.6	127.9	134.8	138.9	139.7
Common, facing and engineering bricks	PARK		104.9	115.3	127.7	133.7	136.9	136.8
Common bricks	PARL		102.2	118.7	136.1	135.6	138.4	137.8 B
Fletton (delivered)	PARN		105.4	118.8	127.7	138.2	147.2	148.7
Facing bricks	PARO		105.8	114.2	123.8	133.2	138.6	138.8
Non-fletton (ex-works) facings	PARP		108.9	118.9	131.0	142.1	145.4	139.9
Fletton (delivered)	PARQ		101.2	107.1	113.0	119.7	128.4	137.1
Clay roofing tiles (plain and single lap) excl. fittings	PART		109.5	122.0	137.9	159.0	175.0	186.4
Cement, lime and plaster	PABF	2420	..	..	105.5	115.5	122.4	128.8
Calcareous cement	PASG		..	..	103.5	113.3	120.2	127.6
Ready-mixed concrete	PABG	2436	100.0	100.2	105.2	118.3	118.0 B	111.4 B
Other building products of concrete, cement or plaster	PABH	2437	104.0	108.7	112.8	121.2	127.8	131.6
Plaster products	PAST		100.1	104.6	108.3	110.1	110.4	118.3
Gypsum plaster products incl. coving	PASU		101.3	104.0	108.4	115.6	118.7	122.5
Plaster board	PASV		100.0	104.7	108.3	109.5	109.5	117.8
Precast concrete goods	PABI		104.0	108.4	112.9	..	..	..
Concrete blocks, bricks, kerbs and edgings etc	PATD		104.5	109.4	114.2	121.6	128.0	127.2
Concrete blocks (all types)	PATE		103.8	109.1	114.3	121.3	127.9	..
Flagstones and paving stones	PATF		106.1	110.4	114.2	122.3	128.9	126.2
Kerbs, edgings, channels, quadrants to BS 340	PATG		105.4	109.2	113.1	121.5	126.5	120.0
Concrete pipes to BS 5911	PATI		102.1	104.6	108.5	116.5	124.2	..
Asbestos goods	PABJ	2440	104.6	108.5	112.0	116.5	123.8	130.4 B
Working of stone and other non-metallic minerals not elsewhere specified	PABK	2450	101.4	106.3	111.0	117.4	129.0	137.5
Ground and processed minerals	PALG		101.3	105.7	109.6	115.4	126.3	131.8
Limestone and dolomite	PAUI		102.6	107.3	111.0	115.4	127.7	133.6
Processed dry limestone and dolomite, ground agricultural and industrial limestone	PAUJ		109.1	115.8	119.5	125.2	138.0	138.8
Limestone and dolomite coated macadam	PABL		94.0	96.0	99.7	102.4	114.0	126.8
Granite	PAUK		101.9	107.9	113.8	122.2	132.6	138.6
Processed granite (classified in accordance with BS group classification as granite, basalt etc)	PABM		103.8	107.4	115.1	123.6	132.9	138.9
Granite coated macadam	PAUL		100.8	108.2	113.4	121.5	132.4	138.5
Building, ornamental and funerary stonework (excl. sculpture)	PAUN		122.5	131.6	151.8	163.5 B	181.1 B	186.0 B
Clays, kaolin, marl	PAUZ		105.6	111.0	121.8	129.2	132.9	137.0
Processed ball and china clays (kaolin)	PAVA		105.6	111.0	121.8	129.2	132.9	137.0

1 Class or activity heading.

Source: Central Statistical Office

Prices

18.4 Producer price index numbers of products manufactured in the United Kingdom (home sales)
continued — Annual averages

1985 = 100

		1980 SIC[1]	1986	1987	1988	1989	1990	1991
Non-metallic mineral products *(continued)*								
Abrasive products	PABO	2460	106.3	113.3	118.4	125.3	134.4	148.6
Abrasive wheels, disc wheels, segments, sharpening stones and other shapes or forms of bonded abrasives (incl. diamond)	KHJS		..	..	..	..	131.3	147.4
Diamond type abrasive wheels	PAVF		104.5	107.4	110.9	115.7	120.8	126.4
Abrasive wheels other than diamond (incl. vitrified and organic type)	KHJT		..	..	..	..	134.3	153.4
Coated abrasives, abrasive paper and cloth and abrasive compounds for metal finishing	KHJU		..	..	..	..	137.6	149.8
Safety glass (laminated or toughened)	KHJV		..	..	..	..	..	149.0
Glass containers	PABQ	2478	99.3	99.6	102.2	105.4	111.0	117.6
Glass containers other than tubular	KHJW		..	..	..	..	110.9	117.5
Other glass products	PABR	2479	102.8	106.0	111.2	116.9	128.1	133.7
Domestic and ornamental glassware	PAVS		106.8	110.9	116.8	127.0	134.6	141.6
Other table, toilet, ornamental and stationery, glassware and kitchenware (excl. heat resisting glassware for cooking purposes)	PAVX		107.0	114.0	117.9	126.1	..	..
Domestic and ornamental glassware mechanically gathered	KHJX		..	..	..	..	..	137.0
Glass envelopes, tubes and illuminating glassware	PAVZ		106.4	106.8	110.6	114.8	127.0	136.2
Refractory goods	PABS	2481	107.1	113.1	116.5	122.8	130.7	136.4
Firebricks and blocks	PAWK		104.4	109.6	115.0	125.0	141.5	154.2
Miscellaneous refractory goods nes	PAWT		105.8	112.3	116.1	122.2	129.7	134.9
Ceramic goods	PABT	2489	105.7	109.9	116.5	126.6	137.9	149.7
Sanitary ware of vitreous china	PAWZ		103.8	105.3	112.1	124.0	135.2	145.8
Domestic china and other pottery	PAXA		106.2	111.8	119.1	130.1	144.5	159.9
China or porcelain	PAXB		105.9	111.8	120.6	130.9	143.4	155.8
Table and kitchenware	PAXC		105.7	112.3	121.4	133.4	146.0	162.6
Domestic stoneware	KHJY		..	..	..	..	..	162.2
Electronic ware wholly or mainly of ceramic material (incl. insulators and insulator fittings)	PAXL		106.8	109.5	113.7	120.3	128.3	..
Chemical industry		25						
Inorganic chemicals except industrial gases	PABU	2511	101.6	104.7	110.5	115.2	122.0	128.0
Chemical elements excluding elemental gases	PAXO		95.1	102.0	105.6	108.3	116.2	110.2
Inorganic acids and oxygen compounds of non-metals	PAXS		101.6	101.5	104.3	110.2	113.2	115.8
Sulphuric acid and oleum	PAXU		96.7	90.4	88.6	97.3	97.0	96.4
Metallic oxides and inorganic bases	KHJZ		..	..	..	..	..	152.4
Metallic salts and peroxy salts of inorganic acids	PAYD		104.4	107.1	111.8	114.8	121.8	131.4
Soda ash	PAYE		105.5	106.2	110.9	110.9	121.7	139.5
Metallic salts and peroxy salts of inorganic acids other than soda ash	PAYF		103.9	107.5	112.2	116.7	121.9	127.6
Basic organic chemicals except specialised pharmaceutical chemicals		2512						
Carboxylic acids and specified derivatives	PAZN		94.4	98.9	108.5	111.8	111.5	110.1
Organo-inorganic and heterocyclic compounds and nitrogen-function compounds	KHVT		..	..	..	..	93.5	..
Fertilisers	PABW	2513	89.2	80.4	82.9	90.0	91.1	88.1
Synthetic resins and plastics materials	PABX	2514	97.8	107.7	118.4	118.8	117.5	111.4
Products of polymerisation and co-polymerisation	PBJA		..	..	..	..	..	..
Acrylic lattices, dispersions and solutions and moulding	KHMP		..	..	..	..	..	133.6
Intermediate forms between the resin and semi-fabricated stages	KHMQ		..	..	..	..	..	127.7
Dyestuffs and pigments	PABZ	2516	107.4	117.1	128.7	140.2	147.1	138.7
Pigments	KHMR		..	..	..	..	..	139.1
Paints, varnishes and painters' fillings		2551						
Building, structural, preservation and decorative products	PBBI		106.4	110.1	116.9	124.0	136.5	154.0
Emulsion paints	PBBP		103.4	105.0	111.2	119.9	134.9	153.6
Paint removers and strippers, and filling and sealing compounds of all types	PBCM		..	..	..	..	..	..
Printer's inks other than lithographic inks	PBCY		..	..	..	..	122.6	132.3 B
Chemical treatment of oils and fats	PACD	2563	71.6	69.4	71.3	79.8	73.9	..
Additives for liquid fuels and lubricating oils, and anti-freeze	PBES		..	..	..	..	154.2	172.3
Wax, refined, blended, bleached etc	PBFI		..	..	..	..	116.0	124.0
Formulated pesticides	PACH	2568	102.6	106.5	110.4	115.1	128.4	143.2
Herbicides	PBFZ		104.8	112.9	121.3	128.3	136.0	..
Herbicides containing phenoxy derivatives of acetic, propionic or butyric acids	PBGB		104.5	104.6	108.2	110.1	113.5	115.0
Herbicides other than than those containing phenoxy derivatives of acetic, propionic or butyric acids	PBGB		104.5	104.6	108.2	110.1	113.5	115.0
Adhesive film, cloth and foil adhesive film, tape etc of plastics or cellulose, adhesive cloth and foil	PACI	2569	95.2	100.1	101.8	103.8	107.1	111.6
Pharmaceutical products	PACJ	2570	106.3	110.4	115.6	117.9	120.6	122.6
Medical preparations as specified	PBGR		101.7	104.8	109.4	111.3	115.0	118.0
Central nervous system	PBGS		101.9	107.2	110.3	114.6	118.7	124.5 B
Analgesics-antipyretics	PBGV		103.2	108.5	113.3	119.4	124.8	130.9
Cardiovascular system	PBHE		102.5	104.8	103.8	101.6	104.6	107.2
Plain hypotensives	PBHF		100.0	100.4	101.9	101.9	101.8	101.8
Plain diuretics	PBHG		100.0	100.8	101.6	102.0	102.5	103.4
Respiratory preparations	KHMS		..	..	..	..	..	117.6
Cough and cold preparations	PBHK		108.4	118.3	127.1	135.8	144.0	152.9
Preparations for the alimentary tract and nutrition	PBHM		102.4	104.8	109.1	113.3	120.8	125.5
Antacids and anti-ulcerants	PBHN		100.8	101.6	105.5	109.6	111.7	..
Laxatives	PHNP		140.1	150.4	131.6	137.4	117.7	94.0
Vitamins and mineral supplements	PBHR		102.1	106.8	112.1	118.3	126.8	134.2
Muscular and skeletal systems (systemic)	PBHU		100.4	101.4	103.2	105.1	107.1	107.5
Topical cortiso-steroids	PBHX		101.4	101.4	107.2	107.9	107.9	..
Antibiotics	PBIA		99.8	100.7	117.6	117.6	118.5	118.8
Preparations for genito-urinary system (incl. sex hormones)	PBIJ		104.3	119.2	122.7	122.7	124.9	132.5
Surgical bandages etc	PBIZ		107.2	113.8	121.8	130.9	142.4	154.0
Adhesive plasters, bandages and self-adhesive first aid dressings	PBJC		103.9	107.4	114.6	..	..	..

1 Class or activity heading.

Source: Central Statistical Office

Prices

18.4 (continued) Producer price index numbers of products manufactured in the United Kingdom (home sales)
Annual averages

1985 = 100

		1980 SIC[1]	1986	1987	1988	1989	1990	1991
Chemical industry (*continued*)								
Soap and synthetic detergents	PACK	2581	103.5	107.9	114.0	119.5	129.9	146.7
Soap (excl. scouring preparations)	PBJO		100.6	101.2	106.8	113.2	122.8	137.1
Toilet soap in tablet form	PBJS		99.7	99.2	104.2	114.6	126.6	143.0
Liquid finished synthetic detergents (excl. scouring preparations)	PBJW		105.6	111.5	116.7	125.1	140.5	163.0
Dishwashing	KHMT		..	..	..	..	..	138.1
Perfumes, cosmetics and toilet preparations		2582						
After shave, cologne and pre-shave lotions	PBKF		107.8	119.6	129.8	134.3	149.3	165.9
Perfumes, cosmetics and toilet preparations other than specifically for men	PBKH		104.4	107.8	112.5	120.1	129.1	139.0
Talc and dusting powders and bath preparations	PBKO		105.5	111.3	114.8	119.8 B	125.8 B	135.6 B
Talc and dusting powders	PBKP		105.9	110.0	115.7	..	..	..
Make-up preparations	PBKS		105.8	110.0	115.4	122.1	132.5	145.8
Make-up preparations for the face	PBKT		..	..	..	..	135.6	..
Lipsticks and lipglosses, including lipsalve	PBKU		103.4	107.0	112.7	119.9	133.8	143.9
Face powders	PBKV		106.4	109.3	115.7	124.5	137.8	..
Liquid and cream make-up for the face	PBKW		104.4	111.8	121.4	128.2	136.7	..
Deodorants, anti-perspirants and depilatories	PBLH		102.7	106.5	111.0	118.9	126.7	135.4
Toothpaste and dental powders	PBLL		103.4	108.0	116.2	130.1	145.0	155.7
Soapless shampoos	PBLM		102.4	..	..	..	..	128.7
Photographic materials and chemicals	PACM	2591	103.4	108.1	113.0	119.9	131.2	140.1
Chemical products, nes	KHMU	2599	..	..	..	..	..	..
Leather and car polishes	KHMV		..	..	..	..	..	118.5
Production of man-made fibres		26						
Production of man-made fibres	PACO	2600	104.7	105.7	106.9	107.9	112.1	115.2
Manufacture of metal goods not elsewhere specified		31						
Ferrous foundry products	PACP	3111	104.3	106.4	113.9	121.7	130.2	139.7 B
Iron castings in the rough or machined	PBSB		104.6	107.0	111.7	119.1	128.5	138.8
Engineers' castings	PBSC		106.0	109.0	114.4	122.0	130.6	138.6
Vehicle iron castings	PBSD		107.0	110.4	115.6	121.9	133.2	140.9
Industrial and marine machinery and plant	PBSE		105.0	107.7	113.2	122.1	127.9	136.2
Light engineering	PBSG		106.3	108.5	114.3	122.1	129.0	137.2
Steel castings	PBSN		101.4	100.4	136.1	147.9	147.6	149.0
Non-alloy steel castings	PBSO		101.3	99.5	136.3	148.7	148.7	149.7
Stainless and heat resisting alloy steel castings	PBSQ		102.6	119.2	126.5	126.6	126.6	126.6
Other alloy steel castings	PBSS		101.6	107.3	135.9	142.6	137.8	146.9
Forging, pressing and stamping		3120						
Steel forgings	PBSX		106.2	111.2	116.2	120.8	124.6	127.9
Bolts, nuts, washers, springs and non-precision chains	PACS	3137	103.7	107.2	111.0	117.4	122.6	126.3
Bolts, nuts, screws, washers, rivets etc. of iron or steel	PBTO		103.5	107.2	110.4	116.6	120.5	122.8
All bolt products including machine screws, studs and socket screws	PBTP		103.7	106.0	109.8	114.9	117.8	115.8
All bolt products of high tensile steel	PBTQ		104.7	107.1	111.1	115.3	119.8	..
All bolt products of mild steel	PBTR		101.9	104.2	107.8	114.1	114.2	..
Heat and surface treatment of metals (incl. sintering)	KHMW	3138	..	107.2	111.0	117.4	..	..
Metal doors, windows etc	PACT	3142	105.6	112.8	121.4	131.0	137.3	145.0
Metal windows and doors (excl. strongroom doors and doors for motor vehicles) door frames, window frames, casements and curtain walling	PBUD		105.6	112.8	121.4	..	..	..
Hand tools and implements	PACU	3161	105.2	109.7	115.4	124.1	134.6	145.2
Agricultural hand tools	PBUH		105.1	109.9	113.4	119.8	127.5	..
Other hand tools	PBVO		105.4 B	110.1 B	117.1 B	126.1 B	138.2 B	150.7 B
Hacksaw blades (other than for machines)	PBUR		104.4	107.4	111.1	120.6	..	..
Bolt cutters, pliers, pincers, nippers and snips	PBUT		105.4	111.6	118.3	..	..	..
Spanners and wrenches	PBUW		106.1	109.8	115.9	..	..	..
Hammers	PBVF		101.7	106.7	112.6	122.7	132.4	..
Cutlery, spoons, forks and similar tableware: razors		3162						
Scissors and tailors' shears including pinking shears	PBWB		104.4	109.4	114.6	121.6	139.0	169.7
Metal storage vessels (mainly non-industrial)	PACW	3163	103.8	109.7	122.5	141.6	153.2	161.5
Packaging products of metal	PACX	3164	102.0	103.8	107.1	110.0	113.0	119.0
Metal cans and boxes	PBWK		101.4	102.3	..	..	..	..
Cans and boxes, covers and components of steel (incl. tinplate and blackplate) and aluminium	PBWL		101.4	102.3	..	..	..	..
Metal kegs, drums and barrels	KHMX		..	..	..	..	..	140.2
New metal kegs, drums and barrels of wrought iron and steel with a capacity exceeding 20 litres	PBWQ		107.5	112.1	118.9	125.5	133.0	141.5
Reconditioned metal kegs, drums and barrels	PBWS		101.5	105.8	109.1	..	..	..
Domestic heating and cooking appliances (non-electrical)	PACY	3165	105.5	109.2	114.8	121.9	130.8	139.9
Gas cookers	PBXD		106.3	110.7	115.5	122.1	129.5	136.8
Gas fires and space heaters (excluding gas central heating equipment)	PBXE		103.9	105.7	112.8	121.2	133.4	146.4 B
Metal furniture and safes	PACZ	3166	105.5	109.9	115.5	123.2	133.3	139.5
Office furniture wholly or mainly of metal	PBXP		104.3	107.4	112.5	116.7	122.3	127.4
Seating	PBXR		104.6	108.7	115.7	123.5	134.3	137.4 B
Adjustable office seating	PBXS		104.4	108.6	116.4	..	..	..
Filing cabinets and other filing containers (incl. parts)	PBXV		104.1	106.4	112.0	113.6	116.5	120.1
Shelving and racking including lateral filing and library shelving	PBXY		105.6	110.8	116.7	125.4	138.5	146.0
Domestic and similar utensils of metal	PADB	3167	105.1	110.6	113.5	119.0	126.6	140.1
Kettles (non-electric) and teapots (including electro-plated and precious metal teapots)	PBYE		102.0	106.1	..	..	..	..
Bakeware, including baking pans, sheets, tins etc	PBYL		103.2	104.6	108.8	114.8	119.6	130.0

1 Class or activity heading.

Source: Central Statistical Office

18.4 Producer price index numbers of products manufactured in the United Kingdom (home sales)
continued — Annual averages

Prices

1985 = 100

		1980 SIC[1]	1986	1987	1988	1989	1990	1991
Manufacture of metal goods not elsewhere specified (*continued*)								
Finished metal products nes	PADC	3169	104.7	110.1	117.5	127.3	137.4	147.8
Locks, padlocks, latches, keys and blanks including bicycle locks (excluding for motor vehicles and time locks)	PBYV		105.6	111.4	118.5	130.4	141.9	154.4
Needles, pins and other metal smallwares	PBYN		..	..	..	..	..	..
Builders' and cabinet makers' ironmongery and hardware	PBZN		103.3	106.6	112.5	120.1	128.8	140.6
Finished metal products - doors and door frames	PBZO		104.8	108.0	113.6	120.8	131.0	142.2
Finished metal products - windows and shutters	PBZP		101.8	106.7	114.3	122.7	131.1	149.8
Sanitary ware and plumbing fixtures and fittings for domestic and similar use	PBZU		104.5	110.3	118.0	128.3	138.4	149.9
Sinks and baths	KHMY		..	..	..	..	..	151.2
Domestic cocks and taps	PBZY		104.7	109.2	118.8	124.4	133.7	145.4
Gate valves, stopcocks and radiator valves	PBZZ		..	..	..	..	119.3	..
Fire extinguishers (hand-operated chemical type)	PCIT		111.1	123.0	133.9	145.4	162.8	..
Mechanical engineering		32						
Agricultural machinery		3211						
Harvesting and threshing machinery	PCJW		107.0	115.0	.. B	.. B	135.8	141.8
Grain and grass dryers	PCKD		103.5	107.4	..	..	..	..
Agricultural elevators and conveyors (including grain augers)	PCKM		101.9	108.5	124.2	133.7	..	..
Soil engaging, soil preparation and cultivation machinery	KHMZ		..	..	..	..	140.3	148.9
Wheeled tractors		3212						
Wheeled tractors, complete (including KD tractors of a minimum value of 50 per cent of a corresponding complete tractor)	PCKP		104.7	105.3	109.5	114.3	120.6	125.4
Metal working machine tools	PADG	3221	104.7	108.1	113.8	120.3	127.7	132.0
Metal cutting machine tools	PCKT		104.7	108.0	114.2	120.9	128.6	131.4
Numerically controlled machine tools complete	PCKU		103.3	106.9	113.0	119.9	126.0	127.3
Machining centres	PCKY		101.2	108.1	115.0	121.7	125.8	124.6
Non numerically controlled metal cutting machine tools complete	PCLM		104.8 B	108.4 B	112.6 B	117.8 B	124.2 B	134.5 B
Non numerically controlled grinding machines	KHVU		105.6	110.2	116.0	..	..	..
Non numerically controlled turning machines	PCLI		106.3	113.5	119.8	126.8	140.1	153.1
Non-turning machines	KHPM		..	..	..	..	127.1	124.6
Engineers' small tools	PADH	3222	106.5	112.2	118.8 B	126.9 B	137.7 B	148.8 B
Hard tipped and other metal cutting tools	PCLS		104.7	110.0	116.6	125.4	135.7	145.1
Hard metal tipped tools	PCLU		106.7	114.6	119.9	122.9	127.8	131.5 B
Hard metal tips and die pellets sold separately	PCLV		103.3	107.9	110.3	..	..	128.1
Diamond tipped tools and diamond dies	PCLY		103.8	106.9	111.1	118.6	123.9	129.2
Threading dies and taps	PCLZ		107.0	111.5	120.4	136.0	152.2	172.3
Saws and saw blades	PCMA		102.7	109.4	116.2	123.6	132.4	137.3
Bandsaws and blades for metal	PCMB		102.4	106.2	113.3	119.2	128.5	136.5
Reamers, end mills and similar shank tools	PCMH		104.0	107.0	113.0	123.6	138.0	152.7 B
Milling cutters	PCMK		102.2	107.5	109.2	..	127.3	140.5
Lathe and planer tools	PCML		106.6	110.5	120.6	137.4	151.8	164.1
Hard metal-tipped tools, taps, dies and die pellets	KHPN		..	..	..	..	127.3	132.4
Twist drills and bit stock drills	KHPO		..	..	..	..	143.1	153.6
Food, drink and tobacco processing machinery; packaging and bottling machinery	PADJ	3244	105.2	111.8	116.4	120.1	128.9	138.3
Food and drink processing machinery	PCNJ		104.1	108.9	112.3	114.8	121.1	127.0
Bakery and confectionery machinery (including parts)	PCNN		101.4	102.1	103.5	105.0 B	109.7 B	..
Drink processing machinery including parts	PCNP		103.7	108.6	112.2	111.4	115.9	120.8
Other machinery and parts for the preparation, processing and sterilisation of food (including oil or fat machinery for food industry)	PCNR		109.0	116.2	120.9	131.0	139.8	151.2
Machines for filling, closing, sealing, capsulating or labelling containers	PCNT		105.3	112.0	117.6	126.3	138.7	150.6
Filling, closing, sealing, etc machines for cans	PCNW		..	..	..	..	..	148.3
Filling, closing, sealing, etc machines for boxes, bags and other containers	KHPP		..	..	..	..	..	148.3
Machines for cleaning and/or drying bottles or other containers	KHPQ		..	..	..	..	..	166.3
Packaging and wrapping machines	KHPR		..	..	..	..	..	166.5
Chemical industry machinery	KHPS	3245	..	..	..	..	..	144.8
Gas, water and waste treatment plant	KHPT		..	..	..	..	125.1	135.2
Water treatment plant (incl. parts)	KHPU		..	..	..	..	..	126.3
Mining machinery	PADL	3251	103.1	105.0	108.6	112.0	120.3	125.3
Mineral transport machinery	PCOT		101.1	102.4	106.4	112.9	121.1	130.4
Mineral cutting and loading machines and parts	KHPV		..	..	..	..	..	121.9
Construction and earth moving equipment		3254						
Wheeled tractor shovels	PCPD		103.6	107.5	110.0	110.4	111.8	115.3
Dumpers and dump trucks	PCPH		103.7	105.9	..	..	..	..
Equipment for concrete, crushing and screening and road works	PCPI		104.7	110.1	115.0 B	121.4 B	130.2 B	138.1 B
Concrete mixing and placing machinery and parts	PCPJ		106.4	107.9	..	..	.. B	149.3
Asphalt, bitumen, tar and tarmacadam plants and parts	PCPL		102.5	105.2	..	..	..	..
Mechanical lifting and handling equipment	PADN	3255	103.2	106.2	110.2 B	119.0 B	130.8 B	139.5 B
Cranes and transporters	PCPU		107.4	111.8	119.1	127.6	134.7	137.0
Lifting and winding devices	PCQC		105.6	111.7	117.9	125.3	137.3	149.2
Lifting jacks, vehicle jacks and lifts	PCQF		107.8	116.4	124.5	134.5	146.2	156.1
Capstans, winches, windlasses	PCQL		103.1	107.1	112.1	117.7	126.6	135.8
Electrically-operated overhead travelling cranes and grabs	KHPW		..	..	..	..	..	139.0
Fork lift trucks	KHPX		..	..	..	..	125.4	134.0

1 Class or activity heading.

Source: Central Statistical Office

Prices

18.4 Producer price index numbers of products manufactured in the United Kingdom (home sales) (continued)

Annual averages

1985 = 100

		1980 SIC[1]	1986	1987	1988	1989	1990	1991
Mechanical engineering (*continued*)								
Precision chains and other mechanical power transmission equipment	PADO	3261	106.1	112.6	118.9	124.4	.. B	147.0
Transmission chains	PCQU		106.0	109.4	115.0	121.0	130.0	139.4
Bearings and bushes other than ball roller and needle roller bearings and parts and chain bearings	PCQV		..	..	..	..	..	..
Helical, spur and bevel gears	PCRA		106.5	111.7	115.6	121.4	134.2	147.0
Ball, needle and roller bearings	PADP		104.9	105.2	111.2	121.6	136.2	140.3
Machinery for working wood, rubber, plastics, leather and making paper, glass, bricks and similar materials; laundry and dry cleaning machinery		3275						
Woodworking machinery	PCRN		..	..	123.5	128.8	139.5	149.7
Leather work and footwear making and repairing machinery	PCRV		105.7	112.3	121.8	131.8	145.4	..
Boot and shoe-making and repairing machinery	PCRN		..	..	123.5	128.8	139.5	149.7
Laundry and dry cleaning machinery	PCSA		100.5	109.4	113.2	122.5	131.2	138.9
Internal combustion engines (except for road vehicles, wheeled agricultural tractors and aircraft) and other prime movers		3281						
Compression ignition IC engines	PCSU		103.5	106.2	110.0	115.9	123.6	137.5
Compressors and fluid power equipment	PADT	3283	105.4	111.8	118.6	128.1	137.4	147.8
Compressors	PCTI		106.4	112.6	119.4	127.7	135.8	145.6
Oil hydraulic pumps	PCTK		104.7	110.6	116.2	123.0	131.2	140.2
Oil hydraulic control valves	PCTM		106.6	114.8	124.1	135.4	149.0	164.0
Pneumatic control equipment	PCTS		104.2	109.1	115.7	130.0	139.4	150.6
Directional control, flow control, check and non-return valves, and moving and non-moving fluidic devices	PCTT		102.9	108.3	113.4	132.9	143.4	154.0
Other pneumatic control equipment (including pressure control valves)	PCTU		105.0	109.5	117.0	128.3	137.0	148.6
Refrigerating machinery, space heating, ventilating and air conditioning equipment		3284						
Space heating equipment	PCUH		104.0	108.1	113.4	121.2	130.7	139.8
Boilers for central heating	PCUJ		104.1	110.1	115.3	121.6	130.5	138.8
Heat emitters other than radiators	PCUQ		103.8	108.9	..	..	139.0	150.1
Ventilating equipment	PCUQ		103.8	108.9	..	..	139.0	150.1
Compressors and condensing units	KHPY		..	..	..	..	..	128.2
Warm air generators	KHPZ		..	..	..	..	149.0	153.2
Scales, weighing machinery and portable power tools	PADV	3285	101.7	105.7	111.7	121.6	126.8	136.9
Scales and weighing machinery complete and parts	PCVF		99.5	98.9	101.5	114.1	119.5	124.1
Portable power tools	PCVG		102.7	109.0	116.7	125.2	130.5	143.2
Pneumatic, petrol, hydraulic and other tools for civil engineering, mining and quarrying	PCVI		104.1	109.9	118.3	137.5	145.2	154.4
Portable power tools (electric)	PCVK		101.4	107.1	114.2	119.2	121.8	135.6
Other industrial and commercial machinery	PADW	3286	104.6	108.6	113.6	119.1	128.7	136.2
Industrial and commercial machinery and service equipment	PCVQ		104.4	108.2	113.3	118.3	127.7	135.0
Lawn mowers powered, including electrical	PCVT		104.6	109.6	115.4	122.4	129.6	135.7
Garage equipment and plant nes	PCVW		105.3	110.7	117.1	128.0	138.7	152.6
Pumps	PADX	3287	105.7	110.6	117.3	127.9	138.7	149.3
Centrifugal pumps	PCWH		105.9	110.8	116.9	126.1	135.2	144.7
Centrifugal pumps with stuffing box or mechanical seal	PCWI		105.7	110.7	118.5	127.3	137.6	148.1
Centrifugal pumps without stuffing box or mechanical seal	KHQP		..	..	..	..	129.8	137.1
Positive displacement pumps	PCWK		105.0	111.4	116.5	125.9	135.0	146.8
Rotary pumps	PCWP		105.5	111.8	117.9	126.7	136.7	148.3
Hand pumps	KHQQ		..	..	..	..	122.6	127.7
Kerbside petrol and oil measuring pumps and parts	KHQR		..	..	..	..	125.4	129.6
Industrial valves	KHQS	3288	..	..	..	..	..	157.3
Metal gate valve units	KHQT		..	..	..	..	..	156.5
Metal globe valve units	KHQU		..	..	..	..	..	166.1
Lubricators and parts	KHQV	3289	..	..	..	..	139.5	148.8
Manufacture of office machinery and data processing equipment		33						
Office machinery	PAEB	3301	103.7	104.5	107.6	111.5 B	121.5 B	127.8 B
Electrical and electronic engineering		34						
Insulated wires and cables	PAED	3410	100.1	101.8	107.5	.. B	113.3	118.8
Mains (power distribution) cables 600/1000 volts and over	PCYX		96.4	92.7	92.1	98.8	..	..
General wiring cable (including. building wires, ship wiring and trailing cables)	PCYY		101.1	104.7	115.6	..	122.5	137.2
Winding wires and strips	PCZA		92.1	89.1	105.7	120.0	111.8	102.1
Basic electrical equipment		3420						
Switchgear and control gear	PCZT		..	..	..	..	..	..
Basic electrical equipment other than machinery for generating and transmitting electrical power, switchgear and control gear	PDIK		..	..	..	..	..	..
Wiring accessories up to 250 volts	PDLJ		..	..	..	..	..	..
Basic electrical equipment	KHQW		..	..	..	..	..	145.5
Generator sets complete	KHQX		..	..	..	..	..	137.2
Transformers	KHQY		..	..	..	..	..	134.3
Transformers over 5 KVA but not exceeding 1500 KVA	KHQZ		..	..	..	..	..	107.5
Starting or control gear	KHRR		..	111.5	117.4	123.8	136.3	145.6
Starting or control gear, complete	KHRS		..	111.5	117.4	123.8	136.2	145.7
Switchgear and switchboards, complete	KHRU		..	..	..	..	..	155.5
Non-traction motors	KHRV		..	109.2	113.8	126.0	136.4	144.0
Non-traction motors AC (incl. AC/DC) 0.75 KW and over	KHRW		..	108.9	114.2	126.4	138.1	145.2
Moulded case circuit breakers	KHRX		..	..	..	..	..	147.5

1 Class or activity heading.

Source: Central Statistical Office

Prices

18.4 continued
Producer price index numbers of products manufactured in the United Kingdom (home sales)
Annual averages

1985 = 100

		1980 SIC[1]	1986	1987	1988	1989	1990	1991
Electrical and electronic engineering (*continued*)								
Batteries and accumulators	PAEF	3432	104.2	110.3	114.7	120.6	134.5	137.2
Primary batteries complete and parts	KHRY		..	..	..	..	..	141.6
Secondary batteries	KHRZ		..	..	..	..	..	137.1
Electrical equipment for motor vehicles, cycles and aircraft	PAEH	3434	107.4	124.0	128.8	138.4	150.7	163.8
Electrical instruments and controls systems	PAEK	3442	102.7	106.3	110.0	115.0	121.6	130.0
Electricity supply meters including prepaid	PDMQ		102.9	105.8	108.7	112.8	120.8	124.6
Instruments and equipment for integrated process control schemes	PDMS		102.7	104.0	104.3	107.6	114.6	125.8 B
Electrical measuring, testing and controlling instruments and apparatus	PDNF		104.3	108.9	115.3	121.6	130.1	140.6
Ammeters, voltmeters, wattmeters	PDNG		106.3	113.4	122.6	131.5	139.9	151.7
Signal and waveform generators	PDNI		103.3	104.4	109.4	115.5	..	130.5
Other electrical measuring, testing and controlling instruments and appliances, incl. telemetering instruments, other than for motor vehicles or aircraft	PDNL		104.9	110.5	117.0	123.4	..	..
Radio and electronic capital goods		3443						
Electro magnetic apparatus	PDOA		111.3	112.9	115.4	120.4	123.9	126.6
Connectors	KHSQ	3444	..	108.0	112.1	117.8	129.0	136.5
Relays	KHSR		..	..	..	..	..	117.4
Resistors	KHSS		..	..	..	..	..	99.4
Terminals	KHST		..	109.2	123.5	130.0	136.7	142.5
Gramophone records and tape recording	KHSV	3452	..	..	..	..	..	135.9
Pre-recorded audio tapes	KHSW		..	..	..	..	..	150.9
Domestic-type electric appliances	PAER	3460						
Electric cooking apparatus	PDPM		104.0	107.7	110.6	112.5	117.4	118.1
Electric kettles	PDPQ		103.9	105.4	106.8	106.9	104.3	..
Electric heating apparatus	PDPT		103.4	105.8	108.2	111.2	117.8	125.6
Electric water heaters	PDPV		105.1	108.6	116.4	..	..	145.5
Deep-freeze units	PDQF		104.4	108.0	112.1	..	..	..
Other domestic-type electric appliances	KHSX		..	107.4	109.8	..	..	124.6
Electric lamps and other electric lighting equipment		3470						
Electric lamp bulbs and tubes	PDQI		105.2	110.4	..	..	129.9	142.3
Discharge lamps, complete	PDQJ		105.0	110.7	..	..	..	..
Electric lamp bulbs, filament type complete	PDQN		105.4	110.2	..	..	..	..
Lamp and lighting fittings and parts thereof	PDQS		106.6	110.2	115.5	122.4	131.1	141.6
For tubular fluorescent lamps	PDQU		105.4	108.1	112.1	117.3	125.0	134.2
Other fittings and parts (other than street and domestic lighting)	PDQX		106.8	111.8	120.1	129.8	141.0	155.7
Discharge lamps complete	KHSY		..	110.7	..	..	..	..
Motor vehicles and parts thereof		35						
Motor vehicles and their engines	PAES	3510	106.8	114.7	123.2	131.9	141.2	150.5
Passenger cars	PAET		106.9	116.1	126.2	136.0	145.1	154.0
Goods vehicles not exceeding 3.5 tons gvw	PAEV		106.7	114.4	123.1	131.8	144.4	154.9
Goods vehicles exceeding 16 tons gvw	PAEX		107.5	115.1	122.3	129.9	136.2	143.8
Passenger cars (inclusive of VAT and car tax)	PARH		..	..	..	..	..	..
Motor vehicle bodies for other commercial vehicles (goods and special purposes)	KHSZ		..	..	..	..	..	145.1
Trailers and semi-trailers (including freight containers)		3522						
Trailers and semi-trailers	PAFC		104.7	111.3	116.4	124.4	129.1	133.8
Motor vehicle parts	KHVW	3530	..	..	..	..	..	138.5
Oil filters	KHTT		..	..	..	..	..	138.5
Fuel pumps (not electric)	PDSP		103.7	108.8	112.0	..	..	..
Railway and tramway vehicles		3620						
Railway and tramway vehicles	PAFF		..	..	..	..	114.2	124.1
Baby carriages and non-powered invalid carriages	KHTV	3650	..	..	..	..	..	152.8
Instrument engineering		37						
Measuring, checking and precision instruments and apparatus	PAFJ	3710	105.4	109.7	115.9	124.8	133.3	142.8
Process measuring and control instruments and equipment	PDTK		106.4	111.6	116.9	124.7	131.1	138.8
Level indicating recording or controlling instruments	PDTL		106.0	114.3	118.9	126.3	135.5	147.8
Temperature measuring and control instruments	PDTN		107.2	113.2	119.2	127.8	134.1	142.1
Thermostats and temperature indicators and controllers	PDTP		108.6	115.6	122.0	130.2	135.1	144.4
Pressure measuring and control instruments	PDTR		108.4	113.6	121.0	128.9	136.9	145.0
Pressure gauges and switches	PDTS		105.4	111.8	118.1	..	135.4	149.1
Other pressure measuring and control instruments	PDTT		114.9	117.2	127.2	..	140.2	136.3
Analytical instruments	PDTU		104.6	107.6	109.5	112.6	118.6	126.0
Ultrasonic instruments and equipment	PDUA		111.2	116.8	117.9	126.5	138.4	..
Counting and velocity measuring instruments	PDUH		104.7	108.0	111.9	116.4	124.7	129.5
Inspection and measuring instruments and tools for measuring and marking out	KHTW		..	..	..	..	..	154.3
Engineers gauges and measuring instruments	PDUO		107.8	114.2	124.2	134.2	142.5	150.0 B
Static gauges	PDUP		108.8	122.3	128.7	137.7	150.6	158.6
Mechanical measuring instruments	PDUQ		107.2	111.6	122.6	134.3	144.6	155.5

1 Class or activity heading.

Source: Central Statistical Office

Prices

18.4 Producer price index numbers of products manufactured in the United Kingdom (home sales)
continued — Annual averages

1985 = 100

		1980 SIC[1]	1986	1987	1988	1989	1990	1991
Instrument engineering (*continued*)								
Medical and surgical equipment and orthopaedic appliances	PAFL	3720	105.2	111.1	114.5	118.9	128.1	140.4
Medical, surgical and veterinary equipment	PDUZ		105.2	112.6	116.1	119.9	130.1	145.3
Other medical, surgical, veterinary and dissecting instruments	PDVD		102.6	106.7	113.4	123.3	136.2	146.7
Aseptic hospital furniture	PDVG		104.3	107.7	111.7	119.0	129.4	136.2
Dental instruments and appliances	KHTX		..	..	..	..	..	124.1
Artificial teeth and dental fillings (incl. complete dentures)	KHTY		..	..	..	..	..	136.0
Orthopaedic appliances and artificial limbs etc	PDVM		105.9	109.3	112.5	117.9	125.6	132.9
Spectacles and unmounted lenses	PAFM		..	..	..	..	105.9	111.1
Finished lenses optically worked, mounted or unmounted	PDVT		..	..	..	..	103.9	106.8
Glass lenses	PDVU		..	..	..	..	103.9	108.0
Glass lenses - single vision	PDVV		..	..	..	..	104.4	108.8
Glass lenses - bifocal	PDVW		..	..	..	..	102.8	106.5
Plastic lenses - single vision	PDVY		..	..	..	..	104.8	102.7 B
Contact lenses	PDWA		..	..	..	..	104.0	..
Contact lenses - hard	PDWB		..	..	..	..	104.0	..
Contact lenses - soft	PDWC		..	..	..	..	104.0	..
Optical meteorological instruments	PDWF		..	..	..	..	137.4	145.1
Spectrophotometers and spectrographs	PDWG		..	..	..	..	122.6	132.9
Photographic and cinematographic equipment	PAFP	3733	104.1	109.7	110.3	108.8	109.0	109.8
Clocks, watches and other timing devices	KHVX	3740	..	..	..	..	..	131.9
Time switches etc	PDWV		104.0	107.9	113.2	119.7	128.0	137.8
Food, drink and tobacco manufacturing industries		41/42						
Margarine and compound fats	PAFR	4115	90.7	87.6	91.6	93.4	97.2	101.5
Processing organic oils and fats (other than crude animal fat production)	PAFS	4116	60.6	57.8	66.5	69.2	64.9	66.6
Slaughterhouses	PAFT	4121	101.0	101.7	109.7	120.9	117.4	111.0
Bacon curing and meat processing	PAFU	4122	101.1	101.2	104.8	113.8	122.6	128.1
Poultry slaughter and processing	PAFV	4123	101.6	102.4	102.8	105.4	113.2	105.2
Animal by-product processing	PAFW	4126	84.7	95.8	91.8	93.2	82.0	78.3
Preperation of milk and milk products	PAFX	4130	101.6	105.3	110.8	117.0	117.8	123.4
Processing of fruit and vegetables	PAFY	4147	104.8	111.0	110.2	116.3	124.5	132.0
Fish processing	PAFZ	4150	105.5	109.6	111.0	109.4	124.1	135.1
Grain milling	PAGA	4160	109.3	109.8	114.4	113.4	112.5	118.8
Starch	PAGB	4180	101.1	100.0	98.6	99.3	102.9	115.1
Bread and flour confectionery	PAGC	4196	106.8	111.3	118.2	123.5	130.8	140.8
Biscuits and crispbread	PAGD	4197	103.6	106.7	112.2	119.3	127.8	136.0
Sugar and sugar by-products	PAGE	4200	100.9	106.2	111.5	116.9	125.1	134.4
Ice cream	PAGF	4213	104.3	111.8	112.7	117.1	124.7	136.2
Cocoa, chocolate and sugar confectionery	PAGG	4214	103.8	106.3	106.7	109.2	113.7	119.2
Compound animal feeds	PAGH	4221	100.3	100.3	106.1	109.7	111.1	113.5
Pet foods and non-compound animal feeds	PAGI	4222	101.5	101.9	102.4	103.7	106.6	108.8
Miscellaneous foods	PAGJ	4239	103.7	106.0	108.5	113.3	120.9	129.7
Potable spirits	PDXF		..	..	..	..	127.3	140.4
Spirits sold duty paid: whisky (blended)	PDXH		..	..	..	..	118.5	129.8
Wines, cider and perry	PAGL	4261	105.6	110.0	116.3	122.4	130.7	142.8
Brewing and malting		4270						
Beer	PDXQ		105.0	108.6	113.8	119.5	129.0	141.7
Soft drinks	PAGN	4283	105.3	109.4	116.1	121.1	130.6	138.0
Tobacco industries	PAGO	4290	110.4	113.8	117.4	120.4	129.0	145.0
Cigarettes	PDXR		110.7	114.0	117.6	120.6	129.5	145.6
Standard cigarettes - sold duty paid	PDXT		110.3	113.8	117.9	121.2	130.2	144.9
Tipped cigarettes - sold duty paid	PDXV		110.7	114.0	117.6	120.6	129.4	145.6
Manufactured tobacco not elsewhere specified - sold duty paid	PDXX		108.2	111.2	114.1	117.1	124.0	137.9
Textile industry		43						
Woollen and worsted industry	PAGP	4310	101.1	107.3	117.7	121.4	119.0	117.3
Spinning on the woollen system	KHTZ		..	..	..	..	..	108.3
All wool yarns spun on the woollen system	PDYT		100.6	107.1	118.5	120.8	113.7	106.0
Worsted yarns, wholly or predominantly of wool, spun on the worsted and semi-worsted systems	PDYY		101.1	109.3	121.0	125.8	123.2	122.9
All wool	PDYZ		100.4	109.9	124.7	129.7	122.3	117.8
Worsted yarns of man-made fibres, spun on the worsted and semi-worsted systems	PDZC		104.8	108.5	112.5	117.0	121.8	129.6
Wholly of man-made fibres	PDYW		..	..	..	..	..	..
Weaving	PDZG		104.4	109.1	121.1	127.2	131.8	133.9
Woven woollen fabrics (excluding blankets)	PDZH		105.0	108.7	119.4	125.1	131.1	136.6 B
Woven worsted fabrics containing 50% or more by weight of wool or fine animal hair	PDZO		103.9	109.8	123.5	130.6	132.3	128.7
Apparel cloths containing 50% or more by weight of wool or fine animal hair	PDZJ		104.5	108.4	118.1	123.5 B	130.8 B	135.2 B
Spinning and doubling on the cotton system	PAGQ	4321	98.2	107.8	106.2	109.2	115.5	116.8
Spinning	PDZW		97.9	110.8	103.9	103.6	108.6	107.4
Single yarns of mm staple fibre nes	PDZY		102.2	106.5	108.5	109.2	..	..
Finished thread for sewing, embroidery etc, doubling and winding	PEAM		106.9	112.2	122.5	129.6	..	..
For industrial uses, of man-made fibre	PEAR		105.1	110.6	118.1	125.8	133.6	140.3
Man-made continuous filament yarns, textured, bulked or crimped								
Of synthetic fibres	PEBF	4336	106.1	108.1	110.5	117.0	122.2	..
Jute and polypropylene yarns and fabrics	PAGU	4350	94.1	94.7	98.3	97.5	95.6	99.7
Woven cloth of polypropylene	PEBR		98.3	97.8	100.9	98.9	..	..

1 Class or activity heading.

Source: Central Statistical Office

Prices

18.4 Producer price index numbers of products manufactured in the United Kingdom (home sales)
continued — Annual averages

1985 = 100

		1980 SIC[1]	1986	1987	1988	1989	1990	1991
Textile industry (*continued*)								
Hosiery and other weft knitted goods and fabrics		4363						
Hosiery including tights and panti-hose	PEBS		107.5	112.8	118.9	125.1	133.5	143.4
Women's socks and stockings	PEBX		..	..	..	..	135.9	147.6
Tights and panti-hose	PECA		107.7	113.6	120.7	..	..	..
Underwear, nightwear and swimwear	PECH		105.6	108.2	117.0	124.5	132.3	141.8 B
Men's knitted underwear	PECI		107.8	109.9	117.1	125.5	134.0	141.5
Men's knitted underwear of cotton	PECJ		..	..	..	..	135.0	142.0
Women's knitted underwear of cotton	PECM		102.1	104.2	113.7	103.5	..	..
Women's knitted underwear other than of cotton or synthetic fibres	PECO		109.0 B	114.1 B	122.6 B	128.4 B	145.2	158.7 B
Men's fully fashioned outerwear of wool	PECW		109.6	113.1	122.7	134.0	143.3	153.5 B
Weft knitted fabrics nes	PEDQ		101.3 B	103.4 B	104.7 B	105.1 B	113.4 B	119.4 B
Of synthetic spun yarn	PEDV		..	..	..	..	107.6 B	115.8 B
Warp knitted goods		4364						
Fashion knitted on raschel and similar machines	KHUP		..	..	..	..	..	140.6
Textile finishing		4370						
Woven fabrics (excl. pile cut), bleached, dyed, printed etc	KHUR		..	..	..	..	..	132.6
Cotton and man-made fibres and mixtures of cotton and man-made fibres	KHUS		..	..	..	..	..	132.8
Pile carpets, carpeting and rugs	PAGX	4384	105.5	112.2	119.0	125.9	133.8	137.9
Woven carpets, carpeting and carpet type rugs	PEEI		106.0	112.6	119.4	127.8	136.2	141.0
Containing 50% or more of wool yarn	PEEM		106.1	112.5	119.0	127.0	134.6	141.0
Figured and plain Brussels and Wilton	PEEN		106.7	113.0	117.0	124.7	131.0	137.5
Spool and gripper Axminster	PEEO		105.8	112.2	120.0	128.0	136.4	142.7
Tufted carpets, carpeting and carpet type rugs, other rugs excluding tufted woven and non woven rugs	PEES		105.2 B	112.0 B	118.7 B	124.9 B	132.5	136.2
Tufted carpets, carpeting and carpet type rugs containing 50% or more by weight of acrylic and polyamide fibres	PEEU		105.5	113.5	119.8	124.6	133.4	137.4
Containing more than 50% by weight of wool	PEEV		106.3 B	110.4 B	117.4	127.2	135.0	139.1
Rope, twine and net	PAHA	4396	103.6	106.8	116.2	123.1	128.6	142.0 B
Twines, cords, ropes, cables and lines of textile materials other than agricultural twine	PEFI		104.1	109.7	116.8	123.3	130.7	..
Narrow fabrics		4398						
Non-elastic and non-elastomeric goods not exceeding 30cms in width - Petersham, galloons and ribbons	PEFV		..	..	..	..	..	..
Miscellaneous textiles nes	PAHC	4399	102.8	108.3	112.6	118.9	130.6	147.4
Felt (and bonded fibre fabrics)	PEGG		102.8	108.3	112.6	118.9	131.5	..
Leather and leather goods		44						
Hair hides and skins, pickled, cured, limed etc (incl. pickled pelts, pickled grains and pickled fleshes)	KHUT		..	..	..	..	..	111.3
Leather (tanning and dressing) and fellmongery		4410						
Fellmongery	PEGS		89.0	114.9	110.9	114.8	80.8	65.4
Footwear and clothing industries		44						
Footwear	PAHF	4510	106.3	110.4	115.4	120.1	125.7	132.4
Outdoor footwear	PEHD		106.0	110.2	115.5	119.9	125.3	131.7
With uppers wholly or mainly of leather	KHVY		..	..	..	..	..	132.0
Men's	PEHF		105.6	110.3	115.8	120.0	127.8	135.0
Women's	PEHG		106.4	109.9	116.1	120.2	125.4	131.1
With uppers wholly or mainly of plastics including poromeric - other than sandals or sandalised shoes								
Women's	PEHI		..	..	..	..	..	..
Children's outdoor footwear with uppers wholly or mainly of leather	KHUU		..	..	..	..	..	128.9
Weatherproof outerwear		4531						
Raincoats (excluding infants)	PEIA		108.8	119.2	..	..	..	..
Raincoats other than of plastic materials	PEIB		108.8	119.2	..	..	..	..
Men's and boys' tailored outerwear		4532						
Men's trousers (sold separately)	PEIM		104.2	106.4	109.0	113.7	117.2	122.0 B
Work clothing and men's and boys' jeans		4534						
Cotton boiler suits, men's and boys'	PEIZ		99.5	102.1	108.2	110.0	118.9	128.2
Men's and boys' shirts, underwear and nightwear		4535						
Shirts (other than industrial shirts)	PEJL		104.2	108.6	114.6	117.7	119.5 B	124.1 B
Men's	PEJN		..	..	..	..	..	..
Gloves	PAHN	4538	107.4	112.3	119.4	127.3	137.2	144.9
Leather/fur gloves, mitten and mitts (leather/fur content exceeding 50% value) women's dresswear	KHUV		..	..	..	..	..	146.0
Fabric gloves, mitten and mitts (fabric content exceeding 50% value)	PELL		106.4	113.4	120.2	131.5	142.4	154.2
Dresswear - other than children's	PELO		108.9	112.9	118.6	131.0	142.8	156.4
Household textiles	PAHR	4557	102.8	103.5	104.7	102.3	.. B	111.1
Bed linen-sheets, pillowcases and bolster cases and duvet cases	PEMV		103.7 B	105.3 B	110.1 B	106.3 B	109.0	112.1 B
Sheets	PEMW		102.3	108.8	117.5	118.4	122.8	..
Bedspreads other than tufted	PENJ		107.9	109.8	..	..	..	..
Tea towels, cleaning and polishing cloths, etc	PENM		102.7	104.7	104.2	106.6	.. B	115.1
Tea towels	PENN		103.7	106.9	109.4	..	..	123.3
Cleaning cloths	KHUW		..	..	..	..	..	..
Hand and bath towels of cotton, terry	PENS		99.8	101.8	107.2	101.6	..	..

1 Class or activity heading.

Source: Central Statistical Office

Prices

18.4 Producer price index numbers of products manufactured in the United Kingdom (home sales)
continued — Annual averages

1985 = 100

		1980 SIC[1]	1986	1987	1988	1989	1990	1991
Timber and wooden furniture industries		46						
Sawmilling, planing, etc of wood		4610						
Sawnwood planed wood - homegrown oak	PEOG		105.6	111.8	116.6	124.6	131.2	135.8 B
Builders' carpentry and joinery	PAHU	4630	103.6	109.8	112.7	117.7	125.0	129.3
Builders' woodwork and prefabricated building structures	PEOU		103.6	109.7	112.5	117.5	124.5	128.2
Doorsets, leaves and frames and window frames	PEOV		103.7	109.7	112.7	118.7	126.2	130.1
Doorsets leaves and frames	PEOW		103.4	110.0	112.6	118.7	126.9	131.5
Door leaves flush	PEOY		103.7	110.9	114.4	119.6	128.0	131.9
Door leaves other than flush including louvre doors	PEOZ		102.0 B	107.6 B	108.5 B	116.0 B	123.0	128.9
Window frames	PEPB		104.0	109.3	112.8	118.6	125.3	128.3
Other wooden articles (except furniture)		4650						
Domestic woodwork	PEPO		107.4	100.1	106.3	113.0	117.8	123.0
Wooden and upholstered furniture		4671						
Upholstered furniture	PEQL		106.0	111.4	118.3	127.4	137.0	144.2 B
Lounge suites and settees, fireside, easy and reclining chairs	PEQO		105.9	111.1	117.9	127.5	137.6	144.3 B
With frames of wood	PEQP		105.9	111.1	117.9	..	..	..
Dining chairs	PERD		109.6 B	115.1 B	122.0 B	131.9 B	142.0 B	151.6 B
Desks and desking	PERR		104.3	110.0	..	..	131.5	136.5
Beds and mattresses	PERZ		105.1 B	118.7 B	127.7 B	134.0 B	142.8	150.5
Interior spring mattresses	PESE		104.3 B	109.3 B	..	..	129.9	140.6
Fully finished interior spring mattresses - 120cm in width or over	PESF		104.3	109.2	..	..	128.2	139.3
Under 120cm in width (excl. cot mattresses)	PESG		104.3 B	109.4 B	..	..	132.3	142.5
Paper and paper products: printing and publishing		47						
Pulp, paper and board	PAIC	4710	100.8	106.5	112.5	119.3	122.1	119.8
Writing and printing papers other than newsprint	PESM		101.0	109.9	115.9	122.5	125.3	121.5
Wrapping and packaging papers	PESN		100.2	101.1	105.8	113.5	115.5	109.1
Flutings and liners for corrugated board	PESR		100.3	99.4	103.2	113.6	114.5	106.8
Industrial and special purpose papers	PEST		100.2	106.9	112.4	..	133.5	137.0
All other products nes	KHUX		..	71.0	80.9	85.8	73.6	60.7
Household and personal hygiene products of paper	PAIE	4722	104.2	113.0	117.2	125.9	137.7	145.8 B
Toilet paper	PETC		103.8	113.8	117.9	..	136.4	..
Sanitary towels and tampons	PETL		106.6	112.7	119.1	..	..	..
Stationery	PAIF	4723	103.6	110.5	116.4	125.5	133.2	135.9
Commercial envelopes	PETP		107.4	114.2	120.2	125.4	131.0	134.1
Listing paper - single part	KHUY		..	..	..	..	..	107.3
Stationery and scholastic books and ruled paper	PAIG		108.4	120.1	126.7	140.4	155.5	156.9
Loose-leaf supplies	PEUB		104.6	107.9	115.8	..	..	144.0
Filing supplies	PEUC		107.7	113.4	119.4	126.3 B	134.4 B	138.7 B
Packaging products of paper and pulp		4724						
Paper sacks	PEUG		98.2	104.7	103.9	109.2	119.2	127.3
Packaging products of board	PAII	4725	103.1	107.3	111.4	119.0	127.5	132.5
Fibre-board packing cases	PEUK		103.2	107.0	111.8	119.3	125.6	128.5
Printing and publishing of newspapers		4751						
Sales of newspapers by printer/publishers	PEUV		102.5	107.8	114.2	120.3	128.7	143.2
National morning	PEUW		101.3	107.3	114.0	119.8	130.2	144.2
National Sunday	PEUX		103.3	108.1	119.7	131.6	137.7	152.8
Regional morning, evening and Sunday	PEUY		103.7	108.3	111.9	115.4	122.2	136.9
Printing and publishing other than of newspapers, periodicals and books		4754						
Atlases, maps, charts and globes	PEWG		108.0	120.5	127.4	134.0	148.5	162.9
Processing of rubber and plastics		48						
Rubber tyres and inner tubes		4811						
New tyre covers	PEWW		105.3	108.1	113.1	115.0	117.8	122.0
Commercial vehicles	PEXA		104.6	107.4	111.9	115.5	118.5	122.0
Other rubber products	PAIP	4812	106.0	108.6	111.0 B	116.6 B	123.1 B	129.3 B
Rubber and plastic hose and tubing	PEXL		106.8	111.8	116.3	126.3	135.3	145.2
Rubber or plastics belting	PEXW		105.1	107.9	103.1	99.7	103.5	106.4 B
Rubber products nes including reclaimed rubber	PEYF		106.0	108.1	111.2 B	117.3 B	123.7 B	129.8 B
Moulded, bonded, extruded, handbuilt, dipped and cast products nes	PEYG		107.4	108.2	109.1 B	115.6 B	124.2 B	132.6 B
Footwear components	PEYU		104.0	108.7	113.5	114.7	118.2	125.4
Rubber linings and rubber flooring	PEZB		106.2	112.7	118.9	128.9	142.8	..
Rubber floorings	PEZC		106.2	112.7	118.9	128.9	142.8	..
Plastics - semi manufactures	PAIS	4832	105.0	111.7	116.2	117.2	123.0	127.8
Plastics floorcoverings	PAIT	4833	104.0	107.6	111.9	116.8	123.6	131.5
Linoleum or plastic (excluding plastic floor covering on a textile base) but including printed felt base	PEZY		104.0	107.6	111.9	116.8	123.6	131.5
Plastics building products	PAIU	4834	103.8	110.3	116.5	122.3	128.8	139.3
Pipes and fittings	PEZZ		104.9	112.9	121.0	128.4	133.5	145.5
Pressure pipes and fittings	KHUZ		..	111.2	..	..	..	144.6
Soil waste pipes and fittings	PFAB		105.7	116.9	129.9	..	..	..
Rainwater pipes and fittings	PFAC		102.7	111.8	120.8	..	..	..
Sanitary ware	PFAH		104.6	112.6	115.6	120.2	131.6	142.3
Open and closed tanks, cylinders, silos and intermediate bulk containers (ie over 250 litres, 439.95 pints)	KHVO		..	..	..	..	..	136.5

1 Class or activity heading.

Source: Central Statistical Office

Prices

18.4 Producer price index numbers of products manufactured in the United Kingdom (home sales)
continued — Annual averages

1985 = 100

		1980 SIC[1]	1986	1987	1988	1989	1990	1991
Processing of rubber and plastics (*continued*)								
Plastics packaging products		4835						
Bottles up to and including one litre capacity	PFAR		104.9 B	109.2 B	116.2 B	119.3 B	122.6	..
Other than of polyethylene and PVC	PFAU		..	..	..	..	139.5	..
Pots and jars	PFAV		101.8	103.0	104.8	106.4	110.4	116.0
Pots and jars up to and including 0.25 litre capacity	KHVP		..	..	..	..	..	115.0
Of polystyrene up to and including 0.25 litre capacity	PFAX		..	..	..	109.4	110.8	114.7
Converted polyethylene film products (excl. laminates)	KHVQ		..	..	..	..	..	135.7
Non-woven sacks and liners - converted polyethylene film products (excl. laminates)	KHVR		..	..	..	..	..	138.1
Plastics product nes		4836						
Industrial hollow-ware of plastics	KHVS		..	..	..	..	..	132.4
Haberdashery (including slide and zip fasteners)	PFCK		102.6	107.5	111.3	118.3	126.7	134.1
Other manufacturing industries		49						
Photographic and cinematographic processing laboratories		4930						
Development and printing of cinematographic film	PFDP		107.6	116.8	129.5	139.0	144.9	152.2
Colour 16 mm	PFDR		106.9	116.2	127.5	138.7	143.8	148.6
Toys and games	PAJA	4941	105.2	111.2	118.3	123.4	134.2	139.0 B
Toys, wholly or mainly of metal, excluding wheeled toys and construction models	PFEG		104.1	110.6	..	..	..	..
Other plastic toys	PFEK		107.4	114.3	..	..	142.1	..
Sports goods	PAJB	4942	101.8	106.5	112.7	122.3	124.8	145.8
Miscellaneous stationers goods	PAJC	4954	105.8	113.8	121.2 B	129.8 B	144.2 B	150.4 B
Pens and pencils	PFFB		106.6	113.0	122.0	129.2	150.9	160.4
Ball pens	PFFD		101.7	113.6	128.6	134.0	169.8	179.7
Fountain pens, stylographic pens, markers and refills	PFFG		108.1	113.5	120.5	131.6	151.8	158.7
Pencils including colour pencils	PFFQ		108.2	110.2	116.1	121.7	133.3	144.0

1 Class or activity heading.

Source: Central Statistical Office

Prices

18.5 Producer price index numbers of commodities wholly or mainly imported into the United Kingdom
United Kingdom; Annual averages

1985=100

		1986	1987	1988	1989	1990	1991
Hides, skins and fur skins, raw							
Hides[1]	PHAQ	93.9	103.0	107.9	116.3	106.0	79.6
Wet[1]	PHAR	94.7	104.0	108.7	117.8	107.4	80.8
Dry[1]	PHAS	82.5	88.5	95.7	92.3	83.6	61.4
Calf skins[1]	PHAT	79.2	71.6	72.1	127.9	102.2	94.7
Oilseeds and oleaginous fruit							
Soya beans, US, cif UK[1]	PHAX	65.8	49.6	57.2	65.0	65.0	63.6
Copra, Philippine/Indonesian cif N. Europe[1]	KHWV	43.0	58.9	70.8	66.3	42.2	52.6
Palm nuts and palm kernels, West African, cif Europe[1]	KHYG	41.4	47.2	63.4	64.9	46.0	54.2
Crude rubber							
Crude rubber (incl. synthetic and reclaimed)	PHBC	..	..	..	99.1	99.5	96.9
Natural rubber (other than latex)[1]	PHBD	93.2	102.3	113.0	99.8	82.7	79.5
Synthetic Rubber latex:							
synthetic rubber	KHWW	..	..	..	..	..	105.2
Synthetic Rubber latex:							
derived from oils	KHWX	..	..	..	..	..	105.2
Other synthetic rubber	KHWY	..	..	..	..	..	101.0
Wood and cork							
Wood sawn lengthwise	PHBS	97.1	105.0	107.9	118.8	135.9	135.0
Wood sawn lengthwise (coniferous)	PHBT	96.7	105.4	110.1	120.3	137.5	136.9
Wood sawn lengthwise (non-coniferous)	PHBV	98.6	103.6	99.7	113.7	130.2	128.1
Mahogany	PHBZ	101.8	114.8	105.1	115.8	138.7	138.6
Meranti	PHCD	92.8	100.7	91.6	118.6	136.7	132.9
Lauan	PHCG	102.8	100.8	91.8	118.4	140.0	140.1
Oak	PHCI	94.2	96.6	101.4	103.1	102.3	94.3
Beech	PHCJ	104.0	107.9	111.5	..	..	..
Pulp and waste paper							
Woodpulp	PHCM	95.8	113.8	120.0	141.7	134.1	105.8
Soda or sulphate chemical wood pulp	PHCP	96.9	120.2	128.6	151.2	143.0	109.7
Bleached or semi-bleached (other than dissolving grades)	PHCS	..	..	..	151.6	..	..
Textile fibres and their wastes	PHCT	91.6	97.8	105.6	121.1	107.8	94.3
Raw cotton[1]	PHCW	69.5	96.6	75.6	98.5	98.5	92.0
Raw jute[1]	PHCZ	45.3	49.9	47.6	53.8	54.3	46.2
Vegetable textile fibres	PHDA	82.8	84.9	82.0	88.9	83.8	79.6
Wool and other animal hair	PHDO	97.4	105.2	122.1	140.7	..	..
Synthetic fibres (discontinuous) not prepared for spinning	KHWZ	..	..	..	..	..	86.5
Crude fertilisers and crude minerals	PHDY	94.7	89.7	86.5	93.3	..	..
Clay[1]	PHEH	99.2	95.0	95.0	95.0	96.9	..
Asbestos, Canadian, fob Quebec[1]	PHEJ	86.0	80.8	80.0	90.4	84.5	86.7
Quartz, mica, felspar, etc[1]	PHEK	100.0	100.0	120.2	122.0	122.0	..
Mineral substances not elsewhere specified[1]	PHEM	106.5	107.6	107.6	107.9	111.0	112.4
Metalliferous ores							
Waste and scrap metal of iron and steel	KHXO	..	..	..	..	..	117.5
Aluminium ores and concentrates (incl. alumina)	PHEP	104.0	104.5	98.7	97.1	96.5	98.5
Zinc	KHXP	..	..	..	..	..	128.2
Tin	KHXQ	..	..	..	..	..	119.0
Manganese ore, 48-50% Mn grade max. 0.1% P, cif Europe[1]	PHED	87.1	73.0	85.9	162.1	205.6	209.6
Ores and concentrates of other non-ferrous base metals	PHER	105.9	113.8	119.2	144.2	156.3	164.1
Chromium ores and concentrates[1]	PHES	73.8	66.2	70.6	92.2	85.1	85.5
Tungsten ore, min. 65%, cif Europe[1]	PHET	61.0	56.2	59.2	65.0	49.3	60.6
Titanium ore[1]	PHEU	110.2	119.9	125.5	151.4	166.1	152.2
Other base metal ores and concentrates n.e.s.	KHXR	..	..	..	..	..	141.1
Copper waste and scrap	KHXS	..	..	..	..	..	120.8
Alluminium waste and scrap	KHXT	..	..	..	..	..	107.5
Lead waste and scrap	KHXU	..	..	..	..	..	100.4
Zinc waste and scrap	KHXV	..	..	..	..	..	117.8
Crude animal and vegetable materials not elsewhere specified							
Gum arabic[1]	PHFC	104.1	98.6	77.2	82.6	61.5	57.2
Petroleum, petroleum products and related materials							
Crude oil[2]	PAKI	48.0	52.0	40.4	49.8	60.6	55.4
Naphtha	PHFK	46.7	52.3	42.3	52.8	65.1	62.5

1 Source of information: trade publications.

2 Includes imported oil and North Sea oil; the imported oil component is based on unit value of imports at their time of entry.

Source: Central Statistical Office

Prices

18.5 continued — Producer price index numbers of commodities wholly or mainly imported into the United Kingdom
United Kingdom; Annual averages
1985=100

		1986	1987	1988	1989	1990	1991
Fixed vegetable oils and fats	PHFS	49.3	50.0	60.4	61.3	52.4	55.6
Fixed vegetable oils 'soft' crude, refined or purified	PHFT	52.1	44.7	55.7	59.8	57.9	58.2
Soya bean oil, Dutch, ex-mill fob[1]	PHFU	51.0	44.4	56.9	58.1	55.7	57.4
Groundnut oil, any origin 2/3% ffa, cif Rotterdam[1]	PHFV	58.7	45.3	49.1	69.7	79.7	74.5
Sunflower seed oil, any origin ex-tk Rotterdam[1]	PHFW	52.6	45.2	55.1	60.7	55.8	54.6
Other fixed vegetable oils fluid or solid, crude, refined or purified[1]	PHFX	46.5	55.6	65.4	62.9	46.6	52.9
Palm oil, crude, cif Liverpool[1]	PHFZ	45.9	54.8	63.6	57.1	44.8	53.0
Coconut oil, Philippine, cif Europe[1]	PHGA	41.4	54.4	63.9	63.3	38.6	49.2
Palm kernel oil, Malaysian, cif Rotterdam[1]	PHGB	43.8	57.6	67.3	64.2	42.3	52.8
Organic chemicals	PHGG	95.1	100.9	101.4	99.9	101.1	104.6
Acrylic alcohols and their derivatives	KHXW	..	..	..	..	..	97.8
Carboxylic acids and their halogenated, sulphonated, nitrated or nitrosated derivatives	PHGS	96.5	95.8	97.7	98.9	102.1	107.0
Monocarboxylic acids and derivatives	PHGT	93.7	86.3	88.2	..	..	..
Amine-function compounds	PHHA	106.1	102.8	95.5	95.7	94.0	86.1
Heterocyclic compounds and nucleic acids	PHHH	99.3	104.1	101.5	..	..	103.0
Aldehyde-ketone and Quinone-function compounds	KHXX	..	..	..	..	..	103.2
Inorganic chemicals							
Inorganic chemical oxides and halogen salts	KHXY	..	..	..	..	..	86.3
Chemical elements	KHXZ	..	..	..	..	..	86.6
Mercury, min. 99.99%, cif Europe[1]	PHHT	58.5	67.5	75.9	68.6	52.8	28.0
Other inorganic bases and metallic ores, hydroxides and peroxides	PHHZ	99.6	99.6	106.3	112.9	..	..
Metallic salts and peroxysalts of inorganic acids	PHID	100.6	103.7	106.3	105.3	107.8	111.9 B
Chlorides, oxychlorides and hydrochloridebromides and oxybromides, iodides and oxyiodides: sulphates (other than sodium) including alums and persulphates	KHYA	..	..	..	..	..	131.2
Inorganic chemical products not elsewhere specified	PHIK	106.4	101.0	103.2	104.0 B	..	..
Dyeing, tanning and colouring materials	PHIN	111.6	131.3	150.9	156.3 B	162.4 B	162.4 B
Essential oils and perfume materials; toilet, polishing and cleansing preparations							
Essential oils, terpenic by-products[1]	PHJF	78.8	91.1	110.1	116.7	95.0	80.1
Mint oil[1]	PHJI	51.6	48.6	76.9	102.0	94.0	92.9
Other essential oils[1]	PHJL	84.3	101.0	119.6	123.2	96.8	77.4
Artificial resins and plastic materials and cellulose esters and ethers							
Polymerisation and copolymerisation products	PHJY	96.3	106.7	117.8	114.4	114.1	107.9
Polyethylene in primary forms	PHKA	84.8	95.6	121.1	112.4	113.7	99.3
Polypropylene in primary forms	PHKC	91.6	106.0	112.4	102.7	..	..
Polystyrene and its copolymers	KHYB	..	..	..	..	..	117.9
Polystyrene and its copolymers in primary forms:	KHYC	..	..	..	..	..	117.9
Polyvinyl chloride	PHKF	107.9	120.1	128.0	131.9	123.5	118.0
Chemical materials and products, not elsewhere specified							
Chemical products and preparations not elsewhere specified	PHKV	113.5	126.7	122.9	117.9	122.7	136.6
Cork and wood manufactures (excluding furniture)							
Plywood and blockboard (delivered to consumers)	PHLA	97.6	103.1	109.3	116.5	128.1	126.7
Paper, paperboard and articles of paper pulp, of paper or of paperboard							
Paper and paperboard	PHLE	103.6	112.4	116.9	122.4	127.8	129.3
Writing and printing paper (excluding newsprint)	KHYD	..	..	..	..	..	131.6
Kraft paper and paperboard	KHYE	..	..	..	..	..	115.2
Paper and paperboard n.e.s.	KHYF	..	..	..	..	..	120.6
Non-ferrous metals							
Silver, gold and platinum and other metals of the platinum group[1]	PHNM	91.1	100.4	88.1	84.2	75.9	68.1
Silver, refined and partly refined[1]	PHNN	78.1	89.6	77.1	70.4	57.4	48.2
Platinum and platinum alloys (unwrought)[1]	PHNP	140.1	150.4	131.6	137.4	117.7	94.0
Other metals of platinum group and alloys thereof (unwrought)[1]	PHNQ	95.2	89.6	77.5	93.5	118.7	114.9
Gold, refined and partly refined[1]	PHNR	101.6	110.4	99.5	94.4	87.6	83.2
Copper, LME settlement price[1]	PHNT	84.8	97.4	131.9	157.0	135.2	119.8
Unwrought nickel, free market price[1]	PHNV	69.8	76.2	195.4	207.0	128.2	119.8
Lead, LME settlement price[1]	PHOA	91.1	119.5	120.9	135.4	150.2	103.5
Zinc, producers' price[1]	PHOD	81.5	76.6	100.2	157.4	129.7	95.3
Zinc, LME settlement price[1]	PHOE	85.7	81.3	116.2	168.1	138.1	106.9
Tin, free market price[1]	PHOG	59.8	58.6	56.5	74.1	50.7	45.5
Magnesium[1]	PHOJ	100.6	100.6	100.6	105.5	83.1	64.2

1 Source of information: trade publications.

Source: Central Statistical Office

Prices

18.6 Internal purchasing power of the pound (based on RPI)[1,2]

Pence

	1976	1977	1978	1979	1980	1981	1982	1983	1984	1985	1986	1987	1988	1989	1990	1991
	BAMI	BAMJ	BAMK	BAML	BAMM	BAMN	BAMO	BAMP	BAMQ	BAMR	BAMS	BAMT	BAMU	BAMV	BAMW	BASX
1976	100	116	125	142	168	188	204	213	224	238	246	256	268	289	317	335
1977	86	100	108	123	145	162	176	184	193	205	212	221	232	250	273	289
1978	80	92	100	113	134	150	163	170	178	189	196	204	214	231	252	267
1979	70	81	88	100	118	132	143	150	157	167	173	180	189	203	223	236
1980	60	69	75	85	100	112	122	127	133	142	146	152	160	172	189	200
1981	53	62	67	76	89	100	109	114	119	127	131	136	143	154	169	179
1982	49	57	62	70	82	92	100	105	110	116	120	125	132	142	155	164
1983	47	54	59	67	79	88	96	100	105	111	115	120	126	136	148	157
1984	45	52	56	64	75	84	91	95	100	106	110	114	120	129	141	150
1985	42	49	53	60	71	79	86	90	94	100	103	108	113	122	133	141
1986	41	47	51	58	68	76	83	87	91	97	100	104	109	118	129	136
1987	39	45	49	56	66	73	80	83	87	93	96	100	105	113	124	131
1988	37	43	47	53	63	70	76	79	83	89	92	95	100	108	118	125
1989	35	40	43	49	58	65	71	74	77	82	85	88	93	100	109	116
1990	32	37	40	45	53	59	64	67	71	75	78	81	85	91	100	106
1991	30	35	37	42	50	56	61	64	67	71	73	76	80	86	94	100

1 To find the purchasing power of the pound in 1980, given that it was 100 pence in 1979, select the column headed 1979 and look at the 1980 row. The result is 85 pence.

2 These figures are calculated by taking the inverse ratio of the respective annual averages of the General Index of Retail Prices. See Table 18.7.

Source: Central Statistical Office

Prices

18.7 General index of retail prices[1]

	All items	All items except seasonal food[2]	Food	Alcoholic drink	Tobacco	Housing	Fuel and light	Durable household goods	Clothing and footwear	Transport and vehicles	Miscellaneous goods	Services	Meals bought and consumed outside the home
15 January 1974=100													
	CBAB	CBAP	CBAN	CBAA	CBAC	CBAH	CBAG	CBAE	CBAD	CBAO	CBAJ	CBAM	CBAI
Annual averages													
1982	320.4	322.0	299.3	341.0	413.3	358.3	433.3	243.8	210.5	343.5	325.8	331.6	341.7
1983	335.1	337.1	308.8	366.4	440.9	367.1	465.4	250.4	214.8	366.3	345.6	342.9	364.0
1984	351.8	353.1	326.1	387.7	489.0	400.7	478.8	256.7	214.6	374.7	364.7	357.3	390.8
1985	373.2	375.4	336.3	412.1	532.4	452.3	499.3	263.9	222.9	392.5	392.2	381.3	413.3
1986	385.9	387.9	347.3	430.6	584.9	478.1	506.0	266.7	229.2	390.1	409.2	400.5	439.5
1987 Jan	394.5	396.4	354.0	100.0	602.9	502.4	506.1	265.6	230.8	399.7	413.0	408.8	454.8

	All items	Food and catering	Alcohol and tobacco	Housing and household expenditure	Personal expenditure	Travel and leisure	All items except seasonal food[2]	All items except food	Seasonal food[2]	Non-seasonal food	All items except housing	Consumer durables
13 January 1987=100												
Weights 1991	1000	198	109	353	101	239	976	849	24	127	808	128
Weights 1992	1000	199	116	344	99	242	978	848	22	130	828	127
Annual averages												
	CHAW	CHBS	CHBT	CHBU	CHBV	CHBW	CHAX	CHAY	CHBP	CHBB	CHAZ	CHBY
1987	101.9	101.4	101.2	102.1	101.4	102.6	101.9	102.0	101.6	101.0	101.6	101.2
1988	106.9	105.7	105.7	108.4	105.2	107.2	107.0	107.3	102.4	105.0	105.8	103.7
1989	115.2	111.9	110.8	121.9	111.2	112.8	115.5	116.1	105.0	111.6	111.5	107.2
1990	126.1	120.8	120.5	139.0	117.6	119.8	126.4	127.4	116.4	119.9	119.2	111.3
1991	133.5	128.6	136.2	142.2	123.6	128.9	133.8	135.1	121.6	126.3	128.3	114.8
1990 Apr	125.1	119.9	118.6	138.5	117.0	118.0	125.1	126.3	123.4	118.0	117.6	111.0
May	126.2	121.2	120.9	139.8	117.6	118.6	126.3	127.4	123.6	119.4	118.8	111.6
Jun	126.7	121.3	121.3	140.7	117.5	119.1	126.9	128.0	118.3	120.3	119.1	111.5
Jul	126.8	120.6	122.4	141.4	116.0	119.6	127.3	128.4	108.1	120.7	119.1	109.7
Aug	128.1	121.7	123.0	142.5	117.2	121.4	128.5	129.6	112.2	121.4	120.3	110.7
Sep	129.3	120.3	123.5	143.6	119.3	123.5	129.8	131.1	111.5	121.8	121.6	112.5
Oct	130.3	122.5	124.4	144.8	120.3	124.6	130.7	132.2	111.8	121.9	122.6	113.2
Nov	130.0	123.4	124.6	143.8	121.1	123.7	130.4	131.7	114.5	122.4	122.7	113.8
Dec	129.9	124.1	125.1	143.8	121.1	122.4	130.2	131.4	119.2	122.6	122.6	114.1
1991 Jan	130.2	124.9	126.0	144.2	118.6	122.8	130.4	131.6	121.2	123.1	122.7	110.7
Feb	130.9	126.2	126.8	145.0	119.7	123.1	131.1	132.2	125.9	124.0	123.5	111.8
Mar	131.4	126.4	127.3	145.5	120.9	123.6	131.6	132.8	124.4	124.4	123.9	113.0
Apr	133.1	128.5	136.9	141.7	123.6	127.5	133.3	134.5	125.6	125.8	127.6	115.2
May	133.5	128.6	137.9	141.5	124.2	128.9	133.8	135.1	122.5	126.2	128.5	116.0
Jun	134.1	129.8	138.4	141.7	124.6	129.4	134.3	135.5	126.0	127.1	129.3	116.1
Jul	133.8	128.8	139.1	141.0	122.3	130.6	134.2	135.4	117.3	126.8	129.2	113.2
Aug	134.1	129.7	139.6	140.9	122.7	130.9	134.4	135.6	121.6	127.3	129.8	113.9
Sep	134.6	129.1	140.0	141.3	125.6	131.6	135.2	136.4	114.9	127.4	130.4	116.2
Oct	135.1	129.4	140.3	141.0	126.7	132.8	135.6	136.9	116.1	127.4	131.1	116.9
Nov	135.6	130.4	140.8	141.3	127.0	133.1	135.9	137.3	121.3	127.8	131.7	117.3
Dec	135.7	130.9	141.0	141.6	127.0	132.9	136.0	137.4	122.7	128.0	131.8	117.6
1992 Jan	135.6	131.9	141.8	141.7	123.5	132.9	135.9	137.1	125.2	129.0	131.6	113.2
Feb	136.3	132.6	142.3	142.2	124.7	133.7	136.6	137.8	126.0	129.7	132.3	114.4
Mar	136.7	133.0	142.7	141.9	126.1	134.6	137.0	138.2	124.8	130.2	133.0	115.7
Apr	138.8	132.8	146.6	144.8	127.3	136.9	139.2	140.7	122.4	130.1	134.4	116.2
May	139.3	133.4	147.3	145.1	127.5	137.5	139.7	141.2	120.9	131.0	134.9	116.4
Jun	139.3	133.1	147.6	145.0	127.7	137.8	139.9	141.3	117.4	131.0	135.0	116.4
Jul	138.8	131.9	148.1	145.0	125.0	137.8	139.6	141.1	105.8	130.9	134.3	113.1
Aug	138.9	132.2	148.4	145.2	125.0	137.7	139.7	141.2	107.0	131.1	134.4	113.5
Sep	139.4	132.0	148.7	145.6	128.2	137.7	140.3	141.8	104.0	131.1	134.9	116.0
Oct	139.9	132.4	149.2	145.8	129.3	138.3	140.7	142.3	106.5	131.1	135.5	116.8
Nov	139.7	132.4	149.5	145.1	129.2	138.4	140.5	142.1	106.3	130.9	135.6	116.8

1 Following the recommendation of the Retail Price Index Advisory Committee, the index has been re-referenced to make 13 January, 1987=100. Further details can be found in the April 1987 edition of *Employment Gazette*.
2 Seasonal food is defined as: items of food the prices of which show significant seasonal variations. These are; fresh fruit and vegetables, fresh fish, eggs and home-killed lamb.
3 For the February, March and April 1988 indicies, the weights for seasonal and non-seasonal food were 24 and 139 respectively. Thereafter the weight for home-killed lamb (a seasonal item) was increased by 1 and that for imported lamb (a non-seasonal item) correspondingly reduced by 1 in the light of new information about their relative shares of household expenditure.
4 From December 1989 the Nationalised Industries Index is no longer published. Industries remaining nationalised in December 1989 were coal, electricity, post and rail.

Source: Central Statistical Office

Prices
18.8 Tax and price index

Tax and price index

	January 1978 = 100 BSAA									January 1987 = 100 DQAB					
	1979	1980	1981	1982	1983	1984	1985	1986	1987	1987	1988	1989	1990	1991	1992
January	106.1	123.2	140.4	162.3	170.7	177.9	184.7	192.9	198.0	100.0	101.4	107.1	113.9	123.6	128.1
February	107.2	125.3	141.9	162.4	171.6	178.8	186.4	193.7	..	100.5	101.8	108.0	114.7	124.3	128.8
March	108.2	127.2	144.3	164.0	171.9	179.4	188.4	194.0	..	100.7	102.3	108.5	115.9	124.9	129.3
April	110.5	130.8	151.3	166.0	171.8	178.8	190.2	192.5	..	99.7	101.4	109.8	118.2	125.4	129.6
May	111.6	132.2	152.4	167.4	172.6	179.6	191.2	192.9	..	99.8	101.9	110.5	119.4	125.8	130.2
June	113.8	133.6	153.5	168.0	173.1	180.1	191.7	192.8	..	99.8	102.3	110.9	119.9	126.5	130.2
July	113.8	134.9	154.2	169.0	174.2	179.9	191.3	192.1	..	99.7	102.4	111.1	120.0	126.2	129.6
August	114.9	135.3	155.5	169.0	175.1	181.8	191.8	192.9	..	100.0	103.7	111.4	121.4	126.5	129.7
September	116.2	136.3	156.6	168.9	176.0	182.2	191.7	194.0	..	100.4	104.3	112.2	122.7	127.0	130.3
October	117.6	137.3	158.2	169.9	176.7	183.5	191.4	194.3	..	100.9	105.4	111.7	123.8	127.5	130.8
November	118.8	138.5	160.1	170.9	177.5	184.1	192.1	196.3	..	101.5	106.0	112.8	123.4	128.1	130.6
December	119.8	139.4	161.2	170.5	178.0	183.9	192.4	197.1	..	101.4	106.3	113.1	123.3	128.2	130.1

	Retail price index: January 1974 = 100 CBAB									January 1987 = 100 CHAW					
	1979	1980	1981	1982	1983	1984	1985	1986	1987	1987	1988	1989	1990	1991	1992
January	207.2	245.3	277.3	310.6	325.9	342.6	359.8	379.7	394.5	100.0	103.3	111.0	119.5	130.2	135.6
February	208.9	248.8	279.8	310.7	327.3	344.0	362.7	381.1	..	100.4	103.7	111.8	120.2	130.9	136.3
March	210.6	252.2	284.0	313.4	327.9	345.1	366.1	381.6	..	100.6	104.1	112.3	121.4	131.4	136.7
April	214.2	260.8	292.2	319.7	332.5	349.7	373.9	385.3	..	101.8	105.8	114.3	125.1	133.1	138.8
May	215.9	263.2	294.1	322.0	333.9	351.0	375.6	386.0	..	101.9	106.2	115.0	126.2	133.5	139.3
June	219.6	265.7	295.8	322.9	334.7	351.9	376.4	385.8	..	101.9	106.6	115.4	126.7	134.1	139.3
July	229.1	267.9	297.1	323.0	336.5	351.5	375.7	384.7	..	101.8	106.7	115.5	126.8	133.8	138.8
August	230.9	268.5	299.3	323.1	338.0	354.8	376.7	385.9	..	102.1	107.9	115.8	128.1	134.1	138.9
September	233.2	270.2	301.0	322.9	339.5	355.5	376.5	387.8	..	102.4	108.4	116.6	129.3	134.6	139.4
October	235.6	271.9	303.7	324.5	340.7	357.7	377.1	388.4	..	102.9	109.5	117.5	130.3	135.1	139.9
November	237.7	274.1	306.9	326.1	341.9	358.8	378.4	391.7	..	103.4	110.0	118.5	130.0	135.6	139.7
December	239.4	275.6	308.8	325.5	342.8	358.5	378.9	393.0	..	103.3	110.3	118.8	129.9	135.7	139.2

	Percentage changes on one year earlier														
	1979	1980	1981	1982	1983	1984	1985	1986	1987	1987	1988	1989	1990	1991	1992

Tax and price index

January	6.1	16.1	14.0	15.6	5.2	4.2	3.8	4.4	2.6		1.4	5.6	6.3	8.5	3.6
February	6.5	16.9	13.2	14.4	5.7	4.2	4.3	3.9	..	2.7	1.3	6.1	6.2	8.4	3.6
March	6.6	17.6	13.4	13.7	4.8	4.4	5.0	3.0	..	2.8	1.6	6.1	6.8	7.8	3.5
April	12.3	18.4	15.7	9.7	3.5	4.1	6.4	1.2	..	2.5	1.7	8.3	7.7	6.1	3.3
May	12.6	18.5	15.3	9.8	3.1	4.1	6.5	0.9	..	2.4	2.1	8.4	8.1	5.4	3.5
June	13.8	17.4	14.9	9.4	3.0	4.0	6.4	0.6	..	2.5	2.5	8.4	8.1	5.5	2.9
July	13.2	18.5	14.3	9.6	3.1	3.3	6.3	0.4	..	2.8	2.7	8.5	8.0	5.2	2.7
August	13.4	17.8	14.9	8.7	3.6	3.8	5.5	0.6	..	2.6	3.7	7.4	9.0	4.2	2.5
September	14.1	17.3	14.9	7.9	4.2	3.5	5.2	1.2	..	2.5	3.9	7.6	9.4	3.5	2.6
October	14.8	16.8	15.2	7.4	4.0	3.8	4.3	1.5	..	2.8	4.5	6.0	10.8	3.0	2.6
November	15.1	16.6	15.6	6.7	3.9	3.7	4.3	2.2	..	2.4	4.4	6.4	9.4	3.8	2.0
December	14.9	16.4	15.6	5.8	4.4	3.3	4.6	2.4	..	1.9	4.8	6.4	9.0	4.0	1.5

Retail prices index

January	9.3	18.4	13.0	12.0	4.9	5.1	5.0	5.5	3.9		3.3	7.5	7.7	9.0	4.1
February	9.6	19.1	12.5	11.0	5.3	5.1	5.4	5.1	..	3.9	3.3	7.8	7.5	8.9	4.1
March	9.8	19.8	12.6	10.4	4.6	5.2	6.1	4.2	..	4.0	3.5	7.9	8.1	8.2	4.0
April	10.1	21.8	12.0	9.4	4.0	5.2	6.9	3.0	..	4.2	3.9	8.0	9.4	6.4	4.3
May	10.3	21.9	11.7	9.5	3.7	5.1	7.0	2.8	..	4.1	4.2	8.3	9.7	5.8	4.3
June	11.4	21.0	11.3	9.2	3.7	5.1	7.0	2.5	..	4.2	4.6	8.3	9.8	5.8	3.9
July	15.6	16.9	10.9	8.7	4.2	4.5	6.9	2.4	..	4.4	4.8	8.2	9.8	5.5	3.7
August	15.8	16.3	11.5	8.0	4.6	5.0	6.2	2.4	..	4.4	5.7	7.3	10.6	4.7	3.6
September	16.5	15.9	11.4	7.3	5.1	4.7	5.9	3.0	..	4.2	5.9	7.6	10.9	4.1	3.6
October	17.2	15.4	11.7	6.8	5.0	5.0	5.4	3.0	..	4.5	6.4	7.3	10.9	3.7	3.6
November	17.4	15.3	12.0	6.3	4.8	4.9	5.5	3.5	..	4.1	6.4	7.7	9.7	4.3	3.0
December	17.2	15.1	12.0	5.4	5.3	4.6	5.7	3.7	..	3.7	6.8	7.7	9.3	4.5	2.6

Note: The purpose and methodology of the Tax and price index were described in an article in the August 1979 issue of *Economic Trends* and in the September *Economic Progress Report* published by the Treasury. The purpose is to produce a single index which measures changes in both direct taxes (including national insurance contributions) and in retail prices for a representative cross-section of taxpayers. Thus, while the Retail prices index may be used to measure changes in the purchasing power of after-tax income (and of the income of non-taxpayers) the Tax and price index takes account of the fact that taxpayers will have more or less to spend according to changes in direct taxation. The index measures the change in gross taxable income which would maintain after tax-income in real terms.

The months April, May and June for the years 1979 and 1980 are affected by the late timing of the 1979 Budget.

Source: Central Statistical Office

Prices

18.9 Index of purchase prices of the means of agricultural production
United Kingdom; Annual averages

1985=100

		Weights	1982	1983	1984	1985	1986	1987	1988	1989	1990	1991
Goods and services currently consumed	BYEA	100	88.9	95.1	98.7	100.0	98.3	132.9	103.3	109.0	113.4	117.6
Seeds	BYEB	3.9	108.7	116.6	122.2	100.0	92.5	113.0	100.7	96.7	102.8	109.0
Animals for rearing and production	BYEC	1.1	78.5	92.1	101.4	100.0	98.8	188.0	111.9	116.1	116.5	109.5
Energy, lubricants	BYED	9.6	81.2	89.3	91.6	100.0	98.8	142.2	73.7	78.0	90.7	95.8
Fuels for heating	KVBA	1.6	75.8	86.4	92.2	100.0	65.0	63.1	54.5	64.0	73.7	72.4
Motor fuel	KVBB	5.5	76.9	86.2	88.8	100.0	73.7	71.7	65.8	74.3	85.2	87.0
Electricity	KVBC	2.1	97.7	101.4	100.3	100.0	102.6	101.5	106.0	113.2	115.0	132.3
Lubricants	KVBD	0.4	80.3	84.3	90.1	100.0	95.5	95.2	92.5	95.9	108.6	122.3
Fertilisers and soil improvers	BYEE	13.8	90.4	91.5	94.1	100.0	90.4	105.6	85.4	92.4	94.1	91.0
Straight fertilisers	KVBE	5.7	89.6	92.7	95.1	100.0	85.4	77.2	84.2	90.0	91.1	85.7
Compound fertilisers	KVBF	7.1	90.7	90.0	93.0	100.0	91.9	82.9	81.6	89.8	90.5	88.8
Lime	KVBG	1.0	92.7	97.0	97.2	100.0	109.1	115.8	119.5	125.2	138.0	138.8
Plant protection products	BYEF	4.8	92.3	93.0	95.8	100.0	102.6	129.1	110.4	115.2	126.8	141.5
Animal feedingstuffs	BYEG	41.0	92.9	100.9	103.6	100.0	101.2	124.0	106.9	112.7	113.6	115.7
Straight feedingstuffs	KVBH	12.3	91.9	99.8	101.1	100.0	105.1	106.1	109.6	112.9	113.5	118.5
Wheat	KVBI	3.3	93.1	102.0	101.4	100.0	103.4	110.4	106.9	110.2	114.6	126.8
Whole barley	KVBJ	3.1	91.2	98.4	100.6	100.0	112.2	114.6	112.2	116.1	120.7	130.2
Flaked maize	KVBK	0.1	93.9	97.8	99.5	100.0	101.2	104.0	100.1	100.0	105.6	122.3
Whole oats	KVBL	0.3	..	..	..	100.0	100.1	119.9	119.7	111.4	120.1	123.0
Oilcake	KVBM	2.9	90.0	98.6	102.4	100.0	100.9	88.9	106.1	116.6	106.7	104.0
White fish meal	KVBN	0.5	88.8	100.3	104.0	100.0	105.7	103.3	126.2	123.2	117.3	113.5
Sugar beet pulp	KVBO	2.0	93.9	100.8	103.2	100.0	103.4	108.6	109.8	105.3	108.3	107.7
Compound feedingstuffs for:	KVBP	28.6	93.2	101.2	104.4	100.0	99.5	99.2	105.7	112.6	113.6	114.5
Calves	KVBQ	1.2	97.6	104.1	104.2	100.0	99.0	100.6	106.3	116.2	120.7	121.2
Cattle	KVBR	10.1	95.6	103.9	106.2	100.0	98.8	97.6	101.6	108.3	109.9	108.2
Pigs	KVBS	6.1	92.0	99.3	103.3	100.0	99.7	100.0	107.4	114.0	115.3	119.2
Poultry	KVBT	9.8	90.7	98.9	102.7	100.0	100.1	99.5	108.8	116.1	115.2	117.8
Sheep	KVBU	1.3	97.8	104.4	109.1	100.0	98.8	104.1	105.3	110.8	115.1	110.6
Material and small tools	BYEH	3.6	84.8	88.6	93.9	100.0	103.8	143.8	114.9	121.6	130.4	139.7
Maintenance and repair of plant	BYEI	7.2	78.1	84.5	91.6	100.0	106.1	169.2	117.7	124.5	136.2	150.6
Maintenance and repair of buildings	BYEJ	4.2	82.3	88.0	93.6	100.0	105.2	161.3	113.2	123.4	129.6	133.6
Veterinary services	BYEK	2.1	86.6	90.9	95.4	100.0	106.6	159.8	112.3	116.1	122.2	127.9
General expenses	BYEL	8.7	84.1	88.9	94.2	100.0	104.9	174.0	119.6	126.4	129.2	138.0
Goods and services contributing to investment in agriculture	BYEM	100	84.0	88.9	94.6	100.0	104.9	154.5	120.8	128.9	131.4	139.3
Machinery and other equipment	BYEN	57.8	84.5	88.8	94.4	100.0	105.2	148.7	116.1	122.9	129.0	136.9
Machinery and plant for cultivation	KVBV	7.8	88.2	90.5	93.7	100.0	112.1	115.5	123.1	133.9	142.5	156.3
Machinery and plant for harvesting	KVBW	13.5	84.1	91.6	97.0	100.0	103.2	109.3	115.4	122.7	128.0	135.8
Farm machinery and installations	KVBX	10.2	91.0	90.8	94.5	100.0	103.2	108.2	113.3	123.4	130.0	138.2
Tractors	KVBY	16.8	79.1	85.5	93.3	100.0	105.8	108.4	113.6	117.1	122.7	128.2
Other vehicles	KVBZ	9.4	83.8	87.5	93.1	100.0	103.8	111.8	118.8	124.2	129.5	136.5
Buildings	BYEO	42.2	83.3	89.2	95.1	100.0	104.5	164.8	127.2	137.0	134.7	142.6
Farm buildings	KVCA	22.5	82.2	88.0	93.6	100.0	104.2	108.7	114.5	122.5	129.9	136.6
Engineering and soil improvement operations	KVCB	19.7	84.9	91.2	97.4	100.0	105.0	111.1	118.0	130.5	140.2	149.5

The movement of Price Indices between 1985 and 1988 differ from those published previously because of the different selection of indicators and weighting patterns.

Source: Ministry of Agriculture, Fisheries and Food.

Prices

18.10 Index of producer prices of agricultural products
United Kingdom: Annual averages

1985=100

		Weights	1981	1982	1983	1984	1985	1986	1987	1988	1989	1990	1991
All products	BYEP	100	89.4	96.5	101.5	101.6	100.0	102.3	104.2	103.5	111.8	113.3	112.0
All crop poducts	BYEQ	37.4	92.7	99.8	113.0	108.8	100.0	106.4	107.7	101.0	107.8	113.8	115.6
Cereals	BYER	19.9	95.3	102.5	113.6	105.0	100.0	100.4	98.9	96.2	97.2	98.8	104.1
Wheat for:													
breadmaking	KVDA	4.4	..	..	..	..	100.0	101.0	101.5	96.1	92.2	93.4	104.1
other milling	KVDB	0.5	94.1	98.5	109.4	100.2	100.0	98.8	98.4	94.7	94.6	96.6	105.5
feeding	KVDC	7.5	98.6	103.6	115.0	104.4	100.0	99.5	96.8	94.9	96.9	99.7	104.3
Barley for:													
feeding	KVDD	5.0	93.2	100.7	110.5	105.2	100.0	99.9	95.2	93.4	96.4	98.3	102.1
malting	KVDE	2.3	93.6	106.1	117.9	108.6	100.0	104.1	107.4	105.7	109.5	106.5	107.2
Oats for:													
milling	KVDF	0.1	99.1	102.8	115.8	123.4	100.0	96.1	114.3	107.8	99.1	105.1	107.5
feeding	KVDG	0.1	96.5	100.4	113.0	124.6	100.0	98.3	113.0	105.2	98.3	104.6	106.2
Root crops	BYES	4.9	116.2	132.2	161.3	157.1	100.0	147.9	152.9	121.0	155.9	171.6	169.5
Potatoes:													
early	KVDH	0.3	166.1	128.1	152.6	217.2	100.0	142.5	156.9	129.3	176.3	101.3	227.6
main crop	KVDI	2.5	130.7	158.8	213.6	196.8	100.0	184.0	196.2	137.6	195.0	230.6	202.1
Sugar beet	KVDJ	2.0	93.0	102.8	103.2	104.0	100.0	104.1	98.5	99.0	104.0	110.5	118.9
Fresh vegetables	BYET	6.4	78.2	80.4	94.0	92.6	100.0	93.5	104.6	100.3	101.9	112.5	112.8
Cauliflowers	KVDK	0.6	78.6	77.2	86.4	82.2	100.0	65.6	86.6	71.2	78.7	84.0	93.6
Lettuce	KVDL	0.6	78.5	76.3	100.5	92.2	100.0	100.4	121.6	105.5	110.0	114.0	111.6
Tomatoes	KVDM	0.5	93.8	86.2	106.9	109.6	100.0	101.8	112.8	113.7	110.9	111.0	98.6
Carrots	KVDN	0.4	84.0	73.2	89.4	87.3	100.0	84.7	106.5	106.7	92.5	126.5	131.6
Cabbage	KVDO	0.6	64.1	84.4	93.2	86.1	100.0	89.4	101.4	105.3	105.8	120.4	122.8
Beans	KVDP	0.3	74.6	78.4	100.8	89.0	100.0	96.1	125.5	111.3	106.7	125.6	117.2
Onions	KVDQ	0.5	82.2	82.2	102.1	112.4	100.0	94.3	121.4	94.3	100.1	131.3	117.6
Mushrooms	KVDR	0.9	86.3	94.6	97.3	100.9	100.0	101.7	101.6	104.2	98.2	103.1	107.4
Fresh fruit	BYEU	1.9	82.7	87.3	93.4	94.4	100.0	117.5	108.3	114.2	120.1	137.0	136.0
Dessert apples	KVDS	0.5	87.0	88.4	90.9	95.8	100.0	110.5	96.3	111.4	108.4	136.7	155.3
Dessert pears	KVDT	0.1	83.3	100.1	99.0	97.1	100.0	110.0	100.9	97.1	125.2	157.6	143.0
Cooking apples	KVDU	0.3	96.2	93.9	93.6	100.4	100.0	117.5	107.3	130.2	107.1	144.1	146.2
Strawberries	KVDV	0.5	72.1	89.5	101.7	94.8	100.0	108.0	100.5	104.6	106.6	99.4	103.7
Raspberries	KVDW	0.2	60.5	65.5	82.1	86.0	100.0	161.1	158.5	126.7	145.2	141.3	118.9
Seeds	BYEV	1.0	109.5	118.3	118.5	135.4	100.0	109.7	124.3	115.2	125.4	131.9	125.9
Flowers and plants	BYEW	1.1	72.4	77.7	82.9	85.7	100.0	99.2	105.5	110.0	108.3	105.8	107.2
Other crop products	BYEX	2.2	91.4	97.6	110.9	109.1	100.0	99.7	88.4	78.8	95.7	102.2	90.5
Animals and animal products	BYEY	62.6	87.9	94.9	95.9	98.1	100.0	99.8	102.2	105.5	114.2	113.0	109.8
Animals for slaughter	BYEZ	36.9	88.4	95.6	97.2	100.2	100.0	99.8	100.4	103.3	112.0	108.2	102.9
Calves	KVDX	0.2	..	..	..	..	100.0	106.7	126.0	160.8	168.1	119.1	110.1
Clean cattle	KVDY	13.4	86.3	95.3	100.9	100.9	100.0	99.8	101.5	114.4	120.4	112.3	112.9
Cows and bulls	KVDZ	3.5	96.1	104.5	99.3	94.3	100.0	93.1	96.3	113.7	118.0	102.9	100.2
Clean pigs	KVEA	8.1	91.4	94.3	89.9	104.9	100.0	96.2	95.0	88.7	110.1	109.7	100.3
Sows and boars	KVEB	0.3	89.3	102.0	84.9	102.5	100.0	96.7	85.7	82.4	113.2	101.0	104.3
Sheep	KVEC	4.9	83.9	94.2	100.7	94.5	100.0	109.3	112.5	101.2	105.1	99.7	83.8
Ewe and ram	KVED	0.4	80.8	89.1	82.0	86.0	100.0	96.8	94.5	105.3	92.5	77.3	67.7
Poultry	KVEE	6.1	85.6	93.6	96.6	98.5	100.0	101.1	98.3	93.4	98.1	109.0	103.2
Chickens	KVEF	4.5	88.9	95.8	98.8	102.2	100.0	99.5	97.9	93.1	98.7	104.8	96.5
Turkeys	KVEG	1.4	77.2	88.0	90.9	88.6	100.0	105.7	98.0	92.6	93.6	121.0	122.0
Cows milk	BYFA	21.0	84.3	92.0	94.3	93.0	100.0	103.5	107.5	115.2	122.7	123.3	125.9
Eggs	BYFB	4.3	101.9	103.4	92.3	106.5	100.0	81.5	94.1	77.5	93.2	106.3	93.0
Other animal products:													
Wool (clip)	BYFC	0.4	88.2	88.0	88.7	92.7	100.0	100.4	99.3	98.9	98.0	93.7	85.7

The movement of Price Indices between 1985 and 1988 differ from those published previously because of the different selection of indicators and weighting patterns.

Source: Ministry of Agriculture, Fisheries and Food

Prices

18.11 Commodity price trends[1]
United Kingdom
Calendar years

			1981	1982	1983	1984	1985	1986	1987	1988	1989	1990	1991
Wheat £ per tonne	KVAA	Average ex-farm price[2]	108.9	113.7	124.7	114.6	112.3	111.1	112.5	105.2	104.9	109.9	116.6
Barley £ per tonne	KVAB	Average ex-farm price[2]	100.5	108.7	119.3	112.4	106.1	105.8	105.5	103.7	106.7	108.8	108.9
Oats £ per tonne	KVAC	Average ex-farm price[2]	97.4	101.2	113.2	123.0	99.2	101.1	115.4	106.5	98.7	106.1	107.4
Rye £ per tonne	KVAD	Average ex-farm price[2]	101.0	108.4	120.7	117.2	110.5	110.6	110.2	108.2	106.8	114.6	118.5
Hops £ per tonne	KVAE	Average farm-gate price	2 636	2 740	3 140	3 306	2 297	2 233	2 299	2 417	2 395	2 400	2 400
Potatoes £ per tonne	KVAF	Average farm-gate price[3]	63.1	78.2	81.9	102.2	48.2	72.8	85.5	67.9	84.4	88.7	90.1
Sugar beet £ per tonne	KVAG	Producer price[4]	27.74	27.15	31.06	30.71	32.81	30.91	30.74	29.65	30.95	31.20	34.43
Oilseed rape	KVAH	Average market price[5]	255	270	310	275	274	284	221	232	286	280	248
Apples £ per tonne		Average market price[6]											
	KVAI	Dessert	335	301	363	369	379	391	368	424	383	500	592
	KVAJ	Culinary	270	279	280	318	299	327	316	385	286	408	..
Pears £ per tonne	KVAK	Average market price[6]	281	331	315	314	325	352	326	321	402	485	468
Tomatoes £ per tonne	KVAL	Average market price[6]	475	466	632	560	502	601	684	571	559	694	604
Cauliflowers £ per tonne	KVAM	Average market price[6]	207	214	243	217	268	203	275	247	257	296	292
Cattle (rearing) £ per head	KVAN	1st quality Hereford/cross bull calves[7,14]	108.0	125.0	124.0	124.0	130.0	133.0	134.0	186.0	188.0	128.5	120.0
	KVAO	1st quality beef/cross yearling steers[14]	275	313	326	330	343	347	360	414	431	395	397
Cattle (fat) p per kg liveweight	KVAP	Clean cattle[8]	88.7	98.3	95.9	95.9	92.7	94.4	96.1	109.2	113.9	101.2	106.9
Sheep (store) £ per head	KVAQ	1st quality lambs, hoggets and tegs[7]	30.2	33.0	33.4	35.3	36.4	36.7	37.5	37.5	38.5	38.4	32.7
Sheep (fat)[9] p per kg estimated dressed carcase weight	KVAR		153.3	152.7[12]	146.5	166.5	167.1	175.3	196.7	177.0	184.5	174.4	143.4
	KVAS		..	173.0[13]	180.5	179.3	177.5	200.1	213.7	208.0	202.5	170.9	179.3
Pigs £ per kg deadweight	KVAT	Average market price clean pigs	93.7	97.1	92.6	107.7	102.8	98.1	97.7	91.0	113.0	113.0	103.0
Broilers p per kg	KVAU	Average wholesale price	91.6	92.8	99.5	104.2	98.9	99.7	98.1	96.2	106.0	121.3	103.7
Milk p per litre	KVAV	Average net return to producers[10]	13.79	14.81	15.02	14.99	15.57	16.07	16.43	17.72	19.16	19.29	19.54
Eggs p per dozen	KVAW	Average producer price[11]	40.7	38.8	35.7	44.7	40.0	32.6	36.6	31.1	37.1	42.6	36.6
Wool p per kg	KHWQ	Average producer price for clip paid to producers by the British Wool Marketing Board	89.50	89.20	90.00	94.00	100.00	97.70	97.40	96.90	95.30	91.04	..

1 This table gives indications of the movement in commodity prices at the first point of sale. The series do not always show to al receipts by farmers; for some commodities additional premiums or deficiency payments are made to achieve support price levels.
2 Weighted average ex-farm prices of United Kingdom cereals.
3 Weighted average price paid to growers for early and main crop potatoes in the United Kingdom.
4 Returns to growers figures.
5 Typical contract price adjusted to delivered basis and 40 per cent oil content.
6 Weighted average wholesale prices for England and Wales. From 1982, for England only.
7 Average prices at representative markets in England and Wales.
8 Based on Meat and Livestock Commission all clean cattle prices.
9 UK weighted average market price for animals certified under the Fat Sheep Guarantee Scheme/Sheep Variable Premium Scheme.
10 Derived by dividing total value of output by the total quantity of output available for human consumption.
11 Average price of all Class A eggs weighted according to quantity in each grade.
12 Great Britain weighted average market price for animals certified under the Sheep Variable Premium Scheme from 1982.
13 Northern Ireland unweighted average market price for clean sheep from 1982.
14 Category change 1988: formerly 1st quality yearling steers beef/dairy cross, now consists of Hereford/cross, Charolais/cross, Limousin/cross, Simmental/cross, Belgian/cross, other continental cross, other beef/dairy cross, other beef/beef cross.

Source: Ministry of Agriculture, Fisheries and Food

Units of measurement

Length
1 millimetre (mm)		= 0.039 370 1 inch
1 centimetre (cm)	= 10 millimetres	= 0.393 701 inch
1 metre (m)	= 1 000 millimetres	= 1.093 61 yards
1 kilometre (km)	= 1 000 metres	= 0.621 371 mile
1 inch (in)		= 25.4 millimetres or 2.54 centimetres
1 foot (ft)	= 12 inches	= 0.304 8 metre
1 yard (yd)	= 3 feet	= 0.914 4 metre
1 mile	= 1 760 yards	= 1.609 34 kilometres

Area
1 square millimetre (mm²)		= 0.001 55 square inch
1 square metre (m²)	= one million square millimetres	= 1.195 99 square yards
1 hectare (ha)	= 10 000 square metres	= 2.471 05 acres
1 square kilometre (km²)	= one million square metres	= 247.105 acres
1 square inch (sq in)		= 645.16 square millimetres or 6.451 6 square centimetres
1 square foot (sq ft)	= 144 square inches	= 0.092 903 square metre or 929.03 square centimetres
1 square yard (sq yd)	= 9 square feet	= 0.836 127 square metre
1 acre	= 4 840 square yards	= 4.046.86 square metres or 0.404 686 hectare
1 square mile (sq mile)	= 640 acres	= 2.589 99 square kilometres or 258.999 hectares

Volume
1 cubic centimetre (cm³)		= 0.061 023 7 cubic inch
1 cubic decimetre (dm³)	= 1 000 cubic centimetres	= 0.035 314 7 cubic foot
1 cubic metre (m³)	= one million cubic centimetres	= 1.307 95 cubic yards
1 cubic foot (cu ft)		= 0.028 316 8 cubic metre or 28.316 8 cubic decimetres
1 cubic yard (cu yd)	= 27 cubic feet	= 0.764 555 cubic metre

Capacity
1 litre (l)	= 1 cubic decimetre	= 0.220 gallon
1 hectolitre (hl)	= 100 litres	= 22.0 gallons
1 pint		= 0.568 litre
2 pints	= 1 quart	= 1.137 litres
8 pints	= 1 gallon	= 4.546 09 cubic decimetres or 4.546 litres
36 gallons (gal)	= 1 bulk barrel	= 1.636 56 hectolitres

Weight
1 gram (g)		= 0.035 274 0 ounce
1 hectogram (hg)	= 100 grams	= 3.527 4 ounces or 0.220 462 pound
1 kilogram (kg)	= 1 000 grams or 10 hectograms	= 2.204 62 pounds
1 tonne (t)	= 1 000 kilograms	= 1.102 31 short tons or 0.984 2 long ton
1 ounce avoirdupois (oz)		= 28.349 5 grams
1 pound avoirdupois (lb)	= 16 ounces	= 0.453 592 37 kilogram
1 hundredweight (cwt)	= 112 pounds	= 50.802 3 kilograms
1 short ton	= 2 000 pounds	= 907.184 74 kilograms or 0.907 184 74 tonne
1 long ton (referred to as ton)	= 2 240 pounds	= 1 016.05 kilograms or 1.016 05 tonnes
1 ounce troy	= 480 grains	= 31.103 5 grams

Energy
	British thermal unit (Btu)	= 0.252 kilocalorie (kcal) = 1.05 506 kilojoule (kj)
	Therm	= 100 000 British thermal units = 25 200 kcal = 105 506 kj
	Megawatt (Mw)	= 10⁶ watts
	Gigawatt hour (GWh)	= 10⁶ kilowatt hours = 34 121 therms

Food and drink
	Butter	23 310 litres milk = 1 tonne butter (average)
	Cheese	10 070 litres milk = 1 tonne cheese
	Condensed milk	2 550 litres milk = 1 tonne full cream condensed milk
		2 953 litres skimmed milk = 1 tonne skimmed condensed milk
	Milk	1 million litres = 1 030 tonnes
	Milk powder	8 054 litres milk = 1 tonne full cream milk powder
		10 740 litres skimmed milk =1 tonne skimmed milk powder
	Eggs	17 126 eggs = 1 tonne (approximate)
	Sugar	100 tonnes raw sugar = 95 tonnes refined sugar
	Beer	1 bulk barrel = 36 gallons irrespective of gravity

Shipping
	Gross tonnage	= The total volume of all the enclosed spaces of a vessel, the unit of measurement being a ton of 100 cubic feet.
	Deadweight tonnage	= Deadweight tonnage is the total weight in tons of 2 240 lb that a ship can legally carry, that is the total weight of cargo, bunkers, stores and crew.

Index of sources

This index of sources gives the titles of official publications or other sources containing statistics allied to those in the tables of this *Annual Abstract*. These publications provide more detailed analyses than are shown in the *Abstract*. This index includes publications to which reference should be made for short-term (monthly or quarterly) series. No entry is made in this index for items where the data have been obtained from departmental records. Further advice on published statistical sources is available from the CSO Library.
Telephone 0633 812973.

Subject	Table number in *Abstract*	Government department or other organisation	Official publication or other source
1. Area and climate			
Area	1.1	Ordnance Survey	Central Statistical Office: Regional Trends
	1.2	Meterological Office	Central Statistical Office: Monthly Digest of Statistics
2. Population and vital statistics			
Population census	2.1-2.3, 2.8	Office of Population Censuses and Surveys	*England and Wales*: Census reports 1911, 1921, 1931, 1951, 1961, 1971 and 1981 Sample census 1966; Registrar General's statistical review of England and Wales, Part II, Tables Census 1971, Great Britain, Summary tables Census 1981, National Report, Great Britain Part 1 Census 1981, Key statistics for urban areas: Great Britain Digest of Welsh Statistics (annual)
		General Register Office for Scotland	*Scotland*: Census reports 1951, 1961, 1971 and 1981 Sample census 1966 Census 1971 Census 1981 Key statistics for urban areas: Scotland
		General Register Office (Northern Ireland)	*Northern Ireland*: Census of population 1951, 1961, 1966 and 1971 The Northern Ireland Census 1981. Summary Report
Mid-year estimates	2.1, 2.2, 2.5, 2.7, 2.9	Office of Population Censuses and Surveys	*England and Wales*: Series FM (Family statistics), DH (Deaths), MB (Morbidity), PP (Population estimates and projections), MN (Migration) and VS (Key population and vital statistics) Series PP1, Population estimates: The Registrar General's estimates of the population of regions and local government areas of England and Wales Population Trends (quarterly)
		General Register Office for Scotland	*Scotland*: Registrar General Scotland, Annual Report Quarterly return of births, deaths and marriages Annual estimate of the population of Scotland
		General Register Office (Northern Ireland)	*Northern Ireland*: Annual report of the Registrar General Quarterly return of births, deaths and marriages
Projections	2.1, 2.2, 2.5	Office of Population Censuses and Surveys	Series PP2, Population projections - national figures
Migration	2.10, 2.11	Office of Population Censuses and Surveys	Series MN (Migration) Population Trends (quarterly)
	2.12	Home Office	Control of immigration statistics United Kingdom (annual)
Vital statistics	2.13, 2.14, 2.16-2.22	Office of Population Censuses and Surveys	*England and Wales*: Series FM (Family statistics), DH (Deaths), MB (Morbidity), PP (Population estimates and projections), MN (Migration) and VS (Key population and vital statistics) Population Trends (quarterly)
		General Register Office for Scotland	*Scotland*: Registrar General Scotland, Annual Report Quarterly return of births, deaths and marriages
		General Register Office (Northern Ireland)	*Northern Ireland*: Annual report of the Registrar General Quarterly return of births, deaths and marriages
	2.15	Lord Chancellor's Department	Judicial statistics, England and Wales (annual)
		Scottish Courts Administration Northern Ireland Court Service	Judicial statistics, Scotland; Civil judicial statistics (annual)
	2.23	Government Actuary's Department	*England and Wales*: 1986-88 Interim Life Table *Scotland*: Interim Life Table: 1986-88 *Northern Ireland*: Annual Report of the Registrar General

Index of sources

Subject	Table number in *Abstract*	Government department or other organisation	Official publication or other source
3. Social conditions			
Social services	3.1-3.6	Central Statistical Office Department of Education and Science	Appropriation Accounts (annual) Northern Ireland Annual Abstract of Statistics
	3.7, 3.8, 3.9, 3.10	Department of the Environment	Housing and Construction Statistics (quarterly) Housing return for Scotland (quarterly)
	3.10	Department of the Environment	Housing and Construction Statistics (quarterly) Welsh Office: Welsh Housing Statistics (annual)
		Scottish Development Department	Housing return for Scotland (quarterly)
		Department of the Environment for Northern Ireland	Northern Ireland Housing Statistics (annual)
Social security pensions, benefits and allowances	3.11, 3.12, 3.14, 3.15	Department of Social Security Department of Health and Social Services, Northern Ireland	National Insurance Fund Account (annual) Northern Ireland National Insurance Fund Account (annual)
	3.13 3.15-3.27	Department of Social Security Department of Health and Social Services Northern Ireland	Social Security Statistics (annual) Health and Personal Social Services Statistics for England (annual) Welsh Office: Health and Personal Social Services Statistics for Wales (annual)
National health service	3.27	Department of Health Welsh Office	Appropriation Accounts (annual) Health and Personal Social Services Statistics for England (annual) Health and Personal Social Services Statistics for Wales (annual)
	3.28	Scottish Health Service, Common Services Agency	
	3.29	Department of Health and Social Services, Northern Ireland	Summary of Health and Personal Social Services Accounts (annual)
	3.30-3.31	Department of Health	Health and Personal Social Services Statistics for England (annual)
Public health	3.32	Office of Population Censuses and Surveys	Communicable Disease Statistics Series MB2 (annual) Population Trends (quarterly)
		Scottish Health Service, Common Services Agency	Scottish Health Statistics (annual)
		General Register Office (Northern Ireland)	Annual report of the Registrar General Northern Ireland: Quarterly return of births, deaths and marriages
	3.33-3.35	Health and Safety Executive DSS	Health and Safety statistics (published as an annual supplement to Employment Gazette) Department of Energy: Digest of United Kingdom Energy Statistics (annual)
		Department of Transport	Casualties to vessels and accidents to men. Vessels registered in the United Kingdom (annual)
		Department of Transport	Railway safety (annual)
		Civil Aviation Authority	Accidents to aircraft on the British Register
	3.36	Office of Population Censuses and Surveys; General Register Office for Scotland	Census 1981 National Report Great Britain Part II
Elections	3.37	Home Office; Scottish Home and Health Department; Northern Ireland Office	Office of Population Censuses and Surveys Electoral statistics (series EL) Return of election expenses Vachers Parliamentary Companion
	3.38	Home Office	Central Statistical Office: Social Trends

Index of sources

Subject	Table number in *Abstract*	Government department or other organisation	Official publication or other source
4. Law enforcement			
	4.2	Home Departments	*England and Wales*: Report of Her Majesty's Chief Inspector of Constabulary (annual) Scotland: Report of Her Majesty's Chief Inspector of Constabulary for Scotland (annual)
		Northern Ireland Office	*Northern Ireland*: Chief Constable's Report (Royal Ulster Constabulary)
	4.1, 4.3-4.11	Home Office	Central Statistical Office: Monthly Digest of Statistics Criminal statistics, England and Wales (annual) Prison statistics, England and Wales (annual) Welsh Office: Digest of Welsh Statistics (annual) Offences relating to motor vehicles, England and Wales (annual bulletin)
	4.12-4.16	Scottish Office Home and Health Department	Criminal statistics, Scotland (annual)
	4.17, 4.18	Scottish Office Home and Health Department	Prisons in Scotland (annual)
	4.19-4.22	Northern Ireland Office	Chief Constable's Report (Royal Ulster Constabulary)
5. Education			
	5.1-5.12 5.19	Education Departments	Scottish Educational Statistics (annual) Northern Ireland Education Statistics (half-yearly) Education Statistics for the United Kingdom (annual) Northern Ireland Annual Abstract of Statistics Welsh Office: Statistics of Education in Wales (annual)
	5.18	Science & Engineering Research Council The British Library Natural Environment Research Council Department of Education and Science Economic & Social Research Council	
	5.13-5.17	University Funding Council	University statistics (Volumes 1 and 3) (annual) Open University (annual) of Statistics, Students, Staff and Finance
6. Employment			
	6.1, 6.2, 6.4, 6.6, 6.8 6.11, 6.14, 6.17	Department of Employment Department of Economic Development (Northern Ireland)	Employment Gazette (monthly) Central Statistical Office: Monthly Digest of Statistics Welsh Office: Digest of Welsh Statistics (annual)
	6.3	Engineering Industries Training Board	Employment Gazette (monthly) Annual Review of the Engineering Industry Training Board
	6.9	Department of Employment	Northern Ireland Annual Abstract of Statistics
	6.5	Ministry of Agriculture, Fisheries and Foods	Agricultural Statistics, United Kingdom (annual)
	6.7	HM Treasury	Civil Service Statistics (annual) Central Statistical Office: Monthly Digest of Statistics
	6.10	Department of Economic Development (Northern Ireland)	
	6.12	Office of Population Censuses and Surveys	Census 1981, Definitions Great Britain

Index of sources

Subject	Table number in *Abstract*	Government department or other organisation	Official publication or other source
employment (contd)	6.13	Central Statistical Office	Size analyses of United Kingdom Businesses (Business Monitor PA1003)
	6.15-6.19	Department of Employment	Employment Gazette (monthly) New Earnings Survey (annual) Central Statistical Office: Monthly Digest of Statistics
	6.18	Department of Economic Development (Northern Ireland)	New Earnings Survey Northern Ireland (annual) (published in Northern Ireland Annual Abstract of Statistics)
	6.20	Department of Employment	Employment Gazette (monthly)
7. Defence	7.1-7.14	Ministry of Defence	Volume II (Defence Statistics) of the Statement on the Defence Estimates (annual)
8. Production			
Census of production	8.1	Central Statistical Office	Report on the Census of Production (Business Monitor PA 1002) (annual)
Fuel and power	8.2-8.13	Department of Energy	Digest of United Kingdom Energy Statistics (annual) Energy Trends (monthly)
Iron and steel	8.14-8.16	Department of Trade and Industry; Iron and Steel Statistics Bureau	Iron and steel industry: annual statistics published by the British Steel Corporation on behalf of the Iron and Steel Statistics Bureau; Regional Trends (annual)
Industrial materials	8.17	World Bureau of Metal Statistics Department of Trade and Industry Aluminium Federation	World Metal Statistics (monthly)
	8.18-8.26	Central Statistical Office Timber Trade Federation British Coal British man-made fibres Federation Wool Industry Bureau of Statistics Textile Statistics Bureau	Business Monitors (quarterly and annual) Monthly Digest of Statistics
	8.22	Fertiliser Manufacturers' Association	
	8.27	Central Statistical Office	Minerals (Business Monitor PA 1007) Natural Environment Research Council: United Kingdom Minerals Yearbook
		Department of Economic Development (Northern Ireland)	Northern Ireland Annual Abstract of Statistics
Building and construction	8.28	Central Statistical Office; Department of the Environment; World Bureau of Metal Statistics	Business Monitor PA 500 Construction (Annual) Housing and Construction Statistics (quarterly and annual) Monthly Digest of Statistics
	8.29, 8.30	Department of the Environment	Housing and Construction Statistics (quarterly and annual)
Manufactured goods	8.18-8.19	Central Statistical Office	Business Monitor (quarterly and annual) Central Statistical Office: Monthly Digest of Statistics
	8.35, 8.36	HM Customs and Excise	Annual report of the Commissioners of HM Customs and Excise
9. Agriculture, Fisheries and Food			
	9.1, 9.2	Agricultural Departments	Agricultural Statistics: England and Wales (annual) Scotland: Agricultural Statistics (annual)
	9.3-9.5	Agricultural Departments	Agricultural Statistics, United Kingdom (annual) Scottish Agricultural Economics (annual) Welsh Office: Welsh Agricultural Statistics (annual)
	9.6	Forestry Commission	Great Britain: Annual Report and Accounts of the Forestry Commission

Index of sources

Subject	Table number in *Abstract*	Government department or other organisation	Official publication or other source
Agriculture, Fisheries and Food (contd)			
		Department of Agriculture for Northern Ireland	Northern Ireland Annual Abstract of Statistics
Agriculture	9.7-9.8	Agricultural Departments	Employment Gazette (monthly)
Food	9.9-9.12	Ministry of Agriculture, Fisheries and Food	Central Statistical Office: Monthly Digest of Statistics
Fisheries	9.13-9.15	Ministry of Agriculture, Fisheries and Food; Department of Agriculture and Fisheries for Scotland	*England and Wales*: Sea fisheries statistical tables (annual) *Scotland*: Fisheries of Scotland report (annual) Scottish sea fisheries statistical tables (annual)
Food supplies		Ministry of Agriculture, Fisheries and Food	MAFF Food Facts (quarterly)
	9.16	National Food Survey Committee	Annual Report of the National Food Survey Committee: Household Food Consumption and Expenditure

10. Transport and communications

Subject	Table number	Department	Source
Road transport	10.1-10.7, 10.11	Department of Transport	Transport Statistics Great Britain (annual) Central Statistical Office: Monthly Digest of Statistics
	10.12-10.14	Department of Transport	Road accidents in Great Britain Central Statistical Office: Monthly Digest of Statistics Welsh Office: Road accidents Wales (annual)
	10.8, 10.9	Department of the Environment for Northern Ireland	Northern Ireland Annual Abstract of Statistics
Rail transport	10.15-10.18	Department of Transport	Transport Statistics Great Britain (annual)
	10.19	Department of Transport	Health and Safety Executive: Industry and Services (annual)
	10.20, 10.21	Department of the Environment for Northern Ireland	Northern Ireland Annual Abstract of Statistics
Air transport	10.22-10.27	Civil Aviation Authority	Central Statistical Office: Monthly Digest of Statistics Civil Aviation Authority; Annual and Monthly Statistics Accidents to aircraft on the British Register (annual)
Shipping	10.29-10.31	Department of Transport	Central Statistical Office: Monthly Digest of Statistics
	10.32-10.35	Department of Transport	Port Statistics (annual) Transport Statistics Great Britain (annual)
Passenger movement	10.36	Department of Transport Civil Aviation Authority	Central Statistical Office: Monthly Digest of Statistics
Communications	10.37	Home Office Post Office Royal Mail	Central Statistical Office: Monthly Digest of Statistics Post Office report and accounts (annual)

11. Distributive trades and services nes

Subject	Table number	Department	Source
	11.1	Central Statistical Office	Business Monitor SDO 25 1984 Retailing Business Monitor SDA 25 - Retailing. Annual from 1986
	11.2	Central Statistical Office	Business Monitor SDM 28 Retail Sales Index (monthly) Monthly Digest of Statistics
	11.3	Central Statistical Office	Business Monitor SDA 27 Motor Trades
	11.4	Central Statistical Office	Business Monitor SDA 28 Catering and Allied Trades Business Bulletin (annual) Distributive and Service Trades
Scientific research and development	11.5-11.9	Central Statistical Office	Industrial Research and Development Expenditure and Employment Business Monitor MO14: Business Bulletin (annual) Central Statistical Office: Economic Trends, September 1983, August 1984, August 1985, August 1986, August 1988, September 1990, August 1991 and August 1992.

Index of sources

Subject	Table number in *Abstract*	Government department or other organisation	Official publication or other source
12. External trade			
	12.1-12.6	Central Statistical Office	Monthly Review of External Trade Statistics Overseas Trade Statistics of the United Kingdom, monthly Business Monitor MM20; annual supplement Business Monitor MA205 Monthly Digest of statistics
13. Balance of payments			
	13.1-13.3	Central Statistical Office	United Kingdom Balance of Payments (annual) Quarterly figures: Economic Trends
	13.3	Bank of England HM Treasury	United Kingdom Balance of Payments (annual) Quarterly figures: Financial Statistics
Overseas aid	13.4, 13.5	Overseas Development Administration	British Aid Statistics (annual)
14. National income and expenditure			
	14.1-14.5	Central Statistical Office	United Kingdom National Accounts (annual) Monthly Digest of Statistics Economic Trends (monthly)
15. Personal income, expenditure and wealth			
	15.1	Central Statistical Office	Economic Trends, May 1990, March 1991, January 1992
	15.2	Board of Inland Revenue	Inland Revenue Statistics (annual) Central Statistical Office: Economic Trends, November 1987, October 1990
	15.3-15.5	Central Statistical Office	Family Expenditure Survey, (annual) (1990 onwards Edition-Family Spending)
16. Home finance			
Central government	16.1, 16.2	Central Statistical Office	Financial Statistics (monthly)
	16.3-16.8 16.11	HM Treasury Central Statistical Office Bank of England	Consolidated Fund and National Loans Fund Accounts Financial Statistics (monthly)
Saving	16.9	Department for National Savings	Accounts of National Savings Bank Investment Deposit Accounts (annual) Ordinary Deposit Accounts (annual)
Central government	16.10, 16.11	Board of Inland Revenue	Inland Revenue Statistics (annual)
Rateable values	16.12	Board of Inland Revenue	Rates and Rateable values in England and Wales (annual) (Up to 1989)
Local authorities	16.13, 16.14	Department of the Environment	Local government financial statistics (England and Wales)(annual) Welsh Office: Welsh local government financial statistics (annual)
		Public Works Loan Board	Annual report of the Public Works Loan Board
		Scottish Office, Central Statistics Unit	Local financial returns (Scotland) (annual)
	16.15, 16.16	Department of the Environment Welsh Office	Local government financial statistics (England and Wales) (annual)
	16.17	Office of Water Services (OFWAT)	Digest of environmental protection and water statistics (annual) Water Facts (up to 1988-89)
	16.18, 16.19	Department of the Environment Welsh Office	Local government financial statistics (England and Wales) (annual)
	16.20-16.22	Scottish Office, Central Statistics Unit	Local financial returns (Scotland) (annual)
	16.23-16.25	Department of the Environment for Northern Ireland	District Council - Summary of Statment of Accounts (annual)

Index of sources

Subject	Table number in *Abstract*	Government department or other organisation	Official publication or other source
17. Banking, Insurance, etc			
Banking	17.1 17.3-17.6	Bank of England	Bank of England Annual Report and Accounts Bank of England Quarterly Bulletin
	17.2	Association of Payment Clearing Services	Annual report of the Bankers' Clearing House
	17.7	Bank of England	Financial Statistics (monthly)
	17.8 17.9	Bank of England Bank of England	Bank of England Quarterly Bulletin Bank of England Quarterly Bulletin Central Statistical Office: Monthly Digest of Statistics Central Statistical Office: Financial Statistics (monthly)
Capital markets	17.10	Bank of England	Central Statistical Office: Financial Statistics (monthly) Interchange (former title
	17.11	Council of The Stock Exchange	Stock Exchange Fact Book) Quarterly
	17.12	Bank of England	Central Statistical Office: Financial Statistics (monthly) Registry of Friendly Societies
Other financial institutions	17.13	Building Societies Commission	Report of the Chief Registrar incorporating the Report of the Industrial Assurance Commissioner (annual)
	17.14, 17.15	Central Statistical Office	Business Bulletin; Credit Business (quarterly)
	17.16	Bank of England	Central Statistical Office: Financial Statistics (monthly)
	17.17, 17.18	Central Statistical Office	Financial Statistics (monthly) Business Monitor MQ5 (quarterly) Registry of Friendly Societies
	17.19, 17.20	Registry of Friendly Societies	Report of the Chief Registrar incorporating the Report of the Industrial Assurance Commissioner (annual) Registry of Friendly Societies
	17.21	Office of the Industrial Assurance Commissioner	Report of the Chief Registrar incorporating the Report of the Industrial Assurance Commissioner (annual) Registry of Friendly Societies
	17.22	Registry of Friendly Societies	Report of the Chief Registrar incorporating the Report of the Industrial Assurance Commissioner (annual) Registry of Friendly Societies
Insurance	17.23, 17.24	Office of the Industrial Assurance Commissioner	Report of the Chief Registrar incorporating the Report of the Industrial Assurance Commissioner (annual)
Companies	17.25	Central Statistical Office	CSO Bulletin, acquisitions and mergers within the UK (quarterly) Financial Statistics (monthly)
	17.26	Central Statistical Office	Business Monitor MA3 (annual) (last edition 23rd issue, published 1992)
Insolvency	17.27, 17.28, 17.29, 17.30	Department of Trade and Industry	Bankruptcy, General annual report Companies Bankruptcy (annual) Central Statistical Office: Financial Statistics (monthly) Civil judicial statistics, Scotland (annual) Ulster Yearbook
18. Prices			
	18.1-18.4	Central Statistical Office	Producer Price Index Press Notice (monthly) Business Monitor MM22, Producer Price Indices Monthly Digest of Statistics
	18.5-18.8	Central Statistical Office	Monthly Digest of Statistics Employment Gazette (monthly)
	18.9-18.10	Central Statistical Office	Agricultural Statistics, United Kingdom (annual) Central Statistical Office: Monthly Digest of Statistics
	18.11	Ministry of Agriculture, Fisheries and Food	Annual Review of Agriculture (annual)

Index

Figures indicate Table number

A

Absolute discharge, 4.7, 4.19, 4.21
Accidents:
 airways, 10.27
 coal-mining, 3.35
 deaths from, 2.20, 3.35, 10.12, 10.13, 10.19, 10.27
 industrial, 3.35
 railway, 3.35, 10.19
 road, 10.12, 10.13
Acetone:
 production, 8.25
Administrative, technical and clerical staff:
 in hospitals, 3.27-3.30
 in manufacturing industries, 6.4
Aerodromes:
 activity, 10.28
Aerospace industry:
 cost of research, 11.6-11.9
Agriculture, fisheries and food, 9.1-9.16
Agriculture:
 crops and grass, 9.4
 index of prices, 18.9, 18.10
 machinery:
  deliveries, 8.31
  sales, 8.31
 numbers employed, 6.5
 output, input and net product, 9.1, 9.2
 sales for food, 9.9
 trading societies, 17.20
Agriculture, forestry and fishing:
 commodity price trends, 18.11
 deaths in accidents, 3.35
 earnings of agricultural workers, 9.7, 9.8
 employment, 6.2
 gross domestic product, 14.7
 index of average earnings, 6.16
 index numbers of output, 14.6
Aid, United Kingdom:
 overseas, expenditure by country, 13.5
 overseas, expenditure on, 13.4
Air transport, 10.2, 10.24-10.28
Airways, UK:
 accidents on, 10.27
 operations and traffic, 10.24, 10.26
 private companies, 10.26
Alcohol, industrial:
 production, 8.25
Alcoholic drink:
 beer, spirits and wine:
  production and consumption, 8.35
  supplies per head, 9.16
 consumers' expenditure, 14.10
 public houses, 11.4
 retail price index, 18.7
Aliens:
 in custody, 4.9
 migration, 2.10, 2.11
 settlement, by nationality, 2.12
Allowance:
 attendance, 3.5, 3.13
 child's special, 3.11
 family - see Child benefit
 guardians' 3.11, 3.13, 3.15
 invalidity, 3.13
 mobility, 3.13
Aluminium:
 exports, 8.17
 fabricated, 8.17
 industry, employment, 6.2
 production and consumption, 8.18
Ambulances:
 licences current, 10.8
 new registrations, 10.9
Anaemias:
 deaths from, 2.20
Animal feedingstuffs:
 agricultural input, 9.1, 9.2
 disposals, 9.12
 exports, 12.3
 imports, 12.4
 prices, 18.9, 18.10
 production, 9.11
 stocks, 9.10
Animals:
 exports, 12.3

imports, 12.4
 on agricultural holdings, 9.5
 sold for slaughter, 9.9
 price index, 18.9, 18.11
Anoxic conditions, deaths from, 2.20
Appendicitis, deaths from, 2.20
Area:
 by country, standard region, 1.1
 cities, 2.8
 conurbations, 2.8
 crops, 9.3
 forest, 9.6
 inland water, 1.1
 land:
  arable, 9.3
  grass 9.3
  total, 1.1
 rural districts, 2.8
 standard regions, 2.8
 urban, 2.8
Armed Forces, *see* Army, Royal Navy and Royal Air Force
Army:
 cadet forces, 7.3
 deaths by cause, 7.11
 defence civilian manpower, 7.7
 defence services and the civilian community, 7.13
 deployment of service personnel, 7.6
 hospitals, 7.9
 married accommodation, 7.7
 medical staff, 7.10
 outflow, 7.5
 pay, Armed Forces, 7.2
 recruitment, 7.4
 reserves and auxiliary forces, 7.3
 strength, 7.3
 uniformed medical staff, 7.10
Army Air Corps, 7.1
Asbestos cement products:
 production, 8.28
Assault offences, 4.3, 4.4, 4.13, 4.20
Asthma, deaths from, 2.20
Asylum applications, 2.12A
Attendance allowance, 3.5, 3.13
Attendance centre order, 4.7
Average earnings: *see also* individual industries
 by age-group, 6.19
 by industry, 6.17
 earnings, manual workers, 6.14
 weekly earnings, 6.15
Aviation, civil:
 deaths from accidents, 3.35
Aviation spirit:
 deliveries, 8.13
 output, 8.12
Awards (educational):
 by research councils, 5.18
 number by type, 5.19

B

Bacon and ham:
 disposals, 9.12
 production, 9.11
Balance of payments, 13.1-13.3
 current balance, 13.1, 13.2
 investment and other capital flows, 13.1
 invisibles:
  civil aviation, 13.2
  government services and transfers, 13.2
  interest, profits and dividends, 13.1, 13.2
  private sector transfers, 13.2
  sea transport, 13.2
  summary, 13.1
  travel, 13.2
 official financing:
  transactions with the IMF, 13.3
  official reserves, 13.1, 13.3
 overseas aid, 13.4, 13.5
 overseas investment, 13.1

Bank advances, 17.5
Bank clearings, 17.2
Banking, insurance, etc, 17.1-17.26
Banking, finance, insurance, etc:
 employment, 6.2
 gross national product, 14.7
Bank of England, 17.1
Bankruptcy:
 number, industry analysis, 17.29-17.30
Banks:
 liabilities and assets outstanding, 17.3
 National Savings, 16.9
 United Kingdom, 17.4
Barley:
 area, 9.3
 disposals, 9.12
 harvested, 9.4
 output, 9.1, 9.2
 sales, 9.9
 stocks, 9.10
Beans for stockfeed, 9.1-9.4
Beef production, 9.11
Beer, production and consumption, 8.35
Benene, production, 8.25
Betting and gaming offences, 4.3, 4.4, 4.20
Bicycles - *see* Cycles, pedal
Bill rates, 17.9
Birth injury, deaths from, 2.20
Births:
 annual changes, 2.2
 by age of mother, 2.17, 2.18
 illegitimate, 2.16
 occurrences, 2.16
 still-births, 2.16
Biscuits:
 employment, 6.2
 production, 9.11
Bitumen:
 deliveries, 8.13
 output, 8.12
Blankets, deliveries, 8.18
Blood diseases, deaths from, 2.20
Board:
 production, 8.19
Boilers and process plant:
 deliveries, 8.32
Books, newspapers and magazines:
 consumers' expenditure, 14.10
Booksellers:
 retail trade, 11.1, 11.3
Borstal training, 4.9, 4.17, 4.19, 4.21
Bread and flour confectionery industry:
 employment, 6.2
Breath tests, on, car drivers, 10.12
Brewing and malting:
 employment, 6.2
Bricks:
 production, 8.28
British Rail, *see* Rail transport and Railways
British wine, home consumption, 8.35
Bronchitis:
 deaths from, 2.20
Building: *see also* Construction
 deaths from accidents, 3.35
 houses, 3.10
 value of output, 8.30
Building boards:
 production, 8.21, 8.28
Building products, glass, ceramics, etc:
 administrative, technical, clerical
 employees:
  percentage employed, 6.4
 employment, 6.1, 6.2
 index of average earnings, 6.16
 size of establishments, 6.13
Building societies:
 balance sheet, 17.13
 current transactions, 17.13
 payment of interest on shares and deposits, 17.13
Bulk carriers:
 analysis by age, 10.30
 tonnage, 10.29, 10.30, 10.31
Burglary offences, 4.1, 4.3, 4.4, 4.10, 4.13, 4.20

Figures indicate table numbers Index (contd)

Buses, coaches, etc:
 fares, indices of, 10.11
 licences current, 10.5, 10.8
 new vehicle registrations, 10.6, 10.9
 passenger journeys, 10.10
 passenger receipts, 10.10
 production, 8.34
 vehicles in service, 10.10
 vehicle miles, 10.10
Butane and propane:
 deliveries, 8.13
 output, 8.12
Butter:
 disposals, 9.12
 production, 9.11
 stocks, 9.10

C

Calcspar:
 production, 8.27
Cameras:
 sales, 8.31
Camping sites, 11.4
Cancer:
 deaths from, 2.20
Capital consumption, 14.1
Capital formation, 14.1, 14.15
Capital issues and redemptions, 17.12
Caravans:
 sales, 8.31
 sites, 11.4
Carbon black:
 production, 8.21
Care orders, 4.7
Cargo liners:
 analysis by age, 10.30
 tonnage, 10.29, 10.31
Cars, passenger: *see also* Motor vehicles
 licences current, 10.5, 10.8
 new registrations, 10.6, 10.9
 production, 8.34
Casualties in road accidents, 10.12, 10.13
Catering trades:
 contractors, 11.4
 employment, 6.2
 holiday camps and hotels, 11.4
 public houses, 11.4
 restaurants, 11.4
 turnover, 11.4
Cattle:
 agricultural output, 9.1, 9.2
 on agricultural holdings, 9.5
 prices, 18.9-18.11
 slaughtered, 9.9
Cement:
 production, 8.28
Central government borrowing requirement, 16.5
Central government expenditure, 3.1
 education, 3.2
 housing, 3.6
 national health service, 3.3
 social security, 3.5
 welfare services, 3.4
Census of:
 distribution, 11.1
 marital condition, 2.6
 population, 2.1, 2.3, 2.8
 production, 8.1
Cereals, *see also* Wheat, Barley, Oats
Breakfast:
 production, 9.11
 area, 9.3
 exports, 12.3
 harvested, 9.4
 imports, 12.4
 prices, 18.9-18.11
 sales, 9.9
Cerebrovascular disease:
 deaths from, 2.20
Chalk:
 production, 8.27
Cheese:
 disposals, 9.12

 production, 9.11
Chemicals:
 exports, 12.3
 imports, 12.4
 inorganic, 8.25
 organic, 8.25
 sales ratio, 12.2
Chemical industry:
 census of production, 8.1
 employment, 6.1, 6.2
 expenditure on research and development, 11.8, 11.9
 index of average earnings, 6.16
 materials and fuels used, 18.1, 18.3
 producer price index, 18.1-18.5
 size of establishments, 6.13
Chemists, retailers:
 retail trade, 11.1, 11.2
Chert and flint:
 production, 8.27
Child benefit, 3.5, 3.13, 3.15, 3.20
Child population, 2.3, 2.5, 5.2
Childbirth:
 deaths in, 2.20
Child's special allowance, 3.11
China clay, production, 8.27
Chocolate confectionery:
 disposals, 9.12
 production, 9.11
 stocks, 9.10
Cholera, deaths from, 2.20
Cider and perry, 8.35
Cirrhosis of liver:
 deaths from, 2.20
Cities:
 population, 2.8, 2.9
Citizens, accepted for settlement, 2.12
Civil aviation:
 accidents, 3.35, 10.27
 activity at aerodromes, 10.28
 airways, 10.23, 10.24, 10.26
 balance of payments, 13.2
 passenger movement, 10.36
Civil service staff, 6.7
Civilian community and defence services, 7.13
Civilian migration, 2.10, 2.11, 2.12
Clay:
 producer price index, 18.3, 18.4
 production, 8.27
Clay roofing tiles:
 production, 8.28
Clearing banks, 17.2
Climate, 1.2
Clothing and footwear:
 administrative, technical and clerical employees:
  percentage employed, 6.4
 employment, 6.2
 expenditure on, 14.10
 exports, 12.2, 12.3
 imports, 12.4, 12.6
 index of average earnings, 6.16
 industrial stoppages, 6.11
 retail prices index, 18.7
 retail trades, 11.1, 11.3
 size of establishments, 6.13
Coaches, buses, etc, *see* Buses, coaches, etc
Coaches (railway):
 in use, 10.15, 10.20
Coal:
 census of production, 8.1
 consumption, 8.2, 8.3
 opencast production, 8.3
 output per manshift, 8.6
 production, 8.3, 8.4
 stocks, 8.3
 supply, 8.3
 wage earners, 8.5
Coal extraction and solid fuels:
 administrative, technical and clerical employees: percentage employed, 6.4
 deaths and injuries, 3.35
 employment, 6.1, 6.2
 gross domestic product, 14.7
 index of average earnings, 6.16
 industrial stoppages, 6.11
 size of establishments, 6.13

Cocoa:
 beans, disposals, 9.12
 powder and drinking chocolate:
  production, 9.11
Coffee:
 disposals, 9.12
 stocks, 9.10
Coke ovens:
 coal consumption, 8.3
Collecting societies, 17.21
Colours, manufactures' sales, 8.23
Commercial vehicles, production, 8.34
Commodity classification, consumers' expenditure, 14.11, 14.12
Commodity price trends, 18.11
Commonwealth migration into and out from the United Kingdom, 2.10, 2.11
 acceptance for settlement, 2.12
Communications industry,
 see Transport and communications industry
Community service order, 4.7
Companies:
 acquisitions and mergers, 17.25
 capital account, 14.5
 capital issues and redemptions, 17.12
 gross trading profits, 14.1, 14.4
 income and finance of large, 17.26
 insolvencies, 17.27, 17.28
Compound feedingstuffs:
 prices, 18.9
Concrete:
 blocks, pipes, etc, production, 8.28
 ready mixed, production, 8.28
Conditional discharge, 4.7, 4.19, 4.21
Confectioners, tobacconists and newsagents:
 retail trade, 11.1, 11.2
Confectionery:
 disposals, 9.12
 production, 9.11
Congenital anomalies, deaths from, 2.20
Consolidated Fund:
 assets and liabilities, 16.7
 prices and yields, 17.10
 revenue and expenditure, 16.4
Construction:
 census of production, 8.1
 cost of research, 11.9
 employment, 6.1, 6.2
 gross domestic product, 14.7
 index of average earnings, 6.16
 industrial stoppages, 6.11
 new orders (value), 8.31
 output:
  index numbers, 14.6
  value, 8.29
 producer price index, 18.1
Consumer credit, 17.14, 17.15
Consumers' expenditure, 14.1, 14.2, 14.8-14.12
Contributory pensions, 3.21
Conurbations:
 area, 2.8
 population, 2.8
Convicted prisoners:
 with previous sentences, 4.8
Co-operative trading societies, 17.20
 index numbers of turnover, 11.3
 number, turnover and persons engaged, 11.1
Copper:
 production, consumption and stocks, 8.18
 tubing production, 8.28
Corn, mixed:
 acreage, 9.3
 harvested, 9.4
Corporate income:
 appropriation account, 14.3
Cotton:
 consumption and stocks, 8.18
 imports, 8.18
 weaving, 8.18
 yarns and woven cloth, production, 8.18
Cream:
 production, 9.11
Criminal damage, 4.1, 4.3, 4.4, 4.13, 4.20, 4.21

345

Index (contd) *Figures indicate table numbers*

Criminal offences:
  age analysis, 4.5, 4.6, 4.10, 4.16
  juvenile offenders, 4.3, 4.4, 4.16, 4.21
  proceedings in court, 4.7, 4.13, 4.19
  sex analysis, 4.5, 4.6, 4.7, 4.10, 4.16, 4.17
  type of offence, 4.1, 4.3, 4.4, 4.10, 4.12, 4.13, 4.20, 4.21
Crops:
  agricultural input/output, 9.1, 9.2
  area, 9.3
  harvested, 9.4
  producer price index, 18.10
Crude oil:
  refinery throughput, 8.12
  supply and disposals, 8.11
Cycles, pedal:
  employees in employment, 6.2
  offences, 4.3
  sales, 8.31

D

Dairy produce:
  disposals, 9.12
  exports, 12.3
  imports, 12.4
  production, 9.11
Dairymen:
  retail trade, 11.1, 11.2
Death grants, 3.5, 3.11, 3.13, 3.15
Death rates:
  by sex and age, 2.22
  infant and maternal, 2.21
Deaths:
  age and sex analysis, 2.19
  average annual changes, 2.2
  by cause, 2.20
  fatal accidents:
    air, 10.27
    due to occupationally related lung disease, 3.33
    industrial, 3.35
    motor vehicle, 2.20, 10.12, 10.13
    rail, 10.19
  service personnel, 7.11
Debt:
  local authorities, 16.13
  public sector, 16.3
Decrees absolute granted, 2.14, 2.15
Deeds of arrangement, 17.29
Defence, 7.1-7.14
Defence:
  armed forces, 7.6-7.14
  civilian manpower-strengths, 7.8
  energy consumption, 7.14
  expenditure on, 7.2, 14.14
  manpower strengths, 7.3
  research, cost of, 11.5
  search and rescue operations, 7.12
  services and the civilian community, 7.13
  sickness and deaths of service personnel, 7.11
Degrees obtained by:
  full-time university students, 5.10, 5.17
Dental services:
  government expenditure, 3.3
  treatment, payments and cost, 3.27-3.29
Dentists:
  numbers on list, 3.27-3.30
  payments, 3.3, 3.27-3.29
Detention centres, 4.7, 4.9, 4.15, 4.17
Diabetes, deaths from, 2.20
Diesel oil, *see* Gas/diesel oil
Diphtheria:
  deaths from, 2.20
  notifications, 3.32
Disablement benefits, 3.11, 3.13, 3.15, 3.28
Discount market, 17.6
Diseases:
  deaths from, 2.20
  industrial, 3.34
  notifications, 3.32
Distribution, hotels and catering repairs:
  employment, 6.2
  gross capital stock, 14.16

gross domestic fixed capital formation, 14.13
gross domestic product, 14.7
index numbers of production, 14.6
Distributive trades, research and development, 11.1-11.9
Dividends, *see* Interest, profits and dividends
Divorce:
  by age and sex, 2.14
  proceedings, 2.15
Doctors:
  numbers on list, 3.27-3.29
  patients per doctor, 3.27-3.29
  payments to, 3.27-3.29
Domestic electric appliances:
  sales, 8.31
Drifter fleet, 9.14, 9.15
Drink industry, *see* Food, drink and tobacco industry
Driving tests, 10.7
Drunkenness, 4.3, 4.4, 4.20
  drunk driving, 4.12, 4.13
Durable goods, 14.6, 14.10-14.12, 15.4
Dwellings:
  completed, 3.10
  demolished, 3.9
  ownership of, 14.7
  renovation, 3.8
  stock of, 3.7
  with usual residents, census, 3.36
Dyestuffs, synthetic:
  production, 8.23
Dysentery:
  notifications, 3.32

E

Earnings, average:
  agricultural workers, 9.7
  manual workers, 6.15
  monthly index of, 6.16
Earnings, distribution of agricultural workers, 9.8
Earnings, gross weekly and hourly, of full-time adults, 6.17-6.19
Earth-moving machinery:
  sales, 8.31
Economic activity, 1981, 6.15
Education, *see also* Schools, Teachers, Universities, 5.1-5.19
  awards, 5.18, 5.19
  central government expenditure, 3.2
  employment, 6.2
  GDP by industry, 14.7
  government expenditure, 3.1, 3.2
  higher and further, 5.1, 5.6-5.13, 5.15-5.18
  index numbers of output, 14.6
  local authorities:
    expenditure, 3.2, 16.15, 16.16, 16.20, 16.23
    grants to, 16.23, 16.25
  postgraduate and special awards, 5.18
  primary and secondary, 5.1-5.6
  pupils' qualifications, 5.5
Eggs:
  disposals, 9.12
  output, 9.1, 9.2
  prices, 18.10, 18.11
  sales, 9.9
Elections, parliamentary:
  by-elections, 3.38
  electorate, 3.37
  number of Members of Parliament elected, 3.37
  votes cast, 3.37
  votes recorded, 3.38
Electrical appliances, sales, 8.33
Electrical and electronic engineering:
  administrative, technical and clerical employees:
    percentage employed, 6.4
  cost of research, 11.9
  employment, 6.2
  expenditure on research and development, 11.8, 11.9
  index of average earnings, 6.16
  producer price index, 18.3, 18.4
  production, 8.1
  sales, 8.31, 8.32
  size of units, 6.13

Electrical machinery:
  exports, 12.3
  imports, 12.4
  sales, 8.31
Electricity:
  capacity of generating plant, 8.9
  consumption, 8.2
  production, 8.8
  sales, 8.10
Electricity industry, *see* Energy and water supply industry
Electronics equipment sales, 8.31
Emigration, 2.10, 2.11
Emphysema, deaths from, 2.20
Employers and self-employed, 6.1
Employment, *see also* individual industries, 6.1-6.20
  by industry, 6.1-6.3
  by size of establishment, 6.13
  income from, 14.1
  occupational analysis, 6.2-6.5
  vacancies unfilled, 6.9, 6.10
Emulsion paint, production, 8.24
Encephalitis, notifications of, 3.32
Endocrine disorders, deaths from, 2.20
Energy, 8.2-8.13
  consumption, 8.2
  expenditure on research, 11.6
  used in agriculture, price, 18.9
Energy and water supply industries:
  bank lending, 17.5
  census of production, 8.1
  consumers' expenditure, 14.10
  employees, 6.2
  producer price index, 18.3, 18.4
  stocks and work in progress, 14.14
Energy consumption:
  defence, 7.14
  total inland, 8.2
Enteritis:
  deaths from, 2.20
Entertainments:
  expenditure on, 14.10
Ethyl alcohol:
  production, 8.25
Ethylene:
  production, 8.25
European Community, acceptance for settlement, 2.12
Exchequer, *see* Consolidated Fund and National Loans Fund
Expectation of life, 2.23
Expenditure on:
  penal establishment, 4.11, 4.18
Exports:
  balance of payments, 13.1, 13.2
  basic materials, 12.2, 12.3
  by destination, 12.5
  food, beverages and tobacco, 12.2, 12.3
  manufactured goods, 12.3
  mineral fuels and lubricants, 12.2, 12.3
  sales and import penetration, 12.2
  value, 12.1
External trade, 12.1-12.6

F

Factories:
  fatal injuries, 3.35
Family allowance, *see* Child benefit
Family Expenditure Survey:
  households and their expenditure, 15.5
  household durable goods, 15.4
  sources of household income, 15.3
Family income supplement 3.5, 3.13, 3.15, 3.22
Family practitioner service, 3.27-3.30
Farming income, 9.1
Feedingstuffs:
  agricultural input, 9.1, 9.2
  disposals, 9.12
  prices, 18.9
  production, 9.11
  stocks, 9.10
Fertiliser industry:

Figures indicate table numbers

employment, 6.2
Fertilisers:
  agricultural input, 9.1, 9.2
  consumption of sulphuric acid for, 8.24
  prices, 18.9
  production and deliveries, 8.22
Fertility statistics, 2.16-2.18
Finance houses, *see* Consumer credit
Fire clay:
  production, 8.27
Fire engines:
  licences current, 10.8
  registrations, 10.9
Fish:
  disposal of fresh, 9.12
  landings, 9.13
  production of canned, 9.11
Fishing fleet, 9.14, 9.15
Fishing industry, *see* Agriculture, forestry and fishing
Flour:
  disposals, 9.12
  production, 9.11
Flowers and plants:
  agricultural output, 9.1, 9.2
  prices, 18.10
Fodder crops:
  area, 9.3
  harvested, 9.4
Food:
  catering, retail trade, 11.4
  consumers' expenditure, 14.9
  consumption, 9.18
  disposals, 9.12
  exports, 12.2, 12.3
  imports, 12.4
  index of producer prices, 18.10
  processed, 9.11
  retail prices index, 18.7
  retail trade, 11.1, 11.2
  stocks, 9.10
Food, drink and tobacco industries:
  administrative, technical and clerical employees:
    percentage employed, 6.4
  census of production, 8.1
  employment, 6.2
  index of average earnings, 6.16
  size of establishments, 6.13
Food poisoning, notifications, 3.32
Food processing:
  machinery sales, 8.31
Footwear, *see* Clothing and footwear
Forces and Women's Services:
  employment, 6.1
  pay in cash and kind, 14.2
  strength, 7.3
Foreign trade:
  imports and exports, 12.1-12.6
  traffic at seaports, by commodity, 10.35
Foreign visitors, *see* Aliens
Forest, area 9.6
Forestry industry, *see* Agriculture, forestry and fishing
Fraud and forgery, 4.1, 4.3, 4.4, 4.10, 4.20, 4.21
Freight wagons, 10.15
Friendly Societies, 17.22
Fresh fruit, producer price, 18.10
Fruit:
  agricultural output, 9.1, 9.2
  area, 9.3
  canned and bottled, 9.11
  commodity prices, 18.11
Fuel and power:
  consumers' expenditure, 14.10
  retail price index, 18.7
Fuel consumption:
  by class of consumer, 8.2
  by type of fuel, 8.2
Fuel oil:
  deliveries, 8.13
  outputs, 8.12
Furniture industry, *see* Timber and wooden furniture industries
Further education, 5.1, 5.6-5.10, 5.13

G

Gas:
  census of production, 8.1
  employment 6.1, 6.2
  gross national product, 14.7
  index of average earnings, 6.16
  index of numbers of output, 14.6
  production, sales, 8.7
Gas/diesel oil:
  deliveries, 8.13
  output, 8.12
Glass industry, *see* Building products
Glucose:
  production, 9.10
Goods transport, railway, 10.1, 10.16,
  road, 10.1
  water, 10.1
Goods vehicles:
  licences current, 10.5, 10.8
  registrations, 10.6, 10.9
Government:
  consolidated fund revenue and expenditure, 16.7
  exchequer financing, 16.4, 16.5
  invisible credits from and debits to overseas, 13.2
  revenue account, 14.3
  securities, 17.1
Government expenditure:
  education, 3.1, 3.2
  housing, 3.1, 3.6
  national health service, 3.1, 3.3
  personal social services, 3.1, 3.4
  school meals, milk and welfare foods, 3.1, 3.4
  social security benefits, 3.1, 3.5
  welfare foods services, 3.4
Government service:
  employment, 6.2
Gramophone records, sales, 8.31
Grass:
  acreage, 9.3
  harvest, 9.4
Gravel and sand:
  production, 8.27, 8.28
Greengrocers:
  retail trade, 11.1, 11.3
Grocery and provision dealers:
  retail trade, 11.1, 11.3
Gross domestic product, 14.1, 14.7, 14.8, 14.13
Gross national product, 14.1, 14.8
Guardians' allowances, 3.5, 3.11, 3.13, 3.16
Gypsum:
  production, 8.27, 8.28

H

Hardwood:
  production, deliveries and stocks, 8.20
Hay:
  harvest, 9.4
Health, *see also* National health service
  central government expenditure, 3.1, 3.3, 3.5
  grants to local authorities, 16.18, 16.21, 16.25
  local authority expenditure, 3.1, 3.3, 16.15, 16.16, 16.20, 16.23
Heart disease:
  deaths from, 2.20
Heavy goods, registration, 10.6
Hire purchase, *see* Consumer credit
Holiday camps, 11.4
Home finance, 16.1-16.25
Home population, 2.1, 2.3, 2.5 2.7-2.9
Hops:
  agricultural output, 9.1, 9.2
  area, 9.3
  harvested, 9.4
  prices, 18.10, 18.11

Horticultural crops, land use, 9.3
Hospitals:
  ancillary staff, 3.31
  central government expenditure, 3.3
  patients treated, 3.31
  selected diagnoses of patients, 3.31
  services, 3.3, 3.27-3.29
Hotels, 11.4
Hours worked:
  by manual wage-earners, 6.15
Housebreaking, offences, 4.13
Household goods:
  consumers' expenditure on, 14.10
  retail price index, 18.7
  retail trade, 11.1, 11.2
Households:
  average incomes, 15.1
  expenditure, 15.5
  private, with usual residents, 3.36
  source of income, 15.2
Houses:
  completed, 3.10
  demolished or closed, 3.9
  stock of dwellings, 3.7
Housing:
  central government expenditure, 3.1, 3.6
  consumers' expenditure, 14.10
  grants to local authorities, 16.19 16.22, 16.25
  local authority expenditure, 3.1, 3.6, 16.15, 16.16, 16.20, 16.23
  output by contractors, 8.29
  renovation grants approved, 3.8
  repair and maintenance, 8.29
  retail prices index, 18.7
  slum clearance, 3.9
Hypertensive disease, deaths from, 2.20

I

Igneous rock:
  production, 8.27
Illegitimate births, 2.16
IMF, official financing, 13.3
Immigration, 2.10-2.12
Imports:
  analysis by source, 12.6
  balance of payments, 12.1, 13.1, 13.2
  food, beverages and tobacco, 12.4
  manufactured goods, 12.4
  mineral fuels and lubricants, 12.4
  penetration and export sales, 12.2
Imprisonments, 4.7, 4.19
Improvement grants, *see* Renovation grants
Income:
  before and after tax, 15.2
  company, 14.13, 17.26
  GDP, income based, 14.1
  local authorities, 16.14, 16.18, 16.19, 16.21, 16.22, 16.24, 16.25
  national, 14.1
  of households, 15.1, 15.3
  personal, 14.2
Income support, 3.23, 3.24, 3.25
Income tax:
  allowances, 16.10
  personal incomes before and after, 15.2
  rates, 16.11
Index numbers of:
  agricultural prices, 18.9, 18.10
  average earnings, 6.16
  gross domestic product, 14.9
  gross national product, 14.9
  industrial share prices, 17.10
  output, 14.6
  producer prices, 18.1-18.5
  retail prices, 18.7
  retail trade, 11.2
  security prices, 17.10
  tax and price, 18.8
Indictable offences:
  juveniles found guilty, 4.21
  offenders cautioned, 4.4, 4.6
  offenders found guilty, 4.3, 4.5
  sentence or order, 4.7, 4.19
Individual voluntary arrangement, 17.27
Industrial:
  and provident societies, 17.19

347

Index (contd)

assurance, 17.24
deaths from accidents, 3.35
disablement pensions, 3.13, 3.15
diseases, 3.34
injuries benefit, 3.5, 3.13, 3.15
production, index of, 8.2
securities, 17.10
spirit:
  deliveries, 8.13
  output, 8.13
stoppages, 6.14
Infant mortality, 2.21
Infectious diseases:
  deaths from, 2.20
  notifications, 3.32
Influenza:
  deaths from, 2.20
Information science research grants, 5.18
Inorganic chemicals:
  production, 8.24
Insolvencies:
  individual, 17.27
  company, 17.28
Instrument engineering:
  administrative, technical and clerical employees:
    percentage employed, 6.4
  employment, 6.2
  index of average earnings, 6.16
  sales, 8.31
  size of establishments 6.13
Insulation board, etc:
  production, 8.28
Insurance, see also National Insurance, 17.22-17.24
Insurance companies balance sheet, 17.18
Interest, profits and dividends:
  balance of payments, 13.1, 13.2
  of large companies, 17.26
International Monetary Fund, 13.3
Intoxication offences, 4.3, 4.4, 4.13, 4.20
Invalidity benefits, 3.11, 3.13, 3.15, 3.17-3.19
Investment overseas, 13.1
Investment trusts, 17.16
Iron and steel:
  exports, 8.14, 12.2, 12.3
  furnaces, 8.15
  imports, 8.14, 12.6
  production, 8.15, 8.16
  scrap, 8.15, 8.17
  supplies, deliveries and stocks, 8.14
Iron and steel industry:
  cost of research, 11.9
  employment, 6.2
  fuel consumption, 8.3

J

Jam and marmalade:
  production, 9.11
Juveniles found guilty, 4.3, 4.16, 4.21

K

Kerosene:
  deliveries, 8.13
  output, 8.12

L

Lamps, electric, sales, 8.31
Land:
  area, 1.1
  held by Ministry of Defence, 7.7
Law enforcement, 4.1-4.22
Lead:
  production, consumption and stocks, 8.17
Leather and leather goods:
  administrative, technical and clerical employees:
    percentage employed, 6.4
  census of production, 8.1
  employment, 6.2
  index of average earnings, 6.16
  size of establishments, 6.13

Letter post, 10.37
Leukaemia:
  deaths from, 2.20
Licences:
  television, 10.37
  vehicle, 10.5, 10.9
Life assurance:
  industrial business, 17.24
  market value of insurance companies, 17.18
  new business, 17.23
Life tables, 2.23
Limestone:
  production, 8.27
Liquidations, 17.28
Livestock:
  agricultural input and output, 9.1, 9.2
  prices, 18.7, 18.10
  purchase for slaughter, 9.9
Local authorities:
  capital account, 14.5
  expenditure on housing, 3.1, 3.6
  expenditure on the national health service, 3.3
  grants by central government, 16.19, 16.22, 16.25
  houses built for, 3.7, 3.10
  income and expenditure, 16.14-16.25
  loan debt, 16.14
  social services expenditure, 3.1, 3.4
  welfare services expenditure, 3.4
Local government service:
  employment, 6.2
Locomotives:
  rolling stock, 10.15, 10.20
London Regional Transport, 10.10, 10.11, 10.18
Lubricating oil:
  deliveries, 8.13
  output, 8.12

M

Machinery:
  sales:
    agricultural, 8.31
    data processing equipment, 8.31
    domestic electric, 8.31
    electricity generating, 8.31, 8.31
    food preparation, 8.31
    machine tools, 8.31
    office, 8.31
    refrigerating, 8.31
  exports, 12.2, 12.3
  imports, 12.2, 12.4
Magnesium and magnesium alloys:
  production and consumption, 8.17
Mail order houses:
  retail trade, 11.1, 11.2
  total business, 17.14
Maize:
  animal feed, 9.12
  disposals, 9.12
  harvested, 9.4
  stocks, 9.10
Malicious damage, 4.2-4.4, 4.13, 4.20, 4.21
Manganese ore:
  consumption, 8.15
Man-made fibres:
  production and consumption, 8.1, 8.18
  size of units, 6.13
Manpower:
  Civil Service, 6.7
  distribution of working, 6.1
  engineering industries, 6.3
  manufacturing industries, 6.4
  national health service, 3.30
  number of employees in industry, 6.2
Manslaughter, offences, 4.3, 4.20
Manual workers' earnings, 6.14, 6.15
Manufactured goods:
  exports, 12.2, 12.3
  imports, 12.2, 12.4
  production, 8.32
Manufacturing industries:
  capital formation, 14.15
  census of production, 8.1
  earnings, 6.15
  employment, 6.1-6.4
  expenditure on research and development,

    11.8, 11.9
  gross domestic product, 14.7
  gross national product, 14.12
  hours worked, 6.15
  index of average earnings, 6.16
  index of materials and fuels used in, 18.1
  units by size, 6.13
Margarine:
  production, 9.11
Marital condition, 2.6, 2.7
Marriages, 2.13
Maternal death rates, 2.21
Maternity benefits, 3.5, 3.11, 3.13, 3.15
Measles:
  deaths from, 2.20
  notifications of, 3.32
Meat:
  disposals, 9.11
  prices, 18.10, 18.11
  production:
    canned, 9.11
    home killed, 9.11
  stocks, 9.10
Mechanical engineering industry:
  administrative, technical and clerical employees:
    percentage employed, 6.4
  employment, 6.1-6.3
  expenditure on research and development, 11.8, 11.9
  index of average earnings, 6.16
  size of establishments 6.13
Mechanical handling equipment:
  sales, 8.31
Medical services:
  Armed Forces, 7.10
  family practitioner services, 3.27-3.30
  public expenditure, 3.3
Mental disorders, deaths from, 2.20
Merchant shipbuilding, see Shipbuilding
Merchant vessels:
  analyses by age, type and size, 10.29-10.32
Metal goods engineering and vehicle industries:
  administrative, technical and clerical employees:
    percentage employed, 6.4
  census of production, 8.1
  employment, 6.1, 6.2
  index of average earnings, 6.16
  industrial stoppages, 6.11
  producer price index, 18.3, 18.4
  size of establishments, total sales 6.13, 8.31
Meteorological services, 7.13
Midwifery staff, 3.27-3.30
Migration, 2.2, 2.11, 2.12
Milk:
  agricultural output, 9.1, 9.2
  prices, 18.10, 18.11
  sales, 9.9
  schools, 3.4
Milk products:
  disposals, 9.12
  production, 9.11
Mineral oil and natural gas, extraction of, 8.1
Mineral oil refining:
  employment, 6.2
Minerals:
  production, 8.27
Mining machinery, sales, 8.31
Ministry of Defence, land holdings, 7.7
Mobility allowance, 3.13
Monetary sector, 17.4
Monetary sector institutions, 17.17
Money and bill rates, 17.10
Money stock M1 and M3, 17.8
Mortality tables, 2.21, 2.23
Motor cycles:
  licences current, 10.5, 10.8
  new registrations, 10.6, 10.9
Motoring offences:
  called for trial, 4.13
  known to the police, 4.12
  offenders found guilty, 4.3

Figures indicate table numbers Index (contd)

Motor spirit:
  deliveries, 8.13
  output, 8.12
Motor trades:
  commodity sales, 11.3
Motor vehicles:
  consumers' expenditure, 14.10
  cost of research, 11.9
  deaths by, 2.20
  employment, 6.2
  gross domestic product, 14.7
  index of average earnings, 6.16
  industrial stoppages, 6.11
  involved in accidents, 10.14
  producton, 8.34
  repairs and servicing, 11.3
Motorways:
  length of, 10.3
Murder:
  persons found guilty, 4.3, 4.20
Musculo-skeletal diseases:
  deaths from, 2.20
Mutton and lamb:
  production, 9.11

N

National debt:
  borrowing and repayment, 16.6
  nominal amount outstanding, 16.3, 16.7
National development bonds, 16.9
National Food Survey, 9.16
National health service, 3.1, 3.3, 3.11, 3.27-3.30
National income and expenditure, 14.1-14.15
National insurance, 3.5, 3.11-3.14, 3.20, 14.3
National insurance fund, 3.11
National Loans Fund:
  receipts and payments, 16.4
National savings:
  amounts remaining invested, 16.9
  receipts, repayments and interest, 16.9
Nationalised industries, 16.13
Natural gas, *see* Gas
Neoplasms, deaths from, 2.20
Nickel:
  production, 8.17
Nitrogen:
  production and deliveries, 8.22
Non-contributory benefits:
  expenditure, 3.5
Non-indictable offences:
  persons cautioned, 4.4, 4.6
  persons found guilty, 4.3, 4.5
Non-manual earnings, 6.15
Non-metallic mineral products, 6.2
Nuclear energy, 8.2, 8.8
Nursery schools, 5.1
Nursing staff in hospitals, 3.27-3.30
Nutritional diseases, deaths from, 2.20

O

Oats:
  agricultural output, 9.1, 9.2
  area, 9.3
  harvested, 9.4
  milled:
    production, 9.11
  prices, 18.9-18.11
  processed, 9.11
  sales, 9.9
Offal:
  production, 9.11
Offences, recorded, 4.1
Offenders cautioned, 4.4, 4.6
Office machinery and data processing equipment:
  producer price index, 18.3, 18.4
Official reserves, 13.1
Off-licences, 11.1, 11.2
Oilcake and meal:
  disposals, 9.12
  production, 9.11
  stocks, 9.10

Oil refining, 8.11, 8.12
Oils and fats:
  disposals, 9.12
  exports, 12.3
  imports, 12.4
  seed crushing production, 9.11
  stocks, 9.10
Oilseeds and nuts:
  agricultural output, 9.2
  harvested, 9.4
  processed, 9.11
  stocks, 9.10
Old age pensions, 3.15
Old persons:
  pensions, 3.13, 3.15, 3.21
  supplementary benefits, 3.5
Opencast coal production, 8.3
Open University, students, 5.6, 5.10
Ophthalmic services, 3.3, 3.27-3.29
Organic chemicals:
  production, 8.24
Organic oils and fats:
  employment, 6.2
Output:
  and expenditure, 14.8
  index numbers of, 14.6
Overseas:
  aid, 13.4, 13.5
  investment, 13.1
  students from abroad, 5.8

P

Packaging products of metal:
  sales, 8.31
Packaging products of paper, etc:
  manufacturers' sales, 8.19
Paint:
  employment, 6.2
  sales, 8.23
Paper, printing and publishing industry:
  census of production, 8.1
  employment, 6.1, 6.2
  exports, 12.2, 12.5
  imports, 12.4
  index of average earnings, 6.16
  producer price index, 18.3, 18.4
  size of establishments, 6.13
Parcels, posted, 10.37
Passenger movement, 10.2, 10.36
Passenger ships:
  analysis by age, 10.31
  tonnage, 10.29, 10.30
Peas for stockfeed:
  agricultural output, 9.2
  harvested, 9.4
Pedal cycles, *see* Cycles, pedal
Pensioners:
  estimated number, 3.15, 3.26
Pensions:
  disablement, 3.11, 3.13, 3.15, 3.26
  funds assets, 17.17
  government expenditure, 3.5
  non-contributory, 3.15, 3.25
  retirement, 3.11, 3.13, 3.15
  war, 3.26
  widows', 3.11, 3.13, 3.15, 3.26
Personal income and expenditure, 14.2
Personal income, expenditure and wealth, 15.1-15.5
Personal social services, 3.1, 3.30, 16.15, 16.16, 16.18
Pesticides, agricultural input, 9.1, 9.2
Petrol, *see* Motor spirit
Petroleum:
  consumption for fuel, 8.2
  exports, 12.3
  filling stations, 11.2
  imports, 12.4
  production, 8.11
Products:
  deliveries of, 8.13
  refined, 8.12
Petroleum coke, deliveries, 8.13
Pharmaceutical services, 3.27-3.29
Phosphate:
  production and deliveries, 8.22
Photographic:
  equipment sales, 8.31

goods retailers, 11.1
Pig iron:
  production, 8.15
Pigs:
  agricultural output, 9.1, 9.2
  on agricultural holdings, 9.5
  prices, 18.9-18.11
  sales, 9.9
Pipelines, goods transport, 10.1
Pitch fibre pipes and conduits:
  production, 8.28
Plaster and plasterboard:
  production, 8.28
Plywood:
  production, deliveries and stocks, 8.20
Pneumonia:
  deaths from, 2.20
  notifications, 3.32
Police:
  establishment and strength, 4.2
  expenditure of local authorities, 16.15, 16.16, 16.20
  grants to local authorities, 16.19, 16.22
Poliomyelitis:
  deaths from, 2.20
  notifications, 3.32
Population and vital statistics, 2.1 - 2.23
Population, *see also* Vital statistics
  age and sex distribution, 2.1, 2.3, 2.5
  aliens, 2.12
  census based, 2.1, 2.3, 2.6, 2.8
  cities, 2.8, 2.9
  changes in, 2.2
  economic activity, 1981, 6.12
  electorate, 3.37, 3.38
  life tables, 2.23
  mid-year estimates, 2.1, 2.5, 2.7, 2.9
  migration, 2.2, 2.10, 2.11
  projections, 2.1, 2.5
  regional distribution, 2.8, 2.9
  summary, 2.1
  working, 6.1, 6.2
Pork:
  production, 9.11
Postal and postal order services, 10.37
Postgraduate awards, 5.18, 5.19
Potash:
  deliveries, 8.22
Potatoes:
  agricultural output, 9.1, 9.2
  area, 9.3
  disposals, 9.12
  harvested, 9.4
  prices, 18.10, 18.11
  sales, 9.9
Pottery industry, *see* Building products and glass
Poultry:
  agricultural output, 9.1, 9.2
  meat production, 9.11
  on agricultural holdings, 9.5
  prices, 18.9-18.11
  sales, 9.9
Pregnancy complications, deaths from, 2.20
Prescriptions:
  average gross cost, 3.27-3.29
  dispensed, 3.27-3.29
Prices, 18.1-18.11
Prices:
  agricultural, 18.9-18.11
  producer, 18.1-18.5
  retail prices index, 18.7
  security, yields and, 17.10
  tax and price index, 18.8
Primary care services, 3.28
Primary schools, 5.1
Printing industry, *see* Paper, printing and publishing
Prisons:
  expenditure on, 4.11, 4.18
  receptions and population, 4.8-4.10, 4.15, 4.17, 4.22
Private sector liquidity, 17.8
Probation, 4.7, 4.14, 4.19, 4.21
Producer price index, 18.1-18.5
Production, 8.1-8.35
Production:
  census of, 8.1
Profits, *see also* Interest, profits and

349

Index (contd) — *Figures indicate table numbers*

dividends, company, 17.26
Propane deliveries, 8.13
Property income:
 from abroad (net), 14.1
Provident societies, 17.19
Public administration:
 employment, 6.2
 gross domestic product, 14.7
Public corporations:
 expenditure on housing, 3.6
 trading surpluses of, 14.1
Public houses, 11.4
Public road passenger vehicles, *see* Buses, coaches, etc
Public sector:
 borrowing requirement, 17.7
 debt, nominal amount outstanding, 16.3
Publishing industry, *see* Paper, printing and publishing industry
Pulpwood:
Pupils:
 in schools, 5.2-5.9
Purchasing power of the pound, 18.6

Q

Qualification obtained:
 by school leavers, 5.5
 degrees and diplomas obtained by students, 5.17
Quarrying, *see* Clay, stone and slate production

R

Radio and electronic goods:
 sales, 8.32
Rail transport, 10.1, 10.2, 10.16-10.21
Railways:
 accidents, 10.19
 fatal injuries, 3.35
 fuel consumption, 8.2, 8.3
 goods traffic, 10.1, 10.15, 10.16
 London Regional Transport, 10.18
 offences, 4.3, 4.4, 4.20
 passenger transport, 10.2, 10.16
 permanent way, 10.15
 rolling stock:
  in use, 10.15, 10.20
 stations, 10.15
Rateable values, 16.12
Rates:
 local authorities' income from, 16.18, 16.21, 16.24
 rebate grant, 16.21
Refinery fuel, 8.12, 8.13
Refinery receipts, 8.11
Refrigerating machinery:
 sales, 8.31
Regional statistics:
 area, 2.8
 population, 2.8, 2.9
 unemployment, 6.6, 6.8
Remand homes:
 sent to, 4.21
Renovation grants, 3.8
Rent:
 corporate income of central government, 14.4
 factor incomes, 14.1
 government grants to rebate 3.6
 imputed - of owner-occupied dwellings, 14.2
 local authorities, 16.18, 16.21, 16.24
Research and development, 11.5-11.9
 analysis by sector, 11.5
 expenditure by industry, 11.9
Research grants by subject, 5.18
Resins, synthetic:
 production, 8.26
Restaurants, 11.4
Retail prices index, 18.7
Retail trade:
 number of establishments, 11.1
 turnover and persons engaged, 11.1

value of sales, 11.2
 volume index numbers, 11.2
Retirement pensions, 3.5, 3.11, 3.13, 3.15, 3.20
Revenue:
 central government, 16.4, 16.5
 local authorities, 16.14, 16.18, 16.19, 16.21, 16.22, 16.25
Rheumatic fever, deaths from, 2.20
Road transport, 10.1-10.14
Roads:
 accidents, 10.12
 casualties, 10.13
 goods transported by, 10.1, 10.14
 length of, 10.3
 traffic on, 10.14
Robbery, 4.1, 4.3, 4.4, 4.10
Roofing tiles, production:
 clay, 8.28
 concrete, 8.28
 slate, 8.28
Royal Air Force:
 cadet forces, 7.3
 deaths by cause, 7.11
 defence civilian manpower, 7.8
 deployment of, 7.6
 hospitals, 7.9
 medical staff, 7.10
 outflow, 7.5
 recruitment, 7.4
 regular reserves, 7.3
 search and rescue operations, 7.12
 service accommodation and land, 7.7
 strength, 7.3
 volunteer reserves and auxiliary forces, 7.3
Royal Navy and Royal Marines:
 cadet forces, 7.3
 hospitals, 7.9
 medical staff, 7.10
 outflow, 7.5
 recruitment, 7.4
 regular reserves, 7.3
 search and rescue operations, 7.12
 service accommodation and land, 7.7
 sickness and deaths, 7.11
 strength, 7.3
 volunteer reserves and auxiliary forces, 7.3
Rubber:
 sales of products, 8.21
 synthetic, 8.21
 tubes, tyres, 8.21
Rural districts:
 area, 2.8
 population, 2.8
Rye (grain):
 acreage, 9.3
 harvested, 9.4

S

Salt:
 production, 8.27
Sand:
 building and concreting, 8.28
 industrial, 8.27
Sandstone:
 production, 8.27
Save As You Earn, 16.9
Savings:
 national, 16.9
 national savings certificates, 16.3, 16.9
 Trustee savings bank, 16.9
Scarlet fever:
 notifications of, 3.32
Scholarships:
 departments of education awards, 5.19
 local education authority awards, 5.19
School:
 assisted special, 5.4
 children by age, 5.2
 children on register, 5.2-.5.4
 meals and milk, 3.1, 3.2
 pupils:
  remaining at school beyond leaving age, 5.6
 teachers in, full/part-time, 5.3, 5.11
School-leavers:
 by qualification, 5.5
Schools:
 number of, by type, 5.1

pupil/teacher ratios, 5.3
Scientific research:
 cost and expenditure, 11.5-11.9
 postgraduate awards and research grants, 5.18
Sea transport:
 balance of payments, 13.2
 fishing fleet, 9.13, 9.14
 goods transport, 10.1
 merchant vessels:
  age and type, 10.30
  deadweight tonnage, 10.31
  fatal injuries, 3.35
  tonnage, by type, 10.29
 trade:
  cargo, 10.32
  carried by principal flags, 10.34
  proportion carried by UK vessels, 10.33
Seaport traffic, 10.35
Search and rescue operations, by services, 7.12
Seat belts, wearing of, by casualties, 10.13
Securities:
 government and government guaranteed, 16.8, 17.11
 prices and yields, 17.10
 London Stock Exchange, 17.11
Seed crushing:
 production, 9.10
Seeds:
 agricultural input and output, 9.1, 9.2
 index of purchase price, 18.9
Sentences:
 offenders found guilty, 4.3, 4.7
Sequestrations:
 number, 17.27
Service trades:
 by kind of business, 11.1
Sewage collection, expenditure on, 16.17
Sexual offences, 4.1 4.4, 4.10, 4.20, 4.21
Sheep and lambs:
 agricultural output, 9.1, 9.2
 on agricultural holdings, 9.5
 prices, 18.10, 18.11
 sales, 9.9
Shipbuilding and repairing:
 completions and orders, 8.33
 employment, 6.2, 6.3
Sickness:
 service personnel, 7.11
Sickness benefit, 3.5, 3.11-3.13, 3.15, 3.17-3.19
Slate:
 production, 8.27
Slum clearance, 3.9
Soap and toilet preparations:
 employment, 6.2
Social conditions, 3.1-3.38
Social services:
 expenditure on, 3.1-3.6, 14.14
Social security benefits:
 expenditure on, 3.1, 3.5
Soft drinks:
 employment, 6.2
 production, 9.10
Softwood:
 production, deliveries and stocks, 8.20
Solid fuels, *see* Coal extraction, etc
Soups, canned:
 production, 9.11
Space research:
 central government expenditure on, 11.7
 research grants current, 5.18
Spectacles:
 supplied, 3.27-3.29
Spent oxide:
 consumption and stocks, 8.24
Spirit, industrial and white:
 deliveries, 8.13
 refining, 8.12
Spirits, alcoholic:
 production and consumption, 8.35
Stateless persons, 2.12
Steel, *see* Iron and steel
Sterling area:
 trade with, 12.5, 12.6
Still-births, 2.16
Stock Exchange, 17.11

350

Figures indicate table numbers Index (contd)

Stocks and work in progress:
  value of physical increase in, 14.1, 14.14
Stone and slate production, 8.27
  employment, 6.2
Straw:
Strikes, 6.11
Students:
  from abroad, 5.8
  further education, 5.1, 5.6-5.10
  Open University, 5.6
  training as teachers, 5.12
  university, 5.6, 5.14-5.19
Subsidies, 14.1, 14.4
Sugar and sugar confectionery:
  disposals, 9.11
  employment, 6.2
  production, 9.11
  stocks, 9.10
Sugar beet:
  acreage, 9.3
  agricultural output, 9.1, 9.2
  harvested, 9.4
  prices, 18.9, 18.10
Suicide:
  deaths by, 2.20
Sulphur and sulphuric acid:
  production, consumption and stocks, 8.24
Summary offences:
  offenders cautioned, 4.4, 4.6
  offenders found guilty, 4.3, 4.5
  sentence or order, 4.6
Superannuation funds:
  assets, 17.17, 3.23-3.25
Suspended sentences, 4.6
Synthetic resins, plastics materials:
  employment, 6.2
  production, 8.26
Synthetic rubber:
  production, 8.22
Syrup and treacle:
  disposals, 9.12
  production, 9.11

T

Take-away food, 11.4
Tankers:
  analysis by tonnage and type, 10.31
  number and gross tonnage, 10.29
  output, 8.34
  percentage and deadweight tonnage, 10.30
Tapes, pre-recorded, sales, 8.32
Tax and price index, 18.8
Taxes:
  on expenditure, 14.1, 14.4
  on income, 14.4
  paid abroad and profits due abroad, 14.1, 14.3
  total income before and after, 15.2
Taxis:
  accidents, 10.12
  licences current, 10.5, 10.8
  new registrations, 10.6, 10.9
  traffic on roads, 10.4
Tea:
  disposals, 9.12
  stocks, 9.10
Teachers:
  full-time, 5.3, 5.4, 5.11, 5.12
  part-time, 5.11
  pupils per, 5.3
  training of, 5.12
  university, 5.11
Telegrams, 10.37
Television:
  licences, 10.37
  sales, 8.33
Temperature:
  daily mean air, 1.2
Temporarily stopped workers, 6.12, 6.13
Textile industry:
  administrative, technical and clerical employees:

    percentage employed, 6.4
  census of production, 8.1
  employment, 6.2
  exports, 12.2, 12.3
  imports, 12.2, 12.4
  index of average earnings, 6.16
  industrial stoppages, 6.11
  production, 8.18
  producer price index numbers, 18.1-18.4
  size of establishments, 6.13
Textile machinery:
  sales, 8.32
Theft, 4.1, 4.4, 4.10, 4.14, 4.20, 4.21
Tiles:
  production, 8.29
Timber and wooden furniture industries:
  administrative, technical and clerical employees:
    percentage employed, 6.4
  employment, 6.1, 6.2
  index of average earnings, 6.16
  producer price index, 18.3, 18.4
  production, consumption, deliveries and stocks, 8.20
  size of establishments, 6.13
Tin:
  exports, 8.17
  production, consumption and stocks, 8.17
Tobacco:
  clearances and stocks, 8.36
  consumers' expenditure, 14.9
  retail prices index, 18.7
Tobacco industry, *see* Food, drink and tobacco industry
Tourists:
  expenditure in United Kingdom, 14.9
Tractors, agricultural:
  licences current, 10.5, 10.8
  registrations, 10.6, 10.9
  sales, 8.31
Tractors, industrial:
  licences current, 10.5, 10.8
  new registrations, 10.6, 10.9
  sales, 8.31
Trade:
  external:
    balance of payments, 13.1
    value, 12.1-12.5
  international seaborne, 10.32
  retail, 11.1, 11.2
  visible:
    of the United Kingdom, 12.1
Trade unions, 6.20
Trading societies, 17.20
Traffic accidents:
  deaths and injuries, 10.14
Traffic offences:
  persons found guilty, 4.3, 4.13, 4.20
Trailers:
  production, 8.34
Tramp shipping, *see* Merchant shipping
Transport and communications, 10.1-10.39
Transport:
  air, 10.24-10.28
  goods, 10.1
  passenger, 10.2
  rail, 10.16-10.21
  road, 10.3-10.14
  sea, 13.2
  shipping, 10.29-10.35
Transport industry, *see* Motor vehicles
Travel:
  balance of payments, 13.2
  consumers' expenditure, 14.9
  passenger movement, 10.36
Trawler fleet, 9.14, 9.15
Treasury bills:
  assets, 17.6
  increase in, 16.5
  outstanding, 16.10
  rates, 17.9
Tuberculosis:
  deaths from, 2.20
  notifications, 3.32
Turbines, sales, 8.31
Typhoid fever:

  deaths from, 2.20
  notifications, 3.32
Tyres and tubes:
  rubber consumption, 8.21

U

Unemployed persons:
  benefit entitlement, 3.16
  supplementary benefits, 3.5
Unemployment:
  benefits, 3.5, 3.11, 3.13, 3.15
  numbers employed, 6.1, 6.7, 6.8
Unit trusts:
  assets, 17.16
Universities:
  awards taken up, 5.19
  CNAA and degrees awarded, 5.10
  courses taken, 5.16
  degrees and diplomas obtained, 5.10
  expenditure on R&D, 11.5, 11.6
  government expenditure, 3.2
  National Diplomas/Certificates, 5.10
  Open University, students, 5.6
  postgraduate and special awards, 5.18
  students, 5.14, 5.15
  teacher training, 5.13
  teaching staff at, 5.11
Urban districts:
  area, 2.8
  population, 2.8

V

Vacuum cleaners:
  sales, 8.31
Vagrancy offences, 4.3, 4.4, 4.20
Value added tax, 3.2, 3.4
Varnish:
  sales, 8.23
Veal:
  production, 9.11
Vegetables:
  agricultural output, 9.1, 9.2
  area, 9.3
  canned:
    production, 9.11
  harvested, 9.4
  prices, 18.10, 18.11
Vehicles, *see* Motor vehicles
Veterinary services:
  prices, 18.9
Violence against the person:
  offender cautioned, 4.4
  called to trial, 4.14
  offence recorded, 4.1
  offenders found guilty, 4.3, 4.12, 4.20, 4.21
  prison population serving sentences, 4.10
Vital statistics, *see also* Population
  birth rates, 2.16-2.18
  death rates:
    by age and sex, 2.22
    infant, 2.21
    maternal, 2.21
  deaths:
    by age and sex, 2.19
    by cause, 2.20
  divorce, 2.14, 2.15
  illegitimate births, 2.16
  life tables, 2.23
  marital condition, 2.6, 2.7
  marriages, 2.13
  still-births, 2.16

W

Wagons, railway, 10.15, 10.20
War pensions, 3.5, 3.13, 3.15, 3.26
Watches:
  sales, 8.33
Water expenditure, 16.17
Water:
  inland area, 1.1

Index (contd)

goods transport, 10.1
Water supply industry, *see* Energy and Water supply
Welfare foods:
  government expenditure, 3.1, 3.4
Wheat:
  agricultural output, 9.1, 9.2
  area, 9.3
  harvested, 9.4
  milled:
    production, 9.11
  prices, 18.9-18.11
  sales, 9.9
  stocks, 9.10
Wheat milling offals:
  disposals, 9.12
  production, 9.11
White spirit:
  deliveries, 8.13
  output, 8.12
Whooping cough:
  deaths from, 2.20
  notifications of, 3.32
Widows' pension and benefits, 3.11, 3.13, 3.15, 3.21, 3.26
Wine consumption, 8.35

Women's Forces:
  nursing services, 7.10
  recruitment, 7.4
  strength, 7.3
Wood chipboard:
  production and stocks, 8.20
Woodpulp:
  consumption and stocks, 8.20
Wool:
  agricultural output, 9.1, 9.2
  exports, 8.18
  imports, 8.18
  prices, 18.9-18.11
  production, consumption and stocks, 8.18
Working population, 6.1
Wounding offences, 4.3, 4.20

Y

Young offenders' centres:
  sent to, 4.15, 4.17, 4.22
Youth custody, 4.7, 4.9

Z

Zinc:
  production, consumption and stocks, 8.17

All The Latest Statistics
from the
Central Statistical Office

0839-338-PLUS

Retail Prices Index 337
Monthly Trade Figures 338
Balance of Payments (quarterly) 339
Public Sector Borrowing Requirement 340
Index of Production 341
Producer Prices 342
Retail Sales 343
Credit Business 344
Gross Domestic Product 345

CSO
STATCALL

Calls charged at 36p per minute cheap rate,
48p per minute at all other times

Central Statistical Office
AN EXECUTIVE AGENCY OF GOVERNMENT

Do you need detailed Product Information?

Do you know about BUSINESS MONITORS?

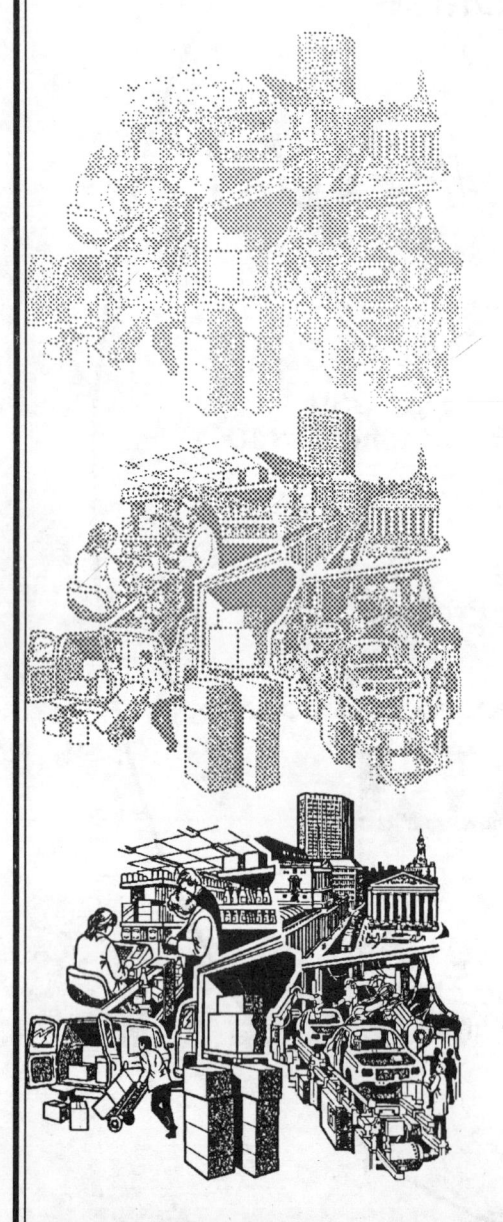

Business Monitors are designed for businesses and others undertaking market research of all kinds. They provide statistics on manufacturing, energy, mining, service and distributive industries. The CSO regularly questions thousands of UK businesses on their output and performance. Some 800,000 inquiry forms are sent out each year, and the statistics are collated and presented by expert government statisticians using accepted statistical techniques.

There are over 300 titles in the series variously published at monthly, quarterly or yearly intervals. Business Monitors are the primary and often the only source of the information they contain.

Business Monitors can help you to:

- ⇨ Monitor business trends
- ⇨ Identify successful products
- ⇨ Assess your efficiency
- ⇨ Identify new markets
- ⇨ Pinpoint seasonal factors in your business
- ⇨ Market your products
- ⇨ Compare the price of your products with those of your industry or sector

HOW TO ORDER BUSINESS MONITORS

Ring the CSO Library on:

0633 812973 and ask for our information brochure, "HMSO Publishes for the CSO". This includes a complete list of Business Monitors and an order form.